THE
PAUL
McCARTNEY
ENCYCLOPEDIA

D0619788

THE

PAUL McCARTNEY

ENCYCLOPEDIA

BILL HARRY

To Virginia Harry:
who had an equal vision in the founding of
Mersey Beat

First published in 2002 by
Virgin Books Ltd
Thames Wharf Studios
Rainville Road
London
W6 9HA

A catalogue record for this book is available from the British Library.

ISBN 0 7535 07161

Typeset by Phoenix Photosetting, Chatham, Kent
Printed and bound in Great Britain by Clays Ltd, St Ives plc

INTRODUCTION

Paul McCartney: Renaissance Man

John Lennon's Aunt Mimi said she'd always remember me because I was the first person ever to call John a genius. There is no doubt that John was one of the most creative figures of twentieth-century popular culture. However, his tragic death elevated him to iconic status, with the result that the undoubted brilliance of his former partner Paul McCartney became overshadowed.

To my mind Paul is also a genius and, when he used to write me letters during the early stages of the Beatles' career, I felt that his writing contained a delightful sense of humour, which, in some ways was equal to John's.

The composer of classic popular songs such as 'Yesterday', 'Hey Jude', 'Eleanor Rigby', 'Sgt Pepper's Lonely Hearts Club Band', 'Lady Madonna' and 'Let It Be' was also the one who conceived a number of the major Beatles projects. Not only was Paul the man responsible for the ideas behind the *Sgt Pepper's Lonely Hearts Club Band* and *Abbey Road* albums, plus the *Magical Mystery Tour* film, but he also sketched and drew the initial designs for a number of the Beatles' album covers.

Paul also composed soundtrack music for the films *The Family Way* and *The Honorary Consul*.

John initially became involved in experimental music when he composed a version of 'Revolution' for the November 1968 album *The Beatles*. However, Paul preceded him, becoming the first member of the Beatles to conduct experiments with sounds when he composed *Carnival of Light*. This was a sound collage lasting 13 minutes and 48 seconds that Paul composed for an event called the 'Carnival of Light Rave' at the Roundhouse in Camden Town, London, which took place on 28 January and 4 February 1967.

John is also remembered as an avant-garde filmmaker, although his collaborations were mainly Yoko Ono's ideas, which he co-produced with her. Their first film was called *Smile*, produced in 1968, a 52-minute film of John smiling. Other projects included *Up Your Legs Forever*, an 80-minute film featuring three hundred pairs of legs, and *Fly*, a film in which a fly crawled across a naked girl's body.

Yet even in the field of avant-garde movies, Paul had beaten John to the punch. In 1966 he made two avant-garde films, *The Defeat of the Dog* and *The Next Spring Then*.

Paul has continued to make film shorts over the years covering subjects ranging from the Grateful Dead to Rupert the Bear.

In the recording studio he conducted a 41-piece orchestra on the 'A

Day In The Life' track on the *Sgt Pepper* album. He is also a multi-instrumentalist who plays not only bass guitar but also lead guitar, steel guitar and acoustic guitar – and bongos, drums, flugelhorn, flute, harpsichord, harmonium, maracas, organ, piano, string bass and trumpet!

He took an interest in composing classical music when Brian Pidgeon, the general manager of the Royal Liverpool Philharmonic, commissioned him to compose *Paul McCartney's Liverpool Oratorio* with Carl Davis.

The work was then given its world premiere at Liverpool's Anglican Cathedral on Friday June 28 1991 before an audience of 2,500 as part of the orchestra's 150th-anniversary celebrations.

Since its debut, during a period of five years, the oratorio has been performed more than a hundred times in twenty different countries.

Liverpool Suite is another classical collaboration by Paul and Carl Davis, which is basically a distillation of the most melodic and songlike segments of *Paul McCartney's Liverpool Oratorio*.

Another work is *Standing Stone*, a symphonic poem by Paul, which marked EMI Records' centenary and was premiered at the Royal Albert Hall on Tuesday 14 October 1997, where it received a standing ovation.

Paul was to say that the origin of *Standing Stone* came about following the death of his friend Ivan Vaughan from Parkinson's disease.

Ivan was the person who first introduced Paul to John Lennon. A television documentary, *Ivan*, portrayed his struggle with the disease and Paul allowed his song 'Blackbird' to be played at the beginning and end of the programme free of charge.

He then invited Ivan to spend Christmas 1984 with the McCartneys at their home in Sussex and continued to keep in touch until Ivan's death.

He said, ' "Jive with Ive, the ace on the bass" was his intro when we played together. Ivan was very important to me. Poetry seemed the right way to express what I felt about his death. Later, I decided to write an epic poem that would serve as the framework for *Standing Stone*. I realised that I wasn't going to write a symphonic work where you take a theme and develop it throughout a movement, partly because I simply didn't know how to do that.'

The theme is basically that of the history of life on earth via the ancient standing stones of the Celts.

Another composition is *Working Classical*, and in August 2000 Paul composed *Liverpool Sound Collage* as a soundtrack to the artist Peter Blake's exhibition at the Tate Liverpool.

In the 27 January 1995 issue of *New Statesman and Society*, Paul made his debut as a published poet with five poems: 'Chasing The Cherry,' 'Mist The Mind,' 'The Blue Shines Through', 'Trouble Is' and 'Velvet Wine'.

On 23 March 1995, at St James's Palace, London, before Prince

Charles and invited guests, Paul was present to hear the debut of 'Leaf', an eight-minute piece for solo piano, which he composed. The event was called 'An Evening with Paul McCartney'.

Paul emerged as a painter with his first exhibition, which opened in Germany on 1 May 1999. He had been passionate about art since he was a child and used to paint his own birthday and Christmas cards. He also designed some of the Beatles' album sleeves.

In London in the mid-sixties, under the influence of the gallery owner Robert Fraser, he became an art collector and particularly liked the work of René Magritte.

Paul also became acquainted with the Dutch painter Willem de Kooning, based in New York, who was a client of Paul's father-in-law. When Paul had turned forty, he was encouraged by de Kooning to take up painting and soon had his own studios in his homes in the South of England, Arizona and Long Island. An added incentive was a Christmas present from Linda – René Magritte's own easel. Since 1983 Paul has produced nearly 600 abstract paintings.

The paintings are in oils and acrylic, and cover landscapes, portraits and abstracts; they include several paintings of Linda. There are also paintings of John Lennon, David Bowie and the British Queen, the last entitled *A Salute to the Queen*. Other titles include *John's Room*, *Yellow Linda With Piano*, *Egypt Station*, *Sea God* and *Tara's Plastic Skirt*.

Singer, songwriter, musician, classical composer, poet, painter, film-maker, Paul McCartney is a true renaissance man. Another example of his creativity in verse is *Blackbird Singing: Poems and Lyrics 1965–1999* (Faber & Faber).

Paul first began to write poetry while at the Liverpool Institute and in his introduction to his book he mentions his desire to have a poem printed in the school magazine – but it was rejected. He doesn't mention it by name, but it could well be 'The Worm Chain Drags Slowly', which was one of his first efforts at poetry. Paul also mentions how the death of his friend Ivan Vaughan led him to attempt to express his feelings in verse.

The volume is introduced and edited by Adrian Mitchell, who also persuaded Paul to include song lyrics in the collection. Mitchell is a major contemporary poet who has given more than a thousand performances of his work around the world. He first met Paul in January 1963, when, as a journalist with the *Daily Mail*, he published the first interview with the Beatles in a national newspaper.

He developed a friendship with Paul and actually performed four of his poems backed by Paul, Linda and the band on the 'Unplugged' tour at Cliffs Pavilion, Southend, on Friday 19 July 1991. (It was Linda who actually phoned Mitchell and suggested that he edit a book of Paul's poems.)

In 1995 Mitchell was poetry editor of the *New Statesman* and published a page featuring five of Paul's poems. Paul was originally inspired to publish his work by Linda, and the book is dedicated to her and their four children.

There are more than a hundred poems written between 1965 and 1999 and a dozen of them are about Linda, written in the months before and after her death in April 1998.

Paul Muldoon, professor of poetry at Oxford University, comments, 'McCartney's new poems confirm that poetry matters to us at times in our lives when we try to make sense of things. We are always reading over the shoulder of the poet and have the moment of opportunity to share the grief.'

Although song lyrics are juxtaposed with the poems, the strength of both approaches is evident: images in the lyrics of 'When I'm Sixty-Four' and 'Eleanor Rigby', for instance, and the powerful words in 'Black Jacket' ('Sadness isn't sadness it's happiness in a black jacket', and its climax 'tears are not tears they're balls of laughter dipped in salt'). Truly evocative are his haunting elegies to Linda, such as 'Her Spirit'.

Paul has received acknowledgment for his undoubted talents, becoming a Freeman of the City of Liverpool, a Fellow of the Royal College of Music and a Fellow of the British Academy of Songwriters, Composers and Authors. He received a knighthood for his services to music. Yet he says that his greatest achievements are his four children.

Paul became pop music's first billionaire and publications have made much copy out of the fact that he is so wealthy. What they don't emphasise are the huge number of contributions he makes to charities. They are not only financial contributions, either: he gives time and makes appearances to promote various causes; he writes and records for charities; and he is particularly unstinting in championing vegetarianism, animal rights and the dangers to the world's ecology.

While writing this book, I have come to realise that Paul's life has been so full of events and music that much might be missed in this volume. There is certainly enough material to double the word count, and no doubt there are a number of unrecorded songs, appearances, people and events that some readers may find missing from this first edition. I would welcome comments, therefore, for future editions.

I have been writing about Paul McCartney since 1961 and during that time have continued my research in newspapers, magazines, fan magazines, television and film. Many of the books included in the bibliography were consulted and of particular value were publications such as *Beatles Monthly*, *Beatlefan*, *Beatles Unlimited* and the *London Beatles Fan Club Magazine*, whose issues contain an incredible amount of information, lovingly compiled by dedicated fans.

I would like to thank Carolyn Thorne and Barbara Phelan for their editorial support and everyone at Virgin Books for making my book a reality.

Bill Harry,
London, July 2002

A Hanney & Co.

The name of a former Cotton Brokers & Merchants, a firm in Chapel Street, Liverpool, where Jim McCartney, Paul's father, first began to work as a sample boy at the age of fourteen. Jim originally earned six shillings a week and by the age of 28 had progressed to the position of cotton salesman earning £250 per annum.

Abbey Road (album)

A Beatles album issued in Britain on 26 September 1969 and in America on 1 October.

The tracks written by Paul were: 'Maxwell's Silver Hammer', 'Oh Darling', 'You Never Give Me Your Money', 'She Came In Through The Bathroom Window', 'Golden Slumbers', 'Carry That Weight', 'The End' and 'Her Majesty'.

The photograph on the cover sleeve, showing the Beatles walking across the zebra crossing outside Abbey Road Studios, has become one of the most famous rock music images. It has been copied on dozens of other album covers and tens of thousands of tourists have had photographs taken of themselves striding over the crossing.

The idea for the sleeve was Paul's and he made a detailed sketch for photographer Iain Macmillan before the picture session took place.

Apart from being imitated and idolised by fans, the *Abbey Road* picture was to assume enormous significance for adherents of the 'Paul is Dead' theory, who avidly analysed the cover for so-called 'clues' to support it – and found a liberal sprinkling of them!

Most important was the fact that Paul is barefoot in the photograph, which was said to be a Mafia/Grecian (take your pick) sign of death. A Michigan journalist, Fred LaBour, reviewing the album, claimed that the group was leaving a cemetery and that John was dressed as a minister, Ringo as an undertaker and George as a gravedigger, and pointed out that Paul was out of step with the others, which apparently meant that it was in fact either his corpse, or, more popularly, a substitute who'd had plastic surgery. Proof positive of the impostor theory was the fact that 'Paul' was holding a cigarette in his *right hand* (Macca is left-handed). The reality, of course, was very different, as two quotes from some of those involved demonstrate.

Photographer Iain Macmillan: 'Paul turned up in his Oxfam suit and sandals and because it was a hot day he decided to do some shots with the sandals on and some with sandals off. Paul checked all the pictures with a magnifying glass.

'I don't think the other three were particularly bothered. He chose the nearest shot with the legs stretched in almost uniform style and it was pure coincidence that it happened to be the one with his sandals off.

'I got the job through John but it was Paul's idea and I was given ten minutes around lunchtime to do it. They came out of the studios, where they were recording, to do it and I managed to take six shots in all.'

Paul himself told disc jockey Paul Gambaccini: 'I just turned up at the photo session. It was a really nice hot day and I think I wore sandals. I only had to walk around the corner to the crossing because I lived pretty nearby. I had me sandals off and on for the session. Of course, when it comes out and people start looking at it and they say: "Why has he got no shoes on? He's never done that before." OK you've never seen me do it before but in actual fact it's just me with me shoes off. Turns out to be some old Mafia sign of death or something.'

But 'Paul is Dead' fanatics were not deterred: in the course of their 'investigations' they discovered that the registration number (281F) of the Volkswagen car in the photo indicated the age Paul would have been *if* he had lived, and that the cracked Abbey Road street sign on the back cover was a mystical omen of the split in the group following Paul's death!

Abbey Road (book)

A book written by EMI Records executive Brian Southall which was first published in Britain by Patrick Stephens Ltd in 1982.

Paul wrote a small introduction for the book in which he mentioned the nostalgia he felt whenever he used the Abbey Road Studios and how he met Sir Malcolm Sargent and Sir Donald Wolfit on the steps outside. Apart from the portrait illustrating the introduction and the photographs of the Beatles, there are more photographs of Paul in the book than of any other artist.

They include Paul and Linda walking across the famous zebra crossing with their pony, Jet; Paul with George Martin and Norman

Smith; Paul drinking a glass of milk; Paul in various disguises for the 'Coming Up' video sessions; giving George Martin a guitar lesson; two further photographs from the 'Coming Up' sessions; two pictures of Paul with boxer John Conteh and Eamonn Andrews when the surprise was sprung for Conteh's *This Is Your Life*; Linda and Jet outside Abbey Road; Wings in Scotland with the Campbeltown Pipe Band; four photographs of the Rockestra sessions; Paul and Linda in the studio's reception area; Paul and Linda at Vera Samwell's retirement party; Linda with Steve Harley and Denny Laine at the studio's fiftieth anniversary party.

In a chapter entitled 'Yesterday – McCartney Remembers', Paul reminisces about his time at Abbey Road from 1962 until the present day. He talks about how the Beatles changed the strict formality which existed at the time, the long hours they spent at recording sessions, the wide range of instruments they could use there and the constant crowds which used to gather outside.

ABC News

An American television news programme, which on Tuesday 1 February 1972 filmed a news story around Paul's controversial new release 'Give Ireland Back To The Irish'. Wings were featured at Paul's farm in Scotland. The line-up comprised Paul, Linda, Denny Laine, Denny Seiwell and Gerry McCullough rehearsing the number. This was followed by an interview with Paul and Linda. Much of the interview concerned the controversy caused by the BBC because they considered it 'clearly politically controversial'.

When ABC TV's London reporter George Watson asked, 'As an entertainer, it doesn't worry you getting a bit into politics?' Paul replied, 'No, you can't stay out of it, you know, if you think at all, these days. We're still humans, you know, and you wake up and you read your newspaper, it affects you. So I don't mind too much about people saying you're too political. I don't mind, it doesn't worry me, like I say. I don't now plan to do everything I do as a political thing, you know, but just on this one occasion I think the British government overstepped their mark and showed themselves to be more of a repressive regime than I ever believed them to be.'

They had also been filmed rehearsing in the music room on the upper floor of Paul's Cavendish Avenue house.

The story was broadcast on Tuesday 7 March 1972.

The promotional clip of Wings rehearsing the number was also broadcast in America on ABC TV's 'David Frost Salutes the Beatles' on Wednesday 21 May 1975.

ABC TV

The American television network. To celebrate Paul and Linda's fifth wedding anniversary, ABC TV filmed Paul at his MPL offices for a two-part interview transmitted in the States on Tuesday 12 March and Wednesday 13 March 1974. Paul discussed the creative process in writing songs such as 'Picasso's Last Words' and 'Eleanor Rigby' and clips from 'My Love', 'Maybe I'm Amazed' and 'Mary Had A Little Lamb' were shown.

During the fifteen-minute interview Paul also answered the question 'Can the Beatles be re-created again?' by saying, 'They might do bits together again, we don't know yet. Every time I say that, some paper prints a headline saying "The Beatles To Reform", so I'm a bit cautious about saying anything. I don't think we'll get together as a band again, I just don't think it'll work actually; it might not be as good. I just saw Jerry Lewis talking the other day about Dean Martin, it's a bit like that.'

About You
A track from the *Driving Rain* album. The number lasts for 2 minutes and 54 seconds and was recorded on Friday 16 February 2001.

Academy, The
A venue in New York where Paul held a press conference on Thursday 11 February 1993. The conference was to promote his new album *Off The Ground* and to announce details of the concert dates of the forthcoming American branch of his New World Tour.

Paul was also asked a number of questions:

Question: One of my favourite songs of the record, actually I don't think it's mentioned is 'Cosmically Conscious'. I was curious about that song – if a long version exists. I also heard that it was written quite a while ago in India.

Paul: Yeah, it was. What it is, it's kind of on the end of the record. It's one of those little kinds of snippets, you know, almost as an afterthought. There is a full-length version and it was written 23 years ago or thereabout, when . . . uh, I think maybe 25, when we were with the Beatles in Rishikesh with the Maharishi and he used to keep saying 'be Cosmically Conscious, peace and joy', so that's pretty much the entire lyrics of that song, which is why it's a snippet on the end.

Question: I was wondering how you might try to top the 184,000 people you had in Rio de Janeiro on the last tour, this time around.

Paul: Probably we're not, is probably the answer. But somebody did invite us back to Brazil and they said there's a bigger place in San Paolo. But it's not on the itinerary this time. Maybe that would top it.

Question: You're doing something as a patron of the arts in Liverpool Institute? What is that?

Paul: OK. A few years ago I went back to my old school in Liverpool and found it kind of going into ruins. So I was hoping that something could be done for it, because it was built in 1825 and even though I hated it when I went there – like most kids I couldn't wait to get away – looking back on it now was a great experience. It gave me a good feeling in the world. What we're going to hope to do in 1995 is reopen it, renovate it and reopen it as a performing arts centre for local and overseas kids. So this is the big dream for 1995.

Question: I'm pleased to see there's a biography of your talented wife Linda in the press kit. I understand there was a documentary about her broadcast in London around Christmas time. Will we have a chance to see that here?

Paul: I'm not sure, but the BBC did make a great documentary on Linda which featured her photography. Because normally she gets a bit eclipsed by the fact that we got married, and I always say I kind of ruined her career. A lot of people think she was free-loading and just hanging on my coat-tails, which was actually not true. She had a very great career, and her *Sixties* book I think proves that. So I'm not sure if it's going to be over here in the States, but I hope so.

Question: It appears that with your recent tour and some of the work you've done since, you've become very comfortable again going into your musical past, particularly the Beatles songs. Another era of your career that was very, very successful and meant a lot to me was Wings. I was wondering how you feel about that, because you really don't delve too much into those songs in your current repertoire.

Paul: No. It's difficult, you know, when you've got as much material to choose from as I have. With a new album you want to do some of your new album, 'cause the new stuff is fresh and you want to do it, and this stuff is pretty live, so it's kind of easy to do live, and if it sounds like the record, so ... but then again you want to do some Beatles stuff, which is probably what I'm most known for and that there'll always be people in the audience who really want to hear that. It is true that the Wings stuff tends to get a little bit squeezed out, and there's always people like you who say 'why don't you do something off *Ram*, man?' It's just there's only so much time, you know. If we were on there for like four or five hours, we could attack that bit of it. Normally you've just got to make some hard decisions. We do a few from that period, but it's true that it gets squeezed out because of the Beatles and the new stuff.

Question: We spoke to Carl Davis recently and he said you might be working on a guitar concerto. Any truth to that, anything classical coming up from you?

Paul: That was a thought we had. That's something I wouldn't mind doing. But in actual fact it turned into some piano pieces. It was a plan to do that, and maybe something we'll do at some point. But what I've just finished with him is six piano pieces. After having done the great full-blown thing, the oratorio, or as someone called it yesterday, the 'oratorio', I've gone back to just one single person sitting at the piano, and it's very simple piano pieces. So that's the next thing, and then I think Carl and I might write something together maybe later in the year.

Question: Can you tell us what is the message of the new song 'Hope Of Deliverance', and the second part of the question, if it was really written in a brief period of time?

Paul: Yeah, it was written quite quickly. You know, if you're lucky, some songs like that just sort of tumble out and you just write them down and you find you've written a kind of thing. They don't all happen like that, but that one just got up into my attic and, as I say, I wrote it quite quickly. The message, you know, I like people to make their own decision as to what the message is. But for me, it is just that these days particularly there's a lot of stuff out there that's dangerous, if you're bringing up kids like I am. Well, they're brought up, mine you know, mine are big, but there's a lot of fears, a lot of worries, a lot of people now homeless, a lot of recessionary stuff going on, disease and stuff. I do mean, really, what I'm saying – hope of deliverance from the darkness that surrounds us, whichever particular bit of darkness yours is, it might just be a girl whose boyfriend has left her or it might be something more serious, you know, some sort of tragedy in the family or whatever, but it's really some kind of prayer I suppose.

Question: I'd like to ask you a little bit about touring. There's an elite handful of people like yourself who sell out stadiums and arenas, but where do you perceive the live concert touring industry going and what kind of trends do you see happening with it, as you've been in the industry for 25 years?

Paul: I don't really know about trends. People always used to ask us what's going to be the next, when we were the Beatles. What's going to be the next thing next year? We'd say, we don't know, you know. I just know what's going on now and what's in the past, but I don't read the future so I couldn't tell you about that. But I think people will always like to hear somebody live, see somebody live. It was really brought home to me before our last tour when I went to see Dustin Hoffman in London in a production of *The Merchant Of Venice*. When he walked on stage it was like – 'Wow, I'm in the room with Dustin.' You got this great feeling – 'I'm Really in the room,' like now, here we are. Welcome into my parlour. You know, it's a special thing, you're not just watching him on video, you're actually there with him and if you shout out 'Hey, Dusty!' he'll hear you. So I just think there is some attraction in that and I think people hopefully will keep going to concerts. I would think they would.

Question: What do you think about the fact that your album is hitting stores the same week as Mick Jagger's latest solo album, and that critics have sort of reviewed them by comparison? Do you consider Mr Jagger competition?

Paul: Competition? Well, yeah, I suppose so. You know, we always used to ring each other when we were in the Beatles and the Stones and sort of say, 'When's your album coming out?' and we used to delay our releases. But I didn't do that this time. He's a good mate, you know, he's a good friend, I like him a lot. I like his music, and he's written great stuff. So you can't really control who you come out with, which week you come out and who's there as your competition. So I don't mind really. I think it's inevitable that certain people will do – it's actually a cheap shot. They don't do their homework, you know, they kind of just review both of them quickly and go, 'Well, he's hard and he's soft,' which is not right. I haven't heard his album but I hear it's good, and I think ours is good. So we'll just see, you know.

Question: Does it bother you that critics continue to say that you haven't been able to get rid of that 'soft' image? Does that still bother you?

Paul: No, not really, no. I mean, there's a lot of people who'd like a soft image, you know. I mean, I don't particularly think I've got a soft image actually. It depends if you know my work or not. If you know what I've been involved in, then things like 'Helter Skelter' is certainly not soft, or 'I'm Down' or some of that stuff. So I think anyone who knows me . . . But maybe I'm known better for songs like 'Yesterday', but listen, I'm not knocking it, it's great to be known for both, you know. I'm quite happy with my reputation at the moment.

Question: Why are you surprised that you're catching so much, if I might use the word, shit, for 'Big Boys Bickering'? I mean, it's just an expression about the environment and everything else. Are you surprised at the attitude?

Paul: Not really. You know, the thing is I've never used swear words in my songs. It just never occurred to me, really, it's just that I've never felt I needed to. I think what's happened is . . . actually, I talked, before we released this, I talked to my sister-in-law about it, she's bringing up young kids, and she was saying 'Oh, you know, you're known as the guy that doesn't swear and now finally you're swearing, it's a kind of letdown.' And I said, 'Yeah, but you know, I'm trying to make a point. This is a protest song about people, men mainly, in smoke-filled rooms sort of running our lives, telling us whether or not we can close this ozone hole.' And I sense that a lot of people, that I meet anyway, would like them to really get on the case and quick. So what I do is say that in the song basically, that they're not 'mucking up for everyone', but I use the F-word, which I'm not going to use now, 'cause there's kids watching. But it doesn't really fuss me, you know, it's no big surprise to me. I hear it in everyday common language. I've heard it since I was a little kid, so I hear it a lot. I mean, even if you go to switch on a movie, there's like fifty times worse stuff than that. I think you know, if it's essential to the plot, it's a bit like nudity in plays, you know, if it's essential for the plot then I think it's valid. I think in this case for what the song was saying, which is like that people ought to get up, get on with it, and stop messing around, I think it's valid.

Question: You have taken a great stance environmentally and an animal rights stance as well. I've read recently about Linda having her own food line of stuff that's not only health-orientated but that is not animal. Are you going to be taking these ideas a bit further than just with that song, onto the tour and translating that mindset as well with the shows on the tour?

Paul: Yeah. The thing is, when you grow up, when you're like a father of four as I am, these things become important: ecology and stuff like that. What we did on the last tour was instead of just saying nothing about it, we tried to be sort of people's voices and try to say we meet a lot of people who are interested in this kind of thing. So really we figure that rather than just being flippant in there, when you're on the TV camera, it's actually allowed to talk a bit of sense and to talk about something you really care about. So, yeah, we'll continue to do this. I don't know about writing songs about it, you can never say whether you'll be able to write another song about that, because they're not easy to write. But certainly we'll be plugging it, and in our tour booklet on the tour, this time we've given a couple of pages to Greenpeace, some to Friends Of The Earth and some to PETA, the animal organisation which we're members of, and we believe in what they have to say. I think going into the next century, I think these ideas are really interesting. Their time has come. So yeah, we'll be plugging them.

Question: What's it like being a pop star and trying to raise normal kids? And also, I know you're counting the minutes until somebody asked you this, but can you tell us anything about this potential project musically with George Harrison and Ringo Starr?

Paul: Yeah, OK. First bit first: the children. The trick is to remember these questions. The three-parter, I'll take the first part – Raising children as a pop star or as anyone famous. Me and Linda, when we got together decided that what we'd try and do was raise the kids with their feet on the ground, even though now we're trying to get off the ground. We made that a big priority because we realised that with having the money that I have, and the fame, that the kids could become snobs real early, and you see a lot of kids like this, you know, rich kids and stuff, and they're really snotty, you know. So we just decided that we'd send them to the ordinary schools like I went to, like she went to and try and give them some good values and really major on that, until they're round about 21 and then, forget it, you've got no control over them anyway. But then at least they've got a grounding and the whole thing. And, touch wood, I think that's worked with the kids. They're really nice kids. I mean, I'm biased. But they are good kids, they're sensible and they're not snobs. And what was the second part of this mammoth question?

Question: Can you tell us anything about this potential project musically with George and Ringo?

Paul: Oh yeah. Well, normally when I'm asked the question, 'Will the Beatles ever get back together?' I just sort of say, 'no, it's absolutely impossible anyway, and without John it wouldn't be the Beatles.' So that's kind of an easy answer, and it's always been true. But at the moment they're making a ten-part series on the Beatles in England, and it's going very well. We've got involved in it, it gives us a chance to say our own point of view rather than everybody speaks for us, you know, and says, 'you know why he was walking across that crossing with no shoes on?' You know, it's like, 'well, because it was hot.' It was like a real hot day and I had some sandals on and I kicked them off. You know, big deal. So we're always answering stuff like that. Like I met some kid, little kid, who had been to a Beatles summer camp, and she was telling me how you turn the record backwards, and I was saying 'no, no, no, I was here . . .' She said, 'No, it's not true!' She wouldn't listen to me, you know. So it's like, we're taking this opportunity with the series to try and put our own point of view. And what happened was we were talking to the director, we were talking together, and he said if there's a piece of film that you've got. I was thinking in terms of maybe like a montage of John material, say, you know, of him just looking great, nice memories of John, I thought – well, you need a piece of music to go with that. So we volunteered to do that. We said, well, you know . . . I kicked it around with the others, would you mind doing that? Would we hate to do that? Is that a definite no-no? And George said, 'Well, that'll be good,' and Ringo as well, you know. So we thought, well, that's a nice start. Rather than trying to get the Beatles back together, there's no touring, we're not thinking anything like that but we'll probably get together, maybe try and write something, record something for this one piece of music and we'll just see where that takes us. We're not looking for anything, I don't think anyone really wants to re-form the Beatles, but just to get together as friends and make a piece of music would be nice.

Question: A lot of your contemporaries like Eric Clapton and Bob Dylan release boxed sets of their outtakes, rarities, B-sides. Have you given any thought to that as far as your solo work and also you've got a lot of videos. How about a video anthology?

Paul: Yeah, well that's one of those things that I think some day will happen. What happens with me is I put a new album out, so I'd rather put out new material than outtakes of old material. But I've got a lot of stuff. But originally we were going to for years, going to try and put together an album called *Cold Cuts*, which was going to be all the things that didn't get on *Ram*, things that didn't get on *Red Rose Speedway*, through the years, you know, which I think would be interesting for collectors and for real fans who've got all the other stuff. But as I say, when you're going on tour, it becomes a nicer possibility to write some new stuff and do that. And plus, *Cold Cuts* is a bootleg, someone's put it together anyway.

Question: Last question. When you write your music now, are you writing for your fans who grew up listening to you or are you writing for younger fans? And if it's for younger fans, how do you stay in touch with the younger generation?

Paul: Well, if I do stay in touch with the younger generation, it will be through my kids, because I've got kids of that age, and that's where you get your clues, just watch them, see what they're into, see what's happening. In truth I don't actually write for anyone but myself. I tried that. You think, I'll write for the, sort of, the moment, or I'll write for the old fans or something. And it's not the way to do it. You shouldn't do anything like that, it's really best to just write for yourself, so what you care about and what you love comes onto the page or onto the demo or whatever you're doing. And then you take your chances with people, you just hope some young people will like it, some older people. So I write for myself really.

Question: Have you already written some new songs?

Paul: Yeah. I've got a couple on the boil. Always got a couple.

Question: What kind?

Paul: Oh, you know: stuff. OK, I think that's it, isn't it? Give it a big wind up. That's a wrap, folks.

Ackroyd, David

A fireman who bought the one-millionth copy of 'Mull of Kintyre' in Britain on Saturday 17 December 1977. As a result he became the first record buyer in the world to receive a gold disc for his purchase. Paul also sent him a Christmas hamper.

Adopt A Minefield

A charity organisation. On Monday 4 June 2001 Paul and Heather Mills launched the British branch of the charity at the Marion Richardson School, Stepney, London.

There was a lunch with 160 guests during which a 25-minute film, made by Heather in Croatia that April, was screened. Paul narrated part of the documentary and commented, 'Imagine living in a country during a terrible war and then peace is declared. You think the killing is over, but when you take your kids to the beach you can't walk on it because the beach blows up if you do. This is the legacy of the land-mine. Landmines take or wreck three lives an hour, every hour of every day of every year. We have come together now to try to stop that.'

Talking of Heather's courage in her ventures into mined areas, he said, 'She's a very brave girl. She will go into earthquake scenes and minefields because she cares very much about it. She's very brave and very courageous. So I admire her, and I worry when she goes to these dangerous places. But we have great discussions about it.'

Later that same month, on Thursday 14 June Paul and Heather took part in the 'Adopt A Minefield' benefit in Los Angeles. Paul presented Radosav Zivovik with a Humanitarian Award. Radosav had part of his leg blown off in Bosnia and later launched the 'Stop Mines' founda-tion. Heather gave a speech, Paul performed a number from his forth-coming album and some films about landmines were screened, including Heather's film with Paul's narration.

The MC at the event was Jay Leno and after dinner Paul Simon performed four numbers. Leno introduced Paul who came on stage with an acoustic guitar and sang 'Yesterday'. His band then joined him and they performed 'The Long And Winding Road' and 'Drive In The Rain'. He recited his poem 'Jerk Of All Jerks' and finished his set with 'Let It Be'. He returned due to a standing ovation to perform 'I've Just Seen A Face' with Paul Simon.

On Thursday 1 November 2001 Paul and Heather attended the launch of a partnership between the 'Adopt A Minefield' charity and the 'Mines Advisory Group'.

Paul also designed a series of six legal postage stamps to raise money for the charity.

They were issued by the Isle of Man Post Office on Monday 1 July 2002. The stamps are colourful floral designs and 170,000 sets were issued.

Pat Tilbury of the Isle of Man Stamp Bureau commented, 'Paul's stamps are truly works of art. We anticipate that the issue will be extremely popular. The stamps have just the look that collectors like and, as art, they can hang on the wall in any décor.'

Paul was to say, 'It's been such a long time since I was on the island, but I can still remember how beautiful the landscape was and how friendly the people were, even to us, a pack of noisy kids from Liverpool. It's no exaggeration to say that it was one of the happiest trips of my childhood.'

African Summer

A BBC 2 documentary that was one of the programmes celebrating the tenth anniversary of 'Live Aid', screened on Saturday 15 July 1995. Paul appeared on a brief pre-recorded interview. The documentary also included part of Paul's concert appearance during his performance of 'Let It Be' and he is seen participating in the 'Do They Know It's Christmas?' finale.

African Yeah Yeah
One of several home demos Paul made in the years 1971 and 1972. This one features Wings band members.

After The Ball
A track on the *Back To The Egg* album lasting 2 minutes and 31 seconds which was recorded at Lympne Castle in September 1978. It was actually part of a medley with 'A Million Miles', which was 1 minute and 27 seconds in length, making the medley 3 minutes and 58 seconds in length. Paul felt that each of the numbers wasn't strong enough on its own, but felt they might work as a medley.

After You've Gone
A number Paul recorded as a demo disc at his Rude Studios in the summer of 1977. It was a number originally composed in 1918 by Henry Creamer and Turner Layton, which is now part of Paul's vast MPL catalogue. Wings member Laurence Juber was to include it on his album *Standard Time*.

Afternoon With Paul McCartney, An
A radio broadcast in America by NBC on Sunday 1 April 1979. Paul Gambaccini interviewed Paul.

Again And Again And Again
A song co-penned by Paul and Denny Laine, lasting 3 minutes and 28 seconds. It was actually the combination of two unfinished songs which Paul suggested should be put together and they recorded it at the Spirit of Ranachan studios. It was included on the *Back To The Egg* album and was one of the numbers included in the repertoire of the Wings British tour in 1979, with Denny Laine as lead vocalist.

Ahoy Sportpaleis, Rotterdam
An arena in Holland where Paul appeared on Saturday 9 October and Sunday 10 October 1993 during his New World Tour.

The show began with a screening of Richard Lester's introductory film. Then Paul came on stage in a pinstripe suit. Paul chatted as he introduced the songs, saying, 'For this next song we're going to take you all on a journey, on a trip to Paris, down the banks of the River Seine' prior to performing 'Michelle' and, 'Here is a song you might recognise,' prior to 'Yesterday'. During 'C'Mon People', Linda's photos of various rock stars from John Lennon to Janis Joplin were projected onto the stage backdrop.

A local paper reported: 'Nostalgia rules in the world of popular music. Nobody is to know better than Paul McCartney, a man who is constantly dragging along his own past. A confrontation in the concert hall can be larger than life. McCartney likes to play with the sentiments of his audience. Doing that he often slips down to a musically critical low level.'

Ain't No Sunshine
A hit for Bill Withers in 1971. It was included in Paul's MTV *Unplugged* and appeared on *Unplugged (The Official Bootleg)*, with Hamish Stuart on lead vocal.

Ain't That A Shame
A number composed by Domino and Bartholomew. Paul's version of the number, lasting 2 minutes and 40 seconds, was included on the *Tripping The Live Fantastic* album. It was recorded live at the Tokyo Dome, Japan on Friday 9 March 1990 during the 1989/90 World Tour.

Air Canada Center
A venue in Toronto, Canada where Paul appeared on 13 April 2002 as part of his 'Driving USA' tour. It was a sell-out show with an audience of 16,169. Prior to the concert, Paul held a 15-minute press conference at the venue. An addition to the show was the introduction of a performance of 'Mull Of Kintyre' played by the Peel Regional Police Pipe Band comprising fourteen pipers and eight drummers. The local newspaper the *Star* reported, 'We should all wear our pasts as well as Paul McCartney. And look as good doing it.'

Alexeyev, Anya
A Russian pianist who Paul first noticed in December 1994 when Prince Charles presented her with the Queen Elizabeth Rose Bowl Award at the Royal College of Music.

When Paul held his charitable event 'An Evening With Paul McCartney And Friends' at the Royal College of Music on Thursday 23 March 1995, his concert opened with Anya playing Paul's new classical composition *A Leaf*.

Anya, who was 22 years old at the time, also recorded the number for release on CD and cassette on Monday 24 April 1995.

All My Loving
Paul thought up this number while he was shaving one day, while the Beatles were appearing on a tour with Roy Orbison. He then worked it out during the afternoon on the tour bus and at the venue he found a piano and set it to music.

He said, 'I wrote 'All My Loving' like a piece of poetry and then, I think, I put a song to it later.'

In fact, 'All My Loving' was the first song Paul had ever written where the words came first.

The Beatles recorded it at Abbey Road Studios on Tuesday 30 July 1963 and the song first appeared on the *With The Beatles* album in November 1963 and was the title track of an EP of the same name in February 1964. It has appeared on many albums, including the American *Meet the Beatles*, *The Beatles 1962–1966* compilation in 1973, the live *The Beatles at the Hollywood Bowl* in 1977 and the mammoth world records *The Beatles Box* and *The Beatles Ballads* in 1980.

The number was also featured in the film *A Hard Day's Night*, and on numerous TV shows including *Sunday Night At the London Palladium*, *The Ed Sullivan Show* and *With the Beatles*.

It has been recorded by almost a hundred artists including Liverpool band the Trends, Count Basie, the Chipmunks, Herb Alpert and the George Martin Orchestra.

A version of the number lasting 2 minutes and 18 seconds was recorded live at East Rutherford, New Jersey on 11 June 1993 and included on the *Paul Is Live* album.

All My Trials

A traditional number, which Paul made an arrangement of and performed during his world tour. This particular track, which Paul also produced, was recorded on Friday 27 October 1989 at Milan, Italy during his 102-concert world tour.

It was an excerpt from the traditional medley 'American Trilogy', which Paul only performed once during the entire tour at this Milan concert. The composer credit on the single read 'Trad. Arr. McCartney' while the production was credited to Paul, Bob Clearmountain and Peter Henderson. Mixing was by Bob Clearmountain and remixing by Matt Butler.

The number featured Paul on vocals and bass, Linda on keyboards, Hamish Stuart on guitar, Robbie McIntosh on guitar, Paul 'Wix' Wickens on keyboard and Chris Whitten on drums.

There were various formats issued, including a 7″ single, also containing the track 'C Moon', taken from the soundtrack of the video documentary 'Put It There'. A cassette version on TCR 6278 included both tracks repeated on both sides of the tape.

The 12″ version (12R 6278) and the first 5″ CD single (CDR 6278) featured both these tracks, plus 'Mull of Kintyre' and 'Put It There' (the latter taken from the *Tripping The Live Fantastic* album), and were issued on Monday 26 November 1990.

Another 5″ CD (CDRX 6278) contained 'All My Trials', 'C Moon' and 'Lennon Medley'. The 'Lennon Medley' had been recorded live in Liverpool on Thursday 28 June 1990 and comprised 'Strawberry Fields'/ 'Help!'/'Give Peace A Chance'.

There was also a 7″ vinyl single, issued on RDJ 6278, which was issued specially to disc jockeys for promotional purposes.

All Shook Up
A track from the *Run Devil Run* album lasting 2 minutes and 6 seconds. Penned by Richard Blackwell and Elvis Presley it was recorded on Tuesday 4 May 1999 at Abbey Road Studios. It featured Paul on lead vocal and bass guitar, Dave Gilmour on electric guitar and backing vocal, Mick Green on electric guitar, Dave Mattacks on drums and Geraint Watkins on Wurlitzer piano.

Paul recalled how he loved Elvis Presley in his pre-Army days. As a teenager he went out with his friend Ian James, both of them dressed in draped, flak jackets. They thought they looked cool and would easily pick up girls. It didn't happen and Paul got depressed, so Ian took him to his Grannie's house in the Dingle and they played 'All Shook Up' on the record player – and it rid Paul of his blues.

All Stand Together
The song which brought George Martin and Paul together again in the recording studios. The number was penned for a short film about Rupert Bear. George produced it in his AIR Studios on Friday 31 October and Monday 3 November 1980. The King's Singers and the St Paul's Boys Choir backed Paul.

'All Stand Together' was eventually released in Britain on Parlophone R6086 on Monday 5 November 1984 and reached No. 3 in the charts.

The flipside was a humming version of the song, credited to Paul McCartney and the Finchley Frogettes.

All The Best
The second Paul McCartney compilation album containing Wings and his solo hits. The double album was issued in the UK on Monday 2 November 1987 and in America on Thursday 5 November 1987 and sported a cover photo by Tim O'Sullivan.

There were 26 tracks in the collection with two previously unreleased numbers 'Once Upon A Long Ago', a song produced by Phil Ramone (which was omitted from the American release) in 1987 and 'Waterspout'.

The tracks were: 'Jet', 'Band On The Run', 'Coming Up', 'Ebony And Ivory', 'Listen To What The Man Said', 'No More Lonely Nights', 'Silly Love Songs', 'Let 'Em In', 'C-Moon', 'Pipes Of Peace', 'Live And Let Die', 'Another Day', 'Maybe I'm Amazed', 'Goodnight Tonight', 'Once Upon A Long Ago', 'Say Say Say', 'With A Little Luck', 'My Love', 'We All Stand Together' and 'Mull Of Kintyre'.

The CD version omitted three tracks: 'Maybe I'm Amazed', 'With A Little Luck' and 'Goodnight Tonight'.

As a promotional measure, EMI issued a limited edition box set containing nine of the singles, featuring tracks from the album, with catalogue numbers from PMBOX11 to PMBOX19.

The American release on Saturday 5 December had a slightly different track listing. Absent were the tracks 'Pipes Of Peace', 'Maybe I'm Amazed', 'Once Upon A Long Ago', 'We All Stand Together' and 'Mull Of Kintyre' and additions were 'Junior's Farm' and 'Uncle Albert/Admiral Halsey'.

The album reached No. 62 in the US charts.

All This Useless Beauty
An album by Elvis Costello & the Attractions, released in 1996. It contained three of the numbers Costello penned with Paul: 'Shallow Grave', 'That Day Is Done' and 'Mistress And Maid'.

All Those Years Ago
George Harrison's tribute to John on which Paul and Ringo also appeared. George and Ringo began recording it at Friar Park in November 1980. George then took out Ringo's vocals and put on his own, with specially written new lyrics. Paul and Linda then recorded backing vocals at Friar Park. It was issued in America on Monday 11 May 1981 with 'Writing's On The Wall' on the flipside and released in Britain on Friday 15 May 1981.

All Together Now
A number penned by Paul that the Beatles recorded on Friday 12 May 1967 at Abbey Road Studios, in the absence of George Martin but with engineer Geoff Emerick at the controls. The number was featured at the close of the animated feature film 'Yellow Submarine' when the Beatles themselves finally make an appearance and sing the song. During the number, the title is repeated around fifty times.

'All Together Now' was recorded during a six-hour session and later became a popular song chanted at football stadiums.

All You Horseriders
One of several tracks Paul recorded for the *McCartney II* album in July 1979 that weren't used on the LP. The number appeared on the film documentary *Blankit's First Show*.

Alpin, Kenny
A classmate of Paul's at the Liverpool Institute.

Paul once used him as a scapegoat. He'd drawn a rather vulgar sketch of a naked woman for the amusement of his classmates, and had put it in his shirt pocket and forgotten about it. His mother discovered it there before washing the shirt and the embarrassed Paul told her that Kenny Alpin was the artistic culprit. His conscience got the better of him and two days later he confessed.

American Music Awards

An awards show that was broadcast on American television on ABC TV on Monday 27 January 1986 to an audience of 50 million viewers.

Taking place in Los Angeles, it was the 13th annual edition of the show. Paul had been given the 'Award of Merit'. The master of ceremonies was Lionel Richie who introduced film clips and tributes from Little Richard, Pete Townshend, Peggy Lee and Chevy Chase. Richie also introduced Julian Lennon who told Paul, 'My father would be as happy as I am to see you honoured in this way tonight. I just want to say congratulations, and here's to the future.'

A pre-recorded satellite transmission of Paul was beamed in from London's Hippodrome club in London where Phil Collins presented him with the award. In his acceptance speech Paul thanked a number of people, ending his speech with the words 'I'd like to thank very specially George, Ringo and Julian's dad, John . . . God bless you all. Peace on Earth.'

American Video Awards

An annual event that is the promotional video equivalent of the Oscars.

When the awards took place in Los Angeles on Wednesday 6 April 1983, Paul received a 'Hall of Fame' award. This special tribute was given for his 'outstanding achievement in video'. The award for the Best Soul Video went to 'Ebony And Ivory' and both awards were accepted on Paul's behalf by John Weaver, a producer at Keefco, the company which made the 'Ebony And Ivory' promotional film and which was established by pop video director Keith McMillan.

Amnesty International

During Amnesty International's fortieth anniversary Paul was presented with a Lifetime Achievement award. The ceremony took place in New York on Monday 28 January 2002 at the organisation's fifth annual Media Spotlight Awards.

The awards honour courageous and principled journalists, filmmakers, writers, musicians and actors who educate the public about human rights through their work.

Amnesty International's American director William F Schultz commented, 'Paul has consistently used his status both as a musician and a public figure to raise awareness of a variety of critical social issues.'

And I Love Her

A number inspired by Jane Asher which Paul wrote when he was living at the Ashers' Wimpole Street house. The Beatles recorded it in February 1964 for *A Hard Day's Night*. Paul was to say that it was the first ballad of his that impressed him, commenting, 'Written at Wimpole Street, it was the first ballad I impressed myself with. It's got nice chords in it. George played really good guitar on it. It worked very well. I'm not sure if John worked on that at all. The middle eight is mine. I wrote this on my own. I can see Margaret Asher's upstairs drawing room. I remember playing it there.'

John Lennon did give him a hand with some of the lyrics. Their publisher Dick James described how that happened. 'They were laying down the tracks and doing the melody lines of the song "And I Love Her". It was a very simple song and quite repetitive. George Martin and I looked at each other and the same thought sparked off in both of our minds. It was proving to be, although plain and a warm and sympathetic song, just too repetitive, with the same phrase repeating. George Martin told the boys, "Both Dick and I feel that the song is just lacking the middle. It's too repetitive, and it needs something to break it up." I think it was John who shouted, "OK, let's have a tea break," and John and Paul went to the piano and, while Mal Evans was getting tea and some sandwiches, the boys worked at the piano. Within half an hour they wrote, there before our very eyes, a very constructive middle to a very commercial song. Although we know it isn't long, it's only a four-bar middle, nevertheless it was just the right ingredient to break up the over repetitive effect of the original melody.'

Apart from appearing on the *Hard Day's Night* album it also appeared on the American Capitol EP 'Four By The Beatles'.

It next appeared on *The Beatles 1962–1966* in 1978; *The Beatles Ballads* and *Beatles Rarities* in 1980; and *Reel Music* and *20 Greatest Hits* in 1982.

One of the most popular of the Beatles' love ballads, it has been recorded by over 300 different artists, covering a range of styles and moods, including Ray Davies, Julie London, Smokey Robinson, Georgie Fame and Connie Francis.

And The Sun Will Shine

A Paul Jones single penned by Robin, Barry and Maurice Gibb and produced by Peter Asher, Jane's brother. The number was issued in Britain on Columbia DB 8379 on 8 March 1968. Paul played drums on the track.

Anderson, Rusty

A session guitarist, former member of the band Living Daylights. He'd played on sessions for the Bangles for producer David Kahne and Kahne recommended him to Paul for the *Driving Rain* album. He also played on *The Concert For New York City* album. He'd previously played on sessions for artists such as Stevie Nicks, Carole King, k.d.lang and Ricky Martin.

Rusty was asked to become part of the band on the 'Driving USA' tour.

Angel In Disguise

A number that Paul had written for Ringo's album *Time Takes Time* in 1991. He commented, 'Ringo's just finished a new album and I wrote a song for that, which I haven't heard yet. It's called "Angel In Disguise" – which is Ringo. He was pleased.'

Paul also revealed that Ringo had asked him for another verse, so Paul told him: '"Let's write the extra verse together. Or you can just write it and we'll have co-written the song." And I understand he has written a third verse. If it's another "With A Little Help From My Friends" great. If it isn't, great.'

However, the number was left off *Time Takes Time* when it was released.

Anglican Cathedral

Situated in Hope Street, Liverpool on St James's Mount, the cathedral is the biggest in Britain and one of the largest in the world. It took seven decades to construct. Architect Sir Giles Gilbert Scott, a Roman Catholic, died 18 years before completion. King Edward VII and Queen Alexandra laid the foundation stone in 1904 and Elizabeth II attended the service of consecration in 1978.

In 1953 Paul auditioned for a place in the Cathedral Choir, but was unsuccessful. He had auditioned because his father had insisted; but he deliberately cracked his voice at the audition. He did become a choirboy for a time – at St Chad's Choir, near Penny Lane, but he soon tired of it.

The Cathedral had a capacity of 2,500 when Paul's first full classical work *Paul McCartney's Liverpool Oratorio* had its world premiere there on Friday 28 June 1991. Carl Davis conducted the Royal Liverpool Philharmonic Orchestra; there was a full choir, a children's choir and four famous singers – Dame Kiri Te Kanawa, Jerry Hadley, Willard White and Sally Burgess.

Angry

A track on the *Press To Play* album lasting 3 minutes and 36 seconds, which also featured Phil Collins and Pete Townshend.

Annie

A hit American musical based on the famous 'Little Orphan Annie' comic strip. It was a major success on Broadway and in London's West End. *Annie* was also turned into a multimillion-dollar movie musical with Albert Finney starring.

Paul purchased the music publishing rights via his MPL Company and took his family to see the musical in both New York and London. He and Linda took 35 friends with them to the London premiere at the Victoria Palace Theatre in May 1978. Paul even bought full-page advertisements in the *Sunday Times* and the *New York Times* to congratulate *Annie*'s success.

When Paul and Linda went to see the musical at the Alvin Theater, New York on Friday 29 April 1977 they went backstage after the show to congratulate Andrea McArdle, who portrayed Annie in the show.

Another Day

Paul's first solo single, to which John Lennon referred to in his song 'How Do You Sleep'. Its theme was about the drudgery of office life.

The songwriting was credited to Paul and Linda, which caused a slight panic at ATV Music who had spent millions purchasing Northern Songs in a deal that included rights to new material from Paul and John. At the time, the *Evening Standard* reported that 'half the copyright is being claimed by Maclen Music Ltd (the first assignees of copyright of all Lennon and McCartney compositions), and the other half by a company called McCartney Inc.'

In a *Rolling Stone* interview with Paul Gambaccini, Paul was to say, 'Lew Grade suddenly saw his songwriting concession, which he'd just paid an awful lot of money for, virtually to get hold of John and I, he suddenly saw that I was claiming that I was writing half my stuff with Linda, and that if I was writing half of it she was entitled to a pure half of it, no matter whether she was a recognised songwriter or not. I didn't think that was important, I thought that whoever I worked with, no matter what the collaboration was, that person, if they did help on the song, should have a portion of the song for helping me. I think at the time their organisation suddenly thought, "Hello, they're pulling a fast one, they're trying to get some of the money back," whereas in fact, it was the truth.'

ATV Music instigated legal action, although the matter was eventually settled amicably. Paul wrote to Lew Grade and Lew replied.

'I can't remember exactly what it said,' commented Paul, 'but it was a very nice letter. He's actually OK, Lew, he's all right.' The action was dropped and Paul agreed to compensate ATV by making a TV spectacular 'James Paul McCartney' for Grade's company.

'Another Day' was released on Apple R5889 in Britain on Friday 19 February 1971 (the day the court case opened to dissolve the Beatles partnership), with 'Oh Woman Oh Why' as the flip. Paul had completed the recording the previous month in New York, backed by Dave Spinozza (guitar), Hugh McCracken (guitar) and Denny Seiwell (drums), in addition to the New York Philharmonic Orchestra. The song topped the British charts. In America it was released on Monday 22 February on Apple 1829 and reached the No. 5 position.

It was also included on the 1978 album *Wings Greatest*.

It was also issued in Germany on Apple/1C600-04758, in Italy on Apple/EMI Italia 3C006-04758, in France on Apple 2C006-04758M and in Japan on Apple AR2771.

Another Girl

A song Paul wrote while he was on holiday at Hammamet, Tunisia in 1965. He recorded it the day after he returned from the holiday on Monday 15 February, while it was still fresh in his mind. The number was included in the film *Help!* and also on the album. Paul sang lead vocal and also played lead guitar.

Anthology Project, The

The Beatles' *Anthology* project had its origins immediately before the Beatles actually broke up. There was a discussion about producing a film of the Beatles' history in which the group themselves would have control. Neil Aspinall actually began work on the project, which was initially called *The Long And Winding Road* and at one point he made a 90-minute film.

Interest faded over the years but around 1989 the concept was revived and Paul recalls that they wrote to ten different film directors including Ridley Scott, Michael Apted, Martin Scorsese and Stephen Spielberg asking if they would be interested in directing a Beatles' anthology.

Steven Spielberg, who was currently directing *E.T.*, contacted them. He told Paul that he was not really the person to do it, but suggested Martin Scorsese. The Beatles eventually decided to do it themselves through Apple and hired Geoff Wonfor who had directed the *Oratorio* film for Paul. Paul, George and Ringo then got together in front of the cameras, individually and in a group. Paul recalled, 'Of course . . . our memories are terrible, which is actually why we wanted to do this thing . . . but we found none of us could remember any of the stories the same. Each one of us, after all those years, has a slightly different story.'

It was suggested that the original title of *The Long And Winding Road* was more appropriate than *Anthology*, but internal politics ruled that out. George Harrison in particular didn't want to use the original title, possibly because it was Paul's. As Paul remarked, 'I have to be ready for my ideas to just mean nothing. And I have to subjugate myself to the common good. That's how the Beatles worked. So you know, George definitely has had a problem with a couple of things that it's just too McCartney.'

Anti-Heroin Project, The

The full title of this charity album was *The Anti-Heroin Project: It's A Live-In World*.

Paul donated a track, 'Simple As That', to the album, which was issued in the UK on Monday 24 November 1986.

Apocalypse Tube, The

A special edition of the 1980s pop show which was broadcast live on Sky Television on Saturday 20 November 1999. It was broadcast from the Newcastle studios of the original show and directed by Geoff Wonfor, who'd directed the Beatles' *Anthology*. The appearance was to promote the *Run Devil Run* album, although Dave Gilmour couldn't be present and was replaced by Chester Kamen. During the performance of 'Party' Fran Healy of Travis joined them. Robbie Williams was originally to have also joined Paul on this number, but didn't make it and Paul said, 'Robbie has left the building.' Paul played 'Party' a second time and also performed 'Lonesome Town', still playing while the credits were rolling.

Appaloosa

A 1992 film follow-up to *Blankit's First Show*. It was a 30-minute film and featured some previously unavailable music from Paul and Linda on the soundtrack. Two of Linda's compositions were 'Love's Full Glory' and 'Appaloosa Jam'. Paul wrote the number 'Blankit' specially for the film, which also included a classical piece arranged by Paul and Carl Davis which incorporated a tune by Linda called 'Appaloosa' and a tune by Paul called 'Meditation'. The number was four minutes in length. The MPL film was given its first screening on BBC 2 on Sunday 16 July 1994.

12 Ardwick Road

A three-bedroom terraced house in Speke, on the outskirts of Liverpool. It was one of the McCartney family homes at the beginning of the 1950s. When the family first moved there it was a new estate on the fringes of Speke where Paul and Mike shared the same bedroom. Their father rigged a set of earphones from the wireless downstairs into their bedroom where they used to listen to one of their favourite programmes, *Dick Barton, Special Agent*. They also had a pet dog called Prince. It was the house the McCartneys lived in prior to moving to 20 Forthlin Road. In 1998 Paul visited this early home with his son James. The owner John Stanley was surprised when he answered a knock on the door and saw Paul and James. His wife Patricia commented, 'Paul said he had passed the house several times but had only just plucked up the courage to knock. He was very down-to-earth – he didn't put on any airs and graces.'

Arrow Through Me

A number penned by Paul which was included on *Back To The Egg* album and issued as a single in America. It was released on Columbia 1-11070 on Tuesday 14 August 1979.

The number was co-produced by Paul and Chris Thomas. 'Old Siam Sir' was on the flipside. The track was very unusual because of the absence of guitars. Moog synthesisers and brass instruments had been used to provide the backing. The single reached No. 29 in the US charts.

A bonus track on the single, 'Arrow Through Me/Old Siam Sir' was issued in Britain and the US. It was included in the repertoire of the 1979 Wings tour of Britain and there was a promotional film clip of the number on the *Back To The Egg* TV special in 1979.

It was also released in Spain on Odeon 10C006-063423.

Arrowsmith, Clive

Photographer who took the cover shots for the albums *Band On The Run* and *Off The Ground*.

Asher, Dr Richard

Jane Asher's father and head of the family group of which Paul became a part when he began to live in their Wimpole Street house. He came to a tragic end. Dr Asher was missing for six days and was then found dead in the basement of Wimpole Street on Saturday 26 April 1969. He was lying on the cellar floor with half a bottle of whisky by his hand. The cause of death was attributed to a mixture of alcohol and barbiturates.

Asher, Jane

An actress/author/TV celebrity. She was born in London on 5 April 1946.

Her father Dr Richard Asher was a consultant in Blood and Mental Diseases at Central Middlesex Hospital in Acton, London in addition to being a writer and broadcaster. (Tragically, he was to die of an overdose of barbiturates and alcohol. His body was discovered on Saturday 26 April 1969.)

Her mother Margaret Augusta Asher was a Professor of Classical Music at the Guildhall School of Music and Drama and had taught George Martin to play the oboe – she was also to teach Paul McCartney to play the recorder. Jane had a brother Peter, who was two years older and a sister, Claire, who was two years younger. All three Asher children had the distinctive Titian-red hair.

Jane was educated at Queen's College, Harley Street. At the age of five she made her film debut in *Mandy* (1952). Her interest in acting began when her parents took their three children to a theatrical agency, thinking it would be fun for them to learn to act.

Her other screen appearances over the years have included *Third Party Risk* (1953); *Dance Little Lady*, *Adventure In The Hopfields* (1954); *The Quatermass Xperiment* (1955); *Charley Moon*, and *The Greengage Summer* (1956); *The Prince And The Pauper* (1962); *Girl In The Headlines* (1963); *The Masque Of The Red Death* (1964); *Alfie* (1966); *The Winter's Tale* (1967); *The Buttercup Chain*, and *Deep End* (1970); *Henry VIII And His Six Wives* (1972); *Runners* (1983), *Success Is The Best Revenge* (1984), *Dreamchild* (1985), *Paris By Night* (1988) and *Closing Numbers* (1995).

Her television appearances are numerous and a brief selection includes 'The Cold Equations' episode of *Out Of This World* (1962);

Nigel Kneale's 'The Stone Tape' (1972); *Brideshead Revisited* (1981); 'A Voyage Round My Father' (1982); 'The Mistress' (1987); 'Wish Me Luck' (1990) and *Murder Most Horrid* (1991). This is in addition to appearances in various series such as *The Adventures Of Robin Hood*, *The Adventurer, The Saint* and *The Buccaneers*, plus prestigious productions including the part of Lisle in *The Brothers Karamazov* and Maggie Tulliver in *The Mill On The Floss*.

At the age of twelve she made her stage debut as Alice in *Alice In Wonderland* at the Oxford Playhouse. In 1960 Jane became the youngest actress to play Wendy in a West End stage version of *Peter Pan*. Her stage roles include the Broadway production of *The Philanthropist*, playing Perdita in *A Winter's Tale* and Cassandra in *The Trojan Women*. She also featured in various productions for the Bristol Old Vic, including the title role in *Cleo* by Frank Marcus, the part of Ellen Terry in *Sixty Thousand Nights* and Eliza in *Pygmalion*.

Her other stage work has included *The Things We Do For Love*, *The Shallow End*, *The School for Scandal*, *Henceforward*, *Blithe Spirit*, *Before The Party*, *Whose Life Is It Anyway?*, *To Those Born Later*, *Strawberry Fields*, *Treats*, *Old Flames*, *Look Back in Anger*, *Romeo and Juliet*, *Measure for Measure*, *Great Expectations*, *The Happiest Days of Your Life*, *Will You Walk A little Faster?*, *Making It Better* and *The Things We Do for Love*.

She was seventeen years old when she first met the Beatles on Thursday 18 April 1963. They were appearing on the BBC radio broadcast 'Swingin' Sound' at the Royal Albert Hall. Jane went along to pose for *Radio Times* photographer Tony Aspler who pictured her screaming in the audience. The article appeared in the Thursday 2 May 1963 edition of the *Radio Times* with Jane commenting, 'Now these I could scream for.'

Jane then approached them while they were having a snack in the Royal Court Hotel in Sloane Square, where they were staying. She mentioned to them that she had been asked to write about them in the *Radio Times*. They were aware of her as she'd been a guest panellist on the TV show *Juke Box Jury* and they were all charmed by her.

Brian Epstein returned to his own hotel and Ringo stayed behind to have an early night. Singer Shane Fenton, who'd also been on the concert bill that day, drove John, Paul, George and Jane to journalist Chris Hutchins' flat, situated on the top floor of King's House on the King's Road. Initially, it was George who seemed to engage most of her attention. During the course of the next few hours Paul began to show his interest in Jane and the others left him to talk to her alone. Later he escorted her home and arranged to meet her again.

The romance became public when a photographer snapped them as they left the Prince of Wales Theatre after attending Neil Simon's play *Never Too Late*.

Cynthia Lennon was to comment, 'Paul fell like a ton of bricks for Jane. The first time I was introduced to her was at her home and she was sitting on Paul's knee. My first impression of Jane was how beautiful and finely featured she was. Her mass of Titian-coloured hair cascaded around her face and shoulders, her pale complexion contrasting strongly with dark clothes and shining hair. Paul was obviously as proud as a peacock with his new lady. For Paul, Jane Asher was a great prize.'

Paul moved into the Asher family home at 57 Wimpole Street, a five-storey terraced house. It happened shortly after Paul had missed his last train home to Liverpool following a date with Jane and stayed the night. Margaret Asher suggested that he regard the house as his London home. Paul had shared a flat in Green Street with Ringo and George, but didn't really like it there. He moved into the top floor, where there were two rooms and a bathroom, the second room being Peter's bedroom. Jane and Claire had the two rooms below.

This relationship with an upper middle-class family broadened his cultural horizons. There were stimulating discussions around the Asher family dinner table and the two of them attended musicals, classical concerts, plays and exhibitions and went on holidays together to exotic places. Paul even opened an account at Coutts, the Queen's bankers, and ordered Jane's birthday cake from Maxim's in Paris, while Jane helped Paul select his new car, a midnight blue Aston Martin DB6.

Paul and Jane were seen frequently in public, but it was noted that Paul gravitated to celebrities when he saw them; often forgetting that he was in the company of Jane.

Film producer Walter Shenson was to observe such a situation and commented, 'Paul and Jane came out to a dinner party with my wife and me one night. Joan Sutherland, the opera singer, just happened to be there. Paul zeroed in on her at once as a big star. He left Jane with me and my wife and stayed talking to Joan Sutherland for the rest of the evening.'

The couple went on a number of holidays together. On 16 September 1963 they flew to Greece for a holiday in company with Ringo and Maureen Starr. On 2 May 1964 they flew to St Thomas in the Virgin Islands with Ringo and Maureen. The two of them went on a 10-day holiday to Hammanet in Tunisia on 4 February 1965. On 27 May 1965 they spent a fortnight's holiday in Portugal. On 6 March 1966 they went on holiday to Klosters in Switzerland. On 6 November 1966 the two travelled through France and Spain and then went on to a safari holiday in Kenya. On 22 July 1967 Paul and Jane, together with John, Cynthia and Julian, holidayed in Greece. Jane also accompanied Paul on the trip to India that year where they studied meditation at the Maharishi Mahesh Yogi's ashram.

The young actress became the inspiration for a number of his songs; initially purely love songs, which changed as the relationship entered stormy patches – primarily because she refused to give up her career. 'She Loves You' was written in the music room at Wimpole Street. Songs inspired by Jane included 'And I Love Her', 'Every Little Thing',

'We Can Work It Out', 'You Won't See Me', 'I'm Looking Through You' and 'Here, There And Everywhere'.

The crisis in their relationship arose from the fact that Jane had a successful career, which she was determined to pursue. Paul wanted his girlfriend to dedicate herself to him in the type of relationship common between men and women in working-class Liverpool. However, Jane came from a different world and had her own strong opinions; extending her own horizons as an actress didn't include becoming a subservient woman and sacrificing her career for 'her man'. At one point she refused to answer his telephone calls, which inspired 'You Won't See Me'. Jane was appearing in *Great Expectations* at the Theatre Royal, Bristol, when he recorded the number.

He obviously tried to give messages to her through his songs and told Beatles' biographer Hunter Davies: 'I knew I was selfish, it caused a few rows. Jane went off and said, "OK, then, leave. I'll find someone else." It was shattering to be without her. That was when I wrote "I'm Looking Through You".'

Jane was appearing at the Bristol Old Vic as Barbara Cahoun in John Dighton's *The Happiest Days of Your Life*, when Paul visited Bristol to see her. While there he noticed the name on a shop, *Rigby & Evans Ltd, Wine & Spirit Shippers*, which he says, gave him the surname for the song 'Eleanor Rigby'.

Jane helped Paul to find the five-storey Victorian house in Cavendish Avenue, St John's Wood, which they moved into in 1966. Jane decorated the house and always kept it in tip-top condition. Unfortunately, during a spring-cleaning session a number of original early Lennon and McCartney songs were lost forever when she threw away a notebook full of lyrics while emptying a cupboard.

It was Jane who, in June 1966, persuaded Paul to buy High Farm, a 183-acre farm in Machrihanish, Campbeltown, suggesting it would be a good idea for them to have a remote retreat to which they could escape from the pressures of being constantly in the public eye.

She embarked on a five-month tour of America in 1967, appearing with the Bristol Old Vic in *Romeo and Juliet* in Boston, Washington and Philadelphia. Paul flew over to America to celebrate her twenty-first birthday, which took place during the tour. It was during this trip that he conceived the idea of 'Magical Mystery Tour'.

On her return, Jane said: 'Paul had changed so much. He was on LSD, which I knew nothing about. The house had changed and it was full of stuff I didn't know about.'

The two decided to get married and during an interview in the *Daily Express* in 1967 she said: 'I love Paul. I love him very deeply, and he feels the same. I don't think either of us has looked at anyone else since we first met.' She was to add: 'I want to get married, probably this year, and have lots and lots of babies. I certainly would be surprised indeed if I married anyone but Paul.'

On New Year's Day 1968 he proposed marriage, gave her a diamond and emerald ring and they travelled up north to tell Paul's father.

But the five-year romance came to an abrupt end, despite the fact that they obviously loved each other. Jane had been a virgin when they met and fidelity to a partner obviously meant a great deal to her. On the other hand, Paul had always been a womaniser. During her absences when touring, he had been dating other girls and began an affair with an American, Francie Schwartz.

Jane arrived home unexpectedly when Paul was in bed with Schwartz. She walked out on him and sent her mother to Cavendish Avenue to collect her belongings.

The couple did meet once or twice after the Schwartz incident, but the split was final, although Jane was to say: 'I know it sounds corny, but we still see each other and love each other, but it hasn't worked out. Perhaps we'll be childhood sweethearts and meet again and get married when we're about seventy.'

The day after her mother had collected her belongings from Cavendish Avenue, Paul and Jane were seen in Hyde Park together and on Paul's birthday, 18 June 1968, they attended the opening of a play together. On 7 July the two travelled to north Wales for the wedding of Mike McCartney and Angela Fishwick.

However, on the 20 July edition of the BBC Television show *Dee Time*, Jane announced officially that their engagement was off. She didn't offer an explanation as to why.

At a later time, commenting on the break-up, Paul said, 'We nearly did get married. But it always used to fall short of the mark and something happened. And one of us would think it wasn't right, for which I'm obviously glad now. Jane and I had a long good relationship, I still like her. I don't know whether she likes me, but I don't see any reason why not. We don't see each other at all.'

Jane met political cartoonist Gerald Scarfe at the tenth anniversary party of *Private Eye* in 1970. The two fell in love and their first child Katie was born on 17 April 1974.

Jane appeared in further acting parts, including a TV production of *Romeo and Juliet*. After the birth of Katie, she curtailed her acting career for a while, but appeared in the stage version of *Whose Life Is It Anyway?*

A son Alexander was born in 1981, and Jane and Gerald were married that year. Their third child Rory was born in 1984.

Jane returned to acting in the 1980s with many television appearances. They included the part of Celia Rider opposite Jeremy Irons in *Brideshead Revisited*, with James Fox in 'Love Is Old, Love Is New', a drama about a couple obsessed with the 1960s which featured a lot of Beatles music; and with Laurence Olivier in John Mortimer's 'A Voyage Round My Father'.

Other TV appearances included the costume drama *Hawkmoor* and an episode of *Tales of the Unexpected*. She teamed up with James Fox once again for the film *Runners*, and in 1985 with Ian Holm and Coral Browne in *Dreamchild*.

Jane has written ten books on entertaining, fancy dress and ornate cake decoration and in 1995 launched her own national publication *Jane Asher's Magazine,* at a time when she was regularly featured on television commercials.

Her books include *Jane Asher's Party Cakes* (1984), *Jane Asher's Fancy Dress* (1985), *Silent Nights for You and Your Baby* (1987), *Keep Your Baby Safe* (1988), *Jane Asher's Calendar of Cakes* (1989), *Jane Asher's Eats For Treats* (1990), *Jane Asher's Costume Book* (1991), *The Best of Good Living With Jane Asher: Creative Ideas For Your Family and Home* (1998) and *Jane Asher's World of Cakes* (1998).

She has also provided the narration to a number of audio cassettes, including *The Snow Spider*, *This Rough Magic*, *My Brother Michael*, *Talk of a One-Way Street*, *Past Eight O'Clock*, *Wildfire at Midnight*, *The Ivy Tree*, *Airs Above Ground*, *Enchantment*, *Haphazard House*, *Lizzy & Co* and *The Skull Beneath the Skin*.

The 1990s was the most successful decade of her career. She had her various cake products sold in Sainsbury's supermarkets and also acted as consultant for the company, her kitchen items were available in the do-it-yourself stores, she had a regular TV show of her own on BBC TV called *Good Living*, and her own weekly column in a national newspaper, in addition to appearing in the McVities biscuits, cakes and desserts advertisements on television. In 1998 she had her first two novels published, *The Longing* and *The Question*. Her new book in 1999 *Tricks of the Trade* was based on her *Daily Express* column. The same year her third novel, *Trying to Get Out*, was published.

Jane met Paul again in 1994 for the first time in more than twenty years.

Asher, Margaret Augusta

Jane Asher's mother, who agreed with Jane that they should invite Paul to use their Wimpole Street home as his residence when in London. He then moved into the Georgian town house in November 1963.

Her father was the Hon. Edward Granville Eliot and she had played in a number of orchestras as an oboist before leaving to raise her children.

Later, she became a music teacher at the Guildhall School of Music, with George Martin as one of her pupils. She also found someone from the Guildhall School of Music to give Paul piano lessons.

In the basement of the house, Margaret also had her own music room with an upright piano in it. 'Eleanor Rigby' was one of the numbers Paul composed on the piano in the room. He also wrote 'Yesterday' during the time he was at the Wimpole Street house and Margaret Asher used the number as a test piece for her students.

She also taught Paul to play the recorder.

Asher, Peter

Jane Asher's brother, he was born in London on 2 June 1944. Margaret Asher had taken all her children to an acting agent and at the age of eight Peter appeared in the film *The Planter's Wife* with Jack Hawkins and Claudette Colburn and *Isn't Life Wonderful?* It was whilst attending Westminster School that he first met Gordon Waller and as the two sang and played guitar, they decided to team up, with their heroes being artists such as the Everly Brothers.

Paul had originally played Peter an uncompleted song 'World Without Love', which he was going to offer to Billy J Kramer. Kramer didn't think it was suitable for him and it wasn't suitable for the Beatles, at least as far as John Lennon was concerned. When Peter & Gordon were offered their EMI recording contract, Peter asked Paul if he could complete the song for them, so he wrote the bridge to the number, which hadn't had one before.

Normal Newall produced the record for them and it topped the British charts.

Peter & Gordon then went on to record two further compositions by Paul, both in 1964: 'Nobody I Know' and 'I Don't Want To See You Again'.

The next composition that Paul wrote for Peter and Gordon was called 'Woman'. Paul asked them if, as an experiment, they could put the record out without saying that he wrote it, so they put it out crediting the writing of the song to Bernard Webb.

Peter & Gordon eventually decided to split up. Gordon was more of a lead singer and Peter felt he was more of a harmony singer, so Gordon was interested in making some records of his own.

Together with John Dunbar and Barry Miles, Peter launched a bookshop and gallery called Indica, which received support from Paul.

Peter was appointed head of A&R at Apple Records and signed up James Taylor.

When Paul signed Mary Hopkin and was putting the session together for 'Those Were The Days', Peter recommended an arranger, Richard Hewson, to Paul and he was hired to arrange the number.

The first record Peter actually produced was a single for Paul Jones called 'And The Sun Will Shine'. The Bee Gees wrote it, Paul McCartney played drums, Paul Samwell-Smith of the Yardbirds played bass, Jeff Beck played guitar and Nicky Hopkins piano.

Following Jane Asher's announcement on the TV programme *Dee Time* that she and Paul had split up, it was said that a furious Paul entered Apple offices the next day and demanded that Peter be given the sack. Ron Kass managed to talk him out of it.

However, Asher resigned from Apple during the Allen Klein regime as he felt that James Taylor wasn't receiving enough promotion and his latest signing, Mortimer, weren't even getting a record released. For a time he joined Ron Kass in the A&R Department of MGM Records, and then went to New York with James Taylor and became his manager. He also went on to manage Linda Rondstadt.

He has since won two 'Producer Of The Year' Grammies.

Asimov, Isaac

The world's most prolific science-fiction author, with over two hundred books to his credit. In one of them, the second volume of his autobiography, he describes how he met Paul McCartney in December 1974. Paul had been toying with an idea of a science-fiction film using Wings and had worked out a rough outline about a terrestrial pop group being replaced by alien imposters. He asked Asimov if he would write a story that would be suitable for a screenplay based on the idea. Asimov obliged and Paul paid him. However, Paul wasn't too happy with the rough draft and decided not to use it. He then asked Asimov if he could develop the idea from a piece of dialogue that he'd written himself, but the author declined.

Aspel And Company

A chat-show series produced by London Weekend Television which was first aired in 1984.

Paul was a guest on the first show, broadcast on Saturday 9 June. He discussed several subjects with host Michael Aspel, including the origin of his 'Picasso's Last Words' song. 'I met Dustin Hoffman and he said could you just write them (songs) like that? He threw me a copy of a magazine story on Picasso the night before his death, and I wrote this song which went on the *Band On the Run* album.'

Aspel asked Paul if he still had an incentive to write songs these days. Paul answered, 'It's just that I like it. I like to sit down with a piano and guitar and just try to write a song.'

Discussing inspiration, he said, 'I just kind of make it up. "Michelle" – I've never met her. I make it up, that's how I write. George Harrison couldn't understand that.'

He discussed his children: 'When I ask them what they think of my music and they tell me they like it, I think it's because they want to stay up late.'

He also commented: 'At home I'm not famous, I'm just Dad,' citing as an example an incident when one of his children turned round to him in Scotland and said, 'Are you Paul McCartney?'

Paul then plugged a contest in which viewers were invited to send in a painting of Buddy Holly to tie in with his 1984 Buddy Holly week. He then sang Holly's 'That'll Be The Day' with Tracey Ullman (also a guest) and Michael Aspel.

Astaire, Fred

A Hollywood singer/dancer, star of films such as *Funny Face* and *Top Hat* who was an inspiration to Paul in his youth. Paul dedicated his song 'You Gave Me The Answer' to Fred Astaire when he performed it on the Wings world tour during 1975/76.

Astaire was also one of the figures featured on the cover of the *Sgt Pepper* album.

Atlantic Ocean
A number recorded at Paul's home studio on Tuesday 10 March 1987, produced by Phil Ramone. Musicians on the track included Phil Picket on keyboards, Louis Jardim on percussion, Stuart Elliott on drums and Martin Barre on guitar. Paul played keyboards, bass and electric guitar. The number finally surfaced as the flipside of the British CD2 'Young Boy' single, issued in 1997. The dance track was also aired on the first programme in the *Oboojoobu* radio series.

Atlantis
A single by Donovan, produced by Mickie Most and issued on Pye 7N17660 on 22 November 1968. Paul played tambourine and also provided some backing vocals on the track.

Attention
A number by Paul, 3 minutes and 23 seconds in length, which he wrote and produced for Ringo for his *Stop And Smell The Roses* album, released in 1981.

The number features Ringo on lead vocal and drums, Paul on bass, piano and background vocals, Linda McCartney, Sheila Casey and Lezlee Livrano Pariser on background vocals, Howie Casey on sax and Laurence Juber on acoustic guitar and electric guitar.

Autodromo Hermanos Rodriquez
A racetrack in Mexico City where Paul appeared for two concerts as part of his New World tour in 1993, attracting capacity crowds of more than 50,000 at each event. The Thursday 25 November concert drew an audience of 52,122. Despite the demeanour of the audience, there were armed guards with automatic weapons, police in full riot gear and security personnel with nightsticks. There were also around seventy unauthorised dealers selling merchandise outside the track. Paul greeted the audience in Spanish with the words '*Hola Mexico, hablo poco Espanol. Estamos contentos de estar en Mexico*,' which means, 'Hello Mexico, I speak a little bit of Spanish. We are very happy to be in Mexico.'

On the afternoon of the second show on Saturday 27 November, the soundcheck jam included the numbers 'A Fine Day', 'Summertime', 'Just Because', 'Be-Bop-A-Lula', 'Honey Don't', 'Every Night', 'All My Trials', 'C Moon', 'Don't Let The Sun Catch You Crying', 'The Long And Winding Road', 'Ain't That A Shame', 'Get Out Of My Way' and 'Twenty Flight Rock'.

During the evening show there was a delay of 40 minutes due to technical problems and prior to performing 'Hey Jude', Paul played '*El Jarage Tapatio*', a Mexican mariachi song.

Average Person

A number by Paul lasting 3 minutes and 34 seconds which was included as a track on the *Pipes Of Peace* album.

Awards

1966: Along with John Lennon, Paul received the Grammy 'Song Of The Year' Award for Paul's composition 'Michelle'.

1966: Paul received a Grammy for 'Best Contemporary (Rock and Roll) Solo Vocal Performance, Male or Female' for 'Eleanor Rigby'.

1967: Paul received an Ivor Novello Award for his composition 'Love In The Open Air', featured in the film *The Family Way* which was voted 'Best Instrumental Theme'.

1973: Paul received a Grammy for 'Best Pop Vocal Performance By a Duo, Group or Chorus' for 'Band On The Run'.

1973: He received a Grammy for 'Best Arrangement Accompanying Vocalist(s)' for 'Uncle Albert/Admiral Halsey'.

1977: He received an Ivor Novello Award for 'Best Selling Single Ever In The UK' for 'Mull Of Kintyre'.

1979: He received a special Ivor Novello Award for 'Outstanding Services to Music'.

1980: Paul was presented with the 'Ivor Novello Special Award For International Achievement' by actor Yul Brynner at a luncheon at the Grosvenor House Hotel in London on Friday 9 May 1980.

1980: Paul received the 'Outstanding Music Personality Of 1979' award at the Café Royal, London during the 'British Rock And Pop Awards'. Pauline McLeod of the *Daily Mirror* presents him with the award, which is the result of votes from *Daily Mirror* readers, listeners to Radio One and viewers of the *Nationwide* TV programme.

1981: He received the prestigious 'International Music Achievement Award' from the Songwriters' Hall of Fame in America.

1982: He received a BPI Award for 'Best British Male Vocalist – Outstanding Contribution to Music' for *Tug Of War*.

1983: On Thursday 10 February Paul attended the British Phonographic Institute annual dinner at the Grosvenor House Hotel where he was presented with a Brit Award as 'Best British Male Artist Of 1982' by George Martin.

1983: On Thursday 5 May 'Ebony And Ivory' was voted 'International Hit Of the Year' at the Ivor Novello Awards ceremony.

1984: On Tuesday 13 March Paul received an Ivor Novello Award for 'We All Stand Together', voted the 'Best Film Theme Song'. (George Martin accepted this on Paul's behalf as Paul couldn't attend the ceremony due to Linda having tonsillitis.)

1985: 'Say Say Say', the number written by Paul and Michael Jackson received a citation at the second annual ASCAP Pop Awards in Beverly Hills, California as one of the five most performed songs in America during 1984.

1986: Paul was awarded a special 'Award of Merit' at the 13th annual American Music Awards. They were held at the Shrine Auditorium in Los Angeles on 27 January 1986. Paul was unable to attend in person but received the award at the Hippodrome in London where he appeared on a live satellite link-up with the Shrine.

1986: On 28 May Paul received an award from ASCAP, the American publishing agency, for 'No More Lonely Nights' as the most performed song of the year from 1 October 1984 to 20 September 1985. As he was unable to attend the ceremony in Los Angeles, Hal David accepted the award on his behalf.

1986: On 16 October Paul received the 'Best Selling Video of the Year' award for 'Rupert And The Frog Song' at the British Video Awards ceremony at the Grosvenor House Hotel, London. David Steel, leader of the Liberal Party, presented him with the award.

1986: On 20 November Paul and Linda attended a reception in Munich, Germany where, at the annual 'Bambi' awards, Paul received the title 'Personality Of The Year' and was presented with his trophy by West German football manager Franz Beckenbauer.

1988: He was inducted into the Rock And Roll Hall Of Fame as a member of the Beatles.

1988: On 24 June he received the Silver Clef Award at the annual luncheon in aid of the Nordoff-Robbins Music Therapy Centre, which took place at the Inter-Continental Hotel in London. The award was for 'Outstanding Achievement in the World of British Music'. (Paul paid $32,000 for a guitar autographed by the Everly Brothers and David Bowie and then gave it back to be re-auctioned.)

1988: Paul attended the Brighton Centre in East Sussex on Tuesday 12 July to receive the title of Doctor of the University from the University of Sussex.

1989: The Performing Rights Society threw a special luncheon at London's Claridge's Hotel on Tuesday 19 December in honour of Paul, presenting him with a 'Unique Achievement Award' – the first time they had honoured an individual member in this way.

1990: On Wednesday 21 February actress Meryl Streep presented him with a Lifetime Achievement Grammy Award.

1990: On 12 December Paul received the Q Merit Award for his outstanding and continued contribution to the music industry in the first presentation of awards by Q magazine, held at Ronnie Scott's nightclub in London.

1991: On 12 June he received the 'Tour Of the Year' award at the International Rock Awards in a ceremony held at the London Arena.

1992: On Monday 18 May Paul became the world's first recipient of 'The Polar Music Prize' from the Royal Swedish Academy of Music. This was in recognition of his 'creativity and imagination as a composer and artist who has revitalised popular music worldwide over the past thirty years'. King Carl Gustaf of Sweden made the award. The honour came with a gift of one million Swedish kronor (around £110,000 sterling) that Paul announced he would give to two projects, the Liverpool Institute of Performing Arts and the campaign to save the Rye Memorial Hospital in Sussex.

1993: In November the US Broadcast Music Inc and the British Performing Rights Society made an award to Paul at the Dorchester Hotel in London. One was for 'Yesterday' with six million broadcasts making it the most performed song ever on American radio and television. 'I Saw Her Standing There' was also acknowledged with two million plays and 'A Hard Day's Night' with one million broadcasts.

1994: On 12 March Paul received the Doris Day award at Century City, California due to his number about animal rights called 'Looking For Changes'. Writing the song was said to have 'showed courage, creativity and integrity'.

1995: On 8 November Prince Charles, president of the Royal College of Music, presented Paul with a Fellowship of the College, their highest award. Paul was to say, 'For a street arab from Liverpool it isn't that bad at all.'

1996: Queen Elizabeth II knighted him. At the Palace he said, 'This brings back memories of 1965. It seems strange being here without the other three.'

1997: Paul received a Lifetime Award from 'Scouseology', an organisation recognising achievements of Merseyside people. The event took place at Liverpool Town Hall. Paul wasn't able to attend the event but sent a fax thanking his 'fellow wackers'.

1997: HMV presented Paul with a Composer of the Century award on Thursday 16 October.

1997: At the Q magazine awards at Park Lane Hotel, London on 4 November, Paul was presented with the 'Best Songwriter Award' for *Flaming Pie*.

1998: Paul was awarded the John Moore's University fellowship for his outstanding achievements and significant contribution to public life.

1999: He was inducted into the Rock And Roll Hall Of Fame as a Solo Artist.

2000: In May, at the Ivor Novello Awards, Paul was given a fellowship by the British Academy of Songwriters, Composers and Authors. The Academy's chairman Guy Fletcher presented the award to Paul. Before an audience that included the Pet Shop Boys, Elton John and Travis, Paul told of his feelings when watching Mozart create music in the film *Amadeus*. 'I remember tears welling up and thinking, "I'm one of them, I'm in that tradition." Maybe not like Mozart, but I'm in that tradition. Everyone who's had a hit is so proud to be a part of it.'

2000: In September Paul received a lifetime achievement award as 'Man Of The Year' from GQ magazine at the Royal Opera House, London. Paul said, 'It's a bit like getting an old git's prize. I was going to say that in my speech, but I didn't think it would have gone down too well.'

2001: On 8 September at the PETA Gala at the Waldorf-Astoria, New York, Paul was presented with a humanitarian award. He said, 'I share this with Linda.'

2001: On 3 November at the Men's World Day Gala 2001 at the Hofburg Palace, Vienna, Paul was presented with an award by former Soviet president Mikhail Gorbachev.

2002: On 11 January Paul was joint winner of the 'Best Song' award at the 7th annual Critics Choice Awards, hosted by Bill Maher in Beverly Hills. He won the award with his theme for 'Vanilla Sky' and the award was shared with Enya.

2002: On Friday 28 January at the 5th annual Media Spotlight Awards in New York on the 40th anniversary of Amnesty International, Amnesty International USA awarded Paul a lifetime achievement award.

Baby Face
Number which closed the unreleased MPL film *One Hand Clapping*. It was recorded at the Sea Saint Studios in 1975 with Paul and the Young Tuxedo Brass Band who comprised Frank Naundorf on trombone, Greg Stafford on trumpet, Ted Reilly on trumpet, Walter Payton on sousaphone, Herman Sherman on alto sax, Joe Torregano on clarinet, Emile Knox on bass drum and Laurence Trotter on snare drum.

Baby Make Love To You
A home recording which Paul made in the summer of 1980.

Baby You're A Rich Man
A song issued as the flipside of 'All You Need Is Love' and which had a similar genesis to 'A Day In The Life'.

Two separate songs, one by John, one by Paul, were fused together. The number penned by John had been called 'One Of The Beautiful People' and the song by Paul, 'Baby, You're A Rich Man'. It was said that the numbers had been merged to provide a song for the *Yellow Submarine* film, but was then rushed out as the B-side to a single. The song is, in fact, heard only in part in *Yellow Submarine*.

Baby, The
Nickname that the 'Exis' (Existentialists) gave to Paul during the Beatles' first trip to Hamburg. The 'Exis' were the students who attended their gigs and who included Astrid Kirchherr and Klaus Voormann. They called George 'the Beautiful One' and John 'The Sidie Man'. Paul says that the 'Exis' liked Stuart (Sutcliffe) the most, with John second, George third, himself fourth and Pete Best fifth.

Baby's Request

A number that Paul wrote specially for the veteran vocal group the Mills Brothers, who he'd met backstage following their performance when he attended one of their shows while on holiday in France. He made a demo disc of the number but when he offered it to them, the Mills Brothers said they wanted him to pay them for recording it, so he included the demo on his *Back To The Egg* album instead.

The Mills Brothers had three basic members, Harry Mills, born in 1913, Herbert Mills, born in 1912 and Donald Mills, born in 1915. John Mills Jr, born in 1889 also performed with them, playing guitar. When John died in 1935 the brothers' father John Mills Sr joined them, in addition to guitarist Bernard Addison. When their father retired the brothers continued as a trio and when Harry died in 1962 the others continued with another singer. They had numerous hits, including 'You Rascal, You', 'You Always Hurt The One You Love', and 'I've Got My Love To Keep Me Warm'.

'Baby's Request' was the last track on the *Back To The Egg* album and the number was also issued as a double A-side single with 'Getting Closer' on Friday 10 August 1979 on Parlophone R6027. Its highest position in Britain was at No. 60 in the BMRB charts.

'Baby's Request', a two-and-a-half minute track, was one of the songs used in the *Band On The Run* promotional video.

Back In The Sunshine

A track on the *Driving Rain* album. It lasts for 4 minutes and 21 seconds. The number was recorded on 28 February 2001 and David Leonard mixed the track.

Paul had written it in Arizona five years previously with the help of his son James, who contributed to the riff and the bridge. James also played rhythm guitar on the track.

Back In The USSR

Paul originally wrote this song for a television documentary about Twiggy that didn't come off. It was a fusion of Beach Boys style with a little bit of Chuck Berry's Back In The USA thrown in. As Twiggy didn't use the number, it was used to open *The Beatles* White Album. Paul handled the lead guitar honours on the track while John and George played bass. Ringo was absent from the track as he'd left the group for several days, frustrated at the arguments which occurred during the making of the album.

The number also appears on *The Beatles 1967–1970* album, the 1980 *Rock And Roll Music* compilation and on *The Beatles Box* set.

Paul's brother Mike at one time suggested that they get the Beach Boys to sing the middle section of the song, but the idea was rejected.

Paul was to comment, 'This just, sort of, came. Chuck Berry once did a song called "Back In The USA", which is very American, very

Chuck Berry, you know. He was "serving in the army and, when I get back home, I'm gonna kiss the ground," you know, "can't wait to get back to the States". It's very much an American thing, I always thought. So, this one, "Back In The USSR", was about, in my mind, a spy who has been in America for a long, long time. Some fellow who's been in America for a long time and he's picked up and he's very American, but he gets back to the USSR, and he's, sort of, saying "Leave it till tomorrow, honey to disconnect the phone", and "come here, honey", with Russian women, and all that. It concerns the attributes of Russian women, a sole element created by George's guitar and heavy bass.'

A version of this number lasting 3 minutes and 16 seconds was included on the *Tripping The Live Fantastic* album. It was recorded live at the Tokyo Dome, Tokyo, Japan on 5 March 1990 during the 1989/90 World Tour.

Back Off Bugaloo
A single by Ringo Starr issued in the UK and US in March 1972. It was rumoured that 'Bugaloo' was a nickname the other Beatles had given to Paul, but Ringo said that the name was influenced by Marc Bolan who Ringo was currently directing a film about.

Back On My Feet
A song co-written by Paul and Elvis Costello and produced by Phil Ramone at Paul's home studio in Rye in June 1987.

Back Seat Of My Car, The
The closing track on the *Ram* album, which was also issued as a single in Britain on Apple R5914 on Friday 13 August 1971 with the credit 'Paul and Linda McCartney'. Paul had actually written the song prior to January 1969 and was seen rehearsing it on 14 January 1969 during the filming of *Get Back* at Twickenham Studios.

'Heart Of The Country' was the flip.

The record failed to make as much impact as Paul's previous single 'Another Day', issued earlier that year, only reaching No. 39 in the British charts, and thus not even registering in a number of the music papers, which only carried a Top 30 chart at the time.

It wasn't issued in America.

Back To The Egg (album)
An album produced during 1978 and 1979 by Paul and Chris Thomas at several locations, including the Spirit of Ranachan Studio in Scotland between 29 June and 27 July, Lympne Castle in Kent from 11–20 September and the Replica Studios and EMI Studios in London in November and December. The master tape was completed on 1 April 1979.

The engineer on the session was Phil McDonald, assisted by Mark Vigars. It was released in 1979, in Britain on Parlophone/MPL PCTC 257 on 8 June and in America on Columbia FC 36057 on 24 May, the first Wings album to be issued on that label. *Back To The Egg* reached No. 4 in Britain and No. 8 in America.

A special half-hour promotional video was made to accompany the album. The album cover featured a fantasy scene, designed by Hipgnosis and depicting Wings in a small living room peering at a space in the floor through which the planet Earth could be seen hovering.

The album featured two tracks from the supergroup Rockestra: 'Rockestra Theme' and 'So Glad To See You Here'. The other tracks were: Side One: 'Reception', 'Getting Closer', 'We're Open Tonight', 'Spin It On', 'Again And Again And Again', 'Old Siam Sir' and 'Arrow Through Me'. Side Two: 'To You', 'After The Ball', 'Million Miles', 'Winter Rose', 'Love Awake', 'The Broadcast' and 'Baby's Request'.

Back To The Egg (TV special)
A 31-minute special which was videotaped between Monday 4 June and Wednesday 13 June 1979. It included promotional film clips for 'Getting Closer', 'Baby's Request', 'Old Siam Sir', 'Winter Rose', 'Love Awake', 'Spin It On', 'Again And Again', 'Arrow Through Me' and 'Goodnight Tonight'. It was syndicated in America during November and December 1979 and screened in Britain on BBC 1 on Wednesday 10 June 1981.

Backyard, The
A film of Paul playing old rock 'n' roll standards on an acoustic guitar, clips of which were originally intended to be included in the documentary short 'One Hand Clapping,' but weren't used. The MPL film of Paul, given the name *The Backyard*, was made in August 1974 but never shown.

The 9-minute short, directed by David Litchfield, showed Paul sitting on a stool in the back gardens of Abbey Road Studios with a couple of mikes in front of him, running through numbers such as 'Twenty Flight Rock', 'Sweet Little Sixteen', 'I'm Gonna Love You Too' and 'Peggy Sue' on acoustic guitar. He also performs an unreleased track called 'Blackpool'. Numbers filmed which ended up on the cutting-room floor were 'Blackbird', 'Country Dreamer', 'Loving You', 'We're Gonna Move' and 'Blue Moon Of Kentucky'. Clips were included in the MPL/BBC TV special 'McCartney' in 1986.

Badfinger
A group who were to become the most successful group on the Apple label, next to the Beatles.

They were originally called the Iveys and were managed by Bill

Collins, father of actor Lewis Collins, who had once worked with Mike McCartney in a Liverpool hairdressing salon. Bill had also known Paul's father Jim McCartney from the days he played in dance bands in Liverpool. Mal Evans, who also knew Collins, invited him to a Beatles recording session for 'Within You, Without You'. At Abbey Road Studios, Collins met Paul and told him about his group the Iveys. Paul said he'd be interested in hearing more about them.

Collins didn't follow through on the invitation. However, when Evans heard that the group wrote their own music he took a tape of them to Apple.

They comprised two members from Liverpool and two from Wales and the line-up at the time was: Pete Ham, vocalist, guitarist, pianist; Tom Evans, rhythm guitarist; Mike Gibbons, bass guitarist and Ron Griffiths on drums.

Mike Berry, who had recently joined Apple Publishing from Sparta Music, actually knew the group and had wanted to sign them to Sparta the previous year. He said, 'I remember telling my Apple publishing partner, Terry Doran, that the Iveys were going to be our first signing. I had actually given Paul McCartney my personal Iveys demo tape, but Paul said he didn't see anything in it. I'd planned to get him another one in the near future.'

Evans brought in the new tape and played it to Paul, Derek Taylor and Peter Asher.

Paul phoned Berry and said, 'Have you heard the new Iveys tape? It's fucking great.' Mike said, 'That's the sign of a good publisher, Paul. To see it before anyone else does.'

Paul had been impressed by a number called 'Knocking Down Our Home' and wanted to hear more of their work, so another demo reel was brought in. There were a few problems. Each Apple signing had to be approved by all four members of the Beatles, although Paul had managed to get Mary Hopkin signed, George had decided to sign up Jackie Lomax and Peter Asher was determined to sign James Taylor – all without necessarily having all four Beatles agree. Asher was to say, 'John Lennon was scathing about everybody. He would say "Who needs James Taylor or the Iveys when you have true artists like Yoko Ono?"'

Mal Evans was determined to secure a contract for them with Apple and brought in a fourth tape and on 23 July 1968 they signed to the label and made their debut with a Tom Evans composition 'Maybe Tomorrow'.

In the meantime, Paul had been asked to write the score for a film *The Magic Christian* which starred Peter Sellers and Ringo Starr.

At the time the Beatles were busy recording *Abbey Road*. He arranged a meeting with the Iveys saying that he had been asked to write the music for the film and was willing to give them a song he had written for it for them to record. The number was 'Come And Get It' and Paul made a demo of the number for them to listen to and he recorded them performing it. He then asked them to take over the assignment for *The Magic Christian* and write the other numbers themselves – and he also recorded them in the studio, advising them and playing some of the instruments. One of the numbers, 'Crimson Ship', contained references to Paul and the Beatles.

Prior to the release it was felt that the Iveys had become too associated with the Merseyside scene and a new name was sought. They thought of names such as Hyena's Nose, the Old, the Glass Onion and Fresh, while Paul suggested Home and John Lennon suggested Prix.

Eventually, Mal Evans remembered 'Badfinger Boogie', a working title for Paul's composition 'With A Little Help From My Friends' and the group were dubbed Badfinger.

Gibbons had left the band, so Evans then took over on bass. They had to find a replacement. The members wanted Scottish guitarist Hamish Stuart of Marmalade to join them and Stuart was interested, but his manager insisted that they would have to pay £10,000 if he was to leave Marmalade, so they looked elsewhere and eventually settled on another Liverpool guitarist, Joey Molland.

Many years later, Hamish Stuart was to join Paul's band.

Despite the success of their hits 'Come And Get It', 'No Matter What', 'Day After Day' and 'Baby Blue', Apple were encountering problems with the advent of Allen Klein. Paul was absent from the offices and had gone to Scotland where he was to begin recording his solo album; Peter Asher left the company, as did his signing James Taylor. Mary Hopkin was also to leave Apple.

On leaving Apple, Badfinger suffered immense financial difficulties, despite writing the international hit 'Without You' and both Pete Ham and Tom Evans were to hang themselves.

Bag O' Nails Club

A club opened on Thursday 24 November 1966 by John Gunnell and Lawrie Leslie at 9 Kingley Street, London. It was here that Francie Schwartz headed for when she arrived in England. She met Mike McCartney at the club and was soon involved in an affair with Paul. It was here that Paul was first introduced to Linda Eastman on the evening of Monday 15 May 1967 during a performance by Georgie Fame & the Blue Flames.

Baker, Celia

A clothes designer who, together with Tony Walker, made and designed the costumes for Wings' first major tour. The only stipulation they were given was that both Paul and Linda wanted the costumes to be in the same colours as those featured on the *Venus and Mars* album sleeve: red, yellow, black and white. Celia and Tony had three weeks in which to complete the entire project.

Baker, Geoff
Paul's long-standing press officer. He was formerly a show business writer for the *Daily Star* and became Paul's press agent at the close of the 1980s after writing a piece about Paul and Linda, which Paul liked.

Bakewell, Gary
The actor who portrayed Paul in the film *Backbeat*. He was also to appear as Paul in the CBS drama 'The Linda McCartney Story' in 2000.

Ballad of James Paul McCartney, The
A track written and recorded by David Peel and featured on his album *Bring Back The Beatles*, issued in America on Orange 004 in 1977.

Ballad of John and Yoko, The
A Beatles single on which only John and Paul appear. On Monday 14 April 1969 John brought the number around to Paul's house in Cavendish Avenue for him to aid in its completion. They finished it quite quickly and then went round to nearby Abbey Road Studios to record it.

At the time Ringo was filming *The Magic Christian* and George was out of the country, but John was in such a hurry to get it recorded that only the two of them appear on the recording.

Paul provided the bass, piano, maracas and drumming sounds.

It was released in Britain on Friday 30 May on Parlophone R 5786 and in America on Apple 2531 on 4 June.

Ballad of Paul
A record by the group Mystery Tour with 'Ballad Of Paul (Follow The Bouncing Ball)' on the flipside. A novelty disc issued on MGM 14097 in 1969.

Ballad of The Skeletons, The
A political poem by Allen Ginsberg, which was set to music. Recording began at Kampo Studios in Greenwich Village, New York when the initial track was cut with Ginsberg and guitarists Mark Ribot and David Mansfield. Lenny Kaye produced it. The tapes were then sent on to Paul McCartney in Britain and Paul added organ, drums and maracas. Then he returned the tapes to America where Philip Glass added further keyboard overdubs.

Executive producer of the project was David Silver, who commented that 'The Ballad of the Skeletons' was: 'a funny, but trenchant political poem, which surveys the US political scene taking a satirical swipe at its hypocrisies'. He also said, 'Paul did a beautiful job. He was wonderful, especially in terms of the priority he gave it.'

When Ginsberg premiered the poem at 'The Return of Forgotten

Poetry' event at the Royal Albert Hall on Monday 16 October 1995, Paul joined him onstage and played electric guitar while Ginsberg recited the poem.

The single was issued in America on Mouth Almighty 697 120 101-2, an imprint of Mercury Records.

Ginsberg died on Saturday 5 April 1997. He was seventy years old.

Band On The Run (12″)

A 12″ interview disc to promote the album was distributed to radio stations in America in 1973. It was an open-end interview, in which local disc jockeys could ask the questions themselves and play Paul's answers on the disc.

The record was sent with a script enclosed. Fred Robbins conducted the interview during Wings' British tour on Monday 9 July 1973.

What follows is a transcript of part of the interview disc, indicating the scripted questions and Paul's reply:

Question: Hi! This is (disc jockey's name) and guess who's our special guest? Paul McCartney and his wife Linda! That's right, and they've got a great new album with their band Wings called *Band On The Run* on Capitol Records. We'll be playing some of the tracks and rapping with Paul and Linda by way of a pre-taped interview recorded while they were on tour in Leicester, England.

I understand when you started Wings you went around like wandering minstrels and played wherever you could, in various towns and colleges. What was behind that strategy?

Paul: Just that I like being in a band, you know? I don't like being out of work, and, in a way, when you're just recording, you can get to feel a bit out of work. You like to have a strum and sing. So that's the main reason behind it.

We had to do it that way because we're a totally new band. We've never played anywhere before, so we couldn't just do big dates and say, 'Hello folks! Here we are, without ever having played together before!' so we chose a few dates that were a surprise to get us worked in.

Question: How did you arrange to play in each place?

Paul: We did a little tour. The first little thing we did, we were in Britain and we went up the motorway. We headed for the nearest nice-sounding town, we didn't book any hotels or any halls or anything. We ended up in Nottingham University and we just said to them, 'OK if we play here tomorrow?' And they kind of put the word round and said, 'Yeah, OK.' So we turned up and played. It was like a kind of little college dance.

Question: No admission charge?

Paul: Oh yeah, 50p. Very reasonable. We actually handled the whole thing ourselves from a mini-van. We just turned up and said

'OK, we're here, we'd like to play, we wanna play our band in, would you like to listen to us while we do it? We don't wanna make too big a deal of this, but, you know, it's only 50p.'

Question: Did you enjoy ad-libbing your way around like that, Linda?

Linda: Oh yeah, very much. It's great. It's good to do that. But I like the other ones, well, where the audience is expecting you.

Question: What a contrast to the frenzied arrivals in town by the Beatles! It's like starting all over again!

Paul: It really is starting all over again. We just all enjoy the idea of being in a band. So here we go lads, one, two, three, off we go!

Question: What had to happen in your own life before you were ready to organise a new band?

Paul: I don't know, really. We had some business problems, you know, and I was getting sick of those. I thought, 'Well, it's not really my gig to go worrying about all the business, I'd rather just play and sing.' So that was it. I thought, 'I'm gonna get back to that, then. Let the business things sort themselves out.' Which they look like they might be going to do.

Question: Did you have any preconceived ideas of what you wanted Wings to sound like, or was it an experimental affair?

Paul: Sort of experimental, yeah. I knew that the people I was getting together had a lot of potential, and we needed to work together and see if we liked each other, and see if we could get on. It's coming together very well, considering. I mean, with the Beatles you couldn't say what the sound was. The press said it was Mersey Beat or whatever, you know. I knew roughly what I wanted – just a rock 'n' roll band, that'll do me.

Question: Did you want to approximate the Beatle sound, or get as far away from that as possible?

Paul: Neither ... I don't mind if it gets near it. They were a pretty good band. But if it gets miles away from it, there are a lot of other good bands that don't sound like the Beatles. We're just aiming to be what we are, which is what any band anywhere wants to be. It's what the Beatles wanted to be.

Question: Linda, isn't it rough for a girl to go on the road, even though she's with her husband?

Linda: So far, no. I like being in a band. I like it all, really. I like playing the best, being on stage, and being with an audience who enjoy it.

Paul: We were up in Scotland and I was saying to Linda, 'Look, we were thinking of going back on the road. Do you think you could kind of enjoy it? There's that feeling when you're behind a curtain waiting to go on, you get that kind of terrible nerves. Once you get on you get the feel of an audience behind you. Do you think you can enjoy all of that?' She's like, 'Sure, show me the curtain!'

Question: It seems that a musical career has been thrust upon you, Linda!

Linda: It has, yeah. I'm just one of the members, though – there's not too much pressure on me. I don't get out and sing main vocal, or anything.

Paul: She's my wife, as you might know, but the thing is that we don't try and play her up as a big member of the band. As you say, she's kind of had it thrust upon her, but the stuff she does is great. It's a bit like Johnny Cash working with June Carter, and June kind of walks over and sings back-up with the Carter Family. She does her own little bit and stuff, but it isn't a big heavy Johnny and June Carter show, it's mainly 'Johnny Cash, ladies and gentlemen'.

Question: Was it always intended, Linda, that you'd be part of any new group Paul would organise?

Linda: Yeah, I'd say so. Just sing harmonies and play a bit of keyboard.

Paul: That's how it started, you know. It started off just as a kind of loon. We were just thinking, 'OK, let's go and make a record. Would you like to sing some harmonies, Linda?' That's how it started off, but it worked itself into a band. So we're just taking it from there and seeing how it goes.

Question: You reached such heights with the Beatles, so is it part of your plan to shoot for the same level of success with Wings?

Paul: No, not really. That's the obvious thing that people will think. But as I say, the main reason everyone's in the band is just to be in a band. All the other things are incidental.

We played Glasgow and got a ridiculous welcome there, and it was really a bit like the Beatles, you know? It was ridiculous, there were police outside and crowds and stuff, the whole bit – in some places you go, it really is like that. But we're just as pleased if the audience in the hall that night just enjoyed it. If they don't enjoy it then we'll be disappointed. But if they like it, it doesn't really matter if it's a pub in the King's Road or Madison Square Gardens to us, you know.

Question: Paul, I suppose you realise that your fans expect you to be as good as you were before . . .

Paul: People do come along kind of thinking that, but that's one of those things, you know. Let them think it. We won't bother about it, we'll just get on playing. And if we start to come together well, and do some great tracks, then we'll just kinda see how we go. Our records sell very well worldwide, so it's not even a kind of comeback. For me, it's like a continuation. If it's as good as the Beatles, then great, obviously. If it isn't, well, hopefully it's as good in another field.

Question: Isn't it amazing, Paul, how well each of you has done on his own since the break-up – when everyone was wondering whether you would be able to get along without each other?

Paul: That's it, you know. A thing can't go on in one form forever. Things are always changing. With the Beatles, it was one of those things, it had to finish, almost. That was then. As you say, everyone's got on with a new type of thing. It's interesting, to say the least.

Question: Do you find more freedom in being able to write on your own now, without needing to collaborate?

Paul: No, I don't think there's any more freedom. It's different, there's no getting away from that, and in fact, I wouldn't like to get away from that. I don't think I'd like to be the Beatles all over again, I don't think there's any point to that.

Question: But you probably wouldn't have written these songs, or recorded several sides in Lagos, if you had still been part of the Beatles. These songs could only have happened on your own, couldn't they?

Paul: Well I suppose so, but you never can tell. I take it myself much more simply, as I say. I just wake up each morning and think, 'Ah, I'm alive. Great! What do we do today?' If I got into all the implications and all the ifs and buts . . . when the Beatles were around, you never caught the Beatles analysing it half as much as the press or the fans did it.

Question: I guess we have to ask you what everyone wants to know – will the Beatles ever play together again?

Paul: The Beatles – I wouldn't think the Beatles would get together and play again. I think if they did, it might be a bit of a comedown on what it was. The Beatles, when they were together, always used to say, 'When it reaches its end, we get out cleanly.' Now we didn't, as it happens, get out quite so cleanly as we wanted to, with all the business stuff. But at least there's a kind of an end to it now, and I think you'll find that's the end of the Beatles.

Question: But you've been playing on each other's albums . . .

Paul: Yeah, that's right. I don't see any reason why that kind of thing shouldn't happen. I played a little bit on Ringo's LP; so did John and George. Obviously, to the press and to fans, when it's put the right way, it looks like the Beatles coming back together again. A lot of people get into all that. But we did what we did and that was it. I think it's best now to forget that and look to the new thing, and see if there's any possibility of enjoying that.

We've got a lot of fans from what we've been doing now, who've written afterwards and said, 'When I came to see you, I thought it really would just be a kind of sentimental evening where I'd think, "Ah! I wish I'd been with the Beatles".' But they write and say, 'It's amazing, I'm really happy. When are Wings coming back to town, as we're really interested?'

It's not this great eternal rift where no-one can come together and work with each other again. It depends what the projects are. We'll be working on each other's albums, keeping the thing together on that kind of level, I think you'll find.

Question: I want to ask about the way you're raising your children. Are you permissive parents or strict parents?

Linda: Honest parents. I think if anything bothers us, we let them know.

Paul: If the kids do anything that really doesn't fit in with what we're doing, then to that extent we'd say 'No,' rather than some parents who'd say 'Yes, OK.' I don't see really how you can do anything else. If someone's going to smash a bottle or something, we say 'No!' If that's being strict, we're strict. But I think they seem to be pretty well-adjusted kids at the moment.

Question: Well, the new band seem to be pretty well-adjusted as well, Paul. May all your future albums be as great as this one, *Band On The Run*!

Paul: OK, thanks, same to you. I must say goodbye to all the listeners in America. Wanna say a big 'hi' to you. Hello, hope you're enjoying yourself as you're listening to this and look us up when we come to your town. Tara.

Band On The Run (album)

Wings' second album was released in America on Wednesday 5 December 1973 on Apple SO 3415 and it was to top the charts the following April. The album was issued in Britain on Friday 7 December (minus the track 'Helen Wheels') on Apple PAS 10007 and topped the charts for seven weeks, although it first reached No. 1 in April 1974.

The reason 'Helen Wheels' was included on the American release was due to Al Corey of Capitol. He phoned Paul prior to the release and said, 'I just did the Pink Floyd thing and we took a single off that and we increased the sales by two hundred thousand units. I think you should do it in America, especially as "Helen Wheels" is doing great guns over here. Put it on the album.' Paul agreed.

Band On The Run was the first Wings album to top the charts on both sides of the Atlantic and the first Wings LP to go platinum.

As Abbey Road Studios were fully booked when Paul wanted to record, he decided to find an available EMI Studio abroad. It was a choice between the EMI Studio in Rio de Janeiro and the one in Lagos. Paul said, 'It was going to be either Brazilian percussion or African percussion and I said African, that would be a great, great vibe.'

There were initial difficulties when Paul set off to record the album in Nigeria. Five days before they were to due leave Henry McCullough resigned from the band and then three hours before the plane was due to take off Denny Seiwell abruptly announced his departure.

Paul, Linda and Denny Laine nonetheless flew out to Lagos and recorded tracks in two studios there – the EMI Studios and Ginger

Baker's ARC Studios. Paul was to reveal that the reason they travelled to Nigeria was that EMI's 8-track studio there was the only EMI studio available during the three-week period he wanted to record.

Discussing the Nigeria trip, Paul said, 'We thought, "great – lie on the beach all day, doing nothing. Breeze in the studios and record." It didn't turn out like that. One night Linda thought I had died. I was recording and suddenly I felt like I had a lung collapse. So I went outside to get some air, and there wasn't any. It was a humid, hot tropical night. So I collapsed and fainted.'

Linda added, 'I laid him on the ground and his eyes were closed and I thought he was dead! We went to the doctor's and he advised Paul that he was smoking too much.'

There was some bad feeling when Nigerian musicians suggested that Paul was trying to capitalise on African music, but Paul had no intention of 'ripping off' the local style. In fact, on their return to London they had percussion added to the 'Bluebird' track at AIR Studios by Remi Kabaka who, by coincidence, had been born in Lagos – but he was the only African musician on the album.

Faced with the last-minute defection of two of his musicians, Paul improvised by playing several instruments himself, including guitar, bass, drums and synthesisers. Tony Visconti, who also did some arrangements, added orchestral backings at AIR Studios. Paul produced the album with the help of engineer Geoff Emerick.

The tracks on the album are: 'Band On The Run', 'Jet', 'Bluebird', 'Mrs Vandebilt', 'Let Me Roll It', 'Mamunia', 'No Words', 'Picasso's Last Words' and 'Nineteen Hundred And Eighty Four'.

Rumour has it that the title track was inspired by a remark George Harrison made about the problems of Apple: 'If we ever get out of here.'

'Picasso's Last Words' was inspired by the Spanish painter's last words: 'Drink to me, drink to my health, you know I can't drink anymore.'

It has also been suggested that Paul took a slightly satirical dig at John Lennon on the 'Let Me Roll It' track. Paul co-wrote 'No Words' with Denny Laine and composed the rest of the material himself.

The album spawned three hit singles. 'Helen Wheels' had been included on the American album but not the British one and was a chart single in the UK. 'Jet' and 'Band On The Run' became hit singles in both Britain and America.

For the *Band On The Run* cover Paul gathered together several celebrities to pose with him, Linda and Denny. The group included American actor James Coburn, Member of Parliament Clement Freud, chat-show host Michael Parkinson, singer Kenny Lynch, horror star Christopher Lee and Liverpool boxing champion John Conteh. All are caught cowering in the beam of a powerful spotlight.

He commented, 'We thought, *Band On The Run*, let's have a group of people caught in a spotlight as if they're trying to escape from jail.

We thought, well, we'll use actors, and then we thought, no, that's not really going to mean much, so we thought, let's try and get different people who are personalities from various walks of life.'

On Monday 22 March 1999, to celebrate its 25th anniversary, the album was re-released throughout the world with some bonus tracks, a booklet and mini poster.

It was issued in France on EMI/Pathe Marconi DC9/2C064 05503.

In Italy it was issued on Apple/EMI Italiana 3C064 05503 on Wednesday 28 November 1973 and on EMI Italiana 3C 064 05503 on Friday 3 October 1980.

There were various reissues in Britain and the initial CD version was released on Parlophone/EMI CDP 7460552 on Monday 4 February 1985, then on Parlophone/EMI 0777 789240 29 on Monday 7 June 1993.

The album was reissued on Parlophone EMI CENT 30/7243 8 2157915 on Friday 14 November 1997 – this was on the occasion of the one hundredth anniversary of EMI Records.

After the initial release in America there was a picture disc issued on Capitol SEAX 11901 in December 1978. The album was also re-released on Columbia FC-36482 on Thursday 22 May 1980 and on Columbia HC-46982 on Thursday 24 April 1981. A CD version was issued on Columbia CK-36482 in 1984.

Band On The Run (movie)

In 1979, Liverpool playwright Willy Russell was commissioned by Paul to write a script for a feature film of *Band On The Run*, in which Paul played a rock star named Jet. EMI Films had agreed to produce, but the project was abandoned.

The basic story concerned a rock star who had walked out in the middle of a concert, fed up with his fame. He finds himself in a café, but after ordering a meal realises he doesn't have the funds on him to pay for it. He notices a local band in the café who have been fired from a gig and decides to team up with them.

Russell spent some time up in Scotland with Wings to study their individual characters for the script.

Band On The Run (single)

The single 'Band On The Run', credited to Paul McCartney and Wings, was released in Britain on Apple R5997 on Friday 28 June 1974 where it reached No. 3 in the charts,

'Zoo Gang' was on the flipside.

It was issued in Spain on Apple 1C006-09683.

In America, where it was to top the charts, the single was issued with a different track on the flipside, 'Nineteen Hundred And Eighty Four' when it was issued on Apple 1873 on 8 April 1974.

This version was also issued in Germany on EMI Electrola/Apple 1C006-05635.

The number was also included on the EMI double CD set *Back To The 70s* issued in Britain on CDEMTV 77 in 1993.

A version of this number, lasting 5 minutes and 10 seconds was included on the *Tripping The Live Fantastic* album. It was recorded live at Wembley Arena, London on 16 January 1990 during the 1989/90 World Tour.

On the origin of the number, Paul told disc jockey Paul Gambaccini, 'It started off with "If I ever get out of here." That came from a remark George made at one of the Apple meetings. He was saying that we were all prisoners in some way, some kind of remark like that. "If we ever get out of here," the "prison" bit, and I thought that would be a nice way to start an album.'

Bardot, Brigitte

Brigitte Bardot, the French actress, was one of the cinema's most potent sex images of the late 1950s and early 1960s.

Paul and John regarded Brigitte Bardot as 'the epitome of female beauty'. They compared every girl with Brigitte and encouraged their own girlfriends to look like her, John with Cynthia and Paul with Dot Rhone. Paul bought Dot a leather skirt in Hamburg and encouraged her to grow her blonde hair long. They even called Astrid Kirchherr 'the Bardot of Hamburg'.

When Paul originally began to sketch out the ideas for the *Sgt Pepper* sleeve he had the four Beatles standing before a wall which was covered in framed pictures of their heroes – and taking prominence was a pin-up poster of Bardot. Although Bardot was drawn ten times larger than any other figure on Paul's original drawing, she was absent from the final tableau, indicating that a number of the Beatles' original suggestions of their own heroes were left off the final set by Peter Blake and Robert Fraser who replaced them with a number of their own selections.

Bates, Simon

A Radio One disc jockey. Paul recorded an interview with him at Broadcasting House on Thursday 16 June 1983 that was transmitted the following day. He discussed his *Pipes Of Peace* album, the *Give My Regards To Broad Street* film and also sang the Radio One jingle.

Baywatch

An American TV show. In 1994 there were rumours that Paul would appear in a cameo role in an episode of the series during which he would give the kiss-of-life to Pamela Anderson. Paul's spokesman Geoff Baker scotched the rumours, saying, 'Paul *was* offered a part in the series, but the answer was an emphatic no!' As to other rumours that Paul was a fan of the series male star David Hasselhof, Baker said, 'He bumped into him at a party – that was about it.'

However, Paul was eventually to turn up on one of Pamela Anderson's TV shows on an episode of *VIP* aired on Saturday 5 February 2000. In an episode entitled 'All You Need Is Val', Pam's character Val is hired to protect an awards ceremony from a bomb scare. Actual footage of Paul at the PETA Awards in September 1999 was used and at the end of the show Paul is seen presenting an award to Val.

BBC America

An American channel available on digital cable and satellite. On 15 April 2000 they held a special Sir Paul McCartney night which included the screening of Paul's appearance on the *Parkinson* chat show and his appearance on *Later With Jools Holland*.

Beatles Album Sleeves

Paul always had aspirations of being an artist and he also had a hands-on approach to every aspect of the Beatles' career, which involved his suggestions and participation in the various Beatles album sleeves, in particular with *Sgt Pepper's Lonely Hearts Club Band*, arguably the most famous sleeve of any album.

Initially, the Beatles debut album was to be called *Off The Beatle Track* and Paul designed a cover for it that included a head and shoulders image of each member of the band, with the 'B' in Beatle sporting an antenna. The idea was dropped and the album became *Please Please Me*.

It was also Paul who came up with the idea for the *Abbey Road* sleeve, another famous image (how many people have had their photo taken on that zebra crossing?). Paul presented his original idea in the form of a sketch to photographer Iain Macmillan and he also selected the final cover shot from the pictures taken by Macmillan.

Beatles At The Beeb, The

The Beatles performed 88 different songs for BBC radio in the 1960s. The numbers on which Paul sang lead vocals were: 'All My Loving', 'And I Love Her', 'Beautiful Dreamer', 'Besame Mucho', 'Can't Buy Me Love', 'Clarabella', 'Dream Baby', 'The Hippy Hippy Shake', 'The Honeymoon Song', 'I'll Follow The Sun', 'I'm Gonna Sit Right Down And Cry (Over You)', 'I Saw Her Standing There', 'Kansas City', 'Hey! Hey! Hey!' 'Long Tall Sally', 'Love Me Do', 'Lucille', 'The Night Before', 'Ooh! My Soul', 'PS I Love You', 'She's A Woman', 'Sure To Fall (In Love With You)', 'A Taste Of Honey', 'That's All Right Mama', 'Things We Said Today', 'Till There Was You' and 'Youngblood'.

Beatles National Lampoon

A special Beatles edition of the American humorous magazine, issued in October 1977, with a cover depicting the Fab Four squashed flat on the Abbey Road zebra crossing by a passing steamroller.

Among the features was a satire on the 'Paul is Dead' affair, entitled 'He Blew His Mind Out In A Car: The True Story Of Paul McCartney's Death,' which relates how, on the morning of 18 January 1967, Paul left a party at Guildford, Surrey. Hours later his body was found in the wreck of the car, having been garrotted, stabbed and shot several times. There was a double-page photograph showing his body on a mortuary slab with a bruise on the temple, knife in the chest and tyre marks across his stomach and shins. Such black humour was probably the best response to the absurdities of the 'Paul is Dead' affair.

Beatles, The (album)

A double album released in November 1968 and often called 'the White Album' because of its plain white cover.

It contained several numbers written by Paul. They are; 'Back In The USSR', 'Martha My Dear', 'Blackbird', 'Ob-La-Di Ob-La-Da', 'Wild Honey Pie', 'Rocky Racoon', 'Why Don't We Do It In The Road?', 'Mother Nature's Son', 'Honey Pie', 'I Will' and 'Helter Skelter'.

He also co-wrote 'Birthday' with John Lennon.

Included with the album were four colour shots of the individual Beatles and a large poster with a montage of photographs. A minute photograph of Paul completely nude, although discreetly posed behind a white column, caused an outcry in the British press at the time, although a larger photograph of John in the nude on the same poster was virtually ignored.

Beatles' Break-Up, The

Paul began proceedings to dissolve the Beatles' partnership because of advice from his legal representative John Eastman, his brother-in-law, that it would be the only way he could break away from Allen Klein, who had been appointed manager of Apple's affairs over Paul's protests.

Paul had originally wanted Eastman & Eastman, his in-law's family firm, to represent Apple, but the other members of the group disagreed. Paul, however, felt very strongly about Klein. There were many decisions, apart from financial ones, which upset Paul. Klein, for instance, brought in Phil Spector to remix the *Let It Be* tapes. This interfered with the artistic control the Beatles had over their own product. It was most obvious in Paul's case when Spector completely altered the atmosphere of 'The Long And Winding Road' by adding lush strings, lots of voices, the usual Spector 'wall of sound'. In other words, he was imposing his own particular style over Paul's music without Paul having any say in the matter.

The Beatles' legal partnership as it stood had originally been set up in April 1967. In 1969 John had privately announced that he would not work with the Beatles again and was annoyed when Paul made a public statement in a newspaper in April 1970 to the effect that the

Beatles had ceased to exist as a group. In an interview with Rolling Stone magazine in December 1970, John said that Paul's attempts to dominate the group had led to its break-up. He said that all the other members of the Beatles had 'got fed up of being side men for Paul'.

The writ eventually issued by Paul was: 'A declaration that the partnership business carried out by the plaintiff and the defendants under the name of "The Beatles and Co" and constituted by a deed of partnership dated 19 April 1967, and made between the parties hereto ought to be dissolved and that accordingly the same be dissolved.'

During the course of the case, Paul was able to point out how Klein had tried to cause discontent and had told him over the phone: 'You know why John is angry with you? It is because you came off better than he did on Let It Be.'

Klein also said to him: 'The real trouble is Yoko. She is the one with ambition.' Paul said, 'I often wonder what John would have said if he had heard that remark.'

David Hurst QC, acting for Paul, said that Allen Klein had instructed his accountants not to give Paul information about the group's finances. 'He is a man of bad commercial reputation. Mr McCartney has never either accepted him as a manager or trusted him. And on the evidence his attitude has been fully justified.'

The reasons put forward for the dissolution were: (1) The Beatles had long since ceased to perform together as a group, so the whole purpose of the partnership had gone. (2) In 1969, Mr McCartney's partners, in the teeth of his opposition and in breach of the partnership deal, had appointed Mr Klein's company ABKCO Industries Limited as the partnership's exclusive business manager. (3) Mr McCartney had never been given audited accounts in the four years since the partnership was formed.

Beautiful Night

A song that Paul had originally written and recorded in 1986. It had been literally lying on a shelf for a decade when Paul became involved in the Beatles' Anthology and suggested that he and Ringo team up once again, after an absence of ten years. Paul made some minor alterations to the lyrics and recorded it, with himself on piano and Ringo on drums. Nine months later he enhanced it with an orchestral arrangement, scored by George Martin and recorded in Studio One of Abbey Road on Wednesday 14 February 1997.

The number was included on the Flaming Pie album and became the third single issued from the album. It was released on Monday 15 December 1997 in three formats, a 7″ picture disc (Parlophone RP 6489) which included 'Beautiful Night' and 'Love Come Tumbling Down' and two CDs.

The two CDs feature extracts from the 1995 American radio series Oobu Joobu.

CD 1 contained: 'Beautiful Night', 'Love Come Tumbling Down' and 'Oobu Joobu Part 5'. There were nine excerpts on the *Oobu Joobu* section: 'And Now' (a jingle), 'Oobu Joobu Main Theme', 'Beautiful Night Chat', 'Paul McCartney and Ringo Starr Chat About Beautiful Night', 'Ringo Starr Chat', 'Beautiful Night (Flaming Pie Mix)', 'Beautiful Night (original version)', 'Goodbyes' and 'Oobu Joobu Main Theme'.

CD 2 contained: 'Beautiful Night', 'Same Love' and 'Oobu Joobu Part 6'. There were 15 excerpts on the *Oobu Joobu* section: 'This One' (a jingle), 'Oobu Joobu Main Theme', 'Oobu Joobu We Love You' (a jingle), 'Paul McCartney Chats About Abbey Road', 'Strawberry Fields Forever' (a Paul solo), 'Come On Baby', 'Paul McCartney Chats About Abbey Road', 'Come on Baby' (continued), 'End Chat Abbey Road', 'OK Are you Ready?' (a jingle), 'Love Mix', 'Wide Screen Radio' (a jingle), 'Goodbye' and 'Oobu Joobu Main theme.'

'Beautiful Night' was 5 minutes and 18 seconds in length and produced by Paul and Jeff Lynne. Engineers were Geoff Emerick and Jan Jacobs with assistance from Keith Smith. Recording began on 13 May 1996 and Paul sang lead vocals and backing vocals and played bass guitar, electric guitar, acoustic guitar, Wurlitzer piano, Hammond organ and additional percussion. Jeff Lynne sang backing vocals and played electric guitar and acoustic guitar. Ringo Starr sang backing vocals at the end and played drums and additional percussion. There was also orchestral backing, conducted by David Snell with orchestration by George Martin. The musicians were: John Barclay, Andrew Crowley and Mark Bennett on trumpets; Richard Edwards and Andy Fawbery on trombones; Michael Thompson, Richard Watkins and Nigel Black on horns; Marcia Crayford, Adrian Levine, Belinda Bunt, Bernard Partridge, Jackie Hartley, Keith Pascoe, David Woodcock, Roger Garland, Julian Tear, Briony Shaw, Rita Manning, Jeremy Williams, David Ogden, Bogustav Kostecki, Maciej Rakowski and Jonathan Rees on violins; Robert Smissen, Stephen Orton, Martin Loveday and Robert Bailey on cellos; Chris Laurence and Robin McGee on double basses; Susan Milan on flute and David Theodore on oboe.

Paul was to comment, 'I'd written it a few years ago and I'd always liked the song, and I'd done a version in New York, but I didn't feel we'd quite pulled it off.

'So I got this song out for when Ringo was coming, changed a few of the lyrics, and it was like the old days. I realised we hadn't done this for so long, but it was really comfortable and it was still there. So we did "Beautiful Night" and we tagged on a fast bit on the end which wasn't there before.'

The official press release for the single read:

Paul McCartney has re-formed the Beatles' rhythm section and made one of the most lavish videos of his career for the release of his Christmas single, 'Beautiful Night'. Parlophone Records will release the single on 15 December.

Much attention around the release is expected to be caused by director Julien Temple's spectacular – and lengthy – video, which includes scenes of actress Emma Moore stripping naked to go skinny dipping in the River Mersey and sees Paul performing with a new band of 16-year-old London schoolboys whilst being 'bombed' by falling TV sets.

'Beautiful Night' – taken from Paul's acclaimed solo album *Flaming Pie* – reunites the Beatles bassist with Beatles drummer Ringo Starr, who plays on the track and provide its Beatle-humoured ending.

'I think everyone who makes a record always has that option, to leave the daft stuff on at the end,' said Paul. 'You nearly always fade it out but at the end of "Beautiful Night", it had been such a good take that Ringo started having fun, acting like he was a doorman, throwing people out. I love that so much, it's very Beatley. It's a very Beatley idea to do that, because we did a bit of that in the group.

'But "Beautiful Night" also actually sounds a bit Beatley too. In fact, I swear that at the end of "Beautiful Night" you can almost hear a sort of very John Lennony voice in there. Listen to it, check it out.

'It was a bit eerie listening to that – and I thought, "wow!" It's so Beatley sounding, that. I love it.'

Working with Ringo on *The Beatles Anthology* projects spurred Paul to hook up in the studio again for 'Beautiful Night', which was in part recorded at Abbey Road and orchestrated by George Martin.

Said Paul: 'Ringo and I had not worked together for a long time before we did "Free As A Bird". Then we did "Real Love" and it was just such a laugh that I said I was doing a new album and I'd love him to drum on a couple of tracks.

'So I got "Beautiful Night" together, Ringo came down to my studio and we did it and it was such great fun. It was really good to see that Ringo and I locked in, the Beatles rhythm section, drum and bass, we just locked in. It would have been kind of disappointing if we'd lost it, but we hadn't. I suppose we'd just played together for so many years with the Beatles that it was still there and really easy to record together.'

Ringo added: 'Paul invited me to play on "Beautiful Night" and I said "sure" because it was a beautiful track. We spent the day recording together and I still feel really comfortable playing with his bass-playing – well, playing with him basically, that drums and bass. We have all that history and it all comes into play when we play together. You just can't dismiss that.'

'I didn't consciously start off trying to make a Beatles sound, although these days I don't try to avoid it,' said Paul.

'There are a lot of other people trying to make that same sound, with great success too. But that's good, it's a turn-on for me. I suppose you could say that when I play it's sort of a Beatles sound anyway. I didn't avoid it or go for it. It just came out that way.'

Beautiful Night (promotional video)

The video for this number, released in December 1997, proved quite controversial as it featured a full-frontal nude scene of actress Emma Moore swimming in the River Mersey. MTV banned the clip and Paul had to have an edited version made which was acceptable to the broadcasters, although the banned version was screened on the Playboy channel in America. The video was directed by Julien Temple who spotted a four-piece group called Spud in a London club and had them appear in the clip performing with Paul. Ringo Starr can also be seen as a night watchman who then begins to play drums.

When Paul appeared on the Oprah Winfrey show, the scenes were censored from the video.

Paul's spokesman Geoff Baker said, 'However, another hot and uncut version of the "Beautiful Night" video will be available worldwide to television programmers who are not restricted by censorship or nudity.'

One of Paul's friends admitted that Paul had taken a chance with the promotional film but said, 'It's without doubt the riskiest thing Paul's done in a long time. People were stunned to discover he had nude women and men frolicking in the Mersey River to promote his single. The jokes have already started about "Hey Nude" but he sees the funny side.'

The five-minute video was screened in Liverpool and London.

Be-Bop-A-Lula

A major hit single for Gene Vincent in the 1950s and the first record which Paul ever bought.

Besame Mucho

A song Paul introduced into the Beatles repertoire in 1961 on which he sang lead vocal. He was influenced by the Coasters' version, released in 1960. Paul also performed it at their Decca audition, on the BBC radio show *Here We Go* and it's also featured on *The Beatles Anthology I* CD.

The number was originally penned by Consuelo Valazquez and Selig Shaftel in 1943.

Best Of Chris Farley, The

A 62-minute video and DVD, released in America on 25 April 2000. Chris Farley was a comedian who made his *Saturday Night Live* debut in 1990 and featured many guests in his sketches, including Paul

McCartney. He died at the age of 33 on Thursday 18 December 1997 of a deadly mixture of opiates and cocaine. Paul is one of the guests included on this compilation.

Best Of Cilla, The
An album by Cilla Black issued in Britain on Friday 8 November 1968 on Parlophone PCS 7065. It contained all three Paul McCartney compositions which Cilla had recorded – 'Love Of The Loved', 'Step Inside Love' and 'It's For You'.

Best Of Paul McCartney And Wings: Wingspan, The
A VHI special that was televised in America on Monday 14 May 2001 and attracted 15 million viewers. The one-hour programme included an exclusive interview between Paul and VHI's Rebecca Rankin.

Beware My Love
A track from the *Wings At The Speed Of Sound* album, 6 minutes and 28 seconds in length.

Bibliography

Body Count, Francie Schwartz, Straight Arrow, 1972.

The Paul McCartney Story, George Tremlett, Futura, 1975.

Paul McCartney: In His Own Words, Paul Gambaccini, Omnibus Press, 1976.

Linda's Pictures, Linda McCartney, Alfred A Knopf, 1976.

The Facts About A Pop Group, Featuring Wings, Dave Gelly, Andre Deutsch, 1977.

Paul McCartney And Wings, Tony Jasper, Octopus Books, 1977.

Paul McCartney And Wings, Jeremy Pascall, Hamlyn, 1977.

Paul McCartney, A Biography In Words And Pictures, John Mendelsohn, Sire Books/Chappell Music Ltd, 1977.

Wings, Rock Fun, 1977.

Paul McCartney: Beatle With Wings!, Martin A Grove, Pyramid Books, 1978.

Hands Across The Water/Wings Tour USA, Hipgnosis, Paper Tiger, 1978.

Paul McCartney und Wings, Klaus Dewes and Rudi Oertel, Bergisch Gladbach, 1980.

Paul McCartney – Composer, Artist, Paul McCartney, Pavilion Books, 1981.

Photographs, Linda McCartney, MPL Communications, 1982.

Remember: Recollections and Photographs of the Beatles, Mike McCartney, Henry Holt & Co, 1982.

The Ocean View, Humphrey Ocean, MPL Communications/Plexus Books, 1983.

Paul McCartney, Alan Hamilton, Hamish Hamilton, 1983.

Paul McCartney: The Definitive Biography, Chris Welch, Proteus Books, 1984.

McCartney: Songwriter, Howard Elson, Comet Books, 1986.

The McCartney File, Bill Harry, Virgin Books, 1986.

McCartney: The Definitive Biography, Chris Salewicz, St Martin's Press, 1986.

Mike Mac's Black And White's Plus One Colour, Mike McCartney, Aurum Press, 1986.

Paul McCartney's Rupert & The Frog Song, adapted by David Hately, Ladybird Books, 1986.

McCartney, Chet Flippo, Sidgwick & Jackson, 1987.

Paul Ist Schuld, Corinne Ullrich Crox, Phantom Verlag, 1987.

Sunprints, Linda McCartney, Barrie & Jenkins, 1988.

Paul Ist Schuld, Corrin Ullrich Crux, Phantom Verlag, 1989.

Paul McCartney, Jurgen Siebold, Moewig, 1989.

Paul McCartney Solo 1970–1990, Rob van den Berg, Loeb, 1989.

Sixties: Portrait Of An Era, Linda McCartney, Reed Books, 1992.

Paul McCartney, Carola Deurwaarder, De Geillustreerde Pers, 1992.

Mike McCartney's Merseyside, Cornerhouse Publications, 1992.

Paul McCartney: From Liverpool To Let It Be, Howard A DeWitt, Horizon Books, 1992.

Paul McCartney, Dominique Grandfils, Zelie, 1992.

Linda McCartney's Main Courses, Bloomsbury, 1992.

Linda McCartney's Light Lunches, Bloomsbury, 1992.

McCartney: 50 Ans, Jordi Sierra I Fabra, Plaza y Janes, 1992.

Paul McCartney – Im Gesprach Für Europa, Christian Frietsch, Radio Victoria, 1992.

Listen To What The Man Said, Judith Philipp and Ralf Simon, Pendragon.

Turn Me On Dead Man: The Complete Story Of The Paul McCartney Death Hoax, Andru J Reeve, Popular Culture Ink, 1994.

The McCartney Interviews: After The Breakup, Paul Gambaccini, Omnibus Press, 1995.

The Walrus Was Paul – The Great Beatles Death Clues of 1969, R Gary Patterson, Dowling Press, 1996.

Roadworks, Linda McCartney, Bullfinch Press, 1996.

Paul McCartney: Many Years From Now, Barry Miles, Secker & Warburg, 1997.

Sir Paul McCartney, Tracks, 1997.

Sir Paul McCartney, Liverpool Echo, 1997.

Paul McCartney: The Standing Stone Premiere, Harriet L Perry, Tracks, February 1998.

Paul McCartney's Oratorio, Festival van Vlaanderen, May 1998.

Wide Open, Linda McCartney (with a foreword by Paul), Bulfinch Press/Little Brown, 1999.

Paul McCartney 1942–1966, Gerrit Wijnne, AO BV, 1999.

Paul McCartney Paintings, Wolfgang Suttner and Nicola van Velsen, Kultur Verlag, 1999.
Paul McCartney, Arturo Blay, Editorial La Mascara, 1999.
Paul McCartney Paintings, Little Brown, 2000.
Performances, Linda McCartney, Little Brown, 2000.
Paul McCartney: I Saw Him Standing There, Jorie Green, Billboard Books/Watson-Guptill, 2000.
Paul McCartney: Faces, Thorsten Schmidt, 2000.
Paul McCartney: Blackbird Singing, Faber & Faber, 2001.
Paul McCartney: 20 Years On His Own, Edward Gross, Pioneer Books, 2001.
Best Of Macca, Paul Nash, Tracks, 2001.
Paul McCartney, Paul Dowswell, Heineman Profiles, 2001.

Big Barn Bed

A number that opened both the *Red Rose Speedway* album and the 'James Paul McCartney' television special. It was recorded at Olympic Studios during the *Red Rose Speedway* sessions.

Big Boys Bickering

The third track on the CD single of 'Hope Of Deliverance', released in January 1993. Due to the use of the F-word in the lyrics, both the BBC and MTV banned the number, with MTV banning it from *Up Close*, the series in which Paul had performed a special show for MTV.

An MPL spokesman said, '"Big Boys Bickering" is a protest song about governments' inability to agree on anything, which results in things like a hole in the ozone layer, and people starving in Africa.' Commenting on the use of the F-word, the spokesman said, 'Paul feels very strongly about this, and he considered using the words "muckin' it up", or even "cockin' it up" in the song, but felt that these words didn't quite capture his anger.'

Paul himself commented, 'People are wrecking our world and the governments are doing nothing to stop it. People are dying in famines and governments are doing nothing. I'm protesting against these men who sit in smoke-filled rooms and tell us what to do, whether we want to do it or not – it's like telling women they can't have abortions or other such nonsense.'

He added, 'I'm protesting against people like George Bush going to the Rio Earth Summit last year and saying, "I'm not signing any agreement".'

On his use of the expletive in the song, he added, 'I sympathise with people who do not approve of swearing, especially those with young children. I must admit I don't like it in front of the kids. I don't normally go for swearing in songs. It has always struck me as a bit gratuitous. But in this case, I felt it was essential to the song. If, like me, you think of that hole in the ozone layer, you don't tend to think, "Oh that flipping great hole in the ozone layer" – you think, "That fucking great hole . . . "'

The song in its entirety was included in a special adults-only version of the ITV programme *Chart Show*. The show's representative Keith Macmillan commented, 'We are happy to take this step because we believe in the sentiments behind Paul's song.'

Big Breakfast, The

An early morning Channel Four show. Paul appeared on the programme on Tuesday 16 November 1999. The subject of Liam Gallagher of Oasis naming his son Lennon came up and Paul joked that he had suggested to his son James that if he had a son he could call him Lennon McCartney. Clips of the 'No Other Baby' video were also screened.

Biker Like An Icon

The third single from the *Off The Ground* album, penned by Paul and lasting 3 minutes and 24 seconds. Parlophone issued it in Britain on Tuesday 20 April 1993. The 7″ was on R 6347, the cassette on TCR 6347 and the CD on CDR5 6347. The flipside was 'Things We Said Today'. The CD also contained the tracks 'Midnight Special' and 'Mean Woman Blues'.

With the exception of 'Biker Like An Icon', all the tracks were from the MTV 'Unplugged' appearance.

A white vinyl version was also issued in America on Capitol /CEMA 17319 on Tuesday 20 April 1993 in a limited edition of 17,000.

Discussing the song, Paul said 'Once I'd messed about with the words, I went up to my attic and wrote it with a 12-string. Robbie (McIntosh) added that great lead guitar break when we cut it, and we got ourselves a good little rocky song.'

Talking about the recording in the studio, he said, 'What I especially like about the record is that the song you hear is the first take. We just did it first time, it rocked along and we thought, "that's it"; we went for the feel, we didn't want to labour over it after that first take.'

In Germany 'Biker Like An Icon' was issued as a 4-track CD on EMI 8810422 along with 'Midnight Special' and 'Things We Said Today', the latter from the 'Unplugged' sessions and also a live version of the title track. A 4-track CD was also issued in Holland, together with a 2-track CD on EMI 8810432 with 'Mean Woman Blues' as the second track. It was issued in Spain as a 7″ vinyl single.

A live version of the number lasting 3 minutes and 40 seconds, recorded in Boulder, Colorado on 26 May 1993, was included on the *Paul Is Live* album.

Bip Bop

A track on Wings' *Wild Life* album that Paul was later to say was 'the weakest song I have ever written in my life.' He also commented, 'It just goes nowhere. I still cringe every time I hear it.' Yet another comment from Paul: 'It's the one our baby likes.'

Bip Bop Link

An instrumental version of 'Bip Bop,' which was included on the *Wild Life* album.

Birthday (single)

The first single to be released from the *Tripping The Live Fantastic* triple album. The number, which was 2 minutes and 43 seconds in length, was recorded during the concert at Knebworth on Saturday 30 June 1990.

The single was available in four formats: 7″ (R 6271), 12″ (12R 6271), cassette (TCR 6271) and CD (CDR 6271). The 7″ and cassette had 'Good Day Sunshine' as the second track. The 12″ and CD had the two tracks plus 'PS Love Me Do' and 'Let 'Em In'.

'Birthday' was the only track of the above numbers that was actually taken from the *Tripping The Live Fantastic* album and was issued in Britain on Monday 8 October 1990 and in America on cassette only on Tuesday 16 October.

The British release of the live recording of 'Birthday' was issued to mark what would have been John Lennon's fiftieth birthday.

MPL issued a statement about the release telling how Paul and John had written the number at Abbey Road one night when Pattie Boyd and other friends were present. Paul remarked, 'It all became a little bit of a party, so rather than get too serious, I just said to John, "Let's just make something up."

'So we worked out this riff and then we just thought of this birthday idea because I remember saying "Some songs are kind of useful, let's do a useful song." What I meant was songs like "White Christmas" are very useful, if you want to get into a Christmas mood, whack that on ... so going on that sort of vibe, I thought, "Well, there's been a Christmas song and an Easter song, how about a birthday song?" Of course, there was "Happy Birthday To You" but we wanted to do a rock song for people who were into rock and roll who could use it as just another way of saying, "it's your birthday". So we came up with this really simple lyric, put a riff in the middle, a little instrumental break and we got the crowd of guests there to sing along to the chorus. And by the end of the evening, we'd done it.'

When it was mentioned that the release coincided with what would have been John's birthday, Paul said, 'That's just a happy coincidence. It's my nod and a wink to an old mate.'

Birthday (song)

A song written and recorded on Wednesday 18 September 1968.

Chris Thomas, who was producing the Beatles at the time,

mentioned that Paul arrived in the Abbey Road Studio first and began playing the 'Birthday' riff. By the time the others had arrived Paul had virtually completed writing the song in the studio.

It was then decided to cut short the recording session because they wanted to rush back to Paul's place to watch the movie *The Girl Can't Help It*. Thomas had told them days earlier that the movie was being given its first British airing on BBC 2 on the Wednesday evening.

Paul said, '*The Girl Can't Help It* was on television. Fats Domino, Gene Vincent and Eddie Cochran were in it, and we wanted to see it, so we started at five o'clock and just did a backing track, a very simple 12-bar blues thing with a few bits here and there. We had no idea what it was going to be. We'd just say, "12 bars in A", and then we'd change to D, then we'd do a few beats in C. Just like that. Then we went back to my house, watched the film, and then went back to the studio and made up some words to go with it all. This song was just made up in an evening. We hadn't even thought of it before then. It's one of my favourites because it was instantaneous. Also, it's a good one to dance to. As for the big long drums break, normally we might have four bars of drums, but, with this, we thought, "No, let's keep it going." We all like to hear drums plodding on.'

John and Paul sang the song together, with Paul playing piano on the track, although the instrument had been adjusted to sound like an electric harpsichord. The number was included on their *The Beatles* double album.

John was later to refer to the number as 'a piece of garbage'. He also said '"Birthday" was written in the studio. Just made up on the spot. I think Paul wanted to write a song like "Happy Birthday Baby" the old '50s hit.'

Black, Cilla

The leading female singer of the Mersey-sound era, born Priscilla Maria Veronica White on 27 May 1943. At the age of seventeen, as Cilla White, she began singing with local groups such as Kingsize Taylor & the Dominoes, the Big Three and Rory Storm & the Hurricanes. In the first issue of the *Mersey Beat* newspaper, published on 6 July 1961, she was mistakenly referred to as Cilla Black and decided to keep the name.

In the evenings she used to work occasionally at the Zodiac coffee bar in Duke Street, Liverpool, where she met her future husband Bobby Willis. The stories about her being the Cavern cloakroom girl are greatly exaggerated as she only unofficially helped out a couple of times.

At the age of twenty she became the only female singer to be signed by Brian Epstein and he immediately placed her with Beatles recording manager George Martin and gave her a Paul McCartney song 'Love Of The Loved' as her debut disc. It was issued in October 1963 on

Parlophone R5065 and was a minor hit, reaching No. 35 in the British charts.

In 1964 she was given another song by Paul, 'It's For You'. It was issued in August on Parlophone R5162 and reached No. 7 in the charts. The number was also issued in the States on 17 August 1974 on Capitol 5258, reaching No. 78 in the American charts. Cilla said, 'Paul sounded great on the demo disc, which he let me hear at the Palladium. He sang the song as a waltz and George Martin put in the jazzy bits for the session arrangement. John and Paul came along to the recording session the same day they arrived back from Australia. George Martin told them they'd better wait outside because I was nervous, and he was right about that. But with John and Paul, I didn't mind. They'd often drop in when I was at the studios, and anyway I was glad to see them back safely from Australia.'

When Cilla was given her own BBC TV series, simply called *Cilla*, Paul was approached to see if he would write the theme tune for it. He agreed and made a demo of the number at his Cavendish Avenue house.

It was 'Step Inside Love', which Paul was to describe as 'not a bad little song'. When Cilla sang it on her first show, which was live, she couldn't remember the words because she didn't have much time to rehearse. She said, 'I'd just forgotten them! I thought since it was the first time on telly and nobody had heard the right words then nobody would know if I sang the wrong words. But one viewer did – Paul himself! He got the impression that my television producer had deliberately changed the lyrics and he rang the BBC to complain.'

'Step Inside Love', was issued in March 1968 on Parlophone R5674 and reached No. 8 in the British charts. It was issued in America on Bell 726, but made no impact.

On Paul's fortieth birthday, Cilla sent him a telegram which read: 'Life begins at forty, what the 'ell 'ave you been doing all these years?'

Black Dyke Mills Band, The

A famous British brass band of international repute, with whom Paul recorded his composition 'Thingumybob', the theme tune of London Weekend Television's comedy series of the same name.

On 30 April 1968, a Sunday afternoon, Paul went up to Bradford, Yorkshire to record the single, which he also arranged.

The band, conducted by Geoffrey Brand, also produced an instrumental version of 'Yellow Submarine' for the flip, which Paul produced.

The single was issued in Britain on Apple 4 on 6 September 1968 but failed to register in the charts. In America, 'Yellow Submarine' became the A-side when the disc was issued on Apple 1800 on 26 August 1968. Although the band never recorded for the Apple label again, Paul was to feature them on a Wings album over a decade later, in 1979, when they performed on 'Winter Rose' and 'Love Awake' for *Back To The Egg*.

Blackbird (song)

Paul taped this track solo on Tuesday 11 June 1968. He used a sound-effects record of birdsong to fill out the track from 'Volume Seven: Birds Of A Feather' taken from the Abbey Road taped sound collection. He sings, plays acoustic guitar and percussion. Three microphones were used on the recording. One for his voice, one for his guitar and one for his tapping feet.

John Lennon was to provide one line in the song, which Paul said he was inspired to write after reading about the American race riots.

It appeared on *The Beatles* double album.

Paul was to say, 'It's simple in concept because we couldn't even think of anything else to put on it. Maybe on *Pepper*, we would have worked on it until we could find some way to put violins on it, or trumpets. But, I don't think it needs it. There's nothing to the song. This is just one of those pick-it-and-sing-it songs. It doesn't need anything else in the backing because, as a song, there's nothing to it. The only point where we were thinking of putting anything on it was where it comes back in the end, stops, and then comes back in. So, instead of putting any backing on it, we put a blackbird on it, so, there's a blackbird singing at the very end. Somebody said it's a thrush, but I think it's a blackbird.

'Blackbird' was one of five Beatles songs that Paul included on his *Wings Over America* tour in 1976.

Blackbird Singing

Paul's first book of poetry, published by Faber and Faber in 2001. Paul was inspired to publish the work by the death of Linda and dedicated the book to their children Mary, Stella and James and to Heather, Linda's daughter by a previous marriage.

It contains more than a hundred poems written between 1965 and 2000, in addition to some of his best-known song lyrics. A dozen of the poems are about Linda and were written in the months before and after her death in April 1998.

Poet and playwright Adrian Mitchell aided Paul in compiling the collection, and commented, 'It was Linda who wanted Paul to get them published. Paul is not afraid to take on the art of poetry, which is the art of dancing naked.'

Paul said he wasn't worried about what critics may say about the book, commenting, 'The critics are always mixed with me. I always say they sharpen their pencils when they see me coming. But I don't care, you know, they criticised *Sgt Pepper* and look what happened to that.'

Blackboard Jungle, The

A famous 1950s film starring Glenn Ford and Sidney Poitier that featured the Bill Haley number 'Rock Around The Clock'. When Paul was sixteen he went along to see the film with George Harrison, who was only fifteen. To make George look a little bit older and thus ensure his entrance to the cinema, they went into the back garden to get some mud to put on George's upper lip to give the impression of a moustache!

Blackpool

One of a number of demo home recordings Paul made in the years 1971 and 1972. It is a band demo rather than the usual solo demo discs he was making around that time. This one features three acoustic guitars, an electric keyboard and drums.

Blair, Tony

British prime minister who, during the first year of office in 1998, said that one of the highlights of his year was meeting Paul McCartney who was, he said, 'a total hero of mine'. He also mentioned that his wife Cherie used to have a picture of Paul by her bed.

Paul was to meet Prime Minister Blair on a number of occasions, although he took him to task during a press conference in London on Thursday 10 June 1999.

He said, 'Tony Blair is wrong to support genetically modified food.

'I can understand what he is doing. He does not want people to panic. But I think he's wrong. I don't think there is enough evidence about the problems that might arise through GM foods. I don't think people are worrying unnecessarily. The last time they got into something like this was BSE when people did swallow it quite literally. This time we have to take time to find out exactly what the implications of GM food are.'

Blake, Peter

A British painter, born in June 1932 in Dartford, Kent.

Art dealer Robert Freeman had introduced Blake to Paul. And Paul later asked Freeman if he could obtain one of Blake's paintings for him. When Paul discussed with Blake what kind of painting he would like, Blake asked Paul what his favourite paintings were. Paul mentioned he liked Sir Edwin Landseer's *Monarch Of The Glen* and Blake painted him a new version *After 'The Monarch Of The Glen' by Sir Edwin Landseer*, Peter Blake, 1966. Paul placed it above his fireplace at Cavendish Avenue.

When Paul showed Freeman his ideas for the cover of the *Sgt Pepper* sleeve, Freeman suggested that they go to Blake's house to discuss it. Following a few meetings, Peter Blake was commissioned to do the sleeve, which was to become the most famous album sleeve of all time.

Paul had also asked Blake if he could give him some painting hints, but Blake forgot about the request.

Peter Blake asked Paul if he could provide a background soundtrack to his 'About Collage' exhibition at the Tate, Liverpool, which ran until 4 March 2001. Paul composed 'Liverpool Sound Collage' and also supplied a picture collage to the exhibition. It was called *The World* and was featured on the cover of the album. The images included a cow, a dog, a screaming man, a corridor, a murder victim and a portrait and photo of a young girl combined to form the shape of a cross.

Commenting on Paul's audio and visual contribution, Blake said, 'Paul surprised me with his offer to do something for this show. Although he is a keen painter, he had never done a collage before.'

There was also a track on the album called 'Peter Blake 2000' which lasted for 10 minutes and 54 seconds.

Blankit's First Show

A 1985 MPL film short in which Linda relates the story of Blankit, son of Lucky Spot, the Appaloosa pony that she had bought in Texas.

In 1976 when Wings were touring America, they were in Texas on the way to a gig when Paul and Linda saw a horse grazing by the roadside. They were so struck by the animal that they immediately made enquiries and bought it.

The movie shows Blankit at Parkhurst Stables with his trainer Peter Larrigan and follows the horse on his first show in front of judges. Included on the soundtrack are several compositions by Paul including 'The Man', 'The Other Me', 'Sweetest Little Show' and 'Hey Hey', mainly from his album *Pipes Of Peace*. In one scene Paul acts as an announcer at a dressage meeting when he sings a number called 'All You Horseriders'.

The documentary was first transmitted on BBC 2 on Saturday 12 July 1986. It was repeated on Thursday 6 November and also on Wednesday 10 May 1989 and Monday 14 June 1993.

Blockbuster Entertainment Corp

The company that sponsored the American leg of Paul's New World Tour in 1993. The company took out television, radio and newspaper advertising and promoted the concerts with in-store posters in all their outlets.

Paul's manager Richard Ogden commented, 'Since Paul started touring again in 1989 we have sought a sponsor who is in the same business as we are. We're pleased that Blockbuster fills the role.'

Blue Angel Club, The

A London club, formerly situated at 15 Berkeley Street, which the Beatles used to frequent during the evenings in 1965. It was during one of these visits that Paul first heard the song 'Those Were The Days', which he was later to record with Mary Hopkin.

Blue Jean Bop
A track on the *Run Devil Run* album lasting 1 minute and 57 seconds. It was penned by Vincent/Levy and originally recorded by Gene Vincent & the Blue Caps in Nashville on 26 June 1956. Paul recorded it at Abbey Road Studios on Friday 5 March 1999. The musicians were Paul on lead vocal and bass guitar, Dave Gilmour on electric guitar, Mick Green on electric guitar and Ian Paice on drums.

The reason why Paul chose this as the first song on the album is that he first heard it when he was at a friend's house near Penny Lane and they played the Vincent album with this track on it. The number immediately brought back memories of those days to him. He also wanted to remain close to the original interpretation of the song.

Blue Moon Of Kentucky
Originally a country hit by Bill Monroe in 1947. Paul was influenced by Elvis Presley's version of the number and first began singing it as a member of the Quarry Men. He included it in his repertoire during his 1972 tour and also featured it on the MTV special *Unplugged* and on *Unplugged (The Official Bootleg)*.

Blue Swat
One of several numbers Paul recorded in July 1979 during sessions for *McCartney II*, which weren't used on the album.

Bluebird
A song, 3 minutes and 21 seconds in length, penned by Paul and included on the 1973 album *Band On The Run*. Paul first performed the number with Linda two years previously on a live radio interview in New York. 'Bluebird' was one of the numbers in the repertoire of the 1975/76 world tour and was also included on the *Wings Over America* album.

Boardwalk
A restaurant at 18 Greek Street, London. Paul and Linda held an 'End Of The World Tour' party there from 6 p.m. to 9 p.m. on 12 December 1990.

A contest had been held by MTV in November called 'The Long And Winding Road'. It was the channel's first global contest and five winners from the USA, Europe, Japan, Brazil and Australia would be flown to London to join the end-of-tour party.

MTV announced the American winner with the news story headed 'MTV To Fly Connecticut Woman To London For Special Private Dinner With Paul McCartney' which read: '5 December 1990, New

York, NY – MTV: Music Television is sending Stacey Eisenberg of Waterbury, CT to London as the grand prize winner in MTV's 'The Long And Winding Road' contest. Stacey and her guest will be having an unforgettable feast on Wednesday, 12 December with Paul and Linda McCartney, and their band, for an end-of-tour celebration.

'Eisenberg is 29 years old and an assignment editor for ESPN. This private dinner party will include selections from Linda's own vegetarian cookbook.

'"The Long And Winding Road" contest was the first global MTV contest, where viewers from MTV affiliates, US, Europe, Japan, Brazil and Australia were able to enter. From these five corners of the world, five grand prize winners were chosen for this once in a lifetime dinner.'

The Brazilian competition proved interesting as this press release illustrates:

Paul McCartney's biggest fan on earth was in tears last night after sending 29,000 personal entries to a 'Meet McCartney' competition – and losing.

Heart-broken waiter Rosalvo Melo was certain that he'd win the MTV competition – after delivering a mountain of envelopes in a truck.

The competition – run by MTV Brazil – drew 31,000 entries in just three weeks. Plus another 29,000 from Rosalvo.

But – when all the entries went into a giant hat, with Rosalvo standing by with a great chance of winning – he blew it.

'I just can't believe it,' he sobbed.

'I spent all the money I have ever saved on this competition. I must be the unluckiest person in Brazil.'

MTV is running a global contest – with winners coming from South America, Australia, Europe, Japan and the USA as special guests for Paul's private End of Tour Party in Soho, London tonight (Wednesday, 12 December).

The party is to mark the presentation to Paul of the *Guinness Book of Records* award for the biggest stadium rock show ever – for playing to 184,000 in Rio de Janeiro in April.

MTV Brazil's Deborah Cohen said: 'This is the most incredible example of a super-fan.

'Rosalvo spent his entire fortune – $400 – on envelopes for the competition and called us to say could he bring in his entries because he couldn't afford the stamps.

'We said, "Well, the rules are that you have to post them … how many entries have you made?" When he said 29,000 we freaked. He ended up driving in an open-back truck to our San Paulo office and dumping them on the pavement.'

But as Rosalvo grew excited at his chance of winning, he was hit by another setback.

'The government rules decree that competition entries must have the PO Box number on them at least,' said Deborah.

'So this guy sits out on the carpet with a mate and a few of our staff who felt sorry for him, frantically writing in the PO Box number.

'In the five hours he had left before the deadline, he got 11,000 entries done.

'So he still had a 25 per cent chance of winning. But another name was drawn out of the hat.

'His face just dropped. I have never seen anyone so sad in my entire life. He was in tears, his friend was in tears, we were in tears.'

Back at work at San Paulo's Crown Plaza Hotel last night, the 23-year-old waiter said: 'It was the biggest dream of my life to meet Paul. I am devastated.'

Cinderella Postscript: On Tuesday, 11 December, Rosalvo went to work as normal and was surprised to find MTV calling on him at the hotel.

'What are you doing tonight, Rosalvo?' Deborah Cohen asked.

'Working,' said Rosalvo.

'No you're not,' said Deborah, 'you're booked on Varig Flight RG760 to London – as Paul McCartney's personal guest. He heard about your hard luck – you're going to the ball after all.'

The Brazilian winner was a twelve-year-old boy, who was accompanied by his father, the others were a young married couple from Australia, two sisters from the Netherlands and a mother and her son from Japan.

The winners had originally been given the impression that they would be among a small group of around 35 people present at Paul's home, with Linda preparing a vegetarian dinner for them.

As it was, the Boardwalk had approximately a hundred people in attendance with the McCartneys and the band, MPL officials, the road crew and personnel connected with the tour, MTV and Capitol/EMI reps, plus a horde of media people due to the fact that Paul was also to be presented with a *Guinness Book of Records* award that night.

This was reported in an official press release issued the next day headed: 'Christmas Comes Early For McCartney As Paul Is Voted No. 1 Rock Star Of The Year'.

The handout read:

Christmas came early for Paul McCartney last night (Wednesday, 12 December) as he was officially declared the world's top live rock and roll star of 1990.

At a series of celebrations in London, Paul received award after award recognising him as the rock record-breaker of the year.

The music industry's official arbiters revealed that Paul's recent

Get Back World Tour beat all-comers – knocking the Rolling Stones off the perch as only runners-up to McCartney.

All day long, Paul was receiving awards and prizes for the record-shattering, ten-month tour.

The most prestigious of the glittering prizes was the *Guinness Book of Records* award for the biggest concert in history by a solo star.

Paul set the new rock and roll attendance record on 21 April, when he played to 184,000 fans at Rio de Janeiro's Maracana Stadium – shattering the previous world best of a crowd of 170,000, held by Frank Sinatra.

Also yesterday, America's prestigious *Billboard* magazine, the rock business's bible, revealed that Paul's USA concerts had also out-sold every other top act. Paul took 5 of *Billboard*'s top 12 concerts of the year – including the No. 1 slot. The Rolling Stones were No. 2 – and Madonna No. 12.

Yet another award followed for McCartney when he received the top honour from the leading British rock magazine, *Q*.

At the *Q* Awards ceremony in London, Paul became the first musician to receive the magazine's Merit Award for 'outstanding and continued contribution to the music industry'.

There were more awards still for the 48-year-old former Beatle when he hosted an end-of-tour celebration in Soho last night.

There he received six awards from rock and roll promoters for breaking attendance records during the world tour at Phoenix, Arizona; Berkeley, California; Ames, Iowa; Cleveland, Ohio; Dallas, Texas; and London's Wembley Arena.

Paul confessed he was amazed and delighted that he'd swept the awards board after thirty years in rock.

He said, 'I'm totally flabbergasted. I don't know why I just don't go straight home and put my feet up. I guess I must be in love with the music business.'

Bogey Music

A number penned by Paul and lasting 3 minutes and 3 seconds which was included as a track on the *McCartney 11* album.

The song was written after Paul had been introduced to the popular British children's book *Fungus The Bogeyman*, a most unusual creation by Raymond Briggs.

Bogeydom exists in dank, subterranean tunnels where Fungus lives with his wife Mildew and son Mould in a place of filth and slime.

Boil Crisis

A punk song written by Paul after he'd seen an 'Oil Crisis!' headline in a newspaper. He slightly changed the headline and made a demo disc of the number at his Rude Studios in the summer of 1977.

Bonzo Dog Doo-Dah Band, The

A highly individual eccentric group of ex-art students who formed a band in 1965. They can be seen in the film *Magical Mystery Tour* performing at Raymond's Revuebar, a Soho strip club. They also played at the Beatles' celebration party at the end of filming, when they were joined by members of the Beach Boys and Fred Lennon, John's dad.

In 1968 the group were having problems recording a single called 'I'm the Urban Spaceman', penned by group member Neil Innes. They approached Paul to produce it for them and he agreed. The saxophonist and group's model maker (they included bizarre models in their stage act) Roger Ruskin Spear, told journalist Chris Welch in an interview: 'We really needed someone we would all respect to produce us, and Paul was asked if he could come down and help us out. We had met him before when we appeared in a scene in *Magical Mystery Tour*.'

Paul turned up for the session at Chappell's recording studio in Bond Street. He showed the bass player Joel Druckman what to play but 'he wouldn't play the bass line on the record. In the end he did play some ukulele. He thrashed at it along with Neil Innes and Viv Stanshall, out in the corridor, and you can hear it plucking in the background.'

Joel had brought a number of names over from America, one of which was Apollo C Vermouth, and it was decided that Paul would use it as a pseudonym.

Roger told Chris: 'Of course, it was cleverly leaked to the press that it was really Paul McCartney. He was only with us for a day but it was extraordinary what he achieved.'

The record was issued in Britain in October 1968 and reached No. 5 in the charts, but it didn't make any great impact when it was issued in the States in December. When the album *Urban Spaceman*, which contained the track, was issued in America in June 1969, Paul's name had replaced the Apollo C Vermouth credit.

Bootlegs

There have been more than 200 different bootleg titles of McCartney/Wings albums that contain unique material, even more if you include different titles that contain the same recordings.

The first McCartney bootleg was probably one called *First Live Show spring '72*, which was a recording of a Wings' concert at Hull University on 11 February 1972. The sound quality was appalling. Paul and his company MPL are completely opposed to bootlegs, although in early issues of the official McCartney Fan Club magazine, fans could openly trade bootleg recordings. Paul also mentioned 'Bootlegs' in the song 'Hi, Hi, Hi' and is on record as saying that he recorded ('bootlegged') several concerts that he attended, such as one for Stevie Wonder.

Bootlegs were declared illegal in Britain and are very difficult to obtain. They are mostly bought on mail order from Europe, the USA and Japan. In Britain, bootleg sellers usually deal at small local record fairs that are held almost every day of the week at venues such as pubs and churches. Bootlegs are now banned from most of the major weekend record fairs, although they are frequently found on the internet on such sites as eBay.

A bootleg CD will sell for anything between £12 and £20 and the latest trend is for CD-R copies, which can be obtained much more cheaply.

In the early 1970s a couple of the bootleg labels offered to pay royalties, but this simply alerted their whereabouts and they were quickly shut down. In the 1980s a label called Great Dane in Italy actually operated officially because of different copyright laws in that country – and they paid royalties to the Italian equivalent of the Performing Rights Society. Since all European law has become standardised, Great Dane is once again operating illegally.

It is very hard to trace bootleggers because as soon as one label is shut down another one starts up. Bootlegging tends to be a very small industry, as the nature of the material only appeals to 'die hard' fans and collectors. The authorities would be better off tracking down the manufacturers of 'pirate' copies of the latest top twenty. These crooks seem to be at every market and boot sale and cost the music industry millions. A bootleg collector would already own an artist's entire catalogue, so bootlegs do not affect the music industry at all.

There is a distinction that must be recognised between 'bootleg' (unreleased) recordings and 'pirate' (released) recordings.

Among the best McCartney bootlegs are 'Cold Cuts', 'One Hand Clapping' and 'Pizza And Fairy Tales' as these three titles would be considered essential listening for McCartney fans.

In 1990 Paul discussed a Beatles bootleg series called *Ultra Rare Trax*.

He said, 'This comes from all the outtakes and all the ... well, the thing is, we were never really very careful. I mean, we went down to EMI to record and when the recording was done, we went home. You know, we didn't watch where they put the tape. So all you needed was one engineer to let a friend in one night, or even take a little copy for himself. You'd be surprised how kind of available that stuff is. You've just got to know where the file is, and get in one evening. It's funny, some guys broke into EMI once to try and get some tapes, but they couldn't find it. They couldn't find all our stuff. I was like amongst all this crazy stuff ... We'd have little demo tapes just to check on whether the mix was the mix we wanted you know. And it falls by the wayside. You move house or something ... and a box goes. I think that is where it all comes from.'

Paul actually admitted that he was a bootlegger of other people's concerts. When he was asked if this fitted in with his attitude of prohibiting others from taping his shows he said, 'Yeah, some guy accosted me on the street the other day and said, "Your Company has just sued me for bootlegging. And I just saw you say you like bootlegs." And I said, "yeah, but you got caught".'

Bored As Butterscotch

A poem composed by Roger McGough when he was a member of the Scaffold. Paul read the poem and wrote a tune around it, which his brother Mike, also a member of the Scaffold, played around with. The group recorded the number, but it remained unreleased by them. Eventually, the number appeared on *Woman*, Mike McGear's (McCartney's) 1972 album issued by Island Records. The track was credited to Mike McGear/A Friend/Roger McGough.

'Woman' was also the title of completely different numbers written separately by John Lennon and Paul McCartney.

Brainsby, Tony

A British publicist who acted as Paul's personal PR for several years in the 1970s. He died in 2000.

Brand New Boots And Panties

A tribute album in honour of the late Ian Dury, issued in Britain on Monday 9 April 2001. It featured every song from Dury's 1977 album *New Boots And Panties*, with the tracks being performed by several different artists. Paul recorded the Dury number 'I'm Partial To Your Abracadabra' for the album, backed by Dury's original band, the Blockheads.

The ten tracks were: 'Wake Up And Make Love With Me', Sinead O'Connor; 'Sweet Gene Vincent', Robbie Williams; 'I'm Partial To Your Abracadabra', Paul McCartney; 'My Old Man', Madness; 'Billericay Dickie', Billy Bragg & the Blokes; 'Clever Trevor', Wreckless Eric; 'If I Was With A Woman', Cerys Matthews; 'Blockheads', Grant Nicholas; 'Plaistow Patricia', Shane MacGowan; 'Blackmail Man', Keith Allen.

The album featured a cover with artwork by Peter Blake, who designed the *Sgt Pepper* cover and was issued as a CD on Newboots 2CD, on cassette on Newboots 2MC and in a limited edition on gold vinyl on Newboots 2LP.

Brat Awards

An awards ceremony presented by the *New Musical Express*. Paul attended the 1 February 2000 ceremony at the Mermaid Theatre, London to accept an award for the Beatles as 'The Best Band Ever'.

Paul thanked John, George, Ringo and God and said, 'I'm delighted. I would much rather attend a ceremony with awards voted for by the readers. I came here because it was the readers' choice, unlike the Brits, which is chosen by a committee. With these awards, you know what's going on. With the others, you don't know what's happening backstage politically.

'I was told that we had won by a landslide, so that's why I wanted to come here today. The Beatles were a good mix of people. We were the coolest. There was a time when I wondered whether I would ever feel like playing again, but I am enjoying it as much now as I did when the Beatles first started.'

Bread
A hit comedy series on BBC 1 TV, penned by Carla Lane. Carla was a friend of the McCartneys and talked Linda into appearing in an episode of the series. Paul and Linda travelled to Liverpool and filmed there on Sunday 26 June and Monday 27 June 1988, with Paul appearing as Linda's driver. Some additional filming took place in front of a live audience at the BBC TV Centre in Wood Lane, London on Sunday 11 September. The episode was first shown on BBC 1 on Sunday 30 October 1988. George Harrison mistakenly watched the BBC show *Howard's Way*, and missed Paul's appearance on *Bread*. He said, 'I'd never seen the show before, and I just couldn't figure out how Paul was going to fit in with all these posh people on boats.'

Breakfast Blues
An unreleased track recorded during the *Wild Life* sessions. Paul played the number when he appeared on WBCS-FM, the New York radio station, on Wednesday 15 December 1971.

Breakfast Time
An early-morning BBC 1 TV programme. Paul appeared on the show on Thursday 17 July 1986 in an interview which had been recorded the previous day at MPL's offices in Soho Square, London. Selina Scott conducted the interview. The interview was 14 minutes in length and was split into two sections, separated by the 8 o'clock news bulletin. The first part saw Paul discussing the subject of hard drugs. During the second half of the programme he discussed his appearance on the Prince's Trust Gala, his making of the 'Press' video, and talked about his movie *Give My Regards To Broad Street*, of which, when considering the critical mauling it received, he said 'I didn't like it that much either.'

Breakfast With Frost
An interview with Paul by David Frost that took place at the MPL offices in London on Friday 28 November 1997. It was pre-recorded and broadcast by the BBC on Sunday 7 December 1997.

During the interview, Paul revealed that during Linda's struggle with cancer he talked to God. He commented: 'It makes you talk to it, or God, or It, a little more often. There's a thing in alcoholism – we have a few friends who are reformed alcoholics – called the 12-step programme, and that's very helpful. When everything is on top of you, and you've really got nowhere to turn, hand it over, give it all up and say "This is too much for me, I'm going crazy, I'm crying, I'm weeping,

I'm frightened." Linda and I both found that very useful, the idea that there is someone to hand it over to. I think that unless you're very religious you live your life not thinking there's anyone you can hand it over to and I think, you know, that was quite a blessing for us to find.'

When asked if he believed in life after death, he said: 'When we were kids we always used to say, "OK, whoever dies first get a message through." Stuart Sutcliffe was the first to die, and I never had a message, and I don't think any of us did. Then when John died, I thought, well maybe we'll get a message from John. So I don't know, I don't know if you can get a message back (after death). Maybe you live but there's no postal service.'

On the subject of drugs Paul mentioned that he has called for the legalisation of cannabis and said that he favoured decriminalisation of the drug. He also recalled the time he spent in jail in Japan after being found in possession of marijuana and said that he would advise people not to take drugs. When his children asked him about drugs he said, 'I always say to them . . . if you want my advice, you know, don't do any.'

Paul also revealed that John Lennon was not to blame for the break-up of the Beatles and that John wasn't as acerbic in private as he appeared to be in public. 'In public, his front would come down. I never needed it, because my family in Liverpool were quite comfortable, so I was always comfortable around people. But John was always having to fight. He had this acerbic wit, so they call it, as a defence mechanism. When we were in private, he had no need of that. I could just as often be the baddie in a situation, and he could be a real soft sweetie, you know. He took everyone by surprise there.'

He also said, 'When we got to America, the first question was, "Who does the words, and who does the music?" Everyone had always done it like that. And we said, "Well, he does them some days, and I do them others. It depends, really, we'll swap around."'

Returning to the subject of John, he commented, 'It's not that John's home life wasn't happy: it was the circumstances – not living with his dad, then his uncle dying, and then his mum being run over when she'd come to visit him and his auntie, who was a lovely lady called Mimi. They were more middle-class than any of us other Beatles had ever met. We thought of John as quite posh. Later, the image was – oh, the Working Class Hero! Power To The People – which he was, and which he believed. But his upbringing was quite posh compared to us. We'd lived in council houses, and they owned their own house. How posh can you get?!

'Aunt Mimi used to take the mickey out of me. She'd say, "Your little friend's here, John," and I'd say, "Thank you" – that was me. But she didn't like George at all – she thought John was scraping the bottom of the barrel there, for some reason.'

When Frost asked Paul who was responsible for the Beatles splitting up, he said, 'I think we'd come full circle, I think we all sort of knew it.

There wasn't really anywhere else to go, except what I suggested, which was to go back to square one, and go out and work little clubs. I thought that might re-energise us, give us an idea of where it was really at – which was the four of us playing music. But to blame any one person, I don't think that's right. I think we all shared whatever blame there was going round.'

Bridge On The River Suite

An instrumental number. While recording 'Country Dreamer', Paul began to play this to get the feel of the 'Country Dreamer' song by playing the guitar for five minutes before starting on the song. Alan Parsons, the engineer on the session, liked the instrumental and edited it together. He then gave it to Paul who overdubbed it with bass, drums, synthesiser and rhythm guitar while recording in Paris in November 1973. Then, during the Nashville sessions on 11 July 1974, Paul and Tony Dorsey added a horn arrangement played by Bill Puitt on sax, George Tidwell and Barry McDonald on trumpets, Norman Ray on baritone sax, Dale Quillen on trombone and Thaddeus Richard on a sax solo. The number, 3 minutes and 12 seconds in length, was then issued as the flipside of 'Walking In The Park With Eloise' by the Country Hams. It was also issued as a bonus track on the 1993 re-release of the *Wings At The Speed Of Sound* album.

Britton, Geoff

A drummer and karate specialist, born on 1 August 1943. Geoff had represented Britain in the first karate international tournament in Japan and held a black belt. He had also been in rock bands such as the Wild Angels and East of Eden and had turned down jobs with Uriah Heep and Curved Air.

Geoff was teaching karate at Maidstone when he was informed by one of his pupils, Clifford Davies, former manager of Fleetwood Mac, that Paul was holding auditions in London for a Wings drummer to replace Denny Seiwell.

On Friday 26 April 1974 Geoff applied and was given an audition at the Albery Theatre, St Martin's Lane, London. There were 52 drummers at that initial audition.

He was to comment, 'You should have seen the people there. It was like a Who's Who of the music industry. But I was a bit disappointed actually because I thought it would be a chance to play with McCartney, but they'd hired session men to play with us instead. Wings just sat out in front in the audience and watched. I wasn't really nervous. I'm never nervous, although I might be a bit apprehensive. We had to play about four numbers – some of it quite advanced stuff for an ordinary rock and roll number. Anyway, I got up there and did my stuff.'

He was to perform at a second audition at a ballroom in Camden and was to add, 'A few days later I got this phone call and they said I was on the short list of five, and this time it would be Paul and the group playing. That time I had a twenty per cent chance, yet I felt it was more hopeless than ever. I met Paul and the group and they were really nice. After that I got a phone call saying they'd narrowed it down to two geezers. Each of us spent a whole day with the group and had dinner with them.'

On Thursday 16 May, after the third audition, he received confirmation that he'd got the job. He said, 'One day the phone rang. It was Paul. He said, "Well, we've decided," and he was mucking about, geeing me up. In the end I said, "Well, who's it gonna be?" and he said, "You got the job".'

Geoff told *Melody Maker*, 'Working with McCartney is such an opportunity, such an eye-opener that you just can't afford to blow it. You can learn so much from him.'

Unfortunately, there were frictions within the band and Geoff didn't get on well with either Jimmy McCulloch or Denny Laine. During recordings in New Orleans the following year he was sacked.

He'd initially been sacked when they were in Nashville, reportedly for fighting with McCulloch. He had also blotted his copybook by telling the British music press that he was the only health nut in the group and didn't use drugs like the others. He also complained that when he'd joined Wings he'd been promised royalties in the order of 'telephone figures', but had only received his scale wages, plus session fees and bonuses.

Recalling the time, he said, 'I was so depressed. I dreaded going to New Orleans with them. It should have been the happiest time of my life. But I was miserable and hated it. There was no sincerity in the band and every day it was a fight for survival, a fight to re-establish yourself. Denny could be very cruel. He and Jimmy were supposed to be close moochers who would go out boozing together and yet, when the chips were down, he tried to get Jimmy shafted out with a knife in the back. He's a bastard. I should have chinned him. I regret it now.'

Britton was later to call *Rolling Stone* magazine to inform them that the *Melody Maker* had misquoted him. He said, 'They said I hate Jimmy McCulloch's guts. What I really said is that he's a nasty little cunt.'

On his return to Britain following his participation in part of the *Venus And Mars* recordings, he said, 'I completed half the tracks on the album and then a local drummer called Joe English did the rest.' He added, 'It's a funny band, Wings. From a musician's point of view, it's a privilege to do it. From a career point of view, it's madness! No matter how good you are, you're always in the shadow of Paul.'

Joe English replaced him.

Other groups Britton was also a member of include Gun, Rough Diamond, Manfred Mann's Earthband, Raphael Ravenscroft and Key.

Broadcast, The

Recorded during the *Back To The Egg* sessions at Lympne Castle in Kent in September 1978. The number was meant to give the effect of a multitude of radio stations weaving in and out of the track and features the poems 'The Sport Of Kings' by Ian Hay and 'The Little Man' by John Galsworthy, both read by Harold Margery.

David Bowie was to say that 'The Broadcast' was his favourite number on the LP.

Broadway Avenue

Situated in Wallasey, L45, 'over the water' from Liverpool. The McCartney family lived in No. 92 for almost two years in 1942 and 1943. Jim and Mary McCartney had moved into the small house with baby Paul, but decided to move back to Liverpool after Mike McCartney was born, because being near the docks the street suffered damage in some of the worst air raids.

Brolly, Brian

The managing director of MPL Communications Ltd and Paul's business manager for five years from 1974 to 1978 when he resigned. He gave no public statement as to the reason for his resignation but later became a director of Andrew Lloyd Webber's Really Useful Company. After leaving the Really Useful Company he formed a partnership with Alan Parsons and Eric Woolfson.

Brother Paul

A disc inspired by the 'Paul is Dead' rumour. Issued in America on Silver Fox 121 in 1969, it was by Billy Shears and the All Americans and had 'Message To Seymour' as the flip.

Brown Eyed Handsome Man

A track from the *Run Devil Run* album lasting 2 minutes and 27 seconds. It was penned by Chuck Berry and recorded at Abbey Road Studios on Friday 5 March 1999 with Paul on lead vocal, bass guitar, percussion and electric guitar, Dave Gilmour on electric guitar, Mick Green on electric guitar, Peter Wingfield on piano, Ian Paice on percussion and Chris Hall on accordion.

Paul felt that the accordion sound gave the number a Cajun feel. Buddy Holly's version of the number is well known, but Paul liked Berry's original version, particularly the humour in the lyrics and his mention of 'Milo De Venus' when referring to the *Venus de Milo*.

Brown, Bryan

An Australian actor whose films include *Breaker Morant*, *Kim* and *Tai Pan*.

Brown has also starred in a number of television epics such as *A*

Town Like Alice and *The Thorn Birds* (during the filming of which he met British actress Rachel Ward whom he would later marry).

Paul was looking for an Australian actor to portray his manager in *Give My Regards To Broad Street* and picked Brown, commenting: 'I had the idea to take some of the elements from my life and slightly exaggerate or change the facts wherever necessary. So, Stephen Shrimpton, mild-mannered Australian manager of MPL in London, became Steve Stanley, tough, outspoken Aussie with a sarcastic streak.'

Bruce McMouse Show, The

In 1974, Paul worked out several ideas for movies that he wanted to make utilising the film arm of his MPL organisation. One of them was to be a television special called *The Bruce McMouse Show*, a documentary of the 1972 Wings tour of Europe that would use actual film clips intercut with animation relating the adventures of a family of mice (Bruce, his wife Yvonne and kids Soily, Swooney and Swat) who lived under the stage.

It was a 50-minute film directed by Barry Chattington. The project was never shown although Paul, in a 1975 interview, mentioned that he was 'just finishing a children's thing we've had for a couple of years now'.

Brung To Ewe By

A 12" promotional one-sided disc to promote the *Ram* album, which was issued in 1971 on SPRO-6210. The disc was sent to radio stations in the US and was accompanied by two notes, one from McCartney Productions, the other from Paul and Linda.

The message from McCartney Productions read: 'The enclosed disc contains fifteen different 30-second and 60-second introductions to *Ram* album tracks. These spots were recorded in the studio by Paul and Linda during their work on *Ram*. This disc is an exclusive limited pressing for radio stations only. We hope you will use and enjoy them. If you have any questions or comments, please contact me at McCartney Productions, 257 Central Park West, New York City, 212-787-3811.

'Regards, Diana Brooks, McCartney Productions Inc.'

The message from Paul and Linda read:

'Dear DJ,

'Here are some introductions you might like to use before *Ram* album tracks.

'We made them while we were doing *Ram* and they're designed to play straight into an album track, or out of it for that matter.

'Anyway, if you'd enjoy using them, we'd enjoy having you. Ram on!

'Paul and Linda McCartney.'

The spots included jingles, the sound of Paul and Linda bleating like sheep and spoof interviews.

B-Side To Seaside

The flipside of 'Seaside Woman', the Suzy And The Redstripes single.

The number was recorded by Paul and Linda at Abbey Road Studios on Wednesday 16 March 1977. Paul produced and the engineer was Mark Vigars. Paul played drums, Mellotron, electric guitars, Moog, congas and banjo, in addition to providing backing vocals.

'B-Side To Seaside' was also included on the *Wide Prairie* album.

Burfitt, Eddy

He is now the Reverend Eddy Burfitt. The Catholic priest had attended Liverpool Institute with Paul. He recalled that he and Paul had a habit of turning up late for school and said that when they found the gates closed they went through the office and mingled with the crowd. This came to an end when they were caught rushing in one day.

He also remembered that another pupil called Neil Harding actually recorded Paul singing 'Pick A Bale Of Cotton'. Burfitt, Harding, Baz Evans and another pupil provided four-part harmony.

Burfitt also remembered George Harrison being a very popular pupil, but also a rebel who would wear a fluorescent tie instead of the standard school tie.

Butlin's

British holiday camps, originally launched by Billy Butlin.

They were particularly popular in the immediate post-war years when few Britons travelled abroad for their holidays. The camps had lots of entertainment provided with theatres and ballrooms, bars, talent competitions and variety shows.

In 1957, the McCartneys went to Butlin's in Filey for their holiday, possibly because their cousin Bett Robbins and her husband Mike were redcoats at the camp. While they were there, Paul and Mike were encouraged to enter a talent competition in the Gaiety Theatre there where they performed 'Bye Bye Love'.

The camps also had 'Rock And Calypso' ballrooms where young groups could perform. Rory Storm & The Hurricanes, with drummer Ringo Starr, were to appear at Butlin's holiday camps.

Paul wrote a letter to Butlin's early in 1960 trying to get work for the group.

'I should like to apply for an engagement at your holiday camp. The group is known as the Beatles and is led by John Lennon. The boys, whose ages range from eighteen to twenty, have a good deal of experience behind them (Ardwick Hippodrome, Manchester, Liverpool Empire, many local ballrooms and clubs too numerous to mention) and, as they have been working together for four years, have acquired three very important things – competence, confidence and continuity. I am sure that the group will completely fill your requirements.

'Yours sincerely,

'JP McCartney.'

Bye Bye Love

The Everly Brothers hit record. This was the first number Paul ever performed in front of an audience, together with his brother Mike. The occasion took place at a Butlin's holiday camp in Filey, Yorkshire in August, 1957.

Jim McCartney had taken his two sons to the camp for a holiday and Mike was nursing a broken arm from an earlier accident.

Bett, one of their cousins, worked at the camp and her husband Mike Robbins was host of a singing contest sponsored by the *People* newspaper. 'Cash prizes of over £5,000 must be won', was the slogan on posters for the nationwide contest in which various heats were taking place.

For the Filey audition Paul, who had brought his guitar with him, entered both himself and his brother Mike, although he hadn't informed Mike about it.

They arrived at the Gaiety Theatre in the camp and Robbins announced, 'Ladies and gentlemen, for the first time on any stage, a really warm welcome for – the McCartney Brothers.'

The 13-year-old Mike was surprised, slightly annoyed, but agreed to get up on stage and sing 'Bye Bye Love', which the two had often rehearsed together at home. Paul then sang 'Long Tall Sally', but they failed the audition because of their tender age, which rendered them ineligible.

C Moon
The B-side of 'Hi, Hi, Hi', issued in Britain on 1 December 1972 on Apple R 5973 and in America on 4 December 1972 on Apple 1857. It received much radio exposure when the BBC banned the A-side. Describing the song, Paul commented: 'Remember Sam The Sham and "Wooly Bully"? Well, there's a line in that that says "Let's not be L7" – and at the time everyone was saying "What's L7 mean?" Well, L7, it was explained at the time, means a square – put L and 7 together and you get a square. So I thought of the idea of getting a C and a crescent moon together to get the opposite of a square. So "C Moon" means "Cool".

C'Mon People (single)
A track from the *Off The Ground* album, penned by Paul, that was issued in Britain as a single on Monday 22 February 1993 on Parlophone R6338 and in America on Monday 12 July 1993.

Paul revealed to the newspaper *The Journal*, 'We figure John's spirit was in the studio with us. We were recording "C'mon People", which feels a bit Beatley, and we were singing the "Oh yeah, oh yeah" part. My guitarist Hamish Stuart and I found ourselves singing it just like John. We couldn't help it. In the end, we just didn't fight it, and went with it. John's spirit *was* in the studio with us. We figured that John visited us on that vocal!'

Paul pre-recorded the number for BBC 1's *Top of the Pops* on Wednesday 17 February 1993 and it was transmitted the following day. The promotional video of the song was premiered on ITV's *The Chart Show* on Saturday 20 February and repeated twice in March.

As usual with Paul's releases, 'C'Mon People' was issued in

different formats. Apart from the 7″ there was the cassette on Parlophone TCR 6339, which featured the title track, and 'I Can't Imagine'. There was a 5″ CD on CDRS 6338 which also included the numbers 'I Keep Coming Back To Love' and 'Down To The River' and an additional CD which featured 'C'Mon People', 'Deliverance' and 'Deliverance Dub'.

A maxi-single was issued in America on 12 June 1993, which had a playing length of 19 minutes and three seconds. It was produced by Paul and Julian Mendelsohn and comprised four tracks: 'C'mon People', 'I Can't Imagine', 'Keep Coming Back To Love' (a McCartney/Stuart composition) and 'Down To The River'.

'C'Mon People' was also included on 'Parlophone February 1993', an 18-track in-house Parlophone sampler cassette. Also in February 1993 on a 2-track CD single for 'C'Mon People' issued to disc jockeys on CDRDJ 6338 which contained a four-minute radio edit and the full-length version at 5 minutes and 45 seconds. Kevin Godley directed the promotional film of 'C'mon People'.

A live version of the number lasting 5 minutes and 59 seconds was recorded during the Kansas City concert on 31 May 1993 and included on the *Paul Is Live* album.

Café On The Left Bank
The first number recorded by Wings when they arrived at the Virgin Islands for the *London Town* album sessions. It was taped on 2 May 1977 on the yacht *Fair Carol* and was inspired by Paul's memories of his trip to Paris, including his first time there in the company of John Lennon in 1961.

Cage
See 'Emotional Moments'.

Caldwell, Iris Violet
Attractive blonde sister of the late Liverpool Beat group leader Rory Storm.

'I was twelve years old when George Harrison was my first boyfriend and that was before he joined any group. The Beatles were just forming then as the Quarry Men. I used to go out with him after school. He went to the Institute, the same school as Paul, and late afternoon he'd come round to our house to see me.'

Iris was one of the Liverpool girls who Paul went out with and their romance lasted for twelve months. For at least six of those months they were serious enough about each other to be what Northerners would call 'going steady'.

Iris trained as a dancer from the age of fifteen and appeared as a showgirl at holiday camps and on variety shows.

When she appeared at the Tower Ballroom, New Brighton on a bill with the Beatles she was wearing a brief costume which highlighted her slim legs in fishnet stockings and Paul couldn't take his eyes off her.

She was seventeen when Paul dated her and when Iris discussed the period in interviews with publications such as *Beatles Monthly*, she commented:

Epstein was not very pleased that I was going out with Paul and I wasn't allowed to go anywhere with the group in case any of their fans saw me. But every night after they'd appeared at the Cavern, Paul would come round to our house – and when they went away to Hamburg he used to write me the most fantastic letters which I wish now I'd kept because they were very funny letters, talking about all the things that happened to them, and sometimes he'd illustrate them with a little cartoon. In those days they had funny names for people and Paul always used to call me 'Harris' and he signed his letters 'Paul McCoobie'. I can remember one letter he'd sent in which he wrote: 'We've been down to London jumping around,' and he illustrated it with a little picture of himself jumping around on his bum.

The first song they recorded together after signing with Epstein, 'Love Me Do', was a song that Paul had written for me – and when the record entered the *New Musical Express* chart at No. 27 I was over the moon and going round saying 'Cor', 'Wow', 'Jeez', because a song written for me was in the charts.

Then there was another time that Paul was round at our house and he started writing out the words for this song he'd written called 'Please Please Me'. I told him the words sounded terrible.

I remember once my Mum told him he had no feelings, so he phoned her up one night and said, 'Listen to this song I've just written,' and sang her 'Yesterday' over the phone. That was when they were appearing at the ABC, Blackpool. After he'd finished the song he said, 'There – and you say I've got no feelings!'

Paul was very hard to dislike. Even in his teens there was something about him, a sort of charisma that used to strike people when they met him for the first time. And he always knew exactly where he was going, even though people often used to tell them they (the Beatles) would never make it.

We used to travel down to the pictures by bus, and then when they started getting successful he went out and bought a second-hand Ford Classic – and I thought, 'Wow – I'm going out with a feller who's got a car!' That was a big thing because we were all broke and not many people could afford cars in Liverpool.

The only present Paul ever gave me was a pair of black leather gloves that he brought me back from Hamburg, but he was always sending me letters and postcards.

When Rory had to go into Broadgreen Hospital in Liverpool to have a cartilage operation, Paul took me into the hospital to see him. There were all these people lying in bed, some of them looking so pale that they could have been at death's door – and then when Paul the Beatle walked in they all started to rise from their beds, carrying sticks and crutches, and hobbling down the ward to shake his hand or ask for his autograph!

I'm quite sure that there were many other girls around at that time, but I didn't know about any of them, and I didn't actually know that he was going out with anyone else, if you see what I mean. I used to say to him, 'Why don't you go out with somebody else?' though I never thought that he did, and then when he came back from London once and said that he had met Jane Asher I didn't want to go out with him anymore, though we remained good friends and kept a good relationship.

Iris married singer Shane Fenton in 1964 and they went on the road as a double act. Shane was to change his name to Alvin Stardust and had the major chart success that had eluded him in the 1960s.

The couple were divorced several years later and Iris remarried in 1983.

Calico Skies

A track from the *Flaming Pie* album lasting 2 minutes and 32 seconds. It was penned by Paul and produced by Paul and George Martin and engineered by Bob Kraushaar on 3 September 1992. Paul sang vocal and played acoustic guitar and knee slap/percussion.

When the McCartneys were in America they became housebound when Hurricane Bob knocked out the power. Paul says, 'I spent a lot of time on my acoustic guitar, making up little bits and pieces. "Calico Skies" was one of them.'

He also commented, 'I wanted to write something acoustic in the vein of "Blackbird", something simple that would stand on its own, so if anyone said, "Give us a song", you could just do it.'

The number was also reworked for the *Working Classical* album.

Call It Suicide

A number that Paul submitted to Frank Sinatra, also sometimes known simply as 'Suicide'. It was rejected.

Campaign For The Protection Of Hunted Animals

An organisation which Paul joined late in 1998 when he called for a ban on fox hunting, stating; 'This activity can in no way be called a sport. It is simply bare-faced cruelty to animals in a so-called civilised society. It is not only outdated but ought to be banned.'

Can't Buy Me Love

John was to say, 'That's Paul's completely. Maybe I had something to do with the chorus, but I don't know. I always considered it his song.'

The number was composed on the upright piano that was situated in the sitting room of the group's suite at the George V Hotel in Avenue George V in Paris. The group recorded it shortly after it was written when George Martin flew over from London to produce the number at the Pathe Marconi Studios in the *Rue de Sevres* on Wednesday 29 January 1964. It was issued in Britain on 20 March 1964. Advance orders were so huge that it leapt straight to No. 1 in the charts. It was issued in America on 4 March 1964 with an advance order of 2.1 million copies and topped the charts for five weeks. It was No. 1 on that historic day, 4 April 1964, when the *Billboard* chart read:

No.1: 'Can't Buy Me Love'. No. 2: 'Twist And Shout'. No. 3: 'She Loves You'. No. 4: 'I Want To Hold Your Hand'. No. 5: 'Please Please Me'. No. 31: 'I Saw Her Standing There'. No. 41: 'From Me To You'. No. 46: 'Do You Want To Know A Secret?' No. 58: 'All My Loving'. No. 65: 'You Can't Do That'. No. 68: 'Roll Over Beethoven'. No. 77: 'Thank You Girl'. That week also saw Beatles albums at No. 1 and No. 2 in the album chart.

Paul was to say how proud he was when Ella Fitzgerald recorded the number.

The song was used in the film *A Hard Day's Night* and a military band played the number at Buckingham Palace when the Beatles received their MBEs.

A version of this number, lasting 2 minutes and 15 seconds, was included on the *Tripping The Live Fantastic* album. It was recorded live on 21 October 1989 at the Olympiahalle, Munich, Germany during the 1989/90 World Tour.

Capitol Records

In 1962, Capitol Records, as the American branch of EMI Records, was offered the Beatles product to release. Alan Livingstone, then head of Capitol, made the much-quoted statement: 'We don't think the Beatles will do anything in this market.' And EMI went on to deal with Vee Jay. It rapidly became obvious that the Beatles were hot property and Capitol did a rapid about-turn, even launching a major promotional campaign when the group arrived in America in February 1964.

After the Beatles disbanded, Paul remained with the label until 1979 when he joined George Harrison, Ringo Starr and Apple Records in a five-million-dollar lawsuit against the company, alleging breach of contract, claiming Capitol had failed to pay them their full royalties.

Paul signed with CBS Records in North America and remained with them until rejoining Capitol on Tuesday 29 October 1985 in a deal negotiated with Bhaskar Menon, the company's chairman, President and Chief Executive Officer.

Commenting on the agreement, he said, 'Paul is a very special part of the EMI music family and I am absolutely delighted that we have renewed our longstanding friendship with him. It is particularly gratifying that McCartney now returns home to Capitol Records in North America where we have greatly missed the privilege of representing his recording career since 1979.'

When asked about the disappointing sales when Paul was with CBS, Menon commented, 'Whether those Columbia albums were successful or not, I really don't know. But we're talking about one of the world's most distinguished musical geniuses. We have every reason to believe he has an enormous career and audience before him.'

Paul sent him a telex: 'Dear Bhaskar, it's great to be back, knowing we can catch up with old acquaintances and hopefully make many new friends. All the best to the lads and lasses in the field – now let's get on with making hits. Warm personal regards, Paul McCartney.'

Paul withdrew his legal battle once he re-signed with Capitol and his first record under the new contract was the 'Spies Like Us' single.

Under the arrangement Paul's CBS albums *Back To The Egg*, *McCartney II* and *Tug Of War* would revert to Capitol Records as from 1 January 1986. *Pipes Of Peace* and *Give My Regards To Broad Street* would also be transferred to Capitol two years hence.

Carlton New Year, A
When Carlton Television obtained the television franchise previously held by Thames Television they decided to herald in their new station, which was to officially launch on 1 January 1993, with a special programme, *A Carlton New Year*.

On Friday 20 November they videotaped Paul and his band performing specially for the show before an audience at the Mean Fiddler in Harlesden, north London.

Paul performed 'Good Rockin' Tonight', 'We Can Work It Out', 'Biker Like An Icon', 'I Owe It All To You', 'Michelle', 'Hope Of Deliverance', 'Can't Buy Me Love' and 'Down To The River'. He also played an impromptu version of 'Auld Lang Syne'.

Only three of the numbers were actually screened when 'A Carlton New Year' was broadcast – 'Hope Of Deliverance', 'Michelle' and 'Biker Like An Icon'.

Carnegie Hall
The Beatles became the first rock-'n'-roll band ever to appear at this prestigious New York concert hall when they performed there on 12 February 1964. Nearly 28 years later, on Monday 18 November 1991, Paul appeared there to attend the American premiere of his *Paul McCartney's Liverpool Oratorio*.

Conducted by Carl Davis, the ensemble was almost identical to the one that performed at the world premiere in Liverpool, although soprano Barbara Bonney had replaced Dame Kiri Te Kawana in the role of Mary Lee. Also there was the Collegiate Chorale and the Boys Choir of Harlem that had replaced the Liverpool Philharmonic Choir and the Cathedral Boys Choir.

Paul's party included Linda and his children, plus his brother Mike. Celebrities in the audience included Steve Martin and his wife Victoria Tennant, Jessica Lang, Mickey Dolenz and Christi Brinkley.

Carnival Of Light

A sound collage lasting 13 minutes and 48 seconds that Paul composed, making him the first member of the Beatles to conduct experiments in sound.

In 1966 Paul commissioned some 'underground' designers Binder, Edwards and Vaughan to decorate his piano in a psychedelic style.

The trio organised various events at 'underground' venues and asked Paul if he would compose a piece of experimental music for a forth-coming promotion of theirs at the Roundhouse in Camden Town, London, which they were to call the 'Carnival of Light Rave'.

Paul then booked Abbey Road on 5 January 1967 for a five-hour session to record his composition, initially completing some overdubs for the 'Penny Lane' track.

Recording the session on a four-track machine were George Martin and engineer Geoff Emerick. The first track had the rhythm backing of drums and organ. Track two included distorted electronic guitar sounds. Track three included the sound of a church organ and John and Paul screaming, with Paul shouting, 'Are you alright?' and John shouting out 'Barcelona!' three times. Further mixed sounds were included on track four, along with the shaking of a tambourine.

George was to tell Emerick: 'This is ridiculous. We've got to get our teeth into something a little more comfortable.'

The composition was only played on 28 January and 4 February 1967 at the Roundhouse. In 1996 Paul suggested that he might use 'Carnival of Light' as background music to an experimental film in which he would use Beatles images in a similar way to that of his film of the Grateful Dead.

George Harrison vetoed 'Carnival Of Light' from appearing on the *Beatles Anthology* CDs.

In 1994, in tribute to Paul's composition, a British band, Ride, named their third album *Carnival Of Light*.

Carolina On My Mind

A track on James Taylor's eponymous debut album for Apple, on which Paul played bass guitar. Produced by Peter Asher, it was recorded between July and October 1968 and issued in Britain on 6 December 1968 on Apple SAPCOR 3 and reissued on 6 November 1970 on Apple 32 and on 25 June 1971. It was issued in America on 17 February 1969 on Apple SKAO 3352 and reissued on 26 October 1970 on Apple 1805.

After Paul inducted Taylor into the Rock 'n' Roll Hall of Fame on 6 March 2000, Taylor held a press conference backstage after the event and was asked about Paul and George recording with him. He said, 'That was great. They were recording the White album at Trident Studios at the time and I was using whatever studio time was left over, just the space in between. I heard rough mixes of "Hey Jude" and "Revolution" and was present when they were recording and overdubbing. They played on "Carolina On My Mind".'

Carry That Weight

This number was originally recorded by the Beatles as one song at Abbey Road Studios on 2 July 1968, along with 'Golden Slumbers' and it was included on the *Abbey Road* album.

Paul commented, 'It's like a story. A bit like "Act Naturally", where a tag line keeps coming up, you know, "So and so and so and so," but all he said was "Act Naturally". It's like your troubles. But it was like a comedy when I first heard it. There was a verse about a drunkard who got drunk, got in trouble with the wife, and, "I woke up the next morning with a weight upon my head and found it was my head." It's like the normal kind of troubles that everyone has. It's one of those songs where you've got everything and you've got everything going great but, you know, "This morning, one of my eggs broke." It's just so trivial. "My bright shoes are a bit tight."'

In 1980 John was to comment, 'I think he was under strain at that period.'

Casey, Howie

A saxophonist from Liverpool. Howie's early band, the Seniors, were popular on Merseyside prior to the Beatles and were the first Liverpool group to travel to Hamburg.

On their return from Germany, Howie told Bill Harry, founder of Mersey Beat: 'Paul had terrific talent and used to play left-handed guitar. He didn't actually play it, he had the amp turned down low.'

Howie's group also became the first Liverpool group to have a record released in Britain, but they never achieved chart success, although one of their vocalists, Freddie Starr, became a successful comedian.

Howie was to team up with Paul in later years, playing on his records and touring with Wings as tenor saxophonist. One of his noted sax solos is to be found on 'Bluebird' from *Band On The Run*. He also appeared on the albums *Wings At the Speed Of Sound* and *Wings Over America*, plus the singles 'Jet' and 'Coming Up'.

Catcall

A tune that Paul composed in the late 1950s, which was occasionally played by the Beatles during appearances at the Cavern. It was an instrumental number which Paul polished up and gave to Chris Barber in 1967, and became Barber's first release on the new Marmalade label in the UK on Marmalade 598-005 on 20 October 1967, with 'Mercy Mercy Mercy' on the flip. At the recording session Paul was one of the people adding vocal 'catcalls' at the end of disc.

It was also included on Barber's album *Battersea Rain Dance*, issued in Britain on 13 March 1970 on Polydor 2384-020.

7 Cavendish Avenue

The St John's Wood house which Paul owns and which he lived in between the years 1966 and 1978.

Paul moved out of Cavendish Avenue in 1970, because he wanted his children to enjoy life in the country outside the pressures of the big city, although he continues to own the house and occasionally finds uses for it. For example, on Saturday 7 July 2001 he held a party at the premises with guests who included Chrissie Hynde, Kevin Godley, Lulu, Twiggy, Peter Blake and Dave Gilmour.

The property is now an officially listed building.

The other Beatles were living out of London, but Paul opted to remain in the city. While still living with the Ashers, he bought the three-storey detached Regency house on Tuesday 13 April 1965 for £40,000 from a physician Desmond O'Neill MD, BCH, MRCP and moved into the premises during the first week of August 1966. Immediately, on Saturday 6 August, it became the setting for a BBC radio interview for a programme called 'The Lennon and McCartney Songbook'.

Paul had commissioned the house to be refurbished at a cost of £20,000 by John and Marina Adams. Marina was the elder sister of Paul's friend John Dunbar.

The house had a high wall and a large black metal electronically operated gate with intercom system. Paul also installed a Victorian streetlamp in the drive.

The property was only five minutes away from Abbey Road Studios.

It also had a sunhouse at the end of the garden with a geodesic dome.

He and John Lennon painted a mural together on one of the walls. When the house was redecorated, Paul preserved it and had the decorators paint around it.

Initially Paul also hired a live-in couple, the Kellys, to act as housekeeper and butler, but they were sacked for selling their story to an Australian magazine.

Under the influence of art-dealer Robert Frazer, Paul began to build up an impressive art collection in the house, which included a specially commissioned version of Landseer's *Monarch of the Glen* by Peter Blake, a statue by Takis and various paintings by Magritte, including one which inspired the Apple logo.

Paul also had a music room in which he worked with John Lennon on compositions for the *Sgt Pepper* album. He also composed numbers such as 'Hey Jude', 'Getting Better' and 'Penny Lane' there.

Cavern Club

The Liverpool cellar club where the Beatles had their first taste of fame. It originally opened as a jazz club on 16 January 1957. The Quarry Men made their Cavern debut on Wednesday 7 August 1957, but Paul was on holiday at the time. Paul made his Cavern debut with the group on 24 January 1958. As the Beatles, Paul, John, George and Pete Best appeared on a lunchtime session on 21 February 1961 and their first evening session took place on Tuesday 21 March 1961.

Ray McFall was the Cavern owner at the time and it was during his reign that the Beatles made all their appearances. Sadly, Ray overextended his capital and declared himself bankrupt in February 1966. Various other owners took over the premises until Liverpool Corporation decided to demolish it to make way for an extraction duct for the underground railway. A replica Cavern was built in Mathew Street in 1984 as part of a new building called Cavern Walks.

Paul commented: 'The Cavern was great. Every gig was more like a private party than a public performance. We knew most of the audience by first name – it was a very personal atmosphere rather than singing and playing to an impersonal crowd.'

Exactly 12,953 days since he last appeared at the Cavern club in Liverpool on 3 August 1963, Paul turned up there again on Tuesday 14 December 1999, saying: 'I can't think of a better way to end the century than with a party at the Cavern, singing the songs of my heroes.'

Paul had formally announced his reappearance at the Cavern on the *Parkinson* TV show on Friday 3 December 1999 and an advance party of his personnel from MPL took over the Cavern for three days from Sunday 13 December.

Eighteen-year-old Ben Lomas, who had changed his name to John Lennon by deed poll three weeks earlier, began a 22-hour wait on the Sunday outside the HMV Shop in order to enter a raffle for 250 tickets for the appearance. A hundred and fifty other fans joined the queue. Four other HMV stores – in London, Birmingham, Glasgow and Newcastle-upon-Tyne – also had queues as each had been given 250 forms, which were to be entered into the draw.

There were only 300 people allowed into the venue for the show, which was broadcast worldwide on the Internet as a live webcast with 3.5 million fans logging in, causing the weblink to be jammed. On the evening of the show, highlights were broadcast on *The Richard Allison Show* on BBC Radio 2. BBC 1 television was to broadcast the show on 15 December.

Paul's backing band were the musicians from his *Run Devil Run* album sessions: Dave Gilmour and Mick Green on guitars, Peter Wingfield on keyboards and Ian Paice on drums. They performed a fifty-minute set with 'Honey Hush', 'Blue Jean Bop', 'Brown-Eyed Handsome Man', 'Fabulous', 'What It Is', 'Lonesome Town', 'Twenty Flight Rock', 'No Other Baby', 'Try Not To Cry', 'Shake a Hand', 'All

Shook Up' and 'I Saw Her Standing There'. The encore was 'Party', after which Paul left the stage after saying, 'See you next time . . .'

The number 'Lonesome Town' was dedicated to 'loved ones past and present' and 'Twenty Flight Rock' was dedicated to the day he met John: 'When I met John, I knew all the words to this song and I think that's why I got to join the band.'

Cayenne
An instrumental number that Paul had penned as a teenager. It was around the same time he composed another instrumental 'Catcall', both songs probably influenced by the Shadows. 'Cayenne' was included on the Beatles *Anthology 1* CD.

CD:UK
A British children's television programme, screened on Saturday mornings. Paul appeared on the show on 24 November 2001, performing 'Freedom' live in the studio and giving a short interview. He was backed by Blair Cunningham on drums, Giles Palmer on guitar and Luke Juby on keyboards.

Celebration
A Granada Television programme, filmed at the Royal Court Theatre, Liverpool on Monday 26 November 1979 at the final Liverpool concert of Wings' British tour, and broadcast on Thursday 29 November 1979 with performances of 'Every Night' and 'Getting Closer'.

Charities
Paul is a great supporter of a number of charities, despite views he made about charities in August 1968 during an interview with Alan Smith of the *New Musical Express*.

Paul commented, 'Starvation in India doesn't worry me one bit, not one iota. It doesn't, man. And it doesn't worry you, if you're honest. You just pose. You've only seen the Oxfam ads. You can't pretend to me that an Oxfam ad can reach down into the depths of your soul and actually make you feel more for those people – more, for instance, than you feel about getting a new car.

'If it comes to a toss-up and getting a new car, then you'd get a new car. And don't say you wouldn't! I know one is morally better than the other one, but to say anything else, I'd be a hypocrite!'

In December 1979, Paul and Linda donated $10,000 to a charity which had been established by the *New York Times* to help the poor at Christmas time.

In 1993, a survey discovered that Paul was among the public figures who most often donated money to charities. However, he preferred to keep his charitable work as discreet as possible, which led London's

Evening Standard to report, 'If McCartney gives you money, and you reveal the fact, he asks for it back!'

Below are just some of the donations Paul has made to various charities.

In May 1990, Paul donated £250,000 to the Sloane-Kettering Cancer Centre and Friends of the Earth.

On 4 February 1997, a London exhibition and charity auction took place at the Saatchi Gallery in which rock stars donated artwork dedicated to musicians who had inspired their own work. Paul contributed a tribute to Buddy Holly for the charity War Child, which ran a music therapy centre for children in Bosnia.

In 1986, Paul was making donations to the Cystic Fibrosis Research Trust.

On Thursday 11 October 1990, Paul and Linda handed out leaflets in support of a fight to save Rye Memorial Hospital from closing. He also headed a march to Rye Town Hall to support the cause on Monday 15 October during which he offered to pay the wages of nurses wishing to work in the casualty department that had recently been closed. Paul and Linda did pay for agency nurses, but the Hastings Health Authority refused permission for them to work in the department.

When the League Against Cruel Sports contacted Paul and Linda in 1991 regarding deer hunting, they then paid £100,000 for 80 acres of Exmoor woodland and banned the Devon and Somerset Staghounds from hunting on the land. Paul commented that stag hunting was 'a barbaric sport which takes civilisation back to the days of the Dark Ages'.

In 1997, Paul contributed to the National Endowment for Science and the Arts, which supports young artists and inventors.

In 1999, he was supporting the Breast Cancer Care charity which were selling limited edition prints of Linda's photograph 'Stallion And Standing Stone'. During April Paul involved himself in a series of auctions for the charity in the American Borders bookshop chain.

In 1994, Paul heard that Gillette was actively involved in vivisection. He sent a letter to the chief executive Alfred Zeien, and parcelled Gillette products including razors, shaving cream, correction fluid and pens and returned them to the company. He wrote, 'Learning that Gillette still blinds and poisons animals to test its products, my wife Linda and I have cleaned our cupboards of anything and everything produced by Gillette. When Gillette modernises its testing practices and abolishes animal testing, I'll happily buy your products again. Until that time, we will boycott Gillette and speak out for animals at every opportunity.' The company's response that it never tests on animals where 'an alternative is available', was not the sort of answer Paul was looking for.

Also in 1994, Paul and Linda contributed to an art exhibition called

'War Child' set up to develop a therapy centre in Sarajevo. Incidentally, during 1994 Paul donated $1,710,000 to various charities.

In 1995, Paul and Linda sent 22 tons of Linda's vegetarian burgers to Bosnia as part of the 'War Child' relief effort.

He gave his first donation to a political party in 2000 when he gave the Liberal Party £10,000 to help in its animal welfare campaign, which included a foxhunting ban.

NESTA (the National Endowment for Science and the Arts) was a trust set up by the Labour government in 1997 in which artists would bequeath copyright or patent royalties to help finance young British artists. Paul was one of the first celebrities to pledge support for the scheme.

In July 2000, Paul donated $1 million to establish the Linda McCartney Endowed Fund for research into breast cancer at the Arizona cancer centre in Tucson, Arizona where Linda had been treated prior to her death. He only made one stipulation – that no animals be used for research.

In December 2000, Paul donated £5,000 to the Hound Cottage Animal Sanctuary in Tichfield, Hampshire, which needed repairs following flood damage.

In March 2001, Paul contributed a drawing of a squirrel which fetched £4,000 for the Calvert Trust and Northumbria Wildlife Trust Charity and he also donated a signed lithograph of Linda to raise money for the Irish Cancer Society.

He contributed £5,000 in 2001, for a violin study for 14-year-old Misha Lindan from Belarus.

On 14 June 2001, the first of a series of Internet auctions was held to raise money for the building of a new cultural centre on the island of Montserrat. Four hundred and ninety reproductions of the original string quartet score for 'Yesterday' were placed for auction, each of them personally signed by Paul and George Martin.

In February 2001, Paul and Stella joined a campaign to save an abused elephant called Rhanee. Paul said, 'Rhanee has suffered for many years at the hands of people who should have known better. Human beings have not respected Rhanee's needs to date. Please let the "Rhanee Appeal" make amends for past abuse and support the campaign to let her live the rest of her life in the sanctuary she deserves.'

These are just a small selection of some of the charities that Paul has supported. He has donated money amounting to millions, has spent a great deal of his time supporting charities and attending functions, even joining protest marches and has also donated musically – and has allowed his recordings to be used on a number of charity albums.

See also: 'Help!' and 'Good Causes'.

Charity Bubbles

A single by the Scaffold, issued in 1969 on which Paul played guitar.

Charley Rose Show, The

An event that took place in New York at the 92nd Street YM-YWHA (Young Men's/Young Women's Hebrew Association), Manhattan on 24 April 2001. Paul took part in his second poetry reading of 'Blackbird Singing' (his first was in Liverpool) at the Kauffman Concert Hall in the building. Charley Rose was introduced and then Rose introduced Paul. Paul spent half an hour reading his various poems, with a story to tell behind each poem and information on what prompted him to compose them. On the poem about Ivan Vaughan he mentioned that since Ivan had studied the classics at Cambridge it was fitting to write a poem in his memory. There were a number of poems about Linda. On one of them he recalled seeing signs of her presence after she had died – of hearing wind chimes when there wasn't a wind, of seeing a rare white squirrel while he was out riding who fixed her gaze on Paul. Another poem was about when Linda was in hospital and Paul set up a camp bed in her room. He recalled a one-eyed dog named Prince in his recollections of early life in Liverpool.

The poems Paul read were 'In Liverpool', 'Dinner Tickets', 'Ivan', 'Jerk Of All Jerks', 'Masseuse Masseuse', 'Chasing The Cherry', 'City Park', 'Trouble Is', 'Tchaiko', 'Blessed', 'Her Spirit', 'Maxwell's Silver Hammer', 'Why Don't We Do It In The Road?' and 'Here Today'.

The onstage interview by Charley Rose followed, although Rose made a couple of mistakes, which Paul had to correct him on. At one point he asked Paul what it was like meeting Paul – and Paul said that he was Paul. Rose also referred to the Quarry Men and the Everymen. Paul related a story of how he took his daughter Stella to meet the Maharishi Mahesh Yogi. He cleared up any misunderstanding in previous reports about the Beatles' attitudes to the Maharishi by stating that he believed the guru was genuine, that he didn't chase women and wasn't obsessed with money. He'd considered that the meeting would be a short one, but it continued for hours and when Stella asked the Maharishi if he could say something on her video camera, he said 'Enjoy'.

Rose asked Paul to name his favourite song. Paul said that it wasn't 'Yesterday', but that he didn't think it would be fair to pick a favourite although he particularly liked 'Here, There And Everywhere'.

Chattington, Barry

A director of Paul's *Appaloosa* film. He also directed the unreleased 'The Bruce McMouse Show' and the 1979 film *Rockestra*.

Children Children

A number from the 1978 *London Town* album that was co-written by Paul and Denny Laine. Originally inspired by a waterfall in Paul's garden, the track was recorded at Abbey Road. It was 2 minutes and 20 seconds in length.

Choba B CCCP: Back In The USSR

An album, recorded in a London studio on Monday 20 July and Tuesday 21 July 1987. During the sessions, Paul recorded eighteen 'oldies'.

Richard Ogden, MD of MPL, had been to Russia to negotiate the exclusive release. He said Paul wouldn't be receiving any royalties, only a one-off payment for the album and would also be paid in roubles, which were non-negotiable outside Russia.

Choba B CCCP, containing eleven of the tracks, was originally released on Monday 31 October 1988 in Russia only, when 40,000 copies were issued on the Melodiya label. A second edition was issued in Russia on Thursday 24 December 1987 in an edition of 350,000 copies.

The first album included eleven tracks, had a gold-coloured back cover sleeve and liner notes by a Soviet writer, while the second included two additional tracks, Paul's version of Fats Domino's 'I'm Gonna Be A Wheel Someday' and George Gershwin's 'Summertime'. The sleeve notes were penned by former *New Musical Express* writer Roy Carr and translated into Russian.

It was later released by EMI on CD on Monday 30 September 1991 on Parlophone CDP 7 976152, in a version containing thirteen tracks. It was issued in America on Tuesday 29 October on Capitol CDP 7976152. The EMI release was retitled *The Russian Album*.

Four of the tracks had previously been released in Britain in 1987. They were: 'Midnight Special', 'Don't Get Around Much Anymore', 'Lawdy Miss Clawdy' and 'Kansas City'. The other tracks had previously been unreleased and were: 'Twenty Flight Rock', 'Bring It On Home To Me', 'Lucille', 'I'm Gonna Be a Wheel Someday', 'That's Alright Mama', 'Summertime', 'Ain't That a Shame', 'Cracking Up' and 'Just Because'.

Paul produced the album, Peter Henderson was the engineer, and apart from Paul, the other musicians were Mick Green on lead guitar, Chris Whitten and Mick Gallagher on bass guitar, Nick Garvey and Henry Spinetti on drums.

Paul had also been interviewed about the album in a Communist Youth League paper and said, 'Since the Beatles days, many of my most loyal fans have been in Russia. It has always concerned me that these people hear our music many years after its release or through illegal importing and home taping. The new spirit of friendship has enabled me to make this gesture to my Russian fans.'

In Russia black-market Western albums usually sold for the equivalent of $85, while Paul's album would be sold officially at around $5.

Chronology

1866

23 November. Paul's fraternal grandfather, Joseph McCartney, is born in Great Homer Street, Everton, Liverpool.

1874

2 June. Paul's fraternal grandmother, Florence Clegg, is born at 131 Breck Road, Everton, Liverpool.

1880

19 January. Paul's maternal grandfather, Owen Mohin, is born in Tullynamalrow, Eire.

1896

17 May. Florence Clegg marries Joseph McCartney at Christ Church in Kensington, Liverpool.

1902

1 July. James McCartney, Paul's father, is born at 8 Fishguard Street, Everton, Liverpool, the son of Joe and Florence McCartney.

1909

29 September. Mary Patricia Mohin, Paul's mother, is born at 2 Third Avenue, Fazakerley, Liverpool, the daughter of Mary and Owen Mohin.

1931

18 December. Allen Klein is born in Newark, New Jersey.

1934

18 February. Yoko Ono is born in Tokyo, Japan, the daughter of Eisuke and Isako Ono.

19 September. Brian Epstein is born at a private nursing home in Rodney Street, Liverpool. His mother, Malka, was the daughter of a furniture manufacturer in Sheffield and his father, Harry Epstein, owned a furniture store in Liverpool.

1938

3 December. Julia Stanley marries Alfred Lennon at Mount Pleasant Register Office, Liverpool.

1939

10 September. Cynthia Powell is born in Blackpool.

15 September. Mimi Stanley, John's aunt, a nursing sister at the time, marries George Smith, a dairy farmer.

1940

23 June. Stuart Sutcliffe is born at the Simpson Memorial Maternity Pavilion in Edinburgh, Scotland. His parents are Charles and Martha Sutcliffe.

7 July. Richard Starkey is born at home at 9 Madryn Street, Liverpool to Elsie and Richard Starkey.

9 October. John Winston Lennon is born at Oxford Street Maternity Hospital, Liverpool, on a night when there was no bombing in the city. His parents are Alfred and Julia Lennon.

25 December. Phil Spector is born in the Bronx, New York.

1941
15 April. James McCartney and Mary Mohin are married in Liverpool. They immediately move into furnished rooms in Sunbury Road, Anfield.

1942
18 June. James Paul McCartney is born in Walton Hospital, Liverpool to James and Mary McCartney.
24 September. Linda Louise Eastman is born in Scarsdale, New York, the daughter of Lee and Louise Eastman.

1943
24 February. George Harrison is born at home at 12 Arnold Grove, Wavertree, Liverpool.
17 May. Priscilla Maria Veronica White is born in Liverpool.

1944
7 January. Peter Michael McCartney is born in Walton Hospital, Liverpool.
22 July. Peter Asher, brother of Jane Asher, is born.
29 October. Denny Laine (real name Brian Hines) is born in Birmingham.

1945
17 March. Pattie Boyd is born.

1946
5 April. Jane Asher is born in London.
4 August. The McCartney family move to a ground-floor flat in Sir Thomas White Gardens, Liverpool.
14 August. Maureen Cox is born.

1949
7 February. Joe English, later to become drummer with Wings, is born in Rochester, New York.

1953
4 June. Jimmy McCulloch, later to become a guitarist in Wings, is born in Glasgow, Scotland.

1956
18 June. Paul's father buys him a trumpet for his birthday.
31 October. Paul's mother, Mary Patricia McCartney, dies of breast cancer. She is 47 years of age.

1957
16 January. The Cavern Club opens in Mathew Street, Liverpool as a jazz club.
6 July. Paul meets John Lennon for the first time at the Woolton Village Fete. He later receives an invitation to join John's group, the Quarry Men.
29 July. Paul and his younger brother Michael attend a Scout camp at Hathersage, Derbyshire.

7 August. The Quarry Men make their debut at the Cavern, but Paul isn't with them as he is on holiday at a summer Scout camp in Hathersage in the Peak District.

18 October. Paul makes his debut with the Quarry Men at the New Clubmoor Hall, Liverpool, but fluffs his chance to become their lead guitarist.

1958

24 January. Paul appears at the Cavern for the very first time as a member of the Quarry Men.

6 February. George Harrison goes to see the Quarry Men at Wilson Hall on the invitation of Paul and plays 'Raunchy' on the bus home to Paul and John.

20 March. Paul and John see Buddy Holly and the Crickets perform at the Philharmonic Hall, Liverpool.

12 July. The Quarry Men record at Percy Philips's studio in Kensington, Liverpool. They perform two numbers, Buddy Holly's 'That'll Be The Day' and 'In Spite Of All The Danger', an original composition credited to McCartney/Harrison, and the first original Beatles number on record.

1959

29 August. The Quarry Men make their debut at the Casbah club in West Derby, Liverpool.

1960

23 April. Paul and John hitchhike to Caversham, Berkshire where they stay at the Fox and Hounds, a pub run by John's cousin Bett Robbins and her husband. They perform as the Nerk Twins during a Sunday lunchtime session at the pub on 24 April.

14 May. As the Silver Beats they perform at Lathom Hall, Seaforth for promoter Brian Kelly.

18 May. As the Silver Beetles they embark on a short tour of Scotland as backing band to singer Johnny Gentle, and three of them decide to use stage names. Paul chooses to call himself Paul Ramon, although they are not acknowledged on the tour under their new names as the billing reads simply 'Johnny Gentle And His Group'. Paul says he chose that name 'because it sounded really glamorous, sort of Valentino-ish'.

6 August. With their appearance at the Grosvenor Ballroom, Birkenhead cancelled, the Beatles drop in at the Casbah Club in West Derby and are impressed by Pete Best's new drums. Paul then phones Pete to invite him to audition for the group. After experiments with the Beatals, the Silver Beats, The Silver Beetles and the Silver Beatles, they decide to simply call themselves the Beatles. Any suggestion that this had anything to do with a Marlon Brando film called *The Wild Ones* is ridiculous because this film was banned in Britain until the late 1960s and the group could not have seen it at the time they devised their name.

12 August. Pete Best auditions for the Beatles and is accepted as their new drummer.

16 August. The Beatles set off for Hamburg.

17 August. The Beatles begin a season at the Indra club in the Grosse Freiheit. Paul comments, 'Hamburg was a good exercise really in commercialism – a couple of students would stick their heads round the door, and we'd suddenly go into a piece of music that we thought might attract them. If we got people in, they might pay us better. That club was called the Indra – which is German for India.'

4 October. The Beatles move to the Kaiserkeller, a larger club in the Grosse Freiheit. Paul was later to write to Bill Harry about his experiences in Hamburg: 'The first time we went to Hamburg we stayed four-and-a-half months. It's a sort of blown-up Blackpool, but with strip clubs instead of waxworks; thousands of strip clubs, bars and pick-up joints, not very picturesque. The first time it was pretty rough but we all had a gear time. The pay wasn't too fab, the digs weren't much good, and we had to play for quite a long time.'

29 November. Paul and Pete Best are arrested for allegedly attempting to burn down the Bambi Kino. (This was probably because they were about to play at a club called the Top Ten and the manager of the Kaiserkeller, who also owned the Bambi Kino, objected. Paul wrote to Bill Harry, 'One night we played at the Top Ten Club and all the customers from the Kaiserkeller came along. Since the Top Ten was a much better club, we decided to accept the manager's offer and play there. Naturally the manager of the Kaiserkeller didn't like it. One night prior to leaving his place, we accidentally singed a bit of cord on an old stone wall in the corridor and he had the police on us.')

1 December. Paul and Pete Best return to Liverpool after being deported from Hamburg, Germany.

27 December. The Beatles appear at Litherland Town Hall and make their names felt on Merseyside for the first time when the show opens and Paul launches into 'Long Tall Sally'. A temporary bass guitarist, Chas Newby, accompanies them.

1961

5 January. At Litherland Town Hall, Paul begins to play bass with the group. (Stuart Sutcliffe, the Beatles' regular bass guitarist, had remained in Hamburg. They had used Chas Newby on their first three Liverpool gigs following their Hamburg appearance, but he turned down this job as he was returning to college. George refused to become the group's bass guitarist, so it fell to Paul to take over.) Promoter Brian Kelly is so impressed with the band that he books them for 36 dates at his various venues. Stuart returned to Liverpool at the end of January 1961, appeared on their Cavern debut and returned to Germany in late February. He played with them at the Top Ten Club in Hamburg before leaving the group.

9 February. The group plays at the Cavern for the first time under the name the Beatles. Their fee is £5. This is the only time that Stuart Sutcliffe makes an appearance with them in Liverpool as the Beatles.

14 February. At Litherland Town Hall on Saint Valentine's Night Paul sings 'Wooden Heart'. He is wearing a red satin heart pinned to his jacket with the names of the group on it. This is raffled off and when the winner climbs on the stage, Paul kisses her.

21 February. The Beatles make their lunchtime debut at the Cavern. They also appear at the Cassanova Club and Litherland Town Hall, the first time they have done three dates in Liverpool on a single day – but it won't be the last.

1 April. The Beatles appear at the Top Ten Club in Hamburg and it is during this period that Stuart Sutcliffe leaves the group.

22 April. The Beatles begin their first professional recording session with Bert Kaempfert, backing Tony Sheridan, but although Stuart Sutcliffe is present, he does not play on the session. The only original number they perform is 'Cry For A Shadow', an instrumental by George Harrison, meaning the first original Beatles composition recorded by a professional A&R man is also credited to George.

1 June. Paul's girlfriend Dot Rhone arrives in Hamburg with John Lennon's girlfriend Cynthia Powell. Paul and Dot then go and stay at the houseboat of Rosa Hoffmann. Paul and John buy their girlfriends leather skirts.

22 June. When the group begin their recording session with Bert Kaempfert at the Friedrich-Ebert-Halle, Hamburg, Paul takes over on bass guitar.

2 July. When the Beatles return to Liverpool, Stuart Sutcliffe elects to remain in Hamburg to study art and Paul is now the permanent bass guitarist with the group.

6 July. Bill Harry coins the phrase Mersey Beat and launches a newspaper of that name. On page 2 he features a piece on the Beatles, which he has commissioned John to write. Harry calls it 'Being A Short Diversion On The Dubious Origin Of Beatles, Translated From The John Lennon'. In it John writes, 'After a few months, Peter and Paul (who is called McArtrey, son of Jim McArtrey, his father) . . .' This misspelling of Paul's surname also appears in a couple of other issues. In this same article is the reference to 'a man appeared on a flaming pie and said unto them "From this day on you are Beatles with an A".' This led to Paul calling a new album *Flaming Pie* decades later.

20 July. The entire cover of the second issue of *Mersey Beat* is devoted to the Beatles recording in Hamburg. Brian Epstein orders 144 copies for his NEMS Whitechapel shop.

3 August. Brian Epstein's first record review column appears in *Mersey Beat*.

17 August. At their appearance at St John's Hall, Tuebrook in Liverpool, the Beatles are joined by bass guitarist Johnny Gustafson of

the Big Three. So Paul takes a microphone and walks among the audience singing.

30 September. John and Paul decide to hitchhike to Spain on £100 which John has been given for his 21st birthday by his Aunt Elizabeth. Once they reach Paris they decide to stay there.

9 October. John and Paul celebrate John's 21st birthday in Paris. During their stay Jurgen Vollmer gives them what becomes the 'Beatles haircut'. Paul recalls, 'Jurgen was in Paris on that trip, and we said, "Do us a favour, cut our hair like you've cut yours." So he did it, and it turned out different, 'cause his wasn't exactly a Beatle cut, but ours fell into the Beatles thing. We didn't really start that. The impression that got over was that it was just us, that we'd started it all. We kept saying, "But there's millions of people in art schools who look like this. We're just the spokesmen for it."'

On their return to Liverpool via London they buy some Chelsea boots from Anello and Davide, which are to become known as 'Beatle Boots'.

19 October. Paul plays rhythm guitar when the Beatles team up with Gerry and the Pacemakers and Karl Terry at Litherland Town Hall to call themselves the Beatmakers.

9 November. Brian Epstein had phoned Bill Harry to arrange for him to visit the Cavern to see the Beatles and he turns up at a lunchtime session, accompanied by Alistair Taylor.

3 December. The Beatles meet Brian Epstein at his office in NEMS, Whitechapel and Epstein is irked that Paul arrives thirty minutes late because he had a bath. George Harrison comments that Paul may have been very late, but he was very clean!

1962

1 January. The Beatles record for Mike Smith at Decca studios in West Hampstead, London. Brian Epstein has advised them not to perform many of their own numbers, so they only record three: 'Hello Little Girl' by John and 'Like Dreamers Do' and 'Love Of The Loved' by Paul.

5 February. Pete Best is ill and can't make the booking, so Ringo Starr sits in for him at the Kingsway Club, Southport.

12 February. The Beatles audition for Pete Pilbeam for the BBC radio programme *Teenager's Turn*. Paul and John sing two numbers each, with Paul performing 'Like Dreamers Do' and 'Till There Was You'. Pilbeam notes 'Yes' for John and 'No' for Paul.

10 April. Stuart Sutcliffe dies in Hamburg following a brain haemorrhage probably caused by an earlier fall down the stairs at Astrid Kirchherr's house.

18 August. Brian Epstein tells Pete Best that the other members of the group have instructed him to sack him as their drummer and hire Ringo Starr. Ringo makes his debut at Hulme Hall, Port Sunlight.

21 August. Ringo Starr makes his debut at the Cavern as a member of the Beatles.

22 August. The Beatles are filmed at the Cavern by a Granada film crew directed by Dick Fontaine.

23 August. Paul acts as best man at the wedding of John Lennon and Cynthia Powell.

4 September. Paul, John, George and Ringo record 'Love Me Do' and 'How Do You Do It?' at Abbey Road Studios. George Martin is dissatisfied with the session and also with the drummer.

6 September. Paul's own version of the Beatles backing a stripper, based on a letter he sent to Bill Harry, is published in *Mersey Beat* under the title 'A Little Bare'.

11 September. When they return to Abbey Road to record their first single they discover that George Martin has booked a session drummer. Ringo Starr thinks, 'They've done a Pete Best on me.'

20 September. Another piece by Paul, based on his letters to Bill Harry, is published in *Mersey Beat* under the title 'Hamburg'.

5 October. 'Love Me Do' is released.

26 October. The Beatles' debut single 'Love Me Do' enters the *New Musical Express* charts at No. 49. Paul recalls, 'If you want to know when we knew we'd arrived, it was getting in the charts with "Love Me Do". That was the one. It gave us somewhere to go.'

30 December. Linda See, née Eastman, gives birth to a baby daughter, Heather.

1963

3 January. The Beatles top the *Mersey Beat* poll for the second time.

11 January. The Beatles' second single 'Please Please Me' is released.

18 April. Paul meets Jane Asher for the first time following a concert appearance at the Royal Albert Hall. Paul and George are heard singing 'Lend Me Your Comb' on Radio Luxembourg.

18 June. Paul's 21st birthday takes place at his Auntie Jin's house at 147 Dinas Lane, Huyton, Liverpool. An incident in which John Lennon attacks Cavern disc jockey Bob Wooler brings them their first national press story when it is reported in the *Daily Mirror*.

27 June. Paul turns up at a recording session at which Billy J Kramer and the Dakotas are recording 'Bad To Me' and 'I Call Your Name'.

6 July. Paul crowns the Carnival Queen at the Northwich Carnival.

26 August. Paul is fined £25 at Wallasey Crown Court and banned from driving for 12 months when he receives his third driving conviction for speeding.

7 September. Rosemary Hart interviews Paul for the BBC Home Service programme *A World Of Sound*.

10 September. Paul and John attend a Variety Club of Great Britain luncheon at the Savoy hotel. They receive an award as 'Top Vocal Group Of The Year'.

13 September. Paul is one of the judges on a 'Miss Imperial 1963' beauty contest at the Imperial Ballroom, Nelson, Lancashire.

16 September. Paul and Ringo set off for a fortnight's holiday in Greece with Jane Asher and Maureen Cox. Paul comments, 'We used to go to Greece because in Greece they never recognised us. Everywhere else, in Germany, in Italy, in the south of France, it was, "There's the Beatles!" and we had to run for our bloody lives.'

27 September. Cilla Black's version of the Paul McCartney composition 'Love Of The Loved' is issued on Parlophone R 5065.

2 October. Paul and Jane and Ringo and Maureen return from Greece.

13 October. The Beatles make their debut on *Sunday Night At The London Palladium*.

17 October. The Beatles are to have lunch at the Old Vienna Restaurant with the winners of a competition in the magazine *Boyfriend*. Paul is the only member to originally turn up, but the other three arrive later on.

26 October. Cilla Black's 'Love Of The Loved' enters the *Melody Maker* charts.

28 October. Anthony Newley's version of Paul's composition, 'I Saw Her Standing There' is issued in America on London 5202.

12 November. Paul is taken ill with gastric flu and the Beatles appearance at the Guildhall, Portsmouth is cancelled. It is rearranged for 3 December.

7 December. The Beatles aren't too happy with their 'It's The Beatles' show at the Liverpool Empire. When they watch a TV broadcast of it, Paul says, 'The sound's all wrong, and they keep showing George and me when John is singing. I think there's a John Lennon hater at the BBC.'

19 December. The Dowlands issue their version of Paul's composition 'All My Loving' on Oriole CB1897.

27 December. Paul and John are named 'outstanding composers of the year' in *The Times* newspaper.

29 December. Music critic Richard Buckle, writing in the *Sunday Times*, proclaims Paul and John 'the greatest composers since Beethoven'.

1964

15 January. Paul and John share a room at the George V hotel in Paris in order to write a number of songs they are committed to – for their forthcoming album and for a Billy J Kramer single.

21 January. Peter and Gordon record 'World Without Love' at Abbey Road Studios.

1 February. Liverpool band the Trends release their cover version of Paul's composition 'All My Loving' on Piccadilly 7N 35171.

9 February. Following their historic *Ed Sullivan Show* appearance, the Beatles are taken to the Playboy Club by disc jockey Murray The K. Paul says, 'The Bunnies are even more adorable than we are.'

28 February. Peter and Gordon's version of Paul's composition 'A World Without Love' is issued in the UK on Columbia DB 7225. Marilyn Power's version of Paul's composition 'All My Loving' is released on Fontana TF 448.

1 April. Paul travels to Liverpool to visit a sick relative at Walton Hospital.

10 April. Paul's composition 'Can't Buy Me Love' tops the *New Musical Express* charts.

11 April. Paul's composition 'Can't Buy Me Love' tops the *Melody Maker* chart.

14 April. Paul's composition 'Can't Buy Me Love' is No. 1 in the American charts.

15 April. David Frost interviews Paul for *A Degree Of Frost*, a BBC TV show.

20–21 April. Paul films his solo spot with actress Isla Blair at the Jack Billings TV School in Notting Hill for the *A Hard Day's Night* movie. The scene ends up on the cutting-room floor.

1 May. Peter and Gordon top the charts in the *New Musical Express* with Paul's composition 'World Without Love'.

2 May. Paul and Jane Asher and Ringo and Maureen Cox fly to St Thomas in the Virgin Islands. Paul assumes the alias Mr Manning, with Jane calling herself Miss Ashcroft, Ringo as Mr Stone and Maureen as Miss Cockroft.

8 May. Paul's composition 'One And One Is Two' is issued in Britain by Mike Shannon and the Strangers on Phillips BF 1335.

18 May. Paul's pre-recorded interview for the TV show *A Degree Of Frost* is screened.

27 May. Paul, Jane, Ringo and Maureen return home from holiday. Paul comments, 'Fantastic scenery in those islands – we really felt we were taking in another world. I remember taking the dinghy out to do some spear fishing. I had this clumsy old spear with me – honestly, it was big enough to catch whales. So I dove – or is it dived? – off the boat and started hunting around for fish. There were lots of little fish kicking around down below, but suddenly I saw some barracudas. Miniature sharks. Nasty fellows these! You can annoy other fish but barracudas are NOT for stirring. They're for avoiding. I tried to get them to go away but it didn't work. So I ran for my life – well, swam for it, anyway! You couldn't see me for bubbles. Of course I didn't catch anything on that trip.'

29 May. Paul attends a Billy J Kramer and the Dakotas recording session where they record his composition 'From A Window'. The same day sees the release in Britain of the Peter and Gordon single 'Nobody I Know', on Columbia DB 7292 written by Paul.

2 June. Paul and Jane Asher see Cilla Black at her London Palladium Show. The Beatles record Paul's composition 'Things We Said Today' and John's 'Any Time At All'.

3 June. Paul records a demo disc of 'It's For You', a number he has written for Cilla Black.

4 June. The Beatles begin their tour with deputy drummer Jimmy Nichol as Ringo is ill in University College Hospital. Paul sends him a telegram: 'DIDN'T THINK WE WOULD MISS YOU SO MUCH STOP GET WELL SOON.'

18 June. During their appearance at Sydney Stadium in Australia, Paul had to stop the show twice because the group were showered with jelly babies. He was to recall, 'I keep asking them not to chuck those damned things, but they don't seem to have the sense to realise we hate being the target for sweets coming like bullets from all directions. How can we concentrate on our jobs on the stage when we are having all the time to keep ducking to avoid sweets, streamers and the other stuff they keep throwing at us?' It is Paul's 22nd birthday and the *Daily Mirror* newspaper throws a party for him.

2 July. Paul and John attend Cilla Black's recording of Paul's composition, 'It's For You'. She was to say: 'Paul was at the recording session when I made "Anyone Who Had A Heart". He said that he liked the composition and he and John would try to produce something similar. Well they came up with this new number, but for my money it's nothing like the "Anyone" composition. That was some session we had when I made the new recording. John and Paul joined me, and George Martin. We made one track and then everyone had a go at suggesting how they thought it should be recorded.'

6 July. Following the world premiere of *A Hard Day's Night*, Paul reveals to his father that he has bought him a racing horse called Drake's Drum for his birthday.

He comments, 'My father likes a flutter – he is one of the world's greatest armchair punters.'

7 July. At Karachi Airport, one of the stopovers on their way to Hong Kong, Paul attempts to buy some souvenirs, but is mobbed by fans.

14 July. Paul is interviewed for *Highlight*, a BBC Overseas Service programme, which is transmitted on 18 July.

17 July. Billy J Kramer's version of Paul's composition 'From A Window' in released in Britain on Parlophone R5156.

29 July. Paul receives an electric shock that makes his hair stand on end during their concert at Stockholm ice hockey stadium.

31 July. Cilla Black's version of Paul's 'It's For You' is issued on Parlophone R5162.

3 August. Paul and Jane Asher visit the Talk Of The Town to see a show by Nina and Frederick.

5 August. Peter and Gordon record Paul's composition 'I Don't Want To See You Again'.

12 August. Billy J Kramer's recording of Paul's composition 'From A Window' is released in America on Imperial 66051.

13 August. The Beatles' 'Long Tall Sally', with lead vocals by Paul, tops the Dutch charts.

17 August. Cilla Black's version of Paul's composition 'It's For You' is issued as a single in America on Capitol 5258.

23 August. In the *New York World Telegram*, Brian Epstein describes the Beatles saying, 'John Lennon is brilliant, I have no doubt of that. Paul McCartney qualifies as brilliant, he's extremely intelligent. Ringo

Starr has blossomed tremendously; I think he has great acting ability, perhaps the greatest of the four. George Harrison is the most practically musical of the group.'

25 August. Paul and John visit Burt Lancaster's house where they watch the screening of the Peter Sellers film *A Shot In The Dark*.

27 August. During a press conference prior to their show at Cincinnati Gardens, Paul is asked what he thinks of gossip columnist Walter Winchell. He says, 'He said I'm married and I'm not.'

31 August. Paul speaks to Elvis Presley by telephone from the Lafayette Motel. Ringo comments, 'Paul had a nice talk with him. Though we haven't met him, we consider ourselves good friends and appreciate what each of us is doing. El and his manager were very generous to us, showering us with presents and keepsakes. These include some very expensive silver guns and holsters which the four of us and our manager Brian received.'

7 September. When they arrive in Toronto for their Maple Gardens appearance, the Beatles are mobbed by fans during which Paul's shirt is ripped. He says, 'I thought I was for it, but an immense copper lifted me up and shoved me into the elevator.'

11 September. Before appearing at the Jacksonville Gator Bowl in Florida, the Beatles insist that they will not appear before an audience that is racially segregated, with Paul commenting, 'We all feel strongly about civil rights and the segregation issue.'

11 September. Peter and Gordon's version of Paul's composition 'I Don't Want To See You Again' is released in Britain on Columbia DB 7356.

18 September. While the Beatles are in Dallas to appear at the Memorial Theater, Paul phones ten-year-old Cheryl Howard at the Methodist Hospital. She had been the victim of a hit-and-run accident. Paul says, 'A pity you can't be with us tonight at the programme'.

21 September. Peter and Gordon's version of Paul's composition 'I Don't Want To See You Again' is released in America on Capitol 5272.

24 September. Roger Webb and his Trio issue their version of Paul's composition 'All My Loving' on Parlophone R 5176.

30 September. The Chipmunks version of Paul's composition 'All My Loving' is issued in America on Liberty LIB 10170.

1 October. Paul goes to see the new James Bond film *Goldfinger*.

2 October. Paul visits Alma Cogan's recording session where she records 'It's You' – and he plays tambourine on the B-side of the record.

8 October. The Beatles record Paul's composition 'She's A Woman'.

26 October. Paul and Jane and Ringo and Maureen visit the Ad Lib club in London, one of their favourite haunts.

30 October. Alma Cogan's single 'It's You', with Paul playing tambourine on the B-side 'I Knew Right Away', is released on Columbia DB 7390.

13 November. In the weekly music paper *Disc* there are track-by-track comments by Paul on the Beatles' latest album *Beatles For Sale*.

24 November. Paul's father Jim, now aged 62, marries 35-year-old Angela Williams. Paul attends the ceremony.

8 December. Paul and Jane Asher see Spike Milligan in the play *Son Of Oblamov* and Paul announces that he will marry Jane. 'When I marry, there will be none of this secrecy stuff. It just wouldn't work out,' he says.

9 December. Paul visits Ringo in hospital where he has had his tonsils removed.

30 December. Paul and Jane Asher visit Rory Storm in Liverpool.

31 December. Paul and Jane Asher and George Harrison and Patti Boyd attend a party hosted by Sir Joseph Lockwood at Normal Newell's apartment.

1965

27 January. Paul and John, together with Brian Epstein, form a company called Maclen (Music) Ltd.

4 February. Paul and Jane Asher set off for a holiday in Hammamet, Tunisia, in a villa provided for them by the British Embassy.

8 February. Music publisher Dick James takes out a £500,000 insurance policy on Paul and John.

11 February. Paul is in Tunisia when Ringo marries Maureen Cox at Caxton Hall in London.

14 February. Paul and Jane fly back from Tunisia.

15 February. Among the numbers recorded by the Beatles at Abbey Road is Paul's composition 'Another Girl'.

17 February. Paul's composition 'The Night Before' is among the numbers recorded by the Beatles at Abbey Road.

18 February. Paul's 'Tell Me What You See' is among the numbers recorded by the Beatles. Del Shannon's album *Handy Man* on Stateside SL 10115 features his version of Paul's composition 'World Without Love'.

30 March. Paul is not happy with the recording of 'That Means A Lot'.

2 April. Glyn John's version of Paul's composition 'I'll Follow The Sun' is issued on Pye 7N 15818.

3 April. Brian Matthew interviews Paul and George on the *Thank Your Lucky Stars* TV show prior to the Beatles appearance.

8 April. Paul and Jane attend the opening of the Pickwick Club in London.

13 April. Paul buys his house in Cavendish Avenue.

14 April. Newspapers report that Paul has sent a message to the Campaign for Nuclear Disarmament marchers: 'I agree with CND. They should ban all bombs. Bombs are no good to anyone. We might as well ban the bomb as be blown up by it.'

17 April. Paul dons a disguise to go shopping in the Harrow Road and Portobello Road.

7 May. The sequence in *Help!* is filmed in which Paul is miniaturised.

18 May. Paul and Jane Asher visit actor Gene Barry following his cabaret show in London. They then go to the Pickwick Club.

27 May. Paul and Jane fly to Portugal and stay at the villa owned by Bruce Welch of the Shadows. During the journey Paul begins to write down the lyrics to 'Yesterday'.

30 May. Paul records 'Yesterday' without the other members of the Beatles.

11 June. Paul and Jane return from Albufeira in Portugal and deny to the press that they are married. Epstein has asked Paul to return from his holiday a day early so that he can attend a press reception at Twickenham Studios the following day to discuss their MBEs.

12 June. The Beatles are awarded MBEs and Paul comments: 'I'm going to wear it in the garden.' At their press reception Paul also says, 'MBE really stands for Mr Brian Epstein.' This quote is also attributed to Princess Margaret.

14 June. Paul records 'Yesterday' at Abbey Road with a string quartet and in the evening Paul and Jane visit the Cromwellian Club.

19 June. There is an announcement that Paul has recorded a solo track without the other Beatles.

29 June. Paul and George spend the day on a yacht owned by promoter Felix Marouani.

2 July. At the Beatles concert in the Monumental Bullring in Madrid, Paul introduces their numbers in Spanish.

5 July. PJ Proby's version of Paul's composition 'That Means A Lot' is released in America on Liberty 55806.

7 July. Paul and Jane and George and Pattie attend a Moody Blues party at Roehampton.

13 July. Paul and John are to be presented with awards at the Ivor Novello Awards at the Savoy Hotel, but Paul turns up late and John doesn't turn up at all.

14 July. Paul goes to the Pilgrim Theatre, Watford to see Jane perform in a play. On his new album *I Have Dreamed*, Matt Monro covers Paul's composition 'All My Loving'.

15 July. Clips of Paul receiving the Ivor Novello award are shown on *Pick Of The Songs* on Rediffusion Television.

2 August. Paul and Jane, together with three members of the Byrds, visit the Scotch of St James club.

6 August. Paul attends the Flamingo Club, London to see the Byrds perform.

9 August. Paul and John attend a recording session by the Silkie who record 'You've Got To Hide Your Love Away'. John produces and Paul plays guitar.

15 August. Jane Asher tells the *Sunday Mirror* newspaper, 'No, I am not Paul's wife – but, yes, we are going to get married.'

27 August. Paul and George attend a Byrds recording session and in the evening the Beatles meet Elvis Presley.

28 August. It is reported that Northern Songs has insured Paul and John for £1 million.

6 September. Paul and Jane see *The Killing Of Sister George* at the Duke Of York's Theatre, London.

10 September. The Silkie's version of 'You've Got To Hide Your Love Away' is released on Fontana TF 603. Paul and John produced it and Paul also contributed musically to the recording.

11 September. Paul, together with John and George, travel to Liverpool to visit relatives. Ringo's wife Maureen is expecting a baby at Queen Charlotte's Hospital, London. (Zak is born on 13 September.)

13 September. 'Yesterday', the Beatles single on which only Paul performs, is issued as a single in America.

17 September. PJ Proby's version of Paul's composition 'That Means A Lot' is issued in Britain on Liberty LIB 10215.

20 September. The Silkie's 'You've Got To Hide Your Love Away' is issued in America on Fontana 1525.

25 September. 'That Means a Lot' enters the *Melody Maker* chart.

1 October. Paul's composition 'Yesterday' reaches No. 1 in the American charts and remains there for four weeks.

3 October. Paul and Jane Asher visit the Talk Of The Town to see Frances Faye.

4 October. Paul and John attend an Alma Cogan recording session during which she covers 'Eight Days A Week'.

9 October. In the evening Paul and the other Beatles attend Lionel Bart's party to celebrate his musical *Twang!*

11 October. Paul attends Marianne Faithfull's recording session at Decca studios where she records 'Yesterday'.

14 October. 'Yesterday' is issued in Australia. John and Paul are at Kenwood working on some songs.

15 October. Paul visits the Scotch of St James club to see Ben E King.

20 October. In America, the single 'Yesterday' goes gold.

21 October. Marianne Faithfull's version of 'Yesterday' is issued in Britain on Decca F 12268.

24 October. 'Yesterday' tops the chart in Hong Kong. Paul, George and Ringo attend a party hosted by Brian Epstein at the Scotch of St James.

26 October. The Beatles receive their MBEs at Buckingham Palace.

1 November. In a newspaper interview, Paul mentions that he is writing a song with the name 'Penny Lane' in it. The Beatles record 'The Music Of Lennon And McCartney' at Granada in which Paul begins to sing 'Yesterday' and Marianne Faithfull finishes the song.

3 November. The Beatles record Paul's composition 'Michelle' at Abbey Road.

6 November. The Beatles record Paul's composition 'I'm Looking Through You' at Abbey Road.

10 November. The Beatles are at Abbey Road recording 'I'm Looking Through You' and 'The Word'.

16 November. Paul attends a Peter and Gordon concert at the Adelphi Cinema, Slough. Gene Pitney is also on the bill. Paul makes some announcements from behind the stage curtains.

22 November. The Scaffold, with Paul's brother under the name Mike McGear, signs an agency contract with NEMS Enterprises.

27 November. Paul attends a Scaffold concert at the Granada, East Ham. Also on the bill are Manfred Mann and the Yardbirds.

5 December. During the Beatles last-ever appearance at the Empire, Liverpool, Paul sits in on drums with Liverpool band the Koobas.

15 December. Peter and Gordon's version of Paul's composition 'World Without Love' is issued in America on Capitol Starline 6076.

16 December. Paul appears on a pre-recorded interview in Radio Caroline's *Pop's Happening* programme.

19 December. Paul and Jane Asher go to see the Lionel Bart musical *Twang!* at the Shaftesbury Theatre, London.

23 December. Paul has four copies of a special record made called *Unforgettable* (also known as *Paul's Christmas Album*) to give to his fellow Beatles as presents.

25 December. Paul announces, 'I suppose I will marry Jane eventually. We've been going together for three years.'

26 December. Paul falls off a moped while spending Christmas with his father in Cheshire and receives a cut to his mouth and a chipped tooth.

30 December. Paul presents his special Christmas record, *Unforgettable* (also known as *Paul's Christmas Album*), to John, George, Ringo and Jane Asher.

1966

1 January. In a *Melody Maker* interview, Paul says that Brian Epstein 'has learned a lot in a very short time and is as straight as they come'.

8 January. Paul visits Liverpool to see members of his family.

10 January. Peter and Gordon's version of Paul's composition 'Woman' is issued in America on Capitol 5579.

13 January. Two singles covering Paul's composition 'Michelle' are released in Britain. One is by David and Jonathan on Columbia DB 7800, the other by the Overlanders on Pye 7N 17034.

17 January. Connie Francis's album *All-Time International Hits*, issued on MGM C 1012, features her version of Paul's composition 'And I Love Her'.

21 January. Paul is the only other Beatle to attend the wedding of George Harrison and Patti Boyd at Esher Register Office. He and Brian Epstein were the best men.

31 January. Paul and Jane and George and Patti attend the Wyndham Theatre for the premiere of the musical *How's The World Treating You?*

2 February. The Overlanders issue their album *Michelle* on Pye NPL 18138 featuring Paul's composition as the title track.

3 February. Paul visits the Scotch of St James to watch a Stevie Wonder performance.

10 February. Paul's composition, recorded by Peter and Gordon, enters the *Billboard* chart.

13 February. Paul attends a party hosted by Brian Epstein. Other guests include John and Cynthia, Ringo and Maureen, Gerry and the Pacemakers, Cilla Black and Peter Asher.

23 February. Paul, together with Barry Miles, attends a performance by Luciano Berio at the Italian Institute in Belgrave Square, London.

24 February. 'Woman', the number Paul wrote for Peter and Gordon, enters the British charts.

6 March. Paul and Jane Asher leave for a holiday at the skiing resort of Klosters in Switzerland and return on 20 March.

7 March. Peter and Gordon's album *Woman*, with the title track by Paul using the alias Bernard Webb, is issued in America by Capitol.

9 March. David and Jonathan issue their debut album on Columbia SX 6031 with their versions of Paul's compositions 'Yesterday' and 'Michelle'.

10 March. 'Yesterday', the Beatles EP, enters the British chart.

13 March. Paul admits that he is the 'Bernard Webb', who penned the current Peter and Gordon hit 'Woman'.

17 March. Pye Records issues the album *The Dancing Sound Of Cyril Stapleton* which features two compositions by Paul, 'Michelle' and 'Yesterday'.

20 March. Paul and Jane return from a holiday at Klosters in Switzerland.

24 March. Paul and George attend the premiere of *Alfie* at the Plaza, Haymarket. The Michael Caine film also features Jane Asher.

25 March. In an interview for the *Evening Standard* in London, Paul says, 'We knew something would happen sooner or later; we always had this blind Bethlehem star ahead of us. Fame is what everyone wants, in some form or other . . . but we don't feel that famous. I mean we don't believe in our fame the way Zsa Zsa Gabor believes in hers.'

26 March. Paul leads Drake's Drum into the winner's enclosure after his father's horse wins the Hylton Plate at Aintree Racecourse in Liverpool.

1 April. Paul and John visit the newly-opened Indica Gallery in Mason's Yard, London.

4 April. The Overlanders version of Paul's composition 'Michelle' is issued on their EP of the same name.

5 April. Jane Asher is twenty years old. Paul presents her with twenty dresses.

7 April. Work begins on the recording of Paul's composition 'Got To Get You Into My Life'.

April 23. Paul spends the day songwriting with John.

25 April. The eponymous *Noel Harrison* album, issued on Decca LK 4783, features a version of Paul's composition 'She's A Woman'.

28 April. At Abbey Road an eight-piece string section is recorded for Paul's composition 'Eleanor Rigby'.

29 April. Vocal dubs for Paul's number 'Eleanor Rigby' are recorded at Abbey Road.

2 May. Paul and Ringo are interviewed for *Pop Profile*, a BBC Overseas Service radio programme.

9 May. David McCallum's album *Music – A Part Of Me*, includes an orchestral version of Paul's composition 'Yesterday'. Paul and Ringo work on Paul's composition 'For No One' at Abbey Road.

11 May. Jan and Dean's album *Folk 'n' Roll* is issued on Liberty LBY 1304 with their version of Paul's composition 'Yesterday'.

16 May. The Morgan James Duo issue their album *Talent Strikes Again* with their versions of Paul's compositions, 'A World Without Love' and 'Things We Said Today'. Paul adds his vocals to 'For No One' at Abbey Road.

26 May. *The Velvet Beat*, an album by the David Rose Orchestra on MGM C 8002, features their version of Paul's composition 'And I Love Her'.

27 May. Paul spends the evening at Dolly's, Jermyn Street with Bob Dylan and the Rolling Stones.

6 June. Paul completes his overdubs for 'Eleanor Rigby' at Abbey Road Studios.

8 June. The Beatles begin recording Paul's composition 'Good Day Sunshine' at Abbey Road Studios.

11 June. In an interview in *Disc*, Paul says, 'I don't like our American image . . . I'd hate the Beatles to be remembered as four jovial mop tops . . . I'd like to be remembered, when we're dead, as four people who made music that stands up to being remembered.'

14 June. The Beatles begin recording Paul's composition 'Here, There And Everywhere'.

16 June. Martha, Paul's sheepdog, is born in High Wycombe.

17 June. The *Daily Mirror* reveals that Paul is buying a 183-acre dairy farm near Machrihanish, Kintyre.

18 June. It is Paul's 24th birthday and his composition 'Paperback Writer' goes straight to the top of the *Melody Maker* charts.

21 June. Paul's composition 'Paperback Writer' tops the American charts.

26 June. A trip down memory lane for Paul and John as they visit some of their old haunts in Hamburg, including the Indra where they first played. Paul also meets up with Doctor Benstein, who was the Beatles' doctor during their Hamburg days.

8 July. Imelda Marcos had told the Philippines promoter of their concerts there to invite the Beatles to the Malacanana Palace to meet her, Ferdinand Marcos and 200 children. When they didn't turn up, the Marcos's were furious. The Beatles hadn't been told, but their explanation wasn't accepted by the President and his wife and the Beatles were

subjected to a hate campaign in the media and literally hounded out the country. Following this harrowing experience in the Philippines, Paul says, 'I wouldn't want my worst enemy to go to Manila.'

12 July. John and Paul receive two Ivor Novello Awards. One is for Paul's composition 'Yesterday', which is declared 'the outstanding song of 1965', the other is for Paul's composition (on which John helped in the middle eight) of 'We Can Work It Out' which had 'the highest certified British sales'. In the evening Paul produces Cliff Bennett and the Rebel Rousers recording his composition 'Got To Get You Into My Life' at Abbey Road Studios.

21 July. The Johnny Mathis album *The Shadow Of Your Smile* includes two of Paul's compositions, 'Yesterday' and 'Michelle'.

1 August. Paul pre-records an interview on the *David Frost At The Phonograph* series, which is broadcast on 6 August.

3 August. Marc Reid issues his new single, a version of Paul's composition 'For No One', on CBS 202244.

5 August. Cliff Bennett and the Rebel Rousers release their single 'Got To Get You Into My Life', written and produced by Paul. Bennett comments, 'He played the number to me on the piano and showed me how to bend the notes.'

6 August. At Paul's home in St John's Wood, he and John are interviewed for the BBC radio programme 'The Lennon and McCartney Songbook'.

10 August. Bobby Goldsboro's latest album *It's Too Late* features his versions of Paul's compositions 'Yesterday' and 'Michelle'.

26 August. In Los Angeles, Paul denies he is planning to marry Jane Asher. 'It's absolute rubbish. We're perfectly happy as we are,' he says.

29 August. Cliff Bennett's version of Paul's composition 'Got To Get You Into My Life' is issued in America on ABC 10842. 'The Lennon and McCartney Songbook' is broadcast on the BBC Light Programme.

8 September. Cliff Bennett and the Rebel Rousers reach their highest position in the British charts at No. 6 with 'Got To Get You Into My Life'.

12 September. The Beatles double A-side single of Paul's compositions 'Eleanor Rigby'/'Yellow Submarine' is certified gold in America.

15 September. Paul attends a concert of free-form music at the Royal College of Art.

16 September. Paul and John are in Paris for the weekend with Brian Epstein.

18 September. The *Sunday Times* features an interview with Paul.

21 September. *The Late Night Sound Of Golden Hits*, an album by Cyril Stapleton on Pye NPL 18152, includes his version of Paul's composition 'Here, There And Everywhere'.

25 September. Rumours begin to spread that Paul and Jane Asher will get married in December.

3 October. Rumours that Paul is to leave the Beatles begin to appear.

13 October. Paul meets John Lennon in Paris and the two spend the weekend there. Denny Laine leaves the Moody Blues.

14 October. The *New Musical Express* reports that Paul is writing the score for a film called *Wedlocked Or All In Good Time*. The film title is later changed to *The Family Way*.

15 October. Paul attends a launch party for the underground newspaper *International Times*. Other guests include Mick Jagger, Marianne Faithfull, Pink Floyd and Soft Machine.

16 October. United Artists announce that *Wedlocked Or All In Good Time* is to be renamed *All In Good Time* and that John Lennon will be helping Paul with the music. The film title eventually becomes *The Family Way* and John doesn't participate in the writing of the theme music.

24 October. 'Mellow Yellow', the Donovan single on which Paul provides some backing vocals, is issued in America on Epic 5-10098.

25 October. The Four Tops new album *On Top*, issued by Tamla Motown, features their version of Paul's composition 'Michelle'.

6 November. Paul flies to France and visits the various chateaux in the Loire valley.

9 November. When the 'Paul Is Dead' rumours begin in 1967, they state that this is the date when Paul was killed in a fatal road accident.

10 November. In the 1967 'Paul Is Dead' affair, this is the date that Paul was 'officially pronounced dead'.

12 November. Paul flies to Nairobi to join Jane Asher on holiday.

18 November. The Escorts single 'From Head To Toe', produced by Paul, is released in Britain on Columbia DB 8061.

19 November. Paul and Jane return from a holiday in Kenya.

25 November. Paul attends a press reception for the Jimi Hendrix Experience at the Bag O' Nails club.

1 December. Paul visits the Scotch of St James to see the Young Rascals make their London debut.

2 December. Paul visits Blaises Club to see the Young Rascals.

5 December. Cliff Richard's EP 'La La La La La', released in Britain on Columbia SEG 8517, contains his version of Paul's composition 'Things We Said Today'.

8 December. Paul overdubs his lead vocal on 'When I'm Sixty-Four' at Abbey Road Studios.

11 December. The George Martin Orchestra record their version of Paul McCartney's theme for the film *The Family Way*.

16 December. The Beatles' fourth Christmas flexi-disc is sent to their fans. Paul comments, 'I drew the cover myself. There's a sort of funny pantomime horse in the design if you look closely. Well I can see one there if you can't.'

18 December. Paul, Jane and George Martin attend the premiere at the Warner Cinema, Cranbourn Street, London of *The Family Way*, which credits Paul as a solo composer. He wrote 26 minutes of music for the

film. John Lennon was to comment: 'I copped money for *The Family Way*, the film music that Paul wrote when I was out of the country filming *How I Won The War*. I said, "You'd better keep that." He said, "Don't be soft." It's the concept. We inspired each other so much in the early days. We write how we write now because of each other.'

19 December. The news that Paul has composed the electronic music for the 'Carnival Of Light' at the Roundhouse is announced.

20 December. George and Ringo join Paul to continue recording 'When I'm Sixty-Four' at Abbey Road Studios.

22 December. Andy Gray, editor of the *New Musical Express*, interviews both Paul and Ringo.

23 December. Two versions of Paul's theme tune from *The Family Way*, 'Love In The Open Air', are issued as singles. The George Martin Orchestra version is issued on UA UP 1165 and a version by the Tudor Minstrels is issued on Decca F 12536.

28 December. The music critic of the American show business publication *Variety* describes Paul's theme for *The Family Way* as 'neat and resourceful'.

29 December. Paul begins working on 'Penny Lane' at Abbey Road Studios.

30 December. Work continues on the recording of Paul's compositions 'Penny Lane' and 'When I'm Sixty-Four' at Abbey Road Studios.

1967

6 January. The soundtrack album for the movie *The Family Way*, which Paul has composed, is released by the George Martin Orchestra on Decca SKL 4847.

7 January. Rumours abound in the UK that Paul has been killed in a car crash.

8 January. Paul and John attend a birthday party at the Cromwellian Club in London, held in honour of Georgie Fame's girlfriend. The *Sunday Times* reports that Paul has turned down an offer from the National Theatre to write the music for a production of Shakespeare's *As You Like It*.

9 January. At Abbey Road Studios, a collection of flutes, trumpets, piccolos and a flugelhorn are overdubbed onto 'Penny Lane'.

12 January. On the eve of her trip to America with the Old Vic Company, Jane Asher has a candlelit dinner with Paul at his Cavendish Avenue home.

13 January. Paul and Ringo see the Jimi Hendrix Experience at the Bag O' Nails club.

15 January. Paul and George attend the Royal Albert Hall to watch a Donovan concert.

17 January. Dave Mason adds his piccolo trumpet solo to 'Penny Lane'.

18 January. Jo Durden-Smith interviews Paul for the Granada Television documentary 'It's So Far Out – It's Straight Down' about the London underground scene.

21 January. Paul attends Julie Felix's birthday party in Old Church Street, Chelsea, London.
24 January. Paul meets playwright Joe Orton at Brian Epstein's Chapel Street house. Orton wishes to discuss a script for a Beatles film with them.
27 January. Parlophone issue *Got To Get You Into My Life*, an album by Cliff Bennett and the Rebel Rousers. It features Paul's composition, which he also produced, as the title track.
28 January. Paul and George visit the Royal Albert Hall to see the Four Tops perform.
29 January. Paul and John attend the Saville Theatre to see The Jimi Hendrix Experience and the Who.
30 January. Donovan's *Mellow Yellow* album is issued in America on Epic BN 26239. Donovan reveals that Paul is one of the backing singers on the title track.
31 January. 'Penny Lane' is given its first airing on the pirate station Radio London.
1 February. The Donovan single 'Mellow Yellow' is issued in Britain on Pye 7N 17267 with Paul providing backing vocals, singing the words 'Mellow Yellow'.
2 February. Petula Clark's album *Colour My World*, issued in Britain by Pet Records, features her version of Paul's composition 'Here, There And Everywhere'.
3 February. Promotional copies of 'Penny Lane' are sent to American disc jockeys. They contain an extra trumpet part not heard on the completed single.
4 February. Paul's experiment in avant garde music 'Carnival Of Light' is played at the Carnival Of Light Rave at the Roundhouse in Camden Town, London.
7 February. Mickey Dolenz of the Monkees visits Paul at his Cavendish Avenue house.
8 February. Review copies of 'Penny Lane' are sent to the British press.
11 February. The BBC TV show *Juke Box Jury* premieres the 'Penny Lane' promotional film.
13 February. The double A-side 'Penny Lane'/'Strawberry Fields Forever' is issued in America on Capitol 5810.
14 February. 'Penny Lane' is issued in Italy on Parlophone QMSP 16404.
16 February. Clips of 'Penny Lane' and 'Strawberry Fields Forever' are screened on *Top Of The Pops*.
17 February. The double A-side 'Penny Lane'/'Strawberry Fields Forever' is issued in Britain on Parlophone R 5570.
18 February. Paul meets up with Micky Dolenz of the Monkees again, who is in London on a promotional visit.
21 February. Recordings begin at Abbey Road Studios on Paul's composition 'Fixing a Hole'.
23 February. Recordings begin at Abbey Road Studios on Paul's composition 'Lovely Rita'.

27 February. 'Penny Lane' is issued in Germany on Odeon 23436.

4 March. 'Penny Lane' tops the charts in the *Melody Maker*.

7 March. Painter Peter Blake and his wife Jann Howarth have supper with Paul and Jane at Cavendish Avenue. Paul plays them an acetate of 'Lovely Rita'.

8 March. 'Michelle' is named 'Song of the Year' in the Grammy awards and 'Eleanor Rigby' is judged the 'Best Solo Vocal Performance by a Male Artist'.

9 March. The Beatles begin to record Paul's composition 'Getting Better' at Abbey Road Studios.

11 March. It is announced that 'Yesterday' has become the most covered song in popular music history with versions by 446 different artists.

14 March. 'Penny Lane' reaches the No. 1 position in the American charts. Paul meets Carla Thomas when she performs at the Bag O' Nails club in London.

15 March. Peter Blake and Jann Howarth have dinner with Paul and John.

17 March. Mike Leander's arrangement for the orchestra backing to Paul's composition 'She's Leaving Home' is recorded at Abbey Road Studios.

20 March. Paul and John record the vocal to 'She's Leaving Home'. In America 'Penny Lane' qualifies for a gold disc.

23 March. 'Michelle' is named the most performed song on radio in 1966 at the Ivor Novello Awards and 'Yellow Submarine' as the best-selling single.

27 March. Paul attends the Fats Domino performance at the Saville Theatre, London.

29 March. Recordings begin at Abbey Road on Paul's composition 'With A Little Help From My Friends'.

3 April. Paul, accompanied by Mal Evans, flies to America to visit Jane Asher, who is on tour with the Bristol Old Vic Theatre Company.

4 April. Paul attends a Jefferson Airplane rehearsal in San Francisco and plays guitar with them.

5 April. Paul flies to Denver to join Jane Asher for her 21st birthday at the Quorum Restaurant. During her American tour with the Bristol Old Vic, Jane says, 'I want to be known as a Shakespearian actress – not as Paul McCartney's girlfriend.'

6 April. Paul and Jane spend the day in the countryside of Colorado.

7 April. Paul, Jane and Mal visit a Greek theatre during their American trip.

8 April. While Jane has matinee and evening performances, Paul and Mal visit some bars, including Paul's Café and the Gilded Garter.

9 April. Paul and Mal fly to Los Angeles in Frank Sinatra's Lear Jet and are met at the airport by Derek and Joan Taylor.

10 April. Paul visits John and Michelle Phillips of the Mamas and Papas and then attends a Beach Boys recording session in Los Angeles during which they record 'Vegetables', a track from the 'Smile' album.

11 April. On his flight back to England, Paul conceives the 'Magical Mystery Tour'.

12 April. Paul arrives back in London.

19 April. Paul, John, George and Ringo sign an agreement to set up 'The Beatles and Co.'

24 April. George Martin's single of Paul's composition 'Love In The Open Air' is issued in America on UA 50148.

25 April. The Beatles begin recording Paul's composition 'Magical Mystery Tour' at Abbey Road Studios.

1 May. Peter and Gordon's versions of Paul's compositions 'I Don't Want To See You Again' and 'Woman' are issued in America on Capitol Starline CS 6155.

5 May. Paul shaves off his moustache.

12 May. Paul and John visit the Speakeasy Club.

15 May. Paul visits the Bag O' Nails Club to see Georgie Fame and meets Linda Eastman. Chas Chandler of the Animals accompanies Linda.

18 May. Paul and John attend a Rolling Stones recording session at Olympic Sound studios and provide backing vocals for 'We Love You'.

20 May. Paul joins John and Ringo on an interview for Kenny Everett's show *Where It's At*.

22 May. Esther Phillip's version of Paul's composition 'And I Love Her', now called 'And I Love Him', is issued in America on Atlantic.

24 May. Paul, John, George and Ringo all visit the Speakeasy club to see Procol Harum.

26 May. The Tremeloes record a version of Paul's composition 'Good Day Sunshine' on their album *Here Come The Tremeloes* issued on CBS 63017.

28 May. Brian Epstein holds a party at his second home in Kingsley Hill. John, George and Ringo attend with their wives, but Paul is absent, which irks Epstein.

29 May. Paul meets Jane Asher at Heathrow Airport on her return from America where she's been touring with the Bristol Old Vic Company.

2 June. Cover versions of three of Paul's compositions are released today: 'When I'm Sixty-Four' by Bernard Cribbins, 'With A Little Help From My Friends' by Young Idea and 'She's Leaving Home' by David and Jonathan.

4 June. Paul and Jane and George and Pattie see the Jimi Hendrix Experience, Denny Laine, the Chiffons and Procol Harum at the Saville Theatre. After the show, Paul throws a party at his Cavendish Avenue house.

5 June. Joe Brown covers Paul's composition 'With A Little Help From My Friends'.

8 June. Paul invites Brian Jones of the Rolling Stones to their recording session at Abbey Road Studios. Jones then plays sax on the recording of 'You Know My Name (Look Up The Number)'.

12 June. The soundtrack for *The Family Way*, which Paul composed, is issued in America on London MS 82007.

17 June. The Beatles are the cover stars of *Life* magazine, but in an article inside the issue, Paul admits that he has taken the psychedelic drug LSD.

18 June. Paul is 25 today. He attends the demo recording studio at Dick James' Music to begin producing the 'McGough & McGear' album.

19 June. Having admitted to *Life* magazine that he'd taken LSD four times, Paul tells the *Daily Mirror*, 'I don't regret that I've spoken out. I hope my fans will understand.'

21 June. Evangelist Billy Graham says, 'I am praying for Paul that he finds what he is looking for. He has reached the top of his profession and now he is searching for the true purpose of life. But I hope he will not find it through taking LSD.'

28 June. The film *The Family Way*, with music by Paul, is premiered in New York.

1 July. *Where It's At*, a BBC Light Programme, airs a pre-recorded interview with Paul in which he discusses 'All You Need Is Love'.

3 July. Paul and Jane, George and Pattie and John attend a party for the Monkees at the Speakeasy Club.

20 July. Paul and Jane Asher attend a Chris Barber recording session at Chappells Studio where Barber records Paul's composition 'Catcall'.

22 July. Paul and Jane, together with John, Cynthia and Julian, fly to Greece where they are considering buying an island in the Aegean Sea.

23 July. In Greece Paul and Jane's taxi catches fire in the intense heat.

31 July. Paul, Jane, John, Cynthia and Julian return from Greece.

18 August. The Rolling Stones single 'We Love You', with backing by Paul and John, is released in the UK on Decca F 12654.

20 August. Paul, together with John Lennon, visits Maureen Starkey at Queen Charlotte's Hospital in London. She'd given birth to her second son, Jason, on 19 August.

22 August. The Beatles begin recording Paul's composition 'Your Mother Should Know' at Chappells Studio in London.

24 August. Paul and Jane, George and Pattie, and John and Cynthia attend a Maharishi Mahesh Yogi lecture at the Hilton Hotel.

27 August. Brian Epstein is found dead at his London home. Paul says, 'This is a great shock. I am terribly upset.'

28 August. The single 'We Love You' by the Rolling Stones, with backing vocals by Paul and John, is released in America on London 905.

1 September. Following Epstein's death, all four Beatles meet at Paul's Cavendish Avenue house to discuss their future.

2 September. Paul reveals to the *New Musical Express* that the Beatles will not appoint a new manager. 'No one could possibly replace Brian,' he says.

11 September. The Beatles set off in their 'Magical Mystery Tour' bus. Paul is the first member of the Beatles to be picked up when he joins the

coach at Allsop Place in London. John, George and Ringo board the bus at Virginia Water.

12 September. Hugh Scully interviews Paul and John for the BBC news programme *Spotlight South West*.

14 September. The Beatles return to Abbey Road Studios to record another version of Paul's composition, 'Your Mother Should Know'.

18 September. The Beach Boys album *Smiley Smile* is released in America on Brother ST 9001 amid claims that Paul is heard munching vegetables on the track 'Vegetables'.

20 September. Ray Charles's version of Paul's composition 'Yesterday' is included on the album *Listen To Ray Charles* issued on HMV CLP 3630.

24 September. Paul's number 'Your Mother Should Know' is filmed at West Malling air station in Maidstone, Kent. There is a huge cast of people involved in the intricate scene and Paul commented, 'That was the shot that used most of the budget.'

25 September. The Beatles begin recording Paul's composition 'Fool On The Hill'.

2 October. The Beatles begin to record Paul's composition 'Hello, Goodbye' which will be their next single.

5 October. Vanilla Fudge issue their cover version of Paul's composition 'Eleanor Rigby'.

12 October. News leaks out that Paul and Mick Jagger have been holding discussions with a view to the Beatles and Rolling Stones becoming partners in the purchase of a London recording studio. Nothing comes of it.

20 October. The Chris Barber Band issue their version of Paul's instrumental composition 'Catcall' in Britain on Marmalade 598 005.

25 October. Paul overdubs his bass on his track 'Hello Goodbye' at Abbey Road Studios.

26 October. Garnett Mimms issues his *Live* album on United Artists ULP 1174, which contains his version of 'Yesterday'.

29 October. Paul flies to Nice in France to shoot the 'Fool On The Hill' sequence for the 'Magical Mystery Tour'.

30 October. Paul and cameraman Aubrey Dewar film Paul miming to 'Fool On The Hill' on mountainside.

1 November. Paul returns from Nice.

2 November. Paul overdubs a second bass part onto 'Hello, Goodbye'.

7 November. Paul spends a two-hour sitting at artist John Bratby's studio and three of his portraits are included in the Bratby exhibition at the Zwemmer Gallery. At Abbey Road he adds new vocals to 'Magical Mystery Tour'.

10 November. Paul directs the Beatles 'Hello Goodbye' promotional film at the Saville Theatre.

19 November. Paul and Jane visit the Saville Theatre to see the Bee Gees, Bonzo Dog Doo-Dah Band, the Flowerpot Men and Tony Rivers and the Castaways.

21 November. Paul tapes a demo disc of his song 'Step Inside Love' with Cilla Black on vocals, prior to her recording the number with George Martin for release as a single.

24 November. Paul and John attend a recording session of new Apple signing Grapefruit at IBC recording studio, Portland Place, London.

29 November. The Scaffold enter the British charts with 'Thank U Very Much'.

3 December. Paul and Jane set off to their Scottish farm on a holiday. Paul comments, 'We shall get married. I think everyone knows this. But when we don't know.'

9 December. Paul's composition 'Hello Goodbye' tops the *Melody Maker* charts.

13 December. Tom Jones's new album *I'll Never Fall In Love Again* features his version of 'Yesterday'.

20 December. Paul and Jane return to London from their brief sojourn in Scotland.

21 December. At the 'Magical Mystery Tour' fancy dress party, Paul and Jane dress up as a Cockney pearly king and queen.

22 December. Paul's composition 'Hello Goodbye' tops the *New Musical Express* charts.

25 December. Paul and Jane Asher officially announce their engagement.

26 December. 'Magical Mystery Tour' is screened on BBC TV and is slated by the critics.

27 December. Paul, who directed 'Magical Mystery Tour', commented, 'We goofed, really. My dad brought the bad news into me this morning like the figure of doom. Perhaps the newspapers are right. We'll have to wait and see.' Paul appears on David Frost's show to discuss 'Magical Mystery Tour' and says, 'the film was badly received because people were looking for a plot – but there wasn't one!'

1968

17 January. Paul, John and Ringo attend a press reception for the group Grapefruit, to celebrate the release of their debut single 'Dear Delilah'.

30 January. Cilla Black's new television series is launched on BBC TV with a song specially written by Paul, 'Step Inside Love'.

1 February. Sharon Tandy's version of Paul's composition 'Fool On The Hill' is issued by Atlantic records.

3 February. The Beatles begin recording Paul's composition 'Lady Madonna' at Abbey Road Studios.

5 February. Paul appears at a press conference at the Royal Garden Hotel, London to publicise the Leicester Arts Festival. This was as a result of a student, John Eades, who talked his way into Paul's Cavendish Avenue house claiming to be a friend. Paul commented, 'I don't know anything about the festival in detail, and this really is a complete publicity gimmick. But it's rather a nice gimmick, don't you think?'

10 February. Paul and Jane Asher attend the Queen Elizabeth Hall to see Paul's brother Mike appear with his group the Scaffold.

14 February. An announcement is made that the Beatles next single will be their version of Paul's composition 'Lady Madonna'.

18 February. Paul is interviewed for the *Evening Standard* newspaper.

19 February. Paul and Jane leave for India, along with Ringo and Maureen.

24 February. Paul discusses Apple in the interview with the *Evening Standard* he made before leaving for India. He says, 'Instead of trying to amass money for the sake of it we're setting up a business concern at Apple – rather like a western Communism.'

26 February. An announcement is made that Paul will appear in Donovan's next film.

28 February. Paul attends Cilla Black's recording session, produced by George Martin, in which she records Paul's composition 'Step Inside Love'.

8 March. Cilla Black's version of Paul's composition 'Step Inside Love' is issued on Parlophone R 5674. Paul Jones's single 'And The Sun Will Shine', issued on Columbia DB 8379, features Paul McCartney on drums.

14 March. The 'Lady Madonna' promo is shown on *Top Of The Pops*.

15 March. The Beatles 17th single, Paul's composition 'Lady Madonna', is issued on Parlophone R 5675.

20 March. The Diana Ross and the Supremes album *Live At The Talk Of The Town*, issued on Tamla Motown TM 11070, features two of Paul's compositions – 'Yesterday' and 'Michelle'.

26 March. Paul and Jane Asher decide to leave the Maharishi's ashram in Rishikesh and set off for London.

28 March. Paul and Jane spend time at home with Jane's family.

3 April. Paul's composition 'Step Inside Love' appears on Cilla Black's new album *Sher-Oo* on Parlophone PCS 7041.

4 April. Paul's composition 'Lady Madonna' is awarded a gold disc in America where it has topped the charts.

8 April. Paul directs the promo for 'Elevator', a single by new Apple group Grapefruit. 'Lady Madonna' is certified gold in the UK.

20 April. Apple takes an advertisement in *New Musical Express* offering to help unknown songwriters and musicians. Paul comments, 'It's ridiculous that people with talent like Dave Mason and Denny Laine have sometimes had to struggle to get their work accepted.'

22 April. The instrumental album by the John Hawkins Orchestra, issued on Polydor 236 244, includes their version of Paul's composition 'Michelle'.

30 April. Paul is in Bradford conducting the Black Dyke Mills Band in a performance of his composition 'Thingumybob', the theme tune to a new television series.

1 May. *More Chartbusters*, issued on Marble Arch MAL 788, is a

compilation of cover versions of hits by anonymous artists and includes cover versions of Paul's compositions 'Lady Madonna' and 'Step Inside Love'.

5 May. The model Twiggy has noticed Mary Hopkin on the TV talent show *Opportunity Knocks* and calls Paul to inform him about her.

6 May. Cilla Black's version of Paul's composition 'Step Inside Love' is issued in America on Bell 726.

11 May. Paul and John fly to New York on a visit to promote Apple.

12 May. Paul and John view the Statue of Liberty from a Chinese junk.

13 May. Following a press conference in New York, Paul meets rock photographer Linda Eastman again.

15 May. Paul and John appear on the American TV show *Tonight*, hosted by Joe Garagiola, to discuss Apple.

16 May. Paul and John fly back to London.

17 May. The album *McGough And McGear*, produced by Paul, is issued on Parlophone PCS 7047.

21 May. Paul and Jane Asher have lunch with Andy Williams in London prior to attending his Royal Albert Hall concert.

23 May. Paul and Ringo are interviewed at Abbey Road Studios for the TV documentary 'All My Loving'.

24 May. *Hits '68*, an album of covers of hits by anonymous artists, is issued on MFP 1226 with a cover of Paul's composition 'Step Inside Love'.

26 May. Paul directs the promo for Grapefruit's 'Elevator' in Kensington Gardens, London.

29 May. Gary Puckett's album *Young Girl* contains his version of Paul's composition 'Lady Madonna'.

31 May. Paul and Jane Asher attend a concert by the Scaffold, the group in which Paul's brother Mike is a member, at the Odeon, Lewisham.

3 June. Kenny Ball's version of the Paul composition 'When I'm Sixty-Four' is featured on the *Stars Of '68* album issued on Marble Arch MAL 762.

4 June. Paul begins seeing Francie Schwartz.

7 June. Paul is best man at the wedding of his brother Mike to Angela Fishwick.

8 June. Paul reveals to the *Melody Maker* that his sojourn in Rishikesh resulted in twenty new songs.

11 June. Paul records his solo version of 'Blackbird' at Abbey Road Studios. Tony Bramwell shoots a promotional film of Paul and Mary Hopkin.

16 June. Paul tapes an interview with David Frost for a programme to be screened in America called 'David Frost Presents ... Frankie Howerd'. Howerd interviews Paul about Apple and then Paul introduces Mary Hopkin who performs two numbers.

18 June. On his 26th birthday Paul hosts a lunchtime party at Apple and attends the opening of a play in London's West End with Jane Asher.

20 June. Paul flies to Los Angeles, accompanied by Ivan Vaughan and Tony Bramwell. He is to address a Capitol Records Sales Conference.

21 June. Paul introduces a film about the Apple project to a conference of Capitol Records salesmen. He also contacts Linda Eastman by phone.

22 June. Paul attends a Capitol Records barbeque and in the evening visits the Whiskey A Go-Go to see Albert King. Linda Eastman has flown out from New York to join him.

24 June. Paul performs several numbers for fans outside his LA hotel before leaving for London.

25 June. Paul returns to London.

30 June. Paul travels to Bradford in Yorkshire to record the Black Dyke Mills Band performing his composition 'Thingumybob'. He is interviewed by Tony Cliff for the BBC TV programme *Look North* and on the way back to London with Derek Taylor and Peter Asher, stops at a village pub and entertains the locals on a piano.

1 July. The *Look North* interview with Paul is broadcast.

2 July. Paul has a lunch date with a number of City businessmen, including Sir Joseph Lockwood and Lord Poole, at which he discusses the Beatles' new business venture – Apple. The meeting takes place at Lazard Brothers & Co in Old Broad Street.

4 July. Paul's composition 'Penny Lane' is the title track of an EP of the same name issued in Australia on Parlophone GEPO 70045.

8 July. Paul is approached by actor David Peel who asks if Paul will pay for a children's beach show at Apple. He says, 'He agreed to help straight away, as well as suggesting our title.' The title was Apple Peel.

12 July. Ray Charles's version of Paul's composition 'Eleanor Rigby' is issued by Stateside Records.

15 July. Paul adds a new vocal to 'Ob La Di, Ob La Da' at Abbey Road Studios.

17 July. Paul, sans Jane Asher, joins John and Yoko and Ringo and Maureen at the London premiere of the *Yellow Submarine* movie. Later that evening, at the Revolution Club, Paul promises Clem Curtis of the Foundations that he will write a number for the group.

20 July. On the BBC TV show *Dee Time*, Jane Asher announces that her engagement to Paul is off.

21 July. When asked about the split in the *Daily Mirror*, Jane Asher says, 'I don't want to say anything about it.' Paul's father comments, 'Paul has never given any hint that he and Jane were parting. They were a really happy couple at their engagement party last Christmas.'

28 July. Paul attends Mick Jagger's 28th birthday party at the Vesuvio Club in Tottenham Court Road and plays an advance pressing of 'Hey Jude'.

30 July. Commenting on the closure of the Apple boutique, Paul says, 'We decided to close down the shop last Saturday – not because it wasn't making any money, but because we thought the retail business wasn't our particular scene. So we went along, chose all the stuff we

wanted – I got a smashing overcoat – and then told our friends. Now everything that is left is for the public.'

31 July. It is announced that Paul's house in St John's Wood is to be the subject of a preservation order as 'having special architectural or historic interest'.

1 August. An interview with Paul appears in the *Daily Mail* newspaper.

2 August. *Thingumybob*, the London Weekend Television series starring Stanley Holloway, for which Paul has written the theme tune, makes its debut.

3 August. Paul and Francie Schwartz visit the Revolution Club in Bruton Place, London. On the Marty Robbins album, *By The Time I Get To Phoenix* issued on CBS 63295, is his version of Paul's composition 'Yesterday'.

7 August. Paul, accompanied by Francie Schwartz, traces the words 'Hey Jude' with white paint on the window of the Apple boutique and says, 'We thought we'd paint the windows for a gas. What would you do if your shop had just closed?'

9 August. Paul records his composition 'Mother Nature's Son' solo at Abbey Road.

10 August. The *New Musical Express* interviews Paul.

15 August. The Beatles begin recording Paul's composition 'Rocky Raccoon'.

19 August. Sergio Mendes and Brasil '66 issue their single of Paul's composition 'Fool On The Hill' on A&M AMS 731.

20 August. Paul adds brass overdubs to 'Mother Nature's Son' and records his composition 'Wild Honey Pie', plus a demo of 'Etcetera' for Marianne Faithfull.

22 August. The Beatles record Paul's composition 'Back In The USSR'.

26 August. The single 'Thingumybob', by John Foster & Sons Black Dyke Mills Band, written and produced by Paul, is issued in America on Apple 1801.

27 August. Paul turns up to watch the Merseyside derby – a match between the Liverpool and Everton football teams.

30 August. The Beatles' 18th single, 'Hey Jude', penned by Paul, is released, becoming the first Beatles single to be issued on the Apple label. On the same day 'Those Were The Days' by Mary Hopkin, produced by Paul, is released. Paul also attends the wedding of Neil Aspinall and Suzy Ornstein.

6 September. Thames Television films Paul and Mary Hopkin for their *Magpie* series. The single 'Thungumybob' by the Black Dyke Mills Band, conducted by Paul, is released in Britain.

7 September. Paul's composition 'Hey Jude' tops the *Melody Maker* charts.

8 September. A clip of 'Hey Jude' is featured on *The David Frost Show*.

9 September. The Beatles record a new version of Paul's composition 'Helter Skelter'. The *Magpie* show featuring Paul and Mary Hopkin is screened by Thames Television.

10 September. Paul appears on the ITV show *Magpie* with his protégé Mary Hopkin.

12 September. *Top Of The Pops* screens the 'Hey Jude' film promo.

13 September. Paul's composition 'Hey Jude' tops the *New Musical Express* charts. Fats Domino issues his version of Paul's composition 'Lady Madonna' on the Reprise label.

16 September. The Beatles begin recording Paul's composition 'I Will' at Abbey Road Studios.

18 September. Paul records 'Birthday' at Abbey Road Studios before the other members of the Beatles arrive. That evening they go to Paul's Cavendish Avenue house to watch 'The Girl Can't Help It' on television.

20 September. The Larry Page Orchestra issue an instrumental single: 'Hey Jude'/'Those Were The Days'.

24 September. Paul's composition 'Hey Jude' tops the American charts.

25 September. Ray Charles's cover version of 'Yesterday' is featured on his *Greatest Hits* album, issued on Stateside SSL 10241.

26 September. Jose Feliciano's debut album, issued on RCA RD7246, features his recording of Paul's composition 'Here, There And Everywhere'.

30 September. Paul visits Liverpool to see his father, who is ill in hospital.

1 October. The Beatles begin recording Paul's composition 'Honey Pie' at Trident Studios, London.

2 October. Paul completes the lead vocal to 'Honey Pie' at Trident Studios.

4 October. Paul records 'Martha My Dear' at Trident Studios with a 14-piece orchestra.

5 October. 'Those Were The Days', Mary's single, produced by Paul, is No. 1 in the *New Musical Express* charts and Paul's composition 'Hey Jude', recorded by the Beatles, is No. 2.

6 October. In America the 'Hey Jude' promo film is shown on *The Smothers Brothers* show.

9 October. A film clip of Paul introducing Mary Hopkin is included in David Frost's TV show in America. While final work is being completed on 'Long Long Long' and 'The Continuing Story Of Bungalow Bill', Paul records 'Why Don't We Do It In The Road?' in the studio next door.

10 October. Paul announces the Beatles plan to perform live in the future.

11 October. 'I'm The Urban Spaceman' by the Bonzo Dog Doo-Dah Band, which was produced by Paul, is issued in America on Liberty LBF 15144.

12 October. In an interview with the *Evening Standard*, Jane Asher says, 'I know it sounds corny but we're still very close friends. We really are. We see each other and we love each other, but it hasn't worked out. That's all there is to it. Perhaps we'll be childhood sweethearts and meet again and get married when we're about 70!'

20 October. Paul sets off on a brief holiday.

22 October. The Beatles single 'Hey Jude', penned by Paul, is No. 1 in the American charts.

23 October. It is announced that the single 'Hey Jude' has sold five million copies worldwide.

24 October. Bobbie Gentry's version of 'Fool On The Hill' is issued on Capitol CL 15566.

25 October. '*Quelle Erand Giorni*'/'Turn! Turn! Turn!' by Mary Hopkin, produced by Paul, is issued in Italy on Apple 2.

26 October. 'Those Were The Days', Mary's single, produced by Paul, is No. 1 in the *Melody Maker* charts and Paul's composition 'Hey Jude', recorded by the Beatles, is No. 2.

31 October. Linda moves to London with her daughter Heather to live with Paul at Cavendish Avenue.

5 November. Paul and Linda travel to his farm in Campbeltown, Scotland for a holiday.

8 November. *The Best Of Cilla Black* is issued on Parlophone PCS 7065 and contains all three songs by Paul that she recorded: 'Love Of The Loved', 'It's For You' and 'Step Inside Love'.

18 November. Two British groups, Marmalade and Spectrum, record cover versions of Paul's composition 'Ob La Di, Ob La Da'.

20 November. Tony MacArthur interviews Paul at home in Cavendish Avenue for a Radio Luxembourg special 'The Beatles'. 'Those Were The Days' qualifies for a gold disc in America.

22 November. Donovan's single 'Atlantis' is issued on Pye 7N 17660. Paul is said to have provided backing vocals.

27 November. *Wort*, an album by Wort Steenhuis, is issued on Studio 2 TWP 231, which features instrumental versions of three of Paul's compositions: 'Michelle', 'She's Leaving Home' and 'Fool On The Hill'.

6 December. James Taylor's eponymous album with the track 'Carolina On My Mind', featuring Paul on bass, is issued in Britain on Apple SAPCOR 3.

7 December. *Disc* reports that Paul has a new girlfriend, Linda Eastman: 'Rumours first began to circulate that she and Paul were good friends about two weeks ago when Paul came to New York for a few days.'

8 December. In the *New Musical Express* Readers' Poll, Paul's composition 'Hey Jude' is voted the Best Single of 1968.

11 December. Paul and Linda arrive at Praia da Luz in the Algarve, Portugal to stay at Hunter Davies's villa.

12 December. Paul conducts a press conference on a beach in Portugal. The Kasenatz-Kats Singing Orchestral Circus issue their latest album on Pye Int. NSPL 28119 with covers of Paul's compositions 'Yesterday' and 'We Can Work It Out'.

25 December. The Beatles promo for their single of Paul's composition 'Lady Madonna' is screened on *Top Of The Pops*.

28 December. An album of cover versions called *Sounds Like This* on Fontana SFGL 13060 includes a cover of 'Hey Jude'.

30 December. Atlantic Records issue Wilson Pickett's version of Paul's composition 'Hey Jude'.

1969

9 January. Sergio Mendes and Brasil '66 issue their album *Fool On The Hill* on A&M AMLS 922, featuring Paul's composition of that name.

16 January. Gerry Lockran issues his version of Paul's composition 'Hey Jude' on Decca F 12873.

17 January. Paul's composition 'Yellow Submarine' is issued as a Beatles single on Apple PCS 7070.

23 January. Work begins on Paul's composition 'Get Back'.

3 February. Paul records 'My Dark Hour' with Steve Miller in London.

7 February. Paul is fined for a speeding offence. The Vic Lewis Orchestra issue an instrumental single of Paul's compositions 'I Will' and 'Blackbird'.

12 February. Paul is the sole director of a new company, Adagrose Ltd, which later becomes McCartney Productions Ltd.

13 February. A launch party for Mary Hopkin is held at the Post Office Tower in London attended by Paul and Linda. Other guests included Donovan and Jimi Hendrix.

17 February. James Taylor's eponymous album with the track 'Carolina On My Mind', featuring Paul on bass, is issued in America on Apple SKAO 3352.

21 February. Mary Hopkin's *Postcard* album, which Paul produced, is issued on Apple SAPCOR 5. Paul also played guitar on several of the tracks and designed the record sleeve. 'Rosetta', a single by the Fourmost, produced by Paul, is issued on CBS 4041.

1 March. Paul is at a recording session at Morgan Studios, Willesden, producing Mary Hopkin's next single.

3 March. Mary Hopkin's *Postcard* album, produced by Paul, is issued in America on Apple ST 3351.

4 March. Paul and Linda visit Ringo Starr on the film set of *The Magic Christian* at Twickenham Studios. Another visitor is Princess Margaret. In the evening he goes to the Odeon, St Martin's Lane to see the film *Isadora* starring Vanessa Redgrave.

5 March. A group called Trifle issue their version of Paul's composition 'All Together Now' on the United Artists label.

7 March. Two of the singles Paul produced with Mary Hopkin are released in Europe: '*Lontano Dagli Occhi*' on Apple 7 in Italy and '*Prince En Avignon*' on Apple 9 in France.

11 March. Paul is producing Jackie Lomax's recording of 'Thumbin' A Ride' at Apple Studios on his wedding eve.

12 March. Paul marries Linda Eastman at Marylebone Register Office.

17 March. Paul and Linda fly to New York to spend three weeks with Linda's family. Linda's daughter Heather accompanies them.

19 March. Noel Harrison reveals to the press that Paul has written a song especially for him, which is to be his next single.

28 March. Apple issue Mary Hopkin's single 'Goodbye', a composition by Paul, who also dueted with Mary on the album and played guitar.

2 April. Paul, John and Allen Klein visit merchant bankers Henry Ansbacher and Company for advice on how to obtain Northern Songs.

4 April. The Gladys Knight and the Pips album *Silk 'n' Soul*, issued in Britain on Tamla STML 11100 includes the group's version of Paul's composition 'Yesterday'.

7 April. Mary's Hopkin's single 'Goodbye' is issued in America on Apple 1806.

10 April. Bing Crosby issues an album called *Hey Jude* on London SHU 8391.

11 April. 'Get Back', the 19th Beatles single, penned by Paul, is issued in Britain on Apple R 5777 and features Billy Preston on piano.

14 April. John and Paul record 'The Ballad Of John And Yoko' at Abbey Road Studios.

17 April. The promotional film for 'Get Back' is featured on *Top Of The Pops*.

18 April. *Atco Chartbusters* on Atco 228 021 features Arthur Conley's version of Paul's composition 'Ob-La-Di, Ob-La-Da'.

26 April. On the trail of the 'Paul Is Dead' rumours, reporters arrive at Paul's Scottish farm. He told them, 'I'm as fit as a fiddle.' Dr Richard Asher, Jane's father, is found dead at his home in Wimpole Street.

2 May. Paul's composition 'Get Back', the latest Beatles single, is No. 1 in the *New Musical Express* charts with Mary Hopkin's 'Goodbye', which Paul wrote and produced, at No. 2.

3 May. Paul's composition 'Get Back', the latest Beatles single, is No. 1 in the *Melody Maker* charts, with 'Goodbye' at No. 2.

4 May. Paul and Linda are among the guests at Ringo Starr and Peter Sellers' party at Les Ambassadeurs in London.

6 May. Paul's composition 'Get Back', the latest Beatles single, is issued in America on Apple 2490. The Beatles also record Paul's composition 'You Never Give Me Your Money' at Olympic Studios in Barnes.

8 May. Asked to comment on the sacking of Alistair Taylor, a long-time member of NEMS and Apple's general manager, Paul says, 'It is not possible to be nice about giving someone the sack.'

12 May. Three Dog Night include their version of Paul's 'It's For You' on their debut album, issued in America on Stateside SSL 5006.

14 May. Ritchie Havens' album *1983* is issued on Verve SVLP 6014 with his versions of Paul's compositions 'Lady Madonna' and 'She's Leaving Home'.

15 May. Roy Corlett of Radio Merseyside interviews Paul, who is visiting his father's house in Cheshire, for the programme *Light And Local*.

16 May. Paul and Linda set off for a month-long holiday in Corfu and announce that Linda is pregnant.

19 May. Paul and John receive an Ivor Novello Award for 'Hey Jude', the top selling British record of 1968.

20 May. The Beatles 20th single 'The Ballad Of John And Yoko' is released. John and Paul are the only members of the Beatles playing on the disc.

27 May. 'Get Back', the Beatles version of Paul's composition, is No. 1 in the American charts.

6 June. Paul and Linda are reported to be house hunting in the Devon area.

8 June. John Bratby's portrait of Paul, which he painted in 1967, is to be included as part of the British trade week in Japan.

9 June. The Bonzo Dog Doo-Dah Band's album *Urban Spaceman*, with its title track produced by Paul, is issued in America on Imperial 12432.

12 June. *This Is Tom Jones*, an album issued on Decca LK 5007, features Tom Jones's version of Paul's composition 'Hey Jude'.

16 June. The Steve Miller Band single 'My Dark Hour', which includes Paul's vocal and instrumental contribution, is issued in the States on Capitol CL 15604. Paul has used the pseudonym Paul Ramon.

17 June. Paul and Linda return from their month-long holiday in Corfu.

1 July. Paul adds a new vocal to 'You Never Give Me Your Money' at Abbey Road Studios.

2 July. Paul records 'Her Majesty' at Abbey Road Studios.

3 July. Paul, George and Ringo are at Abbey Road Studios working on recordings of Paul's compositions 'Golden Slumbers' and 'Carry That Weight'.

5 July. Paul attends the Rolling Stones concert in Hyde Park, London.

9 July. The Beatles begin recording Paul's composition 'Maxwell's Silver Hammer'.

13 July. Paul and Mary Hopkin begin work on her next single.

17 July. Paul adds his lead vocal to 'Oh, Darling!' at Abbey Road Studios.

24 July. Paul records a solo demo disc of 'Come And Get It' as a demo for the Iveys, who are to change their name to Badfinger.

25 July. Work begins on Paul's composition 'She Came In Through The Bathroom Window' at Abbey Road Studios.

21 August. Adagrose Ltd becomes McCartney Productions Limited.

28 August. Paul and Linda's daughter Mary is born at Avenue Clinic in Avenue Road, St John's Wood, London.

19 September. David Wigg interviews Paul for the BBC's *Scene and Heard* programme. 'Que Sera Sera'/'Fields Of St Etienne' by Mary Hopkin, produced by Paul, is issued in France on Apple 16.

21 September. David Wigg's interview with Paul is broadcast on the *Scene and Heard* programme

23 September. *Northern Star*, the Illinois University newspaper, reports rumours of Paul's death.

28 September. The second part of David Wigg's interview with Paul is broadcast on *Scene and Heard*.

13 October. Paul and Linda and Ringo and Maureen attend Mary Hopkin's opening night at the Savoy Hotel, London.

22 October. The 'Paul Is Dead' rumours still persist and Paul tells the *Evening Standard*, 'I'm dead, am I? Why does nobody ever tell me anything?' He and Linda travel to their Scottish farm.

24 October. Chris Drake interviews Paul at his Scottish farm regarding the 'Paul Is Dead' rumours.

26 October. Part of Chris Drake's interview with Paul is broadcast on Radio 4's *The World This Weekend*.

27 October. Excerpts from Chris Drake's interview with Paul are broadcast on Radio 4's *The World At One* and Radio 2's *Late Night Extra*.

30 October. Tom Jones's album *Live At The Flamingo, Las Vegas* is issued by Decca featuring his versions of Paul's compositions 'Hey Jude' and 'Yesterday'.

10 November. 'The Ballad Of Paul' by Mystery Tour is issued in America, one of several such records issued in the wake of the 'Paul Is Dead' rumours.

19 November. Paul and Linda return to London after spending several weeks at their farm in Scotland.

27 November. Aretha Franklin's version of Paul's composition 'Eleanor Rigby' is released as a single by Atlantic.

30 November. Paul talks to the press to scotch the 'Paul Is Dead' rumours, saying that if he is dead, he's the last one to know about it!

5 December. Badfinger's 'Come and Get It', written and produced by Paul, is issued in Britain.

19 December. Anita Harris cover's Paul's composition 'Hey Jude' on her album *Cuddly Toy*.

31 December. Paul and Linda, together with George and Pattie, are guests at Ringo and Maureen's New Year's Eve party in Highgate, London.

1970

9 January. Badfinger's album *Magic Christian Music* is issued in Britain on Apple SAPCOR 12, with one track produced by Paul.

12 January. Badfinger's 'Come And Get It' single, written and produced by Paul, is issued in America on Apple 1815.

14 January. Paul buys extra property in Scotland adjoining his farm.

19 January. A cover version of 'Come And Get It' by the Magic Christians is issued in America on Commonwealth United CU 3006.

8 February. Apple announces that Paul's first solo album will be issued in May.

12 February. Paul books into Morgan Studios using the alias Billy Martin to continue with the recording of his solo album, which he began working on at the end of 1969.

21 February. Paul returns to Morgan Studios as Billy Martin.

22 February. Paul records the tracks 'Every Night' and 'Maybe I'm Amazed'.

25 February. Paul records 'Man We Was Lonely' at Abbey Road Studios.

2 March. *Good Feelin's*, an album by the Happy Day Choir, is issued in America featuring their version of Paul's composition 'Hey Jude'.

6 March. Paul's composition 'Let It Be' is issued as the new Beatles single in Britain on Apple R 5833.

11 March. The 'Let It Be' single is issued in America on Apple 2764.

13 March. Chris Barber's album *Battersea Rain Dance* on Marmalade 2384 020 features Paul's composition 'Catcall'.

16 March. Paul is at Abbey Road Studios listening to playbacks of his solo album recordings.

18 March. Paul announces that his debut solo album will be issued on 17 April.

19 March. Tony Hatch and the Satin Brass feature a version of Paul's composition 'Hey Jude' on their Pye album.

20 March. Karen Young's single '*Que Sera Sera*' is issued on Major Minor MM 691 with adverts stating, 'specially arranged by Paul McCartney'.

23 March. Phil Spector begins mixing *Let It Be* at Abbey Road Studios. Paul finishes his master tapes of *McCartney* at Abbey Road Studios.

25 March. Phil Spector mixes Paul's compositions 'Two Of Us' and 'Teddy Boy'.

1 April. Phil Spector overdubs a choir and orchestra over Paul's composition 'The Long And Winding Road'.

2 April. Actor Edward Woodward issues his album *This Man Alone* on DJM DJPS 405 on which he features his version of 'Eleanor Rigby'. In an interview with the *Evening Standard*, Paul says, 'We all have to ask each other's permission before any of us does anything without the other three. My own record nearly didn't come out because Klein and some others thought it would be too near to the date of the next Beatles album.' He added, 'I had to get George, who's a director of Apple, to authorise its release for me. We're all talking about peace and love but really we're not feeling peaceful at all.'

9 April. London Weekend Television screens the promo film of Paul's solo track 'Maybe I'm Amazed'.

10 April. Paul announces he has left the Beatles, 'because of personal, business and musical differences'. Advance copies of Paul's solo debut album *McCartney* are sent to the press.

11 April. Paul announces that he will not record with John Lennon again.

14 April. Paul obtains the film rights to Rupert The Bear.

15 April. On her new album *This Girl's In Love With You*, issued on Atlantic 2400 004, Aretha Franklin features her versions of Paul's compositions 'Let It Be', 'Eleanor Rigby' and 'Fool On The Hill'.

17 April. Paul's debut solo album *McCartney* is issued in Britain on Apple PCS 7102. Sir Lew Grade describes it as 'absolutely brilliant'.

18 April. The *Melody Maker* runs an article headed 'Paul – The Truth', about his decision to leave the Beatles.

19 April. London Weekend Television screen the promo for 'Maybe I'm Amazed'.

20 April. Paul's debut solo album *McCartney* is issued in America on Apple STAO 3363.

21 April. The first of a two-part interview with Paul appears in the *Evening Standard* during which Paul expresses his feelings about what Phil Spector had done to his composition 'The Long And Winding Road'.

22 April. The second part of Paul's interview is published in the *Evening Standard*.

30 April. *McCartney*, Paul's solo album, is awarded a gold disc for its American sales, while Paul and Linda leave for a holiday abroad. Paul is also featured on the cover of *Rolling Stone* magazine, with a lengthy interior interview with Jann Wenner.

6 May. Three Dog Night's album *Captured Live At The Forum* is released in America on Stateside SSL 5023 with their live version of Paul's composition 'It's For You'.

10 May. Paul's composition 'Ob La Di, Ob La Da' receives an Ivor Novello Award as the most performed song on British radio.

11 May. Paul's composition 'The Long And Winding Road' is issued as a Beatles single in America on Apple 2832.

14 May. Aretha Franklin issues her version of Paul's composition 'Let It Be' on Atlantic Records in Britain.

23 May. Paul's debut solo album *McCartney* tops the American charts.

8 June. The Tony Osbourne Orchestra album *Evergreens Of Tomorrow*, issued on Gemini GMX 5010, includes their versions of Paul's compositions 'Yesterday' and 'She's Leaving Home'.

9 June. 'The Long And Winding Road' tops the American charts.

10 June. Mel Torme issues his album *Raindrops Keep Falling On My Head* on Capitol ST 21585, which features his version of Paul's composition 'She's Leaving Home'.

15 June. Mary Hopkin's '*Que Sera Sera*'/'Fields Of St Etienne' is released in America on Apple 1823. Paul produced both sides of the single. On Paul's behalf Lee Eastman writes to Allen Klein requiring that the Beatles partnership be immediately dissolved officially. He receives no reply.

22 June. Danny Boyle issues his version of Paul's composition 'The Long And Winding Road' on Columbia DB 8698.

2 July. Cissy Houston's album *Presenting* on Major Minor SMLP 80 features her version of Paul's composition 'The Long And Winding Road'.

4 July. The Beatles version of Paul's composition 'Let It Be' tops the *Melody Maker* charts.

8 July. Ray Morgan's version of Paul's composition 'The Long And Winding Road' is released as a single on B&C CB 128.

11 July. The Beatles version of Paul's composition 'Let It Be' tops the *Melody Maker* charts for a second week.

15 July. Another cover version of Paul's 'The Long And Winding Road' is issued as a single, this time by Baskin And Copperfield on the Decca label.

16 July. Cliff Richard's *Live At The Talk Of The Town* album on Regal Starline SRS 5031 features his version of Paul's composition 'When I'm Sixty-Four'.

19 July. Press reports say that Paul intends to collaborate on a television special with Glen Campbell.

20 July. *Four In Blue*, the new Tamla Motown album from Smokey Robinson and the Miracles, features their version of Paul's composition 'Hey Jude'.

2 August. Paul and Linda begin a holiday in the Shetlands that lasts until 20 August.

5 August. The Bonzo Dog Doo-Dah Band compilation album *The Beast Of The Bonzo's*, featuring Paul's production of 'I'm The Urban Spaceman', is issued in America on UA UAS 5517.

13 August. A group called Fickle Pickle issued a cover version of Paul's composition 'Maybe I'm Amazed' on Philips 6006 038.

29 August. A letter from Paul is published in the *Melody Maker* insisting that the Beatles will never get together again.

30 August. Paul is planning a new solo project to take place in New York and begins to book the sessions.

2 September. Joe Cocker's album *Mad Dogs And Englishmen*, issued on A&M SP 6002, features his version of Paul's composition 'She Came In Through The Bathroom Window'.

9 September. Record impresario Mickie Most announces he has asked Paul to star in a movie called *The Second Coming Of Suzanne*.

13 September. Apple issue a denial that Paul will appear in the film *The Second Coming Of Suzanne*.

17 September. The Everly Brothers' double album *Show*, issued on Warner WS 1858, features their version of Paul's composition 'Hey Jude'.

21 October. Paul and Linda travel to New York.

2 November. *Melody Fair*, the new album by Lulu on Atco 2400 017, features her version of Paul's composition 'Good Day Sunshine'.

15 November. Paul files his lawsuit to dissolve the Beatles partnership.

16 December. Johnny Mathis issues his latest album *The Long And Winding Road*, with Paul's composition as the title track.

31 December. Paul begins High Court proceedings to end the Beatles partnership.

1971

2 January. Paul and Linda shoot some 16mm footage at their farm in Scotland.

3 January. Paul and Linda fly to New York where Paul intends to begin work on his *Ram* album.

6 January. Paul tapes a number of tracks with songwriter Leslie Fradkin.

7 January. Paul auditions for a new drummer in New York and selects Denny Seiwell.

8 January. Bob Kerr's Whoopee Band release a cover version of Paul's composition 'Honey Pie'.

9 January. It's reported that Paul has bought another 400 acres of land adjacent to his High Park farm.

10 January. Recording of the *Ram* album begins at Columbia Studios in New York.

11 January. Paul records some orchestral tracks for his debut album.

13 January. Paul begins recording 'Another Day'.

10 February. 'We've Only Just Begun', the new album from Ray Conniff, includes his cover version of Paul's composition 'Let It Be'.

18 February. Paul and Linda return to England.

19 February. Paul and Linda attend the opening day of the High Court case to dissolve the Beatles. Their single 'Another Day'/'Oh Woman Oh Why' is issued in Britain on Apple R 5889.

22 February. Paul and Linda's single 'Another Day' is released in America on Apple 1829.

25 February. In the High Court a statement by Allen Klein is read out which states: 'Paul McCartney never accepted me as his manager, but the partnership did, and I have continued as manager of the partnership. McCartney has accepted the benefits I have negotiated in that capacity.'

26 February. Paul gives evidence in the High Court in his case to dissolve the Beatles partnership. He contradicts John Lennon's statement, 'We always thought of ourselves as Beatles, whether we recorded singly or in twos or threes,' by saying, 'Since the Beatles stopped making group recordings, we have stopped thinking of ourselves as Beatles. One has only to look at recent recordings by John or George to see that neither thinks of himself as a Beatle. On his recent album, John Lennon has listed things he did not believe in. One was, "I don't believe in Beatles".'

12 March. Paul wins the first round in his legal battle to dissolve the Beatles partnership when the High Court appoints James Douglas Spooner as receiver.

15 March. Paul and Linda leave for California.

16 March. Paul receives a Grammy award from John Wayne for the *Let It Be* album as 'Best Original Score Written For A Motion Picture Or Television Special In 1970'.

17 March. Paul tops the *New Musical Express* charts with 'Another Day', his first No. 1 single as a solo artist. Paul's composition 'The Long And Winding Road' is featured on the Four Tops' new album *Changing Times*.

20 March. The *Daily Mirror* runs a story stating that the Beatles will reform with Klaus Voormann replacing Paul.

26 March. Apple issue a press statement that the Beatles will not be reforming with Klaus Voormann.

15 April. The Beatles version of Paul's composition 'Let It Be' wins an Oscar for Best Original Film Song at the 43rd Academy Awards.

12 May. Paul and Linda, with their children, join Ringo and Maureen Starr on a trip to St Tropez for the wedding of Mick Jagger to Bianca.

17 May. The *Ram* album is issued in America.

28 May. Paul and Linda release the album *Ram* in the UK.

10 June. There is a bomb scare at the BBC at Bush House in London over a package sent to Paul. It turns out to be a parcel of birthday presents for his coming birthday.

15 June. Recordings begin at Abbey Road Studios of an instrumental version of Paul's *Ram* album, arranged and conducted by Richard Hewson.

16 June. Recordings continue on the instrumental version of the *Ram* album which is eventually to be released in 1977 as *Thrillington*.

17 June. Recording of the instrumental version of the *Ram* album is complete.

18 June. Tony Clark and Alan Parsons complete the mixing of the instrumental version of the *Ram* album.

24 July. Paul phones Denny Laine to ask him to join a group he is forming.

25 July. Paul is at Abbey Road Studios.

31 July. In a *New Musical Express* interview, John Lennon says, 'The thing with Paul is he wants all the action. He wants it all. It's not just the money. It's the principle.'

2 August. 'Uncle Albert/Admiral Halsey'/'Too Many People' is issued in America.

3 August. Paul officially announces the members of his new band. Apart from himself and Linda they are Denny Seiwell and Denny Laine. He says they have not yet decided on a name.

13 August. Apple issue Paul and Linda's 'Back Seat Of My Car'/'Heart Of The Country' in the UK.

4 September. 'Uncle Albert/Admiral Halsey' tops the American charts.

13 September. Paul and Linda's daughter Stella Nina is born at King's College Hospital, Denmark Hill, London.

7 November. Paul, Linda and family travel from their Scottish farm to London.

8 November. Paul holds a fancy dress party at the Empire Ballroom, Leicester Square, London to announce the launch of Wings. Entertainment is provided by Ray McVay and his Dance Band.

13 November. The first photograph of Wings is published on the front cover of *Melody Maker*.

20 November. *Melody Maker* features an exclusive interview with Paul under the heading, 'Why Lennon Is Uncool'.

4 December. John Lennon attacks Paul in a letter published in *Melody Maker*.

7 December. Wings' first album *Wild Life* is released simultaneously in Britain and America.

15 December. Paul and Linda appear on the New York radio station WCBS-FM to promote Wings' *Wild Life* album.

1972

13 January. Paul begins recording 'Mary Had A Little Lamb'. An interview with Paul and Linda, recorded in December, is aired on the New York radio station WRKO.

17 January. Paul begins twelve days of rehearsals at London's Scotch of St James Club.

29 January. Paul and Linda fly to New York for a meeting with John and Yoko.

30 January. The radio station KHJ in New York interviews Paul.

31 January. Paul and Linda fly back to London.

1 February. Wings record 'Give Ireland Back To The Irish' at Island Studios, London.

2 February. Wings begin rehearsals at the Institute of Contemporary Arts in London.

8 February. Paul, Linda and Wings set off on the motorway intent on appearing at small gigs.

9 February. Paul and Wings perform before 700 students at Nottingham University.

10 February. Wings appear at Goodridge University, York.

11 February. Wings appear at Hull University.

12 February. Kid Jenson conducts a live interview with Paul for Radio Luxembourg.

13 February. Wings appear in Newcastle-upon-Tyne.

14 February. Wings appear at Lancaster University.

16 February. Wings appear at Leeds Town Hall.

17 February. Wings appear in Sheffield.

18 February. Wings appear in Manchester.

21 February. Wings appear at Birmingham University.

22 February. Wings appear at Swansea University.

23 February. Wings appear at Oxford University.

25 February. Wings' controversial 'Give Ireland Back To The Irish' is issued in Britain.

26 February. In a *Melody Maker* interview, Linda says, 'Eric Clapton once said that he would like to play from the back of a caravan, but he never got round to doing it. Well, we have! We've no manager or agents, just we five and roadies. We're just a gang of musicians touring around.'

28 February. 'Give Ireland Back To The Irish' is issued in America on the day that Paul, Linda and Wings fly to Los Angeles.

20 March. Paul is working on the *Red Rose Speedway* album at Olympic Studios, Barnes, London.

17 April. Producer Glyn Johns walks out of the *Red Rose Speedway* sessions following a disagreement with Paul.

12 May. 'Mary Had A Little Lamb'/'Little Woman Love' is released in the UK.

15 May. Paul begins mixing tracks for *Red Rose Speedway* at Manor Studios, Oxfordshire.

22 May. Paul and Wings begin rehearsing for their forthcoming tour at the Scotch of St James, London.

25 May. Wings mime to 'Mary Had A Little Lamb' on *Top Of The Pops*.

29 May. 'Mary Had A Little Lamb' is released in America.

6 June. Wings shoot a new promotional film for 'Mary Had A Little Lamb'.

10 June. Paul and Linda officially end their dispute with ATV Music and sign a seven-year co-publishing deal.

29 June. *Top Of The Pops* screens the 'Mary Had A Little Lamb' promo.

3 July. Wings begin three days of rehearsals at the Institute of Contemporary Arts in London prior to their European tour.

7 July. Paul and Wings travel to France to begin their European tour.

9 July. Paul and Wings begin their seven-week European tour at Chateau Vallon Centre Culturelle.

12 July. Wings appear at Juan Les Pins, France.

13 July. Wings appear at the Theatre Antique in Arles, France.

14 July. A Wings concert in Lyons is cancelled due to poor ticket sales, so Wings go to the EMI Pathe Marconi Studios in Paris to begin recording 'Seaside Woman'.

16 July. Wings perform two shows at the Olympia Hall, Paris.

18 July. Wings appear at the Circus Krone, Munich, Germany.

19 July. Wings appear at the Offenbach Halle, Frankfurt, Germany.

21 July. Wings appear at the Kongresshaus, Zurich, Switzerland.

22 July. 'Mary Had A Little Lamb' reaches No. 28 in the US charts. Wings appear at the Pavilion, Montreux, Switzerland.

23 July. Wings appear at the Pavilion, Montreux, Switzerland.

1 August. Wings appear at the KB Hallen, Copenhagen, Denmark.

4 August. Wings appear at the Messuhalli, Helsinki, Finland.

5 August. Wings appear at Idraets, Kupittaan Urheilli, Turku, Finland.

7 August. Wings appear at the Tivoli Gardens, Kungliga Hallen, Stockholm, Sweden.

8 August. Wings appear at the Idretis Halle, Oerebro, Sweden.

9 August. Wings appear in Oslo, Norway.

10 August. Wings appear at the Scandinavium Hall, Gothenburg, Sweden. Paul, Linda and Denny Seiwell are arrested after the show on drugs offences.

11 August. Wings appear at the Olympean, Lund, Sweden.

12 August. It's reported in the *Daily Mirror* that customs officials in Gothenburg have busted Paul, Linda and Denny Seiwell, who confessed to smoking cannabis.

13 August. Wings appear at Fyns Forum, Odense, Denmark.

14 August. Wings appear at the Wejlby Risskov Hallen, Arkus, Denmark.

16 August. Wings appear at the Stadthalle in Hanover, Germany.

17 August. Wings appear at the Evenmanten, Gronnegan, Rotterdam, Holland.

18 August. Wings appear at Doelan, Rotterdam, Holland.

19 August. Wings appear at Evenementenhal, Groningen, Holland.

20 August. Wings appear at the Concertgebouw, Amsterdam, Holland. During the day they appear on *Popsmuk*, a programme on VPRO radio.

21 August. Wings appear at the Congresgebouw, The Hague, Holland. This was an extra date that had been added to the tour and during the show 'The Mess' was recorded and later issued as the flipside of 'My Love'.

22 August. Wings appear at the Cine Roma Borgerhout, Antwerp, Belgium.

24 August. Wings appear at the Deutschland Halle, Berlin, Germany.

31 August. *Rolling Stone* publishes an interview with Paul which has been conducted backstage at the Theatre Antique concert during the recent European tour.

19 September. Police raid Paul's Scottish farm and discover marijuana plants.

11 October. Paul appeals for the return of a stolen guitar. It was one he'd used on stage with the Beatles. He says, 'If the thief stole it to sell it, he can sell it back to me!'

12 October. The promo clip from 'Mary Had A Little Lamb' is screened in America on *The Flip Wilson Show*.

25 November. The promo films of 'Hi, Hi, Hi' and 'C Moon' were shot at the Southampton studios of Southern Television, directed by Steve Turner.

27 November. Paul and Wings continue work on Linda's 'Seaside Woman' at AIR Studios, London.

30 November. Paul hosts a party at the Village Restaurant, London to celebrate the release of 'Hi, Hi, Hi'/'C Moon'.

1 December. Paul McCartney and Wings release 'Hi, Hi, Hi', which is then banned from BBC Radios One and Two.

2 December. In an interview in *Melody Maker*, Paul says, '"Mary Had A Little Lamb" wasn't a great record, but the funny thing about that is we've got a whole new audience of eight-year-olds and five-to-six year olds – like Pete Townshend's daughter.' 'Hi, Hi, Hi'/'C Moon' is issued in Britain.

4 December. 'Hi, Hi, Hi'/'C Moon' is issued in America.

16 December. The promo for 'Hi, Hi, Hi' is shown on London Weekend Television's *Russell Harty Plus* show.

22 December. Through his solicitor Paul pleads not guilty to charges of growing marijuana at his Scottish farm.

1973

4 January. Wings videotape a performance of 'C Moon' for *Top Of The Pops*.

13 January. Paul and Linda attend the 'Rainbow concert' featuring Eric Clapton.

25 January. The Radio Merseyside programme *Twice The Price*, hosted by disc jockey Peter Price, airs a pre-recorded interview with Paul.

3 February. 'Hi, Hi, Hi' reaches No. 10 in the American chart.

9 February. Mike McCartney's new group Grimms release their eponymous album.

19 February. Paul begins work on his television special 'James Paul McCartney' at ATV Television Studios.

27 February. Paul holds a press conference during which he announces that he will soon begin his first tour of Britain with Wings.

8 March. Paul and Linda are each fined £100 at Campbeltown for growing cannabis on their farm.

10 March. Paul and Wings continue filming for 'James Paul McCartney' and appear on Hampstead Heath performing 'Mary Had A Little Lamb'.

15 March. Filming of the TV special 'James Paul McCartney' resumes at ATV Studios.

18 March. Paul and Linda appear with Wings at the Hard Rock Café, London, raising funds for Release, a charity that aids drug-takers. Earlier in the day they'd recorded songs in front of a live audience for the forthcoming ATV Television special 'James Paul McCartney'.

19 March. Paul and Wings are recording tracks for *Red Rose Speedway* at Abbey Road Studios.

23 March. 'My Love'/'The Mess' by Paul McCartney and Wings is released in the UK.

1 April. Paul and Wings complete the filming of the television special 'James Paul McCartney'.

4 April. Paul and Wings pre-record their third *Top Of The Pops* appearance with 'My Love'.

9 April. 'My Love'/'The Mess' is released in America and becomes Wings' first US chart-topper.

12 April. Paul, Linda and the kids set off for a holiday in the Caribbean.

15 April. Paul and family return from their brief holiday.

16 April. The 'James Paul McCartney' television special is screened in America. Paul aids Ringo in the recording of the track 'Six O'Clock' for the *Ringo* album.

21 April. A two-part feature on Wings appears in *Melody Maker* entitled 'Wings – Anatomy Of A Hot Band'.

30 April. *Red Rose Speedway* is released in America.

4 May. *Red Rose Speedway* is released in Britain.

10 May. The 'James Paul McCartney' television special is screened in Britain.

11 May. Paul McCartney and Wings begin their first major British tour at the Hippodrome, Bristol.

12 May. Wings appear at the New Theatre, Oxford. Paul holds a press conference for forty journalists at the Randolph Hotel and is later interviewed for the BBC radio programme *The David Symonds Show*.

13 May. Wings appear at the Capitol, Cardiff.

15 May. Wings appear at the Winter Gardens, Bournemouth.

16 May. Wings appear at the Hard Rock, Manchester.

17 May. Wings appear at the Hard Rock, Manchester.

18 May. Wings appear at the Empire Theatre, Liverpool.

19 May. Wings appear at Leeds University.

21 May. Wings appear at the Guildhall, Preston.

22 May. Wings appear at the Odeon, Edinburgh.

23 May. Wings appear at the Odeon, Edinburgh.

24 May. Wings appear at Green's Playhouse, Glasgow.

25 May. Wings appear at the Odeon, Hammersmith. In America *Red Rose Speedway* is certified gold.

26 May. Wings appear at the Odeon, Hammersmith.

27 May. The scheduled concert at the Hippodrome, Birmingham is cancelled due to problems caused by a large water tank above the stage installed as part of the musical *The Pajama Tops*, currently running at the theatre. Instead, Wings hold an end-of-tour party at the Café Royal, Regent Street, London.

1 June. 'Live And Let Die', a composition by Paul, is the theme tune for the latest James Bond film. Wings issue it as a single in Britain with 'I Lie Around' on the flip.

2 June. The single 'My Love' and the album *Red Rose Speedway* both top the American charts.

18 June. 'Live And Let Die' is issued in the US.

29 June. The film *Live and Let Die* is premiered in New York.

2 July. The soundtrack for the James Bond movie *Live And Let Die* is released in America featuring the Wings title track and also the Brenda J Arnau version.

4 July. Wings appear at the City Hall, Sheffield.

5 July. Wings attend the premiere of the film *Live And Let Die* at the Odeon, Leicester Square, London. They had cancelled a concert at Trentham Gardens, Stoke-on-Trent because it clashed with the movie premiere.

6 July. The *Live And Let Die* soundtrack album, with Paul's title tune, is issued in the UK. Wings appear at the Odeon, Birmingham. In America 'My Love' is awarded a gold disc.

9 July. Wings appear at the Odeon, Leicester.

10 July. Wings complete their British tour at the City Hall, Newcastle.

27 July. Denny Laine and Henry McCullough join Paul at his Scottish farm to begin rehearsing for the next Wings album.

8 August. Paul reviews Paul Simon's latest album *Paul Simon Songbook* in *Punch* magazine.

29 August. Henry McCullough and Denny Seiwell both leave Wings. Regarding McCullough, a spokesman said: 'He left Wings due to musical differences and by mutual agreement. Everybody thinks it's for the best and wishes each other well in the future.'

30 August. The McCartneys and Denny Laine fly to Lagos, Nigeria, to record *Band On The Run*.

31 August. The 'Live And Let Die' single is issued with a gold disc by the RIAA in America.

1 September. Paul, Linda and Denny Laine begin their recordings for the *Band On The Run* album.

23 September. Paul and Linda arrive at Gatwick airport after six weeks in Lagos, Nigeria. They are a day late due to brake failure on the plane.

26 September. The *Melody Maker* reports that Paul is writing the music for a Twiggy TV special 'Gotta Sing, Gotta Dance'.

5 October. Mike McCartney's band Grimms release their second album *Rockin' Duck*.

15 October. Paul begins a week at Abbey Road Studios mixing tracks for the *Band On the Run* album.

26 October. Paul McCartney and Wings release the single 'Helen Wheels' in Britain, with 'Country Dreamer' on the flip.

12 November. 'Helen Wheels' is released in America.

14 November. Paul, Linda, Denny Laine, Jimmy McCulloch and Davey Lutton fly to Paris to record at EMI's Boulogne-Billancourt Studios for the Suzy and the Red Stripes sessions.

17 November. Paul and Linda return to London.

24 November. Paul is interviewed for the London station Capital Radio.

30 November. The BBC 1 programme *Rockweek* airs a pre-recorded interview with Paul.

5 December. The Paul McCartney and Wings album *Band On The Run* is issued in America.

7 December. The Paul McCartney and Wings album *Band On The Run* is issued in Britain, although it does not contain the track 'Helen Wheels', which is on the American release. It is awarded a gold record in America.

16 December. Paul and Linda record 'Disney Time' at their Cavendish Avenue home.

19 December. Wings mime to 'Helen Wheels' on Granada TV's *Lift Off with Ayshea*.

26 December. Paul and Linda's 'Disney Time' appearance is screened on BBC 1.

1974

4 January. Paul begins recording his brother Mike's album *McGear* at Strawberry Studios, Stockport. The sessions take place at various times over the coming four months and during one of the recording sessions the Carpenters drop in to see Paul at work.

12 January. 'Helen Wheels' reaches the position of No. 10 in the US chart. The *Melody Maker* also suggests that Paul has hinted on a Beatles get-together with the words, 'We have broken up as a band, but I'd like to see us work together on a loose basis – and I think we will.'

28 January. The Paul McCartney and Wings single 'Jet' is issued in America backed by 'Mamunia' – it will reach No. 7 in the charts.

13 February. Jane Asher gives birth to a baby girl at Middlesex hospital.

15 February. Paul McCartney and Wings release the single 'Jet,' with 'Let Me Roll It' on the flip in the UK – again, it will reach No. 7 in the charts.

18 February. Capitol Records in America swap the sides of the 'Jet' single, making 'Mamunia' the A-side.

25 February. Commenting on the fact that the High Court has approved the receiver carrying on running the Beatles' partnership affairs, Paul says, 'As soon as things are sorted out we can all get together again and do something. We've talked about it, but haven't been able to do anything because this has been going on and on.'

8 March. Paul is interviewed for the American network ABC TV at the MPL offices in London.

9 March. Paul and Linda, together with their kids and the other members of Wings, fly to Los Angeles for rehearsals.

28 March. Paul drops in to see John Lennon recording at Burbank Studios and joins John on the track 'Midnight Special'. Paul and Linda receive an invitation to join John the following Sunday.

29 March. Paul's composition 'World Without Love', recorded by Peter and Gordon, appears on a compilation double album *Alan Freeman's History Of Pop Vol 2*.

30 March. Paul and Linda take their kids to the Ringling Brothers and Barnum and Bailey Circus in New York and then fly on to Los Angeles.

31 March. Paul and Linda turn up at John Lennon's beach house for a Sunday evening jam session, with musicians such as Stevie Wonder and Jesse Ed Davis. Paul plays drums and also sings.

1 April. Paul and Linda return to John's beach house and, while John is asleep, Paul jams with Keith Moon and Harry Nilsson.

4 April. Paul and Linda drop by Brian Wilson's house, but he refuses to open the door. They can hear him crying and they leave.

8 April. 'Band On The Run'/'Nineteen Hundred And Eighty Five' is issued as a single in America and tops the US charts.

13 April. The album *Band On The Run* tops the American charts.

26 April. Paul holds an audition at the Albery Theatre in London to find a new drummer and chooses Geoff Britton. Other drummers at the audition included Mitch Mitchell, former member of the Jimi Hendrix Experience, Aynsley Dunbar, a famous Liverpool drummer and Rob Townshend, former drummer with Family.

24 May. Jungle Juice releases Paul's composition 'The Zoo Gang' as a single.

4 June. *Band On The Run* is awarded a gold disc in America.

14 June. *Band On The Run* reaches No. 1 in Australia, Norway and Sweden and receives a gold disc in each country.

15 June. Jimmy McCulloch joins Wings.

17 June. Paul, Linda and Wings fly to Nashville to record. 'God Bless America', a single by Thornton, Fradkin and Unger is released in America. Paul was a guest on the track while in New York three years earlier.

18 June. Paul tells the *Daily Express*, 'I've discovered I'm rather old-fashioned. I believe in the marriage contract.'

28 June. 'Band On The Run' is issued as a single in the UK and reaches No. 3 in the charts. 'Zoo Gang' is on the flip.

4 July. John Christie's single 'July 4', penned by Paul and Linda and produced by Dave Clark, is released.

6 July. The *Band On The Run* album tops the British charts.

14 July. In an interview in the *Evening News*, Denny Laine reveals that he trusts Paul, saying, 'I have signed so many contracts that have got me into so much trouble that I never want to sign anything again.' In Scotland, Paul records several numbers on his studio piano and refers to them as 'Piano Tapes'.

15 July. Paul and Linda set off for New York to meet John and May Pang.

16 July. Paul and Linda visit John and May in their new apartment on East 52nd Street. John recalled that they spent a few 'Beaujolais evenings, reminiscing about old times'.

21 July. Paul and Linda return to England.

1 August. Paul and Linda return to New York City.

15 August. Wings begin recording at Abbey Road and also work on a documentary to be called 'One Hand Clapping'. Willy Russell's play *John, Paul, George, Ringo and Bert*, which Paul feels portrays him in a bad light, makes its West End debut.

16 August. Adam Faith's album *I Survive* is released by Warner Brothers. Paul and Linda are featured on it. Paul plays synthesiser on 'Change', 'Never Say Goodbye' and 'Goodbye'. John and Paul sign a co-publishing agreement with ATV Music.

6 September. Mike McGear's 'Leave It'/'Sweet Baby' is released. Paul produced both sides. The record will reach No. 36 in the British charts.

26 September. Paul is asked to comment on John Lennon's latest album release *Walls And Bridges*. He says, 'It's a very good, great album, but I know he can do better. I heard "I Am The Walrus" today, for instance, and that is what I mean. I know he can do better than *Walls And Bridges*. I reckon "Walrus" is better. It's more adventurous. It's more exciting.'

27 September. Rod Stewart's recording, 'Mine For Me', penned by Paul and Linda, is on his new album release *Smiler*. Mike McGear's solo album *McGear*, produced by Paul, is released on the Warner Brothers label.

1 October. Paul and Linda attend Wembley Arena to watch Liverpool Boxer John Conteh become the world light-heavyweight boxing champion. Peggy Lee issues her album *Let's Love* with the title track written and produced by Paul.

7 October. Peggy Lee's version of Paul's composition 'Let's Love', which Paul also produced, is issued as a single.

14 October. The album *McGear* is released in the States. The British release was on 27 September.

18 October. 'Walking In The Park With Eloise'/'Bridge Over The River Suite' by the Country Hams is issued as a single.

22 October. Paul and Linda hold a press conference in New York to discuss their forthcoming world tour.

23 October. During a press conference, when George Harrison is asked if the Beatles would ever get back together again, even for one night, he said: 'I'd rather have Willie Weekes on bass than Paul McCartney.'

25 October. Paul takes solo billing on the new Wings release 'Junior's Farm'/'Sally G', which was recorded in Nashville. Peggy Lee's 'Let's Love' is issued in the UK.

4 November. 'Junior's Farm'/'Sally G' is issued in America. Rod Stewart's version of Paul's composition 'Mine For Me', is issued in America on Mercury Records.

13 November. Paul and Linda are surprise guests on boxer John Conteh's *This Is Your Life* ITV appearance.

20 November. Wings pre-record a version of 'Junior's Farm' for *Top Of The Pops*. They also back David Essex on 'Gonna Make You A Star'.

21 November. The Wings recording of the group miming to 'Junior's Farm' is aired on *Top Of The Pops*.

27 November. Paul and Linda turn up at Rod Stewart's concert at the Odeon, Lewisham and join him on stage to perform 'Mine For Me'.

30 November. Paul gives details of his forthcoming world tour to *Melody Maker*. Paul films Wings' drummer Geoff Britton at the Michael Sobell Sports Centre in Islington for a projected documentary called 'Empty Hand'.

21 December. The Wings single 'Sally G' enters the American Country Music charts. Advertisements in the British music press announce that *Band On The Run* has received a platinum disc.

22 December. Paul, Linda and the kids arrive back in Britain from America to spend Christmas in Scotland.

1975

9 January. The Beatles' partnership is finally dissolved at a hearing in the High Court in London.

10 January. Paul, Linda and the kids fly off to New York, with Paul telling the press, 'I'm relieved that the legal links between the Beatles have been separated.'

16 January. Wings begin recording the *Venus And Mars* album at Sea Saint Studios in New Orleans.

7 February. The single 'Junior's Farm'/'Sally G' is re-released with the sides reversed.

12 February. Paul appears on *News Scene Eight*, an ABC TV programme that had filmed Paul recording 'My Carnival' at Sea Saint Studios in New Orleans.

25 February. Wings travel to Los Angeles and begin completing tracks for the *Venus And Mars* album at the Wally Heider Studios.

28 February. Paul copyrights an instrumental version of 'Tomorrow', a vocal version of which was included on the 1971 *Wild Life* album.

1 March. Paul and Linda attend the Grammy Awards in Los Angeles and accept two awards for the *Band On The Run* album, the first for 'Best Pop Vocal Performance By A Group', the second for 'Best Produced Non-Classical Recording'.

3 March. In Los Angeles, Linda is arrested for possessing marijuana. The police statement read: 'Mr McCartney and his wife Linda and their three children were driving along Santa Monica Boulevard when their car went through a traffic light soon after midnight. While a patrolman was writing a traffic ticket, he said he smelt the odour of marijuana in the car and ordered the McCartneys out. He found a plastic bag containing a quantity of marijuana which Mrs McCartney had allegedly carried in her purse.'

10 March. Linda appears in a Municipal Court on the charge of possessing marijuana.

24 March. To celebrate the completing of the *Venus And Mars* sessions, Paul holds a party on the *Queen Mary* liner at Long Island, California and has 200 guests. Recordings are made of the two entertainers that night, Professor Longhair and the Meters.

26 March. Paul and Linda attend the Los Angeles premiere of the film *Tommy* and David Frost interviews Paul for the *Wide World Of Entertainments*.

2 April. Paul, Linda and the kids arrive at Heathrow airport.

8 April. Linda, who says she will not fight the marijuana charge, comments that she is 'ready to attend a class on the evils of drug abuse in expiation'.

9 April. Five years after he began his case to dissolve the Beatles, the High Court in London announces, 'All matters in the dispute between Mr McCartney and John Lennon, George Harrison and Ringo Starr have been fully settled.'

24 April. Pete Ham of Badfinger is found hanged at his home in Woking, Surrey.

25 April. Paul and Linda's appearance with Rod Stewart and the Faces at the Odeon, Lewisham on Wednesday 27 November 1974 is featured on the America television programme *Midnight Special*.

5 May. BBC 1 transmits an interview with Paul.

16 May. 'Listen To What The Man Said'/'Love In Song' is issued in Britain and is the first record to feature the MPL logo on the label.

21 May. 'David Frost Salutes The Beatles', an ABC TV show in America, includes a sequence from an ABC News clip in 1972 of Paul and Wings promoting 'Give Ireland Back To The Irish'.

23 May. 'Listen To What The Man Said'/'Love In Song' is issued in America.

27 May. *Venus And Mars* is issued in America.

30 May. The *Venus And Mars* album is issued in Britain.

31 May. A feature on Paul appears in *Melody Maker* under the title 'McCartney: Abbey Road Revisited'.

2 June. *Venus And Mars* is awarded a gold disc in America.

12 June. On *Top Of The Pops*, Pan's People dance to 'Listen To What The Man Said'.

14 June. The album *Venus And Mars* tops the British charts.

24 June. A 60-second commercial promoting the *Venus And Mars* album is screened on the ITV network in Britain.

4 July. Mike McGear's single 'Dance The Do' is issued on the Warner Brothers label. It was produced and co-written by Paul.

19 July. The album *Venus And Mars* and the single 'Listen To What The Man Said' top the American album and singles charts.

23 August. Linda is featured on the cover of *Melody Maker*.

5 September. 'Letting Go'/'You Gave Me The Answer' is released in Britain.

6 September. Wings perform a 'thank-you' concert before 1,200 EMI employees, 100 members of the Wings Fun Club and 100 invited guests at Elstree film studios. Celebrity guests include: Ringo Starr, Elton John, Twiggy, Victor Spinetti, Long John Baldry, Queen, Richard Chamberlain, Harry Nilsson and Dave Mason.

7 September. Paul and Linda attend a concert by Dave Mason at the Odeon, Hammersmith.

9 September. Wings begin a 13-month tour of ten countries at the Gaumont, Southampton.

10 September. Wings appear at the Hippodrome, Bristol.

11 September. Wings appear at the Capitol, Cardiff, following an early press conference at the Post House Hotel, near Bristol.

12 September. Wings appear at the Free Trade Hall, Manchester.

13 September. Wings appear at the Hippodrome, Birmingham. *Record Mirror* features an interview with Paul.

15 September. Wings appear at the Empire Theatre, Liverpool.

16 September. Wings appear at the City Hall, Newcastle.

17 September. Wings appear at the Odeon, Hammersmith.

18 September. Wings appear at the Odeon, Hammersmith. Following the concert, Paul hosts a party. His guests include members of Queen and Pink Floyd, David Frost, Ringo Starr, Alice Cooper, Harry Nilsson and Lynsey De Paul.

19 September. Capital Radio transmits a pre-recorded interview with Paul.

20 September. Wings appear at the Usher Hall, Edinburgh. The *Melody Maker* begins a two-part feature on Wings.

21 September. Wings appear at the Apollo, Glasgow, donning kilts for their encore.

22 September. Wings appear at the Capitol, Aberdeen.

23 September. Wings appear at Caird Hall, Dundee.

25 September. Wings appear in St Mark's Square, Venice performing a concert for UNESCO.

27 September. Second of a two-part series on Wings appears in *Melody Maker*, mainly comprising an interview with Linda. She tells Chris Welch that she is feeling more confident as a musician during the latest tour. She says, 'I never was on any of the other tours. But I think that's because I like it now and know a few chords. Last night a few things kept going out of tune, like the Moog bit on "Band On The Run" and the Mellotron went out a bit – that sort of thing. It happened on "Live And Let Die". During the rehearsals I used to get really, really nervous when a solo bit came up because it all depended on me, but it's funny in front of an audience, I feel more relaxed.'

29 September. 'Letting Go'/'You Gave Me The Answer' is issued in America.

4 October. *Melody Maker* publishes an interview with Paul under the title, 'Just an Ordinary Superstar – Fresh from a highly successful Wings tour, Paul McCartney talks to Chris Welch'.

5 October. Radio One transmits a one-hour documentary 'Wings – The Birth Of A Band', during which Paul is interviewed by Paul Gambaccini.

27 October. The McCartneys are late for their flight to Australia and because they held the flight up they are fined $200 a minute. The single 'Venus and Mars'/'Rock Show'/'Magneto And Titanium Man' is issued in America.

28 October. Wings arrive in Perth, Australia.

29 October. Denny Laine is given a special cake to celebrate his 31st birthday.

1 November. Wings begin a tour of Australia at the Entertainment Centre, Perth. An interview conducted in the afternoon is transmitted that evening on *The Mike Walsh Show* on Channel 7. The concert is also recorded by Radio 3XY and transmitted on 2 November. There is an audience of 8,000 at the opening concert.

2 November. Paul holds a press conference in Perth for more than 200 reporters.

4 November. Wings appear at the Apollo Stadium, Adelaide.

5 November. Wings appear at the Apollo Stadium, Adelaide.

7 November. Wings appear at the Horden Pavilion, Sydney.

8 November. Wings appear at the Horden Pavilion, Sydney.

10 November. Wings appear at the Festival Hall, Brisbane.

11 November. Wings appear at the Festival Hall, Brisbane. Paul also hears that the Japanese minister of justice has banned Wings from appearing in concerts in Japan due to Paul's British drug conviction in 1973.

13 November. Wings appear at Myers Music Bowl, Melbourne before an audience of 14,000. The show is filmed for a TV special and aired in February 1976 on Channel 10.

14 November. Wings appear at Myers Music Bowl, Melbourne.

15 November. Unable to appear in Japan, Wings return to England and Paul and his family then take a holiday in Hawaii.

20 November. As she's completed her psychiatric and drugs counselling course in London, the marijuana charges against Linda are dropped by a Los Angeles judge.

28 November. The single 'Venus And Mars'/'Rock Show'/'Magneto And Titanium Man' is released in Britain.

1976

26 January. The Beatles' contract with EMI expires and Paul is the only former member of the group to re-sign with the company.

14 March. Wings begin rehearsals at Elstree Studios, London.

18 March. Paul's father dies of bronchial pneumonia at his home.

19 March. Paul and Wings hold a press conference at the MPL Offices in London on the eve of their brief European tour.

20 March. Wings appear at the Falkoner Theatre, Copenhagen.

21 March. Wings appear at the Falkoner Theatre, Copenhagen.

23 March. Wings appear at the Deutschlandhalle in Berlin, Germany.

25 March. Wings appear at the Ahoy Sport Paleis in Rotterdam, Holland. The *Wings At The Speed Of Sound* album is issued in America. When they arrive in Holland they are filmed for a special documentary by Veronica Television.

26 March. Wings appear at the Pavillion Du Paris in France. That evening Jimmy McCulloch has an accident that fractures his finger and the American tour has to be postponed for three weeks. Capital Radio in London transmits an interview with Paul.

27 March. An interview with Paul by Chris Welch is published in *Melody Maker*.

29 March. Michael Drucker interviews Paul and Linda in Paris for *Number One*, a French television show.

1 April. 'Silly Love Songs'/'Cook Of The House' is issued in America.

7 April. McCartney Productions Ltd changes its name to MPL Communications Limited.

8 April. Wings had been due to start their American tour today in Fort Worth, Texas, but the tour had been put back for three weeks due to Jimmy McCulloch's accident.

9 April. The *Wings At The Speed Of Sound* album is issued in Britain.

24 April. *Wings At The Speed Of Sound* tops the American charts. Paul visits John Lennon at the Dakota and they both watch the Lorne Michaels offer for the Beatles to appear on *Saturday Night Special* and almost decide to surprise him by turning up.

25 April. Paul drops around to see John again, but John doesn't want to see him, saying he will have to make an appointment next time. They never see each other again.

26 April. Wings begin rehearsals in Dallas.

30 April. 'Silly Love Songs'/'Cook Of The House' is issued in Britain.

3 May. *Wings At The Speed Of Sound* is certified gold. Wings open their American tour at the Fort Worth Tarrant County Convention Center, Texas.

4 May. Wings appear at the Houston Summit, Texas, where Paul narrowly escapes serious injury from a falling piece of scaffolding.

5 May. Paul and Linda buy an Appaloosa stallion that they spot wandering by a roadside.

7 May. Wings appear at the Detroit Olympia, Texas.

8 May. Wings appear at the Detroit Olympia, Texas.

9 May. Wings appear at the Maple Leaf Gardens, Toronto.

10 May. Wings appear at the Richfield Coliseum, Cleveland, Ohio.

12 May. Wings appear at the Spectrum Bowl, Philadelphia. The Veronica Television documentary on Wings is screened in Holland.

14 May. Wings appear at the Spectrum Bowl, Philadelphia.

15 May. Wings appear at the Maryland Capitol Center, Washington. Among the 22,000 strong audience are Peter Asher, Linda Rondstadt and the Eagles.

16 May. Wings appear at the Maryland Capitol Center, Washington.

18 May. Wings appear at the Atlanta Omni.

19 May. Wings appear at the Atlanta Omni. Paul, Linda and Wings leave their hands and footprints in cement for a 'Pavement Of Stars' outside the walkway of Peaches, a record store in Atlanta, Georgia.

21 May. Wings appear at the Nassau Coliseum, Long Island.

22 May. Wings appear at the Boston Garden. 'Silly Love Songs' tops the American charts. On *Saturday Night Live* Lorne Michaels makes another offer for the Beatles to appear, upping the fee to $3,200.

24 May. Wings appear at Madison Square Garden, New York.

25 May. Wings appear at Madison Square Garden, New York.

27 May. Wings appear at the Riverfront Coliseum, Cincinnati.

29 May. Wings appear at the Kemper Arena, Kansas City.

31 May. Wings appear at Chicago Stadium, Illinois.

1 June. Wings appear at Chicago Stadium, Illinois.

2 June. Wings appear at Chicago Stadium, Illinois.

4 June. Wings appear at the Minnesota Civic Center, St Paul. Their appearance is filmed for a television show called 'Wings Over St Paul'.

7 June. Wings appear at McNichols Arena, Denver.

10 June. Wings appear at the Kingdome, Seattle.

12 June. 'Silly Love Songs' reaches No. 2 in the British charts, its highest position.

13 June. Wings appear at the Cow Palace, San Francisco.

14 June. Wings appear at the Cow Palace, San Francisco. An American TV show transmits 'Monday Night Special', which features an interview conducted with Paul at the Kingdome, Seattle on 10 June.

16 June. Wings appear at the Sports Arena, San Diego.

18 June. Wings appear at the Community Centre, Tucson. Linda and the group arrange a special surprise party for Paul's 34th birthday.

19 June. Paul and Linda join Ringo Starr for a four-hour recording session of Paul's composition 'Pure Gold' at the Cherokee Studios in Hollywood.

20 June. Paul and Linda attend a birthday party in Los Angeles for Brian Wilson of the Beach Boys.

21 June. Wings appear at the Forum, Los Angeles.

22 June. Wings appear at the Forum, Los Angeles.

23 June. Wings appear at the Forum, Los Angeles.

24 June. Wings hold an end-of-tour party at the Harold Lloyd Estate in Beverly Hills, attended by several celebrities.

28 June. Paul and Linda appear on *Goodnight America*, where they are interviewed by Geraldo Rivera.

29 June. ABC's *Good Morning America* screens excerpts from the recent Seattle concert of 10 June.

10 July. Paul and Linda attend a Beach Boys concert in Anaheim, California.

16 August. The Melodiya label in Russia issues the *Band On The Run* album.

21 August. As members of the audience, Paul and Linda watch performances by the Rolling Stones and Lynyrd Skynyrd at the Knebworth Festival.

28 August. 'Let 'Em In' reaches No. 3 in the American charts.

7 September. Paul launches his first ever 'Buddy Holly Week' on the 40th anniversary of Holly's birth.

17 September. Ringo Starr's *Rotogravure* album is released in Britain and contains the number 'Pure Gold', which Paul wrote for Ringo and on which he sings backing vocals.

18 September. Paul, Linda and Wings travel to Austria to begin a short European tour.

19 September. Paul and Wings perform at the Wiener Stadthalle, Vienna, Austria.

20 September. Paul is given an American industry award as top male vocalist of the year.

21 September. Paul and Wings perform at the Dom Sportova Hall, Yugoslavia.

25 September. Paul and Wings perform for the 'Save Venice Fund' in St Mark's Square, Venice where they raise $50,000 to aid the restoration work to offset the sinking of the city.

27 September. Paul and Wings perform at the Olympiahalle, Munich, Germany.

27 September. Ringo's *Rotogravure* is issued in the States.

19 October. Wings perform at the Empire Pool Wembley.

20 October. Wings perform at the Empire Pool Wembley.

21 October. Wings perform at the Empire Pool Wembley and Paul says, 'I still love touring and will still be doing it when I'm 99!'

10 December. *Wings Over America*, a triple album, is issued in both Britain and America.

24 December. Paul and Linda attend a Rod Stewart concert at the Olympia, London. Mike McCartney and Denny Laine are among the guests backstage.

1977

8 January. At the *Daily Mirror* Pop Club Readers' Poll Concert at Bingley Hall, Staffordshire, Wings receive awards as Best Pop Group and Best Rock Group. Paul receives an award as Best Group Singer.

22 January. *Wings Over America* tops the American album charts.

3 February. Capital Radio announce an award for Paul for the Best London concert of 1976.

4 February. 'Maybe I'm Amazed'/'Soily' is released in Britain.

6 February. Paul and Linda collect their Capital Radio award.

7 February. Wings begin recording 'London Town' and 'Deliver Your Children' at Abbey Road Studios. 'Maybe I'm Amazed'/'Soily' is issued in America.

20 February. Paul and Linda leave for Jamaica for a fortnight's holiday.

29 April. *Thrillington*, an instrumental version of the *Ram* album, is released in Britain, together with the single 'Uncle Albert/Admiral Halsey'/'Eat At Home'.

30 April. Paul and Linda book into the Stanhope Hotel in New York.

17 May. *Thrillington* is released in America.

31 May. 'Seaside Woman'/'B Side to Seaside' is issued in America.

8 September. Jimmy McCulloch leaves Wings and joins the Small Faces. He says, 'I enjoyed playing with Wings and I learned a lot from Paul, but I felt it was time for a change and the ideal change for me was the Small Faces. They are old friends of mine whose music I have always enjoyed.'

12 September. James Louis McCartney is born at the Avenue Clinic, Avenue Road, St John's Wood, London.

24 September. In a *Melody Maker* poll, Paul is voted No. 5 in the bass player section.

13 October. Director Michael Lindsay Hogg films a promotional clip for 'Mull Of Kintyre' with Paul, Linda and Denny Laine.

25 October. Wings are at Abbey Road Studios for more *London Town* recordings.

11 November. 'Mull Of Kintyre'/'Girls' School' is released in Britain. Paul, Linda and Denny are presented with gold and silver discs at Abbey Road Studios for the album *Wings At The Speed Of Sound*.

12 November. Paul discusses 'Mull Of Kintyre' during a live interview on Radio One.

19 November. Another interview with Paul by Chris Welch appears in *Melody Maker*.

1 December. Paul discusses 'Mull Of Kintyre' with Peter Sharp on ITN News.

3 December. 'Mull Of Kintyre' reaches No. 1 in the British charts. Wings begin further sessions for *London Town* at AIR Studios.

9 December. Wings film a further promotional film of 'Mull Of Kintyre' at Elstree film studios. The first promo makes its American TV debut on *Midnight Special*.

10 December. Wings record an appearance on 'The Mike Yarwood Christmas Show'.

17 December. The millionth copy of 'Mull Of Kintyre' is sold.

1978

4 January. Wings continue recording *London Town* at Abbey Road Studios.

14 January. It is announced that 'Mull Of Kintyre' is the biggest selling record in British recording history. The *TV Times* runs a feature 'Masks Of McCartney'.

15 January. The first of London Weekend Television's new arts series *The South Bank Show* is called 'Paul McCartney: Songsmith'.

23 January. Wings complete the recording of *London Town*.

20 March. 'With A Little Luck'/'Backwards Traveller' is released in America.

21 March. Paul promotes 'With A Little Luck' on Capital Radio. Paul, Linda and Denny Laine shoot a promotional film for 'London Town' at Twickenham film studios.

22 March. There is a great deal of media coverage for Wings' press launch of *London Town* which takes place on a boat sailing on the Thames.

23 March. 'With A Little Luck'/'Backwards Traveller' is released in Britain.

31 March. *London Town* is issued simultaneously in Britain and America.

15 April. Paul and Linda attend a 45th anniversary screening of *Dinner At Eight*, a 1943 film starring John Barrymore.

5 May. Wings record 'Same Time Next Year' at Rak Studios, a number used in the film *Twice In A Lifetime*.

6 May. Paul continues with the recording of 'Same Time Next Year'. An exhibition of Linda's photographs opens at the Baynard Gallery, New York.

9 May. The Granada TV show 'Paul', hosted by Paul Nicholas, includes the promo film of 'With A Little Luck'.

14 May. Paul and Linda appear on the *Simon Bates Show* on Radios One and Two (the shows are broadcast simultaneously) promoting *London Town* and 'With A Little Luck'.

20 May. 'With A Little Luck' tops the American charts.

12 June. 'I've Had Enough'/'Deliver Your Children' is released in America.

16 June. 'I've Had Enough'/'Deliver Your Children' is released in Britain.

19 June. Paul and Linda attend a performance by the Rolling Stones at the New York Palladium.

29 June. Wings begin recording tracks for *Back To The Egg* at Paul's Spirit of Ranachan Studio in Scotland.

7 July. Paul and Linda attend the London premiere of *That's Entertainment II* at the Pavilion cinema.

21 August. 'London Town'/'I'm Carrying' is released in America.

26 August. 'London Town'/'I'm Carrying' is released in Britain.

6 September. Paul and Linda launch their third 'Buddy Holly Week' with a party whose guests include Mary Hopkin, David Frost, Mickey Dolenz, Carl Perkins and George Melly.

11 September. Wings resume recording at Lympne Castle, Kent cutting tracks such as 'We're Open All Night', 'Love Awake' and 'After The Ball'.

3 October. Rockestra sessions take place at Abbey Road Studios.

10 October. More *Back To The Egg* sessions take place at Abbey Road Studios with numbers such as 'Baby's Request' and 'Getting Closer'.

14 October. The design studio Hipgnosis creates the sleeve of *Wings Greatest*.

5 November. Denny Laine marries Jo Jo Wood on a yacht in Boston Harbour.

22 November. *Wings Greatest* is released in America.

1 December. *Wings Greatest* is released in Britain.

1979

15 March. 'Goodnight Tonight'/'Daytime Nightime Suffering' is released in America on the Columbia label.

16 March. The 'Wings Over The World' television special is screened in America by CBS.

26 March. Paul issues a 12″ extended mix of 'Goodnight Tonight'/ 'Daytime Nightime Suffering'.

1 April. 'An Afternoon with Paul McCartney', in which Paul is interviewed by Paul Gambaccini, is broadcast in America. Paul records the Black Dyke Mills Band for his track 'Winter Rose' at Abbey Road Studios.

3 April. 'Goodnight Tonight'/'Daytime Nightime Suffering' is released in Britain. The promotional film for 'Goodnight Tonight' is shot at the Hammersmith Palais.

4 April. A preview of the 'Wings Over The World' documentary takes place at the Bijou Theatre, Wardour Street, London.

5 April. The 'Goodnight Tonight' promo is featured on *Top Of the Pops*.

8 April. The 'Wings Over The World' television special is screened in Britain.

9 April. The 'Goodnight Tonight' promo is featured on Thames Television's *The Kenny Everett Show*.

19 May. Following the marriage of Eric Clapton and Pattie Boyd, Paul, George and Ringo are among the musicians who take part in a jam session.

24 May. The album *Back To The Egg* is released in America.

31 May. Paul commissions Keith MacMillan, Phil Davey and Hugh Scott-Symonds to produce promo clips for the *Back To The Egg* album.

1 June. 'Old Siam Sir'/'Spin It On' is issued in Britain.

4 June. The shooting of the promo for 'Old Siam Sir' begins at Lympne Castle in Kent.

5 June. Promo films for 'Spin it On' and 'Getting Closer' are filmed in a small aircraft hanger in Kent. 'Getting Closer'/'Spin It On' is released in America.

6 June. Promos for 'Winter Rose' and 'Love Awake' are filmed at Lympne Castle.

8 June. The album *Back To The Egg* is released in Britain. Wings film the promo for 'Baby's Request'.

11 June. A press conference to promote *Back To The Egg* is held at Abbey Road Studios during which part of the 'Rockestra' film is screened.

13 June. Wings complete filming their promos for *Back To The Egg* with 'Arrow Through Me'.

15 June. Capital Radio airs Paul's *Back To The Egg* interview.

30 June. Paul is interviewed on Radio Luxembourg about *Back To The Egg*.

30 July. Another interview with Paul discussing *Back To The Egg* is aired on Radio Luxembourg.

10 August. The Suzy and the Red Stripes single 'Seaside Woman' is released in Britain.

14 August. 'Arrow Through Me'/'Old Siam Sir' is issued in America.

3 September. The promo for 'Getting Closer' is screened during the 'Jerry Lee Lewis Muscular Dystrophy Telethon'.

14 September. Paul hosts a Crickets concert at the Odeon, Hammersmith during which he performs 'It's So Easy' and 'Bo Diddley'.

27 September. Jimmy McCulloch, former guitarist with Wings, is found dead at the age of 26.

6 October. The funeral for Jimmy McCulloch is held.

24 October. Paul receives a rhodium medallion from the British arts minister after being declared the most successful composer and recording artist of all time. Between the years 1962 and 1978 he had written or co-written 43 songs that had sold over a million copies each. He had sold 100 million singles and 100 million albums.

1 November. Geraldo Rivera interviews Paul and Linda for the ABC TV programme *20/20*.

16 November. 'Wonderful Christmastime'/'Rudolph The Red Nosed Reggae' is released in Britain.

20 November. 'Wonderful Christmastime'/'Rudolph The Red Nosed Reggae' is released in America.

23 November. Wings open their 19-date British tour at the Royal Court Theatre, Liverpool.

27 November. Wings take a 'ferry 'cross the Mersey' on the *Royal Iris*, the Mersey ferryboat on which the Beatles used to perform.

28 November. Wings appear at the Apollo, Ardwick, Manchester.

29 November. Wings appear at the Apollo, Ardwick, Manchester.

1 December. Wings appear on the TV programme *Tiswas*. Wings appear at the Gaumont, Southampton.

2 December. Wings appear at the New Conference Centre, Brighton.

3 December. Wings appear at the Odeon, Lewisham, London.

5 December. Wings appear at the Rainbow theatre, Finsbury Park, London. Tom Synder interviews Paul and Linda by satellite for the American NBC TV programme the *Tomorrow Show*.

7 December. Wings appear at the Empire Pool, Wembley. They add 'Cook Of The House' and 'Baby Face' into their tour repertoire.

10 December. Wings appear at the Empire Pool, Wembley.

12 December. The 'Wonderful Christmastime' promo is aired on *ATV Today*. Wings appear at the Odeon, Birmingham.

14 December. Wings appear at the City Hall, Newcastle.

15 December. Wings appear at the Odeon, Edinburgh.

16 December. Wings appear at the Apollo, Glasgow.

17 December. Wings appear at the Apollo, Glasgow. The Campbeltown Pipes Band joins them on stage.

21 December. Radio Clyde airs a pre-recorded interview with Paul.

22 December. The show *Saturday Shake Up* features 'Flying With Wings' on Tyne-Tees Television.

25 December. As a special Christmas present, Paul buys a ranch in Arizona for $40,000, one that Linda had fallen in love with when she lived in Arizona during the 1960s.

27 December. The 'Wonderful Christmastime' promo is aired on *Top Of The Pops*.

27 December. The concerts for the people of Kampuchea take place at the Odeon, Hammersmith.

28 December. The second night of the concerts for the people of Kampuchea.

29 December. The last night of the concerts for the people of Kampuchea. There had been rumours that the Beatles would attend and when a toy robot glided across the stage, Paul said: 'No, that's not John Lennon!'

1980

2 January. Wings begin rehearsing for their Japanese tour at Paul's studio, the Mill.

12 January. Paul and his entourage leave London on their journey to Japan, staying overnight at the Stanhope Hotel, New York.

14 January. Paul phones John at the Dakota, hoping to meet him. Yoko intercepts the call and will not allow Paul to speak to John. Paul tells her that they are off to Japan.

16 January. Paul and Wings land in Japan to begin a series of concerts, but Paul is arrested and jailed on a drugs offence. Some people have suggested that it was Yoko Ono who actually tipped off the police.

17 January. Paul, now in a detention centre as Prisoner No. 22, is questioned by police for six hours.

18 January. The Tokyo court grants the prosecutor's request that Paul be held for a further ten days for questioning.

20 January. *Live And Let Die*, with Paul's title theme, receives its television premiere in Britain.

21 January. Laurence Juber and Steve Britton leave Japan for America and Denny Laine travels to Cannes.

22 January. Linda visits Paul in his cell.

24 January. Linda visits Paul in jail once again and states she will remain for 'as long as it takes'.

25 January. Paul is extradited from Japan and flies home via Alaska and Holland.

26 January. Paul and Linda arrive at Lydd Airport in Kent. The *Sun* newspaper reports on Paul's troubles under the headline, 'I'll Never Smoke Pot Again'.

27 January. Reporters hassle Paul at his home in Peasmarsh, pestering him about the incident. He asks them to leave him alone.

29 January. Denny Laine records 'Japanese Tears' at Rock City studios, London.

30 January. The *This Is Your Life* programme honours George Martin and a pre-recorded tribute by Paul is shown.

20 February. Paul gives an interview to *Rolling Stone* magazine.

26 February. At the 'British Rock And Pop Awards' at the Café Royal, Paul receives the 'Outstanding Music Personality of 1979' award.

27 February. The Rockestra Theme wins a Grammy Award. Highlights from the 'British Rock And Pop Awards' are shown on BBC 1.

3 March. Paul begins recording at Abbey Road Studios.

23 March. Paul completes three weeks of recording in both Abbey Road Studios and his own home studios.

26 March. Paul begins filming the promotional video 'Coming Up' at Ewart television studios, with the video being directed by Keith McMillan.

27 March. Recording of the 'Coming Up' promo is completed.

11 April. 'Coming Up' (studio version)/'Coming Up' (live version)'/'Lunch Box – Odd Sox' is released in Britain.

15 April. 'Coming Up' (studio version)/'Coming Up (live version)'/'Lunch Box – Odd Sox' is released in America.

1 May. Paul begins to learn to sail in a boat called *Royal Isis*.

2 May. Denny Laine's 'Japanese Tears' is released in Britain by Scratch Records.

9 May. Paul receives a 'Special International Achievement' award at the Ivor Novello Awards at the Grosvenor Hotel, London.

16 May. *McCartney II* is issued in Britain. Paul and Linda arrive in Cannes to visit the Cannes Film festival where the animated film 'Seaside Woman', based on Linda's song, will receive first prize, the Palm d'Or. The couple stay at the Montfleury Hotel where Ringo asks

Paul if he would like to participate in his new album. Paul agrees to produce and play on it.

17 May. Paul and Linda appear on *Saturday Night Live* by satellite from outside the MPL offices in London. Billy Crystal is the host and the promo of 'Coming Up' is also shown.

19 May. The 'Coming Up' clip opens the MPL show 'Meet Paul McCartney'. During the day Paul is involved in numerous radio and TV interviews including ones for Associated Press and Thames Television.

20 May. Paul records an interview with Andy Peebles for Radio One.

21 May. *McCartney II* is released in America.

23 May. Nicky Horne interviews Paul on Capital Radio for the *Mummy's Weekly* programme.

26 May. The interview Andy Peebles conducted with Paul at Broadcasting House is aired on Radio One.

27 May. Denny Laine appears on the TV programme *Magpie* to discuss his new book, *The Denny Laine Guitar Book*.

31 May. *McCartney II* tops the British album charts.

13 June. 'Waterfalls'/'Check My Machine' is issued in Britain.

14 June. The 'Waterfalls' promo is shown on the children's TV programme *Tiswas*.

22 June. Denny Laine announces that he will go on tour with his wife Jo Jo.

28 June. 'Coming Up' tops the American charts. Wings begin rehearsing at Finston Manor in Kent for a two-week period.

9 July. Wings are filmed on their final day of rehearsals at Finston Manor by a camera crew from *Day By Day*, a Southern ITV programme.

10 July. The *Day By Day* feature on Wings is transmitted and includes an interview with Paul. The animated 'Seaside Woman' film is added to the bill of the Peter Sellers film *Being There* at British cinemas. A *Daily Mirror* feature on Linda is headed 'The Launching Of Linda – Paul's Wife Goes It Alone'.

11 July. Paul and Linda join Ringo at the Super Bear studios in Paris where Ringo records Paul's compositions 'Private Property' and 'Attention'. During their period at the studios, Paul, Linda and Laurence Juber record a number by Linda, 'Love's Full Glory'.

18 July. Paul and Linda are seen in 'Diary Of The Cannes Film Festival', which is screened in America.

22 July. 'Waterfalls'/'Check My Machine' is issued in America.

15 September. Paul's 12″ single 'Temporary Secretary'/'Secret Friend' is released in Britain.

29 September. During a *Newsweek* interview with Barbara Graustark, John Lennon, when asked about Paul, referred to the time in 1976 when 'he turned up at the door. I said, "Look, do you mind ringing first? I've just had a hard day with the baby, I'm worn out and you're walking in with a damn guitar."'

2 October. Paul and Wings begin rehearsing at Finston Manor in Kent.

10 October. Paul and Linda donate £500 to help Liverpool boxer Johnny Owen, who has been injured in a boxing match.

27 October. Paul and George Martin begin recording at AIR Studios on the 'Rupert The Bear' soundtrack.

4 November. Mike McCartney travels to Rijnsburg, Holland to appear on a 'Save The Whales' charity show. In America Paul completes the final edits to the 'Rockestra' film.

6 November. Paul returns to England.

10 November. Paul works with Linda and Denny Laine on demo tracks for a forthcoming album.

26 November. Paul's *Rockshow* film is premiered at the Ziegfeld Theatre in New York.

27 November. Paul and Linda appear on a satellite broadcast from their Sussex home on the American ABC TV programme *Good Morning America*.

28 November. Paul and Denny Laine join George Martin at AIR studios in London to continue work on the next Wings album.

4 December. An interview album *The McCartney Interview* is issued in America.

8 December. John Lennon is fatally shot outside the Dakota building by Mark Chapman.

9 December. In England Paul learns of John's murder. Reporters camp outside his house for quotes. He says, 'I can't take it in at the moment. John was a great man who'll be remembered for his unique contributions to art, music and peace. He is going to be missed by the whole world.' He goes into London to resume working on the next Wings album and phones Yoko Ono in New York to offer his condolences.

1981

4 January. Highlights from the Kampuchea concerts in December 1979 are screened in various ITV regions in a programme called 'Rock For Kampuchea'.

1 February. Paul is in Montserrat to begin recording at George Martin's AIR studios on the island.

2 February. Paul begins recording tracks for forthcoming albums, with George Martin producing and drummer Dave Mattacks backing him.

3 February. Paul continues recording in Montserrat and tracks laid down include 'The Pound Is Sinking', 'Somebody Who Cares' and 'Hey Hey'.

8 February. Bass guitarist Stanley Clarke flies in from Philadelphia to join Paul at his recording sessions in Montserrat.

9 February. With Mattacks having returned to England, Paul is joined by another drummer, Steve Gadd.

15 February. Ringo Starr arrives in Montserrat to join Paul on his recording sessions.

16 February. Work begins on the track 'Take It Away', featuring Ringo on drums.

18 February. Paul, Linda and their kids make a brief visit to the West Indies.

19 February. Ringo Starr and Barbara Bach leave Montserrat to return to Los Angeles.

20 February. Carl Perkins arrives in Montserrat to join Paul on his recording sessions.

21 February. Paul and Carl Perkins begin recording together and tracks laid down over the next four days include 'Get It', 'My Old Friend', 'Honey Don't', 'Boppin' The Blues', 'Lend Me Your Comb', 'When The Saints Go Marching In', 'Cut Across Shorty' and 'Red Sails In The Sunset'.

23 February. The interview album *The McCartney Interview* is issued in Britain. The interview had originally been recorded in May 1980 by Vic Carbarini for *Musician* magazine.

26 February. Stevie Wonder joins Paul in Monserrat and they record a number they have written together, 'What's That You're Doing?'

27 February. Paul and Stevie Wonder begin recording 'Ebony And Ivory'.

3 March. Paul and Linda, having returned from Montserrat, begin recording at the AIR studios in London. During a break in the recordings Paul plays bass on a session with the Michael Schenker Group, on the invitation of drummer Cozy Powell.

30 March. The album *Concerts For The People Of Kampuchea* is released in America.

3 April. The album *Concerts For The People Of Kampuchea* is released in Britain.

8 April. Paul's *Rockshow* film receives its European premiere at the Dominion Theatre, London and Paul holds a party after the screening.

14 April. Paul fills up the tank of his Mercedes with diesel fuel instead of petrol on his way to Scotland. His car breaks down and he calls the AA (Automobile Association) to clear his tank.

27 April. Paul and Linda attend the wedding of Ringo Starr and Barbara Bach at Marylebone Register Office, where they were themselves married. The same registrar, Mr Jevans, conducts the ceremony. There was a reception held at Rags club during which a jam session took place with Paul and Nilsson on piano, George Harrison on guitar and Ringo and Ray Cooper playing spoons. Denny Laine appears on the ATV programme *ATV Today* to announce that he is leaving Wings, ending his ten-year association with the group. This is effectively the end of Wings.

11 May. George Harrison's tribute to John Lennon, 'All Those Years Ago' is released in America. Ringo Starr is on the single and Paul and Linda provide backing vocals.

15 May. 'All Those Years Ago' is released in Britain.

10 June. The 'Back To The Egg' television special, a 31-minute programme featuring promos from eight of the *Back To The Egg* tracks, receives its British TV premiere on BBC 1.

12 June. 'Silly Love Songs'/'Cook Of The House' receives a re-release in America.

18 June. *The Simon Bates Show* on Radio One devotes 50 minutes in celebration of Paul's 39th birthday.

27 September. The *Sunday People* publishes an interview with Paul.

4 October. The rights to the Quarry Men recording of 'That'll Be The Day' and 'In Spite Of All The Danger' pass into Paul's hands.

12 October. Thorn-EMI issue the home video of *Rockshow*. However, six of the tracks featured in the cinema version, issued earlier that year, have been excised: 'Call Me Back Again', 'Lady Madonna', 'The Long And Winding Road', 'Picasso's Last Words/Richard Corey', 'Blackbird' and 'My Love'.

19 November. Paul is unsuccessful in his bid to buy 'Northern Songs'.

21 November. Now joined by Yoko, Paul says that he will sue Grade for breach of trust for not allowing him to buy back the rights to the Beatles' hits.

27 November. Beatles names are given to Liverpool streets in a new housing project. They include a Paul McCartney Way.

1982

3 January. The *Sunday Mirror* features an article on Paul's home in Rye, Sussex.

4 January. *The Times* publishes an interview with Paul in which he says, 'If I could get John Lennon back, I'd ask him to undo this legacy and to tell everybody what he told Yoko – that he still liked me after all!'

8 January. *Nationwide* presents a pre-recorded interview with Paul, which Sue Lawley had conducted at Abbey Road Studios where Paul was spending much of January recording for his *Tug Of War* album.

13 January. Beginning today, Paul, Linda, Ringo and Barbara spend three days filming *The Cooler* at Ewerts Studio, London.

25 January. Paul appears in a short clip for the ATV 'American Music Awards' when he makes an introduction for Stevie Wonder.

30 January. Paul appears on the radio series *Desert Island Discs*. It is the 40th anniversary of the programme and Paul is the 1,630th guest.

11 February. Paul films scenes for the second promo of 'Ebony And Ivory' at the Old Royal Mint, London.

15 February. *Tug Of War* was due to be released on this day, but is postponed until Friday 12 March.

2 March. The first of a three-part interview with Paul appears in the *Daily Star*. The interviewers are Moira Warren and Jan Bendrick.

3 March. Part two of Paul's *Daily Star* interview appears.

4 March 4. The final part of Paul's *Daily Star* interview appears.

12 March. The date when *Tug Of War* is scheduled to be released is postponed again and a new release date is set for 19 April.

15 March. Paul is interviewed by Freddy Hausser for the French station A2.

29 March. 'Ebony And Ivory' is released in Britain.

2 April. 'Ebony and Ivory' is released in America.

8 April. The promo clip for 'Ebony And Ivory' receives its world premiere on *Top Of The Pops*.

11 April. The German TV show *Musicszene* screens a pre-recorded interview with Paul, which had been conducted at his MPL offices in London.

14 April. Paul begins recording 'The Girl Is Mine' with Michael Jackson and Quincy Jones at Westlake Studios.

15 April. Paul continues the recording sessions at Westlake Studios.

16 April. Paul finishes his recordings with Michael Jackson. Paul and Linda visit Universal Studios in Los Angeles. Paul also records an interview for the show *Friday Night Videos*.

17 April. A pre-recorded interview with Paul is included as an audio-cassette with the new British music paper *SFX*.

18 April. A pre-recorded interview with Paul by Andy Peebles is broadcast on Radio One. A two-part interview with Paul, conducted by Tony Fletcher, appears in the *Sunday Mirror*.

19 April. Now at his farm in Scotland, Paul begins to compose some new songs. The release date for *Tug Of War* has been put back again.

20 April. Paul appears in a pre-recorded interview on the American TV show *Entertainment Tonight*.

23 April. Paul spends the day at AIR studios, London. The *Friday Night Videos* show, which Paul filmed on 16 April, is screened, which includes Paul introducing the 'Ebony And Ivory' promo.

24 April. An interview with Paul is published in *Record Mirror*.

25 April. The second part of Tony Fletcher's interview with Paul appears in the *Sunday Mirror*. The *New York Times* also publishes an interview with Paul, written by Robert Palmer. The *LA Times* also publishes an interview with Paul.

26 April. Paul is at AIR studios, London. The first of a four-part interview with Paul, conducted by Brian Grimble, appears on the NBC TV breakfast show *Today*. *Tug Of War* is released simultaneously in Britain and America.

29 April. An interview with Paul appears in the Liverpool publication *Scene*.

1 May. 'Ebony And Ivory' tops the British charts.

6 May. Paul and Linda make a surprise appearance on *Top Of the Pops* following the screening of a promo of 'Ebony And Ivory'. They give a special greeting to Heather, who has recently broken a leg and collar-bone after being thrown off a horse, and they give a brief interview to Simon Bates.

15 May. 'Ebony And Ivory', Paul's duet with Stevie Wonder, tops the American charts.

19 May. Paul meets George Martin at AIR studios.

24 May. *The Cooler* is entered into the 'Best Short Subject' category at the Cannes Film Festival.

29 May. Paul is best man at the wedding of his brother Mike in Liverpool to Rowena Horne. *Tug Of War* tops the American album charts.

13 June. The *Sunday Mail* features a double-page spread entitled 'The Magical Maturity Of Paul McCartney'.

14 June. Paul buys an eighteenth-century windmill.

18 June. Paul begins filming the 'Take It Away' promo at Elstree Studios. And there is a special party to celebrate Paul's 40th birthday with Ringo and Barbara, Eric Stewart, George Martin and Steve Gadd. The *Sun* newspaper features an article 'Fab And Forty'. 'Paul McCartney Today' is the title of a three-part interview, the first part of which is transmitted today on NBC Radio.

19 June. The second part of NBC Radio's three-part interview 'Paul McCartney Today' is broadcast.

20 June. The third part of NBC Radio's three-part interview 'Paul McCartney Today' is broadcast.

21 June. 'Take It Away'/'I'll Give You A Ring' is released in Britain.

23 June. Filming of 'Take it Away' at Elstree Studios is completed.

3 July. 'Take It Away'/'I'll Give You A Ring' is released in America.

5 July. A 12″ version of 'Take It Away'/'I'll Give You A Ring'/'Dress Me Up As A Robber' is released in Britain.

15 July. Paul's 'Take It Away' video is premiered on *Top Of The Pops*.

26 July. The 12″ version of 'Take It Away'/'I'll Give You A Ring'/'Dress Me Up As A Robber' is released in America.

1 August. A pre-recorded interview with Paul, conducted by David Perry and called 'Paul McCartney: The Man and his Music' is broadcast on WGAR-AM Radio in Cleveland, Ohio.

1 September. Paul begins a short spell of recording at Abbey Road Studios.

7 September. Paul and Linda and Ringo and Barbara attend the Buddy Holly Rock 'n' Roll Championship at the Lyceum, London as part of the Buddy Holly Week celebrations.

20 September. 'Tug Of War'/'Get It' is released in Britain.

23 September. Paul films a promo of 'Tug Of War' at AIR studios, London.

24 September. Paul completes the filming of the 'Tug Of War' promo at AIR studios.

25 September. Paul and Linda attend a launch party for the *Guinness Book Of Records* at EMI Studios.

26 September. 'Tug Of War'/'Get It' is released in America.

4 October. To coincide with the 20th anniversary of the release of 'Love Me Do', Paul is interviewed for the *Newsnight* programme on BBC 1. He is asked how likely it would have been for the Beatles to get back together when John had been alive. Paul was to say: 'There were times when we thought "Oh, it would be great, it would be good." But we generally thought that if we did it, it would be a letdown. One of the things we'd been consciously aware of with the Beatles was to go and

have a great career and leave them laughing and we thought we'd done that, you know. We didn't want to come back as decrepit old rockers saying, "Remember us?"'

5 October. Paul is interviewed by Tony Prince for the Radio Luxembourg special 'McCartney Remembers'.

7 October. Paul sends a telegram to British Prime Minister Margaret Thatcher: 'What the miners did to Ted Heath, the nurses will do to you.'

9 October. Mike McCartney appears on BBC 1's *Saturday Superstore* in an interview with Mike Read and the promo of 'Tug Of War' is screened.

18 October. Linda is featured on the cover of *Woman* magazine.

19 October. In New York, Linda buys a pair of doves.

25 October. 'This Girl Is Mine', the Michael Jackson single on which he duets with Paul, is released in America.

29 October. 'This Girl Is Mine' is released in Britain.

5 November. At Elstree Studios Paul begins filming of *Give My Regards To Broad Street*.

23 November. The BBC Radio One programme *Newsbeat* broadcasts a short pre-recorded interview with Paul.

24 November. Paul and Linda arrive in Paris.

25 November. Paul and Linda attend La Galerie Ganon where an exhibition of her photographs is on display.

29 November. Michael Jackson's album *Thriller* is issued in America and features his duet with Paul on 'This Girl Is Mine'.

8 December. Paul appears on a Channel 4 documentary programme about Rupert The Bear.

22 December. Paul attends the rock and pop memorabilia auction at Sotheby's, London.

25 December. Radio Luxembourg transmits 'The Paul McCartney Interview'.

26 December. Paul Gambaccini's *Appreciation* series on Radio One includes an interview with Paul.

1983

2 February. Michael Jackson arrives in Britain and stays with Paul and Linda at their Sussex home. He is here to make a promo with Paul for 'The Man'.

10 February. Paul, Linda and Michael Jackson attend the BRIT Awards. Paul is awarded 'Best British Male Artist of 1982' and receives a Sony Award for 'Technical Expertise' while George Martin and Geoff Emerick receive awards for their work on Paul's album *Tug Of War*.

26 February. An interview with Paul is published in the *Sunday Mirror*.

18 March. Denny Laine's company 'Denny Laine Ltd' is compulsorily wound up.

6 April. At the first American Video Awards, Paul is inducted into the Video Hall of Fame by Mike Nesmith and also receives a second award for 'Ebony And Ivory' as Best Soul Video.

17 April. A three-part series by Jo Jo Laine regarding her association with Paul and Linda begins in the *Sunday People*.

27 April. Paul and Linda join Ringo and Barbara at the St James Club, London to celebrate Ringo and Barbara's second wedding anniversary.

8 May. Filming of *Give My Regards To Broad Street* ends and at the Elstree Studios party the cast and crew are all given a crystal glass tumbler with the message 'With Love From Paul And Linda'.

11 May. A photograph of Paul and Ringo from *Give My Regards To Broad Street* is published in the *Daily Mirror*.

16 May. An interview with Paul is published in the *Daily Mirror*.

5 June. MTV presents a live interview with Paul from Shepperton Studio.

16 June. Paul records an interview with Simon Bates for Radio One.

17 June. The Simon Bates interview with Paul is broadcast with Paul discussing his upcoming album *Pipes Of Peace*.

18 June. 'Paul McCartney – The Solo Years' is a programme broadcast in America by Westwood One radio to celebrate Paul's birthday.

26 June. *Parade* magazine publishes an interview with Paul.

4 July. Paul completes some recordings at AIR studios in London before flying off to Montserrat.

16 July. Paul is seen busking in Leicester Square for an additional scene for *Give My Regards To Broad Street*.

23 July. An exhibition of Linda's entitled 'Photographs' opens in the Barry Stern Gallery in New South Wales, Australia.

25 July. Paul, George and Ringo are spotted at the Gore Hotel, Kensington having a drink together.

26 July. Paul is at Elstree Studios for some post-production work on *Give My Regards To Broad Street*.

6 August. Paul has lunch with his brother Mike in Liverpool before flying to New York.

26 August. Paul begins recording at AIR studios, London with George Martin.

28 August. Paul, Linda and family are in Liverpool.

1 September. The charity single 'The Selection Of Children's Stories', issued by Warwick Records, has sleeve notes penned by Paul and Linda.

6 September. Paul and Linda host their annual Buddy Holly Week.

12 September. A paperback edition of Linda's book *Photographs* is published.

19 September. The *Liverpool Echo* publishes an interview with Paul.

22 September. Paul and Linda attend the Everly Brothers concert at the Royal Albert Hall. Also in the audience are Ringo and Barbara, Eric Clapton and Mickey Dolenz.

27 September. Ruth McCartney makes her American singing debut on NBC's *Fantasy* programme.

29 September. *Time* magazine hosts a 60th anniversary party at the Royal Festival Hall, London. Paul and Linda are amongst the guests, as are Ringo Starr, Elton John, Pete Townshend and Diana Rigg.

3 October. 'Say Say Say'/'Ode To A Teddy Bear', the single on which Paul duets with Michael Jackson, is issued simultaneously in Britain and America.

4 October. Shooting begins on the 'Say Say Say' promotional film in Los Alamos, California and lasts for four days.

14 October. Paul records an interview for Radio One's *Saturday Live Show* in which he discusses *Give My Regards To Broad Street*.

17 October. The release of *Pipes Of Peace* in Britain is delayed.

18 October. The *Enquirer* magazine reports that Paul has bought a $100,000 dollar bed with a built-in stereo system for Stevie Wonder.

22 October. Paul's pre-recorded interview for *Saturday Live Show* is broadcast.

28 October. The 'Say Say Say' promo receives its British premiere on *The Tube*. Linda's 'Photographs' exhibition opens at the Milburn Gallery, Brisbane, Australia.

29 October. Paul and Linda appear on the TV show *The Late Late Breakfast Show*, hosted by Noel Edmonds, to promote their 'Say Say Say' promo.

30 October. The 'Say Say Say' video receives its world premiere on MTV in America.

31 October. *Pipes Of Peace* is released simultaneously in Britain and America.

1 November. Paul, Linda and family return to London from Los Angeles.

4 November. The 'Say Say Say' video receives its network premiere in America on NBC-TV's *Friday Night Videos*.

11 November. MTV announces that Paul will release 'The Man' as his next single.

15 November. Paul composes the theme music for the film *The Honorary Consul*.

24 November. *Smash Hits* publishes an interview with Paul.

1 December. Paul, George and Ringo meet Yoko Ono at the Dorchester Hotel, London to discuss Apple business. The first of a two-part interview with Paul is shown on the American CBS programme *Entertainment Tonight*.

3 December. Paul is interviewed by Simon Bates for his Radio One show.

4 December. The second part of Paul's interview is screened on *Entertainment Tonight*.

5 December. 'Say Say Say' reaches No. 1 in the American charts. Paul's single 'So Bad'/'Pipes Of Peace' is released in America. The British release is 'Pipes Of Peace'/'So Bad'.

6 December. Linda's exhibition 'Photographs' opens at the Molly Barnes Gallery, Los Angeles, California.

11 December. Paul is interviewed on the MTV programme 'MTV In London'.

13 December. A pre-recorded interview with Paul is featured on the ITV show *Razzmatazz*.

14 December. Paul is seen in a pre-recorded interview on the BBC 1 programme *Harty*.

16 December. Paul is interviewed by Leslie Ash for *The Tube*.

23 December. The first of a two-part pre-recorded interview with Paul is included in the *Friday Night Videos* show in America.

25 December. A pre-recorded interview conducted by Allan Banks is broadcast by the British Forces Broadcasting Service.

31 December. The radio station Signal transmits a pre-recorded interview with Paul.

1984

3 January. Paul, Linda and the kids fly to New York on their way to a fortnight's holiday in Barbados.

5 January. An interview with Paul, originally recorded in October 1983, is broadcast on a local NBC station in America, the WKYC news channel.

13 January. Paul, Linda, Stella and James settle in at Potter's House, Bridgetown, Barbados.

16 January. Paul and Linda are arrested for possession of cannabis in Barbados when police raid their villa and discover ten grams of marijuana.

17 January. In court in Barbados Paul and Linda plead guilty to possession of marijuana and are fined 200 Barbados dollars. At the American Music Awards, a message Paul videotaped for Michael Jackson is screened. Cannabis is found in Linda's possession when she arrives back in England.

19 January. Commenting on Linda's search by customs officials at Heathrow, Paul says, 'All our bags were thoroughly searched by police in Barbados after we were busted there. They told us we were clean but they obviously didn't do a thorough job. Most of the time, Linda doesn't know what's in her bag anyway. It wouldn't have been there if they'd done their job properly.'

24 January. Linda appears at Uxbridge Magistrates' Court where her defence counsel tells the magistrates, 'Linda is genuinely sorry, and wishes to make a genuine apology. I urge the court not to make an example of her just because she is famous. Linda is a thoughtful, likeable woman who has done far more for other people than those who sneer at her.' Linda is fined £75 for possession of cannabis.

27 January. The second part of an interview with Paul is screened on *Friday Night Videos*. The London magazine *Time Out* publishes an article in which Paul calls for the legalisation of cannabis.

31 January. The *Sun* newspaper begins a four-part feature by Denny Laine, discussing his association with Paul.

2 February. Humphrey Ocean's portrait of Paul is unveiled at the National Portrait Gallery in London.

10 February. Paul is again featured on *Friday Night Videos*.

11 February. 'So Bad' tops the American charts.

13 February. The Paul/Michael Jackson single 'The Man'/'Blackpool', planned for release in Britain today on Parlophone 6066, is cancelled.

21 February. 'Pipes Of Peace' receives the 'Best Video of 1983' award at the 1983 Rock and Pop Awards. Keith MacMillan picks up the award on Paul's behalf as Paul, Linda and the kids are on a skiing holiday.

29 February. *Tug Of War* is issued on CD in America, while in Britain EMI release a CD of *Pipes Of Peace*.

3 March. The Paul McCartney Fan Club of Scotland organises a two-day Beatles convention.

5 March. Rolf Harris presents Geoff Dunbar with the BAFTA (British Academy of Film and Television Arts) for directing *Rupert And The Frog Song* as 'Best Short Animated Film'.

21 March. On their return from a brief holiday in Switzerland, Paul and Linda attend a reception at St James's Palace and talk to the Queen Mother.

2 April. The first of a three-part series on Paul is featured in the Scottish *Daily Record*.

3 April. The second part of the series on Paul is featured in the *Daily Record*.

4 April. The *Daily Record* completes its three-part series on Paul. An interview with Paul also appears in the *Sun* newspaper.

10 April. Paul begins filming the promo for 'No More Lonely Nights' in Bermondsey, London.

11 April. The first part of a two-part interview with Paul is broadcast on Capital Radio.

14 April. Linda and David Bailey appear on a Radio One programme on photography.

18 April. The second part of Paul's interview is broadcast on Capital Radio.

23 April. Radio Merseyside and Radio Northampton broadcast a pre-recorded interview with Paul entitled 'McCartney: The Man'.

26 April. Bob Marley's 'One Love' video, on which Paul appears in a cameo role, is screened on *Top Of The Pops*. Mike McCartney unveils a statue of the Beatles in Liverpool.

6 May. Paul and Linda have a family get-together with McCartney relatives at 'Rembrandt', their Wirral home.

18 May. The Phipps Plaza Cinema in Atlanta, Georgia holds a sneak preview of the movie *Give My Regards To Broad Street*.

22 May. Linda appears on *Good Morning America*.

3 June. Linda's photographic exhibition at the Barbara Gillman Gallery in Florida closes.

9 June. Paul appears on London Weekend television's *Aspel And Company*, along with Tracy Ullman.

17 June. Stuart Grundy interviews Paul for the Radio One show 'Echoes'.

18 June. The first of a two-part interview with Paul is broadcast on the NBC TV show *Today*.

19 June. The second part of Paul's interview is broadcast on NBC TV's *Today*.

5 July. A colour photograph of Paul with Fairuza Balk, who plays Dorothy in the *Return To Oz* movie, appears in *Rolling Stone* magazine.

28 July. Paul begins mixing a disco version of 'No More Lonely Nights' at AIR studios. The Radio Four programme *Desert Island Discs* makes an apology to Larry Parnes regarding remarks humorously made by Paul when he appeared on the programme in January 1982.

24 August. 'On the Wings Of A Nightingale' by the Everly Brothers is released. It was written and mixed by Paul.

7 September. Paul presents the prizes in a Buddy Holly drawing competition at Hamilton's Gallery, London during his Buddy Holly Week.

8 September. The MPL film *The Music Lives On* is screened by MTV.

24 September. The single 'No More Lonely Nights (ballad version)'/'No More Lonely Nights (playout version)' is issued in Britain, together with a 12″ disc 'No More Lonely Nights (extended playout version)'/'No More Lonely Nights (ballad version)'/'Silly Love Songs'.

2 October. The promotional video for 'No More Lonely Nights' is premiered on MTV. It is directed by Keith MacMillan and includes additional footage with Paul portrayed as a film projectionist who finds no one at home when he calls and wanders out onto a rooftop to gaze at the London skyline. The 12″ single of 'No More Lonely Nights' is also released.

5 October. 'No More Lonely Nights (ballad version)'/'No More Lonely Nights (playout version)' is issued in America.

7 October. Paul is the cover-story subject of the American magazine *Family Weekly*.

10 October. WGN, the Chicago radio station, airs a 30-minute interview with Paul, conducted by Roy Leonard.

14 October. London Weekend Television's *South Bank Show* presents a programme on *Give My Regards To Broad Street*, which includes the first public performance of new versions of 'Eleanor Rigby', 'For No One' and 'Yesterday'.

15 October. Paul arrives in New York to promote *Give My Regards To Broad Street*, beginning with a full day of interviews at the Plaza hotel. He is also honoured at a luncheon by ASCAP at the Jockey Club. Carly Simon and Ashford and Simpson are among the guests. He records an appearance on the *Tonight Show*.

16 October. Paul and Linda leave New York for Chicago.

18 October. Paul and Linda hold a press conference in Chicago to promote *Give My Regards To Broad Street*. The 'No More Lonely Nights' promo is screened on *Top Of The Pops*.

19 October. Paul is interviewed about *Give My Regards To Broad Street* by the Chicago radio station WLS.

22 October. The soundtrack album of *Give My Regards to Broad Street* is issued simultaneously in the UK and America.

23 October. Paul and Linda hold a press conference promoting *Give My Regards To Broad Street* at the Beverly Hills Hotel in Los Angeles.
24 October. Paul appears on the live phone-in radio show *Rockline*. They also host a party at the Bistro Restaurant in Beverly Hills. Paul also appears on *Rocker Special*, an ABC TV programme.
25 October. Paul appears on *Good Morning America* promoting *Give My Regards To Broad Street*. The film opens at the Gotham Theater, New York City.
26 October. Paul appears on *CBS Morning News*, *PM Magazine*, *Hour Magazine* and the *Tonight Show* promoting *Give My Regards To Broad Street*. The film opens nationally in America. Pavilion Books also publish the book of the film.
28 October. Paul appears on the New York radio station WPJL to promote *Give My Regards To Broad Street*.
29 October. Remixed versions of both the 7″ and 12″ versions of 'No More Lonely Nights' are released in Britain.
30 October. The MTV show *Linear Notes* features a pre-recorded interview with Paul.
2 November. Paul and Linda appear on the *A.M. Chicago* radio show while a pre-taped interview with Paul is screened on *Entertainment Tonight*.
5 November. 'We All Stand Together'/'We All Stand Together (humming version)' is released in Britain.
7 November. Paul renews his acquaintance with Julian Lennon after recording an episode of *Friday Night Videos*, an American TV show.
11 November. The first of a two-part interview with Paul promoting *Give My Regards To Broad Street* is broadcast by Capital Radio.
12 November. Paul is heard on two American radio shows, *Top 30 USA* and *Rock Notes*.
16 November. Paul's appearance on *Friday Night Videos* is screened. Paul is also featured on the TV show *New York Hot Tracks*.
17 November. The promo for 'We All Stand Together' receives its world premiere on the BBC 1 show *Saturday Superstore*.
18 November. The second part of Paul's Capital Radio interview is broadcast.
23 November. Paul records a three-part interview with Simon Bates. Paul also pre-records an interview with Russell Harty for a show entitled *Harty With McCartney*. Paul appears on the BBC 1 programme 'Children In Need' and donates £5,000 to the charity.
24 November. A pre-recorded interview with Paul is featured on BBC Radio Two's *Star Sound Extra*. The *Album Time* programme on Radio Two features the *Give My Regards To Broad Street* soundtrack.
25 November. Paul records two spoken messages for the flipside of the 'Do They Know It's Christmas?'/'Feed The World' charity single. Paul and Linda attend the British premieres of *Give My Regards To Broad Street* and *Rupert And The Frog Song* at the Empire Theatre, Leicester Square.

26 November. The first part of the interview with Simon Bates is broadcast on Radio One. The TV show *Harty With McCartney* is broadcast. Linda is interviewed for a regional TV programme *London Plus*. *TV AM* features a pre-recorded message from Paul.

27 November. The second part of Paul's interview with Simon Bates is broadcast on Radio One. In America a pre-recorded interview with Paul is featured on the CBS show *Entertainment Tonight*.

28 November. The gala premiere of *Give My Regards To Broad Street* takes place at the Odeon Cinema, Liverpool and Paul receives the Freedom of the City Award in Liverpool. The third part of Paul's interview with Simon Bates is broadcast. In America a pre-recorded interview with Paul is featured on the TV show *Hour Magazine*.

29 November. *Give My Regards To Broad Street* receives its official London premiere at the Empire Theatre, attended by Paul and Linda, Ringo and Barbara and Olivia Harrison. A pre-recorded interview with Linda is featured on *Good Morning America*.

30 November. 'Entertainment Tonight' in America reviews the film 'Give My Regards To Broad Street.'

1 December. *TV AM* screens a pre-recorded interview with Paul. Paul is in the studios recording 'We Got Married' and 'Lindiana'.

2 December. *Give My Regards To Broad Street* is discussed by Gloria Hunniford and her guests Kenny Everett and Maureen Lipman on ITV's *Sunday Sunday*.

3 December. Westwood One begins syndicating an interview with Paul to various American radio stations.

6 December. The TV documentary 'Paul McCartney, The Man, His Music, His Movies' is screened in Britain in various ITV areas.

8 December. It is the fourth anniversary of John Lennon's murder and Paul discusses him on a pre-recorded 30-minute interview on *Good Morning Britain*. In America a pre-recorded video of Paul introducing the song 'Disco Duck' is shown on *Solid Gold*.

11 December. In a pre-filmed interview, Paul discusses 'Rupert The Bear' on the children's TV programme *CBTV*.

14 December. Paul appears on the American show *Rick Dee's Weekly Top 40 Radio Show*. On the MTV programme *Top 20* Paul introduces his promo for 'No More Lonely Nights'.

15 December. Another clip of Paul's appearance on *Rick Dee's Weekly Top 40 Radio Show* is transmitted. Paul also records another interview for MTV.

16 December. Paul's appearance on *Rick Dee's Weekly Top 40 Radio Show* receives another transmission.

17 December. Paul returns to London from America.

21 December. A pre-recorded interview with Paul is screened on *TV AM*.

25 December. A pre-recorded Christmas message from Paul is screened on *TV AM*. The ITV programme 'Top Pop Videos Of 1984' screens the promo for 'We All Stand Together' plus a Christmas greeting from Paul.

26 December. Paul's *Desert Island Discs* appearance from 30 January 1982 is repeated on Radio Four.

1985
2 January. Paul turns down an offer to appear in the popular American soap *Dallas*. A *Give My Regards To Broad Street* video game is released in Britain.
4 January. Paul, Linda and the kids fly to New York on Concorde.
6 January. MTV screens a repeat showing of Paul's appearance on the Tyne-Tees programme *The Tube*.
9 January. Linda's animated short 'Seaside Woman' receives its British television premiere on BBC 2. Paul and Linda are on the cover of *Weekend* magazine.
11 January. *Give My Regards To Broad Street* goes on general release in Britain.
18 January. Actor Wilfred Brambell dies at the age of 82. He portrayed Paul's grandfather in *A Hard Day's Night*.
19 January. *Night Flight*, a US cable programme, features a 45-minute tribute to Paul and includes the first national screening of the disco version of 'No More Lonely Nights'.
23 February. The ITV series *Freeze Frame* features an interview with Paul that had been recorded a couple of years previously in which he mainly discussed the *Tug Of War* album. Videos of 'Take It Away', 'Coming Up', 'Tug Of War' and 'Ebony And Ivory' are also screened.
2 March. Paul appears on Channel 4's *On The Other Side Of The Tracks* with Paul Gambaccini.
5 March. *Give My Regards To Broad Street* is released on home video in America.
8 March. Paul discusses Little Richard in a pre-recorded interview screened on Tyne-Tees' *The Tube*.
13 March. 'We All Stand Together' receives an award as 'Best Film Theme of 1984' at the Ivor Novello Awards. As Paul is ill, George Martin picks up the award on his behalf.
22 March. The American syndicated radio series *On The Road* presents a one-hour programme on Paul, repeated over the following two days.
30 March. Michael Jackson spends the weekend with Paul and Linda at their East Sussex farm.
15 May. Paul records a brief message for the flipside of Gerry Marsden's single 'You'll Never Walk Alone', which is in aid of the families of the victims of the Bradford City FC disaster.
12 June. A pre-recorded interview with Paul is featured on the MTV programme 'Rock Of The Eighties'.
13 July. Paul appears on the 'Live Aid' concert from Wembley Stadium, London and performs 'Let It Be'.
14 July. Paul overdubs a different vocal onto his 'Live Aid' appearance.

25 July. *Give My Regards To Broad Street* is issued as a video in Britain.

10 August. Michael Jackson outbids the competition in his aim to acquire the Northern Songs catalogue from ATV Music.

29 August. A letter Paul had sent to the *Melody Maker* sells for £10,000 at the Sotheby's auction.

31 August. 'The Beatles – Yesterday', a radio special in honour of the 20th anniversary of Paul's composition 'Yesterday', is syndicated around American stations.

4 September. Traffic warden Meta Davies, who claimed to be the 'meter maid' in Paul's song 'Lovely Rita', retires.

6 September. After eight months of negotiations, Michael Jackson pays $47.5 million for ATV Music, which has the Northern Songs catalogue with 251 Lennon and McCartney compositions, plus 4,000 other songs.

11 September. Paul and Linda host a Buddy Holly Week luncheon in London.

12 September. BBC 2's *Arena* programme plays the Quarry Men's early 'That'll Be The Day' disc. Paul also appears and performs some snatches of Buddy Holly songs.

14 September. Paul and Linda attend another Buddy Holly event in London.

1 October. Paul resumes recordings for *Press To Play* at his Scottish studio which he began in April 1985.

4 October. An exhibition of Linda's photographs opens in Warsaw.

9 October. Paul joins Dan Aykroyd and Chevy Chase at Abbey Road Studios to film a promo for 'Spies Like Us', with John Landis directing.

6 November. Paul is quoted as saying, 'Lennon was a manoeuvring swine' in a *New York Post* interview headed 'Imagine: John Lennon Tries To Steal My Songs'.

14 November. *Rupert And The Frog Song* is issued as a home video in Britain, and also includes 'Seaside Woman' and 'Oriental Nightfish'.

16 November. The 'Spies Like Us' promo receives its British TV premiere on *The Late Late Breakfast Show*. Paul is interviewed on the show by its host Noel Edmonds.

18 November. Paul's single 'Spies Like Us' is issued simultaneously in the UK and USA. It becomes Paul's 100th single to enter the *Billboard* charts.

21 November. Paul is interviewed by Gloria Hunniford on her Radio Two show.

22 November. Paul appears on *Friday Night Videos* promoting 'Spies Like Us'.

6 December. Alan Grimadell of the National Association of Hospital Broadcasting Operations interviews Paul. This is for a broadcast to patients in British hospitals and is called 'Paul McCartney: The Man'.

7 December. Paul appears on *Saturday Superstore*, hosted by Mike Read. He participates in a phone-in and introduces his promos for 'Spies like Us' and 'We All Stand Together'. *The Times* publishes an interview with Paul by Patrick Humphries.

18 December. Paul pre-records a tribute to Gerry Marsden, the subject of this week's Thames television show *This Is Your Life*.

22 December. Paul is interviewed by Janice Long for a Radio One show 'Listen To What The Man Said'.

25 December. TV-AM's 'Caring Christmas Campaign' screens a video message from Paul wishing viewers a 'Happy Christmas.'

1986

6 January. Paul's *Rupert And The Frog Song* becomes the second most successful video released in the UK, Michael Jackson's *Thriller* being the first.

26 January. Paul and Linda attend the Superbowl Party at the Video Café in London.

27 January. Paul receives an 'Award Of Merit' from the American Music awards via a satellite link-up from the Hippodrome club in London.

8 February. *Rick Dee's Weekly Top 40* screens a brief appearance by Paul.

14 February. Paul is the subject of a two-hour *Legends Of Rock* show on NBC radio. The movie *Spies Like Us* receives its British premiere.

15 March. 'Rock For Kampuchea' is screened on American cable television.

28 March. Paul is on the cover of *USA Weekend*.

4 April. Paul appears on the TV show *The Tube*.

8 April. The edition of *The Tube* featuring Paul is repeated.

14 April. Paul begins mixing his new album at AIR studios.

2 May. *Give My Regards To Broad Street* makes its European TV debut on the cable and satellite channel Premier.

26 May. Paul receives an honorary membership in the Guinness Hall of Fame on the BBC 1 show 'Guinness Book Of Records Hall Of Fame', hosted by David Frost.

28 May. Hal David picks up an award for Paul from ASCAP in Los Angeles for 'No More Lonely Nights', the most performed song of the year (October 1984 – September 1985).

13 June. Linda appears live on the BBC Radio Four show *Woman's Hour*.

16 June. Paul films a promo for 'Press', directed by Philip Davey.

20 June. Paul appears at the Prince's Trust Gala at Wembley Arena. It is the 10th anniversary of the Prince's Trust and Paul performs before Prince Charles and Diana, Princess of Wales.

23 June. A pre-taped interview with Paul is aired in America on *Entertainment Tonight*, a CBS TV programme.

28 June. The Prince's Trust concert with Paul performing 'Long Tall Sally', 'I Saw Her Standing There' and 'Get Back' is screened on BBC 2.

4 July. Paul's promo of 'Press' is shown on *The Tube*.

12 July. BBC 2 presents the British TV premiere of the MPL documentary 'Blankit's Last Show'. Paul's 'All You Horseriders', an unreleased composition of his, is heard on the soundtrack.

14 July. The 'Press' single is released in both the UK and the USA with 'It's Not True' on the flip.

16 July. Paul gives a pre-recorded interview to Selina Scott, which appears on the BBC programme *Breakfast Time* the next day.

18 July. Paul films an interview for the BBC 1 special 'McCartney' at Abbey Road Studios. This will be screened on 29 August on BBC 1 and on 30 December on BBC 2 and issued as a home video under the title 'The Paul McCartney Story'.

19 July. Paul's promo for 'Press' receives its premiere on *Off The Wall*, a programme on the Music Box cable channel. *Inside HBO* in America screens a two-minute clip from an interview with Paul.

20 July. MTV screens Paul's promo of 'Press'.

23 July. The American TV show *Entertainment Tonight* features excerpts from 'The Prince's Trust 10th Birthday Party Concert'. It includes an interview with Paul conducted by Selina Scott.

1 August. Paul appears on BBC TV's *Wogan*.

9 August. An interview with Paul conducted by Janice Long is broadcast on *The Saturday Picture Show*.

17 August. Paul and Linda fly to America to promote the album *Press To Play*.

18 August. Paul begins a series of interviews to promote *Press To Play*.

22 August. The *Press to Play* album is issued in America.

24 August. A pre-recorded interview with Paul is broadcast on BBC Radio One's *The Simon Bates Show*.

25 August. Paul begins recording at the Power Station studios New York with Billy Joel's backing band. A pre-recorded interview with Paul is also broadcast on the *David Jenson Show* on Capital Radio. The first of a four-part interview with Paul is screened on NBC TV's *Today* programme.

26 August. The second part of Paul's pre-recorded interview is screened by *Today*. The home video of 'The Real Buddy Holly Story', featuring the Quarry Men performing 'That'll Be The Day' is issued in Britain. This version is thirty minutes longer than the BBC 2 screening on 12 September 1985.

27 August. NBC TV's *Today* screens the third part of Paul's interview.

28 August. The final part of Paul's four-part interview to promote *Press To Play* is featured on the NBC programme *Today*.

1 September. The album *Press To Play* is issued in the UK. It is featured in America on the NBC Radio programme *Album Party*.

5 September. A pre-recorded tape of Paul introducing Tina Turner is screened at the MTV Awards.

10 September. Paul and Linda host a Buddy Holly Week lunch at the Break For The Border restaurant in London during which they present Jerry Allison of the Crickets with a gold disc for 'That'll Be The Day'.

12 September. Linda is featured in the BBC 2 programme *Landscapes*.

13 September. Westwood One radio syndicates a 90-minute broadcast of the Prince's Trust Rock Gala Concert across America.

20 September. The Disney channel screens *Rupert And The Frog Song* for the first time.

21 September. The home video of 'The Real Buddy Holly Story' is issued in America.

24 September. The American Cinemax TV station screens 'The Real Buddy Holly Story'.

27 September. A Radio 1 show 'City to City', about the Liverpool music scene, includes an interview with Paul.

29 September. An interview with Paul is included on *Rock Today*, a syndicated American radio programme. The show is syndicated to various stations around America over the next week.

2 October. Radio 1 repeats 'City To City'.

3 October. *Rock Watch*, a three-hour American radio programme with an interview with Paul, is syndicated in America until 5 October, as is a similar programme, *Hot Rocks*.

4 October. *Les Enfants Du Rock*, a French television show, features a 15-minute pre-recorded interview with Paul.

11 October. The Music Box cable channel show *Off The Wall* reports on Denny Laine's bankruptcy.

12 October. Paul is interviewed on Capital Radio.

16 October. Paul receives the 'Best Selling Video' award for *Rupert And The Frog Song* at the British Music Video Awards.

17 October. Dick Clark's *Rock and Roll Remembers* series syndicates a four-hour radio programme on Paul.

18 October. Paul films a cameo for the promo of 'Pretty Little Head'.

26 October. Paul's single 'Pretty Little Head' is issued in the UK.

27 October. The single 'Pretty Little Head'/'Write Away' is released in Britain. The first of a two-part interview with Paul is published in the new American magazine *Hits*.

29 October. Paul's single 'Stranglehold'/'Angry' is released in America.

3 November. Filming begins on a six-day shoot for a promo of 'Pretty Little Head', which features actors in a story similar to 'She's Leaving Home'. The second of a two-part interview with Paul is published in the new American magazine *Hits*.

6 November. 'Blankit's First Show' is repeated on BBC 1.

17 November. Paul begins three days of shooting for the promotional video of 'Only Love Remains'. The promo is directed by Maurice Phillips and features the actors Gordon Jackson and Pauline Yates.

18 November. Mike McCartney appears on TV-AM promoting his book *Mike Mac's Black And Whites Plus One Colour*.

19 November. *By Request*, an album by Matt Monro who died of cancer in February 1985, is released, with tributes from various stars, including a 22-word tribute from Paul.

20 November. Paul receives the 'Personality Of The Year' Award at the

Bambi Awards in Munich, Germany. West German football manager Franz Beckenbauer presents him with the award.

23 November. Paul and Linda attend the rehearsals for the Royal Variety Command Performance Show.

24 November. Paul appears on stage at the Royal Variety Command Performance Show at the Theatre Royal, Drury Lane, London. The *Anti-Heroin Project: It's A Live-In World* is released in Britain.

28 November. BBC 1 screens the Royal Variety Command Performance Show.

1 December. The single 'Only Love Remains'/'Tight On A Tightrope' is issued in the UK. In America the CD of *Wings Greatest* is released.

9 December. Paul voiced his disagreement over the teachers' strike.

10 December. Paul records an insert for 'Only Love Remains' at the *Top Of The Pops* studios, although it is not shown due to the single's poor chart placing.

11 December. Paul pre-records an interview and performs before a live audience for the Channel 4 series *The Tube*. On the way to the studio in Newcastle Paul and Linda's car bursts into flames.

12 December. The episode of *The Tube* featuring a 14-minute insert of Paul is transmitted.

13 December. Paul appears on the children's programme *Saturday Superstore* and is interviewed by Mike Read. A pre-recorded interview with Paul, conducted by Suni, a female DJ, is screened on the *Off The Wall* programme on the Music Box cable channel. A promo of 'Only Love Remains' is also screened.

14 December. The episode of *The Tube*, which Paul recorded on 11 December, is repeated on Channel 4. *Conspiracy Of Hope*, the Amnesty International charity album, which contains Paul's 'Pipes Of Peace', is issued internationally.

16 December. Denny Laine is officially declared bankrupt in a London court.

25 December. On Noel Edmonds's BBC 1 show, a two-minute Christmas greeting from Paul is screened.

30 December. During Granada TV's 30th birthday celebrations, Channel 4 screens 'The Music Of Lennon and McCartney'.

31 December. The film of 'The Prince's Trust 10th Birthday Party Concert', in which Paul is featured, is repeated on BBC 2. Capital Radio airs a pre-recorded interview with Paul.

1987

3 January. Music Box, the cable channel, presents an exclusive pre-recorded interview with Paul on their series *Private Eyes*.

6 January. Piccadilly Radio, the Manchester station, airs the first of a two-part interview with Paul.

7 January. Piccadilly Radio airs the second part of its interview with Paul.

9 January. *Twice In A Lifetime* the Ann Margret/Gene Hackman film for which Paul wrote the theme music, opens in London.

2 February. Paul is recording at Audio International studios in London, with Phil Ramone producing.

3 February. Paul is recording at Audio International studios.

4 February. Duane Eddy visits Paul at his recording studio in Sussex. He records 'So Glad To See You Here', with Paul on bass. He also records the 'Rockestra Theme' for his forthcoming *Duane Eddy* album, which is released in Britain on 19 June 1987.

5 February. Paul is recording at Audio International studios.

6 February. Paul completes his recordings at Audio International studios.

16 February. Paul and his family set off for a holiday.

27 February. Paul has returned from his holiday and joins George Martin to listen to the recordings produced by Phil Ramone.

28 February. Linda's photographic exhibition opens at the Octagon Gallery, Bath.

4 March. Paul and Linda film a scene for the movie *Eat The Rich* in Moor Park, Hertfordshire.

9 March. Paul's appearance on the Channel 4 programme *The Tube* is screened on MTV.

19 May. Linda's 'Photographs' exhibition opens at the Olympus Gallery, Hamburg and runs until 29 June.

7 April. Linda is a guest at the all-women's lunch for the National Rubella council, although Paul accompanies her.

24 April. The *Prince's Trust 10th Anniversary Birthday Party* album is released in Britain with a free bonus single by Paul.

27 April. CDs of the *McCartney* and *Ram* albums are issued in Britain.

1 May. Richard Ogden becomes Paul's new manager.

26 May. A CD of the *Wings Over America* album is issued in Britain.

30 May. Geoff Baker releases the news that Paul, George and Ringo have recorded together to the British press.

1 June. At a special 20th anniversary party for *Sgt Pepper's Lonely Hearts Club Band* at Abbey Road Studios, Paul and Linda are among the guests – and Linda makes the anniversary cake.

18 June. Vicki Peterson of the Bangles splits her trousers on stage and says: 'It's Paul McCartney's birthday today and I heard he once split his pants in Hamburg, so in honour of him, I split mine.'

30 June. Linda donates the proceeds from her 'Photographs' exhibition in Bath to the Great Ormond Street Children's Hospital.

1 July. Paul is once again at Abbey Road Studios, overdubbing three of his recent numbers.

20 July. Paul begins a two-day recording session during which he records eighteen rock and roll numbers, most of which appear on the *Choba B CCCP* album in 1988. He is accompanied by Mick Green on guitar, Chris Whitten on drums and Mick Gallagher on piano.

21 July. Paul continues recording rock and roll oldies, including 'Crackin' Up', 'Don't Get Around Much Anymore' and 'Ain't That A Shame'. He also records 'I Saw Her Standing There'.

7 September. Paul and Linda attend the EMI Sales conference at the Metropole Hotel, Brighton.

9 September. Paul and Linda hold their Buddy Holly Week luncheon at the Dolphin Brasserie, Pimlico. Paul takes part in a jam session with various guests who include Alvin Stardust and Mick Green.

13 September. Paul's Buddy Holly Week ends with a Rock 'n' Roll funfair at Camden Town Hall, London.

5 October. The CDs of *Red Rose Speedway*, *McCartney II* and *Wild Life* are issued in Britain.

12 October. Disc jockey Mike Read begins recording an interview with Paul at the International Christian Community studios in Eastbourne, Sussex.

13 October. Mike Read finishes recording a lengthy interview with Paul, to be broadcast on Radio One.

16 October. Paul films the promo for 'Once Upon A Long Ago' in the Valley of the Rock in Devon.

20 October. Sony Video issues a 52-minute documentary 'The Paul McCartney Special'. It is taken from a BBC special aired in 1986 and is a retrospective of Paul's career, which includes clips and an interview disc jockey Richard Skinner conducted with Paul at Abbey Road Studios.

21 October. George and Ringo visit Paul at his Cavendish Avenue house.

23 October. The movie *Eat The Rich*, featuring a cameo by Paul and Linda, is premiered in London.

24 October. Radio One broadcasts the first part of Mike Read's three-part interview with Paul.

29 October. A video of 'The Paul McCartney Special' is released.

31 October. The second part of Mike Read's interview with Paul is broadcast on Radio One.

2 November. Paul's second compilation album of hits, *All The Best*, is released in Britain. EMI also release a limited edition box set of nine of Paul's Parlophone singles.

7 November. Radio One broadcasts the final part of Mike Read's interview with Paul.

9 November. The home video of 'The Paul McCartney Story' is issued in America.

16 November. Paul's single 'Once Upon A Long Ago'/'Back On My Feet' is released in Britain. There is a 7", two different 12" releases and a CD release.

17 November. Paul is at Tyne-Tees Television in Newcastle recording for the pop show *The Roxy*. He mimes to a performance of 'Once Upon A Long Ago'.

18 November. Paul promotes 'Once Upon A Long Ago' for the Japanese programme *Yoru No Hit Studio* via a live satellite link.

19 November. Paul and Linda record an appearance on the TV chat show *Wogan*, during which Paul performs 'Jet' and 'Listen To What The Man Said'. A promo of 'Once Upon A Long Ago' is also shown.

20 November. Paul and Linda's appearance on the BBC TV show *Wogan* is broadcast.

24 November. Paul's appearance on *The Roxy* is aired.

30 November. Paul appears on the Dutch TV show *Countdown*.

1 December. A CD of *Band On The Run* is issued in America. Paul is working with George Martin at AIR studios on music for his 'Rupert The Bear' project.

2 December. Paul pre-records 'Once Upon A Long Ago' at the *Top Of The Pops* studio. He later records a sketch for 'Comic Relief', a BBC charity special.

3 December. The 'Once Upon A Long Ago' performance is shown on *Top Of The Pops*.

5 December. Paul's compilation *All The Best* is released in America. Paul and Linda mime 'Once Upon A Long Ago' for *Sacrée Soirée*, a French TV show. They also mime the number for another French show *Annette 2*, during which they make a live appearance.

7 December. The home video 'Once Upon A Video' is released in Britain.

11 December. Paul introduces Madonna's video of 'Open Your Heart' on *Top Of The Pops*.

13 December. Paul is joined by his son James when he appears on the BBC 1 children's TV show *Going Live*.

14–19 December. Paul records his *Rupert The Bear* soundtrack album with George Martin at AIR studios.

21 December. Paul is at his home studio in Sussex where, for the next four days, he records a number of songs including 'Figure Of Eight', '*Ou Est Le Soleil*?', 'How Many People?' and 'Rough Ride'.

25 December. Christmas messages from Paul and Linda are shown on the Italian TV shows *Canale Fantastico* and *Ieri Goggi Domina* and on the BBC 1 show 'Christmas Morning With Noel'.

27 December. An interview with Paul is featured on the Italian TV show *Deejay TV*.

1988

2 January. Paul is working on various tracks at his own home recording studio in Sussex.

4 January. The *Press To Play* album is issued on mid-price CD in Britain.

13 January. 'Paul McCartney Special', a 55-minute interview, recorded at the MPL offices, is broadcast on the Sky Channel.

18 January. The albums *McCartney*, *Ram*, *Tug Of War* and *Wings Over America* are issued on CD in America.

20 January. Paul declines an invitation to attend the 'Rock And Roll Hall Of Fame' ceremony at the Waldorf Astoria Hotel in New York, which George Harrison and Ringo Starr were attending, citing 'still existing business differences amongst the Beatles'.

31 January. The albums *Red Rose Speedway* and *McCartney II* are deleted from the EMI catalogue.

5 February. The sketch for 'Comic Relief', which Paul and Linda filmed on Wednesday 2 December 1987, is screened on BBC 1.

27 February. Paul appears at the San Remo Festival in Italy where he lip-synchs to 'Once Upon A Long Ago' and 'Listen To What The Man Said'.

29 February. A three-minute interview with Paul appears on the Italian programme *Italia I*.

16 April. In New York, veteran guitarist Les Paul presents Paul with a custom-made light guitar designed specially for him.

9 May. Johnny Cash's 'Moon Over Jamaica' is recorded at Paul's studio, the Mill. Linda and Carla Lane are also involved.

14 May. *Give My Regards To Broad Street* is premiered on British television on the ITV network.

24 June. Paul is awarded the Silver Clef for 'Outstanding Achievement in the World of British Music' at the annual Nordoff-Robbins luncheon.

26 June. Paul and Linda arrive in Liverpool to shoot scenes for the comedy TV show *Bread*. Paul is also interviewed by disc jockeys Spencer Leigh, Alan Jackson and Monty Lister.

27 June. Additional scenes for *Bread* are filmed.

12 July. Paul receives an Honorary Doctorate from the University of Sussex.

2 August. Paul directs a promotional video at the Liverpool Institute.

5 September. Paul is interviewed for the launch of 'DEF II – Animation Week' on BBC 2 in which excerpts from 'Oriental Nightfish', *Rupert And The Frog Song*, 'Seaside Woman' and 'Once Upon A Long Ago' are shown.

7 September. The annual Buddy Holly lunch takes place at Stefano's, London, during which Paul joins the Crickets on stage.

8 September. Excerpts from Paul's performance with the Crickets are screened on TV-AM. An interview with Paul from the Buddy Holly lunch, conducted by Rona Elliott is screened in America on NBC TV's *Today* programme.

11 September. At the BBC Centre in London, Linda films her final scenes for *Bread* in front of a studio audience.

10 October. The Johnny Cash album *Water From The Wells Of Home* is released in America containing the track 'New Moon Over Jamaica' on which Cash duets with Paul.

26 October. Paul appears on the BBC 1 programme 'The Power Of Music'.

30 October. The edition of *Bread* featuring Paul and Linda is screened on BBC 1.

31 October. Paul's Russian album *Choba B CCCP* is issued in Russia on the Melodiya label.

1 November. The interview with Rona Elliot, filmed at Stefano's restaurant in London during Paul's Buddy Holly lunch, is shown on NBC News and NBC's *Today* programme.

9 November. An exhibition of Linda's 'Sun Prints' opens at the Victoria and Albert Museum in London.

10 November. Linda's book *Sun Prints* is published.

14 November. The Johnny Cash album *Water From The Wells Of Home* is released in Britain.

27 November. In Britain the Video Collection issue an extended version of the 'McCartney' documentary, originally produced by the BBC and MPL in 1986.

2 December. Paul and his band appear once again on the Dutch TV programme *Countdown*.

12 December. Paul appears on the BBC programme *Going Live!*

24 December. A second edition of *Choba B CCCP* is issued in Russia, which includes two extra tracks.

1989

26 January. Paul holds a live question and answer session lasting 55 minutes for BBC Radio's Russian service programme *Granny's Chest*.

27 January. The BBC World Service programme *Multitrack 3* transmits highlights from Paul's *Granny's Chest* question and answer session.

28 January. The BBC World Service programme *Multitrack 3* transmits highlights from Paul's *Granny's Chest* session once again.

2 February. A pre-recorded interview with Paul is aired on Radio Merseyside.

4 February. Paul is heard on the Buddy Holly commemorative programme 'Not Fade Away' on Radio One.

7 February. 'Not Fade Away', the documentary tribute to Buddy Holly, with comments from Paul, is repeated on Radio One.

24 February. *The Family Way*, the 1966 film for which Paul wrote the theme music, is issued on home video in Britain, as is *The Magic Christian*, which features Paul's composition 'Come And Get It'.

24 March. The first part of an eight-part radio series *McCartney On McCartney* in which Paul is interviewed by disc jockey Mike Read, begins on Radio One, with this initial episode entitled 'Early Beginnings to 1962'.

28 March. The first episode of *McCartney On McCartney* is repeated on Radio One.

1 April. A home video, 'The McCartney Special', is issued in Britain and was originally shown on BBC 1 as 'McCartney' on 29 August 1986.

4 April. Paul receives an award at the Ivor Novello Luncheon for his 'Outstanding Services to British Music' and he recites the 'Ivor Novello Rap'.

10 April. Paul films the promo for 'My Brave Face' at Strawberry Fields in Liverpool.

11 April. Paul completes filming of the 'My Brave Face' promo.

13 April. Final editing on the 'My Brave Face' clip takes place.

20 April. Paul is at PWL studios in south London where he takes part in the recording of the 'Ferry 'Cross The Mersey' charity single for the families of the Hillsborough FC disaster.

3 May. Paul is filmed in an interview by Pedro Bial for Brazilian television, during which he plays parts of 'How Many People', 'Blue Suede Shoes' and 'Distractions' on acoustic guitar.

8 May. The single 'My Brave Face'/'Flying To My Home' is issued in Britain, as is the 'Ferry 'Cross The Mersey' charity single.

10 May. The single 'My Brave Face'/'Flying To My Home' is issued in America.

13 May. The French television show *Champs Elysées* features a nine-minute interview with Paul.

16 May. Rona Elliott, of the NBC *Today* show, records an interview with Paul at his Sussex home studio, which is transmitted the next day.

17 May. Paul appears on *Countdown*, a Dutch television show, and his interview with Rona Elliott is screened on the *Today* show in America. He is also featured on another American television show, *Entertainment Tonight*.

18 May. The second part of Rona Elliott's interview with Paul is screened in America on the *Today* programme. Paul also appears on the German TV show *Mensch Meir* where he mimes to 'Put It There' and 'Figure Of Eight'. *Top Of The Pops* screens the first 'My Brave Face' promo.

19 May. Paul, Linda and the band return from their European promotional tour and appear on the BBC 1 show *Wogan With Sue Lawley*. Paul is interviewed by Lawley and also mimes with the group to 'Put It There' and 'Figure Of Eight'.

21 May. A pre-taped interview with Paul is featured on the American TV show *Entertainment Tonight*.

22 May. Another interview with Paul is featured on *Entertainment Tonight*. Paul and his band appear on the Dutch TV show miming to 'My Brave Face' and 'How Many People'. Paul and Linda also visit the Van Gogh Museum in Amsterdam.

24 May. A Dutch TV station screens an interview with Paul and shows performances of 'How Many People', 'My Brave Face' and 'Mull Of Kintyre'.

25 May. Paul had hoped to perform live on *Top Of The Pops* promoting 'My Brave Face', a promo of which had been shown on the programme the week before. However, due to a *TOTP* ruling which stated that no record could be aired for two weeks in succession, apart from the current chart-topper, his proposed live appearance doesn't go ahead.

26 May. Paul appears in a pre-taped interview on the morning show TV-AM, which also presents a 'Making of "My Brave Face"' video clip. He also appears on the Italian TV programme *Notte Rock*.

27 May. Paul and his band leave London for Los Angeles. The BBC Radio One series *McCartney On McCartney* is premiered in edited form on American radio and runs until 29 May.

29 May. Paul appears on *Rockline*, an American radio phone-in show during which he answers calls from fans and also takes the opportunity to promote *Flowers In The Dirt*. He and Linda then leave America for France.

31 May. Paul and his band appear on the French TV show *Sacrée Soirée* and perform 'My Brave Face'. Paul is also interviewed.

2 June. *The Honorary Consul*, the film for which Paul wrote some incidental music, is shown on BBC 1.

5 June. Paul's album *Flowers In The Dirt* is issued in Britain.

6 June. Paul's album *Flowers In the Dirt* is issued in America.

7 June. Paul performs before a live audience at Twickenham film studios for the Japanese television show *Hunky Dory*.

8 June. Paul and his group arrive in Spain to appear on the TV show *La Luna* and fly back to London the same day.

10 June. The MPL special 'Put It There' is shown on BBC 1. Linda's photo exhibition, containing 76 photographs, opens at the Access Gallery in Manhattan and runs until 26 June.

15 June. Paul and his group arrive in Italy to appear on the RAI TV show *Saint Vincent Estate 89*.

16 June. Paul's appearance on *Saint Vincent Estate 89* is screened in Italy, with Paul and his band miming to 'This One' and 'My Brave Face'. Paul, Linda and the band return to London.

17 June. From a BBC studio in London Paul holds a 2-hour phone-in with the Italian radio station RAI's programme *Stereo 2*, with the station receiving more than 500 calls.

18 June. As a 47th birthday present to Paul, EMI Records had a pink hybrid tea rose grown in the South of France named after him.

19 June. Paul asks Tim Pope to direct the promo of 'This One'.

20 June. CDs of *Wild Life*, *Pipes Of Peace*, *London Town*, *Back To The Egg* and *Wings At The Speed Of Sound* are issued in America.

21 June. The home video 'McCartney' is issued in America.

23 June. Tim Pope begins filming the promo for 'This One' at Albert Wharf in London.

24 June. The promo for 'This One' is completed.

4 July. Paul is not satisfied with the promo for 'This One' and hires director Dean Chamberlain to make another.

5 July. Work continues on the promo for 'This One'.

10 July. The episode of *Bread* featuring Paul and Linda is repeated on BBC 1. *Wings At The Speed Of Sound* is released in Britain.

14 July. Paul begins work on a promo for '*Ou Est Le Soleil?*' at Cliphouse Studios, London.

17 July. The single 'This One'/'Turn To Stone' is released in Britain.
24 July. Paul begins rehearsing with his new band at the BBC Playhouse Theatre, London. Apart from himself and Linda they comprise Hamish Stuart, guitar; Robbie McIntosh, guitar; Paul 'Wix' Wickens, keyboards and Chris Whitten, drums. A limited edition box set of 'This One'/'The Long And Winding Road' is released in Britain.
25 July. Throughout the day Paul pre-records interviews and rehearses his band for several forthcoming TV shows. He also pre-records a performance of 'This One' for *Top Of The Pops* (incidentally, there are already two promos of this number, one directed by Tim Pope, the other by Dean Chamberlain).
26 July. Paul holds rehearsals at the Playhouse Theatre in London for his forthcoming tour, performing before an invited audience. He tells the audience that they were only witnessing a rehearsal, adding, 'so if you see any mistakes, don't!'
27 July. At a press conference at the Playhouse Theatre, London, Paul announces the dates of his European and British tour. Paul and his band also take part in a brief performance. Later they present another concert for an invited audience. A 12″ single and a cassette maxi single of '*Ou Est Le Soleil?*' is released in America.
28 July. A pre-recorded interview with Paul is screened on *The O Zone* programme, together with a clip from his press conference at the Playhouse Theatre.
29 July. A special compilation of Michael Aspel chat-show extracts called 'Aspel In The Best Company' is screened by London Weekend Television and includes excerpts from interviews with Paul, George and Ringo.
30 July. *Ghost Train*, a children's TV show, features a pre-recorded interview with Paul.
1 August. The eight-hour Radio One series *McCartney On McCartney* begins transmissions on the BBC World Service in sixteen half-hour episodes.
2 August. The single 'This One'/'Turn To Stone' is released in America.
3 August. *Top Of The Pops* airs the pre-recorded performance of Paul and his band with 'This One'. Paul and his family leave for Scotland on a short holiday.
4 August. The Italian TV show *Notte Rock* features a special on Paul, including clips from his recent Playhouse Theatre press conference.
10 August. A pre-recorded interview with Linda is featured on the BBC 1 show *But First This* . . . .
12 August. Paul and Linda attend Ringo Starr's concert at the Jones Beach Amphitheatre, Wantaugh, New York. Linda appears on the cover of the *TV Times*.
14 August. The compilation series issues *Now That's What I Call Music* as a double album on NOW 15, a double cassette on TC-NOW 15 and a double CD on CD NOW 15. They contain Paul's 'My Brave

Face' followed by the charity version of 'Ferry 'Cross The Mersey' on which he also appears.

21 August. Paul begins rehearsals at the Lyceum Theater, New York.

22 August. The *O Zone* programme includes scenes of Paul at *Top Of The Pops* rehearsing 'This One' with the band.

24 August. Paul holds a press conference at the Lyceum Theater, New York. There are approximately 400 reporters and 20 camera crews. Paul performs 'Figure Of Eight', 'This One' and 'Coming Up' and holds a question and answer session that lasts for 40 minutes.

25 August. Excerpts from Paul's Lyceum Theater conference appear on CNN's *Showbiz Today*, *USA Today On TV*, *Headline News*, *Entertainment Tonight* and MTV's *Week In Rock*. In the meantime, Paul, Linda and the band return to England.

26 August. Paul and his band continue rehearsals at Paul's Sussex studio.

29 August. The album *London Town* is issued on CD in Britain.

1 September. Paul records a new version of 'Figure Of Eight'.

4 September. Paul and his band continue their rehearsals, this time at Elstree film studios in Borehamwood. Linda appears on the *Wogan* chat show in the evening. The 'Put It There' TV special is issued on home video in Britain.

7 September. Paul and Linda hold their annual Buddy Holly Week luncheon at the Talk Of The Town, Holborn.

11 September. The single 'My Brave Face' is issued as a CD in America.

21 September. A pre-tour concert is held at Goldcrest film studios in Elstree.

25 September. Paul and his band fly to Norway. Mike McCartney is the host of the Yorkshire TV show *Pick Of The Week*.

26 September. Paul holds another pre-tour concert at the Drammenshalle, Dramen, Norway. Channel 4 screens the 1980 concert film *Rockshow*.

28 September. Paul and his band officially open their tour at the Scandinavium, Gothenburg, Sweden.

29 September. Paul and his band appear at the Johanneshows Isstadium, Stockholm, Sweden.

30 September. Paul and his band appear at the Johanneshows Isstadium, Stockholm, Sweden.

3 October. Paul holds a press conference at the Kaiserkeller Club in Hamburg and appears in concert at the Sportshalle, Hamburg. *Wings At The Speed Of Sound* is issued on CD in Britain.

4 October. Paul and his band appear at the Sportshalle, Hamburg.

6 October. Paul and his band appear at the Festehalle, Frankfurt, Germany.

7 October. Paul and his band appear at the Festehalle, Frankfurt, Germany. Paul and Linda are featured on the cover of *Hello* magazine.

9 October. Paul and his band appear at the Palais Omnisport De Bercy, Paris, France.

10 October. Paul and his band appear at the Palais Omnisport De Bercy, Paris, France. The West Berlin radio station SFB2 broadcasts a three-hour Paul McCartney special.

11 October. Paul and his band appear at the Palais Omnisport De Bercy, Paris, France. Paul and Linda then fly home before resuming the tour on 16 October.

16 October. Paul and his band appear at the Westfallenhalle, Dortmund, Germany.

17 October. Paul and his band appear at the Westfallenhalle, Dortmund, Germany.

19 October. An item on Paul is featured on the ITV show *Cover Story*.

20 October. Paul and his band appear at the Olympiahalle, Munich, Germany.

21 October. Paul and his band appear at the Olympiahalle, Munich, Germany.

22 October. Paul and his band appear at the Olympiahalle, Munich, Germany.

24 October. Paul and his band appear at the Palaeur, Rome, Italy.

26 October. Paul and his band appear at the Palatrussardi, Milan, Italy. Nancy Duff of CBS News meets Paul backstage and proposes a *48 Hours* special on him.

27 October. Paul and his band appear at the Palatrussardi, Milan, Italy. He performs the number 'All My Trials' for the first and only time on the tour.

29 October. Paul and his band appear at the Hallenstadion, Zurich, Switzerland.

30 October. Paul and his band appear at the Hallenstadion, Zurich, Switzerland.

2 November. Paul and his band appear at the Palacio De Sportes, Madrid, Spain. He also holds a press conference earlier in the day.

3 November. Paul and his band appear at the Palacio De Sportes, Madrid, Spain.

4 November. The Spanish TV show *Rockopop* includes a report from the Palacio De Sportes concert.

5 November. Paul and his band appear at Le Halle Tony Garnier, Lyon, France.

7 November. Paul and his band appear at the Ahoy Sportpaleis, Rotterdam, Holland.

8 November. Paul and his band appear at the Ahoy Sportpaleis, Rotterdam, Holland. Lawyers for Paul, George, Ringo and Yoko Ono finally settle their multimillion-dollar lawsuit against EMI. An EMI spokesman said that the settlement covers 'all outstanding lawsuits between the artists, Apple, EMI Records and Capitol Records'.

10 November. Paul and his band appear at the Ahoy Sportpaleis, Rotterdam, Holland.

11 November. Paul and his band appear at the Ahoy Sportpaleis,

Rotterdam, Holland. Backstage Mariella Frostrup interviews him and part of the concert is filmed by Channel 4 for their 'Big World Café' programme.

13 November. The single 'Figure Of Eight'/'*Ou Est Le Soleil?*' is issued in Britain in eight different configurations.

15 November. The single 'Figure Of Eight'/'*Ou Est Le Soleil?*' is issued in America on cassette only.

21 November. The Channel 4 programme 'Big World Café' includes an interview with Paul and footage from his rehearsals and concert in Rotterdam.

22 November. Paul, Linda and the band arrive in New York and hold a press conference at the Lyceum Theater.

23 November. Paul and his band appear at the Forum, Los Angeles. In Britain the limited edition *Flowers In The Dirt (World Pack)* is issued with the bonus track 'Party Party'.

24 November. Paul and his band appear at the Forum, Los Angeles. During the day Paul tapes an interview for the music channel VH-1. The Channel 4 'Big World Café' programme is repeated.

26 November. Paul tapes a pre-recorded interview for the Japanese radio show *Super DJ*.

27 November. Paul and his band appear at the Forum, Los Angeles. During a press conference he mentions that he would like to write songs with George Harrison.

28 November. Paul and his band appear at the Forum, Los Angeles.

29 November. Paul and his band appear at the Forum, Los Angeles. 'Mike McCartney's Alternative Liverpool', a 55-minute guide to the city which was written, presented and directed by Mike, is released by the Magnum Music Group. It was completed two years previously.

3 December. Paul and his band appear at the Rosemont Horizon in Chicago. The team from *48 Hours* films him during the next three days.

4 December. Paul and his band appear at the Rosemont Horizon, Chicago.

5 December. Paul and his band appear at the Rosemont Horizon, Chicago.

10 December. Paul is featured on the cover of *Music Connection* magazine.

11 December. Paul and his band appear at Madison Square Garden in New York. Paul also records an interview with the local radio station WNEW and is featured on a *Today* show in America from an interview taped in Toronto, Canada.

14 December. An interview with Paul, conducted by Anne Nightingale, is screened by Central Television, the Midlands television station.

15 December. Paul and his band appear at Madison Square Garden. Following the concert, Twiggy, Sting and Dustin Hoffman join Paul and Linda at Sardi's restaurant. Paul and Linda also donate a cheque for $100,000 to Friends Of The Earth.

19 December. Paul receives an award for his outstanding achievements in the field of popular music from the Performing Rights Society during a lunchtime ceremony at Claridges, London. His award is a miniature copy of his Hofner bass in gold. It is the first time the Society has honoured an individual in 75 years. The home video of 'Put It There' is issued in Britain.

20 December. For four days, in his home studio in Sussex, Paul records music for his *Daumier's Law* film project.

23 December. In America, laserdiscs of *Rockshow*, *Give My Regards To Broad Street* and *Rupert And The Frog Song* are released.

26 December. *Give My Regards To Broad Street* is given a Boxing Day screening on ITV in Britain.

1990

2 January. Paul begins the third leg of his world tour with his UK concerts, starting at the NEC International Arena, Birmingham.

3 January. Paul and his band appear at the NEC International Arena, Birmingham. During the day he takes part in a tree planting ceremony.

5 January. Paul and his band appear at the NEC International Arena, Birmingham. The single 'Put It There'/'Mama's Little Girl' is issued in Britain. The CD and 12″ versions include an additional track, 'Same Time Next Year'.

6 January. Paul and his band appear at the NEC International Arena, Birmingham

8 January. Paul and his band appear at the NEC International Arena, Birmingham.

9 January. Paul and his band appear at the NEC International Arena, Birmingham.

11 January. Paul and his band appear at the Wembley Arena, London.

13 January. Paul and his band appear at the Wembley Arena, London.

14 January. Paul and his band appear at the Wembley Arena, London.

15 January. The limited edition *Flowers In The Dirt (World Pack)* is issued in America.

16 January. Paul and his band appear at the Wembley Arena, London. Backstage at the concert Paul meets Polish teacher Agnieska Czariecka, who has been running the 'Paul McCartney Kindergarten' in Cracow, Poland.

17 January. Paul and his band appear at the Wembley Arena, London. The first of a two-part interview with Paul, conducted by Cathy McGowan, is screened on BBC 1 in the South.

19 January. Paul and his band appear at the Wembley Arena, London.

20 January. Paul and his band appear at the Wembley Arena, London.

21 January. Paul and his band appear at the Wembley Arena, London.

22 January. The first part of a series of pre-taped interviews with Paul is screened on *Good Morning Britain*, a TV-AM programme. Paul directs himself in a promo clip for 'Put It There'.

23 January. Paul and his band appear at the Wembley Arena, London. The second part of the pre-recorded interview with Paul is screened on *Good Morning Britain*.

24 January. Paul and his band appear at the Wembley Arena, London. The third part of the pre-recorded interview with Paul is screened on *Good Morning Britain*. The first of a two-part pre-recorded interview with Paul is screened in America on *Entertainment Tonight*.

25 January. The CBS show *48 Hours* is subtitled '48 Hours With Paul McCartney' and features him during his two days in Chicago in a 90-minute programme.

26 January. Paul and his band appear at the Wembley Arena, London. After the show he holds a party. Guests include Cynthia Lennon, George Martin, Elvis Costello, Neil Aspinall and Dick Lester. The fourth part of the pre-recorded interview with Paul is screened on *Good Morning Britain*. The second part of a pre-recorded interview with Paul is screened in America on *Entertainment Tonight*.

31 January. BBC 1 screens the second part of Cathy McGowan's interview with Paul in its Southern region. The final part of the pre-recorded interview with Paul is screened on *Good Morning Britain*.

2 February. The fourth leg of Paul's world tour returns to America and a concert is held at the Palace of Auburn Hills, Detroit, Michigan.

3 February. Paul and his band appear at the Palace of Auburn Hills.

4 February. Paul and his band appear at the Civic Arena, Pittsburgh.

5 February. Paul and his band appear at the Civic Arena, Pittsburgh.

8 February. Paul and his band appear at the Centrum, Boston. Paul appears on the cover of *Rolling Stone* magazine.

9 February. Paul and his band appear at the Centrum, Boston.

11 February. Paul and his band appear at the Rupp Arena, Lexington, Kentucky. A pre-taped interview with Paul is featured on Capital Gold.

12 February. Paul and his band appear at the Cincinnati Riverfront Coliseum.

14 February. Paul and his band appear at the Market Square Arena, Indianapolis.

15 February. Paul and his band appear at the Market Square Arena, Indianapolis.

18 February. Paul and his band appear at the Omni, Atlanta, Georgia.

19 February. Paul and his band appear at the Omni, Atlanta, Georgia. Paul and Linda are featured on the cover of *US Magazine*.

21 February. Paul and Linda attend the Grammy Awards at the Shrine Auditorium in Los Angeles where Paul is given a Lifetime Achievement Award by actress Meryl Streep.

1 March. Paul and his band arrive in Japan and he holds a press conference at the MZA Ariake Theatre, Tokyo, which is broadcast live on the Japanese TV show *Supertime*.

2 March. Paul and his band rehearse at the Tokyo Dome.

3 March. Paul and his band appear at the Tokyo Dome.

4 March. Paul and Linda pay a visit to Meiji Jinguu.

5 March. Paul and his band appear at the Tokyo Dome.

7 March. Paul and his band appear at the Tokyo Dome. Paul is interviewed by Naoto Kine for the radio show *All Night Nippon*.

8 March. Paul and Linda visit Mount Fuji.

9 March. Paul and Linda visit the Imperial Palace Garden and attend a planting ceremony at the Masago Primary School. Paul and his band appear at the Tokyo Dome and the concert is transmitted to various other Japanese cities by closed circuit television.

11 March. Paul and his band appear at the Tokyo Dome.

12 March. Paul and his band record a promo clip for 'We Got Married'.

13 March. Paul and his band appear at the Tokyo Dome.

14 March. Paul, Linda and the band fly back to England.

24 March. A compilation album *The Last Temptation Of Elvis* is issued in Britain by the *New Musical Express* newspaper and includes Paul's version of the Elvis number 'It's Now Or Never'.

28 March. Paul, Linda and the band arrive in America for the sixth leg of their world tour.

29 March. Paul and his band appear at the Kingdome, Seattle.

31 March. Paul and his band appear at the Berkeley Memorial Stadium, San Francisco.

1 April. Paul and his band appear at the Berkeley Memorial Stadium, San Francisco.

4 April. Paul and his band appear at the Sun Devil Stadium, Arizona State University, near Phoenix.

7 April. Paul and his band appear at the Texas Stadium, Irving. Paul is interviewed by 'Red Beard', a disc jockey with Dallas radio station KTXQ.

9 April. Paul and his band appear at Rupp Arena, Lexington, Kentucky.

12 April. Paul and his band appear at the Tampa Stadium, Florida. Asteroids 4147–4150, originally discovered in 1983 and 1984, are named after Paul, John, George and Ringo.

14 April. Paul and his band appear at the Joe Robbie Stadium, Florida, where he also holds a press conference. Paul is also interviewed for the TV show *The Mike Duccelli Show*.

15 April. Paul and his band appear at the Joe Robbie Stadium, Florida.

19 April. Paul appears on *CBS Evening News* to promote 'Earth Day'. His concert at the Maracana Stadium, Rio de Janeiro is cancelled due to heavy rain.

20 April. Paul and his band appear at the Maracana Stadium, Rio de Janeiro. Paul appears on *CBS This Morning* to promote 'Earth Day'.

21 April. Paul and his band appear at the Maracana Stadium, Rio de Janeiro before the biggest-ever concert for a rock show – 184,000 people. Excerpts from the show are filmed for a TV special 'Paul In Rio' by the Brazilian station GLOBO TV.

23 April. The TV special 'Paul In Rio', with eight of the numbers from the Maracana Stadium show of 21 April, is screened.

1 May. The single 'Put It There'/'Mama's Little Girl' is issued in America on cassette.

5 May. A John Lennon Tribute Concert is held at the Pier Head, Liverpool. Paul sends a video with a greeting and a concert clip of him and the band performing 'PS Love Me Do'. Mike McCartney's third son, Sonny, is born.

8 May. Paul, Linda and Carla Lane support the Towyn Flood Disaster Appeal. This small Welsh town, twenty miles from Liverpool, suffered devastating floods in January.

24 May. The first of a two-part interview with Paul is screened on TV-AM.

25 May. The second of a two-part interview with Paul is screened by TV-AM.

26 May. BBC 1 screens *The Family Way*, for which Paul composed the soundtrack.

13 June. Paul appears live on the *Steve Wright Show* on Radio One.

19 June. Paul and his band begin rehearsals at Paul's Sussex studio.

21 June. Paul and his band begin rehearsing in Glasgow.

23 June. Paul and his band appear at the Scottish Exhibition and Conference Centre in Glasgow. Various ITV regions screen the documentary 'Paul McCartney Now'.

25 June. Paul and Linda attend film sessions at Twickenham Studios.

26 June. Paul and Linda attend film sessions at Twickenham Studios. VH-I presents a video special on Paul.

28 June. Paul and his band appear at the King's Dock, Liverpool, during which he performs a John Lennon medley for the first time. He also hosts a reception for 150 guests.

29 June. Paul and his band arrive at Knebworth Park for a sound check.

30 June. Paul and his band appear at Knebworth Park for a concert in aid of the charity Music Therapy. Radio One broadcasts highlights from the 'Knebworth 90' concert, which features Paul's performance.

2 July. Paul and Linda fly to Washington. The film *Eat The Rich*, with a cameo performance from Paul and Linda, is screened in Britain on Channel 4.

4 July. Paul and his band continue their ten-month world tour at the Robert F Kennedy Stadium, Washington DC. For the 4 July anniversary celebrations, he performs 'Birthday'.

6 July. Paul and his band appear at the Robert F Kennedy Stadium, Washington DC.

8 July. It had been hoped that a concert could take place at Shea Stadium, but it does not take place.

9 July. Paul and his band appear at the Giants Stadium, New Jersey.

11 July. Paul and his band appear at the Giants Stadium, New Jersey.

14 July. Paul and his band appear at the Veterans Stadium, Philadelphia. 'Paul McCartney: Put It There' is screened on Showtime in America. MTV in America airs footage from Paul's Knebworth concert performance.

15 July. Paul and his band appear at the Veterans Stadium, Philadelphia.

18 July. Paul and his band appear at the University Of Iowa Stadium in Aimes, Iowa.

20 July. Paul and his band appear at the Cleveland Municipal Stadium, Cleveland. 'Paul McCartney: Put It There' receives another Showtime screening.

22 July. Paul and his band appear at the Carter-Finley Stadium, North Carolina.

24 July. Paul and his band appear at the Sullivan Stadium, Foxboro, Massachusetts. Paul is interviewed backstage by Boston's radio station WBCN.

25 July. Paul and the band shoot footage for the movie *Get Back* in front of an invited audience of 800 at the Sullivan Stadium.

26 July. Paul and his band appear at the Sullivan Stadium, Foxboro, Massachusetts.

29 July. At Soldier Field in Chicago, Paul introduced 'Twenty Flight Rock' into his repertoire because of its association with the city in the line 'They've sent to Chicago for repairs'. Paul also holds a press conference at the venue.

30 July. 'Paul McCartney: Put It There' receives a third screening on Showtime.

5 August. In the A&E cable channel programme 'My Love Is Bigger Than A Cadillac', Paul is seen talking about the Crickets. The programme is repeated on 11 August.

6 August. *Knebworth: The Album* is issued simultaneously in Britain and America. It features two of the live tracks by Paul, 'Coming Up' and 'Hey Jude'.

25 August. Paul and Linda hold a fancy dress party in the ground of their Sussex home to celebrate their daughter Mary's 21st birthday.

28 August. A home video 'Knebworth: the Event' (Volume One) is released in Britain featuring four numbers by Paul: 'Coming Up, 'Birthday', 'Hey Jude' and 'Can't Buy Me Love'.

1 September. Paul and Linda arrive in America to celebrate Buddy Holly Week in New York for the first time.

2 September. Robert Holmes a'Court dies at the age of 52. He was the man who acquired ATV Music in 1982 and sold it to Michael Jackson.

4 September. At the Buddy Holly lunch at the Lone Star roadhouse, New York, Paul performs several Holly numbers, backed by musicians such as the Crickets and Dave Edmunds.

13 September. Linda's sister Laura Lee Eastman marries Donald James Malcolm in East Hampton, Long Island. Linda, Heather, Stella and Mary are present and Paul is a groomsman.

8 October. The 12″ and CD versions of 'Birthday'/'Good Day Sunshine' are released in Britain and contain the bonus track 'Let 'Em In', originally recorded at the Tokyo Dome in February. Part of Paul's promo of 'Birthday' is premiered on *Entertainment Tonight* in the US.

9 October. The NBC programme *Today* features part of the promo of 'Birthday', plus an interview with Paul, recorded in his London office, talking about the number as a tribute to John Lennon. Paul also performed his Lennon medley.

11 October. Paul and Linda begin to distribute leaflets in Rye, near their home, to help save the Rye Memorial Hospital.

15 October. Paul and Linda lead a march from Rye Town Hall to the Rye Memorial Hospital in a protest to try to save the hospital from closure.

16 October. The single 'Birthday'/'Good Day Sunshine' is issued as a cassette in America.

26 October. Paul appears on the American show *Rockline* in Los Angeles during which he performs an acoustic version of 'Matchbox'.

27 October. Radio One broadcasts 75 minutes of the concert recorded at the King's Dock, Liverpool on 28 June 1990.

29 October–2 November. Radio One broadcasts a five-part, pre-recorded interview with Paul.

5 November. The album *Tripping The Live Fantastic* receives a simultaneous world release.

7 November. Several artists are commissioned to work on an animated promo for Paul's video 'Party Party'.

12 November. MTV Prime in America screens a pre-recorded interview with Paul.

19 November. The CD *Tripping The Live Fantastic . . . Highlights!* is issued in America and Britain. The British version contains 'All My Trials', which is not on the American release.

25 November. Paul appears on the American version of *Desert Island Discs* in Los Angeles.

26 November. 'All My Trials'/'C Moon' is released in Britain in several configurations. The 12″ version also contains 'Mull Of Kintyre' and 'Put It There'. Paul appears in a two-hour radio show *Rockline* in Los Angeles, which is syndicated to other radio stations in the States.

28 November. Paul appears on a one-hour radio phone-in show that is syndicated to more than sixteen countries.

3 December. Yet another configuration of 'All My Trials'/'C Moon' is released in Britain, this time replacing the previous two bonus tracks with the 'Lennon Medley'. A pre-recorded interview with Paul is aired on *The Simon Bates Show* on Radio One.

10 December. 'The 1990 *Billboard* Awards' show on American television includes a pre-recorded insert from Paul who receives an award for the highest-grossing concert during the year.

12 December. Paul's appearance on the American *After Hours* show is

screened on BBC 2. Paul makes an appearance at the *Q* Awards at Ronnie Scott's club in London to receive the Merit Award for his 'outstanding and continued contribution to the music industry'. He holds an end-of-tour party at the Boardwalk Restaurant in Soho.

13 December. Paul and his band are at Limehouse Studios, London, where they mime to songs before an invited audience and are filmed for various European and Japanese TV shows.

14 December. Paul and Linda appear on the *Wogan* chat show during which Paul and the band mime to 'All My Trials'. He also pre-records an interview for *Going Live!* The *Independent* newspaper reports that Paul has resumed collaborating on writing songs with Elvis Costello. MTV in America screens 'Famous Last Words', which include a pre-taped interview with Paul.

17 December. Channel 4 screens the concert documentary 'From Rio To Liverpool'.

18 December. The Limehouse performance of various mimed numbers is shown on the *Countdown* TV show in Holland, and also includes an interview with Paul by Jerone Van Inkel.

22 December. Paul appears in a short pre-recorded interview on the BBC 1 children's programme *Going Live!* which also screens the 'All My Trials' promo. His Limehouse performance is also screened in Italy on the programme *Fantastico*.

24 December. Radio One repeats part of Paul's interview from the *Steve Wright Show* first broadcast in June.

26 December. ITV stations broadcast 'Sounds Like Christmas', a programme of Christmas No. 1's, which includes 'Wonderful Christmastime' and 'Mull Of Kintyre'. The Limehouse performance is screened on the Spanish TV show *Rockopop* and the Dutch TV show *Countdown*. Radio One broadcasts highlights from the 'Knebworth 90' concert, originally broadcast in June and featuring Paul's performance. MTV in America screens the clip of Paul's concert promo of 'Sgt Pepper's Lonely Hearts Club Band'.

30 December. Some ITV stations transmit 'The 1990 *Billboard* Music Awards' with Paul's acceptance speech.

1991

20 January. Paul's Limehouse Studios appearance is screened by the Japanese TV programme *Beat UK*.

25 January. Paul and his group return to Limehouse Studios once again to record *Unplugged* for MTV.

28 January. The American TV show *Pan E! Vision* screens a short pre-taped interview with Paul. The syndicated American radio programme *The Live Show* includes a pre-recorded interview with Paul and plays his 'John Lennon Medley'.

7 March. Paul is voted No. 1 bass guitarist in a *Rolling Stone* magazine poll.

3 April. MTV in America screens Paul's 51-minute *Unplugged* show and includes an interview with Paul called 'Last Word'. It is also simultaneously broadcast on network radio by the Global Satellite Network, which is preceded by a 15-minute interview with Paul.

7 April. MTV repeats Paul's *Unplugged* show.

30 April. Paul and Linda host a press conference in London to launch her new range of vegetarian dishes.

1 May. Paul and Linda make a surprise appearance on Radio One's *The Simon Bates Show*.

8 May. Paul and his band make the first of six surprise concerts to promote *Unplugged* at the Zeleste Club, Barcelona, Spain. Paul and Linda return to England immediately after the concert.

10 May. Another *Unplugged* concert takes place at the Mean Fiddler, London.

13 May. Paul's *Unplugged* show receives its first screening on the European MTV channel.

20 May. *Unplugged (The Official Bootleg)* is released in Britain.

4 June. *Unplugged (The Official Bootleg)* is released in America.

5 June. Another concert in Paul's surprise *Unplugged* series takes place at the Teatro Tendo, Naples, Italy. Paul performs 'The River', playing harmonica, and also introduces the song 'The World Is Waiting For The Sunrise'.

7 June. An *Unplugged* concert takes place at the Cornwall Coliseum, St Austell, England.

10 June. Paul's MTV *Unplugged* show is screened by TSW, a TV station in the southwest of England.

11 June. A letter from Paul voicing his anger at the closure of the Rye Memorial Hospital is published in the *Daily Mirror*.

12 June. The American show *Entertainment Tonight* reports on Paul's *Unplugged* performance at the Cornwall Coliseum.

14 June. The promo for 'Birthday' is issued in Japan as a VSD (video single disc).

19 July. Paul and his band perform another *Unplugged* concert at the Cliffs Pavilion, Westcliffe-on-Sea, Southend, England, slightly altering the repertoire and introducing the poet Adrian Mitchell.

20 June. Paul and Linda host a party to launch a range of her vegetarian foods at the Hard Rock Café in London. Ringo and Barbara Starr are among the guests.

26 June. Linda discusses her vegetarian foods on the ITV show *Good Morning*.

28 June. *Paul McCartney's Liverpool Oratorio* receives its world premiere at the Anglican Cathedral in Liverpool. Paul had earlier shown MP Michael Portillo around the Liverpool Institute.

29 June. A second performance of *Paul McCartney's Liverpool Oratorio* takes place at the Anglican Cathedral, once again with the Royal Liverpool Philharmonic Orchestra conducted by Carl Davis.

7 July. The London premiere of *Paul McCartney's Liverpool Oratorio* takes place at the Royal Albert Hall with Paul and Linda in attendance.

23 July. Paul's MTV show *Unplugged* is screened nationally by Danish television.

24 July. Paul's final *Unplugged* concert takes place at the Falkoner Theatre, Copenhagen, Denmark and Adrian Mitchell appears once again.

26 July. Originally, the Olympia Theatre in Paris, France was to be the final venue in the *Unplugged* tour, but MPL decided to cancel it.

30 July. Linda's father Lee Eastman dies of a stroke. He was 81 years old.

4 August. A documentary 'Power of Music', featuring Paul working with mentally handicapped children, is screened on BBC 2.

26 August. Paul's MTV show *Unplugged* is screened by Channel 4.

3 September. The *Sun* newspaper runs an interview with Paul.

13 September. Paul and Linda hold their annual Buddy Holly Week luncheon at the Orangery in Holland Park, London.

16 September. Paul is interviewed on the Radio Four programme *Kaleidoscope* about his work on *Paul McCartney's Liverpool Oratorio*.

18 September. The *Get Back* feature film receives its world premiere at the Passage Kino, Hamburg, Germany, with Paul and Linda in attendance. Paul also acts as a disc jockey for an hour on the Antenne Bayern radio station.

19 September. The *Get Back* concert film is screened at various Odeon cinemas throughout Britain.

20 September. A single, 'The World You're Coming Into'/'Tres Conejos', from *Paul McCartney's Liverpool Oratorio* is released in Britain. The *Get Back* concert film opens at various other cinema chains in Britain.

30 September. Paul contributes to a new book, *Save The Earth* by Jonathan Porritt, with the royalties going to the Friends Of The Earth. A 14-track version of Paul's Russian album *Choba B CCCP* is issued on CD in Britain.

3 October. Some humorous adverts promoting the *Choba B CCCP* CD release appear in the *Independent* and *Guardian* newspapers.

7 October. The record of the Liverpool premiere of *Paul McCartney's Liverpool Oratorio* is issued in Britain.

8 October. 'Ghosts Of The Past', a documentary on the making of *Paul McCartney's Liverpool Oratorio*, is screened on BBC 1.

13 October. In America the Disney channel screens 'Paul McCartney: Going Home', which is 'From Rio To Liverpool' with a different title.

14 October. Paul and Linda are at the Anuga Exhibition in Cologne, Germany to launch a range of vegetarian menus in Europe.

18 October. On *Six O'Clock Live*, the London Weekend Television show, Paul chats with Michael Aspel while Kiri te Kanawa is seen at the HMV shop signing copies of her Oratorio performance of 'The World You're Coming Into' and her hit single 'World in Union'. Paul is also featured on the American ABC TV programme *In Concert '91*.

19 October. The Disney Channel repeats 'Paul McCartney: Going Home'.
21 October. Paul and Linda fly to New York. *Get Back, The Movie* is issued in Britain on home video.
22 October. The recording of the Liverpool performance of *Paul McCartney's Liverpool Oratorio* is released in America.
23 October. Paul holds a press conference at the Weill Recital Hall, New York City, to promote the *Liverpool Oratorio*. There are 150 representatives from the media and Linda and Hamish Stewart accompany Paul. The 'Ghosts Of The Past' video, showing the making of the oratorio, is screened prior to Paul holding a question and answer session. He is asked how working with Carl Davis compared with writing with John and he says, 'I bossed Carl around more than I bossed John.' Paul is then presented with a platinum disc for sales of *Tripping The Live Fantastic – Highlights*.
24 October. Paul, Linda and Hamish Stuart attend the premiere of *Get Back, The Movie* at the Baronet Theater, New York. During his stay in New York Paul appears on *Good Morning America* and has interviews with Charlie Rose and Bob Costas.
25 October 25. Paul and Linda are in Toronto promoting *Get Back, The Movie*. They hold a press conference at the Sutton Place Hotel. Paul is then interviewed by the *Toronto Star*, appears on CITY-TV's *Movie Television* and is interviewed live on CHUM-AM. Together with Linda he then attends a premiere at the Varsity 11 Cinema. The Disney Channel screens another repeat of 'Paul McCartney: Going Home'.
28 October. PMI release the home video of *Paul McCartney's Liverpool Oratorio*, recorded in Liverpool on 28 June 1991.
29 October. A CD version of Paul's Russian album *Choba B CCCP* is issued in America. MTV feature Paul in their show *Day In Rock*.
30 October. The American television premiere of the *Liverpool Oratorio* takes place on *Great Performances* on PBS. The documentary on the making of the work, 'Ghosts Of The Past', is also shown. The Disney Channel also features another repeat of 'Paul McCartney: Going Home'.
1 November. *Get Back, The Movie* opens at the Canada Square Cinema in Toronto.
2 November. The 25 October interview with Paul is screened on *Movie Television*.
3 November. *CBS Sunday Morning* features a piece on Paul and the oratorio.
5 November. Paul's pre-recorded interview with Bob Costas is screened on *Later With Bob Costas*. Another pre-recorded interview with Paul is featured on ABC TV's *Eyewitness News*.
6 November. Paul's pre-recorded interview with Bob Costas is given another screening.
7 November. The third airing of Paul's pre-recorded interview with Bob Costas is screened.

12 November. Granada Television screens the *Liverpool Oratorio* film in the northwest of England. A single 'Save the World'/'The Drinking Song' from *Paul McCartney's Liverpool Oratorio* is released in America.

16 November. Paul is rehearsing for the *Liverpool Oratorio* with the orchestra at the Carnegie Hall in New York.

18 November. Paul and his family attend the American concert premiere of *Paul McCartney's Liverpool Oratorio* at Carnegie Hall, New York. The single 'Save The World'/'The Drinking Song' from *Paul McCartney's Liverpool Oratorio* is released in Britain.

19 November. Paul appears on Nicky Campbell's Radio One show in a pre-recorded interview to discuss the *Liverpool Oratorio* and to promote his 'Save The Child' single.

20 November. Nicky Campbell interviews Paul on his Radio One show. Toshiba-EMI release a double CD of the oratorio which includes a bonus CD-3 single featuring a six-minute message from Paul in which he discusses the background to the work.

21 November. *Paul McCartney's Liverpool Oratorio* is performed at Ulster Hall, Belfast as part of the Belfast Festival.

24 November. *Paul McCartney's Liverpool Oratorio* is performed at St Patrick's Cathedral, Dublin, Eire.

25 November. Paul begins working with Julian Mendelsohn at his home studios in Sussex on tracks for the *Off The Ground* album.

30 November. *Paul McCartney's Liverpool Oratorio* is performed at St Anne's Cathedral, Belfast by the Northern Ireland Symphony Orchestra and Chorus.

9 December. A laser disc version of *Paul McCartney's Liverpool Oratorio* is released in Britain. Paul continues his recording sessions for the *Off The Ground* album.

11 December. Vestron Video releases *Get Back, The Movie*.

12 December. Paul receives the Q Merit Award for his services to the music industry at a ceremony at Ronnie Scott's club in London.

14 December. *Paul McCartney's Liverpool Oratorio* is performed at the Guildhall, Londonderry. Channel 4 screens the *Paul McCartney's Liverpool Oratorio* concert film. Paul appears in a two-hour Radio Two special discussion about the *Liverpool Oratorio*.

18 December. The *Get Back* concert film is released on home video.

24 December. MTV dedicate their day's programming to Paul with various promo clips, the *Unplugged* performance, 'Famous Last Words' and 'Rockumentary'.

26 December. The BBC series *Arena* screens the documentary 'Linda McCartney: Behind The Lens'.

1992

7 January. Paul appears on *Top Of The Pops* to deliver a live vocal over a recorded version of 'Hope Of Deliverance'.

29 January. The *Daily Mirror* begins a two-part series on Paul ending on 30 January. Paul begins recording a classical piece, which includes Linda's tune 'Appaloosa' and his own 'Meditation', which he has co-arranged with Carl Davis. The recording is to be used in the MPL film *Appaloosa*.

31 January. Paul and Linda attend a party at London's Groucho Club to celebrate the wedding of Paul 'Wix' Wickens who had got married the previous day.

1 February. Paul is interviewed on Radio One.

3 February. MTV and VH-I screen a 90-minute version of Paul's 'Up Close' video.

6 February. MTV repeats the 'Up Close' video, but in an abridged 60-minute version.

7 February. MTV repeats the abridged version of 'Up Close'.

13 February. Paul appears in several comedy sketches on *Saturday Night Live* and performs three numbers with his band, 'Get Out Of My Way', 'Biker Like An Icon' and 'Hey Jude'. VH-I repeats the 90-minute version of 'Up Close'.

14 February. VH-I repeats the 90-minute version of 'Up Close' once again.

21 February. Paul hosts a fundraising lunch at the headquarters of the Performing Rights Society in London on behalf of LIPA.

15 March. The *Sunday Express* runs a cover story on Paul, with a feature to tie in with his forthcoming 50th birthday. Ray Connolly writes, 'Despite everything he has achieved, he is driven to keep proving himself, he has to keep trying, and the harder he tries, the fewer albums sell, the more indifferent the songs become and we get over-produced, over-arranged songs, but McCartney loves rock and roll and loves being in a band.'

9 April. Paul joins George Martin at Abbey Road Studios to be interviewed for the television documentary *The Making Of Sgt Pepper*.

16 April. The rental version of the *Get Back* video is issued.

12 May. Carl Davis conducts the classical pieces *Appaloosa* and *Meditation* with the Boston Pops Orchestra. The performance is filmed by PBS Television.

22 May. Paul's *Liverpool Oratorio* is performed in Sant Jordi, Barcelona, Spain.

23 May. Paul's *Liverpool Oratorio* is performed in Valencia, Spain.

1 June. The *Daily Star* begins a three-day series on Paul.

2 June. Paul is featured on the cover of *Jornal Do Brasil*.

6 June. In an article on 'Sgt Pepper' in *TV Guide* Paul is quoted as saying, 'I was always frightened of the moment when children would say: "we like rap, your music is crap". But it didn't happen that way, they like it, a lot of kids do.'

7 June. The *Independent On Sunday* asks fifty musicians and critics to choose their favourite composition by Paul.

8 June. An interview with Paul appears in *Time* magazine. He says, 'I was thinking, what's this article going to be called. My bet's on "Paul At Fifty" so that everyone can go, "What? Jeez-us Curr-hist! He's fifty! He isn't, is he? Bloody hell! That makes me old!"' The article was called 'Paul At Fifty'.

10 June. Jools Holland films an interview with Paul for the *Anthology* project.

13 June. A souvenir issue of the *Radio Times* celebrates Paul's 50th birthday with a ten-page story.

14 June. The ITV network in Britain screens the documentary *The Making Of Sgt Pepper*.

16 June. Her Majesty Queen Elizabeth II makes a private donation to Paul's LIPA project.

18 June. Paul's 50th birthday. It is 'Paul McCartney Day' on BBC Radio Two, which plays Paul's music throughout the day and features a special documentary, 'Paul McCartney – Rediscovered', narrated by Brian Matthew. *Paul McCartney's Liverpool Oratorio* receives its Japanese premiere in Tokyo with Carl Davis conducting the New Japan Philharmonic Orchestra. Radio Bayern 3 features a three-hour McCartney special. On his 50th birthday Paul says, 'Despite the successful songs I've written, like "Yesterday", "Let It Be" and "Hey Jude", I feel I just want to write one really good song. People say to me, "What's left for you to do?" But I still have a little bee in my bonnet telling me, "Hang on, the best could be yet to come, you could write something, which could be just incredible." That keeps me going. Looking at things now, I don't seem to be over the hill.'

21 June. The career of Richard Hamilton, who worked on designs for *The Beatles* double album, is featured in 'This Is Tomorrow', a programme in the Channel 4 series *Without Walls*. It features a brief interview with Paul.

28 June. In Britain it is National Music Day and BBC 2 features a pre-recorded interview with Paul during which he discusses his LIPA project.

2 July. Paul and Linda fly to Brussels, Belgium on a fundraising trip, which aims to help the LIPA project.

6 July. The *Liverpool Oratorio* is performed in Rome, Italy.

7 July. The *Liverpool Oratorio* is performed in Rome, Italy.

15 July. The *Liverpool Oratorio* is performed in Quebec, Canada.

16 July. The *Liverpool Oratorio* is performed in Quebec, Canada.

18 July. The *Liverpool Oratorio* is performed in Montreal, Canada.

20 August. Paul and Linda visit the Stephen Talkhouse in Amagansett in New York State to see the *Saturday Night Live* band perform. He is persuaded to join them on stage for a rendition of 'Blue Suede Shoes'.

24 August. *Give My Regards To Broad Street* is screened on Nederland 2, Holland.

28 August. *Paul McCartney's Liverpool Oratorio*, conducted by Carl Davis, is performed at the Ravina Festival, Chicago.

5 September. For Stella's 21st birthday, a special party, which includes fancy dress, is held in a marquee at the McCartneys' home in East Sussex. Paul dresses as a highwayman and Linda as Queen Elizabeth I. Ringo and Barbara are among the guests. Providing the entertainment are the Thompson Twins and a ten-piece group called Soul Provider who play a 90-minute set, at the end of which Paul joins them to sing Al Green's 'Take Me To The River'.

7 September. The Dame Kiri Te Kanawa album *Kiri Selection* includes the song 'The World You're Coming Into' which she sang in *Paul McCartney's Liverpool Oratorio*.

9 September. Paul and Linda once again host a luncheon to celebrate Buddy Holly Week. Guests include the Crickets, Leo Sayer, Allan Clarke, Gary Glitter, Mick Green, Big Jim Sullivan and Chrissie Hynde. Paul performs several Buddy Holly numbers.

19 September. Paul and Linda attend the wedding reception of Linda's niece Louise Eastman in Long Island, New York and Paul is persuaded to perform some Buddy Holly numbers.

21 September. Clips of Wings' first European tour are shown on the ITV show 'Memories Of 1972'.

27 September. The Disney Channel in America premieres the documentary *The Making Of Sgt Pepper*.

3 October. BBC 2 features a documentary radio show 'Yesterday Forever' based on Paul's composition and the various artists who have recorded it.

5 October. A 77-minute 'highlights' version of *Paul McCartney's Liverpool Oratorio* is issued as a single CD (CDC 7546422) and cassette (EL 7546424).

8 October. Paul, George and Ringo meet for three hours at Paul's MPL offices.

9 October. Linda's photographic exhibition 'The Sixties: Portrait Of An Era' opens at the Royal Photographic Society in Bath and runs until 15 November.

11 October. The Disney Channel in America screens the documentary 'Paul McCartney: Going Home'.

17 October. The Disney Channel repeats their screening of 'Paul McCartney: Going Home'.

23 October. Linda appears on Ray Cokes' *Most Wanted* show on MTV.

24 October. Paul's *Liverpool Oratorio* receives its West Coast premiere at the Orange County Performing Arts Center. It is performed by William Hall and the Master Chorale of Orange County and the Costa Mesa Children's Chorus with Ruth Golden (soprano), Lucille Beer (mezzo-soprano), Jon Garrison (tenor), Richard Fredericks (baritone), Anthony Kalomas (boy soprano) and Albert Stern (violin solo). Linda appears on MTV Europe promoting her book *The Sixties*.

27 October. Linda appears on *The Late Show* promoting her book *The Sixties*.

1 November. The Disney Channel in America screens the world television premiere of the concert film *Get Back*.

5 November. The concert film *Get Back* receives its first European TV screening on the Filmnet satellite channel.

7 November. The Disney Channel screens *Get Back* once again.

12 November. Yet another repeat screening of *Get Back* is shown on the Disney Channel.

15 November. Paul's *Liverpool Oratorio* is performed in Lille, France by the Royal Liverpool Philharmonic Choir and Orchestra with Choristers of the Liverpool Cathedral, conducted by Carl Davis. The work is performed in the presence of Diana, Princess of Wales and Pierre Mauroy, a former French prime minister who was now Mayor of Lille.

16 November. MTV begin recording Paul at his home studio 'The Mill'.

17 November. MTV continue recording Paul. Paul plays journalists a preview of his forthcoming album *Off The Ground* at EMI House in London. There is also a film crew from Carlton TV present. The Central TV network in the Midlands screens Paul's *Unplugged*.

18 November. MTV complete their recording of Paul at the Mill.

20 November. Paul appears at the Mean Fiddler in Harlesden where Carlton TV films him for their 'A Carlton New Year' special. *Paul McCartney's Liverpool Oratorio* is performed in San Francisco, California.

21 November. Paul's *Liverpool Oratorio* is performed in San Francisco, California.

24 November. MTV Europe screens *Unplugged*.

26 November. The shooting of the promo for 'Hope Of Deliverance', directed by Andy Morahan, takes place at Black Island studios, North Acton, London.

29 November. A pre-recorded interview with Paul and Linda is screened on the Austrian TV show *Yana Lendt*.

30 November. Paul and his band are in San Francisco to shoot the video of 'Hope Of Deliverance', which is completed on 5 December.

3 December. Capitol Records preview the *Off The Ground* album at a Los Angeles luncheon and announce Paul has signed what appears to be a lifelong contract with them. Linda's photographic exhibition 'The Sixties: Portrait Of An Era' opens at the David Fahey Gallery in Los Angeles and guests included Graham Nash, Twiggy and Todd Rundgren. Linda appears on the *Arsenio Hall Show*.

4 December. A pre-taped interview with Linda is screened on the American TV show *Hard Copy*. Another pre-taped interview with her promoting her new book *The Sixties* is shown on CNN's *Showbiz Today*.

9 December. Simon Mayo previews 'Hope Of Deliverance' on his Radio One breakfast show.

10 December. Paul performs before a selected audience at the Ed Sullivan Theater in New York for the MTV series *Up Close*. Linda appears on the American TV show *Vicki!*.

11 December. Paul holds a press conference at the Academy in New York. He performs a second show before a selected audience at The Ed Sullivan Theater for the MTV series *Up Close*. Paul announces the making of a three-part television series on the Beatles history, hinting that the three surviving members were getting together for it. 'We're getting together for this thing and there is a chance that we might do a little bit of music for it. It will just be the three of us. We'll just do that and see how it goes from there. I shouldn't think we'll re-form as a band, but we'll do a bit of work together.'

12 December. Paul and Linda return to England.

15 December. Paul begins recording at Abbey Road with the number 'Is It Raining In London?' Paul also gives a phone interview to Simon Mayo of Radio One.

26 December. BBC TV screens the 50-minute *Arena* special 'Linda McCartney Behind The Lens'.

28 December. 'Hope Of Deliverance'/'Long Leather Coat' is issued in Britain. Apart from the vinyl and cassette versions there is a CD single with the additional tracks 'Big Boys Bickering' and 'Kicked Around No More'.

1993

2 January. The video of 'Hope Of Deliverance' receives its first screening on ITV's *Chart Show*.

7 January. Paul appears live on *Top Of The Pops* performing 'Hope Of Deliverance'. Central Television broadcasts 'From Rio To Liverpool'. Paul pre-records an interview for BBC 2's *The O Zone*.

10 January. Paul appears during a five-minute interview on *The O-Zone* when a clip of 'Hope Of Deliverance' is also screened.

11 January. Paul makes spontaneous calls to various radio shows, beginning with Steve Wright on Radio One.

13 January. Paul makes spontaneous calls to BRMB in Birmingham and Chiltern Radio in Milton Keynes.

14 January. Paul makes a live phone-in call to Kid Jenson at Capital Gold.

15 January. Paul is a guest on the BBC 1 show *Entertainment Weekly* and the video of 'Hope Of Deliverance' is shown. He also makes a spontaneous call to Radio One's *News 93*. A 12" version of 'Hope Of Deliverance' is issued in Britain. The late-night *Chart Show* screens a clip of 'Big Boys Bickering' from MTV's *Up Close*.

16 January. *Paul McCartney's Liverpool Oratorio* is performed in Pretoria, South Africa. The Australian TV show *Rage* shows a clip of Wings performing at Abbey Road Studios in 1977.

17 January. *Paul McCartney's Liverpool Oratorio* is performed in Johannesburg, South Africa. Paul pre-records an interview for a radio special 'Paul McCartney: Off The Ground'.

18 January. 'Hope Of Deliverance'/'Long Leather Coat' is issued in America.

19 January. Paul has to turn down an invitation to play at President Clinton's Inaugural Gala at the Capitol Centre, Landover, Maryland because he was rehearsing for his world tour at the London Arena.

22 January. Paul phones the ITV show *Good Morning With Anne And Nick*. The first of a two-part pre-recorded interview with Paul appears on GMTV. While rehearsing for his forthcoming tour at Pinewood studios, Princess Diana, along with her two sons William and Harry, pay him a visit.

23 January. The German TV station ZDF TV screens a pre-recorded interview with Paul.

25 January. The one-hour pre-recorded radio show 'Paul McCartney: Off The Ground', recorded at his MPL offices on 17 January, is promoted on radio stations throughout the world.

26 January. In an MTV interview Paul says that he has written to Michael Jackson asking if he could buy his songs back and that he now only receives 15 per cent royalties for his early work. The second part of Paul's pre-recorded interview is screened on GMTV.

27 January. Linda's exhibition of photographs, 'Sixties', opens at the Hamilton Gallery in Grosvenor Square, London. Paul and Linda host a party at the gallery with various celebrity guests attending including Elvis Costello and Koo Stark. Paul and Linda's daughters Mary and Stella are there, along with Ringo's children, Lee and Jason.

28 January. Linda appears on Carlton TV's *Big City* in an interview recorded the previous evening at the Hamilton Gallery.

29 January. A number of radio stations in Britain and America will not play 'Bad Boys Bickering' because of Paul's use of a four-letter word.

1 February. Paul appears on Radio One's *The Simon Bates Show* and 'Biker Like An Icon' is aired.

2 February. Paul's latest album, *Off The Ground*, his 18th solo LP, is released in Britain.

3 February. MTV screens *Up Close*, the concerts Paul recorded at the Ed Sullivan Theater in December 1992. Paul moves from Pinewood Studios to continue his rehearsals at the Docklands Arena.

5 February. Paul hosts a 25-minute press conference at the Docklands Arena and then holds a 90-minute tour rehearsal before an invited audience of 3,000.

6 February. Paul, Linda and the band fly to Los Angeles.

7 February. Paul records a special programme about his *Off The Ground* album for 'The Official World Premier Special', which is a radio special syndicated across America. He also records an interview for *Up Close*, another syndicated radio show.

9 February. Paul's album *Off The Ground* is released in America. Paul continues his rehearsals at the Docklands Arena.

10 February. Paul, Linda and the band fly to New York.

11 February. Paul holds a press conference at the Academy in New York. He also holds a live phone interview with *Rockline*, the Los Angeles radio show.

12 February. Paul rehearses for his appearance on *Saturday Night Live*. He also engages in some pre-recorded interviews for two NBC shows, *Nightly News* and *Today*.

13 February. Paul appears live on *Saturday Night Live*, appearing in some comedy sketches and performing 'Biker Like An Icon', 'Get Out Of My Way' and 'Hey Jude'.

15 February. Paul officially launches *Off The Ground*, his 18th album, at a press conference at the Docklands Arena, London.

17 February. Paul and the band pre-record an appearance for *Top Of The Pops*, lip-synching to 'C'Mon People'.

18 February. The *Top Of The Pops* show includes the pre-recorded 'C'Mon People'. Paul, Linda and the band fly to Italy. The RAI TV network interviews Paul.

18 February. Paul and the band begin the first leg of their European tour with a concert at the Forum, Assage, Italy.

19 February. Paul and the band appear on their second concert at the Forum, near Milan, Italy.

20 February. The promo of 'C'Mon People' receives its premiere in Britain on *The Chart Show*, an ITV networked programme.

21 February. *Big E!*, a programme on the Carlton and Meridian regions in Britain, screens excerpts from Paul's Docklands conference.

22 February. Paul and the band appear at the Festehalle, Frankfurt, Germany where he is presented with a gold disc for his *Off The Ground* album. The single 'C'Mon People' is released in Britain.

23 February. Paul and the band appear at the Festehalle, Frankfurt, Germany.

24 February. 'The Making Of C'Mon People' is screened on the Carlton and Meridian TV regions in Britain. Paul's *Up Close* is given its European premiere on MTV.

25 February. *Inside Music*, a programme on VH-I, includes news of Paul's forthcoming American tour.

28 February. An interview with Paul, conducted by Andrea Babrato on 18 February, is broadcast on the RAI TV network. Another interview, pre-recorded on the same day by Rolando Giambelli of the Radio 10 Network is aired on RAI UNO.

3 March. Paul, Linda and the band arrive in Perth for the second leg of their world tour. The TV channels Channel 9 and Channel 10 feature Paul's arrival in Australia.

4 March. MTV's *3 From 1* spot features Paul and screens the promotional videos of 'Birthday', 'No More Lonely Nights' and 'Hope Of Deliverance'. Paul is also heard on the Radio 96FM show with Bob Geldof. Australian programme *Eleven AM* show a number of McCartney TV clips.

5 March. Paul and his band appear at the Subiaco Oval, Perth. During a press conference Paul refuses to be drawn on political issues due to the Australian election campaign. He says, 'I think Australians are more

worried about the economy but someone has to talk about the environment. I would happily shut up if the politicians would do something about it.' The ITV programme *The Chart Show* screens the 'C'Mon People' promo. A special four-CD box set *The New World Collection* is issued to coincide with the Australian/New Zealand Tour. In America the NBC programme *In Concert '93* presents a two-part feature on the world tour and the *Off The Ground* album, part of which had been recorded at Paul's Docklands press conference on 5 February.

6 March. The ITV programme *The Chart Show* screens the 'C'Mon People' promo for the third time. An advert appears in the American publication *Billboard*, paid for by Paul and Apple, in which they congratulate George Martin on the opening of AIR studios in London.

7 March. MTV Europe presents 'Paul McCartney Sunday', a day devoted to documentaries and promotional videos of Paul.

9 March. Paul and his band appear at the Cricket Ground, Melbourne. He holds a 30-minute press conference. Linda visits the cast of the TV show *Neighbours*. Perth's Radio 96FM show in which Bob Geldof interviewed Paul is repeated. Paul also pre-records an interview for 3AW-AM, a Melbourne radio station.

10 March. Paul holds a press conference at Melbourne Cricket Ground prior to his second concert there. The press conference is featured on the television news show *Live Eye*. Paul's pre-recorded interview for 3AW-AM is broadcast.

11 March. *Paul McCartney's Liverpool Oratorio* is performed in Linkoping, Sweden.

12 March. Paul's *Liverpool Oratorio* is performed in Stockholm.

13 March. Paul and his band appear at the Oval, Adelaide.

16 March. Paul and his band appear at the Entertainment Centre, Sydney. Channel 7 screens the concert film *Get Back*. Backstage, Paul and Linda are visited by actor Bryan Brown, who portrayed Paul's manager in *Give My Regards To Broad Street*.

17 March. Paul and his band appear at the Entertainment Centre, Sydney. Ian Rogerson and Debbie Spillane of 2JJJ FM, a Sydney radio station, interview him. Channel 9 screens clips of 'Drive My Car' and 'Coming Up'.

19 March. 12,000 people join a queue outside Brash's record store in Pitt Street, Sydney after it has been announced that Paul will do a 30-minute signing session. Queuing begins five hours before Paul arrives and it is his first record-store signing since his Liverpool days. Linda appears on a Channel 9 midday show hosted by Ray Martin to discuss her 'Sixties' photographic collection. She creates controversy when she is interviewed by Roland Roccheccioli for the Channel 7 programme *Real Life* by verbally attacking Australian Prime Minister Paul Keating, a pig farmer, who she describes as a 'pig slaughterer'. She says, 'The only way to be a good leader is to be kind and fair. And you're not kind and fair if you're murdering animals for profit.'

20 March. Paul and his band appear at the Entertainment Centre, Sydney.

22 March. Various Australian news reports screen Paul and Linda's visit to the Rainbow Warrior, the Greenpeace vessel docked in Sydney Harbour. In the evening Paul and his band appear at the Parramatta Stadium, Sydney.

23 March. Paul and his band appear again at the Parramatta Stadium, Sydney.

25 March. Paul and the band arrive in New Zealand.

26 March. Paul holds a press conference and a rehearsal with the band. Linda is interviewed for the TV show *Prime Time*.

27 March. Paul and his band appear at the Western Springs Stadium, Auckland, New Zealand. The Continental Airlines Pipe Band joins him on stage for 'Mull Of Kintyre'. Paul appears on the Channel 9 show *Hey Hey It's Saturday*. After the show Paul and Linda return to England.

2 April. The *Off The Ground* promotional clip receives its American premiere on the TV show *Friday Night Videos*.

8 April. Paul attends the Mayfair Hotel, London for a press conference in which Grundig announce that they will become one of the sponsors to LIPA.

9 April. Paul, Linda and the group set off for Nevada and the next leg of their world tour.

12 April. The documentary about the Nordoff-Robbins music therapy charity, with its introduction by Paul, is repeated on BBC 2. In America the VH-I show *Inside Music* features a pre-recorded interview with Paul and screens the 'Hope Of Deliverance' promo and clips from *Up Close*. Paul's MTV *Up Close* programme is screened on BBC 1.

14 April. Paul and his group appear at the Sam Boyd Silver Bowl, Las Vegas. Prior to the concert Robert Hilburn of the *LA Times* interviews Paul, who mentions his current activism: 'The strange thing about activism is it's not easy. It's so much easier for me to go off and hibernate with my money, but I'm an older guy, one of the planet's elders almost – and I figure there is a sort of responsibility to either just tell everyone to "tune in, drop out, turn on, man," if that's what you think, or give them some ideas.'

16 April. Paul appears at the Hollywood Bowl, Los Angeles, for the Earth Day For The Environment concert and is joined on stage by Ringo for the finale. CNN's *Showbiz Today* screens clips from Paul's Las Vegas concert.

17 April. Paul and his group appear at the Anaheim Stadium, California.

18 April. Channel 4 screens Paul's 'Movin' On' documentary, directed by Aubrey Powell, filmed in June 1992.

19 April. Paul's single 'Off The Ground' is released in America.

20 April. Paul and his band appear at the Aggie Memorial in Las Cruces, New Mexico. Capital release a vinyl single of 'Biker Like An Icon'.

22 April. Paul and his band appear at the Astrodome, Houston, Texas. The American VH-I music channel screens clips from Paul's performance on the 'Earth Day' event at the Hollywood Bowl and is immediately followed by a re-edited version of *Up Close*.

24 April. Paul and his band appear at the Louisiana Superdome, New Orleans.

26 April. The American show *Entertainment Tonight* features a peek at Paul's current tour by Pat O'Brien.

27 April. Paul and his band appear at the Liberty Bowl in Memphis, Tennessee. Before the concert, Paul is filmed with Carl Perkins performing 'Blue Suede Shoes', 'Maybelline', 'Matchbox' and 'My Old Friend' for the HBO programme 'Go Cat Go'.

29 April. Paul and his band appear at the Busch Memorial Stadium in St Louis, Missouri.

30 April. The *Hollywood Report* programme on ITV features excerpts from Paul's Hollywood Bowl concert for 'Earth Day'.

1 May. Paul and his band appear at the Georgia Dome in Atlanta, Georgia.

2 May. The music programme *VH-I to I* features a pre-recorded interview with Paul and a rare clip from the '3 Legs' promo. *Paul McCartney's Liverpool Oratorio* is performed at the St Elizabeth Seton Catholic Church, Indianapolis, Indiana by the Carmel Symphony Orchestra and Chorus, conducted by David Hunter, who was formerly an Abbey Road Studios employee.

5 May. Paul and his band appear at the Riverfront Stadium in Cincinnati, Ohio.

7 May. Paul and his band appear at the Williams-Bryce Stadium, Columbia, South Carolina. Backstage, Paul records an interview for the NBC show *Today*.

9 May. Paul and his band appear at the Citrus Bowl in Orlando, Florida.

10 May. VH-I provides a competition for a prize winner to join Paul at one of his American concerts. The competition is called the 'Backstage With Paul Sweepstakes'.

11 May. Linda appears in a pre-recorded interview on the CBS TV show *This Morning*. The *Liverpool Oratorio* is performed at Linkopings Konserthus.

12 May. The *Liverpool Oratorio* is performed at Stockholm Konserthus.

19 May. Paul's pre-recorded interview from backstage at his Columbia South Carolina gig is featured on the *Today* show.

21 May. Paul and his band appear at the Winnipeg Stadium, Winnipeg, Manitoba, Canada, during which the Heatherbelles Ladies Pipe Band joins him onstage for 'Mull Of Kintyre'. The local radio station 103 UFM interviews him. The Meridian TV region screens the *Give My Regards To Broad Street* film.

23 May. Paul and his band appear at the HHH Metrodome, Minneapolis, Minnesota.

26 May. Paul and his band appear at the Folsom Field Stadium in Boulder, Colorado.

27 May. Linda's book *The Sixties* is reprinted in Britain.

29 May. Paul and his band appear at the Alamodome, San Antonio, Texas.

31 May. Paul and his band appear at the Arrowhead Stadium, Kansas City, Missouri.

2 June. Paul and his band appear at the County Stadium, Milwaukee, Wisconsin.

4 June. Paul and his band appear at the Pontiac Silverdome in Pontiac, Detroit, Michigan.

6 June. Paul and his band appear at the CN Exhibition Stadium in Toronto, Canada.

7 June. Re-mastered CDs of the albums *McCartney*, *Band On The Run*, *Venus And Mars*, *Wild Life*, *London Town*, *Ram* and *Red Rose Speedway* are released in Britain.

9 June. A proposed concert at the Carrier Dome, Syracuse, New Jersey, is cancelled.

11 June. Paul and his band appear at the Giants Stadium in East Rutherford, New Jersey. NBC/Fox and ABS News in America report on the Giant's Stadium concert and include snippets of an interview with Paul. MTV Europe reports that Paul is going to team up for recording sessions with Sting.

12 June. Paul and his band appear at the Giants Stadium in East Rutherford, New Jersey.

13 June. Paul and his band appear at the Veterans' Stadium in Philadelphia, Pennsylvania.

14 June. BBC 1 screens the MPL film 'Blankit's First Show', which includes several numbers by Paul: 'The Man', 'The Other Me', 'Sweetest Little Show', 'Hey Hey' and 'All You Horse Riders'. It is the third time the BBC has screened the 1984 documentary. In America the Fox channel airs the first of a two-part interview with Paul.

15 June. 'Live In The New World', the concert by Paul given at the Blockbuster Pavilion in Charlotte, Carolina is broadcast on the Fox channel in the States. It attracts 9.54 million viewers, a record for the Tuesday night spot on the channel.

24 June. Paul Cooper of the Bootleg Beatles performs a concert at the Royal Court Theatre, Liverpool in aid of LIPA.

27 June. MTV Europe screen Paul's 1991 *Unplugged* once again.

10 July. The Australasian premiere of *Paul McCartney's Liverpool Oratorio* takes place at the Aotea Centre, Auckland, New Zealand. Paul is featured on the cover of *Hor Zu*, the German TV guide.

11 July. Another performance of *Paul McCartney's Liverpool Oratorio* takes place at the Aotea Centre, Auckland.

12 July. *Paul McCartney's Liverpool Oratorio*, at the Aotea Centre, New Zealand, is staged by the Auckland Choral Society, the Auckland

Boys' Choir and the Auckland Philharmonic Orchestra for the third and final time. MTV Europe screens 'Paul McCartney Up Close'. The single 'C'Mon People' is released in America.

14 July. Disc jockey Chris Tarrant interviews Paul live by phone for Capital Radio.

20 July. Paul appears in a pre-recorded interview on *London Tonight*, a Carlton ITV programme.

22 July. Paul poses on the Abbey Road zebra crossing for the cover of his *Paul Is Live* album.

28 July. *MTV News* on MTV Europe reveals that Paul is writing classical pieces for piano.

9 August. A new set of re-mastered CDs of Paul's albums are released in Britain: *Wings At The Speed Of Sound, Back To The Egg, McCartney II, Tug Of War, Pipes Of Peace, Give My Regards To Broad Street, Press To Play, Wings Greatest* and *Flowers In the Dirt*.

3 September. Paul and his group begin the fourth leg of their world tour at the Waldbuehne, Berlin, Germany.

5 September. Paul and his group appear at the Stadhalle, Vienna.

6 September. Paul and his group appear at the Stadhalle, Vienna.

7 September. Paul and Ringo are at Abbey Road Studios where they record a special message for 'Cilla – A Celebration', a programme on Cilla Black's career.

9 September. Paul and his group appear at the Olympiahalle, in Munich.

11 September. Paul and his band appear at Earl's Court, London. Backstage, Paul tapes a speech for 'Cilla – A Celebration'.

12 September. The Disney Channel in America screen 'Paul McCartney: Going Home'. They screen further showings of the documentary on 18, 24 and 30 September.

13 September. Paul's son James is swept out to sea near Winchelsea, Sussex when he falls off his surfboard. An RAF helicopter rescues him.

14 September. Paul and his band appear at Earl's Court, London.

15 September. Paul and his band appear at Earl's Court, London.

18 September. Paul and his band appear at the Westfalenhalle in Dortmund, Germany.

19 September. Paul and his band appear at the Westfalenhalle in Dortmund, Germany.

21 September. Paul and his band appear at the Westfalenhalle in Dortmund, Germany.

23 September. Paul and his band appear at the HM Schleyer-Halle in Stuttgart, Germany.

25 September. Paul and his band appear at the Scandinavium in Gothenburg.

27 September. Paul and his band appear at the Spektrum in Oslo.

1 October. Paul and his band appear at the Globen Arena, Stockholm.

2 October. The MTV documentary *Up Close* is screened on local American television stations.

3 October. Paul and his band appear at the Maimarkthalle, Mannheim.
5 October. Paul and his band appear at the HM Schleyer-Halle, in Stuttgart, Germany.
6 October. Paul and his band appear at the Festhalle, Frankfurt, Germany.
8 October. The Brazilian premiere of the *Liverpool Oratorio* takes place at Curitiba.
9 October. Paul and his band appear at the Ahoy Sportpaleis in Rotterdam, Holland
10 October. Paul and his band appear at the Ahoy Sportpaleis in Rotterdam, Holland.
13 October. Paul and his band appear at the Palais Omnisports de Bercy in Paris, France.
14 October. Paul and his band appear at the Palaise Omnisports de Bercy in Paris, France. During the day he makes a personal appearance at the FNAC record store. Whilst in the store he renews acquaintance with Tony Sheridan.
17 October. Paul and his band appear at the Flanders Expo, Ghent.
18 October. The planned concert in Metz, France is cancelled due to the fact that Paul has strained his voice.
20 October. Paul and his band appear at the Zenith in Toulon, France.
22 October. Paul and his band appear at the Palasport in Florence, Italy.
23 October. Paul and his band appear at the Palasport in Florence, Italy.
26 October. Paul and his band appear at the Palau San Jordi in Barcelona, Spain.
27 October. Paul and his band appear at the Palau San Jordi in Barcelona, Spain.
30 October. The MTV show *First Look* on MTV Europe screens the European premiere of the 'Biker Like An Icon' promo.
31 October. MTV repeats *First Look*, with the 'Biker Like An Icon' promo.
1 November. MTV Europe hosts a Beatles Day, which includes a pre-recorded interview with Paul.
4 November. The US Broadcast Music Inc honours 'Yesterday' as the most performed song in history. At this time the song has been covered by 2,500 artists and has received six million plays on American radio and television alone.
12 November. Paul begins the fifth and final leg of his world tour with an appearance at the Tokyo Dome, Japan.
13 November. An alternative version of the 'Biker Like An Icon' promo is screened on MTV in Japan. Channel 4 screen the UK premiere of the Fox TV 'Paul McCartney Live', which was taken from the 5 June concert at Charlotte North Carolina.
14 November. Paul and his group appear at the Tokyo Dome, Japan.

15 November. Paul and his group appear at the Tokyo Dome, Japan. The album *Paul Is Live* is released in Britain. The album *Strawberries Oceans Ships Forest* by the Fireman (Paul and Youth) is released in Britain.

16 November. The album *Paul Is Live* is released in America.

18 November. Paul and his group appear at the Fukuoka Dome, Fukuoka, Japan.

19 November. Paul and his group appear at the Fukuoka Dome, Fukuoka, Japan.

25 November. At a press conference in Mexico City Paul announces that he will be getting together with George Harrison and Ringo Starr in January to work on *The Beatles Anthology*. That evening Paul and his group appear at the Autodromo Hermanos Rodriquez racetrack.

27 November. Paul and his group appear at the Autodromo Hermanos Rodriquez racetrack in Mexico City.

3 December. Paul and his group appear at the Pacaembu Stadium, San Paolo.

5 December. Paul and his group appear at the Paulo Leminski Rock in Curitiba, Brazil.

10 December. Paul and his group appear at the Estadio River Plate, Buenos Aires.

11 December. Paul and his group appear at the Estadio River Plate, Buenos Aires.

12 December. Paul and his group appear at the Estadio River Plate, Buenos Aires.

16 December. Paul and his group appear at the Estadio Nacional, Santiago.

1994

1 January. The *Paul Is Live* concert video is released in Japan.

19 January. Paul makes his induction speech for John Lennon's entry into the 'Rock And Roll Hall Of Fame' during a ceremony at the Waldorf Astoria in New York.

28 January. Paul and Linda attend the premiere of *Wayne's World II* at the Empire, Leicester Square, London and then visit the Hard Rock Café where Mike Myers presents them with a cheque for LIPA for £25,000 from the sale of Linda's vegetarian burgers.

29 January. 'El Especial de Paul McCartney', a 50-minute excerpt from the *Unplugged* show is screened on Channel 5 in Peru.

7 February. An all-star 'Recording Artists Against Drunk Driving' video, with the artists singing 'Drive My Car', featured Paul as the main vocalist when the clip was screened on US TV.

10 February. An interview with Paul appears in *Rolling Stone* magazine.

11 February. Paul, George and Ringo get together at Paul's studio, the Mill, to begin recording 'Free As A Bird'. The 'In Concert' show on American TV, hosted by Dan Marino, features clips from Paul's 'New World' tour.

22 February. Capitol releases Paul's 'Fireman' album in America.

7 March. A feature on Paul and Linda's 25 years of marriage is published in the *Liverpool Echo*.

12 March. Paul receives the Doris Day Award at the Genesis Awards in Century City, California.

21 March. The 85-minute *Paul Is Live* home video is released in Britain.

10 April. The *Sunday Times* estimates Paul's fortune as being £400,000,000.

5 May. Paul, George and Ringo visit a vegetarian restaurant in Chiswick High Road.

11 May. Paul and Linda fly to America to promote Linda's vegetarian foods.

24 May. Mike McCartney appears in a charity concert at the Empire Theatre, Liverpool and sings a new song he has composed, 'You're Never Too Old To Rock And Roll'.

8 June. Paul, George and Ringo, with their wives, return to the vegetarian restaurant in Chiswick High Road, during their discussions about *The Beatles Anthology*.

22 June. Paul, George and Ringo record at George's studio in Henley.

1 August. *People* magazine run a colour photo of Paul in Australia in 1993.

27 September. An art exhibition called 'Little Pieces From Big Stars' opens in Hackney, London. Among the contributions for a charity auction are a wood sculpture by Paul and a photograph by Linda.

28 September. Paul sends a statement to the press conference being held at LIPA in Liverpool, which reads: 'I want this to be the best school of its type in the world. Let's aim high with this, because I'm very optimistic of what we can do here.'

7 October. Linda's press conference on her vegetarian range is filmed and shown on GMTV in Britain on 10 October.

8 October. The German Channel 3 screen an extended version of Paul's 'Live In The New World' concert, which had taken place at Charlotte, North Carolina on 15 June 1993.

3 November. Paul is involved in a car accident, but is unhurt.

13 November. 'Paul McCartney Live' is shown on Channel 4.

21 November. The cast of *Baywatch* appear on the *Geraldo Show* in America. David Hasselhoff announced, 'Paul McCartney will be our next big guest star.' It didn't happen!

3 December. Paul is featured on *Top Of the Pops 2* on BBC 2, with an excerpt from 'Once Upon A Long Ago'.

8 December. The 'Hope Of Deliverance' video is screened on the ITV networked *The Album Show*.

11 December. *Liverpool Suite* is performed at St John's Square, Smith Street, London by the New London Orchestra.

24 December. Fuji Television in Japan air a 90-minute Paul McCartney special, which includes 16 songs.

26 December. MTV Europe repeats a screening of 'Paul McCartney Up Close'.

31 December. The German channel SWF screen 'Movin' On'.

1995

14 January. *McCartney Unplugged* is repeated on Sat-3 in Europe, with German subtitles.

29 January. 'Memories Of 1984' on Sky News shows clips of Paul receiving the freedom of the city in Liverpool, attending the premiere of *Give My Regards To Broad Street* and Linda's drugs bust, which took place that January.

6 February. Paul, George and Ringo begin recording 'Real Love' at Paul's Mill Studios.

7 February. Paul, George and Ringo continue with their recording of 'Real Love'.

12 February. Linda's 'The Sixties' exhibition opens at the Kunsthalle zu Kiel, in Germany and runs until 26 March.

4 March. Paul, Linda and Mary attend a Booksellers Association convention reception at Marc Restaurant in Chicago to promote Linda's latest book *Linda's Kitchen*. They arrive at 6 p.m. in a limousine and shake hands and sign autographs for some of the 200 guests. They leave the reception at 8 p.m. and go to a restaurant called Charley Trotters.

11 March. Paul, Linda and their children record Yoko Ono's 'Hiroshima Sky Is Always Blue' with Yoko and Sean at Paul's home studio in Sussex.

15 March. A press conference promoting LIPA takes place at Planet Hollywood, New York. Paul sends a message: 'I'm sorry I can't be there with you, but I've got the best possible excuse. I'm working in the studio on a couple of tracks from a sixties beat group you may have heard of – called the Beatles. These tracks will be released at the end of this year as a couple of cherries on the cake of the *Beatles Anthology*.'

20 March. Paul, George and Ringo begin work on the track 'Now And Then' at the Mill, but decide to abandon the number.

23 March. Paul appears at the Royal College of Music where 22-year-old Anya Alexeyev premieres his piano piece *A Leaf*. He also performs 'Mistress And Maid' with Elvis Costello and 'For No One' and 'Yesterday' backed by the Brodsky Quartet. Prince Charles is among the 300 attendees.

25 March. 'MTV Unplugged – The Rock And Roll Hall Of Fame Edition' is screened by MTV. This includes acoustic sets from past and present inductees of the Rock And Roll Hall Of Fame and Paul was featured.

29 March. Paul, George and Ringo are in Chiswick, working on *The Beatles Anthology* project.

31 March. A photograph of Paul, George and Ringo together appears on the cover of the *Daily Mirror*. They are referred to as 'The Threetles'.

6 April. Paul and Linda attend the ceremony marking the completion of the new Rye Memorial Care Centre.

24 April. A *Panorama* report on drugs features a clip of Paul from a 1984 interview saying that cannabis was less harmful than alcohol. Paul's piano piece *A Leaf* , played by Russian pianist Anya Alexeyev, is issued in the UK on EMI Classics.

25 April. Linda is at the Amstel Hotel, Amsterdam promoting her line of vegetarian foods.

30 April. Details of Paul's finances are published in the magazine *Night And Day*, which mentions his interests in Apple Corps, Maclen Music and MPL Communications, pointing out that they generated £30 million in 1992 and a further £25 million in 1993. The accounts showed that Paul paid himself £837,000 in 1992 and £310,000 in 1993. During 1993 MPL had a turnover of £14.3 million, with costs of £11.7 million.

1 May. The CD of *Thrillington* is released in Britain.

3 May. James McCartney is airlifted to the Conquest Hospital, Hastings after being rescued by a police helicopter when he breaks his ankle after his Land Rover overturns.

4 May. Together with Steve Miller, Paul records 'Broomstick' at the Mill in Hog Hill.

5 May. Paul and Steve Miller begin recording 'Used To Be Bad' at the Mill.

8 May. David Mirkin, producer of *The Simpsons*, flies to London with the scripts for Paul and Linda's appearance on the show, in order to tape their voices.

11 May. Paul and Steve Miller record 'If You Wanna' at the Mill.

14 May. Paul is listed at No. 20 in the *Sunday Times* annual list of the wealthiest people in Britain, with his fortune quoted as being £420,000,000.

15 May. Paul, George and Ringo are at the Mill, completing 'Real Love'.

17 May. Paul, Linda, son James and Geoff Emerick fly to America to record for a week at Steve Miller's studio in Sun Valley, Idaho.

22 May. Paul and Linda are promoting National Vegetarian Week, with Paul narrating a 'Devour The Earth' video in which he says, 'I am convinced that vegetarianism will become the future way of life. Therefore, I'm very happy and proud that I'm able to participate in it now.'

23 May. Paul and Linda are the subject of a double-page spread in the 'Woman Extra' section of the *Liverpool Echo*. They mention the animals at their home in Sussex – the cows Lavender and Vanessa who had been brought to them when their pregnant mothers were on their way to the slaughterhouse; their flock of sheep; seventeen horses; two deer; a golden pheasant; and three Old English sheepdogs.

24 May. Paul returns from America and appears on the ITV *London Tonight* show in tribute to former British prime minister Harold Wilson who'd died the previous day. He says, 'He was very canny. The

last time we met him, somebody from the press tried to put a microphone in our faces and tried to get us to say something indiscreet with
him. But he put the microphone in his pocket and just carried away
puffing on his pipe. I liked him a lot, he seemed a nice man.'

29 May. The first of the 13-part *Oobu Joobu* series is aired with a two-
hour special by Westwood One and syndicated to stations across
America.

1 June. Steve Miller returns to America.

2 June. Paul begins overdubbing the tapes he has recorded with Steve
Miller at Abbey Road Studios.

4 June. Paul, Linda and Mary attend a reception at the Marc
Restaurant in Chicago for the book *Linda's Kitchen*.

12 June. 23-year-old Stella presents her graduation collection at the
Central St Martin's Design School in London. Paul writes a song,
'Stella', for the soundtrack. Naomi Campbell, Kate Moss and Yasmin
Le Bon model her creations. The *Daily Telegraph* describe it as 'a
strong collection'. Paul, Linda and James are present and Paul says,
'I'm the proudest dad in the world. I thought that it was brilliant, and
Stella has come such a long way since she first started out.'

20 June. The CD of *Thrillington* is issued in America on the EMI
Records Group (North America) label.

22 June. Paul meets producer Chips Chipperfield and director Geoff
Wonfor to discuss the Beatles *Anthology* documentary.

15 July. Paul and Linda lead a march through Rye to celebrate the
opening of the local 16-bed hospital. Paul also appears on a BBC Radio
4 programme 'Remembering Live Aid'.

16 July. Cole Moreton interviews Paul in an *Independent On Sunday*
feature in which he discusses the Rye Memorial Care Centre. He also
mentions the *Anthology* series.

28 July. Paul and Linda visit the site of the Liverpool Institute of
Performing Arts.

6 August. 'Hiroshima Sky', the Yoko Ono number Paul and his family
recorded with Yoko and Sean, receives its world premiere on *Good
Morning Japan* on the Japanese television station NHK.

25 August. The *Liverpool Suite* receives its American debut in
Cleveland.

4 September. Paul, together with Paul Weller, Noel Gallagher and the
Mojo Filters records 'Come Together' at Abbey Road Studios for the
charity album *Help!*

7 September. For the Buddy Holly Tribute Show at the Shepherd's Bush
Empire, London, Paul appears on stage with the Crickets, Bobby Vee
and Carl Perkins.

10 September. Channel 4 screens the documentary on the making of
'Come Together', filmed at Abbey Road Studios on 4 September.

14 September. At Sotheby's auction in London, Paul's handwritten
lyrics to 'Getting Better' sell for £161,000.

2 October. Paul and Linda fly to America to spend a week promoting Linda's new book, *Linda's Kitchen*. Her publishers, Little Brown, comment: 'Linda McCartney is today recognised as one of the most influential vegetarian campaigners. She is determined to persuade more of us to adopt a healthier and more caring way of life by cutting back on the amount of meat in our diet, and ultimately becoming vegetarian.'

3 October. Paul and Linda, on their five-day promotional tour for Linda's range of vegetarian foods, appear in Detroit, Seattle and Los Angeles, with Linda conducting press conferences. An exhibition of Linda's 'Sixties' photographs ends at the Reiss Museum, Mannheim, Germany.

4 October. Linda holds a press conference at the Ritz Carlton in Dearborn, Michigan to discuss her vegetarian foods. Paul is in the audience and is asked, 'What does your husband think of the dinners?' He then joins her on stage. Paul and Linda appear on *Live! With Regis and Kathie Lee* and Linda appears on *Late Night With Conan O'Brien*. Paul's wood sculpture 'Wood One' realises £12,500 at the charity auction held at the Royal College of Art.

7 October. Linda's press conference on her vegetarian range was filmed and shown on GMTV in Britain on 10 October.

11 October. *The Album Show* features a clip from the Abbey Road sessions on 4 September when Paul recorded 'Come Together' with Paul Weller and Noel Gallagher.

15 October. The McCartney episode of *The Simpsons* is shown on Fox TV. Paul reveals to Lisa that if you play 'Maybe I'm Amazed' backwards you will hear a recipe for a really ripping lentil soup. To celebrate World Food Day, People for the Ethical Treatment of Animals distributes Linda's range of vegetarian foods to the homeless in the Farringdon district of London.

16 October. Paul joins poet Allen Ginsberg on the stage of the Royal Albert Hall, London to provide backing for Ginsberg's poem 'The Ballad Of The Skeletons' during the 'Return Of The Forgotten Poetry' event. Only half of the 5,000 seats are filled.

17 October. BBC 1's *Newsroom South* features a clip of Paul backing Allen Ginsberg at the Royal Albert Hall, together with a short interview with Paul. *Help!*, the benefit album for the 'War Child' charity that features Paul, is released.

19 October. The BBC 2 programme *Today's The Day* includes a clip of Paul and Wings at a press conference at Wembley following the end of their 1975/76 tour. Linda's book *Linda's Kitchen* is published in Britain.

24 October. The BBC 2 programme *Today's The Day* includes a clip of Paul from his 'Guinness Book Of Records Investiture' in 1979.

28 October. The *Paul Is Live* special makes its American debut on VH1. In an interview in the *Daily Express*, Paul says, 'There are those who think John *was* the Beatles. That is not true and he would be the first to tell you that.'

2 November. Paul's Grateful Dead film is scheduled for the London Film Festival.

8 November. Paul holds a private viewing of his nine-minute *Grateful Dead – a Photofilm* at the Metro Cinema, Rupert Street, London. Guests include Paul's family and friends. Paul is honoured with the fellowship of the Royal College of Music and is presented with the award by Prince Charles.

10 November. The American TV show *Day and Date* screens the 14 May 1968 interview with Paul and John discussing Apple with journalist Larry Kane.

12 November. The *Sunday Mirror* reports that Paul is angry with his 66-year-old stepmother Angie McCartney because she sold Paul's birth certificate. The birth certificate has actually been sold a couple of times at different auctions.

16 November. *Grateful Dead – a Photofilm* is premiered at the Odeon, Leicester Square as part of the London Film Festival.

19 November. The Beatles *Anthology* series premieres on the ABC network in America.

21 November. The Beatles *Anthology 1* is released worldwide.

26 November. The Beatles *Anthology* documentary series is premiered in Britain on the ITV network.

4 December. The single 'Free As A Bird' is issued in Britain.

7 December. A hospital scan reveals that Linda has a malignant tumour in one of her breasts.

9 December. *The Family Way* soundtrack is reissued on CD in America.

11 December. Linda undergoes surgery at the Princess Grace Hospital, London to remove a lump from her breast. Paul comments, 'We're very optimistic about the future and, for the moment, everything goes on as normal. The doctors have said she will need a couple of months of recuperation – she just needs peace and quiet at the moment.'

1996

8 January. The Liverpool Institute of Performing Arts opens in Liverpool.

30 January. Paul hosts the press launch for LIPA. Guests include his son James, his brother Mike, Gerry Marsden, Neil Aspinall and George Martin.

6 February. Paul and Linda are featured in the Woman Extra supplement of the *Liverpool Echo*.

13 February. A new promo of 'Real Love' is completed.

14 February. The *Sun* newspaper claims that two robbers, now in custody, revealed that there had been a plot to kill Paul.

26 February. Sky Movies screens *Give My Regards To Broad Street*.

4 March. Paul and Ringo appear on BBC 2's *Pebble Mill* discussing 'Real Love', which has been released on this day. It is reported that Paul has turned down an offer on behalf of the three remaining Beatles to tour Europe, Japan and America for £147 million.

9 March. Paul writes an article in the *Daily Mirror* newspaper condemning Radio One's decision not to play 'Real Love'.

18 March. The Beatles *Anthology 2* is released internationally.

13 May. Paul and Ringo work on the number 'Beautiful Night' at Paul's studio at the Mill.

18 May. Paul appears on *The Steve Wright Show* on BBC Radio Two.

7 June. Her Majesty Queen Elizabeth II officially opens LIPA and is shown around the school by Paul, who comments, 'This is a very proud day for me. It's exciting that we have saved this fine old building of my school, and that Her Majesty has taken such an interest in our new school.'

8 June. 'The Fame Game', a documentary about LIPA, is shown on BBC 1.

26 June. Paul visits the site for the forthcoming Prince's Trust Gala at Hyde Park.

29 June. Newspapers anticipate a Beatles reunion at the Prince's Trust Gala and the *Evening Standard* newspaper even prints a headline 'Beatles Lined Up For Hyde Park Surprise'.

23 August. The *Liverpool Echo* publishes an exclusive interview with Paul.

21 September. The 100th performance of the *Liverpool Oratorio* takes place at the Philharmonic Hall, Liverpool, with Paul and Stella in attendance. Geoff Baker, Paul's spokesman, comments, 'The funny thing about it, when it was premiered, one of the critics said it would never travel. It's played 20 countries, 14 states of the US and has travelled 195,504 miles. They ought to call it *Paul McCartney's Peripatetic Oratorio*!'

24 September. Excerpts from an interview with Paul are included on the BBC Radio 2 programme 'The Beatles In Scotland'.

28 September. Paul and Linda's photo film of the Grateful Dead receives its American premiere at the New York Film Festival.

4 October. Abbey Road Studios holds its 65th anniversary party. Paul is unable to attend due to Linda's chemotherapy treatment, but his brother Mike deputises.

6 October. The *Daily Mail* reports on its front page that Linda is in Los Angeles undergoing 'a new intensive course of chemotherapy treatment'. Mike McCartney also confirms the treatment and says, 'She has more stamina than all of us and Paul is there for her.'

11 October. Paul and Linda's Grateful Dead film is shown again at the Angelika Film Center, New York.

22 October. Paul, Linda and Mary attend a private party at Heather's pottery exhibition at Felissimo, New York, where her new range of Tulip, Sunflower and Crocus vases is on display. Each vase is in a numbered box and limited to 100 signed pieces.

28 October. The Beatles *Anthology 3* is released around the world.

7 November. Linda's book *Roadworks* is published by Little Brown.

8 November. Linda's 'Roadworks' photographs exhibition opens at the International Center of Photography in New York. A photograph of Paul is entitled 'My Love'.

9 November. An interview with Linda promoting 'Roadworks' appears in the *Guardian* newspaper.

23 November. Linda's 'Roadworks' photographic exhibition opens at the National Film and Television Museum in Bradford.

24 November. A performance of the *Liverpool Oratorio* takes place at the Sorbonne in Paris.

4 December. A clip of Paul, George and Ringo jamming on 'Blue Moon Of Kentucky' at Friar Park in June 1994 is shown on ABC's *Good Morning America*.

7 December. The *Daily Mail* newspaper publishes profiles of Mary and Stella McCartney.

14 December. Paul and Linda are awarded a Lifetime Achievement Award at the PETA Gala in Hollywood. They send a 45-second acceptance video. The two take turns thanking PETA for the award, with Linda saying, 'You've certainly brightened up my year.' Paul wished everyone peace and love from himself, Linda and the kids and they both added, 'and from the animals'.

16 December. Paul is informed that he will be awarded a knighthood in the next honours' list and he videotapes an acceptance speech.

17 December. Linda appears with Paul for the first time since her cancer scare.

25 December. An interview with Paul is broadcast on London's Talk Radio.

31 December. Paul's knighthood is announced in the New Year's Honours List. Paul is on holiday in America but had been informed a few weeks previously and made a tape of acceptance during a visit to LIPA: 'It's a fantastic honour and I am very gratefully receiving it on behalf of all the people of Liverpool and the other Beatles, without whom it wouldn't have been possible. So I hope I can be worthy of it. I would also like to thank my wife and kids and wish everyone a Happy New Year.'

1997

2 January. RTL, the German TV channel, reports on Paul's knighthood.

8 January. EMI hold a press conference at the Royal Lancaster Hotel, London, during which they announce that there will be a world premiere of Paul's classical work that he is writing to celebrate the EMI centenary at the Royal Albert Hall on 14 October.

9 January. The BBC programme *Watchdog* covers the story of Paul banning the sale of the handwritten lyrics to 'With A Little Help From My Friends', which had been put up for auction by Lily Evans, wife of former Beatle aide Mal Evans. Paul gave *Watchdog* a statement: 'The programme is trying to make the Beatles out to be widow beaters. Nothing could be further from the truth. I would like to meet Mrs

Evans and discuss this and come to some arrangement to see that she is taken care of, and the lyrics are returned.' He added, 'To show how ridiculous this whole memorabilia market has become, there is someone in the US who owns my birth certificate. How people can feel that is right is beyond my comprehension.'

27 January. The *Jornal Do Brasil* reports that Paul is furious about Beatles memorabilia sales in London and Japan.

4 February. Paul donates a portrait of Buddy Holly to an auction at the Saatchi Gallery on behalf of the charity War Child.

14 February. Paul is at Abbey Road Studios for the orchestral overdubs on 'Beautiful Night'.

3 March. Paul is at Abbey Road Studios recording demos for *Standing Stone* with the London Symphony Orchestra and a school choir.

4 March. Paul spends a second day at Abbey Road Studios making demos.

10 March. The *Daily Mail* publishes a feature on Paul under the title 'The Reclusive Beatle'.

11 March. Paul is knighted by Queen Elizabeth II at Buckingham Palace. On the BBC's *6 O'clock News* they erroneously refer to him as 'the man who gave his MBE back'.

13 March. Paul and Linda voice their support for a vigil in memory of the children who were gunned down in Dunblane in 1996. The two send a fax, 'We will be lighting a candle in memory of the beautiful children and their teacher whose lives were so tragically snatched away. Hopefully, in some small way, this will help relieve the pain of their loved ones.'

17 March. In a *Daily Mirror* interview Jane Asher was asked if she was sick of people asking her about Paul. 'No, I get sick of people asking me if I get sick of people asking me about it.'

24 March. Paul is featured in *People* magazine.

2 April. Record retailers are invited to a playback of Paul's *Flaming Pie* album. In the press kit, he states, 'I came off the back of the *Beatles Anthology* with an urge to do some new music. The *Anthology* was very good for me, because it reminded me of the Beatles' standards and the standards that we reached with the songs. So, in a way, it was a refresher course that set the framework for this album.'

4 April. Allen Ginsberg dies at the age of seventy.

5 April. In the *Liverpool Echo*, Glen Campbell says that he cried when he first heard 'Mull Of Kintyre' and comments, 'Playing in Liverpool is a must for me – the home of the Beatles. I'll play "Mull Of Kintyre" in honour of Sir Paul, he is one of the greatest songwriters in the world and Liverpool should be rightly proud of his achievements. His songs such as "Michelle" with that great French verse, "Yesterday" and "Fool On The Hill" are classics.

6 April. Paul features on a pre-recorded interview on Capital Radio during their *Chart Show* and the number 'Young Boy' is aired.

10 April. Paul performs two numbers from *Flaming Pie* on the roof of his MPL building – 'Young Boy' and 'The World Tonight'.

12 April. A promo for 'Young Boy' is made. The *Daily Mirror* publishes a story by Maggie McGivern about her affair with Paul in the 1960s. Stella is made chief designer of Chloe. She comments, 'I felt really honoured, but I was sure I could handle it. I knew Chloe clothes because my mum used to wear them.' An interview with Paul by Thom Duffy appears in the American *Billboard* magazine, where he discusses his new album. Paul also comments, 'I've really started to say to myself, look, what's it been worth to do all that Beatles career, earn all this money, get all that fame, if at some point, I don't go, "That was great, now I can have a good time."'

15 April. International journalists are invited to a press launch for *Flaming Pie* at the Metropolis Studios in Chiswick, London.

18 April. A promo for 'The World Tonight' is made.

19 April. Paul appears on a phone interview for Steve Wright's Radio Two show. Melanie Coe, the inspiration for Paul's song 'She's Leaving Home', appears on the Radio Four programme 'You Probably Think This Song Is About You'.

21 April. VH-I invites viewers from around the world to submit questions for Paul to answer during a forthcoming event at Bishopsgate Town Hall in London. Three million questions are received.

23 April. Stella is featured in the *New York Times*.

25 April. The London edition of *The Times* publishes an interview with Paul.

28 April. The single 'Young Boy' is released in Britain in three different formats. Stella is featured in *Newsweek* magazine.

30 April. The recording sessions for Paul's *Standing Stone* begin at Abbey Road Studios.

1 May. Paul appears on *ITN World News*. Little Brown publishes Linda's book *Linda McCartney's Summer Kitchen*. A pre-recorded interview with Paul is used during various parts of the day on the Sky News channel.

2 May. *The Times* publishes a very critical review of the *Flaming Pie* album.

3 May. Paul's video of 'Young Boy', which had been banned by *Top Of The Pops*, appears on ITV's *The Chart Show*.

4 May. An extended version of Paul's pre-recorded interview, first screened by Sky news on 1 May, is included in the Sky news programme *Newsmakers*. The *Sunday Times* reviews *Flaming Pie*.

5 May. The album *Flaming Pie* is issued in Britain. BBC Radio Two airs a *Flaming Pie* special.

6 May. Robert Katz and Bill Flanagan of VH-I meet Paul at the Mill to discuss the forthcoming meeting at Bishopsgate Town Hall, London, where Paul is to answer questions on the Internet from all around the world.

9 May. The film *Father's Day* opens in America and includes two *Flaming Pie* numbers on the soundtrack – 'The World Tonight' and 'Young Boy'.

11 May. Paul has a look at the forthcoming documentary 'The World Tonight'.

12 May. VH-I begins a week of programmes about Paul and is committed to screening the promo of 'The World Tonight' 25 times during the week.

13 May. 'The World Tonight' documentary is screened at a press launch in London.

14 May. VH-I in America has been running a 'Paul McCartney Week' and screens a one-hour programme, hosted by John Fugelsang, called 'The Paul McCartney Video Collection'. It features ten of Paul's promos. They also screen *Paul Is Live*.

15 May. On the BBC programme *And I Quote*, Paul says, 'I'm a chain saw man. No tree is safe. I apologise to them, though.' VH-I screens *Rockshow*.

16 May. VH-1 in America screens the TV premiere of Paul's documentary under the title 'Paul McCartney In The World Tonight', and also screens 'Wings Over The World'. An interview with Paul appears in the *Daily Telegraph* under the heading 'The Superstar Next Door'.

17 May. Paul is filmed at Bishopsgate Town Hall, London in an interview with John Fugelsand which is screened live by VH-1 in Europe and America under the title 'Paul McCartney's Town Hall Meeting'. Paul also takes part in a netcast. *Flaming Pie* reaches No. 1 in the British album charts. VH-1 in America screens 'Wings Over The World' and *Rockshow*.

18 May. 'The World Tonight' receives its British television premiere on the ITV network.

20 May. The *Flaming Pie* album is issued in America.

22 May. The single 'The World Tonight', a track from the *Flaming Pie* album, is issued in America. In the *Liverpool Echo* Paul reveals he has an exercise book with five or six songs in it. 'It's got "Love Me Do" and four other songs that were never recorded,' he says.

24 May. Radio Two airs a programme on the making of the *Sgt Pepper* album with interviews with Paul, George Martin, Geoff Emerick and Peter Blake. MJI Broadcasting in America begins airing a two-hour special on *Flaming Pie*, which is broadcast on 100 affiliated stations. It was recorded at Paul's studio, features music from the new album in addition to previously unrecorded material, and also has interviews with Ringo Starr, Jeff Lynne and Steve Miller.

27 May. Paul spends the afternoon at Abbey Road Studios where he tapes a one-hour interview for VH-I Europe, which is screened on 18 June.

1 June. Paul becomes 'Artist Of The Month' on VH-1. Paul is the cover star of the June edition of *Q* magazine and is featured inside in an eight-page interview.

16 June. A second promo for 'Young Boy', this time directed by Alastair Donald, is completed.

18 June. VH-1 Europe celebrates Paul's birthday with a selection of programmes on their 'Paul McCartney Day'.

22 June. A one-hour television special on Paul is broadcast on the *Manchete* network in Brazil.

23 June. 'From Rio To Liverpool' is screened on the MCM TV channel in France. A pre-recorded interview with Paul is screened on the programme *In Control* on the Italian TV station RA13.

24 June. Matt Lauer of NBC's *The Today Show* interviews Paul at the Mill for a three-part series. He asks if he should refer to him as Sir Paul. Paul says, 'I prefer "Paul". My dad would have said, "Sir? Do we spell that C-U-R?"'

26 June. Paul rehearses at Riverside Studios, Hammersmith for his appearance on *TFI Friday* the next day.

27 June. Paul appears on the show *TFI Friday*, interviewed by the host Chris Evans and performing 'Flaming Pie' and 'This Boy'. Ringo Starr sends in a question for Paul to answer: 'Who is your favourite Beatle?!'

2 July. Following a suggestion from PETA, Paul and Linda send an autographed copy of *Veganissimo*, a PETA vegetarian cookbook, to Chancellor Kohl of Germany who, along with his wife Hannelore, had just published a book of German recipes *Kulinarische Reise durch Deutsche Lande, A Culinary Tour Of Germany*. Paul and Linda also enclose a letter in which they write, 'Linda and I think PETA's new vegetarian cookbook makes the perfect complement to the Kohl cookbook. After all those heavy, meaty recipes, you may be ready to lighten up in the kitchen. There are more than four million vegetarians in Germany – won't you and your wife be the two newest?'

6 July. On the 40th anniversary of the day when Paul first met John Lennon, a special celebration is held at St Peter's Church Hall in Woolton, Liverpool. Paul sends a special message. Paul pre-records an interview for the *Late Night With Conan O'Brien* show.

7 July. The first of a three-part interview with Paul is featured on NBC's *The Today Show*. The others follow on 8 and 9 July. Paul is also featured in an interview in the *Independent* newspaper discussing *Standing Stone*. He says, '*Liverpool Oratorio* came off the back of my normal music and stretched it a bit. This time, I wanted to go further, to acknowledge in my own way, as best I could, the end of the twentieth century. There's a passage in the narrative, a sea voyage, which takes the form of a kind of Celtic jazz – except that it all goes horribly wrong and the Everyman figure at the centre of the piece finds himself lost at sea. So here it is: my first atonal music. One of my colleagues suggested that I might be putting in for my doctorate with this one!'

'The World Tonight' becomes the second single from the *Flaming Pie* album to be released in America.

10 July. Paul appears on *Late Night With Conan O'Brien* in an interview recorded at the MPL office in London. In America several pretaped interviews are shown on various programmes, including NBC's *Internight*.

30 July. 'Paul McCartney In The World Tonight' is screened on the Veronica TV channel in Holland.

18 August. VH-I features an edited version of the 'Rock For Kampuchea' concert.

22 August. There is a memorial service at Liverpool Town Hall to mark the 30th anniversary of Beatles manager Brian Epstein's death. Paul sends a message, 'Brian was a wonderful man who had an exceptional talent for guiding the careers of young people. I'm eternally grateful for the loving guide that he gave to the Beatles. Brian, your show goes on.'

23 August. The first of a three-part interview with Paul is aired on the weekly American syndicated radio series *Up Close*.

29 August. Chancellor Kohl of Germany replies to Paul regarding his letter about vegetarianism: 'I read the many recipes and ideas with great interest. Cookery, like life in general, depends upon the right balance. As with music, composition is the key.' Paul records 'Kansas City' solo on acoustic guitar.

5 September. Paul visits Derek Taylor at his home. Derek has been a close associate for many years and is dying of cancer. Paul also writes another letter to Chancellor Kohl: 'Thank you very much for sending me your cookbook of favourite recipes. I am afraid it is much too full of meat dishes for our tastes, and we can't help thinking of the unnecessary suffering that must inevitably have taken place for these recipes to reach your plate.'

7 September. Derek Taylor dies and Paul makes the statement: 'He was a beautiful man. It is time for tears and words may follow later.'

10 September. Paul holds his annual Buddy Holly Week lunch at a Mexican restaurant in London, but it is very subdued due to the death of Princess Diana a few weeks earlier. No Buddy Holly numbers are played and Roger McGough reads some poetry.

12 September. Mike McCartney attends the funeral of Derek Taylor. In New York a '*Flaming Pie* Night' is held at Shea Stadium.

14 September. 'In The World Tonight' is shown on the Fox cable channel in Brazil. The *Observer* newspaper begins a three-part serialisation of 'Paul McCartney: Many Years From Now'. Paul and Linda send a bouquet of flowers for the unveiling of a Jimi Hendrix blue plaque in London. Paul once again voices his opinion in the British press that cannabis should be legalised, saying, 'You're filling all the jails and yet it's when you're in jail that you really become a criminal. That's when you learn all the tricks.'

15 September. The Concert For Montserrat, organised by George Martin, is held at the Royal Albert Hall with guests who include Paul, Elton John, Sting, Eric Clapton and Mark Knopfler. The show is

broadcast live by Heart FM. It is also filmed for the pay-to-view Sky Box Office channel and screened on 16, 17, 18 and 19 September.

18 September. Stella McCartney is named Best Young Designer at the *Elle* Style Awards.

23 September. *Paul McCartney's Standing Stone* is released in America on CD and cassette on EMI Classics 7243 556484 26. *Standing Stone* is featured on the American National Public Radio's *Performance Today* programme.

25 September. In an article in the *Sun* newspaper, Paul discusses the Manchester group Oasis.

28 September. Paul, along with Richard Branson, supports the *Independent On Sunday* newspaper's call for cannabis to be made legal.

29 September. *Paul McCartney's Standing Stone* is issued in Britain in a limited edition vinyl LP boxed double album with a gatefold sleeve.

30 September. Photographs from Linda's *Sixties* book are on display at the Museum of the City of San Francisco.

2 October. *Paul McCartney: Many Years From Now* is published in America by Henry Holt and in Britain by Secker & Warburg.

8 October. The home video of 'The World Tonight' is released in Britain. EMI classics release Paul's *Standing Stone* in Britain.

10 October. Paul once again discusses the decriminalisation of cannabis, this time in the *Daily Mirror* saying, 'My own view is that we should decriminalise cannabis – like the authorities have in Holland – rather than legalise it.' In an interview in *USA Today*, Paul says that he hates being called 'sir' and didn't use the stationery with it on that Linda bought, although, 'It's a great honour but I'm intelligent enough to find it easy to be cynical about these things.'

12 October. Paul is interviewed on *Parkinson's Sunday Supplement* programme on BBC Radio Two.

14 October. Paul holds a press conference at the Mayfair Hotel and in the evening the London Symphony Orchestra performs *Standing Stone* at the Royal Albert Hall. Paul meets with Tony Blair, the prime minister, to discuss government help in the funding of LIPA.

15 October. Linda joins Paul and Ringo and Barbara at Stella's first show for Chloe, her 1998 Spring/Summer collection, held in the Grand Salon of the Paris Opera House. Heather, Mary and James are there, along with celebrities such as Kylie Minogue, Naomi Campbell and Meg Matthews. Paul says, 'I loved it. It's so beautiful and elegant. She's a very talented girl.'

16 October. Paul was present at the HMV store in London signing copies of *Flaming Pie* and *Standing Stone* and unveiling a statue of the HMV trademark – Nipper. 2,000 people turned up, some having queued for 24 hours, but only 250 were lucky enough to have one of the albums signed. Paul also received a 'Composer of the Century' Award.

23 October. On the BBC Radio One show *Evening Sessions*, Liam Gallagher of Oasis talks about *Standing Stone*, saying, 'Sitting around

with a bunch of old lesbians writing doesn't sound classical to me. I've written three classic albums.'

27 October. Paul was at Alexandra Palace, London for the *Gramophone* magazine awards and presented the Young Artist Of The Year Award to Isabelle Faust, a German violinist. He also met Luciano Pavarotti and they discussed a possible collaboration. The evening closed with a performance of 'Celebration' from *Standing Stone*.

28 October. Paul performs with a teenage band called Spud in Hackney for the video of 'Beautiful Night'.

4 November. Paul receives a Best Songwriter Award for *Flaming Pie* at the annual *Q* Awards in London. He then walks out on the event as a protest against Phil Spector receiving a special award, allegedly saying, 'He fucked up *Let It Be* and I'm not a man who forgets.'

6 November. Paul and Linda arrive in New York to attend rehearsals for the Carnegie Hall premiere of *Standing Stone*.

17 November. Rehearsals for the *Standing Stone* premiere are held at Riverside Church on New York's West Side.

18 November. Rehearsals for *Standing Stone* continue at the Riverside Church. Rhino Home video issue 'Paul McCartney: In The World Tonight' in America.

19 November. The US live premiere of *Standing Stone* takes place at Carnegie Hall. The concert is performed by the Orchestra of St Luke's, conducted by Lawrence Foster, with the New York Choral Artists, directed by Joseph Flammerfelt. Paul pre-records an interview for NPR, a radio station. The promo for 'Beautiful Night', directed by Julian Temple, is ready for distribution.

20 November. Paul videotapes an appearance on *Oprah*, the Oprah Winfrey chat show, during which he also performs 'Flaming Pie' and 'Young Boy'. The promo for 'Beautiful Night' is also shown, but has been edited.

23 November. The Royal Albert Hall performance of *Standing Stone* is broadcast on the A&E cable network in America.

24 November. A home video version of the Royal Albert Hall performance of *Standing Stone* is issued in Britain.

7 December. Paul appears in a pre-recorded interview on *Breakfast With Frost* on BBC 1.

14 December. Paul's appearance on the *Oprah* chat show is repeated, with additional footage, including that of Paul fielding questions from the studio audience. A promo for 'Little Willow' replaces 'Beautiful Night'.

15 December. 'Beautiful Night' becomes the third single from the *Flaming Pie* album to be issued in Britain. The promo causes controversy due to a nude swimming scene.

17 December. Paul speaks to fans on the Internet, discussing Linda's *Wide Prairie* album and revealing his recipe for mashed potatoes.

23 December. Sky One in Britain screens the *Oprah* show featuring Paul.

25 December. Channel 5 screens Paul's *Standing Stone* concert.

26 December. BBC 1 screens 'The Making Of *Standing Stone*' documentary.

28 December. Channel 5 screens 'Paul McCartney Talks With David Frost', a 58-minute programme.

1998

4 January. *Flaming Pie* is nominated for 'Best Album Of 1997' at the 40th Annual Grammy Awards ceremony, but is beaten by Bob Dylan's *Time Out Of Mind*.

18 January. The *News of the World* reports on two letters Paul and Michael Jackson sent to each other in an attempt to end their 12-year-old feud.

19 January. Carl Perkins dies at the age of 65 in Nashville. Paul's spokesman issues a statement, 'Paul is saddened to hear of Carl's death. They were close friends and had the greatest respect for each other.' Paul also sends a video message to be played at the memorial service.

1 March. Paul contributes a video message, which includes a performance of 'Calico Skies', to the ABC TV special 'Christopher Reeve – A Celebration Of Hope'.

7 March. The *Daily Express*, in a story headlined 'Gangster Hatched £1m Plot To Shoot Sir Paul', relates how Jimmy Phillips intended to have someone wound Paul so that he could fake a rescue and receive a reward. He was found guilty and jailed.

11 March. Paul and Linda are in Paris to attend Stella's latest catwalk show for Chloe, which Stella has dedicated 'to my mum'. Linda tells reporters, 'Right now, I'm feeling great. I'm feeling fit and well and looking forward to having lunch together as a family before we go back to London.'

19 March. Linda and Mary are photographed with the vegetarian cycling team which Linda has sponsored.

15 April. Paul takes Linda riding in Arizona.

17 April. Linda McCartney dies with Paul at her side at their ranch near Tucson, Arizona. The news of her death is kept secret for a few days.

18 April. A pre-recorded item featuring Paul's merging of 'Yesterday' with the Goons' 'Ying Tong Song' is screened during 'Spike Night' on BBC 2 – a tribute to Spike Milligan.

19 April. Paul, with Heather, Mary, Stella and James, scatter Linda's ashes over their Sussex farm and Paul has his spokesman declare that she died in Santa Barbara, California.

20 April. John Eastman, Linda's brother, together with Linda's sisters Laura and Louise, arrive at the McCartneys' farm.

21 April. Paul writes a moving tribute to his late wife.

22 April. The media announce that Linda died in Arizona on the previous Friday and not in Santa Barbara as had previously been announced.

26 April. The Boston Beatles Expo '98 is dedicated to Linda and a special memorial service is organised in her honour.

3 May. BBC 1 repeats the documentary 'Behind The Lens' as a tribute to Linda.

4 May. *People* magazine devotes seven pages to 'Paul's Tragic Loss'.

9 May. Linda is posthumously awarded with the Ellis Island Medal of Honor. This was given by the National Ethnic Coalition of organisations who honour people who have enriched society with their actions or ideas.

22 May. Paul takes out a full-page advertisement in a number of newspapers thanking everyone for their support following Linda's death.

26 May. The *Liverpool Oratorio* is performed in Antwerp, Belgium.

27 May. The *Liverpool Oratorio* is once again performed in Antwerp, Belgium.

28 May. The *Liverpool Oratorio* is performed at the Limburghal, Genk, Belgium. The conductor is Dirk Brosse.

4 June. Linda's photo exhibition 'Wide Open' is held at the Bonni Benrubi Gallery, New York, running until 2 July. It features black-and-white shots of landscapes and still lifes.

8 June. A special memorial service for Linda is held at St Martin in the Fields church in Trafalgar Square, London. Paul, Heather, Mary, Stella and James are in attendance, along with George, Olivia and Dhani Harrison.

18 June. Paul receives a present from his late wife Linda for his 56th birthday. He says, 'She gave me a beautiful box with a picture of the two of us in the lid. It was just a little box to keep things in. She'd planned everything over the last couple of years. She said the sweetest things to the kids – private things to help them through if anything happened.' VH-1 is dedicated to 'Paul McCartney Day' and they include a repeat of an Abbey Road Studios interview with Paul, plus 'Ten Of The Best: Paul McCartney's Greatest Hits' and 'Town Hall Meeting'.

20 June. *Hello* magazine publishes nine pages devoted to Linda's London Memorial Service.

22 June. Linda's American memorial service takes place at the Riverside Church on Riverside Drive, New York. Paul and his family attend (Heather, Mary, Stella, James) and others in attendance include Chrissie Hynde, Twiggy, Laurence Juber, Steve Holly, Neil Young and Paul Simon. Yoko Ono tells *People* magazine, 'Sean and I were not invited. We were a bit hurt, but I know that Paul is dealing with a tragedy as best he can, so he is allowed. We sent flowers for Linda to the memorial.'

20 July. Paul was originally to have appeared at the John Moore's University in Liverpool to be bestowed with an honorary fellowship, but he pulls out of it.

21 July. All TV news bulletins in Britain report on the opening of Paul's former home in Forthlin Road, Liverpool as a National Trust property.

22 July. BBC 2 screens 'The Birthplace Of The Beatles', a documentary about the Forthlin Road house.

30 July. The media reveals that Paul paid Lily Evans, widow of Mal Evans, £100,000 for the handwritten lyrics of 'With A Little Help From My Friends'.

2 August. Paul is featured on the cover of the *People* newspaper.

5 August. Paul discusses Linda's passionate fight for animal rights in interviews with two publications, *Viva Life* and *Animal Times*. He says, 'Animal rights is too good an idea for the next century to be suppressed. I think it's time we got nice.'

8 August. An interview with Paul is featured in the *Daily Express*.

23 August. Paul berates pig farmers in an interview in the *News Of The World*.

9 September. Paul attends the Buddy Holly Week event at the Empire, Leicester Square, but does not perform.

16 September. Paul's original draft lyrics to 'Hey Jude' are sold at Sotheby's sale at the Hard Rock Café for £115,000.

19 September. The *Sun* newspaper announces that Paul is in discussions with Chrissie Hynde to set up a tour as a tribute to Linda.

21 September. *Rushes*, the album Paul made with Youth, using the pseudonym the Fireman, is released in Britain.

22 September. It is announced that Paul has been nominated as an inductee to the 'Rock and Roll Hall of Fame'.

23 September. Radio Merseyside broadcasts a pre-recorded interview with Paul.

24 September. Linda's cookbook *On Tour* is issued on what would have been her 57th birthday.

26 September. Paul attends the wedding of his daughter Mary to Alistair Donald at the church of St Peter and Paul in Peasmarsh, East Sussex. Stella and Heather are bridesmaids.

27 September. The documentary 'Clive James Meets the Supermodels' on ITV includes scenes of Paul, Linda, Ringo and Barbara at Stella's fashion show filmed in October 1997.

2 October. Paul appears on a special live webcast, disguised in a ski mask, answering questions about the Fireman album *Rushes*.

12 October. Linda is honoured with an 'empty chair' tribute at the 43rd 'Woman Of The Year' lunch at the Savoy Hotel, London. Paul sends each of the guests a floral tribute and a message regarding the honour, adding, 'It was a shame us blokes can't go.'

14 October. At her fashion show in Paris, Stella dedicates her latest collection to her mother, saying, "This collection is dedicated to my mum. She was everything. Also, to my dad, brother and sisters, who have kept me strong. Everything. Always. Stella.' She later added further comments about Linda. 'She was incredible. Everyone who met her for even ten minutes thought the same. She was strong, motherly, normal, warm. She had all the right values. People thought that animals thing was just her sympa-

thising with a cute beagle, but it was much more intelligent than that. I'll never meet anyone like her – I just hope I have some of her qualities.'

Paul says of Stella, 'I am very proud of her because she is a serious English designer more than holding her own at the heart of Paris fashion. It is beautiful, just beautiful. It's a credit to the family. Here we are seeing real clothes for real women to look really good in.'

19 October. Paul releases some previously unpublished photographs by Linda, which are featured on the Sky News channel.

20 October. The *Daily Mirror* features the photographs by Linda that Paul has released.

23 October. Sir George Martin was given an 'outstanding achievement' award at the annual dinner of the Music Industry Trust. Guests included Paul, George, Ringo and Prime Minister Tony Blair. Paul says, 'Congratulations on getting the man of the year, man of the minute, the man of the hour, the man for me. Thanks for everything you've done for us all. We love you.' A pre-recorded interview with Paul by Des Lynam is featured on BBC Radio Two.

24 October. BBC 2's *TOTP2* includes the British TV premiere of the animated clip for Linda's 'Wide Prairie'.

26 October. Linda's posthumous album *Wide Prairie* is released simultaneously around the world. A pre-taped interview with Paul is also sent to various TV stations.

30 October. The Fireman Internet website repeats the interview with the Fireman (Paul in disguise).

1 November. An interview with Paul, conducted by Chrissie Hynde, is published in *USA Weekend*.

6 November. The first of a two-part interview with Paul is published in the *Sun* newspaper. He discusses the possibility of playing some benefit concerts in aid of vegetarianism.

7 November. The second part of Paul's interview is published in the *Sun* newspaper in which he discusses Linda's album *Wide Prairie*.

9 November. Linda's single 'Wide Prairie' is released in Britain.

10 November. Linda's single 'Wide Prairie' is released in America. An announcement is made that Paul and George Martin will be inducted into the Rock And Roll Hall of Fame in 1999.

14 November. *Paul McCartney's Liverpool Oratorio* is performed at the Alte Oper Frankfurt in Frankfurt, Germany.

20 November. The Fireman Internet website once again repeats the interview with the Fireman.

25 November. An interview with Paul, conducted by Edna Gundersen, is published in *USA Today*.

29 November. The media announce that Paul's daughter Mary is pregnant.

6 December. The *News of the World* publishes a story that Paul intends to buy Everton football club.

7 December. The media announce that Paul has turned down the chance of buying Everton.

17 December. Paul appears on the Internet for one hour in a show called 'The McCartney Wide Prairie Show'.

1999

7 January. Paul attends a trade fair in Atlanta, Georgia to promote his stepdaughter Heather's new range of Homeware Designs.

25 January. Paul takes advertisements in several newspapers to protest about the banning of Linda's single 'The Light Comes From Within' by the BBC because of some of the strong language in the lyrics.

26 January. Paul contributes an article to the *Sun* newspaper to discuss Linda's single 'The Light Comes From Within'.

27 January. Paul discusses the banning of Linda's single on GMTV and also, by satellite, on *Good Morning America*. He also meets the prime minister's wife, Cherie Blair, to discuss a campaign to fight breast cancer.

30 January. Linda's veggie burgers are given free to supporters of Birmingham City football club.

2 February. VH-I Europe screens an unedited version of Linda's 'The Light Comes From Within'.

4 March. *Paul McCartney's Liverpool Oratorio* is performed at the theatre Royal de Liege in Belgium.

6 March. The Royal Opera Company of Belgium performs *Paul McCartney's Liverpool Oratorio* at the Palais Des-Arts de Charleroi in Belgium.

7 March. Once again the Royal Opera Company of Belgium performs *Paul McCartney's Liverpool Oratorio* at the Palais Des-Arts de Charleroi in Belgium.

10 March. At the 'Freedom For Tibet' rally at Westminster Hall, London, Paul goes on stage to read the lyrics to 'Blackbird'.

13 March. Linda's photographic exhibition 'Sixties: Portrait Of An Era' opens at the Bruce Museum, Greenwich, Connecticut.

15 March. Paul is inducted as a solo artist into the Rock And Roll Hall Of Fame at a ceremony at the Waldorf Astoria in New York. He later attends a party hosted by Bruce Springsteen.

19 March. An announcement that 'Here, There And Everywhere – A Concert For Linda' will take place at the Royal Albert Hall in April results in all tickets being sold within an hour.

20 March. A computer-enhanced version of the 'Helen Wheels' promo receives its first screening on BBC 2's *TOTP2*.

21 March. The German ADF television channel screens a feature on Paul's career in its *Pop Gallerie* series.

22 March. A 25th-anniversary issue of *Band On The Run* is released simultaneously worldwide, with previously unreleased bonus tracks.

31 March. Paul's former house in Forthlin Road, Liverpool is once again open to the public.

2 April. The *Daily Mail* publishes a story that Paul has found a new romance with Sue Timney, a designer.

3 April. Paul becomes a grandfather as his daughter Mary gives birth to a baby boy. A furious Paul gives an interview to the *Sun* newspaper attacking the *Daily Mail* for its story on Sue Timney, which is completely false. 'The story is a pack of lies,' he says.

9 April. Paul is rehearsing at the Royal Albert Hall.

10 April. 'Here, There And Everywhere – A Concert For Linda' takes place at the Royal Albert Hall with a star-studded bill of guest artists. Paul performs 'Lonesome Town', 'All My Loving' and 'Let It Be'.

26 April. The *Sun* newspaper runs a story about Paul's forthcoming art exhibition in Germany.

30 April. Paul holds a press conference in Hamburg, Germany to launch his art exhibition.

1 May. Paul's art exhibition opens at the Kunstforum Lyz Gallery in Siegen, Hamburg.

10 May. Paul, together with Sir Chris Bonnington and David Bellamy, writes an open letter supporting MP Maria Eagles' fur farm prohibition bill.

17 May. The media announce an eight-piece 'Garland for Linda' musical tribute with eight composers contributing, including Paul with 'Nova'.

18 May. The Fox network in America screens the movie *Give My Regards To Broad Street*.

19 May. The Fox network repeats its screening of *Give My Regards To Broad Street*.

20 May. Paul attends the 'Pride Of Britain Awards' at the Dorchester Hotel, London to present the Linda McCartney Award for Animal Welfare to Juliet Gellatley of the Viva animal rights organisation.

6 June. Paul agrees to participate in a campaign by the British Union for the Abolition Of Vivisection.

10 June. Paul holds a press conference in London to discuss genetically modified (GM) foods and to announce that Linda's range of foods were now GM free. He said: 'Sales of Linda McCartney foods dropped after the BBC revealed in February that they contained a tiny trace – 0.5 per cent – of GM soya. The company has now removed soya from its products and has replaced it with wheat for which there is no GM alternative grown.'

11 June. Paul continues his stance against GM foods with an interview in the *Daily Mail* during which he says, 'We have to work out what the dangers of GM foods are before we put them in the public arena. How do we know what we are eating? I've got a grandson and I want him to eat good foods. As far back as 1995, Linda was saying, "I'd rather have my own food grown by Mother Nature than by the chemical industry," and we are sticking to that benchmark.' Paul also pre-tapes an interview of his opinions on GM food for GMTV.

12 June. Paul's pre-recorded interview appears on GMTV and he also talks about Linda and his grandson Arthur.

13 June. An exhibition of Linda's 'Sixties' photographs begins a three-year tour of America when it opens at the Bruce Museum, Greenwich, Connecticut.

16 June. Paul is upset to hear the news that CBS TV will make a mini-series about his life with Linda, based on the Danny Fields biography of Linda. A spokesman comments, 'What man would want to see the memory of his beloved wife cheapened like this? Let's just say Paul *won't* be watching. If the film gets anything badly wrong they can be sure that Paul will not remain silent.'

17 June. Paul's *Give My Regards To Broad Street* is screened in America on the ENC PLEX channel.

18 June. VH-I in Europe celebrate Paul's birthday with another day of programmes which include the film of his New World concert at Charlotte, North Carolina and 'Ten of the Best' and 'Greatest Hits'.

19 June. Linda's 'Sixties' photographic exhibition opens at the Rock And Roll Hall Of Fame in Cleveland, Ohio.

20 June. VH-I Europe screens various clips of Wings.

18 July. A Garland For Linda concert is held at Charterhouse School in Surrey.

7 September. Paul joins the Crickets to perform 'Rave On' at his Buddy Holly Dance Party.

9 September. Paul and Madonna present an award to Lauryn Hill at the MTV Music Video Awards.

18 September. Paul performs at the PETA Millennium Gala at Paramount Studios in Hollywood. The event holds a tribute to Linda.

21 September. Stella McCartney receives the *Elle* magazine award as Best International Designer.

3 October. Paul's *Standing Stone* is performed in Siegen, Germany.

16 October. The London Symphony Orchestra performs *Working Classical*, Paul's latest classical collection, at the Philharmonic Hall, Liverpool.

2 November. Paul performs four numbers live at the BBC Centre, Wood Lane for the programme *Later With Jools Holland*. His backup musicians are Dave Gilmour and Mick Green on guitars, Pete Wingfield on keyboards, Ian Paice on drums and Chris Hall on accordion.

13 November. Paul appears on the *Red Alert for the National Lottery* show, hosted by Lulu.

16 November. Paul appears on Channel 4's *Big Breakfast* show.

18 November. Paul performs 'No Other Baby' on *Music First*, a VH-I programme.

20 November. Paul appears on Sky One's *The Apocalypse Tube* programme.

21 November. The *Sunday People* newspaper reports that Paul will be playing gigs at small venues such as pubs in the New Year.

22 November. Paul attends the world premiere of the latest James Bond film *The World Is Not Enough* at the Odeon, Leicester Square, London.

23 November. Paul attends a press launch for Heather Mills's single 'Vo!ce' on which he plays and provides backing vocals. The event takes place at the IMAX Cinema, London. Stella McCartney tells how she was affected by her mother's death to an audience at the International Breast Cancer conference in Montreaux, Switzerland.

4 December. A Garland For Linda concert is held at the Riverside Church, Riverside Drive in New York.

12 December. Linda's 'Sixties' photographic exhibition opens at the Tampa Museum of Art, Tampa, Florida.

14 December. Paul appears at Liverpool's Cavern Club.

2000

14 January. Paul, Stella and James fly to Havana for the day during their holiday in the Providenciales Islands in the Bahamas.

27 January. The London premiere of 'A Garland For Linda' takes place at St Andrew's church. Paul attends a press conference during the day, along with Sir John Tavener, Roxanna Panufnik, Judith Bingham and David Matthews. In the evening he attends the concert, accompanied by his brother Mike.

1 February. At the *NME* Premier Awards ceremony at the Mermaid Theatre, London, his son James and daughter Mary accompany Paul. On behalf of the Beatles he accepts the 'Best Band In The World Ever' award, saying, 'Can I just say thank you to John, George, Ringo and thank you God.'

5 February. A cameo appearance of Paul appearing on the Pamela Anderson series *VIP* is launched in syndication. The footage of Paul has been taken from the PETA special.

7 February. The album *A Garland For Linda* is issued in Britain.

13 February. The 'A Garland For Linda' concert of 27 January is aired on BBC Radio Three.

14 February. The *Daily Star* newspaper reports that Paul and Heather Mills have spent ten days of a Caribbean holiday at the Parrot Cay resort on the Turks and Caicos Islands, 575 miles southeast of Miami. Initially his daughter Stella had been staying with him at the £8,000-a-week beachside cottage, but Heather joined him when Stella returned to Paris.

18 February. Stella McCartney is named 'Glamour Designer Of The Year' at London's Fashion Week.

21 February. *People* magazine publish photos of Paul and daughter Mary at the *NME* Awards.

1 March. Paul is in Paris to see his daughter Stella unveil her Chloe collection. Sean Lennon also attends and comments, 'I think it's just great how she has managed to carve out her own separate career. She's ever so talented and I'm pleased she has done so well.'

6 March. Paul inducts former Apple artist James Taylor into the Rock 'n' Roll Hall of Fame at the Waldorf Astoria, New York.

10 March. Linda's will is filed for probate at the Manhattan Surrogate's Court, New York.

15 March. Paul admits that he and Heather Mills are an item. He says, 'Yes, we're very good friends. She's a very impressive woman. We've done charity work together and we've grown close. We have been on holiday together and that's it.' He was also to say: 'What we don't need at this stage is photographers lurking in bushes. If this is to develop, then give us a chance. I'm not a politician and we're not spies. I don't want to be surrounded by photographers because that could wreck something.'

19 March. Linda McCartney's first husband Joseph Melville See Jr is found dead.

3 April. Paul and Heather Mills are on the cover of *People* magazine.

6 April. Paul attends Peter Blake's exhibition at Liverpool's Tate Gallery.

15 April. BBC America presents a special Paul McCartney night which includes his appearances on *Parkinson* and *Later With Jools Holland*.

25 April. The album *A Garland For Linda* is issued in America.

27 April. Paul appears at a benefit dinner for the Garland appeal in New York. It raises $150,000.

4 May. Paul appears at a concert by Sir John Tavener at The Church of St Ignatius, New York.

8 May. It is announced that while Paul is in Italy he will visit the ailing George Harrison.

9 May. Paul holds a press conference at the Cannes Film Festival to promote the release of 'Wingspan'. He says that despite the fact that Linda said she was unable to play a musical instrument, 'she made a tremendous difference to the band and quickly learned to play keyboards and harmonise beautifully'.

10 May. The *Daily Mail* publishes a special photo spread on Wings, including some photographs of Paul and Linda that had previously been unpublished.

11 May. Paul and his daughter Stella attend the opening of the Tate Modern in London.

12 May. An early car of Paul's, his 1966 Aston Martin DB6, is put up for auction at Bonham's in London.

19 May. Paul is featured in the *Radio Times* where he airs his comments about the credits to 'Yesterday'. *Paul McCartney's Liverpool Oratorio* is performed at Napier Cathedral, New Zealand by the Napier Civic Choir.

21 May. The CBS drama 'The Linda McCartney Story' is screened in America by CBS with Elizabeth Mitchell as Linda.

23 May. Paul hosts a special edition of *TOTP2* on BBC 2, during which ten promos of his records are screened, with Paul making comments on each of them.

25 May. Paul is honoured with a fellowship at the Ivor Novello Awards in London.

26 May. Paul arrives in Liverpool to conduct a master recording class at LIPA until 30 May.

3 June. The 'A Garland For Linda' concert is performed at the Riverside Church, New York.

4 June. Mary and Stella McCartney meet up with Anoushka Shankar at the Tibetan Peace Garden Appeal in London.

5 June. Virgin issue the *Maybe Baby* soundtrack album in Britain, with Paul's version of the title track.

11 June. Paul signs copies of *Blackbird Singing* at Barnes & Noble's book store in the Rockefeller Center. PBS stations in America screen a Charlie Rose interview with Paul.

12 June. Paul and Heather appear on CNN's *Larry King Live*.

15 June. Paul inducts Brian Wilson at the 31st annual Songwriters Hall of Fame Induction Awards at the Sheraton New York Hotel and Towers.

16 June. A German television station screens the 'Wingspan' documentary.

23 June. Paul acts as chauffeur at his cousin Sally Harris's wedding in Wallasey.

18 July. Capitol releases Peggy Lee's *Rare Gems And Hidden Treasures* collection, with a foreword by Paul: 'She has the power to move the heart and soul quite unlike any other artist. Her music has always given me a thrill.'

4 August. Paul buys a house by auction, situated in East Hampton, Long Island, New York.

6 August. VH-I in America holds a 'Paul McCartney Night'.

10 August. The European VH-I screens an evening themed around Paul, including the PETA awards ceremony and his 'Live at the Cavern' show.

11 August. The *Sun* newspaper reports that Paul has threatened to boycott his favourite restaurant unless it changes its menu, having discovered they were offering ostrich and wild boar. He writes a letter to owner Aldo Zilli: 'I enjoyed my last visit to your wonderful restaurant but was surprised to see that you are now offering wild boar and ostrich. I was wondering if there is so much profit in including these on your menu that you feel you could not consider removing them.'

14 August. The *Daily Mirror* reports that Paul's children, particularly Mary and James, were unhappy about Paul's relationship with Heather Mills.

21 August. *Liverpool Sound Collage*, the music that Paul composed for Peter Blake's Liverpool Tate Gallery exhibition, is released on CD.

3 September. In a *Sunday Times* interview, Paul discusses various topics, including his thoughts about his painting and poetry. Discussing his painting of Queen Elizabeth II, *The Queen After Her First Cigarette*, he says, 'I don't know if she will like it. I don't care, really. It is affectionate. It is not meant to be anti-royalist.' He adds, 'She is often ready with a little joke. The first time I met her was in a Beatles line-up

at a Royal Command Performance, and she said, "Where are you playing tomorrow night?" I said, "Slough, Your Majesty," and she goes, "Oh, just near us."' (Paul was wrong – it was the Queen Mother who said that.)

5 September. Paul arrives at the *GQ* Man Of The Year awards with Heather Mills and controversial artist Tracey Emin.

9 September. In *The Times* newspaper, art critic Brian Sewell confesses he is not impressed by Paul's paintings, saying, 'It's an infuriating tendency amongst clapped-out pop stars to become artists – they usually reproduce unmitigated garbage and should stick to what they were doing. I don't think anyone should move into the visual arts at that age and expect to be taken seriously.' BBC 2 repeats the *Later With Jools Holland* show featuring Paul.

11 September. Paul is in Geneva, Switzerland at a United Nations conference where he calls for a ban on landmines. He urges every country to sign the Ottawa treaty against the use of landmines, saying, 'We want to see an end to the use, manufacture, production, stock-piling and export of landmines. We applaud governments that have already joined. The treaty is a vital step forward. But there is still an urgent need for greater effort to clear mined land and help the victims. Not enough is being done. Too many people are still being killed and maimed, too much land can't be used. Every minute counts.'

12 September. *The Times* publishes a feature on Paul and his activities as a painter, entitled 'My Fear Of Being Branded A Celebrity Painter'. He says, 'When I was in the Beatles and began to be interested in collecting art, meeting artists through my friend Robert Fraser, I still couldn't get around this idea that the likes of me didn't paint on canvas, we were allowed only to paint bits of wood or toilet seats. It was Linda who helped me to get around the problem. When I turned forty she introduced me to the great American painter William de Kooning. It was a great experience to watch him paint and chat about his work. At the end of our visit he said that he'd like to give us a present of one of his paintings and that we should take our pick. Being friends, we didn't want to take one of the big million-dollar jobs, so we selected a small one, which he had framed himself. To me, it looked like a painting of a purple mountain, but, being unsure, I said to de Kooning, "At the risk of appearing gauche Bill, what is it?" And he replied, "I dunno, looks like a couch, huh?" That "huh?" at that moment liberated me. I'd thought his painting looked like a mountain and he thought it looked like a couch – but the fact that he said that it didn't matter was such a liberation. And so, at the age of forty, I grew up and realised that I could paint if I wanted to. It was allowed.'

14 September. Little Brown publishes the book *Paul McCartney, Paintings*.

16 September. The *Daily Telegraph* publishes an interview in which Paul discusses his paintings.

17 September. The *Electronic Telegraph* features a report in which Paul discusses his painting career.

21 September. Jack Douglas, producer of *Double Fantasy* tells the *Liverpool Echo* that John received a phone call from Paul during the *Double Fantasy* sessions. He said: 'From what I heard and from what I heard from John as well, he was looking to get hooked up with Paul before Paul went to Japan to do some writing.'

24 September. Capital Gold airs a pre-recorded interview with Paul.

27 September. Paul and Heather are at Gilda's Club charity photography exhibition at Sotheby's. *Now* magazine reports that Paul claims he still speaks to Linda and says she would have told him, 'If I was there, you'd be dead meat, sucker. But I'm not and I want you to be happy.'

28 September. An exhibition of Paul's paintings opens at the Arnolfini Gallery in Bristol and runs until 1 October. Paul is interviewed on the BBC 2 programme *Newsnight*.

6 October. Paul is nominated in the Lifetime Achievements category of the BBC's People Awards, but the winner is heart surgeon Sir Magdi Yacoub.

8 October. Paul and Heather Mills attend the Castelli Animati Animated Film Festival in Venice where Linda's 'Shadow Cycle' animation receives its world premiere. Paul is the guest of honour.

11 October. Paul is in Paris attending Stella's fashion show.

19 October. Paul holds a netcast to discuss his art and painting.

20 October. Paul presents the 'Designer Of The Year' award to his daughter Stella at the VH-I/*Vogue* fashion awards at Madison Square Garden, New York.

22 October. Heather Mills appears on the 'Stars In Their Lives' TV programme, hosted by Carol Vorderman, during which Paul makes an appearance and publicly declares his love for her.

25 October. *Now* magazine reports that Paul and Heather were romancing in Rome.

27 October. Barbara Walters interviews Heather Mills in ABC TV's *20/20* programme.

2 November. Paul is interviewed on ABC TV's *Prime Time* during his American trip and also attends the opening of his 'Paintings' exhibition at the Matthew Marks Gallery in New York.

11 November. The exhibition of Paul's paintings at the Matthew Marks Gallery ends. Proceeds from the exhibition were donated to the Memorial Sloan-Kettering Centre and the Garland Appeal.

24 November. Prime minister's wife Cherie Blair opens the £4 million Linda McCartney cancer centre at the Royal Liverpool Hospital. A letter from Paul is read in which he writes that he was sorry that he couldn't come to the opening. Mrs Blair says, 'I know it's wonderful for them to know Linda's name lives on in a place so associated with McCartneys.'

26 November. An article discussing Mary McCartney's photography is featured in the *New York Times* magazine.

8 December. ZDF, the German television station, screen the 'Paul Is Dead' film, directed by Hendrik Handloegten. Paul is at Abbey Road Studios.

13 December. Paul holds a signing for his *Paintings* book at Waterstone's in Piccadilly, London. It is his first-ever book signing.

31 December. Samples of Paul's poems dedicated to Linda are published in the *Sunday Times*.

2001

12 January. Paul holds a party for Heather at the Club 10 in London.

21 January. Paul is in India and stays at the Taj Mahal Hotel in Mumbai.

28 January. The *Sunday People* reports that rumours of Paul and Heather marrying in the summer are false. Paul's PR Geoff Baker also has a telephone message on his answering machine: 'If you are calling on that story about Paul marrying Heather, no, it's not true. It's just a flier that has been doing the rounds. So discount that one.'

31 January. The *Daily Mirror* reports Paul as saying, 'Look, I'm not getting married. I am NOT getting married in the same church as Mary. I am NOT going to the Mull of Kintyre or Jamaica for my honeymoon.'

2 February. Paul's 1999 Cavern concert appearance is broadcast on the Norwegian Television channel NRK.

8 February. The *Liverpool Echo* reveals details of the forthcoming signing by Paul of *Blackbird Singing* at the WH Smith Church Street branch.

10 February. The *Daily Mail* begins a week-long series of articles on the contemporary ex-members of the Beatles. The writer considers that Paul, 'far from being the nice Beatle, possesses a monstrous ego and ruthless desire to control others – whatever the cost.'

13 February. A new version of Paul's composition 'Nova', which he recorded with the London Symphony Orchestra, is included on the charity album *Music Of Hope*, proceeds of which go to the American Cancer Society.

21 February. Paul is nominated for 'Best Alternative Music' in the Grammy Award but loses out to Radiohead.

11 March. The annual Paul McCartney Day in Liverpool includes a party at the new Clubmoor Hall, the venue where Paul made his debut with the Quarry Men.

17 March. Mike McCartney's photographs go on display at the National Portrait Gallery, London.

21 March. Paul holds a book signing session for *Blackbird Singing* at WH Smith in Church Street, Liverpool and gives his first public poetry reading at the Everyman Theatre.

23 March. Paul donates a signed lithograph of Linda to the Irish Cancer Society to raise money in an Internet auction. He also contributes a

drawing of a squirrel to the Calvert Trust and Northumbria Wildlife Trust charity, which receives a top bid of £34,000 at auction.

26 March. Paul arrives at Kew Gardens, London to promote sales of scarves based on Linda's design. Proceeds will go to the Millennium Seed Bank Project. He talks to the press in the temperate house at Kew Gardens, discussing the Eco-scarves which were based on photographs Linda took at Kew Gardens in February 1998 for a project to support the Seed Bank Project. There are three designs for the scarves – 'Daisy Chain', 'Loving Memory' and 'Flower'. There is also an exhibition of Linda's work which is to be displayed from 27 March to 16 April 2001.

1 April. The *Sunday Times* runs a feature on Heather Mills and her relationship with Paul, quoting Heather as saying, 'Because I am going out with a very well-known person my reputation has gone down. The association has not been positive. Before I was "Heather the amazing survivor", or "Heather Mills, campaigner", or at least "Heather Mills, model". Now I am just Paul McCartney's girlfriend.'

9 April. The Ian Dury tribute album *Brand New Boots And Panties* is issued, featuring Paul's version of 'I'm Partial To Your Abracadabra'.

10 April. *Hello* magazine features a nine-page illustrated feature on Heather Mills in which she discusses her recent trip to India in March. Heather says, 'It was a terrific shock the day we arrived home to hear about the Gujarat earthquake. It was so close to where Paul and I had been. I just couldn't believe it had happened and my immediate instinct was to get back there straight away, because I knew that where there were earthquakes there were always amputees.'

19 April. Paul and Heather Mills meet US Secretary of State Colin Powell. They then appear on the CNN show *Inside Politics* and are honoured in New York for their work with the Adopt-A-Minefield charity.

20 April. Paul and Linda remain in New York to raise funds for the Adopt-A-Minefield campaign.

22 April. The *Sunday Express* features an interview with Paul. When chatting about Heather, he says, 'She's more Wings. She didn't hear much Beatles stuff when she was growing up. She had a strange childhood, involving all sorts of deprivation and stuff, so she didn't have much chance to hear the music then. But now, having heard quite a bit of it, she likes the Wings stuff. It's a generational thing and I like that layering of generations. It's great to me to realise that I've spanned quite a few – and now with the Beatles *1*, it's come full circle. People say to me, "You know, my eight-year-old son loves you".'

24 April. Paul appears on Charlie Rose's chat show at the YM-YWMA on 92nd Street in Manhattan New York.

25 April. Paul hosts the American radio show *Rockline*, during which listeners phoned in to ask him questions.

3 May. The *New York Times* runs an interview with Paul and also reports

on his poetry reading appearance at the 92nd Street YM-YWMA in Manhattan on 24 April. There was a teenage girl in the crowd who wore a button reading, 'I slept with Paul McCartney'. When he saw it, an amused Paul commented, 'Oh, really. When was that?'

7 May. *Wingspan* is issued in Britain. Paul attends a signing session in the Adagio Club, Marlene Dietrich Platz, Berlin, Germany, where he is promoting *Wingspan*. Following a press conference he signs autographs in the foyer of the Stella Musical Theatre.

8 May. *Wingspan* is issued in America. Paul attends a signing session in Milan, Italy. An interview with Paul is broadcast on Simon Mayo's BBC Radio Five Live show.

9 May. Paul attends a signing session in Cannes, France and tells the press conference, 'There is a good chance I will get married in the future. But that is a decision we will make in private and only then will we make it public.' In America the *Rockline* radio show with Paul answering questions from listeners is repeated. Michael Jackson makes an official statement that he will not sell the Beatles catalogue. 'I want to clarify a silly rumour: the Beatles catalogue is not for sale, has not been for sale, and never will be for sale.'

11 May. 'Wingspan: The Story Of Wings', the documentary, receives its world premiere on television when it is screened by ABC TV in America. Paul was originally due to appear on Chris Evans' Virgin breakfast show but declines due to the show being sponsored by McDonald's. Paul's spokesman Geoff Baker said: 'It doesn't take a genius to work out that McCartney and McDonald's don't mix. We don't sleep with the enemy so we're certainly not going to wake up with them on a breakfast show.' An interview with Paul discussing his *Blackbird Singing* book is published in the *Observer* newspaper.

18 May. Paul holds an on-line chat on the Internet on his www.paulmccartney.com website.

19 May. 'Wingspan' is televised in Britain.

23 May. Paul presents a 45-minute BBC 2 *TOTP2* show special on Wings, introducing several of the promo clips.

30 May. Paul appears at the Hay Festival Of Literature and the Arts at Hay-on-Wye and performs a reading from *Blackbird Singing* in the Gerrard Marquee before an audience of 1500. He recites the poems 'In Liverpool', 'Dinner Tickets', 'Ivan', 'Jerk Of All Jerks', 'Masseuse Masseuse', 'Chasing The Cherry', 'City Park', 'Trouble Is', 'A Billion Bees In The Borage', 'Anti Alarm Call', 'Black Jacket' and 'Her Spirit'. Song lyrics included 'Here Today', 'Eleanor Rigby', 'Maxwell's Silver Hammer' and 'Why Don't We Do It In The Road'. Stella appears at the BP Lecture Theatre at the British Museum to lecture about her life and work in 'An Evening With Stella McCartney'.

2 June. The *Sunday People* newspaper reports that Paul and Heather Mills have been visiting Ireland to trace relatives of his mother. Paul said: 'I really want to trace my mother's family. I don't know why it has

taken me so long. She was a lovely Irish lady. I've always wanted to look them up, but I've never got round to it before.'

4 June. Paul and Heather launch the British branch of the 'Adopt-A-Minefield' charity at the Marion Richardson Primary School in Stepney, London.

12 June. Paul and Heather appear on the CNN show *Larry King Live*. Paul is initially interviewed and is then joined by Heather who discusses her campaign against landmines.

13 June. Paul makes a guest appearance at the Paul Simon, Brian Wilson concert at the Greek Theater, Los Angeles. When Paul enters the theatre, Wilson introduces him to the audience and says that the next song is one of Paul's favourite numbers – 'God Only Knows'. Paul later appears on stage with Paul Simon and they sing 'I've Just Seen A Face'.

14 June. Paul and Heather Mills attend the Adopt-A-Minefield charity gala at the Beverly Wilshire Hotel, Los Angeles.

17 June. The *Mail On Sunday* quotes Paul as saying 'I don't worry because the moment the man upstairs wants me, I'm his.'

19 June. 'Paul McCartney: Live at The Cavern' is issued on video. The 63-minute tape features the concert, together with two music videos, 'No Other Baby' and 'Brown Eyed Handsome Man', and a 20-minute interview. Roy Harper's compilation album *Hats Off* is issued by the Right Stuff (72435-27640-2/0) and contains the backing track of Paul and Linda singing on 'One Of Those Days' which was originally included on Harper's 1977 album *Bullinamingvase*.

20 June. The 'Wingspan' documentary is screened on RTLA, the Dutch television station.

23 June. *Paul McCartney's Liverpool Oratorio* is performed at the Silesian Music Festival in the Czech Republic.

25 June. Paul's return to the Cavern on 14 December 1999 is released on video.

7 July. Paul hosts a party at his Cavendish Avenue house with guests including Lulu, Chrissie Hynde, Peter Blake, Twiggy, Dave Gilmour and Kevin Godley.

13 July. Paul and Heather Mills attend the Institute of Directors annual dinner at Winchester Guildhall, Hampshire, where Heather was a guest speaker.

20 July. Paul attends the graduation ceremony at LIPA in Liverpool.

23 July. Paul proposes marriage to Heather Mills at the Sharrow Bay Hotel in the Lake District, and she accepts.

26 July. Paul and Heather announce their engagement to the media outside the Cavendish Avenue house. Paul says, 'We are standing here for the cameras and we are very happy. We will get married sometime next year. When I proposed I was a bit nervous but I managed. We've had a good reception from relatives and friends and from the media.' Heather said she would not take up the title Lady McCartney, 'I am not into all that pretence.'

4 August. 'Saturday Night Live Remembers Chris Farley' includes a sketch with Paul.

9 August. Paul and Heather visit the Book Soup bookstore on Sunset Boulevard in Hollywood and dine at the Ago Restaurant in West Hollywood, which is owned by Robert de Niro and Christopher Walken. VH-I screens Paul's film 'Live At The Cavern'.

10 August. *OK* magazine devotes a six-page feature to Paul and Heather's engagement.

12 August. Paul and Heather dine at the Earth Café on Melrose Avenue, Hollywood.

19 August. Paul and Heather visit Snug Harbour, the New Orleans Jazz Club.

3 September. Paul and Heather attend The Garage in London to see Denzel, a group in which Heather's cousin is a member.

4 September. Paul and Heather arrive in Venice for the premiere of *Tuesday*.

7 September. The episode of *The Simpsons* featuring Paul and Linda is repeated on BBC 2.

8 September. Paul presents the Linda McCartney Memorial Award to Chrissie Hynde at a PETA 21st Anniversary And Humanitarian Awards event at the Waldorf Astoria in New York.

9 September. Paul and Heather watch the men's singles tennis final at Flushing Meadow, New York, between Pete Sampras and Lleyton Hewitt.

10 September. Paul and Heather attend the 'Movers And Shakers Awards' in New York, which are presented by Hillary Clinton. Heather is one of the award winners. Paul and Heather also appear on the *Today* show.

11 September. Paul and Heather are due to fly back to London when a horrific terrorist attack destroys the World Trade Center. Soon after the tragic events, Paul makes a statement.

20 September. Paul and Heather take a cab to visit 'ground zero' in New York and he announces his charity concert. Paul says, 'America saved Europe in World War II and Britain is behind the US one hundred per cent.'

4 October. Paul reads from *Blackbird Singing* at the National Poetry Marathon at the Queens Theatre, Shaftesbury Avenue, London on National Poetry Day.

8 October. Paul, Heather Mills and Chrissie Hynde attend Stella's latest fashion show in Paris.

11 October. Paul and Heather attend Yankee Stadium in New York for the baseball game between the Yankees and Oakland Athletics.

15 October. Paul and Heather are involved in a car collision in East Hampton, Long Island, but neither require hospital treatment.

16 October. The album *Good Rockin' Tonight (The Legacy Of Sun Records)*, on which Paul sings 'That's Alright Mama', is released in America.

18 October. Paul appears on the *Howard Stern Show* and among the subjects discussed are Paul's disagreements with Yoko Ono and Michael Jackson. Stern plays two songs from Paul's *Driving Rain* album, 'From A Lover To A Friend' and 'Lonely Road'.

19 October. Paul hands out tickets for 'The Concert For New York' at two Manhattan fire stations, the Ladder Company 55 on Broome Street and Ladder Company 6 on Canal Street. Paul comments, 'We found out that some of the guys here didn't have tickets. This concert is happening to honour brave guys like these, so when Heather told me they didn't have tickets, I thought, "Well, we've got to fix that, haven't we."' He appears on MTV's 'Remember'/'Rebuild' show.

20 October. Paul performs 'Freedom' at the 'Concert For New York' at Madison Square Gardens. The show is screened on VH-I, which had its highest-ever audience of 16 million viewers.

21 October. Paul and Heather attend the Yankee Stadium to see the New York Yankees and the Seattle Mariners.

24 October. Dan Rather interviews Paul for the *60 Minutes* TV show. The *Jonathan Ross Friday Night Chat Show* is repeated.

30 October. Image Entertainment releases 'Paul McCartney & Friends: The PETA Concert For Party Animals' on video and DVD.

1 November. Paul and Heather attend the launch of a partnership between the Adopt-A-Minefield charity and the Mines Advisory Group.

3 November. Paul receives the World Arts Award from the International Jury of Men's World Day at the Hofburg Palace in Vienna, Austria. The Ardent Productions documentary *Paul McCartney* is shown on the Biography Channel.

4 November. VH-I screens the six-hour 'Concert For New York'.

6 November. The Cavern Club in Liverpool holds a playback evening for *Driving Rain*, and also features a tribute to Paul by Bob Bartley.

7 November. Paul is seen buying jazz records at a collectors' shop near to the MPL office in London.

10 November. Paul and Heather attend the premiere of Paul's new classical work *Ecce Cor Meum* at Magdalen College, Oxford.

12 November. Paul's album *Driving Rain* is released in Britain.

13 November. *Driving Rain* is released in America. The 'Wingspan' video and DVD is released in America. The DVD contains additional footage not included in the original documentary. There are vintage videos of 'Jet' from 1973, 'Let 'Em In' from 1976 and 'Rockestra' from 1979. There are 22 minutes of out-take material not seen by the public before, a gallery of 100 of Linda's photographs and a specially designed complete interactive discography.

16 November. TV France 2 screened an edited version of 'The Concert For New York' lasting two hours.

19 November. The *News Of The World* prints the story of Paul's attempt to rescue Hound Cottage Animal Sanctuary under the heading 'Macca Rescues Animal Sanctuary'.

20 November. Paul appears on Capital Gold to promote his *Driving Rain* album. 'Wingspan' is released on video and DVD in Britain.

21 November. Paul appears on *GMTV* to promote his *Driving Rain* album.

23 November. Paul appears on *Top Of The Pops* for the first time since 1993. He also appears on *Friday Night with Jonathan Ross* the same evening.

24 November. Paul appears on the Saturday morning children's TV show *CD-UK* performing 'Freedom'.

25 November. Penny Smith interviews Paul for the TV programme *GMTV* and in the evening Paul gives a poetry recital at the University of East Anglia.

28 November. The 'Freedom' video is screened on *Top Of The Pops*. The television documentary 'Good Rockin' Tonight: The Legacy Of Sun Records', which also features Paul, is screened.

29 November. The tragic death from cancer of George Harrison. Linda's photographic exhibition 'The Light From Within' opens at the Bonne Benrubi Gallery in New York. It runs until 5 January 2002.

30 November. Paul was due to appear at the '*Top Of The Pops* Awards' to become the first entrant in the 'Top Of The Pops Hall Of Fame.' He decides not to attend due to the death of George Harrison, although a message from him is read out in his absence.

1 December. The 'Freedom' video is shown on *Top Of The Pops* again.

2 December. Paul and Heather attend Madison Square Garden in New York City to view the New York Knicks game.

7 December. Paul and Heather attend the memorial service for Desmond Wilcox at St Martin's Church in London.

8 December. Paul records at Abbey Road Studios.

11 December. At the Nobel Concert in Oslo, Paul performs 'Your Loving Flame', 'Freedom' and 'Let It Be'.

13 December. Paul attends a signing for his book *Paintings* at Waterstones in Piccadilly, London. He is also interviewed on Radio One during which he performs 'Freedom', with accompaniment from disc jockeys Marc Riley on guitar and Mark Radcliffe on drums.

14 December. Paul and Heather arrive in Dresden, Germany and appear on the television programme *Wetten Dass* . . .

26 December. Paul sends an open letter to Prime Minister Tony Blair requesting a vote on the banning of fox hunting.

2002

1 January. Paul and Heather are in Merseyside and are seen shopping in Heswall.

11 January. Paul is joint winner of the 'best song' award at the Critics Choice Awards in Beverly Hills, California for 'Vanilla Sky'.

12 January. Paul and Heather celebrate her birthday during their holiday in India at the Coconut Lagoon, Kumarakom.

18 January. At the celebrity auction 'Hands Up For Hedgehogs', Paul's drawing of a hedgehog, donated in aid of the British Wildlife Fund, is sold for £3,012.

22 January. Paul attends Brian Wilson's concert at the Royal Festival Hall, London.

24 January. Linda's exhibition 'The Light From Within' opens at Hackelbury Fine Art, London and runs until 1 February 2002.

25 January. The George Harrison tribute 'All Things Must Pass' on the French Canal channel includes an interview with Paul.

27 January. Linda's 'Sixties' photographic exhibition opens at the Manitoba Museum of Man and Nature in Winnipeg, Canada and runs until 30 March 2002.

28 January. Prior to receiving his Lifetime Achievement Award in New York, Paul, together with Heather and her sister Fiona, attend a reception at Chateau in Greenwich Village where Heather is to launch her modelling career for INC International Concepts. Heather appears on the TV shows *Good Morning America* and *The View*. Paul receives his award from Amnesty International.

29 January. Heather Mills appears on the TV show *Entertainment Tonight* in which she says that rumours that she and Paul were to marry at Skibo Castle in Scotland were untrue. 'If you always listen to rumours, you've got a lot to learn,' she says.

3 February. Paul and Heather attend Super Bowl XXXVI and at the pre-game show he performs 'Freedom'.

13 February. Paul is among the guests at Sir Richard Branson's party in honour of former New York Mayor Rudy Giuliani, to celebrate his honorary knighthood. The reception is held at the Kensington Roof Garden, London.

14 February. It is announced that Paul's composition 'Eleanor Rigby' is to be inducted into the Recording Academy Hall of Fame.

20 February. Paul and Heather visit Dublin for a day during which Heather is guest speaker at a disability conference at Dublin Castle.

23 February. Paul takes Heather to visit his old home in Forthlin Road, but although he knocks on the door, no one is in to show them around.

24 February. Paul attends the George Harrison tribute concert at the Empire Theatre, Liverpool and performs an a cappella version of 'Yesterday'.

6 March. *Paul McCartney's Liverpool Oratorio* is performed in Switzerland

7 March. Paul is interviewed by satellite on NBC's *Today* show, discussing the death of George, his Oscar nomination for 'Vanilla Sky', his forthcoming American tour and upcoming wedding to Heather Mills.

11 March. Paul and Heather Mills attend Stella's latest fashion show at the Beaux Arts School in Paris.

12 March. *Paul McCartney's Liverpool Oratorio* receives another performance in Switzerland.

21 March. *Paul McCartney's Liverpool Oratorio* is performed at Ruhr University, Bochum, Germany by the Bochumer Symphoniker.

24 March. Paul performs 'Vanilla Sky', a nominated song, at the 74th Academy Awards ceremony in Los Angeles. It is his performance debut at the Oscars, although the song fails to win. Paul is pleased that the Best Song Oscar goes to Randy Newman and says, 'If I had to lose to anyone, Randy was the man because he has been nominated sixteen times. He's a great guy and I am a big fan of his anyway. This year, with what happened in America, I think maybe it was kind of important that a lot of Americans won. And you know I don't blame them, I wouldn't take that away from them. If I was an American voting, which most of the voters were, it is the year for America and why not?'

24 March. An exhibition of Paul's paintings opens at the Walker Art Gallery, Liverpool and runs until 4 August.

25 March. Paul launches a new radio station 'Real Radio'. When the Yorkshire station goes on the air, Paul's voice is the first to be heard. John Myers, a company executive, comments, 'There is something for everyone in our schedule, but above all, the station will have a real sense of fun that doesn't exist elsewhere on the airwaves. Entertainment is what brings listeners to Real Radio in droves and to have a legend such as Sir Paul McCartney launch the station for us is the icing on the cake.'

29 March. *Standing Stone* is performed in Lucerne, Switzerland by the Handel Chor Luzern and the Luzerner Sinfonieorchester.

1 April. Paul appears at the Oakland Arena, Oakland.

3 April. Paul appears at the San Jose Arena, San Jose. In the audience is Graham Nash, former member of the Hollies and a member of Crosby, Stills, Nash and Young, who are to appear at the venue later that week.

6 April. Paul becomes the highest paid British artist of all time when he appears at the MGM Grand in Las Vegas for a fee of $4 million. Celebrities who are in the audience include Tony Curtis, Alice Cooper, Roger Daltrey and Tony Orlando.

7 April. *Paul McCartney's Liverpool Oratorio* is performed in Bielfeld, Germany.

8 April. Paul and Heather Mills appear at the Center For International Rehabilitation awards dinner in Chicago, where Heather is honoured.

9 April. Paul appears on *Entertainment Tonight*.

10 April. Following his appearance at the United Center, Chicago, Paul is visited backstage by George Harrison's sister Louise.

12 April. Paul appears on *E! News Live*.

13 April. Paul appears at the Air Canada Center, Toronto, Canada. 'Mull Of Kintyre' is included in his set and the Peel Regional Police Pipe Band backs him.

16 April. Paul appears at the First Union Center, Philadelphia. Prior to the concert Paul and Heather have a three-hour session at a spa,

including haircuts, facials, manicures, pedicures, massages and yogic deep-breathing sessions. *Hello!* magazine features an article on the *Driving Rain* tour.

17 April. Paul appears at the Continental Arena, Rutherford.

19 April. Paul appears at the Fleet Center, Boston.

20 April. 'Sixties: Portrait Of an Era', Linda's photographic exhibition, opens at the Dayton Art Institute, Dayton, Ohio and runs until 23 June.

21 April. Paul and Stella are featured on the cover of the *Sunday Times* magazine.

22 April. *People* magazine devotes three pages to the *Driving Rain* tour. Stella attends 'Viva Glam IV' at the Criterion Theatre in London. Proceeds from the fundraising benefit go to M.A.C. AIDS Fund Campaign.

23 April. Paul appears at the MCI Center, Washington.

25 April. Paul appears on *Access Hollywood* and NBC's *Today*.

26 April. At the Madison Square Garden Concert, the CityKids Foundation join Paul on stage. They were the youngsters who designed the backdrop that was issued for his performance of 'Freedom'. Paul's daughter Stella and his brother-in-law John Eastman also attend the concert.

27 April. Paul's brother Mike attends the Madison Square Garden Concert.

29 April. Paul appears at Gund Arena, Cleveland. The appearance on *Access Hollywood* is screened again.

1 May. Paul appears at the Palace at Auburn Hills, Detroit. The *Daily Mail* features a two-page story alleging that Paul's children were against his forthcoming marriage to Heather Mills. It says that Paul had originally hoped that Stella would design Heather's wedding dress, Mary would take the wedding photographs and James would play music at the event – but it was not to be.

2 May. Paul and Heather tape *The Tonight Show With Jay Leno*.

3 May. *The Tonight Show With Jay Leno*, which Paul and Heather had taped the previous evening, is screened. Paul originally intended to perform two songs, but had a sore throat and didn't want to aggravate it prior to his next concert. The show includes the network television premiere of 'Your Loving Flame'.

4 May. At Paul's concert at the Staples Center, Los Angeles, Geoff Emerick, Jeff Lynne and the former Wings drummer Denny Seiwell are in attendance, along with Tom Cruise and Penelope Cruise, John Cusack, Cameron Crowe, Mickie Dolenz, Ted Danson, Jack Nicholson, Sylvester and Frank Stallone, Paul Stanley and Gene Simmons of Kiss and Brian Wilson.

5 May. At Paul's concert at the Pond, Anahein, the former Wings guitarist Laurence Juber is in attendance.

7 May. Paul appears at the Pepsi Arena, Denver.

9 May. Paul participates in an online event, 'MSM Chat'. At his concert at the Reunion Arena, Dallas, that evening, George Martin is in attendance.

12 May. Paul participates in a jam session with apes at the Language Research Facility in Atlanta, Georgia. In the evening, following his concert at the Philips Arena, Paul performs a set on piano in the lounge of the Four Seasons Hotel.

15 May. Paul appears at the Ice Palace, Tampa. Lulu's new album, which includes her duet with Paul on 'Let 'Em In', is released.

18 May. The 'Driving USA' tour ends in Fort Lauderdale and Paul and Heather host an end-of-tour party at the house in Biscayne Bay, where they have been staying.

21 May. Paul is in a video production studio in London working on a DVD of his *Driving Rain* tour.

22 May. Paul is at the Walker Art Gallery in Liverpool inspecting the exhibition of his paintings. There are seventy paintings and photos and six sculptures. They included *Hottest Linda*, a 1992 nude in acrylic on canvas, the inkjet printings of *My Eye* and *Larry King 2* and the driftwood sculptures *Running Legs With Penis*, *Large Cheetah*, *African Bust* and *Small Cheetah*. Peter Blake is also in attendance and Paul returns to the gallery in the evening for a two-hour reception.

23 May. *The Art of Paul McCartney*, an exhibition, opens at the Walker Art Gallery in Liverpool, with Paul and Heather in attendance.

24 May. Public Radio International interviews Paul for its show *World Café*. The *Daily Mail* publishes the opinions of three critics on Paul's exhibition paintings. John Monks comments: 'I found his paintings more interesting than I thought, as there is a genuine quality that ultimately prevents any sense of pretension or concoction.' Dave Lee says: 'McCartney is potentially better than a chancer. He has promise. This said, none of these pictures is on any artistic merit.' Robin Simon writes: 'Stick to the day job, Macca. That is the message of these wholly talentless daubs. Perhaps endless adulation has made McCartney deaf to the voice of criticism.'

28 May. The Ardent documentary *McCartney On McCartney* is screened by Channel 5.

1 June. Heather Mills begins presenting 'Diana Forever', a season by BBC America, running from June to August, which honours Princess Diana. It begins on this date with 'Diana: Story Of A Princess'. Paul's 60th birthday is celebrated by a new series about him on the BBC World Service.

2 June. The BBC screens the one-hour documentary, *There's Only One Paul McCartney*.

3 June. Paul is among the performers at the Golden Jubilee Concert for the Queen in the grounds of Buckingham Palace, during which Eric Clapton joins him for a duet on 'While My Guitar Gently Weeps' in tribute to George Harrison. Paul also leads a host of artists in a singalong of 'All You Need Is Love'.

5 June. Paul and Heather attend Brian Wilson's concert at the Brighton Centre. They spend half an hour with him backstage following his performance.

8 June. BBC America begin two evenings of programmes to celebrate Paul's forthcoming 60th birthday, called 'Paul McCartney Forever'. They include 'Here There And Everywhere: A Concert For Linda', which had been recorded on 10 April 1999 at the Royal Albert Hall, London, and *Later With Jools Holland*.

9 June. VH-I screens 'The Queen's Jubilee: Party At The Palace' in which Paul appears. BBC America continue their tribute to Paul with his 1999 appearance on *Parkinson* and 'Live At The Cavern'.

10 June. A new album *The Very Best Of MTV Unplugged* is released in Britain, which includes Paul performing 'Every Night'.

11 June. Paul and Heather are married at Castle Leslie in Ireland.

14 June. Linda's exhibition 'The Sixties' opens at the Ella Sharp Museum in Jackson, Michigan and runs until 14 September 2002.

15 June. To celebrate Paul's forthcoming 60th birthday, a 'Paul McCartney Day' is held in Liverpool.

18 June. BBC World Service interviews Paul, who comments that he never imagined he would be famous for forty years.

24 June. The *Party At The Palace* album is released by EMI in conjunction with the BBC. Various charities nominated by the Queen are to be the beneficiaries.

27 June. PETA (People for the Ethical Treatment of Animals) issue a copy of a letter that Paul sent to the top one hundred shareholders of McDonald's, asking them to encourage the fast-food chain to extend its standards. It reads: 'Although McDonald's had made laudable efforts on behalf of farmed animals in the United States and the United Kingdom, it now needs to do the same in other countries. Abuse is abuse, whether it goes on in Sussex or San Salvador, Toronto or Tijuana.'

29 June. Linda's 'Sixties' exhibition opens at the Southern Vermont Art Center, Manchester, Vermont and runs until 24 August.

1 July. The Isle of Man has requested that Paul design a series of six stamps for them based on simple floral designs. A hundred and seventy thousand of the stamps are issued today and money raised will go to the Adopt-A-Minefield charity.

2 July. Paul and Heather dine at Paul's favourite vegetarian restaurant, Manna, in Primrose Hill, London. Their meal comprises organic brie and leek strudel and a tarte tatin.

4 July. Paul and Heather make their first public appearance since their wedding at Carlton TV's *Britain's Brilliant Prodigies*. Paul presents a prize to the Best Young Pop Singer and Heather to the Young Person Who Made a Difference. The press ask Paul if he is going to have any more children and he says: 'Oh, here we go, the British press. I mean, Jesus, isn't that so typical? I think we can nix that question and try to get on with what we are here for, which is Sarah's charity and the

charity work done.' Heather's friend Sarah, the Duchess of York, had invited the couple to present awards.

7 July. Paul and Heather attend the men's singles final at Wimbledon.

11 July. Paul is spotted in Union Square, New York. *Entertainment Tonight* includes a brief clip of Paul from his AOL interview. Hamish Stuart, former sideman in Paul's band, appears at the Cavern in Liverpool with his band.

15 July. *US Weekly* reports that there is a feud between Heather Mills McCartney and Paul's children.

16 July. Paul officially announces the resumption of his American tour, now called 'Back in the US'. He says: 'I'm excited to be starting up again in Milwaukee. They're a loud crowd there and the beer's good, too.'

19 July. Paul and Heather attend the Liverpool Institute of the Performing Arts graduation ceremony at the Philharmonic Hall, Liverpool.

25 July. Paul escorts the Queen around his exhibition of paintings at the Walker Art Gallery, Liverpool. He says: 'I think she liked them. She said they were very colourful and I took that as a great compliment.' Not included in the exhibition were three paintings Paul had done of the Queen: *The Queen After Her First Cigarette*, *The Queen Getting a Joke* and *A Greener Queen*.

4 August. Linda's *Roadworks* exhibition is on show at the Washington County Museum of Fine Arts in Hagerstown, Maryland.

18 September. Paul and Heather host an Adopt-a-Minefield benefit gala at the Century Plaza Hotel, Los Angeles. Paul, Brian Wilson and the Wondermints are among the performers on a show emceed by Jay Leno.

19 September. Linda's exhibition 'The Sixties' opens at the Lakeview Museum of Arts and Sciences, Peoria, Illinois and runs until 30 November 2002.

21 September. Paul's 'Back In The US' tour begins at the Bradley Center, Milwaukee, Wisconsin.

23 September. 'Back In The US' appears at the Xcel Energy Center, Minneapolis, Minnesota.

24 September. 'Back In The US' appears at the United Center, Chicago, Illinois.

27 September. 'Back In The US' appears at the Hartford Civic Center, Hartford, Connecticut.

28 September. 'Back In The US' appears at the Boardwalk Hall, Atlantic City, New Jersey.

1 October. 'Back In The US' appears at the Fleet Center, Boston, Massachusetts.

4 October. 'Back In The US' appears at the Gind Arena, Cleveland, Ohio.

5 October. 'Back In The US' appears at the Conseco Field House, Indianapolis, Indiana.

7 October. 'Back In The US' appears at the Sports Center, Raleigh, North Carolina.

9 October. 'Back In The US' appears at the Savvis Center, St Louis, Missouri.

10 October. 'Back In The US' appears at the Schottenstein Center, Columbus, Ohio.

12 October. 'Back In The US' appears at the New Orleans Arena, New Orleans, Louisiana.

13 October. 'Back In The US' appears at the Compaq Center, Houston, Texas.

15 October. 'Back In The US' appears at the Ford Center, Oklahoma City, Oklahoma. Linda's 'Roadworks' exhibition ends at the Washington County Museum of Fine Arts.

18 October. 'Back In The US' appears at the Rose Garden, Portland, Oregon.

19 October. 'Back In The US' appears at the Tacoma Dome, Tacoma, Washington.

21 October. 'Back In The US' appears at the Arco Arena, Sacramento, California.

22 October. 'Back In The US' appears at the Compaq Arena, San Jose, California.

25 October. 'Back In The US' appears at the Arrowhead Pond, Anaheim, California.

26 October. 'Back In The US' appears at the MGM Garden Grand Arena, Las Vegas, Nevada.

28 October. 'Back In The US' appears at the Staples Center, Los Angeles, CA.

29 October. 'Back In The US' appears at the America West Arena, Phoenix, Arizona.

21 November. *Paul McCartney's Liverpool Oratorio* is performed by the Association Choeur et Orchestra de Assistance Publique-Hopheaux de Paris in Paris, France.

26 November. The *Driving USA* DVD set is released and also contains footage of Paul and Heather's wedding.

28 November. *Paul McCartney's Liverpool Oratorio* is once again performed in Paris.

Cimarons, The

A long-established British reggae band that originally formed at a youth club in Harlesden in 1967. They made their debut album in 1973 with *In Time* and became the first reggae band to tour Africa.

When Paul had the idea of a reggae band performing pop standards, particularly those from the MPL catalogue, the Cimarons fitted the bill. Paul's company sponsored the recordings and their first release from the project was a single of Paul's song 'With A Little Luck', issued in Britain on 29 January 1982 on I.M.P. IMPS 50, with Buddy Holly's 'Peggy Sue' on the flip.

The album *Reggaebility* was issued on 25 February of the same year on Pickwick SHM 3106. Tracks on the album included the Lennon and McCartney composition 'Love Me Do' and three of Paul's songs – 'With A Little Luck', 'Mull of Kintyre' and 'C Moon', and he personally directed the group's video for the 'Big Girls Don't Cry' single.

The group's line-up is: Locksley Gichie, guitar; Winston Reid, vocals; Sonny Binns, keyboards; Jah Bunny, drums and percussion; Elroy Bailey, bass.

Citrus Bowl

Venue in Orlando, Florida where Paul made his tenth stop in a 15-city tour on Sunday 9 May 1993. Prior to the concert he held a 15-minute press conference which was televised live, during which he mentioned that 'Paul McCartney Live In The New World', to be filmed in Charlotte, North Carolina on 15 June, would be screened on Fox television. The Citrus Bowl has a capacity of 43,000 and 40,000 people attended the concert. The concert started 45 minutes late and Paul told the audience, 'If you've got any hair, I want you to let it down – we're going to have a party here.'

Clarke, Brian

An artist who designed the *Tug Of War* album cover. Paul and Linda attended an exhibition of his work at the Mayfair Art Gallery on Tuesday 14 June 1983, where they met an old friend, Marianne Faithfull.

Clarke, Stanley

One of the world's most respected bassists. When George Martin and Paul discussed the recording of the *Tug of War* album, to be produced in Montserrat, George suggested that he include some of the world's top musicians on their particular instruments.

They included Paddy Maloney of the Chieftains, acknowledged as the best living exponent of the Uilleann pipes; Britain's major clarinettist Jack Brymer, and Stanley Clarke.

It was while they were jamming in the studio during the recording of *Tug Of War* that Stanley and Paul collaborated on 'Hey Hey', an instrumental which was to be included on *Pipes of Peace*.

Classical Music

In an interview with *MTV News* in 1993, Paul said, 'I'm writing some single piano pieces – the complete opposite to three hundred people, a massive choir, massive orchestra, kids' choir and soloists. This is for one bloke or bloke-ette at a piano. So it doesn't rely on me or my personality. It's got to be in the notes.'

Discussing classical music, he said, 'I don't know much about classical. If it came on the radio, my dad, who was a jazz fan, would say, "Bloody classical, turn it off!"

On 6 October 1997, BBC's Ceefax featured a quote from Paul: 'While I am not a serious classical freak, it's a bit pompous of people to assume that I'm interested in nothing other than loud guitars and drums.'

Paul has since become associated with composing various classical pieces ranging from *Paul McCartney's Liverpool Oratorio*, *Standing Stone* and *Working Classical* to *A Leaf* and *Ecce Cor Meum*.

Classical Paul McCartney

A two-hour special that was aired on various commercial classical music stations in America by the Concert Music Network in September 1995. It featured the American premiere of Paul's *A Leaf*, performed by Anya Alexeyev, excerpts from *Paul McCartney's Liverpool Oratorio* and an interview with Paul.

Clean Machine

An instrumental number, which Paul composed and recorded exclusively for the Linda McCartney Pro Cycling Team, which was sponsored by Linda McCartney Vegetarian Foods and launched in February 1999. The ceremony began in Trafalgar Square, London. Paul recorded the number at Abbey Road Studios on Friday 28 May 1999 and said he'd called the team 'The Clean Machine' because all fifteen members were vegetarian.

The number could be heard on the team's website. www.lindamccartney-pct.co.uk.

Cliff Bennett & the Rebel Rousers

A group formed in 1961 and led by Cliff Bennett, who was born in Slough. They appeared at the Star Club, Hamburg and became friendly with many of the Liverpool bands. Their first hit came in 1964 with 'One Way Love', issued on the Parlophone label. Their biggest hit was in 1966 with 'Got To Get You Into My Life', which reached No. 6 in the British charts. The number was written and produced by Paul.

Cliffs Pavilion, Westcliff

On Friday 19 July 1991, Paul performed one of the six *Unplugged* concerts before 1,000 fans at Cliffs Pavilion, Westcliff, near Southend.

Paul and his band took the stage at 8.30 for a 130-minute show. Music based around his *Unplugged* album for the first hour, followed by an intermission and then an hour of music from Paul's world tour of the previous year. Announcing, 'The weekend starts here ... ' Paul went into an acoustic set with 'Mean Woman Blues', followed by 'Be-Bop-A-Lula', 'We Can Work It Out', 'San Francisco Bay Blues', 'Every Night', 'Here, There And Everywhere', 'That Would Be Simple', 'Down To The River', 'She's A Woman', 'I Lost My Little Girl', 'Ain't No Sunshine', 'Hi-Heel Sneakers' and 'I've Just Seen A Face'.

Then poet Adrian Mitchell came on stage to recite four of his recent poems. Paul and the band supported him musically on three of the poems, beginning with 'Song in Space'. He recited 'I Like That Stuff' without musical backing, then while he recited 'Maybe Maytime' Paul and the group performed an instrumental version of 'Junk' as the backing music. The final poem was 'Hot Pursuit', about R&B star James Brown.

They then performed 'Good Rockin' Tonight' before the ten-minute interval.

They changed their outfits and played the next set with electric instruments, opening with 'Twenty Flight Rock'. This was followed with 'Band On the Run', 'Ebony and Ivory', 'I Saw Her Standing There', 'Coming Up', 'Get Back', then Paul sat at the piano to perform 'The Long and Winding Road', which was followed by 'Ain't That A Shame' and 'Let It Be'. The encore saw him perform 'Can't Buy Me Love' and 'Sgt Pepper'.

Club Sandwich

The official title of Paul's Fun Club magazine. It was a quarterly magazine chronicling current progress as part of the membership of the Paul McCartney Fun Club. The final issue was published in 1998 following Linda's death. It was the 86th issue and was a 44-page special filled with pictures of Linda. There was the announcement: 'Paul and Linda McCartney created *Club Sandwich* together almost 21 years ago now. It was their joint project, with Paul as executive editor and Linda as picture editor. Paul now feels that it is not appropriate to continue without her, and therefore we will stop publishing *Club Sandwich* and will wind up the Paul McCartney Fun Club as well.'

MPL has now created an archive of *Club Sandwich* on the web at: http://www.mplcommunications.com/mccartney/club/

Cogan, Alma

One of Britain's leading female vocalists of the 1950s, with a huge string of hits to her credit, including the chart topper 'Dreamboat' and novelty discs such as 'Never Do A Tango With An Eskimo' – which topped the charts in Iceland! Alma was born in London on 19 May 1932.

The Beatles met her for the first time on Sunday 12 January 1964 following their appearance together on *Sunday Night at the London Palladium* and they began to attend the soirées at her first-floor flat at 44 Stafford Court on Kensington High Street. Brian Epstein, Lionel Bart, Michael Caine, Sammy Davis Junior, Tommy Steele and Terence Stamp were among the regular visitors. In 1963 Paul told her he had a tune he wanted her to hear. He recalls: 'I played the melody for her and she said, "It's lovely". It was a little bit embarrassing because I think she thought I'd written it for her. Maybe I didn't make it very clear by saying, "here's a song I've written, what do you think of it?"'

Alma's sister Sandra was present and their mother Fay (who the Beatles referred to as Mrs Macogie) walked into the room while Paul was at the piano and said, 'Anyone like some scrambled eggs?' which prompted Paul to begin singing 'Scrambled eggs . . . oh my baby how I love your legs.' As a result, for some time, the working title of 'Yesterday' was 'Scrambled Eggs'.

When Paul played tambourine on one of her singles, Alma returned the favour by recording 'Yesterday', which was issued on Columbia DB7757 on 11 November 1965 and a few weeks later, on 28 November, her double A-side single 'Eight Days a Week'/'Help!' was released on Columbia DB 7786. She'd recorded it on 9 October and both Paul and John had attended her recording session.

Cancer was diagnosed in March 1966 and she died at the Middlesex Hospital on Wednesday 26 October of that year. She was only 34 years old.

In 1988 EMI issued a double album *Alma Cogan: A Celebration* which featured a gatefold sleeve photograph of Alma with the Beatles. Paul also penned a sleeve note for the release.

In October 2000 a blue plaque was placed on Alma's former home in Kensington High Street.

Cold Cuts

A projected album in which Paul had intended to compile a number of his hit tracks. He'd originally begun the project under the name *Hot Hitz and Kold Kutz* until someone from the record company asked him, 'Why have cold cuts on a hot hits album?' and he changed the title to *Cold Cuts*.

In the autumn of 1974 he announced that he would be releasing it under the title *Hot Hits and Cold Cuts* and said it would feature unreleased Wings tracks, together with A and B-sides of Wings singles which had not been available on an album before. He intended it to be a budget-priced release, issued around Christmas 1974. It wasn't released then, but plans were still kept alive and following the release of *McCartney 11* in 1980 Paul began preparing what was to be *Cold Cuts*. He even had the American artist Saul Steinberg draw a cover for him. However, the death of John Lennon seemed to delay his plans for a few more years.

In 1986 Paul told *Hits* magazine that he was working on the much-delayed *Cold Cuts* project. 'You know, it's something I've been threatening the fans with for a long time,' he said. 'If they all mix up great, it may be something sooner rather than later. I get a lot of fans who write to me and say, "hey, when is that *Cold Cuts* coming out?" So I figured it would be nice to finish that up, and the release can come at any time. There's always tracks knocking around. I just don't like to have too much hanging around. So I'm going to finish that up.'

At around the same time he was discussing finishing the project, in

1986 *Cold Cuts* by Paul McCartney and Wings was issued on Club Sandwich SP-11. It was a bootleg whose release led Paul to decide against releasing his own *Cold Cuts* album.

The bootleg *Cold Cuts* contained twelve of Paul's outtakes recorded between 1971 and 1980. The tracks were: Side One: 'A Love For You', 'My Carnival', 'Waterspout', 'Momma's Little Girl', 'Night Out', 'Robbers Ball'. Side Two: 'Cage', 'Did We Meet Somewhere Before?', 'Hey Diddle', 'Tragedy', 'Best Friend', 'Same time Next Year'.

Collaborators

The most famous songwriting partnership is that of Lennon and McCartney, although Paul was to co-write various songs with a large number of different people.

They included Linda McCartney; Roger McGough; Denny Laine; Eric Stewart; Elvis Costello; Carl Lewis; Mike McGear (Mike McCartney); Michael Jackson; Stevie Wonder; Hamish Stuart; Steve Miller; Stanley Clarke; James McCartney; and, arguably, Mal Evans and Alistair Taylor (who both claim they contributed to Paul's songs).

When Paul and Linda wrote 'Another Day' together, Sir Lew Grade filed a lawsuit, alleging that Linda wasn't a competent songwriter and couldn't be the co-composer of the song.

Many years later Paul was to tell journalist Tim White, 'I had a contract with Northern Songs for me and John as writers. As I wasn't collaborating with John anymore, I looked for someone else to collaborate with. I assumed there wouldn't be any sweat ... They were so wonderful to me after all the success I'd brought them with me and John – more than they ever dreamed of earning anyway – then they immediately slapped a million-dollar lawsuit on us. So they were charming pals who shall be remembered ever thus ... If my wife is actually saying, "Change that," or "I like that better than that," then I'm using her as a collaborator. I mean, John never had any input on "The Long And Winding Road" and Yoko still collects royalties on it.'

The case went to court and Linda had to testify that she felt competent to collaborate on a song with Paul. A settlement was agreed with Paul making the television special 'James Paul McCartney' for Grade.

Paul and Eric Stewart collaborated on writing six of the ten tracks on the *Press To Play* album. Discussing his writing with Stewart, Paul said: 'We enjoyed the experience; I remember the old way I'd written with John, the two acoustic guitars facing each other – like a mirror, but better! I'd never really tried to do that again: I'd either sit on my own with a guitar or a piano, or with Michael Jackson doing lyrics, or Stevie and I just made that other one up. But it was never across the acoustics, which I'd always found a very complete way of writing.'

During the summer of 1987 Paul phoned Elvis Costello and suggested they write and record together. Paul helped Costello to write 'Veronica' which was to appear on Elvis's album *Spike* and Costello helped Paul to write 'Back On My Feet', which appeared as the flipside of 'Once Upon A Long Ago'.

Paul collaborated with bassist Stanley Clarke on 'Hey Hey' on the *Pipes Of Peace* album; Steve Miller on 'Souvenirs' and Ringo Starr on 'Really Love You' on the *Flaming Pie* album, while Roger McGough worked with Paul on some numbers for the *McGear* album and Hamish Stuart collaborated with Paul on numbers such as 'Keep Coming Back To Love' and 'The First Stone'.

Paul was also to collaborate with his son James on the *Driving Rain* album. Paul and his son co-wrote 'Spinning On An Axis' and 'Back In The Sunshine Again', making it the first time that the credit McCartney and McCartney has appeared on a record.

Columbia

An American record label, more popularly known simply as CBS. Paul signed with the company in 1979 for an advance of two million dollars, making him the highest paid recording artist in the industry. His first release with the label was 'Goodnight Tonight'/'Daytime Nightime Suffering' on Thursday 15 March 1979. He left Columbia to return to Capital in October 1985.

Come And Get It

A number composed by Paul as the theme tune to the Peter Sellers/Ringo Starr movie *The Magic Christian*. In September 1969 Paul recorded the number with Badfinger and it was issued in Britain on Friday 5 December 1969 on Apple 20 and in America on Monday 12 January 1970 on Apple 1815. 'Rock Of Ages' was on the flip. It was also the lead track on the Badfinger album *Magic Christian Music*, which Paul also produced. The LP was issued in Britain on Friday 9 January 1970 on Apple SAPCOR 12 and in America on Monday 16 February 1970 on Apple ST 3364. The number was also included on *The Magic Christian* original soundtrack album, issued in Britain on Friday 10 April 1970 on Pye NSPL 28133 and in America on Commonwealth United CU 6004 on Wednesday 11 February 1970.

Coming Up

A Wings single issued in the UK on Parlophone R6035 on Friday 11 April 1980 and in America on Columbia 1-11263 on Tuesday 15 April 1980. The full track listing was 'Coming Up', (studio version); 'Coming Up' (live version recorded in Glasgow), plus the tracks 'Lunch Box' and 'Odd Sox'. The British single reached No. 2 in the charts and the American version topped the US charts.

Columbia in America liked the tune of 'Coming Up', but didn't like the way Paul had recorded it, with a tinny vocal sound that they felt was not typical of him. They preferred his version of 'Coming Up' from a recording of a live show at the Apollo Theatre, Glasgow.

The 'Lunch Box'/'Old Sox' track had been recorded five years prior with a Wings line-up which had included Jimmy McCulloch and Geoff Britton.

It was released in Germany on Odeon 1C006-63794.

A version of this number lasting 5 minutes and 18 seconds was included on the *Tripping The Live Fantastic* album. It was recorded live at the Tokyo Dome, Tokyo, Japan on 3 March 1990 during the World Tour.

Coming Up (tribute album)

The second tribute album of Paul's music to be issued by the American record label Oglio in October 2001, with funds donated to the American breast cancer charity, the Susan G Komen Breast Cancer Foundation.

The full title of the album, issued on 23 October 2001, was *Coming Up: Independent Artists Pay Tribute To The Music Of Paul McCartney*. The tracks were: 'Let 'Em In', Starbelly; 'Take It Away', Jellybricks; 'Every Night', Marc Bacino; 'This One', Cliff Hillis; 'My Brave Face', Star Collector; 'Temporary Secretary', the Andersons; 'Mull Of Kintyre', Kyf Brewer; 'With A Little Luck', the Masticators; 'Somedays', Phil Keaggy; 'Getting Closer', Michael Carpenter; 'Maybe I'm Amazed', Gadget White Band; 'Helen Wheels', the Shazam; 'Oh Woman, Oh Why', Ray Paul with Emit Rhodes; 'Another Day', Cherry Twister; 'Back On My Feet', Cockeyed Ghost.

Commercials

When National Panasonic began a television advertising campaign using a cover version of 'All You Need Is Love', Paul once again publicly condemned the use of Beatles songs in commercials. He instructed his manager Richard Ogden to issue a statement in October 1989: 'Paul cannot stop Northern Songs doing this but he is nonetheless opposed to it. Paul and John Lennon always believed that it devalues the songs both as property in the long run and in the hearts and minds of the fans. If we could stop it, we would.'

The use of Beatles numbers for TV commercials has always upset Paul and Ringo, who issued a joint statement making clear they did not want any Beatles music to be used in advertisements, declaring; 'We are not in the business of singing jingles. We do not peddle sneakers, pantyhose or anything else.'

The fact that Michael Jackson, who beat a bid by Paul and Yoko Ono to buy the Beatles back catalogue, has allowed the numbers to be used in commercials caused a rift between Paul and Jackson. Paul is furious at the times Jackson has allowed the numbers to be used in advertisements. Nike paid £166,000 in 1987 for the use of 'Revolution' in one advert to promote trainers. Apple sued Capitol-EMI and Nike stating that although Capitol had the right to exploit the

Beatles' goodwill and persona to advertise their records, this did not include commercial purposes such as television jingles. Nike even took out a full page newspaper advertisement stating, 'Can we talk? The last thing we want to do is upset the Beatles over the use of their music. That's why we've asked them to discuss the issue with us "face-to-face" without all the lawyers and spokesmen.'

Capitol said that Yoko Ono had given permission and her representative Sam Havadtoy had assured them that Paul had also given his consent. They also said that Yoko had insisted that the original Beatles version and not a soundalike be used.

Apple said that Paul had not agreed and that Capitol had nothing in writing from Yoko. They also pointed out that the Apple board had to agree unanimously on such matters. Paul said, 'I don't like this commercial thing. It's a pity, but we don't have any say in the matter.'

Jackson also allowed Oriole Cooking to use 'Good Day Sunshine' in their advertisements, in addition to the National Panasonic use of 'All You Need Is Love'.

Paul has personally appealed to Jackson to stop allowing the songs to be used in this way, without success. He says, "What Michael is doing cheapens songs which mean a lot not only to me but to a generation of Beatles fans.

'I thought "Revolution" was a serious song with a serious meaning – not a jingle to sell sneakers.'

In 1994 Michael Jackson gave permission for Paul's composition 'Come And Get It' to be used on commercial TV in Japan – not performed by Badfinger, but by a soundalike group.

In January 2002 Paul had occasion to be upset again by Jackson's permission for the American insurance giant Allstate to use 'When I'm Sixty-Four' in a 30-second commercial – sung by Julian Lennon.

It is particularly frustrating for Paul as that particular song, despite the Lennon and McCartney credit, was a number he originally wrote himself at the age of sixteen for a proposed musical. He then added new lyrics and recorded it largely solo, with George Martin aiding on the arrangement of clarinets.

Complain To The Queen

During his Wings tour of Holland in 1972 Paul appeared on a number of radio shows to promote the tour. On Sunday 20 August, prior to his appearance at the Concertgebouw in Amsterdam he appeared on the programme *Popsmuk* during which he performed this number that was a song he said he composed specially for the Netherlands. When he appeared at the Congresgebouw the next day, 21 August, the number was recorded during his live show and released in Britain on 23 March 1973 as the flipside of 'My Love'. It was released in America on 2 June 1973, where 'My Love' was to top the charts.

Concert For Bangla Desh, The

The famous concert organised by George Harrison that took place at Madison Square Garden, New York on Sunday 1 August 1971.

George had invited John, Paul and Ringo to appear. Ringo immediately accepted. John arrived in New York with Yoko, but when Yoko discovered that George only wanted John to appear and not her, there was such an unholy row that John fled to the airport and returned to Europe. Paul also rejected the offer, feeling that the Beatles had only recently disbanded and it wouldn't be logical for them to get together again so soon.

In an interview with Chris Charlesworth of *Melody Maker* in November 1971, Paul mentioned that he was asked to play at the concert by George, but declined. He said, 'Klein called a press conference and told everyone I had refused to do so for the Pakistani refugees – that's what he called them. It wasn't so. I said to George the reason I couldn't do it was because it would mean that all the world's press would scream that the Beatles had got back together again, and I know that it would have made Klein very happy. It would have been an historical event and Klein would have taken the credit.' Paul said that if it hadn't been for Klein he might have had second thoughts about the offer.

Concert For New York, The

On the New York radio station WPLJ on 21 September 2001, Paul announced that he'd planned a benefit concert in aid of the families of firefighters involved in the Twin Towers tragedy, commenting, 'I was here in New York when the disaster happened. I was actually on a plane, on the tarmac, when the pilot said it'd all been closed down. I've been here in New York ever since and, in a way, I was pleased to be here to witness all the heroism. At the time of the disaster I was flying home in order to plan a concert that I was going to do in Russia, in Red Square in October. But that doesn't seem appropriate now, so I've postponed that.'

He later released an official statement on his reasons for the concert: 'I'm doing this benefit concert because, in short, I love New York. I was there when the tragedy occurred and I witnessed the last moments of the World Trade Center Twin Towers. Heather and I were sitting on a plane at the airport waiting to take off. Suddenly the captain announced that all the planes had been grounded. From our side of the plane we could see the Towers smoking and in flames, we couldn't believe what had happened.

'A tragedy like this affects everyone and everything. A few days after the attack we went down to the Canal Street area and you could smell it and feel it, people were still in a daze. At first I felt useless. I thought, "What can I do?" I knew I had to do something to help, so I'm going to do this concert. Although the events are dreadfully sad, in a way I was glad I was in New York when it was all happening because I was able to witness the tremendous heroism that has come out of the city since the disaster.

'This concert will honour those heroes and heroines and I'm very proud to be doing that. It will benefit the families of the victims, including the families of the firefighters involved. I feel a connection with the firefighters because my dad was a volunteer fireman in Liverpool during World War Two.

'So I'm going to do this benefit show to show solidarity. The thing is that people may disagree with how we live, but this attack has crossed the line; it is a real no-no and you have to show the people who have done this that we are not going to put up with it. You've got to stand up and do something. I can't fight fires, but I can do a concert. It will be a difficult night, but it needs doing and I hope to help raise a lot of money for the families of the victims.'

When the tickets went on sale from 7 October 2001, Paul personally delivered a hundred tickets to two Manhattan fire stations.

The concert took place at 8 p.m. on Saturday 20 October 2001 at Madison Square Garden with Paul headlining. David Bowie opened the show singing the Paul Simon song 'America', and was followed by Bon Jovi, Jaz-Z, the Goo Goo Dolls, Billy Idol, Destiny's Child, Eric Clapton, the Backstreet Boys, Melissa Etheridge, the Who with Zak Starkey on drums, Mick Jagger and Keith Richards, Macy Gray who sang 'With A Little Help From My Friends', James Taylor and Elton John. Paul closed the show performing 'I'm Down', 'Lonely Road', 'From A Lover To A Friend', 'Yesterday', and 'Freedom', a number he had written specially for the concert. The artists joined him on stage to perform 'Let It Be' and he then reprised 'Freedom' and 'Let It Be'. He sang 'Freedom' again as an encore.

Paul told the audience, 'This is one of the greatest nights for me. I want to thank you guys for everything you've done, on behalf of the British, on behalf of America, on behalf of the world.'

A number of Hollywood stars also came on stage, including Meg Ryan, Jim Carrey, Susan Sarandon, Mike Myers, John Cusack and Michael J Fox. The show was televised.

The concert had been produced by VHI, Cablevision, Miramax and AOL. There were more than 6,000 firefighters, police officers and rescue workers attending as guests.

Paul and Heather then attended an after-show party at the Hudson Hotel. He said, 'I think it went really well. Now I just want everyone to let their hair down and have some fun. Everyone pulled together and we've raised a lot of money.'

Paul then joined the Hudson's bar band and sang 'I Saw Her Standing There' with Jim Carrey and Dan Aykroyd.

A four-hour edited version of the concert was televised live by VHI and seen in more than 80 million American homes. There was also a live simulcast on radio stations across the country on the VH1 network and Westwood Inc. It was also carried on the digital channels VHI Classic, VHI Soul and VHI Country. There was a live webcast by AOL on the Internet.

Over $30 million was raised for the Robin Hood Relief Fund established by the Robin Hood Foundation with funds to be distributed to the Twin Towers fund and other charities directly affected by the World Trade Center tragedy.

A 2 CD set was also issued and Sony Music's net proceeds from the sale of the album went to the Robin Hood Relief Fund. There were four tracks by Paul at the end of the second CD – 'I'm Down', 'Yesterday', 'Let It Be' and 'Freedom'.

Concerts For Kampuchea, The

A double-album issued on Friday 3 April 1981 on Atlantic K60153 in Britain, which had been recorded at the series of Hammersmith Odeon concerts from 26–29 December 1979 in aid of the suffering people in Kampuchea.

The entire fourth side of the album comprises six tracks: three with Paul and Wings and three with Paul and the Rockestra.

The tracks are: 'Got To Get You Into My Life', 'Every Night', 'Coming Up', 'Lucille', 'Let It Be' and 'Rockestra Theme'.

There was also a television special of the concert in which Paul performed, simply called 'Concerts For The People Of Kampuchea'. Directed by Keith McMillan, the 90-minute film networked on Independent Television in Britain on Sunday 4 January 1981.

Conspiracy Of Hope

A compilation album to celebrate the 25th anniversary of Amnesty International. Paul donated the track 'Pipes Of Peace' to the LP, which was issued in Britain on Mercury MERH 99 and in America on USAM 830 588-1 on 14 November 1987. A UK cassette was issued on MERHC99 and a CD on 839 588-2 on 5 December 1987.

Conteh, John

A famous Liverpool boxer, born in the Toxteth area in 1951. His mother was of Irish descent and his father came from Sierra Leone. He was to become one of Britain's most glamorous boxers and was, for a time, the light-heavyweight champion of the world.

In his biography *I, Conteh* he describes one of the highlights of his life: the 1964 civic reception of the Beatles. A boy in short pants, he was jostling among the crowds in Lime Street and managed to duck under a policeman's horse in order to get a better view.

He later got to know Paul personally and was included on the *Band On The Run* album cover and had personal greetings from Paul when he was spotlighted on Thames Television's *This Is Your Life*.

Paul and Linda were actually at the ringside at Wembley on Tuesday 1 October 1974 when Conteh became the first British boxer in a quarter of a century to become the World Light-heavyweight Champion. Prior to the bout, Paul and Linda had sent the 23-year-old fighter a telegram that read: 'You made me Number One. Now *You* be Number One!' This was a reference to Conteh's appearance on the *Band On the Run* sleeve.

Cook Of The House

Linda's track on *Wings At The Speed Of Sound*, which Paul described as 'the first British cooking on record'. Linda sang lead vocal and the number was 2 minutes and 38 seconds in length.

Cooler, The

An intriguing film short starring Paul, Linda, Ringo Starr and Barbara Bach, made as a promotional video for 'Private Property', which was written and produced by Paul and was the second single issued from Ringo's album *Stop and Smell the Roses*.

Paul wanted to help Ringo in the promotion of the album and arranged for MPL to make the 11-minute video.

The result was described as a surrealist musical and concerned a prison camp of the future patrolled entirely by women, with Barbara as the Camp Commandant and Linda as a prison guard.

Ringo is an escaped prisoner who is recaptured and thrown into solitary confinement. He has visions. Paul appears as a country music bass player, as a fellow prisoner and as Ringo's father.

The video was directed by Kevin Godley and Lol Crème and was the official British entry in the Short Film category at the Cannes Film Festival on 24 May 1982. It featured three numbers from the *Stop and Smell the Roses* album: 'Private Property' and 'Attention', both written by Paul, and 'Sure To Fall' by Carl Perkins, Quinton Claunch and William Cantre.

Coquette

A track from the *Run Devil Run* album lasting 2 minutes and 43 seconds. Paul had originally heard it when it was the B-side of a Fats Domino single. It was penned by Green/Kahn/Lombardo. Paul recorded it at Abbey Road Studios in March 1999 with himself on lead vocal and bass guitar, Dave Gilmour on electric guitar, Mick Green on electric guitar, Pete Wingfield on piano and Ian Paice on drums.

Corfu

Paul, Linda and Heather holidayed in Corfu during June 1968. They rented a villa on the Greek island. As Paul had been working hard in the studios when he and Linda got married the previous March this must have been a kind of belated honeymoon for them.

Cornell, Lyn

A blonde-haired singer from Liverpool who'd lived quite close to Paul. She became a member of the Vernons Girls and married musician Andy White. It was Andy who was hired by Ron Richards and George Martin to play drums on 'Love Me Do', although Ringo was also allowed to cut a version of the number. Andy's performance is included on the British and American albums. Lyn was booked for the special all-British edition of the American television series *Shindig*, on which the Beatles appeared, and during rehearsals at the Granville Theatre, Fulham, was able to talk over old times with Paul.

Cornwall Coliseum

A venue in St Austell, Cornwall, England, which was one of the several 'surprise' concert appearances Paul made between May and July 1991. It was the first time Paul had ever performed in Cornwall – he hadn't even appeared there during his years with the Beatles. His line-up for the show comprised himself, Linda, Robbie McIntosh, Hamish Stuart, Paul 'Wix' Wickens and Blair Cunningham.

The show took place on Friday 7 June 1991 and it saw the largest audience of the 'surprise gigs' tour, with an audience of 3,326. As with the other 'surprise' concerts, the set was divided into one acoustic and one electric set. The acoustic set comprised: 'Mean Woman Blues', 'Be-Bop-A-Lula', 'We Can Work It Out', 'San Francisco Bay Blues', 'Every Night', 'Here, There and Everywhere', 'That Would Be Something', 'Down To The River', 'And I Love Her', 'She's A Woman', 'I Lost My Little Girl','Ain't No Sunshine', 'I've Just Seen A Face', 'Hi-Heel Sneakers' and 'Good Rockin' Tonight'. The electric set comprised 'My Brave Face', 'Band On The Run' 'Ebony and Ivory', 'I Saw Her Standing There', 'Get Back', 'Coming Up', 'The Long And Winding Road', 'Ain't That A Shame' and 'Let It Be'. The encores were 'Can't Buy Me Love' and 'Sgt Pepper's Lonely Hearts Club Band'.

Entertainment Tonight, the Paramount TV programme, screened a report of this concert in America on Wednesday 12 June 1991.

Cosmically Conscious

A number penned by Paul, lasting 1 minute and 42 seconds, which was the final track on the *Off The Ground* album.

Costello, Elvis

A singer/songwriter, who was born Declan McManus in 1955. His father was a professional singer and his mother worked for a time in Brian Epstein's NEMS record store. He was to say, 'My parents loved the Beatles and all those beat groups because my dad had to sing a lot of those songs.' Elvis started singing in Liverpool in the 1970s.

Writing about his association with Paul in the sleeve notes of *Bespoke Songs, Lost Dogs, Detours & Rendezvous*, a compilation of his songs, issued by Rhino Records on R2 75273 in 1998, Costello commented, 'I first met Paul when we opened the show for Wings during the 1979 Concerts for Kampuchea series in London. He was very friendly and good at putting people at ease who might have been a little overwhelmed. He was also singing and playing tremendously.'

During the 1980s they bumped into each other regularly at AIR Studios and then Paul invited Elvis to write songs with him.

Elvis commented, 'Our writing sessions could not have been more enjoyable or instructive. We set up in a room above Paul's studio with two acoustic guitars, an electric piano and a big notebook, and worked at great speed for about five hours a day. Once we had finished writing, we would go downstairs and knock off a demo recording.

He added that Paul was very sympathetic in his handling of Elvis's personal lyrical details in 'Veronica' and 'That Day Is Done' and felt that their work together was well illustrated by a series of 'character songs': 'Mistress And Maid', 'So Like Candy', 'Tommy's Coming Home' and 'My Brave Face'.

The Rhino Records album included 'My Brave Face' as the final track.

Paul and Elvis Costello wrote ten joint compositions in 1998, including 'Back On My Feet', for the B-side of 'Once Upon A Long Ago' and two others for Elvis's own album. Their co-written songs include 'My Brave Face', 'Flying To My Home', 'Don't Be Careless Love', 'You Want Her Too', 'That Day Is Done', 'Lovers That Never Were', 'So Like Candy', 'Playboy To A Man', 'Twenty-Five Fingers' and 'Tommy's Coming Home'.

They did sessions together at Paul's home studio in Sussex in September and late October 1987. 'Flying To My Home' appeared on the 'My Brave Face' single, while 'Lovers That Never Were', 'So Like Candy' and 'Playboy To A Man' appeared on Costello's album *Mighty Like A Rose*.

Countdown

A Dutch television programme. Paul and his band appeared on the show on Monday 30 November 1987 for 27 minutes during which they mimed to 'Once Upon A Long Ago'. They also appeared on the show on Monday 22 May 1989 when they mimed to 'My Brave Face' and 'How Many People'.

On Thursday 13 December 1990 Paul videotaped 'All My Trials', 'The Long And Winding Road' and 'Let It Be' at Limehouse television studios in Wembley for the show, which was screened in Holland on Wednesday 26 December 1990.

Country Dreamer

A number that appeared on the B-side of 'Helen Wheels'. An acoustic version which Paul recorded in his garden backyard and which was to be used in a short called *The Backyard* has found its way onto several bootlegs.

Cow

A number about animal rights which Linda wrote with Carla Lane. The two had recorded two numbers with Paul, the other being an anti-vivisection song called 'White Coated Man', the latter included on an American charity CD *Animal Magnetism*. 'Cow' was to appear on a promotional CD *Oobu Joobu – Ecology* in 1997.

Crackin' Up

A number composed by McDaniel. Paul's version, lasting only 49 seconds, was included on the *Tripping The Live Fantastic* album. It was recorded live at the Great Western Forum, Los Angeles on 23 November 1989 during the 1989/90 World Tour.

Crickets, The

Buddy Holly's backing band were the inspiration for the name the Beatles. Basically, the group had had various names since their Quarry Men days. Early in 1960 they were discussing a suitable name and Stuart Sutcliffe mentioned they could have a name similar to the Crickets (the group had included several Buddy Holly numbers in their repertoire). They began to think of insects and the word 'beetle' came up. John Lennon was to add the 'a', although there were initial variations over the next couple of months, including Beatals, the Silver Beats, the Silver Beetles and the Silver Beatles.

Holly had originally formed a duo with Bob Montgomery called Buddy & Bob. Drummer Jerry Allison joined them in 1955. The following year, for his Decca recording sessions in Nashville, since the trio had split up, Holly recruited Sonny Curtis on guitar and Don Guess on bass. The group that backed him on his first release 'Blue Days, Black Nights' on 16 April 1956 was Holly, Allison, Curtis and Guess. The Decca sessions didn't work out and in February 1957 Holly began recording with Norman Petty and formed a new backing band with Allison, Niki Sullivan on rhythm and Joe B Mauldin on bass. They chose the name the Crickets for themselves. Together they recorded numbers such as 'That'll Be The Day', 'Peggy Sue', 'Oh Boy!' 'Listen To Me' and 'Maybe Baby'. Holly split from the Crickets and began recording without the group in 1958.

After Paul had acquired the publishing rights to the Buddy Holly catalogue he instigated his annual Buddy Holly Week on what would have been Buddy's fortieth birthday, 7 September 1976. The following year he invited Allison, Mauldin and Curtis to perform at his Buddy Holly Week as the Crickets.

At the finale of Buddy Holly Week on Friday 14 September 1979, Paul appeared on stage with members of the Crickets at the Odeon, Hammersmith.

Paul recorded the Crickets performing the winning song from his 1987 Buddy Holly Week. The number was 'Got The Tee Shirt', written by Jim Imray, and Paul also contributed backing vocals and piano to the track. He also performed 'Rave On' with them at the 1999 Buddy Holly event in New York.

Crossroads

A popular soap opera on British television that ran from 1964 to 1987.

Tony Hatch penned the theme tune (he was an A&R man for Pye Records, who went to Liverpool in 1963 and recorded several Mersey bands, including the Undertakers and the Chants). Paul rearranged Hatch's theme tune from *Crossroads*, including it on his 1975 album *Venus and Mars*. The television company later used Paul's version as their theme for a time.

The number was recorded during the January/February sessions at Sea Saint Studios in New Orleans and, when asked at a press conference why he had recorded the *Crossroads* theme, he said, 'It's a joke. It's after "Lonely Old People", you see. They are sitting there in the park, saying, "Nobody asked us to play". It's a poignant moment. Then there's a little break and then *Crossroads* starts up. It's lonely old people. It's just the kind of thing that lonely old people watch. It could just as easily have been *Coronation Street*, but we knew the chords to *Crossroads*. I just thought that it would be nice to do it.'

Incidentally, the soap has been responsible for a few pop hits.

Stephanie De Sykes appeared on the show in 1974 as pop singer Harriet Blair who was staying at the hotel while recovering from a nervous breakdown. She sang 'Born With A Smile On My Face', which featured heavily on the show for a couple of weeks – and it went on to top the British charts (Stephanie later married Stu James, former lead singer with Liverpool band the Mojos). In 1982, Paul's cousin Kate Robbins sang on the soap and also had a chart hit from *Crossroads* with 'More Than In Love', which reached No. 2 in the charts.

Crowder, Alan

A long-time MPL staffer, hired by Paul in 1973 to administer the furtherance of his music publishing company and who became head of the publishing division. In the *Oobu Joobu* radio series there is the track of a jam which is called 'Alan Crowder At Caesar's Palace'. This was recorded during a tour rehearsal in 1989 when Alan walked into the room and they named this jam in tribute, although Alan was to tell them, 'Could you do it in tune next time?'

Cummins, Jeff

An artist from the Hipgnosis design group who drew the colourful illustration on the sleeve of the special limited edition 12″ single 'Temporary Secretary' issued in Britain in September 1980.

The cover showed Paul in a knitted V-necked sweater, jeans and sneakers, holding a telephone while balancing a bespectacled secretary on his knee – she is taking shorthand. Jeff also designed the inner sleeve of *Wings Over America*.

Cunningham, Blair

A former drummer with Echo & the Bunnymen, Haircut 100 and the Pretenders, born 11 October 1957 in Memphis, Tennessee. He replaced Chris Whitten in Paul's backing band in 1991 when Whitten returned to Dire Straits. He also recorded a number of TV shows with Paul in December 1990 and appeared on the albums *Unplugged (The Official Bootleg)* and *Paul Is Live*.

Dahner, Bert

One of Paul's cousins. He devised crosswords for the now defunct *Club Sandwich* magazine. He also compiled crosswords for the *Daily Telegraph*, the *Guardian* and *The Times* newspapers. He died on 4 March 2002. He was 75 years old. Paul wrote to the *Daily Telegraph* thanking them for their obituary, saying, 'All of us in the family loved Bert and were very proud of his achievements.'

Dallas

One of the most successful American television soap operas of all time. Produced by Lorimer Productions, *Dallas* was the saga of an oil-rich family called the Ewings who lived in a sprawling ranch called Southfork, situated on the outskirts of the Texas city of Dallas. In the 1980s, due to the popularity of another American soap opera, the *Dallas* spin-off *Dynasty*, the producers of *Dallas* began looking for internationally known celebrities to appear in the series. Late in 1984, they offered Paul McCartney almost one million pounds to make a series of appearances in the role of a wealthy British landowner, spread over eight episodes at £110,000 each. Paul declined saying that he didn't want to be separated from his children.

Quite frankly, if Paul wanted to be reduced to appearing in soap operas to make money, the Beatles might as well have appeared in a string of second-rate movies in the 1960s as Elvis did. No, the legend would surely have suffered a severe blow if Paul had actually accepted that *Dallas* role.

Daniel, Jeffrey

An American singer, a former member of the group Shalamar. He made his screen debut in *Give My Regards To Broad Street* and commented:

'That's all about Paul's real life versus his unconscious dream life. I play myself in one of the dream sequences.'

He appeared as the robot dancer prior to the 'Silly Love Song' sequence.

Daumier's Law

A 15-minute animated short directed by Geoff Dunbar, and produced by MPL's Juggler Films Company. It was premiered at the Cannes Film Festival in March 1992. The short was based on the works of French artist Honore Daumier, who lived from 1808 to 1879. Basically re-creating the drawings of Daumier, the animation was in six acts, telling the tale of an Everyman who is abused and discarded by a tyrannical system.

Paul and Linda had been working on the project for four years. Paul wrote and produced the musical score for the film, performing himself and recording it in December 1989. He also co-wrote the short with Dunbar and it was to win the top prize at the British Academy of Film And Television Arts in 1992.

David Frost At The Phonograph

A radio series on the BBC Light Programme. Paul was the show's guest and recorded the programme on Monday 1 August 1966 at Broadcasting House in London's West End. Frost interviewed him in Studio B14 and the programme was transmitted a few days later on Saturday 6 August from 12 noon to 1.30 p.m.

The series took one personality and interviewed them on various matters, in between playing specific records.

David Symonds Show, The

A BBC Radio One show hosted by disc jockey David Symonds. Symonds interviewed Paul for the show following the appearance by Wings at the New Theatre, Oxford on Saturday 12 May 1973. During the interview Symonds mentioned that his daughter referred to Paul as 'Paul McCarpet'.

Davis, Carl

An American composer, born in Brooklyn, New York on 28 October, 1936. He is married to Liverpool actress Joan Boht, the star of the sitcom *Bread*.

A classically-trained composer, Davis originally arrived in Britain in 1959 to appear at the Edinburgh Festival with a revue he'd co-written called *Diversions*. As a result he was offered a commission by Ned Sherrin to compose music for the TV series *That Was The Week That Was*. Other commissions poured in for radio, stage and film work and he settled in Britain in the early 1960s. He composed for the Royal Shakespeare Company, the National Theatre, worked with artists such as Laurence Olivier and John Gielgud, wrote the scores for films such as *The French Lieutenant's Woman* and for numerous other film and television productions.

He was even the musical director of the American made-for-TV film *The Birth Of The Beatles*.

Paul read an article about Carl in 1988 in which the composer said, 'If it moves, I can score it.' Paul was impressed.

A short time later, when Davis was conducting the Royal Liverpool Philharmonic Orchestra in a performance of his and Carla Lane's *Pigeon's Progress*, featuring his wife Joan, Paul and Linda sent a good luck message.

Brian Pidgeon, the general manager of the RLPO then had an idea that resulted in Davis approaching Paul on his behalf to write a composition for the 150th anniversary celebrations of the orchestra.

Paul and Carl were then officially commissioned to compose the work that became *Paul McCartney's Liverpool Oratorio*. The two sat down and spent hundreds of hours at their respective homes writing, scoring and re-scoring over a two-year period.

Although Paul had written around 400 recorded songs, he had no musical training, but Carl had studied in the classical tradition, which led Paul to comment, 'I prefer to think of my approach to music as primitive, rather like the primitive cave artists, who drew without training. Hopefully, the combination of Carl's classical training and my primitivism will result in a beautiful piece of music. That was always my intention.'

When he was asked how working with Carl differed from working with John Lennon, Paul replied, 'I bossed Carl around more than I bossed John.'

On Tuesday 12 May 1992 Davis was in America where he conducted the Boston Pops in a performance of Linda's *Appaloosa* and Paul's *Meditation*. The performance was filmed by PBS (Public Broadcasting Service) and screened in America in August of that year.

Davis, Meta

The meter maid who claims to have inspired Paul's song 'Lovely Rita.'

She retired after nineteen years as a traffic warden on Wednesday 4 September 1985, when the media gave her story maximum coverage. She appeared on both BBC and ITV news programmes that evening, pictured walking across the Abbey Road zebra crossing and discussing how she gave Paul his ticket (although she called him Paul 'McCarthy' in the interviews).

In 1967 Miss Davis, who lived in St John's Wood before her death, was once giving Paul's car a ticket in Garden Road, when he turned up. She comments: 'He saw that my name was Meta and he laughed and said "That would make a nice jingle, I could use that." We chatted for a few minutes and then he drove off. I didn't think any more of it, but later the song came out and although I knew the record was about me I never bought a copy.'

Paul didn't recognise her when, a few years later, she met him in the reception room of the local vet where she'd taken her cat. Paul was there with his dog and Meta says: 'We chatted about animals and he didn't recognise me out of uniform and I didn't tell him who I was.'

When the record was originally released in Australia it included Meta's name in the lyrics, but this was changed to Rita in other versions.

Day In The Life, A

A collaboration between Paul and John, but one in which they each wrote separate parts, John penning the beginning and end of the number and Paul composing the middle section.

Paul had already written some of the lyrics for another song, but decided to incorporate them into the number that John had been writing. There is a long chord at the end of the song that lasts for 42 seconds and it has been suggested that it was only intended to be heard by Martha, Paul's dog!

John's section was inspired by two separate items: the death in a car crash of Guinness heir Tara Browne, a friend of the Beatles, and a story that he'd read in the *Daily Mail* newspaper concerning holes in the roads in Blackburn, Lancashire.

Paul's rather cheery section, according to Stephen Norris, a former schoolmate who became Conservative MP for Oxford East, was based on a bus journey they used to take to school together. In a *Daily Mirror* interview in 1985, Norris commented: 'Everyone says that "A Day In The Life" was about drugs, but Paul always claimed it was about catching the bus to school. I agree. It's exactly what we used to do. "Went upstairs and had a smoke, somebody spoke and I went into a dream." That's just how I remember it. Getting sleepily out of bed, dragging a comb across your head, then going out and catching the bus, upstairs to the top deck like we all did, still not properly awake and having an untipped Woodbine.'

In fact, it was only ever John's part of the song that was said to be about drugs. The BBC banned it nonetheless. It has never been clear why they assumed a drug connection – one suggestion was that they thought the holes in the road referred to holes caused by a drug addict's hypodermic needle.

The number, which has a classical 'feel' and was recorded with 42 musicians from the London Philharmonic Orchestra, first appeared on *Sgt Pepper* and was also included on *The Beatles 1967–1970* compilation.

Paul was to say, 'We were being influenced by avant-garde composers. For "A Day In The Life", I suggested we should write all but fifteen bars properly so that the orchestra could read it, but where the fifteen bars began we would give the musicians a simple direction: "Start on your lowest note and eventually, at the end of the fifteen bars, be at your highest note." How they got there was up to them, but it all resulted in a crazy crescendo. It was interesting because the trumpet players, always famous for their fondness for lubricating substances, didn't care, so they'd be there at the note ahead of everyone. The strings all watched each other like little sheep: "Are you going up?" "Yes." "So am I." And they'd go up. "A little more?" "Yes." And they'd go up a little more, all very delicate and cosy, all going up together. You listen to those trumpets. They're just freaking out.'

Daytime Nighttime Suffering

A number penned by Paul that was 3 minutes and 19 seconds in length. It had been written over a weekend break and recorded in Replica Studios, situated in the basement of MPL. During the sessions Linda had stepped into the mike range and the sound of baby James McCartney giving a cry is heard.

The number was issued as the flipside to 'Goodnight Tonight' in March 1979.

Dazzlers, The

One of the names, along with Turpentine that Paul considered calling the band he eventually named Wings.

De Doelen, Rotterdam

A venue in Rotterdam where Wings played the first of four concert dates in Holland during their 1972 European tour. A concert planned for Breda was cancelled due to poor ticket sales. The group travelled around Europe on a brightly painted double-decker bus (WNO 481).

The group's repertoire on the concerts were: 'Eat At Home', 'Smile Away', 'Bip Bop', 'Mumbo', '1882', 'I Would Only Smile', 'Give Ireland Back To The Irish', 'Blue Moon Of Kentucky', 'The Mess', 'Best Friend', 'Soily', 'I Am Your Singer', 'Seaside Woman', 'Henry's Blues', 'Say You Don't Mind', 'Wild Life', 'Mary Had A Little Lamb', 'My Love', 'Maybe I'm Amazed', 'Hi, Hi, Hi' and 'Long Tall Sally'.

There have been various bootleg releases of recordings of this particular concert.

De Kooning, Willem

A Dutch artist based in New York. He and his wife, the painter Elaine De Kooning, lived at the Springs, East Hampton, close to the Long Island home of Linda's father, Lee, who was De Kooning's attorney. Paul first met him in the late 1970s. Paul also visited him in his studio in 1981 and Linda took a photograph of them together. The picture was used on the cover of the issue of *Art News* magazine in which Paul discussed De Kooning during an interview. He was to say, 'I saw him draw Linda and her brother and her two sisters, for a present to give to their dad on his sixtieth birthday. We went round to his studio and they knew him well enough to say, "Would you do us a quick drawing to give to Lee?" and he did.'

At one time, De Kooning offered Paul the pick of the paintings in his studio and Paul picked a modest work that he particularly liked.

It was obviously the influence of De Kooning that led Paul to work on his first oil painting while he was staying at Long Island.

Dear Boy

A song Paul co-wrote with Linda for the *Ram* album. The song was about Paul finding Linda as an important part of his life, although John Lennon thought it might have been an attack in song against him.

Paul was to use the song during memorial services to Linda in 1998.

Dear Friend

A song written about John Lennon and included on the *Wild Life* album. Paul had been upset by all the disagreements and when John began to slag him off in public he considered his response. Instinctively he felt he shouldn't play tit for tat and begin to slag John off in public, so he wrote 'Dear John' as a message saying that they should 'lay the guns down, let's hang up our boxing gloves'.

It was recorded in New York in April 1971.

Death Of Variety, The

A concept Paul had during the Apple days, prior to Allen Klein joining the company. He thought of organising something similar to a 'battle of the bands' at the Royal Albert Hall with a rock and roll orchestra competing with a classical orchestra. Paul approached Sir Lew Grade with the idea and also discussed it with Glyn Johns (see Johns, Glyn), but it didn't come to fruition. He eventually utilised part of the idea when he created the Rockestra, a collection of leading British guitarists and drummers.

Defeat of the Dog, The

One of two avant-garde films that Paul made in 1966; the other was called *The Next Spring Then*. Paul screened the films for journalist Patrick Skene Catling and they were mentioned in his article, which appeared in *Punch* magazine on 23 November 1966.

Catling commented: 'They were not like ordinary people's home movies. There were over-exposures, double-exposures, blinding orange lights, quick cuts from professional wrestling to a crowded car park to a close-up of a television weather map. There were long still shots of a grey cloudy sky and a wet, grey pavement, jumping Chinese ivory carvings and affectionate slow-motion studies of his sheepdog Martha and his cat. The accompanying music, on a record player and faultlessly synchronised, was by the Modern Jazz Quartet and Bach.'

Paul was also to show the films to Italian movie director

Michaelangelo Antonioni. Both films were lost when Paul's Cavendish Avenue house was burgled.

Degree of Frost, A

Paul appeared on this BBC Television programme, hosted by David Frost, discussing his song writing. It was transmitted on Monday 18 May 1964 and repeated on Tuesday 1 September 1964.

Deliver Your Children

A *London Town* album track, 4 minutes and 17 seconds in length, which was co-written by Paul and Denny Laine in 1978. It was the flip-side of the June 1978 single 'I've Had Enough'.

Dera, Joe

Paul's American publicist and spokesman, who has acted as press agent for over thirty years. Apart from Paul, his clients have included Elton John, David Bowie and Rod Stewart.

Dera originally represented Paul as a member of the American branch of the public relations company Rogers & Cowan. He left Rogers & Cowan to form his own company Dera and Associates Public Relations in 1989 and Paul moved with him.

Desert Island Discs

A popular British radio show conceived by Roy Plumley, who died in 1985, which has run for more than fifty years.

The show's format is deceptively simple: celebrities are asked to imagine being stranded on a desert island and to select the records they would take with them. In between their choices being played, they discuss their lives and give reasons for their record selection.

Paul McCartney was the first and only ex-Beatle to appear on the show: on Saturday 30 January 1982, he became the 1,629th castaway. Each castaway selects eight records and also identifies one particular record that they would keep if they were only allowed a single disc. They also have to suggest a luxury item and a book they would want with them on a desert island.

Paul's eight selections were: 'Heartbreak Hotel' by Elvis Presley; 'Sweet Little Sixteen' by Chuck Berry; 'Courtly Dances From Gloriana' by the Julian Bream Consort; 'Be Bop A Lula' by Gene Vincent; 'Searchin'', by the Coasters; 'Tutti Frutti' by Little Richard; 'Walking In The Park With Eloise' by the Country Hams and 'Beautiful Boy' by John Lennon. The last became his special selection. His luxury was a guitar and the book he picked was *Linda's Pictures*.

When Paul appeared the host was Michael Parkinson who appears on the cover of *Band On The Run*.

When Paul was on his way to the BBC to record the programme, Paul Massey, an 18-year-old news photographer, attempted to take photographs of Paul. Paul gave him a fierce shove that knocked him to the ground. Paul regretted the incident and apologised, saying, 'I'm sorry I blew my top, mate. I knew there was only one way to stop you taking pictures and that was to lay into you.'

During his conversations on the programme, Paul said that the Silver Beetles had never been paid for their appearance when they backed Johnny Gentle on a tour of Scotland. As a result, impresario Larry Parnes filed a suit against Paul and the BBC for slander. Eventually, the matter was resolved when a formal apology was read out on the programme by Roy Plumley prior to the 28 July 1984 edition, also pointing out that Paul's comment had been made as a joke.

Paul appeared on the American edition of *Desert Island Discs* whilst in Los Angeles on Sunday 25 November 1990.

Devour The Earth

A 20-minute video produced by the Vegetarian Society in 1995 when Paul and Linda were patrons. The video looked at the impact of meat-eating on the environment. Paul provided the voice-over for the video and bought a number of copies that he sent to friends such as Prince Charles.

Paul was to comment, 'I'm convinced that the vegetarian way is the way for the future for many people and Linda and I are pleased to be part of it.'

DeWilde, Brandon

An American actor who appeared as the young boy in the classic Western *Shane* in 1953. Ten years later he appeared in another acclaimed film, *Hud*, with Paul Newman.

When the Beatles were filming *Help!* in the Bahamas, they stayed in a rented house and DeWilde was one of the visitors. He was fascinated when Paul began to compose the song 'Wait' in his presence.

DeWilde died in a car crash in June 1972 and Gram Parsons based his song 'In My Hour Of Darkness' on the actor.

Diary Of The Cannes Film Festival

An ITV television programme, hosted by American film critic Rex Reed. Reed interviewed Paul and Linda in Cannes while they were there for the screening of *Seaside Woman* on Friday 16 May 1980. The programme was sreened on Friday 18 July.

Reed asked Paul: 'Do you think there'll ever be the chance of another Lennon and McCartney song?'

Paul answered, 'Well, I wouldn't say there would be actually, 'cause the last time I spoke to John, I just happened to ask him about whether he was writing songs and stuff, just out of my curiosity, and he told me he was kind of finished doing that and that he's not really into that, which when you say it to people, they say, "Oh, it's a big disappointment," or "He must have gone crazy," but if you think about it, most of us do our jobs to arrive at a point where we no longer have to do our jobs and we can put our feet up and we can enjoy life for a change. I think John's probably reached that point.'

Didn't We Meet Somewhere Before?

A song recorded by Paul and Wings for the Ramones' film *Rock 'n' Roll High School*. The number wasn't included on the soundtrack album of the film and is unavailable on disc.

147 Dinas Lane, Huyton, Liverpool

The address of Paul's Aunt Jin, where Paul's 21st birthday party was held in a marquee in the back garden on Tuesday 18 June 1963.

Paul had asked the Fourmost to play at the party and offered to pay them their normal performance fee, but they said they'd accept only fourpence halfpenny each – although they were never paid anything!

Other guests included the Shadows, who were currently appearing in Blackpool. Brian Bennett, Hank Marvin and Bruce Welch travelled from Blackpool by car and rendezvoused with Paul and Jane Asher outside the Empire Theatre, Liverpool and they all set off for Dinas Lane together.

During the course of the evening, John Lennon beat up Bob Wooler, the Cavern disc jockey. Wooler made a remark alluding that the recent trip John had made to Spain with manager Brian Epstein had been a 'Honeymoon'.

Billy J Kramer, one of the guests, said that John was very drunk and they had to pull him off Wooler, and that John had also tried to hit a girl.

Discography

Singles releases:
'Another Day'/'Oh Woman, Oh Why'. UK Apple R5889, 19 February 1971. US Apple 1826, 22 February 1971.

'Eat At Home'/'Smile Away'. Issued in Germany on Apple IC006-04864 in August 1971 and in France on Apple 2C006-04864M.

'Uncle Albert-Admiral Halsey'/'Too Many People'. Credited to Paul and Linda McCartney, issued in America on Apple 1827 on 2 August 1971.

'Back Seat Of My Car'/'Heart Of The Country' by Paul and Linda McCartney, issued in the UK on Apple R5914 on 13 August 1971.

'Give Ireland Back To The Irish'/'Give Ireland Back To The Irish' by Wings. Issued in the UK on Apple R5936 on 25 February 1972 and in America on Apple 1847 on 28 February 1972.

'Mary Had A Little Lamb'/'Little Woman Love', a Wings single issued in the UK on Apple R5949 on 12 May 1972 and in America on Apple 1851 on 29 May 1972.

'Hi, Hi, Hi'/'C Moon'. A Wings single issued in the UK on Apple R5973 on 1 December 1972 and in America on Apple 1857 on 4 December 1972.

'My Love'/'The Mess'. A Paul McCartney and Wings single issued in the UK on Apple R5985 on 23 March 1973 and in America on Apple 1861 on 9 April 1973.

'Live And Let Die'/'I Lie Around'. A Wings single issued in the UK on 1 June 1973 on Apple 5987 and in the US on Apple 1863 on 18 July 1973.

'Helen Wheels'/'Country Dreamer' by Paul McCartney and Wings. Issued in the UK on Apple R5987 on Friday 26 October 1973 and in the US on Apple 1869 on Monday 12 November 1973.

'Mrs Vandebilt'/'Bluebird', a single by Paul McCartney and Wings, was issued in Germany on EMI Electrola/Apple 1 C006-05529 in January 1974 and also in Spain on Apple IJ006-05529 and France on Apple 2C006-05529.

'Jet'/'Let Me Roll It' by Paul McCartney and Wings, was released in the UK on Apple R5987 on Friday 15 February 1974 and in the US on Apple 1871 on Monday 18 February 1974.

'Band On The Run'/'Zoo Gang', a single by Paul McCartney and Wings, was issued in the UK on Apple R5997 on Friday 28 June 1974. It was also issued in Spain on Apple C006-09683.

'Band On The Run'/'Nineteen Hundred and Eighty Eight' by Paul McCartney and Wings was issued in America on Apple 1873 on 8 April 1974 where it reached the No. 1 position in the charts. It was also issued in Germany on EMI Electrola/Apple 1C006-05635 in June 1974.

'Walking In The Park With Eloise'/'Bridge Over The River Suite' by the Country Hams was issued in the UK on EMI 2220 on Friday 18 October 1974 and in the US on EMI 3977 on Monday 2 December 1974.

'Junior's Farm'/'Sally G' by Paul McCartney and Wings was issued in the UK on Apple R5999 on Friday 25 October 1974 and in America on Apple 1876 on Monday 4 November 1974.

'Listen To What The Man Said'/'Love In Song', a single by Wings which was issued in the UK on Capitol R6006 on Friday 16 May 1975 and in America on Capitol 4091 on Friday 23 May 1975.

'Letting Go'/'You Gave Me The Answer', a single by Wings that was issued in the UK on Capitol R6008 on Friday 5 September 1975 and in the US on Capitol 4145 on Monday 29 September 1975.

'Venus And Mars – Rockshow (medley)'/'Magneto & Titanium Man' was a Wings single issued in the UK on Capitol R6010 on 28 November 1976 and in the US on Capitol 4175 on 27 October 1975.

'Silly Love Songs'/'Cook Of The House'. A Wings single issued in the UK on Capitol R6014 on Friday 30 April 1976 and in the US on Capitol 4256 on Thursday 1 April 1976.

'Let 'Em In'/'Beware My Love', a Wings single, was released in the UK on Capitol R6015 on Friday 23 July 1976 and in America on Capitol 4293 on Monday 28 June 1976.

'Maybe I'm Amazed'/'Soily' was issued in Britain on Capitol R6017 on 4 February 1977 and in the US on Capitol 4385 on 7 February 1977.

'Uncle Albert/Admiral Halsey'/'Eat At Home' was issued in Britain on Regal Zonophone EMI 2594 on 22 April 1977.

'Seaside Woman,'/'B Side To Seaside' by Suzy & the Red Stripes was released in America on Tuesday 31 May 1977 on Epic 3-50403.

'Mull Of Kintyre'/'Girls' School', by Wings, was issued in Britain on Capitol R6018 on Friday 11 November 1977 where it topped the charts and in the US on Capitol 4504 on Monday 14 November 1977 (the American version had the tracks reversed).

'With A Little Luck'/'Backwards Traveller – Cuff Link', was issued in the UK on Parlophone R6019 on Thursday 24 March 1978 and in the US on Capitol 4559 on Monday 20 March 1978.

'I've Had Enough'/'Deliver Your Children', a Wings single which was issued in the UK on Parlophone R6020 on Friday 16 June 1978 and in the US on Capitol 4594 on Monday 12 June 1978.

'London Town'/'I'm Carrying' was issued in the UK on Parlophone R6021 on 11 August 1978 and in the US on Capitol 4625 on 21 August 1978.

'Goodnight Tonight'/'Daytime Nightime Suffering' was a Wings single issued in the UK on Parlophone R6023 on Friday 23 March 1979 and in the US on Columbia 3-109 39 on Thursday 15 March 1979. A 12″ extended mix was issued in America on Monday 26 March 1979 and in the UK on Tuesday 3 April 1979.

'Old Siam Sir'/'Spin It Out', a single by Wings, was issued in the UK on Parlophone R6026 0n Friday 1 June 1979.

'Getting Closer'/'Spin It On', a single by Wings that was issued in the US on Columbia 3-11 020 on Tuesday 5 June 1979.

'Seaside Woman'/'B Side To Seaside', a single by Suzy And The Red Stripes (Linda McCartney and Wings), was issued by A&M Records on AMS 7461 on Wednesday 10 August 1979.

'Arrow Through Me'/'Old Siam Sir', a single by Wings, was issued in the US on Columbia 3-11070 on Tuesday 14 August 1979.

'Getting Closer'/'Baby's Request', a single by Wings, was issued in the UK on Parlophone R6027 on Thursday 16 August 1979.

'Wonderful Christmastime'/'Rudolph The Red Nosed Reggae', a single by Paul McCartney, was issued in the UK on Parlophone R6029 on Friday 16 November 1979 and in the US on Columbia 3-11162 on Tuesday 20 November 1979.

'Coming Up'/'Coming Up (Live At Glasgow)'/'Lunch Box'/'Odd Sox' was a Paul McCartney single issued in the UK on Parlophone R6035 on Friday 11 April 1980 and in America on Columbia 1-11263 on Tuesday 15 April 1980.

'Waterfalls'/'Check My Machine', a single by Paul McCartney, was issued in the UK on Parlophone R6037 on Friday 13 June 1980 and in America on Columbia 1-11335 1847 on Tuesday 22 July 1980.

'Seaside Woman'/'B-Side to Seaside' was issued in the UK on A&M AMS 7548 on 18 July 1980.

'Ebony And Ivory'/'Rainclouds' was a single by Paul McCartney and Stevie Wonder which was issued in the UK on Parlophone R6054 on Monday 29 March 1982 and in the US on Columbia 18-03018 on Monday 29 March 1982.

'Take It Away'/'I'll Give You A Ring', a single by Paul McCartney, was issued in the UK on Parlophone R6056 on Monday 21 June 1982 and in the US on Columbia 18-03018 on Saturday 3 July 1982.

'Tug Of War'/'Get It', a single by Paul McCartney, was issued in the UK on Parlophone R6057 on Monday 20 September 1982 and in the US on Columbia 38-03235 on Sunday 26 September 1982.

'Say Say Say'/'Ode To A Koala Bear', a single by Paul McCartney and Michael Jackson, was issued in the UK on Parlophone R6062 on Monday 3 October 1983 and in the US on Columbia 38-04168 on Monday 3 October 1983.

'Pipes Of Peace'/'So Bad', a single by Paul McCartney, was issued in Britain on Parlophone R6064 on Monday 5 December 1983. In America the A and B-sides were reversed when the single was issued on Columbia 39149 on the same day.

'No More Lonely Nights (ballad)'/'No More Lonely Nights (playout version)' was issued in the UK on Parlophone E6080 on Monday 24 September 1984 and in the US on Columbia 38-04581 on Friday 5 October 1984.

'No More Lonely Nights (ballad)'/'No More Lonely Nights (Special Dance mix)' was issued in the UK on Parlophone 6080 on Monday 29 October 1984.

'We All Stand Together'/'We All Stand Together (humming version)', a single by Paul McCartney and the Frog Chorus which was issued in the UK on Parlophone R6086 on Monday 5 November 1984.

'We All Stand Together'/'We All Stand Together (humming version)' was issued in the UK on Parlophone RP 6086 on 3 December 1984.

'Spies Like Us'/'My Carnival' was a single by Paul McCartney issued in the UK on Parlophone R6118 on Monday 18 November 1985 and in the US on Capitol B-5537 on the same day.

'Spies Like Us'/'Carnival', a shaped picture disc, was issued in the UK on Parlophone RP 6118 on 9 December 1985.

'Seaside Woman'/'B-Side to Seaside' was issued in Britain on EMI 5572 on 7 July 1986.

'Press'/'It's Not True', by Paul McCartney, was issued in the UK on Parlophone R6118 on Monday 14 July 1986 and in the US on Capitol B-5597 on the same day.

'Pretty Little Head (Remix)'/'Write Away' was issued in the UK on Parlophone R6145 on Monday 27 October 1986.

'Stranglehold'/'Angry (Remix)' was issued in the US on Capitol B-5636 on Wednesday 29 October 1986.

'Only Love Remains (Remix)'/'Tough On A Tightrope' was issued in the UK on Parlophone R6148 on Monday 1 December 1986 and in the US on Capitol B-5672 on Tuesday 17 January 1987.

'Long Tall Sally'/'I Saw Her Standing There' were live recordings of Paul performing at the Prince's Trust Concert on 20 June 1986. The single was issued in the UK as a free bonus with the album *Prince's Trust Tenth Anniversary Birthday Party* on A&M FREE 21 on Friday 24 April 1987.

'Once Upon A Long Ago'/'Back On My Feet' was a Paul McCartney single issued in the UK on Parlophone R6160 on Monday 16 November 1987.

'My Brave Face'/'Flying To My Home' was a single by Paul McCartney issued in the UK on Parlophone R6213 on Monday 8 May 1989 and in the US on Capitol B-44367 on Wednesday 10 May 1989.

'This One'/'The First Stone' was a single by Paul McCartney issued in the UK on Parlophone R6273 on Monday 17 July 1989 and in the US on cassette only on Capitol 4JM44438 on Wednesday 2 August 1989.

'This One'/'The Long And Winding Road' was issued in a limited edition in Britain on Parlophone RX 6223 on 24 July 1989.

'Figure Of Eight'/'Ou Est Le Soleil?', a single by Paul McCartney, was issued in the UK on Parlophone R6235 on 13 November 1989 and in the US on Capitol 4JM44489 (in cassette form only) on 15 November 1989.

'Party Party' was a one-sided single on vinyl on Parlophone R6238 that was issued as a bonus in a limited edition repackaging of the album *Flowers In The Dirt* (World Tour Pack) on Thursday 23 November 1989. It was issued in the US on Sunday 15 January 1990.

'Put It There'/'Mama's Little Girl' was a Paul McCartney single issued in the UK on Parlophone 6246 on Monday 5 February 1990 and in the US on Capitol 4JM44570 (in cassette form only) on Tuesday 1 May 1990.

'Birthday'/'Good Day Sunshine', a single by Paul McCartney, was released in the UK on Parlophone R6271 on Monday 8 October 1990 and in the US on Capitol 4JM44645 (in cassette version only) on Tuesday 16 October 1990.

'All My Trials'/'C Moon', a single by Paul McCartney, was issued in the UK on Parlophone R6278 on 26 November 1990.

'The Long And Winding Road'/'C Moon', a single by Paul McCartney, was issued in Germany on Parlophone 066-2041747 on Friday 4 January 1991.

'Hope Of Deliverance'/'Long Leather Coat' by Paul McCartney was issued as a single in the UK on Parlophone R6330 on Monday 28

December 1992 and in the US on Capitol 41CM0777 74490443 in a cassette version only on Monday 18 January 1993.

'C'mon People'/'I Can't Imagine' was a single by Paul McCartney issued in the UK on Parlophone R6338 on 22 February 1993 and in the US on Monday 12 July 1993.

'Off The Ground'/'Cosmically Conscious' was a single by Paul McCartney, and was issued in America only on Capitol S7-17318 on Monday 6 April 1993.

'Biker Like An Icon'/'Things We Said Today' was originally to be issued in the UK on Parlophone CDRDJ 63471 on Monday 26 April 1993 in a 7″ vinyl format, cassette and CD. It was issued as a vinyl single on Capitol/CEMA on Tuesday 20 April 1993.

'Young Boy'/'Looking For You', a single by Paul McCartney, was issued in the UK on Parlophone R6462/7243 8 8378673 on Monday 28 April 1997. One version was a picture disc, another was a jukebox issue.

'The World Tonight'/'Used To Be Bad', a single by Paul McCartney, was issued in the UK on Parlophone RP6472 on Monday 7 July 1997.

'Beautiful Night'/Love Came Tumbling Down', a single by Paul McCartney, was issued in the UK on Parlophone RP 6489 on 15 December 1997.

'No Other Baby'/'Brown Eyed Handsome Man' was a Paul McCartney single issued in the UK on Parlophone R6527 on 24 October 1999.

'Run Devil Run' was part of an 8-single box set issued in the UK on Parlophone 523 221 on Monday 6 December 1999.

Album releases:
The Family Way. Released on 6 January 1967 on Decca SKL 4847 (UK) and 12 June 1967 on London MS 82007(US).

McCartney. Released on 17 April 1970 on Apple PCS 7102 (UK) and 20 April 1970 on Apple STAO 3363 (US).

Ram. Released on 17 May 1971 on Apple 33 (UK)and 28 May 1971 Apple PAS 10003 (US).

Wings' Wild Life. Released on 7 December 1971 on Apple PCS 7142 (UK) and 7 December 1971 on Apple SW 3386 (US).

Red Rose Speedway. Released on 4 May 1973 on Apple PCTC 251 (UK) and 30 April 1973 on Apple SMAL 3409 (US).

Band On The Run. Released on 7 December 1973 on Apple PAS 10007 (UK) and 5 December 1973 on Apple SO 3415 (US).

Venus and Mars. Released on 30 May 1975 on Capitol PCTC 254 (UK) and 27 May 1975 Capitol SMAS 11419 (US).

Wings At The Speed Of Sound. Released on 26 March 1976 on Capitol PAS 10010 (UK) and 25 March 1976 on Capitol SW 11525 (US).

Wings Over America. Released on 10 December 1976 on Capitol PCSP 720 (UK) and 10 December 1976 on Capitol SWCO 11593 (US).

Thrillington. Released on 29 April 1977 (UK) on EMI EMC 3175 and 17 May 1977 on Capitol ST 11642 (US).

London Town. Released on 31 March 1978 on Parlophone PAS 10012 (UK) and 31 March 1978 on Capitol SW 11777 (US).

Wings Greatest. Released on 1 December 1978 on Parlophone PCTC 256 (UK) and 27 November 1978 on Capitol S00-11905 (US).

Back To The Egg. Released on 8 June 1979 on Parlophone PCTC 257 (UK) and 11 June 1979 on Columbia FC 36057 (US).

McCartney II. Released on 16 May on Parlophone PCTC 258 (UK) and 26 May 1980 on Columbia FC 36511 (US).

Tug Of War. Released on 26 April 1982 on Parlophone PCTC 259 (UK) and 26 April 1982 on Columbia TC 37462 (US).

Pipes Of Peace. Released on 3 October 1983 on Parlophone 12R 6062 (UK) and 10 October 1983 on Columbia 44-04169 (US).

Give My Regards To Broad Street. Released on 22 October 1984 on Parlophone EL 260 278 (UK) and on 13 October 1984 on Columbia SC 396 13 (US).

Press To Play. Released on 1 September 1986 on Parlophone PCSD 103 (UK) and 25 August 1986 on Capitol PJAS-12475 (US).

All The Best. Released on 2 November 1987 on Parlophone PMTV 1 (UK) and 1 December 1987 on Capitol CLW-48287 (US).

Choba B CCCP. Released on 31 October 1988 on Melodia A60 00415 006 (USSR), 30 September 1991 on Parlophone PCSD 117 (UK) and 29 October 1991 on Capitol CDP 7 97615 2 (US).

Flowers In The Dirt. Released on 5 June 1989 on Parlophone PCSD 106 (UK) and 6 June 1989 on Capitol C1-91653 (US).

Flowers In The Dirt – Special Edition. Released on 1 March 1990 on EMI TOCP 6118/6119 (UK).

Tripping The Live Fantastic. Released on 5 November 1990 on Parlophone PCST 73461-3 (UK) and 6 November 1990 on Capitol C1-9 4778 (US).

Tripping The Live Fantastic – Highlights. Released on 19 November 1990 on Parlophone CDPCSD 114 (UK) and 20 November 1990 on Capitol CDP 7 95379 2 (US).

Unplugged (The Official Bootleg). Released on 20 May 1991 on Hispa Vox PCSD 116 (UK) and 4 June 1991 on Hispa Vox 7964 131 (US).

Paul McCartney's Liverpool Oratorio. Released on 7 October 1991 on EMI Classics LP PAUL 1 (UK) and 22 October 1991 on EMI Classics CDS 7 54371 2 (US).

Selections From Paul McCartney's Liverpool Oratorio. Released on 5 October 1992 on EMI Classics 7 54642 2 (UK).

Off The Ground. Released on 1 February 1993 on Parlophone PCSD 125 (UK) and 9 February 1993 on Capitol CDP 7 80362 2 (US).

Off The Ground – The Complete Works. Released autumn 1993 on Parlophone CDEQ 5010 (UK).

Paul Is Live. Released on 8 November 1993 on Parlophone PCSD 147 (UK) and 16 November 1993 on Capitol CDP 8 27704 2 (US).

Strawberries Oceans Shops Forest. Released on 15 November 1993 on Parlophone PCSD 145 (UK) and 22 February 1994 on Capitol CDP 8 27167 2 (US).

Flaming Pie. Released on 5 May 1997 on Parlophone PCSD 171 (UK) and 15 July 1997 on Capitol C1 56500 1 (US).

Standing Stone. Released on 1 December 1997 on EMI Classics 5 56484 1 (UK) and 23 Septembe 1997 on EMI Classics 5 56484 2 (US).

Rushes. Released on 21 September 1998 on Hydra 4 97055 1 (UK) and 20 October 1998 on Hydra 4 97055 2 (US).

Run Devil Run. Released on 4 October 1999 on Parlophone 5 223521 1 (UK) and 5 October 1999 on Capitol CDP 5 22351 2 (US).

Working Classical. Released on 6 December 1999 on EMI Classics 5 56897 1 (UK) and 19 October 1999 on EMI Classics CDQ 5 56897 2 (US).

Driving Rain. Released on 12 November 2001 on EMI 7243 5 35510 2 5 (UK) and 13 November 2001 on Capitol 7243 5 35510 25 (US).

Disney Time

A British television special that has been shown annually on BBC 1 in the UK during the Christmas/New Year holiday season for a great number of years. The show, hosted by British celebrities, features a selection of clips from Disney films, old and new, with a linking narrative from the celebrity. The 42-minute programme was recorded at Paul and Linda's house in Cavendish Avenue, St John's Wood, on Sunday 16 December 1973 with the two as hosts, surrounded by their children, Heather, Mary and Stella.

The programme was transmitted on Boxing Day, 26 December between 6.16 p.m. and 6.58 p.m.

There were clips from *Pinocchio*, *Mary Poppins*, *Wild Geese Calling*, *Run Cougar Run*, *Bambi*, *The World's Greatest Athlete*, *101 Dalmatians*, *Snow White & The Seven Dwarfs*, *Herbie* and *Robin Hood*.

Incidentally, the Disney Channel's showing of 'Paul McCartney: Going Home' won the Ace Award (Cable TV's equivalent to the Emmy awards) for best musical special on 12 January 1992.

Distractions

A number by Paul lasting 4 minutes and 47 seconds, which was included on the *Flowers In The Dust* album.

Do They Know It's Christmas?

A charity single recorded as part of the project to raise money for the starving people of Ethiopia. Paul recorded a message on the flipside of the record. He also participated in singing along with the song at the finale of the 'Live Aid' concert on Saturday 13 July 1985.

'Do They Know It's Christmas?' was the single that overtook his own 'Mull Of Kintyre' as Britain's biggest-selling single of all time.

Docklands Arena

A venue in London, where Paul chose to hold a press conference, primarily to announce details of his New World Tour and his 18th solo album release *Off The Ground*. The event took place on Friday 5 February 1993.

The initial press conference began at 6.30 p.m. and lasted for 25 minutes, with Paul's press agent Bernard Doherty hosting the questions.

They covered various subjects from the drug Ecstasy to Eastern Europe. He was also asked whether the Beatles would re-form and in which places he would be touring.

Paul was asked: 'Why did you decide to go back to your roots in recording *Off The Ground*?'

He replied: 'I was talking to the co-producer of this album, and I'd remembered that the easiest and most pleasant days I'd ever had in a recording studio were in the mid-Beatles period. John and I would go in with a couple of guitars, and play the song we'd written to the guys.

'In about an hour we'd have a pretty decent version of it. We'd then use that live take to build upon. And it was good to have this very strong foundation of a good take, rather than what can happen these days with little (makes an onomatopoeic sound imitating drum machine noises) and everyone saying, "Don't worry, it'll sound great when we mix it." With that you never get the feel as you're recording it. That was why I went back to the roots.'

Another journalist asked him, 'What can you tell us about the songs on the album written in partnership with Elvis Costello?'

Paul replied: 'Of the two songs with Elvis, one of them was a recent collaboration, 'Mistress And Maid', which was originally supposed to be a sexy title, slightly kinky – but it turned out to be a feminist title. The other one is 'The Lovers That Never Were' which is the first song we actually wrote together. But it wasn't that easy to record – on the last album we made a record of it but it wasn't too good. I like the song, so I brought it back for this album.'

He was also asked, 'Why do you keep pushing green issues on your albums?'

He replied: 'Look at all these people here today. If I just came here and said, "Hey, great", and it was all very frivolous, I feel like I would have wasted this occasion. I think people like to hear people standing up for things like human rights and ecology, and against some of the disasters that we've got in the world. So I'll keep pushing them. If the governments sort it out, then I'll sit down, because I don't really want this job. It's just that as I've got all this attention from the media, I feel like I ought to use it wisely rather than just fritter it away.'

Another question was: 'Can you comment upon Michael Jackson owning Northern Songs and your attempts to buy back the company?'

Paul replied: 'When John and I were kids, probably under the age of twenty, we were signed to a song deal. We didn't know that you could own songs. It was a surprise to us. We thought they were just in the air. We could see how you could own a house, but not a song. I think the publisher saw us coming. We got signed to a very old-fashioned deal – pretty much a slave deal, which I'm still under to this day.

'My argument is that it should have been varied a bit because we've been rather successful for the company! Michael was able to buy the company because it was just up for sale on the open market. And he had a lot of money after the record *Thriller*. And in actual fact I advised him to get into music publishing. And he said, "I'm going to buy your songs." And I said, "Good joke!" I thought he was joking! And then someone rang and said, "yeah, he's bought them." So that's that.'

Following the press conference Paul and his group then began a 'rehearsal' before an audience of 3,000 people, comprising media, members of his fan club and 25 winners of a *Daily Mirror* competition.

Paul performed for ninety minutes with five of the thirteen numbers from his forthcoming *Off The Ground* album with his band, which comprised Linda, Hamish Stuart, Robbie McIntosh, Paul 'Wix' Wickens and Blair. He began with 'Drive My Car' and followed with 'Coming Up', 'Get Out Of My Way', 'Another Day', 'All My Loving', 'Let Me Roll It', 'Peace In The Neighbourhood', 'Off The Ground' and 'I Wanna Be Your Man'. Then, while the group left the stage, Robbie McIntosh played a guitar solo. Then Paul and the rest of the group rejoined him for a series of acoustic numbers: 'Good Rockin' Tonight', 'We Can Work It Out', 'And I Love Her', 'Every Night', 'Hope Of Deliverance', 'Michelle', 'Biker Like An Icon', 'Here, There And Everywhere' and 'Yesterday'.

Then, from beneath the floor rose Paul's baby grand piano and the performance continued with 'My Love', 'Lady Madonna', 'Live And Let Die' and 'Let It Be'. The encore was 'Sgt Pepper's Lonely Hearts Club Band'.

Dom Sportova Hall

A venue in Zagreb, Yugoslavia where Paul appeared during his second 1976 European tour on Tuesday 21 September. This was the first show behind the 'Iron Curtain' by any member of the Beatles. Speaking on 'Tonight', a BBC documentary, Paul said that the appearance at the Dom Sportova Hall was 'the best show we've ever had'.

Don't Be Careless Love

A composition by Paul and Elvis Costello, 3 minutes and 17 seconds in length, which was included on the *Flowers In The Dust* album.

Don't Break The Promises

A number co-written by Paul and Eric Stewart during the time they were recording the *Press to Play* album, although it didn't appear on the finished album. The number was recorded by 10cc, who comprised Eric Stewart, Graham Gouldman, Kevin Godley and Lol Crème, in 1992 for their reunion album. This time the song included a credit for Gouldman, who had added to the number.

Don't Dig No Pakistanis

A number that was intended to be another of Paul's political statements in song. He initially wrote the lyrics using the tune of 'Get Back'. He recorded it during the *Let It Be* sessions, but it was never released and eventually became 'Get Back'.

Don't Let It Bring You Down

Another song recorded in the Virgin Islands for the *London Town* album and another Paul McCartney/Denny Laine joint work. On the track both musicians play Irish whistles.

It was 4 minutes and 34 seconds in length.

Don't Let The Sun Catch You Crying

A song composed by Joe Greene that was originally recorded by Ray Charles. Gerry & the Pacemakers popularised the number. Paul's version, lasting 4 minutes and 31 seconds, is the last track on the *Tripping The Live Fantastic* album and was recorded during the sound-check at the Forum, Montreal, Canada on 9 December 1989 during the 1989/90 World Tour.

Donald, Alistair

Paul's son-in-law, the husband of Paul's daughter Mary. He had been Mary's partner for three years before the marriage. Alistair is a TV producer and his projects for Paul included the documentary 'Wingspan' and Paul's solo project 'Anthology'.

Donald, Mary Alice McCartney

Paul and Linda McCartney's first child. She was born at the Marie Louise Hospital in London on Wednesday 28 August 1969 at 1.30 a.m. and weighed six pounds and eight ounces. Paul and Linda chose the hospital because it reflected the names of Mary's paternal and maternal grandmothers, Mary and Louise. In fact, Mary was named after Paul's mother who died of breast cancer when he was fourteen.

A picture of Mary appeared on the cover of Paul's first solo album *McCartney*.

Together with her sister Stella and younger brother James, she enjoyed an idyllic childhood on the family farm in Sussex. They were protected from publicity and Paul and Linda had ensured that despite their wealth and privileged position, their children would grow up to be 'ordinary'.

Rather than being steered towards academic careers, the children were encouraged in their artistic pursuits, resulting in Stella becoming a renowned fashion designer.

Mary began to work as her mother's personal photographic assistant in 1992. She studied her mother's techniques and supervised her photographic library. Yet she decided on a low-key approach to her career and enjoyed a degree of anonymity, even though she received an award and her photographs were displayed at the National Portrait Gallery.

Her boyfriends included musician Paul Weller and Giles Martin, son of George Martin.

She worked from MPL's Soho offices and her pictures have been featured in magazines around the world, including the Australian edition of *Elle* and the German edition of *Vogue*.

In April 1998, a few days after Mary had announced her plans to marry film director Alistair Donald, her mother died from breast cancer.

She married Alistair six months later on Saturday 26 September at a twelfth-century church near to the family home in Peasmarsh, near Rye, East Sussex. The Rev. Christopher Hopkins conducted the 40-minute ceremony. Mary and her TV producer fiancé Alistair Donald had intended getting married in the same register office as her parents, the Marylebone Register Office. She had moved the date of her wedding to early summer 1998 in order for her mother to be present, but Linda died in April. They abandoned the idea of a Marylebone wedding and were married at St Peter and St Paul Church in Peasmarch. Mary was 29 years old at the time. The guests, who numbered almost a hundred, were transported to the church in two coaches. Paul and Mary drove up to the church in an antique blue Rolls Royce.

Mary wore a strapless rose-coloured dress made of linen with trimmed cream antique lace, designed by her sister Stella, and Stella and Heather both wore mint-green dresses. James was dressed in a brown suit, Paul in a grey suit and Alistair in a beige one.

Paul took her into the church along a path scattered with petals.

In April 1999 Mary gave birth to a son, Arthur, Paul's first grandchild. Paul was to say: 'He's brought a lot of joy into the family. A grandchild immediately ennobles a lot of people. He makes me into a granddad, he makes my son into an uncle and he makes my daughter into an auntie. He's really lovely, we're all really proud of him – he's a good looking boy.'

It was while Mary was engaged in fund-raising work for the charity Breast Cancer Care that she first met the British Prime Minister's wife Cherie Blair in 1999. As a result, Mary was personally chosen by Mrs Blair to take photographs of her new baby, Leo, in May 2000.

Mary was thirty years old at the time and was to say: 'They (Tony and Cherie Blair) thought it would be nice to have a female photographer for these pictures and I was very complimented to be asked to take them. Leo was only 38 hours old when I took the pictures. He's a lovely baby and a gentle little soul.'

Publication fees for the photographs went to Breast Cancer Care and Sargent Cancer Care for Children.

Paul was obviously proud of the honour paid to Mary and commented, 'I'm really proud of Mary. It's a great tribute to her talent. Her mother would, to say the least, have been incredibly proud of her – and she probably is.'

She was the official photographer for the Brit Awards at Earls Court, London on 26 February 2001.

Mary was attacked and mugged in June 2002 near her home in Maida Vale. She was two months pregnant at the time when two attackers grabbed her from behind and covered her mouth to stifle her screams while one of them pulled out her diamond earrings and ripped off her engagement ring and watch.

After the attack she was taken to hospital for precautionary checks on her unborn child.

A friend commented, 'Mary never dresses in flash clothes or expensive jewellery. She likes the fact that she can walk around unrecognised. She had always avoided the public eye.'

Donovan

A singer/songwriter, born in Glasgow, who enjoyed a series of chart successes.

Paul made a guest appearance on Donovan's 'Atlantis' single playing tambourine and providing some backing vocals. He'd also dropped into the studio during Donovan's recording of 'Mellow Yellow'. A fifteen-minute session between the two artists, also from 1968, has been captured for all time on an American bootleg album *No. 3 Abbey Road, NW8*. The interlude was taken from a studio warm-up between Donovan and Paul and in their book *The End Of The Beatles*, authors Castleman and Podrazik mention that the two stars sat down together with acoustic guitars and exchanged songs-in-the-works, with Paul offering 'Blackbird' and 'Heather' and Donovan selecting numbers from what eventually became the album *HMS Donovan*.

In February 1968 it was announced that Donovan had written a script for a film to be made by Ingmar Bergman and that Paul had agreed to make a guest appearance in it. However, the film was never made.

Dorsey, Tony

The leader of the Wings horn section during the 1975/76 World Tour. The trombonist first worked for Paul in New Orleans during the recording of *Venus and Mars*. Paul asked him to lead the horn section for his next tour and Tony chose Steve Howard on trumpet and flugel-horn, Thaddeus Richard on soprano and alto saxophones, clarinet and flute, and Howie Casey on tenor saxophone. He played trombone in addition to writing the arrangements.

Drake's Drum

A racehorse that Paul bought for £1,200 as a present for his father's 62nd birthday on Monday 6 July 1964.

During that evening there was a private party following the premiere of *A Hard Day's Night* at the London Pavilion, attended by Princess Margaret and the Beatles. It was during the party that Paul told his father of the present. He was to say, 'My father likes a flutter – he is one of the world's greatest armchair punters.'

The horse came second on its very first race after the purchase. The most exciting moment occurred on Saturday 26 March 1966 when both Paul and his father were at Liverpool's famous Aintree Racecourse to watch Drake's Drum win the Hylton Plate, coming in at 20-1. Paul was particularly pleased at the pride his father felt, leading the horse into the winner's enclosure. In later years, Paul retired the horse to his High Park Farm in Scotland.

Drammeshalle

A theatre in Dramen, Norway. Immediately prior to his official world tour, Paul held a special pre-tour concert at the venue on Tuesday 26 September 1989.

Paul and his band performed 'Figure Of Eight', 'Jet', 'Rough Ride', 'Got To Get You Into My Life', 'Band On The Run', 'Ebony And Ivory', 'We Got Married', 'Maybe I'm Amazed', 'The Long And Winding Road', 'The Fool On The Hill', 'Sgt Pepper's Lonely Hearts Club Band', 'Good Day Sunshine', 'Can't Buy Me Love', 'Put It There', 'Things We Said Today', 'Eleanor Rigby', 'Back In The USSR', 'I Saw Her Standing There', 'This One', 'My Brave Face', 'Twenty Flight Rock', 'Coming Up', 'Let It Be', 'Live And Let Die', 'Hey Jude' and 'Get Back'. For the encore he performed 'Golden Slumbers', 'Carry That Weight' and 'The End'.

Dream Baby

The first number by the Beatles to be performed on the radio. Paul sang lead vocal on this song during their radio debut on *Teenager's Turn* on 8 March 1962. A few weeks earlier Roy Orbison had released his version of the Cindy Walker penned number and other artists who had recorded it included Del Shannon and Bruce Channel.

Dreams

Paul revealed the nature of his dreams to journalist Alan Smith in July 1966, including a recent dream of his in which he was queuing up at the Labour Exchange to collect his dole money. His dreams sometimes included visions of violent death, plane crashes, various disasters, dreams of him being pursued. He also recalled that before the success of the Beatles he constantly had dreams of being on holidays.

Drive My Car

The opening track on the *Rubber Soul* album.

Paul said, 'I arrived at the studio with this fairly good tune, but it had crappy lyrics, like: "I can give you diamond rings, I can give you golden rings, I can give you anything," and John said, "Oh!" He didn't like them and we had a deep sad moment. So, I said to him, "I'll tell you what, let's have a cup of tea and a ciggie and we'll just relax for a minute." After that we just jollied up and I said, "I'll tell you what then, how about this girl in LA who wants a chauffeur?"'

George Harrison was to comment, 'We laid the track because, what Paul would do, if he had written a song, he'd learn all the parts for himself and then come into the studio and say, "Do this." He'd never give you the opportunity to come up with something. But, on "Drive My Car", I just played the line, which is really like a lick off "Respect", you know, the Otis Redding version. I played that line on the guitar and Paul laid that with me on bass. We laid the track down like that.'

The Beatles recorded the number on Wednesday 13 October 1965.

'Drive My Car' was also included on the 'Nowhere Man' EP, the compilations *The Beatles 1962-1966* and *Rock 'n' Roll Music* and the American album *Yesterday And Today*.

A live version of the number lasting 2 minutes and 33 seconds, which was recorded in Kansas City on 31 May 1993, was included as a track on the *Paul Is Live* album.

Driving Rain (album)

A 15-track album released in Britain on Monday 12 November 2001 and in America on Tuesday 13 November 2001. It was Paul's first album of new songs in four years and he recorded it at Henson Studios in Los Angeles between March and July 2001 with a new band comprising three American musicians, Rusty Anderson, guitar, Gabe Dixon, keyboards and Abe Loboriel, drums. He also worked with a new producer David Kahne, who'd produced numerous major artists ranging from Tony Bennett to the Bangles. During the sessions he recorded 22 new songs, 15 of which were included on the album.

To keep the music fresh the album was recorded in two weeks and Paul said, 'We didn't fuss about it. I didn't even tell the producer or any of the guys what we were going to do until the morning of the day we were going to do it. Nobody knew what I was going to pull out of the hat. I just said, "OK, guys, what do you think of this one? Let's go do it."'

He had originally used the provisional title *Blue Skies*.

Paul was to comment: 'One of the things that began when we were doing *Run Devil Run*, the rock and roll album, was me remembering that I'm mainly the bass player. Talking about the old way the Beatles used to record brought that back to me. So although I've played a bit of guitar and stuff on the occasional track, I've basically been the bass player. That's my role. It's simple and satisfying. I sing and I play bass.'

He also explained the system of recording he employed, which was like the Beatles' recording technique and didn't include rehearsing. It was the method he'd employed with *Run Devil Run*.

'We did the same thing with this album; we came into the studio on Monday morning, I'd show them a song, and we'd start doing it. We recorded eighteen tracks in the first two weeks in February, and then I went back to LA in June and recorded another couple of tracks and mixed the album. So making the whole album from beginning to end has taken about five weeks. That's still pretty good going, but that is the kind of work rate we'd do in the Beatles.'

The cover of the album depicts Paul at a urinal in a photograph taken by him using a miniature camera built into his Casio watch.

The tracks were: 'Lonely Road (Nu Nu)', 'From A Lover To A Friend', 'She Given Up Talking', 'Driving Rain', 'I Do', 'Tiny Bubble', 'It Must Have Been Magic', 'Your Way', 'Spinning On An Axis', 'About You', 'Heather', 'Back In The Sunshine Again', 'Loving Flame', 'Riding Into Jaipur' and 'Rinse The Raindrops'.

Driving Rain (single)

The title track from the *Driving Rain* album, lasting 3 minutes and 26 seconds. It was recorded on 27 February 2001.

Drugs

Paul's flirtations with drugs began, as far as anyone can tell, with mild 'uppers' such as purple hearts, in Liverpool. In Hamburg, the Beatles were known to take similar stimulants, such as Preludin and Captogen, which could be obtained in local chemist's shops without a prescription, but which they used to buy from Rosa, the lavatory attendant at the Kaiserkeller and, later on, the Top Ten club.

Singer Bob Dylan introduced the Beatles to marijuana in 1964 and at the time Paul was quoted as saying: 'I'm thinking for the first time, really *thinking*.'

However, it was for his use of LSD that Paul first hit the headlines in connection with drugs. LSD or 'acid' is a chemical hallucinogenic and Paul was to admit that he'd taken it in an interview that appeared in *Life* magazine in America on 16 June 1967. This created such a furore that Paul was interviewed on the subject for a TV news programme broadcast on 19 June. The same day the *Daily Mirror* also published an interview in which Paul discussed taking LSD. The confession led to Evangelist Billy Graham declaring he would pray for Paul's salvation!

The interview on television went as follows:

Q: Paul, how often have you taken LSD?

A: Er, four times.

Q: And where did you get it from?

A: Well, you know, I mean, if I was to say where I got it from, you know, it's illegal and everything, it's silly to say that so I'd rather not say it.

Q: Don't you believe that this was a matter which you should have kept private?

A: Well, the thing is, you know, that I was asked a question by a newspaper and the decision was whether to tell a lie or tell the truth, you know. I decided to tell him the truth but I didn't really want to say anything because if I'd had my way I wouldn't have told anyone because I'm not trying to spread the word about this but the man from the newspaper is the man from the mass medium. I'll keep it a personal thing if he does too, you know, if he keeps it quiet. But he wanted to spread it so it's his responsibility for spreading it. Not mine.

Q: But you're a public figure and you said it in the first place. You must have known that it would make the newspapers.

A: Yes, but to say it, you know, is only to tell the truth. I'm telling the truth. I don't know what everyone is so angry about.

Q: Well, do you think you have encouraged your fans to take drugs?

A: I don't think it will make any difference, you know, I don't think my fans are going to take drugs just because I did. But the thing is that's not the point anyway. I was asked whether I had or not and from then on the whole bit about how far it's going to encourage is up to the newspapers and up to you, you know, on television. I mean you're spreading this now at this moment. This is going into all the homes in Britain and I'd rather it didn't, you know. But you're asking me the question and if you want me to be honest, I'll be honest.

Q: But as a public figure, surely you've got a responsibility not to say any . . .

A: No, it's you who've got the responsibility not to spread this now. You know I'm quite prepared to keep it as a very personal thing if you will too. If you'll shut up about it, I will!

However, it was his association with cannabis that continued to dog him. In August 1972, during the Wings tour of Europe, Paul found himself in trouble when the group appeared in Sweden. As soon as Wings had finished their set at the Scandinavian Hall, Gothenberg, the police stepped in and cut off the PA system. They were waiting to question Paul, Linda and Denny Seiwell and took them to the local police headquarters, together with Paul's secretary Rebecca Hinds.

Customs officers had apparently intercepted seven ounces of marijuana that had been sent from London addressed to Paul.

A senior police officer commented: 'We told them we had found the cannabis in a letter and at first they said they knew nothing about it. But after we had questioned them for about three hours they confessed and told the truth. McCartney, his wife and Seiwell told us they smoked hash every day. They said they were almost addicted to it. They said they had made arrangements to have drugs posted to them each day they played in different countries so they wouldn't have to take any drugs through the customs themselves.'

John Morris, the tour operator, said, 'Paul, Linda and Denny did admit to the Swedish police that they used hash. At first they denied it but the police gave them a rough time and started threatening all sorts of things. The police said they would bar the group from leaving the country unless they confessed.'

Gothenberg's public prosecutor, Lennart Angelin, released them after a preliminary fine of £1,000. He said: 'They were not arrested since it was obvious that they were going to use the cannabis for themselves and not pass it on.'

Paul, Linda and Denny were fined on 12 August 1972. Not too long after the Swedish incident a police constable, Norman McPhee, set off to Paul's two farms in Campbeltown ostensibly to check the security in Paul and Linda's absence. McPhee had been on a drugs identification course in Glasgow and when he visited High Park, one of Paul's farms, for some reason he checked one of the greenhouses where he said he became suspicious of some plants. He returned to his station, later to return to the farm with six other policemen. A thorough search turned up no further evidence and in December Paul was charged on three counts, including those of possessing cannabis and cultivating cannabis plants. Paul was asked to appear in court the following year, in March 1973. The hearing took place on Monday 8 March and the court was told that in September 1972 a crime prevention officer had gone to the farm to check that it was secure. He had noticed some plants in the greenhouse with the tomatoes and had returned to the station to consult a reference book. To the charge of knowingly cultivating the plants, Paul pleaded guilty. To the two other charges of possessing cannabis he pleaded not guilty – and the charges were dropped. His lawyer told the court how Paul had received the seeds in the post and, being interested in horticulture, had planted them. The Sheriff, convicting him on the first count, commented, 'I take into account that you are a public figure of considerable interest, particularly to young people, and I must deal with you accordingly. The fine will be £100.'

Paul said: 'I was planning on writing a few songs in jail. You have to be careful. I look on it like Prohibition but you have to recognise the law. I think the law should be changed – make it like the law of homosexuality with consenting adults in private. I don't think cannabis is as dangerous as drink. I'm dead against hard drugs.'

Due to the various drug convictions, Paul had been repeatedly refused an American visa, but was finally given one in December 1973.

The next drugs affair happened in 1975. Wings had begun recording *Venus And Mars* in America between January and April. They were using the Sea Saint Studios in New Orleans and the Wally Heider Studios in Los Angeles. One night, shortly after midnight, on their way home from the Wally Heider Studios to Malibu, the trouble began. It was Monday 3 March and Paul was driving a silver Lincoln Continental with Linda at his side and their three children in the back seat.

Driving along Santa Monica Boulevard, Paul failed to stop for a red light and a Highway Patrol motorcyclist flagged him down. The motorcyclist approached their vehicle and said that he smelled a strange substance as he put his head inside the car. He then found a smouldering joint on the floor and discovered a small amount of marijuana, between 16 and 18.5 grams, in Linda's purse. Linda immediately admitted that the joint had been hers and that Paul had no part in it. They were taken to West Los Angeles police station and Paul was told he was free to take the children home. Linda was detained for two hours before bail was arranged; in April she was taken to court after being charged with possession. In May, the judge, Brian Cuhan, said that he would be prepared to have the charges dropped if Linda agreed to have six sessions with a psychiatrist. She said she would and the case was dismissed. The judge also agreed that she could have the sessions in London. The arrangement was not unusual, as a Los Angeles police officer commented: 'After six months instruction by approved counsellors, first offence drug charges – like that facing Mrs McCartney – are usually dropped.'

Paul was later to comment: 'The only really unfortunate thing about it is that it starts to get you a reputation as a kind of druggie. It's really only a minor offence. It isn't something we take too seriously, and of course the press image is really far worse. We're not serious drug addicts or anything. The fact is that it's illegal, and if a thing's illegal you're liable to get caught doing it.'

A year later, Paul's convictions were to catch up with him. As part of the Wings World Tour of 1976, Paul intended to make appearances in Japan. These would be his first performances there for ten years, since the Beatles appeared at the Budo Kan Hall in Tokyo in July 1966.

All arrangements had been made and tickets for all the concerts had been sold out in advance, lavish programmes had been printed, but just as Paul and company were due to fly from Australia to Japan, they were told that Paul's visa had been cancelled at the last minute by

Japan's Minister of Justice due to Paul's drug convictions in Sweden and Scotland in 1972 and 1973 respectively.

However, this incident was to prove minor in comparison with their next, horrific experience in Japan.

Wings had finally confirmed that they would be allowed to tour the world's second biggest record market and were to appear at eleven concerts in Japan in January 1980. Once again, all the tickets were sold out well in advance. All the main equipment for the tour had been sent on ahead to Japan and Paul, Linda and the children had gone to New York for Christmas to visit Linda's family. They set off from the Big Apple on a 14-hour flight to Tokyo with just their personal baggage. As they went through Customs at Narita airport, they were asked to open their luggage. In the first case opened there was a polythene bag which, when examined, was found to contain almost half a pound of marijuana.

Jo Jo Laine was to say: 'Linda had left twenty Thai sticks of grass in her make-up bags ... Paul took the rap.'

The Customs officials called the police and Paul was led away handcuffed. Narcotics officers questioned him and after five hours of interrogation he admitted that he had smoked pot for eleven years and had obtained the grass that had been found in his bag from a friend in America. Linda and the three children were taken to a hotel in Tokyo and the tour was cancelled, disappointing the 100,000 who had been lucky enough to obtain tickets.

Paul was told that he could be in jail for up to twenty days before being charged. He was initially shocked when Albert Marshall, the British Vice-Consul visited him on the first night. Paul believed the situation was a storm in a teacup until Marshall told him otherwise. Paul recapped: 'I thought, fantastic, good old consul, he is going to get me out. He just sat down and said, "Well, it could be eight years, you know".'

As he was not Japanese, Paul was allowed coffee and bread rather than the usual rice and green tea given to detainees. He had to sleep on a mat on the floor, Japanese style, and was awakened by a guard at 6 a.m. each morning. He also had to retire to bed each night at 8 p.m., was only allowed half an hour of exercise in his cell each day and was denied access to his guitar and writing material.

In all, Paul was to spend ten days in the Japanese prison. Linda was first able to visit him on the fifth day and told him that she was worried he might be sentenced to three months. She saw him again on the eighth day (she made three visits in all) when her lawyer brother John accompanied her. Linda brought Paul a cheese sandwich, some fruit and science-fiction books. Paul had been allowed a change of clothes and some blankets, but it was a week before he was able to take a bath. He was offered the option of bathing alone or in the communal prison bathhouse. He chose the latter. He commented: 'Life in jail isn't so bad. The prison wasn't the rat-infested hole I thought it was going to be. For the first few days I was worrying all the time. For eight days I didn't see any daylight at all. I had to eat seaweed and onion soup for breakfast. I shared a bath with a man who was in for murder and all because I didn't think.'

He also commented: 'At first I thought it was barbaric that they put handcuffs on me twice a day when I went to see the investigators. There seemed to be a different lot each time. I had made a confession on the night I was arrested and apologised for breaking Japanese law but they still wanted to know everything. I had to go through my whole life story, school, father's name, income, even my medal from the Queen. Perhaps they decided to deport me because I was totally frank with them.'

Paul was deported, carted off from prison directly to the airport, still in handcuffs and surrounded by twelve policemen.

Linda was to say that Paul had been released because of a loophole in the law – since his visa had been taken from him at the airport on arrival he was, in fact, an illegal alien. The Japanese authorities said that they released him because he showed signs of repentance. In fact, he did seem to repent his actions to reporters on his flight back home, via Anchorage, Alaska and Amsterdam, Holland.

On the plane to Alaska he told the press: 'I have been a fool. What I did was incredibly dumb. My God, how stupid I have been. I had just come from America and I still had the American attitude that marijuana isn't too bad. I didn't appreciate how strict the Japanese are about it. I was really scared thinking I might be in prison for so long. I've made up my mind. I've been smoking marijuana for more than eleven years and I'm never going to touch the stuff again.'

Despite this declaration, Paul again made the headlines after being busted in Barbados.

Paul, Linda, James and Stella had been staying at a luxury nineteenth-century villa on the holiday island. On the evening of Saturday 14 January 1984 three police cars arrived at the villa. Drug squad officers produced a search warrant and discovered 10 grams of marijuana. Alan Long, the local police inspector, commented, 'We received a tip-off that they were in possession of marijuana. Four uniformed officers went round to the McCartneys' holiday villa with a search warrant. Mr McCartney freely admitted his guilt and accompanied the officers to the police station.'

At the police headquarters in Bridgetown, the capital, they were questioned for two hours. Their passports, together with £1,000 in cash, were confiscated when they were released on bail for the sum of £1,400.

Paul and Linda were ordered to appear at Holetown Magistrate's Court the next day, where they both pleaded guilty to the charge.

Their defence attorney, David Simmons, told the magistrate: 'The male accused is of considerable international standing. He is a very talented and creative person. People who have this talent sometimes need inspiration. I'm instructed that Mr McCartney and his wife obtained the vegetable matter from someone on Holetown Beach. They are not pushers.'

The Assistant Police Commissioner, Keith Whittaker, commented: 'The law is for everybody on the island – and that includes McCartney. We are treating this as a very serious case. I don't know if he'd be welcome here again.'

Police inspector Alan Long also commented, 'By their example the McCartneys are encouraging our young people to use drugs.'

Judge Haynes Blackman fined them 200 Barbados dollars each.

When he left the court, Paul said, 'I've got absolutely no grudges and no complaints. It was a small amount of cannabis and I intended to use it, but the police came to my place and I gave them 10 grams of cannabis. Linda had another small carton of cannabis in her handbag.'

When they arrived back in London on Tuesday 17 January Paul made a statement to the press at Heathrow Airport, commenting, 'This substance cannabis is a whole lot less harmful than rum punch, whisky, nicotine and glue, all of which are perfectly legal. I would like to see it decriminalised because I don't think, in the privacy of my own room, I was doing anyone any harm whatsoever.'

Paul and Linda then went to board a private aircraft when they were asked to return to the airport Customs hall where they were questioned and some marijuana was discovered in Linda's handbag. She was arrested but released on unconditional bail and was required to appear at Uxbridge Magistrate's Court on Tuesday 24 January.

The hearing lasted thirteen minutes during which Linda pleaded guilty to illegally importing 4.9 grams of marijuana. Mr Edwin Glasgow, Linda's defence counsel appealed to the magistrates, 'Linda is genuinely sorry, and wishes to make a genuine apology. I urge the court not to make an example of her just because she is famous. Linda is a thoughtful, likeable woman who has done far more for other people than those who sneer at her.'

She was fined £75.

The two busts so close together caused a furore in the British press, with many people airing their views on both sides of the marijuana question.

Paul's brother Mike, coming to their defence, said: 'As kids, Paul and I were taught moderation and toleration by my dad. Other people could do with the same lesson. The idea that marijuana leads to heroin is rubbish. It's like saying a few drinks makes you an alcoholic.'

Gerry Marsden, leader of Gerry and the Pacemakers, commented, 'Paul has said too much really. In any case I don't agree with him.' He added, 'Kids tend to do whatever people they admire are doing. He should set an example whether he wants to or not.'

In the edition of London's *Time Out* magazine, published on Friday 27 January 1984 there was a feature by Paul in which he expounded his reasons why he considered that cannabis should be legalised.

Denny Laine has made several statements in some newspaper articles regarding Paul's use of cannabis, claiming that Paul and Linda got through two ounces of cannabis each day, the equivalent of £1,000 worth of marijuana per week. He also claimed that they had once smuggled a small amount through customs in the hood of baby James's coat.

In an interview with *New Statesman* magazine in 1997, Paul commented about marijuana stating that he supported decriminalisation. He said, 'People are smoking pot anyway and to make them criminals is wrong. You're filling up all the jails and yet it's when you're in jail that you really become a criminal. That's where you learn all the tricks. When I was jailed in Japan, there was no rehabilitation. They just stuck me in a box for nine days. Decriminalisation would take the sting out of the issue.'

Several national newspapers in Britian picked up his comments. Labour MP, Lin Golding, a member of the Commons Drugs Misuse Group commented, 'I've never seen a shred of evidence to suggest it would be safe to legalise cannabis. Soft drugs tempt youngsters to try other harder drugs. It could be very damaging to educate children about drugs.'

Dunbar, Geoff

A British animation specialist. He co-wrote a script with Paul for the *Rupert Bear* film and collaborated with Paul on other animated film ventures such as *Rupert And The Frog Song*, *Daumier's Law* and *Tuesday*.

Dunbar, John

A man who had a part to play in Paul's cultural education in London in the mid-1960s, particularly during the time that Paul was residing at the Ashers' house in Wimpole Street.

Dunbar was married to Marianne Faithfull and the couple lived at 20 Lennox Gardens where Paul and Jane were often invited. The couple were introduced to various people from the world of the arts and it was Dunbar who introduced Paul to Robert Fraser, the art gallery owner.

It was Dunbar, together with Peter Asher and Barry Miles, who opened Indica, the art gallery/bookshop, to which Paul provided some financial backing – and he was actually the bookstore's first customer.

Dunbar was also a link in the romance between John Lennon and Yoko Ono. It was Dunbar who organised Yoko's exhibition 'Unfinished Paintings and Objects' at the gallery.

Durband, Alan

A former head teacher at Liverpool Institute who was originally educated at Cambridge University, his tutor being F R Leavis. When

Paul was attending the Institute, Durband was his sixth-form English teacher. Paul claimed that he was the only teacher he liked and mentioned that he told the boys about books such as *Lady Chatterley's Lover* and Chaucer's *The Miller's Tale*, pointing out that they weren't dirty books but examples of good literature.

He was one of those unique teachers who actually made a difference to the lives of their pupils. He died in September 1994 at the age of 67.

A plaque was unveiled in his memory at the Everyman Theatre in Liverpool in a ceremony attended by playwright Willy Russell, whose plays were first presented at the theatre and who said that Durband was an 'extraordinary man'.

Durband was a board member of the Everyman Theatre and is credited with putting the theatre on the map. Paul was unable to attend the ceremony but said that he had always remembered Durband for his wit and wisdom.

Russell said, 'He was an inspiration to me; he was an inspiration to so, so many people.'

Another former pupil, Brian Jacques, who became a successful children's author, commented, 'I wouldn't be here if it wasn't for Alan Durband. He was always interested in people and in talent. I gave him my first ever manuscript in a plastic Tesco bag. He went away and sent it to a publisher. He believed in me. He believed in passion.'

Earth Day For the Environment Concert

A concert held before an audience of 30,000 at the Hollywood Bowl, Los Angeles on Friday 16 April 1993. It took place during the third leg of Paul's North American tour. Paul performed an 85-minute set during which he gave an acoustic performance of 'Mother Nature's Son' and also added 'Blackbird' to the repertoire of this particular concert. Paul also announced, 'Your friend and mine, Ringo Starr,' and Ringo appeared on stage to participate in the chorus finale of 'Hey Jude'.

The repertoire of that particular performance was: 'Coming Up', 'Looking For Changes', 'Fixing A Hole', 'Band On The Run', 'All My Loving', 'We Can Work It Out', 'Hope Of Deliverance' (which was performed as a duet with kd lang), 'Mother Nature's Son', 'Blackbirds', 'Peace In The Neighbourhood', 'Off The Ground', 'Can't Buy Me Love', 'Magical Mystery Tour', 'C'mon People', 'Live And Let Die', 'Let It Be' and 'Hey Jude'.

£250,000 was raised from the concert and charities receiving donations from Paul's performance were Friends of the Earth, Greenpeace and People For the Ethical Treatment of Animals.

Earthrise – The Rainforest Album

An album issued to coincide with the Earth Summit. All the proceeds of the album were donated to the registered charity the Earth Love Fund, formed to provide aid to people trying to save the endangered rainforests.

Paul contributed his *Flowers In The Dirt* track 'How Many People?' to the album, which also had contributions from Ringo Starr and Julian Lennon.

Polygram issued the album in Britain on Monday 1 June 1992 on

CD (Polygram 419-2), cassette (Polygram 515 419-4) and vinyl (Polygram 515 419-1). On the same day Weinerworld issued a compilation tape *Earthrise – The Rainforest Video* on WNR 2027. As Paul hadn't made a promotional film for 'How Many People?', scenes of forest destruction were shown.

The CD was reissued in Britain in 1994 and also in America for the first time on Rhino/Pyramid (R2 718030).

East Gate Farm

The 160-acre farm that Paul and Linda bought from Jim Higgs in 1978 for a fee in excess of £100,000. Situated near the village of Peasmarsh, near Rye in East Sussex, it is close to the two-bedroom cottage that they first moved into in that area in 1975.

In 1982 the couple had the farmhouse demolished and a five-bedroom house built on the site. There is also a swimming pool, stables and a paddock for their horses. The estate is called Waterfall and is surrounded by a six-foot fence, constructed in a way that makes it very difficult for any intruder to scale. There is also a 65-foot tower. These security measures prompted journalist Chris Hutchins to dub the property 'Paulditz'.

Paul, on the other hand, maintains that the fence was erected to prevent foxes from getting in to attack his pheasants and peacocks and that the tower enables the family to look over the surrounding countryside.

The cottage found an ideal use in 1983 when it became the setting for Linda's daughter Heather's 21st birthday party. More than a hundred local people were invited and a marquee was erected on the grounds. Fun Boy Three provided music and guests included Ringo Starr and Barbara Bach. The main food was vegetarian stew; there was ample red and white wine and the party continued until 5 a.m.

Eastman, Jay

Linda McCartney's nephew. In September 2001, Jay married Katama Guernsey and Paul and Heather attended the wedding. During the reception Paul played 'When The Saints Go Marching In' on a trumpet. He also sang 'The Very Thought Of You' and 'I Saw Her Standing There' to the newlyweds.

Eat At Home

One of the tracks from the 1971 album *Ram* which was co-penned by Paul and Linda. Wings performed the number during their European tour. The single wasn't released in either Britain or America but it was issued as a single in Germany in August 1971 on Apple IC006-04864 and in France on Apple 2C006-04864M.

'Smile Away' was on the flip.

When asked about the number in 1975 Paul said that it was 'a plea for home-cooking – it's obscene'.

Eat the Rich

A British comedy film by Michael White Productions and the Comic Strip, which was premiered on Friday 23 October 1987. Paul and Linda made a brief cameo appearance in the movie, filming their scene at Moor House, Moor Park, near Rickmansworth, Herts on 4 March 1987. Also in the film were Lemmy of Motorhead, French and Saunders and Rik Mayall.

Ebony And Ivory

Paul's song about racial harmony on which he shared vocals with Stevie Wonder. The plea for racial harmony used the black and white keys of a piano to symbolise the way in which races can live together.

The two of them recorded the number at Air Studios on the island of Montserrat on Friday 27 February 1981 during the *Tug Of War* sessions.

Paul had been in his home studio in Scotland sitting at his piano when he remembered a title he'd had in his head for some years after hearing Spike Milligan using the black and white notes on the piano as an analogy of harmonious race relations.

Paul recalled, 'He'd said, "you know, it's a funny kind of thing – black notes, white notes, and you need to play the two to make harmony, folks".'

The song developed from there, with Paul visualising it being performed by a black artist, his first choice being Stevie Wonder, with the two of them sitting side by side at a piano. The arrangements were made and the recording took place at Montserrat with recording manager George Martin suggesting that Paul and Stevie do the number without additional musicians and singers.

The single was issued in Britain on Parlophone R6054 on Monday 29 March 1982 and topped the charts for three weeks from 24 April, giving Stevie his first British No. 1. The American release on Columbia 18-02860 was on Sunday 2 April and also went to No. 1. There was a 12″ version of the number that was issued in the States on Columbia 44-02878 on Thursday 16 April 1982. The flipside was a number that Paul co-wrote with Denny Laine called 'Rainclouds'.

The number was also the last track on the *Tug Of War* album and was produced by George Martin.

It was released in Germany on 1C006-64749.

A version of this number, lasting 4 minutes and 1 second, was included on the *Tripping The Live Fantastic* album. It was recorded live at the Ahoy Sportpaleis in Rotterdam, Netherlands on 8 November 1989 during the 1989/90 World Tour.

Ecce Cor Meum

A classical composition by Paul, which received its world premiere on Saturday 10 November 2001 at the 800-seater Sheldonian Theatre, Magdalen College, Oxford.

Paul had visited the college in 1997 with his late wife Linda and had promised to write an oratorio especially for Magdalen College's new chapel.

'Ecce Cor Meum' means 'Behold My Heart' and the theme was that of finding love within music. It had been scored for a choir and small orchestra and was in four movements – 'Spiritus Spiritus', 'State of grace', 'Ecce Cor Meum' and 'Musica'.

Paul, accompanied by Heather Mills, was in the audience when the Magdalen College Choir, accompanied by a 23-piece orchestra conducted by Bill Ives, performed the choral piece, which lasts for 48 minutes.

After the performance Paul went on stage to thank the conductor and choir, joking that the choirboys should be in bed and the rest of the choir in the bar with him.

Echoes

A BBC Radio London show. On Sunday 17 June 1984, Paul appeared on the show in a live interview conducted by Stuart Grundy. The interview was syndicated in America during October of that year as part of the promotion for the film *Give My Regards To Broad Street*.

Eddy, Duane

Famous rock guitarist, born in Corning, New York on 26 April 1938. His hits included 'Rebel Rouser', 'Shazam' and 'Peter Gunn'.

Duane recorded with Paul at Paul's Sussex studio on Wednesday 4 and Thursday 5 February 1987. He recorded a version of the Wings 'Rockestra Theme' for his Capitol album *So Glad To See You Here*. Paul produced the track and also played bass on it.

Edmunds, Dave

A musician and record producer who was born in Cardiff, Wales on 15 April, 1944. His first group was the Raiders in 1966 and over the years he appeared in a large number of different bands including the Human Beans, Love Sculpture and then had a solo hit with 'I Hear You Knocking' in 1970. He appeared in the film *That'll Be The Day* and formed a band called Rockpile in 1977. On 29 December 1979 the group appeared with Wings in the Concert For Kampuchea at the Odeon, Hammersmith.

In 1983 he appeared in *Give My Regards To Broad Street* as a member of Paul's band in the film, joining Ringo Starr and Chris Spedding on several live numbers which were included on the movie soundtrack.

In June 1983 he produced 'On The Wings Of A Nightingale' with the Everly Brothers, a number penned by Paul for the Everly Brothers' comeback and in June 1984 he produced the Everly Brothers' first studio album for eleven years.

Edmunds also joined Ringo Starr's All Starr Band for tours in 1992 and 2000. He was also musical director for 'The Lennon Tribute' concerts in Liverpool and Tokyo in 1990.

Edwards, Jack
The headmaster of Liverpool Institute when Paul was a pupil. He became the inspiration for 'The Headmaster's Song' in *Liverpool Oratorio*. He died at a nursing home in Formby on 8 January 1992. He was 95 years old.

1882
A solo piano demo that Paul recorded in 1970. It lasts for approximately three and a half minutes and is one of the many unreleased numbers by Paul that has found its way onto bootleg releases.

Eight Days A Week
A song Paul and John composed at Kenwood, John's house in Weybridge. On occasion, Paul would journey there in a chauffeured car because he had lost his licence due to a speeding offence. At one time Paul asked the driver what kind of a week he had, had he been busy? 'Busy, I've been working eight days a week,' the driver told him. As soon as Paul arrived at John's house he related the expression to him as neither had heard it before. They decided it would be a good title for a song.

However, John didn't have much enthusiasm for it and was to say, '"Eight Days A Week" was never a good song. We struggled to record it and struggled to make it into a song. It was his initial effort, but I think we both worked on it. But it was lousy anyway.'

The number was included on the *Beatles For Sale* album and EP in Britain and was issued as a single in America.

Eleanor Rigby
The song was recorded on 28 and 29 April and 6 June 1966 and issued on Parlophone R5493 in Britain on 5 August and in America on Capitol 5715 on 8 August. The No. 1 single was a double A-side with 'Yellow Submarine', the second time they had issued a double A-side, and remained in the No. 1 position in Britain for four weeks and topped the American charts for six weeks.

'Eleanor Rigby' was also featured on the *Revolver* album, issued in Britain on the same day. A few months later, in December, it resurfaced on *A Collection Of Beatles Oldies (But Goldies)* and also appeared on several albums, including *The Beatles 1962–1966* and *The Beatles Box*. It was re-released among a batch of singles to celebrate the group's twentieth anniversary, in 1982, of their first EMI record release.

The version found on Volume One of *Anthology 2* was simply a backing track.

In an interview with the *Sunday Times* Paul revealed how the song came about. He said, 'I was sitting at the piano when I thought of it. Just like Jimmy Durante. The first few bars just came to me. And I got this name in my head – Daisy Hawkins, picks up the rice in the church where a wedding has been. I don't know why. I can hear a whole song in one chord. In fact, I think you can hear a whole song in one note, if you listen hard enough.

'I couldn't think of much more, so I put it away for a day. Then the name Father McCartney came to me – and all the lonely people. But I thought people would think it was supposed to be my dad, sitting knitting his socks. Dad's a happy lad. So I went through the telephone book and I got the name McKenzie. I was in Bristol when I decided Daisy Hawkins wasn't a good name. I walked round looking at the shops and saw the name Rigby. Then I took it down to John's house in Weybridge. We sat laughing, got stoned and finished it off. All of our songs come out of our imagination. There never was an Eleanor Rigby.'

It's not strictly true that all of the Lennon and McCartney songs came from the imagination; a number of them were autobiographical. Paul wrote songs relating to ups and downs in his romance with Jane Asher, John wrote about an affair of his in 'Norwegian Wood' and songs such as 'Penny Lane' and 'Strawberry Fields Forever' were about real places.

However, the genesis of this particular song does apply to Paul's words about a song coming from the imagination and that there never was an Eleanor Rigby.

When it was discovered that in the churchyard of St Peter's Church in Woolton there was a gravestone to an Eleanor Rigby, everyone assumed that that was where Paul got the name, although his explanation of the development of the song proves that this was not the case. The late Tom McKenzie, a Liverpool compere who was master of ceremonies on some Beatles gigs at the Memorial Hall, Norwich, believed that Father McKenzie referred to him and began calling himself Father McKenzie. He was also mistaken. This is a common mistake when people attempt to analyse Beatles songs too literally, expecting them to refer to particular people – some said that 'the man from the motor trade' referred to in Paul's 'She's Leaving Home' was Terry Doran, a former Beatles' associate who was a car dealer. Paul has denied this – and Judith Simonds of the *Daily Express* believed that 'Hey Jude' referred to her, but of course Paul began writing it with Julian Lennon in mind.

The *Sun* newspaper printed a story about the song in 1984, when it published a photograph of Tom McKenzie posing at the side of the gravestone and commented that Tom was also the Father McKenzie referred to. Yet Paul was adamant that the character was fictitious.

McKenzie died at the age of 75 in July 1991. Paul was to say, 'He was a funny old man. It's sad.'

If we refer once again to detailed comments Paul made about the song: 'It started off with sitting down at the piano and getting the first line of the melody, and playing around with words. I think it was "Miss Daisy Hawkins" originally; then it was her picking up the rice in a church after the wedding. That's how nearly all our songs start, with the first line just suggesting itself from books and newspapers.

'At first I thought it was a young Miss Daisy Hawkins, a bit like "Annabel Lee", but not so sexy; but then I saw I'd said she was picking up the rice in church so she had to be a cleaner; she had missed the wedding, and she was suddenly lonely. In fact she had missed it all – she was the spinster type.

'Jane (Asher) was in a play in Bristol then, and I was walking round the streets waiting for her to finish. I didn't really like "Daisy Hawkins" – I wanted a name that was more real. The thought just came: "Eleanor Rigby picks up the rice and lives in a dream" – so there she was.

'The next thing was Father MacKenzie, and he was just as I had imagined him, lonely, darning his socks. We weren't sure if the song was going to go on. In the next verse we thought of a bin man, an old feller going through dustbins; but it got too involved – embarrassing. John and I wondered whether to have Eleanor Rigby and him have a thing going, but we really couldn't see how. When I played it to John, we decided to finish it.

'That was the point anyway. She didn't make it, she never made it with anyone, she didn't even look as if she was going to.'

Despite there being no link with people like Tom McKenzie or the St Peter's Church gravestone, the name 'Eleanor' was actually inspired by actress Eleanor Bron, who appeared in the film *Help!* with the Beatles. Paul said, 'I think Eleanor was from Eleanor Bron, the actress we worked with in the film.' He mentioned that the Beatles knew her well and that he'd seen her at Peter Cook's Establishment Club in Greek Street.

It's interesting that songwriter Lionel Bart also came up with an erroneous assertion that the name came from a gravestone.

He said, 'Paul has always thought that he came up with the name Eleanor because of having worked with Eleanor Bron in the film *Help!* but I am convinced that he took the name from a gravestone in a cemetery close to Wimbledon Common where we were both walking. The name on this gravestone was Eleanor Bygraves and Paul thought the name fitted the song. He then came back to my office and began playing it on my clavichord.'

There is no doubt that the song was Paul's and the actual input by John Lennon on this particular number was minute. Yet John was to claim several years later, 'I wrote a good half of the lyrics or more.' He persisted in the claim, telling *Hit Parader* magazine, 'I wrote a great deal of the lyrics, about seventy per cent.' Even in his interview in *Playboy* magazine he said, 'The first verse was his and the rest are basically mine.'

John's close friend Pete Shotton, who spent time with John at his Weybridge home, says, 'Though John was to take credit, in one of his last interviews, for most of the lyrics, my own recollection is that "Eleanor Rigby" was one Lennon–McCartney classic in which John's contribution was virtually nil.'

Paul was to say; 'I saw somewhere that (John) says he helped on "Eleanor Rigby". Yeah. About half a line.'

Apart from the backing vocals, Paul was the only member of the group featured on the track, accompanied by a string section that had been arranged by George Martin. The session musicians comprised four violins, two violas and two cellos.

The number was animated in a marvellous scene in the film *Yellow Submarine*.

'Eleanor Rigby' has also become one of the most popular Beatles songs to be recorded by other acts with over two hundred recorded versions, including those by Diana Ross & the Supremes, Paul Anka, Frankie Valli, Aretha Franklin, the Four Tops, Johnny Mathis and Vanilla Fudge.

Incidentally, Paul was delighted when poet Allan Ginsberg told him that 'Eleanor Rigby' was one hell of a poem.

A version of this number lasting 2 minutes and 36 seconds was included on the *Tripping The Live Fantastic* album. It was recorded live at the Worcester Centrum, Worcester, Massachusetts on 8 February 1990 during the 1989/90 World Tour.

'Eleanor Rigby' was inducted into the Recording Academy Hall of Fame in February 2002.

Elevator

A single by Grapefruit. Despite being discovered by Terry Doran, head of Apple Music, the group's releases were issued by RCA. For their 1968 single 'Elevator', Paul produced a promotional film of the group. He took them to Hyde Park and filmed a three-minute sequence.

Ellis, Richard

One of the photographers used by Paul when Wings were still extant. Ellis took the shots that appeared on the covers of the albums *Red Rose Speedway*, *Wings At The Speed Of Sound* (he also took the photo used as a poster and included with the LP) and *Wings Over America*.

Emerick, Geoff

A recording engineer and producer, born in 1946. He first began his studio career as a disc cutter and started work at EMI in 1962. He was twenty years old when Norman Smith took him on as second engineer for Beatles recordings, which mainly meant that he operated the tape machines. His first session as second engineer was on 'She Loves You' and he graduated to first engineer on the *Revolver* album when

Norman Smith was promoted to the position of producer. His final work with the Beatles was on the *Abbey Road* album.

He has won Grammy awards for 'Best Engineered Recording' for *Sgt Pepper's Lonely Hearts Club Band*, *Abbey Road* and *Band On the Run*.

Geoff has been engineer or producer on a number of Paul's records, including the albums *Band On the Run*, *Venus And Mars*, *London Town*, *Tug Of War*, *Pipes Of Peace*, *Flowers In The Dirt*, *Paul Is Live*, *Flaming Pie* and Paul also phoned him up to ask him to work with him on the MTV acoustic project *Unplugged*.

He also produced albums by a variety of artists including Ringo Starr, Elvis Costello, Badfinger and Cheap Trick.

Paul was best man at the wedding of Emerick to Nicole Graham at the register office in Rye, East Sussex in early January 1989.

Tragically, Geoff's wife died of cancer. When Geoff and Paul were engaged in the studio sessions for *Wide Prairie*, they both expressed their grief, sometimes crying at the console and sometimes laughing while listening to Linda's tapes and remembering her.

Paul said, 'He lost his wife to cancer, too. So the pair of us were just crying on the console. But then we'd listen to Linda's spirit and we'd laugh and remember her. So it was the "Tears and Laughter" sessions.'

Emotional Moments
A number also referred to as 'Cage'. Paul made a demo of the song at his Rude Studio in Campbeltown in 1978, using drums, keyboard and electric guitar. It was considered for *Back To The Egg*, but rejected.

Empire Ballroom
A large ballroom situated below ground level in Leicester Square, London, and part of the Moss Empire group. On Monday 8 November 1971 Paul invited a thousand guests to the ballroom to celebrate the release of Wings' first album *Wild Life*. Guests were requested to wear conventional dress and the tone of the affair was similar to that of a typical night at the Empire, with music by the Ray McVay Band, entertainment from the Peggy Spencer Formation Dancing Team and guests able to buy their own drinks over the bar.

Among the celebrity guests were Elton John, John Entwistle, Keith Moon, Ronnie Lane, Ronnie Wood, Kenny Jones, Ian McLagen and Jimmy Page.

Empty Hand
Produced by Paul and directed by David Litchfield, this short film was the first project from McCartney Productions, Paul's film company, in 1977. It was a 32-minute documentary featuring the current Wings drummer George Britton, who was a karate expert, at the Amateur Karate Championships where he appeared with the British Amateur Karate Association team.

The filming took place on Saturday 30 November at the Michael Sobell Sports Centre, Islington, London. Britton fought in two bouts, losing the first and winning the second. Paul also wrote incidental music for the documentary.

End, The

A number by Paul included on the *Abbey Road* album, which only lasted for a minute. It was recorded at Abbey Road on 23 July 1969 and John Lennon was to comment, 'That's Paul again, the unfinished song, right? He had a line in it, "The love you take is equal to the love you make," which is a very cosmic, philosophical line. Which again proves that if he wants to, he can think.'

The number includes the only recorded drum solo by Ringo as a Beatle, which led Paul to comment, 'We could never persuade Ringo to do a solo. The only thing we ever persuaded him to do was that rumble in "The End" on *Abbey Road*. He said, "I hate solos".'

English, Joe

It was ironic that drummer Geoff Britton was replaced by an American drummer called Joe English in the Wings line-up.

Joe was born in Rochester, New York on 7 February 1949 and became a rock drummer at the age of eighteen when he joined a band called the Jam Factory. For six years the band toured America numerous times supporting acts of the calibre of Jimi Hendrix, Janis Joplin and the Grateful Dead, until they split up in 1973. The demise of the group marked a dark period in Joe's life during which his wife left him, taking their two children with her. He didn't have any gigs and was completely broke.

'I was on the bottom,' he said. He managed to get through his bad patch with encouragement from a girlfriend called Dayle and had settled in Georgia where he found regular work as a session musician.

When Geoff Britton left Wings during the *Venus and Mars* sessions, Tony Dorsey, leader of Paul's horn section, recommended Joe. At the time he was rehearsing with Bonnie Bramlett and intended touring with her, but when he received the offer from Paul he found a replacement for the tour and immediately went to New Orleans to record on *Venus and Mars*.

The album was mixed at the Wally Heider Studio in Los Angeles, and it was on the way there that Paul asked Joe if he'd like to become a member of Wings. He was delighted to accept.

Britton stayed with the band until late in 1977 and quit after completing part of the *London Town* sessions. He'd also contributed to the albums *Wings At The Speed Of Sound* (on which he sang lead vocals on the track 'Must Do Something About That') and *Wings Over America* and had joined the world tour. During Wings' appearances at the Omni in Atlanta (18–19 May 1976), Paul introduced Joe from the stage saying he was 'from just down the road in Juliette, Georgia'.

When he left the group, Joe stated, 'I enjoyed being in Wings and I learned a lot, but I got tired of the months and months sitting in recording studios. I wanted to come home and see if I could make it as Joe English and not off Paul McCartney.'

He told the American *Beatlefan* magazine that he liked Linda but didn't consider her a good musician or vocalist and that Denny Laine tended to sing off-key. He also commented: 'I was continually promised a share of the record royalties, but I never received any,' although he qualified the statement by adding that he was very well paid when he was with the band.

After leaving Wings (1975–77) he joined the group Tall Dogs, and later Sea Level. In 1981 he had become a born-again Christian and was living in Nashville where he issued his first gospel album *Lights In The World* on Refuge Records.

Entertainment Centre

A venue in Sydney, Australia where Paul performed concerts on the second leg of his world tour on Tuesday 16, Wednesday 17 and Saturday 20 March 1993.

TCN 9, the Sydney TV station, which screened highlights from the shows, filmed his Tuesday and Wednesday performances. During the sound check on the Tuesday Paul performed 'Get Out Of The Rain' and also part of the Paul Simon song 'Fifty Ways To Leave Your Lover'. Paul was also visited backstage by Australian actor Bryan Brown who portrayed Paul's manager in the film *Give My Regards To Broad Street*.

During his performance of 'Mull Of Kintyre' the Blackwood Pipe Band joined Paul on stage.

Epaminondas, Andros

A London-born Greek-Cypriot, Andros gained his experience in the film world with Stanley Kubrick on such films as *A Clockwork Orange*, *Barry Lyndon* and *The Shining*. He worked for Kubrick for eleven years and has said that he did 'everything from scouting locations to organising the money for doing the washing up'.

Paul made him producer of *Give My Regards To Broad Street* and was to say: 'Andros took a lot of slagging-off during production. People were always coming up to me and saying, "that bastard Andros, he's so tight-fisted". He was the scapegoat because he's little and Greek and he took it all in his stride. What better whipping boy? But I tell you, I look at the budget now and I'm glad to have been involved with him.'

Epstein, Brian

The Beatles' first manager, born in Liverpool on 19 September 1934.

He first heard about the Beatles in the pages of *Mersey Beat*, the newspaper he stocked from July 1961 and for which he wrote record reviews. After visiting the Cavern during a lunchtime session on 9 November 1961 to see the group, he decided to sign them up and arranged for them to meet him at his office on 3 December 1961.

Epstein was punctilious and he was very irked when Paul turned up late for the meeting. George Harrison apologised saying, 'Sorry Mr Epstein. He's just been having a bath.' Epstein was not amused. 'This is disgraceful. He is going to be very late.'

'Late,' said George, 'but very clean.'

In 1961, when asked about the individual Beatles, Brian's comments on Paul were that he was 'probably the most changed Beatle. He's mellowed in character and thought. A fascinating character and a very loyal person. Doesn't like changes very much. He, probably more than the others, finds it more difficult to accept that he is playing to a cross-section of the public and not just to teenagers, or sub-teenagers, whom he feels are the Beatles' audience.'

In 1964 he commented, 'Paul can be temperamental and moody and difficult to deal with but I know him very well and he me. This means that we compromise on our clash of personalities. He is a great one for not wishing to hear about things, and if he doesn't want to know he switches himself off, puts one booted foot across his knee and pretends to read a newspaper.'

Brian also considered that Paul was very musical and his voice was more melodic than John's, commenting, 'Also, and this is vital to me, he has a great loyalty to the other Beatles and to the organisation around him. Therefore, I ignore his moods and hold him in high esteem. I would not care to lose him as a friend.'

Of the relationship between Brian and Paul, Beatles press agent Tony Barrow was to comment, 'Paul learned to conduct himself quickly and Brian felt overpowered. He recognised Paul as very forceful and was, on a personal basis, a little scared and uncertain of him. Paul was very much a social climber in those days. He liked to learn the etiquette of life from Brian.'

In June 1967, when the story that Paul had admitted to taking LSD was about to be published in the British press, Paul phoned Brian the evening before the story appeared to tell him. Epstein had a sleepless night and then decided he would back Paul and also admit to taking LSD himself. He said, 'There were several reasons for this. One was certainly to make things easier for Paul. People don't particularly enjoy being lone wolves and I didn't feel like being dishonest and covering up, especially as I believe that an awful lot of good has come from hallucinatory drugs.'

On hearing of Brian's death on 27 August 1967, Paul said, 'This is a great shock. I am terribly upset.'

In 1997, when he heard that the Beatles Store in Liverpool planned a plaque to Brian Epstein, Paul sent a message: 'This event will ensure that Brian will be remembered for many years to come by people he cared about so much – his fellow Scousers. Having known and loved him, I feel I can say on his behalf, to the people of Liverpool, thank you very much.'

Equinox Club
A club in London's Leicester Square. On Thursday 30 September 1999 Paul made a special public appearance to promote his *Run Devil Run* album. He talked to the audience and presented them with a short behind-the-scenes film of the making of the album. He also had a question-and-answer session with the audience during which he admitted that there was a 'final' Beatles song in the vaults which hadn't been released yet. He was also presented with original 45s of two of the numbers he covered on the album, 'No Other Baby' by the Vipers and 'Shake a Hand' by Little Richard.

Escorts, The
A popular Liverpool band who never quite made the major league. They comprised Terry Sylvester (guitar), John Kinrade (guitar), Mike Gregory (bass) and Pete Clarke (drums).

Paul took an interest in the band and produced their single 'From Head to Toe'/'Night Time', issued in Britain on Columbia DB 8061 on 18 November 1966, but it fared no better than their previous releases. Paul also played tambourine on the A-side.

Elvis Costello recorded both numbers in the 1980s.

The Escorts disbanded towards the end of the 1960s and Terry and Mike joined the Swinging Bluejeans for a time, then Terry later became a member of the Hollies.

Incidentally, their first Liverpool residency in 1962 arose as a result of a helping hand from Ringo Starr.

Evening With Adrian Mitchell, Willy Russell and Very Good Friends, An
An event that took place before an audience of 400 at the Everyman Theatre in Liverpool on Wednesday 21 March 2001.

The Oxford Union, the Royal National Theatre and the Los Angeles Festival of Books had offered Paul readings of his new book *Blackbird Singing*. He said: 'If I'm going to do this, I want to do it in Liverpool first.'

It also allowed him to pay tribute to Liverpool poet/painter Adrian Henri who had died a few months previously.

Only three poets had been advertised for the reading – Tom Pickard, Willy Russell and Adrian Mitchell. Paul Bell of the Everyman commented, 'Paul wanted a group of people who wanted to see poetry – not him.'

Paul was on stage for thirty minutes and was introduced by Adrian Mitchell, who had aided Paul in the editing of *Blackbird Singing*.

He told the audience that he'd first become interested in poetry when his English teacher at Liverpool Institute had told him about the 'dirty bits' in Geoffrey Chaucer's poems.

Paul recited 'Ivan', 'In Liverpool', 'Jerk Of All Jerks', 'Maxwell's Silver Hammer', 'Day With George', 'City Park', 'Black Jacket', 'Dinner Tickets', 'Masseur', 'A Billion Bees In The Borage', 'Tchaica', 'Why Don't We Do It In The Road?' and 'Without You'.

At the end of the evening Paul, Mitchell, Russell and Pickard each read a line from Adrian Henri's poem 'Without You'.

Evening With Paul McCartney, An

Title of a fundraising event in aid of the Royal College of Music which took place at St James's Palace, St James's, London SWI on Thursday 23 March 1995.

Admission was limited to 300 invited guests and although the admission was free, the guests were expected to make their own donations to the College of approximately £250 each.

Also present at the event was the College's patron, Prince Charles.

The occasion marked the debut of *A Leaf*, an eight-minute piece for solo piano. Paul introduced the number and a former member of the College, 22-year-old Russian pianist Anya Alexeyev, performed it. Paul sang three numbers, 'For No One', 'Yesterday' and 'Lady Madonna', backed by the Brodsky Quartet. Michael Thompson guested on French horn. Paul then sang a duet with Elvis Costello on 'Mistress And Maid', co-written by them both, and Costello then performed four of his own songs. The Brodsky Quartet next played a brief recital that included 'Ticket to Ride'. Also performing were baritone Willard White and mezzo-soprano Sally Burgess, who had performed on *Liverpool Oratorio* and sang selections from it.

Everton

An area of Liverpool where Paul's grandparents lived. They moved several times within Everton, from their original home in Fishguard Street where Paul's father was born to Lloyd Street and Salva Street before eventually moving out of the area to Scargreen Avenue in West Derby.

Every Night

A number which Paul originally performed in January 1969 during rehearsals for the *Get Back* project, although it wasn't completed at the time. Later that year, while on holiday in Greece, he completed the lyrics, recorded it and finally mixed the track at Abbey Road Studios on 22 and 24 February before including it on his solo *McCartney* album.

The number lasted 2 minutes and 29 seconds, with Paul playing the various instruments himself and double-tracking part of the vocal track. He also performed it on the Wings tour of Britain in 1979, and in the same year Phoebe Snow recorded it, giving her a minor hit.

Fair Carol

The yacht, which Paul hired in the Virgin Islands, on which he and Wings recorded part of their *London Town* album in 1977.

It was a pleasant experience although the musicians weren't seamen and the rolling of the waves caused a number of accidents, with Paul slipping and cutting his knee badly. Jimmy McCullough also injured his knee in a fall, which also left him deaf in one ear. Geoff Emerick, the engineer, electrocuted his foot and MPL's Alan Crowder fell down a stairway and broke his heel. The band and the crew also suffered from sunburn!

Faithfull, Marianne

She was born in Hampstead, London on 29 December 1946, the daughter of Baroness Erisso von Sacher-Masoch and Dr Glynn Faithfull.

As a schoolgirl she met John Dunbar at a Valentine's Ball at Cambridge and he became her boyfriend. He invited her to London to stay with his parents and took her to Wimpole Street where she met the Asher family and Paul. She thought Paul looked incredibly handsome and asked Dunbar if Paul and Jane had sex. 'Of course they do!' he told her. The same evening she went to a party attended by the Rolling Stones and their manager Andrew Loog Oldham spotted her and thought that she had the virginal looks that would have an appeal to young pop fans, so he recorded her with a Mick Jagger/Keith Richards song 'As Tears Go By', which became a hit.

Marianne married John Dunbar on 6 May 1965.

While the couple lived at 29 Lennox Gardens, Paul used to visit them regularly at their flat.

Marianne turned down the song 'Etcetera' which Paul had offered to her, but she wanted to record 'Eleanor Rigby', although Paul told her he wanted to record it himself. She decided on recording 'Yesterday', although Paul told her that various artists had already planned several other versions.

Matt Munro's version of 'Yesterday' was already climbing the charts when she was recording her version. She invited Paul along to her recording session at Decca's West Hampstead studio on Monday 11 October 1965 in which a 100-voice choir backed her. Her version was rush-released and entered the British chart on Thursday 4 November 1965 but only managed to reach the No. 36 position.

Paul attempted to promote Marianne's version of the number and included her as one of the guests on the Granada TV special *The Music of Lennon and McCartney*.

Paul began singing 'Yesterday' seated on a stool and strumming his guitar, then after thirty seconds the song faded into Marianne's version, with the sound of orchestra and choir. At the time Marianne was eight months pregnant and the cameras mostly viewed her head and shoulders.

Her son Nicholas was born on 10 November 1965.

Marianne and Dunbar were divorced in 1970 and she went on to marry Ben Brierly in 1979 and Giorgio Dellaterza in 1988.

Falkoner Theatre

A venue in Copenhagen, Denmark, where Paul appeared on Wednesday 24 July 1991 on the last of six surprise concerts promoting his *Unplugged – The Unofficial Bootleg* album.

All 3,000 seats in the theatre had sold out in 75 minutes and seating had to be removed prior to the show to facilitate standing room for the large audience.

Falling In Love Again

A song that Paul performed after introducing it into the Beatles repertoire in 1962. Marlene Dietrich originally sang the number in the classic German film *The Blue Angel*. Paul sang it at the Star Club in Hamburg and it can be heard on the *Star Club* recordings, first issued in June 1997 as a two-album set by Lingasong.

Fame Game, The

A BBC 1 documentary which was basically a history of Paul's efforts to establish his LIPA (Liverpool Institute Of Performing Arts) project, which included some of Paul's own monochrome film, rare footage which he taped while visiting the derelict site in the 1980s. He was also seen jumping on a desk and singing 'Tutti Frutti'. The film was produced by Rob Rohrer and screened on Saturday 8 June 1996.

Family Way, The (album)

The original soundtrack album for the film *The Family Way*, by the George Martin Orchestra, was issued in Britain on 6 January 1967 on

Decca SKL 4847 and in America on Monday 12 June 1967 on London MS-82007. This mainly comprised of thirteen variations on the Paul McCartney theme 'Love In The Open Air'.

The album was 25 minutes and 19 seconds in length.

It was Paul's first solo outing and produced by George Martin at CTS Studios in London.

Paul had been asked to pen the soundtrack in the late summer of 1966. After watching the film he composed the theme 'Love In The Open Air', which was orchestrated by Martin.

The soundtrack resulted in Paul receiving his first solo Ivor Novello Award for 'Best Instrumental Theme'.

Family Way, The (film)

A British film starring Hayley Mills, John Mills and Hywel Bennett, produced by the Boulting Brothers. The movie gave Paul his first credit as a solo composer. He had produced 26 minutes of music for the film, arranged for him by George Martin. A soundtrack album was issued on Decca SKL 4847 on 6 January 1967; two singles from the album were also issued – 'Love In The Open Air'/'Theme From The Family Way' on United Artists UP 1165 on 23 December 1966 and 'Love In The Open Air'/'Bahama Sound', on United Artists UA 50148 on 24 April 1967.

Paul, Jane Asher and George Martin attended the film's premiere at the Warner Theatre, London on 18 December 1966.

The film had been based on the play *All In Good Time*, penned by Bill Naughton, a former Liverpool lorry driver. Due to the theme of an unconsummated marriage, it was given an X certificate.

Famous Groupies

A number written by Paul in Scotland and recorded in the Virgin Islands for the *London Town* album.

Faron

Noted Liverpool singer and group leader during the era of the Mersey Sound. With his group Faron's Flamingos he recorded a blistering version of the Contours 'Do You Love Me?', but the record company in London put it on the B-side. The Dave Clarke Five and Brian Poole & The Tremeloes then issued the number, almost identical to Faron's version – and it established their careers. Dejected, the Flamingos broke up.

Faron appeared on a number of gigs with the Beatles on Merseyside, one of which took place at Litherland Town Hall. Faron always packed his stage clothes neatly in a suitcase and that night, as it was pouring with rain, Paul asked if he could put his leather trousers in Faron's case. Faron agreed and said he'd meet them later at Joe's Café in Duke Street. When he arrived the Beatles had eaten and left and Joe Davey, the owner, presented Faron with a bill for five pounds, saying the Beatles said he'd pay it. Faron was furious and decided not to return Paul's leather trousers to him. He left them in the house and promptly forgot about them.

Over ten years later he was searching the attic and came across a pair of leather trousers, covered in green mould. He polished them up and happened to mention his find to Allan Williams, a local club-owner. Williams said they would be worth a fortune and asked Faron to give them to him and he would get a good price for them both.

Faron phoned his brother, who now lived in America, to tell him about the trousers and his brother revealed that they did not belong to Paul. He told Faron that he had found the trousers soon after Faron had put them away and began wearing them when he went out on his motorbike. One day he had an accident, skidding along the road and ripping the leather trousers so badly he had to throw them away. He bought another pair of leather trousers and when he left Liverpool had put them away in the attic.

Faron told Williams but Williams put them up for auction in October 1976 claiming that they were Paul's.

Fascher, Horst

The former bouncer, then manager, of the clubs the Beatles worked in during their early Hamburg gigs. He was with them at the Kaiserkeller, the Top Ten Club and the Star Club. He was even captured singing with them on stage at recordings made at the Star Club.

Sadly, Horst was to suffer a number of tragedies. In 1992 his two-year-old son Rory was suffocated when a fold-up wall bed trapped him in his sleep and suffocated him. His mother was Alison, daughter of Liverpool rock star Faron, and their son had been named after Liverpool music legend Rory Storm.

Horst and Alison became estranged and Horst and his next partner had a baby daughter, Marie-Sophie. The baby was born with heart problems and when the one-year-old girl needed a heart operation, Horst called Paul for help. Paul generously paid for a team of heart specialists to fly to London from New York and arranged for Horst and his family to bring the baby to London for the operation. Unfortunately, Marie-Sophie didn't survive.

Fashion For Ecology

A venture that Paul launched at Kew Gardens, London on 26 March 2001. He was promoting the sale of scarves with designs inspired by Linda's photographs. These were based on images from Kew Gardens that Linda photographed in February 1998. Linda's friend Sue Timney designed the scarves. Proceeds from the sale of the scarves went to the Millennium Seed Bank Project, a conservation charity, based in West Sussex, which Linda had supported.

The scarves were made of satin devoré, velvet devoré, silk and Viscose and came in three designs – 'Daisy Chain', 'Loving Memory' and 'Flower Garden'.

Feed The World

The flipside of the Band Aid charity single, 'Do They Know It's Christmas?' which took over from 'Mull Of Kintyre' as the biggest-selling British single ever.

The proceeds were in aid of the Ethiopian Appeal fund. Although Paul donated his services, he was unable to make the actual studio session when 'Do They Know It's Christmas?' was recorded, so he sent in a spoken message that appeared on the B-side 'Feed The World'.

The 7″ pressing was issued on Saturday 7 December 1985 on Mercury FEED 1 and a 12″ version was released the following week on Saturday 14 December on FEED 112.

Fellows, Graham

An actor who portrayed Paul in the Everyman Theatre, Liverpool production of the play *Lennon*.

Ferry 'Cross The Mersey

One of the major British football disasters took place when Liverpool FC was playing Nottingham Forest at the Hillsborough football ground in 1989. Ninety-five people were crushed to death.

Gerry Marsden decided to make a benefit record to aid relatives of the victims. He'd made a special version of 'You'll Never Walk Alone' four years previously in aid of another football disaster at Bradford. On that particular record, in which Gerry had fifty artists participate under the name the Crowd, he had Paul contribute a few words on the B-side of the record, called 'Messages'.

That record topped the British charts. It also gave Gerry another unique record achievement: the first time that an artist had topped the British charts with a different version of the same number.

For the 'Mersey Aid/Hillsborough Fund', Gerry approached Pete Waterman of the hit production team Stock, Aitken and Waterman, who agreed on Gerry's choice of the number 'Ferry 'Cross The Mersey'. Paul McCartney, Holly Johnson of Frankie Goes to Hollywood and another Liverpool band, the Christians, were approached to participate in the recording.

Gerry recorded his part first and Paul and the Christians went in the studios together. Holly Johnson was in Germany at the time and recorded his vocals after the others had all finished. Waterman had to explain to Gerry that their recording technique was different from what he had in mind. He was to comment, 'He (Gerry) wrote it as a *pop song*. When we produced it with four artists, we did it as a *tribute*, which changed the whole meaning of why the song was being recorded. Gerry had recorded it with George Martin as a hit; we were now recording it with Paul McCartney and everybody else to raise money for a charity. We were creating an emotional message to wrench money out of people's pockets. Our job was to make money for an appeal and for that we had to be mercenary.'

In the middle of the record, Paul lets out a wail. Waterman commented, 'He goes out of tune and he wanted me to take it off and do it again and I wouldn't let him. I said, "Why did you do it?" and he said, "Well, it's just how I felt." And I said, "Then it stays!" Linda McCartney called me up afterwards and said, "You know, you're probably the only person who's ever told Paul McCartney that he couldn't have his own way. But all of us down here think you're absolutely right; we think it's marvellous to hear him showing some emotion."'

Waterman made some additional comments. 'He [Paul] wanted to make it perfect which, of course, because he's Paul McCartney, he would do. But we knew the song had got to him at that point, the emotion of the tragedy had got to him, and when you see the video it definitely gets your throat, catches you and gives you a tear in the eye. McCartney did capture the spirit of it – and that's down to the fact that Gerry wrote a great song that does stand up to that treatment.'

The record topped the British charts on 20 May 1989.

Gerry Marsden was to comment, 'It was fun to think that Paul McCartney had returned, with me, to the top of the charts with a Marsden composition.'

Festehalle, Frankfurt, Germany

Paul appeared at this venue on the first European leg of his World Tour on Friday 6 October and Saturday 7 October 1989.

He was to return to the venue three and a half years later on Monday 22 and Tuesday 23 February 1993.

On the Monday Paul held a press conference at the venue during which he was presented with a gold disc for the *Off The Ground* album.

Paul was initially asked why he continued to perform when he could just relax and enjoy life. He answered, 'When I was about fifteen I thought that's what would happen. I wanted to win the football pools, the lottery. Buying a house, a car and a guitar. That was all I needed to make this a happy world for me. So when I got those three things, you don't just stop.

'I enjoy my work and if, like tomorrow, I'd have some time off, and I'd be OK for about a month. But after three or four weeks I'd want to play my guitar again, want to start to write a song again and take it into the studio and record it, coming out and playing it to the people, really, that's what I enjoy most. That's what I couldn't do without.'

He was asked about the controversy surrounding 'Big Boys Bickering'.

'This song really contains only one swear word which, everyone has pointed out, happens fourteen times. I was watching this film last night on TV. The language in that ... forget my song! It was like all the language you've ever heard. I don't like changing a song once I've written it. It's like when the Stones were asked to sing their 'Let's Spend The Night Together'. Harmless now, but that was shocking once. 'A Day In The Life' was banned – and 'Give Ireland Back To The Irish'.

'It's too much of a cop-out, I think, to change your song just because somebody doesn't like it.

'Big boys like the BBC or MTV sure, they had to ban my song. They may have some young listeners whose parents may be offended. My kids, they weren't offended. I didn't have to explain to them. It's a fact of modern life, going round swearing. I just wanted to protest against certain political conditions, so removing that word would be like removing the protest.'

He was then asked about 'Hope Of Deliverance'.

'This hope of deliverance is what you want to make it. It can take on a different significance. If you're falling out with your husband or your girlfriend, then you want deliverance from that situation. If it's someone in your family becoming ill, then it's that. It's really deliverance from whatever your own personal problem is that you're going through. Deliverance from all our polluting earth? I couldn't offer any answers on that, I'm as puzzled as we all are. Don't know any real answer, just being optimistic. The only answer, I think, is for people to openly communicate about it. Having faith in young people, give them the information hoping they will be sensible. That's my hope of deliverance for the future – a lot of crossed fingers.'

He was asked about using Wings material in his stage act and replied: 'The stuff I made with Wings has always received a lot of criticism. People have always said this was, like, not a good period for us. I don't believe that, but I'm afraid such a policy does have its effect. If someone keeps telling you you're stupid, in the long run, you tend to believe that. It's a pity. It now so happens that the Wings material gets squeezed out between the new stuff and me reliving the success of my Beatles songs.

'Still, there's "Live And Let Die", "Another Day" and "Let Me Roll It". We don't miss it out completely. I used to desperately try being different from the Beatles then, seeking for a new thing. Now, I'm much more happy with the Beatles style, playing it back and I enjoy singing it. The main change is that the words are a little bit more involved with grown-up issues now. Where it used to be "she loves you, yeah, yeah yeah", now that's changed to include a bit more serious matter.'

Paul was then asked what he considered made a good song.

He said, 'I don't know what makes a good song. Luck, I think. Good luck. Some of my best songs, they just wrote themselves. You can sit down behind the piano, guitar in hand, for hours and maybe come up with an average song.

'A song like "Hope Of Deliverance", I wrote that in like two or three hours. I don't know how, but you can tell when you're writing, it just feels good. What's the use of asking yourself "where is this coming from?" I mean, if "Yesterday" was a song which I just woke up with one morning, then stop asking. I don't know. It's coming from some source above us – or below us. Who knows?'

He was then asked if he'd be doing some more shows in Germany.

'I hope so. They haven't fixed any further dates for Europe yet. We're going to Australia first, then to America and after that, who knows. But, yes, we will be coming back to other cities in Germany soon. Berlin or Munich. Which ones exactly, that's still to be decided.'

Figure of Eight

A single by Paul which was released in Britain on Parlophone R6235 on Monday 13 November 1989 where it reached No. 42 in the charts and in the US on Capitol 4JM44489 (on cassette only, with both tracks in a shorter version than the British release) on Wednesday 15 November 1989. It reached No. 92 in the American charts.

'Ou Est Le Soleil?' was on the flipside.

Paul had been releasing multiple versions of his singles releases and there were no less than eight different 'Figure Of Eight' singles issued in Britain, including three different CD versions.

There was a 7" version at 4 minutes and 1 second in length issued with 'The Long and Winding Road', which was the live version from the 'Put It There' video and 'The Loudest Thing'. This was released in Britain on Monday 20 November 1989 on CDS Parlophone CD3R 6235 in a gatefold edition. Another version issued in Britain on Monday 27 November 1989 on 3D3 Parlophone CD3R 6235 contained the 7" version of 'Figure Of Eight' with a live version of 'Rough Ride' from the 'Put It There' video and 'Ou Est Le Soleil?' Another release that day was in a standard jewel case on CDS Parlophone CDR 6235.

The single was also issued in Germany on CD3 Parlophone CDP 552 203653 3.

A version of this number lasting 5 minutes and 33 seconds was included on the *Tripping The Live Fantastic* album. It was recorded live at the Ahoy Sportpaleis in Rotterdam, Netherlands on 10 November 1989 during the 1989/90 World Tour.

Filmography

Paul has always been interested in films and was a regular cinemagoer in his youth. He particularly remembers the time he went to see *The Blackboard Jungle* with George Harrison.

Paul revealed details of eight of his favourite rock movies to journalist Jan Etherington in a feature in the Saturday 13 October 1984 issue of the British magazine *TV Times*. The films were *Rock Around The Clock*, *The Girl Can't Help It*, *Loving You*, *A Hard Day's Night*, *Gimme Shelter*, *Woodstock*, *Let The Good Times Roll* and *The Song Remains The Same*.

Of *A Hard Day's Night*, he commented: 'I hate to say it but when you see the girls in their miniskirts and white floppy hats it does look dated.'

Of *Let The Good Times Roll*: 'Chuck Berry was the main writing influence on John and me – together with Buddy Holly.'

Of *Gimme Shelter*: 'It was made by the Maysles Brothers who made *Beatles In the USA* in 1964. I remember the Maysles well.'

And of *The Girl Can't Help It*: 'I think it was the best rock-'n'-roll film ever made.'

Paul actually suggested *What Little Old Man?* as the title of the Beatles debut film. This was in reference to Wilfred Brambell's character, John McCartney, Paul's screen grandfather who was referred to in an early sentence in the film as 'What little old man?' The group settled on *A Hard Day's Night*.

Paul also suggested *Where Did the Ringo?* as the title of their second film, which ended up with the title *Help!*

Over the years, Paul has not only appeared in various films, ranging from features to documentaries to animated shorts, but has also composed the scores, produced, directed and also contributed as a writer. Paul's filmography is:

A Hard Day's Night (1964).
Help! (1965).
The Next Spring Then (1966).
The Defeat Of The Dog (1966).
Yellow Submarine (1966).
The Family Way (composer) (1967).
Magical Mystery Tour (1967).
Let It Be (1969).
Live and Let Die (composer) (1973).
Empty Hand (producer) 1974.
Rockshow (1980).
The Cooler (1982).
Give My Regards To Broad Street (1984).
Rupert & The Frog Song (writer) (1985).
Daumier's Law (composer) (1992).
Grateful Dead (director) (1995).

Find A Way Somehow

A Denny Laine track which he originally featured on his 1973 album *Ahh . . . Laine!* A new version was recorded during the *London Town* sessions with Laine on keyboards, Paul on bass, Jimmy McCulloch on guitar and Joe English on drums. It was considered for the *London Town* album but then rejected.

Finston Manor

A concert hall near Tenterton in Kent. Wings began two weeks of rehearsals at the venue on Saturday 28 June 1980 and were filmed rehearsing by a team from *Day To Day*, an ITV programme. They returned to the venue on Thursday 2 October for recording sessions for *Hot Hits And Cold Cuts* and *Rupert The Bear*, which lasted until Saturday 25 October. They also recorded tracks, which were to appear on forthcoming albums such as *Tug Of War* and *Pipes Of Peace*.

Among the numbers they recorded were: 'Rainclouds', 'Average Person', 'Keep Under Cover', 'Ebony And Ivory', 'Twenty Flight Rock', 'Ballroom Dancing', 'Cage', 'Old Man Lovin'', 'Sure To Fall', 'Movie Magg', 'Blue Moon Of Kentucky', 'Summertime', 'Good Rockin' Tonight', 'Shake, Rattle And Roll', 'Cut Across Shorty', 'Stealin' Back To My Same Old Used To Be', 'Singin' The Blues', 'Johnny B. Goode', 'Dress Me Up As A Robber', 'The Pound Is Sinking', 'Sweetest Little Person', 'Wanderlust' and 'Take It Away'.

Wings also jammed on a number of unreleased tracks, 'Take Her Back, Jack', 'The Unbelievable Experience', 'Here's The Chord, Roy', 'Seems Like Old Times' and 'Boil Crisis'.

Fireman, The

Paul had made records using pseudonyms in the past, as with Percy Thrillington, and an instrumental album by the Fireman was eventually revealed as a duet with Paul and remix specialist Youth.

The project had taken over a year to make. Dance promoter Steve Anderson had collaborated with Paul on the mix of 'Deliverance 12'. Paul then decided to contact another studio technician known as Youth, a former bass guitarist with Killing Joke who had become an expert remixer and had helped to launch the careers of ambient dance music artists such as the Orb and KLF.

Paul invited Youth to the Mill, his home studio in East Sussex where he had been completing *Off The Ground*. The original idea was to come up with several *Off The Ground* 12″ remixes, as Anderson had done with *Deliverance*. This eventually developed over a period of time into a 77-minute CD that they named *Strawberries Oceans Ships Forest*.

Paul decided to use the pseudonym the Fireman for himself and Youth, and chose the name because his father had been a volunteer firefighter during the Second World War.

The Fireman could be referred to as an ambient dance duo. The debut album *Strawberries Oceans Ships Forest* was issued in Britain on Monday 15 November 1993. The CD was issued on Parlophone CDPCSD 145, the vinyl double album on PCSD 147 and the cassette on TCCD 145. The tracks on the 77-minute release were: 'Transpiritual Stomp', 9 minutes, 1 second; 'Trans Luna Rising', 9 minutes, 9 seconds; 'Transcrystalline', 8 minutes, 39 seconds; 'Pure Trance', 8 minutes, 40 seconds; 'Arizona Light',

8 minutes, 39 seconds; 'Celtic Stomp', 8 minutes, 34 seconds; 'Strawberries, Oceans, Ships, Forest', 8 minutes, 37 seconds; '444', 7 minutes, 35 seconds and 'Sunrise', 8 minutes and 16 seconds.

Paul's company MPL had tried to keep Paul's involvement in the CD secret and had sent a number of pre-release copies to various clubs around Britain.

An MPL spokesperson was to say, 'We never thought we'd manage to keep it a secret throughout its release. There was no danger of that succeeding! But we didn't want people to pre-judge the album. We didn't want anyone to run out and buy it just because it was Paul. This was partly because we wanted to see how the album would stand up on its own two feet, and partly because we didn't want anyone to be disappointed. I think people who are generally fans of what Paul does are unlikely, in the main, to appreciate this. On the other hand, we didn't want people to write the entire project off simply because Paul was behind it.

'We wanted dance audiences to listen to it with open minds, and to a large extent that succeeded. We had very good responses from the specialist DJs. They have been playing it, mixing it, and making nice comments about it.'

In a *Melody Maker* review, Michael Bonner wrote, 'Paul McCartney has discovered dance music – and the results are as staggeringly brilliant as those which came from John Lydon's similar road-to-Damascus-like conversion last year. Truly, we live in an age of miracles.

'Eschewing the easy option of making a remix album, McCartney and his collaborator, Youth, have chosen to follow the likes of Brian Eno down a more experimental and cerebral path. They take a melody and, with dextrous genre-hopping through ambient, trance and house, evolve a number of breathtaking variations. Like snowflakes, each song seems identical to the last, until closer inspection reveals that it has its own unique shape.'

The album was issued in America on Tuesday 22 February 1994 on CD and cassette on Capitol CAP 27167.

On Friday 2 October 1998 Paul appeared on a netcast on the Fireman web site. He disguised himself in a ski mask and glasses, wore a floppy yellow hat and headphones. Dressed completely in black, save for a pair of white shoes, he played guitar, bass and keyboards and sang alone with a live remix of some of the *Rushes* music. His real identity became obvious when he gave the familiar Macca thumbs-up sign.

There was also a ten-minute question and answer section. The Fireman (Paul) was to answer questions sent online in advance. He sat on a couch with the young woman who had appeared naked on the *Rushes* sleeve, this time she was fully clothed, and handed her the answers, which had been written down.

To the question asking when the Fireman would be appearing live, the answer was: 'When the cosmic seasons are right.'

A question asked how the Fireman classified his music. The answer was: 'Ambient dreams in rainbow arches describe the circles of the Fireman.'

The question asking what was the significance of the naked woman on the *Rushes* cover, brought the answer: 'The symbolism of the unknown naked woman is an ancient mystery. We do not have her number.'

To the question asking what had inspired the album, the answer was: 'Night skies, flowing streams and whipped cream fire extinguishers.'

The question, 'How did the Fireman get his name?' earned the reply, 'The Fireman is no nickname – simply a warm place in the head!'

The netcast lasted for seventy minutes and ended with a slide saying, 'The Fireman loves you.' It was repeated on Friday 30 October and Friday 20 November.

First Stone, The

Paul said an American television evangelist inspired this number. He wouldn't name him, although it is likely that he was referring to Jimmy Swaggart.

It was recorded during sessions at the Mill between April and July 1988 and Hamish Stuart helped Paul with the lyrics. Paul produced and arranged the song and Geoff Emerick engineered it.

The number was chosen as the flipside of 'This One'. It was released in Britain on Monday 17 July 1989 and in America on Wednesday 2 August 1989 (as a cassette single only).

Fixing A Hole

A track from the *Sgt Pepper* album on which Paul sings lead, in addition to playing the harpsichord.

Paul was to comment: 'This song is just about the hole in the road where the rain gets in; a good old analogy – the hole in your make-up which let's the rain in and stops your mind from going where it will. It's you interfering with things; as when someone walks up to you and says, "I am the Son of God." And you say, "No you're not; I'll crucify you," and you crucify him. Well that's life, but it is not fixing a hole.

'It's about fans too: "See the people standing there/who disagree and never win/and wonder why they don't get in/ Silly people, run around/they worry me/and never ask why they don't get in my door." If they only knew that the best way to get in is not to do that, because obviously anyone who is really going to be straight and like a real friend and a real person to us, is going to get in; but they simply stand there and give off, "we are fans, don't let us in".

'Sometimes I invite them in, but it starts to be not really the point in a way, because I invited one in, and the next day she was in the *Daily Mirror* with her mother saying we were going to be married. So we tell the fans, "forget it".

'If you're a junky sitting in a room *fixing* a hole then that's what it will mean to you, but when I wrote it I meant if there's a crack or the room is uncolourful, then I'll paint it.'

Perhaps the explanation is not as complicated as all that. Paul wrote the song after repairing the roof on his Scottish farm. The number was recorded on Thursday 9 February 1967 at Regent Sound Studio in London and overdubbed on Tuesday 21 February at Abbey Road Studios.

Paul was to tell *Playboy* magazine, 'The night we went to record that, a guy turned up at my house who announced himself as Jesus. So I took him to the session. You know, couldn't harm, I thought. Introduced Jesus to the guys. Quite reasonable about it. But that was it. Last we ever saw of Jesus.'

Flaming Pie (album)

Paul's first studio album in almost five years, following *Off The Ground*. He was to comment, 'I wanted to have some fun and not sweat it. That's been the spirit of making this record. You've got to have a laugh, because it's just an album. So I called up a bunch of friends and family and we just got on and did it. And we had fun making it. Hopefully you'll hear that in the songs.'

It was recorded over a period of four years at various locations – Paul's own studio in East Sussex, George Martin's AIR Studio in London and Steve Miller's studio in Sun Valley, Idaho and is 53 minutes and 46 seconds in length.

Geoff Emerick and Jan Jacobs, assisted by Keith Smith, engineered the album and recording began on 6 November 1995. It was produced by Paul, Jeff Lynne and George Martin and sported a cover photograph of Paul by Linda McCartney. There was a 24-page booklet enclosed with personal notes about the tracks from Paul and photographs by Linda.

Flaming Pie was issued in Britain on Monday 5 May 1997 and topped the charts. The British release was in three formats: LP on Parlophone PCSD 171, cassette on TCPCSD 171 and CD CDPCSD 171. It was issued in America on Tuesday 20 May 1997 on Capitol CDP 8 56500-2 and reached No. 2 in the charts. *Flaming Pie* remained in the US charts for 18 weeks.

The album broke Paul's own world record for gold discs by getting his 81st, which went gold both sides of the Atlantic, taking only three days to pass the 500,000 sales mark in America.

Paul commented, 'None of the fourteen songs were written with an album in mind. They were written for my own pleasure.'

The tracks were: 'The Songs We Were Singing', 'The World Tonight', 'If You Wanna', 'Somedays', 'Young Boy', 'Calico Skies', 'Flaming Pie', 'Heaven On A Sunday', 'Used To Be Bad', 'Souvenirs', 'Little Willow', 'Really Love You', 'Beautiful Night' and 'Great Day'.

To coincide with the 5 May release in Britain BBC Radio 2 presented a *Flaming Pie* radio special that day.

The Times commented on the album: 'this is the sound of rock 'n' roll with its teeth in a glass of water by its bedside.' The *Independent On Sunday* described it as 'woeful stuff', saying, 'what is effectively a bunch of mash notes to the wife, jams with old friends and family members and throwaway doodles of songs mostly written on his holidays.'

Commenting on the negative reviews in the *Daily Express*, Paul said, 'I really don't give a shit if this album is a hit or not. I've been saying that and I mean it. Sure, everyone likes to have a hit – but not at the expense of having fun.'

On 17 May 1997 Paul went on to the internet 'live' for a question-and-answer session held at the Bishopgate Memorial Hall, London before an audience of a thousand as part of the *Flaming Pie* campaign. The event was screened live on VH-I, the music cable channel. Prior to the session taking place there were 2,476,092 questions put forward. This would have taken Paul almost two years to answer. He said, 'It's an awful lot to ask of anyone. I don't think we'll get through all the questions – but we'll give it a go.'

Flaming Pie was nominated for a Grammy on 6 January 1998 as 'Album Of The Year', but lost out to Bob Dylan's *Time Out Of Mind*.

Flaming Pie (song)

The title track of the *Flaming Pie* album. It was 2 minutes and 30 seconds in length. The number was penned by Paul and produced by Paul and Jeff Lynne. The recording engineers were Geoff Emerick and Jan Jacobs, assisted by Keith Smith.

'Flaming Pie' was recorded on Tuesday 27 February 1996. Paul sang lead vocal and harmony vocal and played piano, drums, bass guitar and electric guitar while Jeff Lynne sang harmony vocal and played electric guitar.

Flaming Pie Night

An event that took place at Shea Stadium, Flushing, New York on Friday 12 September 1997. WNEN-FM and Nobody Beats the Wiz sponsored it and the master of ceremonies was Pat St John of WNEN.

The evening was devoted to Paul's music and included numbers from throughout his career, through the Beatles, Wings and solo years. There were also special video messages from Paul, who was unable to attend due to prior engagements.

Among the many prizes on offer to members of the audience was a trip to London and Liverpool.

Flaming Pie Radio Show, The

A two-hour radio special hosted by Paul, which included interviews with Jeff Lynne, Steve Miller and Ringo Starr on the making of the album.

The show was broadcast in May 1997 by Mji Radio Network Worldwide. It was taken up by 67 stations in America, 25 in Canada and by stations in South Africa, Japan, Hong Kong, Austria, France, Spain, Portugal, Switzerland and Holland.

Flanders Expohal, Ghent

A venue in Belgium with an 11,000 capacity where Paul appeared during his New World Tour on Sunday 17 October 1993. Due to Paul's influence, vegetarian snacks were available, together with a stall for the GAIA Foundation (Global Action in the Interest Of Animals: Stop the Animal Holocaust). Prior to the concert Paul attended a special reception, which included a vegetarian meal for the guests, with the ticket funds going to LIPA.

Paul began his introduction on stage in the Belgian language, then lapsed back to his own, saying, 'And now I'd better speak in English, 'cause it's so much easier.'

Flowers In The Dirt (album)

The title of a 53 minute 44 second album released in Britain on Monday 5 June 1989 on Parlophone PCSD (album), Parlophone CDP 7 91653 2 (compact disc) and TD PCSD106 (cassette) with a cover by Brian Clarke and Linda McCartney. It was issued in America on Tuesday 6 June 1989 on Capitol CDP 791653 2. It reached No. 21 in the American charts.

Paul had originally considered calling it *Distractions*. The title actually comes from the lyrics of one of the songs on the album called 'That Day Is Done', which he wrote with Elvis Costello. A painter friend of Paul's suggested that he use that phrase as the title of the album.

On this album Paul's main collaborator was Elvis Costello and the two co-wrote a number of songs together including 'My Brave Face', the duet 'Don't You Want Her Too?' and 'That Day Is Done'.

There were a great many other people involved in the making of the album – musicians, engineers and producers. Apart from Paul, the main artist, there was Elvis Costello: vocals, keyboards, and producer; Linda McCartney: harmony vocals; Hamish Stuart: harmony vocals, acoustic guitar, electric guitar; Chris Whitton: drums; Guy Baker: trumpet; Dave Bishop: saxophone; Chris Davis: saxophone; Dave Foster: keyboards, producer; Mitchell Froom: keyboards, producer; Dave Gilmour: guitar; Tony Goddard: cornet; Ian Harper: alto horn; Nicky Hopkins: piano; Trevor Horn: keyboards, producer; Judd Lander: harmonica; Steve Lipson: bass, guitar, engineer, producer; Dave Mattocks: keyboards; Robbie McIntosh: acoustic guitar, electric guitar; Ian Peters: euphonium; David Rhodes: guitar; John Taylor: cornet; Chris White: saxophone; Jah Bunny: contributor; Ross Cullum: producer; Neil Dorfsman: engineer, producer; Peter Henderson: producer; Chris Hughes: producer; Eddie Klein: producer.

The album tracks were: 'My Brave Face', 'Rough Ride', 'You Want Her Too', 'Distractions', 'We Got Married', 'Put It There', 'Figure Of Eight', 'This One', 'Don't Be Careless Love', 'That Day Is Done', 'How Many People?', 'Motor of Love' and 'Ou Est le Soleil?'.

There was a special limited edition *Flowers In The Dirt* World Tour Pack, released in Britain on Thursday 23 November 1989 on EMI CP-PCSDX 106. This included a 'Party Party' CD or vinyl single, a poster, family tree, bumper sticker, six postcards and a tour itinerary. The tour pack was issued in America on Monday 15 January 1990 on EMI CD-PCSDX-106.

Flying

A number credited to all four members of the Beatles which was included in the *Magical Mystery Tour* film and EP. Paul was to say, '"Flying" was an instrumental. In the studio one night, I suggested to the guys that we made something up. I said, "We can keep it very, very simple. We can make it a 12-bar blues. We need a little bit of a theme and a little bit of a backing." I wrote the melody.'

Flying To My Home

A composition by Paul, 4 minutes and 15 seconds in length, which was included on the *Flowers In The Dirt* album.

Fool On The Hill, The

The number was recorded at Abbey Road Studios on 25 September 1967 with overdubbing taking place on 26 September and 20 October. Paul sang lead vocals and played piano, acoustic guitar, bass and recorder, John played harmonica and jew's-harp, George played acoustic guitar and harmonica and Ringo drums, maracas and finger cymbals. Three flautists were also used – Christopher Taylor, Richard Taylor and Jack Ellory.

In his *Playboy* interview, in which he discussed the Beatles' songs, John Lennon commented, 'Another good lyric. Shows he's capable of writing complete songs.'

Alistair Taylor, Apple's 'Mr Fixit', seemed to think that the number was inspired by an incident on Primrose Hill. He was to comment: 'Paul and I were having an early morning walk on Primrose Hill with his dog, Martha. We watched the sun rise, before realising that Martha had gone missing. We turned round to go, when suddenly there was a man standing behind us. He was a middle-aged man, very respectably dressed in a belted raincoat. There's nothing in that, you may think. But he had come up behind us over the bare top of the hill in total silence.

'We were sure that the man hadn't been there seconds earlier, because we had been searching the area for the dog. The man just seemed to have appeared miraculously. We exchanged greetings, and the man commented on the beautiful view and then walked away. When we looked round, he'd vanished! There was no sign of the man. He'd just disappeared from the top of the hills, as if he'd been carried off into the air. No one could have run to the thin cover of the nearest trees in the time we had turned away from him, and no one could have run over the crest of the hill. Strangely enough, immediately before the man's appearance, Paul and I had been mulling over the existence of God. We both felt the same weird sensation that something special had happened. We sat down, rather shakily on the seat, and Paul said, "What the hell do you make of that? That's weird! He was there, wasn't he? We did speak to him?"

'We both felt that we'd been through some mystical religious experience, yet we didn't care to name, even to each other, what or who we'd seen on that hilltop for a few brief seconds.'

However, Paul says that he was sitting at the piano in his father's house, hitting a D-6th chord and then began to compose the number. He played it to John Lennon at Cavendish Avenue in March 1967 while they were working on 'With A Little Help From My Friends' and John encouraged him to write the words to the song down.

Paul believes he was writing about someone like the Maharishi Mahesh Yogi because people called him a fool because of his giggle (he was often referred to as 'the giggling guru'). Paul was also intrigued with the idea of a hermit in a cave.

The sequence for 'The Fool Of The Hill' was filmed for *The Magical Mystery Tour* in Nice on 30 October 1967. However, when travelling to the location Paul discovered that he'd not only forgotten his passport, but his wallet too, which placed him in some difficulty with the French officials. Hurried phone calls were made before documents arrived by air freight several hours later. Unfortunately, the person from the Beatles' management company, NEMS (originally, North End Music Stores), who had sent the documents and passport forgot to enclose any money with the package. As a result the hotel he was staying in refused to accept his signature for the room and wouldn't give him any credit. More hurried phone calls were made to resolve the problem.

The wrong lens for the camera had also been delivered and the correct ones had to be sent for. The two-and-a-half minute sequence ended up costing £4,000.

There were a couple of successful cover versions of the number. Sergio Mendez and Brasil '66 reached No. 6 in the American charts with the song in 1968 while Shirley Bassey was to reach No. 48 in the British charts with the number on 2 January 1971 when her version was issued on United Artists UP 35156.

The number was included on the *Magical Mystery Tour* EPs and album, the compilations *The Beatles 1967–1970* and *The Beatles Ballads* and two versions of the number were included on *The Beatles Anthology 2*.

The song won a certificate of honour in the 1968/69 Ivor Novello Awards and there have been over one hundred covers of the song with versions by artists such as Petula Clark, the Four Tops, Aretha Franklin, Lena Horne and Count Basie.

Wings performed the number on their British tour in 1979.

A version of this number, lasting 5 minutes and 2 seconds, was included on the *Tripping The Live Fantastic* album. It was recorded at Wembley Arena, London on 13 January 1990 during the 1989/90 World Tour.

Footprints
The fourth track on the *Press To Play* album. It was co-written by Paul and Eric Stewart. The number lasted for 4 minutes and 32 seconds. Paul and Hugh Padgham produced it.

For No One
A song Paul wrote while he was on a skiing holiday with Jane Asher at Klosters in Switzerland. The two had rented a chalet between 6 and 20 March 1966. Paul had originally called the number 'Why Did It Die?'

The Beatles recorded 'For No One' on 9 May 1966 at Abbey Road Studios.

It was one of John Lennon's favourite Beatles tracks and was included on the *Revolver* and *Love Songs* albums. Cilla Black recorded the song but didn't achieve chart success with it.

Paul also included the number in his film *Give My Regards To Broad Street*, commenting: '"For No One" I'd never done anywhere, ever. I'd written the song, took it to the studio one day, recorded it, end of story. It's just a record, a museum piece. And I hated the idea of them staying as museum pieces.'

Only Paul and Ringo were at the recording and Paul played bass, piano and harpsichord. Dennis Brain had been booked to play the French horn solo on the track but died in a car accident before the session and Alan Civil was booked in his place. George Martin scored the number.

20 Forthlin Road, Liverpool
This was the McCartney home from 1955 to 1964. Because Paul's mother was a midwife, a phone was installed, which was a rare treat in working-class areas of Liverpool in those days. The number was: GARston 6922.

Numbers such as 'Love Me Do' and 'I Saw Her Standing There' were composed here.

John Birt, then Director General of the BBC, was in Liverpool to show his children his birthplace and noticed the house was up for sale. He then contacted Martin Drury, the Director of the National Trust.

For 34 years it had been the home of Mrs Sheila Jones who moved in with her husband and children when the McCartneys moved out. At the age of 66 Mrs Jones decided to move out of the house and live with her daughter. She said that she'd regretted cleaning off the words of a song that had been written on a door, although Paul's initials still remained scrawled on a bedroom wall.

The National Trust purchased it for £55,000. The restoration took three years at a cost of £47,000, from Heritage lottery funding, with fixtures and fittings, wallpaper and paintwork, furniture and fireplace all restored in a 1950s style.

Paul said, 'My dear mother Mary had great aspirations for our family and was very proud when we moved to Forthlin Road. She and my dad would have found it very hard to believe that the house is now National Trust property. You expect them to own places like Blenheim Palace, not a little terraced house like ours. But they would have been chuffed about it and so am I.'

He was also to say, 'I was living at 20 Forthlin Road when I first met John Lennon and it was here that he and I rehearsed with the Beatles. John and I would sometimes sag off school to go back to my house to write many of our early songs. I was still living at the house when the Beatles found worldwide fame, so my memories of it are closely connected with those times.'

The house is open to the public from 11 a.m. to 5 p.m. Wednesday to Saturday. There are no more than six tours per day and each tour is limited to fifteen people. The official brochure states what the visit includes: 'Powerful, evocative photographs of family life at 20 Forthlin Road displayed with kind permission of Sir Paul and Michael McCartney. Audio tour music and memories from the people who were there. Beatles' memorabilia collection kindly loaned by Hunter Davies, the Beatles' only authorised biographer. Minibus trip with introductory video. Tours direct from Albert Dock and Speke Hall.'

It was realised that the house was an example of 'the social impact that the provision of municipal housing has had throughout the twentieth century, both on individuals and society as a whole'.

The National Trust's Keith Halstead said, 'This house is a major part of the culture of the twentieth century. We also own the homes of Sir Winston Churchill and Thomas Hardy, and Paul's former home should be a huge attraction.'

The live-in custodian is 50-year-old John Halliday who lives in the house rent-free and shows around parties of fifteen fans at a time. They arrive in bus tours four days a week from nearby Speke Hall.

It was officially opened to the public on Wednesday 29 July 1998.

Forum, Assago, Milan, Italy

A recently built arena where Paul made his first public appearance as a try-out for his New World Tour on Thursday 18 and Friday 19 February 1993. He arrived at Linate Airport near Milan by private jet and was taken immediately to the Forum for a sound check and then to the VIP section to meet 300 media people during which he did interviews for RAI TV and the radio 105 Network He then stayed at the Principe di Savoia Hotel, Piazza Della Republica. There was an audience of 20,000 at the arena.

The show opened with film clips on a huge screen, merging Paul's career with world events over the past thirty years. It was basically the same film that opened Paul's first world tour, with a few additional clips added.

Paul appeared on stage and began with 'Drive My Car'. On finishing the number, Paul said, '*Grazie, ciao cari Italiani, ciao Milanesi, buona sera. Parlo pochissimo Italiano. Adesso parlo Inglese.*' He then performed 'Get Out Of My Way', 'Another Day' and 'All My Loving'.

He then took off his Hofner guitar and picked up his electric guitar to perform 'Let Me Roll It', then played two songs from his latest album, 'Peace In The Neighbourhood' and 'Off The Ground'. He then played 'I Wanna Be Your Man' and the band then left the stage, with the exception of Robbie McIntosh who performed a lengthy guitar solo.

Paul and the band returned to perform an acoustic version of 'Good Rockin' Tonight'. He followed with 'We Can Work It Out', 'And I Love Her' and 'Every Night'. The audience began to join in on 'Hope Of Deliverance' and when he performed 'Michelle' the audience began to hold up matches and flickering cigarette lighters.

The next song was 'Yesterday', followed by 'My Love', 'Lady Madonna', 'Live And Let Die' and 'Let It Be'.

A piano then appeared on stage and Paul performed 'Magical Mystery Tour', 'The Long And Winding Road' and 'C'Mon People'.

He then took up his Hofner bass again and performed 'Paperback Writer', followed by 'Fixing A Hole' and 'Penny Lane'.

Paul then told the audience that he was too tired to play anymore, but the audience wouldn't accept that and he launched into 'Sgt Pepper', then the band sang, 'We're sorry but it's time to go' and all left the stage.

Paul then returned on stage to a wild audience response and the band followed him. He next performed 'Band On the Run' and 'I Saw Her Standing There'.

The finale proved to be 'Hey Jude', with Paul seated at the piano with the audience singing along, while Linda and the band threw paper flower-petals into the audience.

Forum, Los Angeles

The last venue of the American leg of the Wings World Tour of 1975/76. They appeared there on Monday 21 June, Tuesday 22 June and Wednesday 23 June 1976, the last date being an added extra date, due to the fact that 40,000 tickets were sold in less than four hours.

Ringo was in the audience and came onto the stage to present Paul with a bunch of flowers. Other celebrities at the concerts included Dennis Wilson, Elton John, Dustin Hoffman, Jesse Ed Davis, Diana Ross, Adam Faith, Leo Sayer, Harry Nilsson, Robbie Robertson, John Bonham and Candy Clark.

The shows were taped and much of the material made up the album *Wings Over America*, while the performances on Tuesday and Wednesday were filmed and provided over two-thirds of the footage for the 1980 concert movie *Rockshow*.

Following the final show there was an end of the tour party at the Harold Lloyd Estate in Benedict Canyon, Beverly Hills on Thursday 24 June. Among the guests were Jack Nicholson, Tony Curtis, David Cassidy, Rod Stewart and members of the Beach Boys. Music was provided by the Nelson Riddle Orchestra. The party cost Wings $75,000.

Paul was to comment on the tour's success: 'After the Beatles you would have thought it would have been pretty much impossible for me to follow that and to get anything else going. At least I thought that. This tour convinced us that we're a group and I think it has convinced audiences too. This wasn't just a one-time trip. This is going to be a working band. We'll be back.'

Foster, David

A session musician turned record producer, who Paul had first worked with during the tracking of 'This Girl Is Mine'. In September and October 1984 Paul and Foster worked on some recordings and taped three songs, although it was to be several years before two of the numbers were released.

On Monday 24 September 1984 they recorded 'I Love This House' with Paul, Foster, Dave Gilmour on guitar and Dave Mattacks on drums. Another track was 'Lindiana'. The third number was actually the backing music for 'We Got Married'.

When Paul was asked why his collaboration with Foster didn't work out, he said, 'It came at that bad time for me when I was really burned out. I think under better circumstances we could have done a lot better.'

(4148) McCartney

The name of a minor planet. It was discovered on Monday 11 July 1983 by E Bowell at the Anderson Mesa Station of Lowell Observatory and it was decided to name it in honour of Paul.

Fourmost, The

A popular Liverpool band who performed in the same local halls as the Beatles and were to sign with Brian Epstein and appear on the Beatles Christmas shows in 1963. Their first hit, a Lennon and McCartney number, 'Hello Little Girl', reached No. 9 in the British charts and was followed by another Lennon and McCartney song which had been specially written for them, 'I'm In Love', which went to No.17.

In 1969, Paul produced their single 'Rosetta', a number that he had found and thought would be suitable for the band. It was issued on CBS 4041 on 21 February but failed to make any impact on the charts.

Drummer Dave Lovelady told journalist Spencer Leigh: 'Paul liked the way we could mimic instruments with our voices, our "mouth music", if you like. Brian O'Hara was a trumpet and we were the trombones. We used it on "Rosetta" and the Beatles did the same thing on "Lady Madonna". There were proper instruments on our record as well. I was playing the piano at the session, but Brian O'Hara told me to play it badly. I soon found out why. Paul said, "Look, I'll do the piano bit", and so he ended up playing on the record.'

Sadly, Brian O' Hara committed suicide in 2000.

4th Of July

A single by John Christie, written by Paul and Linda and produced by Dave Clark. It was issued in Britain on 28 June 1974 on Polydor 2058-496 and in America on 1 July 1974 on Capitol 3928. The flipside was 'Old Enough To Know Better, Young Enough To Cry'. Dave Clark had asked Paul if he could provide him with a number for Christie to record and Paul sent him a home demo of the song.

48 Hours

A weekly CBS Television News programme. Although the programme is normally sixty minutes in length, it was expanded to a 90-minute edition of the programme, devoted to Paul, on Thursday 25 January 1990. The show included onstage footage from his December 1989 concerts in Chicago, plus an exclusive backstage interview with Paul. Donna Dees of *48 Hours* commented, 'We're all Beatles fans – and McCartney fans – on the show. So we're doing everything the best we can. We have so much music that we're having some trouble with licensing fees. We have to be careful about review tapes getting out, so there won't be a bootleg album before the show airs.'

Initially, the programme's anchorman Dan Rather was scheduled to do the interview with Paul on 2 December 1989, but he had to report on the Malta Summit instead, although he did visit Paul backstage at Madison Square Garden and discussed a number of serious topics with him, although their conversation wasn't filmed.

Replacing Rather was Bernard Goldberg, who interviewed Paul and Linda.

Rather was to say that he was pleased with the way it worked out. 'I'm from a time and place – if Hank Williams didn't sing it, I didn't know it.'

48 Hours With McCartney

A television special on Paul which first appeared as an MTV rockumentary special on Paul's career in 1989 and the following year it was repeated and included film of his tour.

Fraser, Robert Hugh

An art dealer, born in London in August 1937, who Paul met in the spring of 1966 at John Dunbar and Marianne Faithfull's flat in Lennox Gardens. He was an old Etonian and a heroin addict who opened his gallery at 69 Duke Street in August 1962 and had a nearby apartment at 20 Mount Street.

Through Fraser Paul met Andy Warhol, Claes Oldenberg, Richard Hamilton and Peter Blake.

Paul began to frequent Fraser's gallery and often dropped into his flat for discussions about art and to meet some of the artists Fraser represented, as well as a variety of other talented people including author Terry Southern, Italian director Michaelangelo Antonioni and American comedian Sid Caesar. Fraser's knowledge of the arts was to boost Paul's appreciation in such a way that in his autobiography *Many Years From Now*, he wrote, 'The most formative influence on me was Robert Fraser. Obviously the other Beatles were very important, but the most formative art influence for me was Robert.'

In fact, Paul sought Fraser's advice as consultant regarding the sleeve of the *Sgt Pepper* album. Simon Posthuma and Marijke Koger of the Fool had already prepared a centrefold design. Fraser told the Beatles that it was no good. Fraser drafted in artist Peter Blake and the classic sleeve was brought to life.

Fraser was at Keith Richards house during the famous drug bust in 1967, when Marianne Faithfull was caught wearing only a fur rug, having just had a bath. When the police raided the premises Fraser fled through the garden and two policemen chased and caught him, discovering he was in possession of heroin.

In May 1967 he appeared in court, along with Mick Jagger and Keith Richards.

The three were then put on trial at Chichester Crown Court on Monday 27 June. Richards was sentenced to a year in prison; Jagger was sentenced to three months and Fraser to six months. Jagger and Richards were released on bail and eventually appealed and were never interred, while Fraser was sent to Wormwood Scrubs.

Fraser was to die of AIDS-related pneumonia and meningitis in January 1986. A biography of him called *Groovy Bob: The Life And Times Of Robert Fraser*, penned by Harriet Vyner, was published in October 1999.

Free As A Bird

The Beatles 28th official single which became their first new single in 25 years when it was issued in Britain on 4 December 1995 on two-track 7″, cassette and four-track CD and released in America the following day.

John originally wrote it in 1977 and the 1995 release was recorded at Paul's Sussex studios during February and March 1994.

When the three surviving Beatles were working on the *Anthology* project, it was decided to approach Yoko Ono to see if any of John Lennon's home demo tapes could be utilised into a new Beatles single, with the participation of Paul, George and Ringo.

When Paul visited New York in January 1994 to make the induction speech for John Lennon's entry into the Rock And Roll Hall Of Fame, Yoko gave him four of John's demo tapes: 'Free As A Bird', 'Real Love', 'Girls And Boys' and 'Grow Old With Me'.

Yoko claimed that it was George Harrison and Neil Aspinall who had originally approached her with the idea of adding new vocals and instrumentation to John's demo tapes. She commented, 'People have said it was all agreed when Paul came over to New York to induct John into the Rock And Roll Hall Of Fame, but it was all settled before then. I just used that occasion to hand over the tapes personally to Paul.'

John had recorded at least three demos of 'Free As A Bird', although the demo Paul was given was unfinished and he wrote fairly extensive additional lyrics.

Paul was to say, 'We took the attitude that John had gone on holiday saying, "I finished all the tracks on my album except this one. I'm sorry that I can't make the last session but I leave it to you guys to finish it off. Do what you'd normally do. Don't get fussy; just do your normal thing. I trust you." So we fixed the timing and then added some bits. John hadn't filled in the middle-eight section of the demo so we wrote a new section for that, which, in fact, was one of the reasons for choosing the song: it allowed us some input.'

Paul discussed the recording in a telephone interview with WNEW-FM, New York on 15 March 1995 and said that the beginning was originally just John on piano and his voice on mono tape. Then George added some guitar and they all did harmonies. Ringo said, 'It sounds like the bloody Beatles.'

Paul did admit that there were some arguments during the recording of 'Free As A Bird' and said, 'George Harrison and I competed on who actually had the better lyrics to the unfinished Lennon song.'

Freedom

A song Paul composed for his appearance at the 'Concert For New York City'.

He said that Heather inspired him to write the number, commenting, 'We were watching President Bush talking on TV about the attack on our freedom and she said it'd be good to write something about it.'

Paul also commented, 'Immediately after the disaster, I wrote this song about our right to live in freedom against any who would attack that right. The attacks on New York were an attack on that freedom, and we have to make a stand against threats like that. We are not going to buckle under to threats from anyone, and all of us here are united in our desire to make this a show of solidarity. Freedom is our right and we are pulling together tomorrow in defence of it.'

After performing 'Freedom' at the concert, Paul remained in New York and recorded a studio version of the number, accompanied by Eric Clapton on guitar. The number was then added as a bonus track to the *Driving Rain* CD.

The first CD single release from *Driving Rain* was issued on 29 October 2001 on Parlophone CDRS 6565 with 'From A Lover To A Friend' and two David Kahne remixes of 'Freedom'. A second CD single followed this on Parlophone CDRS 6567 on 5 November 2001, which featured only one David Kahne remix. On 13 November 'Freedom' and 'From A Lover To A Friend' was issued as a double A-side in America. With a playing time of 12 minutes 52 seconds it featured 'Freedom (studio mix)' and 'From A Lover To A Friend'. The B-side featured 'From A Lover To A Friend (David Kahne Remix 2)', produced by David Kahne and was issued on Capitol 5-50291-2.

All the profits from the singles were donated to the families of the New York Firemen and Police who were killed in the disaster.

Freeze Frame
An album by Godley and Creme, issued in Britain by Polydor on Friday 30 November 1979 and in America on Monday 21 January 1980. Paul made a guest appearance on the album, providing backing vocal on the track 'Get Well Soon'. It was re-issued as a CD on Polydor 831555 2 on 10 May 1991.

From A Lover To A Friend
The first track from the *Driving Rain* album. The number lasts for 3 minutes and 45 seconds. It was recorded at the Henson Recording Studio in Los Angeles on 20 February 2001. David Kahne produced it and the engineer was Mark Dearnley.

Paul sang lead vocal and played bass, guitars and piano. Rusty Anderson provided backing vocals and played guitars, Abe Laboriel Jr provided backing vocals and played drums and percussion, Gabe Dixon provided backing vocals and played keyboards and David Kahne provided programming, orchestra samples, synth and guitar.

It was the first single issued from the album and released globally on Monday 29 October 2001 as a charity single. In Britain it was issued on Parlophone R 6567 and CDR 6567 and TCR 6567. It reached No. 45 in the charts with a two-week chart life.

The record was the 53rd single to be issued under the 'Paul McCartney' name.

All proceeds from the sale of the record went to help the families of the firemen who died in the attacks on New York's World Trade Center on 11 September 2001. More than 300 men from the fire service went missing, believed buried under the rubble of the buildings.

Paul commented, 'I have great admiration for the courage those guys showed. I hope that the sales of this new single will help raise money for the firemen and their families.'

The number was also used in the Tom Cruise film *Vanilla Sky* and the album's producer David Kahne commented, 'His voice is very emotional in that song. It starts kind of quietly but has a great "Come Together"-type bass line in the bridge. He sings, "How can I walk when I can't find my way?" and there's a really good sound he makes. It has a sadness to it, but it's actually a real hopeful song.'

From A Window

A number penned by Paul, which was recorded by Billy J Kramer and the Dakotas in May 1964. It was issued in Britain on Parlophone R 5156 on 17 July 1964 with 'Second To None' as the flipside.

From Rio To Liverpool

A 50-minute television documentary which was a behind-the-scenes look at Paul's 1990 world tour, featuring interviews and live footage from concerts in Rio, Philadelphia and Glasgow, with an emphasis on the 'Get Back To Liverpool' concert at the King's Dock, Liverpool.

It was first broadcast on Channel Four in Britain on Monday 17 December 1990.

The documentary received its American premiere on the Disney Channel on Sunday 13 October 1991, where it had undergone a name change to 'Paul McCartney: Going Home'. The Disney Channel repeated it three further times that month on Saturday 19, Friday 25 and Wednesday 30 October.

Frost, David

A television celebrity who first rose to fame in the early 1960s with the satirical show *That Was The Week That Was*. Frost became a prominent TV interviewer and hosted several of his own shows on both sides of the Atlantic.

Paul made his first solo television appearance on *A Degree Of Frost* when he taped an appearance before a live audience at BBC Television Centre, White City on Wednesday 15 April 1964. The show was transmitted on Wednesday 18 May 1964.

At one time Frost had a BBC radio programme, *David Frost At The Phonograph* on which Paul appeared on Saturday 6 August 1966.

Paul also appeared on *The Frost Programme* in Britain on Wednesday 27 December 1967, during which he discussed the critical reaction to *Magical Mystery Tour*. He told Frost: 'People were looking for a plot, but there wasn't one.'

On Sunday 16 June 1968 Paul filmed a one-hour interview with Frost for *David Frost Presents*, recorded in England, but specifically for an American audience, which was transmitted in the States on Sunday 23 February 1969. During the show comedian Frankie Howerd also interviewed Paul and Paul introduced his protégée Mary Hopkin, who performed two numbers.

Frozen Jap

A composition by Paul, 3 minutes and 35 seconds in length, which was included on the *McCartney 11* album.

Fukuoka Dome Stadium

An indoor baseball stadium in Japan, which opened in 1992. Paul appeared in two concerts there as part of his New World Tour in 1993. The first was held on Thursday 18 November, although the venue was not completely sold out, as there were a few thousand empty seats. The following concert on Friday 19 November did attract a capacity audience.

Paul and his party left for Los Angeles the following afternoon and Paul told reporters at the airport, '*Sayonara. Mata kimasu!*'

Gabriel, Peter

A former member of Genesis who enjoyed a successful solo career. In 1986 Gabriel announced that he was collaborating with Paul on a song for Amnesty International's 'International Day of Peace'. The two wrote and recorded a demo disc of 'The Politics Of Love', which was intended for a compilation in aid of Costa Rica's University of Peace.

Gambaccini, Paul

An American disc jockey domiciled in Britain.

Gambaccini has interviewed Paul on a number of occasions for both press and radio.

His series of interviews with Paul for *Rolling Stone* magazine were gathered together in book form for *Paul McCartney: In His Own Words* published by Omnibus Press.

On Sunday, Christmas Eve 1982 he broadcast a programme about Paul on Radio One at four o'clock in the afternoon, as part of his *Appreciation* series. This was previewed in the *Radio Times* with the comment: 'Paul McCartney is the greatest tunesmith of our time – almost superhumanly so – he is erratic, depending on the discipline he imposes on himself and the degree to which he is willing to work with people who will appreciate his talent.'

Garland For Linda, A

A classical music tribute to Linda. Stephen Connock, who is chairman of the Ralph Vaughan Williams Society, first suggested the idea. Connock himself had contracted liver cancer in December 1996. He says the concept was inspired by the 1953 tribute *A Garland for the Queen* in which ten British composers wrote a piece in honour of the Coronation.

The Linda tribute was formally announced on Monday 17 May 1999. Eight British composers had written an eight-song cycle for an unaccompanied choir. Each of the composers contributed one song, beginning with Paul's 'Nova', which he wrote between November 1998 and May 1999.

The other compositions, from which the composers donated their royalties to charity, were: 'A Good Night' by Sir Richard Rodney Bennett, 'The Doorway Of The Dawn' by David Matthews, 'Farewell' by Michael Berkeley, 'Water Lilies' by Judith Bingham, 'Musica Dei Donum' by John Rutter, 'I Dream'd' by Roxanna Panufnik, 'The Flight Of The Swan' by Giles Swayne and 'A Prayer For The Healing Of The Sick' by John Tavener.

The Joyful Company of Singers premiered the production on Sunday 18 July at the chapel of Charterhouse School in Surrey. There were also new choral arrangements for five Beatles songs, written by Paul – 'Lady Madonna', 'Fixing A Hole', 'And I Love Her', 'Here, There and Everywhere' and 'Let It Be'.

The American premiere of *A Garland for Linda* took place at the Riverside Church, Riverside Drive, New York on 3 June 2000. The venue had been the scene of Linda's American memorial service.

It was performed at Bridgewater Hall, Manchester on 28 May 2000, the Anvil, Basingstoke on 9 June, the Deal Festival, Deal on 6 August and St Bartholomew's Church, Brighton on 21 September 2000. The British performances were by the Joyful Company of Singers conducted by Peter Broadhurst.

The idea was also to hold 200 concerts worldwide for the work over a three-year period in choral societies, cathedrals, churches and universities.

The CD was issued on EMI Classics 7243 5 56961 2 0 and contained the added work of a tenth composer. It was recorded during August and September 1999 at the All Saints church in London.

A 24-page booklet came with the CD and a portion of the purchase price was donated by EMI to the 'Garland Appeal', a charity.

The British magazine *Classic FM* featured Paul and Linda on the cover of their March 2000 issue, which contained an article 'A Time to Heal', which was all about *A Garland for Linda*.

Genealogy

In the early 1960s the Beatles commissioned the Society of Genealogists in London to trace their family trees. In Paul's case the McCartneys were traced back to 1663 when his ancestors lived on the Isle of Man. His father had worked as a cotton salesman and previous generations of the family had been fishmongers, a tobacco cutter, boilermakers and plumbers. Paul's great-great-grandfather had been a coroner in Victorian England.

Paul's ancestors also sported Irish names such as Danher and Mohin, although the name McCartney has only been known in Northern Ireland for a few centuries. A branch of the Scottish clan Mackintosh, the McCartneys settled in Ulster in the early seventeenth century and became the principal family in Belfast.

Paul's younger brother Mike also researched and drew a family tree that he called 'Maclineage', which was featured in his book *Thank U Very Much* (known as *The Macs* in the US). The tree traces the family back to the 1840s, with James McCartney, upholsterer, on his father's side, and Michael McGergh on his mother's. A boilermaker, coroner, plumber, fishmonger, tobacco cutter, coal merchant and nursing sister represent other professions.

General Certificate of Education (GCE)
A British educational certificate awarded following the passing of examination in particular subjects. Now known as General Certificate of Secondary Education (GCSE). The certificates are in two grades: ordinary (O level) and advanced (A level).

Paul took his GCE exams at Liverpool Institute and passed in six O level subjects, including French, German and Spanish. He had intended to study for a further two years for the A level in English Literature in order to pursue a career as a teacher, but his career with the Beatles intervened.

Georgia Dome, Atlanta, Georgia
The venue where Paul appeared on Saturday 1 May 1993. The performance of 'Lady Madonna' that evening is included on the album *Paul Is Live*.

Paul held a press conference at the Dome, opening it by saying, 'Thank you very much. Good afternoon everybody. I called you here today . . . for the case of the flying fruit . . . Hi there. I'm obviously starting off with a little silliness. OK, let's get serious.' The press conference continued after a question had been asked about Paul and John as songwriters:

Q: Regarding the songs you are going to play: what role do you feel is played in the songwriting, the competitiveness?

Paul: It was very useful, as you said, if I wrote a good one and I'd play it to him and he'd go right, I'll write one better, whatever. Then I'll hear his and I'd think, whooo, I'll write one better. So it is very handy. In a nice way, we are never vicious. But we are always trying to go one better than each other. But when we came together on songs, then you got a different kind of song again. You got things like 'I Wanna Hold Your Hand', 'Help!' and stuff like that. So it was very good, it was very handy to have someone to compete with like that in a friendly way.

Q: It is good to have you back in Atlanta. What is it about

touring that turns you on, that makes you come back time and time again? Whereas in *Wings Over America* in 1976, you took a break from touring for a while. What is it that excites you about touring?

Paul: It's the audience, really. Not that it ... when I laid off for a little while ... not that I went off audiences. I was raising kids. I have four kids, the youngest is fifteen now. So he is kind of getting there now. He'd love me to say that. He is very mature, very grown-up. Raising them took a lot of time. When we got back a couple of years ago, it was just so good to see the audience. You are in isolation when you write your songs or record them. But when you come to play to this many people, it's great, it's instant feedback. So you don't have to be asking yourself if I wrote a good song. They are telling you it's good. Whereas if it is just a record, you have to go and read the critics and some of them tell you it's terrible and you failed the exam Paul. And I say I didn't enter an exam, did I? Yes. So that can be really dodgy. So it really is the people, the fans themselves. The best bit about it.

Q: Do you enjoy playing the large gigs or do you prefer the smaller ones?

Paul: I like all sizes of gigs actually. Some people don't like these big gigs because they are a bit too remote. I've been to see people in gigs this big and I've not enjoyed them. I went to Genesis in London. I couldn't see if Phil Collins was on stage or not! So it kind of defeats the purpose of it. We tried to learn lessons from things like that when we brought this show out. We are basically trying to satisfy the person in the 500th row right in the back there. That's why we got the big screens, we've got a few tricks. I try to take time out to sort of reach those people. Try and get some kind of intimate atmosphere. It's not easy in front of forty thousand people. We get a really good fire going in the show and the audience gives us a lot of feedback. Yeah, I really do enjoy these big things. They are an event. It's not so much an intimate show anymore. It's a big huge event. The circus came to town. I like that.

Q: Do you find yourself relying on a lot of outside influences?

Paul: I get a lot of outside influences, because you just can't help it. You'll be driving along in your car and somebody's got the radio on and that stuff comes in. I absorb that and take what I like out of it. Basically, I rely on instincts. Never having been trained, I really don't know how to do this stuff. I wrote my first song when I was fourteen and I still approach it the same way each time. It's like magic to me. It's like WOW, I wonder if I'll be able to do it today. I sit down with a little guitar and I'm still amazed when something comes out that looks like a song. And if you are very lucky you get a special song. Those don't happen all the time, but every so often something comes out that is a little more special. If you keep at it as long as I have, you end up with a few special ones.

Q: I know you are very enthusiastic about promoting environmental concerns. Are there any things that make you feel better about it?

Paul: I'll tell you what makes me feel more optimistic, is that the present administration in America, with Clinton and Gore. Because there has been a change and because we know Gore has written a book on it. I think that's far better for my tastes than the outgoing President who, I really think he blew it in the last campaign when he called Gore 'Mr Ozone'. I mean, what a mean-spirited statement. I suppose that was really stupid. I don't think that it helped him a lot in the election. I mean like, I don't agree with it, fine – but don't make fun of it. That's not a joke. I'm not an optimist. I think the kids are the hope. That's why we do this on the show. We give out the free booklet and in it we promote people like Greenpeace, Friends of the Earth and the American PETA, Organisation for the Ethical Treatment of Animals. I think that's the way it should be done. I really think man as hunter has been played out. We'll get to the end of the twentieth century and that's kind of interesting – we had to blast off all the animals to be top dog. I think we won that. I think we can't keep blasting them. We have to look at other ways now. I think those ways are there. People have just got to realise that we have to change from that stuff now.

Q: Do you think hemp might help?

Paul: Get out of here! Who is this guy? I think he is a plant from the narcotics bureau.

Q: In the early seventies you wrote a song called 'Give Ireland Back To The Irish'. With all the things going on in London now, with the bombings, do you ever think they are going to give Ireland back?

Paul: It's just the most difficult subject. It's like the Middle East. If we had three hours to discuss it in depth, I think we should do it, but to just give it a quick answer is too difficult. Why I wrote that song, it was the first time our army, our paratroopers, had actually killed someone in our name, in the British people's name, in Ireland. It was a sort of accident. It is known as 'Bloody Sunday'. I wrote the song about that. So many things have changed, and it is just such a difficult subject, that you couldn't begin to get into it unless you have hours.

Q: What is the age range of fans that are coming to your concerts?

Paul: I don't really know. Since the last tour, we had people out more my age who were grown-ups with families who were coming largely, I think, for the nostalgic things. But it changed near the end of the tour and we started to get a lot of college kids. This time it's really mixed. We have a lot of really young kids. People bring babies. I like that, I have no problem about age. In fact we did a show, one of our first try-out shows and we got an old lady. I mean a really old lady; she must have been seventy to eighty years old. Not a spring chicken. She is sitting there and I'm playing the piano and I just started into 'Live And Let Die' and there is a big bang in there and I thought, 'Oh, no!' I'm trying to think, 'Can I stop the song, no, it's too late now.' It happened and I looked at her and she was grinning from ear to ear. I mean young – old, I don't really know why they come, I'm just glad they do.

Q: Looking back on the spectrum of your career, can you pick out any one project that you are most proud of, that satisfied you the most?

Paul: That is very difficult. To give you an answer – *Sgt Pepper*. There are a lot of others. That was very complete. I am very happy with the song 'Yesterday' because I dreamed it. That is my argument of, like, not really knowing where it comes from. I just woke up one morning and had this tune in my head. How lucky can you get? Those are two instances that I am really proud of. There are a lot of others. It is like talking about your babies. You don't want to favour one over the others. They are all good.

Q: About a year and a half ago you wrote the *Oratorio*. How did that come about?

Paul: I was asked to do that by the Liverpool Philharmonic Orchestra to celebrate their 150th anniversary. So that was a big sort of party thing. That was a big celebration and three hundred people were involved in the production of that. So that was a big deal. At the moment I am working on piano pieces. Just for a single pianist. So it is right at the other end of the scale. They are just little instrumental pieces that I am enjoying working on. Maybe towards the end of the year after the tour we might get into something like the *Oratorio*. I would like to do that again. It was good fun.

Q: You are one of the few major artists who have never put out a promo video compilation. Have you ever thought about doing that?

Paul: Yeah, we have never done it. It's one of those things that people ask us, when are you going to do that. I suppose we will soon. There are enough of them. They go back quite a while. Do you want the job?

Q: It is very unusual to be left-handed and I would like to know how you got started playing left-handed.

Paul: My Dad gave me a trumpet when I was fourteen and I figured out that I couldn't sing with this in my mouth. I asked him if he minded if I traded it in and he said he didn't mind. So I went and traded it in for a guitar. I started to play it the normal, correct way around until I saw a picture of Slim Whitman, who is an old Country star.

He had his guitar the left-handed way. So I thought there is a hint there. So I turned all the strings around and I could play it better because of that. Then when I went on to play the bass in Hamburg, because our bass player left, I spotted a violin-shaped bass . . . very similar to the one you have there, can you hold that up! It looks like we are working together! I spotted something like that. Because it was so symmetrical it looked like a violin, that helped me get over the left-handed right-handed thing. So that was really it. It hasn't really bothered me. The only time it bothered me was when I was in school and they encouraged me to write with my right hand and I wrote my name starting with the Y. I wrote it backwards. It had never bothered me, actually. There are quite a lot of people who are left-handed. Leonardo Da Vinci.

Q: Have your children's musical tastes gone one way or the other?

Paul: I have always expected my children's musical taste to go directly against mine and for the generation gap to show up in a big way. You figure it can't go on forever. But it hasn't happened. As you were saying before, I think the young kids now are looking at the sixties, re-examining it. My son, for instance, is a big fan of Jimi Hendrix, people like James Brown, and he is heavily into all that stuff. Which is great by me because I'm into all that stuff. I love it, I can relate to it all. We don't live in America so he's not into rap. I think he's great. My kids are very supportive. I'm just lucky they actually like coming to shows. They seem to enjoy the music. It's Dad's music. They support me. The generation gap's never happened in my family yet.

Q: I hear your son plays guitar.

Paul: Yes, he plays a little guitar. I never really pushed him into it. It's not easy being a famous guy's kid. If any of them are really desperate to get into music, then of course I'll help them, but I'm not going to push them into it. If they just can't stop, then of course I'll help them.

Q: Atlanta's invited some constructive criticisms. What are your impressions of this town, strengths and weaknesses?

Paul: Well I haven't really been here long enough to tell you. I usually come from the airport to the Dome.

Q: Have you never come here before?

Paul: Yes I have, but only to tour, really, but you don't really get an impression. What I do know is that you have the Braves and that it's one of the fastest growing towns in the South. Other than that, I really don't know a whole lot about it. I'll tell you what, I'll stay here for a few days and work it all out and tell you.

Q: Will we be lucky enough to hear 'Big Boys Bickering' tonight?

Paul: It's not in the set tonight. No. Thanks for the interest.

Q: What do you think about the return to live music recently?

Paul: Yeah, I think it's a natural thing like when synthesisers came out. People get interested in them for a few years and then someone eventually says, 'Wait a minute, a piano sounds as good as that.' Or what about an accordion, which we used to use? I think there is a return to live music. The other stuff was interesting for a little while, but it was a little shallow. A little bit thin. I think people are returning to warmer acoustic instruments. We certainly are. I've noticed a lot of other bands, a lot of the current young bands are into, it's the real thing.

We've got to go. Thank you. Goodbye.

Get Back (film)

The feature film of Paul's 1989/90 World Tour was premiered in London on Friday 20 September 1991. The US premiere took place on Thursday 24 October 1991 at the Baronet Theatre, at 3rd Avenue and 60th Street in New York. Paul and Linda attended. They also flew to Canada for the premiere at the Varsity 11 Cinema in Toronto on Friday 25 October. The film was screened twice in November in the US on the Disney cable channel and released on home video there on Wednesday 18 December 1991.

It was an Allied Filmmakers/MPL/Front Page Films presentation, produced by Henry Thomas and Philip Knatchbull. The executive producer was Jake Eberts, who originally founded Goldcrest Films.

Director Dick Lester introduced diverse newsreel footage as a background to some of the numbers and the various songs were taken from different concerts during the mammoth 102-show tour, attended by 3 million fans in 13 countries, with a particular number including shots from various concerts, resulting in Paul and band appearing in different clothes while performing the same song.

The 89-minute film included footage from concerts in the UK, the US, Holland, Japan, Italy, Canada and Brazil, with a great deal of footage concentrating on the Rio de Janeiro show with its audience of 184,000.

The film featured twenty songs performed live during the 1989/90 World Tour, opening with 'Band On The Run', followed by 'Got To Get You Into My Life', 'Rough Ride', 'The Long And Winding Road', 'Fool On The Hill', 'Sgt Pepper's Lonely Hearts Club Band', 'Good Day Sunshine', 'I Saw Her Standing There', 'Put It There', 'Hello Goodbye', 'Eleanor Rigby', 'Back In The USSR', 'This One', 'Can't Buy Me Love', 'Coming Up', 'Let It Be', 'Live And Let Die', 'Hey Jude', 'Yesterday', 'Get Back', 'Golden Slumbers/Carry That Weight' and 'The End'.

Newsreel footage included shots from the Vietnam War, the Apollo moonwalk and the Beatles receiving their MBEs during 'The Long And

Winding Road', scenes of Liverpool in 'Eleanor Rigby', soldiers marching in Red Square, Moscow during 'Back In The USSR', Tiananmen Square in China, Middle East turmoil and conflict in Northern Ireland in 'Live And Let Die' and the fall of the Berlin Wall in 'Put It There'.

The film did garner some bad reviews, mainly of Lester's direction. The *Toronto Star* critic wrote, 'The film is an embarrassment that ranks right up there with some of the worst of McCartney's misfires. Whatever value there may be in a straight concert documentary is ruined by director Richard Lester, who intersperses ludicrous stock library footage of 1960s newsreels within the songs – it's puerile social commentary.' The *Hollywood Reporter* said that Lester's newsreel 'intrusions feel slapdash, with the footage seldom matching the music'.

Get Back (song)

A number that Paul wrote in Apple Studios during the recording of *Let It Be*. 'We were sitting in the studio and we made it up out of thin air,' he said, as the number was recorded shortly after he finished writing it.

He was also to comment, 'I originally wrote it as a political song: "Don't dig no Pakistanis taking all the people's jobs, Wilson said to the immigrants, You'd better get back to your commonwealth homes, Yeah, yeah, yeah, you'd better get back home, Now Enoch said to the folks, Meanwhile back at home, too many Pakistanis, Living in a council flat."'

The point Paul was trying to make was an anti-racist one. At this time there was a huge public debate about immigration into Britain and politician Enoch Powell was saying that it would lead to 'rivers of blood'.

However, the words were misinterpreted in some quarters as racist.

Paul was to comment, 'When we were doing *Let It Be* there were a couple of verses of "Get Back" which were actually not racist at all – they were *anti*-racist. There were a lot of stories in the newspapers then about Pakistanis crowding out flats – you know, living sixteen to a room or whatever. So in one of the verses of "Get Back", which we were making up on the set of *Let It Be*, one of the outtakes has something about "too many Pakistanis living in a council flat" – that's the line. Which to me was actually talking out *against* overcrowding for Pakistanis.'

The single was issued in Britain on 11 April 1969 on Apple R5777 with 'Don't Let Me Down' as the flipside and in America on 5 May.

It topped the charts in Britain and America and several other countries throughout the world, including Australia, Belgium, Canada, Denmark, France, Holland, Malaysia, New Zealand, Norway, Singapore, Spain and West Germany. It was re-released on 6 March 1970 when EMI issued 23 Beatles singles at the same time. It reached the No. 55 position. The track has also been included on a number of album compilations, including the 1982 *20 Greatest Hits*. There was another version of the song that featured on the *Let It Be* album and which has also been used on a number of compilation LPs. At the end of the number on the album, Paul can be heard saying, 'Thanks, Mo.' He is referring to Maureen, Ringo's wife, who was clapping.

Another version of this number, lasting 4 minutes and 11 seconds was included on the *Tripping The Live Fantastic* album. It was recorded live at the Tokyo Dome, Tokyo, Japan on 13 March 1990 during the 1989/90 World Tour.

Get On The Right Thing

A track on the *Red Rose Speedway* album lasting 4 minutes and 19 seconds. Paul sang lead vocal and played bass, piano and acoustic guitar. Linda provided background vocals and David Spinozza was on electric guitar and Denny Seiwell on drums. The number was actually recorded during the *Ram* sessions.

Get Out Of My Way

A track from the *Off The Ground* album, penned by Paul and lasting 3 minutes and 29 seconds.

Getting Better

A track on *Sgt Pepper* that was penned by Paul with some aid from John on the lyrics of the middle eight.

Paul had driven to Primrose Hill in the spring of 1967 to take his dog Martha for a walk. It was a sunny day and Paul recalled a phrase often used by Jimmy Nicol, the drummer who stood in for Ringo during part of their world tour in 1964. Jimmy's phrase was a bit of positive home-spun philosophy: 'It's getting better.' Paul mentioned to John at their next meeting that 'It's Getting Better' sounded like a good title for a song.

Paul was to say, I wrote that at my house in St John's Wood. All I remember is that I said, "It's getting better all the time", and John contributed the legendary line, 'It couldn't get much worse", which I thought was very good. Against the spirit of that song, which was all super-optimistic – then there's that lovely little sardonic line. Typical John.'

The number was recorded at Abbey Road Studios on 9 March 1967. During the overdubbing of the song on 21 March, John couldn't continue recording. George Martin realised something was wrong and took him onto the roof above No. 2 studio. He said, 'I remember it was a lovely night, with very bright stars. Then I suddenly realised that the only protection around the edge of the roof was a parapet about six inches high, with a sheer drop of some ninety feet to the ground below, and I had to tell him, "Don't go too near the edge. There's no rail there, John."'

John couldn't go on with the recording. He said, 'It dawned on me I must have taken acid.' So Paul offered to take him home and when they arrived there he took some LSD to keep John company. It was the first time Paul had ever taken the hallucinogenic.

Getting Closer

The last British single to be credited to Wings. It was issued as a double A-side with 'Baby's Request' on Parlophone R6027 on Thursday 16 August 1979. Both tracks were taken from the *Back To The Egg* album. The number only managed to reach No. 60 in the UK charts. In America 'Getting Closer' was issued on Columbia 3-11020 on Tuesday 5 June with 'Spin It On' as the flip and reached No. 20 in the US charts. Wings included the number as part of their repertoire on their British tour in 1979.

The 'Getting Closer'/'Spin It On' version was also issued in Germany on Odeon 1C006-62945 and in France on Parlophone 2C006-62945.

Paul had penned 'Getting Closer' several years earlier, although he'd recently written 'Spin It On' in Scotland.

Ghosts Of The Past

A 1991 BBC/MTV/MPL documentary on the making of the *Liverpool Oratorio*, which was filmed over a three-month period. It included various rehearsals at the Mill with artists such as Kiri Te Kanawa and Sally Burgess, Jerry Hadley rehearsing with the Liverpool Philharmonic Orchestra, the initial 18 March 1991 rehearsal with the Royal Liverpool Philharmonic Choir, clips of Paul and Carl Davis composing the work, a rehearsal with the concert master Malcolm Stewart and various other highlights during the run up to the premiere of the work.

The documentary was broadcast in Britain by the BBC on Tuesday 8 October 1991 and received its American premiere on the *Great Performance* series on PBS (Public Broadcasting Service) on Wednesday 30 October 1991, shortly after the American CD was issued.

Giants Stadium

An arena in East Rutherford New Jersey where Paul appeared on Monday 9 and Wednesday 11 July 1990 during his world tour. There were combined audiences of 105,082 at the shows.

Paul introduced the Lennon medley saying that it was something he had 'worked up for Liverpool and is also quite special to this area'. He was referring to the fact that the Dakota building was less than ten miles distance from the stadium. Scott Muni of WNEW-FM interviewed Paul before the 11 July concert and when Paul addressed the audience, welcoming everyone to New York, Linda corrected him that it was New Jersey. Paul then got the New Yorkers to boo New Jersey and also asked if there was anyone from Liverpool in the audience.

Gibbs, Russ

A disc jockey and programme controller with the Detroit radio station WKNR who, on 12 December 1969, reported that Paul had been dead since 1966 when he was killed in a road accident and had been replaced by a lookalike.

He'd received information from a listener who had told him that the Beatles had been hinting to the world what had happened via clues on their album covers and in the lyrics of their songs.

Gibbs became inundated with thousands of calls and the 'Paul is Dead' rumours swept America like an epidemic.

Gibbs pointed out that one of the clues had been on the *Magical Mystery Tour* album sleeve. The stars, which composed the word 'Beatles', became a telephone number when studied upside down, he said. Gibbs presumed that the number, 537 1438, was in London and called up. A journalist who didn't know what Gibbs was talking about answered the phone. When Gibbs tried the number the following week, it had been disconnected.

Giddy

A number penned by Paul for Roger Daltrey's album *One Of The Boys*, which was released in Britain on Friday 13 May and in America on Thursday 16 June 1977. Part of the song came from the refrain of a number 'Rode All Night', recording during the *Ram* sessions.

Gilmour, Dave

Born David Jon Gilmour in Grantchester Meadows, Cambridge on 6 March 1946, he was in a group with Syd Barrett called Jokers Wild and then took Barrett's place in Pink Floyd in 1968.

He worked extensively with Paul in 1999 as part of Paul McCartney And Friends, recording *Run Devil Run* and making various live appearances with the band.

Giraldi, Bob

The director of the 'Say Say Say' promotional video that starred Paul and Michael Jackson. Giraldi commented, 'Michael could upstage anybody else but Paul McCartney. There was only one star on that set.'

Girl Is Mine, The

The single on which Paul sang a duet with Michael Jackson.

Paul was in Los Angeles in May and June 1982 when Jackson was recording his *Thriller* album and joined him on this track, which was produced by Quincy Jones.

It was the first collaboration between Paul and Michael.

The number was penned by Michael Jackson and included as the third track on his *Thriller* album, produced by Quincy Jones.

The flipside was the Jackson/Quincy Jones number 'Can't Get Outta The Rain'.

The single was issued in America as a 7″ on Monday 25 October 1982 on Epic EPC A2729 where it reached No. 2 in the charts. There was also a 7″ picture sleeve version issued the same day on Epic EPCA 11-279 with a photograph of Paul and Michael taken by Linda McCartney. A 12″ maxi single was also issued the same month on Epic EPCA 12-2729. The British release was issued on Friday 29 October on Epic EPC A2729 where it reached No. 4 in the charts.

Girlfriend

It was not by accident that this track sounded like a Jackson Five number because Paul actually wrote it with Michael Jackson in mind.

The number was featured on Wings' *London Town* album and was recorded by Michael Jackson the following year for inclusion on his album *Off the Wall*. Jackson then issued it as a single in 1980 when it reached No. 30 in the charts.

Girlfriends

Paul was only fifteen when he lost his virginity. The girl was older than he was and the occasion occurred when he was baby-sitting at her house when her mother was out. He wasn't able to repeat the experience with her because he had eagerly told his schoolmates all about it the next day and she was furious that he'd tarnished her reputation.

Val (surname not known) was, according to Mike McCartney, the first girl that Paul ever liked. He was at a tender age at the time and began to notice Val on the school bus, staring at her long hair. 'Then one night word came along the grapevine that Val liked him,' said Mike. 'You should have seen the way he went on! He was completely knocked out! He took Val out once or twice – to the cinema, visiting friends, that sort of thing. Then the whole affair suddenly fizzled out.'

Another early Liverpool girlfriend was called Sheila. One day he accidentally broke her nose by throwing a ball into her face. Sheila was later to become a member of the Vernons Girls and married singer Tommy Bruce.

Paul also dated Julie Arthur, the niece of Liverpool comedian Ted Ray and he also recalls a girl called Layla, who he went out with soon after joining the Quarry Men.

When Paul was sixteen he had a girlfriend called Celia who was attending Liverpool College of Art. One night when he went on a date with her, to Paul's embarrassment, John Lennon turned up and tailed along with them. Later, the girl told Paul that she didn't like John.

Paul was also to date one of John's former girlfriends from the art college, Thelma Pickles, who later married Mersey poet Roger McGough.

A serious romance had been going on for some time between Paul and Dorothy Rhone, an attractive young blonde. Paul seemed to have a penchant for blondes in Liverpool. Prior to going out with Jane Asher he was dating Iris Caldwell.

Liane (surname not known) was a blonde-haired German barmaid who Paul dated during the Beatles' season at the Kaiserkeller. Iain Hines, member of the Jets, recalls, 'I personally struck up quite a friendship with Paul McCartney. He was at the time going out with a barmaid called Liane, whilst I was going out with her friend Gerda. Every morning at two Paul would arrive from the Kaiserkeller, which was closed at that hour, and would listen to our last session. The four of us would go in Gerda's VW to Liane's flat where we would cook hamburgers and listen to Everly Brothers records that Paul had got hold of from seamen who had been to the States.'

Cattia (surname not known) was a German girl who was one of Paul's girlfriends from the early Hamburg days. When the group returned to Hamburg for a concert at the Merck Halle in June 1966, Cattia turned up backstage to visit them, along with several other friends, including Astrid and Gibson Kemp, Bert Kaempfert and Bettina Derlin, former barmaid at the Star Club.

Paul obviously had several girlfriends in Germany, but a question mark hovers over Erika Heubers.

She worked in a Hamburg club and said that as a result of an affair with Paul she became pregnant. She also claimed that Paul encouraged her to have an abortion. Paul said that he didn't remember her or any affair they were reputed to have had in 1961.

Heubers sued Paul in 1966 and although Paul didn't admit paternity, he paid up, commenting at a later date: 'It was 1966 and we were due to do a European tour. I was told that if the maintenance question wasn't settled we couldn't go to Germany. I wasn't going to sign a crazy document like this, so I didn't. Then we were actually on the plane leaving for the tour when they put the paper under my face and said if I didn't sign, the whole tour was off. They said the agreement would deny I was the father and it was a small amount anyway. I've actually seen a letter from Brian Epstein saying it would be cheaper to sign than not to go to Germany where we would make a lot of money.'

Paul paid up £2,700, which would be the equivalent of £10,000 today, and claimed that he was virtually tricked into paying for Erika's support until her daughter Bettina was 18. When Bettina came of age her mother instigated an action.

From 1981 the publicity began to plague Paul because everyone acted as if the case against him had been proven – regular newspaper coverage about Bettina kept referring to her as 'Beatle Girl' and similar phrases. Paul commented: 'What I object to most is the effect on my children. It's not fair to them. Why should they suffer? She (Bettina) was on the cover of *Time* magazine in 1983 and there was a picture of her holding one of my record covers with the comment, "Dad says . . ." Not even *alleged* father. My kids had to read that. You have to put it down to life being tough at the top.'

The case was first heard at the District Court, Schoeneberg, Berlin on

22 February 1983, and Paul appointed a German lawyer, Dr Klaus Wachs, to represent him. The Heubers were asking for maintenance of 1,500 Deutschmarks per month (approximately £375) and an official declaration from Paul that he was the father. Under German law, if it were proven that Bettina was Paul's daughter, she would be entitled to inherit ten per cent of any money he might leave. This would only be enforceable in Germany – but all German royalties could be frozen.

Paul had agreed to have blood and tissue samples taken and his first blood test was in February 1983. A blood test proves paternity with ninety per cent certainty. It identifies proteins and enzymes in the child that must be present in the mother or father's blood. In March 1983, he was ordered to pay the £180 per month interim maintenance by the German court who rejected the evidence of the blood test, which had indicated that Paul was not the father.

Paul said: 'It seems the girl's blood contains something that is not in mine or the mother's, so it must have come from the third person and he is the real father.'

In April 1983 the German court finally awarded full maintenance. Paul commented: 'One thing I think is very unfair is that the judge is a woman and is pregnant herself. But I'm not going to ask for a different judge. I just want to get the whole thing settled.'

In June 1983, stories began to appear in the press with headlines such as 'Beatle Girl Strips To Raise Cash'.

Bettina was then twenty and had posed naked for the sex magazine *High Society*. There were eight pages of her wearing only leather gloves and carrying a glass guitar. It was disclosed that she received £600 for the session and said she was forced to do it because Paul refused to pay the maintenance that had been awarded by the court in April. She'd worked as a kindergarten teacher until then and had hoped to start a new job in September. Her mother, now 39, commented: 'The pictures are very tasteful . . . she did the session because she is broke and Paul hasn't paid her any maintenance money yet.' In fact it seemed rather naïve of her to accept only £600 when the pictures were syndicated throughout the world and must have generated tens of thousands of pounds in reproduction fees.

By the time Bettina was 22 and settled in Berlin as a hairdresser, she had lost two cases concerning her claim and Paul had had a further blood test which once again indicated that he was not her father. As Bettina had lost the case, she was liable to pay Paul's legal costs of £60,000. Dr Wachs advised Paul that he pay the money, commenting: 'I advised Paul, and he agreed, for psychological reasons he should by no means enforce his right for costs. It was my opinion that if he did this, it would give Miss Heubers another cause to make bad publicity for him.'

However, after Paul had made the generous gesture, Bettina announced that she would bring another paternity case against him, saying: 'I think it is very odd that Paul paid these costs for us and this will be prominently brought forward in our new case.'

Paul had had similar problems with another ex-girlfriend. Anita Howarth was a Liverpool girl who, in 1964, claimed that her son Philip was the result of her affair with Paul. Her mother told the press: 'They would go out together regularly, although it was not really serious. Then one day she confessed she was pregnant by Paul. It was a bombshell to the family.'

When the Beatles returned to Liverpool for their Civic Reception, her uncle began to put notices in Liverpool telephone boxes and fliers around the city announcing that Paul was the father of his niece's child.

In 1997 she asked Paul to take a DNA test.

Her son Philip, 37 years old in 2001, revealed that his mother had admitted to him that she had another lover at the time she went out with Paul and he could have been the father. Philip tracked the man down and asked him to take a DNA test, which he did – and it proved positive, proving that Paul was not his father.

Philip announced, 'I never wanted Paul McCartney to be my father and I am happy that he isn't. I rang him to tell him the news.'

Another paternity claim was made in 1993 when Paul was touring America on his New World Tour. A 33-year-old American woman, Michelle Le Vallier (who had changed her name to Michelle McCartney) claimed to be Paul's daughter, saying that Paul had had an affair with her mother in London in the late 1950s. She produced a birth certificate that stated she was born in Paris on 5 April 1959 and her parents were Monique Le Vallier and a man named James Paul McCartney. At that time, however, that would mean her mother was only fourteen years old when she was born and Paul would have been seventeen.

The ridiculous claim was dismissed.

When Paul was in America during February 1964 he had a relationship with actress Jill Haworth, who he first met at a press conference at the Plaza Hotel. He then began to visit her at her apartment. 'He wanted a good cup of tea and he couldn't get it at the Plaza and he came to my apartment,' she said.

He next called her up and invited her to stay in Miami while the Beatles were there. Paul arranged for payment of her trip, although she was booked into another hotel while they stayed at the Beauville. 'A car would be sent for me to take me over there,' she said. Paul wanted to keep the relationship out of the press, as Jane Asher was still his girlfriend.

When Paul's long romance with Jane Asher came to an end in 1968, Paul often frequented the Revolution Club in Bruton Place, London. He took a shine to one of the waitresses there, Maggie McGivern, and the two of them went off for a holiday in Sardinia together. News of the couple on holiday appeared in the Sunday newspaper, the *People*.

Many years later, in the *Daily Mail* newspaper dated Saturday 12 April 1997 there was a four-page interview with her in which she described a clandestine affair with Paul which lasted between 1966 and 1969.

See also: Asher, Jane; Caldwell, Iris; McGough, Thelma; Rhone, Dorothy; Schwartz, Francie.

Girls' School

A number mainly recorded in London in March 1977 with Paul, Linda, Denny Laine, Jimmy McCulloch and Joe English. The song was said to have been inspired by the famous St Trinians, the girls' school created by Ronald Searle and subject of several British comedy films. Paul also claimed to have received added inspiration from adverts in American newspapers for soft-porn films with such titles as *School Mistress*, *Curly Haired* and *The Woman Trainer*. The original title was 'Love School'.

The number was issued as a double A-side with 'Mull of Kintyre' in Britain on Capitol R6018 on Friday 11 November 1977, although it was 'Mull of Kintyre' which got the credit for making the record the biggest-selling British single of all time up to that date. With home sales surpassing the two million mark, the record lasted until the release of the Band Aid charity single seven years later.

In America it was 'Girls' School' which received the major promotion, although the single only managed to reach the No. 33 position. It was issued in America on Capitol 4504 on Friday 4 November 1977.

Paul discussed his decision to make the record a double A-side. He said, 'The idea of it was that if someone had bought the single and decided they wanted to have a dance, all they had to do was flip it over and there they had something to dance to, rather than put two songs that were the same sort of thing on the record.

'The idea of having a double A-side was so that if someone thought we were only into ballads, there was the opposite to prove we do all kinds of songs. I think there may be some people who prefer the more rocking side, which is the 'Girls' School' one. So, for those people, we made it a double A, because B-sides get swallowed. B-sides never get played on the radio or anything like that, so you have to say it's a double A even if you really think it's an A and a B.

'The song came about when we'd finished our tour of Australia and were coming back via Hawaii for a sort of holiday after the tour. We were supposed to go to Japan, but the Japanese Minister of Justice decided we couldn't get in, because we'd been naughty. So we went to Hawaii instead, on the way back to England. Anyway, I was looking through one of these American newspapers and the back page, at the end of the entertainments section, is always the porno films.

'I rather liked the titles, so basically I took all the titles and made a song out of them. For example, there was a film called *School Mistress*, another called *Curly Haired*, one called *Kid Sister* and another called

The Woman Trainer and I liked those titles so much I just wove them into a song. It's kind of like a pornographic St Trinians.'

Give Ireland Back To The Irish

A single by Wings issued in Britain on Friday 25 February 1972. The number had been recorded at Island Studios, London on Tuesday 1 February 1972. Paul had written the song in protest at the British army's involvement in Northern Ireland. It followed what was referred to as 'Bloody Sunday', the tragic events which took place on Sunday 30 January 1972 when thirteen Catholic protestors were shot dead during a civil rights demonstration in Londonderry. The paratroopers involved said that they had come under sniper fire. As a result Paul wrote this song. Paul had roots in Northern Ireland and his mother had been baptised a Catholic, so his sympathies were with the Catholics in this instance. It was also Paul's first major political statement in songs and was the first single on which new guitarist Henry McCullough, who was Irish, performed.

On Thursday 10 February Paul's assistant Shelley Turner announced, 'EMI are one hundred per cent behind it and are very keen to put it out. As soon as they have got the final lacquer, they will put it out. It will probably be in the shops by next week. Paul has strong feelings about the Irish situation.'

Apple had prepared a 30-second TV commercial for the single in which Paul was featured, but the Independent Television Authority banned it from the ITV Network as they said it contravened the ITV Act. ATV also banned the disc, together with the BBC, Radio One, Radio Luxembourg and even the GPO.

When he heard that the BBC had banned the record, Paul said, 'Up them! I think the BBC should be highly praised ... preventing the youth from hearing my opinions.'

BBC press officer Rodney Collins explained that it wasn't played on Radio One because it made a political point.

The single was issued in Britain on Apple R5936 on Friday 25 February 1972; it entered the Top 20 despite the lack of plays, but only reached No. 15 in the charts. In America, where it was released on Apple 1847 on Monday 28 February it fared even worse, only reaching No. 21 in the charts.

Both the British and American releases had an instrumental version of the number on the flipside.

The single was also issued in Germany on EMI Electrola/Apple 1C006-05007 and in France on Apple 2C006-05007M.

Posters were to proclaim that BBC radio and television, Radio Luxembourg and the GPO had banned the record.

The single topped the charts in Ireland and Spain.

When George Watson, a reporter for ABC TV, asked Paul if he were worried about making a political point, he answered, 'No. You can't stay out of it, you know, if you think at all these days. We're still humans, you know, and you wake up and read your newspaper, it affects you. So I don't mind too much, it doesn't worry me, like I say. I don't now plan to do everything I do as a political thing, you know, but just on this one occasion. I think the British Government overstepped their mark and showed themselves to be more of a sort of repressive regime than I ever believed them to be.'

'Give Ireland Back To The Irish' was taken off Paul's two-disc set in 2001 due to a terrorist bomb, which killed a number of people in London earlier in the year. Paul said, 'I support the idea of Ireland being free and being handed back. I feel, like a lot of people, but I don't support their methods. I certainly don't want to support when a bomb goes off in London and people are killed. I would have a hard time supporting that. So when EMI rang me up and said, "Look, you know, we're pretty nervous and you don't have much time on the album. We should pull that one," that was really why it got pulled.'

Give My Regards To Broad Street (album)

The vinyl version of the film soundtrack was issued on EL2602781 and the compact disc on CP 2702782. They were released simultaneously in Britain on 22 October 1984 by EMI records. The album reached No. 1 in the British charts and No. 21 in the US.

The tracks were: 'No More Lonely Nights', 'Good Day Sunshine', 'Yesterday', 'Here, There and Everywhere', 'Wanderlust', 'Ballroom Dancing', 'Silly Love Songs', 'Not Such A Bad Boy', 'No Values', 'For No One', 'Eleanor Rigby'/'Eleanor's Dream' and 'The Long And Winding Road'.

Paul had originally chosen a shortlist of thirty songs. He commented: 'A lot of them were put in for reasons of the plot; we wanted a long one like "Yesterday", the director wanted that more than me, because I'd sung it a lot of times!'

He also said: 'We did a special orchestral arrangement that takes new themes based on the *mood* of "Eleanor Rigby", and we extended it for something like nine minutes without a vocal, which for me is quite a departure ... The bit we needed the images for was after "Eleanor Rigby", which was conjured up by the song's mood. So it went to altars and churches, Dickensian characters, carriages, Victorian picnics. I just threw out a lot of images, the director picked them up and made them into this big anxiety dream.'

'Good Day Sunshine', 'Here, There and Everywhere', 'For No One' and 'Eleanor Rigby' all originally appeared on the Beatles' *Revolver* album and 'Eleanor Rigby' was also a double A-sided single with 'Yellow Submarine'. 'Yesterday' originally appeared on *Help!* and gave the Beatles their eleventh No. 1 in the States when issued as a single. 'The Long And Winding Road' first appeared on the *Let It Be* album, and Paul also included a new version of the number on his *Wings Over*

America album. 'Silly Love Songs' was Wings' first British No. 1 single and also appeared on the album *Wings At The Speed Of Sound*. 'Wanderlust' and 'Ballroom Dancing' originally appeared on Paul's fourth album *Tug Of War*; the film version of 'Ballroom Dancing' includes an extra verse which Paul added at the director's request. *Wanderlust* was also the name of one of the yachts that Wings chartered when they were recording the *London Town* album. 'No More Lonely Nights' was the first single to be released from the film project and there were several versions of it. 'Not Such A Bad Boy' and 'No Values' were brand new and appeared on the *Give My Regards To Broad Street* album for the first time anywhere.

Give My Regards To Broad Street (film)

Paul's ambition to produce a feature film came to fruition with *Give My Regards To Broad Street*, an original idea of his.

He'd initially commissioned playwright Willy Russell to write a script.

'It was a nice idea and one it may be possible to resurrect at some point,' he has said, 'but I felt it wasn't quite right for me at the time.'

Paul also had discussions with another playwright, Trevor Nunn, before finally deciding to write the script himself.

The idea for the plot came to him when his chauffeured car was held up in a traffic jam and he jotted down the idea on the spot. He'd remembered a story record producer Chris Thomas had told him about how an assistant had left the master tapes of the Sex Pistols *Never Mind The Bollocks* on a station platform. He'd been due to take them to the factory and rushed back to the station to find that although the case had been soaked in the rainfall, the tapes were still intact and undamaged.

Paul said, 'I thought just over three million dollars would see us through. In the first week alone, we'd spent nearly all that and I was ordering new cheque books.' He then realised he didn't have to spend his own money and did a deal with 20th Century Fox who provided funds of between $6 and $8 million.

Paul originally didn't write a part for Linda in *Give My Regards To Broad Street*, but added one for her after she'd protested to him about it.

The film was two years in the planning and pre-production. Shooting eventually began in August 1982, and lasted for 28 weeks. When it opened in 1984, the film was given a number of premieres. The American one was held at the Egyptian Theater, Los Angeles, on 22 October with a special party at the Bistro Club. The New York premiere at the Gotham Theater was followed with a party at Club A. The Liverpool premiere took place at the Odeon cinema on 28 November and Paul was presented with the Freedom of the City at a special ceremony earlier in the day. The London premiere took place at the Empire Leicester Square, on 29 November, with a pre-premiere party at the Hippodrome.

Paul became involved in major promotion for the film in both America and Britain and travelled to the US early in October 1984 for three weeks to promote it, appearing on shows such as *Good Morning America* and *The Johnny Carson Show*.

In Britain he appeared for one hour on a *South Bank Show* special, on the chart show *Harty* and on *Film '84*.

Paul had originally intended using the finances of his MPL company, but 20th Century Fox stepped in with funding in exchange for world-wide distribution rights.

When it opened in 311 cinemas across America, it was savagely panned by the critics and was an initial box-office disappointment. The show business magazine *Variety* described it as: 'Characterless, blood-less and pointless'.

Paul commented, 'I wanted to make the sort of movie that I like to see. It's an old-fashioned musical, a good night out, nothing heavy. Like most people, I go to the cinema to be entertained, not to see my own problems on the screen.'

On the film's release, Paul held several press conferences to promote it. Here is the transcript of one of the conferences, although he didn't seem to take the opportunity of plugging the film, since most of the queries related to topics apart from the movie:

Question: Did you have a hard time picking the old songs to re-record?

Paul: I pulled out about fifty songs that I fancied singing and I gave a list of these to the director and said, 'Let's just choose.' So some of them got chosen for pure story reasons. Like 'Yesterday' was included on the director's request because he wanted to set up the thing that happens toward the end of the movie where I become a busker. But something like 'For No One', that was just because I love that song and I realised I hadn't sung it since that twenty years ago we're talking about. I never ever did it in public. I did it only once on the record. And I thought, 'Well, it's a pity that songs can just come and go that quickly.' I wanted that one in just for my own pleasure. And then 'Ballroom Dancing', for instance, was put in because it's a very visual number. So it was a mish-mash of reasons.

Why shouldn't I sing 'em? Just because I once recorded them with the Beatles? They're not sacred, not to me, anyway. I wouldn't say I do a better version of those. Maybe those are the definitive versions, maybe not. You know, I think 'Long And Winding Road' in this is better than the original version. Just that particular song. So that was it really, I fancied singing them and didn't see why not.

John and I once tried to write a play when we were just starting out, even before we wrote any songs. We got two pages and just couldn't go any further, we just dried up. It would have been great, actually, because it was like a precursor to *Jesus Christ Superstar*. It was about this guy called Pilchard who you never actually saw. He was always upstairs in a room, praying. And the whole play was about the family saying, 'Oh God, is he prayin' again?' It was quite a nice idea, but we could never get him out of that room and downstairs.

Question: There are so many books out on the Beatles. Do you have any plans to write an autobiography?

Paul: The only thing that would make me do it is that round about this age, you do start to forget, you know. After twenty years, you don't remember it so well. And that would be the motivating factor, to actually get it down. But I haven't actually thought of doing it, really. But it's beginning to sneak into my mind that maybe I ought to get it down even if it isn't going to be like Mick's. It's more a publicity stunt rather than a book.

Question: In the early press accounts, you were the good guy. But in later biographies, you're cast as the bad guy. Do you feel a need to give your side?

Paul: Well, like anyone, I wouldn't mind being understood rather than misunderstood. It's very tempting when someone like John was slagging me off in the press. There was a period there when he was really going for me. It's very tempting to answer back, but I'm glad I didn't, I just thought, 'The hell with it, he's going over the top like he does.' He was a great feller, but he had that about him. He'd suddenly throw the table over and on to a new thing. And I was the table. But, I mean. A lot of it was talk and I think John loved the group. I think, though, he had to clear the decks for his new life. That was my feeling at the time. And there's nothing really you could say. But I don't think I was the bad guy or the good guy. I think what originally happened is that I'm from a very close, warm family in Liverpool, and I was very lucky to come from that kind of family. John wasn't. John was an only child. His father left home at three. His mother was killed when he was sixteen. My mum died when I was fourteen, so we had that in common. But when it came to meet the press and I saw a guy in the outer office shaking, I'd go in and say, 'Want a cup of tea?' because I just didn't like to be around that tension, that nervousness. So it fell to me to go and chat to the guy and put him at ease. Which then looked like PR. So I became known as the sort of PR man in the group. I probably was. The others would say, 'I'm not bloody doing that interview, you do it.' So I tended to look a bit the good guy in the media's eyes, because that's who I was being nice to. And I suppose the others may have resented that a little. But eventually, I've got this wild, ruthless ambition kind of image. If you do well, you get a bit of that. I don't really think it's that true. I think everyone was just as ruthless and ambitious as I was.

Question: What do you think of the exploitation of Lennon's death?

Paul: I think it's inevitable. You're talking about the West and capitalism. Exploitation's part of the game, really. I prefer to remember him how I knew him. I was in Nashville and saw a John Lennon whiskey decanter. AARGH! He didn't even drink it. So, yeah, it's a bit yucky. But you can't do anything about it. This is America, folks.

Question: There have been reports you might bid upwards of $60 million for Northern Songs. How important is it for you to regain control of your old material?

Paul: I'd really like to do it. Just because it seems natural that I should be allowed to own my own songs eventually. And I figure whoever's been publishing them has made a lot of money on me. But if you sign them away, you sign them away. That's the law of the land. And I signed them away, so I can't really blame the feller who bought them. But I'd like to get them back just because they're my babies, John's and my babies.

Like 'Yesterday'. I think if you tell the man in the street that Paul doesn't own 'Yesterday', it would surprise him. And the trouble is having to ask permission to sing it in the movie. That gets you. But actually, the publishers were quite fair. I think they only charged me a pound. I think they saw the irony too.

Question: Your current work will always be compared to your past work with the tendency to devalue the current. Is that difficult to live with? Do you ever just want to get rid of the Beatles?

Paul: Not really. I know what you mean, though. I have to admit, looking at all the songs I've written that probably there's a little period in there that was my hottest period. 'Yesterday', 'Here, There And Everywhere', a little bunch of stuff that just came all in a few years. I suppose it was because we were at our height and the novelty became a very important factor. What's happened with me over the past ten years is I've tended to assume that the critics were right. 'Yeah, you're right. I'm not as good as I used to be.' But in actual fact, recently I've started to think, 'Wait a minute, let's check this out. Is this really true?' And I don't think it actually is. For instance, a song called 'Mull Of Kintyre', which sold more records than any other record in England, is from my 'bad period'. The song 'Band On The Run', that's also from my bad period. I think what happens is after such a success as the Beatles, everyone, including me, thinks there's no way we can follow that, so you just tend to assume it's not as good. I think, as a body of work, my ten years with the Beatles, I would say, is probably better than this stuff. I do tend to be a bit gullible and go along with whoever's criticising me and say, 'Yeah, you're right, I'm a jerk.'

Question: Do you feel as if you're competing with your past work?

Paul: Yeah, a little bit. I think this new song, 'No More Lonely Nights', I felt good about that. There are, I think, some decent things in there. It's not all rubbish. But I think it's a natural thing after the Beatles to assume he must be on a losing streak now. And I tend to go along with it. But I don't think it's really true.

Question: Do you just sit and wait for the songs to come to you?

Paul: No, I just tend to sit down and try and write a song, I think the best ones come of their own volition. 'Yesterday', I just fell out of bed and that was there. I had a piano by the side of my bed. I mean, that particular song I woke up and there was a tune in my head. And I thought, 'Well, I must have heard it last night or something.' And I spent about three weeks asking all the music people I knew, 'What is this song? Where have you heard this song before?' I just couldn't believe I'd written it.

George Martin was drafted in to work on the arrangements for the film and also to appear as himself. The musicians who were featured included Dave Edmunds, Chris Spedding, John Paul Jones, Eric Stewart, Steve Lukather, Jeff Porcaro, Jody Linscott, Louis Johnson, Dave Gilmour, Dave Mattocks and Herbie Flowers.

Songs featured were: 'Good Day Sunshine', 'Here, There And Everywhere', 'Wanderlust', 'No More Lonely Nights', 'Ballroom Dancing', 'Silly Love Songs', 'Not Such A Bad Boy', 'So Bad', 'No Values', 'For No One', 'Eleanor Rigby', 'Band On The Run', Zip-A-Dee-Doo-Dah', Bless 'Em All', 'Give My Regards To Broad Street' and 'Sleepy Lagoon'.

Prominent among the cast were Sir Ralph Richardson, Tracey Ullman, Bryan Brown and the wrestler 'Giant Haystacks'. Peter Webb was the director.

The plot was basically a simple one with Paul sitting in the back of a black limousine on his way to meet his manager Steve (Bryan Brown) for an important meeting. The car is stuck in a long traffic jam and Paul dozes off. He finds himself driving along a country road in his customised Ford, which has its own computer. He receives a call on the car phone from Steve who tells him that the master tapes of his new album have vanished. Harry (Ian Hastings), an assistant, hasn't turned up with them. Paul arrives in the boardroom where the sinister banker Rath (John Bennett) makes an appearance. He is seeking to make a takeover bid for Paul's company and will be successful if the tapes are not recovered.

Steve estimates that the missing tapes are worth five or six million pounds and Paul sets off with him to a recording studio, dismissing Steve's fears that Harry may have absconded with the tapes to bootleg them.

At the studio Paul tells Ringo Starr and George Martin about the missing tapes and then goes to Elstree Studios where he joins Linda and the band to record the 'Ballroom Dancing' sequence. After a short break in the studio canteen it's off to the make-up room to apply a futuristic look for the 'Silly Love Songs' scene, and then the search for Harry and the missing tapes continues. Paul later fits in some rehearsals in a warehouse before setting off to the BBC for an interview.

During a rendition of 'Eleanor Rigby' we are taken back to Victorian times as Paul, Linda, Ringo and Barbara Bach picnic on a riverbank. Another scene is Dickensian as Harry is pursued by a giant figure with a bull terrier (shades of Bill Sikes!) and is eventually stabbed by Rath.

The visions fade and Paul makes his way to visit the Old Justice, an East End pub where Harry had been spotted the previous evening. He chats to Jim, the landlord, and then drives into central London as the deadline for the takeover nears. Paul comes to Broad Street station and remembers that Harry had mentioned the station when he left with the tapes. Paul wanders along the deserted platform and discovers Harry, who had been accidentally locked inside a hut. Paul is able to return to his office with the tapes in time to beat the deadline of the Rath takeover.

Commenting on the 'Ballroom Dancing' sequence, Paul said: 'I wanted to do it in either Hammersmith Palais or the Lyceum, but the director said that the reason they don't like doing that in films is that if the lighting man suddenly says "Take that wall out", it's all right on a set, but you could imagine the manager of the Hammersmith Palais being a bit upset!

'It was great that, we had the band on stage – John Paul Jones on bass, Ringo on drums, Dave Edmunds and Chris Spedding on guitars, Linda and me on piano, so we had that element, which was nice enough anyway. We had the back-up guys, who were like the Palais band, then we had the dancers. All the formation dancers, three specialist dancers, then we had another back-up of young dancers, who were like the rock-'n'-roll kids. One of the couples were the people who won our Buddy Holly competition, the guy who had been on the dole in Liverpool until then. So all of these elements, pulling them together, and still trying to have a laugh, I think that works really well in the film.'

The video was originally released in America in May 1985 and in Britain on 25 July. The home video was issued in Britain on CBS/Fox 1448-50 (VHS) and 1448-40 (Beta).

Givin' Grease A Ride

A number which Paul co-wrote with his brother Mike for the 1974 *McGear* album, which Paul also produced. Paul also plays on this track.

Glasses

A track on Paul's 1970 debut album *McCartney*. Lasting only 48 seconds, it features the sounds of multi-tracked wine glasses.

GMTV

GMTV – Good Morning Television – a British morning TV show. The programme screened an interview with Paul on Monday 26 November 2001. Paul was originally to have been interviewed on Wednesday 21 November, but he felt that 33-year-old Kate Garraway was too old and he requested a younger interviewer. Penny Smith – who was a few years' older than Paul's fiancée Heather Mills – finally interviewed him.

Go Cat Go

A HBO (Home Box Office) programme on Carl Perkins. Paul participated in it during his American tour. Following his concert in Memphis on Tuesday 27 April 1993, he jammed backstage at the Liberty Bowl performing with Carl on the numbers 'Blue Suede Shoes', 'Maybelline', 'Matchbox' and 'My Old Friend'. 'My Old Friend' was an unreleased number at the time, which had been penned by Carl and recorded during the *Tug of War* album sessions in 1981.

An album of the same name was issued by Dinosaur Records in America on 15 October 1996. It included 'My Old Friend' and also tracks with participation by John Lennon, George Harrison and Ringo Starr. Other artists on the album were Paul Simon, Bono, Johnny Cash, Tom Petty and the Heartbreakers, Jimi Hendrix and Willie Nelson.

God Bless America

A single by Thornton, Fradkin and Unger and the Big Band, issued in America in June 1974. The track was originally recorded in January 1971 and issued in America on Monday 17 June 1974 on ESP-DISK ESP 45-63019. Wings' drummer Denny Seiwell had introduced Paul and Linda to Paul Thornton, Leslie Fradkin and Bob Unger and Paul agreed to make a guest appearance on this track. He played bass guitar and also provided backing vocals.

The track was also included on the group's album *Pass On This Side*, issued in America on Monday 8 July 1974 on ESP-Disk ESP 63019.

Going Home

An MPL documentary, screened in Britain as 'From Rio To Liverpool'. It was named 'Best Music Special' in the annual ACE awards for US cable television programmes. (See 'From Rio To Liverpool'.)

Going Live

A BBC children's programme on which Paul appeared for fifteen minutes on Saturday 12 December 1987. The programme went out live and during his interview he revealed that he and George Martin were going to record a new song for Paul's planned feature-length film about Rupert Bear. Paul was also accompanied by his son James when he took some phone calls live from viewers. Paul also mimed to 'Once Upon A Long Ago' to the studio audience, backed by his band, which included Stan Salzman and Nigel Kennedy.

Goldcrest Film Studios

On Thursday 21 September 1989, prior to his world tour, Paul held a special pre-tour concert in Studio 6 at the Goldcrest Film Studios in Elstree, Hertfordshire, before an invited audience of 750 people, mainly members of the Wings Fun Club and the winners of a Radio One contest. Prior to the concert the 11-minute pre-concert film, directed by Richard Lester, was screened and Paul and the band then performed the thirty songs they would be performing on the forthcoming tour.

Golden Earth Girl

A track from the 1993 album *Off The Ground*, penned by Paul and lasting 3 minutes and 43 seconds. The number was also featured on the 1999 classical CD *Working Classical*.

Golden Slumbers

Paul used to work on songs at 'Rembrandt', the house he'd bought for his dad as a retirement present, using a piano in the lounge.

Paul's stepsister Ruth was nine years old at the time and taking her music lessons at school seriously. One day she brought home the music of 'Golden Slumbers' to practise on the piano. She was playing it quite badly, so Paul sat down and spent the rest of the evening trying to teach her the left-hand bass notes.

This resulted in Paul deciding to make his own 'Golden Slumbers', taking the verse lyrics from the traditional ballad and creating a new melody, which ended up on *Abbey Road* the next year.

Paul said, 'I can't read music and I couldn't remember the old tune, so I started playing my tune to it, and I liked the words so I just kept that.'

The original 'Golden Slumbers' was an English hymn based on a 400-year-old poem by Thomas Dekker. Some of Dekker's original lines were:

Golden slumbers kiss your eyes
Smiles awake you when you rise
Sleep pretty wantons do not cry
And I will sing a lullaby
Rock them rock them, lullaby.

The Beatles recorded the number at Abbey Road on 2 July 1969 and it was included on the *Abbey Road* album.

Another version by Paul of this medley was included on the *Tripping The Live Fantastic* album. At 6 minutes and 41 seconds in length, it was recorded live at the Skydome in Toronto, Canada on 7 December 1989 during the 1989/90 World Tour.

Good Causes

On Friday 10 October 1980, Paul and Linda donated £500 to an appeal for the Liverpool boxer Johnny Owen, who had been injured in a bout.

In 1986 Paul became a patron of the 'Million Minutes Of Peace' campaign, which aimed to promote racial, religious and international harmony throughout the world.

During 1988 Paul and Linda became patrons of the Cinnamon Trust, a charity which helps the elderly cope with problem pets. Paul and Linda also contributed to a collection of charity Christmas cards organised by Yves St Laurent in aid of the Save The Children fund. Paul contributed a drawing of a snowman and Linda one of her photographs. Paul also contributed a drawing of Santa Claus for a charity book 'The Childline Christmas Book'.

In 1989 Paul and Linda allied themselves with Greenpeace in a campaign against acid rain. Paul wrote a letter to be distributed widely, which read, 'Do you remember "Norwegian Wood"? Who would have guessed that the title would call to mind an image of dying forests. If your family loves the countryside, I urge you to help.' In December they donated $100,000 to Friends Of The Earth.

In 1992 Paul and Linda made a donation to Crosby Action Aid, which raises cash for immunising children in Africa against infectious diseases.

During the same year the couple, along with Carla Lane, paid £4,000 to prevent a number of animals and birds from being auctioned off at Guilsborough Grange Wildlife Park, Northants.

Together with Carla, Paul and Linda also took part in a rescue attempt to try to save a Beluga whale. The 900lb whale had escaped from an experimental station in the Ukraine and was in the Black Sea where fishermen had dubbed it 'Brightness'. There were fears for the safety of the whale unless it was returned to its natural habitat in the Arctic, a venture that required raising £200,000. In the meantime, the Ukrainian scientists were demanding that the whale be returned to them.

Paul established a scholarship fund at Iowa State University in 1990 for students studying environmental issues. When he played Aimes, Iowa in 1990 he raised $15,000 that went straight into the fund. The first recipient of the scholarship was Melissa Veylupek of Omaha in 1992.

In 1993 Paul and Linda issued a statement to the International Whaling Commission. They were concerned that Japan, Iceland and Norway had requested that the ban on commercial whaling should be lifted. Japan had said that their current license was for scientific purposes, but Paul disagreed, saying, 'These must be the fastest experiments going because pretty soon after the whaling ships dock in Japan, the whale meat is served up in restaurants.'

He also stated, 'The people of the planet are depending on you to keep the sea blue, not red.' The Whaling Commission ignored Paul's plea and lifted the ban.

During the same year Paul and Linda gave their support to Dr Vernon Coleman's 'Plan 2000' campaign. This was a campaign that was seeking to stop experimentation on animals by the year 2000. Dr Coleman pointed out that a thousand animals are killed by scientists every thirty seconds. In supporting the campaign, Paul commented, 'Vernon is absolutely right. We're with him all the way.'

1993 also saw him donate a collection of children's books which were auctioned to raise funds for 'Gimme Shelter', a campaign for homeless people, and he donated an autograph doodle to Relate North Wales, a crisis counselling charity.

In his concern for whales, Paul returned to the fray in 1996 when it was known that Norway would begin the slaughter of 425 whales. Paul wrote an open letter to the people of Norway:

Dear People of Norway,

On Monday 20 May a small group of your countrymen will once again take up the 'tradition' of whaling and will hunt down and kill 425 minke whales. By this action, this minority is going to earn your country the contempt and the scorn of the rest of the world and we believe you should realise that.

The whalers say that they are doing this because it is a long-established Norwegian tradition. You know and we know that this is nonsense. The cloak of 'tradition' is being used to disguise the fact that this whole bloody exercise is being done for a huge profit. But who will really profit from this massacre? Probably not the people of Norway. A few whalers will make a lot of money and a few rich businessmen in Japan will be able to grotesquely impress their dinner guests. But the losers will be you and your country. Just as, years ago, the right-thinking world condemned slavery, so too your beautiful land will be stained and despised on account of a handful of traditionalists who are going to tarnish Norway's name through their action.

When we have toured there, it is one of the best places to be. In our experience, the overwhelming majority of Norwegians – especially young Norwegians – are kind and forward thinking. They are concerned about ecology and open to new, better ideas like whale-watching. Our friends in Norway have told us that most Norwegians don't eat whale meat anyway and, as Greenpeace has alerted, this whole sad and sick exercise is being conducted not to uphold tradition but for greed.

Last year the Norwegians slaughtered 232 minke whales. This year they intend to double the slaughter. Last year the International Whaling Commission called on Norway to 'halt immediately all whaling activities'. That's not just men in suits passing a resolution. The IWC ruling is the world calling. The whole of the rest of the planet – with the exception of a few hypocrites who whale for the 'scientific purposes' that don't fool or impress anybody – is imploring Norway to stop or be shamed. We don't believe that the people of Norway want or deserve that shame. We believe that you have it within your power to stop this killing. Call on your leaders to write to Mrs Brundtland, and demand a ban on Norwegian whaling. You could earn the praise and respect of the world.

With love, Paul and Linda McCartney.

Paul's concern for the survival of whales also appeared in a two-page foreword to the book *On the Trail Of The Whale* by zoologist Mark Carwardine, published by Thunder Bay Publishing Company in 1994.

He wrote, 'On a recent concert tour of the world I met a woman who said to me, "My ambition in life is to see a whale before I die." I believe she is typical of a growing number of people who feel the same way – and who realise that it is becoming more and more possible to make this great ambition come true.

'For many years now, my wife Linda and I (and our kids for that matter) have been strongly opposed to the killing of whales and, like many people, have been doing our utmost to save the largest creatures ever to grace our fair planet.

'In Norway, traditionally a whaling nation, we spoke out against what we see as the unnecessary slaughter of these precious animals. We were met with the objection that people had been making their living from whaling for countless generations.

'But our argument was that people once sold slaves for a living and children were forced to work in mines. At the time, this was all thought to be perfectly acceptable. But we have moved on. We have learned that such behaviour is brutal and can lead only to the lack of regard for life in general.

'Obviously, no one wants to see people thrown out of work, particularly in these recessionary times, so an alternative way of making a living has to be found. Nowadays, there is a real alternative to whale slaughter – whale-watching. I believe that well-organised whale-watching will provide a perfectly acceptable method of making money for the whaling communities. It will also offer an opportunity for the people of the world to learn about these great creatures and to experience them living wild and free in their natural environment. I hope Mark's book will inspire more people to achieve this great dream for themselves and that it will help to show us the way to a more peaceful and happier future.'

In 1995 Paul and Linda sent a letter to the French President Mitterand asking him to end the disgraceful way animals were transported in Europe.

In 1996 Paul, together with Cliff Richard, launched a £6 million appeal for the Music Sound Foundation, to help future stars.

In 1997 Paul was among several artists who signed a petition asking China to release the Tibetan music student Ngawang Choepel who had been jailed for eighteen years. Other signatories were Peter Gabriel, Sting and David Bowie. Annie Lennox delivered it to the Chinese embassy in London.

In August 1997 Paul and Linda sent a message of support to an anti-hunt rally in London where 20,000 protesters had gathered.

In 1998 Paul signed a petition for the League Against Cruel Sports against the three-day Waterloo Cup tournament at Altcar in which two greyhound dogs chase a field hare which is usually ripped to pieces. Paul addressed his petition to the landowner Lord Leverhulme, writing, 'Is it not symbolic that although we live in the heart of the countryside we have never had the privilege of seeing a hare? Hare coursing is one of the most cruel of so-called sports.'

In December 1998 at his home studio, Paul recorded the number 'Little Children', penned by Peter Kirkley, the proceeds of which were to benefit street children in Brazil.

On 26 December 2001 Paul wrote an open letter to British Prime Minister Tony Blair urging him to stick to his promise of allowing a free vote on hunting. Paul's two daughters Stella and Mary also signed the letter. Paul wrote, 'All around the country today people on horseback will be marking Boxing Day by following packs of hounds chasing and savaging hundreds of wild animals in the name of sport. We want to live in a country where it is illegal to inflict pain and suffering by hunting wild animals with dogs; an activity that we, along with most British people, believe is cruel, unnecessary, unacceptable and outdated. Your government has promised to give the House of Commons an "early opportunity to express its view", to have a "free vote" and to "enable Parliament to reach a conclusion on this issue". The time to do this has come.'

Paul and Linda also supported the League Against Cruel Sports. Linda was to say, 'As you can imagine, I'm really anti-hunting – as most people are. I think that chasing innocent creatures with horses and hounds is a barbaric thing. It is old-fashioned and outdated, and with the help of the League Against Cruel Sports, it will soon be banned.'

Paul and Linda donated the 200-acre site of St John's Wood in Upton to the league in 1991 in order for them to use it as a deer sanctuary.

Following Linda's death, Paul decided to establish an area of woodland to commemorate her and her work for animal protection.

In 1999 he wrote in the League's newsletter: 'I understand that many League supporters have written asking whether there is any way in which they may pay tribute to Linda's life and work for animal protection. The League have suggested the planting of a new woodland adjacent to St John's Wood, and a memorial plaque to those who contribute at their St Nicholas Priory HQ. I think that this is a splendid idea to benefit wildlife and would like to thank you for your kindness in naming the wood in my dear Linda's memory.'

In 2001 Paul participated in a 'Hands Up For Hedgehogs' campaign by the Surrey Wildlife Trust. The charity had been raising funds by auctioning off pictures of hedgehogs, which a number of celebrities had supplied. They included Hayley Mills, Joan Collins, Joanna Lumley, Helena Bonham Carter, Britt Ekland, Charlie Dimmock, Rolf Harris, Twiggy, Wendy Richard, Prunella Scales and Alan Titchmarsh.

Paul donated an original piece of his artwork depicting a hedgehog, personally signed, and it raised £3,012 at the Internet auction held at QXL.COM between 17 December 2001 and 25 January 2002.

In June, Paul donated £1,000 to help a sick seventeen-year-old donkey, Humphrey, which had been found dying in a field with its hoofs hacked off. He sent the cheque to the Willows Animal Sanctuary, where Humphrey was being looked after.

See also 'Charities'.

Good Day Sunshine

A track on the *Revolver* album, composed by Paul and recorded at Abbey Road Studios on 8 and 9 June 1966. Paul actually wrote it during a visit to John's house in Weybridge. He said, 'The sun was shining. Influenced by the Lovin' Spoonful.' Paul was referring to the Lovin' Spoonful's hit 'Daydream'. There was some input from John who said, 'Paul wrote this, but I think maybe I helped him with some of the lyric.'

The number was a particular favourite of composer Leonard Bernstein who praised the song on a CBS news documentary in 1967.

Good Morning America

An American breakfast show on ABC TV on which Paul and Linda appeared on Thursday 27 November 1980. They appeared live on the show but it was by satellite from their Sussex farmhouse. Dan Hartman interviewed the two for approximately ten minutes.

Paul appeared on this major American television show for five consecutive weekday mornings from Thursday 25 October until Wednesday 31 October 1984. He was in America to promote his film *Give My Regards To Broad Street* and when he initially appeared, he attracted the biggest studio audience applications ever for the show.

Good Morning Policeman

A song Paul was said to have written when he was interred in a Japanese prison in January 1980.

Good Rockin' Tonight

A number by Roy Brown, which Paul has performed on numerous occasions. Paul recorded a medley of the number, along with 'Shake, Rattle And Roll' during a *Tug Of War* rehearsal at Pugin's Hall in Tenterden, Kent on Thursday 30 October 1980. He also recorded the number for his MTV *Unplugged* appearance in 1991 and it was included on his album *Unplugged – The Official Bootleg* and in his acoustic set during his short *Unplugged* tour. It was also included in the set he performed at the Mean Fiddler, London on Friday 20 November 1992 for the 'A Carlton New Year' TV show broadcast on Thursday 1 January 1993. He included it in the acoustic set of his Australian/New Zealand tour in March 1993 and the acoustic set of his North American tour from April to June 1993. A live version of the song, lasting 2 minutes and 52 seconds and recorded at the Blockbuster Pavilion, Charlotte on Tuesday 15 June 1993, was included on the *Paul Is Live* album.

Good Rockin' Tonight – The Legacy Of Sun Records

An album issued in America on Sire/WEA 31165 on 30 October 2001. Disc One opens with 'That's All Right Mama' by Paul McCartney.

Good Times Coming/Feel The Sun

The first of Paul's solo compositions to feature on the *Press To Play* album, lasting 4 minutes and 56 seconds. It comprises two separate songs that Paul ran together into each other because they had a similar theme. He commented, 'There's a nostalgic air about summers that have gone. It's a pretty strong feeling, even for people who are only seventeen; they can remember a summer when they were ten. In Britain, you tend not to get too much of that stuff, so you tend to remember them.'

Goodbye

A number composed by Paul which was recorded by Mary Hopkin on Saturday 1 and Sunday 2 March 1969 at Morgan Studios in Willesden, London. Although Paul was the sole writer, the Lennon and McCartney songwriting credit remained. Paul also produced it, sang a duet with Mary and played guitar on the number. The flipside was 'Sparrow', a number penned by Gallagher and Lyle. Apple's Tony Bramwell was in the studio and filmed the production on 16mm film.

Apple issued the single simultaneously in 28 countries, accompanied by a promotional film showing Paul and Mary making the record. It was released in Britain on Friday 28 March 1969 on Apple 10 and in

America on Monday 7 April 1969 on Apple 1806. The number reached No. 2 in the British charts and No. 13 in the American.

Paul made a demonstration record of the tune on which he sang and played acoustic guitar. The disc came up for auction at Sotheby's London branch on Wednesday 22 December 1982.

Goodnight America

An American television show hosted by Geraldo Rivera. Rivera interviewed Paul, Linda and Wings on the show on Monday 28 June 1976 to discuss the success of their recent American tour. Excerpts of the performances of 'Band On The Run' and 'Yesterday' from the concert in Seattle on 10 June were shown and the group also promoted their new single 'Let Em In', which had been issued in America that day.

Goodnight Tonight (promotional film)

A promotional video filmed at the Hammersmith Palais on Tuesday 3 April 1979 by Keef & Co. Wings appeared in 1930s-style clothes and then changed to modern dress during the instrumental break. The video was screened on *Top Of The Pops*, *The Kenny Everett Show* and on the American programme *Midnight Special*.

Goodnight Tonight (single)

A Wings single issued on Parlophone R6023 on Friday 23 March 1979. There was also a special extended disco version issued on Tuesday 3 April. The number reached No. 6 in the British charts. It had been issued in America some days before, on Thursday 15 March on Columbia 3-10939 and reached the No. 5 position. The British 12" version was issued on Parlophone 12Y R6023 and the American on Columbia 23-10940.

'Daytime Nightime Suffering' was the flipside on all versions.

It was the first Wings single on the Columbia label and Paul had been given an advance of two million dollars against a royalty of 22 per cent, which made him the highest paid recording artist in the world.

Columbia had wanted Paul to include the number on the *Back To The Egg* album, but Paul refused, saying the song didn't fit the album. 'I'm making records, I'm not running a record store,' he added.

The single was also issued in Germany on Odeon 1C006-62579 and in France on Parlophone 2C006-62579.

Got To Get You Into My Life

A song penned by Paul and featured on the Beatles' *Revolver* album, issued on 5 August 1966. It featured a 'soul' sound, probably inspired by the music of Stax records artists and included a five-piece brass section. On the same day the Cliff Bennett and the Rebel Rousers version was issued in Britain on Parlophone R 5489, which Paul personally produced. It was released in America on 29 August 1966 on

ABC 10842. It was also the title of the Rebel Rousers' album, issued in Britain on 27 January 1967 on Parlophone PCS 7017.

American group Earth, Wind and Fire recorded a version for the Robert Stigwood film *Sgt Pepper's Lonely Hearts Club Band* and this reached No. 4 in the American charts in August 1978, although it only reached the position of No. 20 in Britain.

Paul said, '"Got To Get You Into My Life" was one I wrote when I had first been introduced to pot. I'd been a rather straight working-class lad, but when we started to get into pot, it seemed to me to be quite uplifting. "Got To Get You Into My Life" is really a song about that, it's not a person, it's actually about pot. It's saying, "I'm going to do this. This is not a bad idea," so it's actually an ode to pot, like someone else might write an ode to chocolate or good claret.'

Regarding the trumpet sound on the track, Paul commented, 'We put trumpets on because it sounded like a trumpet number. None of the others did, so we haven't used them on any other tracks, so it's a nice novelty.'

A version of this number, lasting 3 minutes and 21 seconds, was included on the *Tripping The Live Fantastic* album. It was recorded live at the Westfalenhalle in Dortmund, Germany on 17 October 1989 during the 1989/90 World Tour.

Gotta Sing, Gotta Dance

A song Paul originally wrote for Twiggy in 1973. The TV special in which she was to sing it was never made, but Paul was able to utilise the number as the highlight of his 'James Paul McCartney' TV spectacular.

A Swedish trio, First Mistake, recorded the number and issued a single at the end of 1986 with a party mix of the same number on the flipside.

Gracen, Jorie B

A photojournalist from Chicago who has taken more than a thousand photographs of Paul at record signings, private parties, press conferences, backstage, award ceremonies and at concerts.

She first met Paul and Linda on the *Wings Over America* tour in 1976 when she was still a student photographer. She next met them when she flew over to London in 1978 and took photographs of them in Abbey Road where they were recording *Rockestra*.

Jorie was then commissioned to cover the 1989/90 World Tour and at the end of the 45-week tour she presented Paul with a book of 40 10x8s of her pictures.

She has continued to photograph Paul ever since.

Grammy Awards

In America the Recording Academy and the Grammy awards were founded in 1957.

There are various categories of awards, a number of which have been presented to the Beatles as a group or to Paul as an individual.

They include the Trustees Award that the Beatles won in 1972.

The Grammy Hall of Fame Awards was established in 1973. This was to honour recordings of lasting, qualitative or historical significance that were recorded more than 25 years ago.

Awards in this category won by the Beatles include *Abbey Road* in 1995; 'Yesterday' in 1997; 'I Want To Hold Your Hand' in 1998; 'Strawberry Fields Forever' and *Revolver* in 1999; *The Beatles (White Album)*, *A Hard Day's Night* and *Rubber Soul* in 2000; 'Hey Jude' and *Meet The Beatles* in 2001.

Joe Cocker also received the Hall of Fame Award for his performance of Paul's composition 'With A Little Help From My Friends' in 2001.

Other awards included: Best New Artist of 1964, the Beatles; Best Performance by a Vocal Group: 'A Hard Day's Night', 1964; Best Contemporary (R&R) Solo Vocal Performance, Male or Female: Paul McCartney, 'Eleanor Rigby', 1966; Song of the Year: 'Michelle', John Lennon and Paul McCartney, 1966; Best Contemporary Album: *Sgt Pepper's Lonely Hearts Club Band*, 1967; Album of the Year: *Sgt Pepper's Lonely Hearts Club Band*, 1967; Best Original Score Written for a Motion Picture or a Television Special: *Let It Be*, 1970; Best Arrangement Accompanying Vocalist(s): 'Uncle Albert/Admiral Halsey', 1971; Best Pop Vocal Performance by a Duo, Group with Vocal: 'Band On The Run', 1974; Best Rock Instrumental Performance: Paul McCartney & Wings with the Rockestra Theme, 1979; Best Pop Performance by a Duo or Group with vocal: 'Free As a Bird', 1996; Best Music Video, Long Form: 'The Beatles Anthology', 1996; Best Music Video, Short Form: 'Free As A Bird', 1996.

Paul made his personal appearance at the 32nd annual Grammy Awards (Academy of Recorded Arts and Sciences) at Shrine Auditorium, Los Angeles on Wednesday 21 February 1990 to receive his Lifetime Achievement Award. He accepted the award from actress Meryl Streep and made a small speech. Streep recalled that she was in the audience of the Shea Stadium in 1965 and held up a sign that read 'I love you forever Paul'. Ray Charles performed 'Eleanor Rigby' and Stevie Wonder performed 'We Can Work It Out'.

The Lifetime Achievement Award is presented by vote of the Recording Academy's national trustees to performers who, during their lifetimes, have made creative contributions of outstanding artistic significance to the field of recording.

The academy was to announce: 'Paul McCartney who, as a member of the Beatles, had an impact not only on rock and roll but also on Western culture, and who, as a solo performer and songwriter continues to develop and grow after three decades.'

Granny's Chest

A BBC Russian Service programme. On Thursday 26 January 1989 Paul became only the second person to participate in a live radio phone-in between the West and the Soviet Union. The first had been by Margaret Thatcher the previous summer.

Paul was guest in Studio 57 at Bush House, London when the show was broadcast to an estimated 18 million listeners in the Soviet Union from 6.05 p.m. to 7 p.m. GMT.

On the morning of the show, the Soviet newspaper *Komsomolskaya Pravda* had printed the London telephone number to call. Over one thousand calls were received, although only fourteen callers were actually included in the broadcast.

The questions were translated into English by the show's host Sam Jones and an interpreter in a nearby studio in Bush House translated Paul's answers into Russian.

During the broadcast, three tracks from Paul's *Choba B CCP* album were broadcast.

The BBC world service programme *Multitrack 3* transmitted edited highlights from the programme on Friday 27 and Saturday 28 January 1989.

Grapefruit

An Apple band, mainly comprising members of the former Tony Rivers and the Castaways, who had been signed to Nems NEMS Enterprises. John Lennon gave them the name Grapefruit.

Paul produced their promotional film for the single 'Elevator'.

On Sunday 26 May 1968 he filmed them in Hyde Park for a three-minute film sequence, during which onlookers surrounded them while they were filming around the Prince Albert Memorial. Around fifty Beatles fans sought an autograph from Paul, so he signed some for them.

Grateful Dead – A Photofilm, The

A nine-minute short film by Paul, which he had worked on for two years. It used some animation techniques to utilise photographs Linda took of the Grateful Dead in the 1960s and bring them to life, with a soundtrack of music by the Grateful Dead. The film was completed in 1995, the year in which Grateful Dead leader Jerry Garcia died. Paul was invited to preview the film at the London Film Festival that year.

The film received its American premiere at the New York Film Festival on Sunday 28 and Monday 29 September 1997 and was also shown as a support to the feature *Trainspotting*. It was screened at the Angelika Film Center in New York on Friday 11 October 1997 and also in cinemas in Santa Monica and San Francisco. In Los Angeles it was shown as support to the film *Microcosmos*.

When Paul talked to fans on the Internet on 17 December 1999, he mentioned this film and another film of the Beatles he had considered making utilising Linda's photographs.

'She actually did one of the Grateful Dead and I noticed on the contact sheet that the shots were similar and if you looked through them quickly, it looked like a film. So I got the idea to flip through them quickly. The other I'm working on, they aren't all unpublished photos of the Beatles, but I'm hoping to do some sort of photofilm with it. But it's a long project and will take some time. Hopefully it will go on general release.'

Great Cock And Seagull Race, The

A number Paul recorded at the A&R Studios in New York in December 1971 on which he played lead guitar and drums. Shortly after the recording a 45 acetate was given to the New York radio station WCBS-FM to play on Wednesday 15 December – it was played at a speed of 33⅓. Paul had originally considered using it as a B-side to one of his singles, but decided against it and it remained unreleased. When he appeared on WCBS with the record he commented, 'This is when we got up and ate our cornflakes,' resulting in the number being referred to as 'Breakfast Blues' on some bootlegs.

Great Day

The final track on the *Flaming Pie* album. It was penned by Paul and lasted for 2 minutes and 9 seconds. It was produced by Paul and George Martin and engineered by Bob Kraushaar when it was recorded on 3 September 1992. Paul sang lead vocal and played acoustic guitar and leg slap/percussion while Linda provided backing vocals.

Paul said, 'I wanted a short song for the album and I remembered this one, which goes back twenty years or so when the kids were young. Linda and I used to sing it around the kitchen. It's just a little upbeat song of hope, to the point and in the spirit of the whole album.'

Greenham Common

The site of a Cruise Missile base in the Berkshire countryside. Large groups of women camped out there in the early 1980s for several months in order to demonstrate their opposition to the weapons. In December 1983 Paul and Linda sent the women some expensive food hampers from London's Fortnum & Mason's, a high-class grocery store in Piccadilly, with the message: 'You are doing a great job. Keep it up and don't give in.'

Grillo, Oscar

An Argentine artist, born in Buenos Aires in 1943. As a child he first saw *Snow White And The Seven Dwarfs*, which inspired him and he was later to recall, 'No one explained it was animation, but I knew they were moving drawings and I knew I wanted to be an artist.' At the age of sixteen he began working in a studio making commercials and moved to Britain in 1970 where he has been living ever since.

He became an advertising and children's book illustrator, and as a film animator he won the Palm d'Or Award for Best Short with his film based on Linda McCartney's song 'Seaside Woman'. Paul also commissioned him to participate in the animation of a Rupert the Bear cartoon, but another artist finally did it. Grillo then went on to create animated films for Linda's 'Wide Prairie' and 'Shadow Cycle'.

He was to form an animation studio Klacto with his partner Ted Rockley.

Groucho Club, The

A trendy club for media people situated in London's Soho. On Thursday 1 October 1992 Paul and Linda held a special fundraising lunch at the club on behalf of LIPA (Liverpool Institute of Performing Arts). Among those present were Lord Palumbo, chairman of the Arts Council, Robert Key of National Heritage and Peter Bounds, chief executive of Liverpool City Council.

Guildhall, Portsmouth

A venue where the Beatles were due to appear on Thursday 12 November 1964 during a British tour. The show was cancelled as Paul was suffering from gastric flu. The booking was rearranged and the Fab Four were due to appear there a few weeks later on 3 December, but that appearance was also cancelled due to a television appearance on the programme *Day By Day*.

Guinness Book of Records Hall of Fame

A BBC 1 television programme transmitted on Monday 26 May 1986.

The show was hosted by David Frost and Norris McWhirter and broadcast from the BBC Television Centre in Wood Lane, London.

The occasion was to present the first six people to be inducted into the Guinness Book Of Records Hall Of Fame and Paul appeared to receive his acclaim as the most successful musician of all time.

The other five inductees were Billie Jean King, Sir Ranulph Fiennes, Vesna Vulovic, Colonel Joe Kittinger and Vernon Craig.

Guinness Superlatives

The company that publishes the world's biggest selling book, *The Guinness Book Of Records*. To celebrate a new edition in 1979 they organised a special promotional reception at London's Les Ambassadeurs club, announcing that the event was to honour Paul. The date was Wednesday 24 October and Norris McWhirter, co-founder of the book, presented Paul with a rhodium-plated disc (at the time the metal was worth £345 an ounce). This unique metal is twice as valuable as platinum and makes a handsome award. It was announced that Paul had been honoured because he was 'The Most Successful Composer And Recording Artist Of All Time'. For the following three reasons: 1) he'd written 43 songs between 1962 and 1978 which had sold over a million copies; 2) he'd been awarded sixty gold Discs, forty-two with the Beatles, seventeen with Wings and one with Billy Preston; and 3) he'd sold more records worldwide than anyone else, his estimated record sales at that time being 100 million albums and 100 million singles.

At the presentation ceremony, McWhirter commented, 'Since, in the field of recorded music, gold and platinum discs are standard presentations by recording companies, we felt we should make a fittingly superlative presentation of the first ever rhodium disc with a special label listing Paul McCartney's three achievements.'

Guitars

Paul's first musical instrument was a trumpet, which he gave up in order to buy a guitar, saying, 'It (the trumpet) used to hurt my lip and I didn't fancy the thought of walking around like a beat-up boxer, so I decided to buy myself a guitar.'

The instrument he chose was a Zenith.

Paul recalled, 'I couldn't figure out what was wrong at first, until I realised the strings were all in the wrong place for me, being left-handed. This was the first time I was conscious of finding left-handedness any sort of handicap as far as everyday gadgets were concerned.'

He said, 'I started bashing away and pretty soon I had the basic chords well and truly learned. Then I got a bit more ambitious and bought a solid Rosetti. It only had two strings and, when I played it, it didn't produce a very melodic sound. But I kept the volume right down and it seemed OK to me.'

He was also to say, 'Before we went to play in Hamburg, I'd bought myself a Rosetti Solid Seven electric guitar from a store in Liverpool. It was a terrible guitar! It was really just a good-looking piece of wood. It had a nice paint job, but it was a disastrous, cheap guitar. It fell apart when I got to Hamburg, because of the sweat and the damp and continually getting knocked around, falling over and stuff. So, in Hamburg, with my guitar bust, I turned to piano.'

Paul was able to add more detail about the incident in a *Beat Instrumental* interview, saying, 'Actually, I had that old Rosetti a long time. I used it all through the early days – in the Cavern – and only changed it when we went to Hamburg for the first time.

'I didn't want to get rid of it, but I had to, because it got smashed when I dropped it one day. It wasn't a complete write-off, but I didn't think it was worth repairing so all of us – George, Stu, Pete and John (especially John) had a great time smashing it to bits by jumping up and down on it! . . . I couldn't afford to buy a new guitar, so I became the Beatles' official piano player.'

When Stuart Sutcliffe left the group, Paul decided to take up the bass guitar. He said, 'I had a big problem, though. I'm left-handed and it was very difficult because it was the only left-handed bass available and I thought, I'd better have a spare.'

In 1958 he bought an Epiphone Casino. Paul stripped his Rickenbacker down to natural wood.

In the days when Stuart Sutcliffe was a member of the band Paul had a white Hoffner 200 guitar and from 1962 he also used a Sunburst Hoffner 500 bass guitar which he later used as a spare on live performances. From late 1963 up until the Beatles' final live performances he used a Sunburst Hoffner 550/1, often called a Hoffner violin bass or a Hoffner Beatle bass. He stopped using it around 1965, when the group began their studio recordings in earnest, and started using his Rickenbacker.

In 1974 he commented, 'The violin bass doesn't record well.' However he did use it during the *Let It Be* recordings. In 1965 he acquired a Sunburst Rickenbacker 400 stereo bass guitar in the States, which was a specially built left-hand model. He used it in the studios, but not on stage – until the formation of Wings. He also acquired another guitar in America during 1965, a Sunburst Epiphone E23OT semi-acoustic electric six-string, with a Bigsby tremolo. It was a right-hand model so Paul had to play it upside down. He was later to remove the scratch plate, because it was on the wrong side of the guitar for him, and occasionally used the guitar on live gigs with Wings. Also in 1965 he used a Martin D18 acoustic guitar, which he used on Beatles recordings and on the TV special 'The Music Of Lennon And McCartney' during his performance of 'Yesterday'. It was a right-hand model so he had to play it upside down with the strings reversed.

The Rickenbacker was used in 'Magical Mystery Tour', 'Our World' and the promotional film for 'Hello Goodbye', by which time the Fool had painted it in psychedelic colours.

During the recording of *Sgt Pepper* he used a right-hand Sunburst Fender Esquire.

On the solo *McCartney* album Paul played a left-handed Sunburst Fender Telecaster. He used an Epiphone E150 acoustic guitar on the *Wild Life* album and a black Gibson Hummingbird acoustic guitar on the 'James Paul McCartney' TV special – also using the guitar on stage performances. On the *Ram* recordings he used a left-handed green Gibson Firebird with Bigsby tremolo arm. He used a right-handed black Danalectro bass guitar on the Wings 1972 tour and a brown Fender Precision bass for the *Venus And Mars* album, once again a right-hand model with the strings reversed.

Discussing guitars in the June 1990 edition of *Guitar* magazine, Paul said that his favourite instrument was the acoustic guitar, 'If I couldn't have any other instrument, I would have to have an acoustic guitar,' he said. Praising guitarists such as Eric Clapton, Eddie Van Halen and Dave Gilmour, he said, 'I still like Hendrix the best.'

Gunston, Norman

An Australian comedian, real name Garry McDonald, who hosted his own show, *The Norman Gunston Show* on Channel 9.

He was one of 200 media people who attended a press conference for Wings in Perth on Sunday 2 November 1975.

When Wings first entered the room for the conference, they found Gunston asleep in a chair.

He then put a question to Linda: 'It must be difficult Mrs McCartney, being married all day, you know the two of you, and then at night having to perform together on stage.'

Linda answered, 'We're about to have a fight on stage one night.'

Gunston continued, 'Do you ever feel like sometimes saying, "Not tonight, thanks darling, I've got a headache?" They'd slow hand-clap you if you did.'

He continued, 'Would you coax one of your children to go into the "overnight sensation" world of the music industry?'

Paul answered, 'Well, if they wanted to, Norman, I'd let them.'

Gunston then said, 'I suppose anyway, if they didn't do too good they could always open up a sandwich shop using your name, you know, something like "Paul McCartney's Sons Takeaway Foods", except that fruit shop of yours didn't do too good in London did it?'

A puzzled Paul asked, 'The McCartney fruit shop?'

Then he seemed to realise and said, 'Apple! . . . Oh, Apple!'

Gunston said, 'That didn't do too good.'

Paul countered, 'Give that man a drink.'

Gunston continued, 'Was that one of John's ideas.'

Paul said, 'It was, Norm, yes.'

Gunston then said, 'There are two sides to every story, but I've heard the other Beatles used to get a bit annoyed because Mrs McCartney used to invite them over for long, boring slide evenings all the time.' He paused while reporters laughed and continued, 'When you did that LP *Abbey Road*, was there any truth in the rumour that you were dead?'

Denny Laine answered, 'He's not really here.'

Gunston then turned to Linda, 'Did you have any Beatlemania, Mrs McCartney?'

Linda answered, 'Constantly.'

Gunston continued, 'Which was your favourite, before you was related?'

Linda replied, 'Er . . . Mick Jagger!'

Gunston turned to the camera to say, 'I think she got him,' pointing to Paul, 'on the rebound.' Then he said, 'The marriage is OK?'

Paul answered, 'It's all right, but you're not helping it, Norm.'

Gunston then turned to Linda and said, 'It's funny, you know. You don't look Japanese.'

Hamburg

Paul originally used to write letters to Bill Harry informing him of the Beatles activities. Bill used an excerpt from one of the letters in the 12 September 1962 issue of the *Mersey Beat* and titled it 'Hamburg'. It was Paul's observations on his first visit to the German city.

The first time we went to Hamburg we stayed four and a half months. It's a sort of blown-up Blackpool, but with strip clubs instead of waxworks: thousands of strip clubs, bars and pick-up joints, not very picturesque.

The first time it was pretty rough, but we all had a great time. The pay wasn't too fab, the digs weren't much good, and we had to play for quite a long time. The club was a small place called the Indra and was owned by the proprietor of the Kaiser Keller, where we also played.

One night we played at the Top Ten Club and all the customers from the Kaiser Keller came along. Since the Top Ten was a much better club we decided to accept the manager's offer and play there. Naturally, the manager of the Kaiser Keller didn't like it. One night prior to leaving his place, we accidentally singed a bit of cord on an old stone wall in the corridor, and he had the police on us. He'd told them that we'd tried to burn his place down, so they said: 'Leave please, thanks very much, but we don't want you to burn our German houses.' Funny, really, because we couldn't have burned the place if we had gallons of petrol – it was made of stone.

There was an article on the group in a German magazine. I didn't understand the article, but there was a large photograph of a South African Negro pushing the jungle down. I still don't quite

know what he has to do with us, but I suppose it has some significance.

Hammell, John
Paul's chauffeur, a former road manager for Humble Pie. On Thursday
3 November 1994, when he was driving Paul to his home in Rye,
Sussex in the dark blue, customised Mercedes, which cost £60,000,
Hammill pulled over to the near side of the road to let a lorry pass. The
lorry skidded on wet leaves coming down a hill and crashed into the
side of the car. Paul and Hammill were unhurt, but there was extensive
damage to the car.

Hammersmith Odeon
A major London concert venue that presented the Beatles' Christmas
Concerts. Paul and Wings appeared there on Friday 25, Saturday 26
and Sunday 27 May 1973. The Sunday date was an additional date,
entered into because the planned concert at the Hippodrome,
Birmingham had been cancelled. They returned to the venue in 1975
during their World Tour to appear on Wednesday 17 and Thursday 18
September. Paul had commissioned a 30-second television commercial
to promote the two dates, although they had already been sold out. A
special party was held after the final concert with members of Queen,
Pink Floyd, David Frost, Alice Cooper, Harry Nilsson, Ringo Starr and
Lynsey De Paul.

The venue was used for the Concerts for Kampuchea on Saturday 29
December 1979 in which several leading musicians joined Wings in a
'Rockestra' encore.

Hands Of Love
The third part of a four-number 11-minute 15-second medley that
closed the *Red Rose Speedway* album and was 2 minutes and 12
seconds in length. Paul sang lead vocal and played acoustic guitar.
Linda provided vocal, Denny Laine electric guitar, Henry McCullough
percussion and Denny Seiwell drums and percussion.

Hanglide
An instrumental by Paul and Eric Stewart recorded during the *Press to
Play* sessions at Hog Hill Mill studios. The mixing was credited to
'Mac 'N' Matt', who were Paul and Matt Butler.

Hard Day's Night, A (film)
The Beatles' debut film has become a classic, which basically revolved
around a fictional day in the life of the group. They arrive in London
along with the mischievous grandfather John McCartney, played by
actor Wilfred Brambell, famous for his role in the TV series *Steptoe
And Son*.

Paul said: 'Wilfred Brambell was great. The only terrible thing for us was that Wilfred kept forgetting his lines. We couldn't believe it! You see we expected all the actors to be very professional and word perfect. We couldn't imagine that an actor like Wilfred could ever do a thing like forget his lines. So, we were very shocked and embarrassed by this.'

Paul's major contributions to the film soundtrack were 'And I Love Her', 'Things We Said Today' and 'Can't Buy Me Love'. He also co-wrote 'If I Fell', 'Tell Me Why' and 'I'll Cry Instead' with John.

Discussing how they first came to make the film, Paul commented, 'We'd only released a few singles and a couple of albums but we'd now reached the position where the Beatles were big enough for producers to approach us and ask if we'd like to make a full-length movie on our own terms. Not bad going for a bunch of scruffs who'd only recently come down south to London from Liverpool. We discussed this with Brian (Epstein) on a number of occasions and he asked if we had any ideas of our own. The only person we could think of was whoever made that *The Running Jumping And Standing Still Film*. Who did that? 'Cause it was brilliant!

'The thing was, we all really loved the Goons film so, right away, that was an indication of the kind of direction we were all interested in. It might look a bit dated now, but it was fabulous back then. Basically, it was just what we liked. We could relate to the humour wholeheartedly. Brian discovered that it had been made by Richard Lester and so we said, well he's all right by us.'

Paul's recollections in hindsight may not be entirely accurate. It's doubtful whether the Beatles came up with the idea of having Richard Lester direct their first movie.

Lester had recently directed the films *Mouse On The Moon* for producer Walter Shenson and it was Shenson who decided on hiring him for the Beatles movie. He did approach the Beatles for their agreement on the hiring of Lester and was to say that the main reason they had accepted him was because he had worked on *The Running Jumping And Standing Still Film*.

The film's scriptwriter, Alun Owen, had written a scene for Paul during the episode when members of the group set out individually to track down the missing Ringo. Paul filmed the scene with young actress Isla Blair, but the entire sequence ended up on the cutting-room floor because it was felt that Paul seemed too self-conscious in it.

The dialogue for the missing sequence is as follows:

Interior, Rehearsal Room
Paul goes into the room. The girl is in mid-flight. She is very young and lovely and completely engrossed in what she is doing. The room is absolutely empty except for Paul and herself. She is acting in the manner of an eighteenth-century coquette, or, to be precise, the

voice English actresses use when they think they are being true to the costume period ... her youth however makes it all very charming.

GIRL: If I believed you, sir, I might do those things and walk those ways only to find myself on Problems Path. If I believed you, sir, I might like you or even love you, but I cannot believe you and all those urgings, pleadings and the like serve only as a proof that you will lie and lie again to gain your purpose with me.

She dances lightly away from an imaginary lover and as she turns she sees Paul who is as engrossed in the scene as she was.

GIRL: (surprised) Oh!

PAUL: (enthusiastically) Well ... go 'head, do the next bit.

GIRL: Go away! You've spoilt it.

PAUL: Who, me?

GIRL: Yes, you.

PAUL: Oh, sorry I spoke.

He makes no effort to go. He simply continues to look steadily at the girl; then he smiles at her. She is undecided what to do next.

GIRL: Are you supposed to be here?

PAUL: I've got you worried, haven't I?

GIRL: Of course not. I asked you who you are, that's all.

PAUL: No you didn't, you asked me, 'Was I supposed to be here?'

GIRL: It's the same thing.

PAUL: It isn't you know.

GIRL: Well, you've obviously no right to be here.

PAUL: Aah, that's more like it. Do I look like a trespasser, like?

GIRL: I'm warning you, they'll be back in a minute.

PAUL: D'you know something, 'they' don't worry me at all.

GIRL: They'll throw you out!

PAUL: Is that a gentle hint I won't be missed, like if I go?

GIRL: (haughtily) I want to go on rehearsing.

PAUL: Well, I'm not stopping you.

GIRL: (hotly) Don't be rude.

PAUL: You had the first go, not me. Anyroad, I only fancy listening to you ... that's all but if it worries you ... well ...

GIRL: Of course it doesn't worry me, I can ... (she interrupts herself) ... Who are you?

PAUL: (smiling cheekily) Another worrier.

GIRL: (accusingly) You're from Liverpool, aren't you?

PAUL: (comically) How'd you guess?

GIRL: (seriously) Oh, it's the way you talk.

PAUL: (innocently) Is it ... is it, really?

GIRL: (suspiciously) Are you pulling my leg?

PAUL: (looking her straight in the eye) Something like that.

GIRL: (unsure) I see ... (airily) do you like the play?

PAUL: Yeah ... I mean, sure, well, I took it at school but I only ever had boys or masters say those lines, like, sounds different in a girl (smiles to himself) Yeah, it's gear on a girl.

GIRL: Gear?

PAUL: Aye, the big hammer, smashing!

GIRL: Thank you.

PAUL: Don't mench . . . well, why don't you give us a few more lines, like?

GIRL: (points) Oh, there isn't much point. Anyway, I was only doing it for myself.

PAUL: You don't half slam the door in people's faces, don't you? I mean, what about when you're playing the part, like, hundreds of people see you and . . .

GIRL: (cutting in) I'm not . . .

PAUL: What?

GIRL: Playing the part.

PAUL: Oh, you're the understudy, sort of thing?

GIRL: (aggressively) I'm a walk-on in a fancy-dress scene. I just felt like doing those lines.

PAUL: Oh, I see. You are an actress though, aren't you?

GIRL: Yes.

PAUL: Aye, I knew you were.

GIRL: What's that mean?

PAUL: Well, the way you were spouting, like (he imitates her) 'I don't believe you, sir . . .' and all that.

GIRL: I don't sound like that.

PAUL: Yes you do.

GIRL: Do I really?

PAUL: Yeah, it was gear.

GIRL: (dryly) The big hammer?

PAUL: (smiling) Oh aye, a sledge.

GIRL: But the way you did it then sounded so phoney.

PAUL: No . . . I wouldn't say that . . . just like an actress . . . you know.

He moves and stands about like an actress.

GIRL: But that's not like a real person at all.

PAUL: Aye well, actresses aren't like real people, are they?

GIRL: They ought to be.

PAUL: Oh, I don't know, anyroad up, they never are, are they?

GIRL: (teasingly) What are you?

PAUL: I'm in a group . . . well . . . there are four of us, we play and sing.

GIRL: I bet you don't sound like real people.

PAUL: We do, you know. We sound like us having a ball. It's fab.

GIRL: Is it really though?

PAUL: What?

GIRL: Is it really fab or are you just saying that to convince yourself?

PAUL: What of? Look, I wouldn't do it unless I was. I'm dead lucky 'cos I get paid for doing something I love doing. (He laughs and with a gesture takes in the whole studio.) All this and a jam butty too!

GIRL: I only enjoy acting for myself. I hate it when other people are let in.

PAUL: Why? I mean, which are you, scared or selfish?

GIRL: Why selfish?

PAUL: Well, you've got to have people to taste your treacle toffee.

She looks at him in surprise.

PAUL: No, hang on, I've not gone daft. You see, when I was little me mother let me make some treacle toffee one time in our back scullery. When I'd done she said to me, 'Go and give some to the other kids.' So I said I would but I thought to myself, 'She must think I'm soft.' Anyroad, I was eating away there but I wanted somebody else to know how good it was so in the end I wound up giving it all away . . . but I didn't mind, cos I'd made the stuff in the first place. Well . . . that's why you need other people . . . an audience . . . to taste your treacle toffee, like. Eh . . . does that sound as thick-headed to you as it does to me?

GIRL: Not really but I'm probably not a toffee maker.

PAUL: Oh sorry.

GIRL: You are though, aren't you?

PAUL: Yeah.

GIRL: How would you do these lines of mine?

PAUL: Who, me? Oh, I'd make a giggle and it'd be all wrong . . . funny, but all wrong.

GIRL: Yes, but how?

PAUL: Oh, definitely, it sticks out a mile, she's trying to get him to marry her but he doesn't want . . . well . . . I don't reckon any fella's ever wanted to get married, they just do it to keep the girl-friend quiet and by the time you've quietened her, she's the wife.

GIRL: That's not very romantic.

PAUL: Oh, I dunno, getting pulled for marriage when all you want's a bit of fun, I think that's very romantic and clever too. That's what, but girls are like that, clever and cunning. You've got to laugh.

He laughs.

GIRL: Well, it's nice to know you think we're clever.

PAUL: (grinning) And winning.

GIRL: And what do you think about it?

PAUL: Me? Oh, I don't have the time, I'm always running about with the lads . . . no, we don't have the time.

GIRL: Pity.

PAUL: (not noticing the invitation) Aye, it is but as I say as you get by, it's all right, you know ... bask on, happy valley; when they let you stop. Anyroad, I'd better get back.

GIRL: Yes.

PAUL: (going) See you.

GIRL: Of course.

Paul stands at the doorway, shrugs, then goes out. After a moment the girl starts to act her speech. She is still using her actress voice.

GIRL: If I believe you, sire, I might do ... (she breaks off and smiles) ... clever and cunning ...

She starts again but this time she delivers the lines in a saucy teasing manner.

Paul pops his head back round the door.

PAUL: Treacle toffee ... wowee!

Recalling the scene, Paul said, 'There was a sequence that I was going to do and, to this day, whenever I go past the pub in Shepherd's Bush – on the corner by the old BBC TV Theatre – I remember going in with Isla Blair and filming on the second floor.'

The venue was the Jack Billings School of Dancing.

'She was supposed to be the object of my desire or I was of hers – that was the idea behind this little scene-ette. I had to sort of wander around her with the camera going round and round in circles – all very sixties, all very French and I had to repeat these very quirky lines. We had a whole day of doing that, but it didn't work because it wasn't the kind of thing we would have done in everyday life. It was all a little bit too contrived.'

Although DVDs include missing scenes and additional material, this particular scene is likely to have been destroyed. In June 1970 director Richard Lester went to Twickenham Studios to look at the film's outtakes in the studio library and discovered that all the footage which hadn't been included in the original film had been destroyed due to the studio's policy of getting rid of such material five years after the completion of a film.

A Hard Day's Night received a Royal Film Premiere at the London Pavilion on Monday 6 July 1964 and was premiered in America on Wednesday 12 August 1964.

Hard Rock Café

Paul and Wings made a special live appearance at the café, a fashionable American-style venue situated in Piccadilly, London. On Sunday 18 March 1973, Paul and Wings played a one-hour set at the Hard Rock Café before two hundred guests, who paid £5 per head. The occasion was a charity show to raise money for Release, the London-based organisation that helps victims of drug abuse. At the time, Paul had been convicted of possessing cannabis only ten days previously.

Paul also hosted a private party there on Thursday 20 June 1991 to celebrate the launch of Linda's vegetarian burgers. Apart from Paul and Linda, Ringo and Barbara Starr were also in attendance.

On Friday 28 January 1994 Paul and Linda were at the Hard Rock again where Mike Myers presented them with a Hard Rock Foundation cheque for £25,000 from the proceeds of Linda's vegetarian burgers, which were on sale at the café.

Harris, Sally

Paul's second cousin. Paul acted as chauffeur for the day at her wedding to Kevin Murphy at Wallasey Town Hall on Friday 23 June 2000. He wore a charcoal-grey suit and blue and grey trainers.

Mike McCartney acted as official photographer at the ceremony and Mike's wife Rowena made the bride's pale gold wedding dress. Heather Mills was also in attendance.

Mike was to comment: 'It was a real family affair and lovely to see Sally on her big day. She looked beautiful in her dress and drew gasps from the crowd when she stepped out of the car. Paul hired a nice car for the day and drove Sally to the Town Hall. The only thing missing was a chauffeur's cap!'

Harrison, George

George was born on 24 February 1943 at 11.42 p.m. at 12 Arnold Grove, Wavertree, Liverpool 15. His parents were Harold and Louise Harrison.

In 1948 he began attending Dovedale Primary School, which John Lennon also attended. However, as John was three years ahead of him, George never met him there.

In 1949 the family moved to a new home at 25 Upton Grove, Speke.

In 1954 George enrolled at Liverpool Institute, where he was to meet Paul, who had started at the school the previous year. George recalled: 'It took from four o'clock to five to get home in the evening to the outskirts of the Speke estate and it was on that bus journey that I met Paul McCartney, because he, being at the same school, had the same uniform and was going the same way as I was so I started hanging out with him.'

George's mother first bought him a guitar for £3 in 1957 and that year he formed his first group, the Rebels, with his brother Pete and a friend called George Kelly. The group performed only one gig, at the British Legion club in Speke. George said: 'I remember the Rebels had a tea chest with a lot of gnomes around it. One of my brothers had a five-shilling [25 pence] guitar, which had the back off it. Apart from that it was all fine. Just my brother, some mates and me. I tried to lay down the law a bit, but they weren't having any of that.'

The next day George told Paul about the gig and they decided to practise together, with Paul joining George in the front room of the

Harrison house, where they played their way through chord books. George recalled: 'Paul was very good with the harder chords, I must admit. After a time, though, we actually began playing real songs together, like "Don't You Rock Me Daddy-O" and "Besame Mucho".

'Paul knocked me out with his singing especially, although I remember him being a little embarrassed to really sing out, seeing as we were stuck right in the middle of my parents' place with the whole family walking about. He said he felt funny singing about love and such around my dad. We must have both been really a sight. I bet the others were just about pissing themselves trying not to laugh.'

Paul was to say: 'I knew George long before John and any of the others. They were all from Woolton, the posh district, and we hailed from the Allerton set, which was more working-class. George and I had got together to learn the guitar and we were chums, despite his tender years, as it seemed to me then. In fact George was only nine months younger than I was but to me George was always my little mate. But he could really play the guitar, particularly a piece called "Raunchy", which we all loved. If anyone could do something as good as that, it was generally good enough to get them in the group.'

Paul wanted George to become a member of the group, but it was up to the leader John Lennon to make the decision. Arguably, the day George Harrison became a Quarry Man was following a gig at Wilson Hall, Garston, on 6 February 1958. George joined Paul and John on the bus home. Paul recalled: 'George slipped quietly into one of the seats on the almost empty bus we were on, took out his guitar and went right into "Raunchy". Some days later I asked John: "Well, what do you think about George?" He gave it a second or two and then replied: "Yeah, man, he'd be great." And that was that. George was in and we were on our way.'

In the summer of that year, Paul and George hitchhiked to Wales. George remembered: 'We ran out of cash again, and Paul had the idea that we could sleep at the police station in one of the cells. Unfortunately the police refused but did suggest we could kip in the grandstand of the local football club. With great difficulty we climbed the wall surrounding the football ground, and with even greater difficulty got to sleep on the concrete steps of the grandstand. Just as day was breaking, I woke to see the caretaker standing over us. "What are you doing in my grandstand?" he demanded. "Sleeping," Paul croaked. "Well, you're not any more." We didn't need telling twice.'

It was also the summer that the Quarry Men made their first ever record at Percy Phillips's studio at 53 Kensington, Liverpool. The A-side was a version of Buddy Holly's 'That'll Be The Day' with John on lead vocal, and the other track was the first original number ever recorded by the group who were to evolve into the Beatles. It was called 'In Spite Of All The Danger' and was credited to Harrison-McCartney. So the first songwriting team was actually George and Paul!

Following the Quarry Men appearance at Woolton Village Club on 24 January 1959, the group seemed to disband. John and Paul got together at Paul's house to compose songs, but they had, to all intents and purposes, finished playing as a band. George then joined a group called the Les Stewart Quartet. This group was booked to become resident at a new club to be opened in West Derby Village called the Casbah, but Les Stewart refused to play there. Another member of the group, Ken Brown, who had originally obtained the residency for the band, asked George if he knew any other musicians. George contacted Paul and John and they obtained the Casbah residency, opening the club on 29 August 1959. This Quarry Men line-up comprised Paul, George, John and Ken Brown. They had no drummer, saying that 'the rhythm's in the guitars'.

On 10 October there was a dispute with Ken Brown and Paul, George and John walked out of the residency and continued as a trio, using various names such as Johnny & the Moondogs. Stuart Sutcliffe joined them on bass guitar in January 1960.

They briefly toured Scotland as a backing band to the singer Johnny Gentle, and when their drummer, Tommy Moore, left them they found another drummer, Pete Best, to join them on their first trip abroad, a season in Hamburg beginning in August 1960.

Their initial residency in Hamburg was the Beatles' 'baptism of fire' and George was to recall: 'In my opinion our peak for playing live was Hamburg. At the time we weren't so famous, and people who came to see us were drawn in simply by our music and whatever atmosphere we managed to create. We got *very* tight as a band there. We were at four different clubs altogether in Germany. Originally we played the Indra, and, when that shut, we went over to the Kaiserkeller and then, later on, the Top Ten. Back in England, all the bands were getting into wearing matching ties and handkerchiefs, and were doing little dance routines like the Shadows. We were definitely not into that, so we just kept doing whatever we felt like.'

It was while they were playing at the Kaiserkeller that they were second on the bill to another Liverpool band, Rory Storm & the Hurricanes, whose drummer was Ringo Starr.

George was to say: 'I didn't like the look of Rory's drummer myself. He looked the nasty one with his little grey streak of hair. But the nasty one turned out to be Ringo, the nicest of them all.'

Because of his age, George was known as the 'baby of the Beatles' at the time. The police decided he was too young to play after the 10 o'clock curfew that existed for youngsters in the St Pauli district and he was forced to return to Liverpool, alone.

Although John Lennon got on with Pete Best, it was basically George and Paul who wanted to get rid of him and he was replaced by Ringo. Brian Epstein was to write about this in a letter to a friend, saying:

Didn't fit well as a drummer or a man. Beat too slow, or George thought so. I liked him though he could be moody. Friendly with John, but Paul and George didn't like him. I wasn't too happy about Ringo. I didn't want him, but then as now I trusted the Beatles' judgement.

Perhaps word got around that it was George in particular who insisted that Best leave, because, when the Beatles appeared at the Cavern with the crowd shouting 'Pete for ever, Ringo never!', George was given a black eye.

An interesting insight into George happened when Brian Epstein managed to secure the Beatles a recording contract in 1962, sending them a telegram: 'Congratulations boys. EMI requesting recording session. Please rehearse new material.' They sent postcards in reply. Paul wrote: 'Please wire £10,000 advance royalties.' John wrote: 'When are we going to be millionaires?' But George wrote: 'Please order four more guitars.'

During the Beatles' phenomenal career during the 1960s, George felt overshadowed by John and Paul. He was to say: 'The usual thing was that we'd do fourteen of their tunes and then they'd condescend to listen to one of mine.'

George introduced the sitar into Western music when he played it on 'Norwegian Wood'. He became intensely interested in Eastern philosophy and became involved with the Indian sitarist and composer Ravi Shankar and the Maharishi Mahesh Yogi (who introduced transcendental meditation into Western society), initially travelling to India in 1966 and continuing to visit there frequently over the years.

After mammoth success throughout the world, the Beatles ceased touring to concentrate on recording. However, George always seemed to have problems in placing his songs with the Beatles, owing to the dominance of Paul and John. He also had to suffer criticism from Paul about his ability as a guitarist.

Recalling the recording of 'Hey Jude', Paul said: 'I remember telling George not to play guitar on "Hey Jude". He wanted to echo riffs after the vocal phrases, which I didn't think was appropriate. He didn't see it like that, and it was a bit of a number for me to have to dare to tell George Harrison – who's one of the greats, I think – not to play guitar. It was like an insult.'

George walked out on the group at one point on 10 January 1969 during the filming of the 'Get Back' project, an incident that eventually emerged as the *Let It Be* film. There had been an argument in the studio canteen and George had walked out, saying he'd see the other Beatles around the clubs. He then drove to Liverpool.

The tension had already been witnessed during the filming of the recordings. At one point, during the recording of 'Two Of Us', Paul had been making comments to George, who turned to him and said: 'I'll play whatever you want me to play, or I won't play at all if you don't want me to play. Whatever it is that'll please you, I'll do it.'

George recalled: 'Paul and I were trying to have an argument and the crew carried on filming and recording us. Anyway, after one of those first mornings, I couldn't stand it. I decided: This is it; it's not fun any more; it's very unhappy being in this band; it's a lot of crap; thank you, I'm leaving.'

Ringo was to say: 'George had to leave because he thought Paul was dominating him. Well, he *was* because Michael Lindsay-Hogg liked Paul, I would think, more than the rest of us. So, it's like Paul's film, actually.'

On his return George insisted that he'd left because of Paul. He said: 'That period was the low of all time. In normal circumstances, I had not let his attitude bother me and, to get a peaceful life, I had always let him have his own way, even when it meant that songs, which I had composed, were not being recorded. In front of the cameras we were actually being filmed. Paul started to get at me about the way I was playing. Everybody had left at one time or another, but I left during "Let It Be". When I left, there's a scene where Paul and I are having an argument and we're trying to cover it up. Then, the next scene, I'm not there and Yoko's just screaming, doing her screeching number. Well, that's where I left, and I went home and wrote "Wah Wah". It'd given me a wah-wah, like I had such a headache with that whole argument. It was such a headache.'

George had actually agreed to return only if Paul would stop his plans to have them make a major live performance – and they settled for the Beatles' rooftop appearance on the Apple building.

Since the Beatles had stopped touring, George had been writing more and more songs. He'd been to the United States, where he'd played with other top musicians and appreciated how cooperative the atmosphere had been. He said: 'This cooperation contrasted drastically with the superior attitude which for years Paul had shown towards me musically. In normal circumstances I had not let this attitude bother me and to get a peaceful life I had always let him have his own way, even when this meant that songs, which I had composed, were not being recorded.

'When I came back from the United States ... I was in a very happy frame of mind, but I quickly discovered that I was up against the same old Paul. In front of the cameras, as we were actually being filmed, Paul started to "get at" me about the way I was playing.'

George also felt that not only did Paul criticise how he played his solos, but he was also resentful about George's compositions and the fact that he had become a fine songwriter and deserved more of his songs on Beatles recordings. John was to comment that the reason why Paul never liked the double album *The Beatles* was that George had three compositions on it. He said: 'He was always upset over it because on that one I did my music, he did his, and George did his. And first, he didn't like George having so many tracks, and second, he wanted it to be more of a group thing, which really means more Paul.'

Ringo was to observe: 'George was writing more. He wanted things to go his way, where, when we first started, they basically went John and Paul's way. George was finding his independence and wouldn't be dominated as much by Paul.'

When it came to the recording of 'The Ballad of John and Yoko', only John and Paul appeared on the record. Ringo was filming *The Magic Christian* and George was disenchanted with being a Beatle and was recording the Radha Krishna Temple. He said: 'I feel as though all that is far behind me. It all seems so trivial, it doesn't matter any more, none of it. What I am interested in now is finding out the answers to the real questions. The things which really matter in life.'

After the Beatles split up, George became the first solo Beatle to top the charts with his No. 1 single 'My Sweet Lord' and chart-topping album *All Things Must Pass*.

With this success he felt vindicated and told *Rolling Stone* magazine: 'By the time *All Things Must Pass* came, it was like being constipated for years, then finally you were allowed to go.'

In 1971 he organised the 'Concert For Bangla Desh', which was a triumph, and set the template for all other major rock-for-charity events that were to follow.

Fortunes seemed to change in 1974. His tour of the US and Canada was bashed by the critics and not well attended. His wife Pattie left him for his friend Eric Clapton. 'I'd rather she was with him than some dope,' George commented. Then, in 1976 he was ordered to pay £10 million in damages for 'subconsciously plagiarising' the Chiffons' hit 'He's So Fine' with 'My Sweet Lord'.

There was a positive side to his romantic life when he fell in love with Olivia Trinidad Arias, a secretary at the office of his record label Dark Horse. 'I fell for her immediately. I told her that I didn't want her doing all that typing,' he was to say.

Their son Dhani was born in August 1978 and the couple married the following month.

It was in 1978 that George instigated a move that virtually made him a saviour of the British film industry. He teamed up with an American investment banker, Denis O'Brien, to bail out the Monty Python film *The Life of Brian*. This led to the formation of Handmade Films, which was to produce a series of major British movies such as *The Long Good Friday* and *Time Bandits*. However, he wasn't so successful with *Shanghai Surprise*, which starred Madonna and her then husband Sean Penn.

George sold Handmade at a loss in 1994, but was later successful in suing his former partner O'Brien for $11 million after a lengthy lawsuit.

Following the murder of John in 1980, George retreated to his mansion Friar Park, saying: 'You don't know who's crackers and who isn't.' Which was prophetic when one considers the events of December 1999 (see below).

In 1987 he had a chart-topping single, 'Got My Mind Set On You', and later teamed up with Tom Petty, Bob Dylan, Roy Orbison and Jeff Lynne in the Traveling Wilburys, an outfit many compared, or preferred, to the Beatles.

With the constant demands of the press for the Beatles to re-form, George would say: 'Having played with other musicians, I don't even think the Beatles were that good. It's all a fantasy, this idea of putting the Beatles back together again. The only way it will happen is if we're all broke. Even then, I wouldn't relish playing with Paul. He's a fine bass player but he's sometimes overpowering. Ringo's got the best backbeat in the business and I'd join a band with John Lennon any day. But I wouldn't join a band with Paul McCartney. That's not personal: it's from a musician's point of view. The biggest break in my career was getting in the Beatles. The second biggest break since then was getting out of them.'

Discussing George with the journalist Chris Welch in 1975, Paul said: 'George is so straight. He's so straight and ordinary and so real. And he happens to believe in God. That's what's wrong with George, to most people's minds. He happens to believe in God, you know, which is a terrible crime and that's so mad. There's nothing freaky about George at all. Some people think he's freaky because he's grown a beard. All George is – he's a grown-up teenager, and he refuses to give in to the grown-up world. He won't do it – just because everyone says: "You're a freak. You're a recluse." '

Discussing George in 1986, Paul said: 'If we don't talk about Apple, then we get on like a house on fire. I had a great day the other day when George came down to visit me for the first time in billions of years; we had a really nice time. George was my original mate in the Beatles.'

In the late eighties, Paul had mentioned that he'd like to write some songs with George. When asked about this in 1990, George said: 'He's left it a bit late, is all I can say to that. I'm entrenched with Bob Dylan, Tom Petty and Jeff Lynne and I don't see any reason to go back to an old situation.'

George also felt the same way about any suggestion of reviving the Beatles and kept denying that a reunion would ever happen in his various interviews. When Paul was asked about a reunion in 1990 he said: 'What's it matter what I think about that? George has taken the liberty of answering that question with shocking regularity for you media guys. He's had a field day getting publicity from his negative responses. So, obviously, it's never going to happen, no matter what I think.'

In 1993 George attended one of Paul's concerts at Earls Court, London. Paul said: 'He came back afterwards and criticised the show in a sort of professional way. "A bit too long," George reckoned. Well, fuck you. And the old feelings came up. But George is a great guy. Even with old friends, this shit happens.'

In 1994 Paul mentioned the reunion sessions planned with George, Ringo and himself. He said: 'We're looking for a completely unpressurised situation to get together, because nobody wants to revive the Beatles. If we hate it the first day, then we'll just can it, nothing lost. But if we quite enjoy it, then we'll say, "See you tomorrow." It could be a laugh.

'I've never even tried writing with George before, so that's exciting. Still, there's no way we're going to get back together and just be all smiley-smiley. At one of our last meetings, my hackles started to rise because I was sort of being told what to do, and I've been solo for so long I'm not used to compromising. I mean, there's going to be some psychiatric crap from *way* back. We've all grown up, and we've been through a lot.'

When Paul, George and Ringo got together again to work on *The Long and Winding Road*, a documentary history of the band, George objected that the Beatles' history was being lumped under the title of one of Paul's songs and it was changed to *Anthology*.

In fact, Paul found that George resisted various of his ideas, including the use of Paul's 'Carnival Of Light' on the Beatles *Anthology* CD set. Paul commented: 'George doesn't like avant-garde music. It was considered for the *Anthology* album but he vetoed it.'

In the June 1997 issue of *Mojo* magazine, Paul was asked if he would consider collaborating with George. He said: 'When we were working together on "Free As A Bird", there were one or two little bits of tension, but it was actually cool for the record. For instance, I had a couple of ideas that he didn't like and he was right. I'm the first one to accept that, so that was OK.

'We did say then that we might work together, but the truth is, after "Real Love", I think George has some business problems. Er, it didn't do a lot for his moods over the last couple of years. He's been having a bit of a hard time; actually, he's not been that easy to get on with. I've rung him and maybe he hasn't rung back. No big deal. But when I ring Ringo, he rings back immediately; we're quite close that way. You know, I'll write George a letter and he might not reply to it. I don't think he means not to reply to it, but it makes me wonder whether he actually wants to do it or not. And if you're not sure, you back off a little. But I love him, he's a lovely guy and I would love to do it. It'd be fun, he's good.'

It was in July 1997 that a lump was discovered on George's neck. It initially seemed that radiation treatment for throat cancer had proved successful and in 1998 George said: 'I'm not going to die on you folks just yet.'

In December 1999 Michael Abram, a schizophrenic, viciously attacked George at his home in Friar Park. Abram had broken into the Harrisons' mansion and he attacked George, plunging a knife in and out of George's chest, puncturing his lung and narrowly missing his heart. George's wife Olivia saved her husband's life by smashing a lamp over Abram's head.

Then, in March 2001, George flew to the Mayo Clinic in Rochester, Minnesota, to have a cancerous growth removed from his lungs. The following month he underwent radiotherapy for a brain tumour.

As his health began to deteriorate, he moved to an Italian lakeside villa for a while until his wife Olivia arranged for him to have treatment at the Staten Island University Hospital.

In 2001, while Paul was in Italy during his *Wingspan* promotional tour he visited George, who told him that he was cheered by Paul's visit and had no plans to die. An aide commented: 'Paul really wanted to see how George was and thought it was an ideal opportunity for them to get together. It was quite a moving meeting for both of them.'

Paul visited George a few weeks before his death and held his hand for a couple of hours. Describing the visit on BBC Radio 1 on 13 December 2001, Paul said: 'The best thing for me was seeing him for a couple of hours and laughing and joking and holding his hand. Afterwards, I realised I'd never, ever held his hand. We'd been to school together and got on buses together and we didn't hold each other's hands. It was like a compensation; he was rubbing his thumb up and down my hand and it was very nice.'

The experimental treatment in New York didn't seem to be working and George and his family left for Los Angeles, where he undertook radiation treatment at UCLA Medical Center.

George died from cancer on 29 November 2001. He was 58 years old. On George's death, Paul issued a statement:

We are all devastated by this news, it's deeply sad to lose such a beautiful guy. Luckily Heather and I saw George a couple of weeks ago and true to form he was laughing and joking.

George was a very brave man with a heart of gold but also someone who didn't suffer fools gladly. I'll always remember that without George it all wouldn't have been possible.

I'll miss him dearly and I'll always love him – he's my baby brother.

Paul attended a special tribute concert in George's memory that took place at the Empire Theatre, Liverpool, on Sunday 24 February 2002, with proceeds going to the Macmillan Cancer Relief charity. He spoke on stage, sharing his memories of George with the audience of 2,300 people, who included Heather Mills and Paul's brother Mike.

He said: 'It is always lovely to come back to my home town. I have so many memories – and, of course, a lot of them are of George.

'We go way back. We both used to live in Speke and he used to get on the bus one stop after me. We used to have half an hour on the bus to talk about guitars and music and stuff like that.

'He was a lovely bloke. He gave a lot to the world – his music, his spirituality. He was always a very strong man. I think he would have been delighted with this.'

Ralph McTell, Steve Harley and Pete Wylie were among the artists who appeared that night.

Harty
A BBC 1 television chat show hosted by Russell Harty. Paul made a pre-recorded interview that was included in the programme aired on Wednesday 14 December 1983.

Have You Got Problems?
Paul co-wrote this number with his brother Mike for the 1974 *McGear* album.

Haven't We Met Somewhere Before?
The number that Paul wrote for the Warren Beatty/Julie Christie film *Heaven Can Wait*. The song was rejected by Beatty, but was used as the opening song for the film *Rock 'n' Roll High School*, released in August 1979.

Hay-On-Wye Literary Festival
An annual British literary event. On Wednesday 30 May 2001, Paul read a selection of his poems to an audience of 1,300 people. He recited poems and song lyrics for ninety minutes, during which he seemed very self-assured and told anecdotes that amused the crowd, also giving a brief explanation regarding each of the poems.

The poems Paul read out included: 'In Liverpool', 'Dinner Tickets', 'Ivan', 'Jerk Of All Jerks', 'Masseuse Masseuse', 'Chasing The Cherry', 'City Park', 'Trouble Is', 'A Billion Bees In The Borage', 'Anti Alarm Call', 'Black Jacket' and 'Her Spirit'. He also recited an unpublished work. Then he recited the song lyrics, 'Here Today', 'Eleanor Rigby', 'Maxwell's Silver Hammer' and 'Why Don't We Do It In The Road?'. Then he answered questions from the audience.

Heart Of the Country
A track from the *Ram* album that was issued in Britain as a single with 'Back Seat of My Car', but it made little impact, only managing to reach No. 39 in the charts. The number was also featured on the 'James Paul McCartney' television special.

Paul produced a 16mm promotional film of this number in Scotland, along with a promotional film for '3 Legs'.

Heart That You Broke
A number that Wings recorded during their sessions in Nashville in 1974.

Heather

An unreleased song dedicated to his adopted daughter, which Paul wrote and recorded in 1968. During the sessions for Mary Hopkin's *Postcard* album, Paul sat around with Donovan and they both played each other songs on their acoustic guitars, including 'Heather' – which later appeared on bootleg albums.

Heather

A track from the 2001 *Driving Rain* album lasting 3 minutes and 26 seconds. Tracks from Paul's original demo tape were transferred to 16-track analogue on 2 March 2001. The song was Paul's tribute to the new love of his life, Heather Mills.

Heaven Can Wait

An Oscar-winning movie directed by and starring Warren Beatty. Paul composed a song specially for the film soundtrack entitled 'Haven't We Met Somewhere Before?' The number wasn't used then, but re-emerged later as the first number in the film *Rock 'n' Roll High School*.

Heaven On A Sunday

A track from the *Flaming Pie* album lasting 4 minutes and 27 seconds. It was produced by Paul and Jeff Lynne and engineered by Geoff Emerick and Jan Jacobs with assistance from Keith Smith. Recording began on 16 September 1996 and Paul sang lead and backing vocal and played drums, bass guitar, electric guitar, acoustic guitar, Fender Rhodes, harpsichord, vibraphone and percussion. Jeff Lynne sang backing vocal and played acoustic guitar. James McCartney played an electric guitar solo and Linda McCartney provided additional backing vocal.

Paul was to comment, 'I wrote this on holiday, and when I'm on holiday I like to sail – not a big boat, just a little Sunfish. It's a great relaxation for me, away from the high-profile stuff. That's often when I come up with that kind of song, relaxed, peaceful. I wrote it and was playing it at home. Linda was singing along with the chorus and it was getting nice.'

This track was a family affair, with three McCartneys present. On the presence of his son James, Paul said, 'I thought it would be a nice idea to play with him, as he's getting really good on guitar. When you've been in a band with someone for twenty years, you read them and they read you. I thought, "Well, I haven't been in a band with James for all those years, but I've known him for all those years. I've heard him play and he's heard me play. We've got so much in common that I bet we could do it."'

Helen Wheels

A single, 3 minutes and 44 seconds in length, issued in Britain on Friday 26 October 1973 on Apple R5987 and in America on Monday 12 November on Apple 1869.

'Country Dreamer' was featured on the flipside.

The number went to No. 12 in the British charts and No. 10 in the American.

Paul's Land Rover inspired the title of the song, which was about a trip from Scotland to London in the vehicle. (Hell On Wheels! – get it?). 'Helen Wheels' was included on the American album *Band on the Run*, but not the British version.

It was released in Germany on EMI Electrola/Apple 1C006-05486.

Hello

A celebrity magazine, published in Britain. In January 2002 they conducted an online poll to discover their readers' 'Favourite Veteran Rocker'. Paul topped the poll with 27,000 votes. Coming in second was Tom Jones with 24,000 votes.

Hello Goodbye

A number penned by Paul that was recorded by the Beatles at Abbey Road on Monday 2 October 1967. It was released as a single in Britain on Saturday 25 November 1967 and topped the charts. It also topped the charts in America following its release there on Wednesday 29 November.

John Lennon's 'I Am The Walrus' was the flipside and John resented the fact that his number had been relegated to the B-side.

Alistair Taylor disputes Paul's sole authorship.

He claims that when Jane Asher had left Paul, Paul used to phone him saying that he was fed up and wanted Alistair to come round to his Cavendish Avenue house to keep him company.

Alistair says, 'So, this night we were sitting, and he said to me, "Have you ever thought about writing music?" So I said, "Good grief, no." So he said, "It's dead easy. Anybody can write a song." So I said, "Oh, come on, Paul. Don't be silly. If that were the case, everybody would be writing." He said, "Come on, we'll write a song."

'In his dining room, he had this old, hand-carved harmonium, you know, a little organ, that you pumped to get the air into it, with big pedals at the bottom. He lifted the lid off this and said, "Right, you get on that end, and I'll get on this end." I was at the treble end, and he was at the bass end. And, as we were peddling like mad, he said, "What I want you to do is hit any note, any note at all. Don't worry about what ones; just hit notes with both hands, as you feel like it. I'll do the same this end, and I'm going to shout out a word, and I want you to shout out the opposite word. That's all, and then we'll write a song."

'So I said, "Yes, all right." We started this, and we got the rhythm going, just banging the keys. Then he shouted "White"', and I shouted, "Black", and so it went on. "Come", "Go", "Hello", "Goodbye", we did a few more, and it lasted about five minutes. Then we packed up. He said, "There you go, we've got a song." Several weeks later, he came waltzing into the office and he said, "Here's our new single." He put it down on the desk, and I looked at it. It was "Hello Goodbye", a song written by Taylor-McCartney. I am, in fact, the co-writer of the song.'

However, when the Beatles first began recording the number, the title was actually 'Hello Hello'.

Hello Goodbye (promos)

Paul directed three promotional films for this single on Friday 10 November 1967. They were filmed at the Saville Theatre, with the Beatles wearing their *Sgt Pepper* uniforms on the first of the promos. Girls wearing Hawaiian-style grass skirts and garlands also appeared on stage with them.

Due to a ban implemented by the Musician's Union on Friday 10 June 1966, which prevented artists lip-syncing to their records on British TV shows, the film could only be shown outside the UK.

Help!

A charity album in aid of the 'War Child' charity to aid children in Bosnia. At Abbey Road Studios on Monday 4 September 1995 Paul recorded the track 'Come Together' for the album, along with Paul Weller and the Mojo Filters and Noel Gallagher. The album was issued on Monday 11 September and a single featuring the track was issued on Go-Discs on Monday 4 December.

Discussing the session, which was completed in an afternoon, Paul commented, 'It reminded me a little of the Beatles' recordings, although with more drugs and booze!'

A documentary on the recording of the album was made and the session featuring Paul was also filmed and shown on Channel 4 on Saturday 10 September 1995.

Helter Skelter

A strong rock-'n'-roll track composed by Paul which, when it was first recorded at Abbey Road Studios on 18 July 1968 was 25 minutes long. The number was recorded on an eight-track machine that EMI had just installed at Abbey Road. The track was for *The Beatles* double album and the album version was recorded on 9 September 1968 with an overdub added the following day. Brian Gibson, a technical engineer on the session, was to comment, 'The version on the album was out of control. They were completely out of their heads that night. But, as usual, a blind eye was turned to what the Beatles did in the studio. Everyone knew what substances they were taking, but they were really a law unto themselves in the studio.'

Paul had been inspired to write the number after he'd read an interview by Pete Townshend in *Melody Maker*. He commented, 'He said the Who had made some track that was the loudest, most raucous rock 'n' roll, the dirtiest thing they'd ever done. It made me think, "Right.

Got to do it." I like that kind of geeking up. And we decided to do the loudest, nastiest, sweatiest rock number we could. That was "Helter Skelter".'

At the end of the number Ringo screamed, 'I got blisters on my fingers!'

'Helter Skelter' was one of the numbers Charles Manson claimed had inspired him to send his acolytes out to murder people. At the murder scene at Rosemary and Leno LaBianca's house, the title 'Helter Skelter' was smeared in blood along the wall, along with 'Revolution No. 9'.

At his trial, Manson garbled, 'Like, Helter Skelter is a nightclub. Helter Skelter means confusion. Literally, it doesn't mean any war with anyone. It doesn't mean that those people are going to kill other people. It only means what it means. Helter Skelter is confusion. Confusion is coming down fast, you can call it what you wish. It's not my conspiracy, it is not my music. I hear what it relates. It says, "Rise!" It says, "Kill!" Why blame it on me? I didn't write the music. I am not the person who projected it into your social consciousness.'

Manson seemed completely ignorant of the fact that Helter Skelter refers to an amusement ride in Britain.

Her Majesty

The closing track on the *Abbey Road* album and the shortest Beatles track on record at 23 seconds in length. Paul composed the number in tribute to Queen Elizabeth II and copies of the album were sent to Buckingham Palace. Paul played acoustic guitar and sang solo on the number.

Paul had quickly recorded the number at Twickenham one morning before the other members of the Beatles had arrived. When it was placed between 'Mean Mr Mustard' and 'Polythene Pam' as part of a medley, Paul wasn't happy with it and ordered it to be scrapped. Since the engineer John Kurlander had been instructed never to throw anything away that had been recorded at a Beatles session, he cut the song from the master tape of the medley and placed it on the end, following twenty seconds of silence. Paul was pleased with the effect and the song remained on the album.

Paul sang the number before Queen Elizabeth II during the Golden Jubilee concert at Buckingham Palace on 3 June 2002.

Here Today

A ballad, featured on the April 1982 *Tug Of War* album that Paul wrote as his tribute to John Lennon. On it, Paul sings and plays acoustic guitar. Jack Rothstein and Bernard Partridge on violins, Ian Jewel on viola and Keith Harvey on cello provided the backing.

Paul was to comment: 'One of the feelings you always have when someone close to you dies like that is that you wish you could have seen him the day before to square everything up and make sure he knew how much you really cared. The song is about saying to John: "Do we really have to keep this sort of thing up?" but we never got around to doing it. I guess we never felt any urgency about it. We were behaving like we were going to live forever . . . I was kind of crying when I wrote it.'

Paul included the number on his 'Driving USA' tour and said it had received the biggest reaction of any song on the tour. He said, 'I think a lot of the audience didn't know the song so it's kind of cool when they hear it for the first time. I'm rediscovering it myself. I hadn't sung it live ever until this tour. It's quite emotional – it's a reaffirmation of how much I love him.'

Here, There And Everywhere (concert)

A Linda McCartney tribute concert held at the Royal Albert Hall on Saturday 10 April 1999. The backdrops to various songs comprised a series of slides of Linda's photographs.

The concert had been organised by Linda's friend, singer Chrissie Hynde, who opened the show with her group the Pretenders performing 'Message Of Love', which was dedicated to Linda.

Johnny Marr sang 'Meat Is Murder' and was followed by Lyden David Hall performing 'Here, There And Everywhere', backed by a string quartet, the Duke Quartet. He also sang 'Abraham, Martin And John' and 'Foxy Lady'. Des'ree performed 'Blackbird' with the Duke Quartet and was joined by Ladysmith Black Mambazo on a medley of 'Amazing Grace' and 'Nearer My God To Thee'.

Sinead O'Connor sang 'I Believe In You' followed by Neil Finn with 'She Goes On' and 'Don't Dream It's Over'. The first half closed with a rendition of 'Wonderful World' by Heather Small of M People.

After a 20-minute interval the Pretenders opened the second half backing Johnny Marr on 'Back In the Chain Gang'. Next to take the stage was Tom Jones, who performed 'She's A Woman', 'The Green, Green Grass Of Home' and 'When A Man Loves A Women'. Paul had made a request to Jones that he sing 'The Green, Green Grass Of Home'. On his last song he was joined by Chrissie Hynde, Sinead O' Connor and Des'ree.

Marianne Faithfull next appeared performing 'Vagabond Way' and Johnny Marr joined her, providing backing for her rendition of 'As Tears Go By'. Chrissie Hynde then sang 'I Wish You Love'.

The following artist was Elvis Costello who told the audience how kind Linda had been to him when he first began writing songs with Paul. He then performed a number written by Paul called 'Warm and Beautiful' on which he was backed by Steve Nieve on piano and the Duke Quartet. He said, 'It's one of the most beautiful songs that Paul ever wrote for Linda.'

Elvis then performed 'That Day Is Done' and '(What's So Funny 'bout) Peace, Love And Understanding'.

George Michael then appeared and sang 'Eleanor Rigby' and 'The

Long And Winding Road', backed by the Duke Quartet. Other performers joined him for a rousing rendition of 'Faith'.

Compere Eddie Izzard then introduced Paul.

Paul told the audience that when he'd first been approached by Chrissie Hynde to take part in the show, he didn't know if he could, but promised to try. When he noticed the response of the fans to Linda's death he was so moved that he decided on taking part. He thanked the other acts and said, 'Linda'd probably, if she knew this was going on, she'd say, "What? For me?" She was a very unassuming lady.' He then added, 'She's with us, she's loving it.'

Next he said, 'This is a song which Linda and I used to listen to. I was in Liverpool, she was in New York. We both listened to it in the fifties.' He then performed the Ricky Nelson number 'Lonesome Town', backed by the Pretenders. He followed with 'All My Loving'.

When he performed 'Let It Be', Hynde, Costello and Des'ree joined him. He then thanked the audience and left the stage.

The concert was broadcast on BBC Radio 2 on Saturday 17 April 1999 and was screened on Sunday 18 April 1999 on BBC television at 10.35 in the evening. Kevin Godley directed it.

Here, There And Everywhere (song)

One of Paul's favourite songs. He said, 'This one was pretty much mine, written sitting by John's pool. Often I would wait half an hour while he would do something – like get up. So I was sitting there tootling around in E on the guitar.'

John was to say, 'Paul's song completely, and one of my favourite songs of the Beatles.'

The number was included on the *Revolver* album in 1966 and on the *Love Songs* compilation in 1967. Paul re-recorded the number for *Give My Regards To Broad Street*.

It was said that the song was inspired by the Beach Boys' 'God Only Knows' and was recorded at Abbey Road Studios on 14 June 1966 with overdubs added on 16 and 17 June. When Paul recorded it, he was to admit that he decided to sing it in the studio in the style of Marianne Faithfull.

A live version of the number lasting 2 minutes and 30 seconds, recorded at Paramalla in Sydney Australia on 22 March 1993, was included on the *Paul Is Live* album.

Hewson, Richard

A conductor and arranger who was commissioned by Paul to work on some of his projects. He'd orchestrated 'Those Were The Days', 'Goodbye' and 'Let My Name Be Sorrow' for Mary Hopkin's *Postcards* album and he'd also arranged the James Taylor album for Apple. In addition, he'd arranged 'The Long And Winding Road' and 'I Me Mine' for the Phil Spector version of the *Let It Be* album.

In May 1971 Paul contacted him to commission him to conduct and orchestrate an instrumental version of the *Ram* album, which hadn't been released at the time. When the album was eventually released several years later, Hewson was surprised to find his work credited to Percy 'Thrills' Thrillington.

Hey Diddle

A number recorded during the *Ram* sessions which has found its way onto bootleg releases and is also referred to as 'Hey Diddle Diddle'. While trying to add percussion sounds at a later date, Paul used an ashtray. He also made home recordings of the number in Campbeltown, Scotland, along with 'Bip Bop' in June 1971.

Hey Hey

An instrumental, which Paul co-wrote with bass guitarist Stanley Clarke, which was included on the *Pipes Of Peace* album.

Hey Jude

John Lennon was to say, '"Hey Jude" is Paul's. It's one of his master-pieces.'

The Beatles spent two days rehearsing the number at Abbey Road Studios in July 1968 and on the second day they were filmed for the film documentary *Music!* They then moved to Trident Studios to begin recording the next day and on the day following they employed the services of a 36-piece orchestra.

Paul said that the song began life as 'Hey Jules' and was a message of encouragement to Julian Lennon at a time when his father and mother had parted the ways.

Paul was driving to Weybridge to visit Cynthia and Julian when he began singing 'Hey Jules'. He recalled, 'I happened to be driving out to see Cynthia. It was just after John and she had broken up, and I was quite a mate with Julian. He's a nice kid. I was going out in my car, just vaguely singing this song, and it was like "Hey Jules". It was just this thing, you know. "Don't make it bad, take a sad song . . . " And then I thought a better name was Jude. A bit more country and western for me. I finished it all up in Cavendish and I was in the music room upstairs when John and Yoko came to visit and they were right behind me over my right shoulder, standing up, listening to it as I played it to them.'

George Harrison wanted to answer each of Paul's vocal lines with an electric guitar, but Paul vetoed it – and they were still arguing about it while making the *Let It Be* film. Paul commented, 'I remember on "Hey Jude" telling George not to play guitar. He wanted to echo riffs after the vocal phrases, which I didn't think was appropriate. He didn't see it like that, and it was a bit of a number for me to have to *dare* to tell George Harrison – who was one of the greats – not to play. It was like an insult. But that's how we did a lot of our stuff.'

The single was issued in both Britain and America on Monday 26 August 1968 and topped the charts for three weeks. In the United States it topped the charts for nine weeks.

It was also a No. 1 hit in Belgium, Denmark, Holland, Ireland, Malaysia, New Zealand, Norway, Singapore, Sweden and West Germany.

The number was the first Beatles release on the Apple label and was also the group's longest single, at 7 minutes and 11 seconds in length. The fade to it took three minutes. Paul commented, 'We liked the end. We liked it going on. The DJs can always fade it down if they want to. If you get fed up with it, you can always turn it over. You don't always have to sit through it. A lot of people enjoy every second of the end and there really isn't much repetition in it.'

The Apple boutique had closed, but Paul went to the shop and whitewashed the name 'Hey Jude' on the windows to promote the single. Neighbouring shopkeepers then objected, thinking it referred to *Juden* and was an anti-Jewish slogan. Before an explanation could be given a brick was thrown through the window.

Julian Lennon bought Paul's recording notes for 'Hey Jude' for £25,000 at Sotheby's rock-'n'-roll memorabilia auction held at the Hard Rock Café in September 1996.

Another version of this number, lasting 8 minutes and 4 seconds was included on the *Tripping The Live Fantastic* album. It was recorded live at Riverfront Coliseum, Cincinnati, Ohio on 12 February 1990 during the 1989/90 World Tour.

Paul had to apply to the High Court in April 2002 to prevent the auction house Christie's from selling the handwritten lyrics to 'Hey Jude'. Paul's representative stated that the lyrics were either stolen during one of several burglaries at Paul's house or had been taken by someone working for him.

The single sheet from a notebook had been put forward by a Frenchman Florent Tessier, who said he'd bought them in Portobello Road for £10 in the early seventies.

Hi, Hi, Hi (promotional film)

Two videos of this number and 'C Moon' were filmed at the Southampton Studios of Southern ITV by Steve Turner. Although shot in video they were transferred to 16mm film for international distribution.

Hi, Hi, Hi (single)

A single issued by Wings in Britain on Apple R5973 on Friday 1 December 1972. Paul co-wrote the number with Linda, and they also jointly composed the B-side 'C Moon'. It reached No. 3 in the charts.

BBC Radios One and Two banned 'Hi, Hi, Hi' declaring the lyrics were sexually suggestive.

Rodney Collins, a publicity officer at the BBC, commented on the band at the time, saying: 'The ban has nothing to do with drugs. We thought the record unfit for broadcasting because of the lyrics. Part of it goes: "I want you to lie on the bed and get you ready for my body gun and do it, do it, do it to you". While another part goes: "Like a rabbit I'm going to grab it and do it till the night is done".'

The BBC and Collins seemingly hadn't listened to the lyrics properly. Paul and Linda had written 'get ready for my polygon', not 'get you ready for my body gun'.

Paul explained, 'We wrote "Hi, Hi, Hi" in Spain, because we had this tour coming up. Purposely as a nice easy rocker. It's basically a rock and roll thing written on three rock and roll chords to give us something aside from the rest of our material. The general reaction is that "Hi, Hi, Hi" is a kind of strong side, but the reason we made it a double A is that "C Moon" is one of those songs that catches up on you after a while. I can hear "C Moon" in a year's time, people saying, "Yeah, I like that one." There's things to listen to on that one, put it on headphones and it's quite a trip.'

Most disc jockeys played 'C Moon' instead and the single reached No. 3 in the British charts despite the ban.

It was issued in the States on Apple 1857 on Monday 4 December and reached No. 10 in the charts.

'Hi, Hi, Hi' was included on *Wings Greatest* album and a live version of it was also featured in the UK version of the 'James Paul McCartney' TV special and in the repertoires of the 1972 European, the 1973 British and the 1975/76 world tours.

It was also released in Germany on EMI Electrola/Apple 1C006-05208 and in France on Apple 2C006-05208.

Higgins, Gertrude
The name that Paul sometimes used to introduce Linda on stage during the 1989/90 World Tour.

High Park Farm
At the height of their romance, Jane Asher recommended to Paul that he invest in a farm that they could use as a retreat. In June 1966 they went to view High Park Farm in Scotland.

Farmer's wife Janet Brown, who had lived there since 1947, commented: 'Our farm has been up for sale for a while now but what a surprise my husband and I had when we saw the famous pair – Paul told me that it had always been his ambition to own a farm in Scotland.'

Paul said, 'It's desolate, very desolate. It's two hundred acres in a valley and thirty miles from Ireland. It's in Scotland, but I mean it's just off the coast of Ireland, it's nice. It's cold, very cold in winter and gets lots of snow. Anyway, I didn't really pick Scotland, it's just that I wanted a farm and I said to my accountant, "What's happening with my money," and he said, "Well, the best thing you can do is buy a house." I mean, he's thinking about the safety of the money because if you put it in other things, it sort of goes. I told him I'd like it with a bit of land and would he look out for me. And he found this farm in Scotland, which was cheap. It's nice and quiet. What I'm going to do is let the trees grow on it, because it's very desolate at the moment, and build a small house on it and go there for a couple of months in the year.'

Paul purchased the farm and Jane helped him to furnish it. The farm comprised 183 acres near Machrihanish, the nearest town being Campbeltown. The affair with Jane over, Paul continued to enjoy relaxing at the faraway retreat, which was greeted with equal enthusiasm by Linda when the couple were married.

The area was too bleak and hilly for cows, so Paul bought sheep, almost two hundred of them. However, he couldn't bear the thought of killing them and rarely sent any to market, allowing them to breed. For some time Paul sheared the sheep himself with hand shears, sending the wool to the Wool Marketing Board.

The couple also grew lots of vegetables on the farm and stabled horses such as Drake's Drum, Honor and Cinnamon, along with ponies Coconut, Cookie and Sugarfoot.

Paul took to the farming life and Linda once bought him a tractor as a Christmas present.

Highlight

A BBC radio Overseas Service programme. When the Beatles arrived at Broadcasting House to record for a new BBC radio show *Top Gear* on Tuesday 14 July 1964, Michael Smee interviewed Paul for *Highlight*. The interview lasted for thirteen minutes but only five minutes and forty five seconds of it was used when the programme was broadcast on Saturday 18 July. It was repeated on the Home Service on Tuesday 22 December in a longer version lasting eleven minutes and eleven seconds under the title 'A Beatle's eye View'.

Hipgnosis

A London-based design firm who specialise in music-related work and have been responsible for hundreds of critically acclaimed album sleeves.

Aubrey Powell (nicknamed 'Po') and Storm Thorgerson covered the Wings 1976 tour of America and put together a book *Hands Across The Water*.

Storm and Gordon House designed the sleeve of *Band On The Run*. The company won *Music Week*'s Album Cover of the Year Award in 1975 for *Venus and Mars*. The photograph of Wings used in the centre-fold of the sleeve was taken by Aubrey Powell, and the graphics for the cover and inner sleeve were supplied by George Hardie.

Other covers designed by the company include *Wings At The Speed Of Sound*, *Wings Over America*, *Thrillington*, *Back To The Egg* and *Tug Of War*. They also assisted Paul with the design and finished artwork for the *London Town* and *Wings Greatest* albums.

Hiroshima Sky Is Always Blue

A number written by Yoko Ono as a memorial to the fiftieth anniversary of the dropping of the atomic bomb on Hiroshima.

The lyrics basically consisted of the title words being repeated in different ways.

The recording was initially said to have healed the rift between Paul and Yoko when it was recorded at Paul's own studio at his home in Rye.

Yoko and Sean spent a weekend at the McCartneys' home and on Saturday 11 March 1995 Yoko and Sean performed alongside Paul while Linda accompanied them on organ. Paul's three daughters, Mary, Stella and Heather, played percussion and son James played guitar.

Paul presented Yoko with the master tape and was later to comment on the number, describing it as 'Quite strange. Lovely strange.' He also said, 'It was a cool way to cement our friendship. We've been through so much shit over the years that inevitably people look at these things and suspect some ulterior motive. It isn't like that any more.'

Paul played the Bill Black double bass and his studio included the Mellotron used on 'Strawberry Fields Forever' and the harmonium used on 'We Can Work It Out'. Paul said, 'I showed Sean an old electric spinet that we used on the old Beatle track "Because", which John had sung on. Then he sat down and started to play it. So I said, "Hey, do you fancy making a track?"'

The song received its premiere on the programme *Good Morning Japan* on NHK-TV on Sunday 6 August 1995, alongside a ten-minute interview with Yoko.

The number was a seven-minute piece.

Hoffman, Dustin

The acclaimed American actor, known for his roles in films such as *The Graduate*, *Midnight Cowboy*, *Kramer Versus Kramer* and *Tootsie*.

While Paul and Linda were on holiday in Jamaica they were staying in a house just outside Montego Bay. They read in the Jamaican newspaper the *Daily Gleaner* that Dustin Hoffman and Steve McQueen were in town filming *Papillon*. Paul thought it would be great to meet them and Linda phoned Hoffman's wife Annie suggesting they meet for dinner. Annie invited them to their house.

Dustin began asking Paul about songwriting and Paul described his creative processes in writing a song. When they returned to the house a few days later, Hoffman told Paul he'd seen something in *Time* magazine about Picasso and it struck him that it would be ideal if set to music.

The article told how Picasso had said, 'Drink to me, drink to my health, you know I can't drink anymore.' He then did some painting, went to bed at three in the morning and died in his sleep.

Dustin said to Paul that they were Picasso's last words, could he do something with them.

Paul had a guitar with him at the time and began singing 'Drink to me, drink to my health' and Hoffman leapt out of his chair and shouted 'Annie! Annie! The most incredible thing! He's doing it! It's coming out!'

The result was the song 'Picasso's Last Words'.

Hog Hill
The name of a windmill that Paul bought in 1982, in Icklesham, quite close to his house in Peasmarsh, East Sussex.

Hold Me
A number on the *Red Rose Speedway* album that formed the beginning on an 11-minute and 15-second medley closing the album, preceding three other tunes. It was 2 minutes and 24 seconds in length. Paul sang lead vocal and played piano and bass. Linda provided background vocal, Denny Laine played electric guitar and background vocal, Henry McCullough electric guitar and background vocal and Denny Seiwell drums and background vocal.

Holly Days
The tribute album to Buddy Holly made by Paul and Denny Laine at Paul's Rude Studios in Scotland.

Denny sang lead vocals, Paul produced, played guitar and drums and provided backing vocals with Linda.

The album was issued in 1977 in Britain on EMI 781 on 6 May and in America on Capitol ST 11588(LP) on 19 May.

The tracks were: 'Heartbeat', 'Moondreams', 'Rave On', 'I'm Gonna Love You Too', 'Fool's Paradise', 'Lonesome Tears', 'It's So Easy', 'Listen To Me', 'Look At Me', 'Take Your Time' and 'I'm Looking For Someone To Love'.

Holly, Buddy
American singer/songwriter, born Charles Harden Holley in Lubbock, Texas on 7 September 1936.

The Quarry Men and the Beatles included several of his numbers in their repertoire, including 'It's So Easy', 'Maybe Baby', 'Peggy Sue', 'That'll Be The Day', 'Think It Over', 'Words Of Love' and 'Crying, Waiting, Hoping'.

John and Paul saw Buddy Holly & the Crickets at the Philharmonic Hall, Liverpool on 20 March 1958.

When the group were considering a new name early in 1960, Stuart Sutcliffe suggested they find a name like Buddy Holly's backing group the Crickets. They thought of various insects and Sutcliffe suggested Beetles. There were variations over a matter of months – Beatals, Silver Beats, Silver Beetles, Silver Beatles (with John Lennon adding the 'A') and finally, the Beatles.

Paul acquired Buddy Holly's song publishing in 1971. It was Lee Eastman, Linda's father, who was responsible. Paul commented, 'He said originally, "If you are going to invest, do it in something you know. If you invest in building computers or something, you could lose a fortune. Wouldn't you rather be in music? Stay in music." I said yeah, I'd much rather do that. So he asked me what kind of music I liked and that first name I said was Buddy Holly. Lee got on to the man who owned Buddy Holly's stuff and bought it for me because the Buddy Holly stuff was up for sale. Norman Petty just happened to be selling it. EMI was interested in it. Chappells was interested in it, Allen Klein was interested in it and I think, secretly, that's what got me interested. I had always said I liked Buddy, he was one of my big influences when I started writing. When it came up for sale, I had to spend my money somehow and I thought, "Well, I'd rather have that than anything else." Not so much to be greedy, but to just, kind of, be able to look after those songs and do stuff for them, because it's stuff that I'm really interested in.'

Paul has been particularly upset that the Beatles song catalogue is owned by others and was particularly galled when Michael Jackson allowed Lennon and McCartney compositions to be used for television commercials. When he saw that George Harrison's composition 'Something' had been used in a TV ad for Chrysler, he said, 'The other day I saw "Something", George's song, in a car ad and I thought, Eww, yuck! That's in bad taste.'

Yet Paul could be accused of doing the same himself by allowing Buddy Holly's 'Oh Boy!' to be reworked as 'Oh Buick!' in a car commercial.

When quizzed on this, he commented, 'It's very difficult because I do feel differently in both cases. As far as the Beatles' stuff is concerned, in actual fact what has happened is some people have used it without the right to use it. People who haven't got the right have been giving away the right. So it's a different affair with the Buddy Holly stuff, where I do have the right to let people use it because we're the publishers of that. But the most difficult question is whether you should use songs for commercials. I haven't made up my mind where I stand.'

On Tuesday 7 September 1976 Paul launched the first of his annual Buddy Holly Weeks on the fortieth anniversary of Buddy's birth. That day Paul and Linda hosted a party with Holly's manager Norman Petty as the guest of honour. Petty presented Paul with a pair of cufflinks that Buddy had worn on the plane on the day of his crash. The luncheon was attended by numerous show business celebrities who included Freddie Mercury of Queen, Eric Clapton and Pattie Boyd, Steve Harley of Cockney Rebel, 10cc and Roger Daltrey. On Thursday 9 September there was a Buddy Holly Night at the Lyceum, London featuring Mike Berry & the Outlaws, Flight 56 and Flying Saucers. Paul also released three Buddy Holly maxi-singles that week.

On Wednesday 14 September 1977 Paul hired the Gaumont State Theatre in Kilburn for the celebration before an audience of rock stars and rock 'n' rollers. On stage were the line-up of Crickets who backed Holly on 'That'll Be The Day' – Jerry Allison, Sonny Curtis and Joe Mauldin. Among the audience were Mick Jagger and Ronnie Wood of the Rolling Stones, Kevin Godley and Lol Creme of 10cc, Eric Clapton and Denny Laine.

In 1978 Paul and Linda hosted their third Buddy Holly Week with several guests who included Mary Hopkin, George Melly, Carl Perkins, the Monkees and David Frost.

Friday 14 September 1979 saw Paul presenting a free Crickets concert at which Wings turned up at the Odeon, Hammersmith. Denny Laine sang 'Raining In My Heart' with Don Everly of the Everly Brothers, Paul sang 'It's So Easy' and everyone joined in for the finale, 'Bo Diddley'. Guests in the audience included Christopher Reeve, David Frost, Kevin Godley, Victor Spinetti, Alan Freeman, Micky Dolenz and Ronnie Laine. The event was captured on videotape to be used in the MPL documentary 'The Music Lives On' which was eventually screened on 8 September 1984.

In 1980 Paul didn't hold a Buddy Holly Week although he appeared on a 'Buddy Holly Special' aired by Capitol Radio in London.

Tuesday 7 September 1982 saw the launch of Buddy Holly Week with a Buddy Holly Rock 'n' Roll Championship at the Lyceum, London. Among Paul and Linda's guests were Ringo and Barbara Starr.

The 1983 week was a low-key one due to the fact that Paul had been involved in a number of projects. It ran from Tuesday 6 September to Monday 12 September, although Paul and Linda did host the event. However, Buddy Holly Week was to be celebrated in America and MPL manufactured an EP which was sent to America, catalogue number MPL 2. It was a 7″ record entitled 'Buddy Holly Week America '83' and contained the tracks: Side One: 'Peggy Sue', 'Rave On'. Side Two: 'Maybe Baby', 'That'll Be the Day', 'Heartbeat'. The record came with a press pack and a message from Paul:

'Welcome to America's first "Buddy Holly Week". In England "Buddy Holly Week" has been a regular feature on the rock calendar since 1976. It all began when I organised a party to cele-brate what would have been Buddy Holly's fortieth birthday on 7 September 1976. Actually, it really began in Liverpool in 1957 when I first heard Buddy Holly's "Peggy Sue". I was fifteen years old and like millions of others a great fan of Buddy's records. Over the years it seems ironic that Buddy has been more popular in England than his home country, which is why this year we have decided to inaugurate America's first "Buddy Holly Week". Since the beginning it has been great to see so many young fans enjoying the same sort of music their parents did. It is hard to believe that it is nearly a quarter of a century old, but the great thing about Buddy Holly – the great thing about rock 'n' roll – is that it is timeless. Some people say that rock 'n' roll died with Buddy Holly. Rock 'n' roll dead? That'll be the day. Enjoy yourselves.

    Paul McCartney, 1983.'

The 1984 Buddy Holly Week ran from 8 to 14 September with MPL having run a nationwide competition for drawings, sketches and paintings of Buddy. The seven best entries judged by Paul and artists Humphrey Ocean and David Oxtoby were to be used as sleeve designs on MCA Records limited edition releases of Holly singles. The top hundred designs were also displayed throughout the week at the Hamilton Gallery, Carlos Place, Mayfair, London.

Wednesday 11 September 1985 saw Paul and Linda hosting a luncheon for thirty guests. The following day BBC's *Arena* programme screened the MPL special 'Buddy Holly'.

Paul and Linda hosted their lunchtime party on the tenth anniversary of Buddy Holly Week on Wednesday 10 September 1986 at the Break For The Border, a Tex-Mex restaurant off Charing Cross Road, London. Guests included boxer Frank Bruno, George Martin, Dave Edmunds, Eric Stewart, Alvin Stardust and Bill and Virginia Harry.

In 1987 Paul launched a songwriting competition in which a song had to be written in the Holly style. The first prize was £1,000, plus the chance of having the song recorded by an established artist. The winner was Jim Imray who composed a song called 'Got The T-Shirt'. Paul held his annual private party at the Dolphin Brasserie in Pimlico, London on Wednesday 9 September with guests who included disc jockey Tony Prince, Alvin Stardust and Mick Green, all of whom joined Paul on stage in the performance of three numbers, 'What'd I Say', 'Mean Woman Blues' and 'Twenty Flight Rock'. Members of the invited audience included Twiggy, Joan Collins, Adam Faith and Jonathan Ross.

On 7 September 1988, Paul celebrated Buddy Holly Week with a lunchtime party at Stefano's in Holborn with the Crickets playing a set which included 'T-Shirt', the number produced by Paul, who joined them on stage. Guests at the event included Linda McCartney, Chrissie Hynde, Mike Berry, Tony Prince, Mike Read and Bill and Virginia Harry.

On Thursday 7 September 1989, Paul and Linda hosted their Buddy Holly party at the Talk Of The Town in Parker Street, London.

The 1990 Buddy Holly Week took place in New York City on 4 September at the Lone Star Café, with the Mayor of New York in attendance. It was held there primarily to promote the opening of the musical *Buddy*. Former Wings drummer Steve Holly was present, as was Tony Visconti and his wife May Pang and Buddy's widow Maria Elena.

Everyone who turned up was given a pair of Buddy Holly-style glasses, without lenses. The cast of *Buddy*, led by Paul Hipp, who portrayed Holly, began the entertainment, followed by the Crickets, Tommy Alsup, Ricky Van Shelton, Steve Forbet, Joe Ely, Henry Gross and Pat Dinizio of the Smithereens and Max Weinberg and Gary Tallent. Then Paul took the stage for a 25-minute jam session, backed by Dave Edmunds, Ely, Van Shelton, Hipp, Tallent, Weinberg, Joe B Mauldin and Jerry Allison, beginning with 'Rave On'. Paul then said, 'Here's another well-known Buddy Holly tune: "Lucille"',' and they performed the Little Richard number, followed by 'Oh Boy'.

1991 saw Paul and Linda return to a venue that had been used for their first Buddy Holly party in 1976 when they hosted a lunchtime party at the Orangery in Holland Park on 13 September.

Paul once again hired a London restaurant and invited 300 people from the music business to join him at lunchtime on Wednesday 9 September 1992. An album sponsored by MPL called *Buddy's Buddies* was also promoted which featured 25 tracks of Holly numbers performed by a variety of artists, who included Blondie, the Crickets, Blind Faith, Steeleye Span, Paul Anka and Mud – although Paul didn't appear on the album. It was issued by Connoisseur Collection.

Paul performed 'Rave On' and 'Oh Boy', backed by Big Jim Sullivan, with Willie Austin (vocals), Andy Crossheart (bass) and Malcolm Mortimer (drums). Gary Glitter also joined him on stage. Paul returned to the stage shortly after to perform 'Mean Woman Blues' and 'Shake Rattle and Roll', accompanied by Gary Glitter, Leo Sayer and Allan Clarke of the Hollies on vocals with Mick Green on guitar, Henry Spinetti and Blair Cunningham on drums and percussion and Linda McCartney, Chrissie Hynde, Hamish MacIntosh, and Tony Prince on backing vocals.

The 1993 Buddy Holly Week saw the final of the 'Rock 'n' Roll Brain Of Britain' trivia contest. This was held on the stage of the *Buddy* musical at the Victoria Palace Theatre, London on 9 September. Paul attended the event and MPL had flown in Bobby Vee from America to present the winner with a prize of £1,000.

The 19th Buddy Holly Week event took place on 7 September 1994 at Deals restaurant, London. Awards were given for the competition, which comprised making a promotional video to a Buddy Holly song. Advertising executive Graham Fink won this.

The twentieth event on 7 September 1995 took place at the Shepherd's Bush Empire which ended in Paul joining the other artists on stage – they included Carl Perkins, the Crickets featuring Sonny Curtis, Bobby Vee, Mike Berry and disc jockey Tony Prince – in a finale of 'Rave On'.

The 1996 Buddy Holly Week celebration featured a competition to find the best British singer of a Buddy Holly song, with a £5,000 prize for the winner, £2,000 for the runner-up and £1,000 for the third-placed singer. The annual luncheon took place at the Texas Embassy Cantina in London on 11 September. Paul got on stage to join in on one number.

Paul wrote the foreword to *A Poem For Buddy*, a book of poems about Buddy Holly, published by Stride Publications in 1997. The book comprised the fifty best entries from a competition marking MPL's 1997 Buddy Holly Week.

Paul was to write, 'Years ago, we inaugurated Buddy Holly Week as a doff of the cap to the memory of the great man and his great music. Over the years this has become the platform for many wonderful and wacky ways of marking that memory. We'd had competitions for sing-a-likes and look-a-likes, we've had a Paint a Buddy Painting and contests to write a song in his style, and now we've done poetry inspired by Buddy. Good golly, it's Holly.'

Wednesday 9 September 1998 saw Paul attend the National Rock 'n' Roll Dance Championship at the Empire Ballroom, Leicester Square, London, which was the culmination of the annual Buddy Holly Week.

Paul was present in New York on Tuesday 7 September 1999 for the special event of his Buddy Holly Week. That year it was a roller-skating dance party at the Roseland Ballroom, New York called 'The Buddy Holly Rock 'n' Roller Dance Party'. The three hours of music included the Crickets, led by Sonny Curtis, Nanci Griffith, Bobby Vee and Stan Perkins, son of Carl Perkins.

Disc jockey Cousin Brucie announced, 'What you've been waiting for is about to happen,' and Paul came on stage to join the Crickets. He said, 'I wasn't even supposed to be doing this, you know,' but he felt he should do something because the spirit of Buddy Holly lived on, he mentioned. 'We didn't rehearse a thing,' he added, before performing 'Rave On' with the Crickets. He only performed the one number and was followed by Bobby Vee who sang his hits such as 'Devil Or Angel' and some Holly numbers. The Crickets performed 'Oh Boy', 'Maybe Baby' and 'Everyday' and were joined by country folk singer Nanci Griffith who sang 'Well All Right'.

In September 2001 Paul had intended to attend a special reception in London for Elena Marie Holly who had flown into London to attend the *Buddy* stage show at the Aldwych Theatre, but he was stranded in New York when the disaster of the Twin Towers occurred.

Holly, Steve

The drummer who replaced Joe English in Wings in 1978 on the recommendation of Denny Laine. He appeared on the album *Back To The Egg* and on the Concerts For Kampuchea at the Odeon, Hammersmith. Steve had previously worked with artists such as Elton John and Kiki Dee and has appeared on albums for several artists including Elton John and Julian Lennon.

Interestingly, when he was a kid he saved up his pocket money and bought his first ever record, 'Sgt Pepper's Lonely Hearts Club Band'.

Hollywood Bowl
Paul appeared at the Hollywood Bowl on Friday 16 April 1993 before an audience of 30,000 and performed an 85-minute set. Ringo Starr was in the audience and came on stage to join in the finale of 'Hey Jude'. Paul also performed an acoustic version of 'Mother Nature's Son' and duetted with k.d. lang on 'Hope Of Deliverance'.

His full repertoire for the concert was: 'Coming Up', 'Looking For Changes', 'Fixing A Hole', 'Band On The Run', 'All My Loving', 'We Can Work It Out', 'Hope Of Deliverance', 'Mother Nature's Son', 'Blackbird', 'Peace In The Neighbourhood', 'Off The Ground', 'Can't Buy Me Love', 'Magical Mystery Tour', 'C'mon People', 'Live And Let Die', 'Let It Be' and 'Hey Jude'.

The occasion was the Earth Day For The Environment Concert. Paul's contribution went to the charities People for the Ethical Treatment of Animals, Greenpeace and Friends of the Earth. Prior to the concert he attended a press conference.

The American branch of the VH-1 music channel held an 'Earth Day' concert programme on Thursday 22 April in which they screened Paul's renditions of 'We Can Work It Out', 'Hope Of Deliverance' and 'Hey Jude'. Excerpts were also shown in the Carlton and Meridian ITV regions in England on 30 April 1993 with excerpts from Paul's press conference and clips of his performance.

Honey Hush
A track from the *Run Devil Run* album lasting 2 minutes and 36 seconds. It was penned by Big Joe Turner and recorded at Abbey Road Studios on Tuesday 2 March 1999 with Paul on lead vocal and bass guitar, Dave Gilmour on electric guitar, Mick Green on electric guitar, Pete Wingfield on piano and Ian Paice on drums.

Paul first heard the original Johnny Burnette recording when he stayed overnight at Stuart Sutcliffe's flat in Gambier Terrace.

Honey Pie
A song penned by Paul about a girl from the North of England who becomes a movie star. The Beatles began recording it on 1 October 1968 with overdubbing on 2 and 4 October at Trident Studios, with a brass arrangement scored by George Martin.

The night they started working on it, Jim Webb popped into the studio. Paul sings vocal and plays piano, John is on electric guitar and George is playing bass again. There were also fifteen session musicians whose contribution was scored by George Martin.

It was included on *The Beatles* double album.

The number had a 1920s flavour and the sound of scratches from an old 78 rpm were added to the beginning of the record to add to the period atmosphere.

Paul was to comment, 'My dad's always played fruity old songs like this, and I like them. I would have liked to have been a 1920s writer because I like that top hat and tails thing.'

Paul's original demo was included on the *Anthology 3* CD.

Honorary Consul, The

A film starring Richard Gere and Michael Caine, based on a Graham Greene novel of the same name. John McKenzie, director of Paul's 'Take It Away' video, directed the movie and Paul was commissioned to compose the title music. Paul produced an instrumental theme for the film and it was issued as a single by guitarist John Williams under the title 'Paul McCartney's Theme From The Honorary Consul' on 13 December 1983 on Island 1S/155. The film's name was changed to *Beyond The Limit* in America.

Honours

In 1981 Paul received the prestigious 'International Achievement Award' from the Songwriter's Hall of Fame in America.

Paul received the 'Freedom of the City' in Liverpool on Wednesday 28 November 1984. On Wednesday 7 March 1984 Liverpool City council passed a resolution that each surviving member of the Beatles be given the Honorary Freedom of the City, the highest honour they could bestow to an individual. Paul was the only member to formally accept.

The ceremony took place in the Picton Library, William Brown Street, Liverpool.

On 12 July 1988 he was awarded an Honorary Doctorate from Sussex University.

On Tuesday 19 December 1989 Paul received a Unique Achievement Award from the Performing Rights Society at a presentation at Claridges Hotel in London.

In June 1993 Paul was honoured at the first Annual Earth Day International Awards. He was presented with an award for his efforts to raise public consciousness over environmental issues.

Paul was honoured with a fellowship of the Royal College of Music for his distinguished services to music. The ceremony took place at the Royal College of Music in London on Wednesday 8 November 1995 when Prince Charles, President of the College, presented Paul with the award. Other recipients had been Placido Domingo and Yehudi Menuhin. Paul said, 'For a street arab from Liverpool it isn't that bad at all.'

In December 1996 it was announced in the Honours List that Paul would receive a knighthood.

The investiture ceremony took place at Buckingham Palace, London on Tuesday 11 March 1997. There were 1,000 fans outside the palace as Paul arrived to be knighted by Queen Elizabeth II. He spent two and a half hours inside the Palace, accompanied by his three children, Mary, Stella and James. Linda was too ill to attend. When Paul left, the fans outside had been singing 'A Hard Day's Night' and 'Hey Jude'. When they saw him they began to sing 'Yesterday', with the title altered to 'Yes Sir Day'.

Paul commented, 'This is the best day of my life. To come from a terraced house in Liverpool to this house is quite a journey and I am immensely proud.

'I would never have dreamed of this day. If we had that thought when we started out in Liverpool it would have been laughed at as a complete joke. Today is fantastic, there is a blue sky and it's springtime. My mum and dad would have been extremely proud today and perhaps they are.'

In 1999 Paul was named 'The Greatest Composer Of The Last 1,000 Years' in a BBC poll, beating Mozart, Bach and Beethoven.

On 25 May 2000 Paul was honoured with a Fellowship at the annual Ivor Novello Songwriting Awards at the Grosvenor House Hotel in London, in recognition of his four decades in the music business. It was the 45th year of the awards.

The Fellowship was awarded by the British Academy of Composers and Songwriters (BACS) and Paul received a minute-long standing ovation. BACS Chairman Guy Fletcher referred to Paul as 'an exemplary role model for young people the world over'.

Paul was to say, 'I remember coming here the very first time with my mates John, George and Ringo and looking back then, it was just fantastic to be part of this whole songwriting thing. It was always just the greatest award, the greatest thing to get for songwriters and it still is many years later.'

Before an audience, which included Elton John, Travis and the Pet Shop Boys, he recalled how touched he was watching Mozart composing in the film *Amadeus*. He said, 'I remember tears welling up and thinking, "I'm one of them. I'm in that tradition." Maybe not like Mozart, but I'm in that tradition. Everyone who's had a hit is so proud to be part of it.'

Paul had previously won Ivor Novello awards for 'Michelle', 'Yellow Submarine' and 'Yesterday'.

On 23 September 2000 Paul attended the 16th Annual TEC (Technical Excellence & Creativity) Awards at the Regal Biltmore in Los Angeles. He received the Les Paul Award from legendary guitarist Les Paul himself. This particular award recognised 'individuals who have set the highest standards in the creative application of recording technology'.

Also in September at the annual *GQ* Magazine 'Men of the Year' award ceremony at the Royal Opera House, London, Paul received a

'Lifetime Achievement Award'. He commented, 'It's a bit like getting an old git's prize, I was going to say in my speech, but I didn't think it would have gone down well.'

On 26 April 2002, backstage at Madison Square Garden, New York, he was made an honorary detective by the New York Police Department.

Hope Of Deliverance (promotional film)

The promotional film of 'Hope Of Deliverance' was directed by Warren Hewlitt and filmed at Island Studios, Acton, London on 21 November 1992.

The film was to prove controversial due to the fact that Paul paid £20,000 to 350 New Age travellers to appear in the video.

They were allegedly from a mid-Wales group of travellers who were said to have damaged farms in Wales, uprooting fences, ruining grass with excrement and setting their dogs on sheep. One farmer claimed they had caused £20,000 worth of damage to his farmland.

Hewlitt was to say, 'They see Paul as just another hippie and they like the vegetarian and green life style he promotes.'

Tory MP David Amess was to describe the payment to the travellers as 'a disgraceful waste of money'. He also said, 'I can think of many better uses for his spare cash than paying people who live in a disgusting manner and leave rubbish everywhere.'

Paul said, 'I like the fact that these kids are harking back to the values of the sixties.'

A set with the appearance of a forest setting had been built in the studio and members of Paul's fan club were also present. However, fans complained at the treatment they received, being separated from the New Age travellers and feeling that they received rather cavalier treatment compared to that of the travellers. They also mentioned that they signed release forms for which they received nothing, while the travellers received £25 for each release form they signed.

Hope Of Deliverance (single)

A track from the *Off The Ground* album, penned by Paul and 3 minutes and 20 seconds in length.

A single was released on Parlophone R 6330 on Monday 28 December 1992. 'Long Leather Coat' was on the flipside. In addition to the vinyl and cassette release, there was also a CD single on CDR 6330 with the extra tracks 'Big Boys Bickering' and 'Kicked Around No More'. It was released in the US on Tuesday 18 January 1993 on Capitol 4KM0777 in a cassette version only.

The single was released in France on EMI France 8804542.

Andy Morahan directed the 'Hope Of Deliverance' promotional film.

There was also a maxi-single, produced by Paul and Julian Mendelsohn, which was issued in America on Capitol 7-15950-2 on Tuesday 18 January 1993. It was 15 minutes and 49 seconds in length and featured four tracks: 'Hope of Deliverance', 'Big Boys Bickering', 'Long Leather Coat' (co-written with Linda) and 'Kicked Around No More'.

CEMA, the special markets label from Capitol, issued a limited edition of 22,000 in America on Capitol/CEMA 56964.

A live recording of the number lasting 3 minutes and 33 seconds, which was recorded live at East Rutherford, New Jersey on 11 June 1993, was included on the *Paul Is Live* album.

Hopkin, Mary

A Welsh singer born in Pontardawe, South Wales on 3 May 1950 who was spotted on Hughie Green's television talent show *Opportunity Knocks* by Twiggy.

Paul was to comment, 'I heard of Mary Hopkin first in Liverpool. Twiggy and Justin had come up in their new car and we were eating our pudding, later that evening, and we talked about *Opportunity Knocks* and discovery shows in general and I wondered whether anyone really got discovered, I mean *really* discovered in discovery shows. Then, Twiggy said she had seen a great girl singer on *Opportunity Knocks*.

'When I got back to London next day, several other people mentioned her, so it began to look as if Mary really was something. So, I got her phone number from the television station and rang her at home in Pontardawe, somewhere in Wales, and this beautiful little Welsh voice came on the phone, and I said, "This is Apple Records here. Would you be interested in coming down here to record for us?" She said, "Well . . . er . . . would you like to speak to my mother?" And then, her mother came on the line and we had a chat and two further conversations, and, later that week, Mary and her mum came to London.'

They all had lunch together and then went on to Dick James's Studios in New Oxford Street, situated above a branch of the Midland Bank, for Mary to audition.

She performed five numbers before one of her guitar strings snapped and she was unable to continue. Paul was delighted with her and remembered a song that would suit her. It was called 'Those Were The Days'.

Paul was to recall, 'A long time earlier, maybe a couple of years ago, I'd first heard 'Those Were The Days' when the American singers, Gene Raskin and Francesca, sang it in the Blue Angel in London and I had always remembered it. I'd tried to get someone to record it because it was good. I'd hoped that the Moody Blues might do it, but it didn't really work out and later, in India, I played it to Donovan who loved it, but didn't get around to doing it. We rang Essex Music, the publishers of the song, but they didn't know anything about it other than that they owned the song.'

Mary herself recalled, 'There was only ever one song in mind for the first single. I didn't record anything else. Paul sang it to me in the office and I recorded it straightaway. I thought it was a bit too pop, you know, in the way that he sang it, but it was nice. Paul has been so nice and kind to me all along in producing my record. He knew exactly what to do. He worked very hard. I was frightened of recording, and I kept saying, "I can't do it," and he kept telling me, "Of course you can."'

Paul produced Mary singing the Gene Raskin song 'Those Were The Days' in English, Italian, Spanish, French and German.

The English version was issued in America on Monday 26 August 1968 on Apple 1801 and in Britain on Friday 30 August 1968 on Apple 2 with Pete Seeger's 'Turn! Turn! Turn!' on the flipside. '*En Aquellos Dias*' was the Spanish language version of 'Those Were The Days', issued in Spain on Friday 25 October 1968 on Apple 3 with Pete Seeger's 'Turn! Turn! Turn!' on the flip. '*Quelli Erand Giorni*' was the Italian version, issued on Saturday 5 October 1968 on Apple 2 with 'Turn! Turn! Turn!' on the flip. The French version was '*Le temps des Fleurs*' issued on Odeon FO-131 on Friday 25 October 1968 and the German version was '*An Jenem Tag*' issued on Odeon O-23910 also on Friday 25 October 1968.

Paul produced Mary's debut album *Postcard*. He also thought of the title, designed the cover and wrote out the featured postcards on the reverse of the sleeve, which listed the songs on the album. It had an eclectic mix of songs, including three written by Donovan. Paul also suggested one of the tracks, 'The Honeymoon Song', which the Beatles used to perform at the Cavern. Linda took the cover photograph. Paul plays guitar on the three tracks penned by Donovan – 'Lord Of The Reedy River', 'Happiness Runs (Pebble And The Man)' and 'Voyage Of The Moon'. Other tracks were Harry Nilsson's 'The Puppy Song'; 'Young Love', a pop song from the 1950s; 'Inchworm', a song from the Danny Kaye musical *Hans Christian Anderson*; George Gershwin's 'Someone To Watch Over Me'; 'Love Is The Sweetest Thing', '*Y Blodyn Gwyn*', 'Lullabye Of The Leaves', '*Prince En Avignon*', 'The Game' and 'There's No Business Like Show Business'. For the American release, the Gershwin number was dropped in favour of the inclusion of 'Those Were The Days'. Paul had written some new arrangements to standards such as 'There's No Business Like Show Business'.

The album was issued in Britain on Friday 21 February 1969 on Apple SAPCOR 5 and in America on Monday 3 March 1969 on Apple ST 3351. It reached No. 28 in the American charts.

Incidentally, on a postcard Paul sent to Derek Taylor, he referred to Mary as 'Hairy Mopkin'.

The next release, which Paul produced, were two singles issued on Friday 7 March 1969. The first was in the Italian language and issued in Italy on Apple 7. It was 'Lontano Dagli Occhi' with 'The Game' on the flip. The second was in French and issued in France on Apple 9. It was 'Prince en Avignon' with 'The Game' on the flip.

Paul produced her next single 'Goodbye'/'Sparrow'. 'Goodbye' was a number Paul composed and Bernard Gallagher and Graham Lyle wrote the flipside. This was issued in Britain on Apple 10 on Friday 28 March 1969 and in America on Apple 1806 on Monday 7 April 1969. It reached No. 2 in the British charts.

Paul's next production for Mary was 'Que Sera Sera (Whatever Will Be Will Be)', the Jay Livingston and Ray Evans number that Paul rearranged. The flipside was another Gallagher and Lyle composition, 'Fields Of St Etienne.' This single was issued in France on Friday 19 September 1969 on Apple 16 and in America on Monday 15 June 1970 on Apple 1823. It was Paul's last production for Mary.

Mickie Most then took over the production of Mary's singles, although the next release 'Temma Harbour' had Paul's production of 'Lontano Dagli Occhi' on the flip.

Following Mickie Most, Tony Visconti began to produce her records. Mary had announced in March 1972 that she would not remain with Apple, so the final release on the label was a compilation of her previous recordings, her album Those Were The Days, which was issued in America on Monday 25 September 1972 on SW 3395 and in Britain on 24 November 1972 on SAPCOR 23, the tracks produced by Paul being: 'Those Were The Days', 'Que Sera Sera', 'Fields Of St Etienne', 'Sparrow', 'Lontana Dagli Occhi' and 'Goodbye'.

The album was reissued as a CD in 1994 with a revised running order chosen by Mary, which also included some tracks from her 1971 album Earth Song – Ocean Song.

For the Apple press reception for Mary, the Post Office Tower in London was hired in February 1969 and each of the guests was given an apple as they entered the reception suite.

Mary married producer Tony Visconti and had a son Morgan and daughter, Jessica. After her divorce from Visconti she joined Sundance and Oasis, the latter a middle of the road group with Peter Skellern, Julian Lloyd Webber, Bill Lovelady and Mitch Dalton. She also provided backing vocals for Thin Lizzie's 'Dear Lord' and David Bowie's 'Sound and Vision'.

Commenting on her role as a backing singer she said, 'I enjoyed working like that rather than on my own stuff because I still found my public image nauseating. I had no motivation to return.'

Incidentally, Visconti was then to marry John Lennon's former lover, May Pang, although that marriage also became estranged.

In August 1970 Mary was made a Bard at the Welsh Eisteddfod for her skills as 'an interpreter of contemporary folk music'.

Mary has appeared as a back-up vocalist on records by David Bowie, Ralph McTell and Tom Paxton, although she was uncredited.

In 1972 she recorded 'Summertime Summertime' with Visconti under the name Hobby Horse.

On 27 February 27 1976, Mary sang in a new style with her single of the Edith Piaf number, 'If You Love Me'/'Tell Me Now'.

As a tribute to her fiftieth birthday on Wednesday 3 May 2000, Channel Four Wales, S4C, screened the documentary 'Mary Hopkin' at 8.15 p.m. on Monday 1 May 2000.

In 2001 Mary had a small part in the film *Very Annie Mary*.

Hopkins, Nicky

One of Britain's former leading session musicians, who appeared on 14 Rolling Stone albums, plus albums by Rod Stewart, the Who, the Jeff Beck Group, Jefferson Airplane and numerous other artists.

When he played on Paul's *Flowers In The Dirt* album, he became the only session musician to appear on studio recordings by all four of the individual members of the Beatles in addition to recording with the Beatles as a group.

Hopkins first met the Beatles in Hamburg, Germany in 1962 when he was a member of Cliff Bennett & the Rebel Rousers at the Star Club. His first recording session with the Rolling Stones was on the single 'We Love You' on which Paul and John provided the backing vocals.

In 1968 he was asked to play piano on the Beatles recording of *Revolution*. He was to join George Harrison and Ringo Starr on Jackie Lomax's album *This Is What You Want* in 1969 and in 1971 played on John Lennon's *Imagine* album and on the single 'Happy Xmas (War Is Over)'. He also played with Harrison and Starr on Harry Nilsson's *Son Of Schmilsson* in 1972 and Lennon's *Sometime In New York City* and Ringo's *Living In The Material World*.

George Harrison also played guitar on Hopkins' own album *Tin Man Was A Dreamer*.

Other albums he appeared on by ex-Beatles included *Goodnight Vienna*, *Dark Horse*, *Walls And Bridges* and *Extra Texture*.

Hopkins performed on 'That Day Is Done' on the *Flowers In The Dirt* album.

He died in Nashville on 6 September 1995. He was fifty years old.

Horn, Trevor

A record producer, born in Hertfordshire, England on 15 July 1949. He founded the Buggles and then began to record dozens of major names including ABC, Yes, Frankie Goes To Hollywood, Rod Stewart, Simple Minds and Tina Turner. One of the world's most successful record producers, he was voted 'Producer Of the Year' by *Rolling Stone* magazine in 1983.

Paul worked with him early in 1988 when Horn produced the *Flowers In The Dirt* album, including the numbers '*Ou Est Le Soleil?*' and 'Figure Of Eight'.

Horne, Nicky

A British disc jockey. He interviewed Paul in his 'Nicky Horne's Music Slot' on the *Thames At Six* news programme on Monday 19 May 1980 and on his Capitol Radio show *Mummy's Weekly* on Friday 23 May 1980.

Hot As Sun

An instrumental, 1 minute and 28 seconds in length, which Paul used on his *McCartney* album. Paul recorded the number at Morgan Studios and played acoustic guitar, electric guitar, drums, organ, bass, maracas and bongos.

He'd originally begun composing the tune in the late 1950s and there was a brief appearance of the number during the *Let It Be* sessions, when Paul ad-libbed a few lines. It was never developed as a number for the Beatles although lyricist Tim Rice added a complete set of lyrics to the number and it was issued as a single by Noosha Fox on Earlobe Records (ELB-S-105) on Friday 24 July 1982. The Tim Rice lyrics were also used on Elaine Paige's cover version on her *Hot As Sun* album, issued by WEA (K58385) on Tuesday 2 November 1982. The sleeve notes on Elaine's album claimed that Paul had written the number especially for her, but he actually wrote it in 1958/59.

On the *McCartney* album the number segued into 'Glasses' and ended with a chorus of a song called 'Suicide' which Paul had originally penned with Frank Sinatra in mind.

Hotel In Benidorm

A number lasting 2 minutes recorded during the sound check before the concert at Boulder, Colorado on 28 May 1993 and included on the *Paul Is Live* album.

Hour With Paul McCartney, An

A feature on Paul included in the American CBS TV show *Entertainment This Week* in August 1986. It was an interview, which Paul recorded at his London offices in Soho Square.

How Do You Sleep?

A track on John Lennon's *Imagine* album, which was an attack on Paul. John listened to Paul's album *Ram* and believed that Paul was taking digs at himself and Yoko in the songs 'Too Many People' and 'Dear Boy'.

Adding insult to injury, John had included a picture of himself fondling a pig, similar to the pose on the cover of *Ram* of Paul holding a sheep. Another slight was the fact that George Harrison also played on the number.

Paul was upset when he read about the number in *Melody Maker* and John's references to Paul's songwriting being 'rubbish'. He commented, 'I never came back at him, not at all, but I can't hide my anger about all the things he said at the time about "Muzak" and Engelbert Humperdinck. I was in Scotland when I read this in *Melody Maker*. I was depressed for days. When you think about it, I've done nothing really to him, compared to what he said about me. John is the nice guy and I'm the bastard! It's repeated all the time. But what did I do to John? OK, let's try to analyse this. Now, John was hurt. So, what was he hurt by? What was the single biggest thing we could find in all our research that hurt John? Well, the biggest thing I could find was that I told the world that the Beatles were finished. But I don't think that's so hurtful.'

When Paul gave an interview to *Melody Maker* in November of that year he commented on John's reference in 'How Do You Sleep?' that the only decent number Paul had ever written was 'Yesterday'.

Paul said that it was silly of John to make such a reference. 'So what if I live with straights? I like straights. I have straight babies. It doesn't affect him. He says the only thing I did was "Yesterday". He knows that's wrong. He knows and I know it's not true.'

However Absurd

The final track on the August 1986 *Press To Play* album, lasting 4 minutes and 58 seconds. It was co-written by Paul and Eric Stewart.

Hunky Dory

The English name for the Japanese television programme *Yoru No Hit Studio*. On Wednesday 7 June 1989, before an audience of members of the Wings Fun Club, Paul performed a satellite link-up to the programme from Twickenham Film Studios in Middlesex. Apart from miming to 'This One' and 'My Brave Face' he also gave an interview.

Hydra

An EMI label that issued Paul's two Fireman albums, *Strawberries Oceans Ships Forest* in 1993 and *Rushes* in 1998 and also *Liverpool Sound Collage* in 2000.

Hynde, Chrissie

Chrissie Hynde, a close friend of the McCartneys and an active animal rights campaigner.

Chrissie was born in Akron, Ohio on 7 September 1951 and moved to London in 1970. She helped form the Pretenders in 1978, two former members of which – Robbie McIntosh and Blair Cunningham – were to back Paul in groups he formed.

At the time she had her first baby, Chrissie had never met Paul and Linda and was surprised when she received a present for the baby and some baby clothes with the note: 'Love – Paul and Linda and the kids.' A month later, Paul was in the next studio to where Chrissie was recording and she walked in and thanked him for the present. A few weeks later she met Linda for the first time. The year was 1983.

She became a close friend and she persuaded Linda that she should become a spokesperson for animal rights.

In 1998 Chrissie had an idea for a pose she wanted for the photograph of her forthcoming album *Viva el Amor*. She believed Linda was too ill for her to approach and, knowing that Mary had become a photographer like her mother, asked Mary if she could take the shot. The next thing was a call from Linda making arrangements for the photo shoot, which took place at Linda's home studio in Rye. It was the last photograph Linda took.

It was Chrissie who read out a eulogy at Linda's New York memorial on 21 June 1998, saying:

Linda McCartney was a pal and an ally
She wasn't an avant-garde intellectual bully
And she sure wasn't here for the fame or the money
She didn't cry 'Peace!' in a room full of furs
She thought animals' skins were theirs, and not hers.

When Chrissie first moved to Britain she was former journalist with the *New Musical Express*, although she never interviewed Paul when she worked on the paper. However she has interviewed Paul a number of times over the years. She conducted an interview with Paul, which was published in *USA Weekend* on Sunday 1 November 1998. During the interview he mentioned why he did not invite Yoko Ono to Linda's American memorial service. 'We decided to stay true to Linda's spirit and only invite her nearest and dearest friends. Seeing as Yoko wasn't one of those, we didn't invite her. People who were maybe doing it out of duty weren't asked. Everyone who went remarked that there were so many friends there and it was such a warm atmosphere. Everyone who spoke, spoke from the heart, genuinely. Linda would have hated anything else.'

Chrissie also organised the Royal Albert Hall tribute to Linda, 'Here, There And Everywhere – A Concert For Linda' on Saturday 10 April 1999.

In September 1998 Chrissie asked Paul to help her organise a series of concerts in 1999 to promote animal rights. Paul said, 'Good animal activists around the world might think, "Oh, God, we've lost a very powerful voice when we lost Linda." Well, we have. But my voice is there now, and I'm going to try to use it. We are going to keep up her good work.' But after a while he told the *Sun* newspaper, 'I might not be able to get up on stage again. I don't know whether I can go up there and sing, thinking about Linda. If I can manage it, then I will. But I've said that if I can't do it, Chrissie'll just have to forgive me.'

In September 2001, at the annual PETA gala, Paul presented the 'Linda McCartney Award' to Chrissie.

I Am Your Singer
A track on the *Wild Life* album, with Paul and Linda alternating on the vocals, with acoustic guitar sounds in the background. The number was later recorded by David Cassidy.

There were plans to issue it as the B-side of 'Love Is Strange', as a single release from the *Wild Life* album, but the idea was abandoned.

Paul and Linda performed it on a New York radio station in December 1971 and on Wings' European tour of 1972. They dedicated the song to their respective fathers.

I Can't Write Another Song
A home demo that Paul recorded at his Rude Studio in 1979 playing acoustic guitar and using a drum machine. It is also known as 'Believing'. The number was heard on the *Oobu Joobu* radio series.

I Do
A track from the *Driving Rain* album. The number lasts for 2 minutes and 56 seconds. David Leonard, who overdubbed orchestral samples onto the track, also mixed it.

I Don't Want To See You Again
A number Paul wrote specially for Peter and Gordon. This was the third number he had given to the duo, although it was the least successful of the Lennon and McCartney numbers they recorded. Norman Newall produced it. The Beatles never recorded this number, although Paul is likely to have given Peter and Gordon a demo disc of it. The record was issued in Britain on Columbia DB 7356 on 11

September 1964, but failed to register in the charts. It was issued in America on Capitol 5272 on 21 September 1964 and reached No. 19 in the charts.

It was also the title of the Peter and Gordon album issued in Britain on Friday 11 December 1964 on Capitol ST 2220. The album also contained another Paul McCartney composition, 'Nobody I Know'. The number was also included on the duo's *In Touch With Peter And Gordon* album, issued on Friday 18 December 1964 on Columbia 33SX 1660.

It was reissued as a single in America on 1 May 1967 on Capitol Starline 6155, with another McCartney composition, 'Woman', on the flipside.

I Got Love
One of a number of compositions Paul wrote while on holiday in Jamaica in January 1995. It remains unreleased.

I Got Stung
A track from the *Run Devil Run* album lasting 2 minutes and 40 seconds. A former hit for Elvis Presley, it was penned by Aaron Schroeder and David Hill and recorded at Abbey Road Studios on Monday 1 March 1999 with Paul on lead vocal and bass guitar, Dave Gilmour on electric guitar, Mick Green on electric guitar, Pete Wingfield on piano and Ian Paice on drums.

This was a number which Elvis had recorded soon after he got out of the army. Paul initially wasn't keen on the number, but it grew on him because he liked the intro to the number so much.

I Got Up
A Suzy and the Red Stripes track, recorded in Paris in November 1973 with Paul, Linda, Denny Laine, Jimmy McCulloch and Davey Lutton. Linda added her vocals to the track on 20 March 1998 at Paul's home studio in Hog Hill shortly before her death. Paul added final overdubs in July 1998 and the track was finally included on the *Wide Prairie* album.

I Lie Around
A number penned by Paul and sung by Denny Laine which was issued as the flipside of 'Live and Let Die' in 1973. It was the only single by Wings on which Paul didn't sing lead vocals.

I Lost My Little Girl
The first number Paul ever wrote. He was fourteen years old and it was shortly after the death of his mother. This was the number that Paul first played to John Lennon and probably set the seal on their idea of becoming a songwriting partnership.

Paul could be heard busking the number while he was working at home in the late 1970s on a bootleg tape and in a brief part of his interview with Melvyn Bragg for the *South Bank Show*.

He performed it in public for the first time on Friday 25 January 1991 when he appeared before a studio audience for the MTV show *Unplugged*, asking the audience to gather round and listen to the first song he wrote. It was then included as track two on his *Paul McCartney: Unplugged – The Official Bootleg* release.

I Owe It All To You

A number penned by Paul, lasting 4 minutes and 50 seconds, which was included on the *Off The Ground* album.

I Saw Her Standing There

A song Paul thought up when he was driving home from a concert in Southport and wrote in the living room of his Forthlin Road house in September 1962 under the working title of 'Seventeen'. John was present and made a small contribution although the song is generally considered as one mainly written by Paul.

Paul was to say, 'Originally the first two lines were "She was just seventeen, Never been a beauty queen." When I played it through the next day to John, I realised that it was a useless rhyme and so did John. John came up with "You know what I mean", which was much better.'

Paul was to admit that he took the bass line from the Chuck Berry number 'I'm Talking About You', commenting, 'I played exactly the same notes as he did and it fitted our number perfectly. Even now, when I tell people about it, I find few of them believe me. Therefore I maintain a bass riff doesn't have to be original.'

John himself was to comment on the song in a *Playboy* interview: 'That's Paul doing his usual good job of producing what George Martin used to call a potboiler. I helped with a couple of the lyrics.'

The Beatles included the number in their repertoire between 1962 and 1964, including their appearance on the *Ed Sullivan Show* on 16 February 1964.

The Beatles recorded the number on 11 February 1963 and it was the opening track of their debut album *Please Please Me* and was issued in America as the flipside of 'I Want To Hold Your Hand' on 13 January 1964. It is also to be found on the Star Club recordings.

John Lennon performed the song with Elton John on stage at Madison Square Garden on 28 November 1974 and Paul was to perform it at the Prince's Trust Concert in 1986.

A version of this number lasting 3 minutes and 20 seconds was included on the *Tripping The Live Fantastic* album. It was recorded live at the Forum, Montreal, Canada on 9 December 1989 during the 1989/90 World Tour.

I Survive

An album by Adam Faith, his first for more than a decade, on which Paul plays synthesiser on three tracks: 'Change', 'Never Say Goodbye' and 'Goodbye' and provides backing vocal, along with Linda, on 'Star Song'. The album was issued in America on 2 September 1974 on Warner Brothers BS 2791 and in Britain on 20 September 1974 on Warner Brothers K 56054. A single from the album, 'Star Song', was issued in Britain on 6 December 1974 on Warner Brothers K 16482.

I Wanna Be Your Man

A song mainly written by Paul, with a little help from John.

The number had originally been written with Ringo Starr in mind, as they wanted to give him a song to sing on each album.

Paul said, 'We wrote "I Wanna Be Your Man" for Ringo because we wanted him to have a song on our album. "I Wanna Be Your Man" was trying to give Ringo something like "Boys", an up-tempo song he could sing on the drums. "I wanna be your ma-an", that little bit is nicked from "Fortune Teller", a Benny Spellman song. We were quite open about our nicks.'

The number hadn't actually been completed when Andrew Loog Oldham bumped into John and Paul one day and asked if they had a number suitable for the Rolling Stones to record, although Paul's version is slightly different.

Paul said, 'We were in Charing Cross Road, where we often used to go to window-shop at the guitar shops and daydream. Dick James was on the Charing Cross Road and we'd go to his office and daydream on the way. Coming out of his office one day, John and I were walking down Charing Cross Road when passing in a taxi were Mick and Keith. They shouted from the taxi and we yelled, "Hey, hey. Give us a lift," and we bummed a lift from them. So there were the four of us sitting in a taxi and Mick said, "Hey, we're recording. Got any songs?" and we said, "Ah, yes, sure. We've got one. How about Ringo's song, you could do it as a single."'

Paul's version differs from other details of how the number came about. The occasion was 10 September 1963 and John and Paul had been at the Variety Club lunch at the Savoy Hotel where they'd received an award as Top Vocal Group of the Year.

In Jermyn Street they bumped into Rolling Stone manager Andrew Loog Oldham who told them he was on his way to a Stones rehearsal, although the group were having difficulty finding suitable material for their second single.

The two of them went with Oldham to Studio 51 where the Stones were recording and completed the number in about ten minutes. It proved to be a hit for the Stones and, many years later, a minor hit for the Rezillos when it reached No. 71 in the British charts on 18 August

1979. The Beatles version was included on *With The Beatles* in Britain and *Meet The Beatles* in the States.

A live version of the number lasting 2 minutes and 37 seconds was recorded during the sound check of the Paramatta concert in Sydney, Australia on 29 March 1993 and included on the *Paul Is Live* album.

I Will

A track on *The Beatles* double album. Paul commented, 'I wrote quite a few songs in Rishikesh. I was doing a song "I Will" that I had as a melody for quite a long time. But, I didn't have lyrics to it. I remember sitting around with Donovan, and maybe a few others. And I played him this one and he liked it and we were trying to write some words. We kicked around a few lyrics. I kept searching for better words and I wrote my own set in the end, very simple words, straight love-song words, really. I think they are quite effective.'

There were actually 67 takes of this number, recorded at Abbey Road Studios on 16 September 1968.

Paul said that it was a love song dedicated to Linda.

I Would Only Smile

A Wings track with the original line-up of Denny Seiwell and Henry McCullough which Denny Laine included on his album *Japanese Tears*. It was composed by Laine and recorded in 1973.

I'll Be On My Way

A number penned by Paul early in his career that was recorded by Billy J Kramer and the Dakotas in 1963 and appeared on the flipside of their chart-topper 'Do You Want To Know A Secret?' Although the Beatles didn't record the number, they performed it on the BBC radio show *Side by Side* on 24 June 1963.

Paul was to comment, 'It's a bit too June-moon for me, but these were very early songs and they worked out quite well.'

I'll Follow The Sun

An early composition by Paul that eventually surfaced on the *Beatles For Sale* album and EP, the American *Beatles '65* album and the 1977 *Love Songs*.

Paul recalled, 'I wrote that in my front room in Forthlin Road. I was about sixteen. I seem to remember writing it just after I'd had the 'flu. I remember standing in the parlour, with my guitar, looking out through the lace curtains of the window, and writing that one.'

The Beatles recorded it on 18 October 1964.

In his *Playboy* interview, John Lennon was to comment, 'That's Paul again. Can't you tell? I mean – "Tomorrow may rain so I'll follow the sun." That's another early McCartney, you know, written almost before the Beatles, I think. He had a lot of stuff.'

I'll Give You A Ring
A song by Paul, which Wings recorded at Abbey Road Studios on Thursday 15 August 1974 during their sessions for the documentary 'One Hand Clapping'. It remained unreleased until June 1982 when it was issued as the flipside to 'Take It Away'.

I'll Keep You Satisfied
A number by Paul which Billy J Kramer & the Dakotas recorded on 22 July 1963 and released as a single in the UK on 1 November 1963 on Parlophone R 5073 with 'I Know' on the flipside. It was issued in America on Liberty 55643 on 11 November 1963. It was also the title of Kramer's EP, issued in Britain on 20 March 1964 on Parlophone GEP 8895. The four tracks were: 'I'll Keep You Satisfied', 'I Know', 'Dance With Me' and 'It's Up To You'.

The Beatles never recorded the number.

I'm Carrying
A track from the *London Town* album, penned by Paul, which lasted 2 minutes and 44 seconds.

It was issued as the flipside of the 'London Town' single in August 1978.

Inspired by a former girlfriend of Paul's, it was recorded in the Virgin Islands on 5 May 1977. George Harrison said it was his favourite track on the album. An unusual instrument, a sort of souped-up synthesiser called a 'gizmo' is featured. This was invented by Kevin Godley and Lol Creme, former members of 10cc.

I'm Down
A composition by Paul, recorded by the Beatles on Monday 14 July 1965 and issued as the flipside of the 'Help!' single. It was also included on the *Rock and Roll Music* and *Rarities* compilations. The group performed the song on their 'Ed Sullivan' television appearance in September 1965 and on their 1965 and 1966 world tours when they often closed their concert performances with it.

Paul was to say, 'I could do Little Richard's voice, which is wild, hoarse and a screaming thing. It's a funny little track and, when you find it, it's very interesting. A lot of people were fans of Little Richard, so I used to sing his stuff, but there came a point where I wanted one of my own, so I wrote "I'm Down".'

He was to add, '"I'm Down" was my rock-'n'-roll shouter. I ended up doing it at Shea Stadium. It worked very well for those kind of places, it was a good stage song.'

I'm Looking Through You
A song of lost love that Paul penned following a row he had with his girlfriend Jane Asher, ironically writing it in the music room of the

Asher house in Wimpole Street. Jane was in Bristol appearing with the Old Vic. Initially he just wrote a verse and a chorus that the Beatles taped in October 1965 during their *Rubber Soul* sessions. The Beatles re-recorded it on 6 and 10 November and overdubbed the vocals on 11 November 1965.

Paul was to say, 'My whole existence for so long centred around a bachelor life. I didn't treat women as most people do. My life generally has always been very lazy and not normal. I knew I was selfish. It caused a few rows. Jane went off to Bristol to act. I said, "OK then, leave, I'll find someone else." It was shattering to be without her. That's when I wrote "I'm Looking Through You" – for Jane.'

The number first surfaced on the 1965 *Rubber Soul* album and has also been featured on the 1978 *The Beatles Collection* and the 1980 *The Beatles Box*. There was an interesting version of the number sung by Vincent Price to the accompaniment of spectral figures in a spoof horror edition of *The Muppet Show*.

I'm Partial To Your Abracadabra

Paul's contribution to the Ian Dury tribute album, a remake of Dury's *New Boots And Panties* called *Brand New Boots And Panties*. Produced by Laurie Latham, Paul was backed by Dury's original band the Blockheads. The CD single was issued in April 2001. The album cover was designed by Peter Blake of *Sgt Pepper* cover fame.

I'm The Urban Spaceman

A single by the Bonzo Dog Doo-Dah Band, penned by Neil Innes and produced by Paul McCartney under the name Apollo C Vermouth. It was issued in Britain on Friday 11 October 1968 on Liberty LBF 15144 and in America on Wednesday 18 December 1968 on Liberty 66345. 'Canyons Of Your Mind' was on the flipside. It was reissued in America on Monday 19 July 1971 on United Artists UA 50809.

It was the first track on the album *Urban Spaceman*, issued in America on Monday 9 June 1969 on Imperial 12432 and in Britain on the album *I'm The Urban Spaceman* on Sunset SLS 50350 on Friday 7 September 1973.

The number was also included on the 1970 compilations *Progressive Heavies* and *The Beast Of The Bonzos*.

I've Got A Feeling

The combination of two separate songs, one by Paul, one by John. John's song was called 'Everybody Had A Hard Year', Paul's was 'I've Got A Feeling'. It was decided that they would collaborate and make the two separate songs into one, with it probably being the last true collaboration between the two writers. The Beatles taped the number at Abbey Road at three separate sessions and the number was featured in the *Let It Be* album and film.

I've Had Enough (single)

A song recorded in the Virgin Islands for the *London Town* album. It was issued as a Wings single on Parlophone R6020 on Friday 16 June 1978 in Britain, but only reached No. 42 in the chart. In America it was released on Monday 12 June on Capitol 4594 and reached No. 25 in the charts.

'Deliver Your Children' was the flipside.

It was also released in Germany on EMI Electrola 1C600-61260.

I've Had Enough (promotional film)

The promotional film for this record featured new Wings members Laurence Juber and Steve Holly, although neither of them had played on the track.

I've Just Seen A Face

A folk-rock number. The Beatles taped this song by Paul on Monday 14 June 1965, the same day they recorded 'I'm Down' and 'Yesterday' and it was included on the *Help!* album. Paul later revived it for Wings' 1975/76 World Tour.

Its original working title was 'Auntie Gin's Theme' and the George Martin Orchestra actually recorded it under this title when he issued his *Help!* album in America.

Paul wrote the number in the Asher's Wimpole Street house and commented, 'I think this is totally by me. It was slightly country and western from my point of view. I was quite pleased by it. The lyrics work. It keeps dragging you forward, it keeps pulling you to the next line.'

Iachimore, Ian

A pseudonym Paul assumed when friends wanted to contact him by letter in order to differentiate them from the vast fan mail that came his way.

See 'Pseudonyms'.

If I Were Not Upon The Stage

A number composed by Sutton/Turner/Bowsher. Paul's version of this number, lasting only 36 seconds, was included on the *Tripping the Live Fantastic* album. It was recorded live at the Riverfront Coliseum, Cincinnati, Ohio on 12 February 1990 during the 1989/90 World Tour.

If You Wanna

A track from the *Flaming Pie* album which Paul originally began composing when he had a day off in Minneapolis during his New World Tour in May 1993. He then had Steve Miller record it with him.

Paul also produced the number, which lasted 4 minutes and 38 seconds. Geoff Emerick and Jan Jacobs, assisted by Keith Smith, engineered it.

Recording began on 11 May 1995 with Paul on lead vocal, drums, bass guitar, electric guitar and 12-string acoustic guitar. Steve Miller provided harmony vocal and electric piano and electric guitar.

If You've Got Trouble

A number that Paul mainly wrote which was recorded on Thursday 28 February 1965. It was originally intended for Ringo to sing as a contribution on the *Help!* album. Only one take was made and it was not included in the final selection and remains unreleased.

In Spite Of All The Danger

The first original composition ever recorded by the group who were to become the Beatles. The Quarry Men recorded it on 12 July 1958 at Percy Philips's studio at 53 Kensington, Liverpool. The group at the session were Paul McCartney, John Lennon, George Harrison, Colin Hanton and John Lowe.

They recorded two songs that day, Buddy Holly's 'That'll Be The Day' and 'In Spite Of All The Danger' which was credited as a Harrison/McCartney composition. Paul sang lead on the latter.

They could only afford one copy of a two-sided shellac disc between them and Philips was to wipe out the tape.

The disc was passed around to each member for a while and ended up in the hands of Lowe, who put it in a drawer and forgot about it for a number of years. When he eventually realised its potential value, Lowe put it up for auction, but Paul prevented its sale and then bought it from Lowe for an undisclosed sum.

Paul had both sides placed on a master disc at Abbey Road Studios. The master tapes were then taken to Orlake pressing plant in Dagenham where Paul ordered two dozen copies to be produced in shellac at 78 rpm.

'In Spite Of All The Danger' was included on *The Beatles Anthology 1* CD.

Indeed, I Do

One of a number of home recordings made by Paul in 1971 and 1972. This was a demo track with Paul on acoustic guitar and himself and Linda on vocals.

India

Paul wasn't really as enthusiastic about the Indian influences of the Maharishi Mahesh Yogi and Ravi Shankar as George was, although he went along with the others on their forays into meditation and also decided to travel to Rishikesh with Jane Asher and remained there for five weeks.

When the two returned on Tuesday 25 March 1968, they were interviewed at London airport.

A reporter asked Paul how he felt after five weeks of meditation. Paul said, 'Yes, yes, I feel a lot better, except for the flight, you know. That's quite long. I'm a bit shattered, but the meditation is great!' He then mentioned the meditation: 'You sit down, you relax, and then you repeat a sound to yourself. It sounds daft, but it's just a system of relaxation, and that's all it is. There's nothing more to it. We meditated for about five hours a day in all. Two hours in the morning and maybe three hours in the evening, and then, for the rest of the time, we slept, ate, sunbathed and had fun.'

The reporter said, 'One Indian MP accused the camp where you stayed as being an espionage centre, and you, in fact, of being a spy for the West.'

This amused Paul, who replied, 'Yes, it's true. Yes, we are spies. The four of us are spies. Actually, I'm a reporter and I joined the Beatles for that very reason. The story is out next week in a paper which shall be nameless.'

The reporter asked Jane whether she'd gone to India for a holiday or to meditate, and she said, 'Oh, to meditate.' When asked what effect it had on her and whether this was her first big meditation experience, she replied, 'Yes, I think it calms you down. It's hard to tell because it was so different, you know, the life out there. It'd be easy to tell now that I'm back, or when we're doing ordinary things, to see just what it does.'

When Paul was asked if he'd actually seen any examples of the extreme poverty that existed in India, he replied, 'Yes, oh yes. I don't equate it, you know, because it's nothing to do with it, you know. The idea is to stop poverty at its root. You see, if we just give handouts to people, it'll just stop the problems for a day, or a week, you know. But, in India, there's so many people, you really need all of America's money to pour into India to solve it, you know, and then, they'll probably go back the next year, and just lie around, you know. So, you've got to get to the cause of it and persuade all the Indians to start working and, you know, start doing things. Their religions, it's very fatalistic, and they just sit down and think, "God said, this is it, so it's too bad to do anything about it." The Maharishi's trying to persuade them that they *can* do something about it.'

One good result of the Indian trip was the number of songs written by the individual Beatles. Paul said that they'd written twenty songs when they were in Rishikesh.

In later years, Paul began to visit India to holiday. Whilst in Goa in January 2001 he wrote 'Lonely Road', 'I Do' and 'About You', which became tracks on the *Driving Rain* album. Another track on the album shows an India influence, 'Riding To Jaipur'.

On Friday 11 January 2002 Paul and Heather arrived in southern India to enjoy a vacation at the Coconut Lagoon hotel, in Kumurakom, but on Monday 14 January they were discovered by the local press and decided to leave, also cancelling the next step of their holiday, which was to have been at the Ashtamudi Resorts.

Indica Books & Gallery

A specialist bookshop and art gallery, launched in March 1965 by Barry Miles, Peter Asher and John Dunbar, trading under the business name MAD. It was situated at No. 6 Mason's Yard, next door to the Scotch Of St James club, which was frequented by the Beatles.

As all three were friends of Paul, he gave them £5,000 to help build shelves, buy book stock and pay wages. He also designed the bookshop's wrapping paper and helped in the shelf-building and decorating.

The bookshop was situated upstairs and the gallery downstairs. The bookshop was later moved to 102 Southampton Row, which also housed *International Times* where Paul had helped to decorate the office.

It was on 9 November 1966 that John Lennon turned up at the gallery, on the invitation of Dunbar, for the exhibition 'Unfinished Paintings And Objects', by Yoko Ono.

Ingrained Funkiness

An unreleased number recorded by Paul and his daughters Heather and Stella in his Sussex studio in November 1992 as part of a surprise Christmas present for Linda.

Inner City Madness

A track on the *Tripping The Live Fantastic* album, which lasts for 1 minute and 23 seconds. It was composed by Paul, Stuart, McIntosh, Wickens and Whitten and was recorded during the soundcheck at the NEC International Arena in Birmingham, England on 2 January 1990 during the 1989/90 World Tour.

Internet, The

Paul has taken an interest in utilising the Internet and has made several on-line 'Netcasts'. His first on-line chat took place at the Bishopsgate Memorial Hall, London on Saturday 17 May 1997, which was organised by VH1 as part of 'Paul McCartney Week' during which Paul answered fifty questions which had been put to him by fans.

Here is a transcript, although there are some gaps due to parts of the netcast becoming inaudible:

Question: Picked up the *Oobu Joobu* CD this morning. Will there be more editions?

Paul: Ahhh, yeah. That was released as a radio show, but in England, we're releasing it as the B-side of the singles – that is probably the best place to get hold of it at the moment.

Question: It is known that you paint for relaxation. Do you ever plan to exhibit or sell your paintings?

Paul: I've been painting for about fourteen years now. I didn't really want to exhibit because of the sort of thing that people say like, 'Oh he's just a singer that paints a bit' and I have had offers from people who have said, 'I'll give you a show', but I said, 'but you haven't seen my paintings yet,' and they've replied, 'doesn't matter'. But funnily enough I am going to get an exhibition this year in Germany so this will be my first exhibition ever.

Question: How do you feel about teenagers buying your CDs rather than modern ones.

Paul: I feel very good about that, Lisa. Very good indeed.

Question: You are still breaking boundaries and trying new projects – but what do you consider to be your greatest achievement?

Paul: My children – it's basically that. It's not easy to have good kids when you are in a high-profile show business thing like I am and Linda and I reckon that is our greatest achievement.

Question: Sir Paul, where do you keep your knighthood medal?

Paul: By the side of the bed.

Question: Who took all the wonderful photographs that accompany the new album?

Paul: Thanks for asking that Marsie. It was actually Linda that took all those wonderful photos.

Question: I wouldn't go veggie for health reasons, but you make a good point about the animal rights. When did you go vegetarian?

Paul: Approximately twenty years ago, after eating leg of lamb one Sunday.

Question: What do you do when you have free time, Paul?

Paul: One of my favourite hobbies is to make trails in the woods. There are a lot of woods where I live and Linda and I like horse riding. So I go out and make trails – it's the complete opposite of what I do for a living.

Question: I loved your concert in Buenos Aires in 1993. When are you going to come back?

Paul: Well, at the moment there are no plans for a tour but we all enjoyed being in Argentina, we had a great time. So, if we do come back someday, we'll stop there again. You were a great audience by the way.

Question: Hello Paul, I have a question for you: do you wear boxers or briefs?

Paul: Steady on, Rosie! Luckily we are on the Internet so I can't show you! You wouldn't believe the answer actually. I'll stay enigmatic on that one.

Question: How many Hofner basses do you own? Is the one you have now the original Beatles bass?

Paul: Yeah, I have one main one that I use and a backup. But in the sixties a couple of them got nicked, as we say in England. Nicked, which is stolen.

Question: Didn't one get sold?

Paul: One did, but they said I'd played it a lot but I managed to prove I didn't.

Question: Do you believe mankind can save itself – or do we need divine intervention?

Paul: I don't know about divine intervention, but I think we are always in the need of divine help. All we can do is get serious and tell our politicians that we want a future and make sure they listen – I think it is possible, with a little divine help.

Question: Will you and George and Ringo ever record together again?

Paul: We don't know, really. We had some ambitions to after 'Free As A Bird' and 'Real Love', but it didn't come to anything. The nearest we got is, Ringo and I record on the new album together. So we will have to wait and see.

Question: Is it true that there was a notebook of fifty unrecorded songs written by you and John that were accidentally thrown away?

Paul: No. There was a book, and to tell the truth, we used to exaggerate. There was never fifty songs in it but we used to tell people we had fifty songs in it because it sounded much better. There was probably five or six – and I do believe somewhere I've still got that book. It has got 'Love Me Do' in it and a couple of very early songs that we didn't really want to develop. So somewhere . . . It was a school exercise book.

Question: Do you plan to record any songs from that time that you didn't record?

Paul: I don't know. Sometimes you think about it, but you find yourself writing a new song and you always favour that.

Question: How were you introduced to Steve Miller?

Paul: I think it goes back to the original session at Olympic studios where we'd had an argumentative Beatles meeting and the session got cancelled due to a business thing. Steve was in the studio and we asked if a studio was free and he and I stayed up all night making the track called 'My Dark Hour'.

Question: Which three human qualities do you respect most?

Paul: I think honesty is probably top, I think kindness is next, then humour third. It's difficult to pull three out of a hat.

Question: Did you or Frank Clarke play the bass on 'Penny Lane'?

Paul: Get serious man. It was I and not said Frank Clarke!

Question: What is the greatest gift?

Paul: That's a hard question. Tolerance of other people, perhaps.

Question: What happened to the 27-minute version of 'Helter Skelter'?

Paul: We edited it for the original version, I think. I'm not absolutely sure. When you make these songs, you don't keep track of the different versions. I'm sure it exists somewhere. EMI has probably still got it.

Question: What is yours and Linda's greatest love?

Paul: Our main love is horse riding. Linda was a great rider in her teens and she actually rode in Madison Square Garden when she was about sixteen I think. So she taught me how to ride.

Question: I'm fourteen and became a fan when I saw *Help!* Will you possibly do another movie with that kind of humour?

Paul: Ummm. I think what you saw in *Help!* was Beatles humour, caused by the four of us together. So it would be difficult to do that again. I like the sense of humour, though. Possibly it might happen one day.

Question: Do you have anything planned for the anniversary of *Sgt Pepper*?

Paul: No I don't actually. The thing with being in the Beatles is that we were so busy making the music we never kept track of the dates, it is more the fans do that. So I am always surprised it's the thirtieth anniversary. It feels about three years ago to me.

Question: I'm from the Ukraine. Are you going to come to see us in the future?

Paul: Well, one of my ambitions has always been to play in Russia and sing 'Back In The USSR'. There are a lot of people who go there to sing it. I'd like to do that myself, but no plans just yet.

Question: Is Linda doing another cookbook?

Paul: Yes, she is at the moment. She is working on a cookbook, a photography book, and an exhibition of stained glass in Switzerland. She has a friend who mounts her photographs in stained glass, it's an amazing process. That is happening later this year in Switzerland.

Question: What was your legacy of the sixties?

Paul: I like to think it was promoting peace with the Beatles. We've obviously had some long-term effect – and that was it.

Question: How long did you work on *Flaming Pie*?

Paul: It was made over a couple of years, while we were preparing for *The Beatles Anthology*.

Question: Will you ever work with Wings again?

Paul: I don't know – it's an interesting thing – when I go out on tour I guess I could call my band Wings, we didn't think to do that with the last band but it may be something we'd do in the future.

Question: What do you really think of Oasis?

Paul: I like the fact that they play live. I think they sing well, and, if they have to tribute anyone, I'm proud it's the Beatles.

Question: Have you thought about releasing a 'Paul McCartney Anthology'?

Paul: I've never thought to do it, but after *The Beatles Anthology* people have started to talk about a Wings retrospective. So I suppose after that we could do a solo retrospective. No plans at the moment, but who knows.

Question: What are you wearing right now?

Paul: I'm wearing a rather attractive ensemble, with a feather boa, large wide-brimmed hat and nylon stockings – and boxer shorts. That's the answer to that one!

Question: Who is playing the heavy guitar on *Flaming Pie*?

Paul: It's a few of us. Sometimes it's me, sometimes it's Steve Miller, sometimes it's Jeff Lynne, and sometimes it's my son James.

Question: Do you listen to music when you paint? If so, what?

Paul: I don't actually. I think a lot of people do . . . It's not something I seem to need.

Question: If you were a fruit, which fruit would you be?

Paul: A great big watermelon.

Question: How has being knighted changed your life?

Paul: Not a lot really, except that it's a huge honour. We carry on just as before. It is good that I get to make my girlfriend a Lady.

Question: Were there other John demos you were given by Yoko other than 'Free As A Bird' and 'Real Love'?

Paul: Yes, there was a couple of tracks that were offered, but because of the quality of the demos it's a difficult job. 'Free As A Bird' and 'Real Love' were difficult records to make, although they were enjoyable. But there were one or two . . . one in particular that I still have my eye on a little bit, but I'm not sure whether we'll get around to it.

Question: What would you say is the biggest difference between music in the US and the UK?

Paul: I'm not sure there is a huge difference. You have a lot of live bands; so have we. You've got a lot of techno; so have we. I suppose rap is the biggest difference. You are the home of rap. We've got a few rappers over here. Though, actually, Jamaica is the original home of rap.

Question: What Beatles song was the most difficult to write?

Paul: The only one John and I really had a problem with was 'Drive My Car'. I had the original idea, but I had a bad set of lyrics that were about golden rings and they were terrible, and we got stuck on them. But we had a cup of tea and somehow we came up with the woman that needed a chauffeur and we made it quite quickly after that. But it was nearly a dry session.

Question: What was the first record you ever bought?

Paul: The first record, Chris, was 'Be-Bop-A-Lula' by the great Gene Vincent.

Question: What is your favourite book?

Paul: I don't know – *Foundation* by Isaac Asimov, I like a lot. I like *Far From The Madding Crowd* by Thomas Hardy. You'll have to give me a few weeks on that one. There are so many choices I'd have to whittle that down.

Question: I'm 28 and an owner of a multimedia company. What advice can you give me about getting a lot of creative people to work together.

Paul: Good humour – and staying on top of it yourself, thus letting them know how it goes, and then, giving them their head.

Question: What was your reaction to the Beatles getting the Grammy awards?

Paul: It's always great to get any award, and it was lovely after so many years to get a Grammy as the four Beatles which is something you would have said was completely impossible – but it happened.

Question: Is there any chance of you doing any more straight rock and roll?

Paul: Yes, there is a chance. The last one I did, the Russian album, was done very quickly over a couple of days. So there's every chance. I actually recently compiled a list of my favourite rock and roll songs with a view of doing that, but I haven't got around to it yet. I've been busy.

Question: What is the single most important thing we can do to help animals?

Paul: Go veggie. Because if you don't eat them, that sure helps them.

Question: What is the most memorable thing a fan has done?

Paul: That's a difficult question. I can't immediately think of an answer to that. Someone once tried to take a snippet of my hair which didn't go down well at all.

Question: What is your favourite Elvis song?

Paul: I have a few, really. 'Jailhouse Rock' is a masterpiece. 'All Shook Up' was always a great favourite. 'Love Me Tender' was another.

Question: Are you planning any special events for the end of the century?

Paul: No. Everyone keeps asking me this but I haven't even thought what I am going to do. The thought that keeps occurring to me is it's only if you count by Jesus's birth that there's even a millennium going. I'm sure for the Chinese it's not the millennium. So I haven't any plans at the moment but I'll probably think of something.

Question: In which key do you play 'Don't Get Around Much Anymore'? I really like it and would love to learn it.

Paul: E major, dude.

Question: Sir Paul, a lot of celebs are doing online stuff. Bowie's single 'Telling Lies' was available only online, and now here you are. Does the new medium excite you particularly?

Paul: To tell you the truth, I'm not an onliner. But I think I could easily become addicted. The nearest I've become to being a computer freak is the music program I used to write a recent large-scale orchestral piece.

Question: Does your son James play on *Flaming Pie*?

Paul: Yes, on the track 'Heaven On Sunday'.

Question: What does 'Love Me Do' mean?

Paul: 'Love Me Do' means 'Love Me Do'.

Question: I am fifteen and I'm in a band. What does it take to become famous?

Paul: Talent, dude.

Question: Paul, do you ever sit down and listen to old Beatles albums? And, if so, how do they make you feel?

Paul: I do sometimes, yeah. And they make me feel great, because I have so many great memories of that period and the guys.

Question: Did listening to your earlier work on the *Anthology* help you with *Flaming Pie*?

Paul: Yeah, I think it did. It reminded me how simple and direct the Beatles songs were, so I tried to be careful that all the songs on the new album were simple and direct.

Question: Have you watched the whole ten hour *Beatles Anthology* movie?

Paul: No, I haven't Heather.

Paul: Shall we just wind this up with one more?

Question: Is this your first time chatting online?

Paul: Yes, this is my first time chatting online and as we are going to have to wind it up, I want to say thanks to all you computer freaks out there for tuning in to this global hook-up. It's been a blast.

In 2000 Paul also became a major Internet investor by buying an undisclosed stake in Magnex Holdings plc, a company which has created software allowing online purchases and sale of music and other content that prevent unauthorised copying.

Is It Raining In London?

An unreleased number, which Paul co-wrote with Hamish Stuart. He recorded it at Abbey Road Studios on Tuesday 15 December 1992. The track is heard on the 1993 documentary 'Movin' On'.

It's For You

A composition by Paul. He gave the number to Cilla Black to record in 1974. At the session, which took place on 2 July, Paul, together with John Lennon, turned up and Paul played piano on the track. It was released in Britain on Friday 31 July 1964 on Parlophone R 5162 and in America on Monday 17 August 1964 on Capitol 5258. Produced by George Martin, it had 'He Won't Ask Me' on the flipside. It reached No. 8 in the British charts.

It was also the title track on her EP 'It's For You', issued in Britain on Parlophone GEP 8916 on Friday 23 October 1964. The other tracks were 'He Won't Ask Me', 'You're My World' and 'Suffer Now I Must'.

'It's For You' notched up advance orders of 200,000 copies, but didn't top the charts as her two previous discs had, although it made a respectable Top 10 entry. Cilla was to say, 'I couldn't keep getting a number one every time, people'd think I was a freak.'

It's So Easy/Listen To Me

A Buddy Holly medley by Denny Laine, which Paul produced. It was issued as a single in Britain on EMI 2523 on 3 September 1976 and in America on Capitol 4340 on 4 October 1976. The flipside was another Holly number, 'I'm Looking For Someone To Love'.

It's So Far Out It's Straight Down

A Granada Television documentary about the 'Counter-Culture' thriving in London during the 1960s that was screened on Tuesday 7 March 1967. It included an interview with Paul, which he'd pre-recorded on Wednesday 18 January 1967.

During the interview he commented, 'I really wish the people that look, sort of, in anger at the weirdos, the happenings, and at the psychedelic freak-out, would instead of just looking with anger, just look with nothing, with no feeling, and be unbiased about it. They really don't realise that what these people are talking about is something that they really want themselves. It's something that everyone wants. You know it's personal freedom to be able to talk and be able to say things, and it's dead straight. It's a real sort of basic pleasure for everyone, but it looks weird from the outside.'

It's You

An Alma Cogan single issued in Britain on Columbia DB 7390 on 30 October 1964. Paul played tambourine on the flipside, 'I Knew Right Away'.

Ivor Novello Awards Luncheon

Paul attended the Ivor Novello Awards luncheon on Tuesday 4 April 1989. He received an award for his 'Outstanding Services to British Music'.

During the presentation he recited a piece he composed for the occasion called 'Ivor Novello Rap', saying:

This Ivor Novello was a pretty fine chap,
But just one thing he didn't know, was how to rap.

Cause if he was living in the present day,
He'd have to think of something to say.
I think I know what it might just be,
He'd say whatever happened to the melody!

Ivory Impact

A double album by American pianist Roger Williams produced by Paul's brother-in-law John Eastman in 1983 and containing several numbers written by Paul.

Jackson, Michael

Michael Jackson was born on 28 August 1958 into a musical family in Gary, Indiana. By the age of five he had teamed up with his brothers in their group the Jackson Five. They signed to Detroit's Motown Records and began their climb to fame. They changed their name to the Jacksons in 1976 when they signed to Epic Records

In his autobiography *Moonwalk* he writes that he first met Paul at a party aboard the Queen Mary, moored at Long Beach, California.

They shook hands and Paul told him that he'd written a song for him. Jackson was surprised, but thanked him and Paul then sang a song for him. They exchanged telephone numbers, but unfortunately Paul mislaid the song for a time and didn't call Michael. When he found the composition again he included it on the *London Town* album, calling it 'Girlfriend'.

When Michael began working on his first solo album for Epic, Quincy Jones brought the number to his attention, saying it would be ideal for him to record. At one time the album was going to be called *Girlfriend*, but became *Off The Wall*. The album sold seven million copies and launched Michael into solo superstardom. 'Girlfriend' became the fifth single issued from the album in Britain in July 1980 and reached No. 30 in the *NME* charts.

Michael then wrote a number for his next album, *Thriller*, called 'The Girl Is Mine'. He thought it would make a suitable duet for him and Paul, and they recorded it in Los Angeles between sessions for Paul's *Tug Of War*. *Thriller* was issued in 1982 and became one of the biggest-selling albums of all time. 'The Girl Is Mine' was issued as a single in Britain on Epic EPC A2729 on 29 November 1982 and reached the No. 4 position. In the US it was issued on Epic 34-03288 on 3 October 1982 and reached No. 2. The song was co-credited to both Michael and Paul, as Paul had helped with the finishing touches.

On Christmas Day 1981 Jackson rang Paul and said that he wanted to come over and write some hits with him. Paul didn't believe it was Jackson. Michael persisted and when he phoned again, Paul said he'd think about it. In May 1981 Jackson travelled to Britain and met up with Paul and the two began to work on a number they called 'Say Say Say'. Then Paul invited Michael to his Sussex home where Linda took photographs of him riding one of their horses.

The two worked on several numbers in the studio and 'Say Say Say' was issued simultaneously in the UK and US as a single on Monday 3 October 1983, with 'Ode To A Koala Bear' on the flipside. A 12″ single with an extended mix and an instrumental version of 'Say Say Say' was also issued at the time. Another number, 'The Man', appeared on *Pipes Of Peace*.

Paul renewed their acquaintance backstage at a Los Angeles gig of Paul's during his 1989 tour.

In February 1990 when Paul was in Los Angeles to receive his Lifetime Achievement Award at the Grammys, he met up with Michael to discuss the future of Northern Songs. Jackson then agreed to increase Paul's share of the royalties. This was probably due to changes in the copyright laws in America which would have meant a huge loss in royalty payments to Paul when the Beatles numbers came up for renewal, beginning with 'Love Me Do' that year. The 1978 copyright law revision allowed for retroactive provisions for widows and orphans which would have meant that Yoko would start to take back half of Jackson's portion of royalties in America. Up until then, Jackson was splitting the royalties equally – 50/50 with the Lennon estate and McCartney. This meant that the Lennon estate and Paul received 25 per cent each with Jackson receiving 50 per cent. Under the new law Yoko's share could rise to 62.5 per cent, with Jackson receiving 25 per cent and Paul only receiving 12.5 per cent.

In 1994 Jackson was sued by Eric Kolper and Jay Bildstein of 57 Inc who claimed that Jackson had originally lent his support to their plan for a *Beatles Rap* album which they intended to record with artists such as the Beastie Boys, Ice-T and Run DMC to raise money for HELP, an American charity for the homeless, only to find that Jackson then blocked the project. The New York Court ruled in favour of Michael and his ATV music Group. It's believed that Jackson decided to withdraw permission for the album to use Beatles numbers due to Paul McCartney's dislike of Jackson's handling of the Beatles' songs.

Also during 1994, while Paul was touring South America, he gave an interview to the Argentina newspaper *Clarin*. Discussing the reports that Michael Jackson was addicted to painkillers, Paul said he felt that Jackson couldn't handle the pressures of fame. He admitted that the Beatles had been affected by Beatlemania at its height, but said, 'The

Beatles were ordinary guys. When fame arrived we went a bit crazy. But even so, we had our feet on the ground. We had roots, we knew about life.' On the fact that Jackson took painkillers, he said, 'It's very LA! I mean Judy Garland, Elizabeth Taylor – these are people who became stars at a very young age.' When he was queried about the accusations of child abuse which Jackson had been accused of, he said, 'Linda and I are parents, and it's clear to us that Michael isn't *that* kind of person.'

Shortly prior to his New Orleans Show on Saturday 24 April 1993 Paul complained about Michael Jackson allowing Beatles songs to be used for commercials, saying, 'I don't like it and the fans don't like it. I get a lot of letters saying they don't like to hear Beatles songs advertising sneakers or soft drinks. I think it cheapens the songs.'

On 28 July 1987 Leonard Marks, the Apple lawyer, had filed a lawsuit against Nike and Capitol Records due to the use of the Beatles' 'Revolution' in Nike TV commercials. There had been anger at the use of Beatles music in TV commercials since early 1985 when Ford used 'Help!' in a commercial.

Marks stated, 'The Beatles' position is that they don't sing jingles to peddle sneakers, beer, pantyhose or anything else. Their position is that they wrote and recorded these songs as artists and not as pitchmen for any product – use of the Beatles' voices constitutes unauthorised exploitation of the Beatles' persona and good will.'

At the time Paul had written to Jackson several times stating that he wanted to get the rights to his songs back and wanted to discuss it with Jackson, but all he'd received was a standard answer suggesting that he should talk to his lawyers.

In 1995 Paul said, 'I am not happy with the way Michael has handled it (the Lennon and McCartney catalogue). He was the first of all the owners of the songs to use them in commercials. I think this is a bad move commercially, not just morally. It cheapens the songs. When people come to my concerts, they often hold candles when we do "Let It Be". I don't think they'd do that anymore if the song suddenly became part of an Oldsmobile ad.'

Paul is to be found on one track of Michael Jackson's summer album *HIStory:Past, Present & Future Book 1*, released on Epic E2K-59000 on 20 June 1995. The 1992 recording of 'The Girl Is Mine' was included.

Paul was also to comment during the following month that he had requested increased royalty payments from Jackson on a number of occasions. He said, 'I've written to him three times. I'm the only living songwriter in the company, and he hasn't even replied.'

However, contact must have been made because on 24 June 1997 the text of some private letters between Paul and Jackson were published in *Flair*, a Belgian magazine.

In one letter Paul wrote:

'I know it has been a long time, but isn't it a time to forget the past? As a peace offer, my new CD. I think it's a pretty good one (haha!). Especially "Souvenir" and "Great Day".

'So, friends again?

'Paul.

'ps. but keep your hands off the rights this time!'

Jackson replied:

'Paul, my dear friend, just a short note to let you know me, myself and I are doing fine on the mystery tour. Come and see for yourself on 31 August in Oostende or on 8 or 10 June in the Amsterdam Arena. Bring Linda and the kids too, so they can meet my little boy. Let's reunite, make up and forget the past. I'll promise not to remix "Yesterday". Remember, I'm a lover, not a fighter!

'Hugs and kisses,

'Your Michael.'

In 1999 it was rumoured that Jackson was to sell off the Northern Songs catalogue, as he needed extra money to fund future projects. Jackson had bought ATV music in August 1985 for $47.5 million. Both Paul and Yoko Ono wanted to buy the company at the time but weren't able to match Jackson's offer.

In 1993 Jackson had signed a deal granting EMI's publishing division managerial control over the catalogue and he received $70 million in advances. The previous licence holders had been MCA. EMI took over on 1 January 1994 for a five-year period. When the contract terminated, Jackson was able to license his ATV Music catalogue, which included the rights to 251 Beatles songs, to Sony for £60 million.

In 2001 it was reported that Jackson was planning to sell the rights to cover his legal bills and to aid the upkeep of his 'Neverland' ranch. Jackson denied the rumours, saying, 'I want to clarify a silly rumour. The Beatles catalogue is not for sale and will never be for sale.'

Jailed In Japan
Paul spent time in a Japanese jail in January 1980.

Wings were to appear in eleven concerts in Japan between Monday 21 January and Saturday 2 February. Paul had previously been refused a visa for Japan in 1976 due to his drugs conviction, but had now been allowed to enter the country to make appearances with the band.

On the journey to Tokyo they had stopped off in New York to stay at the Stanhope Hotel and Paul attempted to contact John Lennon who he hoped to meet. When Paul phoned the Dakota, Yoko Ono refused to allow him to speak to John. He told her that they were off to Japan and would be staying at the Okura Hotel, which was John and Yoko's favourite hotel in Tokyo.

Arriving at Narita Airport on Wednesday 16 January, customs men searched Paul and discovered 8 ounces of marijuana. Sources were later to voice their suspicions that it was Yoko Ono who had tipped the police off about Paul.

Paul was arrested, handcuffed and questioned by narcotics officers and was then taken to spend the night in a local jail, being designated as Prisoner No. 22. The following day he was questioned for over six hours in the presence of his Japanese lawyer, Tasuko Matsuo. When the narcotics officers attempted to take him from the jail they were besieged by 200 fans and had to leave him behind for another night.

On Friday 18 January the prosecutors requested that they be allowed to detain Paul for a further ten days for questioning and the Tokyo district court agreed. They said that after that time they would either free him or charge him with possessing cannabis.

Paul requested that he be given a guitar in his cell, but this was rejected. Meanwhile a cable was sent to Paul and Linda at the hotel: 'Thinking of you all with love. Keep your spirits high. Nice to have you back home again soon. God bless. Love, George and Olivia.'

Senator Edward Kennedy made several calls to Tokyo enquiring about Paul's arrest. He expressed concern that if Paul intended to appear in concerts in America, a conviction in Japan would mean he would be unable to get a permit for the US. It has been suggested that Kennedy's calls helped to persuade the Japanese to release Paul without charge.

Since Paul wasn't allowed either guitar or tape recorder, Linda visited him on Thursday 24 January with some science-fiction books for him to read. She commented, 'He looks incredibly well. He was managing to smile and crack jokes. In fact, he was laughing so much, he even got me laughing and believe me, I haven't been able to do much laughing during the last week.'

On Friday 25 January the prosecutor's office announced, 'Charges were not brought against Mr McCartney because he had brought in the marijuana solely for his own use and that he has already been punished enough as a result of the incident.'

He was taken to the airport and deported. During his trip back home, at the various stops, Paul was surrounded by reporters and made various statements.

He confessed, 'I have been a fool. What I did was incredibly dumb. My God, how stupid I have been! I was really scared, thinking I might have been imprisoned for so long and now I have made up my mind never to touch the stuff again. From now on, all I'm going to smoke is straightforward fags and no more pot.'

Asked about his experiences in jail, Paul said, 'I sang "Yesterday" to a killer in the bath! I joined my fellow inmates for a dip in the baths and they asked me for a singsong. I gave them the old ones like "Red Red Robin" and "Take This Hammer". Their favourite, though, was "Yesterday".'

Enlarging on his experience, he said, 'I communicated with other prisoners by knocking on the walls and shouting. I became quite matey with the chap next door. He could speak a bit of English. Funnily enough, he was inside for smuggling pot. We told each other the worst jokes in the world. They were really dreadful, but they helped to relieve the tension. Discipline in the prison was very strict, but I made friends among the prisoners and guards. We sang and laughed together as if we had been mates for ages. But I was never allowed to see sunlight or get a breath of fresh air. That was depressing.'

At the time of his arrest, nearly 100,000 tickets had been sold and it was said that money amounting to the equivalent of £800,000 had to be returned to ticket holders. In addition, Paul's insurance had lapsed shortly prior to the Japanese trip.

Denny Laine was very critical of Paul due to what he considered he had lost financially with the collapse of the tour and wrote a bitter song 'Japanese Tears'. Paul was also angry with Laine because he flew to Cannes to make deals for himself while Paul was still detained in jail.

As a result of the charge Wings' records were banned from Japanese television and radio for three months.

Jamaican Hilite
An unreleased instrumental which Paul made a demo disc of at his Rude Studio in Scotland in the summer of 1977.

James Bond Greatest Hits
A compilation album of theme songs and soundtrack music from the twelve James Bond movies that had been issued up to the time of the album's release on Liberty EMTV 007 on 8 March 1973.

It reached No. 6 in the British album charts and 'Live And Let Die' by Paul McCartney and Wings was Track 2 on Side 2 of the LP.

James, Ian
A classmate of Paul's during his days at Liverpool Institute. The two friends virtually taught each other to play guitar, passing tips, playing together. They also used to wander round the visiting funfairs, trying to pick girls up. They began to look and dress alike, sharing the same hairstyle (like Tony Curtis's, nicknamed the DA, duck's arse), which was popular at the time, and both wore white sports jackets and drainpipe trousers. Paul said they wore the jackets because of the song 'A White Sports Coat' and described his jacket as having 'speckles in it and a flap on the pockets'. It was Ian who taught Paul the chords he played to John on their first meeting.

Paul was to say, 'We used to go round to the fairs, listening to the latest tunes on the Waltzer. Occasionally we'd get really depressed, so we'd maybe go back to his house and put on an Elvis record – "Don't Be Cruel" or "All Shook Up" – and five minutes later we'd feel good again.'

James Paul McCartney (TV interview)

A 31-minute television special recorded at AIR Studios, London on Monday 15 March 1982. This was Paul's first major interview since John's murder and was for the French television station A2. During the interview, conducted by Freddy Hausser, Paul talked about his idols, which included footballer Kenny Dalglish, who had been playing for Liverpool FC. He mentioned his new album *Tug Of War*, discussed music publishing and played an excerpt from the very first song he ever wrote, 'I Lost My Little Girl', on piano. Footage from *Rockshow* was also screened, together with the promotional video for the 'Ebony And Ivory' single.

James Paul McCartney (TV special)

An hour-long televison special made by Sir Lew Grade's company ATV. It was described in the promotional blurb as: ' . . . a personal project of Sir Lew, realised through the genius of Paul McCartney and the expertise of producer Gary Smith and director Dwight Hewison'.

Smith and Hewison had produced Elvis Presley's 'Comeback Special' in 1968.

In fact, Paul agreed to do the show in a deal struck to heal the breach caused between him and Sir Lew when Paul shared the composing credits with Linda on 'Another Day'. Grade initially believed it was a ruse to cut into the royalties due to his company through its ownership of Lennon and McCartney material.

The TV show was filmed on videotape in various places: on location in Scotland; in a Liverpool pub where Gerry Marsden, leader of Gerry & the Pacemakers joined Paul and locals in a rousing singalong and at ATV's Boreham Wood studios in front on a live audience.

It opened with 'Big Barn Bad' from the recently released *Red Rose Speedway* and followed with a medley of 'Blackbird'/'Bluebird'/ 'Michelle'/'Heart Of The Country', with Linda taking photographs and Paul singing the medley with an acoustic guitar. 'Bluebird' was edited out of the medley when it was screened in Britain. 'Mary Had A Little Lamb' had overdubbed animal noises to add to the effect and was followed by another medley, this time of 'Little Woman Love'/'C Moon', followed by 'My Love'. The 'Uncle Albert/Admiral Halsey' number is played before the 'Pub sequence' in which Paul, Linda and relatives appear in a Liverpool pub for a singalong with such numbers as 'It's A Long Way To Tipperary', 'April Showers', 'Come Along', 'California Here I Come' and 'You Are My Sunshine'.

The next song was one Paul had originally written for Twiggy, 'Gotta Sing, Gotta Dance'. This featured a long-haired Paul, complete with moustache, dressed in a white tail-suit, dancing with a host of showgirls whose costumes and make-up were half-male, half-female.

'Live And Let Die' followed and then a street sequence in which cappella versions of Beatles numbers were sung – 'When I'm Sixty

Four', 'A Hard Day's Night', 'Can't Buy Me Love', 'She Loves You', 'Ob-la-di Ob-la-da', 'Yesterday' and 'Yellow Submarine'. A live performance of numbers filmed at ATV Elstree Studios came next – 'The Mess', 'Maybe I'm Amazed', 'Long Tall Sally' and 'Hi, Hi, Hi'.

Finally, Paul ended the show singing 'Yesterday' to his own acoustic guitar accompaniment.

The programme was first screened in America on ABC-TV on Monday 16 April 1973. It was broadcast in Britain on Thursday 10 May 1973. For the British version, there was a live performance on 'Hi, Hi, Hi' that replaced 'Long Tall Sally', which had been the closing song in the American transmission.

Paul was to comment: 'You could say it's fulfilling an old ambition. Right at the start I fancied myself in a musical comedy. But that was before the Beatles. Don't get me wrong. I'm no Astaire or Gene Kelly and this doesn't mean the start of something big. I don't want to be an all-rounder. I'm sticking to what I am.'

The reviews in general were not exactly enthusiastic, *Melody Maker* calling it 'overblown and silly'.

Japanese Jailbird

Title of 20,000-word manuscript, which Paul penned himself and completed in 1984. It was based on his thoughts and experiences during the time he spent in a jail in Tokyo, Japan, in 1980, when he was arrested at the airport for possession of marijuana.

Paul wrote the book in secret and deposited it in a bank vault. It was a project strictly 'not for publication' (although he did have one copy privately printed for himself). He was to comment 'The mercifully short time I spent in jail cured a block I've experienced as a writer ever since schooldays. It's always been my ambition to write a book.'

When he was interviewed for the 1989 radio series *McCartney On McCartney* he mentioned the manuscript and said, 'I did it for my children immediately I got home. I thought, one day when we're all old and my son's a great big thirty-year-old and says, "Dad, what about that Japanese thing?" I'll be able to say: "There you are. Read that." I've just got one copy at home. It's called *Japanese Jailbird*.'

Paul was 37 years old when he arrived at Narita Airport and customs officers discovered 8 ounces of marijuana in a plastic bag at the top of his suitcase.

Twenty-one years after the event, Paul revealed his experiences of the nine-day ordeal in the Japanese prison cell in the 2001 documentary 'Wingspan'.

Due to the fact that he realised he was facing the possibility of a seven-year sentence of hard labour, he couldn't sleep at night. When he did manage to get some sleep he had disturbing dreams.

Paul was required to sweep his cell each morning with a reed brush, had to fold up his bedding and blanket and only then was allowed to wash and brush his teeth. He was also allowed a cigarette break during the day, which allowed him to speak to some of the other prisoners, one a murderer, another a Marxist student.

On release he went home, had a cup of tea and never spoke to anyone of his experiences, preferring to write about them in *Japanese Jailbird*.

However, with 'Wingspan' he began to discuss them for the first time during an interview with his daughter Mary.

He said:

I do not know what possessed me to stick this bloody great bag of grass in my suitcase. Thinking back on it, it almost makes me shudder.

I think, 'I don't believe that, how could I do that? How could Linda – who was much smarter than me – let me do that?' I must just have said, 'Oh baby, don't worry, it'll be alright.'

I was thrown into nine days of turmoil. It was very, very scary for the first three days. I don't think I slept much at all. And when I slept, I had very bad dreams.

I really thought I was such an idiot. I didn't have a change of clothes. I couldn't see anyone. I couldn't even have a book. And of course they were all speaking Japanese and I couldn't understand a word of it.

It took me three days to realise that you were allowed a change of clothes. I'd just worn this green suit that I'd arrived in and hadn't taken it off.

I was scared because the actual penalty for what I did was seven years hard labour. After a few days I started to see lawyers, but nobody actually said they would be able to get me out.

After a few days I became like Steve McQueen in *The Great Escape*. My sense of humour and natural survival instinct started to kick in.

I realised from all the movies I'd ever seen and from all the books I'd ever read that the gig in the morning is that you've got to clean your cell.

They'd put a reed brush and a little dustpan through the grill in the cell door.

I started to realise, 'Right, I'm going to get up when the light goes on, I'm going to be the first up, I'm going to be the first with his room cleaned, I'm going to roll up my bed, I'm going to do this, I'm going to do that.'

You had to clean your room and then sit cross-legged on your blanket, and you went 'Hai' and the guard came and said, 'OK, you can get washed.'

The first couple of days I'd been the last to get washed because

I hadn't figured it out. But once I understood what was needed I started to become the guy who was cleaned first, who got to do his teeth first.

During what they used to call the exercise period I'd squat down with all the other prisoners and you were allowed to have a cigarette. You squatted around a tin can, like a baked-bean can, smoking your cigarette and tapping the ash in the can.

There was one guy who spoke English. He was a student, in for social unrest. He was quite clever – a bit of a Marxist. I could talk to him.

There was another guy who was in for murder, a gangster guy. He had a big tattoo on his back, which is the sign of gangsters in Japan.

I started to become one of the lads. I started doing games with these guys. One of my games was something we'd played in the studio with the Beatles. It was who can touch the highest part of the wall. Of course, because I was taller than the other prisoners as they were all Japanese, I tended to win that game.

So I was going all of that, almost enjoying it by the end. When I got out Linda said I'd got institutionalised.

Japanese Tears (album)

A solo album issued by Denny Laine following the lack of action on the Wings front in the months following Paul's Japanese drug bust. A number of the tracks had been recorded some time previously, and three of them were actually Wings tracks – 'I Would Only Smile', first recorded in 1973, 'Send Me The Heart', recorded in 1974 and co-written with Paul, and 'Weep For Love', from the 1979 *Back To The Egg* sessions.

The album was issued in Britain on Scratch SCR L 5001 on 5 December 1980, but it was not until 8 August 1983, some time after Wings had officially disbanded, that it was released in America on Takoma TAK 7103. It did not reach the charts in either Britain or America. Artists appearing on the album, apart from Denny, included Paul and Linda, Howie Casey, Steve Holly, Jo Jo Laine, Henry McCullogh and Denny Seiwell.

It was re-released under the title of *In Flight* in May 1984 by Breakaway Records (BLY 110) and again on 31 May 1985 by President Records on PRCV 135 under the title *Weep For Love*. In June 1990 it was issued as a CD under the new title *Denny Laine Featuring Paul McCartney*.

Japanese Tears (single)

When the Wings' tour of Japan was cancelled due to Paul's drug bust in 1980, Denny Laine decided to write a song about the event, which he called 'Japanese Tears'. The flipside was a number he had recorded in 1978 with Steve Holly called 'Guess I'm Only Fooling'. The single was issued in Britain in 1980 on Scratch HS 401 on 2 May and in America on 5 May on Arista AS 0511.

Its name was changed to 'Denny Laine Featuring Paul McCartney' when it was issued as a CD in Britain in June 1990.

The number was recorded at Rock City. It followed the arrest of Paul in Tokyo and tells the story of a young Japanese fan's reaction to the cancellation of the tour.

Jazz Piano Song

A number credited to McCartney/Starkey. It was a spontaneous piece that arose during the *Let It Be* recording sessions and is seen being created in the early part of the *Let It Be* film. Paul had sat at the piano and begun playing an improvised boogie-woogie song and was immediately joined by Ringo. The two played for a couple of minutes and, since the piece was included in the film, it had to be copyrighted. As a result it was given the title 'Jazz Piano Song' and credited to Paul and Ringo.

Jazz Street

An eight-minute jam session recorded during the *Red Rose Speedway* sessions.

Jet (promotional film)

The MPL promotional film of this first track from *Band On The Run* to be issued as a single included animated line drawings of Paul and Linda, lyrics flashing onto the screen and a montage of images of Paul and Linda.

Jet (song)

Although the lyrics of this song mention a suffragette, Paul insists a black Labrador puppy inspired the title.

Paul and Linda were driving in the country one day when they came across a small roadside pet shop. On impulse they bought a little bitch puppy, the runt of the litter.

As she grew up, she got into the habit of jumping over the wall of the garden in St John's Wood and would disappear for long periods of time. On one of these walkabouts she got pregnant and some months later gave birth to nine little puppies in the garage.

Paul gave names to each of them, including Jet, Brown Megs and Golden Molasses.

The song, 4 minutes and 8 seconds in length, made its bow on the *Band On The Run* album, and was issued as a single on Friday 15 February 1974, on Apple R5996 in Britain where it went to No. 6 in the charts, and on Apple 1871 in America on Monday 18 February 1974, where it got to No. 7.

'Let Me Roll It' was the flipside on both sides of the Atlantic, with fellow Liverpudlian Howie Casey playing sax.

A live version of the number was included on the *Wings Over America* album, recorded during the 1975/76 tour, and the song was also on the *Wings Greatest* compilation. On 4 December 1980 it was issued as the flipside of 'Uncle Albert/Admiral Halsey' in America on Columbia Hall of Fame 13-33408.

The single was issued in Germany on EMI Electrola/Apple 1C006-05529, in France on Apple 2C008-05555 and in Japan on Apple EAR-10520.

A version of this number lasting 4 minutes and 2 seconds was included on the *Tripping The Live Fantastic* album. It was recorded live at the Wembley Arena, London on 17 January 1990 during the 1989/90 World Tour.

Jim Mac's Jazz Band

Jim McCartney, Paul's father, formed his own ragtime band at the age of seventeen in 1919. The initial name they used at rehearsals and on their debut was the Masked Melody Makers. Jim was on piano and trumpet, his brother Jack on trombone and a cousin was also in the group.

On that first appearance they wore highwaymen's masks, but they were sweating so much during the performance that the dye from the masks ran down their faces. After that they became known as Jim Mac's Jazz Band.

Their repertoire included 'The Birth Of The Blues', 'Stairway To Paradise', 'Chicago', 'Lullaby Of The Leaves' and 'After You've Gone', together with a Jim McCartney original composition, 'Walking In The Park With Eloise'.

The semi-professional band wore dinner jackets and appeared at local venues such as Oak Hall and St Catherine's Hall and they were booked to perform during the first showing in Liverpool of the silent film *Queen Of Sheba*. They played 'Thanks For The Buggy Ride' during the chariot race sequence and 'Horsy Keep Your Tail Up' during the Queen of Sheba's deathbed sequence.

Jim Mac's Jazz Band lasted until the mid-1920s.

John, Paul, George, Ringo ... And Bert

A play about the Beatles, penned by Willy Russell. It originally made its debut at the Everyman Theatre, Liverpool, then opened at the Lyric Theatre, London on Thursday 15 August 1974.

Paul was furious when he read the original script that portrayed him in a bad light and, as a result, he refused to allow Robert Stigwood to obtain the film rights.

In an interview, Paul was to say, 'I certainly appear to come out as the one saying, "No. No. Don't do Klein, and don't do this." I think I did have a good idea of what was going on there, because no one seemed to spot the Klein thing, and there was me left in a big, bad situation ... .he's (Russell) got me saying, "I'm leaving. I'm leaving the group," and the rest of the group saying, "Oh no, come on Paulie. It's the group. Let's stick together." In fact, that is physically wrong. I was actually the last to leave the group.'

Johnny Walker Show, The
A Radio One FM show which played the soundtrack of Paul's first UK gig of his 'New World Tour' on Saturday 11 September 1993. It included the numbers 'Good Rockin' Tonight', 'We Can Work It Out' and 'Biker Like An Icon'.

Johns, Glyn
A leading British producer/engineer. Glyn's first association with the Beatles occurred when he acted as an assistant engineer on Jack Good's television special 'Around the Beatles'.

A few years later Glyn received a phone call from Paul in December 1968, inviting him to work with the Beatles. Paul explained that they were producing their own television show and intended making a documentary and an album from it. The project turned out to be *Let It Be*. The tapes that Glyn recorded, together with George Martin, were later given to Phil Spector to mix. Glyn was to comment: 'I cannot bring myself to listen to the Phil Spector version of the album – I heard a few bars of it once, and was totally disgusted, and think it's an absolute load of garbage.'

Paul called Glyn again, this time to work on the *Red Rose Speedway* sessions, but it was said that he felt Paul's work on the album was too slow and he walked out on the sessions.

Jones, John Paul
Leading British guitarist and former member of supergroup Led Zeppelin. John appeared on the Rockestra recordings for *Back To The Egg* and also performed with the Rockestra at the Hammersmith charity concert on 29 December 1979. He appears in some scenes in the film *Give My Regards To Broad Street*, performing during the 'Ballroom Dancing' sequence and at a rehearsal session.

Jones, Shelagh
Paul's personal assistant for almost sixteen years. When she left his employ in 2000 she was given a bonus of £160,000 – on the stipulation that she did not publicly discuss the time she spent working for Paul.

Jones, Tom
During Paul's tour of Australia in 1993, he received the following note from Tom Jones:

Dear Paulboyo,

It's bad enough following in your wake around Australia, trying to get an audience going with 'Delilah' when they've just OD-ed on 'Sgt Pepper's, but now I hear you're nicking part of my act as well. Paulbach, this ain't fair. Lingerie is my line. Can you please have a word with your fans to discourage this bra-bunging and tell them ... have the last pants for me.

Yours,
Tomo.

In 2000 Paul promised to write a song for Tom Jones. Jones had mentioned in an interview that he'd been given the opportunity to record 'The Long And Winding Road' before the Beatles' version had been released, but had turned it down. Paul read what he'd said and decided to write him a new song.

Paul explained, 'He was telling the story of how I offered him "Long And Winding Road". He had to turn it down at the time because I stipulated it had to be his next single, and he had something like "Delilah" coming out, so they couldn't stop it.

'He was telling me this in private, and said, "Come on boy, write us a song then." I just think he's cool, and when someone asks like that, if I like them I'll give it a try and if something comes, great. If not, I'll just ring them up and say, "couldn't do it", but something came.'

Joseph Williams Primary School

A school in Liverpool. It was the school where both Paul and Mike were moved to when Stockton Wood Road became overcrowded. Paul was an apt pupil and came top in most subjects regularly. He did not have any difficulty in passing his 11-Plus examinations and gaining entrance to Liverpool Institute.

Liverpool Council announced they were closing the school down in 1996.

Paul joined a campaign to prevent the school closing, saying, 'It's a shame because I have many good memories of the school. I remember it as a good school and I hate to see any school anywhere closing down. I would like to request that the authorities rethink this decision.'

There was a reprieve.

Juber, Laurence

It was hearing the Beatles' 'I Want To Hold Your Hand' which inspired Juber to become a guitarist and he particularly wanted to become a studio musician. He joined a group and was also a member of the National Youth Jazz Orchestra.

He was working on a television show with David Essex and Denny Laine, who was present, liked the way he played. Juber had worked with artists such as Cleo Laine and also backed Denny on a TV show performing 'Go Now'.

A few months later, when he was recording at Abbey Road, he received a call from MPL saying, 'Denny Laine wants you to come over and play. Oh, by the way, Paul and Linda will be there too.'

He recalled, 'Paul was one of my earliest influences. I have tremendous respect for him. When I went for the audition I was surprised – I wasn't nervous.'

After the audition, Denny Laine approached him and said, 'What are you doing next year?' 'What do you mean?' Juber said. 'Well, you know, do you want to join us?'

So, at the age of 25, the session musician became a member of Wings (the line-up known as Mach VII) in June 1978, along with drummer Steve Holly, after initially recording with the group on their 5 May session for 'Same Time Next Year'.

Laurence toured with Wings in 1979, but mainly his time with the group was spent in the recording studios. When the Wings tour of Japan was cancelled, he spent his time making some solo recordings, mainly instrumentals.

In 1982 he released five of them on an album called *Standing Time* issued by Braking Records on BRAK 1 on 9 July. Among the tracks was 'Maisie', an instrumental he wrote for *Back To The Egg*, recorded by Wings but left off the album itself by Paul. On the track, Paul plays bass guitar.

Juber moved to California and married Hope Schwartz, daughter of Hollywood producer Sherwood Schwartz, producer of such shows as *Gilligan's Island*.

Juber occasionally appears at Beatles conventions in the States with his wife Hope, and at one of them he told the American magazine *Beatlefan* his thoughts about Paul: 'He treated me very well. He's a very gentlemanly person, very clever, very demanding and very competitive. He's a good source of information, a brilliant musician and a very nice man, I can't say anything bad about him.'

His recordings as a member of Wings were: 'Goodnight Tonight'/ 'Daytime Nighttime Suffering', 'Old Siam Sir'/'Spin It On', 'Back To The Egg', 'Getting Closer'/'Baby's Request', 'Wonderful Christmastime', 'Rudolph The Red-Nosed Reggae', 'Concerts For The People Of Kampuchea', 'Put It There'/'Same Time Next Year'.

Jungle Juice

A band that issued a version of Paul's 'Zoo Gang' in Britain one month before Wings issued their own. The record was released on Pye-Bradley BRAD 74071 on 24 May 1974.

Junior's Farm

When Paul and Linda were recording in Nashville in 1974 they stayed at a farm owned by Curly Putnam, also called Junior, and decided to immortalise him in this song.

Famed Country musicians Chet Atkins and Floyd Cramer joined Wings on the track. It was also the first Wings single to feature Jimmy McCulloch and Geoff Britton.

The number was issued in Britain on Apple R5999 on Friday 25 October 1974 and in the States on Apple 1875 on Monday 4 November. The single reached No. 3 in America and No. 16 in Britain.

The flipside was 'Sally G', a number reputed to have been written in honour of a Country singer whom Paul had met.

In 1975 Paul decided to reverse sides, releasing 'Sally G' as the A-side with 'Junior's Farm' on the flip. He commented, 'We flipped the single and I thought it might seem like we were trying to fool the public, but it isn't. It's only to get a bit of exposure on that song. Otherwise, it just dies a death, and only the people who bought 'Junior's Farm' get to hear 'Sally G'. I like to have hits, that is what I am making records for.'

It was issued in Britain on Apple R5999 on Tuesday 7 January and in America on Apple 1875 on Friday 7 February. It only reached No. 39 in the US. It was the last Paul McCartney and Wings single to be issued by Apple in both Britain and America.

'Junior's Farm' was included on the *Wings Greatest* compilation.

The single was released in Germany on EMI Electrola/Apple 1C006-05753 and in France on Apple 2C004-05752.

Junk

A number that Paul originally began to write during a trip to India in March 1968, with an early working title of the song being 'Jubilee'. It has also been known as 'Junk In the Yard'. In May of that year Paul completed a demo at George's bungalow 'Kinfauns', completing the song in time for *The Beatles White Album* sessions, although it wasn't used. The number was recorded again during the *Abbey Road* sessions but was one of six numbers that were not included on the final selection. Paul was initially seen running through a version of the number in January 1970 at Twickenham Studios during the filming of *Let It Be*.

It eventually appeared on Paul's solo debut album *McCartney*, lasting 1 minute and 53 seconds; he played all the instruments on the song himself, part of which he recorded at his home and part at Morgan Studios in London. Paul also released an instrumental version called 'Singalong Junk'.

Kahne, David

An American record producer, the A&R head of Warner Brothers Records, who has worked on albums with a range of artists including Tony Bennett, the Bangles, Fishbone, Sugar Ray and Sublime. Paul chose him to produce his *Driving Rain* album in 2001.

Commenting on the album, Kahne said, 'It's a more aggressive record, definitely. It's got real energetic guitar songs. They're all original and there's a lot of power there. I think he really loved doing that because he hadn't done it in a while.'

Kaleidoscope

A BBC Radio 4 programme. Paul went to Broadcasting House on Monday 16 September 1991 to be interviewed live on the programme discussing *Paul McCartney's Liverpool Oratorio*. Parts of the programme were repeated later that day.

Kansas City/Hey Hey Hey

A medley which Paul sang, utilising Jerry Leiber and Mike Stoller's 'Kansas City' and Little Richard's belter 'Hey Hey Hey'. The Beatles recorded the track for the *Beatles For Sale* album on 18 October 1964. Recalling the session, Paul said, 'John always used to egg me on. He used to say, "Come on, Paul, knock the shit out of 'Kansas City'," just when the engineers thought they had a vocal they could handle.'

The number 'Kansas City' was originally known as 'K.C. Loving' and had originally been a single by Little Willie Littlefield in December 1952. Under his real name of Richard Penniman, Little Richard had penned 'Hey Hey Hey' and he recorded the two songs as a medley in 1959, which is what inspired the Beatles to add the number in their repertoire.

A live version of the number lasting 3 minutes and 54 seconds was recorded live in Kansas City on 31 May 1993 and included on the *Paul Is Live* album.

Karate Chaos
A number recorded during Wings' sessions for *Venus And Mars*, and inspired by Geoff Britton, Wings drummer and a karate champion. However, Geoff left the group during the recording sessions for the album and was replaced by Joe English, which is probably why this number was never released.

Keep Coming Back To Love
A number written by Paul and Hamish Stuart and recorded at The Mill At Hog Hill Studios in Paul's Sussex home during the *Off The Ground* sessions in 1992. Julian Mendelsohn produced it. The song was five minutes in length.

Keep Under Cover
First recorded as a studio demo at Park Gate Studios, Sussex in August 1980, the number was eventually recorded during sessions in Montserrat on 7 and 8 December 1980 when Stanley Clarke added bass to the track. It was included on the *Pipes Of Peace* album.

Kellys, The
A husband and wife domestic team who Paul hired when he moved into Cavendish Avenue. Mrs Kelly was the housekeeper and her husband acted as butler and manservant.

Paul had never employed a housekeeper before and had engaged her as an experiment.

They were a live-in couple who worked for Paul for two years, but he had to fire them in January 1967 when they sold their story of life at Cavendish Avenue to an Australian magazine.

However, Paul did provide her with a handwritten reference, which read:

'Mrs Kelly worked for me and was a very capable and trustworthy housekeeper. She is an excellent cook and generally very efficient.

'Paul McCartney.'

She sold the reference in 1993 for £250.

At the time, Paul was to say, 'Mr and Mrs Kelly are looking for another place and I'm getting another couple to replace them. There have been disagreements over the running of the household. I haven't asked them to leave instantly because that would be unreasonable.'

A Mr and Mrs Mills replaced them.

Kenwright, Bill

A major West End theatrical producer, Bill attended Liverpool Institute at the same time as Paul. He commented: 'I first knew Paul when we travelled on the same bus to school. He always used to wear a big overcoat with a huge fur collar. We were both keen on acting and on one occasion were both in crowd scenes in a school production of *Saint Joan*.'

Bill briefly flirted with a career as a singer before turning to acting; he appeared in the TV soap *Coronation Street* before becoming successful as a theatrical producer.

Kicked Around No More

A number recorded during the *Off The Ground* sessions which was later used as an extra track on a *Hope Of Deliverance* CD.

King, Larry

The famous host of CNN's *Larry King Live*. King interviewed Paul and Heather for an hour on 12 June 2001.

Commenting on the current music scene, Paul said, 'I like some of the Eminem stuff because it's kind of clever. I like the rhythm, I like the attitude, and I can imagine if I was a young kid now, I'd like that.' On his musical heroes, he noted, 'Little Richard is fantastic, Jerry Lee Lewis, Gene Vincent, all of them. And then the next wave was Motown, Marvin Gaye and Smokey Robinson and Nat King Cole.'

Mentioning the Beatles, he said, 'People say, "Are you going to reunite?" and stuff like that. But for me, if we were on stage, the three of us, there'd be someone missing. I'd look over there and there'd be someone missing and that'd be John.'

On his relationship with Yoko Ono he said, 'We don't get along. But some people you may be destined to not become great buddies with. So it's not that we don't get along, just we don't talk much. We talk if we have to. I don't ring up and say: "Hey, Yoko, what's happening, babe?" We don't do that.'

He mentioned his book *Blackbird Singing*, and a poem he'd written when thinking about John Lennon, '"Here Today" is a song I wrote after John died. I was just thinking about him and remembering the good times and not so good times and having an imaginary conversation with him. What happened was that on the day that John got shot, there was this horror that someone we loved could just be mown down. At the end of the day, after all the tears and all the newscasts and all the pundits, who said: "John Lennon was . . . " and I'd really said nothing, the phrase that came to me was "jerk of all jerks". So I ended up writing a poem about it.'

Paul was to create an image of King that he included in his exhibitions of paintings, prints and photographs.

For his portrait of Larry King, Paul snapped pictures of King during his interview with him on the *Larry King Live* show, using his wrist-watch camera. The original photographic print was used as one of 28 deliberately grainy shots that appeared on the cover of Paul's *Driving Rain* album, released in November 2001.

Paul then turned the image into a portrait in its own right by enlarging the print several times and painting a wash of light colour over it.

King's Dock

A site in Liverpool, near to the famed Pier Head and Liver Buildings, where Paul performed a historic concert on Thursday 18 June 1990 as part of his World Tour.

A press release regarding the appearance was issued on 23 May headed: 'Paul McCartney Announces UK "Thank You" Shows'.

It read:

Paul McCartney is going home to Liverpool with his record-breaking world tour – as a personal 'thank you' to the people he says 'are so special to me'.

Paul is to stage the biggest rock show ever seen on Merseyside, taking a massive 240ft-wide, 100ft-high stage to his home town on Thursday 28 June. His 140-minute show will feature 15 Beatles songs and new material especially for Liverpool.

It will be the first time in 11 years that Paul – currently on an all-sold-out, year-long tour – will have played in the city that matters so much to him.

In the same week, Paul will also play in another of his favourite towns, Glasgow, on Saturday 23 June.

'It's all a home-coming for me,' Paul said today.

'There's just certain cities in the world that you try to play because the people there are so special.

'I've travelled everywhere but I've never found anyone to beat the people I grew up with. Obviously, Liverpool means a lot to me and the people there always will do. But we always had a great welcome in towns like Glasgow too.

'It's because of the people, they're working-class people and they are the sort I get off on – they're canny lads and I can relate to 'em.'

Paul had initially planned to play Liverpool and Glasgow earlier in the year, when his World Tour did a record-breaking eleven shows at London's Wembley Arena, but he was unhappy that the only venues available were too small.

'The people from Liverpool and Glasgow really got behind us when I started off in this business with the Beatles. I wanted to say thank you properly to them,' he said.

'We've been taking this show all around the world, playing huge gigs, and yet it looked as if I would have to scale it all down – take out some of the lights and the video screens and special effects – to get in the halls available in Liverpool and Glasgow at the time.

'And that would have been disappointing to me, I didn't want to take this really big gig across America and then do a crummy little show in Liverpool.'

It was Paul who personally found the open-air Liverpool site for the critically-acclaimed show that last month set a new rock and roll attendance record – when Paul played to 180,000 fans at Rio De Janeiro's Maracana Stadium.

He drove around Liverpool and spotted the ideal site for the new show – the arena, King's Dock, Liverpool. The Glasgow gig – at the Arena, Scottish Exhibition Centre, Queen's Dock – is a similar open-air venue. Both shows are supported by TDK.

'Both shows are by the water, which I like. Both shows are by docks, which used to fascinate me as a kid, and both should be a good laff,' he said.

'I'm really looking forward to seeing all those fans again – for me it's Get Back to Glasgow and Let It Be Liverpool.'

Paul last played Liverpool in November 1979, during Wings' last UK tour.

For this new show, the McCartney band will be Linda and Paul, 'Wix' Wickens on keyboards, Robbie McIntosh and Hamish Stuart on guitars and Chris Whitten on drums.

'They're a fairly silly lot and that's one of the attractions of going out on the road with this group, because we have a good time. It's a bit of a party,' said Paul.

McCartney has insisted that the ticket prices be kept to a realistic level and he will be donating money from the shows to local charities.

In Liverpool, profits from the show will go to: Alder Hey Hospital's 75th Birthday Appeal, The Women & Children's Aid Centre, Kids In Need & Distress (KIND), The Netherley Youth Trust, Sunnybank Appeal (The Marie Curie Hospital), the Merseyside Play Action Group (MPAG) and Liverpool Institute for the Performing Arts (LIPA).

In Glasgow, a substantial donation will be shared between: The Yorkhill Children's Trust for sick children, Scottish Women's Aid for battered wives, The Simon Community for the homeless and destitute and Scotcare – a consortium of charities that incorporate helping family conciliation, alcoholics, single parents, marriage guidance and victim support schemes.

'It's just my way of giving a little back,' Paul commented.

There was a press conference backstage at the King's Dock prior to the Liverpool concert, which began at 5.30 p.m.

Mark Featherstone-Witty took the stage to announce the campaign for the Liverpool Institute for Performing Arts and was followed by Vicky Roberts, chairperson of the Finance and Strategy Committee to confirm that the City Council had approved plans to make the Liverpool Institute for Performing Arts a reality.

George Martin then appeared, saying, 'This is where it all began.' He expressed his support for LIPA and said, 'Music, like love, is a human emotion. Paul and the other boys knocked the world sideways back then. Congratulations, Liverpool . . . do it again!'

He then introduced Paul, who began to answer questions from the press.

When asked how he felt being back in Liverpool thirty years on, he replied, 'I'm here often. It's just another visit. But to actually be playing is unbelievable. Great.' When he was asked about the John Lennon memorial concert which had taken place on the King's Dock on 5 May that year, he squirmed slightly, said he sent a video to it 'because John was a mate' but talking of the memorial concert itself he said, 'I think John might not have liked it.'

There were numerous questions about the tour, his family, LIPA and the fact that the Yale Bowl concert was cancelled. Paul said, 'I won't go anyplace where I'm not wanted. Yale University was a choice, but too many people in the city didn't want the noise.'

During the concert, which was attended by 50,000 people, Paul performed a John Lennon medley of 'Strawberry Fields Forever', 'Help!' and 'Give Peace a Chance', the first time he had ever done so and the first time he'd performed a solo Lennon composition in public.

Seventy-five minutes of the concert performance was transmitted on BBC Radio One on 27 October. Film of the concert was included in the documentary 'From Rio To Liverpool' and also in the Disney Channel documentary 'Paul McCartney – Going Home'.

Following the show, Paul hosted a reception backstage at the concert and the 150 guests included George Martin, Mike McCartney and family and various friends, relatives and media personnel.

Kingdome, The

The venue in Seattle, Washington where Wings appeared on Thursday 10 June 1976 before an audience of 67,053 people. This created a world record for a single act. Prior to the show, Paul was filmed during an interview for 'Monday Night Special', a TV show which then aired on Monday 14 June 1976. The Kingdome concert was filmed and part of the performance is included in the 1980 film *Rockshow*. Footage from this concert was also shown on *Good Night America* on Wednesday 28 June 1976 when Geraldo Rivera interviewed Paul; the clips from the Kingdome concert were 'Band On The Run' and 'Yesterday'.

Paul made his final appearance at the Kingdome on Thursday 29 March 1990 when he opened the sixth leg of his World Tour there. He arrived in Seattle on Wednesday 28 March and held a press conference the following day. The Kingdome was demolished on 26 March 2000.

Klein, Allen

An American music entrepreneur and accountant who was president of ABKCO Industries Inc. when he became business manager for John Lennon, Ringo Starr and George Harrison.

The son of a poor Jewish butcher, he was born in Newark, New Jersey on 18 December 1931. He initially entered the show business world as an accountant and was hired by artists such as Bobby Darin. He also became a manager of Sam Cooke, the Shirelles and Bobby Vinton and represented several 'British Invasion' groups such as the Rolling Stones, Herman's Hermits, the Animals and the Dave Clark Five.

Klein had a reputation for playing hardball with record companies and approached artists saying: 'Whaddya want? Money? You got it.'

Klein also arranged a deal in which the Rolling Stones received a $1,250,000 advance against 25 per cent of the wholesale price of their records – 75 cents per album. At the time the Beatles were receiving only 15 per cent in Britain and 17.5 per cent in America. Ironically, this led to Paul's becoming the first member of the Beatles to suggest that Klein should act on their behalf, although nothing came of that original suggestion.

When he read an interview Ray Coleman had conducted with John Lennon saying that Apple was going bust, Klein seized the opportunity, and contacted Apple by transatlantic call to arrange an appointment with John. A meeting was eventually arranged for Klein to meet John and Yoko at the Dorchester Hotel in London.

Ray Coleman was to say: 'When I interviewed John in January 1969, he told me that Apple was "losing £50,000 every week and if it carried on like this we'll be broke in six months." My report that went round the world's media caught the eye of Allen Klein, a New York terrier in pop management who was then encouraged into Apple by Lennon, Harrison and Starr with a brief to sharpen its activities. Paul resisted this and rebuked me for reporting John's loose-tongued admission of Apple's problems.'

The canny Klein had done his homework and at the meeting his knowledge of the Beatles impressed John, who said: 'He knew all about us and our music. I knew right away he was the man for us. I wrote to Sir Joseph Lockwood that night. I said: "Dear Sir Joe: From now on Allen Klein handles all my stuff." '

Describing that first meeting, John said: 'We were both nervous. He was nervous as shit and I was nervous as shit and Yoko was nervous. We met at the Dorchester. We went up to his room and we just went in, you know. He was all alone. He didn't have any of his helpers around, because he didn't want to do anything like that. He was nervous – you could see it in his eyes. When I saw that, I felt better. We talked to him for a few hours, and we decided that night, "He was it!" He knows the lyrics to every fuckin' song you could ever imagine from the twenties on! He not only knew my work, and the lyrics that I had written, but he also understood them, and from way back. He is a very intelligent guy. He told me what was happening with Paul and George and Ringo. He knew every damn thing about us.'

Here is Paul's version of his first meeting with Klein: 'The very first thing that made me suspicious about him was meeting him, because he is a bit of a boy. I thought, OK, and treated it ordinarily. It was nine o'clock, and we had been meeting all day, so I said: "I think I'll go home to Linda," and everybody said: "Oh no, man. How can you be so uncool? We are meeting this great guy and you are going home." I thought: He's a businessman, and you don't do business past nine o'clock at night, do you? The crunch was when we came to discuss percentages. I thought: We are big stars now, and Brian Epstein asked twenty per cent in the beginning. I even argued with him then. I said: "Twenty? I thought that managers only took ten per cent." He said: "No, it's twenty these days." So, I said: "OK, maybe I'm not very modern." But, we were pretty unknown in those days and Klein asked for the same. I said to the others: "He'll do it for five. We are big boys now." Well, I thought we had had a bit of success. So, there would be John, George and Ringo with Klein and there would be me. I would be saying: "Listen, Allen, you said that that was going to happen. Where is it now?" And he would say: "Oh, well, we can't do it today. That was two weeks ago. We could do it then." I think they were using this whole Eastman–Klein bit, and playing me off against the others.'

Yet this is in contrast to another statement he made: 'We called in Klein, which was John's idea. We needed top advice and Klein gave it to us. The people who complain against him are mostly the people who have come off second best in deals with him because he is such a good negotiator.'

John Lennon was to say: 'Paul's criticisms of Allen Klein may reflect his dislike of the man, but I don't think they are fair. Klein is certainly forceful to an extreme but he does get results. He didn't sew discord between us.'

It was the Stones who originally suggested Allen Klein to the Beatles. The London group first met him on 24 August 1965 and within four days he was co-managing the group with Andrew Loog-Oldham. Then they shed Loog-Oldham in September 1967. However, like other creative artists, they had their differences with Klein and on 30 July 1970 they informed him that neither he nor ABKCO Industries Inc., nor any other company, had any authority to negotiate contracts on their behalf in the future.

A person such as Klein, whose prime motivation seemed to be 'money' and 'litigation', didn't appear to be the sort of person to consider the creative or cultural needs of artists, which is why it was so strange that creative artists signed with him, because, in a number of cases, it ended in disaster.

Take the case of the film director Alejandro Jodorowsky. John Lennon saw his film *El Topo* and he was so impressed he contacted Klein to finance Jodorowsky's next film *Holy Mountain*. As a result, Klein acquired the rights to *El Topo* and *Holy Mountain*. This did, indeed, prove disastrous for Jodorowsky, as Klein destroyed the original negatives and prevented the films being shown.

In the 1990s, Jodorowsky issued a statement headed 'Jodorowsky vs. Klein', the text of which read:

Allen Klein insists to prevent my movies from being shown. Now he's trying to bring me into a trial for having shown my movies in some festivals and pirate copies. It would be good that all the people who admire my work demand lifetime jail for Klein, under the charge of cultural murder. Killing a work of art is as monstrous as killing a human being. For 25 years Klein has prohibited the public to see 'El Topo' and 'The Holy Mountain'. He has destroyed the original negatives. It would be necessary to have a worldwide campaign against him and his crimes. Please translate this message in all possible languages and send it to as many people as you can. We will establish the existence of cultural crime against humanity. Allen Klein is a criminal, together with his accomplice lawyers. All of them deserve punishment and prison.

Paul wrote a letter to Klein because he was furious that Phil Spector had added strings, voices and horns to his number 'The Long And Winding Road'. The letter read:

In future no one will be allowed to add to or subtract from a recording of one of my songs without my permission. I had considered orchestrating 'The Long And Winding Road' but decided against it. I therefore want it to be altered to these specifications: 1. Strings, horns, voices and all added noises to be reduced in volume. 2. Vocal and Beatles instrumentation to be brought up in volume. 3. Harp to be removed completely at the end of the song and original piano notes substituted. 4. Don't ever do it again.

Although Paul strongly objected to Allen Klein, he was told that under his contract he would have to let him be his manager. Paul didn't want that and sought advice. He was told that he could sue Klein. 'Great, I'll sue him,' he said. Then he was told that he would also have to sue Apple.

Paul didn't want to do this and it took him two months to make up his mind. Eventually he decided to go ahead.

Paul was to describe Klein as 'nothing more than a trained New York crook'. He was able to point out that on 29 January 1971 in the US District Court, Southern District of New York, Klein was found guilty on ten counts of 'unlawfully failing to make and file returns of Federal income taxes and FICA taxes withheld from employees' wages'.

Paul was to say: 'Klein was not the exclusive reason why the Beatles broke up. We were starting to do our own things before he arrived, but it certainly helped. There were various reasons why we split. I don't think even the four of us know all the reasons, but Klein was one of the major ones.'

Paul's suspicions were vindicated on Saturday 31 March 1973, when John, George and Ringo decided not to renew his contract. Klein then issued a statement on Monday 2 April 1973, saying that his company ABKCO was severing its links with Apple and the three former Beatles. John, George and Ringo finally fired him in November of that year.

It was John Lennon, the one who originally insisted on Klein's taking over the management of the Beatles, who was to make a public statement on Friday 6 April, when he was interviewed by John Fielding for the London Weekend Television programme *Weekend World*.

Fielding asked him: 'Can you tell me what happened with Allen Klein? Why did you and the other two decide finally to get rid of him?'

John replied: 'There are many reasons why we finally gave him the push, although I don't want to go into the details of it. Let's say possibly Paul's suspicions were right – and the time was right.'

In June 1973, the litigious Klein sued Apple. For John, George and Paul actually to rid themselves of Klein they had to pay him a settlement of $4 million.

Paul's suspicions about him were further consolidated when Klein was jailed for two months in May 1979 for tax evasion relating to the income he'd derived from illegal sales of the *Concert For Bangla Desh* album.

Knebworth Festival

A concert that took place on Saturday 30 June 1990. There was an audience of 120,000 at the festival, which was in aid of the Nordoff-Robbins Music Therapy Centre and the Brit School for Performing Arts.

This particular concert was known as the 'Silver Clef Award Winners Show'. The charity had awarded 'silver clef' awards over the years to outstanding performers of British music and it was decided to invite previous winners of the award, including Paul McCartney, Robert Plant, Genesis, Eric Clapton, Elton John and Pink Floyd to appear in order to raise funds for a much needed new centre for the charity. The charity itself provided 'a way of communicating with, developing and enhancing the lives of mentally, physically and autistically handicapped children, through music'.

An album of the event was issued in which Dave Dee, in the liner notes, wrote: 'The concert sold out instantly and it became evident that our target would be exceeded. To gratefully acknowledge the support that Nordoff-Robbins has received from the music industry it was agreed that the proceeds would be shared with a new venture – The Brit School for Performing Arts – currently being established by the British Phonographic Industry Institute.

'And so to the day itself – as host for the concert, I represented Nordoff-Robbins Music Therapy. Onstage, I was overwhelmed by the size, the appreciation and the sheer good humour of the huge audience. Offstage, I was equally impressed by the professionalism and goodwill of the artists and their crews. A magnificent show, a terrific day – one of the best of my life.'

Knebworth: The Album

Album issued by Polydor Records in Britain and America on Monday 6 August 1990 weeks after the original 30 June 1990 festival at Knebworth at which Paul had appeared. The proceeds of the album were donated to the Nordoff-Robbins Music Therapy charity and the Brit School for Performing Arts. Two of the numbers from Paul's live set, 'Coming Up' and 'Hey Jude' were featured on the release, which was a double album, Polydor 843 921-1, a double-cassette, Polydor 843 921-4 and double CD, Polydor 9843 921-2. The concert was also transmitted in Britain on the ITV network on 6 August and included Paul performing four numbers, 'Coming Up', 'Birthday', 'Hey Jude' and 'Can't Buy Me Love'.

Knebworth: The Event (Volume One)

A home video of the Knebworth concert of Saturday 30 June 1990. It was issued in the UK by Castle Video (CMP 6006) on Tuesday 28 August. The video featured Paul performing four numbers, 'Coming Up', 'Birthday', 'Hey Jude' and 'Can't Buy Me Love'. Profits from the sale of the video were shared between the Nordoff-Robbins Music Therapy charity and the Brit School for Performing Arts.

Knight, Ian

A stage designer who specialises in rock shows. Ian designs the complete stage setting for bands, including the scenery, lighting and special effects. His assignments have included shows for the Who, Led Zeppelin and Wings. For the Wings shows he also designed some special backcloths, one featuring a giant-sized copy of a René Magritte painting to illustrate the number 'C Moon' and another the David Hockney painting of a chair which was displayed during the number 'Chair'.

Knighthood

George Martin was honoured with a knighthood when he was named in the New Year's honours list at the end of 1995. Cliff Richard also received a knighthood. Commenting on the fact that he'd been overlooked in the honours list, Paul said, 'All the Beatles are MBEs – Members of the British Empire – except John, who sent his back. It's the lowest honour you can have from Britain. George (Martin) has a higher honour than we have.

'You can't sit around saying, "God, I wish they'd make me a sir." Or, you know, "I wish they'd put me in the Rock And Roll Hall Of Fame." Funnily enough, in his early days, John was very much wondering how he would be remembered. I said, "You're crazy, man. What are you talking about? Number one, you'll be remembered as something fantastic. You'll be out in the cosmos somewhere."'

Paul was 54 years old when it was announced in the Queen's New Year's honours list (there were 1,035 names on the list) on Monday 30 December 1996 that he would receive a knighthood. He was abroad at the time of the announcement, but said, 'It is a fantastic honour, and I am very gratefully receiving it on behalf of all the people of Liverpool and the other Beatles – without whom it would not have been possible.

'So I hope I can be worthy of it. I would also like to thank my wife and kids and wish everyone a Happy New Year.'

On the same honours list, other Liverpool artists were named. Frankie Vaughan, already an OBE, received a CBE, Cilla Black received an OBE and Roger McGough also received an OBE.

Paul's brother Mike commented, 'It is an excellent day and absolutely deserved by all concerned. Our kid told me a while back that this was going to happen, and so did Roger, so I had to swear that I'd keep my mouth shut. Liverpool people have always had loads of talent. They are always there, and always will be.'

When the news of the New Year's honours list was first announced, the caption writers on the British national press had a field day with punny titles and headlines. *The Times* headed it 'A Hard Day's Knight', the *Daily Mirror* titled it 'Dub Me Do – Happy New Yeah Yeah Yeah', the *Daily Express* described Paul as a 'Hard Dazed Knight' and the headline on the *Sun* newspaper was 'YesSirday'

Paul arrived for the ceremony at 10.15 a.m. in a dark-blue chauffeur-driven Mercedes.

The investiture took place at Buckingham Palace at 11.00 a.m. on Tuesday 11 March 1997 and lasted approximately two and a half hours. Linda was too ill to attend and his children, James, Stella and Mary, accompanied Paul. Paul was initially briefed on protocol before entering the Palace ballroom into the presence of Queen Elizabeth II. He knelt in front of the Queen who placed King George VI's sword first on his right shoulder, then the left, dubbing him with the title 'Sir Paul'.

After the ceremony, wearing his black morning suit, he went to the Palace quadrangle to pose for photographs and addressed the gathered reporters, saying, 'Today is fantastic, there is a blue sky and it's springtime. My mum and dad would have been extremely proud – and perhaps they are.

'I would never have dreamed of this day. If we'd had that thought when we started off in Liverpool it would have been laughed at as a complete joke. Proud to be British. A wonderful day. It's a long way from a little terrace in Liverpool.'

He was asked if he'd spoken to any of the other Beatles about it and he said, 'Yep. They make fun of me. They keep ringing me up and calling me "your holiness", but they're having a good time. It seems strange being here without the other three. I keep looking over my shoulder for them.'

Linda was at home in Cavendish Avenue with her daughter Heather and the reporters asked after her health. Paul said, 'She's doing fine, thanks. We drew straws, 'cos we could only get three tickets. So I've got my three youngest kids with me.'

He was asked again about Linda's state of health and said, 'Linda is fine. She's doing very well. I would have loved my whole family to have been here, but as we only had three guest tickets, Linda and Heather decided to stay out of the limelight today.'

Paul left the Palace at 12.45 p.m.

Knite, Hilda

A former midwife at Walton Hospital where Paul was born. She became a midwife in 1936 and retired in 1965.

As a senior midwife at Walton Hospital she helped to deliver both Paul and his brother Mike into the world.

She was to say, 'Paul and Mike's mother was one of my pupils and I trained her to be a midwife. She came back to have her babies at Walton Hospital.

'I used to take most of the ex-staff on my small block. I remember Paul had to be delivered by a doctor because it was a tricky delivery.'

At a celebration at the hospital in 1997, anyone who was born on the same day as Paul was presented with a special certificate.

Knoc-Turn'al

A Los Angeles rapper. In 2002 Paul allowed him to use the Wings track 'Old Siam Sir' on his single 'Musik.' Initially, Paul wasn't going to allow him to use the sample. Knoc said: 'But, when he heard it and realised it was a positive song, he cleared it. So I just explain that to them in the song. I think Paul appreciate that, because he understands that he sacrificed a lot, seeing that he's been here for thirty-five, almost forty years.'

Kramer, Billy J

A singer, born William Ashton in Bootle, Liverpool, who was signed up by Brian Epstein. His original Liverpool band, the Coasters, wouldn't turn professional and as Epstein couldn't convince another Liverpool band, the Remo Four, to back him, he engaged a Manchester outfit, the Dakotas, to be his backing band.

Together with the Dakotas, Kramer recorded four Lennon and McCartney numbers, three of them written by Paul. His first number was the John Lennon composition 'Do You Want To Know A Secret?' which was released in the UK on 26 April 1963 and replaced the Beatles 'From Me To You' at the top of the British charts. The flipside was Paul's composition 'I'll Be On My Way'.

John's 'Bad To Me' was specifically written for Kramer, with another Lennon composition, 'I Call Your Name' on the flipside. His next release was the Paul composition 'I'll Keep You Satisfied'. Paul also penned his next single, 'From A Window', which was released in the UK on 17 July 1964.

Kramer didn't accept everything John and Paul gave him and had originally turned down Paul's 'A World Without Love', which became a chart-topper for Peter and Gordon. One number, mainly written by Paul, which he recorded but never released, was 'One And One Is Two'. Kramer was unhappy with the number and when John Lennon told him, 'Release that and your career is over,' he decided not to release it. The number was then recorded by Mike Shannon & the Strangers, but failed to make any impact on the charts.

When Kramer was searching for another hit he approached Paul and asked him if he had a song for him to record. Paul offered him 'Yesterday', but Billy turned it down, as he didn't think it was suitable for him.

Kreen Akrore

The final track on Paul's solo debut album *McCartney* lasting 4 minutes and 8 seconds. Paul was to comment, 'There was a film on TV about the Kreen-Akrore Indians living in the Brazilian jungle, and how the white man is trying to change their way of life. The next day, after lunch, I did some drumming. The idea behind it was to get the feeling of their hunt. The end of the first section had Linda and I doing animal noises (speeded up) and an arrow sound (done live with bow and arrow – the bow broke), then animals stampeding across a guitar case. We built a fire in the studio but didn't use it (but used the sound of the twigs breaking).'

Paul recorded the song at Morgan Studios, aided by engineer Robin Black.

Kumbh Mela

The world's largest religious gathering. The festival takes place each decade and lasts for 42 days during which devotees wash away their sins at the point where the holy rivers the Ganges and Yamuna converge. The 2001 gathering attracted 30 million people.

Paul and Heather Mills attended the festival, booking into the Tony Maurya Hotel, New Delhi on 9 January 2001 at the invitation of the sitar virtuoso Nishat Khan. It was reported that the couple stayed in their room for most of the visit.

La Luna

Paul travelled to the TVE TV Studios in Barcelona, Spain on Thursday 8 June 1989 to promote the *Flowers In The Dirt* album. He appeared on the *La Luna* programme. He mimed to 'My Brave Face', 'Distractions', 'We Got Married' and 'This One'. He was also interviewed, during which he spoke some Spanish: '*Tres conejos en un arbul tocando et tambor; que si, gue no, que si lo he visto yo.*' The rough translation is: 'Three rabbits in a tree playing the drum; why yes, why no, why yes, I have seen it.' He was to use this Spanish item in the *Liverpool Oratorio*. When the programme was aired, 'Distractions' had been edited out.

Laboriel Jr, Abe

An American session drummer who backed Paul on the *Driving Rain* album and tour. He is the son of the famous jazz bassist Abraham Laboriel.

Lady Madonna

Apart from writing the song, Paul also designed the press advertisements to promote it.

The single was issued in Britain on Parlophone R5675 on 15 March 1968 and was the last Beatles single on that label. It was also the last American single to use the Capitol label.

The flipside was George Harrison's 'The Inner Light'.

While the number topped the charts in Britain it only reached No. 2 in *Cashbox* and *Record World* and No 4 in *Billboard*. There is a brass section of four saxophones, with jazzman Ronnie Scott leading Harry Klein, Bill Povey and Bill Jackson. The track was included on a number of compilations, including *The Beatles 1967–1970*, *Hey Jude* and *The Beatles Box*. A live version of the number is also included on *Wings Over The World*.

At the time of the original release, the Beatles mentioned that the arrangement of the number was based on an old song called 'Bad Penny Blues'.

Paul initially sat at a piano and attempted to write a bluesy boogie-woogie number and it reminded him of Fats Domino.

The song originally began as the Virgin Mary, and then became a working-class woman in Liverpool. Paul mentioned that he was brought up among Catholics and there were a lot of Catholics in Liverpool to whom the Virgin Mary was very important and he considered the number as a tribute to the ordinary working-class woman.

A live version of the number lasting 2 minutes and 31 seconds was recorded live at the concert in Atlanta, Georgia on 1 May 1993 and included on the *Paul Is Live* album.

Lady Madonna
The promotional film was premiered on BBC TV's *All Systems Freeman*.

Laine, Denny
A former member of the Moody Blues who joined Wings in 1971. Paul and Linda first hired drummer Denny Seiwell, who had performed on the *Ram* album. They then asked Denny Laine, who became the fourth member.

Born Brian Frederick Hines in Birmingham on 29 October 1944, he first met Paul when his band Denny & the Diplomats were on the same bill as the Beatles at the Old Hill Plaza, Staffordshire on Friday 5 July 1963. Denny later found fame as a member of the Moody Blues and his vocal rendition of 'Go Now' with the band became a No. 1 hit in Britain. Denny had co-written the number with Bessie Banks.

After leaving the Moodies he tried a few projects, one of which was the Electric String Band, a group of classically trained violinists and cellists. Brian Epstein booked them to appear at the Saville Theatre, but they weren't a success.

In 1967 he wrote and recorded 'Say You Don't Mind', regarded as one of his best recordings, although it wasn't until Colin Blunstone had a hit with it in February 1972 that it was recognised as such. Later Denny joined bands such as Balls, and Ginger Baker's Airforce.

He then went to Spain and spent a year living in a shack and learning to play flamenco guitar.

When he returned to England he began putting together songs for a solo album, but was so broke he was sleeping on a mattress on the floor of his manager's office.

When Paul asked him to join Wings in August 1971, he'd already begun working on the solo album, but he dropped everything to go to

Scotland to rehearse with Wings and to begin recording the band's debut album *Wild Life*. Denny performed 'Go Now' on the Wings World Tour and it's to be found on the triple album *Wings Over America*.

Denny and Paul became close friends, Denny helping in the composition of 'Mull Of Kintyre'.

His solo album *Ahh . . . Laine* didn't prove to be a big seller, but he continued with further solo ventures.

To celebrate the 1976 Buddy Holly Week Denny issued the Holly number 'It's So Easy' as a single. The following year saw the release of his complete album of Holly numbers *Holly Days*.

The tribute album by Paul and Denny was made at Paul's Rude Studios in Scotland. Denny sang lead vocals; Paul produced, played guitar and drums, and provided backing vocals with Linda. The album was issued in 1977. In Britain it was released on EMI 781 (LP) on Friday 6 May and in America on Capitol ST 11588 (LP) on Monday 19 May. The tracks were: 'Heartbeat', 'Moondreams', 'Rave On', 'I'm Gonna Love You Too', 'Fool's Paradise', 'Lonesome Tears', 'It's So Easy', 'Listen To Me', 'Look At Me', 'Take Your Time', 'I'm Looking For Someone to Love'.

With the American release, Capitol issued an interview with Denny:

Q: Whose idea was it to do an album of Buddy Holly songs?

DL: Originally, Linda's father, Lee Eastman, suggested it. It was my idea a long time ago to do something like that because I'd done one solo album just before I joined the band, and instead of this being just my second solo album, I wanted it to be a Buddy Holly album, or a folk album – something a bit different. But it's obviously not me leaving the group to do a solo album. You don't get that feeling about it. It was Lee's original idea, but as I say, it's always been in the back of my mind anyway. He just sparked it off.

Q: Why Holly?

DL: Because I like his stuff. We were playing it back in the good old days. It was the first stuff I listened to.

Q: How did you go about choosing the songs that you would do on the album?

DL: Well, the ones I liked, really. Also, the more obscure ones like 'Mood Dreams'. These are the songs that Paul had anyway, 'cause he's got Buddy Holly songs, a lot of them. So it was half to do with what they've got in the catalogue and half picking out the best ones.

Q: With great respect, do you not think some of the more cynical journalists would question your motives, knowing that Paul has the publishing of the Holly catalogue?

DL: I'm sure they will. I mean, I could say that I did a Buddy Holly album because we've got the copyright, but that's ridiculous. I wouldn't do it if I didn't like his stuff. It's as simple as that, so they can say what they like.

Q: Do you consider this a solo Denny Laine album or a tribute to Buddy Holly by Denny Laine?

DL: It's a tribute to Buddy Holly really, because I got to know Norman Petty, who wrote most of the songs anyway. I got very friendly with the guy, you know. It was like I'd known him for years. He was one of those sort of guys. So that's what it turned out to be, a tribute. Originally, it was that I liked Buddy Holly songs. I wanted a package album, wanted to do a set album of a certain thing, not just all separate songs like it's away from the group. I knew if I did a solo album it would be, first of all, in holiday time, so I didn't fancy it. I'm busy enough, but I thought it would be a fun sort of thing if I did it at home. This is how this Holly thing was. It was just done in Scotland in a little shack, a place called Rude Studios.

Q: Why did you choose to do it in that form rather than going into a studio with the musicians?

DL: Because we were fed up with going into a studio. That's all we ever do. We always do it normally, twenty-four track. This is just a little four-track studio. Well, it wasn't a studio, it was a shack which we hired stuff for and gave it a name.

Q: And it was only yourself, Paul and Linda who were actually involved?

DL: Yes. Paul did the backing tracks, ninety per cent of them, and then I just did my ten per cent – little guitar bits and vocals, etc., with Linda on harmonies.

Q: Were you in Scotland at the time?

DL: Yes. It was a holiday idea to just do it rough and ready. It is probably the same environment that all groups start out with. As I said, we just had enough time to mess around in a regular studio anyway, but I didn't particularly want to do it that way, purely because of boredom, I suppose, or change.

Q: How long did it take?

DL: It took about three weeks, I suppose. It was certainly no longer. Paul laid down all the backing tracks before I went in to do the vocals. In the morning he would be working on the backing track and I would go over in the afternoon and help him finish them off and then do the vocals. Then we added more to the tracks in a bigger studio to make them a little more professional, stuff like strings, etc.

Q: What about that decision?

DL: We tried it on one track. It sounded good, so we did it with most of them.

Q: How is it working with McCartney as the producer?

DL: Well, I've worked with him for a long time. As a producer, he produces all the Wings stuff as well, so it was no problem.

Q: Do you think the album will cause a lot of criticism?

DL: Yes, because it's Buddy Holly, because of the hardcore fanatics. But they weren't there doing it. If you get fun out of it, that's it.

Q: When do you think you will start doing another solo album and what sort of project do you envisage?

DL: I envisage it to be probably a folk album or something in that vein. Something like the Buddy Holly things, rough and ready. It'll probably be the same kind of thing, but a different style of music. That's what I want to do, something different – different styles on each album that I put out. But I really don't have any plans.

Q: How did you come to join forces with McCartney originally?

DL: I knew him from the Beatles days. After the Moodies and String Band I was trying to make it again, but not really going out of my way as I was not getting the kind of results that I wanted. I started to make this *Aah Laine* album, but again it wasn't being believed. Let's put it this way, I am the sort of person that, if I'm not believed, I'll be stubborn to the point of being a maniac. It was just a mock-up to prove myself. Anyway, Paul just happened to call me up and it was the weekend that I had just finished some of the mixes from that album. So when he called me up I just said, 'Thank Christ for that. Now I have somebody to work with whom I don't have to explain everything to.' So that was the decider really . . . just one of those things of fate. I think I've some idea of the way Paul feels about things. I know the kind of pressure he's under because I've been through a lot of the same stuff myself. The longer you go on, the tougher it is in a lot of ways. People expect more and more of you. For Paul, having been part of the best rock-'n'-roll band in history . . . it must be very heavy. I admire him so much for the way he handles it and doesn't let it interfere with his music.

Q: It has been a remarkable relationship, to say the least.

DL: No problems. None whatsoever.

Unfortunately, Denny's relationship with Paul was soured by the fiasco of the cancelled Japanese tour and Paul's imprisonment in 1980.

Denny released a single called 'Japanese Tears' which pointed a critical finger at Paul. The flipside was a number he had recorded in 1978 with Steve Holly called 'Guess I'm Only Fooling'. The single was issued in 1980. The British release was on Scratch HS 401 and issued on Friday 2 May and the American on Arista AS 0511 was issued on Monday 5 May.

On Monday 27 April 1981, on the same day as Ringo and Barbara's wedding, Laine announced that he was leaving Wings, citing the absence of touring. The group were supposed to be appearing in concerts but due to the murder of John Lennon, Paul was reluctant to expose himself and Linda in public. Laine was already rehearsing with a new band and said, 'I wanted to go back on the road, but Paul is a studio person.'

Denny was to appear on George Harrison's tribute to John Lennon, 'All Those Years Ago' and also appeared with George on stage at Birmingham's NEC five years later for a 'Heartbeat' charity concert.

In 1982 Denny split up with his wife Jo Jo and moved to Spain for a time. In 1984 he wrote a series of articles for the *Sun* newspaper, ghosted by Dan Slater and called 'The Real Paul McCartney', which were highly critical of Paul.

On 30 October 1985 he released his first album since leaving Wings. 'Hometown Girls' was issued on President PTKS 1080, and among the musicians were two drummers – Zak Starkey, Ringo's son and Steve Holly, former member of Wings.

He was declared bankrupt at the London Bankruptcy Court on Tuesday 16 December 1986, with debts of £76,035. Since quitting Wings in 1981 he'd had no commercial success and had alienated fans with his series of articles knocking Paul and Linda in the *Sun* newspaper.

Although co-author of 'Mull Of Kintyre', he had elected to receive £135,000 for his remaining rights in the song, but the money was swallowed up in his divorce settlement and his company Denny Laine Ltd went into liquidation, leaving Denny penniless.

Denny continues to record, both as a solo artist and in collaboration with other artists.

Laine, Jo Jo

The ex-wife of Denny Laine. Jo Jo first met Denny in Cannes in 1972 when Wings were in the South of France. The couple lived together for a number of years and had two children – a son, Laine, born in Kintyre, then a daughter, Heidi Jo. The couple were married for a brief time but divorced in 1982.

As Denny's 'old lady', Jo Jo spent eight years travelling with him, often in the company of Paul and Linda, and she sold her memoirs to the *Sunday People* newspaper in a series published on 17 April and 1 May 1983. The series was illustrated with some raunchy shots of a bare-breasted Jo Jo, and carried headlines such as 'My Galaxy Of Pop Star Lovers' and 'Lust At First Sight'.

The main bulk of the series, however, concerned the private life of Paul and his family. Jo Jo seemed irked that Linda regarded her as a 'groupie' when she first began to go out with Denny – but she admits in the series that she slept around with a host of pop stars, including Rod Stewart, even during the time she was married to Denny. She complains of the Spartan conditions when they stayed at Paul's farm in Scotland, yet talks of the plush hotels and champagne life she had as the wife of a Wings member. She intimates that Paul was very mean with Denny, yet talks of the mansion Denny bought in Laleham and how Denny's royalties on one album came to £50,000, and on another £100,000. She admits that Denny was treated like one of the family by the McCartneys, but continually refers to the fact that she personally didn't get on well with Linda.

Lane, Carla

A Liverpool-born comedy scriptwriter and animal welfare campaigner. She married in her teens and had two sons. In 1970 the first of her scripts, *The Liver Birds* was accepted for television and a successful series followed. Her other television series have included *Solo*, *Mistress*, *Bread*, *Screaming* and *Luv*.

Carla first met Linda at Chrissie Hynde's house. She became a close friend of Linda's because both were passionately concerned about animal welfare.

Carla asked Paul and Linda if they would appear in an episode of *Bread*. Paul told her, 'You write it, luv. I'll tell you then.' Carla then wrote a scene for Linda and one line for Paul. The episode was screened in October 1988.

In her autobiography *Instead Of Diamonds*, published in 1996, Carla wrote, 'As for Linda she, like me, carries the pain of knowing what happens in laboratories, in slaughterhouses, in dark corners where dehumanised people earn their living, sometimes their kicks, harming and terrifying creatures which ask no more than a little space on this planet.'

During the same year, in June, Carla was to say, 'Paul does so much to help animals that no one knows about. He buys land which he doesn't want or need just to stop hunting. He and Linda are the biggest "animal people" I know. They constantly rescue animals and if I can't take a particular animal for my sanctuary they will always take it. Linda is always being undermined, but she's the kindest, nicest, most humble woman I know.'

Her numbers 'Cow' and 'The White Coated Man' appear on Linda's *Wild Prairie* album.

Carla says, 'It was such a surprise to me that these songs were recorded in the first place. They both started off as poems that I'd written and sent to Linda. I was just passing on my thoughts to another animal lover.

'Out of the blue, I got a call from Linda asking if I'd like to pop over to Paul's recording studio for a chat. They sent a car for me, I arrived and discovered that she and Paul had turned my poems into these beautiful songs.

'I didn't even realise what they had done at first. They began playing this song, I was thinking, "that's a lovely tune" and then I thought, "hang on, those are my words, my poetry, it's been transformed." The next thing I know, Paul's saying, "Come on, our kid, walk up to the mike, you're on, record your verse."'

Language Research Facility

Located in Atlanta, Georgia. Paul spent four hours there on 12 May 2002, performing a jam session for monkeys. Peter Gabriel, the former Genesis singer, had informed Paul about the facility, in which apes were being taught to understand English.

Paul sang 'Eleanor Rigby' and a new composition with the apes and said, 'The fact that they could recognise and understand eight hundred words was pretty astounding and we found ourselves actually communicating with them easily. We played some music. The male ape and I jammed a little and his sister joined in with us. He played keyboards and she played drums. It was wild.'

The jam session was filmed for inclusion in the *Driving USA* DVD set for November 2002 release.

Larry King Show, The

A CNN TV show in which Larry King interviews prominent guests. On Tuesday 12 June 2001, Paul appeared live on the show for one hour. Towards the end of the interview Heather Mills joined him to discuss their anti-landmine campaign.

Paul revealed that his thirty-year relationship with Linda continued to place a strain on Heather. He commented, 'I think she's handled it particularly well. It's obviously not easy when someone's loved someone for thirty years. I think it's different if it was a divorce because you can say, "Ah, the old bird, get rid of her. Come on honey."'

He also talked about death and said he didn't fear it, despite the fact that John Lennon was murdered, an attacker had stabbed George Harrison and Linda had died of cancer. 'I don't worry because the moment the man upstairs wants me, I'm his. I know that,' he said.

'At one point I'm going to die so I don't worry about it. Of course, I try and avoid it! I'm not deeply religious, but I have a spiritual feeling about these things. I know Linda is still around me, in another dimension, but I feel her.'

He also mentioned the poems in his book *Blackbird Singing*, which were about Linda. 'We loved each other. Quite simple. We'd both sown our wild oats before we got together and we were kind of fed up with playing the field.'

He then talked about his new love, Heather. 'I was at an awards ceremony and Heather was giving a speech. I thought, wow, she looks good. It was a looks thing.'

Paul mentioned that he'd recently been to see George Harrison who had been recovering from surgery for throat cancer. 'He's great. He's gorgeous,' he said.

On the subject of Yoko Ono he commented, 'Some people are destined not to become great buddies. It's not that I don't get along with her, it's just that we don't talk to each other.'

He confessed that he couldn't read or write music, that unless he and

John were able to keep the tunes in their head, they were lost for good. 'When we started it was before anything like the tape cassettes. I had to remember it. I can't read or write music. Me and John used to say, if we forget it, then it can't be much good. How can we expect others to remember the music if we can't?'

Heather wouldn't be drawn into questions about her personal life and said, 'I'm here to talk about clearing landmines, not our personal lives.'

See also, **King, Larry.**

Last Resort with Jonathan Ross, The

Paul appeared live on the Channel 4 programme on Friday 27 November 1987 in a 15-minute spot. With Steve Nieve and the Playboys he performed 'Don't Get Around Much Anymore', 'I Saw Her Standing There' and 'Lawdy Miss Clawdy'.

Clips from this performance appeared on a Jonathan Ross compilation programme 'Phew! Rock 'n' Roll' on Sunday 24 April 1988 and also on the German television programme 'Ohme Filter' on Wednesday 30 March and Thursday 31 March 1988.

Last Temptation Of Elvis, The

A charity compilation album on behalf of the Nordoff-Robbins Music Therapy Centre, originally available only in Britain by mail order via the *New Musical Express* from Saturday 24 March 1990. This contained a track by Paul, 'It's Now Or Never', from among the eighteen 'oldies' he recorded in London on Monday 20 July and Tuesday 21 July 1987, with most of the other tracks later being issued on the Russian release *Choba B CCCP*.

The album was released in America in April of that year.

Late Late Breakfast Show, The

A BBC 1 television show, hosted by Noel Edmonds. Paul and Linda made their first live television appearance in ten years when they appeared on the programme on Saturday 29 October 1983.

Edmonds introduced the pair, asked them some questions and then aired the promotional film of 'Say Say Say'.

The decision to arrange for Paul and Linda to do the show was taken following a problem with an original *Top Of The Pops* plan to air the video.

The video featuring Paul and Michael Jackson was due to appear on *Top Of The Pops* the week it was No. 10 in the British charts. Paul felt that the video soundtrack was not quite right and decided to postpone the *Top Of The Pops* appearance until the following week while he adjusted the promotional video soundtrack. It was ready the following week, but the record had slipped to No. 13. As it was the policy of *Top Of The Pops* never to feature a record that was slipping down the charts, it couldn't be shown.

MPL and the BBC had discussions resulting in the arrangement for Paul and Linda to appear on *The Late Late Breakfast Show*, which would also screen the promotional film. It had dropped to No. 14 in the charts, but following the show it leapt to No. 3.

Later With Jools Holland

A late night television music show hosted by Jools Holland and broadcast on BBC 2. Paul recorded four numbers live for the show at the BBC Centre in Wood Lane, London on 2 November 1999 and it was broadcast on 6 November.

The numbers were 'Honey Hush', 'No Other Baby', 'Brown Eyed Handsome Man' and 'Party'.

Paul was backed by the band who'd supported him on *Run Devil Run*: Dave Gilmour and Mick Green on guitars, Pete Wingfield on keyboards, Ian Paice on drums and Chris Hall on accordion.

Lawley, Sue

A popular British television newscaster. She interviewed Paul for BBC's *Nationwide* TV programme (no longer broadcast) at Abbey Road Studios where he had been completing the recording of *Tug Of War* with George Martin, late in 1981. He mentioned that he was working with different musicians on the album rather than with Wings. Sue asked him if Wings had disbanded, but he said they hadn't, that he was keeping it loose and they could be reformed should the need arise. At that moment he wanted a change and the opportunity to work with other people. She mentioned that he hadn't brought out a record for some time and Paul said that he and George were taking their time and not working to a deadline. Asked if John's death had made him think again about his fame, Paul said he had thought about it, but concluded: 'There's nothing you can do.' Sue asked if the murder had altered his lifestyle, and he said he'd continue as he was.

Lazy Dynamite

The second number of a four-number 11-minute 15-second medley that closed the *Red Rose Speedway* album. It was 2 minutes and 48 seconds in length with Paul singing lead vocal and playing piano, bass and Mellotron. Denny Laine was on harmonica and Henry McCullough on electric guitar.

Leaf, A

A classical composition by Paul, which he premiered at the Royal College of Music on Thursday 23 March 1995. EMI's classical division released 'A Leaf' as a CD single and cassette on April 24 1995. The CD was issued on EMI Classics CD LEAF 1 (7243 8 82176 2) and on cassette on TC LEAF 1 (7243 8 82176 4). Although it was credited to Paul, Anya Alexeyev played the piece. The single was divided into seven movements: i) Andante semplice; ii) Poco piu mosso; iii) Allegro ritmico; iv) Andante; v) Allegro (man non tanto); vi) Moderato; vii) Andante semplice.

League Against Cruel Sports, The

An organisation that Paul supports. In July 1991 Paul and Linda paid £100,000 for 80 acres of woodland in Exmoor after an appeal from the league. This parcel of land had been used by the Devon and Somerset Staghounds to hunt deer. Once Paul and Linda had bought the land they announced that stag hunting would no longer be allowed on the land.

As the League Against Cruel Sports owned 135 adjoining acres, they agreed to manage Paul and Linda's land by employing wardens to prevent the hunters using it.

Leave It

A single by Mike McGear from the *McGear* album sessions, with 'Sweet Baby' on the flipside, both sides of which were produced by Paul and feature instrumental work by Wings. Paul wrote 'Leave It' and he co-wrote 'Sweet Baby' with his brother. The single was issued in Britain on Warner Brothers K 16446 on Monday 2 September 1974 and reached No. 36 in the British charts. It was issued in America on Monday 28 October 1974 on Warner Brothers 8037.

Lee, Peggy

A celebrated jazz singer, born Norma Engstrom in Jamestown, North Dakota on 26 May 1920. She had a number of hits in the 1940s and 1950s such as 'Manana', 'Lover' and 'Fever'. Paul had always admired the blonde-haired singer and was inspired by her 1961 hit ''Til There Was You', a song from the musical *The Music Man*, which he performed during early Beatles gigs.

When Paul and Linda were invited to join Peggy Lee for dinner, Paul took along a song he'd written for her as a present. He also produced her recording it in June 1974, recording an album, *Let's Love*, on which there were two versions of the title song. It was issued in America on 1 October 1974 on Atlantic SD 18108 and in Britain on 8 November 1964 on Warner Brothers K50064.

Peggy was to say, 'Paul and Linda McCartney are two people I sincerely like. I remember once when I was playing London I invited them up to the Dorchester for dinner when Paul said to me, "I'm bringing you a song." It was called "Let's Love", and I was very thrilled about it.

'Anyway, when I got back to the United States, he and Linda came over to help record it with me, which was lovely. Later in the studio he played on the song for me and even conducted it; that whole side was all his. Unfortunately, due to an unexpected merger between my label

Atlantic, and Electra Asylum, the tune never quite made it out as a single, but one thing's for sure, that man has loads of class and we had a wonderful time working together.'

Peggy was wrong on that score because the single 'Let's Love' was issued in America on October 7 1974 on Atlantic 3215 and in Britain on October 25 1974 on Warner Brothers K 10527.

Paul also wrote the foreword to the liner notes of the Peggy Lee CD *Rare Gems And Hidden Treasures*, issued in 2001.

Lennon and McCartney Songbook, The

A BBC Light Programme special recorded at Paul's Cavendish Avenue house on Saturday 6 August 1966. Derek Chinnery produced it and Keith Fordyce was the interviewer.

Paul and John discussed fifteen recordings by artists who had covered their work on record, including Ella Fitzgerald, Peggy Lee, the Mamas And Papas and the Band of the Royal Irish Guards. The interview was broadcast on 29 August, Bank Holiday Monday, between 4.30 and 5.30 p.m.

A condensed version of the programme was pressed onto disc and sent to various overseas radio stations, although it had been cut to only thirteen minutes.

Lennon, John

John Winston Lennon was born at Oxford Street Maternity Hospital, Liverpool, at 6.30 p.m. on Wednesday 9 October 1940. Contrary to what has appeared in numerous books, he was not born during an air raid. The raids had ceased by 23 September and didn't resume until 16 October.

At birth he weighed seven and a half pounds and had blonde hair. His 27-year-old mother Julia had been in labour for thirty hours. His father, Alfred (a.k.a. Freddie), was a merchant seaman, currently at sea.

It was Freddie who chose the name John and Julia who chose the middle name Winston.

While Freddie was away on one of his voyages, Julia gave birth to a baby daughter by a Welsh soldier, Taffy Williams. She refused Freddie's attempts at reconciliation and began to live with another man, John Albert Dykins, with whom she had two daughters. Freddie wanted to bring up John himself and pondered emigrating to New Zealand; but, when John was five years old and asked whether he wanted to be with his father or mother, he first chose his father, then changed his mind and opted for his mother – and when he went with his mother she placed him with her sister Mimi Smith for her to rear him and didn't see her son until a number of years later.

When Julia and her new family moved into Blomfield Road, which was not a great distance away from Menlove Avenue, where he lived with his Aunt Mimi, John began to visit her more frequently.

At the time John was a student at Quarry Bank School, where he'd formed a skiffle group called the Quarry Men. A friend, Ivan Vaughan, brought Paul along to see John and his group, which has become a historic moment in music history.

John recalled: 'I had a group, I was the singer, I was the leader. Meeting Paul meant making a decision about having him in the line-up. Was it good to make the group stronger, by bringing in someone better than the ones we had, or to let me be stronger? The decision was to let Paul in and make the group stronger.'

That was John's recollection of meeting Paul for the first time. The occasion was the village fête at St Peter's Church, Woolton, Liverpool on 6 July 1957.

In a message sent to the organisers of the fortieth anniversary of that meeting on 6 July 1997, Paul set out his own memories of that first meeting:

Ah yes, I remember it well.

I do actually. My memory of meeting John for the first time is very clear. My mate Ivan Vaughan took me along to Woolton here and there were the Quarry Men, playing on a little platform. I can still see John now – checked shirt, slightly curly hair, singing 'Come Go With Me' by the Del Vikings. He didn't know all the words, so he was putting in stuff about penitentiaries – and making a good job of it.

I remember thinking, 'He looks good – I wouldn't mind being in a group with him.' A bit later we met up. I played him 'Twenty Flight Rock' and he seemed pretty impressed – maybe because I *did* know the words.

Then, as you all know, he asked me to join the group, and so we began our trip together. We wrote our first songs together, we grew up together and we lived our lives together.

And when we'd do it together, something special would happen. There'd be that little magic spark.

I still remember his beery old breath when I met him here that day. But I soon came to love that beery old breath. And I loved John. I always was and still am a great fan of John's. We had a lot of fun together and I still treasure those beautiful memories.

Paul was also to recall: 'I was impressed with the band and with John's performance. So backstage, later that day in the church hall, I wrote down the words of various songs for John and showed him how I played "Twenty Flight Rock". I sang a couple of other old things.'

He bumped into John's friend Pete Shotton and says: 'Pete saw me cycling one day and shouted that John wanted me to join the band. It was as simple as that. I met them at a Conservative club and I was in. I goofed a big solo, on "Guitar Boogie". I couldn't play at all that night and became awfully embarrassed. This was the reason I was shifted over from lead guitar to rhythm in the group.'

When John was reunited with his mother Julia, she became an influence on his music. He recalled: 'The first tune I ever learned to play was "That'll Be The Day". My mother taught it to me on the banjo, sitting there with endless patience until I managed to work out all the chords. I remember her slowing down the record so that I could scribble out the words.' Julia also bought John his first guitar.

She taught both John and Paul some numbers and Paul recalled: 'Oddly, one of them was "Wedding Bells Are Breaking Up That Old Gang of Mine" while another was definitely "Ramona". Much later, during the Beatle years, John and I attempted to write a few songs with a similar feel, with "Here, There And Everywhere" coming immediately to mind.'

Recalling the origins of the songwriting partnership, John said: 'When we started off, we were uncertain as to exactly where our writing would take us. Paul was a rocker with one eye on Broadway musicals, vaudeville, and shit like that. I, on the other hand, was inspired by Buddy Holly's songwriting and was determined to show I was as capable as any Yank. To me Buddy was the first to click as a singer-songwriter. His music really moved and his lyrics spoke to us kids in a way no one ever bothered before. It was youth speaking to youth. Which was exactly what people said about the Beatles years later.'

In 1980, John recalled: 'Paul and I made a deal when we were fifteen. There was never a legal deal between us, just a deal we made when we decided to write together that we put both our names on it, no matter what.'

Paul was to observe: 'Which didn't mean we wrote everything together. When I first began writing songs I started using a guitar. "I Lost My Little Girl" is a funny little song, a nice song, a corny little song based on three chords: G, G78, and C. Later on we had a piano and I used to bang around on that. I wrote "When I'm Sixty-Four" when I was about sixteen. I was vaguely thinking it might come in handy in a musical comedy or something. I didn't know what kind of career I was going to take.'

In 1960 the group underwent various name changes, settling on the Beatles in August of that year on the eve of their first trip to Hamburg. The group now comprised John, Paul, George, Stuart Sutcliffe and Pete Best. They changed their image, began to wear black leather clothes and developed a dynamic style, which made its impact in Liverpool when they returned in December 1960.

They began to build up a loyal following at the Cavern club and John saw his work in print for the first time when the *Mersey Beat* newspaper was launched on 6 July 1961.

Once Brian Epstein took over the group, he smartened up their image, making them dispense with the black leathers that John loved so much. He was to say: 'In the beginning it was a constant fight between Brian and Paul on one side and me and George on the other. Brian put us in neat suits and shirts and Paul was right behind him. I didn't dig that and I used to try and get George to rebel with me. I'd say to him, "Look, we don't need these fucking suits. Let's chuck them out of the window." My little rebellion was to have my tie loose, with the top button of my shirt undone, but Paul'd always come up and put it straight.'

Their recording manager, George Martin, was to comment on the rivalry between John and Paul. 'The truth is, deep down they were very, very similar indeed. Each had a soft underbelly, each was very much hurt by certain things. John had a very soft side to him. But, you see, each had a bitter turn of phrase and could be quite nasty to the other.

'It was like a tug of war. Imagine two people pulling on a rope, smiling at each other and pulling all the time with all their might. The tension between the two of them made for the bond.'

At another time, Martin commented on Paul: 'He's the sort of Rodgers and Hart of the two. He can turn out excellent potboilers. I don't think he's particularly proud of this. All the time he's trying to do better, especially trying to equal John's talent for words. Meeting John has made him try for deeper lyrics. But for meeting John, I doubt Paul could have written "Eleanor Rigby".

'Paul needs an audience, but John doesn't. John is very lazy, unlike Paul. Without Paul he would often give up. John writes for his own amusement. He would be content to play his tunes to Cyn [Cynthia, his first wife]. Paul likes a public.'

John appeared to be the dominant partner initially, speedily writing 'A Hard Day's Night' on a matchbox cover to beat Paul to the title song of their movie, commenting: 'There was a little competition between Paul and I as to who got the singles. If you notice, in the early days the majority of singles, in the movies and everything, were mine. And then only when I became self-conscious and inhibited did Paul start dominating the group a little too much for my liking.'

Paul had the ability to write songs swiftly and said: 'I've developed a system of how to write "McCartney kind of stuff". I just sit down when I'm in the mood, grab a guitar and I get lucky. I'll hit some chord that interests me, and, in that, there is the opening chords. I've got a gift. If you said, "Do a tune now," I could go off; in five minutes I could guarantee I'd come back with a tune.'

John concurred: 'Paul has a special gift when it comes to making up tunes. I find myself using tunes which already exist and fitting my words to them. I realise I'm pinching an old American hit. With me, I have a theme which gets me started on the poetry side of the thing. Then I have to put a tune to it, but that's the part of the job I enjoy least.'

John married his pregnant art-school sweetheart Cynthia Powell on 28 August 1963, although the marriage was originally hushed up on the orders of Epstein. Cynthia gave birth to a baby boy, Julian, named after John's mother, on 8 April 1963. Their marriage came to an end after John had met Yoko Ono, a Japanese avant-garde artist, on 9 November 1966.

The affair was to change John as a creative artist. Influenced by Yoko, he became involved in a number of bizarre avant-garde films and was to document his romance in an almost obsessive fashion with a Beatles single called 'The Ballad of John and Yoko', the changing of his name to John Ono Lennon and albums such as *Two Virgins* and *Life With The Lions*. In his solo career, his singles appeared with Yoko Ono compositions and performances on the B-sides.

'The Ballad of John and Yoko' was recorded on Monday 14 April 1969 with only John and Paul participating, because Ringo was filming *The Magic Christian* and George was busy recording the Radha Krisha Temple. Paul played bass, drums and piano.

Two Virgins was an experimental album by John and Yoko, the sleeve of which featured the two of them in a full frontal nude pose. John and Yoko had to visit Sir Joseph Lockwood of EMI with the nude photos to ensure that he would allow their use and there wouldn't be any censorship problems. Although he personally didn't like the album or photographs, Paul accompanied the two of them to their meeting.

Sir Joseph thought that the fans would be outraged and the Beatles' reputation would be damaged, but Yoko told him: 'It's art.'

Lockwood said: 'Well, I should find some better bodies to put on the cover than your two. They're not very attractive. Paul McCartney would look better naked than you.'

Later, Sir Joseph was to say: 'Paul McCartney was not in favour of it, I'm sure. He just wanted to prevent me from blowing up with them, which I had no intention of doing.'

The break-up of the Beatles seemed imminent. The other members of the group, and George in particular, resented Yoko, who became omnipresent at their recordings and meetings. Paul was at odds with the other three regarding representation by Allen Klein. Ringo and George had both walked out on the group at one point and the relationship between John and Paul was becoming strained.

Paul would say: 'By the time we made *Abbey Road*, John and I were openly critical of each other's music. I felt he wasn't interested in performing anything he hadn't written himself.'

John was to say: 'We were never really close. We were working so hard and so long, that's all we were ever doing. I thought very highly of him, of course, but ours was the sort of relationship I imagine soldiers develop during wartime. The situation forces them together and they make the most of it.'

There now seemed to be a different sort of rivalry between John and

Paul. Paul married Linda on 12 March 1969 and, as if in response to that, John and Yoko decided to get married a little over a month later. Their wedding took place in Gibraltar on 20 April 1969.

Paul, still adamant that he didn't want Klein to represent him, took his legal advice from Linda's father Lee Eastman, who was amazed to find that Dick James owned half of Northern Songs, and all four Beatles shared only what was left. He advised Paul to buy more shares in Northern Songs himself, saying: 'You should be reaping the rewards of your creativity, not anybody else.'

As a result, Paul began buying up shares in the company, but didn't inform John. He eventually owned 751,000 shares while John owned 644,000. Naturally, John was infuriated when he found out and felt that Paul had betrayed him.

Around the time of the break-up, when Paul released his solo album *McCartney*, John described it as 'rubbish'. The two then sniped at each other in some of their songs. In the *Ram* album they were 'Too Many People' and 'Dear Boy'. Paul said: 'OK, there was a little bit from my point of view, certain little lines, I'd be thinking: Well, this will get him. You do, you know. Christ, you can't avoid it. "Too Many People" – I wrote a little bit in that. He'd been doing a lot of preaching and it got up my nose a bit. It was a little dig at John and Yoko.'

Then John attacked Paul in song with 'How Do You Sleep?' on his *Imagine* album, saying that the only decent thing Paul had written was 'Yesterday'. A feud began in which Paul referred to John as 'a manoeuvring swine' and John called Paul 'Engelbert Humperdinck'.

Paul was upset by the feud. 'I hated it. You can imagine, I sat down and pored over every little paragraph, every little sentence. "Does he really think that of me?" Gradually I started to think: Great, that's not true. I'm not really like Engelbert: I don't just write ballads. And that kept me kind of hanging on, but, at the time, I tell you, it hurt me.'

To repair the damage, Paul wrote a song called 'Dear Friend' on his *Wild Life* album, commenting: 'It was written for John, to John. It was like a letter. With the business pressures of the Beatles breaking up it's like a marriage. One minute you're in love, the next minute you hate each other's guts. It's a pity, because it's very difficult to cut through all that. So you do what we all seemed to do, which was write it in songs. I wrote "Dear Friend" as a kind of peace gesture.'

In 1971 John wrote a six-page letter to Paul and Linda filled with swearwords and grammatical errors. John had been furious about comments made by Linda in a recent interview and in the letter, on Bag Productions notepaper, he wrote:

I hope you realize what shit you and the rest of my kind and unselfish friends laid on Yoko and me since we have been together. Linda, if you don't care what I say, shut up! Let Paul write or whatever.

I know the Beatles are 'quite nice people', I'm one of them. They're also just about as big bastards as anyone else, so get off your high horse.

The letter continued:

They ask me about Paul, and I answer I know some of it gets personal, but whether you believe it or not, I try to answer straight, and the bits they use are obviously the juicy bits. I don't resent your husband. I feel sorry for him.

Addressing Paul, John wrote:

Do you really think most of today's art came about because of the Beatles? I don't think you're that insane, Paul, do you believe that? When you stop believing it you might wake up. Didn't we always say we were part of the movement – not all of it?

Despite the rancour, he signed it, 'Love to you both, from us two'.

The letter was sold for £61,000 at a Los Angeles auction house on Saturday 3 December 1994.

Discussing their relationship with Tom Snyder on the American NBC-TV show *Tomorrow* on 28 April 1975, John said: 'We're very good friends and we'd known each other since we were fifteen, you know, and we'd gotten over all the actual fighting, you know, the real nitty-gritty dirty stuff, which had nothing to do with how popular we were. The same popularity, meaning Paul was always more popular than the rest of us, was going down in the dance halls in Liverpool, so it didn't come as any big surprise, you know. I mean, the kids saw him, the girls would go, "Ooh! Ooh!" right away, so we knew where the score was there, but it was the music that was interesting. It was important. As long as we were going forward and going somewhere, it didn't matter.'

During an interview with David Frost in 1998 Paul discussed John and his reputation for having an abrasive manner. 'In public, his front would come down. I never needed it, because my family in Liverpool were quite comfortable, so I was always comfortable around people. But John always had to fight.

'He had this acerbic wit, so they call it, as a defence mechanism. When we were in private, he had no need of that. I could just as often be the baddie in a situation, and he could be a real soft sweetie, you know. He took everyone by surprise there.'

He also commented: 'It's not that John's home life wasn't happy: it was, in the circumstances – not living with his dad, then his uncle dying, then his mum being run over when she'd come to visit him and his auntie, who was a lovely lady called Mimi. They were more middle-class than any of us other Beatles had ever met. We thought of John as quite posh. Later, the image was, Oh, the Working-Class Hero! Power to The People – which he was, and which he believed. But his upbringing was quite posh compared to us. We'd live in council houses, and they owned their own house. How posh can you get?

'Aunt Mimi used to take the mickey out of me. She'd say, "Your little friend's here, John," and I'd say, "Thank you" – that was me. But she didn't like George at all – she thought John was scraping the bottom of the barrel there, for some reason!'

Paul had attempted to see John after John and Yoko had moved permanently to New York and received a rebuff when he turned up at the Dakota apartment block, where John and Yoko lived, and was told, 'We're not in Liverpool any more. Do you mind calling before you come round next time?'

Paul persevered and was to recall: 'I happened to be on my way to the Caribbean, so passing through New York I rang John up. But there was so much suspicion even though I came bearing the olive branch. I said: "Hey, I'd like to see you." He said: "What for? What do you *really* want?" It was very difficult. Finally he had a great line for me: he said: "You're all pizza and fairy tales." He'd become sort of Americanised by then so the best insult I could think of was to say: "Oh, fuck off, Kojak!" and slam the phone down. That was about the strength of our relationship back then, very, very bitter, and we didn't get over that for a long, long time.

'At the very end we suddenly realised that all we had to do was not mention Apple if we phoned one another. We could talk about the kids, talk about his cats, talk about writing songs. The one paramount thing was not to mention Apple. I remember he once said to me: "Do they play me against you like they play you against me?" Because there were always people in the background pitting us against each other. And I said: "Yeah they do. They sure do."'

Bridges were made and John was to say: 'He visits me every time he's in New York like all the other rock 'n' roll creeps. He comes over and we just sit around and get mildly drunk and reminisce.'

Paul and Linda dropped round to visit John and Yoko at their Dakota apartments on Saturday 24 April 1976. They all watched *Saturday Night Live* on TV together, during which the producer, Lorne Michaels, made a tongue-in-cheek offer for the Beatles to turn up and appear at the programme performing three numbers. Paul and John felt tempted to take a cab to the studio and surprise everyone, including the 22 million viewers of the show, but then decided they were too tired, missing out on what could have been a historic piece of television. The following day Paul decided to visit John again, but was surprised to receive a rejection.

John recalled the incident in his *Playboy* interview: 'That was a period when Paul just kept turning up at our door with a guitar. I would let him in, but finally I said to him, "Please call before you come over. It's not 1956, and turning up at the door isn't the same any more. You know, just give me a ring." That upset him, but I didn't mean it badly. I just meant that I was taking care of a baby all day, and some guy turns up at the door with a guitar.'

John and Paul were never to meet each other again. Yet it was also reported that on that last meeting John patted Paul on the shoulder and said, 'Think about me every now and then, old friend.'

Paul recalled his last telephone conversation with John. 'He was padding around his apartment, feeding the cats. That was very John. He was a great cat lover, like my son. I'm not. I'm a dog person.'

Admitting that John and he had a stormy relationship, Paul said: 'I'd go through it all again and have him slagging me off again just because he was so great; those are all the down moments. There was much more pleasure than has really come out. I had a wonderful time, with one of the world's most talented people.'

The 1970s hadn't been a very productive decade for John and he spent five years being a house-husband for his son Sean, almost as if in atonement for the fact that he'd deserted and ignored his elder son, Julian.

He then began to have the confidence to return to music and recorded the album *Double Fantasy*, although, even here, Yoko insisted on having a number of her tracks on John's album.

Tragically, John was shot to death outside the Dakota building on 8 December 1980.

In Liverpool it was 9 December at the time of John's murder. Paul was quoted as saying: 'It's a drag', which drew criticism. He was to explain: 'When John was killed somebody stuck a microphone at me and said: "What do you think about it?" I said, "It's a dra-a-ag" and meant it with every inch of melancholy I could muster. When you put that in print it says, "McCartney in London today when asked for a comment on his dead friend said, 'It's a drag.' " It seemed a very flippant comment to make.'

He was also to recall: 'I talked to Yoko the day after he was killed and the first thing she said was, "John was really fond of you." The last telephone conversation I had with him we were still the best of mates. He was always a very warm guy, John. His bluff was all on the surface. He used to take his glasses down, those granny glasses, and say, "It's only me." They were like a wall, you know? A shield. Those are the moments I treasure.'

In 1983 Paul said: 'I would not have been as typically human and standoffish as I was if I knew John was going to die. I would have made more of an effort to try and get behind his "mask" and have a better relationship with him.'

Paul discussed John in a series of articles in the *Daily Star* tabloid newspaper in June 1992. He mentioned that John 'wanted me to bore a hole in my head; he had been reading about trepanning, boring holes in the skull, which is supposed to relieve stress.' He also revealed that 'he once wanted to jump off a cliff – and suggested that I should try it as well.'

When Paul emerged publicly as a painter in 2000 he mentioned that John was often the subject of his work, commenting: 'John is a central figure in my life. I will always be grateful for having so much intimate time with him. The more distant his stuff becomes, the greater it seems. I used to do caricatures of John. He was the only person I knew with an aquiline nose. When I painted him recently, I found myself saying: "How did his lips go? I can't remember." Then I would think: "Of course you know, you wrote all those songs facing each other." '

On the anniversary of John's death in 2001 Paul was in Abbey Road Studios recording. He says he was there 'because it's what we always enjoyed best together. It is shocking to think that John was killed twenty years ago. If he were alive, I'd be chuffed to let him know that his album has gone to No. 1 in twenty-eight countries. I know he'd be tickled by that. I'll be thinking of all the great times that we had together, and I'll be remembering him with all the love in my heart.'

In the 100th edition of *Mojo* magazine in 2002 Paul nominated John as his ultimate hero. He said: 'I've got a few heroes, but if I really have to plump for one, well how's about John?'

Lester, Dick

Film director Richard Lester was born in Jenkinstown, Philadelphia in 1932. He moved to Britain in 1955 and was to direct the two Beatles feature films *A Hard Day's Night* and *Help!*

The idea of filming Paul's 1990/91 World Tour was Lester's. He said he wanted to climax his 25-year relationship with Paul by filming his return to the road.

Lester became involved in the tour from the very beginning and made the 11-minute film that began each concert. It was shown on a giant split screen behind the stage and included documentary archive and McCartney home footage of Paul's career from the 1960s until the present day. Intercut with the footage of Paul with the Beatles and Paul and Linda with Wings, Lester included images of significant world events of the previous thirty years.

Lester also developed the theme of balancing Paul's music against images of his times for the film.

He was to say, 'What I most wanted to put on film was the genuine connection between Paul McCartney and his audience, who obviously had such a highly emotional response to him.

'There was such a wonderful sense of exuberance, such good spirit between each member of the band, and between the band and the audience that my primary aim became to convey that.

'I used to say that this had to be a kind of love affair, a love story.

'Paul's audience brings a lot of romantic and nostalgic baggage with it and with the use of 25 years of music, including classic Beatles songs, and the extraordinary newsreel footage that we were able to obtain, we tried to recreate that feeling of romantic nostalgia that hopefully makes the film work well on an emotional, as well as a musical, level.'

On its release, the film was called *Get Back*.

Let 'Em In

The first track on the album *Wings At The Speed Of Sound*, 5 minutes and 10 seconds in length. It was also issued as a single in Britain on Parlophone R6015 on Friday 23 July 1976, where it reached the No. 2 position. The flipside was 'Beware My Love'.

It was also included on the *Wings Greatest* compilation. In America the single was issued on Capitol 4292 on Monday 28 June and reached the No. 3 position. It was performed on the 1975/76 Wings tour and a live version can be heard on *Wings Over America*. Joe English had given the doorbell heard at the beginning of the song to Paul and Linda as a present.

Paul had immortalised his own Aunty Jin in the song by mentioning her in the lyrics, in addition to his 'brother Michael', 'Phil and Don' of the Everly Brothers, 'brother John' Lennon and 'Uncle Ernie', a character Ringo Starr played in *Tommy*, the Who rock opera. Paul had originally composed the number with Ringo in mind.

The single was also issued in Germany on Capitol 1C006-98062, in France on Parlophone 3C006-98062 and in Japan on EMI EPR-20070.

Let It All Fall Down

A single by James Taylor, issued in America on Monday 22 July 1974 on Warner Brothers 8015. Paul provided backing vocal on the track.

Let It Be (album)

The Beatles' final album issued in Britain on PXI on 8 May 1970 as part of a special boxed set which included the book *The Beatles Get Back*. The album sans the book was then released on PCS 7096 on 6 November 1970. It was released in America on AR 34001 on 18 May 1970.

The album had the highest advance orders of any album up to that time – 3,700,000.

Originally, the album title was to be *Get Back*, a reference to the Beatles returning to their roots and producing an album with basic sounds. Initially, a release date of August 1969 had been planned, but there were numerous hours of tapes to edit and the Beatles seemed to lose heart in the project, although they did commission engineer Glyn Jones to edit a 44-minute master tape. Then, Allen Klein intervened and brought Phil Spector on board. This pleased John, George and Ringo but dismayed Paul.

The album tracks were – Side One: 'Two Of Us', 'Across The

Universe', 'I, Me, Mine', 'Dig It', 'Let It Be' and 'Maggie May'; and, Side Two: 'I've Got A Feeling', 'One After 909', 'The Long And Winding Road', 'For You Blue' and 'Get Back'.

Let It Be (song)

A song that Paul dedicated to his late mother, actually mentioning her by name in the lyric, and on which he took lead vocals. It was released as a single in Britain on Apple R5833 on 6 March 1970 and went to No. 1, and in America on Apple 2764 on 11 March 1970, also reaching No. 1. The version on the eponymous album (released in May 1970), mixed by Phil Spector, was a contributing factor in the group's eventual split.

A version of this number lasting 3 minutes and 54 seconds was included on the *Tripping The Live Fantastic* album. It was recorded live at the Joe Robbie Stadium, Miami, Florida on 14 April 1990 during the 1989/90 World Tour.

Let Me Roll It

A Wings number, 4 minutes and 47 seconds in length, which was included on the album *Band On The Run*, issued in December 1973.

Paul was to comment, 'I wrote that up in Scotland one day. It was a nice day. I was just sitting outside, plonking my guitar and I got this idea for a song. We took it off to Lagos and put down a backing track with Linda playing organ, me playing drums and Denny playing guitar. Then we overdubbed the big guitars you can hear right the way through it, going through a PA amp, not a guitar amp, but a vocal amp, which was a big powerful amp.'

In an interview with Timothy White for the 17 March 2001 issue of *Billboard* magazine, Paul commented that the number 'was a riff, originally, a great riff to play, and whenever we played it live, it goes down great. We'd play it on two guitars, and people saw it later as a kind of John pastiche, as Lennon-ish, Lennon-esque. Which I don't mind. That could have been a Beatles song. Me and John would have sung that good.'

A live version of the number, lasting 4 minutes and 12 seconds, which was recorded in Boulder Colorado on 6 May 1993, appears on *Paul Is Live* and it was covered as a B-side by Grapes Of Wrath.

Letter To Paul

A novelty disc by Arlen Sanders issued in America on Faro 616 in 1964 with 'Hopped Up Mustang' on the flip.

Letting Go

A Wings single that was issued in Britain on Capitol R6008 on Friday 5 September 1975 where it reached No. 41 in the charts. It was issued in America on Capitol 4145 on Monday 29 September 1975 where it reached No. 39 in the charts.

'You Gave Me The Answer' was on the flipside.

The single was also issued in Germany on Capitol 1C600-96940 and in France on Capitol 2C006-96940.

Life

A major American news magazine that, in June 1967, featured an interview with Paul that caused a controversy on both sides of the Atlantic. They asked him whether he used the hallucinogenic drug LSD and he admitted he'd taken it. The story was splashed across the national press in Britain and Paul had to make an appearance on a TV news programme in Britain to explain what he'd meant.

Life And Times Of Little Richard, The

Little Richard's biography, penned by Charles White and published by Harmony Books in America in October 1984.

Paul was asked to write the foreword in which he said, 'I have these fantastic memories from a very early age, singing "Tutti Frutti" at school – it was a big rave at the time. The first song I ever sang in public was "Long Tall Sally" in a Butlin's holiday camp talent competition. When the Beatles were first starting, we performed with Richard in Liverpool and Hamburg and we became close friends. Richard is one of the greatest kings of rock 'n' roll. He's a great guy and he's my friend today.'

Light Comes From Within, The

One of Linda's last recordings, which was included on her posthumous *Wide Prairie* album. 'The Light Comes From Within' was the second single to be released from the album, but when it was issued in January 1999, radio and television stations were reluctant to feature it because it contained some swear words. Paul considered that the record was 'universally banned' and took out advertisements in national newspapers complaining about the ban.

Paul wrote: 'PARENTS! We need your guidance. In what age are we living? Is this the nineties or the twenties? Should you decide that your children must not hear this record, we would be grateful for your wisdom and good sense and will put our fingers in our ears whenever we hear it played.

'If, on the other hand, you feel that no harm will come to your children by being exposed to this song, give the guidance so sorely needed and tell them it's OK to do so.'

Radio One disc jockey Chris Moyles commented, 'I feel sorry for Paul, and I was upset when Linda died, but these are stupid lyrics and we can't play it for that reason alone.'

Like Dreamers Do

A song Paul originally wrote in 1960. It became part of the Beatles repertoire and they continued to perform it until 1962. It was one of

the few original numbers from their repertoire that they performed
during the recording for their Decca audition on 1 January 1962.

In 1964 the Applejacks, a group from Solihull, Birmingham,
recorded it. The single was issued on Decca F11916 on 5 June and
reached No. 20 in the British charts. Interestingly enough, Decca A&R
man Mike Smith recorded their audition session in which the number
was included – and he was also the person who recorded the
Applejacks version of the number.

Limehouse Studios

Studios situated at 128 Wembley Park Drive in Wembley, London
which were formerly used by Redifusion Television for the recording of
TV shows such as *Ready, Steady Go!* Paul had appeared there with the
Beatles and returned to the studios for the first time in twenty years on
Thursday 13 December 1990 to perform at a five-hour session before a
live audience of members of Wings Fun Club for a series of overseas TV
shows, which were later screened in Italy, Denmark, Spain and Japan.
Paul and his band performed three numbers, 'Let It Be', 'The Long And
Winding Road' and 'All My Trials'.

Blair Cunningham had replaced Chris Whitten in the drum seat.

When the Dutch show *Countdown* was broadcast in Holland on
NED 2 TV on Tuesday 18 December it also included an interview with
Paul by Jerone Van Inkel and a promotional video of the number 'Once
Upon A Long Ago'. RAI UNO in Italy also screened the recording on
the programme *Fantastico* on Saturday 22 December, and it was shown
by TVE in Spain on Wednesday 26 December and in Denmark on the
same day. It was also broadcast on the Japanese programme *Beat UK*
on Sunday 20 January 1991.

Paul returned to Limehouse Studios on Friday 25 January 1991 to
once again record before an invited audience. This time it was for the
MTV series *Unplugged*.

Linda

A four-hour CBS Television mini-series starring Elizabeth Mitchell as
Linda and Gary Bakewell as Paul. Mitchell had previously starred in
the television soap *Loving* and the TV movie *Gia*, while Bakewell
featured as Paul in the film *Backbeat* in 1993. The other main characters included George Segal as Lee Eastman, Tim Piper as John Lennon,
Chris Cound as George Harrison and Michael McMurty as Ringo
Starr. Armand Mastroianni directed the biography.

The TV movie began filming in Vancouver, Canada early in 2000
and moved on to Britain. It was based on the biography, *Linda* by
Danny Fields. Paul was not consulted about the film and a spokesman
said, 'Sir Paul can't comment as he has not seen it nor been asked for
any input.'

The series made its debut in America on 21 May 2000.

Linda (song)

Linda's father Lee Eastman represented a number of show business clients, including songwriter Jack Lawrence. In lieu of a bill, Eastman asked Lawrence if he would write a song dedicated to his daughter Linda, who was then six years old. Together with Ann Rochell, Lawrence penned 'Linda'. The number was included in the Robert Mitchum movie *The Story of GI Joe* in 1945 and was recorded by former member of the Benny Goodman Band, Buddy Clark. Perry Como and Charlie Spivak and his Orchestra also recorded versions and it was a hit for Jan and Dean in 1963. The record was covered in Britain by a number of artists, including Jimmy Young, later to become a prominent disc jockey, and Dick James, later to become the Beatles' music publisher.

Paul recorded the song for Linda's 44th birthday in September 1986. He composed and recorded two versions of 'Linda', which he then had pressed as a double-sided single. There was a Latin-style arrangement on one version and a Big Band version, with fifteen session musicians, on the other. Paul had one copy pressed for Linda and it was a record he declared he wasn't going to issue commercially.

The number was played at Linda's memorial service on 8 June 1998.

Linda McCartney Centre, The

A section of the Royal Liverpool Hospital dedicated to cancer research, established after the death of Linda, which raised £4 million in donations. Among the donors was photographer Jorie Gracen, who donated more than 20 of her photographs of Paul and Linda to the hospital.

Prime Minister Tony Blair's wife Cherie Blair QC officially opened the centre on Friday 24 November 2000. Roger James of the Royal Liverpool University Hospital read out a letter from Paul, who couldn't attend, but wrote, 'Fellow Scouser Cherie will do a good job.'

Linda McCartney: Behind The Lens

A one-hour BBC television documentary screened in 1992 covering Linda's career as a photographer. It included interviews with her and Paul, plus friends and associates, and showed a selection of her rock photos of the Beatles, Doors, Stones, Hendrix, Who, Joplin and others.

Lindiana

A number recorded on Saturday 1 December 1984, a day when Paul also recorded 'We Got Married'. 'Lindiana' was originally considered as the flipside of 'Figure Of Eight', but remained unreleased although, like many of Paul's unreleased numbers, it can be found on various bootleg albums.

Listen To What The Man Said (single)

A Wings single recorded in New Orleans in 1975.

It was issued in Britain on Capitol R6006 on Friday 16 May 1975, with 'Love In Song' on the flipside, and reached No. 6 in the charts. It was also the first record to include the MPL logo on the label.

The number was included on *Venus And Mars*.

The same single was issued in the States on Capitol 4091 on Friday 23 May 1975, where it reached No. 1. A live version appears on *Wings Over The World*.

The single was also issued in Germany on 1C006-96638 and in France on Capitol 2C06-96638.

Listen To What The Man Said (tribute album)

This was a tribute album issued on 9 October 2001 by Oglio Records in America. This was one of two Paul McCartney tribute albums issued by the company in a project to raise funds for the Susan G Komen Breast Cancer Foundation, the other album being *Coming Up*, issued on 23 October 2001.

The full title of the album was *Listen To What The Man Said: Popular Artists Pay Tribute To The Music Of Paul McCartney*. The track listing was: 'Band On The Run', Owsley; 'My Brave Face', SR-71; 'Junk', Barenaked Ladies, Steven Page, Kevin Hearn, Stephen Duffy; 'Jet', Semisonic; 'No More Lonely Nights', the Merrymakers; 'Let Me Roll It', Robyn Hitchcock; 'Too Many People', Finn Brothers; 'Dear Friend', The Minus 5; 'Every Night', Matthew Sweet; 'Waterfalls', Sloan; 'Man We Was Lonely', World Party; 'Coming Up', The John Faye Power Trip; 'Maybe I'm Amazed', Virgos; 'Love In Song', Judybats; 'Warm And Beautiful', Linus of Hollywood; 'Ram On', They Might Be Giants.

The Finn Brothers, who recorded 'Too Many People', were Neil and Tim Finn of the band Crowded House. Tim was to comment, 'I fell in love with the Beatles and let them change my world. Falling in love tends to do that, and Paul and Linda's love story was one for our times.'

John Flansburgh of They Might Be Giants, who recorded 'Ram On', was to say, 'It is daunting to try and reinterpret any McCartney song. I was always a huge fan of the first couple of McCartney solo albums because, like the Stevie Wonder albums of the same era, they were great examples of the intensity of home-made recordings. You can hear a lot of the experimentation and discovery right in the tracks, and that makes the recordings a kind of event in themselves.'

Listen To What The Man Says (radio)

A two-hour programme broadcast on Radio One from 10 a.m. on Sunday 22 December 1985. Liverpool disc jockey Janice Long interviewed Paul and excerpts from a number of his records were also played.

Little Bare, A

This is the title Bill Harry gave to a *Mersey Beat* item published in September 1962. This was another excerpt from a letter that Paul had written to him. It recounted the time the Beatles backed a stripper in a club run by Lord Woodbine.

Paul wrote this epistle while the period was still fresh in his memory and referred to the striptease artist as Janice.

Paul's letter read:

John, George, Stu and I used to play at a Strip Club in Upper Parliament Street, backing Janice the Stripper. At the time we wore little lilac jackets ... or purple jackets, or something. Well, we played behind Janice and naturally we looked at her ... the audience looked at her, everybody looked at her, just sort of normal. At the end of the act she would turn round and ... well, we were all young lads, we'd never seen anything like it before, and we all blushed ... four blushing red-faced lads.

Janice brought sheets of music for us to play all her arrangements. She gave us a bit of Beethoven and the Spanish Fire Dance. So in the end we said, 'we can't read music, sorry, but instead of the Spanish Fire Dance we can play the Harry Lime Cha-Cha, which we've arranged ourselves, and instead of Beethoven you can have "Moonglow" or "September Song" – take your pick ... and instead of the "Sabre Dance" we'll give you "Ramrod".' So that's what she got. She seemed quite satisfied anyway ....

The Strip Club wasn't an important chapter in our lives, but it was an interesting one.

Little Eddie

The title of an unfinished song that Paul wrote. The title was the name of one of his dogs and is also known as 'There You Go Eddie'. It has appeared on bootleg albums.

Little Lamb Dragonfly

A track from the 1973 album *Red Rose Speedway*. The song was originally inspired by the death of one of Paul's sheep on the farm. This was actually recorded during the *Ram* sessions and features Hugh McCracken on guitar. Paul had also considered the number as a track for his planned *Rupert* album. Denny Seiwell is said to have aided Paul in composing the number, but went uncredited.

Little Pieces From Big Stars

An exhibition that opened at the Flowers East gallery in Hackney, London on 27 September 1994. Fifty celebrities donated items which were to be auctioned off in aid of the War Child charity which aimed to raise money for an arts and music therapy centre in Sarajevo. Paul's contribution was a piece of wood sculpture entitled *Wood One* while Linda donated one of her photographs. Other stars contributing items included Kate Bush, David Bowie, and U2's the Edge.

When the auction was held at the Royal College of Art on Tuesday 4 October, Paul's sculpture raised £12,500, the highest amount in the auction.

Little Willow

A track on the *Flaming Pie* album which Paul had written as a tribute to Ringo's late ex-wife Maureen. He said, 'I wanted to somehow convey how much I thought of her. For her and her kids.'

He contributed the track to *Diana – A Tribute*, a double-album in honour of Princess Diana, which was issued on 1 December 1997 by V2 records. Other artists who also contributed tracks included Eric Clapton, Bruce Springsteen, U2, George Michael and Queen.

'Little Willow' was penned by Paul and is 2 minutes and 58 seconds in length. Engineers were Geoff Emerick and Jan Jacobs, assisted by Keith Smith. Recording began on 21 November 1995 and Paul was on lead vocal, backing vocals and played bass guitar, acoustic guitar, Spanish guitar, electric guitar, piano, harpsichord, harmonium and provided Mellotron percussion effects. Jeff Lynne provided backing vocal and electric spinet harpsichord.

Recalling that the song was a message to Maureen's children after her death, Paul commented, 'The morning I heard the news I couldn't think of anything else, so I wrote this to convey how much I thought of her. It's certainly heartfelt and I hope it'll help the kids. Instead of writing a letter I wrote a song.'

The promotional video was shot at Lydd Primary School with sixty children appearing it in. The school was presented with £1000 to buy musical instruments.

Little Woman Love

Linda and Paul co-wrote this song. It was issued as the flipside of 'Mary Had a Little Lamb'. Wings performed the number on their British tours in 1973 and 1975 where it was included in a medley with 'C Moon'.

The number had been recorded in New York during the *Ram* sessions and was included on the *Wild Life* album. A stand-up bass sound was provided by Milt 'The Judge' Hinton.

Live Aid Concert, The

One of the most spectacular concerts in the history of popular music, which took place simultaneously on Saturday 13 July 1985 at Wembley Stadium, London and John F Kennedy Stadium, Philadelphia, the two venues linked by satellite.

There was a live audience of 90,000 at the Wembley event.

It was organised by Bob Geldof to raise money for the Ethiopian famine appeal. The concerts were televised throughout the world to over one billion people and raised almost fifty million pounds to help the starving people of Ethiopia.

Paul's name was not included in the first bill presented to the press, but Geldof talked him into appearing, arguing that if Paul were to make an appearance he would be able to arrange for the concert to be beamed to more countries than had originally been planned.

Paul was the closing act at the Wembley concert and took to the stage shortly after ten o'clock in the evening. He sang 'Let It Be', but unfortunately, the sound system was acting up and the vocals of the first half of the song couldn't be heard properly, severely reducing its impact. By the time the mikes were in order, various stars and the entire audience had joined in the big singalong with Paul. This was followed by the rendition of the Band Aid hit 'Do They Know It's Christmas?' in which most of the stars appeared on stage and Paul and Pete Townshend hoisted Geldof onto their shoulders in an emotional finale.

Live And Let Die (song)

A song that Paul wrote for the James Bond movie of the same name, the first to star Roger Moore. This was the eighth Bond movie and, traditionally, it was generally a female vocalist who had sung the theme song over the credits.

Paul had originally been asked to pen the theme for the 1971 Bond film *Diamonds Are Forever*, starring Sean Connery, but it didn't work out.

Paul said he would only compose the number if his version, recorded with Wings, was used in the film.

George Martin played Paul's finished version of the number for producer Harry Saltzmann. Saltzmann thought that the record was a demo and suggested that Thelma Houston should record the number. Martin assured him that the number was a finished production by an ex-Beatle. It was agreed to use Paul's version, although a version by singer Brenda Arnau was introduced at the end of the film.

Paul called on George Martin to help score and produce the song with the George Martin Orchestra supplementing the Wings track. The film producers then asked Martin to compose a score for the entire film.

'Live And Let Die' was included on the movie soundtrack album, issued in Britain on United Artists UAS 28457 on 6 July 1973 and in America on United Artists LA 100-G on 2 July 1973. The American album rose to No. 17 in the charts, but the British album didn't chart at all.

A few days before the soundtrack release, the Wings single had been issued on Apple R5987 on Friday 1 July, reaching No. 9 in the British charts. In America it had been released on Monday 18 June on Apple 1863 and reached No. 2.

The number was nominated for an Oscar and George Martin was awarded a Grammy for his arrangement.

'I Lie Around' was on the flipside. The number had been written by Paul but sung by Denny Laine.

Paul was to comment, 'I liked doing the Bond music. I'm rather like

Bach, really. I mean, he was asked to write especially for a medium. His was the church, mine is the cinema. Very little difference when you come to think about it.'

The single was also issued in Germany on EMI Electrola/Apple 1C600-05365.

A version of this number lasting 3 minutes and 12 seconds was included on the *Tripping The Live Fantastic* album. It was recorded live at the Scandinavium, Gothenburg, Sweden on 28 September 1989 during the 1989/90 World Tour.

Another live version, lasting 3 minutes and 51 seconds, recorded in Boulder, Colorado on 26 May 1993, was included on the *Paul Is Live* album.

Live At The Cavern

A DVD released by Aviva International on IX0384MBXD in June 2001. The release came with a four-page booklet and 14 scenes: 1. Opening Party/'Honey Hush'. 2. 'Blue Jean Bop'. 3. 'Brown Eyed Handsome Man'. 4. 'Fabulous'. 5. 'What It Is.' 6. 'Lonesome Town'. 7. 'Twenty Flight Rock'. 8. 'No Other Baby'. 9. 'Try Not To Cry'. 10. 'Shake A Hand'. 11. 'All Shook Up.' 12. 'I Saw Her Standing There'. 13. 'Party'. 14. End Credits/'Run Devil Run'.

The DVD contained a number of extras: 1. A 17-minute 12-second interview with Paul conducted by Jools Holland. 2. A 21-minute 59-second documentary on the making of the *Run Devil Run* album. 3. The Cavern Club – a basic history and list of the artists who have appeared there. 4. The 'Brown Eyed Handsome Man' promotional film. 5. The 'No Other Baby' promotional film. 6. Biographies of the band members – Dave Gilmour, Ian Paice, Chris Hill, Peter Wingfield and Mick Green. 7. 'Run Devil Run'.

Live In The New World

The title of a full-length live concert by Paul that was televised on primetime American television on Tuesday 15 June 1993. It was filmed at the last gig of Paul's American tour that took place at the Blockbuster Pavilion in Charlotte, North Carolina. The two-hour show was broadcast on the Fox Network television station with simultaneous stereo sound on the Westwood One radio network. Due to the fact that there were advertising breaks on the television, several of the numbers weren't transmitted.

Paul's official sponsor for his tour, Blockbuster Entertainment Corps, presented the extravaganza, which was the first time Paul had performed a full-length concert on television.

Being on network television, it was free to viewers, unlike previous filmed concerts such as the Rolling Stones 'Steel Wheels' tour and Michael Jackson's 1992 TV concert, both of which were screened only on cable channels and had to be paid for.

Paul's manager Richard Ogden commented, 'Paul wanted as many people as possible to have access to this show, which is the biggest rock and roll production of his life. With the support of Blockbuster, we're going prime-time on a network, and you can't get any bigger than that.'

Due to the fact that a number of the songs were edited out due to the amount of commercials on American television, a longer version of the show, including the missing songs and with a remixed sound, was featured on Channel 4 in Britain on Saturday 13 November.

Three of the numbers from the show, 'Robbie's Bit (Thanks Chet)', 'Good Rockin' Tonight' and 'Paperback Writer' appeared on the album *Paul Is Live*.

Live-In World Anti-Heroin Album, The

A charity double album, proceeds of which went to the Phoenix House charity for heroin recovery centres. It was issued in Britain by EMI on AHPLP 1 (LP) and TC-AHPLP 1 (double cassette) on Monday 24 November 1986 and contained thirty tracks. Paul contributed a specially composed song 'Simple As That' which lasted 4 minutes and 15 seconds, which he produced alone following the completion of the *Press To Play* album.

Liverpool Institute

A former High School for boys, situated in Mount Street, Liverpool. It was founded in 1825 as a Mechanics Institute and was officially opened as a school on 15 September 1837.

Charles Dickens lectured there in 1844 and famous pupils have included Sir Charles Lamb, Lord Mersey, Sir Henry Enfield and Sir Macalister of Talbert.

In 1890 one half of the school became an art college and brick walls were built to separate the two buildings internally.

The Institute was changed from a fee-paying school and became a free grammar school in 1944, making it the oldest grammar school in Liverpool.

The school motto was '*Non Nobis Solum, Sed Toti Mundo Nati*', which means, 'Not for ourselves alone but for the whole world were we born'.

Paul entered the Institute from Joseph Williams Primary School when he passed his 11-plus exams.

His brother Michael was also to gain entrance to the 'Innie' and the two used to travel to school by the No. 86 bus. George Harrison also became a pupil of the school and others included Colin Manley and Don Andrew, who formed the Remo Four, Neil Aspinall, who became the Beatles' road manager and MD of Apple, Les Chadwick who joined Gerry & the Pacemakers, Bill Kenwright who became a theatre impresario, Stephen Norris who became a prominent politician and Peter Sissons who became a newscaster.

In September 1957 Paul took two O level exams and passed in Spanish, but failed in Latin. He took six further subjects in order to move up into the Sixth Form in 1958. He passed in five and seemed to have a penchant for languages – apart from Spanish, he also has O levels in German and French.

On his last day at the Innie, Paul stood on his desk and performed 'Good Golly Miss Molly'.

Bertram Parker was the incumbent headmaster of the Liverpool Institute in 1979 when Wings performed a free concert for pupils and faculty of the school at the Royal Court Theatre on 23 November.

Mr Parker had been Paul's geography teacher when he attended the school in the 1950s. Pupils had nicknamed him 'Blip' and during the Royal Court concert, Paul was to announce from the stage: 'Hello "Blip" – nice to see you.'

Jack Edwards, the previous headmaster of Liverpool Institute, died at the White House nursing home in Formby on 8 January 1992. He was 95 years old. His memory was immortalised by Paul in his 'Headmaster's Song' in *Liverpool Oratorio*.

After the school had closed down, Paul became determined to turn it into an internationally recognised 'fame' school, the Liverpool Institute of Performing Arts. At the close of 1994 he was to express his feelings about the project.

'The whole idea of LIPA was first born in my mind a few years back after the inner-city riots that we had in Liverpool. I was at a party and I got talking to this black guy from Toxteth, the area of Liverpool where all the riots were, and he said, 'You know, what Liverpool needs is a 'Fame' school.'

That got me thinking about maybe there was some way in which I could help give something back to my home town. You see, after the riots, various people had suggested to me that I should help the city by taking the kids off the street in some way. But none of these ideas sounded right to me – somebody suggested I should open a car factory but what do I know about making cars? That wouldn't have worked and I'd have just created more unemployment.

But this thing about a 'Fame' school – like the school in the TV series, *Fame* – really did appeal to me. The idea was particularly attractive because my old school, the Liverpool Institute, had been closed down by the City Council in the 1980s and this wonderful building, which was built in 1825, was becoming derelict.

So I figured that if we had this 'Fame' school housed in my old school, at the very least we would be saving this great old building.

Four years ago, just before a gig we did in Liverpool, I announced the plan to build LIPA and we started fund-raising. We needed to raise about £13 million to open the school. I didn't want to get like Paul Getty and just *provide* the school because I figured that if it was going to work, Liverpool had to want it. We all had to work together to achieve this if it was going to be worthwhile.

Anyway, I put in some money to get it going and we got a lot of help from a lot of different people – Eddie Murphy sent us some money, so did Jane Fonda and Ralph Lauren, David Hockney and Chevy Chase, Apple helped us, as did the Queen. I wrote to Buckingham Palace and I got this letter back with a cheque from the Keeper of the Privy Purse.

We also got a lot of money from Grundig and the EC and, what was also heartening, little kids from Liverpool sent us their pocket money.

So, now, we're opening our doors to audition the first students, be they from Liverpool, Long Island or Tokyo or whatever. The great thing about LIPA is that it will be open to all kids from wherever they live in the world.

For me, doing all this is kind of strange because when I was actually *at* this school, I didn't want to be there at all. I was pretty lazy at school and all I really enjoyed was playing round and sagging off to bolt across the road to the cathedral and sunbathe and have a kip on the gravestones there.

When I first went to the Institute, I was living in a working-class area of Liverpool. I'd have to catch a bus to school and all the other kids would call me 'college pudding'. It was just a jibe; anyone who went to a grammar school, a posh school like that, was called a college pudding. So that was me. I'd be off to school and all the kids would be shouting, 'Get off the bus, you,' at me.

I was just like the schoolboys I wrote about in the *Liverpool Oratorio*, overtired, overworked, overhomeworked. I remember scuttling around the bus depot with my mates, collecting cigarette packets that people'd dropped and hoping there would be a couple of ciggies left inside. That was my introduction to the exotic world of smoking.

Anyway, as I said, I was pretty lazy at school and apart from liking a couple of subjects like English and art, I just loved playing around. I just wanted to mess about with my mates. There were a thousand boys at the school then and some nuthouse that was. We used to mess around throwing water bombs ... well, not exactly water bombs. These days you see kids doing that, filling a balloon and throwing them. I hate to tell you what we filled them with, guys.

And now, all these years on, I'm going to go back to the building and now *I'll* teach a lesson or two. Although I'm not quite sure yet how I'm going to do that. I know how I *won't* be doing it, though. When I was at school there were a couple of teachers I liked but the rest were just maniacs with punishment complexes who would whip you and cane you.

I remember this one guy, a big guy, he had a huge sneaker and boy, he used to take it out of your ass! I used to get whacked with that just for something like talking out of line. But I don't believe in all that corporal punishment. I don't think it does you any good. All it does in the end is to get some guys liking to be punished but I've never been into that.

Now it may be that I may teach a class in songwriting but I won't be telling the kids how to do it because I don't know how to do it. I really don't know how to write songs. I can't notate songs. To me, music is something much more magical than simply a series of black dots on a page.

John Lennon and I taught each other when we wrote songs and if I'm teaching a class in songwriting, that's how I'll want to do it with the students. I'll walk in the classroom and say 'Good morning. I don't know how to do this.' Because I think it is part of my skill that I don't know exactly how to write a song and the minute I do know how to do it, I'm finished. Every time I sit down to write a song, it's a new occasion for me and I value that freshness. The minute I know how to do it, it'll get boring.

So, I would want to explain to the students that I don't agree that there is an accepted method of writing a song. I certainly don't want to dictate to them. If I got like some of the teachers who taught me, that would be the end. There's no way I would walk into a class and say, 'Sit down. Take your notebooks out. Write this down: Paul McCartney was a great composer. He was born in Liverpool in 1942,' like dictation. My God, that would be mind-numbing.

The way I would want to do it is to tap *their* talent, and the excitement for me would be if I can learn while they are learning. I'm not particularly interested in my students learning how to write a song in the style of somebody else. I'll tell them that what I'm interested in is the style of *you*.

And, as I say, I don't believe there's an accepted method of teaching songwriting. I'll tell the students that if they want, they can write a song called 'Shit' and I won't have a problem with that. Or they could write a song called 'Love' and I won't have a problem with that. The spectrum will be pretty broad with me and it won't matter how simple their song is. It could be just a couple of words, just a tune three seconds long that they put on a loop to make a song, and then we'll discuss that. Basically, I want to find out what *they* want.

Of course, you can pass on a few tricks. For instance, when I write, I start by getting a chord that I just fancy that day; and then you get a chord structure and you strum for a bit to see what sort of mood you're in and then babble for a bit and then you get the odd word coming out of this babbling and then you're beginning.

But, as I say, I'd want them to do it their way. Now, that may mean that they want to collaborate with a partner. And that's OK with me, too. Well, it would be – when I worked with John, he was such a witty and clever guy that he'd turn you on so much that we wrote all those Beatles songs in an afternoon, none of those songs took more than three hours to write – except, I remember, 'Drive My Car', we really got stuck for a while on that one. We started out writing it about golden rings – 'I can give you golden rings', but that seemed so bad to us so we had another ciggie and another coffee and John was getting all impatient which is good for the creative process, and out of sheer desperation we got into this surreal image of this woman who didn't actually have a car but who wanted a chauffeur. And once we got into that surreal land, we finished it in half an hour.

It's not as easy now to write a song as it was to write with John, nor was it as easy for him to write without me. But then, I don't know of any collaborations that were as good as John and me. I was the one in the room with him and I know how easily it came to us and although I wrote a lot of Beatles songs on my own, like 'Yesterday' and 'Hey Jude', there was always that thought that John was there if I got stuck and we'd be able to find a way to do it.

But I hope that in a lot of ways, collaboration will be what this performing arts school will be all about. What was good about the *Fame* series was the crossover, where the synthesiser player got with the dancer, got with the comedian and they got a show on together.

In the same way, I entertain a little romantic idea that our students at LIPA can do that – but the difference will be that because we'll have all these other courses in the behind-the-scenes side of performing, at our show, the student lighting engineer will be there and the prospective manager will be there, all working on it.

We're not trying to just have a school of stars at LIPA. If you want to go into the performing industries, then there's a lot of other things you can do besides dance or sing or play a guitar. And we want our students to have the opportunity to learn about the others sides of the business.

And there's a lot of other sides to it. For instance, if I take my band on a world tour – as I have been doing over the past five years – then we take about 140 guys with us in the crew. That's 140 guys doing their job to put six of us on stage. And those 140 jobs are all proper, professional jobs and necessary to putting on the gig. So it's an interesting prospect that we may be able to teach our students some of the new skills that you need for these jobs now, like knowing computer skills to run the lighting, because it's not just a matter of pointing a spot any more.

In fact, we are actually going to train roadies at LIPA. Now that makes some of my friends smirk because you've really arrived in the nineties when there are roadies schools. But it's going to be needed; people think of roadies and they may think of *Spinal Tap*, but it's actually a lot more complicated than that now.

As far as the students needing certain qualifications for LIPA goes, we'd like them to have them but John Lennon didn't have any and I only had a smattering that would have only got me to teacher training college. I didn't get music. I didn't pass my music exam. And so I can't sit down and teach someone the violin but I will have certain uses and there will be people at LIPA with degrees in music who can basically balance my insanity.

So, we'll have auditions for the students and what we want to be is flexible. For instance, if someone shows at the auditions that he is a hell of a dancer but has no qualifications, then that will be noted. Similarly, if some girl has got a hell of a voice but hasn't got perfect pitch or can't play an instrument, then that will be noted. What we're essentially looking for is some form of talent.

As I've said, although I'm not in the prospectus, I'll certainly teach a class and I want to get other people who actually *do* it to turn up and tell our students *how* they do it. I've asked Elvis Costello and he's said yes and I want to ask a lot of other friends in the business, not just performers but promoters and directors, too.

And I'm very optimistic about this school. I think there's a lot of interesting talent out there that we can help.

Of course, some may say, 'Do we need another music college?' and that's like saying do we need another baby in the world. The official answer may be no but the real answer is yes.

There may be people who doubt what we're trying to do but a lot of what I've done has been pretty good and I won't let the doubters discourage me. It's too easy to be discouraged. What you've actually got to do is grab ideas like this by the balls and say we're *going* to do it.

In December 1994 Paul even appeared in a television commercial to promote LIPA, dressed in Shakespearian costume, a painter's smock and a school headmaster's mortarboard and gown.

Following a refurbishment costing £12 million and seven years of planning, LIPA opened on 8 January 1996 with the first 200 of a planned 700-student intake. Paul held a special event on 30 January before an audience of special guests, patrons and the world's media in which he related the history of his dream.

There were over 200 fans outside the building that mobbed his car when Paul arrived. His son James, his press agent Geoff Baker and his assistant John Hammell accompanied him.

The inauguration ceremony opened in the Paul McCartney Auditorium when a short film about LIPA was screened, with Paul's 'C'Mon People' on the soundtrack.

Chief Executive Mark Featherstone-Witty was the first to speak and George Martin, who had been one of the main supporters of the LIPA project, followed him.

Martin said, 'I'm absolutely delighted to be here today at the inauguration of the Liverpool Institute for the Performing Arts. I think that it is a marvellous project, and I know that it will do a great deal for Liverpool – and not only Liverpool, but the whole country.

'You know, there has always been a popular misconception about our business, the entertainment business, that it's an easy place to be. I suppose the feeling is, well, a bit of talent, we've all got that, haven't we? A little bit of luck and anybody could be Sean Connery or even Paul McCartney. It's easy stuff.

'But it's not like that at all, it really isn't. It's a lot of hard work. Of course, there's fame and there's glamour and money at the end of it. But it doesn't happen to everybody, and the difficult thing is that it does need a lot of talent, a lot of hard work and a lot of dedication, plus the resilience to take knocks when they come – and plenty come!

'Above all, though, it takes education and experience, and I can't think of a finer place for getting that than this place, LIPA. I think that it is going to do a great deal for the young people of this country, and eventually for the country as a whole, because these young people are going to carry the torch in the future.

'I should add that this business of talent that we should be nurturing is something that I'm lucky enough to have been involved with my whole life. A few years after he was a student at this school, an extraordinary man whose talent turned into genius became a friend of mine and we worked together for many years.

'And it was his inspiration and his generosity that led to LIPA. Of course, I'm talking about Paul McCartney. Together with his mates, he altered the perception of the British performing arts around the world. And he made a breakthrough in the United States that remains today. I should add that as a result of that breakthrough, many billions of pounds of foreign exchange was earned for this country, and our music business continues to be a vital part of British industry.

'So to all of the students who are going to pass through these doors, I'd like to say good luck to you all, in continuing that work, and may you all do well and prosper.'

Paul then took the stage to say, 'I haven't got a speech, you're probably glad to know! But I've got a lot of memories of this place. When I first came here, I sat up there somewhere (pointing to the left side of the stage upstairs). I was aged about eleven in 1953, and I was filled with awe. There were a thousand boys going to this school and I realised that I was going to get quite a special education. And that's what really happened, the school gave me the kind of chance that a boy of my background was not really likely to get.

'So I've got memories, as I say. Just out here was the Headmaster's office (he pointed to a door on his left) – one or two painful memories there!' (He was referring to canings, an action which he mimed.)

He noticed newscaster Peter Sissons, a former pupil, and remarked, 'I'm glad to see one or two mates of mine who went to the school, old boys, back here today.

'On the whole it was fantastic, and looking back at it at this great, venerable age that I am now, it was very, very special. It gave me the idea that I could succeed, and that I could go from a place like Speke, where I was brought up, and go and conquer the world, if you had enough love, enough passion, in what you were going to do, and you were prepared to put in enough hard work.

'Obviously, one of my great feelings now is how proud my mum and dad would have been if they could have been here. But I won't go into that, or I'll start crying. So let's just look to the future, let's say to all these kids and all of the people who come through these doors, from me, from everybody who's supported us, all these wonderful people here – the very best of luck. You will need it, but keep at it. Even though it was a hard day's night, as someone said earlier on, we can work it out.'

A short press conference followed and then Paul and James mingled with the guests. They included Apple's managing director Neil Aspinall, Mike and Rowena McCartney, Gerry Marsden, Joan Armatrading, Ben Elton and Wayne Sleep.

Joan Armatrading had also been quoted in the LIPA souvenir programme, stating, 'I wish I had some training because it would have made life easier, instead of searching all the time. If there had been training, I would definitely have gone for it, in both the guitar and the piano. Understanding contracts is also very important. I signed my first contract but I couldn't tell you any part of what I signed, because the artist is the innocent party at this stage, everyone else has the knowledge and they keep it to themselves.'

Paul had also contributed to the souvenir and was quoted as saying, 'The word that comes to mind when I try to sum up my feeling about LIPA is – PROUD. Jim and Mary, my parents who are unfortunately no longer with us, would have been extremely proud to see this day arrive. Being born in Liverpool, I, myself, was very proud to go to the Liverpool Institute High School for Boys, the original school on this site. And I'm also very proud of the team, led by Mark Featherstone-Witty, who have put in so much hard work to help make this dream come true.

'The Liverpool Institute of Performing Arts – sounds a bit lofty, perhaps, but the idea is that it won't be. As I see it, LIPA is going to help those with talent, in various fields, realise and develop it. LIPA is here to help realise the dreams of many people working in many different areas of study.

'There's more to creativity than being young and having success. I come across so many people who simply love being involved in the arts and entertainment and don't realise the breadth of employment and tasks that exist. They also don't realise that there are many forms of success.

'I like the idea of being involved with a place which opens people's eyes and ears and where skills and experiences can be passed on – lessons which have been learned the hard way. I see LIPA as being that place.

'I'm proud that my old school is now back in use helping the next generations. It's exciting that once again my home town will be the world's target for tomorrow's talent.

'To those who get a place at LIPA, I want to say: good luck, trust your instincts and follow your passion and enjoy yourselves. I feel sure that the students attending this wonderful new school will make us all proud by their efforts and the eventual success I hope many of them will have.'

George and Olivia Harrison were believed to have made a very large financial contribution to the school and other patrons included: Peter Sissons, Wayne Sleep, André Previn, Ronnie Scott, Richard Branson, Lenny Henry, Melvyn Bragg, Dr Jonathan Miller, Paul Scofield, Michael Crawford, Dudley Moore, Judi Dench, Victoria Wood, George Martin, Carly Simon, Vangelis, Mark Knopfler, Toyah Willcox and Glyn Johns.

On Friday 7 June 1996, Her Majesty Queen Elizabeth II officially opened the Liverpool Institute for the Performing Arts. Paul had first announced his dream of such a venue in 1990. Over 2,000 individuals had made private donations to the school, including the Queen.

The Chief Executive was Mark Featherstone-Witty. Paul and Featherstone-Witty showed the Queen around the building and she watched a performance by the Salvations, one of the school's rock bands. The Queen was also taken to a recording studio, saw a 15-strong contemporary dance class and heard a choral recital in the Paul McCartney Auditorium which included Stephen Sondheim show tunes and Paul's 'Blackbird'.

Paul was to say, 'She was very impressed and she was very entertained by all of it.'

The Queen unveiled a plaque commemorating the opening and also signed the visitors' book.

Featherstone-Witty was to comment, 'The motto of Paul's old school – and this, his new school – remains the same: "Not for ourselves alone, but for the whole world were we born".'

Paul was to add, 'This is a very proud day for me. It's exciting that we have saved this fine old building of my school, and that Her Majesty has taken such an interest in our new school. I'm also proud that so many people have helped in so many ways to make this dream come true, and I'm sure that the students will one day make us proud by the eventual success that I hope many of them will find. LIPA has been built to help those with talent realise their dreams. I hope that LIPA will become the finest school of its type in the world and, if it does, it'll be with thanks to all the many people – especially the people of Liverpool – who have helped us work this out.'

Paul also attended the first LIPA graduation ceremony at the school on Tuesday 21 July 1998, accompanied by his daughter Mary and son James, saying, 'This is just one day I couldn't miss.'

After making a speech he shook hands with each student and presented them individually with a special commemorative pin.

Liverpool Lou

A folk song by Domenic Behan. Paul produced the number in June 1974 for his brother Mike's group the Scaffold. It was issued on the Warner Bros label in Britain on K16400 on Friday 24 May 1974. It reached No. 7 in the British charts, but didn't have much luck in America where it was issued on Warner Bros 8001 on Monday 29 July 1974. The flipside of the disc was a number penned jointly by Paul and Linda called 'Ten Years After On Strawberry Jam'.

The number was also included on the Scaffold album *Sold Out*, issued in Britain on Friday 7 February 1975 on Warner Brothers K 56097.

Liverpool Oratorio

Brian Pidgeon, the general manager of the Royal Liverpool Philharmonic commissioned Paul McCartney and Carl Davis to compose *The Liverpool Oratorio*.

When Davis had originally approached Paul to suggest they collaborate on the venture and base it around a character similar to Paul himself, Paul asked what an oratorio was. It is defined as 'a dramatic but unstaged musical composition for soloists, chorus and orchestra, based on a religious theme'.

The work was then given its world premiere at Liverpool's Anglican Cathedral on Friday 28 June 1991 before an audience of 2,500 as part of the Orchestra's 150th anniversary celebrations (although their 150th anniversary actually fell on the previous year).

A second performance took place at the cathedral on Saturday 29 June.

The first performance, which lasted for ninety minutes, was recorded and issued in the UK on 7 October and in the US on 22 October.

A videotape of the performance was also issued in Britain on 28 October, followed by a laser disc version on 9 December (LDB 99 1301 1). A single 'The World You're Coming Into'/'Tres Conejos' was issued only in Britain on 20 September. A second single 'Save The World'/'The

Drinking Song' was released in the US on 12 November and the UK on 18 November.

The television premiere of the performance took place on the PBS network in America on 30 October and in Britain on Channel 4 on 14 December.

The American premiere took place at Carnegie Hall, New York on Monday 18 November 1991. Paul and his family were in the audience. The performers were basically the same as those from the Liverpool Anglican Cathedral debut with the exception of Kiri Te Kanawa who was replaced by Barbara Bonney.

Since its debut, during a period of five years, the Oratorio was performed 99 times in 20 different countries: Eire, Hungary, Sweden, Italy, Germany, Brazil, Spain, Poland, Norway, Slovakia, Japan, the Czech Republic, South Africa, New Zealand, France, Britain, Canada, Finland, Venezuela and in 14 states of America: Colorado, Iowa, Arizona, New York, California, Minnesota, Indiana, Rhode Island, Florida, Wisconsin, Connecticut, Maryland, Michigan and Texas. The one hundredth performance took place at the Philharmonic Hall, Liverpool on Saturday 21 September 1996. Paul was in attendance. The performers were: Carl Davis, conductor; Anne Dawson, soprano; Bernadette Cullen, mezzo soprano; Bonaventura Bottone, tenor; Michael George, bass; the Royal Liverpool Philharmonic Orchestra; the Royal Liverpool Philharmonic Choir and the Liverpool Cathedral Choristers.

Paul and Carl Davis had worked on and off for eighteen months on the work which began with the words 'non nobis solum sed toti mundo nati'. The Liverpool Institute motto, 'Not for ourselves alone but for the whole world we were born'.

It told the story of 'Shanty', born in Liverpool during the Second World War in the middle of an air raid. This was the first movement, called 'War'. At the age of eleven, Shanty sags off school to sunbathe in the graveyard of Liverpool Cathedral. This is the movement called 'School', during which Shanty, his schoolmates and teachers all celebrate the fact that they were born in Liverpool.

The teenager Shanty goes to a church dance in the crypt where he meets Mary Dee, who is to become his wife. He tells her that his father has died. This is the movement called 'Crypt'.

Shanty comes to terms with the loss of his father in the movement called 'Father.' A few years later Shanty marries Mary in the movement called 'Wedding'.

Mary runs an office staffed entirely by women and has a heavy schedule and then discovers she is pregnant in the movement called 'Work'.

A drunken Shanty rows with his wife and says he doubts her love for him. She runs out on him, telling him she is pregnant, and is knocked down by a car and taken to hospital. Shanty prays that she will be saved, saying that he will change his ways if she is.

The Oratorio has a happy ending with Shanty, Mary and their child happily reunited in a movement called 'Peace'.

The *Guardian* newspaper published a critical review of the work, which led to Paul writing in his defence in a letter published in the paper on 4 July.

'Thank you for your review of the *Liverpool Oratorio*. I fear there is some danger of misleading your readers with some of the remarks made by your critic, so I would like to make the following points. He states that the music is "afraid of anything approaching a fast tempo". This is nonsense and a quick perusal of the score will prove my point (Movements 2, 3 and 6 in particular). He goes on to suggest there is "little awareness of the need for recurrent ideas that will bind the work into a whole".

'Having spent two years putting this together I can assure him further study will reveal a plethora of recurrent themes throughout the piece, two examples being the Narrator's theme and "Ghosts Of The Past" which recur often.

'Happily, history shows that many good pieces of music were not liked by the critics of the time so I am content to point out the afore-mentioned errors and let people judge for themselves the merits of the work.'

Liverpool Oratorio (film)

The film of the 28 June Liverpool premiere of Paul's *Liverpool Oratorio* was issued on home video in the UK by PMI on Thursday 28 November 1991. It was also screened in the northwest of England on Granada Television on Tuesday 12 November and nationally on Channel 4 on Saturday 14 December between 8.00 and 9.55 p.m.

Liverpool Sound Collage

A 58-minute CD issued on 21 August 2000 on EMI's Hydra LSC 01.

It was compiled by Paul for Peter Blake as a soundtrack to his exhibition 'About Collage' that ran at the Tate Liverpool until 4 March 2002.

The cover of the CD also features a collage by Paul called 'The World', which contains images of a screaming man, a cow, a corridor, a dog, a murder victim and a photograph of a young girl. The images are combined to form the shape of a cross.

Commenting on both the soundtrack and the collage, Blake said, 'I think both works are very good and complement each other. Paul surprised me with his offer to do something for this show. Although he is a keen painter, he had never done a collage before.'

Titles on the five-track album were: 'Plastic Beetle' by Paul, which included outtakes from Beatles recording sessions from 1965–69, mixed with unheard cuts of Beatles guitar work; 'Peter Blake 2000' by the group Super Furry Animals and the Beatles, a collaboration with the Welsh indie stars who Paul invited to remix the Beatles material;

'Real Gone Dub Made Manifest In The Vortex Of The Eternal Wheel', by Youth, Paul's collaborator on *The Fireman*; 'Made Up' by Paul and the Beatles and 'Free Now' with Paul, the Beatles and Super Furry Animals.

The CD featured recordings made on the streets of Liverpool where Paul interviewed shoppers, chatted with LIPA students and even talked to 'the lady who gets me chips when I'm back in the Pool'.

There were also two promotional discs issued, each featuring the song 'Free Now'. The CD was nominated for a Grammy in the Best Alternative Music category.

Liverpool Suite

A classical collaboration by Paul and Carl Davis. It is basically a distillation of the most melodic and song-like segments of *Paul McCartney's Liverpool Oratorio*. The nine-minute piece incorporates 'School', 'Save The Child', 'Let's Have A Drink!' 'Spanish Dance' and 'Finale' from the Oratorio. Its world premiere took place in December 1992 in Stoke, with a performance by the BBC Philharmonic Orchestra, conducted by Carl Davis. It then made its London debut in St John's Church, Smith Street, SW1 on 11 December and a third performance took place on 16 December 1993 at the Royal Northern College Of Music, Manchester where it was performed by the Northern Choral Orchestra.

London Tonight

An ITV programme focussing on current events in London. When Paul turned up at Waterstone's bookstore in Piccadilly on Wednesday 13 December 2000 to attend a signing session for his new book *Paintings*, he gave a brief interview to Ken Andrew of *London Tonight*, which was broadcast that evening, along with footage of the book-signing.

The interview went:

Ken Andrew: People might not know you've got this string to your bow.

Paul: It's something I've been doing in a closet for about seventeen years.

Ken: The Beatles number *1* is selling like hot cakes.

Paul: Not doing too bad.

Ken: You've got a future in this business.

Paul: I know, I think I'm going to stick with it.

Ken: You're back in the recording studio. What sort of stuff are you doing at the moment?

Paul: Just new music. I did a little thing with an orchestra the other day, some new songs. Enjoying it, that's the main thing.

Ken: And you're still bringing Piccadilly to a standstill after all these years.

Paul: I know. We were round the block there and there's people in Jermyn Street. We said, 'What are you queuing for?' I thought it was a market or something.

London Town (album)

A working title was *Water Wings*, because it had partly been recorded on board a yacht.

The actual work on the album initially began on Monday 7 February 1977 at Abbey Road Studios, where Wings began recording the tracks 'London Town' and 'Deliver Your Children'. The weather in London at the time was cold, windy and dismal and Paul decided they should choose a warm and sunny clime in which to record, so he arranged for Wings to travel to the American Virgin Islands.

He recalled, 'We originally started the recordings here at Abbey Road Studios in London, coming in for the usual album sessions, and it was pouring rain as usual and things were becoming a bit boring. Geoff Emerick, our engineer, had just returned from Hawaii where he'd been working on America's latest album, and he was telling us how beautiful and sunny it had been around those parts. So we got a bit jealous about the weather and I thought maybe we could fix a little excursion and record in a foreign place.'

On Saturday 30 April, a yacht *The Fair Carol* set off from St Thomas, the capital, to Francis Bay on the island of St John, where it awaited the arrival of Wings. The yacht had been equipped with a 24-track recording system, which had been converted by the Record Plant in New York, and was joined by two other vessels, the *Samala* and the *El Toro*.

The *Samala* was a converted British minesweeper which the group were to use for eating and sleeping and the *El Toro* was reserved for the McCartney family.

Later in the year the group returned to Abbey Road to complete the album on Tuesday 25 October on sessions lasting until 14 December.

During November 1977, Paul discussed the making of the album with Chris Welch of *Melody Maker*.

He commented; 'We hired a charter boat that people use for holidays. The captain went spare when he saw all the instruments. We remodelled his boat for him, which he wasn't too keen on.

'We converted his lounge into a studio and we turned another deck into a sound control room, and it was fantastic! We had a recording boat and two others we stayed on. We didn't have any problems with salt water in the machine or sharks attacking us. At night, there was much merriment, leaping from top decks into uncharted waters and stuff. I had a couple too many one night and nearly broke something jumping from one boat to another. But then you always break yourself up on holiday. The studio worked out incredibly well and the very first day we got a track down. There was a nice free feeling. We'd swim in the day and record at night.

'We've come back to Abbey Road here to finish it all off. We're over-dubbing and putting on main vocals.'

To promote the album on its release, Wings held a press reception on a boat sailing from Charing Cross Pier to Tower Bridge and back again on Wednesday 22 March 1978. The album was issued simultaneously in Britain and America on Friday 31 March 1978.

The Capitol Records press release produced a commentary on the individual tracks:

The title track is a mid-tempo number with pensive lyrics talking about ordinary people and everyday life in London.

'Cafe On The Left Bank' is a straight-ahead rocker describing an evening on the town in Paris, and the guitar work on the track is simply ripping.

'I'm Caring' is an acoustic ballad backed with beautifully arranged strings, and it's about someone who is taking gifts of love to a lover after they've been away from each other for a long time.

Paul is the 'Backwards Traveller', a punch rock-'n'-roll number with a retrospective storyline, and after a connecting synthesiser passage, the funky 'Cuff Link' instrumental completes the two-song medley.

'Children Children' is a bright, nicely textured acoustic tune with a bit of Caribbean flavour about children playing hide-and-seek in a forest by a waterfall.

'Girlfriend' is a mid-tempo rocker, and the lyrics are about a girl who belongs to another guy, but not for long. Paul sings the first couple of verses in falsetto, and the instrumental break features some great guitar and synthesiser lines.

Side One closes with 'I've Had Enough', a driving rock-'n'-roll tune that lyrically describes an artist's ultimatum to the tax man, a self-serving manager, or both.

'With A Little Luck' opens Side Two. It's a bouncy pop number that's lyrically an update on the 'We Can Work It Out' theme. Nearly six minutes long, 'With A Little Luck' has a nice classically influenced synthesiser passage before the final chorus.

'Famous Groupies' is a crazy tongue-in-cheek number talking about the real stars of rock – the groupies. Turnabout's fair play, you know.

'Deliver Your Children' is instrumentally a bit of English folk-rock, with acoustic rhythm guitars and an acoustic solo guitar.

'Name And Address' is Wings rockabilly, believe it or not – a really wild track featuring a Sun Records-style echo effect used on Paul's Elvis-flavoured lead vocals. The neo-Medieval tones of 'Don't Let It Bring You Down' follow, it's an acoustic contrast to the previous track. It's about never giving up. Very pretty vocal harmonies on that one.

The album closes with 'Morse Moose And The Grey Goose', a funky rocker with hot and nasty guitar lines and intense lead vocals by Paul as he tells a mystical sea story.

London Town (promotional film)

The promotional film was shot at Twickenham Film Studios on 21 March 1978 with Paul, Linda and Denny Laine and was directed by Michael Lindsay-Hogg. It also included an appearance by Victor Spinetti, who mimed his part.

London Town (single)

The opening track on the *London Town* album, issued in March 1978. The number, which lasted 4 minutes and 10 seconds, was co-written by Paul and Denny Laine.

Paul had originally conceived the number while in Perth, Australia, although it wasn't about London then, as he'd only worked on the opening line. He developed the number in Scotland and London and roughly finished it during a holiday in Mexico. He then had Denny Laine work on it with him for the completed version.

It was also issued as a Wings single in Britain on Parlophone R6021 on Saturday 26 August 1978 and in America on Capitol 4625 on Monday 21 August 1978 – it was Paul's final single for Capitol.

The flipside was 'I'm Carrying'. The title track from the album only reached No. 60 in the British charts and No. 39 in the American.

It was also issued in Germany on EMI Electrola 1C600-61540 and in France on Parlophone 2C008-61540.

Lonely Road

A track from the *Driving Rain* album. It lasts for 3 minutes and 16 seconds. It was written in Goa, India in January 2001 and recorded on 16 February 2001.

Lonely Road (promotional film)

The promotional video for 'Lonely Road' was directed by Jonas Akerlund and featured Paul driving a fiery red Ford Thunderbird convertible. The promotional film was initially screened by VHI on 8 April 2002.

Lonesome Town

A track from the *Run Devil Run* album, lasting 3 minutes and 31 seconds. It was a number originally recorded by Ricky Nelson and was a hit in 1958. Paul's version was produced at Abbey Road Studios on Wednesday 3 March 1999. It featured Paul on lead vocal and bass guitar, Dave Gilmour on electric guitar and backing vocal, Mick Green on electric guitar, Pete Wingfield on piano, Geraint Watkins on piano, Ian Paice on drums and Dave Mattacks on percussion.

On 10 April 1999, at the Linda tribute at the Royal Albert Hall, Paul made an unannounced appearance on stage and performed three numbers, 'Lonesome Town', 'All My Loving' and 'Let It Be'. Commenting on 'Lonesome Town', he said the song was 'one Linda and I used to listen to – I was in Liverpool, she was in New York, we both listened to it in the fifties.'

Long And Winding Road, The

Paul's composition from the *Let It Be* sessions on which he sings lead vocal.

Recordings initially began on Sunday 26 January 1969 and again on Friday 31 January 1969. Further recordings were made in March 1970.

The number was featured in the *Let It Be* film and Paul had OKed this version for release. However, Allen Klein gave the tapes of the recording sessions to Phil Spector for remixing. On 'The Long And Winding Road' track Spector included an orchestra with violins, a harp and female choir.

Paul was to comment, 'I couldn't believe it. I would never have female voices on a Beatles record.'

George Martin was to say, 'It was a very good McCartney song, but when it came back from being handled by Phil Spector, it was laden down with treacle and choirs and the scoring and so on.'

In an interview with Paul Gambacchini in 1973 Paul remarked, 'I'm not struck by the violins and ladies' voices on 'The Long And Winding Road'. I've always put my own strings on. But that's a bit of spilled milk. Nobody minded except me, so I shut up.'

The number was first featured on *Let It Be* and then on the *The Beatles 1967–1970* and the *Love Songs* compilations. Paul performed a new version on the Wings 1975/76 tour, which was included on the *Wings Over America* album and he also re-recorded the number for his *Give My Regards To Broad Street* movie project.

The live version from his tour was issued as a single in Germany on Parlophone 066-2041747 with 'C Moon' on the flip on Friday 4 January 1991.

A version of this number, lasting 4 minutes and 19 seconds, was included on the *Tripping The Live Fantastic* album. It was recorded live at the Maracana Stadium, in Rio de Janeiro, Brazil on 21 April 1990 during the 1989/90 World Tour.

Long Haired Lady

A track from the *Ram* album. Paul had joined together 'Long Haired Lady' with another song 'Love Is Long' to produce the longest track on the album.

Long Tall Sally

The first number Paul ever sang on stage. While holidaying at a Butlin's camp in Wales, Paul and his younger brother Mike were asked up on stage by a cousin-in-law who was a redcoat (an official camp steward). The duo sang the Everly Brothers hit 'Bye Bye Love' and then Paul went solo, singing Little Richard's 'Long Tall Sally', a number which he had already practised singing 'in one of the classrooms at school'.

In issue No. 214 of *Record Collector*, Paul discussed the *Backbeat* film in which they had John singing 'Long Tall Sally'; 'There's revisionism as we speak,' Paul said. 'Yeah, I was really pisssed off when the John character sang "Long Tall Sally". There's no need for that. I sang "Long Tall Sally". There are a million songs that John sang just as well, which they could have given him. But they just didn't bother . . . it was just slack of them, really. It's not too clever, a young kid watching that will think, "Yeah, John did sing 'Long Tall Sally'. Great!" It's a bit of a nuisance . . . they're robbing you of your history.'

Paul performed the number at the Prince's Trust concert on 20 June 1986 and the live recording was issued as a free bonus single, together with 'I Saw Her Standing There' with the *Prince's Trust Tenth Anniversary Birthday Party* album issued by A&M Records on A&M FREE 21 on 24 April 1987. The free single wasn't included with the album when it was issued in America on Monday 11 May 1987, although it was available in Germany on A&M 390 190-7.

The song had originally been penned by Enotris Johnson, Richard Penniman (Little Richard) and Robert Blackwell under the name 'The Thing'. They then changed the title to 'Bald Headed Sally' and finally to 'Long Tall Sally'.

The Beatles recorded it in a single take at Abbey Road Studios on Sunday 1 March 1964.

Looking For Changes

A number penned by Paul and lasting for 2 minutes and 45 seconds that was the second track on the *Off The Ground* album. It was a protest song about Paul's passion for animal rights.

A live version of the number lasting 2 minutes and 41 seconds, which was recorded in Kansas City on 31 May 1993, was included on the *Paul Is Live* album.

Loup (First Indian On The Moon)

An instrumental track on the *Red Rose Speedway* album lasting 4 minutes and 23 seconds. Paul was on bass guitar, Moog and chant, Linda on organ and chant, Denny Laine on electric guitar and chant, Henry McCullough on electric guitar and chant and Denny Seiwell on drums and chant.

Love Comes Tumbling Down

A song written by Paul. The track was co-produced by Paul and Phil Ramone at Paul's home studio in March 1987 and issued with the CD singles of 'Beautiful Night' in December 1997.

Love For You, A

A number that Paul recorded during the *Ram* sessions.

Love In Song

The flipside of 'Listen To What The Man Said' single and a track on the *Venus and Mars* album. This track wasn't recorded during the New Orleans sessions of *Venus And Mars*, but had been recorded at Abbey Road in 1974 with Geoff Emerick as engineer. Paul used the Bill Black stand-up bass he'd acquired on this track – it was the same one used on Elvis Presley's recording of 'Heartbreak Hotel'.

Love In The Open Air

A theme tune for the film *The Family Way* which Paul wrote and passed on to George Martin to embellish, score and record. It was the first piece of music to bear only one name from the Lennon and McCartney songwriting partnership.

The George Martin Orchestra single 'Love In the Open Air'/'Theme From *The Family Way*', was issued in Britain on 23 December 1966 on United Artists UP 1165 and in America on 24 April 1967 on United Artists UA 50148.

In March 1967 Sounds Sensational issued a cover version of the number.

'Love In The Open Air' was voted the year's best instrumental theme at the Ivor Novello Awards in March 1968.

Love Is Strange

A track on the *Wild Life* album. The number was originally written and recorded by Mickey and Sylvia, a husband-and-wife duo and then recorded by the Everly Brothers, who had a hit with it in 1966. There was even a posthumous Buddy Holly version issued in 1969.

Paul and Linda sang it on this track.

They had recently returned from Jamaica and gave the number a reggae flavour.

EMI and Apple wanted to issue a single from the *Wild Life* album with 'Love Is Strange' as the A-side and 'I Am Your Singer' on the flip. The single was even given the catalogue number Apple R 5932, but Paul objected and the idea was dropped. At the last minute he'd decided to rush-release his one and only protest song 'Give Ireland Back To The Irish'.

Love Me Do

The Beatles' first Parlophone single. Paul wrote the main structure of the song in 1958 when he sagged off school; John later helped him a bit with the middle part. An initial version was recorded on 4 September 1962 at Abbey Road. George Martin wasn't too happy with the drum sound and the Beatles hadn't realised that what they could play on the studio floor sounded different in the control room. At that time recording managers used session drummers a lot because, as George Martin admitted, it didn't matter too much about the vocals and guitars, but there had to be a certain drum sound in the studios. This was actually used as an excuse to sack Pete Best, although when they went into the studios on Tuesday 4 September to record the number with Ringo, neither Paul, nor George Martin, nor Ron Richards liked Ringo's drumming and they booked yet another session for Tuesday 11 September, hiring Andy White to play on drums.

When the single was released on Friday 5 October 1962 it was rumoured that Brian Epstein had bought 10,000 copies for his store. This is untrue. Epstein denied this ever took place and it's strange that this silly rumour has continued because a single store buying 10,000 copies of one particular record wouldn't affect its position in the charts because of the system by which the charts were devised in those days – and Brian Epstein, being a record store manager, would have been aware of this at the time.

There were three basic British national charts at the time, one compiled by *Record Retailer*, another by the *New Musical Express* and a third by *Melody Maker*. The single went straight to No. 1 in *Mersey Beat*.

Together with 'PS I Love You' it is the only Beatles number which Paul's MPL company owns the copyright to.

Love Of The Loved

This was one of the earliest of Paul's compositions. It was even included in the repertoire of the Quarry Men skiffle group. The Beatles also performed the number during their Decca Records audition.

At Liverpool's Blue Angel club one night Bill Harry asked John Lennon if he had a song for local singer Beryl Marsden to record. John said that there was a number called 'Love Of The Loved' that would be ideal for her. A few days later he told Harry that Brian Epstein had vetoed him giving the number to Beryl as Epstein wanted to utilise the Lennon and McCartney numbers for his own acts. Epstein gave the song to Cilla Black as her debut record and Paul attended the recording session.

The single was issued on Parlophone R 5065 on Friday 27 September 1963. The highest position it reached was No. 30 on Saturday 19 October 1963, and then it began to drop down the charts. 'Shy Of Love' was on the flip.

Cilla was to say, 'I'd heard the song many times in the Cavern and I was ever so disappointed when I got into the studio and heard this jazzy brass sound. Paul did the same thing with 'It's For You' later on. He sounded great on the demo he gave me and then turned it into a jazz waltz by the time I came to record it. Still, I can't complain because both records were successful for me in the end even if they weren't Number Ones.'

The review in *Disc* read: 'Cilla Black is a young woman with a hard-trumpeting vocal manner that's not unlike the sound of Shirley Bassey at times. It's a song with an urgent strut to it – as if it's in a hurry to reach the best sellers. Which it may.'

Lovely Linda, The

A song dedicated to Paul's wife, and his first love song to her, which was recorded in December 1969. It was the first track on his solo debut album *McCartney*, issued in April 1970. The acoustic number on the album only lasted for 20 seconds, with Paul claiming that it was 'a trailer to the full song, which will be recorded in the future'. The number was reworked and included on the *Working Classical* album.

Lovely Rita

Commenting on his inspiration for this song, Paul has said: 'I was bopping about on a piano in Liverpool when someone told me that in America they call parking meter women meter maids. I thought it was great and it got to be "Rita, Meter Maid" and then "Lovely Rita, Meter Maid", and I was thinking it should be a hate song, but then I thought it would be better to love her and if she was freaky too, like a military man, with a bag on her shoulders. A foot stomper, but nice.'

In Paul's song, the narrator sees Rita filling in parking tickets and notices that she has an almost military look with her cap and bag. He invites her out to tea, and then takes her out to dinner – although Rita ends up paying the bill. He then takes her home, but doesn't quite make it with her as his two sisters are sharing the sofa.

Visually, artists interpret Rita as a very sexy woman. In the David Bailey colour photograph in *The Beatles Illustrated Lyrics*, she is a sluttish figure, smoking a cigarette, her cap askew, face heavily made up and her left hand pulling aside her jacket to reveal an ample cleavage. The Robert Rankin illustration in *Behind the Beatles Songs* depicts her clothed only in a hat and black stockings.

The number was featured on the *Sgt Pepper's Lonely Hearts Club Band* album. Several other artists, including Fats Domino and Roy Wood, have recorded it.

Lovers That Never Were, The

A track on the *Off The Ground* album, lasting 3 minutes and 41 seconds, which was co-penned by Paul and Elvis Costello.

Low Park Farm

A farm that Paul bought in 1970 to add to his Scottish acres and to stop trespassers gaining access to the adjacent High Park Farm.

Low, Mr

A Merseyside journalist, first name unknown, who Paul wrote to in 1959.

The Beatles had met a journalist called Low in a public house and Paul, always conscious of the value of publicity, wrote him a letter about the group, although facts had been altered to make himself seem more colourful.

There is no record of whether Low ever replied, nor any details of which paper he worked for, although it seems likely that it was the *Liverpool Echo* or *Liverpool Daily Post*, neither of which would have entertained the idea of writing about an unknown local rock group.

Paul had still retained notes from his original letter, although there were gaps. Parts of it read:

Dear Mr Low,

I am sorry about the time I have taken to write to you, but I hope I have not left it too late. Here are some details about the group:

It consists of four boys: Paul McCartney (guitar), John Lennon (guitar), Stuart Sutcliffe (bass) and George Harrison (another guitar) and is called the . . .

This line-up may at first seem dull but it must be appreciated that as the boys have above-average instrumental ability they achieve surprisingly varied effects. Their basic beat is off-beat, but this has recently tended to be accompanied by a faint on-beat; thus the overall sound is rather reminiscent of the four in the bar of traditional jazz. This could possibly be put down to the influence of Mr McCartney who led one of the top local jazz bands (Jim Mac's Jazz Band) in the 1920s.

Modern music is, however, the group's delight, and, as if to prove the point, John and Paul have written over fifty tunes, ballads and faster numbers during the last three years. Some of these tunes are purely instrumental (such as 'Looking Glass', 'Catswalk' and 'Winston's Walk') and others were composed with the modern audience in mind (tunes like 'Thinking Of Linking', 'The One After 909', 'Years Roll Along' and 'Keep Looking That Way').

The group also derive a great deal of pleasure from rearranging old favourites ('Ain't She Sweet', 'You Were Meant For Me', 'Home', 'Moonglow', 'You Are My Sunshine' and others).

Now for a few details about the boys themselves. John, who leads the group, attends the College of Art, and, as well as being an accomplished guitarist and banjo player, he is an experienced cartoonist. His many interests include painting, the theatre, poetry, and of course, singing. He is nineteen years old and is a founder member of the group.

Paul is eighteen years old and is reading English literature at Liverpool University. He, like the other boys, plays more than one instrument – his specialities being the piano and drums, plus of course . . .

Lowe, John
A former member of the Quarry Men, nicknamed 'Duff', who was with the group when they recorded their first record 'That'll Be The Day'/'In Spite Of All The Danger' at Percy Philips Studio in Kensington, Liverpool. The group only bought one copy of the disc, which was passed around to each of them and Lowe was the last to receive it. He rediscovered the disc in a drawer and put it up for auction in 1981. Paul took out a High Court writ to ban the sale and was successful. He then paid Lowe an undisclosed sum for the original.

Lucky Spot
The name of an Appaloosa stallion that Paul bought for Linda in 1976. The Appaloosa is a native American steed of the Nez Perce Indian tribe. Wings were touring America and they were in Texas on the way to a gig when Paul and Linda saw the horse grazing by the roadside. They were so struck by the animal that they immediately made enquiries. Paul bought the horse as a surprise for Linda and had the stallion flown to Britain.

Linda said, 'When we were on our farm in Scotland, I looked out of the window one day and there was Lucky Spot.

'Some people could look at him and think he looks like a puppy dog compared to a great thoroughbred, but I say, "I could trade you for any horse in the world, I could trade you for the greatest hunting thoroughbred or whatever – but it's you I want."'

Lulu
British singer born Marie MacDonald McLaughlin Lawrie on 3 November 1948 in Glasgow, Scotland.

Her numerous hits have included 'Shout', 'The Boat That I Row', 'To Sir With Love' and 'The Man Who Sold The World'.

Paul was a guest on Lulu's national lottery show 'Red Alert' on Saturday 13 November 1999. He was promoting his *Run Devil Run* album and was backed by the same team who had backed him on the album, with the exception of Dave Gilmour, who was unable to appear. The house guitarist from the show took his part.

Paul and Lulu sang a duet on 'Brown Eyed Handsome Man' and 'Party' and the band backed Paul on 'No Other Baby'.

Paul was later to team up with Lulu to record a track for her comeback album in 2002 in which she recorded duets with a number of other artists including Cliff Richard, Elton John, Sting, Joe Cocker, Bobby Womack, Samantha Mumba, Westlife, Diana Ross, Gladys

Knight and Marti Pellow. The number she performed with Paul is 'Inside Thing', which runs for 5 minutes and 2 seconds and was produced by Lukas Burton. It's a club-style dance track based on 'Let 'Em In'.

The album *Lulu Together* was released on 20 May 2002 on Mercury 063021 2.

Lulu was also one of Paul's guests when he hosted a party at Cavendish Avenue on Saturday 7 July 2001.

Lunchbox & Odd Sox

A number recorded for the *Venus And Mars* album during the Los Angeles recording sessions in February 1975. It didn't find its way onto that album but was released as a track on the flipside of the 1980 single 'Coming Up'. A second version of 'Coming Up', which had been recorded in Glasgow, had been placed on the flipside and was followed by the 3-minute 47-second 'Lunchbox & Odd Sox'.

Lutton, Davy

A drummer who played on the recording session for Linda's 'Seaside Woman' in France in 1972. Paul, Linda, Denny Laine and Jimmy McCulloch were also on the session. Lutton later auditioned for the drum spot in Wings, but didn't get it.

Lyceum Theater, New York

A theatre in the Broadway district of New York where Paul held a press conference and rehearsals on 24 August 1989.

The conference began at 2.30 p.m. and Paul and the Paul McCartney Band previewed some numbers from their forthcoming tour, performing 'Figure Of Eight', 'This One' and 'Coming Up' before 400 reporters and around 20 camera crews. Following the performance he returned to the stage for a question and answer session which lasted for approximately 40 minutes.

Paul revealed that he had thought of having young bands from each city he visited opening up the concert, but decided against it. He mentioned that he'd asked director Richard Lester to compile a film retrospective of his career that would be shown on large screens prior to his performance. He talked about performing Beatles numbers such as 'Hey Jude' and 'Sgt Pepper', commenting, that what was 'interesting about some of the Beatles stuff was that I'd never actually performed it on stage before, something like 'Sgt Pepper', we only recorded that and we never got to do it with the Beatles 'cause we'd stopped touring at that time. And I didn't realise that when I chose them and then we'd get up on stage and I'd say, "I've never done this one before." So that's nice, because they're fresh for me even though they're older songs.'

Discussing the lawsuit he'd filed against the Beatles to dissolve the partnership and his current relations with the surviving members, he said, 'I think we're settled. Everything's there, ready to be signed, and we finally, after about twenty years, have sorted it all out. So we're hoping to sign that very soon.'

With the tour, Paul had given a forum to Friends Of The Earth to present their views with literature and merchandise at the concerts. A 100-page colour souvenir booklet would be available free of charge and the name 'Friends Of The Earth' would appear on all tickets and merchandise.

He also mentioned that he was looking for a sponsor for the tour, which would cost in the region of $24 million. 'We're really looking around for a sponsor that kind of fits rather than just taking the first one that comes along and says we'll offer you a lot of money,' he said. 'On this tour, we're offering a platform to these people in England called Friends Of The Earth in an effort to make the tour mean something. You know, once we've been round this world, I'd like to kind of get back and think, well, we said a few important things rather than just "drink this product". So it's not that we're against sponsors. I just want to find somebody who we're kind of proud to be associated with rather than just sheer commercialisation.'

Paul discussed merchandising. 'We'll do merchandising and stuff. Because the idea is, if you don't, there'll be people at the gig who will have it and it'll be just cheap, shoddy stuff. So you've kind of got to do it. But the booklet we're giving away is just an idea that was cooked up by my manager when we were planning the tour. It's basically that you're just going to have on everyone's seat a free kind of groovy programme. And in it we can sort of address certain issues, tell them about the band and stuff. We're just going to see if it works. I think it's quite a nice idea, myself. You know, rather than having to buy a $10 programme. There's just one there. It's included in the ticket price.'

He was asked about the possibility of performing in Russia. 'Yeah, I'd like to go to Russia and there's every chance of getting over there, particularly now that we've released the album over there and it did well. We looked into doing dates there, but it's the weather. It really is. It's like Napoleon and Hitler both had the same problem. We opted for Italy instead. It's just warmer! But one of these days we'll get there when they have a warm spell.'

Paul was also asked if he'd have any guest performances during the forthcoming tour. 'It's really down to who shows up. If somebody like Elvis Costello shows up at a gig, or even Elvis Presley . . . no, no, come on, that's a cheap shot. But he's been spotted you know . . . I'll play with anyone who wants to sort of get up and have a bit of fun, but there's no plans for that. That just happens of its own accord. At one point we were thinking of doing some dates with an orchestra. It's something I've never done and I'd quite like to do it, some of the songs would lend themselves to it, but we decided not to do that on this tour. We just may later do one or two special gigs, you know, like Carnegie

Hall with George Martin and orchestra would be good. But we haven't got plans for that. Maybe in the future.'

Regarding the songs he'd picked for the tour repertoire, he said he'd sat down and asked himself: 'What would I like to see him play if I was just somebody coming to the show ... and I wrote a list of about 35 songs that were what I considered to be some of my best songs. And we just chose from that. So, basically, we chose from the rock-'n'-roll period: pre-Beatles, then Beatles period, Wings period and then the new album.'

A 6 p.m. rehearsal concert took place at the theatre with an audience of 800. They included a hundred people who'd been queuing outside the theatre, together with members of the Wings Fun Club. They joined celebrities, radio contest winners and Capital Records personnel. Celebrities included Axl Rose, Raquel Welch, Ralph Laurel and Lorne Michaels.

Paul and his band played 18 songs during an 80-minute rehearsal and the numbers were: 'Figure Of Eight', 'Jet', 'Rough Ride', 'Got To Get You Into My Life', 'Band On The Run', 'We Got Married'. Paul then played acoustic guitar on 'Put It There' and 'Hello Goodbye'. He then played lead guitar on 'Summertime' and shared lead with Robbie McIntosh on 'Can't Buy Me Love'. He played his Hofner bass on 'I Saw Her Standing There', with Hamish Stuart on lead. 'This One', 'My Brave Face' and 'Twenty Flight Rock' followed and then Paul played piano on 'The Long And Winding Road', 'Ain't That A Shame' and 'Let It Be'. During 'Let It Be' he sang 'Julie Andrews comes to me' rather than 'Mother Mary comes to me'. He encored with 'Coming Up'.

Lympne Castle

A medieval castle, which overlooks the English Channel, built near to an old Roman fort in Kent. Paul and Wings recorded tracks for their *Back To The Egg* album at the castle between Tuesday 11 and Thursday 20 September 1979. They recorded 'We're Open Tonight' in the well of an old stone spiral staircase and Steve Holly's drums were situated in the fireplace of the great hall. A number of songs were recorded in the kitchen and Paul performed an acoustic guitar solo at the foot of a spiral staircase.

Other numbers recorded there included 'Love Awake', 'After The Ball' and 'Million Miles'. The castle's owners at the time were Harold and Deirdre Margary who made several literary readings that were also recorded and their voices were mixed in with two group instrumentals, 'Reception' and 'The Broadcast'.

Paul and the band returned to Lympne Castle for further recordings in May 1979.

Lynne, Jeff

A musician/record producer born in Birmingham on 30 December 1947. His first band was Mike Sheridan and the Nightriders, followed by the Idle Race and the Move. In the bands a co-member was Roy Wood, who he teamed up with to form ELO (the Electric Light Orchestra). During the 1980s he began to involve himself more in studio production and produced albums for various artists, a breakthrough coming in 1987 when he was asked to produce George Harrison's comeback album *Cloud Nine*. He also produced albums by artists such as Tom Petty and Roy Orbison and was also a member of the Travelin' Wilburys.

Lynne was asked to produce the new Beatles singles 'Real Love' and 'Free As A Bird'. Later on, this led to Paul McCartney requesting him to work with him on the album *Flaming Pie* and Jeff co-produced eight of the tracks with him. He also produced Paul performing the Buddy Holly number 'Maybe Baby' in Los Angeles in 1999, a number used in the film soundtrack of *Maybe Baby*.

Macca

Nickname by which Paul is known and one which is frequently used in the musical press. He was given the nickname when he attended Liverpool Institute High School.

Madison Square Garden, New York

Wings appeared at Madison Square Garden on Monday 24 May and Tuesday 25 May 1976. The concerts had been announced on the radio and all 40,000 tickets were sold within 24 hours.

The *Daily Mirror* 'Pop Club' had flown a specially chartered plane from Britain with member of Wings Fun Club, who were present at both shows.

Following the Tuesday show there was a special party at the venue, although no press were allowed to attend due to the fact that Jackie Onassis stressed that she would only turn up if no press people were present. She was photographed backstage with Paul and Linda.

Paul gave four concerts at this venue during the final part of the first leg of his American tour, appearing there between 11 and 14 December 1989. All four concerts sold out rapidly, with around 18,000 seats at each concert. There were initially such large queues outside Madison Square Garden that the management decided to put the tickets on sale one hour earlier than announced.

On the Tuesday, Paul held a press conference. He commented, 'Some audiences fall right over. Here last night we had to work a bit harder. I noticed some pinstripe suits with the folded hands saying, "entertain me" and that's all right, we will. I don't read reviews because I always find the worst line. In LA they told me I had to read one because it was so great. And I was reading, and saying, "Uh-huh" and "Oh yeah" and then it said the low point of the show was "Ebony And Ivory". Every night since then I've worked the death out of that song.'

On the Thursday he introduced Linda as Gertrude Macgillicuddy rather than introducing her as Miss Gertrude Higgins. During the Friday night performance, as he put on his Hofner bass to play 'Get Back' he said, 'I picked up this new bass yesterday. You like it? It's the latest model.' After the show Paul and Linda went out with Dustin Hoffman and his wife.

There were numerous celebrities at the shows. During the first night members of the audience included James Taylor, Patricia Hearst Shaw, Robin Williams, Jane Pauley, Ralph Lauren and Paul 'Kiss' Stanley.

The following night celebrities included Billy Joel and Bill Murray.

There were a number of celebrities who commented favourably on the first leg of the tour, Paul's first for thirteen years. Jack Nicholson was to comment, 'It was one hell of a concert. I've never seen anything like it. McCartney is the ultimate professional. When I heard "Jet" and "Live And Let Die" in the same hour, I wanted to die.' Tom Hanks said, 'I was a Beatles fan but I never saw them live, so this was a chance I couldn't miss. "Back In The USSR" was the best number for me.'

Actress Meryl Streep said, 'I arrived with Tracy Ullman and we were on our feet all night long. I've never enjoyed a rock show so much,' while Raquel Welch commented, 'Paul may be forty-seven but he is still one of the sexiest men in rock. I loved every minute of the show. "Hey Jude" was out of this world.'

Fellow musicians were also out in force. Axl Rose summed it up, 'Fucking great!' while Chrissie Hynde said, 'When Paul played "The Long And Winding Road" I almost cried. What a show!' Lionel Ritchie said, 'I had a great, great time. Everyone loved the Beatles and it was such a thrill to hear their songs played live again. Paul is the greatest.' Stevie Wonder said, 'McCartney is and will always be the best in the business. The old songs like "Let It Be" and "Sgt Pepper" brought back some great memories.' Michael Jackson said, 'Wow! I had a good time. Paul is a great friend and his show proved that he is one of the world's best performers.'

Paul also appeared at Madison Square Garden in October 2001 in the tribute to the victims of the World Trade Center.

As part of his 19-city *Driving USA* Tour Paul appeared at Madison Square Garden on Friday 26 April 2002. He performed 21 songs by the Beatles and 10 songs by Wings. The biggest cheer of the night went to his rendition of 'Here Today', the song he wrote for John Lennon after John's murder. It had received the most reaction of any song during the brief tour. He also paid tribute to George Harrison by performing 'Something', played 'My Love' for Linda and also sang a song for his fiancée Heather Mills.

Prior to the show he was visited backstage by members of the New York Police Department who made him an honorary detective.

Magic

A track from the *Driving Rain* album. The number lasts for 3 minutes and 59 seconds and was recorded on 25 February 2001.

Magical Mystery Tour (TV special)

Paul always harboured the vision of becoming a film producer and made some avant garde films during the mid-1960s. He had also always wanted to produce a Beatles movie.

Paul first had the idea of creating a Beatles special when he travelled to Denver, Colorado to celebrate Jane's 21st birthday in April 1967.

On the plane back to Heathrow on 11 April he began working on the idea of 'Magical Mystery Tour' and songs he'd include in the film.

John Lennon was to comment, '"Magical Mystery Tour" was something Paul had worked out with Mal and he showed me what his idea was and this is how it went. It went round like this, the story and how he had it all . . . the production and everything. Paul had a tendency to come along and say well he's written these ten songs; let's record them now. And I'd say, "Well, give us a few days and I'll knock a few off," or something like that.'

Within a week of Brian Epstein's death, Paul arranged a meeting at his Cavendish Avenue home to discuss the project, saying that he wanted the project to be completed by the end of September and to have an album in the shops by Christmas. He did his best to convince the other members that they should get to work immediately on the project and showed them a drawing he'd made of the plan – circular, like a cake, it was divided into segments, each of which contained details of what they needed to do to make the film.

When Paul showed John the notes he had made and asked John for some ideas to expand them, John commented, 'What does he mean? I've never made a film! I don't know how to write a film script!'

Paul wanted the title 'Magical Mystery Tour', rather than John's tongue-in-cheek suggestion that it be called 'Leaving No Turn Unstoned'.

Once it had been agreed, Paul wanted the film to have a start date of 4 September; this was considered to be too soon, so 11 September was agreed upon.

The special was initially screened on BBC 2 on 26 December 1967, with an audience of 13 million, but it received virtually universal criticism. The *Daily Mirror* commented, 'If they were not the Beatles, the BBC would not have fallen for it.'

The following day, 27 December Paul said in an *Evening Standard* interview, 'We goofed, really. My dad brought the bad news into me this morning like the figure of doom. Perhaps the newspapers are right – perhaps we're right. We'll have to wait and see.' He also appeared on *The Frost Programme* that day to say, 'the film was badly received because people were looking for a plot – and there wasn't one.'

Paul also commented that if the film had been shown in colour as intended, rather than black and white, it might have made more sense.

The BBC repeated the show on BBC 2 on 8 January 1968, this time in colour.

Magneto And Titanium Man

A track on the *Venus And Mars* album.

Paul was to say, '"Magneto And Titanium Man" is about Marvel Comics. When we were on holiday in Jamiaca we'd go into the supermarket every Saturday, when they got a new stock of comics in. I didn't use to read comics from eleven onwards. I thought I'd grown out of them, but I came back to them a couple of years ago. The drawings are great. I think you'll find that in twenty years time some of the guys drawing them were little Picassos. I think it's very good. It's very clever how they do it.'

Magpie

A Thames Television children's show networked to all ITV stations in Britain. Paul appeared on the programme with Mary Hopkin in a special insert called 'A Day In The Life Of Mary Hopkin' in which he played piano. The crew then filmed Mary at the Apple offices in Savile Row and at other locations, although Paul wasn't present then as he was at Abbey Road Studios recording. The filming took place during the day on Friday 6 September 1968 and was screened on Tuesday 10 September 1968. The Friday filming had been edited down to 3 minutes and 45 seconds and the Mary Hopkin spot took a total of 6 minutes of the show, during which she appeared live.

Magritte, René

Surrealist painter. Robert Fraser, who advised Paul on the acquisition of artworks, took him to Paris to meet Alexandre Iolas in 1966. Iolas acted as agent for Magritte and Paul was shown a number of Magritte's works. He chose two oils *Cibria* and *The Countess of Monte Christo*, which he bought.

Magritte died the following year, in August 1967. One of his last works was a painting *Le Jeu de Mourre (The Guessing Game)*, which he completed in 1966. Fraser brought the painting to Paul's house in Cavendish Avenue and placed it on a table. Paul bought it. This was the work that inspired the Apple logo. It was a painting of a large apple and Paul suggested that the Beatles' new company use the apple sign as their logo.

Magritte's widow Georgette held a number of studio sales and at one of them Linda purchased Magritte's double-sided easel, some blank canvases, brushes, Magritte's palette, a small painting table and other items as a Christmas present for Paul.

Maisie

A track on Laurence Juber's 1983 album *Standard Time* on which Paul plays bass guitar for the former Wings member.

Maitland Smith, Geoffrey

The man who acted as Paul's accountant in the late 1960s. In 1982, as chief executive of Sears Holdings, he expressed interest in buying Northern Songs for his company.

Major McCartney

A character played by Paul in a cameo scene in 'Magical Mystery Tour'.

Costume advisors must have been absent that day as he was actually wearing the uniform of a Colonel.

Paul sits at a desk in an army recruitment office with two little Union Jacks decorating the wall behind him. The scene was in fact created for Victor Spinetti who plays the recruiting sergeant.

Making Of My Brave Face, The

Title of a promotional video, filmed on Monday 10 April and Tuesday 11 April 1989 in Strawberry Fields in Liverpool. Paul made two videos at the time, directed by Roger Lunn. One was a straightforward promotional film in monochrome for 'My Brave Face' that featured the group performing the number, intercut with vintage archive clips and the second, which also included a colour film of the making of the promotional video, was called 'The Making Of My Brave Face'.

The promotional film was distributed to various European television stations from Wednesday 10 May 1989.

Making of Sgt Pepper, The

A television documentary first screened by ITV in Britain as a *South Bank Show* special on Sunday 14 June 1992. Paul, George and Ringo each participated and Paul was the first to shoot his contribution. This took place on Thursday 9 April 1992 at Abbey Road Studios where he joined George Martin and was filmed in Studios One and Two listening to some of the original four-track tapes and was interviewed discussing the album.

Soon after the ITV screening it was shown in America on the Disney cable channel on Sunday 27 September.

It was independently made by Isis Productions, the Really Useful Company, London Weekend Television and Walt Disney.

George Martin also wrote a book of the same title to accompany the documentary.

Mama's Little Girl

A number originally recorded at Olympic studios during the *Red Rose Speedway* sessions. It is credited as being co-produced by Paul and

Chris Thomas and was included as the flipside of the 'Put It There' single. A version was also included on *Flowers In the Dirt – Special Edition* and as a bonus track on the 1993 release of *Wild Life*.

Mamunia
A track, 4 minutes and 49 seconds in length, from the 1973 Wings album *Band On The Run* recorded in Lagos. During his trip to Nigeria, Paul noticed a phrase on a plaque that inspired him to think up the theme for the number. The title was adapted from the name of a hotel in Marrakech which Paul had stayed in. In Arabic the word means 'safe haven'.

A video of the number was produced by Jim Quick in July 1974, which has only appeared on *The Dave Cash Radio Show* on ITV Wales in 1975.

Man We Was Lonely
A track on Paul's 1970 debut album *McCartney* lasting 2 minutes and 55 seconds. He wrote the number during the actual recording sessions on 25 February 1970 and Linda joined him on the harmony. Paul played guitar, bass drum, bass and achieved a 'steel guitar' sound by playing a telecaster with a drum peg.

Man, The
A McCartney-Jackson collaboration. It was originally due to be released in Britain on Parlophone R 6066 on Monday 13 February 1984, with 'Blackpool' as the flip. There was also a 12″ due for simultaneous release, with an instrumental version of the number on the flip and an extended remix of the number by an American disc jockey. Shortly prior to the release date, the single was cancelled.

It was eventually featured as the second track on the *Pipes Of Peace* album.

Many Years From Now
Paul's authorised biography, penned by Barry Miles, first published by Secker & Warburg in 1997. Author Miles explained that the book intended to dispel some of the inaccuracies that were passed on from biography to biography, pointing out that the book particularly focussed on Paul in the 1960s when he was the only member of the Beatles living in London, the only one who was single and the one regularly attending theatre first nights, clubs and gallery openings. As a result Paul was also the first member of the Beatles to produce experimental music and avant garde films.

Paul lived with the Asher family for a time and reveals how fascinated he was by them. Also important to Paul's appreciation of the arts was Barry Miles himself who, in the 1960s, ran the Indica bookshop and gallery. One of his partners was John Dunbar, who was also an influence, as was gallery owner Robert Fraser.

Commenting on the book, Miles said, 'The idea is not to repeat what's been printed in other books, but to tell new stories, and to correct mistakes and inaccuracies which are often regarded as fact. This will be the inside story from Paul's point of view. The book will be discursive and anecdotal, a serious study of what I consider to be the Beatles' most exciting period, when Paul was living in London from 1965 to 1970.

'London at that time was rather like Paris in the 20s, only with musicians and singers at the centre of it all, rather than poets, writers and artists – and the Beatles, and Paul, were at the heart of that scene.'

He was also to say, 'This book will be surprisingly frank about the drug-taking the Beatles did, especially about Paul's friendship with Robert Fraser, the London art dealer whom Mick Jagger was arrested with in the 60s for possession.'

Maple Leaf Gardens

Venue in Toronto, Canada where Wings appeared during their 1975/76 tour on Sunday 9 May 1976. There had been rumours once again that the Beatles would turn up for a reunion at this concert which was, of course, nonsense – although George and Ringo were among the 18,000 strong audience.

Maracana Stadium

The largest stadium in the world, situated in Rio de Janeiro, Brazil. Promoters Mills and Mierneyer together with Rio de Janeiro Municipal Government and Raymond Ribero handed Paul a letter from the Mayor of Rio de Janeiro inviting Paul to Rio saying he would be made very welcome. Paul arrived from Miami on Monday 16 April 1990. He was scheduled to appear at the stadium on Thursday 19 and Saturday 21 April. Paul, Linda, James and Stella stayed at the Rio Palace Hotel. There were terrible storms, which resulted in some deaths, so the Thursday concert was postponed until the Friday. It was still raining on the day of the concert. There was a press reception during which Paul discussed various subjects including ecology, the rain forests and the Beatles.

It didn't rain on Saturday and among the attendees at the concert were famous actors, musicians and politicians.

The President of Brazil had sent Paul letters and gifts. Paul sent the President an autographed copy of 'Put It There' and Linda sent him an autographed copy of her cookbook.

At the concert, Paul said some words in Portuguese and introduced Linda in Portuguese.

The numbers performed on the show were; 'Figure Of Eight', 'Jet', 'Got To Get You Into My Life', 'Rough Ride', 'Band On The Run', 'We Got Married', 'Let 'Em In', 'The Long And Winding Road', 'Fool On The Hill', 'Sgt Pepper's Lonely Hearts Club Band (Reprise)', 'Good Day Sunshine', 'Can't Buy Me Love', 'Put It There', 'Things We Said Today',

'Eleanor Rigby', 'This One', 'My Brave Face', 'Back In The USSR', 'I Saw Her Standing There', 'Coming Up', 'Let It Be', 'Ain't That A Shame', 'Live And Let Die', 'Hey Jude', 'Yesterday', 'PS Love Me Do', 'Get Back', 'Golden Slumbers', 'Carry That Weight' and 'The End'.

The *Guinness Book Of Records* acknowledged that Paul's second show on 21 April 1990 had broken the world attendance record for a rock concert with 184,000 attendees.

On Monday 23 April, TV Globo screened 'Paul In Rio', featuring ten of the numbers performed at the Friday show.

Marsden, Gerry

The leader of Gerry & the Pacemakers, the first British band ever to have three No. 1 hits with their first three releases.

When 'Mull Of Kintyre' was released in 1977, Gerry was touring Australia and was appearing on a radio show when 'Mull Of Kintyre' was played. He was asked what he thought of the number and said, 'Well, I've never heard such a load of crap in my life. It won't be a hit. You're a mug, Paul, making that!'

When Gerry celebrated the twentieth anniversary of his recording career with a party at Stringfellows club in London in 1983, Paul, who was recording at the time, sent him a birthday cake.

When Gerry gathered together a group of recording artists to make a charity record for the relatives of those killed in the Bradford City Disaster (a fierce fire at a soccer club in which a number of spectators were killed), he gave them the name the Crowd and they re-recorded one of his No.1 hits, 'You'll Never Walk Alone', which also reached the top of the charts following its release on 20 May 1985 on BRAD 1.

Paul was invited to participate and he recorded a 17-second message that appears on the flipside of the single, which is called 'Messages'. Gerry also recorded an album of Lennon and McCartney numbers that was released in England by K-Tel Records in 1986.

Gerry was also Paul's special guest on the TV special 'James Paul McCartney'.

Martha

The most famous of Paul's pets and the first real pet that he ever had. He acquired Martha when he moved into Cavendish Avenue from Ann Davis, a breeder in High Wycombe. This Old English sheepdog gained immortality when Paul used her name in the song 'Martha My Dear'.

Martha was born in 1966 and died at the age of fifteen in August 1981 at Paul's farmhouse in Scotland.

Martha My Dear

A song by Paul in which the name of his sheepdog Martha was used, although the song is not about a dog, it's a love song. There was a solo vocal by Paul, although he is double-tracked.

Recording began at Trident Studios on 4 October 1968. When the Beatles started recording the track, Ringo bashed a hole in his new bass drum skin.

The number was featured on *The Beatles White Album*.

Martin, George

The Beatles' record producer for eight years.

Martin had joined the Parlophone label in 1952 and became label head in 1955. He remained with Parlophone until 1965 when he formed the Association of Independent Record Producers (AIR) with John Burgess, Peter Sullivan and Ron Richards. Although he'd officially left Parlophone, he continued to produce the Beatles right up to the *Abbey Road* album.

During the 1960s he also recorded Beatles material in his own right, contributing arrangements and orchestral and instrumental tracks to the soundtracks of *A Hard Day's Night*, *Help!* and *Yellow Submarine*. He released a number of instrumental singles and also two albums – *Off The Beatles Track* in August 1964 and *The Beatle Girls* in 1967, the latter featuring songs such as 'Eleanor Rigby' and 'Michelle'.

Paul had also asked George to help him on the theme music for the film *The Family Way*, in particular on the track 'Love In The Open Air'.

Although ten years were to pass between *Abbey Road* and *Tug Of War*, the album that Paul asked George to produce for him, Paul also called in George to help him when he composed the theme for the 1973 James Bond movie *Live And Let Die*. As a result George was asked to compose further background material for the soundtrack.

The team was also reunited on the *Pipes Of Peace* and *Give My Regards To Broad Street* albums.

Martin has been the subject of a *This Is Your Life* programme, has had his autobiography *All You Need Is Ears* published, and also edited the book *Making Music* in which he interviewed Paul about songwriting and playing the bass guitar.

Martin, Rose

A housekeeper employed by Paul in 1967. Her Christian name was the inspiration for the album title *Red Rose Speedway*.

Mary Had A Little Lamb (promotional films)

There were four clips of this particular song. Nicholas Ferguson, who had first met Paul when he was working on *Ready. Steady. Go!*, directed the first three.

The first promotional film had Wings performing in a barnyard setting, with a hen sitting on Paul's piano and with Linda cuddling a lamb. This was the promotional film that received the main plays and was featured on *Top Of The Pops* on Thursday 29 June 1972 and was later to turn up on 'Beatles Story', a programme on the Australian Channel 7 in 1974.

The second promotional film was known as the 'psychedelic' version due to the swirling patterns of vivid colours used in the background and the matching orange T-shirts and dungarees worn by Wings. This time the group weren't in a barnyard and no animals were present. It was included on *The Flip Wilson Show* in America on Thursday 12 October, with comedian Wilson introducing it with the words, 'Wings singing a different tune – Paul and wife Linda on bongos singing "Mary Had A Little Lamb". Go kill 'em, Paul.'

The third version had the group performing at the bottom of a hill with Paul at the piano, Linda sitting on a wall and playing bongos, Denny Laine lying on his back and the other members of Wings standing against a painted backdrop of a hill. This promotional film was featured on BBC 1's *The Basil Brush Show* on Saturday 24 June.

The fourth clip of the number was actually taken from the ATV special 'James Paul McCartney' filmed on Saturday 10 March 1973 and featured Wings on an outside location with various little scenes – Linda riding a horse, Wings with a flock of sheep and so on.

Mary Had A Little Lamb (single)

The single that followed Paul's controversial 'Give Ireland Back To The Irish' was recorded at Olympic Studios, London in March 1972. It was issued as a single in Britain on Apple R5949 on Friday 12 May 1972 and in America on Apple 1851 on Monday 29 May. It reached the position of No. 6 in Britain and No. 28 in the US.

It was issued in Germany on EMI Electrola/Apple 1C600-050058.

Paul and Linda described it as 'A song for spring to make people happy'.

At the height of Beatlemania, people often said that there was so much adulation aimed at the Beatles that they could have a hit recording passages from the Bible or singing nursery rhymes. It looks as if Paul took them at their word with this adaptation of the familiar children's rhyme.

'Little Woman Love' was the flip.

Following the highly controversial single 'Give Ireland Back To The Irish', this seemingly lightweight number incurred heavy flack from the music press and Paul was later to admit: 'It wasn't a great record.'

In an interview he commented: 'It was written for one of our kids, whose name is Mary, and I just realised if I'd sang that, she'd understand. That's it with us, that's what you might expect from us – just anything. The quote that sums up that song for me is I read Pete Townshend saying that his daughter had to have a copy. I like to keep in with the five-year-olds!'

The track was to be included on *For Our Children*, a 20-track collection from Disney Records released on Disney 60616-2 on 28 May 1991. Proceeds from the album went to the Pediatric AIDS Foundation. Paul waived all royalties.

A version of Paul rehearsing the number on a piano is to be found on some bootleg albums. This arose from an interview Paul recorded for the radio station WRKO in New York in December 1971. The interview was conducted in the apartment offices of Paul's MPL Productions Ltd and broadcast on 12 January 1972. During the interview Paul discussed how he now considered Wings to be a proper band, Linda mentioned her own composition 'Seaside Woman' and there was talk of a forthcoming Wings tour.

Massey & Coggins
A Liverpool firm of electrical engineers.

Following the Beatles first trip to Hamburg in 1960, Paul, who had left school against the advice of his father, abandoning his idea of becoming a teacher, felt guilty about not getting a regular job and approached the Labour Exchange. Initially he worked temporarily for a parcels delivery service, being laid off after the Christmas rush. He was then sent to Massey & Coggins where he received a wage of £7 per week. He admits he was not very good at the job which consisted of him winding electrical coils all day long. While fellow labourers would complete between eight and fourteen coils per working day, Paul confessed he was lucky if he managed one and a half. One of his workmates called him 'Mantovani' because of his long hair, and his boredom with the job was such that after two months he didn't bother turning up one morning.

Matchbox
A version of this number, composed by Carl Perkins, lasting 3 minutes and 10 seconds, was included on the *Tripping The Live Fantastic* album. It was recorded live on 21 January 1990 at Wembley Arena, London during the 1989/90 World Tour.

Mattacks, Dave
A musician born in Edgeware, Middlesex in March 1948 who joined Fairport Convention in 1969, replacing Martin Lamble, who had been killed when the group's van crashed. He left and rejoined the group over a period of years. Mattacks became a freelance performer in 1978 and played on a number of tracks Paul recorded at Montserrat in early February 1981 for his *Tug Of War* album. He worked with Paul on other recordings, including the *Pipes Of Peace* album and performed on Paul's version of 'The Long And Winding Road' in *Give My Regards To Broad Street* and on the track 'We Got Married' for *Flowers In The Dirt*. He was also one of the musicians used on the recording of the *Run Devil Run* album.

Maxwell's Silver Hammer

Paul wrote this number in the late summer of 1968, originally for *The Beatles* double album, but it wasn't recorded then. The Beatles rehearsed it during the *Let It Be* sessions, but actual recording began on 9 July 1969 and it was included on the *Abbey Road* album.

This was the first session John played on immediately after his car crash in Scotland. Balance engineer on the session was Phil McDonald, who commented, 'We were all waiting for him and Yoko to arrive. Paul, George, Ringo downstairs and us upstairs. They didn't know what state he would be in. There was a definite "vibe" they were almost afraid of Lennon before he arrived, because they didn't know what he would be like. I got the feeling that the three of them were a little bit scared of him. When he did come in it was a relief, and they got together fairly well.'

John was very critical of this song.

He said, 'I hate it, 'cause all I remember is the track. He made us do it a hundred million times. He did everything to make it into a single and it never was and it never could've been, but he put guitar licks on it and he had somebody hitting iron pieces and we spent more money on that song than any of them in the whole album.'

Paul was to comment, '"Maxwell's Silver Hammer" was my analogy for when something goes wrong, out of the blue, as it so often does, and I was beginning to find that out at that time in my life. I wanted something symbolic of that, so, to me, it was some fictitious character called Maxwell with a silver hammer. I don't know why it was silver, it just sounded better than "Maxwell's Hammer".'

In the song he used the words, 'pataphysical science'. The word came from a drinking club in Paris which was called the Pataphysical Society.

Paul added moog synthesiser.

Maybe Baby

A cover of the Buddy Holly number, recorded in September 1999. Following a PETA performance Paul met Jeff Lynne at Capitol Records and they recorded the number in Los Angeles. Paul's version of the number was released on Virgin Records CDV 2916 on 5 June 2000 on the soundtrack of the British film *Maybe Baby*.

Maybe I'm Amazed (promotional film)

David Puttnam directed this promotional video of the Paul/Linda number, which featured a montage of Linda's still shots of Paul, herself and Heather. London Weekend Television took the unusual step of screening the promotional film at 6 p.m. on Sunday 19 April 1970. It was also screened that night on *The Ed Sullivan Show* in America. Charlie Jenkins produced it.

Maybe I'm Amazed (single)

Highly praised as the outstanding track on Paul's first album in 1970 and Paul's first major song written for Linda. Despite the encouraging airplays this particular track received, Paul decided not to issue it as a single at the time. It resurfaced in 1976 on the *Wings Over America* album. This later version was a live cut from their American tour and it was issued as a single in Britain on 4 February 1977 on Parlophone R6017 and in the US on Capitol 4385 on 7 February.

Capitol, in fact, issued a promotional 12″ record for American radio stations that included four different versions of the number. It reached No. 27 in the British charts and No. 11 in the American.

The flipside was 'Soily'.

Rod Stewart and the Faces featured it on live concerts and recorded 'Maybe I'm Amazed' on *Long Player*, their 1971 album. Wings performed it on their European, world and both of the British tours. It was also one of the numbers included in the TV spectacular 'James Paul McCartney'.

The number was also reworked for inclusion on *Working Classical*.

The single was issued in Germany on Capitol 1C600-98701 and in France on Capitol 2C006-98701.

A version of this number, lasting 4 minutes and 41 seconds, was included on the *Tripping The Live Fantastic* album. It was recorded live at the Ahoy Sportpaleis in Rotterdam, Netherlands on 8 November 1989 during the 1989/90 World Tour.

American singer Carleen Anderson covered the number in 1998 and her version reached No. 12 in the US charts.

Mayles, Albert

A documentary film-maker who, together with his brother David, was commissioned by Granada Television in Britain to film the Beatles first visit to America in 1964. It resulted in 'What's Happening – The Beatles In the USA'. Another notable Mayles Brothers documentary was 'Gimme Shelter', filmed at the Rolling Stones concert at Altamont which brought a vicious end to the 1960s, as a brutal murder was captured on film.

David had died in 1987, but in 2000 Paul approached the 75-year-old Albert to ask him to film a documentary of his Concert For New York City at Madison Square Garden.

McCartney

There was some internal wrangling at Apple concerning Paul's first solo album release. Paul had kept a relatively low profile while working on it at his Scottish farm, overdubbing instruments and using a Studer 4-track recorder. With the exception of some vocal help from Linda, it was a one-man album with Paul playing all the instruments: toy xylophone, electric and acoustic guitars, bass, drums, Mellotron and organ.

Recordings began in December 1969 and other locations during the recordings were Abbey Road's Studio Two and Morgan Studios in Willesden.

Tension between Paul and the other Beatles was already in the air, particularly because of the Allen Klein affair, and this was unfortunately exacerbated by the release date that Paul wanted for the album. This roughly coincided with the *Let It Be* release and was also close to the release date of Ringo's debut album *Sentimental Journey*. Paul felt that the *Let It Be* project had been around for some time and didn't see why he should alter his plans because of it. Ringo was sent to Paul's St John's Wood house to 'reason' with him. Ringo took two letters along, one from John, the other from George. Paul opened them and vented his anger on Ringo. Ringo was to say later: 'I could see the release date of his record had a gigantic emotional significance for him. Whether he was right or wrong, I felt that since he was our friend and since the date was of such immense significance to him, we should let him have his own way.'

It was decided that there should be a three-week gap between the release of *McCartney* and *Let It Be* and the release of Ringo's album was brought forward.

McCartney was issued on Apple PCS7102 on Friday 17 April 1970. It reached No. 2 in the British charts and No. 1 in the US charts, selling over two million copies.

Not content with showing the world that he was capable of working on a musical project without the other three, Paul was also at pains to put across his viewpoint about the entire Beatles situation as it stood. He prepared his own press release with members of the Apple staff, Peter Brown, Derek Taylor and Mavis Smith, issuing it in the form of a questionnaire to the Fleet Street papers, radio disc jockeys, and in a limited run on the inner sleeve of the album itself. It read:

Q: Why did you decide to make a solo album?
A: Because I got a Studer 4-track recording machine at home – practised on it (playing all instruments) – liked the results and decided to make it into an album.

Q: Were you influenced by John's adventures with the Plastic Ono Band, and Ringo's solo LP?
A: Sort of, but not really.

Q: Are all the songs by Paul McCartney alone?
A: Yes sir.

Q: Will they be so credited: McCartney?
A: It's a bit daft for them to be Lennon-McCartney-credited, so 'McCartney' it is.

Q: Did you enjoy working as a solo?
A: Very much. I only had me to ask for a decision, and I agreed with me. Remember Linda's on it too, so it's really a double act.

Q: What is Linda's contribution?

A: Strictly speaking she harmonises, but of course it's more than that because she is a shoulder to lean on, a second opinion, and a photographer of renown. More than all this, she believes in me – constantly.

Q: Where was the album recorded?

A: At home, at EMI (No. 2 studio) and at Morgan Studios (Willesden!).

Q: What is your home equipment (in some detail)?

A: Studer 4-track machine. I only had, however, one mike, and, as Mr Pender, Mr Sweatham and others only managed to take six months or so (slight delay), I worked without VU meters or a mixer, which meant that everything had to be listened to first (for distortion, etc ...) then recorded. So the answer – Studer, one mike and nerve.

Q: Why did you choose to work in the studios you chose?

A: They were available. EMI is technically good, and Morgan is cosy.

Q: The album was not known about until it was nearly completed. Was this deliberate?

A: Yes, because normally an album is old before it comes out. (aside) Witness *Get Back*.

Q: Why?

A: I've always wanted to buy a Beatles album like 'people' do and be as surprised as they must be. So this was the next best thing. Linda and I are the only two who will be sick of it by the release date. We love it really.

Q: Are you able to describe the texture or the feel of the theme of the album in a few words?

A: Home, Family, Love.

Q: How long did it take to complete – from when to when?

A: From just before (I think) Christmas, until now. 'The Lovely Linda' was the first thing I recorded at home, and was originally to test the equipment. That was around Christmas.

Q: Assuming all the songs are new to the public, how new are they to you? Are they recent?

A: One was 1959 ('Hot As Sun'), two from India ('Junk', 'Teddy Boy'), and the rest are pretty recent. 'Valentine Day', 'Momma Miss America', and 'OO you' were ad-libbed on the spot.

Q: Which instruments have you played on the album?

A: Bass, drums, acoustic guitar, lead guitar, piano and organ-Mellotron, toy xylophone, bow and arrow.

Q: Have you played all these instruments on earlier recordings?

A: Yes – drums being the one that I would normally do.

Q: Why did you do all the instruments yourself?

A: I think I'm pretty good.

Q: Will Linda be heard on all future recordings?

A: Could be; we love singing together, and have plenty of opportunity for practice.

Q: Will Paul and Linda become a John and Yoko?

A: No, they will become a Paul and Linda.

Q: Are you pleased with your work?

A: Yes.

Q: Will the other Beatles receive the first copies?

A: Wait and see.

Q: What has recording alone taught you?

A: That to make your own decisions about what you do is easy and playing with yourself is difficult but satisfying.

Q: Who has done the artwork?

A: Linda has taken all the photos, and she and I designed the package.

Q: Is it true that neither Allen Klein nor ABKCO have been nor will be in any way involved with the production, manufacturing, distribution or promotion of this new album?

A: Not if I can help it.

Q: Did you miss the other Beatles and George Martin? Was there a moment eg, when you thought, 'wish Ringo was here for this break'?

A: No.

Q: Assuming this is a very big hit album, will you do another?

A: Even if it isn't, I will continue to do what I want – when I want to.

Q: Are you planning a new album or single with the Beatles?

A: No.

Q: Is this album a rest away from the Beatles or the start of a solo career?

A: Time will tell. Being a solo album means it's 'the start of a solo career . . .' and not being done with the Beatles means it's a rest. So it's both.

Q: Have you any plans for live appearances?

A: No.

Q: Is your break from the Beatles temporary or permanent, due to personal differences or musical ones?

A: Personal differences, business differences, musical differences, but most of all because I have a better time with my family. Temporary or permanent? I don't know.

Q: Do you see a time when Lennon-McCartney becomes an active songwriting partnership again?

A: No.

Q: What do you feel about John's peace effort? The Plastic Ono Band? Giving back the MBE? Yoko's influence? Yoko?

A: I love John and respect what he does – it doesn't give me any pleasure.

Q: Have you plans to produce any other artists?

A: No.

Q: Were there any of the songs on the album originally written with the Beatles in mind?

A: The older ones were. 'Junk' was intended for *Abbey Road*, but something happened. 'Teddy Boy' was for *Get Back* but something happened.

Q: Were you pleased with *Abbey Road*? Was it musically restricting?

A: It was a good album. (No. 1 for a long time.)

Q: What is your relationship with Klein?

A: It isn't – I am not in contact with him, and he does not represent me in any way.

Q: What is your relationship with Apple?

A: It is the office of a company which I part-own with the other three Beatles. I don't go there because I don't like the offices or business, especially when I'm on holiday.

Q: Have you any plans to set up an independent production company?

A: McCartney Productions.

Q: What sort of music has influenced you on this album?

A: Light and loose.

Q: Are you writing more prolifically now? Or less so?

A: About the same. I have a queue waiting to be recorded.

Q: What are your plans now? A holiday? A musical? A movie? Retirement?

A: My only plan is to grow up.

Paul also prepared his own track-by-track commentary on the album:

'The Lovely Linda'. When the Studer 4-track was installed at home, this was the first song I recorded, to test the machine. On the first track was vocal and guitar, second – another acoustic guitar – then overdubbed hand slaps on a book, and finally bass. Written in Scotland, the song is a trailer to the full song which will be recorded in the future.

'That Would Be Something'. This song was written in Scotland in 1969 and recorded at home in London – mixed later at EMI (No. 2). I only had one mike, as the mixer and VU meters hadn't arrived (still haven't).

vocal, guitar

tom-tom and cymbal

electric guitar

bass

'Valentine Day'. Recorded at home. Made up as I went along – acoustic guitar first, then drums (maybe drums were first).

Anyway – electric guitar and bass were added and the track is all instrumental. Mixed at EMI. This one and 'Momma Miss America' were ad-libbed, with more concern for testing the machine than anything else.

'Every Night' (Blues). This came from the first two lines, which I've had for years. They were added to in 1969 in Greece (Benitses) on holiday. This was recorded at EMI with:

vocal
acoustic guitar
drums
bass
lead guitar (acoustic)
harmony to the lead guitar
double-tracked vocal in parts
electric guitar (not used)
track

'Hot As Sun'. A song written in about 1958 or '59 or maybe earlier, when it was one of those songs that you play now and then. The middle was added in Morgan Studio, where the track was recorded recently.

acoustic guitar
electric guitar
drums
rhythm guitar
organ
maracas
bass
bongos

'Glasses'. Wineglasses played at random and overdubbed on top of each other – the end is a section of a song called 'Suicide' – not yet completed.

'Junk'. Originally written in India, at Maharishi's camp, and completed bit by bit in London. Recorded vocal, two acoustic guitars, and bass at home, and later added to (bass drum, snare with brushes, and small xylophone and harmony) at Morgan.

'Oo You'. The first three tracks were recorded at home as an instrument that might someday become a song. This, like 'Man We Was Lonely', was given lyrics one day after lunch, just before we left for Morgan Studios, where it was finished that afternoon. Vocals, electric guitar, tambourine, cow bell, and aerosol spray were added at Morgan, and it was mixed there.

On the mix, tape echo was used to move feedback from guitar from one side to another.

'Momma Miss America'. An instrumental recorded completely at home. Made up as I went along – first a sequence of chords, then a melody on top.

Piano, drums, acoustic guitar, electric guitar.

Originally it was two pieces, but they ran into each other by accident and became one.

'Teddy Boy'. Another song started in India, and completed in Scotland and London, gradually. This one was recorded for the *Get Back* film, but later not used.

Recorded partly at home ... (guitar, voices and bass) ... and finished at Morgan.

Linda and I sing the backing harmonies on the chorus, and occasional oos.

'Singalong Junk'. This was take 1, for the vocal version, which was take 2, and a shorter version.

Guitars and piano and bass were put on at home, and the rest added at Morgan Studios.

The strings are Mellotron, and they were done at the same time as the electric guitar, bass drum, and sizzle cymbal.

'Maybe I'm Amazed'. Written in London, at the piano, with the second verse added slightly later, as if you cared.

Recorded at EMI, No. 2 studio

1. piano
2. vocal
3. drums
4. bass
5. and vocal backing
6. and vocal backing
7. solo guitar
8. backing guitars

Linda and I are the vocal backing group. Mixed at EMI.

A movie was made, using Linda's slides and edited to this track.

'Kreen-Akrore'. There was a film on TV about the Kreen-Akrore Indians living in the Brazilian jungle, their lives, and how the white man is trying to change their way of life to his, so the next day, after lunch, I did some drumming. The idea behind it was to get the feeling of their hunt. So later piano, guitar and organ were added to the first section.

The second had a few tracks of voices (Linda and I) and the end had overdubbed breathing, going into organ, and two lead guitars in harmony.

Done at Morgan. Engineer, Robin Black.

The end of the first section has Linda and I doing animal noises (speeded up) and an arrow sound (done live with bow and arrow – the bow broke), then animals stampeding across a guitar case.

There are two drum tracks.

We built a fire in the studio but didn't use it (but used the sound of the twigs breaking).

At the time of release, Langdon Wiiner of *Rolling Stone* wrote: 'Its explicit and uniform message is that Paul McCartney, his wife Linda and family have found peace and happiness in a quiet home away from the city, and away from the hassles of the music business.'

Some years later, Roy Carr and Tony Tyler in *The Beatles Illustrated Record* were to comment: 'It is also extremely hastily made, and the very unpretentious qualities which McCartney tried to emphasise were badly misconstrued as ineptitude. Hindsight displays its charms.'

Generally, most reviewers considered 'Maybe I'm Amazed' as the outstanding track, although ten years were to elapse before it was issued as a single.

The album cover featured a photograph of a bowl and various cherries on a strip and a gatefold sleeve sported 23 of Linda's photographs of the McCartney family life.

McCartney was re-released in both album and cassette versions in Britain on Tuesday 17 April 1990 to celebrate the twentieth anniversary of the original release.

McCartney (promotional record)
This was a special 12″ record pressing in white vinyl sent to radio stations in 1982 to coincide with the release of the 'Ebony And Ivory' single. Apart from 'Ebony And Ivory', two further tracks were included on the promotional disc: 'Ballroom Dancing' and 'The Pound Is Sinking'.

McCartney (TV special)
The title of an MPL/BBC co-production that was first transmitted on BBC 1 on Friday 29 August 1986.

Produced by David G Croft, it featured a lengthy interview with Paul at Studio Two, Abbey Road, conducted by Richard Skinner, filmed on Friday 18 July. Paul also conducted a guided tour of the Abbey Road Studios for the cameras. He discussed his post-Beatles career, beginning with the 1970 *McCartney* album, mentioned all his albums since, plus his reunion with George Martin for three of the albums, his formation of Wings and his various tours. He also performed 'Press', from his new album *Press To Play* and there was a clip from the unreleased film *The Backyard*.

The special was repeated on BBC 2 on Tuesday 30 December in an extended version lasting for 59 minutes and on Saturday 1 April 1989 it was released as a home video in Britain under the title 'The Paul McCartney Story' and on home video and laserdisc in America on Wednesday 21 June 1989.

See also '*Paul McCartney Story, The*'.

McCartney, Florence
Paul's paternal grandmother who was born in the Everton district of Liverpool at 131 Breck Road on 2 June 1874. On 17 May 1896,

21-year-old Florence, née Clegg, married Joseph McCartney at Christ Church in Kensington. She was known as Florrie and had seven children, two of whom died in early childhood. She died on VE day in 1945.

McCartney, Heather (stepdaughter)

She was born on 31 December 1963. Her mother was Linda, her father Melvin See. When Linda began staying with Paul in London, she used to phone her daughter, who was in New York, each night. Paul was also encouraged to talk to Heather on these occasions and he remembers the first time he spoke with her on the phone and was worried that she might not like him.

He said to her: 'Will you marry me?'

Heather said: 'I can't. You're too old!'

Paul then said: 'Well, maybe I should marry your mummy – that'd be good.'

Around October 1968 Linda was feeling guilty about leaving Heather in New York. Paul was aware of this and he suggested that they both travel there, since he wanted to see Heather and meet Linda's family.

It was during the two weeks he spent in New York that Paul began to develop a relationship with Heather at Linda's apartment on the tenth floor of 140 East 83rd Street. Heather was five years old at the time and Linda went off, leaving them together with Paul playing games and cooking for the little girl.

At the end of the visit, on 31 October, all three of them flew back to London. When Heather passed her A-level exams in November 1982, she asked her parents for a car.

Ringo, who was filming with Paul on *Give My Regards To Broad Street* at the time, talked Paul into buying her one, saying: 'Give the kid a break. All her friends have cars. It's not as if she wanted a BMW or a Roller. We're only talking about a Volkswagen.'

Like her sisters and brother, she attended local state schools and became independent at the age of twenty, paying her own bills (although Paul and Linda occasionally helped her out) and taking a variety of jobs, including washing up in kitchens and in a pub.

Soon after, she went to Mexico to visit her blood father, who has been a lifelong influence and his career as a geologist has given her a love for crystals, quartz and turquoise.

Heather is a potter, and the firm of Wedgwood once said she was 'one of Britain's most exciting new talents'. Her pottery work has been the subject of exhibitions in New York, Phoenix in Arizona, Tokyo, Paris and Sydney.

In October 1997 the British Council selected her to head a showcase launch in Los Angeles, opened by Princess Anne. At the time Heather described herself as a country person and said that there was no man in her life. She commented: 'Can't imagine I'd meet one who fits in with me. And I'm not the sort who can adapt.' Admitting to having had emotional troubles, she said: 'I was on a quest to find my own individuality. Living up to other people's expectations can cause such stresses.'

Commenting on her family, she said: 'They're all exceptionally talented people. My brother, James, is a very special person, a gentle soul, and a brilliant guitarist. He's going to have problems, like I have.'

Heather is also known as a gentle soul with a love for animals and seems rather reclusive. She is not married and has no steady relationship, although she used to go out with Billy Idol in the early 1980s. She has a home in the English countryside with her Airedale dog and two cats and grows organic vegetables. Her studio is two miles away from her home.

In 1996 a pottery exhibition of Heather's work was staged at the New York Department store Felissimo. It included three vases: the Sunflower (in yellow), the Crocus (in purple) and the Tulip (in blue). Paul and Linda attended the private opening in October. On Thursday, 7 January 1999, Paul joined Heather at the opening of an exhibition of her work at the America's Mart, Atlanta, Georgia. It was called the Heather McCartney Housewares Collection, and included candles, clocks, cushions and rugs in designs inspired during the time she spent with the Huichol and Tarahumara Indians.

Paul and Heather took part in a press conference and here are some of its edited highlights:

Paul: 'Good evening all. This is my daughter, Heather.'
Q: 'How do you guys feel?'
Paul: 'Fine.'
Heather: 'We feel welcomed, we're very comfortable, it's a special place here.'
Paul: 'And we are not at all nervous!'
Heather: 'No.'
Q: 'Heather, why did you choose Atlanta?'
Heather: 'It's a golden opportunity for me because all the exclusive interior designers launch their collections here and it's an opportunity to show what we've been working on for the past few months.'
Q: 'Paul, why did you want to be here with her?'
Paul: 'I'm a daughter supporter. That's who I am. And she's my big baby, you know, so she's got a big blow and she asked, so I thought, Come on, come ahead.'
Heather: 'And it's the home of the blues, I've been told.'
Q: 'Heather, is there any piece that your mother inspired?'
Heather: '*All* of it.'
Q: 'Why so?'
Heather: 'That's inside us, the colour, the strength, compassion for this earth, that's everything that we are – all of us, you know – Mary, Stella, James and my dad, that's it.'

Q: 'Did you intentionally design the C moon logo into your logo?'

Heather: 'No. It was very lucky the way it all evolved. I was born on the Southwest of America and I've borrowed the indigenous sun symbol and I've united that with the colours that I gathered when I was in Mexico with the Huichols and Tarahumaras. And they are very special people and we need to help them. We need to watch after them – all the indigenous people.'

Q: 'What do you hope people take away from your collection when they see it and what do you hope they learn about you as a woman and an artist?'

Heather: 'The freshness and the use of colour; and the feel is lighter and that it makes people think in an instinctive way, just colour: colour very much.'

Q: 'Paul, when did you first realise that Heather had a talent for design?'

Paul: 'She's always been very talented that way. When she was very little she started off as a potter and made pots and such, and she's now moved into this interior-design world. She's been doing that for the last couple of years now, and I think she's brilliant – but, then again, I would, wouldn't I?'

Q: 'Paul, do you have a favourite design of Heather's?'

Paul: 'No, I really like it all, you know. This is quite new to me. Heather keeps it quite close to herself, you know, so I'm really experiencing this for the first time, like you are. But it looks fantastic.'

Q: 'Heather, the business is based in London. Will there be a US base for your business?'

Heather: 'I don't know. We're very lucky that this is English and uniting America, because of the fact that I was born here, so there is a union between the two.'

Q: 'Why the Mexican/Spanish influence?'

Heather: 'I was very, very lucky. I went off with a close friend of mine and I didn't really know about all of this and I was in ceremonies with these people. They have nothing, but they'll give you anything that they have – they're very generous. I just saw all these colours, and everything is very intricate in ceremonies – it is very, very intricate and very fragile.'

Paul: 'Heather went to stay with the Huichol Indians so she kind of got first-hand knowledge of it all, so it's inspired a lot of it by now.'

Heather: 'And it's all symbolic, everything is symbolic, and there's a lot of ancestry to it.'

Q: 'Heather, in what ways has Paul inspired you?'

Heather: 'As a father, is what is most important to me. To help me through everything that we're dealing with. That's really, that's what's important, to have a real daddy.'

Q: 'Paul, do you see yourself as a daddy?'

Paul: 'Yeah, man.'

Q: 'Paul, I understand before long you're going to be a "dandaddy!" '

Paul: 'Yeah, I'm going to be a granddaddy too.'

Q: 'Heather, I love your logo. How did you come up with that? It's beautiful.'

Heather: 'Again, I was very lucky. I very much work on my own and occasionally the energy is there and it was. The M is symbolic of a mountain and then, as you say, the crescent moon and the sea. It was very, very lucky the way it's all evolved. It's a golden opportunity for me.'

Q: 'It's been such a tough year for your family. Is it exciting, Paul, to see Heather and the other kids moving out in their own direction? It's probably a little bittersweet, too.'

Paul: 'You know, it is great. You know, it's been obviously a very difficult time for us, over this last year. But you know, we're drawing on the energies, as Heather says, and we're moving forward, you know. You've got to move forward, and so this is all really up stuff and very vibrant and what Linda would have liked. I know that.'

Q: 'Heather, how do you think this will help the Indians?'

Heather: 'To say that their ancestry and their symbols are important in our modern lives, that we can unite their ancient world with the modern world and that the two can be together.'

Paul: 'And bring attention to them, you know, that's what this is all about.'

Q: 'Are all the colours that you have here represented in the original art and artefacts that you drew upon?'

Heather: 'Yes, they were very bright. This is the sun symbol, the Southwestern sun symbol, and then all the colours. This is the lightning happening here and those colours are from Mexico, so the two are together. I haven't seen myself lucky having gone there over about ten years. The first time I went, the rivers were lean, it was glorious. The last time I went, the rivers were foul, polluted. Lumber – all I saw was lumber going out, timber, everything being cut. The people are having to go further and further into the canyons. They have nothing, they have no help and they have nothing.'

Paul: 'Until you came along.'

Heather: 'Yes. We are here.'

Q: 'Will you donate a portion of your proceeds to the Indian tribes?'

Heather: 'The last exhibition that we had, we worked with an organisation, an English organisation, called Survival, and they work only to support indigenous peoples. So they had a stand there, leaflets and their posters and everything, were there. So that's what we did. We invited them along to our exhibition.'

Heather was also to say: 'The Huichols have greatly influenced my work. When I first met them some years ago, they introduced me to many things, including the bold use of colour, which is evident in my new designs.

'The Huichols allowed me into the centre of their circle and revealed to me ceremonies that originated thousands of years ago. Drawing on this experience and launching my designs at this, the dawn of the third millennium, I aim to synergise the ancient and modern in this collection.'

Paul was asked how he felt to have two designers in the family, and answered: 'We never pushed them into anything when they were younger. They're all over twenty-one now, so they're ready to work themselves.'

Heather was asked if her mother had inspired any of her work. She said: 'Her strength, her passion, everything that we are, all of it is in Mary, Stella, James and me and my dad.'

Of Paul, she said: 'As a father, he's most important to me to help deal with everything we're dealing with. It's obviously been a very difficult time for us this past year; but, you know, we're drawing on our energies and we're moving forward.'

On 28 November 1999, in an interview in the *Sunday Times*, Heather said: 'When my mother died 19 months ago, I could see no reason for living any more. Today I am stronger, partly because her legacy lives with people. Now I, too, am campaigning.'

Another tragedy occurred on Sunday, 19 March 2000, when Melvin See, Heather's blood father, was found dead of self-inflicted shotgun wounds.

McCartney, Heather Mills (wife)

Heather was born in January 1967, the daughter of John and Beatrice Mills. She endured a penniless childhood in Washington, near Newcastle-under-Wear, with a violent father and absentee mother. She had two siblings: an older brother, Shane, and a younger sister, Fiona.

Her father, a former paratrooper, abused his wife and the children, beating up the mother, throwing the children against walls and through glass doors. Beatrice almost lost her leg when her husband, in an irate mood, crashed the car and wouldn't allow her injured limb to heal properly by causing her to work continually before she'd recovered from the injury.

In 1977, when Heather was nine, her mother ran away to London with an actor from the *Crossroads* television soap. They didn't hear from their mother and later discovered that her father had intercepted all her letters to the children.

'We came home from school one day to find the house empty,' Heather recalled. Three years later her father was jailed for fraud.

Heather then travelled to London with her sister to join her mother (who was working as a hospital psychologist) and her partner, Charles Stapley. Her mother told Heather to lie to the school authorities that she was having home tuition. At the age of thirteen she had a furious row with Charles and left home, beginning to sleep rough. She joined a funfair and slept in a caravan at night, existing on leftover hot dogs. Her fairground friend died of a drug overdose and she took to sleeping in Waterloo arches in a cardboard box.

This period lasted for four months. She decided to stop living rough following an incident: 'There was this stench and I realised my hair was soaked. A tramp was urinating on my head.' She went to Victoria station and paid 10 pence for a shower and found a job in a croissant shop.

Heather returned to the northeast when an aunt and uncle heard of her plight. They took her into their home and arranged for her to have a Saturday job at a jeweller's shop. She was furious when the owner accused her of stealing a Rolex watch, so in an act of revenge she stole a number of gold chains from him and sold them for £1,000 and bought a moped with the proceeds. She was arrested, jailed overnight and placed on probation.

Heather lost her virginity at sixteen and commented: 'Lovemaking was incredible. Sex was everything I'd ever dreamed of.'

She began to live with her boyfriend, Stephen, but became fed up with the domesticity and ran away to London again, recalling: 'I knew who I was and who I wanted to be and it wasn't a stay-at-home housewife. I dreamed not just of money now, but also of success, of new experiences. I dreamed of being the next prime minister, of being a TV presenter. I wanted to try everything life had to offer.'

After answering a newspaper advertisement, she became a showroom model and travelled to Delhi to try on dress samples before they were mass-produced.

She was modelling topless at the age of seventeen and the next year was running her own model agency, ExSell Management UK Ltd. Her friend Diane introduced her to her brother Alfie Karmal, who sent photographs of Heather to the *Daily Mirror* 'Dream Girl' contest, resulting in her winning it.

Heather had started up a few small businesses, one that supplied self-adhesive breast supports for backless dresses, another that sold frozen yoghurt; but she sold both of them and for a time hung around rich Arabs such as Adnam Khashoggi.

A reconciliation with her mother began when Heather was 21, but her mother had an accident when a shopping trolley opened up her old leg wound, which wouldn't heal. This led to the formation of blood clots on her heart and lungs, resulting in her death at 45 in February 1989.

Another string to Heather's bow was television work, and she presented or produced a number of programmes, including *That's Esther*, *Wish You Were Here* and *First Say*.

On 6 May 1989, Heather married Alfie Karmal, who was now the sales director of a computer company, a middle-aged man who had children from a former marriage.

Karmal, who had showered her with gifts such as gold Cartier earrings and a £20,000 BMW car, said that he was disturbed by her temper tantrums and her difficulty telling the truth, and recalled: 'It got so bad that I told her I would not marry her unless she saw a shrink to stop the lies and curb her temper.'

Shortly before they were married she disappeared for three months with a man called George, then returned and married Karmal.

Two years later she had lost two babies through ectopic pregnancies. She went to northern Yugoslavia, fell in love with a Slovenian ski instructor called Milos and went to live with him, serving divorce papers on her husband.

On her return to England she became engaged to City bond dealer, Rafaelle Mincione, who she met at Stringfellow's.

She said: 'The intensity of our life was incredible. This was the man of my dreams and my soul mate.' Two weeks after their first meeting she was hit by a motorcycle.

Her accident occurred on 8 August 1993, in Kensington. She was with her boyfriend Rafael Mincione. They were about the cross the road when two police motorcycles sped past. They waited, and then people began to cross the road. As Heather stepped into the road a third police motorcycle came 'from out of nowhere' and she was hurled ten feet across the road. She recalled: 'My training shoe lay on the road, and inside was my left foot. What remained of my left leg pumped out blood.' She passed out and was taken by air ambulance to Mount Vernon Hospital, Northwood, where they failed to re-attach her foot. During a five-hour operation they had to remove more of her leg.

Heather was said to have died four times in the wake of the accident.

When she woke up in hospital the doctor told her that it might affect her sex life, implying that few would want to make love to her. She said: 'I feel sorry for your wife if that's the only position you know.'

Selling her story to the *News of the World*, she said she and Mincione had made love in the hospital bed. Within weeks she discarded her crutches and was playing tennis, swimming and dancing. She then called off her wedding to Mincione 24 hours before she had the fitting for her £3,000 wedding dress.

Within days she was with Marcus Stapleton, a tennis tournament organiser, saying: 'We are madly, madly in love.' She then had a whirl-wind but short romance with a New Zealander and then took up with

Chris Terrill, a TV director. An August wedding was planned and *Hello!* magazine agreed to pay £40,000 to photograph the event. But Terrill called it off, saying she was 'too bossy'. One of the guests who were to have been invited to the wedding was Paul.

The police motorcyclist involved in the accident was Simon Osbourne. When he was cleared of careless driving he then launched a suit against Heather for damages for stress and injuries. As a result, in response to his suit, Heather went to court against Scotland Yard, who eventually agreed to an out-of-court settlement with her of £200,000.

Heather heads the Heather Mills Trust, a charity aiding those who have lost limbs in war areas. It was while she was being fitted for artificial limbs that she realised that earlier artificial limbs have to be abandoned because the stump shrinks over time, and she had the idea of collecting old ones and shipping them out to countries that needed them. The trust was soon helping more than 27,000 amputees in countries that included India and the former Yugoslavia.

She was also nominated for the Nobel Peace Prize in 1996 for her work in Bosnia. Heather has received more than twenty awards for her work and in 1999 the Royal Association for Disability and Rehabilitation also honoured her. Her other awards include the John Major Gold Award for Outstanding Achievement; the *Times* Human Achievement Award; the British Chamber of Commerce Outstanding Young Person of 1996 award; the 1999 People of the Year Award; the Cosmopolitan Human Achievement 2000 Award; the Pantene Spirit of Beauty Award; Woman of the Year – Blue Drop Group, Sicily; Redbook Mothers and Shakers Award 2001; the 2001 Victory Award by the National Rehabilitation Hospital, Washington, DC.

Heather's autobiography, *Out on a Limb*, written in collaboration with Pamela Churchill, was published on 6 June 1996.

Heather and Paul first met on Thursday May 20 1999 at the Pride of Britain Awards at the Dorchester Hotel, London, in which Heather was a presenter. Paul saw her present an award to Helen Smith, who had lost her hands and feet through meningitis.

Paul was there to present the Linda McCartney Award for Animal Welfare and had chosen Juliet Gellatley, founder of the vegetarian charity, Viva.

Heather and Paul had been in the lift shortly before the ceremony and Heather recalled: 'I got into a lift and just felt these eyes in my back. I turned round and saw him peeping around the corner. I said: "I think you're eyeing my bum."'

Later, Paul would say: 'I didn't even know Heather had a limb missing. I didn't know who she was, you see, and to see her running on stage, well, it's hard to believe she's disabled. I thought Heather's speech was great and it got me thinking.'

Heather recalled: 'He was up at the top table with Tony Blair and I only spoke to him for a moment when I made the presentation, but

Paul told me later he really thought the work I was doing was important and he wanted to help.'

At a ceremony on 22 October Paul presented her with a cheque for £150,000 for her charity.

Heather would later say: 'I've never been offered such an enormous donation before and this time there was enough to set up a trust. It's an amazing thing for him to do. And it's all happened so quickly. He's changed the lives of hundreds of disabled people because of it. And he's changed my life, too.'

She had to catch a plane to Cambodia that day, where she was making a documentary about the victims of landmines. She'd gone with the TV producer Chris Terrill, whom she almost married.

After the charity meeting in which Heather had delivered a speech, Paul was impressed and said: 'So I found her telephone number – like you do – and rang her up and suggested we should talk about the charity and I realised I fancied her.'

On Heather's return from Cambodia she found several messages from Paul asking her to contact him. She was actually sitting with Terrill one Sunday afternoon waiting for their film to be shown when Paul rang. 'Hello, this is Paul McCartney. I've been trying to get hold of you about this charity you organise' he said.

She said: 'Are you near a television set? Switch it on, and call me back when you've seen the film.'

Paul watched the film and called her back.

During the next four weeks the two began to meet frequently to discuss how best to use the money Paul had donated and also to work on a single. By that time her romance with Terrill, which had lasted for only three months, was over.

The rumour of her romance with Paul began following a Guy Fawkes party at Paul's house in Sussex in November 1999.

At the time Paul had lent her his recording studio there to work on her charity single 'VO!CE', launched later that month. When he'd given her £150,000 for the Heather Mills Health Trust, he said: 'Why don't you come to my Bonfire Night?'

It was at the party that people began to realise that the two felt strongly about each other. One of the guests would later comment: 'Paul's keen on Heather and she's keen on him. You just have to see them together to realise that.'

She was to say then: 'It's true we have a lot in common: the way we think, the things we do, liking children, playing music. It doesn't even bother me that he's much older than me. Not at all. We get on really well.'

When Heather was spotted the next morning walking the grounds of Paul's house with her dog Oliver, people assumed that the two had become lovers, although Heather said that following her acceptance of the invitation to the party: 'He has the party every year and it seemed the most natural thing in the world to do. So I stayed in his guesthouse.'

The couple went on a ten-day holiday to Parrot Cay in the Turks and Caicos Islands in February 2001, and, when the media began to question him on their relationship, he said: 'It started with us doing charity work together and then it moved on. We have been great friends for a while, but now we are an item. We have been on holiday together, which was wonderful. It's very early days for us and it's a wait-and-see situation. I find Heather a very impressive woman. She is incredibly committed and determined and I admire her greatly.'

In an interview with the *Sunday Times*, published on 1 April 2001, she said: 'Because I am going out with a very well-known person my reputation has gone down. The association has not been positive. Before I was "Heather the amazing survivor", or "Heather Mills, campaigner" or at least "Heather Mills, model". Now I am just Paul McCartney's girlfriend. If it gains attention for landmines, that's great.' She also said: 'They say every great man has a great woman behind him, and he had a great woman behind him for 30 years.'

While in a London restaurant in 2001 they alarmed the diners with a stand-up row. Later he commented: 'She's a bit bossy and she thinks she's cleverer than me.'

In July 2001 the couple were on holiday at the Sharrow Bay country house hotel in the English Lake District. During dinner on their last day at the hotel, Monday July 23 2001, Paul went down on one knee to propose. She wept and immediately said yes. Paul then presented her with a large sapphire and diamond ring, set in white gold, which he'd bought secretly in February when they were in Jaipur, India.

On Tuesday 24 July 2001 they travelled to London to break the news to his children, Stella, Mary, James and his adopted daughter Heather. They were said to be delighted. His office ran a short statement: 'Paul and Heather are pleased to announce their engagement. They are looking forward to being married "some time next year".

'Paul and Heather say they would like to thank their relatives and friends for all the great support they have shown them.

Paul was 59, Heather 33.

The couple talked briefly to the press outside the Cavendish Avenue house. Paul said: 'I'm still in shock. It's all happened all of a sudden. We're both very much in love and we're just looking forward to it all.' The photographers asked if he could kiss Heather for the cameras, but he said: 'We don't kiss on demand, we're spontaneous.' He ended by saying: 'I'm over the moon. We are very happy. We've had a good reception from friends, relatives and the media.'

Heather caused some raised eyebrows in December 2001 during an interview on the BBC Radio 4 programme *The Choice*. It was only months after Paul had been declared to be the richest man in pop with an estimated fortune of £713 million and she said: 'If I was going to go out with anyone for their money, it would be someone a lot richer.'

At the beginning of the week prior to the wedding, the British press were reporting some discord in the relationship, saying that the couple had been in an argument at the Turnberry Isle Resort and Club in Miami following Paul's final American show in Fort Lauderdale. It was rumoured that, during the furious row, Paul threw her £15,000 diamond and sapphire engagement ring out of the window. It was said that he asked the hotel staff to search for it and it was later delivered to his London home by one of the hotel employees.

One of the hotel's security guards said that Paul 'kept yelling that he wanted to call it off'. The reports also suggested that Paul's daughter Stella was reluctant to welcome Heather into the family and hadn't spoken to her father for a month. It was alleged that a friend of hers had commented: 'She thinks Heather saw that Paul was vulnerable and pounced on him like a preying mantis.'

In fact, there have been many rumours regarding the relationship that 'friends' or 'associates' have suggested. One was that Paul had hoped that Stella would create Heather's wedding dress, that Mary would shoot the wedding pictures, that James would perform for the guests and that stepdaughter Heather would create a centrepiece for the banquet. None of these seem to have occurred.

Paul must have been aware of the family tension as he commented: 'A second marriage is hard for children. They find it difficult to think of me with another woman, but it's how it is and how it must be, and I think that, more than anything, they want me to be happy – and this is what makes me happy.'

He was also to say: 'They know this is my life and I will continue to live it the way I wish until I run out of time myself. My kids are all that's left to me of the love of my life, Linda, but they have to realise there's a point at which you do pick up and resume life. That's what I'm trying to do. Will I ever love anyone the way I loved Linda? Never, but there will be other loves that are just as special and, right now, Heather is very special.'

Heather's former husband Alfie Karmal was to say: 'She should have "Buyer beware" stamped on her forehead. I just hope for Paul's sake that it doesn't end in heartbreak like our marriage did.'

Heather was aware of the amount of criticism she was receiving from people from her past and the media and said, 'People say I am hardline. They either feel threatened by me or they admire me. Those that criticise tend to be those who do the least for others.'

There was massive press coverage building up to the wedding. One of the newspaper spreads made a comparison between Paul's two weddings. The later one was said to be the most expensive and extravagant show business wedding ever with the papers estimating the cost at £2.5m. London's *Evening Standard* pointed out that it was a world apart from his simple marriage to Linda 33 years before. Then, the wedding party retired to Paul's house for champagne and then went to the Ritz for lunch, while the 2002 wedding would see a vegetarian meal with an Indian theme served to 300 guests in two marquees erected beside a lake. At the 1969 wedding Linda wore a bright yellow maxi-coat and a beige dress while Heather was to wear a £10,000 wedding dress. At the 1969 wedding Mike McCartney was best man and the only other people in attendance were Peter Brown and Mal Evans of Apple, a journalist, Paul's driver and Linda's daughter Heather. A host of international celebrities were invited to the 2002 nuptials. The 1969 wedding costs were between £1.75 and £4 at the register office, lunch for £2 per head and a ring that cost Paul £12. The 2002 wedding had an estimated cost of £2.5 million and the wedding ring cost £15,000. The 1969 civil ceremony lasted five minutes, the 2002 was extensive.

Shortly before the wedding, Heather had £50,000 worth of renovation work done on the £1 million house in Brighton, which Paul had bought for her. Paul had also converted a floor of the MPL offices in Soho as an apartment for the two of them and he was also spending £150,000 on 'panic rooms' in his Cavendish Avenue and Long Island homes.

The couple were married at the seventeenth-century Castle Leslie in County Monaghan, Ireland. It has a thousand acres of grounds and there was tight security with 45 security guards on horseback and 30 guards on foot.

On Monday 11 June 2002 parties were held at the castle until 4 a.m., when the families of Paul and Heather met for the first time to start the wedding celebrations. There were twelve McCartneys and twelve Millses, together with four members of Paul's recent 'Driving USA' tour. They all had a vegetarian meal and Paul's brother Mike toasted the couple before everyone joined in with Irish dancing. Paul also sang and played piano for the guests.

Heather retired early to her room in a separate wing of the castle. Geoff Baker explained: 'They are doing the traditional thing of sleeping in separate rooms while still sleeping under the same roof.

'Paul will be up bright and early regardless of the previous night's festivities – he's an early riser anyway; and remember, he's sleeping on his own so there will by no lying in together. Heather will be up really early, too, as she has so much to do, like any bride. All the talk of there being animosity between Heather and Paul's kids is nonsense – they just want them both to be blissfully happy.'

There were a total of 300 guests invited to the wedding, many of whom were given pink embossed invitations informing them to meet at Heathrow airport at 8.30 a.m. sharp. Two privately charted aircraft then left Heathrow at 11 a.m. with the guests, arriving in Belfast shortly before noon. They were then ferried by six coaches to Castle Leslie, about sixty miles away. Some guests had hired helicopters to fly them directly from the airport to the castle grounds. The guests included Ringo and Barbara Starr, Sir George and Lady Martin, Bob Geldof, Jools Holland, Chrissie Hynde, Sir Elton John, Eric Clapton, Sting, Lulu, Dave Gilmour, Twiggy and Mike Batt.

Paul commented: 'It is basically a family wedding for family and friends. It will be a lot of fun and we won't worry about the rain.

'There will be about ten people there you will have heard of. My mother was born in Monaghan, which is why we're having it here. We're just going to have a great time.'

Geoff Baker's official statement read: 'No expense has been spared. Paul has truly built a castle for his bride. Every girl would want to get married here. It is one of the most romantic places in the world.'

Baker also announced that they had turned down an offer of £1 million from *OK! Magazine* for the rights to photograph the wedding. They had also rejected an offer of £1.5 million from *Hello!* magazine. He said: 'Instead we are asking for a donation of £1,000 from newspapers to use a photo of Paul and Heather. That will go to Adopt A Minefield UK, which is Heather's charity, to help landmine victims and support mine clearance. The guests can get wedding presents from a list or give the money to the charity.'

The wedding took place in St Salvator's church in the castle grounds and the two marquees in which the reception was held were of white and gold, situated on the banks of a lake.

Paul had already persuaded Heather to become vegetarian and the wedding banquet was an Indian-inspired vegetarian buffet, prepared by Noel McNeel, the Castle Leslie chef.

There were 300 bottles of vintage Cristal and Laurent Perrier champagne at £180 a bottle, 150 bottles of Chardonnay, 100 bottles of Merlot and an untold amount of beer. A ten-piece band, Celtic Ragas, provided entertainment. Paul had also booked a thirteen-piece band from Englewood, New Jersey, whom he had first seen at the Miramax party in New York following the Concert for New York in 2001. The band, Soul Solution, hadn't been informed that they were to play at the wedding, believing they'd been booked for a corporate bash. They were told when they were flying across the Atlantic. The band performed a two-hour set with songs such as 'Let's Stay Together' and 'Simply The Best', along with their own number 'Here We Are'. When it was over, the singer, Greg Denard, said: 'I think it's only now hitting me. We played at Paul McCartney's wedding. We're professionals, we do a good show. We know how to play and how to conduct ourselves. Sir Paul was wonderful to us. He's very down to earth.'

After the wedding Paul and Heather stayed in the castle's Red Room. This was the room that was alleged to be haunted by the castle's former owner, Sir Norman Leslie, who had been killed in France during the first World War.

The day after the wedding the *Daily Mail* featured a colour cover of the newlyweds with the headline, THE NEW LADY McCARTNEY SIGNS A PRE-NUPTIAL CONTRACT: HEATHER'S £20M DEAL. The inside story related that Paul hadn't wanted to ask Heather for such a deal in case it upset her, but he changed his mind owing to pressure from Stella, who was opposed to the marriage. A friend of Stella commented: 'She said that she was pushing her father to get Heather to sign something for ages before the wedding because she was worried about him. She has made no secret of the fact that she despises Heather and she is angry that Heather has made little attempt to be friendly to towards her either.'

Following her marriage to Paul, Heather announced that she would be writing her second autobiography, to be called *A Single Step*. This would focus on her romance with Paul and her charity work.

There were some quite savage attacks on Heather in the British press following the wedding. In particular from Lynda Lee-Potter of the *Daily Mail*. In one of her columns headed ONLY PAUL CAN SAVE HIS FEUDING FAMILY NOW, she wrote: 'The bride is young and ruthless with a besotted husband' and pointed out that Paul had taken off Linda's wedding ring. She was also to write:

> She wants Paul to love only her. She can't tolerate what she sees as competition and her stepchildren increasingly feel sidelined and peripheral in their father's world.
>
> His houses, which were once their homes and full of Linda's vital presence, must feel like alien territory. They've lost their mother and now they're in danger of losing their father to his driven and bossy bride.

The *Sunday Times* on 16 June had Heather's former husband Alfie Karmal discussing his ex-wife and saying: 'She lived in a dream world, desperate for fame and fortune.'

Even her stepfather, Charles Stapley, made disparaging remarks about her to the tabloids.

Owing to such adverse coverage, Heather's family and friends rushed to her defence. Her sister Fiona arrived from Athens, declaring: 'For the record, my sister is a truly thoughtful, giving and loving person who has always devoted herself to others, whether that be via her charity works or simply helping her family and friends.'

A friend, David Nix, commented: 'I could relate countless good works that she has carried out mostly with no one knowing and also mostly out of her own finances.'

Members of various charities remarked on Heather's unstinting devotion to charities and her remarkable courage.

This is perhaps indicated in Heather's own philosophy: 'The overcoming of adversity, and ultimately denying it the rite of passage, has been a constant and perpetual motive throughout my life.'

On Thursday July 4 2002, at the invitation of Sarah, the Duchess of York, a friend of Heather's, Paul and Heather made their first public appearance following their marriage a month before at Carlton Television's the *Britain's Brilliant Prodigies* awards show to present some awards.

Heather revealed that she is to be known as Heather Mills McCartney and not Lady McCartney. A member of the television team commented: 'Heather has been known as Heather Mills McCartney throughout our dealings with her on the programme. We've been told that's what she wants to be known as now.'

When asked about their honeymoon in the Seychelles, Paul said: 'Thank you very much. We don't want to talk about that – we're going now.' And the couple left the hall, with Paul playfully slapping Heather's behind.

McCartney II

Paul's second solo album, issued in Britain ten years after his first, on 16 May 1980 on Parlophone PCTC 258. It was released in America on 21 May 1980 on Columbia FC 36511.

The album reached No. 1 in the British charts and No. 3 in the American.

As with the first album, Paul composed all the songs and played all the instruments himself. He took six weeks to record the album in 1979, starting in his Sussex farm, completing it at his Scottish farm and producing and engineering everything himself.

The tracks were: Side One: 'Coming Up', 'Temporary Secretary', 'On The Way', 'Waterfalls', 'Nobody Knows'. Side Two: 'Front Parlour', 'Summer's Day Song', 'Frozen Jap', 'Bogey Music', 'Darkroom', 'One Of These Days'.

The album spawned three hit singles: 'Coming Up', 'Waterfalls' and 'Temporary Secretary'.

The only song which had been written prior to the actual recording sessions was 'Waterfalls'.

McCartney Interview, The

A unique album which originally saw life as an interview for the American magazine *Musician: Player & Listener*.

The publication's managing editor, Vic Garbarini, travelled to London and held an extensive taped interview with Paul at MPL's Soho Square offices.

The interview initially appeared in print in 1980, in the August issue of the publication. Paul gave his permission for the tapes to be used on a special two-record promotional set by Columbia in the States to be sent to various radio stations for use by their disc jockeys. It worked so well that Columbia was able to issue an album of the edited interview on Columbia PC 36987 in December of that year in a limited issue of 57,000 copies.

The disc was, in fact, nominated for a 1982 Grammy Award in the 'Best Spoken Word, Documentary, or Drama Recording' category but this section was won by Orson Welles narrating the science-fiction classic *Donovan's Brain*.

In Britain EMI issued limited numbers of the album on Parlophone CHAT 1 on 23 February 1981 and deleted it the same day, a gimmick which created an immediate collectors' item.

The sleeve of the British and American releases both carried two photographs of Paul by Linda.

Paul touches on many topics in the interview: his decision to make a solo album; Stevie Wonder; his reaction to the critical reviews of *Back To The Egg*; the making of various Beatles albums, including *Sgt Pepper*, *Abbey Road*, *Rubber Soul* and *The Beatles*; his interest in the bass guitar; Wings' British university tour of 1972; the Beatles' American visit in February 1964; the break-up of the Beatles; British 'New Wave' music; and his 'Mary Had A Little Lamb' single. The track-by-track breakdown of subjects covered on the album is as follows:

Side One – *McCartney II*; Negative Criticism Of Beatles and Wings; His influences; *Venus and Mars/Wild Life/Band on the Run*; Musical direction/Ringo/George/'Hey Jude'; The White Album; 'Helter Skelter'; *Abbey Road*; Musical background/trumpet, guitar, piano/Learning bass in Hamburg; early Beatles mixes/Motown and Stax influences; The *Sgt Pepper* story/The Beach Boys; 'Pet Sounds'; *Rubber Soul/Revolver*; Fame and success/his and John's reactions; Stage fright during the Beatles and Wings; how Wings started; New Wave/early Beatles; and Creating the Beatles sound/ 'Love Me Do' and early songs.

McCartney, James (father)

Paul's father was born on 7 July 1902 at 8 Fishguard Street, Everton to Joseph and Florence McCartney. He had five sisters – Edith, Ann, Millie, Annie and Jin and two brothers, Jack and Joseph. Another brother Joe had died and a sister Alice had passed away at the age of eighteen months the year before James's birth.

In his early years he was reared in Solva Street in Everton, a tiny cobbled street of terraced houses.

He attended Steer Street School in Everton and while still at school was given employment at a local music hall, the Everton Theatre Royal, as a lampboy.

Paul was to say, 'He actually burned bits of lime for the limelights.'

Jim was hired to sell programmes before each performance. He would then collect discarded programmes at the end of the show and rush home so that his sister Millie could iron them out in time for the second show, then he'd sell them again, but this time pocketing the money.

The family had an old second-hand piano, originally from NEMS (the Epstein family store, North End Music Stores), which they had been given. It was installed in the McCartney's parlour and Jim taught himself to play, pounding out tunes he'd heard the night before at the music hall.

The family even had what they called 'pound nights' when friends or relatives would arrive for a singsong bringing along a pound of something or other such as sugar or tea.

At the age of ten Jim had broken his right eardrum falling off a wall, but he continued with his love of music and taught himself to play chords.

He left school at the age of fourteen in 1916 for full-time employment at A Hannay & Company, Cotton Merchants, in Chapel Street, where he earned six shillings a week as a sample boy. At the age of 28 he was promoted to cotton salesman at the Cotton Exchange, earning £5 a week.

It was towards the end of the First World War that Jim started a swing band with his brother Jack on trombone to play at local functions. They called themselves the Masked Melody Makers and had a gimmick of wearing black harlequin masks. At one engagement the high temperature made the black dye trickle slowly down their faces, so they abandoned the masks and the name. They became Jim Mac's Jazz Band and wore dinner jackets with paper shirtfronts and cuffs. They were playing at dances, socials and occasionally in cinemas, and provided music at one cinema for the silent movie *The Queen Of Sheba*.

Tunes that Jim selected to play for the movie included 'Thanks For The Buggy Ride', played during the chariot scene and 'Horsey Keep Your Tail Up' for the Queen's deathbed sequence.

The band's repertoire included 'Birth Of The Blues', 'Some Of These Days', 'Chicago', 'Stairway To Paradise' and Jim's own composition 'Walking In The Park With Eloise'.

In addition to being pianist, Jim also began to play trumpet, but when his teeth gave out, he just performed on piano.

Jim loved a flutter and gambling once got him into trouble. When the family were now living in West Derby, he wanted to raise some money to send his mother on holiday, but had a dreadful losing streak and found himself heavily in debt.

When his boss Mr Hannay heard of it, instead of sacking him he loaned him enough money to pay off his debts and send his mother on a holiday to Devon. Jim then repaid the cash, saving the money by walking the five miles to work and back every working day for a full year.

World War Two saw the end of the band's engagements. The Cotton Exchange also closed down for the duration of the war and Jim went to work as a lathe operator at Napier's, the munitions factory that specialised in building the Sabre aircraft engine. Jim was 37 years old at the time, basically too old to be called up for military service, and he'd also been exempt from National Service due to his hearing disability.

One night he met Mary Mohin, a nursing sister at Walton Hospital, at his sister Jin's house and on 15 April 1941 the pair were married at

St Swithin's Roman Catholic Chapel, Gill Moss, although Jim was agnostic. Jim was 38 while Mary was 31.

While working at Napier's he felt he should participate in some further work to help the war effort and became a volunteer fireman at night.

The couple's first son James Paul McCartney was born in Walton Hospital. To Jim's initial horror, 'he looked awful ... like a horrible piece of red meat,' he said, and went home where he broke down and cried.

They lived in furnished rooms at the time and when Mary put her baby son in a pram in the warm weather that summer, she was horrified to find his face coated with flecks of dust and insisted that they move house. Since Jim's work at Napier's was classified as work for the Air Ministry they were eligible to move into a government sponsored house and moved into 92 Broadway Avenue in Wallasey Village.

The job at Napier's came to an end and Jim began to work at the Liverpool Corporation cleansing department. The pay was notoriously low, so Mary had to return to work.

She stopped work again temporarily when the couple's second son Michael was born, but by that time they had moved to a prefab house in Roach Avenue on the Knowsley Estate.

Due to Mary's work, they were able to move again to 72 Western Avenue, Speke.

Since the war had ended Jim had left the cleansing department for his old job at the Cotton Exchange, although the pay remained poor at £6 a week.

The family then moved to 12 Ardwick Road and later settled down at 20 Forthlin Road.

Paul confirms that his father was a major influence on his life. 'Never overdo it. Have a drink, but don't be an alcoholic. Have a cigarette, but don't be a cancer case,' he told him.

He was also to say, 'My Dad was a pianist by ear and then a trumpeter until his teeth gave out. He was a good pianist, you know, but he would never teach me, because he felt that you should learn properly. It was a bit of a drag, because a lot of people have said that I do chords a lot like he used to do. I'm sure I picked it up over the years.'

At another time he commented, 'Dad used to play the cornet a lot, just for fun, at home. This was my earliest musical influence at, say, the age of five. This and the radio, listening to Luxembourg under the bedclothes, the Top Twenty Show on a Sunday night.'

Naturally, Jim was devastated when Mary died. 'I missed my wife – it knocked me for six when she died,' he said. 'The biggest headache was what sort of parent I was going to be.'

Milly and Jinny, two of his sisters, regularly came around the house to help out with the cleaning and his younger son Mike was to remark,

'He had to decide to be a father or a mother to his two growing lads. Luckily, he chose to be both, a very hard decision when you've got used to being the man around the house.'

When the Silver Beetles were given the opportunity to tour Scotland backing Johnny Gentle, Paul lied to his father.

On his return from Germany, Jim insisted that Paul get a job and he signed on at the labour exchange. He found work at a local firm, but soon gave it up.

Jim didn't think much of the Cavern and told Paul, 'You should have been paid danger money to go down there.' He was also suspicious of Brian Epstein at first, referring to him as 'a Jew boy'.

Early in the Beatles' career, Paul was to say, 'Dad always encouraged me to take up music. He likes our sound, I think – but sometimes says we're away from home a bit too much. He put up with my practice sessions for years which shows he's a brave man.'

Commenting on his father, Mike McCartney said, 'My dad taught me a lot of things; we both owe him a lot. He's a very good man, and he's a very stubborn man. He looks more like Paul than me, but I've got him inside me.

'Of course, it would have been easy for him to have gone off with other birds when Mum died, or to have gone out getting drunk every night. But he didn't. He stayed at home and looked after us.

'He's a brilliant salesman with a very fine business brain and he could have gone right to the top in business if he had played the rules like they are now, if he had wanted to kill. He knew that to be a good businessman you have to have that killer streak, and he just wasn't prepared to be like that. And it would have meant neglecting us, and he wasn't prepared to do that, either. He told us that you have to be prepared to kill if you are to get to the top, and if he'd been prepared to pay that price he could have got there. But he was not prepared to do that – and that is the big lesson he taught us. It has rubbed off on to both of us; neither of us has really got that killer streak.'

On 6 July 1964, following the premiere of *A Hard Day's Night* in London, it was the eve of Jim's birthday. While they attended the after-show party at the Dorchester Hotel, Jim was introduced to Princess Margaret. At midnight Paul said, 'Happy Birthday, Dad' and handed him a painting of a horse.

'Thank you, son, very nice,' Jim said, thinking, 'It's very nice, but couldn't he have done better than that,' when Paul revealed that the painting was of a £1,050 racehorse called Drake's Drum which he'd bought as his father's present.

Jim was delighted, 'You silly bugger,' he said.

Also in 1964, when Jim was 61 years old, Paul asked his father if he wanted to retire from his £10 a week job at the Cotton Exchange. He said he'd maintain him for the rest of his life and buy him a nice house in Heswall, 'across the water' from Liverpool. Jim was delighted.

1964 was also the year that Jim remarried. His bride was Angela Lucia Williams, a widow of Northwood, Kirby, who was 28 years younger than him and mother of a five-year-old daughter, Ruth.

They married on 24 November at St Bridget's Church in Carrog, North Wales. At the time Jim owned a house, 'Afon Rho' in Carrog and the vicar of the church was the Reverend D J Bevan, a former chaplain of Walton Hospital, Liverpool, where Paul and his brother Mike had been born and where Mary McCartney had worked.

Jim had been affected by arthritis for some time and for eight years before his death the attacks were crippling. He had to move into a bungalow and Paul bought 'Rembrandt', his house, back from him. Jim died at his home in Heswall on 13 March 1976. His final words were, 'I'll be with Mary soon.'

Jim was 73 years old. John Lennon, in New York, was one of the first people to hear of Jim's death and he was the one who actually phoned Paul to tell him the sad news.

The funeral took place on 22 March and Jim was cremated at Landican Cemetery.

Paul didn't attend his father's funeral. His brother Mike said, 'It was no coincidence that Paul was on the Continent at the time. Paul would never face that sort of thing.'

McCartney, James (son)

Born on 12 September 1977. He was delivered by Caesarean section and weighed six pounds and one ounce. Paul and Linda issued their official photograph of James eight days after his birth and Paul was able to comment, 'I'm over the moon! When I knew the baby was a boy I really flipped. I was waiting outside the door while he was being born. He has fair hair and looks like Linda. She's still a bit tired, but otherwise smashing. I don't know how she does it.'

On Monday 13 September 1993 James had a lucky escape while bodysurfing off the coast of east Sussex. He was celebrating his sixteenth birthday. His partners lost sight of him for forty minutes and a lifeboat and helicopter took part in a search. He was found drifting off the entrance to Rye Harbour. Paul rushed to the hospital and said, 'We are all distressed by this, and the most important thing is to get back and look after him.'

Linda was to say, 'It was scary for a parent. He was out there not even knowing we were all panicking. It was a panic, as you can imagine. But everything is well – his friends and everyone were great. I just count my blessings!'

There was some criticism about the air-lift rescue of James and a furious Paul was to say, 'After the sea rescue, some people said, "Oh, why's his bloody son got the helicopter?" I say, "What do you mean? My son's entitled just like your fucking son." Would they say, "Hang on, leave him because he's rich?" Would they say, "Hang on, check his Barclaycard. Oh no, he's flush. Leave the bastard to drown?" It's not on!'

In May 1995 the 17-year-old James was involved in an accident on farmland near Peasmarsh.

He was driving his Land Rover when it hit a rut and overturned and James was trapped beneath it. His leg was caught beneath the three-and-a-half-ton vehicle for half an hour while a friend ran for help. Doctors, an ambulance and a fire crew rushed to the scene and the Land Rover was lifted by air bags. He was immediately treated for a broken ankle and then airlifted by helicopter to the Conquest Hospital, Hastings.

James has followed in his father's footsteps, taking up the guitar, and he co-wrote and performed on two tracks on the *Driving Rain* album, 'Spinning On An Axis' and 'Back In The Sunshine Again'. He played percussion on the first track and guitar on the second.

McCartney, Joan

One of Paul's aunties. When he appeared in Liverpool on 21 March 2001 to sign copies of his poetry book *Blackbird Singing* his Auntie Joan was waiting for him in the WH Smith branch in Church Street and hugged him as he entered. She said, 'It's always lovely to see him and I am always very proud. I've had a quick scan of his poems and they seem very good.'

McCartney, Joseph

Paul's fraternal grandfather, who was born on 23 November 1866. He was a tobacco cutter at Cope's in St Vincent Street. Joseph had played the E-flat bass in Cope's band and the Territorial Army Brass Band, and was also noted for his ability as a singer.

At the age of 29 he married Florence Clegg.

Joe encouraged his children to take music seriously and also to learn to play an instrument.

He died before Paul was born.

McCartney, Josh

The first son of Mike and Rowena McCartney who was born at Arrowe Park Hospital in the Wirral, Merseyside on 18 August 1983. At the time, the 22-year-old Rowena, a dress designer, was suffering from a rare disease that causes convulsions during pregnancy. Josh was born nine weeks prematurely and was immediately placed in an incubator and life-support machine. He weighed only 2lb 8oz at birth. Fortunately he battled for his life and put on weight, causing Mike to comment, 'He's absolutely marvellous – a real McFighter.'

Paul's nephew was also to enter a career as a musician and Josh became a drummer and in 2001 was performing with an indie band, the trio Trilby.

McCartney, Linda Louise (née Eastman)

Linda was born in Scarsdale, New York State, on 24 September 1942. Her paternal grandparents fled from Russia and set up a little furniture store in New York. Her father, Leopold ('Lee'), the son of Mr and Mrs Louis Epstein, was poor, but won a scholarship to Harvard, graduating from the law school there in 1933. He eventually became a lawyer for prestigious clients such as Tennessee Williams and the artist Willem de Kooning.

Her mother, Louise Sara Linder Eastman, born in Cleveland on 9 November 1911, was the only child of Max and Stella Dreyfous Linder, who owned major department stores. She married Leopold Veil Epstein in 1937 and on the birth of their first child, John, changed the family name to Eastman. Linda was their next child, followed by Laura and then Louise Jr.

When Linda was a child, the songwriters Jack Lawrence and Ann Rochell composed a song, 'Linda', for her in 1948. Her father was a specialist in copyright law in the show business field and agreed to undertake some legal work for Lawrence in exchange for his writing a song dedicated to his six-year-old daughter. It was first recorded by Buddy Clark and then by Jan and Dean in 1963 and Jimmy Young and Dick James, the Beatles' music publisher, also recorded it.

Linda had a privileged upbringing, since her parents lived in Scarsdale, Westchester County, in upstate New York. They also owned a house in East Hampton and an apartment in Park Avenue. Many celebrity guests were invited to dinner parties at their home including the songwriter Hoagy Carmichael, the jazz legend Tommy Dorsey and the actor William Boyd, who portrayed Hopalong Cassidy on the silver screen.

Her education was also privileged, for she followed a period at Scarsdale High School by moving to the exclusive Sarah Lawrence School in nearby Bronzville.

When she graduated from Scarsdale High, her senior year entry in the yearbook noted that she belonged to Advertising Club 4, Chorus 1, 2, 3, 4 and Pep Club 3, 4. She was also described as 'strawberry blonde ... [with a] yen for men. Shetlandish.'

Linda loved music and commented: 'All my teen years were spent with an ear to the radio.' She would often play truant to attend concerts at the Paramount Theater in Brooklyn and recalled: 'They'd have twenty acts on, twenty-four hours a day. Alan Freed was the MC, but sometimes they'd get Fabian or Bobby Darin to MC. I remember seeing Chuck Berry sing "School Days" for the first time.'

She also remembered: 'At home in Scarsdale, New York, which was out in the countryside then, although it's a suburb now, I listened to the Alan Freed rock-'n'-roll show on the radio every night of the week, seven to ten. He never played a bad record. The Dells, the Doves, the Moonglows – I was into them all. I wasn't in a band but some of the girls used to sing doo-wop together for fun up in our school's music tower.'

Louise Eastman died in a plane crash on 1 March 1962 on an American Airlines flight from New York to Los Angeles. She and her husband had made a pact never to travel on a plane together in case an accident left their children orphans. It was a prophetic decision. Louise was 50 years old.

Linda was a fine-arts major at the University of Arizona, where she met Joseph Melvin ('Mel') See Jr. Linda felt that the traumatic effect of her mother's death precipitated a hasty marriage in 1962. She was to say: 'My mother died in a plane crash and I got married. It was a mistake.'

Linda and her new husband continued their studies at the University of Colorado and then moved to Tucson, Arizona, where she discovered she was pregnant. She gave birth to her first daughter, Heather, on 31 December 1962.

See became a geophysicist. Linda, who realised that the marriage wasn't working, said: 'When he graduated he wanted to go to Africa. I said, "Look, if I don't get on with you here I'm not going to Africa with you. I won't get on with you there." '

See went to Africa, still hoping that Linda would follow, but she wrote to him saying she was going to get a divorce.

It was while in Arizona that Linda studied art history at the University of Arizona. While she was there she began taking an interest in photography following a short course in the subject given by wheel-chair-bound Hazel Archer at Tucson Art Center. Linda said: 'Arizona opened up my eyes to the wonder of light and colour.'

In an interview, Linda was to say: 'When my marriage broke up, I decided to get away from everything I had ever known before. I moved down to Tucson, staying with friends, studying photography at a local college and spending much of my time riding on the edge of the desert. For the first time I started going round with artists, actors and writers, and all that helped me to discover who I am. It changed my life, meeting so many interesting, intelligent people.'

Her divorce from Melvin See was finalised in June 1965, and the following year Linda reverted to her former name, Eastman. (Mel was to commit suicide in March 2000 at the age of 62, and it was rumoured that this was caused by the depression he suffered as a result of Linda's death.)

Linda and her daughter moved to New York to join her father and brother John and she became a receptionist with *Town and Country* magazine. When an invitation arrived to cover a Rolling Stones reception on the SS *Sea Panther* on the Hudson River, Linda snapped it up, grabbed her Pentax, jumped in a cab and went down to the boat. She said: 'I stood there on the quay with my long blonde hair and, I guess, a miniskirt. I must have caught the band's eye because a woman came down the gangway and said I was the only photographer they would allow on board. I got well into it, using black and white. Then back on the quay all the journalists came up and gave me their cards because they needed the pictures. I got them back from the lab and, lo! they were wonderful.

'After that I started to get a lot of work with bands like the Jimi Hendrix Experience, Lovin' Spoonful, the Doors, Jefferson Airplane, the Grateful Dead and the Beatles. One reason is, I was the cheapest photographer in town. Give me a credit and pay for the film and I'd do it.'

The Stones were No. 1 in the American charts with 'Paint It Black' that week of the *Sea Panther* reception, and Linda discovered she was the only photographer on board. The photographs established her reputation and she became friends with Mick Jagger and also with other British artists such as Eric Burdon of the Animals, while she continued taking photographs of the bands. When the Fillmore East opened in New York she was invited to become the official photographer for the venue. Linda wasn't actually paid any money for the job, but it gave her the opportunity to photograph a host of major stars, including Janis Joplin, Jim Morrison and Pete Townshend.

Discussing her method of work, she said: 'I've always liked to spend a day with someone if I'm going to take their photograph. If you have a really nice day, having lunch together, going to the zoo maybe, the pictures can't fail to turn out well.'

The first time she met the Beatles was at Shea Stadium in 1966. She recalled: 'It was John who interested me at the start. He was my Beatle hero. But when I met him the fascination faded fast and I found it was Paul I liked.'

The author J Marks was preparing a book to be called *Rock and Other Four Letter Words*, and, on his invitation, Linda flew to London to photograph some of the major groups. It was during that trip that she met Paul at a fashionable 'in' club.

Paul was to say in 1993: 'The night Linda and I met, I spotted her across a crowded club, and, although I would normally have been nervous chatting her up, I realised I had to. So when she passed our table I asked her to come with us to another club, and she said yes.

'I realise now that, if she had said no, we wouldn't have married, and our four beautiful children would not have blessed our lives. Pushiness worked for me that night!'

The club at which they met was the Bag O' Nails in Kingley Street and Linda was in the company of Chas Chandler of the Animals. Georgie Fame & the Blue Flames were performing that night.

Interestingly enough, Linda would later recall: 'I was quite shameless really. I was with somebody else at the Bag O' Nails Club in Soho to see Georgie Fame & the Blue Flames and I saw Paul at the other side of the room. He looked so beautiful that I made up my mind I would have to pick him up.'

Linda's photographs were much appreciated by the leading acts and Jimi Hendrix wanted her to shoot the cover of his *Electric Ladyland* album. He was disappointed when the record company rejected Linda's picture and used one of a group of naked girls instead.

Brian Epstein's assistant, Peter Brown, admired Linda's photographs and asked if he could buy some of her shots of Brian Jones of the Rolling Stones. Linda gave them to him as a present and he put her on the list of exclusive guests invited to the *Sgt Pepper* party Epstein was hosting at his home on 19 May 1969, where she met Paul for the second time.

In his book *The Love You Make*, Brown was to write:

> The girl that turned up at Chapel Street that May nineteenth wasn't the same sloppily dressed girl I had seen in my office a few days before. She wore impeccably applied make-up, including long, fluttering false eyelashes. It wasn't long before she zeroed in on Paul. He watched as Linda sank to her knees in front of his chair and began snapping photos of him. Although she tried to manage otherwise, she left with all the other photographers.

The two met for the third time when Paul arrived in New York with John Lennon to promote Apple in May 1968. As there were so many people around when they saw each other again, she slipped a piece of paper in his hand. It had her phone number on it. Paul phoned her that evening and spent a few days with her, during which he babysat for Heather when Linda went to take some photographs at a gig.

Paul returned to London and a few weeks later invited Linda to join him on a business trip to Los Angeles. The couple spent a week together at the Beverly Hills hotel on Sunset Boulevard. Linda then returned to New York with Paul and an entourage, who included the Apple Records boss Ron Kass and Paul's childhood friend Ivan Vaughan. Paul then returned to London and Linda remained in New York.

Five months after Paul had split with Jane Asher, he asked Linda to join him in London. She recalled: 'I came over and we lived together for a while. Neither of us talked about marriage. We just loved each other and lived together. We liked each other a lot, so, being conventional people, one day I thought: OK, let's get married, we love each other, let's make it definite.'

The two of them had had their share of lovers and they sat down and discussed their past affairs together. Some years later, Paul said: 'You prove how much you love someone by confessing all that old stuff. Both Linda and I were ravers back then. But that's one of the reasons our marriage has worked. We had both sown our wild oats and gotten it out of our system. We got it all out before we were married.'

When they were married at Marylebone Register Office on 12 March 1969, Linda was 27 years old and four months pregnant. The previous day, she had rushed to the register office to give notice of their wedding plans, booking the ceremony for 9.45 a.m. the next day. That evening, Paul was recording the Liverpool singer Jackie Lomax performing 'Thumbing A Ride' and realised he'd forgotten to buy a ring. He managed to talk a jeweller into opening his shop specially that evening and he bought a plain gold ring for £12. Paul and Linda spent that night at his Cavendish Avenue house. On the morning of the wedding, the press began to gather outside Cavendish Avenue at 6 a.m. An hour later a group of fans stole Paul's mail and telegrams. The police then escorted Paul and Linda to the register office, where a crowd of about 300 had gathered.

Paul's best man was his brother Mike. Unfortunately, his train from Liverpool was delayed and he arrived an hour late. He rushed into the register office apologising: 'Forgive me, it wasn't my fault. Have you been done?' Since there were no other weddings booked for that morning, Paul was able to say: 'No, we've been waiting for you.'

Linda wore a yellow maxi-coat, a beige dress, brown stockings and buckled shoes. Paul wore a dark-grey suit, made by Dougie Millings, the former Beatles tailor, along with a lace shirt and a yellow tie to match Linda's coat.

Apart from Mike, the only other people present at the ceremony were Linda's daughter Heather, who was bridesmaid, Peter Brown and Mal Evans of Apple, Paul and Linda's driver Don Murfet and the journalist Mike Housego. No other members of the Beatles were present, owing to the fact that Paul was taking legal action to dissolve the group.

The magistrate, ER Sanders, and the superintendent registrar, JL Jeavons, performed the ceremony. The couple later received a blessing from the Rev. Noel Perry-Gore at St John's Wood Parish Church, with Paul commenting: 'I'm a lapsed Catholic, but I would like our marriage to be blessed in church.'

The party then moved to Cavendish Avenue, where the press had gathered, and Paul gave them champagne to sip and answered various questions.

Linda told them: 'No. I'm nothing to do with the Eastman-Kodak family.' Paul said: 'What? I've been done. Where's the money?'

Commenting on the marriage years later, Paul said: 'To the world, of course, she was a divorcee, which didn't seem right. People preferred Jane Asher. Jane Asher fitted. She was a better Fergie. Linda wasn't a very good Fergie for me and people generally tended to disapprove of my marrying a divorcee and an American. That wasn't too clever. None of that made a blind bit of difference. I actually just liked her, I still do, and that's all it's to do with.

'I mean, we got married in the craziest clothes when I look back on it. We didn't even bother to buy her a decent outfit.'

After the wedding, Paul and Linda then went on to the Ritz Hotel in Piccadilly to join their friends for their reception.

That evening Paul and Linda spent time in the recording studio where Paul finished the recording of Jackie Lomax's disc. Five days later they flew to New York to visit Linda's family.

Paul had taken Linda to see High Park Farm shortly before their wedding and they returned to the 180-acre Scottish farm to find some refuge. After they'd returned from New York, the female fans who'd hung around the Beatles' haunts began booing and hissing Linda, taunting her with remarks such as 'ugly face' and 'hairy legs'.

Linda said: 'I just wasn't ready for all of it. I married Paul because we loved one another and I didn't even think about the attacks that were going to be made on me. All I could do was just go on being myself and let people either take me or leave me.'

She would also recall: 'The girls went to war when I married Paul. Looking back I think I took on a battle when I should have just said that I understood, and tried to talk to them. But it was difficult. I had been a free woman in New York. When I married Paul I suddenly felt fenced in. We would go home at night and find about twenty girls outside who had been standing there for five years! They each felt as though they were Paul's wife. They would say: "I hate you. You're horrible. Why didn't he marry Jane Asher? At least we knew her." They painted nasty things all over our walls and played their radios real loud at night outside our house.'

Fans actually broke into the Cavendish Avenue house, stealing Linda's clothes and ripping up her photographs.

One of the first songs that Paul wrote after the couple were married was 'The Lovely Linda'. Another was 'Maybe I'm Amazed'. Both songs were included on his solo debut album *McCartney*.

Linda loved High Park Farm and said: 'The light in Scotland is the best light in the world for me. The incredible beauty in old rocks and moss, the sky, the changes in the weather. It's good.'

They were to remain there for a time with Heather, their new baby daughter Mary and the sheepdog Martha.

Paul and Linda would have two further children, Stella and James.

When Paul decided that he wanted to return to the active music scene by forming a new band, he wanted Linda to become part of it, even though she hadn't played a musical instrument since her school-days. She protested, but Paul insisted. He told her he could teach her a few chords on the electric organ. Looking back on that, she would say: 'I really tried to persuade Paul that I didn't want to do it.'

Although Linda had loved the music scene, she had formerly eschewed learning an instrument and recalled: 'I was forced to learn piano and, like a lot of children forced to do something against their will, I rebelled against that, learned nothing and finally got away.'

When they appeared at their first university gig, Paul introduced the band and told the audience they were going to begin with a song called 'Wildlife'.

'One, two, three . . .' he began. But nothing happened. Linda was supposed to begin the song with a few simple chords on the electric piano. 'I've forgotten the chords,' she told him.

'OK, Linda,' he said. 'Just put that finger on C, that one on F sharp, like this, that's right, and then you'll remember the rest.'

That evening Linda broke down and cried and she was aware that Henry McCullough and Denny Seiwell were unhappy with her being in the band.

Recalling the incident, Linda said: 'I cried. The first time when I hit the stage with Paul I was terribly nervous, that I cried. I didn't know what I was doing over there. I can remember the time when I had forgotten the intro of a song completely. Paul gave me a clue and then there was silence: I couldn't remember the music. He looked at me, but it was useless: I couldn't remember anything at all. Paul realised that something was wrong, so he came to my keyboard to show me the intro, but then he forgot the music as well and it became one big laugh.'

Paul told her: 'If you think of any group or musician, there has to be a time when they're learning. George Martin didn't want Ringo to play on our first Beatles record because he thought he wasn't good enough and Ringo must have felt like giving up then. But he stuck it out and pretty soon he became a great drummer.'

During the Wings tour in 1975 Linda was asked if she ever saw herself as a musician. She replied: 'Not even when I married Paul I didn't. If he hadn't said anything I wouldn't have done it. It was his idea – it wasn't like me saying: "Listen I can do this. I never tried to sing or play or anything." '

Linda wasn't initially happy about being a member of the band as her first calling was photography. In 1998 she was to comment: 'Playing in a band totally stopped me from being a working photographer; my career just stopped. Before that I was taking pictures for all sorts of magazines and I was also working on photographs for a book about rock 'n' roll . But I joined a band and all the time that I was in that band I would have been taking photographs. Photography was more important to me than music, but my husband and my family were more important to me than photography, and I was prepared to give up photography for them.'

On another occasion she said: 'When the Beatles broke up Paul said: "Let's you and me do a band." It was like a tennis pro asking me if I wanted a game. I said: "Well, I don't play an instrument. I love music, but I'm a photographer"; and he said: "Well, here's middle C on the piano – you can learn and then you can play keyboards." So I learned. Nobody taught me the keyboards. I just learned twelve bars; I taught myself. In Wings they said I sang out of tune – big deal! Most punks do and I love punk music. I don't like things to be perfect and beautiful. I like rough music, so I'm the rough edge.'

Paul was to say: 'It was OK for me to have her on stage. Linda is the innocence of the group. All the rest of us are seasoned musicians – and probably too seasoned. Linda has an innocent approach, which I like. It's like when you hear an artist say: "I wish I could paint like a child again." That's what she's got. That is very easily made fun of and if an artist does a naïve drawing people say: "Ooh, he can't draw." But if you talk to an artist like Peter Blake he'll tell you how much great artists love the naïveté of aboriginal paintings. Linda's inclusion was something to do with that. She was a mate. I wanted her on stage and so I thought: We'll have her on stage. We didn't do badly. We took a lot of flak with Wings; but you look at the hits we had.'

Linda developed a growing authority as a musician during the world tours she embarked on with Paul. She also appeared in a cameo role in the popular BBC TV series *Bread*, scripted by her friend Carla Lane.

The only time Paul and Linda were ever parted during their years of marriage was the nine days that Paul spent in a Japanese jail.

In 1985 Paul recalled: 'Most people thought I was due to marry Jane Asher. I rather thought I was, too. But I just kept remembering Linda, this nice blonde American girl. I twisted her arm and finally she agreed to marry me. Linda was afraid it wouldn't work out. And I kept telling her: "Aw, come on, it'll be fine." I'm still telling her that.'

Of her life as a vegetarian, Linda would comment: 'I love cooking. I find it artistic and sensual. My kitchen is the sexiest, most creative room in the whole house – apart from my bedroom!'

Yet none of her dishes contain meat. She was to say: 'I want to convert people from demanding flesh on their plates. For every bit of meat they eat, an animal has been killed.'

For her efforts in promoting vegetarianism and animal welfare, she was presented with a Lifetime Achievement Award by PETA (People for the Ethical Treatment of Animals) in December 1991.

What aided Linda in her veggie ventures was TVP – textured vegetable protein. Linda pointed out: 'It looks, chews and tastes like meat, but it's made from soya bean or wheat.'

After her death, the Vegetarian Society announced: 'Her contribution to vegetarianism was tremendous. Linda had a passion and a desire to change people's attitudes. Her positive outlook and dedication to promoting a diet that would bring about the end of animal suffering was absolute.'

Linda had been successful in the publishing world with her books of photographs. Over the years they included *Linda's Pictures*, *Sun Prints*, *Linda McCartney's Sixties*, *Roadworks* and *Wide Open*.' Her photographs were exhibited in galleries in more than fifty countries around the world, including the Victoria and Albert Museum in London.

Linda also became a publishing phenomenon with her cookbooks.

In 1998 she published her book of vegetarian cooking, *Linda's Home Cooking*, which was to sell over 400,000 copies and become the world's biggest-selling vegetarian cookbook. This encouraged Linda to begin to produce her own range of healthy vegetarian dishes in 1991. On 16 May 1995 she opened a new £10 million factory in Fakenham, Norfolk, where her products were manufactured. When production began she sold over 100 million units and her dishes became the best-selling vegetarian deep-frozen foods in the United Kingdom. She began to market them on a worldwide basis and in 1994 her products were named 'Best New Meat' by the American food industry.

By the end of 1997 her vegetarian food company, MacVege Ltd, already successful in Britain, had expanded to six other European countries. Linda McCartney's Frozen Foods had also been available in America since October 1994 and included vegetarian lasagne and meatless beef stroganoff.

The managing director of MacVege was Tim Treharne, who helped Linda implement his ideas while he handled the business side of the company.

In 1997 Linda commented: 'I've taken profits from the sale of my food and used them to set up a food-development kitchen. In this development kitchen, we're making meals from Indian recipes, Chinese recipes and dishes from all over the world.'

Linda was not only a vegetarian, but also supported organisations such as Greenpeace, Friends of the Earth and the Council for the Protection of Rural England.

Sadly, what is arguably the most romantic marriage in rock-'n'-roll history became tragic.

On Saturday 9 December 1995 a routine scan revealed that Linda had a small malignant cancer on one of her breasts. Paul said: 'Linda had a scan at the Princess Grace Hospital in London and was found to have a small lump. She has had an operation to remove the lump, which was performed successfully. Luckily it was caught in time.

'Fighting breast cancer is something we've been keen to promote and we would urge anyone with a worry about this to check it out at an early examination with their doctor.'

Early in 1996 she began having chemotherapy sessions once or twice a week. By the summer of that year the McCartneys cancelled a holiday in the South of France with Ringo Starr because Linda was too ill to travel, although on 3 September Paul said: 'Linda is not seriously ill. She's recovering from cancer and doing incredibly well.' In October she visited Los Angeles for a high-dose chemotherapy treatment. By December 1996 it seemed as if her health was improving and she was pictured with cropped hair.

She had been having treatment, which seemed to have worked, but in March 1997 it was discovered that the cancer had also spread to her liver. She was unable to accompany Paul to Buckingham Palace when he received his knighthood on 11 March 1997.

Linda continued to fight against the cancer and on Wednesday October 15 1997 she was able to appear at her daughter Stella's fashion show. Linda declared herself 'fit and well' and applauded Stella, saying: 'We flew into Paris this morning and came straight here. Right now I'm feeling great. I'm looking forward to having lunch together as a family before we go back to London.' After the show Stella collapsed into her mother's arms and said: 'I'm so happy Mum and Dad could make it today.'

Linda also rallied enough to be present at the *Standing Stone* premiere at the Royal Albert Hall in November 1997.

In her last interview Linda felt that she'd won her battle; and, of her relationship with Paul, she said: 'We're like boyfriend and girlfriend again, like love-struck teenagers, enjoying life at the Scottish farm. I've always thought life is to be lived. I know that Paul and I are coming up to our thirtieth wedding anniversary, but some days it feels like we have just got together and I love that. I love it when there's a power cut, no light, no heat and I'm having to cook over an open fire while Paul serenades me on guitar. I love that simple life.

'Yeah, I'm back. Now the kids have flown the nest it's meant that Paul and I have become like boyfriend and girlfriend again. We're doing those little things together that you do when you're first dating – going to the theatre or just walking hand in hand through the fields. How many married couples of thirty years' standing do you know who walk about holding hands? In some ways we haven't grown up. I guess it must be love!

'When Paul was knighted he said at the time it was great because he got to make his girlfriend a lady. But nobody called me Lady Linda or Lady McCartney. I'm still just Linda and he's Paul. Sure, it's a great honour for Paul and I'm proud of him. But it doesn't seem real that my boyfriend is a knight – although he's always been a hero. We're enjoying life, but then we always have. I have always said that life is to be lived. I know a lot of people say that but I really do mean it. I'm busier now than I've ever been.

'My intention is to develop meat-free versions of every food we currently get from animals. All my life I have cared for animals. I'm aiming to save the bacon of a lot of pigs right now. One of the secret projects I've been working on is to develop meat-free bacon that cooks and tastes like the real thing. That will be a real treat for Paul: he's always said that's one of the things you miss most when you give up meat – a bacon buttie!'

In the last two years of her life Linda compiled her third vegetarian cookbook, *Linda McCartney On Tour*, took photographs for two further exhibitions of her photography, produced a short animated film and worked on finishing her solo album, *Wide Prairie*.

There were sixteen tracks on the album, thirteen written by Linda herself and three that were cover versions of R&B and reggae numbers. Writing in the sleeve notes, Paul comments: 'The sweet innocence of this song made many of our friends decide to "go veggie". Linda has done more than anyone else to bring vegetarianism into the dietary mainstream of our society.'

Linda wrote two of the numbers in collaboration with Carla Lane, who said: 'She worked at it until the end. She wanted to get this record out no matter what she was going through. This is the bravest album ever made.'

The two numbers they wrote together were 'Cow' and 'The White Coated Man'. Six of the songs on the album were in defence of animals and one number, 'The Light From Within', saw her lashing at the critics who carped at her beliefs. Paul said: 'It was her answer to all the people who had ever put her down and that whole dumb male-chauvinist attitude that to her had caused so much harm in our society. God bless her, my little baby literally had the last word.'

When asked how she coped with those critics who wrote about her, she answered: 'By not caring about it. Critics can destroy artists; I read criticisms about people I love and think: Have we met the same person? I know that a lot of my critics have never met me even though they write as if they know me. I am too busy living life to really get hung up about what they say.'

Shortly before she died she was having treatment at the Sloane Kettering Cancer Center in New York. The centre practises an experimental new treatment called 'aggressive high-dose chemotherapy'.

Linda died at 5.04 a.m. on Friday 17 April 1998 at the ranch in Arizona that she and Paul bought in 1979. Of the last hours, her friend Carla Lane reported that Paul 'got into bed with her and lay with her and said everything was going to be all right. He held her and talked to her through the night.' Paul was to tell friends: 'There was no better way for her to go.'

Mary, Stella and James had remained with Linda throughout the night, but her eldest daughter Heather arrived minutes too late.

Linda was 56 years old at the time of her death and was cremated within hours. There had been reports that she had died in Santa Barbara, although the death was not registered in the Santa Barbara district. This resulted in officials from the Santa Barbara coroner's office investigating as to why no death certificate had been filed and no cremation permit sought. It was then revealed that the death had occurred in Arizona and the Santa Barbara story had been concocted to allow the family to grieve in private.

Paul brought Linda's ashes home and scattered part of them in the countryside near their home in Peasmarch, East Sussex. Stella, James, Mary and Heather accompanied him. He retained some of the ashes to keep by him, saying: 'She will always be with me. I have the little urn and she is here with me now.'

Paul also made an official statement:

This is a total heartbreak for my family and I. Linda was, and still is, the love of my life, and the past two years we spent battling her disease have been a nightmare.

She never complained and always hoped to be able to conquer it. It was not to be.

Our beautiful children – Heather, Mary, Stella and James – have been an incredible strength during this time, and she lives on in all of them.

The courage she showed to fight for her cause of vegetarianism and animal welfare was unbelievable. How many women can you think of who would single-handedly take on opponents like the Meat and Livestock Commission, risk being laughed at, and yet succeed?

People who didn't know her well, because she was a very private person, only ever saw the tip of the iceberg. She was the kindest woman I have ever met, the most innocent.

All animals to her were like Disney characters and worthy of love and respect. She was the toughest woman who didn't give a damn what other people thought. She found it hard to be impressed by the fact that she was Lady McCartney. When asked whether people called her Lady McCartney, she said: 'Somebody once did – I think.'

I am privileged to have been her lover for 30 years, and in all that time, except for one enforced absence, we never spent a single night apart. When people asked why, we would say – 'What for?'

As a photographer there are few to rival her. Her photographs show an intense honesty, a rare eye for beauty.

As a mother she was the best. We have always said that all we wanted for the kids was that they would grow up to have good hearts, and they have.

Our family is so close that her passing has left a huge hole in our lives. We will never get over it, but I think we will come to accept it.

The tributes she would have liked best would be for people to go vegetarian, which, with the vast variety of foods available these days, is much easier than many people think. She got into the food business for one reason only, to save animals from the cruel treatment our society and traditions force upon them.

Anyone less likely to be a businesswoman I can't think of, yet she worked tirelessly for the rights of animals, and became a food tycoon. When told a rival firm had copied one of her products, all she would say was, 'Great, now I can retire.' She wasn't in it for the money.

In the end, she went quickly with very little discomfort, and surrounded by her loved ones.

The kids and I were there when she crossed over. They each were able to tell her how much they loved her.

Finally, I said to her, 'You're up on your beautiful appaloosa stallion; it's a fine spring day, we're riding through the woods. The bluebells are all out, and the sky is clear blue.'

I had barely got to the end of the sentence, when she closed her eyes and gently slipped away.

She was unique and the world is a better place for having known her. Her message of love will live on in our hearts forever.

I love you Linda.

George Harrison paid tribute to Linda: 'Linda will be missed not only by Paul, her children and brother John, but by all of us who knew and loved her. She was a dear person with a passionate love of nature and its creatures and, in her passing, has earned the peace she sought in life. God bless her.'

Ringo paid their tribute, saying: 'Both Barbara and I would like to say how sorry we are. We were privileged to have known her. Her positive courage throughout her illness was truly inspiring. We send all our love to Paul, Heather, Mary, Stella and James. It was a blessing that she was in our lives.'

Denny Laine was to say: 'Her endless love for nature and God's creatures was a guiding light for even a hardened rocker like me who just went with the flow and never really had any radical principles. She was always an inspiration to both Paul and myself as musicians – she loved everything about art and creativity, and mainly because she told the truth. This is a quality that few except her close friends gave her credit for and I enjoyed her wit and sense of humour so much I feel sorry for the many that never really knew her. She never relented and she deserves a place in history as a saint, and not just as Paul's wife who happened to be in a band called Wings.'

The British Prime Minister, Tony Blair, praised Linda for her 'tremendous contribution to British life. Cherie and I are very saddened for Paul and all his family. Linda showed extraordinary courage throughout her illness.' Tim Angel, chairman of the British Film Academy Awards said: 'Paul and Linda had strong and loyal connections to the film industry and I know that everyone here, from Sean Connery to Sigourney Weaver, was left simply speechless when they were told Linda had died.'

Sir George Martin commented: 'We have lost a good friend who was a very special person.'

Yoko Ono said: 'I'm very saddened. I've spoken to Linda over the past year and she seemed to be her usual powerful self. I can't believe it.'

Carl Davis said: 'I'm totally shocked. We knew Linda had been ill, but it's terrible news. It was Linda who first encouraged Paul to do the oratorio. I used to call her my good fairy. She was very committed to the causes she was interested in. She introduced Paul to things he wouldn't have dreamed of doing before he met her. I will always remember her as a very warm motherly figure. She will be missed by everyone who knew her.'

The Times published details of Linda's will:

Linda Louise McCartney of Tucson, Arizona, US, left estate valued at £3,884,731 net. She left her estate to a trust fund, the net income of which is to be paid at least quarterly to her husband, James Paul McCartney, for as long as he lives and then to her children, Heather, Mary, Stella and James.

The first memorial service for Linda was held in London on Monday 8 June 1998 with a congregation of 700 gathered inside St Martin-in-the Fields church in Trafalgar Square, London. More than 4,000 people had gathered outside in the cold and rain, comprising not only fans but also animal protesters, who were paying tribute to Linda's dedication to animal rights.

Paul arrived with Stella, Mary, Heather and James, Ringo with Barbara and George with Olivia and Dhani.

Among the church congregation were Spike Milligan, Sting and Trudi Styler, Neil Tennant, Elton John and David Furnish, Billy Joel, Peter Gabriel, Dave Gilmour, John Thaw and Sheila Hancock, David Bailey, Joanna Lumley, Kevin Godley, Tracey Ullman, Marie Helvin, Michael Parkinson, Carla Lane, Pete Townshend, George Martin and Ken Townsend.

The walls of the church were decorated with photographs of Linda, which Paul had selected.

The ninety-minute service began at 8.30 p.m. and, prior to the ceremony, Paul gave a ten-minute speech about Linda, telling how they first met. 'I'm privileged to have been her lover for thirty years,' he said. 'Except for one enforced absence, we never spent a single night apart.' He described her as 'the first lady of animals', telling of her being a champion for animal rights, and he then led in and up the aisle two Shetland ponies, Schoo and Tinsel, which he'd given to Linda as a Christmas present.

The service then began with a pipe solo of 'Mull Of Kintyre' from Jim McGeachy, who was pipe major of the Campbeltown Pipe Band. He had performed on the original Wings recording.

The Rev. Clare Herbert welcomed the congregation and led them in the hymn 'All Things Bright and Beautiful'.

Ken Townsend, the former head of Abbey Road Studios, then gave an address and was followed by the Brodsky Quartet, who performed four songs that Paul had written specially for Linda: 'The Lovely Linda', 'You Gave Me The Answer', 'Maybe I'm Amazed' and 'Warm And Beautiful'.

The actress Joanna Lumley, herself an animal-rights supporter, then read the moving poem 'Death Is Nothing At All' by Henry Scott Holland, who'd been a Canon of St Paul's Cathedral in the nineteenth century. The line 'I have only slipped into the next room' touched many.

Students of the Liverpool Institute of the Performing Arts (LIPA) performed the next songs. They sang Paul's number 'Blackbird', followed by the gospel song 'His Eye Is On The Sparrow.'

Brian Clarke, a friend of Linda's, next addressed the congregation. The Brodsky Quartet then returned to perform another selection of songs that were special to Paul and Linda: 'Golden Girl', 'Dear Boy', 'Calico Skies' and 'My Love'. David Bailey then read a Spike Milligan poem called 'Lyric'.

Linda's close friend Carla Lane, an active animal-rights campaigner, then paid tribute to Linda as a person and also to her support of animal rights in an address called 'For Linda from the People in the Square'. This was mainly addressed to the thousands of animal-rights supporters outside in Trafalgar Square and she said: 'Cranks, they called us. But you took the path where no one had gone; you promised them a voice and you held their terror close . . . Lady Linda, we cannot see you but we can still hear you.' The entire congregation then sang 'Let It Be'.

Pete Townshend next made an address in which he pointed out the long and loving relationship between Paul and Linda.

The LIPA students then received support from the St Martin-in-the Fields choir when they performed 'Celebration' from *Standing Stone*.

A prayer was followed by an address from Paul, who said: 'She was my girlfriend. I've lost my girlfriend and it's very sad. I still can't believe it but I have to, because it's true.' He also said: 'I thought of her after she died as a diamond – she was as great as them all.'

The service ended with a performance of 'Linda', a song written by Jack Lawrence for Linda when she was a little girl.

The second memorial service took place at the Riverside Church, Riverside Drive, New York on 22 June 1998.

A spokesman for Paul said: 'It was something that had been in the back of Paul's mind for a while, because of Lin coming from New York. There were a lot of people over there who couldn't get to the first one.'

In the church they brought in Linda's favourite Appaloosa stallion, Blankit.

Friends attending the service included Chrissie Hynde, Paul Simon, Ralph Lauren, Twiggy, Neil Young, Diane Sawyer, Mike Nicols.

Twiggy read a poem by William Cooper, and then the Harlem Boys' Choir sang 'Blackbird' and 'His Eye Is On the Sparrow'. The Loma Mar string quartet performed 'The Lovely Linda' and 'My Love' and the congregation sang 'Let It Be'.

There were 45,000 flowers in the church and eight blown-up colour photographs of Linda displayed.

Paul told the congregation: 'It's a very sad time for all of us, but she wouldn't want it to be sad, but to count our blessings, as there are so many of them. We have four gorgeous kids and she lives on in all of them, and through them she's here. I was so lucky to be the one she chose.

'She was a friend, a beautiful friend to so many people. You know I love her and you all love her, too – that's why we're here tonight.'

The main thrust in newspaper reports the following day was that Yoko Ono and Sean Ono Lennon hadn't been invited, with her spokesman saying: 'She was saddened by it.'

In October 1998, to promote Linda's solo album, *Wide Prairie*, Paul discussed Linda, who had left Christmas presents for all the members of her family, which she'd bought and wrapped before her death.

He said: 'Somehow Lin's spirit is helping me see my way through the days. It hurts, but that's the way of life.

'I've said to a lot of my friends: "Remember, you've got a finite amount of seconds left on the planet and the next time you're going to argue with your missus, think of Linda."

'I've had my finite amount of seconds with her and it's really, really difficult to be without my best friend.'

Another tribute took place at the Royal Albert Hall, London, on Saturday April 10 1999. It was a concert called *Here, There and Everywhere: A Concert for Linda*. All profits were donated to Animaline.

The artists appearing were Des'ree, the Duke String Quartet, Eddie Izzard, Elvis Costello, George Michael, Heather Small, Johnny Marr, Ladysmith Black Mambazo, Lynden David Hall, Marianne Faithfull, Neil Finn, Sinead O'Connor, the Pretenders and Tom Jones.

In an interview in the *Guardian* on 11 September 2000 Paul said: 'People say time is a healer, and time heals by erasing. That is a sad fact. When Linda died, all of us in the family expected her to walk in the door, and we don't now.'

On Monday 12 October 1998 Linda was honoured at the 43rd Woman of the Year lunch at the Savoy Hotel, London, with an 'empty-chair' tribute. Paul sent each of the guests a floral tribute with the message, 'Linda would have been chuffed at this honour. It is a shame that us blokes can't go.'

Paul found it very hard to cope with Linda's death. In an article in the *Daily Mail* he said: 'I got a counsellor because I knew that I would need some help. He was great, particularly in helping me get rid of my guilt. Whenever anyone you care about dies, you wish you'd been perfect all the time you were with them. That made me feel very guilty after Linda died. The guilt's a real bugger. But then I thought, hang on a minute. We're just human. That was the beautiful thing about our marriage. We were just a boyfriend and girlfriend having babies.'

He also confessed that he didn't let Linda know that the treatment she was having didn't work. 'I knew a week or so before she died. I was the only one who knew. One of the doctors said she ought to be told, but I didn't want to tell her because I didn't think she'd want to know.'

Paul noted her courage and said: 'It was amazingly difficult, but Lin was really strong. We had many laughs during the two and a half years that she was going through treatment.'

Two days before her death, Linda and Paul went riding. He said: 'She was a bit tired, but riding had always been one of those things with us. The crowning moment was when this big rattlesnake stretched across the track. We just looked at it and felt awed. Like it was some sort of magic sign.'

Linda was too tired to get out of bed the next day. Paul said: 'I joked and said: "You just fancy a lie in." The doctors had warned me that she would slip into a coma. I went to bed that night with her and though things looked kind of serious, but I kept hoping. Thank the Lord, she went into a coma as they had predicted.'

The coma lasted only a day and Paul recalled: 'It was as if she was so smart that something in her said, "We can't lick this one. Let's get the hell out of here, quick." And she didn't hang about. In her last moments she got very peaceful.'

Linda participated in the following films and videos: *Crickets*, *My Love Is Bigger Than A Cadillac*, *Get Back*, *Give My Regards To Broad Street*, *Going Home*, *In The World Tonight*, *The Making Of Flaming Pie*, *Knebworth, The Event*, *Let It Be*, *Liverpool Oratorio*, *Movin' On*, *Once Upon A Video*, *Paul Is Live In Concert*, *Put It There*, *Buddy Holly Special*, *Rockshow*, *Oriental Nightfish*, *Seaside Woman*, *Standing Stone*.

Her books include: *Home Cooking*, *Light Lunches*, *Linda McCartney on Tour*, *Linda's Kitchen*, *Linda's Pictures*, *Linda's Summer Kitchen*, *Main courses*, *Photographs*, *Roadworks*, *Sixties* and *Sunprints*.

McCartney, Mary (daughter)

See 'Donald, Mary Alice McCartney'.

McCartney, Mary Patricia (mother)

The former Mary Patricia Mohin, the daughter of Owen Mohin, a coal merchant, was born at 2 Third Avenue, Fazarkerley on 29 September 1909. Her mother was Mary Teresa Mohin, nee Danher.

Mary had an elder brother, Wilf, and a younger brother and sister, Bill and Agnes. Agnes died at the age of two. Mary's mother also died giving birth in January 1919 and the baby died with her.

Mary became a nurse at Alder Hey Hospital at the age of fourteen. When her father remarried, Mary couldn't get on with Rose, her stepmother, and she moved out of the family home at the age of eighteen and settled in with other relatives.

Mary was to become a nursing sister at the age of 24 after she'd moved to Walton Hospital.

Mike McCartney recalls that her patients knew his mother as 'the Angel'.

It was while Mary was a nurse at Walton Hospital that she was acquainted with Jim's sister Jin, who had recently been married to Harry Harris, and she dropped by to see them at the McCartney family home in 11 Scargreen Avenue, West Derby where she met Jim McCartney. There was a Luftwaffe air raid that night, so Mary and Jim spent the evening huddled together downstairs in the house.

On 15 April 1941 she married James McCartney at St Swithins Roman Catholic Chapel in Gill Moss, Liverpool. Mary was 31 years old while James was 38. The couple moved into furnished rooms at Sunbury Road, Anfield, which was Paul's first home.

Mary gave birth to her first son, James Paul McCartney, on 18 June 1942 and was given a private ward at Walton Hospital due to the fact that she'd previously been the sister in charge of the maternity section. The baby was named after his father, great-grandfather and great-great-grandfather.

She gave up her job for a time and gave birth to her second son, Peter Michael McCartney, on 7 January 1944. The family then moved to a 'prefab' bungalow in Roach Avenue, Knowsley.

Because Mary was a Catholic, both her sons were baptised as Catholics, but they weren't sent to Catholic schools.

Due to the family's limited finances as Jim's job was not a well-paid one, Mary returned to her profession and became a part-time health visitor. She then became a domiciliary midwife, which meant that the family were given a council house at a nominal rent. Initially this was at 72 Western Avenue, Speke.

Paul was to say, 'My mum was the upwardly mobile force. She was always moving us to a better address; originally we had to go out to the sticks of Liverpool because of her work as a midwife. Roads were unmade but the midwife's house came free. So economically it was a good idea. She always wanted to move out of rough areas.'

He also said, 'I had a broad scouse accent, talking real broad like the rest of the kids round our way. She told me off about it.'

Paul remembered that his mum whistled a lot and recalled, 'That's one of my fond memories of my mum. You don't hear many women whistling. She was quite musical.'

She also travelled to her duties (she was on call 24 hours a day) by bicycle in her navy-blue uniform and hat as the family couldn't afford a car.

Mary had aspirations for her sons, wanting them to move up in life and she encouraged Paul to speak properly, which resulted in him not having a strong Liverpool accent. She also had dreams of Paul becoming a doctor.

Due to Mary's job, the family were able to move into Forthlin Road in the Allerton area in 1955, which was much nearer to Liverpool centre than Speke.

In the summer of 1955 she began experiencing pains in her chest and started taking large doses of BiSodol, which was merely an antacid powder. The following summer her 12-year-old son Michael came into the bedroom and found her crying. When he asked her what the matter was, she said, 'Nothing, love.'

Breast cancer was diagnosed and she was taken to the Northern Hospital, where she underwent a mastectomy operation, which actually exacerbated the condition. When Paul, Mike and their father went to visit her in hospital they were startled by her appearance. Paul said that it was 'a huge shock to us, suddenly she was ill, we were very young'. Paul and Mike then went to stay with their Uncle Joe and Auntie Joan.

Mary was to tell her sister-in-law, 'I would have liked to have seen the boys grow up.'

On 31 October 1956 when the boys woke up to get ready for school, Joan told them, 'Love, your mum's dead.'

Mary was 47 years old; Paul was 14 and Mike 12.

On 3 November 1956 Mary was buried at Yew Tree Cemetery in Finch Lane, Huyton.

On hearing of his mother's death, Paul cried himself to sleep and prayed for her to come back. He described them as: 'Daft prayers, you know, if you bring her back I'll be very, very good for always. I thought, it just shows how stupid religion is. See, the prayers didn't work when I really needed them.'

But his mother's death caused Paul to find solace in a guitar his father had recently bought for him as his brother Mike recalls. 'It was just after Mother's death that it started. It became an obsession. It took over his whole life. You lose a mother – and you find a guitar.'

Paul was to pay tribute to her in 'Let It Be' with the reference to 'mother Mary' and in 'Lady Madonna' when he sings about 'children at her feet'. Mike McCartney also paid tribute when he placed a photograph of her on the cover of his first solo album.

Paul's first daughter Mary was also named after his mother.

In 1984, during a television interview, Paul discussed his mother's death. 'I was fourteen. It's a very difficult age, fourteen, because you are growing up and you're getting your act together. So it was a tough time to have something as devastating as that happen. I think I probably covered a lot of it up at the time, as you would, a fourteen-year-old boy.'

McCartney On McCartney (documentary)

A television documentary produced by Ardent Productions and originally screened on the Biography Channel. It was to receive a larger audience when it was screened on Channel 5 on 28 May 2002.

It basically revolved around Paul, sitting by a piano and discussing the history of the Beatles, covering mainly the years 1957 to 1970. It featured interviews with various people who knew Paul, including Pete Best, Bill Harry, Bob Wooler, Brian Wilson, Julia Baird, Klaus Voormann, Tony Barrow, George Martin, Alistair Taylor, Donovan, Steve Miller and Peter Asher.

Brian Wilson recalled the 'Vegetables' recording session and Miller said that the Beatles' songs were the most important body of work ever recorded.

At the end of the programme, Paul admitted that he'd secretly wished that the Beatles had got together again at the end of the 1970s.

McCartney On McCartney (radio)

A series of eight one-hour radio programmes in which Mike Read interviewed Paul. *McCartney On McCartney* was produced by Paul Williams and recorded in a tiny studio in Eastbourne. Paul was to put the record straight about many events in his life including his meeting with John Lennon, his romance with Jane Asher, Brian Epstein's death, the formation of Wings, his marriage to Linda, the incident when he was mugged in Lagos and the failure of his movie *Give My Regards To Broad Street*.

Paul was to give his reasons for such an in-depth interview by commenting, 'Twenty years after the Beatles all the little stories become legendary; they tend to be distorted, so that you find yourself reading stories as told by the friend of a man who once worked at the Cavern, or something. Suddenly you find that you want it to go down more truthfully, for people like your own children, as well as for general edification.'

He added, 'In a way it's a bit like being on a psychiatrist's couch, except that I'm not paying them.'

The eight-part series began broadcasting on Saturday 25 March 1989 and ran to Saturday 13 May 1989. Each programme was also repeated on the Thursday following the Saturday broadcast.

An edited version of the series was also broadcast in America between Saturday 27 May and Monday 29 May, Memorial Day weekend.

The series was also repeated in Britain on 25–28 December 1989 and 1–4 January 1990.

Discussing the fact that people tended to have the misconception that he only wrote 'the sentimental stuff', he explained, 'Occasionally I have to say, now look fellas, "Helter Skelter" was fairly hard, "Give Ireland Back To The Irish" was pretty activist, but they just notice the record after it, which was "Mary Had A Little Lamb". You can't blame them for forming an opinion, but I think it's best that I should try to correct it.'

Discussing John Lennon, he said, 'When I think of him now, it's the little things I remember, all the inconsequential things, not the big ones.

'I have a recollection of arguing with John, and of getting fairly hot under the collar about some Beatle thing, and he swore at me and I must have looked a bit dismayed. He had his round glasses on, and he took them off and said: "It's only me." Then he put the glasses back up, and it was Mr Front again.

'When we were in Switzerland doing the ski sequences for *Help!*, I remember, it was that nice bit of the evening when you take your ski boots off and feel the lead weights falling from your feet, and we had a tape of, I think it was *Revolver* or *Rubber Soul*. The way the side was sequenced there were two songs of John's and two songs of mine, which were nice and maybe sentimental.

"We were listening to them in this twin bedroom at the hotel and, again symbolically, the glasses were lowered, the defences lowered, and he said: "I probably like your songs better than mine, you know." End of subject.'

He was also to add: 'You see, the whole thing about the John that I grew up with was that he'd had a tragic life, being left by his father when he was three, then his mum being knocked over and killed by a drunken policeman at sixteen, right in front of the house where he was staying with his maiden aunts. His mother was living in sin with this guy, a waiter whom we used to call Twitchy. A waiter! John was enough of a snob to say, a waiter, come on love . . . at least his dad had been a sailor. You could hold your head up.

'John was very civil, but he loved his mum. She was a dish, very beautiful, with red hair, and she played the ukulele. How many women do you know who do that? I've got a cousin who's the same. I was eleven, right? I had a mum and dad – till I was fourteen, then my mother died, and that brought John and me closer together. Our mothers died within a couple of years of each other, so that was something we had against the world. It was part of our bond.

'Teenage lads are cruel. We used to have this thing, when people said "How's your mum then?," we'd say, "Oh, she died," and we'd know that we were kind of embarrassing them with it, and we'd watch them squirm. This is how real life is, isn't it?'

McCartney, Peter Michael

Paul's younger brother. He is a multi-talented solo performer, photographer and author who was born at 10 a.m. on 7 January 1944 at Walton Hospital, Liverpool.

He recalled, 'Although Paul and I were baptised Catholics (and circumcised Jewishly) our parents preferred a non-Catholic education. Paul and I would sag from school to swim nude in the Mersey.'

Paul and Mike's father Jim recalled the relationship between the two brothers:

Michael and Paul did everything together, especially anything that they were told specifically not to do. As children they were inseparable. Wherever one went so did the other. I remember that amongst their friends they were known as the 'Nurk Twins', but I never did find out why. I believe that John and Paul used the name for one of their first playing dates.

Paul was eighteen months older than Michael so naturally, he was the leader. I remember that he always seemed to know exactly what he wanted and usually knew how to get it. He didn't moan or nag in any way, but persuaded us in the nicest possible manner. I think he was a born diplomat.

Although Paul was a typical tearaway, ragamuffin, he was very close to Mike. I always remember one incident when they were caught stealing apples. Paul, Mike and another boy went scrumping from a farm in Speke. They were only twelve and ten at the time, and they called the place Chinese Farm, although I don't know why.

Apparently they were just about to climb the trees when the farmer appeared. They all ran away, but Paul got stuck and Mike went back to help. The first thing I knew about it was when the farmer rang me up and told me that my two sons were locked up in his barn. I went along to the farm to see him and he was very reasonable about it, so we decided to scare the boys a bit before we let them off. We stood outside the barn door and said things like, 'Do you think they'll get a long sentence?' or 'Shall we just spank them now and not tell the police?' When we thought they had had enough, we opened the barn door to let them out only to find we'd been completely wasting our time. The two boys trotted out and greeted me with, 'Hello Dad, about time you got here.' I was really amazed that both of them seemed so completely unconcerned by the whole proceedings.

When I talked to them afterwards, I found that because they didn't actually steal any apples, they considered that they had done nothing wrong and therefore were not worried. I did the usual thing and sent them to bed without any supper, although at the time I didn't think it would do the slightest good. I believe that a few years later, they did realise that they had done wrong.

Both Mike and Paul attended Stockwood Road Infants School and were then moved to Joseph Williams Primary School in Gateacre. In 1957 the two boys were members of the Nineteenth City Boy Scouts and went on summer camps with them. On their second camp trip Mike had his arm broken in an accident.

At the age of thirteen, while at Butlin's holiday camp in Filey, Yorkshire, Mike was dragged on stage by Paul to duet 'Bye Bye Love' and had stage fright.

Paul recalled, 'We went to stay with our parents at Butlin's and one of my cousins-in-law was one of the camp's redcoat entertainers. He called us up to do a turn during one of these talent shows. Looking back, it must have been a put-up job – I had my guitar with me. I probably asked him to get me up with my brother who had just recovered from breaking his arm and looked all pale. He had his arm in a big sling.'

They didn't win anything, as they were both ineligible due to their tender age.

Paul was very protective of his brother, ensuring that no one bullied him. Paul's own pranks, however, often caused Mike some pain; such as the time Paul dangled him by his ankles above the back door of the yard of their house. When Mike wanted to be let down, Paul did so literally, letting go of him, leaving Mike to fall face down on the concrete, breaking several of his teeth!

Mike then attended Paul's grammar school the Liverpool Institute, although his ambition was to become an artist, but he was turned down when he applied to the Liverpool College of Art, because of the introduction of new rules that made it mandatory to have five General Certificate of Education passes.

On leaving the grammar school, he trained as an apprentice hair-dresser, with Jimmy Tarbuck and Lewis Collins (Tarbuck became a leading comedian and Collins starred as Bodie in *The Professionals*) and in 1962 became involved with the Merseyside Arts Festival, along with Roger McGough (then a teacher) and John Gorman (then a post office engineer). After the event the trio continued as 'The Liverpool One Fat Lady All Electric Show', performing poetry and satirical sketches at local clubs.

In 1963 the three of them, Mike, Roger and John were approached to provide material for Granada TV's *Gazette*. They then changed their name to Scaffold – and Mike changed his surname to McGear, coming to the decision in his Uncle Bill's pub The Eagle Hotel in Paradise Street, Liverpool. He had been billed at the Merseyside Arts Festival as Michael Blank and considered the names Mike Dangerfield (from JP Donlevy's 'Ginger Man') and Mike McFab. He felt that Mike McGear sounded Irish. Mike changed his name to McGear when he was eighteen and adopted it for eighteen years before reverting back to Mike McCartney.

The name Scaffold came from Roget's *Thesaurus* – and they'd also noticed a Miles Davis album of that name which had recently been released.

Brian Epstein's company NEMS Enterprises briefly managed the trio and George Martin became their recording manager, issuing singles on Parlophone such as '2 Day's Monday' and 'Three Blind Jellyfish'.

Their first top five hit, which was Prime Minister Harold Wilson's favourite song, was 'Thank U Very Much', written by Mike. He said the inspiration for the song came from a Nikon camera given to him one birthday by Paul. As he couldn't play any instruments, he composed the song by humming into a tape recorder. During the recording session at Abbey Road Studios, Paul dropped by and suggested to Mike that he leave out reference to the 'Aintree Iron' as it was too oblique. When the record reached No. 5 in the charts Paul phoned Mike and admitted that he'd been wrong.

Incidentally, Mike also became a noted photographer. His father lent him a Kodak box camera and the first photograph he took was of Paul outside the Butlin's hot-dog corner in Pwllheli, North Wales. When Paul returned from Hamburg he brought back a Rollei Magic for Mike. His first published photographs appeared in *Mersey Beat* under the pseudonym Francis Michael and at the turn of the twenty-first century his photographs were being exhibited at the National Portrait Gallery in London. His photographic exhibition 'Mike Mac's White and Blacks' was staged at the Walker Art Gallery, Liverpool and the Jill Youngblood Gallery, Los Angeles. The exhibition then opened at the Photographer's Gallery in London in November 1968 to tie in with his book *Mike Mac's Black And Whites, Plus One Colour*, published by Aurum Press. His exhibition was to tour Britain and Japan in 1987.

On 7 June 1968 Mike married Angela Fishwick at a ceremony in Wales, with Paul and Jane Asher in attendance, and set up home in a dream cottage in Little Heswall, Cheshire they called 'Sunset', which was a present from the family. Mike was also best man at Paul's wedding to Linda, although the ceremony had to be delayed because Mike was late.

The Scaffold's follow-up to 'Thank U Very Much' was 'Lily The Pink' which reached the top of the British charts and stayed there for five weeks. This led to an amusing incident. Paul and Mike were walking down a street in London when an excited girl shrieked, 'Oooh, look. There's Mike McGear!'

Although they could have had their pick of major venues once they had hit the top of the charts, they decided to appear for a month at Ronnie Scott's Jazz Club, along with Stan Getz.

The Scaffold had their own children's television show *Score With The Scaffold*, they sang the theme tune to the popular *Liver Birds* TV series and composed music for feature films including Alf Garnett's *All The Way Up* and the horror film *Burke And Hare*.

They also appeared at the Bitter End in New York and appeared on network television shows hosted by Merv Griffin and David Frost. The Scaffold also hosted the centenary at the Royal Albert Hall and performed before the Queen and various Royal Family members.

Between 1967 and 1974 Scaffold made around twenty recordings, including 'Do You Remember', 'Gin Gan Goolie' and 'Liverpool Lou',

Producer David Puttnam approached Mike to play the lead in *The Virgin Soldiers*. Mike turned it down because he didn't like the idea of his daughters seeing him in the sex scenes.

Following Mike's solo debut album *Woman* in 1972, Paul decided to produce Mike's second album *McGear*, commenting, 'It's a singing thing because he's quit comedy for the moment. We're going to do it at Strawberry Studios in Stockport. We'll play it by ear, it's Mike's album.'

This had been inspired originally when Mike had visited Paul in London and the two of them had written 'Leave It' together. Lee Eastman heard the song, liked it and suggested, 'Why are you stopping here? This is good. Don't stop here.'

In 1974 Paul also produced the Scaffold's Top Ten single 'Liverpool Lou'.

On 9 February 1973 his latest group Grimms released their eponymous debut album in Britain. Mike had penned 'Jellied Eels' for the LP.

His second album with Grimms was *Rockin' Duck*, released on 5 October 1973. On it he penned the track 'Take It While You Can'.

On 25 May 1973 he reformed the Scaffold and released the album *Fresh Liver* on which he co-wrote seven of the songs.

Mike divorced Angela Fishwick on St George's Day 1979. At the time he still lived in 'Sunset' in Heswell, with his three daughters, Abbi, Benna and Theran.

In 1985 he embarked on a speaking tour of American colleges. His presentation was called 'Mike McCartney Reflects' and began with a general history of Liverpool, illustrated by lots of his own personal photographs and also closely followed the text of his book *Thank U Very Much* (called *The Macs* in America).

1987 proved a busy year for Mike, who was working on a children's book *The Ringdom Rhymes* (his first children's book had been called *Roger Bear*). He was commissioned to take photographs of Liverpool and the east coast of Scotland by 3i (Investment In Industry) and in November flew to America to launch the Penguin book of his photographs. He had an exhibition at the Howard Greenberg Photofind Gallery in SoHo, New York and appeared on several television shows, including the *Larry King Talk Show*, *Sonya Live In LA* and the CBS *Today* show.

He had further photographic exhibitions the following year in Washington and New York and in December 1988 flew to Florida to open his first Silk Screen Exhibition.

At one time he planned to write a cookbook, *Auntie Jin's Liverpool Cookbook*. His books included *Thank U Very Much*, published in 1981 and *Remember: The Recollections And Photographs Of Michael McCartney*, published in 1992.

In 1990 he produced a 47-minute video 'Mike McCartney's Alternative Liverpool', issued by Skyline/MMcC Ltd. The video includes a rare interview with Ivan Vaughan, the promotional film of the Scaffold's 'Thank U Very Much' and some music from the *McGear* album. Mike has also acted as recording manager to Liverpool groups. He was appointed to the Board of Management for the Institute of Popular Music at Liverpool University and continues to work on books, animation and photography.

Mike's son Josh became drummer with an indie trio called Trilby. Here is a selected discography of Mike's recordings:

Singles:

'2 Days Monday'/'Three Blind Jellyfish'. Parlophone R 5443, May 1966.

'Goodnight Batman'/'Long Strong Black Pudding'. Parlophone R5548, December 1966.

'Thank U Very Much'/'Ide B The First'. Parlophone R 6543, November 1967.

'Do You Remember?'/'Carry On Krow'. Parlophone R5679, March 1968.

'1-2-3'/'Today'. Parlophone R5703, June 1968.

'Lily The Pink'/'Buttons Of Your Mind'. Parlophone R5734, October 1968.

'Charity Bubbles'/'Goose'. Parlophone R5784, June 1969.

'Gin Gan Goolie'/'Liverbirds'. Parlophone R 5812, October 1969.

'All The Way Up'/'Please Sorry'. Parlophone R 5847, June 1970.

'Busdreams'/'If I Could Start All Over Again'. Parlophone R 5866, October 1970.

'Do The Albert'/'Commercial Break'. October 1971.

'Liverpool Lou'/'Ten Years After On Strawberry Jam'. Warner Bros K 16400, May 1974.

'Leave It'/'Sweet Baby'. Warner Bros K 16446, September 1974.

'Mummy Won't Be Home For Christmas'/'The Wind Is Blowing'. Warner Bros K 16488,

'Sea Breezes'/'Givin' Grease A Ride'. Warner Bros K 16520, February 1975.

'Leaving Of Liverpool'/'Pack Of Cards'. Warner Bros K 16521, March 1975.

'Dance The Do'/'Norton'. Warner Bros K 16521, July 1975.

'Simply Love You'/'What Do We Really Know?' Warner Bros K, November 1975.

'Doing Nothing All Day'/'A to Z'. EMI 2485, June 1976.

'The Womble Bashers'/'Womble Bashers Wock'. Virgin VS 154, June 1976.

'Wouldn't It Be Funny If I Didn't Have A Nose?'/'Mr Noselighter'. Bronze BRO 33, October 1976.

'How D'You Do'/'Paper Underpants'. Bronze BRO 39, April 1977.

'All The Whales In The Ocean'/'I Juz Want What You Got: Money'. Carrere CAR 144, May 1980.

'No Lar Di Dar (Is Lady Di)'/'God Bless The Gracious Queen'. CONN 29781, July 1981.

The releases on Parlophone and Bronze were with the trio Scaffold, as were the Warner Bros titles on K 16400, 16488 and 16521. The Virgin single was under the name the Bashers and all the others were credited to Mike McGear.

Albums:
McGough & McGear. Parlophone PCS 7047, May 1968.
The Scaffold. Parlophone PCS 7051, July 1968.
L The P. Parlophone PCS 7077, May 1969.
Woman. Island ILPS 9191, April 1972.
Grimms. Island HELP 11, February 1973.
Fresh Liver. Island ILPS 9234, May 1973.
Rockin' Duck. Island ILPS 9248, October 1973.
McGear. Warner Bros K 56051, September 1974.
Sold Out. Warner Bros K , February 1975.

McCartney, Rowena

Née Home, the second wife of Paul's brother Mike.

Rowena, a dress designer, was 21 when she married the 38-year-old Mike at St Barnabas Church in Penny Lane, Liverpool, on Saturday 29 May 1982. Over six hundred fans gathered outside the church in the morning and waited for Mike to arrive at 2.30 p.m. and Rowena about ten minutes later.

Paul was Best Man, dressed in casual style with grey jacket, blue trousers and white sneakers, and there were five bridesmaids: Mike's three daughters (Benna, 13, Theran, 11, and Abbi, 8) and Rowena's two sisters.

The Rev. Harrington, who conducted the ceremony, recalled when Paul was a choirboy at the church and commented: 'He used to sit up there in the choirbox, making some kind of noise.'

After the ceremony the wedding party left the church and headed for Hoylake for the reception. Later, Mike and Rowena flew to Malta for their honeymoon.

McCartney, Ruth

Paul's stepsister. She was born and raised in Liverpool. She began studying singing and dancing at the age of four, began learning the piano at the age of seven and the guitar at the age of twelve.

Her name had been Ruth Williams when her widowed mother, 34-year-old Angela Williams, married Paul's father, 62-year-old Jim McCartney on 24 November 1964. Ruth was five years old at the time, was given the McCartney surname and went to live at the McCartney home in the Wirral, Cheshire.

Paul had always had an affinity with children and bought her a pet dog, which she called Hamish, when she suffered a broken leg. She also grazed her knees so often that Paul referred to her as 'Scabby'.

When she was nine years old she was playing the piano one day, but her efforts to perform the traditional hymn 'Golden Slumbers' wasn't going well and she asked Paul if he could read music. Paul couldn't, but he was intrigued by the number and composed his own lyrics to one of the verses. As a result he recorded the number and it appeared on the *Abbey Road* album.

Ruth spent twelve years with the McCartney family, but the situation changed when Jim McCartney died.

She attempted a career in show business and led a dance trio called Talent, but they were unsuccessful and in 1981 she moved to King's Lynn with her mother and worked as a salesgirl in Debenham's store.

Unfortunately, relations with Paul soured when her mother sold his birth certificate and there has been no communication between them since.

However, Ruth went on to become a highly successful singer, song-writer and businesswoman.

As a singer she toured Russia nine times, with over a million people buying tickets for her concerts, although she donated most of the proceeds to a fund for Armenian refugees. Her East European appearances took in Russia, Lithuania, Armenia, Uzbekistan, Turkmenistan and Siberia. Ruth has lived in Sydney, London, Liverpool, Munich, Moscow, Hollywood, Nashville and Los Angeles.

While in Australia in 1982 she met David Skinner and they penned a single for Tina Cross called 'New Blood', which reached No. 17 in the Australian charts.

She relocated to Los Angeles in 1983 and formed a writing partner-ship with Barry Cotting and they have penned numbers for several feature films. She settled in Hollywood in 1983 with her husband Martin Nethercutt, her mother Angie and her four cats. She wrote a song for Randy Crawford which became a gold single.

She later married Dieter Bockmeier in Germany in 1990. A Russian documentary 'Picture Of Ruth' was screened on Russian television in January 1998.

In 1992 she released an album on BMG Jupiter *I Will Always Remember You*.

In 1995 she issued a cassette, *Ruth McCartney*, in Russia featuring ten songs, most of them co-written by Ruth and musicians from Nashville. They included numbers such as 'Kidnap Your Heart', 'Russian Nights', 'Swimming Pool Music' and 'Overnight Success'. One of the numbers on the cassette was 'The Casket', penned by Mike McCartney and Roger McGough and featured on Mike's 1973 album *McGear*.

She is also Artist Relations advisor and CEO of McCartney Music & Media Inc, founded in Nashville in 1995.

Currently she is working on a book called *In My Life* with Dan Altieri.

McCartney, Stella Nina

Paul's second daughter was born on Monday 13 September 1971 at King's College Hospital, London. It was a difficult pregnancy as Stella was three months premature and, as with the birth of Mary, Paul moved into Linda's room, sleeping on a camp bed. There were some complications and Stella was delivered by Caesarean section. She weighed five pounds nine ounces and was named in honour of Linda's grandmothers, Stella Epstein and Stella Dryfoos.

Stella's birth gave rise to the name Wings.

Paul was not allowed into the operating theatre and sat outside. He recalled, 'I sat next door in my little green apron praying like mad . . . the name Wings just came into my head.'

He was also to say, 'Our baby was in intensive care, so rather than just sitting round twiddling my thumbs, I was thinking of hopeful names for a new group, and somehow this uplifting idea of Wings came to me at exactly that time. It just sounded right.'

Linda confirmed it, saying that Paul had been thinking of 'the wings of angels'.

Like many children of famous personalities, Stella has had to put up with the pressure of being accused of living off a famous name. She was to comment, 'I'm so sick of this "my parents" thing. It's not my fault. It's been that way my whole life. When I would do a good drawing in primary school, it was because my dad was famous. Or if I got a part in a school play, it was because Dad was a Beatle. What do I do? Do I become a smack-head and live off my parents' fortune, or do I have my own life?'

Stella had always had ambitions of becoming a fashion designer and at the age of sixteen Paul and Linda sent her to Paris during the summer to help couturier Christian LaCroix in the preparations for his show. After four days of running errands she commented, 'I'm not sure I want to be a designer now. It's so much work. I never imagined it like that.'

In June 1995 at the age of 22 Stella was one of 72 young designers to display their designs at the Central St Martin's College student fashion show at the Business Design Centre in Islington, London. Her clothes were paraded on the catwalk by a clutch of supermodels – Kate Moss, Naomi Campbell and Yasmin LeBon – during a two-hour fashion parade.

Paul and Linda were in the audience and Paul commented, 'I am the proudest dad in the world. I thought it was brilliant. Stella has come a long way since she first started out.'

In 1997 Stella secured a £100,000 per year job as head designer at the Paris fashion house, Chloe, only 18 months after she left St Martin's School of Art.

On the occasion of her fashion show on Wednesday 14 October 1998, Stella said, 'This collection is dedicated to my mum. She was everything. Also to my dad, brother and sisters, who have kept me strong. Everything. Always, Stella.' Paul, together with his son James, Barbara Bach and Lee Starkey, were in attendance at the show during which models walked along the catwalk to the tune of 'Hey Jude'. Barbara was wearing one of Stella's suits, Paul wore a suit from Edward Saxton, the Savile Row tailor where Stella had been an apprentice and James had a new shaved-head look.

Commenting about Stella's designs, Paul said, 'I am very proud of her because she is a serious English designer more than holding her own at the heart of Paris fashion. It is beautiful, just beautiful. It's a credit to the family. We are seeing real clothes for real women to look really good in.'

When Paul attended Stella's fifth fashion show for the house of Chloe on 6 October 1999 at the Petite Palais in Paris he noted how skimpy the outfits were and was to comment, 'It's hot, sexy and chic. It will make all the men sweat. Stella means "star", and she is. I'm very, very proud of her.'

The show was called 'She's A Woman' and Stella dedicated it to 'my family, friends and my beautiful mum'. On 18 February 2000, Stella was named glamour designer of the year at the London Fashion Awards. On 1 March 2000 at the opera in Paris she unveiled her new collection with her father in the audience, also in attendance were Jerry Seinfeld and Sean Lennon. Sean commented: 'I'm so proud of Stella. I think it's just great how she has managed to carve out her own separate career. She's ever so talented and I'm pleased she has done so well.'

Stella became a millionairess in her own right and an A1 celebrity.

Stella's close friends include Madonna, Gwyneth Paltrow, Liv Tyler and Kate Moss and she designed Madonna's wedding dress in 2000.

On 30 May 2001 she gave a lecture called 'An Evening With Stella McCartney' at the BP Lecture Theatre in the British Museum in London.

In June 2001 Stella left her job as chief designer at Chloe to join the Gucci Empire, where she was given her own label. Between 1997 and 2001 when she worked at the once-ailing Chloe label, she quadrupled their profits.

In August of that year her name was romantically linked with Alasdair Willis, publisher of *Wallpaper* magazine. Her name had previously been linked with several other young men, including Lenny Kravitz.

In November 2001 she bought a farm at Bishampton, Worcestershire for £1.3 million.

April 2002 saw media attention surrounding her £4 million house in Notting Hill. Neighbours were concerned about a ramshackle structure she had erected on the roof and her plans to entertain friends on the roof. The *Daily Mail* reported: 'She plans to do a great deal of entertaining on the roof in the coming summer months, and has been boasting of plans to dance naked and take a shower in the open-air cubicle provided.

'But wealthy neighbours have failed to be impressed by the prospect of 30-year-old Miss McCartney cavorting in the altogether and have flooded Westminster Council with complaints.'

McCartney Today
An American television special screened by NBC on Friday 18 June and Sunday 20 June 1982. The 90-minute show was to celebrate Paul's fortieth birthday.

McCartney Wide Prairie Show, The
An Internet broadcast, on Thursday 17 December 1998, marking Paul's only public appearance in 1998, the year of Linda's death. The one-hour exclusive show had Paul fielding questions from fans from around the world. His spokesman commented, 'Paul is not exactly an Internet buff, but he is very excited, and a bit nervous. He chose the format over several TV offers because he wants to go directly to the fans without the use of an interviewer.'

In addition to answering questions, Paul discussed the making of *Wide Prairie*, previewed video clips and showed his favourite pictures of Linda.

McCulloch, Jimmy
A young guitarist who had a brief, but glorious, spell with Wings.

Jimmy was born in Glasgow on 4 June 1953. At the age of thirteen he joined a band called One In A Million. He was sixteen when he performed on a No. 1 record, 'Something In The Air' by Thundercap Newman. For a short time he was a guitarist in John Mayall's band, following in the footsteps of such musicians as Eric Clapton and Jeff Beck. After the tragic electrocution on stage of Les Harvey (also a Glaswegian), Jimmy replaced him in Stone The Crows. In 1973 he joined the band Blue, managed by Robert Stigwood.

Jimmy had originally met Paul when he first played with Paul, Linda, Denny Laine and Davy Lutton in Paris in 1972, backing Linda on the record 'Seaside Woman'. He next met Paul in 1974 when he was hired to play on Mike McCartney's album *McGear*, which Paul was producing. Paul then asked him to join in on some recording sessions with Wings in Nashville in June 1974, and Jimmy became a member of the band.

He recorded on *Venus And Mars*, *Wings At The Speed Of Sound*, *Wings Over America*, *London Town* and on the single 'Junior's Farm'. He also appeared on tour with the band.

Following his appearances on the British gigs, Linda McCartney commented: 'Jimmy is great and I think he'll improve a lot, he'll get better and better and really get his own style.' He went on the 1975/76 World Tour and also on the 1977 tour of America. The American tour had originally been set to begin in either May or June 1976, but Jimmy dislocated his left hand after a concert in Paris and the US trip was postponed.

Two numbers which Jimmy co-wrote with Colin Allen, a former member of Stone the Crows, were included in Wings' repertoire. 'Medicine Jar' appears on *Venus And Mars* and *Wings Over America*. Jimmy provided lead vocals for the number and performed it on the world tour. 'Wino Junkie', said to be a nickname for himself, and like 'Medicine Jar' about drugs, was included on the 1976 album *Wings At The Speed Of Sound*.

Jimmy drank a lot and was often abrasive and argumentative with people. He argued frequently with Geoff Britton, until the latter left the band. There were even rumours of arguments between him and Paul. Jimmy finally left Wings on 8 September 1977, joining the Small Faces for a short time, until he formed his own band, the Dukes.

When he hadn't turned up for rehearsals on two consecutive days, his brother Jack visited Jimmy's Maida Vale flat and found his body on the floor. An open verdict was recorded on his death, although the pathologist reported that he had traces of cannabis, alcohol and morphine in his body. Yet there were some mysterious circumstances. The flat contained no evidence of drink or drugs, there was no money to be found and a security chain on the door had been broken.

Jack was to comment, 'I'm sure someone was in the flat after my brother died and I'd like to find out who he was.'

The mystery has never been solved.

McCullough, Henry

An Irish guitarist who was a member of Wings for almost two years.

His career began with the Skyrocket Showband, one of the many 'showbands' popular in Ireland. He then joined the rock group Jean & the Gents before becoming a member of Eire Apparent in 1967. The group began to play in England and were spotted at London's UFO Club by Chas Chandler, who was manager of Jimi Hendrix at the time. The group's road manager was Dave Robinson (later to launch the successful Stiff Records) and their PR was Bill Harry.

They played a number of gigs with Jimi Hendrix, but the group never achieved the success they deserved. Henry moved on to Sweeny's Men and then Joe Cocker's Grease Band. He was already friendly with Denny Laine, but it was Paul's road manager who informed him that Paul was holding auditions for a new lead guitarist. Henry auditioned on a Tuesday, and was asked to return to audition again the following Thursday. Later Paul rang him to ask him to join the band, in time to contribute to Wings' first single, appropriately 'Give Ireland Back To The Irish'.

Discussing this chain of events in *New Musical Express*, Henry revealed, 'In fact it was Paul's roadie who rang, saying do you fancy sitting in? After the Grease Band I didn't know what the hell was going on so I went down and had a play. That was Tuesday and afterwards things were left at that – nothing was said. Then I had another call on Thursday to go down again and afterwards Paul said, "Do you want to join our group?" Although I knew Denny Laine, I'd never met McCartney before. Once I got used to seeing him there in person, he turned out to be a great bloke, I guess I was a bit nervous but I had a couple of pints of Guinness before I went along the first time. That helped.

'McCartney wants to play everything. Surely that's the point of music – to have enough different material to play in audiences of twelve-year-olds or old age pensioners. Paul just wants to play the whole lot – heavy numbers, rock numbers, everything.'

Henry toured with Wings in Europe in 1972 and in the UK in 1973. He can also be heard on the 1973 album *Red Rose Speedway*. However, at the end of the year, just before the recording of *Band On The Run*, he quit the band.

In an interview with Paul Gambaccini, Paul commented, 'Henry McCullough came to a head one day when I asked him to play something he really didn't fancy playing. We all got a bit choked about it, and he rang up later and said he was leaving. I said, "Well, OK". That's how it happened. You know with the kind of music we play, a guitarist has got to be a bit adaptable. It was just one of those things.'

Henry told the press that he had quit because he and Paul didn't see eye to eye musically and that he considered Linda an amateur and wasn't too happy with her being in the band.

He later signed with George Harrison's record company, Dark Horse records. Over the years he provided backing for many artists, including Donovan, Joe Cocker, Marianne Faithfull, Leon Russell and Ronnie Laine.

The *Melody Maker* once described McCullough as: 'The eternal drifter, wandering from gig to gig, following his nose with his guitar to pay the rent. The future's never too clear when you talk to Henry, and his past is a blurred trail of events.'

In the early 1980s he had an accident with a knife that severed the tendons in his playing hand and he retired to Ireland for several years. He eventually recovered and was able to perform again.

McDonald, Arthur

Paul's first grandchild, born on Saturday 3 April 1999 to his daughter Mary and her husband Alastair McDonald. Paul immediately drove from his farmhouse to be by his daughter's side and see his 7 lb grandson. Sadly, Linda never saw her first grandchild, as she'd died the year previously.

McDonald, Phil

A recording engineer who worked with Paul on *Wings Over America*. Phil was used to working with Paul, having been an engineer on *Abbey Road*. He also engineered six George Harrison and two John Lennon albums.

McGear

Title of a solo album by Mike McGear, the pseudonym of Paul's brother Mike McCartney, a former member of the British hit group the Scaffold.

Paul produced the album, which was recorded between January and May 1974. It was issued in Britain on Friday 27 September 1974 on Warner Brothers K 56051 and in America on Monday 14 October 1974 on Warner Brothers BS 2825.

The tracks were: Side One: 'Sea Breezes', 'What Do We Really Know?', 'Leave It', 'Have You Got Problems?'. Side Two: 'The Casket', 'Rainbow Lady', 'Simply Love You', 'Givin' Grease A Ride', 'The Man Who Found God On The Moon'.

Paul composed the numbers 'What Do We Really Know?' and 'Leave It'. He also co-wrote 'Have You Got Problems?', 'Rainbow Lady', 'Simply Love You' and 'The Man Who Found God On The Moon' with Mike. He co-wrote 'The Casket' with Roger McGough, also a former Scaffold member.

In addition to producing the album, Paul also played a number of instruments in addition to co-mixing it with Mike and engineer Peter Tattersall. He is also pictured on the cover sleeve. Other figures featured on the cover include Jim and Mary McCartney, Mike's two daughters, a baby Paul, Linda, Pete Strawberry, Brian Jones from the Liverpool band the Undertakers, Robert Doogle, an announcer, Paddy Maloney, Denny Seiwell, Paul and Mike, Kevin Godley and Lol Creme of 10cc, Denny Laine, Jimmy McCracken, Melvin Edwards who cut the album and engineers from Strawberry Studios.

10cc played on the track 'The Man Who Found God On The Moon' and 'Givin' Grease A Ride', although they used the alias the Gysmo Orchestra.

A single from the album, 'Sea Breeze'/'Givin' Grease A Ride', was released in Britain on Friday 7 February 1975 on Warner Brothers K 16520.

The album was issued as a CD for the first time on Monday 24 September 1990 when Rykodisc issued it in America, with 'Dance The Do' as a bonus track. It was issued in Britain as a CD on 6 April 1992 on the See For Miles label on SEECD 329, with two bonus tracks, 'Dance The Do' and 'Sweet Baby', both compositions co-written by Mike and Paul.

McGivern, Maggie

One of Paul's former girlfriends. She revealed details of their affair in an article in the *Daily Mail* on 12 April 1997. She claimed that her relationship with Paul began in 1966 when she was working as a nanny for Marianne Faithfull and John Dunbar. Paul was a friend of the couple and regularly visited their flat where he met Maggie on a number of occasions. This developed into a secret love affair lasting for three years, occurring during the period Paul was engaged to Jane Asher. After Jane found Paul in bed with Francie Schwartz and ended their engagement in the summer of 1968, Paul asked Maggie to accompany him on a trip to Sardinia. She says that while they were there Paul discussed marriage with her, but she was unsure whether to accept. They continued to see each other, but after Paul met Linda they drifted apart.

Maggie had an affair with Denny Laine and later married Mel Collins.

McGough And McGear

An album by Roger McGough and Mike McGear, recorded in January 1968. Paul produced it. The album was issued in Britain on Friday 17 May 1968 on Parlophone PCS 7047. It was re-released in Britain on Monday 10 April 1989, the album on Parlophone PCS 7332 and the cassette on Parlophone TC-PCS 7332. A mid-price compact disc of the album was also available on Parlophone CDP 7 91877 2.

The tracks were: Side One: 'So Much', 'Little Bit Of Heaven', 'Basement Flat', from *Frink* (a book of poems by McGough), 'A Life In The Day Of' and 'Summer With Monika', 'Prologue', 'Introducing: Moanin'', 'Anji', 'Epilogue'. Side Two: 'Come Close And Sleep Now', 'Yellow Book', 'House In My Head', 'Mr Tickle', 'Living Room', 'Do You Remember?', 'Please Don't Run Too Fast' and 'Ex Art Student'.

At a small press lunch, a select number of journalists were presented with the album and also a typed press release from Derek Taylor which read:

HELLOW.
   Thank you for coming to lunch.
   It is very nice of you and we are your friends.
   Now then, what do you want to know about it all?
   'Oh well of course' you may say.
   'How do we know what we want to know; surely you would be the best judge of that. After all is said and done, what is there to know?'
   It is so much a case of guessing, for there's no knowing what anyone would want to know.
   No.
   Let us guess.
   Eyes down.
   Our father, all the eights, 88 . . .
   We are already confusing the issue.

This approach is what the psychiatrists call 'maze making' or 'problem posing' or 'crisis creating' brought about in order to find a solution, or an exit line.

Now ... some names ...

Jane and Mrs Asher ... William I Bennet (WIB) ... Spencer Davis (is) ... Barry Fantoni ... Mike Hart ... Jimi Hendrix ... Vera Kantrovitch ... Gary Leeds ... Dave Mason and Carol ... MIKE McGEAR ... ROGER McGOUGH ... John Mayall ... Paul McCartney ... John Mitchell ... Zoot ... Graham Nash ... Viv Prince (yes) ... Andy Roberts ... Prince 'Stash' de Rola ... Paul Samwell-Smith ... Martin Wilkinson ...

What have they in common? What have they not? They are all beautiful. The two in capital letters are here today. They made the album. You have in your hand or adjacent. They are in the Scaffold (the capital letters were mine not theirs. McGear and Mc Gough have no egos).

The other people are friends. Friends. Friends who all contributed to the album in one way or many or all or a little.

At any rate they all went into the recording session and sang or played or beat some tangible thing or simply waved their arms to create in the air some benign (we mean, of course, benign) turbulence.

McGear and McGough are from Liverpool poetic and funny, concerned and open ...

Well listen, we are all here together now aren't we? In circumstances such as these, who needs a press release?

Have we no tongues to speak.

You are kind.

Thank you.

Derek.

McGough, Roger

Liverpool-born poet who was educated at St Mary's College and the University of Hull. He became a member of the Scaffold, along with Mike McGear and Roger Gorman.

In January 1968 Paul produced an album by Roger and Paul's brother Mike called *McGough And McGear*. In 1964, when Paul produced the *McGear* album, he co-composed the number 'The Casket' with Roger.

Roger, who contributed to the script of the *Yellow Submarine* movie, although he was not credited, was to become one of Britain's major poets with numerous books to his credit, including *Summer with Monika*, *Blazing Fruit* and *Defying Gravity*.

McGough, Thelma

Née Pickles. Thelma was a former student at Liverpool College of Art. Whilst there she became one of John Lennon's early girlfriends and was privy to some of the John and Paul rehearsals in Menlove Avenue.

John had poor eyesight and wore glasses at the time, but when he went out with Thelma he wouldn't wear them. When they went to the cinema to see Elvis Presley in *Love Me Tender*, he couldn't actually see what was happening on the screen and had to ask Thelma to tell him.

Soon after the recording of 'Love Me Do' she began dating Paul. She later married Roger McGough, a Liverpool poet who was a member of Scaffold with Mike McGear. They later split up.

Thelma became a TV producer and produced Cilla Black's *Blind Date* before leaving England to settle in New Zealand.

McIntosh, Robbie
A musician who appeared in Paul's band from 1989 to 1993.

Robbie was born on 25 October 1957 and in 1975 he joined his first group, 70% Proof. The following year he joined the Foster Brothers, an outfit which lasted for eighteen months. When they disbanded he was disillusioned and began driving a lorry for a building supplies company, but music still obsessed him and he joined a band called Night. His next group, Chris Thompson & the Islands, had a keyboards player called Wix, who was later to also become a member of Paul's band.

During this time, Robbie also did a lot of session work for artists who included Kirsty MacColl, Marilyn, Tears For Fears, Haysi Fantayzee and the Inspirational Choir of the First Church of the Living God.

In September 1982 he joined the Pretenders, a spell which lasted until late 1987. It was Chrissie Hynde who recommended him to Paul. On leaving the Pretenders he became involved in some session work, also played with Custer's Last Blues Band and a year had passed since leaving the Pretenders and joining Paul.

When McIntosh joined Paul's band, Chrissie said, 'That was Robbie's dream come true, because he knew every Beatles song. His lifestyle also fits in well with Paul's, because he's a country person and loves to ride horses. It's really worked out for him . . . the bastard!'

After leaving Paul's band he resumed session work with numerous artists including Paul Young, Rod Stewart and Joe Cocker. He later released a blues-country-rock album *Emotional Bends* and also issued an album of guitar instrumentals, which was only available on the Internet.

McKenzie, John
A Scottish film director who was responsible for a series of critically acclaimed TV plays and movies from 1967 when he made his directorial debut with a BBC Wednesday night play 'Voices In The Park'.

His films include *One Brief Summer*, *Unman, Wittering & Zigo* and

The Long Good Friday (which George Harrison had a hand in distributing).

He was hired by Paul to direct the video film for the single 'Take It Away', based on a treatment written by Paul. The film took five days to shoot from Friday 18 June 1982 at EMI's Elstree Studios in Hertfordshire.

On the first day of filming there was a celebratory party hailing Paul's fortieth birthday. Among the guests were Ringo and his wife Barbara, George Martin, Steve Gadd and Eric Stewart.

A telegram from Cilla Black was read out. It read: 'If life begins at forty, what the 'ell 'ave you been doing all these years?'

McMillan, Keith
Videofilm director. He made the 'Ebony And Ivory' promotional video in which Paul and Stevie Wonder are featured on piano. The two stars were not filmed simultaneously. Keith filmed Paul in London and then flew to Los Angeles to complete the Stevie Wonder section, then merged the two on the completed film.

McPeake, Family, The
An Irish band from Belfast that performed at the 'Magical Mystery Tour' party at the Royal Lancaster Hotel on Thursday 21 December 1967.

Paul had seen them perform on television and was so enthusiastic that when he arrived at Apple the following day he commented, 'They're fantastic, too much. There's an old guy, two younger guys and a girl. They play this incredible fairy music on some weird pipes. I've never heard anything like it, it just blew my mind.'

He then instructed Alistair Taylor to contact them and book them for the party.

McQuickly, Dirk
Dirk was the Paul figure in the Beatles TV spoof 'The Rutles', which was later released on a videocassette as 'All You Need Is Cash'. Eric Idle portrayed Dirk. In the lampoon, when the Rutles split up he joins a group called the Punk Floyd.

Mean Fiddler
A rock music venue in the London district of Harlesden where Paul and his band gave a live performance on Friday 10 May 1991 as part of a six-venue 'Surprise Gigs' tour to promote *Unplugged – The Official Bootleg*.

When news of the appearance was announced on Capitol Radio, all tickets to the 600-capacity venue were sold within an hour.

He made his second appearance at the Mean Fiddler on Friday 20 November 1992 when he was filmed for a television special, 'A Carlton

New Year', due to be screened on New Year's Day. Carlton had received the television franchise previously held by Thames Television.

Meet Paul McCartney

An MPL programme, 25 minutes in length, which was produced to promote Paul's *McCartney II* album. The 'Coming Up' clip, videoed in March 1980, was used and the rest was filmed at Trilion studios in Soho on Monday 19 May, opening with an interview with Paul conducted by Tim Rice. A promotional film for 'Waterfalls' was also shown. Perhaps to recall the recent Japanese drug bust for which Paul was jailed, there was a short sketch in which actor Victor Spinetti, dressed as a punk rocker, handcuffs Paul and takes him away, although the sketch was dropped from the televised showings.

It was shown in the Thames TV region on Thursday 7 August 1980 and the Granada region on Monday 27 October 1980.

Mellow Yellow

A single by Donovan, issued in Britain on Pye 7N-17267 on 13 January 1967 and in America on Epic BN 26239 on 30 January 1967. Paul can be heard on the backing vocal. Donovan was to comment, 'I went to the Beatles' *Yellow Submarine* session and helped a little with the lyrics. Then Paul came to the session for my "Mellow Yellow" single. In the middle of the take, he suddenly yelled out, "Mellow Yellow!" and it's still there on the single somewhere.'

Melody Maker

A British musical weekly, which ceased publication in 2000.

During the period when Ray Coleman edited the publication, Paul and John used it to cross swords. In an interview published in November 1971 Paul discussed the Beatles break-up, John, and Yoko and John's song 'How Do You Sleep?' The feature infuriated John who wrote a letter to the *Melody Maker* insisting that it be published in its entirety, taking the opportunity once again to slag Paul off.

Mess, The

The B-side of 'My Love' released on 23 March 1973. The number is a live recording from a performance at the Congresgebouw in Holland which took place on 21 August 1971 during Wings' European tour. The number was also featured on their British University tour in 1972, their British tour of 1973 and in the 'James Paul McCartney' television special.

Meters, The

A band hired by Paul to play at a party he organised for the press in New Orleans in February 1975 during the recording of *Venus And Mars*. He rehired them the following month when he threw another party aboard the *Queen Mary*. The ship was docked at Long Beach in California and the occasion was the completion of the album. George Harrison was among the star-studded array of guests, as were Dean Martin, Bob Dylan, Ryan O' Neal, Cher, Carole King, Micky Dolenz and Michael Jackson.

MGM Grand

Venue in Las Vegas where Paul appeared on Saturday 6 April 2002 as part of his 'Driving USA' tour.

Paul was paid a staggering $4 million to play at the venue. This was mainly due to the fact that his appearance was to replace the cancelled world heavyweight fight between Lennox Lewis and Mike Tyson, which the State authorities had banned and which had been transferred to a New York venue.

Tickets at the 15,000-seater venue were priced at $250 each.

The appearance made Paul the highest paid British performer of all time, during which he earned an estimated £500 per second.

Michelle

A number by Paul, although John helped him with the bridge. Paul had originally composed the tune while he was still at Liverpool Institute. The track was featured on the *Rubber Soul* album and within a month of the LP's release there were more than twenty different cover versions of the song, with the Overlanders and David & Jonathan both reaching the British charts with their singles.

When Ivan Vaughan and his wife Jan were visiting Paul at the Ashers' house in Wimpole Street Paul asked Jan, who taught French, if she could help him with some lyrics. He asked her for some French words to rhyme with Michelle and she said '*ma belle*', and she helped him with the other French words included in the song. Some years later Paul sent her a cheque for her help with the number.

A live version lasting 2 minutes and 57 seconds and recorded on 26 May at Boulder, Colorado, was included on the *Paul Is Live* album.

Mighty Like A Rose

An Elvis Costello album released in Britain on 13 May 1991 on Warner WX419. The cassette version was on WX419C and the CD on 7599 265752. The album featured two songs that Costello co-wrote with Paul, 'So Like Candy' and 'Playboy To A Man'. It was issued in America on cassette (Warner Bros 4-26575) and CD (2-26575).

Mike Yarwood Christmas Show, The

Paul and Wings appeared in this British TV show on Christmas Day 1977, performing 'Mull Of Kintyre', backed by the Campbeltown Pipes Band. Filming took place on Saturday 10 December at the BBC

TV Theatre in Shepherd's Bush. They also appeared in a comedy sketch with Yarwood, a leading impressionist, in a routine in which he acted as Dennis Healey, then chancellor of the exchequer.

Miller, Steve

An American rock guitarist born in Milwaukee, Wisconsin on 5 October 1943. His single 'The Joker' topped the charts on both sides of the Atlantic.

On Friday 9 May 1969 the Beatles were booked to record at Olympia Studios, Barnes. John, George and Ringo began to argue with Paul about Allen Klein who wanted them to sign a management agreement immediately. Paul wanted time to get advice about it. He also felt that Klein should only get 15 per cent and not the 20 per cent that he demanded. The other three Beatles supported Klein and said he should have 20 per cent; they then told Paul to 'fuck off!' and left the studio without completing the session.

Steve Miller was in Olympia recording that night and Paul bumped into him. Paul asked if he could drum for him and became a guest on Miller's track 'My Dark Hour'.

They kept in touch and Paul phoned him early in 1995 inviting him to join him in recording a few tunes. On Wednesday 17 May Paul, Linda, their son James and engineer Geoff Emerick flew to Miller's Sun Valley Studio where they began recording, mainly with Paul and Steve playing standards on acoustic guitars, until Tuesday 23 May. Paul then invited Steve to join him at his own studios in Sussex where they spent from Thursday 25 May until Wednesday 31 May recording six new songs, which included original numbers by both Paul and Miller, who both took turns singing lead. Paul was also to play various instruments including bass, drums, guitar and piano. Among the numbers penned by Paul that they recorded were 'Used To Be Bad', 'Broomstick' and 'If You Wanna'.

Miller was to comment, 'People don't know the real Paul McCartney. The man is a great blues artist and he can play jazz with the best of them.'

He also said, 'Paul, in one session, wrote a song in about five minutes. He even had my parts laid out for me. He is a genius. There has never been anyone else like him. I was thrilled to be working with a Beatle. Paul is very relaxed, yet was also professional and quite focussed.'

Milligan, Spike

A British comedian and former member of the Goons. In 1981 he asked if Paul and George Harrison could contribute to a fund to set up a sanctuary for otters in Gloucestershire. They chipped in with £800 each.

Paul had once taken Jane Asher to see Spike in *Son Of Oblomov* on 8 March 1964. Spike also inspired Paul to write 'Ebony And Ivory'.

In mid-1995, when the three remaining Beatles were recording at Paul's studio, near Milligan's house, they decided to pay him a visit.

When they turned up at his door he refused to see them, shouting to his wife, 'tell them to fuck off!'

At the *Q* Awards on Tuesday 4 November 1997, Spike presented Paul with an award as 'Best Songwriter' for *Flaming Pie*. He said, 'In my case he gave me £25,000 to restore the Elephant Oak in Kensington Gardens. If he did nothing else, he wrote 'Yesterday'. Mind you, I wrote 'Ying Tong Yiddle I Po'.'

Paul said, 'This means a lot because there is a lot of competition out there, a lot of brilliant music being made at the moment. And I want to thank Spike for being older than me.'

Spike died on 27 February 2002. He was 83 years of age.

Millings, Dougie

A London tailor who made the Beatles collarless suits in 1963. He also appeared as the Beatles personal tailor in *A Hard Day's Night*.

Millings made the special costumes for Paul's 1972 Wings tour as well as the special outfits used in the photography shoot for the *Band On The Run* album cover.

He died on 20 September 2001 at the age of 88.

Million Miles

A number penned by Paul and included on the 1979 *Back To The Egg* album and the flipside of the 'After The Ball' single. On it, Paul plays the concertina.

Mills, Heather

See McCartney, Heather Mills.

Mine For Me

This song had its origin during a press conference in Oxford on Saturday 12 May 1973 when Paul was asked why he had written 'Six O'Clock' for Ringo Starr's *Ringo* album. Paul replied, 'I would do it for any friend. I would do it for Rod Stewart if he rang up.' As a result Rod Stewart did ring Paul up and Paul wrote 'Mine for Me'.

At another time, when asked why he wrote the song for Rod, he said, 'It was just the result of another drunken night, I suppose! It's nice to write for someone like Rod, because he's got such a distinctive voice. You can hear him singing it as you are doing it. Certain people . . . well, they are just a bit boring, and you write boring songs for them.'

Paul, along with Linda, sang the number with Rod Stewart during a concert by Stewart at the Odeon Theatre, Lewisham on Wednesday 27 November 1974. Paul admitted that he'd only gone along to watch and never intended to sing, but Rod called him and Linda on stage. Their appearance with Rod was filmed and shown on the programme *Midnight Special* on 25 April 1975.

Stewart had included the track on his *Smiler* album, issued in Britain on 27 September 1974 on Mercury 9104-001 and in America on 7 October 1974 on Mercury SRM 1-1017. He then issued it as a single. It was issued in America on 4 November 1974 on Mercury 73636, with 'Farewell' on the flip.

Mirror Mirror

A 1995 album by 10cc. Paul is featured on two of the tracks. 'Yvonne's The One' is a number he co-wrote with Eric Stewart, who he collaborated with on his *Press To Play* album. Eric was a founder of 10cc. On the other track, 'Code Of Silence', Paul plays strings, Rhodes piano, percussion and contributes frog and insect noises.

Mistress And Maid

A number co-written by Paul and Elvis Costello, which was included on the *Off The Ground* album.

Mitchell, Adrian

A British poet and journalist, born in London in 1932. Mitchell first met Paul in January 1963 when he became the first journalist to interview the Beatles for a national newspaper. The interview appeared in his column in the *Daily Mail* on 1 February 1963.

He said, 'I went back to write about them whenever my paper would give me the space. Paul was interested that I was a published poet and novelist, so I came to know him best. We maintained a friendship that became closer over the years, especially when our families met.'

In 1991, when Paul, Linda and their band were appearing at Cliffs Pavilion, Southend on Friday 9 July 1991 as part of their *Unplugged* tour, they backed Mitchell on stage, performing four of his poems.

The poems were 'Song In Space', 'I Like That Stuff', 'Maybe Maytime' and 'Hot Pursuit'. For the musical backing to 'I Like That Stuff', Paul played an instrumental version of 'Junk'. The final poem was about rhythm and blues star James Brown.

Mitchell was able to return the favour in 1995 when he was poetry editor of the *New Statesman*. He published five of Paul's poems.

It was Linda who originally suggested to Mitchell that he edit a collection of Paul's poems and he eventually did so in 2001 when Faber & Faber published *Paul McCartney Poems and Lyrics 1965–1999*. It was also Mitchell who suggested that Paul juxtapose the poems with his song lyrics.

Mitchell has had several books of poems published and has given more than a thousand performances of his poems around the world.

Mohin, Owen

Paul's maternal grandfather. He was born in Tullynamalrow in 1880 and married Mary Danher of Toxteth, Liverpool in 1905.

Momma Miss America

A track on Paul's debut album *McCartney* lasting 4 minutes and 3 seconds. Paul recorded the number at home and played piano, drums, acoustic guitar and electric guitar. The original title was 'Rock 'n' Roll Springtime'. The instrumental is included in the soundtrack of the 1996 film *Jerry Maguire*.

Money, Zoot

A British musician, real name George Bruno, who established himself on the London scene in 1964 with his Big Roll Band which had the hit single 'Big Time Operator' in 1966.

The band became Dantalion's Chariot in 1967, but Zoot had no great success on the music scene so he became an actor and also appeared in a number of TV commercials.

He worked with Paul on the *McGough And McGear* album and also worked with Mike McCartney in the group Grimms.

In April 1977 he teamed up with Paul, Denny Laine and Vivian Stanshall to record with Mike McCartney. A number of tracks were cut at the sessions, but they remain unreleased.

In 1980 Paul suggested that Zoot did an album of MPL numbers. Zoot said, 'I leaped at the chance. There was a list of songs as long as Oxford Street. I picked out those I'd fancied and Paul paid for the session. Also, Paul helped to design the sleeve.'

The album *Mr Money* was issued in Britain on Magic Moon Records Lune 1 on Monday 15 September 1980, and a single 'The Two Of Us'/'Ain't Nothin' Shakin' But The Bacon' was also issued on Friday 5 June 1981 on Magic Moon Records Mach 6.

Monkberry Moon Delight

A track on the *Ram* album. Perhaps inspired by Screamin' Jay Hawkins's 'Love Potion No. 9' because 'monk' berry means 'milk' and 'moon delight' is a fantasy drink. In fact, Hawkins actually recorded Paul's 'Monkberry Moon Delight' on his 1979 album *Screamin' The Blues* and Paul included Hawkins's version of the number in the soundtrack played before his 1993 concerts. Also included were other versions of his songs by different artists, including 'Live And Let Die' by Guns N' Roses, 'My Love' by Junior Walker, and 'Let 'Em In' by Shinehead.

Hawkins died at the age of seventy on 12 February 2000 due to an internal haemorrhage.

Montserrat

The Caribbean island where George Martin built his AIR Studios in 1978, although it wasn't until Paul had recorded there that the stars began to flock to the place.

Paul and Linda recorded *Tug Of War* there in February 1981.

Paul commented, 'I wanted to work with George again. We hadn't worked together since Beatle days and it was something I had wanted to do for ages. I suppose I could have done that in London, but wouldn't you rather go to a paradise island if you had a choice?'

Paul arrived with Linda and his four children on 1 February and was soon followed by Ringo Starr, Carl Perkins and Stevie Wonder, who were guesting on the album.

Stevie was so impressed with Montserrat that he composed a number about the island and spent his last night there listening to a steel band at the only local club bar, the Agouti.

During sessions from Monday 2 February until Tuesday 3 March Paul recorded 'Somebody Who Cares', 'The Pound Is Sinking', 'Hey Hey' and 'Rainclouds'.

Morse Moose And The Grey Goose

At 6 minutes and 27 seconds, the longest track on the *London Town* album. During Wings' recording sessions in the Virgin Islands, Paul and Denny Laine were fooling around, Paul poking away at an electric piano and Denny thumping on a standard piano. They enjoyed the unusual sound, which Paul likened to Morse code, and began to write a song around it which they completed in London.

Mother Nature's Son

One of the songs Paul began composing during his sojourn in India.

It was recorded after John, George and Ringo had gone home, so Paul recorded it playing acoustic guitar at around three o'clock in the morning of 9 August 1968. Brass backing was added later and the number appeared on *The Beatles White Album*.

Engineer Ken Scott was to comment: 'Paul was downstairs going through the arrangement with George Martin and the brass players. Everything was great, everyone was in great spirits. It felt really good. Suddenly, halfway through, John and Ringo walked in and you could cut the atmosphere with a knife. An instant change. It was like that for ten minutes and then as soon as they left it felt great again. It was *very* bizarre.'

Paul was to say, '"Mother Nature's Son" was inspired by a lecture given by the Maharishi, but mostly written in Liverpool when we got back. The same lecture inspired John to write "I'm Just A Child Of Nature".'

Mother's Pride

Trade name of a loaf of bread produced in Britain. Dusty Springfield was among the pop stars who had appeared in the Mother's Pride television commercials and Paul and Wings were hired to appear in 1974. Paul wrote and recorded a Mother's Pride jingle, but the jingle and the TV spot with Wings were never aired due to a bread strike which had halted production at the time the TV spots were due to go out.

Move Over Busker

A number from the *Press To Play* album, lasting 4 minutes and 5 seconds, which had started life with the title 'Move Over Buster'.

Movie Magg

A track from the *Run Devil Run* album lasting 2 minutes and 12 seconds. It was penned by Carl Perkins and recorded at Abbey Road Studios on Tuesday 2 March 1999 with Paul on lead vocal, acoustic guitar and bass guitar, Dave Gilmour on electric guitar, Mick Green on electric guitar and Ian Paice on drums.

Paul had become friends with Perkins, who told him amusing stories about the songs he wrote. This song, as described to Paul by Perkins, was about him trying to take his girlfriend Maggie to the movies on a horse called Becky. The horse turned out to be a mule and they both rode to the movies on Becky's back.

Movin' On

An hour-long behind-the-scenes documentary directed by Aubrey Powell, which began with the working title 'What It Takes'. The documentary covered Paul's recordings of *Off The Ground* at Abbey Road Studios; the special-effects work undertaken at Industrial Light and Magic Studios in Los Angeles for the 'Off The Ground' single; Kevin Godley's work on the 'C'mon People' video; Paul and Linda visiting Linda's exhibition in Los Angeles; Paul performing with Angelo Badalamenti, the soundtrack composer, and a 52-piece orchestra; Paul rehearsing with his band; Paul working with photographer Clive Arrowsmith and sculptor Eduardo Paolozzi.

The soundtrack to the documentary included seven tracks from the *Off The Ground* album, together with new versions of 'Penny Lane' and 'I Wanna Be Your Man'. It featured a live excerpt of a 'Live And Let Die' performance; a studio rehearsal of 'Drive My Car'; the filming of the video of 'C'Mon People'; a studio rehearsal of 'Penny Lane'; the promotional film of 'Off The Ground', a live rehearsal of 'Twenty Flight Rock', a live rehearsal of 'Looking For Changes'; the filming of the video of 'Hope Of Deliverance'; a live version of 'Get Out Of My Way' and a live version of 'Biker Like An Icon'.

With a name change to 'Movin' On' and pruned down to only 27 minutes, it was premiered on Channel 4 in Britain on Sunday 18 April 1993 and on the Fox Television network in America on Thursday 10 June 1993, with slightly different footage from the British version. The full-length version was aired in Germany later that year.

The MPI home video was issued in America on 26 July 1993.

MPL Communications

An abbreviation of McCartney Productions Limited. Paul had originally formed a company called Adagrove Limited on 12 February

1969, which was then changed to McCartney Productions. On Wednesday 7 April 1976 McCartney Productions changed its name to MPL Communications Ltd.

It was originally established as a management company for Paul and Linda's projects including songwriting, recordings, books, films and videos. The company secured several music catalogues and by 1997 owned the copyrights to 25,000 songs.

It was first established at 12–13 Greek Street in 1976 in a small two-roomed office above the Cucaracha Mexican restaurant and later moved to 1 Soho Square. The company initially had one office there, but gradually took over the entire building on the advice of Lee Eastman. The bullet-proof glass windows cost £2,000 and a replica of Abbey Road's Studio Two was built in the basement.

MPL is involved in various activities although the main bulk of its millions comes from the vast music publishing catalogue which Paul has been purchasing over the years.

The first music catalogue they bought was that of EH Morris, who owned the songs of Buddy Holly.

In 2000 MPL acquired 28 per cent of Mills Music Trust, which owns the rights to songs by Duke Ellington and other jazz artists.

MPL already owns the music from hit musicals such as *Guys And Dolls*, *Grease*, *La Cage Aux Folles*, *Bye Bye Birdie*, *Mame*, *Hello Dolly!*, *The Music Man* and *A Chorus Line*. It also owns classic numbers such as 'Unchained Melody', 'Autumn Leaves', 'Tenderly', 'Stormy Weather' and 'After You've Gone' and Four Seasons classics such as 'Walk Like A Man', 'Sherry' and 'Big Girls Don't Cry'.

The company is generally more interested in obtaining catalogues rather than individual songs.

The only Beatles numbers MPL owns are 'Love Me Do' and 'PS I Love You'.

Paul also purchased the music catalogues of songwriters and composers such as Scott Joplin and Ira Gershwin.

MPL has seventeen different companies responsible for song publishing, films, tours and video. Affiliated MPL companies include Arko Music, Barwin Music, Claridge Music, Conley Music, Desilu Music, Edwin H Morris & Company, Frank Music, Frank Music & Meredith Willson Music, Harwin Music, Jerryco Music, Morley Music, Remsen Music, Winmore Music and Wren Music.

In 2002 it was revealed that Paul had an apartment refitted on the top floor of the offices in Soho that he used as a one-bedroom hideaway after being hounded by fans and the press at his other homes. The flat has an estimated value of £1.5 million.

A friend of Paul's commented, 'The flat has proved convenient since the paparazzi think he's just going into the offices to work late.'

Although not a record company, MPL has issued several discs, mainly to advertising and entertainment companies. MPL 1 was a 7″

disc called 'We Moved', informing clients of the change of address from
12–13 Greek Street to 1 Soho Square. MPL 2 was a 7" disc called
'Buddy Holly Week America '83' with six Holly numbers on it.

Other releases have included *Galaxy Of Songs*, *Wow Mom*, *Listen
To This*, *MPL's Treasury Of Songs – The Standards*, *MPL's Treasury
Of Songs: The Rock 'n' Roll Classics* and *The MPL 25th Anniversary
Collection*.

MPL Presents

A hand-numbered box set of seven albums, only 25 of which were
produced. Paul decided to produce this limited-edition set, which could
be auctioned for charity, in 1979.

Paul had originally decided that the box set should contain all his
solo and Wings albums up to that date, a total of eleven. He also
wished them to be presented in a card box with the title *MPL Presents*,
on the box cover. However, he had forgotten that some of his albums
had gate-fold sleeves which, because of their thickness, would mean
that the box that had been designed couldn't accommodate them all.

As a result Paul rethought what he would include and decided on
seven albums from his solo career: *Ram*, *Red Rose Speedway*, *Wings
At The Speed Of Sound*, *Wings Over America*, *London Town*, *Wings
Greatest* and *Back To The Egg*.

Mr H Atom

One of several numbers Paul recorded in July 1979 during sessions for
McCartney II, which weren't used on the album.

Mr Sandman

The backing track for this number was recorded at the Black Ark
studios in Kingston, Jamaica, destined for a solo album by Linda, who
added her vocal track at Rude Studios in Scotland in August 1977. The
tune had originally provided the Chordettes with a No. 1 hit in January
1955 and it was included on the *Wide Prairie* album.

Mrs Vanderbilt

A single by Paul McCartney and Wings, 4 minutes and 37 seconds in
length, which was included on the *Band On The Run* album. It was
issued as a single in Europe with 'Bluebird' on the flip.

The single was released in Germany on EMI Electrola/Apple 1C600-
05529, in France on Apple 2C006-05529 and in Spain on Apple
1J006-05529.

MSN Webchat

On 9 May 2002, while appearing in Dallas, Texas, during his 'Driving
USA' tour, Paul agreed to participate in a question-and-answer session
online.

HOST: 'Welcome to MSN Live. Paul joins us tonight live from the sound check in Dallas.'

PAUL: 'Thanks. Lovely to be here, virtually and really.'

HOST: 'Paul, since you are about to go on stage, let's talk about your tour.'

QUESTION: 'What exactly was the pre-concert show, and where did the idea come from?'

PAUL: 'Originally we were thinking of having a support act, but it gets difficult because you have to move their stuff off stage and yours on. So I thought of having the audience come in rather than have them feeling like an auditorium. Then it turned into having them seem like they didn't know how they got there. Then I worked with Youth, and that was it basically. It just gets the audience in and gets them into the atmosphere.

QUESTION: 'Are you planning any other live dates in the UK in the near future and if so do you know where?'

PAUL: 'There are no plans at the moment, but I'm looking into taking the band to Britain, but I don't have any dates yet.'

QUESTION: 'Do you think you will record more songs with Ringo, possibly including more unreleased songs by Lennon or Harrison, like "Real Love"?'

PAUL: 'I don't know about that. It's an interesting idea. When we did "Free As A Bird" and "Real Love" there was another track under consideration for us to work on but we didn't get around to it, so I wonder if there will be a chance in the future. I wouldn't mind doing it.'

QUESTION: 'Songs become relevant to people at a particular time and place in their lives. What song is relevant to you at the moment? What do you play on the acoustic when alone?'

PAUL: 'When I'm touring I don't really find myself sitting around playing acoustic, because you're doing so much in the day that time off is time off. I really just play whatever comes into my mind. It could be an old song that I learned when I first learned guitar, or something new, or someone else's song. Or I'm writing a song when I have time off. I play nothing in particular and just see if an interesting idea comes out of that. It just depends on the mood you're in. I like doing it and always have one with me, but on tour I don't always use it that much.'

QUESTION: 'Do you have any plans to release a DVD music video collection?'

PAUL: 'That's one of those things that have been cooking for a while. Often something gets in the way of it. There's been talk of a DVD or live record of this tour, so that would mean the DVD would be put into next year. I would love to do them and look at them back to back. So I would like that for myself so one day we'll get around to that. But, like I said, there may be a DVD from this tour coming at the end of the year.'

HOST: 'So many of your fans here seem to go to one show after another.'

PAUL: 'I love that. It's a tribute, really. Sometimes when you go to see someone you get enough. But I love when they can't get enough. And that's a tribute to the band and to us. I do think that the people on the tour with us say you can watch the show more than once and always see something new.'

QUESTION: 'Your version of "Something" on your current tour is beautiful. Did you talk to George about covering his song?'

PAUL: 'As I say on stage, what happened was, I actually played it for George, kind of half a joke after dinner. I'd been sitting around and playing around with it on the ukulele. I found myself singing it, so I didn't say to George that I was going to sing it on stage because I didn't know I was going to. But I played it for him and he got a laugh from that.'

QUESTION: 'Will Paul like to do *Today*, a sequel to his famous *Yesterday* anthology?'

PAUL: 'I did a song called "Tomorrow" and "Yesterday" so the next should be "Today".

QUESTION: 'What is your favourite genre of book and your favourite author? Great concert in Boston. Thank you.'

PAUL: 'Thanks for the compliment. You know I think the kind of book I enjoy most is sort of old novels by Dickens, Wilkie Collins or Thomas Hardy because they transform you out of this world. I love the descriptions and characters of Dickens. I just get immersed in them. I don't read them all in one go, but I enjoy being transported to a different place and time.'

QUESTION: 'Hi, Paul. Your concert at the Garden in NYC was awesome. My husband works for the NYC fire dept and this concert was the best for all of us.'

PAUL: 'Oh, yeah. There was no doubt about it. The Concert for New York was a high spot in our year and we were all very proud of it because of the coming together, standing and being counted, and the emotion of the evening. So, if we had to do it again, I would do it.'

HOST: 'If you had to do it all over again, would you do it the same way?'

PAUL: 'It was a very special concert for us. I think it was great to assist in lifting the spirits of New Yorkers and Americans, especially firefighters and Port Authority.'

HOST: 'Paul, best of luck with the tour and thanks for being here tonight on MSN Live.'

PAUL: 'I just want to say thank you for being so wonderful and your support. Not just on the tour, but me personally. Thank you for the good vibes that you've been sending me. So from the dressing room here in Dallas from me, my fiancée Heather, Sir George Martin, we send our best wishes to everyone around the world.'

Mull of Kintyre

For a number of years this was Britain's biggest selling single ever, taking over the honours from 1963's 'She Loves You' until finally over-taken itself in 1984 by the Band Aid single 'Do They Know It's Christmas?'

It was originally issued as a double A-side with 'Girls' School' in Britain on Capitol R6018 on Friday 11 November 1977 and swiftly became the most rapid-selling single in Britain, passing its millionth pressing a month later in December.

'Mull Of Kintyre' was recorded in August 1977 at Paul's 'Spirit of Ranachan' house in Scotland with the RAK mobile recording unit brought up from London.

Discussing the number with Chris Welch of the *Melody Maker*, Paul commented, 'It's Scottish. It sounds so different from the songs we did on the boat (referring to the boat charted for the recording of the *London Town* album), we thought it should be a single and it sounds very Christmassy and New Yeary. It's kind of a "glass of ale in your hand, leaning up against the bar" tune. We had the local pipe band join in and we took a mobile studio up to Scotland and put the equipment in an old barn. We had the Campbeltown Band and they were great – just pipes and drums. It was interesting writing for them. You can't write any old tune, because they can't play every note in a normal scale. It's a double A-side.'

On Friday 23 December this millionth pressing was purchased by David Ackroyd who discovered a slip in the sleeve with a message from EMI informing him that he had won a Christmas hamper, to be presented by Denny Laine. He also received a specially pressed gold disc.

Denny had helped Paul with the song's composition in 1976. The title referred to a point on the southern tip of the Kintyre peninsula, near Paul's farm in Campeltown. At the time of the release, Wings comprised Paul, Linda and Denny, who made a promotional film at the Mull featuring the Campbeltown Pipe Band, a 21-piece group of bagpipers who also performed on the record.

It was issued in Germany on Capitol 1C600-60154 and in France on 2C006-60154.

In America the single was issued on Capitol 4504 on Monday 14 November but failed to make anything resembling the impact that it had in Britain. In fact, the single promoted in America was 'Girls' School', a number that Paul referred to as 'pornographic St Trinians'. St Trinians was the famous anarchic girls' school created by cartoonist Ronald Searle and featured in several British comedy films.

With 'Girls' School' as the A-side it reached No. 33 in the American charts.

In the 'Wingspan' television documentary, first screened in May 2001, Paul was to make further references to the remote Mull of Kintyre itself, saying that the peninsula helped save him from a nervous breakdown after the Beatles broke up.

He said, 'When the Beatles finished at the end of the sixties, it was such a shock to my system.

'Suddenly I was feeling totally redundant. I felt washed up and it was a very traumatic time.

'I'd lost the framework for my whole working life. I just didn't know what to do. I started staying up all night and staying in bed all day. There didn't seem any point in getting out of bed.

'I stopped shaving. I started drinking Scotch and I sort of went a little crazy for a few weeks. Looking back, I guess I nearly had a breakdown.

'I just had to get out of London and get in the mist and mountains, just to walk round and get some air and get away from this trauma.'

He found that the privacy and isolation in Scotland restored his self-confidence and led him to writing the number.

'I wasn't trying to write a big hit, I just wanted to write a love song to the area really,' he said.

During an interview with Steve Meyer, a national promotions manager for Capitol Records, it was pointed out that the record didn't have much success in America.

Paul explained, 'No. You have to remember, it's a record about a place that is totally alien to almost ninety-five per cent of the people in the US. They don't know what it is or what it means or anything. We had calls from radio stations asking us what it meant. What is "Mull Of Kintyre"? Then you have to say it's a place in Scotland and Paul vacations there etc., etc. He wrote this song out of love for the place. And over there, the English know what it is. It would be like writing a song about Yellowstone Park or the Grand Canyon here, and having someone in Europe not know what it means. Geography has a lot to do with it, and the melody really had a lot to do with it. But we did have about eighty per cent of all the radio stations in the US playing the record. It did respectable in the charts, but it didn't have the same meaning to the American people that it did over in England.'

Mumbo

A song that Paul co-wrote with Linda. It was the opening track on the first Wings album, *Wild Life*, issued in December 1971, and the number consisted of a string of nonsense words. No doubt a lot of mumbo jumbo.

Paul explained, 'Tony Clarke engineered it for us, and we told him we wanted it fat and funky. "Mumbo" just bombed along. We took it on the first take.'

Mumbo Link
An instrumental track from the *Wild Life* album, although it was unnamed on the initial release. It was missing from the Columbia album release in 1985 but included and credited when *Wild Life* was issued on CD in 1988.

Murphy, Eddie
Popular film actor, who also makes records. His album *It's Alright*, released on Motown 374636354-2/4 in 1993, featured Paul on the track 'Yeah', which was a one-word-lyric tune. The album also contained a version of 'Good Day Sunshine'.

Murphy had asked Paul to appear on the all-charity track 'Yeah', which was also issued as a single and proceeds of which were to go to an educational trust. Other artists on the track included Bon Jovi, Stevie Wonder, Patti Labelle, Michael Jackson and Aretha Franklin.

Murphy had said that he was inspired to make the record after watching *Yellow Submarine* on video.

Paul agreed to appear on the track if Murphy agreed to become a vegetarian for a week – which he did.

Commenting on Paul, Murphy said, 'So many people who amass a great deal of wealth and get really famous destroy themselves. This cat has everything, and he could have gone down any road. But he wound up on his feet, with a beautiful family, still making beautiful music. That really inspired me.'

Music For Montserrat
The title of a benefit concert held at the Royal Albert Hall on Monday 15 September 1997. George Martin had organised it in order to raise money for the residents of the island of Montserrat that had recently been devastated by volcanic activity. Martin had established a studio on the island and many British artists had recorded there, including Paul.

George Martin was to announce, 'I am delighted that we look set to raise so much money for the long-suffering people of Montserrat. I am very grateful to all the wonderful musicians who will perform in the concert. I'm going to Montserrat in the next few weeks to see for myself where the money raised should be spent to the best effect.'

Paul performed a solo acoustic version of 'Yesterday' and was then joined by Mark Knopfler, Eric Clapton and Phil Collins to perform 'Golden Slumbers', 'Carry That Weight' and 'The End'. He then sang 'Hey Jude', duetting on the piano with Elton John, and then all the other musicians, who included Sting, Carl Perkins and Midge Ure, joined them on stage in a rendition of 'Kansas City'/'Hey Hey Hey'.

Sky Box Office, the pay-to-view TV channel, filmed a 2-hour 15-minute programme of the event that was broadcast each day from Tuesday 16 to Friday 19 September.

During rehearsals Sky's Tania Bria interviewed Paul and the interview was also broadcast with screenings of the concert.

Here is a brief transcript:

Tania: How did you get involved in the concert?

Paul: I was on holiday and George Martin rang me up and said, 'Have you heard what's happening on Montserrat?' I said, 'Yes, I've seen the stuff on television about the volcano and it looks serious.' He said, 'Yes, it is, and I'm trying to put together a concert.' He let me know who was on the bill – the guys he'd approached – and I said, 'Yeah, I'll do it.' And that was it.

Tania: Everyone seems so enthusiastic about Montserrat and memories of recording there. Do you feel the same way, Paul?

Paul: Yeah, it's beautiful. I had a great time recording there. It's a beautiful island. The people are lovely, and of course, then there was no threat from the volcano at all. I recorded there with Stevie Wonder, we had a great time. We did 'Ebony and Ivory' together and Carl Perkins was there too. I recorded with some good friends and we had a nice stay out there.

Tania: What was so special about the island do you reckon?

Paul: Well, for me it was the opportunity to enjoy a Caribbean island and a recording studio. George had a really fine studio, which is now under ash, I believe. It was a combination of having a holiday and recording during the day and, after having a swim, waltz in and do some music. It was a nice laid-back feeling for everyone.

Tania: Was it pretty relaxed? Would the local people leave you alone?

Paul: It was really good. I always get left alone on a Caribbean island pretty much which is great for me because some places I get no privacy. Those islands are great really. There was a nice lady. We were down a market and I had longer hair then. She said, 'Are you American?' On learning that I am British she said, 'Ah, you're a subject like us!' I was just a subject, that's all I am.

Tania: Mark Knopfler and Jimmy Buffet said they went to a nightclub there. It seems a small place to have one.

Paul: They've got some jumping little places there – yeah.

Tania: What about the concert – are you excited by it?

Paul: Yes, I've seen these guys in the corridors at recording studios, or at festivals you may cross when you go on and they come off. I know them all very well – most of them anyway. But we've never really worked together. Apart from 'While My Guitar Gently Weeps', he played on that Beatle record, I've never worked with Eric. Elton I've never done anything with and Sting and the rest of them ... Mark. I've seen them, we've had cups of tea together, but not much more, so it's exciting to play together.

An edited ninety minutes of the show was included on a video/CD package of the show that was released the following year, also called 'Music For Montserrat'. Paul is seen performing 'Yesterday', 'Hey Jude', 'Golden Slumbers' and 'Kansas City'. The 3-track CD issued with the video included Paul's rendition of 'Hey Jude'.

Music Lives On, The

The film made its debut on Saturday 8 September 1984 on Channel Four in Britain and MTV in America. Unadvertised, it was slipped in on the tail-end of the evening's programmes at 12.40 a.m. (so, strictly speaking, Saturday morning), following 'The Making Of The Company Of Wolves'.

It was Buddy Holly Week and MPL Communications produced the fourteen-minute documentary as a tribute to Buddy Holly.

It begins with a black-and-white film of Buddy Holly and the Crickets performing 'Oh Boy'. Buddy's mother, Mrs Ella Holly, then relates how he thought his fame wouldn't last. A group of Buddy Holly fans dressed in colourful teddy boy costumes then wax enthusiastic, followed by Scottish comedian Billy Connolly talking about the durability of Holly's music.

A black-and-white film of couples jiving and jitterbugging to 'Brown Eyed Handsome Man' is followed by Buddy's brother Travis showing off a guitar that Buddy bought in 1951, a second-hand instrument and one of the first of many guitars. He mentions that he only taught Buddy to play a few chords.

More archive film of a performance of 'Peggy Sue' is followed by Ella talking about his early career playing locally at high school and graduation dances, then going to Norman Petty's studio in Clovis.

A still photograph of Buddy with the tune of 'Think It Over' in the background is followed by Ella mentioning that she wrote a song herself, which Buddy performed. The number was 'Maybe Baby'. The Crickets are seen performing the number at one of Paul's Buddy Holly Week concerts.

Buddy's other brother Larry talks about the number 'That'll Be The Day' and how Buddy, being flat broke, called New York to enquire about how the song was doing. He was told it was getting airplay and would sell a million, so he asked if he could have a cheque for $500.

Archive film of Buddy performing 'That'll Be The Day' is followed by his widow Maria Elena Holly mentioning that he'd been talking about expanding his career, producing other artists, seeking new talent, and recording with artists such as Paul Anka and Phil Everly.

Don Everly and Albert Lee are seen performing 'Bye Bye Love' at Paul's Hollywood concert.

There is a monochrome wedding photograph and Maria mentions the songs 'It Doesn't Matter Anymore', 'True Love Ways' and 'Raining In My Heart'.

Denny Laine then performs 'Raining In My Heart'.

Roy Orbison is interviewed and mentions that Buddy was a kindred soul and that they had a friendly rivalry.

Paul McCartney next appears performing 'It's So Easy To Fall In Love'. Then he performs 'Bo Diddley' with the Crickets (Sonny Curtis, Joe Maudlin, Jerry Allison), Don Everly and Denny Laine; both numbers were from the show at the Odeon, Hammersmith on Friday 14 September 1979. Bo Diddley briefly utters the sentence, 'God bless rock and roll,' and Maria Elena mentions that her favourite song was 'True Love Ways'. The number is played as a photograph of Buddy appears on the screen and the credits roll.

The film was also screened in America by MTV on Saturday 8 September 1984.

Must Do Something About It

A number recorded during the *Wings At The Speed Of Sound* sessions. Once the backing track had been laid down, Paul had the idea of getting Joe English to sing lead vocal on it. It is the only lead vocal by English on a Wings album. Paul, in fact, decided to give each member of the group the opportunity to sing on the 1976 album. It was 3 minutes and 39 seconds in length.

My Brave Face (promotional film)

A first promotional film of this number, directed by Roger Lunn, took place at Strawberry Fields, Liverpool on Monday 10 and Tuesday 11 April 1989. Apart from filming Paul and his group performing, there was archive footage included taken from the MPL archives. Paul also commissioned another promotional film of the same song which he called 'The Making Of My Brave Face'.

My Brave Face (song)

One of four songs Paul wrote with Elvis Costello (who is credited under his real name, Declan MacManus) for the album *Flowers In The Dirt*. Paul describes it as basically about a man who has been left by his woman and starts off the song in a happy frame of mind because he has his freedom – and then after a time, with the woman gone, he doesn't feel too happy about having to wash the dishes. Paul said that in a way it was a love song, but it's about someone who is not too pleased and he has to put on a brave face.

The single was released in Britain on Parlophone R6213 on Monday 8 May 1989 where it reached No. 18 in the charts and in the US on Capitol B-44367 on Wednesday 10 May 1989 where it reached the position of No. 25.

There were actually three other releases available apart from the 7″. They were a 12″ on Parlophone 12R 6213, a compact disc on CDR 6213 and a cassette on TCR 6213. The 12″, CD and cassette versions included two bonus tracks, 'I'm Gonna Be A Wheel Someday' and 'Ain't That A Shame'.

'Flying To My Home', a number composed by Paul, was on the flip. Neil Dorfsman and Mitchell Froom produced it.

A version of this number, composed by Paul and Elvis Costello, lasting 3 minutes and 8 seconds, was included on the *Tripping The Live Fantastic* album. It was recorded live at the Wembley Arena on 19 January 1990 during the 1989/90 World Tour.

My Carnival

A single recorded during the *Venus And Mars* album sessions at Sea Saint Studios in New Orleans on 12 February 1975. It was intended to issue it on the planned *Cold Cuts* album, but that album was never released. Instead, 'My Carnival' wound up as the flipside of 'Spies Like Us', issued in 1985.

The number was inspired by a boat trip down the Mississippi on the *Voyager*, which Paul and Linda undertook on their visit to the Mardi Gras Festival, where they performed on stage with the Tuxedo Jazz Band. It was also inspired by a Professor Longhair number 'Mardi Gras In New Orleans'.

Apart from Paul and Linda, those participating in the recording included Jimmy McCulloch, Joe English, Gene Porter, Benny Spellman and the Meters.

My Dark Hour

A single issued by the Steve Miller Band and released in the US on Capitol 2520 on Monday 16 June 1969 and in Britain on Capitol CL 15604 on Friday 18 July 1969. It was re-released in Britain on 25 February 1972 on Capitol CL 15712.

'My Dark Hour' was recorded at Olympic Sound Studios in London on Friday 9 May 1969. Paul played drums, bass guitar and sang backing vocals, and used his old pseudonym Paul Ramon for the session. The track was also included on the band's album *Brave New World*, issued on 16 June 1969 on Capitol SKAO 184 in America and in Britain on 10 October 1969 on Capitol E-ST 184. It resurfaced on the Steve Miller Band double album *Anthology*, issued in America on 6 November 1972 on Capitol SVBB 11114 and in Britain on 9 February 1973 on Capitol E-ST SP12.

My Little Girl

Sometimes called 'I Lost My Little Girl'. The first song that Paul ever wrote.

My Love

This Wings single was issued on Apple R5985 in the UK on Friday 23 March 1973. Although it was a studio cut, the flipside 'The Mess' was taped during Wings' French concerts in August 1972. The single reached No. 9 in the British charts. It was issued on Apple 1861 in America on Monday 9 April and topped the charts for four weeks, becoming Wings' first chart-topper.

'My Love' was recorded during the preparation of *Red Rose Speedway* and is included on the album. It's also on *Wings Greatest*. The song was included in the repertoire of Wings' 1972 tour of Europe, the British tour of 1973 and the world tour in 1975/76.

Commenting on his writing of the number, Paul said, 'I just sat down at the piano and wrote a love song, and that's the kind of tune that came out and it worked, luckily. I can't really say much more about it than that. If we had a computer monitoring my every thought and getting it down, I'd be able to tell you, but it happens too quickly. It's like, what makes a dog bark? You can analyse it. Roughly speaking, it's a bit like that. Roowf!'

The number became the first of his songs that Paul owned outright following the end of the 1963 Northern Songs contract.

Wings taped an appearance for *Top Of The Pops* performing the number on 4 April 1973 and a promotional film was also shot.

The single was also issued in Germany on EMI Electrola/Apple 1C600-05301 and in France on Apple 2C006-05301.

A live version of the number, lasting 4 minutes and 7 seconds, was recorded in San Antonio, Texas on 29 May 1993 and included on the *Paul Is Live* album.

My Love Is Bigger Than A Cadillac

A film about Buddy Holly's backing band the Crickets which was first aired on American television in two parts on 5 and 11 August 1990. It was also released as a home video in Britain in October. Paul makes a brief appearance in the film.

Myers, Mike

Actor/comedian, born in Scarborough, Canada on 25 May 1963. His parents had immigrated to Canada from Liverpool, England. He became a star of of *Saturday Night Live* with creations such as Wayne Campbell who was successfully translated to the big screen in *Wayne's World*. Myers also became successful with movies such as *Austin Powers*.

Paul and Linda attended the premiere of *Wayne's World II* at the Empire, Leicester Square, London on Friday 28 January 1993 and the northern premiere at the Cannon Cinema, Lime Street Liverpool the following day. Mike Myers, the star of the film, was in attendance at both events, which were held on behalf of LIPA and raised a total of £35,000 for Paul's project.

Following the Leicester Square event, Myers was also at the Hard Rock Café in Piccadilly with Paul and Linda and presented them with a Hard Rock cheque for £25,000 for the sales of Linda's veggie burgers.

Name and Address

A track on the *London Town* album. It was recorded at Abbey Road Studios and featured Paul on lead guitar. Jimmy McCulloch and Joe English had already left Wings at the time this track was recorded.

Hank Marvin, guitarist with the Shadows, dropped in on the session, although he didn't play. The number was Paul's tribute to Elvis Presley.

Nashville Diary 1979

A bootleg album (PRO 1234) containing tracks recorded by Wings during rehearsal sessions in Nashville in the summer of 1974. They included numbers such as 'My Love', 'One Hand Clapping', 'Hi, Hi, Hi' and 'Soily'.

National Poetry Day

Paul appeared at the Queen's Theatre, Shaftesbury Avenue, London on Thursday 4 October 2001 to read his poetry on the 21st anniversary of 'Poetry Olympics'; it was also the eighth year of National Poetry Day, which had originally been launched at Westminster Abbey to celebrate excellence in British poetry.

Paul read excerpts from *Blackbird Singing*, his first time in London, having read his poetry previously in Liverpool and at the Hays Festival.

Also at the Queen's Theatre event were Adrian Mitchell, Michael Horovitz and Frieda Hughes, daughter of the late Poet Laureate Ted Hughes and Sylvia Plath.

New Clubmoor Hall

A Liverpool venue run by local promoter Charlie McBain, situated to the rear of Broadway, Norris Green. This is the venue where Paul made his debut as a member of the Quarry Men on Friday 18 October 1957.

The other members of the band were: John Lennon on guitar, Len Garry on tea-chest bass, Eric Griffiths on guitar and Colin Hanton on drums.

The group travelled to the venue by bus and began their set at 9 p.m. Paul was to make his debut as the group's lead guitarist and began by singing 'Long Tall Sally'. However, when he began to perform the Arthur Smith number 'Guitar Boogie', it proved something of a disaster and he never played lead guitar with them after that.

This was probably due to the fact that Paul was playing his guitar upside down and backwards, as he still didn't know how to string a guitar for a left-handed person.

Years later, he was to comment, 'I went into the Quarry Men as the lead guitarist, really, because I wasn't bad on guitar. When I wasn't on stage I was even better, but when I got on stage, my fingers all went stiff. I had a big solo, on the song 'Guitar Boogie', and when it came to my bit . . . I blew it! I just blew it! I couldn't play at all and I got terribly embarrassed. My fingers found themselves underneath the strings instead of on top of them. So I vowed that first night that that was the end of my career as the lead guitarist. I goofed on that one terribly and so, from then on, I was on rhythm guitar.'

John was to comment, 'He really cocked up on this lone song. It was Arthur Smith's 'Guitar Boogie', a tune we all especially liked. When it came time for the big solo Paul lost his bottle and was all thumbs. The rest of the evening actually went down pretty smooth. We all had a good laugh about it afterwards; everyone, that is, except Paul.'

Promoter McBain wrote his opinion on the group's visiting card: 'Good & Bad.'

However, that particular night proved to be an extremely important one in the life of John and Paul and sparked off what was to become one of the greatest song writing teams of all time.

As if to atone for the mess he'd made as lead guitarist he decided to impress John by playing him an original song he'd written himself, 'I Lost My Little Girl'. John then responded by playing a few of the numbers he'd written and asked for Paul's opinion. It was the beginning of their songwriting partnership.

New Moon Over Jamaica

A number Paul co-wrote with country music artists Johnny Cash and Tony T Hall. Paul also sang a duet with Cash on the track when it was featured on the Johnny Cash album *Water From The Wells Of Home*, issued in America on Monday 10 October 1988 by Mercury Records. The album was issued in Britain on Monday 14 November 1988.

New Statesman And Society

A British political journal, with left-wing leanings. In the 27 January 1995 issue, Paul made his debut as a published poet with five poems:

'Chasing The Cherry', 'Mist The Mind', 'The Blue Shines Through', 'Trouble Is' and 'Velvet Wine'.

The accompanying text read: 'Paul McCartney is one of the great songwriters, never afraid to experiment with words or music. In 1994, he took a sabbatical from touring and has been writing new songs and a large-scale orchestral piece as well as mounting an exhibition of paintings for Germany.

Paul was also to cause some controversy in a *New Statesman* interview in September 1997 in which he supported decriminalisation for marijuana and knocked the currently popular group Oasis. Giving his verdict on the Manchester band, Paul said, 'They're derivative and they think too much of themselves. I hope for their sakes they're right. But really they mean nothing to me. They're not my problem. Oasis's future is their problem. I sometimes hear their songs and think, "That's OK", but I hope they don't make too much of it and start to believe their own legend because that can cause problems as others discovered. I wish them luck. I don't want to see them as rivals.'

New Theatre, Oxford
Venue where Wings appeared on Saturday 12 May 1973. Prior to the performance, Paul held a press conference attended by forty journalists, who were invited by Paul to bring along their wives or girlfriends. During the conference there was a reference to the number 'Six O' Clock' which Paul had recently written for Ringo and Paul said he'd write a song for any friend – and would write a number for Rod Stewart if he were asked. As a result Rod rang Paul and asked for a number and Paul wrote 'Mine For Me' for him, which Stewart released the following year. Following the show Paul was interviewed for *The David Symonds Show*.

New World Collection, The
A special four-CD box set, which was released to tie in with Paul's March 1993 tours of Australasia, which included *Wings Greatest*, *Band On The Run*, *Tripping The Live Fantastic: Highlights* and *Unplugged*.

New York Philharmonic Orchestra, The
Paul hired this orchestra to perform on three tracks of the *Ram* album, which he recorded in New York in 1971, his first recording stint outside Britain. He personally conducted the orchestra on the tracks 'Uncle Albert/Admiral Halsey', 'Long Haired Lady' and 'Back Seat Of My Car'.

Newman, Randy
An American singer/songwriter. In August 1967 Paul said that Newman was one of the best songwriters he had ever heard and hoped to be able to find time to team up with Newman and produce his first

album for him. He was pleased when Newman won the Academy Award for Best Song in 2002, even though it meant that Paul's 'Vanilla Sky' was the loser.

Newsfront

An American television show on which Paul appeared with John Lennon on Wednesday 15 May 1968. This was during their special trip to America to promote Apple. In addition to discussing their new project they also touched on a number of political subjects. The interview was repeated a week later on Wednesday 22 May.

Newsroom At Six

A news programme transmitted in London and the South East of England on BBC 1. Paul was interviewed during his 1989 Wembley concerts by former *Ready, Steady, Go!* host Cathy McGowan and the interview was shown in two parts on Wednesday 17 January and Wednesday 31 January 1990.

Night Before, The

A song penned by Paul for the *Help!* album and recorded in a single session at Abbey Road Studios on Wednesday 17 February 1963. In the film it was used during the Salisbury Plain sequence. It was also included on the *Rock And Roll Music* album. John Lennon played electric piano for the first time on the track.

Night Out

A number recorded by Wings in 1972. It was a track considered for the proposed *Cold Cuts* project, which was never issued.

Night Owl

A track featured on Carly Simon's *No Secrets*, released in 1972. The number was penned by her husband James Taylor, a former Apple artist and both Paul and Linda provided backing vocals, together with Doris Troy and Bonnie Bramlett. Paul and Linda provided their vocals following a recording session at AIR Studios for 'Live And Let Die'.

Nineteenth City School Scouts, The

A Boy Scout troop which Paul and his brother Mike joined soon after they entered their teens. Their first camping trip with the scouts took them to North Wales. Their second, in July 1957, took them to Hathersons in Derbyshire. There was an accident during the trip in which Mike broke his arm.

No More Lonely Nights (single)

The theme song to Paul's film *Give My Regards To Broad Street*, which was issued in Britain on Monday 24 September 1984 on Parlophone

R6080 and entered the charts on 6 October where it was to reach the No. 2 position, with a chart life of thirteen weeks.

After its release it was discovered that around 100,000 copies of the single said 'Lonley' on the label. Paul insisted that all copies be returned to the pressing plant so that the spelling could be corrected. Obviously, copies of the single that slipped away with the misspelling have become collectors' items.

The song was written specially for the film, and was effectively the theme tune, being played throughout the movie.

This was known as the 'ballad' version, as the song is played in two tempos.

Paul commented: 'Twentieth Century Fox asked for an upbeat play-out as people leave the cinema, so I was happy to arrange it in an up-tempo version as the play-out: that's more of a dance version.'

Two pressings of this double A-side were issued which featured both versions of the number. There was the normal 7″ single on Parlophone R6080 and a special 12″ pressing on Parlophone 12R 6080. Then on 8 October the 12″ pressing was issued as a picture disc in a special limited edition on Parlophone 12RP 6080. Writer Mark Lewisohn in a special article in the January 1985 issue of *Beatles Monthly* entitled 'It's All Too Much', bemoaned the fact that there were so many versions of this particular song. He pointed out that it would cost the collector, and in particular the completist, a small fortune to catch up with all the different editions of the same number. Mark reckoned that it would cost a collector £33.34 to buy the different British versions of the single, which included the 7″ ballad version; a 7″ special dance mix of the ballad version; a 12″ extended version, over eight minutes long; the 12″ picture disc; and a 12″ extended ballad version, with 'Silly Love Songs' and two versions of 'No More Lonely Nights'. This was in addition to the versions on the album, cassette and compact disc.

When the single was issued in America on Columbia 38-04581 on Friday 5 October 1984 it had a different flipside – the Arthur Baker 'Special Dance Mix'. It reached No. 6 in the charts. It was also issued in Germany on Parlophone 1C600-2002497.

'No More Lonely Nights' was also included on the compilation *Now That's What I Call Music 1984* on CDNOW 84.

The record received an American award from ASCAP for being the most performed song in America between Monday 1 October 1984 and Monday 30 September 1985. At a celebration dinner in Los Angeles on Wednesday 28 May 1986 songwriter Hal Davis accepted the award on Paul's behalf.

No Other Baby

A track from the *Run Devil Run* album lasting 4 minutes and 17 seconds. Penned by Bishop/Watson, it was recorded at Abbey Road Studios on Friday 5 March 1999. It featured Paul on lead vocal, bass guitar and electric guitar, Dave Gilmour on electric guitar and backing vocal, Mick Green on electric guitar, Peter Wingfield on Hammond organ ands Ian Paice on drums.

Paul had come across the song in the late 1950s but couldn't remember who had written it or recorded it and he never bought a copy of the record, but he remembered the words. When he came to record it, none of his fellow musicians knew of it either. He was later to discover that it had been recorded by an English skiffle group, the Vipers, and their version had been produced by George Martin.

No Other Baby
A single by Paul McCartney issued in Britain on Parlophone R6527 on 24 October 1999 with 'Brown Eyed Handsome Man' on the flip.

No Values
A track from *Give My Regards To Broad Street*. The song came to Paul in a dream. He'd been on holiday and was just waking up and he found he was still dreaming and was watching the Rolling Stones perform a number called 'No Values'. He remembered the chorus quite clearly when he woke up. He was sure that his own mind had created it in the dream. To make sure he checked that the Stones hadn't done a song of that title and when he found they hadn't, wrote the number and included it in the film and album.

No Words
A collaboration between Paul and Denny Laine. Denny had started off writing the song and Paul helped him to complete it. They shared writing credits when it appeared on the Wings 1973 album *Band On The Run* and performed the number during their British tour in 1979. Paul, Linda and Denny provided vocal harmony.

Nobel Peace Prize Concert
On 11 December 2001 Paul appeared at the Nobel Peace Prize 100th Anniversary concert at the Spektrum Arena in Oslo, Norway, before an audience of 6,000. Actors Meryl Streep and Liam Neeson hosted the concert. Norway's Crown Prince Haakon, Crown Princess Mette-Marit and Princess Martha were also in attendance.

Rusty Anderson backed Paul on guitar and Blair Cunningham was on drums. Paul performed 'Your Loving Flame', playing piano, and 'Freedom' on acoustic guitar. He said, 'The first one I wrote for my fiancée Heather, and the second one I wrote for the American people after 11 September, but tonight I'd like to dedicate them both to my friend George.' He finished his spot playing 'Let It Be' on piano and was joined on stage by some of the other artists who'd been appearing that night, including Natalie Imbruglia, rapper Wyclef Jean and Anastacia.

Prior to the concert, Paul commented, 'I have always felt that the strength of peace and love can give the world hope upon which to build our future. Peace has long been the theme of many of my songs. Although I believe that the world could not simply ignore the events of 11 September, I remain a pacifist and am happy to play for peace.'

The concert was televised on the cable/satellite channel Trio on 16 December 2001 and in America on USA Network on 21 December. Trio repeated the broadcast on 26 and 27 January 2002.

Nobody I Know
A composition by Paul, which he wrote for Peter & Gordon as a follow-up to 'World Without Love'. They recorded it at Abbey Road Studios in April 1964.

It was produced by Norman Newall and issued in the UK on 29 May 1964 on Columbia DB 7292 and in the US on June 15 1964 on Capitol 5211, with 'You Don't Have To Tell Me' on the flip.

It was also the title track on Peter & Gordon's EP *Nobody I Know*, released in the UK on Columbia 8348 on 24 July 1968.

Norton
A number penned by Paul and Mike McCartney and produced by Paul for the *McGear* album. It was included as a track on *The Force*, a mail-order double album, available only in America and released on Friday 14 February 1975 on Warner Brothers PRO 596. It was also issued as the flipside of the 'Dance The Do' single by Mike McCartney, also produced by Paul, which was issued in Britain on Friday 4 July 1975 on Warner Brothers K 16573.

Note You Never Wrote, The
This was a track from *Wings At The Speed Of Sound* and the first song recorded for the album in September 1975. Although Paul wrote the number, it was sung by Denny Laine.

Nottingham University
The venue for Wings' first ever gig which took place at lunchtime on Wednesday 9 February 1972 and was hurriedly arranged the previous day. Notices announcing: 'Tonight! Guest group: Paul McCartney and Wings! Admission 50p' drew an audience of 700 students. It was Paul's first live gig in nearly six years and the group's share of the take was £30.

Paul was to recall, 'It was a spur of the moment thing. One of the group had said he had played at Nottingham University and liked it so that's where we ended up. It was fifty pence at the door, and a guy sat at the table taking money. The kids danced and we all had a good time. The Students' Union took their split and gave us the rest. I'd never seen money for at least ten years. The Beatles never handled money . . . we walked around Nottingham with thirty pounds in coppers in our pockets.'

In an interview in *Melody Maker*, Paul was to comment, 'It was very good for us. We will go on touring the country for a while, playing more of these concerts when we feel like it.'

Trevor, one of Wings' road managers, was to comment: 'We went into Nottingham University students' union at about five o' clock and fixed it up for lunchtime the next day. Nottingham was the best because they were so enthusiastic. No hassles. No one quite expected or believed it.'

Commenting on the brief series of university gigs, Linda told *Melody Maker*: 'Eric Clapton once said that he would like to play from the back of a caravan, but he never got around to doing it. Well – we have! We've no manager or agents – just we five and the roadies. We're just a gang of musicians touring around.'

Nova
The composition by Paul that he wrote for *A Garland For Linda*. The reviewer in *Classic FM* magazine commented that 'Nova': 'certainly speaks directly to the listener. The repeated question, "Are you there?" from the sopranos and altos rises in intervals. The appeal to the listener is both potent and passionate.'

Paul was also interviewed in the magazine and commenting on his grief at the death of Linda, said, 'I thought I might be dead at the end of the year, it would just be so unbearable. I half-prepared for that to happen. The nearest I did get to that was with grief and crying. But I thought, no, that's a slippery path. So I tried to counteract that by just going from day to day.'

Discussing 'Nova', he said, 'I thought, "I'll write something, and if it's no good, I'll just say sorry." So I got on my computer and put up the choral settings that I use and just thought, "Well, now do I want to start it?" And just thought it all through.'

Now Hear This Song Of Mine
One of the numbers written and recorded by Linda and Paul in 1971 at the time of the *Ram* sessions. It was not included on the album and was never released as a single, although a thousand copies were pressed and circulated within the music industry to aid the promotion of *Ram*.

Now It's Paul McCartney, Stevie Wonder, Alice Cooper, Elton
A single by Clive Baldwin issued in America in 1975 on Mercury 73680. I Levine and L Russell Brown penned it and the flipside was 'Disco Rag'.

Now That's What I Call Music 11
Now That's What I Call Music is a series of British chart compilation double albums. The 11th release in the series issued by EMI/Virgin on NOW 2 on 26 March 1984 included the track 'Pipes Of Peace'.

Nurk Twins, The

Paul and his brother Mike first thought up this name when they were kids and used it when they entertained friends or family with a duet. In 1960 John and Paul made an appearance as a duo at the Fox and Hounds pub in Caversham, Berkshire in April 1960 and called themselves the similarly sounding Nerk Twins.

Nutwood Scene

A number that Paul had originally penned for a projected animated movie of *Rupert The Bear*. The 2-minute 10-second song has surfaced on several bootlegs and was included in the *Oobu Joobu* radio series.

Nutwood was the name of the area where Rupert the Bear and his friends lived.

O'Connor, Des

A British singer, comedian and chat-show host. Des appeared on the bill of Buddy Holly's last tour, two weeks before his tragic death, and Buddy made a present of his guitar to him. Paul, being one of Buddy Holly's staunchest fans, tried to buy the guitar from Des, who said, 'I won't sell unless I'm really hard up! I value it not only as a souvenir of a good friend but because it has memories of so many good times. Paul can borrow it if he likes – but only if he comes on my TV show and plays it!'

Oakland Coliseum

A venue in San Francisco, with a capacity of 14,000, where Paul opened his 'Driving USA' tour on Monday 1 April 2002. San Francisco was the city in which the Beatles played their last ever concert performance.

Paul decided on the venue for the first night of his tour.

During this concert, Paul paid tribute to Linda, John Lennon and George Harrison.

He performed George's 'Something' on a ukulele. He said 'George was a great ukulele player and whenever you went to his house, he'd play it at the end of the night. I showed him I could play the song on the ukulele and tonight I'd like to do it now as my tribute.'

Towards the close of the song he introduced some humour by saying, 'Of course, if George was here, he'd say, "No, it doesn't go like that, it should be like this," and he doubled the tempo of his playing in the style of George Formby.

He also received a standing ovation when he performed 'Here Today' for the first time before an audience, the song he wrote after

John's murder. He announced it following his rendition of 'Fool On The Hill', saying, 'When people are around, it's not always easy to tell them what you feel. After my dear friend John passed on, I wrote this song.'

The number had originally been included on his 1982 album *Tug Of War*.

Another tribute was 'My Love', the song he wrote for Linda.

During the two-and-a-half-hour show Paul performed 36 songs, including 21 by the Beatles and 10 by Wings. They included 13 No. 1 hits.

He said, 'When I was picking what song to play I imagined myself sitting in the audience and thinking, "Right, what would I want to hear him play?"'

Paul also played his first live performance of 'Getting Better' which had his fiancée Heather Mills dancing in the aisles.

Other numbers included 'Back In The USSR', 'Can't Buy Me Love', 'All My Loving', 'Live And Let Die' and 'Jet'.

Paul's group comprised Rusty Anderson on guitar and Abe Laboriel Jnr on drums, both of whom played on his *Driving Rain* album, plus Paul 'Wix' Wickens on keyboards and Brian Ray on guitar and bass.

At a press conference prior to the show, some journalists were wondering whether the tour would be Paul's farewell tour. He said, 'I'm a little cynical about saying something is a farewell tour because so many people have said they were gone and they came back. Besides, I always thought I would live until about ninety, and the estimate is going up! I will probably be wheeled on stage, singing "Yeeeessss-teeer-daaaay"!'

Oasis

A Manchester group, popular in Britain in the 1990s, led by the brothers Liam and Noel Gallagher, whose music showed an obvious homage to the Beatles.

In the *New Statesman* dated 26 September 1997, Paul made some comments about Oasis. He said, 'They mean nothing to me. They're derivative and they think too much of themselves.'

He was to add, 'They're not my problem – Oasis's future is their problem. I sometimes hear their songs and think, "that's OK". But I hope they don't make too much of it and start to believe their own legend because that can start to cause problems, as others have discovered.'

Despite this, when Paul made a special limited edition run of 200 copies of *Flaming Pie* he sent one to various friends in the music business, including Liam and Noel Gallagher.

When Noel and Meg Mathews were married in Las Vegas, the organist played 'Yesterday' and 'All My Loving'.

In 1999 Paul commented on the fact that Liam Gallagher and his actress wife Patsy Kensit had named their son Lennon, after John.

He said, 'I think it's a cool name. It's a nice tribute. Liam has always been a mega-fan of John's.

'I suppose it's like calling your baby after the Liverpool football team. I think it's a good name – but then I would, wouldn't I?'

Ob-La-Di Ob-La-Da

Paul was inspired to use the title of the song from the name of a reggae band: Jimmy Scott and his Obla Di Obla Da Band.

Paul said, 'A fella who used to hang around the clubs used to say, "ob-la-di, ob-la-da, life goes on," and he got annoyed when I did a song of it, 'cause he wanted a cut. I said, "Come on, Jimmy, it's just an expression. If you'd written the song you could have had the cut." He also used to say, "Nothin's too much, just outta sight." He was just one of those guys who had great expressions, you know.'

The number was recorded over five sessions during July 1966 and appeared on *The Beatles* double album.

Paul had wanted it to be a single but John Lennon and George Harrison voted against it. John actually hated the song. They were also annoyed at the length of time it had taken to record the number.

Second engineer Richard Lush was to comment, 'After about four or five nights doing "Ob-La-Di, Ob-La-Da" John Lennon came to the session really stoned, totally out of it on something or other, and he said, "All right, we're gonna do 'Ob-La-Di Ob-La-Da'." He went straight to the piano and smashed the keys with an almighty amount of volume, twice the speed of how they'd done it before, and said, "This is *it!* Come on!" He was really aggravated. That was the version they ended up using.'

John's friend Peter Shotton was to describe the scene when Paul, after what seemed like a flawless performance, then burst out laughing and said they'd have to do it again.

'Well, it sounded OK to me,' John yawned.

'Yeah!' George agreed. 'It was perfect.'

'But didn't you notice?' Paul demanded.

'Notice what?' said John.

'I just sang "Desmond stays at home and does his pretty face . . . " I should've sung "Molly"!'

The others refused to believe him – until George Martin played back the tape and proved Paul right.

'Oh, it sounds great anyway,' Paul concluded. 'Let's just leave it in – create a bit of confusion there. Everyone will wonder whether Desmond's a bisexual or a transvestite.'

The number was actually covered by two British bands, Marmalade and the Bedrocks, both of whom entered the British charts with the number. Marmalade topped the charts and the Bedrocks reached No. 20. Capitol actually issued it as a single in America on Capitol 4347 on 8 November 1976 and it only reached No. 36 in the American charts, becoming the first Beatles single on Capitol not to break into the American Top 30.

Ocean View, The
A book published by MPL Communications/Plexus Publishing in 1982.

It is a collection of paintings and drawings by Humphrey Ocean from the Wings American Tour that took place between April and June 1976.

Paul commissioned the works, as he wanted pictorial documentation of the tour.

He explains in a preface to the book that Captain Cook, who took an artist to record the discovery of Australia for posterity, inspired him. As Humphrey actually managed to do the work during the tour, it is hard to see why six years should have passed before publication.

There are sixty illustrations in the book ranging from brief sketches to completed paintings. A number of them are Hockneyesque, but they serve as a fresh visual record of the momentous tour.

Humphrey also kept a diary and his entries are reproduced in eight pages of text. They also illuminate life on the road.

The entry for Friday 18 June, which was Paul's 34th birthday, reads: 'The road-crew gave a birthday party with tortillas, enchiladas and a ten-piece Mexican band.'

Wings were in Tucson, Arizona at the time.

Ocean, Humphrey
A former member of Kilburn & the High Roads, who became a painter.

Ocean contributed to the inner sleeve of the *Wings At The Speed Of Sound* album and Paul commissioned him to join the Wings tour of America and document it as 'artist in residence'.

The result was the book *The Ocean View*.

Humphrey was also commissioned to work on a painting by the Imperial Tobacco Portrait Award. This turned out to be a portrait of Paul.

Paul sat for him for a total of thirty hours in six separate sittings in his Sussex home. The painting was unveiled at the National Portrait Gallery, London on 2 February 1984.

A gallery spokesman commented, 'This is a painting that puts the singer in a very unusual light. He looks nothing like he does on the record sleeves – it's bound to cause a few surprises.'

Humphrey said, 'I'm happy with it. I believe it shows Paul in a relaxed setting.'

Off The Ground – The Complete Works
The 1993 album *Off The Ground* was reissued in Germany in 1994 as a double CD set with eleven bonus tracks under the title *Off The Ground – The Complete Works*. Issued on Parlophone 8282772, it was exclusive to Germany.

The album included all of Paul's B-sides and CD-single tracks from 1993, with the exclusive of remixes such as 'Deliverance' and 'Off the Ground (Bob Clearmountain Remix)'.

The bonus CD contained: 'Long Leather Coat', 'Keep Coming Back To Love', 'Sweet Sweet Memories', 'Things We Said Today' (from the 1991 *Unplugged* sessions), 'Midnight Special' (also from *Unplugged*), 'Style Style', 'I Can't Imagine', 'Cosmically Conscious' (the full length version), 'Kicked Around No More', 'Big Boys Bickering', 'Down To The River' and 'Soggy Noodles'.

Off The Ground (album)

Paul's 18th solo album was released in Britain on Tuesday 2 February 1993 and in America on Tuesday 9 February 1993. It reached the position of No. 19 in the US charts. The cover was photographed by Clive Arrowsmith and showed the feet of, from left to right: Robbie McIntosh, Linda, Paul, Blair Cunningham and Hamish Stuart.

Paul asked his friend, the poet Adrian Mitchell 'to look through the lyrics as if he was an English teacher checking my homework'. Mitchell then advised him on a number of things. On the number 'C'mon People', for example, he suggested that Paul find a stronger adjective than 'coming' in his line 'we got a future and it's coming in'. Paul revised it to 'rushing' and in another verse, to 'changing'.

The tracks were: Side One: 'Off The Ground', 'Looking For Changes', 'Hope Of Deliverance', 'Mistress And Maid', 'I Owe It All To You', 'Biker Like An Icon'. Side Two: 'Peace In The Neighbourhood', 'Golden Earth Girl', 'The Lovers That Never Were', 'Get Out Of My Way', 'Winedark Open Sea', 'C'mon People'. There is also an uncredited fade-out track. This is 'Cosmically Conscious' which Paul wrote in 1968 in India.

Paul and Julian Mendelsohn produced the album and two of the tracks 'Mistress and Maid' and 'The Lovers That Never Were' were collaborations between Paul and Elvis Costello.

EMI Toshiba released *Off The Ground* in a double CD case with a bonus 3″ CD of 'Long Leather Coat' and 'Kicked Around No More' on TOCP 7580.

Off The Ground (single)

The title track of the album, penned by Paul and lasting 3 minutes and 38 seconds in length. The single was issued in America on Monday 19 April 1993 as two versions had been prepared for the US market, one 'The Bob Clearmountain Remix', the other 'The Keith Cohen Remix'. It was not released in the UK.

The flip was 'Cosmically Conscious'.

A limited edition in white vinyl was issued on Capitol/CEMA 17318. CEMA was a special markets label.

Mathew Robbins directed the 'Off The Ground' promotional film.

Ogden, Richard

Record company executive, former PR for United Artists in Britain, who became managing director of Paul's management and publishing companies on 5 May 1987 after a period as managing director of Polydor Records.

When he took over as Paul's manager he commented that before taking up his position: 'I wanted to know that Paul wanted to have a full-time career, including playing concerts, which are very important in the overall picture. I was convinced that he did.'

He also said that he wanted: 'to get Paul back on the road, to see his records in the charts and to encourage and help him find inspiration as a musician and a writer. We're having weekly "get-togethers" with musicians and Paul's playing the bass and singing great.'

There was controversy surrounding his leaving Paul's employ in July 1993. MPL maintained that his contract had run out, stating, 'He resigned because his contract ended and the departure was quite amicable.' Ogden claimed that he had resigned. The situation probably resulted from the claim that there were disagreements regarding the high costs and poor publicity on the New World Tour.

Ogungboro, Adi

The man who inspired Paul to conceive the idea of LIPA. The Toxteth man told the *Liverpool Echo* that Paul had promised him that a special bursary scheme to help unemployed people, especially the black and working-class youngsters, would be named after him, although LIPA management denied this.

Oh Woman, Oh Why?

A number that developed from a studio jam session and ended up on the flipside of 'Another Day' and as a track on *Wild Life*.

Oh, Darling!

A blues ballad, penned by Paul, part of which appears in the *Let It Be* film. The Beatles recorded it at Abbey Road in April 1969 with John on piano and George running his guitar through a Leslie speaker.

John was later to comment, '"Oh, Darling!" was a great one of Paul's that he didn't sing too well. I always thought I could've done it better – it was more my style than his.'

Alan Parsons, who was second engineer on the recording, said, 'He'd come in, sing it, and say, "No, that's not it. I'll try again tomorrow." He only tried it once per day, I suppose he wanted to capture a certain rawness which could only be done once before the voice changed. I remember him saying, "Five years ago I could have done this in a flash," referring, I suppose, to the days of "Long Tall Sally".'

Paul was to explain, 'When we were recording this track, I came into the studios early every day for a week to sing it by myself because at first my voice was too clear. I wanted it to sound as though I'd been performing it on stage all week.'

The number was included on the *Abbey Road* album.

In the Robert Stigwood movie *Sgt Pepper's Lonely Hearts Club Band* the number was sung by Robin Gibb of the Bee Gees and issued as a single, which reached No. 24 in the American charts in 1978.

Old Siam Sir
A Wings single released in Britain on Friday 1 June 1979 on Parlophone R6026 with 'Spin It On' on the flip. The number reached No. 27 in the British charts.

On Our Way Home
A number Paul wrote specially for a teenage trio from New York called Mortimer, who comprised Guy Masson, Tony Van Benschoten and Tom Smith. The trio played acoustic guitars and conga drums. Paul recorded them performing the number in April 1969. Apple intended releasing it as a single, but never did. The number eventually re-emerged, with a different title 'Two Of Us', in the film *Let It Be* and was recorded by the Beatles for the album.

On The Wings Of A Nightingale
A number Paul wrote specially for the Everly Brothers, who had reunited after being estranged for ten years. Paul also remixed the track and played acoustic guitar on it. Phil and Don issued the song as a single in a picture bag by Mercury Records on MER 170 on Friday 24 August 1984. The flipside was a non-McCartney composition, 'Asleep'.

The song was also included on *EB '84*, their first studio album since 1972, which was produced by Dave Edmunds and issued on Friday 5 October 1984 on MERH 144.

Once Upon A Long Ago
A single by Paul that was issued in Britain on Parlophone R6170 on Monday 16 November 1987 where it was to reach No. 10 in the charts.

'Back On My Feet' was on the flipside.

There was no US release of the disc although in Britain there was a 7", two 12" vinyls and one CD version.

It was released in Germany on Parlophone 1C006-2021857.

Interestingly enough, a composer called Pat Doyle adapted the tune of 'Once Upon A Long Ago' and used it in a TV play of *Twelfth Night* in a BBC Shakespeare season in which he set Shakespeare's lyrics to music. The credits named the song 'Come Away Death' and credited it to Pat Doyle and Paul McCartney.

'Once Upon A Long Ago' was a track from the *All The Best* album, produced by Phil Ramone, orchestrated by George Martin and featuring classical violinist Nigel Kennedy.

One And One Is Two

A number originally written for Billy J Kramer. It was a collaboration between Paul and John, although Paul was responsible for most of the composition. When the two of them had taped a demo of the number for Billy J, John commented, 'Bill J's career is finished when he gets this song.' Billy J rejected the number and chose to record 'Little Children', which took him to the top of the charts. The number was eventually recorded by Mike Shannon & the Strangers in 1964, but failed to make the charts.

Oddly enough, in his book *Many Years From Now*, when discussing the number 'One And One Is Two' Paul says, '"One And One Is Two" is OK, it's a memorable title, it's not wonderful. The Strangers were mates of ours from Liverpool.'

The Strangers with Mike Shannon were a group totally unconnected to the Liverpool band the Strangers, whose lead singer was Joe Fagin.

One And Only, The

One of the numbers Paul wrote during a holiday in the Virgin Islands in 1964. It remains unreleased.

One Hand Clapping

A 50-minute 1974 film from McCartney Productions, directed by David Litchfield, who had previously directed another MPL film *Empty Hand*. It was a short documentary of Wings rehearsing and recording in Nashville, Tennessee, which opens with a motion of a hand and then has the group perform 'Jet' and 'Soily'. The group then listen to the playback in the control room, which was manned by Geoff Emerick.

'C Moon' is the next performance and Paul says, 'I like a little team. I like the fun of all having a cup of tea together, getting your heads down and working on a piece of music. I've never been a solo performer.'

His little team on this venture includes himself and Linda, Denny Laine, Jimmy McCulloch, Geoff Britton and Howie Casey.

Voice-overs are used and Geoff Britton asks Denny, 'Do you think parents are important?'

Denny says, 'If I hadn't been pushed by my old man, if he didn't take me down to the Jackie Cooper School Of Dancing, then I wouldn't have started 'cause I was not interested in going. I was interested in music, yeah, but I wasn't interested in going through all the crap that you have to go through to get there.'

McCulloch's voice-over is partly biographical telling how he practised guitar while getting ready to go to school and how he left Scotland to arrive in London.

The band performs 'Maybe I'm Amazed' and 'My Love' and when Paul sits at the piano and plays he mentions a song 'Suicide', which he wrote for Frank Sinatra.

There is also a voice-over from Linda who says, 'Paul shows me what to play on some of them. On others, I just get the chords and find out what the chords are, and pick it up from there. If you don't do it, nobody can do it for you.'

Denny refers to Paul, 'He's an old man. He has his own band. His family are as talented as he is.'

The band performs 'Band On The Run', 'Live And Let Die' and '1985'.

One Love
A single by the legendary Bob Marley. It was issued posthumously by Island Records (IS 169) on 6 April 1984. It leaped high into the British charts and Paul made a fleeting appearance on the accompanying video. He is seen clasping Don Leets, who directed the video, and his lips voice the words 'one love'. The video was also included on the video compilation 'Legend', issued by Island Video in May 1984.

One More Kiss
A track from the *Red Rose Speedway* album. It was copyrighted under the title 'Only One More Kiss'.

One Of Those Days In England
A track on the Roy Harper album *Bullinamingvase*, originally issued in February 1997. Paul and Linda were featured on backing vocals on the track, on which former Wings guitarist Henry McCullough also played. It was re-released by EMI Records in their mid-price range on Monday 24 August 1987 and also reissued on Harper's compilation album *Hats Off*, on 19 June 2001.

One To One
A British weekly television series. Disc jockey Anne Nightingale's 24-minute interview with Paul was featured on the series and screened on some parts of the ITV network on Thursday 14 December 1989 prior to a repeat screening of 'The Birth Of The Beatles' TV movie and on London Weekend Television on Sunday 21 January 1990.

Only Love Remains (remix)
A track from the *Press To Play* album, recorded live at Paul's 48-track studio, Hoghill, East Sussex. Tony Visconti arranged it.

Commenting on the number, Paul said, 'People ask if I feel an album's incomplete without a ballad, and I do think so, a little bit. I know there are people who like them who will inevitably gravitate towards the track. People who've heard the album say, "That's the McCartney I like," so I sorta put it on for them – and for myself, because I'm pretty romantic by nature.'

The song, 4 minutes and 16 seconds in length, was released as a single in Britain on 1 December 1986 where it reached No. 34 in the charts. It was issued in America on Capitol B-5672 on Tuesday 17 January 1987.

In Britain the 7″ was issued on Parlophone R 65148 and the 12″ on Parlophone 12R 6148.

'Tough On A Tightrope' was on the flipside.

Ono, Yoko

Yoko Ono first met Paul at a gallery opening for the artist Claes Oldenburg in 1966. She also went to Paul's Cavendish Avenue house to ask if he had any spare manuscripts of Beatles lyrics that she could give as a present to John Cage for his fiftieth birthday, as he collected musical scores. Paul regarded his own lyrics sheets as too precious, but referred her to John and gave her John's address – and this was prior to her Indica Gallery exhibition, which puts paid to the false story that Yoko had never heard of John until he turned up at the exhibition.

John actually gave her the lyric sheet of 'The Word', which was reproduced in Cage's book *Notations*. Cage had been collecting a diverse range of musical scores for the Foundation of Contemporary Performance Arts.

Paul recalled the incident vaguely, saying, 'There was a charity thing – it was rather avant-garde, something to do with John Cage . . . .She wanted lyrics, manuscripts. I really didn't want to give her any of my lyrics – you know, selfish, or whatever, but I just didn't want to do it. So I said, "But there's a friend of mine who might want to help – my mate John." I kind of put her on to John and then they hit it off – it was like wild fire.'

It was suggested that when Yoko began her omnipresence at Beatles recording sessions, Paul got back at her in the song, 'Get Back'. It was said that when Paul was singing, 'Get Back! Get Back! Get Back to where you once belonged!' he was looking at Yoko. However, Paul has said that the song was about the Beatles 'getting back' to their roots in rock 'n' roll.

Paul was the only other member of the Beatles on 'The Ballad Of John And Yoko'.

It was John, under Yoko's influence, who brought Allen Klein into the Beatles' lives, against Paul's wishes. Paul blamed Yoko. He said, 'We were pretty good mates . . . until Yoko came into it. The thing is, in truth, I never really got on well with Yoko anyway. It was John who got on well with her – that was the whole point.'

He was to add, 'Klein, so I heard, had said to John – the first time anyone had said it – "What does *Yoko* want?" So, since Yoko liked Klein because he was giving Yoko anything she wanted, he was the man for John.'

Apple executive Peter Brown was to say, 'McCartney was placed in an impossible position. John wanted to go in another direction and McCartney couldn't follow him because there was Yoko in the middle and Yoko didn't want them to continue. Yoko wanted John for herself. And she was very single-minded.'

Paul gave an interview to Ray Connelly and said, 'John's in love with Yoko and he's no longer in love with the other three of us.'

In the same interview he also talked about his songwriting collaboration with John. 'It simply became very difficult for me to write with Yoko sitting there. If I had to think of a line, I started getting very nervous. I might want to say something like, "I love you, girl," but with Yoko watching I always felt that I had to come out with something clever and avant-garde. She would probably have loved the simple stuff, but I was scared.'

Paul had been in the habit of sending anonymous cards, notes and letters to people, which caused one particular strain between himself and John Lennon. John and Yoko were staying at Cavendish Avenue at the time and a card arrived one day addressed to John and Yoko. It said, 'You And Your Jap Tart Think You're Hot Shit.' John placed it in front of Paul, who confessed that he'd written it as a joke. John and Yoko then packed their bags.

Paul was living with Francie Schwartz at the time and she was to comment, 'One morning I noticed there was an envelope with a typed address on it. No stamp or return address, it just said "John and Yoko". They thought it was a piece of fan mail and they opened it up and it was a typed unsigned note that said, "You and your Jap tart think you're hot shit," and John was wounded by it. He loved her and couldn't understand why people would hate her, and Paul came into the living room and he says, "Oh, I just did that for a lark!" The letter was from Paul, and John looked at him and that look said it all, "Do I know you?"'

In 1970, Hunter Davies, the Beatles' official biographer, stated that Yoko Ono was the main cause of the Beatles break-up. 'If there was one single element in the split, I'd say it was the arrival of Yoko,' he claimed. He said that under Yoko's influence, Lennon began taking charge at Apple and this 'was a blow to Paul's pride . . . Paul fell by the wayside and . . . they were no longer bosom buddies . . . George Harrison and Ringo Starr are not exactly dotty over Yoko either.'

In a statement he read to the court on Friday 26 February 1971 Paul said that one of the reasons George Harrison left the group was 'he could not get on with Yoko'. He also said that Allen Klein had told him on the phone, 'The real trouble is Yoko Ono. She is the one with ambition.'

When Geraldo Rivera, ABC television journalist, wanted John and Yoko to perform at a benefit concert at the end of August 1972 for the One to One Foundation, Yoko suggested that they phone Paul and ask him to appear. Paul refused.

In 1981 Paul had an opportunity to purchase the Beatles' songs from ATV. Lew Grade's company had been having problems over the astronomical costs of the film *Raise The Titanic*, and seemed set to sell ATV

Music. Paul had lunch with him and asked if he would be willing to separate Northern Songs from ATV Music and sell Northern Songs to him. As Northern Songs was the jewel in ATV Music's crown, Grade was advised against it, but he told Paul, 'I'll pull it out for you. I'll sell it separately. Only to you. The price is going to be twenty million pounds.'

Grade gave Paul one week to accept the offer. He took advice from his lawyers and felt that the money could be raised and also felt a moral twinge if he took control himself as that would mean bypassing Yoko, Sean, Julian and other parties. 'There was no way I was going to be seen as the guy who had stolen John's songs.'

He decided he'd call Yoko and the two of them could own the company. He said, 'I rang her up and I said: "Lew Grade has just offered me the company. He said it's twenty million pounds. We should do it. You'll have half of it; I'll have half of it. That will feel good to me. John will have his half back. It's ten to me and ten to you. I don't know how easy it's going to be to find it. But that's the deal."

'And she said: "No, no. Twenty is way too high a price."

'I said: "Well, you may be right. Certainly as I wrote 'Yesterday' for nothing! It certainly seems a little expensive for me, but that's the ball game and we can't ignore it."

'And she actually did say to me: "No, we can get it for five."

'I said: "Well, I'm not sure that's right. I've spoken to the man who's selling them. He says twenty million. But you'd better get back to me."

'She said: "No, let me talk to a few people. I can do something here."

'And of course, it fell through, obviously,' said Paul. 'We couldn't get it for five.'

In 1990, when recalling these events again, he said, 'She's since denied that. I don't want to have friction with anyone. Particularly not John's widow. I loved John. If John loved her, I'd like to love her. That's the way I'd like it to go. But that is the truth as far as I can see it. If she wants to deny it, fine . . . I know in my mind what happened.'

In November 1983 Yoko brought Sean to London, primarily to discuss Apple business with the three remaining Beatles. The meeting didn't go well. A witness commented, 'The tension was still there. Yoko was not forgiven. Oh, Ringo was nice. He always was nice. And Paul was charming in the way that he could always be when he chose to. He knew how to turn it on and off, and Yoko saw right through it. George still didn't care. He didn't like Yoko when John first met her and he didn't like her in London three years after John was dead.'

It seemed that the long feud between Paul and Yoko had ended in 1994 when John Lennon was inducted into the Rock And Roll Hall of Fame as a solo artist on Wednesday 19 January. Paul made the induction speech and Yoko picked up the award. The two were then photographed hugging each other and during the following press conference it was announced that the three surviving Beatles would be recording together again, with Yoko saying, 'Give the three of them a chance.'

Yoko also presented Paul with four of John's demos for them to use in their comeback recording sessions.

Discussing how they got together again for the awards ceremony, Paul commented, 'Yoko was a little surprised to get a phone call from me, because we'd often been a bit adversarial because of the business stuff. She told me she had three tracks, including "Free As A Bird". I'd never heard them before, but she explained that they're quite well known to Lennon fans as bootlegs.'

When he received the cassettes of John's songs, Paul told Yoko, 'Don't impose too many conditions on us, it's really difficult to do this. We don't know, we may hate each other after two hours in the studio and just walk out. So don't put any conditions, it's tough enough. If it doesn't work, you can veto it.'

Paul once recalled how Yoko had contacted him to say that she needed him and asked him to come to New York. Paul remembered, 'I said I was going through New York and so I stopped off and rang her, and she said she couldn't see me that day. I was four hundred yards away from her. I said, "Well, I'll pop over anytime today – five minutes, ten minutes, whenever you can squeeze me in." She said, "It's going to be very difficult." I said, "Well, OK, I understand. What is the reason by the way?" She said, "I was up all night with Sean." I said, "Well, I understand that. I've got four kids, you know. But you're bound to have a minute today, sometime." She'd asked me to come. I'd flown in specially to see her and she wouldn't even see me. So I felt a little humiliated, but I said, "OK, nine-thirty tomorrow morning. Let's make an appointment." She rang up about nine and said, "Could you make it tomorrow morning?" So that's the kind of thing. I'm beginning to think it wasn't all my fault.'

On Saturday 11 March 1995 Yoko and Sean spent a weekend visiting Paul and his family at their home in East Sussex. Whilst there, Yoko and Sean went into Paul's home studio, the Mill, and, together with Paul, Linda, Mary, Heather, Stella and James recorded a track called 'Hiroshima, It's Always A Beautiful Blue Sky' commemorating the fiftieth anniversary of the dropping of the atomic bomb on Hiroshima.

Yoko took the lead on her composition, with Paul providing backing vocals and playing the upright bass, which formerly belonged to Bill Black. Linda played celeste, Sean and James played guitars and Mary, Heather and Stella provided percussion and backing vocals.

Prior to Yoko returning to America, Paul gave her a copy of the tape.

Yoko was able to comment, likening the feud between the families to that in Shakespeare's *Romeo And Juliet*, 'Montague and Capulet coming back together was beautiful. It was a healing for our families to come together in this way. The feeling was very special.' Sean said that the spontaneous recording session was 'the result of our reconciliation after twenty years of bitterness and feuding bullshit. Here were these people who had never played together actually making music. It was incredible working with Paul.'

On Friday 16 January 1998 Yoko appeared on *The O-Zone*, a children's programme on the BBC, where she took the opportunity of sniping at Paul on a number of points during a 20-minute programme subtitled 'The Ballad Of John and Yoko'.

Yoko attacked him by implying that he was just a second fiddle to John's genius. 'I know Paul thinks he was leading, or something like that. The way John led the band was very high-level, on some kind of magical level. Not a daily level like Paul said, "Oh, but I was the one who told them all to come and do it. I made the phone calls." John did not make the phone calls. He was not on that level as a leader – he was on the level of a spiritual leader,' she said. 'He was the visionary and that is why the Beatles happened.'

In response to a claim by Paul early in 1997 in which he said that he was responsible for initiating reconciliation between John and Yoko following their 18-month separation in the 1970s, Yoko dismissed this saying, 'Let him say what he wants to say. I feel that he has to say all of those things. But if he wants to get credit about it, why not? That's fine, I know that it wasn't true. I know that he didn't come back because Paul said a few words. Let him say what he wants to say. I feel sad he needs to say it but if he wants to get credit for it, why not? That's fine. I know that it wasn't true. I know that he didn't come back because Paul said a few words, or something like that. He's put in the position of being a Salieri to a Mozart.'

She also claimed, 'Because John passed away, people have this incredibly strong sentiment for him. Paul is always just encouraging people, not given the same compliment that they give John now. And naturally, they do that because he passed away. It's a high price for Paul, to be in the same position as John.'

A clash occurred once again when Paul requested that his name be placed before John's on the credit for 'Yesterday' on the *Beatles Anthology*. Yoko refused.

Paul was to say, 'At one point Yoko earned more from 'Yesterday' than I did. It doesn't compute, especially when it's the only song that none of the Beatles had anything to do with.

'I asked as a favour if I could have my name before John's on the anthology credits for 'Yesterday' and Yoko refused.

'I could question her, but I'm a civil person and life isn't long enough.'

Yoko was not invited to Linda's memorial service in New York. Paul explained, 'We decided to stay true to Linda's spirit and only invite her nearest and dearest friends. Seeing as Yoko wasn't one of those, we didn't invite her. People who were maybe doing it out of duty weren't asked. Everyone who went remarked that there were so many friends there and it was such a warm atmosphere. Everyone who spoke, spoke from the heart, genuinely. Linda would have hated anything else.'

At one point during his CNN interview with Larry King in June 2001 Paul was asked how he got on with Yoko. He said, 'We don't not get along, but you know, it's like some people you may be destined to not become great buddies with.

'It's not that we don't get along, just we don't talk much. We talk if we have to.'

Paul refused to invite Yoko as his guest at his Madison Square Garden Concert in New York on 26 April 2002 and he was to admit publicly that they did not get on with each other. He said, 'Yoko Ono and I are just not the greatest of buddies. Everyone has a family, and sometimes your Uncle Eddie is not your greatest friend. It's like that with us. Too many things have gone down in the past.'

Oo You

A track on Paul's debut album *McCartney* lasting 2 minutes and 47 seconds. The number opened the second side of the album and Paul initially recorded it at his home as an instrumental, adding the lyrics later on. He completed the recording at Morgan Studios. Paul played electric guitar, tambourine and cow bell – he also used an aerosol spray!

Oobu Joobu

On Monday 29 May 1995 Westwood One began their McCartney radio series called *Oobu Joobu* with a two-hour special followed by a series of one-hour shows and climaxing with a two-hour show on Labor Day weekend.

Paul had been planning such a series for a long time and had originally discussed it with the executive producer Eddy Pumer in 1981.

The name came from a BBC Third Programme radio production of Alfred Jarry's play *Ubu Cocu*, which Paul had heard in January 1966. He was to say, 'It was the best radio play I had ever heard in my life, and the best production, and Ubu was so brilliantly played. It was just a sensation.'

The title *Oobu Joobu* was inspired by the character of Monsieur Ubu created by the playwright. Paul was acting as deejay and introduced rare live recordings, studio outtakes, home recordings from Paul's own Rude Studios, excerpts from interviews and previously unreleased material from his own 250 hours of archives.

Linda also featured with her cooking recipes and Paul had conversations with various musicians – duetting with one of them, Carl Perkins, on 'Honey Don't'. Other musicians he interviewed were Brian Wilson of the Beach Boys, the Pretenders' Chrissie Hynde, Little Richard, Stevie Wonder, Jeff Beck, Elvis Costello, John Entwistle and Pete

Townsend. He also chatted with Mike Myers, creator of *Wayne's World*, and Kim Basinger There were eleven one-hour programmes and the final one in the series was another two-hour one, broadcast on Monday 4 September 1995.

Paul made a six-minute promotional video expressing his ideas about the series for the staff of Westwood One. He made the video at his home in Peasmarsh in 1995.

'Hello there, how are you all doing, all you radio people assembled there today,' he began.

He then discussed the origination of the series: 'When I was a kid I used to listen to the radio a lot. I used to sit on the floor and enter a world where your imagination went wild. In Britain, they used to have a lot of plays and music and comedy shows. I was a big fan, still am. In those days, you'd think to yourself, one day I might be able to put together my own radio show. Through the years I've had the idea on and off, and a couple of years ago, I thought I really should do it.'

On the subject of the series title he said, 'For no particular reason we called the idea "Oobujoobu". What is "Oobujoobu" you ask me – I can hear you, radio people! Well, it's just a title. Get off my back! What do you want?'

He then referred to Westwood's previous series, 'The Lost Lennon Tapes' which included previously unissued tapes that had been provided by Yoko Ono, stating that he would be providing unissued tapes of his own.

'We started off by getting hold of a few favourite records of mine, and looking for outtakes and rehearsal tapes from some of the recordings we'd done. After saying some silly things into the microphones, we finally edited the whole thing down into what you're going to hear as "Oobujoobu" – which we think of as widescreen radio.'

Paul mentioned that there would be humorous stories of his own and snippets from comedy shows, saying, 'We have some jams and some rehearsal tapes that haven't been heard before – certain things from soundtracks and stuff, which never got to be released at the time and which we can't really put out on album, 'cos people will feel a bit cheated. But in a radio show, I think they're quite interesting.

'Now this isn't the kind of show that can just fit into an easy little format. You have quite a variation in music styles. You'll have world music, there could be some African music, some reggae, some rock 'n' roll, old-fashioned rock 'n' roll; coming more up to date with some soul. You get odd silly moments, with, for instance, quite a bit of reggae.'

Paul then talks about Caribbean music, using a Jamaican accent. 'I got introduced to that many years ago on holiday in Jamaica, when we used to go to a little record shop called Tony's – Tony's Records, Fostick Road, man, Montego Bay! I remember Linda and I discovering this place where they had big speakers outside blasting out the reggae.

There were lots of kids on the pavement checking it out, and we used to go into the shop and leaf through all the 45s. You'd have some pretty crazy sounding titles on them. I remember finding one called "Poison Pressure". I said, "'Poison Pressure', what's that?" "Lennon-McCartney." I said, this can't be so; we've never done a song called "Poison Pressure". It must be another Lennon-McCartney. There are a lot of them about, you know!'

Paul continued describing the show, 'We even, would you believe it, have a cookery spot with my wife, Linda. It's nice, it's easy, because she's the cook of the house. And so, as you see, it's a kind of magazine programme. My idea is that when you're settled and you've got a little moment to put your feet up, this is the kind of programme that you could listen to. I think there's a lot of interesting stuff in it.'

He returned to his Jamaican accent, 'So that ya gonna do, 'cos you're assembled here to listen to the radio and listen to all the shows, 'cos you've got to check it out, because it's "Ooobujoobu" on Westwood One. You check it out, man! Come along listen to widescreen radio for the first time in your life, man. Why I'm talking Jamaican I have no idea. But it's that kind of show and so welcome, radio people, to "Oobujoobu!" Check it out, man.'

Paul commented, 'We started off by getting hold of a few favourite records of mine, and looking for outtakes and rehearsal tapes from some of the recordings we'd done. After saying some silly things into the microphones, we finally edited the whole thing down into what you're going to hear as *Oobu Joobu* – which we think of as wide-screen radio.'

The programmes included a mix of jokes and jingles, music reminiscences, studio rehearsals, demos, outtakes from sound checks, excerpts from recording sessions and unreleased masters. In the introductory two-hour special Paul explained how, in his youth, he lost himself in the world of radio and that was the spirit he was trying to recapture. He was also influenced by the anarchy in Radio One shows with Keith Moon and the Bonzo Dog Doo-Dah Band's sketches and songs. During the first show he included material from 'Ebony And Ivory', the previously un-issued dance track 'Atlantic Ocean', 'Boil Crisis' and other songs such as 'Don't Get Around Much Anymore', 'Put It There', 'C Moon', 'Biker Like An Icon' and 'I Wanna Be Your Man'.

Oprah Winfrey Show, The

When Paul was in New York preparing to conduct the 'Standing Stone' performance at Carnegie Hall, the ABC TV chat show *Oprah*, hosted by Oprah Winfrey, was being moved to New York that week and Sir Paul had agreed to be a guest.

His appearance was taped on Tuesday 20 November 1997 and aired on Monday 24 November 1997. The show lasted 44 minutes.

Oprah appeared first and said she was overwhelmed to be introducing

Paul. 'I was the only black girl who was into a group other than Motown sounds. I used to kiss Paul's picture I had hung next to my bed everyday.'

She had tears in her eyes as she introduced him and he joined her.

Among the subjects he discussed were Linda, the knighthood ceremony and the Beatles. He mentioned that Michael Jackson had approached him for advice and he told him three main things – first, to have somebody he trusted to look after his money, second, to make more promotional videos and third to get into publishing.

Paul played acoustic guitar on 'Young Boy' and piano on 'Flaming Pie'.

The world premiere of two *Flaming Pie* videos also took place on the show – 'Beautiful Night' and 'Little Willow', although 'Beautiful Night' was censored to excise the nude swimming scene and 'Little Willow' was cut out of the initial transmitted show.

On Sunday 14 December a slightly different version of the show was aired. In this one, Paul answered questions from the studio audience and a clip of 'Little Willow' replaced the 'Beautiful Night' video.

The first version of the show was screened in Britain on Sky One twice on Tuesday 23 December.

Oriental Nightfish, The

A three-and-a-half minute cartoon directed by Ian Emes and Linda McCartney and produced by MPL Communications Ltd in 1978. The film was a fantasy in which an extraterrestrial force descends to Earth from outer space. It went on general release in Britain in October 1978 supporting the Ryan O'Neal feature film *Driver*.

Orton, Joe

A talented British playwright who was murdered by his lover Kenneth Halliwell on 9 August 1967. Orton's play *Loot* had won the *Evening Standard* award as the best play of 1966 and in 1967 Walter Shenson contacted Orton to see if he could re-write a script he had received as a possible third film for the Beatles – *Shades Of A Personality* by Owen Holder. This was a script about a multiple personality and the Beatles were supposed to play the four different aspects of personality of the same person. Orton changed the script radically, utilising material from a first novel that he had written with Halliwell in 1953 called *The Silver Bucket*. He ended up with a completely different script than the Holder one, which he now called *Up Against It*.

Orton wrote in his diary, 'Basically, the Beatles are getting fed up with the Dick Lester type of direction. They want dialogue to speak. Also, they are tired of actors like Leo McKern stealing scenes. Difficult this, as I don't think any of the Beatles can act. As Marilyn Monroe couldn't act.'

In January 1967 Orton was invited to meet Paul and Brian Epstein at Epstein's house to discuss the script. Orton considered that Paul looked just like his photographs, apart from the fact that he'd now grown a beard and his hair was much shorter. Paul played him 'Penny Lane', which he liked, although he didn't like the other side of the record 'Strawberry Fields Forever'.

Paul told Orton that he'd seen his play *Loot* and said that it was the only play he hadn't wanted to leave before the end. Paul also chatted on about various topics, including tattoos and drugs. Epstein's assistant Peter Brown, together with a French photographer joined them.

The *Up Against It* script was rejected.

Over The Rainbow

An evergreen tune immortalised by Judy Garland in the film *The Wizard Of Oz*. Paul used to sing the number in the Beatles' early days, although he'd been inspired by the Gene Vincent version of the number rather than Garland's.

Pads, Paws And Claws

A number co-written by Paul and Elvis Costello and included on Costello's 1989 album *Spike*.

Commenting on the collaboration of the number, Costello says that Paul 'was like, "We've got two verses, now we need a bridge!" He really writes like that, he really thinks about telling the story – that it's all very good to have a good hook line but maybe you need to explain what it means. I got an education in that, about being a bit more disciplined about these things. I always take for granted that people are going to understand everything I'm saying. Though he's not pedantic. He'll also go, "I like that," when you suddenly throw in something for effect that might not otherwise seem to make sense.'

Paice, Ian

Born in Nottingham on 29 June 1948, Paice was given a violin at the age of ten, but at the age of fifteen opted for playing drums and joined his father's dance band. In the mid-60s he joined Georgie and the Rave-Ons and during his career has appeared with numerous groups and solo artists. He is a mainstay of Deep Purple, having been in at least eight of the re-formed line-ups since he first became a member of the band in 1968.

He has performed or recorded with George Harrison, the Velvet Underground, Jackson Heights, Paice Ashton & Lord, Whitesnake and many other artists and groups.

He became a member of Paul McCartney And Friends in the spring of 1999 and recorded the album *Run Devil Run* with the group. Paice had never played with Paul before and was chosen after Ringo Starr was unable to make the sessions.

He also appeared on various live shows, including the PETA concert on Saturday 18 September 1999 and the Cavern appearance later that year. He also appeared with the band on TV shows such as *Later With Jools Holland* and the German *Wetton, dass . . . ?*

Palace of Auburn Hills

Venue in Auburn Hills, near Detroit, Michigan where Paul appeared on the fourth leg of his world tour on Thursday 1 and Friday 2 February 1990.

On the second night he held a press conference.

Question: You made a comment last night about how you took a lot of your musical roots from this city. Were you referring to Motown or were there other things?

Paul: I mainly meant Motown, yeah. We were major fans of black American music, a lot of which came from this city.

Question: You've met a lot of the Motown people over the years; any particular favourites?

Paul: Oh, I love them all, you know. They kind of happened alongside us happening. The English people and the black Motown boom was great. So we were good mates, like Diana Ross and the Supremes. We were kind of contemporaries happening together.

Question: Did you think of having any Motown artists do a guest slot with you last night?

Paul: It's kind of difficult to work in guests. We've sort of got the show set now. Really, the only person who's guested so far is Stevie in LA, who is very much Motown, as you know. But that was easy because we do 'Ebony And Ivory' in the set. It's not too easy to open up the set when you get to this stage with the production.

Question: What made you decide to tour after thirteen years?

Paul: Maybe the fact that I got a good band. You know, I've been recording and doing solo stuff and little guest spots like Live Aid and shows like that but during the recording of the *Flowers In The Dirt* album the band felt really good. We've got a sense of humour in common and they're good musicians, too. So it was either a question of saying, 'Goodbye, see you next album,' or like, 'Should we stay together, and if we stay together, what should we do? Let's go on tour.'

Question: A lot of critics are quick to judge anything that you or any of the other Beatles do. How did you get into this LP mentally? Do you ever get to the point where you thought, 'To heck with them. I'm going to shove one down your throat?'

Paul: Yeah, I get to that point. I was not that pleased with the album before it, which is *Press To Play*. So I wanted to make this one better and shove it down a few people's throats. I'm quite happy with the album itself. It has some of my best songs on it.

Question: Has coming out on the road re-inspired you to go back in the studio a little earlier than you have in the past?

Paul: Not really, but it's good for you, getting on the road. It's a stimulating thing, actually seeing your fans instead of just getting letters from them. It really lifts you.

Question: In your programme last night, I noticed you said the best thing about touring is the audience. Was the audience last night as good as you expected?

Paul: It was a serious audience last night, really, because we've always been playing . . .

Question: What do you mean by that?

Paul: Seriously good, seriously fab. Seriously doody. We've just come from England and Wembley, which was a great series of concerts. We did eleven on the truck, I think, but the English are a little bit more reserved, you know. They get going, but it takes them like half an hour. This audience, it didn't take them but a second, and then the screams.

Question: Paul, a lot of the people said your show was an emotional experience. Why did it take twenty years for you to come back out and finally play the classic Beatles songs?

Paul: When the Beatles broke up, it was a little difficult, it was a bit like a divorce and you didn't really want to do anything associated with the ex-wife. You didn't want to do *her* material. So all of us took that view independently and John stopped doing Beatles stuff, George, Ringo, we all did. Because it was just too painful for a while. But enough time's gone by now. On the last tour I did in 1976 with Wings, we avoided a lot of Beatles stuff because of that. So now it feels really kind of natural to do those songs. It's a question of either getting back to those songs or ignoring them for the rest of my life. And, as I say, some of them I haven't actually done before and I didn't realise that until we were rehearsing with the band and I said, 'This feels great, "Sgt Pepper". I mean, why is this so great?' And someone reminded me, they said, 'You've never done it.' It's like a new song to me. It's just the right time to come back with that stuff.

Question: Will there be a time when you get together with George and Ringo? Not really a reunion without John but kind of a jam maybe?

Paul: I don't know. That's always on the cards but a reunion as such is out of the question because John's not with us. The only reunion would have been with John. But, like you say, we might easily get together. There's a couple of projects that are possible now that we've solved our business differences. I don't know, I haven't actually seen them. I've been living this whole thing through the press. People say to me, 'George said he won't do it.' I haven't spoken to him yet.

Question: Why did it take so long to resolve your business differences?

Paul: Have you ever been in a lawsuit? I was in one for the last twenty years. It just took forever. What happens is you get your advisors and they get theirs and then lawyers, I think, are trained to keep things like that going. The first rule in law school, you know, 'Keep it going.'

Question: Do you regret that the four ex-Beatles never got together again before John died?

Paul: Well, I regret it, you know, but I mean, this is life. It just didn't happen for a number of reasons. It would have been great, but John not dying would have been even better.

Question: What's going on in Eastern Europe?

Paul: I think it's very exciting. To me it seems like the sixties kicking in again. That's my point of view. It's all the stuff that was said in the sixties: peace, love, democracy, freedom, a better world and all that stuff. It's finally kicked in. The way I look at it, people like Gorbachev grew up with the sixties and I don't think you can be unaffected by it and I think it's all kicking in now. Look at those people who are coming across the border and a lot of them are wearing denim. It's *us* coming across that border. I think it's very exciting. I think China's next.

Question: Are you going to play any dates in Eastern Europe now that the Iron Curtain is history?

Paul: I'd like to, but we've got so many dates on this tour and they don't include Eastern Europe. I'd like to go to Russia, but the promoters say it's too cold, so we went to Italy.

Question: What are your plans after the tour?

Paul: I'll be writing after the tour. I've got a lot of writing I want to do. I'm doing a very interesting thing. It's a classical thing for an orchestra which is due to be performed by the Liverpool Philharmonic Orchestra in the Liverpool Cathedral in 1991 and that's like a serious work, so I've got a lot of writing to do.

Question: Why don't you write your memoirs?

Paul: I don't know, really. I always thought that you had to be like about seventy before you did.

Question: What new things are you listening to right now?

Paul: Um, I listen to everything. I listen to all sorts of things.

Question: James and Stella are travelling with you right now. Would you ever invite either of them on the stage?

Paul: Not really. It's too sort of showbizy, that kind of thing. I know a lot of people do that. If they really wanted desperately to do it then I'd help them, but it's got to come from them. I'm not going to push them on stage because it's a tough game.

Question: How do you compare the thrill of performing in the sixties with performing today?

Paul: It's very similar, actually. That crowd last night was strangely sixties. It's very good, you know.

Question: But now you can hear yourself.

Paul: With the new technology, yeah. I mean, you compare all this equipment here and you've got like Cape Canaveral. But when we started out it was like two guitars and a bass and one amp.

Question: There's a big controversy now over garbage, there's too many landfills and it's causing a lot of toxic . . .

Paul: I think they're basically just trying to address some of the more serious problems we got ourselves into. We're the only species of animals on earth that fouls its own nest. Everybody else, all the other birds, they go over *there* to take a dump. But we don't; we do it *right here*, right where we live. We put all our toxic waste into our lakes and stuff. I mean, Britain's got this great business where we accept waste from, like, Japan and we put it in cans and put it under the sea. And they said, 'It'll be all right for a hundred years.' Well, I say, 'What about a hundred and one years when it blows up? What's going to happen?' So, I mean, I think we've got to be clever. I think we're clever enough to address all of that, but it's going to take some doing.

Question: What was your inspiration for the film presentation before the concert? How did you go about putting the film footage together?

Paul: I talked to Richard Lester, who made *A Hard Day's Night* and *Help!* and we were thinking of having a support act before our act, but the promoters told me that it was going to get difficult. So I suggested, 'Well, how about if we do a film?' So I rang Dick Lester and said to him, 'Could you do a film that says, "First there was the Beatles, then there was Wings and then there was now?"' He said, 'Let me think about it,' and he came back with the film, which I like. It's kind of uncompromising, it's a very grown-up film, gives people something to think about.

Question: Are you going to change the show when it comes to stadiums?

Paul: Yeah, we will magnify it a little bit. This style of show is fine in an arena like this, but when you get into a forty-thousand arena it starts to look a little small, so we'll just make it bigger. But basically keep the same show.

Question: There's been a flood of unreleased Beatles recordings, very high quality like the *Ultra Rare Trax* you probably heard about. What are your feelings on the release of those things and would you like to see EMI release them officially?

Paul: That's kind of a difficult question. It's like, as far as the Beatles were concerned we released all our good material, except for maybe one or two little things that at the time we didn't like. And there are one or two tracks I think are worth looking at.

'Leave My Kitten Alone', John sings, which I think is very good. But in the main we released all our best material, so now you know, it's like memorabilia. People just like to hear tracks that were the takes we didn't use or something. If people are interested it's fair enough. I mean, I don't get uptight about bootlegs. What are you going to do?

Question: I just wondered if you plan to tour again after this.

Paul: Yeah. It's funky because I think a lot of people come to the show and think, 'Well, it's the last time you'll see him.' I don't know why they think that, but, yes, the Stones and I, well, we're 'getting up there' kind of thing, but as far as I'm concerned I feel twenty-seven, not forty-seven.

Question: Will you rock and roll after you're fifty, do you think?

Paul: I think there probably is like after fifty, yeah.

Question: Paul, of all the songs you've written, what would be your favourite, if you still have one.

Paul: That's a very difficult question. I mean, musically, I might say 'Here, There And Everywhere', but as far as success is concerned, it has to be 'Yesterday', because it's just done more than I could have ever hoped for.

Question; Does 'Yesterday' mean something different to you now that you're forty-seven?

Paul: Yes, it sure does. When I wrote it I was a twenty-year-old singing, 'I'm not half the man I used to be'. It's like, it's very presumptuous for a twenty-year-old. At forty-seven, however, it *means* something.

Question: At that time did you ever think you'd be rocking now?

Paul: I didn't think we'd still be rocking now. The great thing, as I say, is you look at what a lot of us have done recently and you look at people like Muddy Waters and think, 'It didn't matter that he was seventy, he'd still be singing the blues.' Instead of a youth-orientated thing, it's become a music-orientated thing, so I think as long as you can still deliver . . . I mean, you look at the age of these audiences. I'm very surprised, the sort of young people, I thought it just would be my age group mainly, but there's a lot of young kids and they know the material.

Question: Are they simply looking for nostalgia?

Paul: I don't know, I'm always talking to my kids about that. You tell me. What songs are going to be remembered? It's going to be, I don't know. Some rap song . . .

Question: Are you enjoying all of this, Paul?

Paul: Yes, it's great. I really am.

Question: How do you like your music today?

Paul: My music? I still like it.

Question: How do you feel when you look out into the crowds and you see parents holding their children to see you?

Paul: It's really beautiful because I've got four kids and the great thing about me and my kids is that there isn't this generation gap that I thought would be there.

Question: Do they listen to any music that bothers you?

Paul: No. But I know what you mean. I thought that they'd get into some odd punk music and I'd be saying, 'Well, the sixties was better,' but they're not. My son loves the Beach Boys. His big new turn-on album that I turned him on to is *Pet Sounds*. And he loves James Brown, Otis Redding, the Commodores, he's got some good taste.

Question: Are your children musically inclined?

Paul: Yeah, they are, but Linda and I have always said that we'd never push them because it's a tough game and unless they're really keen . . . But they're all very good, they're all very interested in music and they can all carry a tune and stuff.

Question: Are you surprised how many young people on this tour are responding to your music?

Paul: Well, kind of. But a couple of years ago I started to notice how kids like my nephews, who are eighteen now, but who I've known since they were two or whatever, started getting into the Grateful Dead. Now they're all Deadheads, it's incredible. I think maybe it is because modern music is a little bit synthetic and shallow that they're looking back to the sixties. And the great thing about a lot of that sixties stuff is that it does stand up still.

Paul returned to the venue on 1 May 2002 as part of his 'Driving USA' tour.

Palais de la Musique, Lille, France

The venue that hosted the French premiere of Paul's *Liverpool Oratorio* on Sunday 15 November 1992.

Paul, Linda and their children attended the performance, arriving in their private Lear jet at Lesquin Airport a few minutes before Diana, Princess of Wales also touched down. Diana was in France for three days and attended the performance.

The event was part of a 'British Festival' in Lille and was also attended by Pierre Mauroy, the local Mayor, who had once been Prime Minister.

The performance was by the Royal Liverpool Philharmonic Choir and Orchestra with Choristers of the Liverpool Cathedral, conducted by Carl Davis. The other artists were Marie McLaughlin, soprano, as Mary Dee; Sally Burgess, mezzo-soprano as Miss Inkley, chief mourner and nurse; Thomas Randle, tenor, as Shanty; William White, bass, as Headmaster, Preacher and Mr Dingle, and Andrew O'Connor, soprano, as boy soloist.

Paolozzi, Eduardo

Internationally renowned Scottish sculptor who tutored former Beatle Stuart Sutcliffe at Hamburg Art College. Paul bought one of his works called *Solo* and used another on the cover of *Red Rose Speedway*. Paolozzi also designed the artwork for Paul's *Off The Ground* album.

Paperback Writer

Paul had the idea for the song on his way to Weybridge to meet John. He thought he'd read something in the *Daily Mail* that morning about people who were paperback writers. He told John of the idea of trying to write to publishers, wanting to be a paperback writer and suggested that the song be in the form of a letter. Paul began to work on the number in front of John, finished it and they both went upstairs and put a melody to it.

John Lennon confirmed that this number was mainly penned by Paul saying, 'Paul wrote this. I think I might have helped with some of the lyrics. Yes, I did. But it was mainly Paul's tune.'

George Harrison was also to say, 'The idea of "Paperback Writer" is Paul's. I think John gave him some of the chords, but it was originally Paul who came up with the story line.'

Some sources claim it was written in connection with John's two books, hence the mention of nonsense writer Edward Lear in the fourth line.

A young man working for the *Daily Mail* wants to become a paperback writer. It is also suggested that Paul even worked out the man's name, a character called Ian Iachimore, which he devised because it sounded like his own name after it had been played backwards on a tape loop. The number was used quite successfully as the theme tune to a television book series in Britain called *Read All About It*.

Apart from singing lead vocal, Paul played Rickenbacker bass on the track. Recording engineer Geoff Emerick commented, '"Paperback Writer" was the first time the bass sound had been heard in all its excitement. For a start, Paul played a different bass, a Rickenbacker. Then we boosted it further by using a loudspeaker as a microphone. We positioned it directly in front of the bass speaker and the moving diaphragm of the second speaker made the electric current.'

The single was recorded at Abbey Road Studios on Wednesday 13 April 1996 and issued in the UK on Parlophone R 5452 on Friday 10 June 1966 where it entered the chart at No. 2, topping the chart in the second week and remaining at the top for a further two weeks. The flipside was 'Rain'.

It was issued in the US on Capitol 5651 on Monday 30 May 1966 and was also No. 1 for two weeks.

Other countries in which it topped the chart included Australia, New Zealand, West Germany, Austria, Holland, Denmark, Ireland, Hong Kong, Singapore and Malaysia.

It was also later featured on several album compilations, including 'A Collection Of Oldies (But Goldies)', 'The Beatles 1967-1970', the 1979 'Hey Jude' album and 'The Beatle Box.'

Michael Lindsay-Hogg made a promotional film of the number on 20 May 1966 at Chiswick House in London, which was screened on *Top Of The Pops* on Thursday 9 June 1966.

A live version of the number, 2 minutes and 37 minutes in length, was recorded at the Blockbuster Pavilion, Charlotte on 15 June 1993 and included on the *Paul Is Live* album.

Parkinson

Michael Parkinson, a Yorkshire-born former journalist who became a television chat-show host, was one of the celebrities featured on the cover of Wings' *Band On The Run*.

When the photograph was taken in 1973 Parkinson told Paul he could return the favour by appearing on his show and Paul agreed.

The long-standing promise was eventually honoured on Friday 3 December 1999 when Paul was the sole guest for one hour on *Parkinson*.

A studio performance with Paul's new band on 'Honey Hush' opened the show.

Paul then sat with Parkinson and played 'Twenty Flight Rock' and 'Yesterday' with an acoustic guitar. He also played an unreleased number, 'When The Wind Is Blowing', which was intended for the full-length movie Paul had wanted to make about Rupert Bear. Paul then went to the piano and played 'The Long And Winding Road' followed by three unreleased songs, including 'Suicide', which had once been rejected by Frank Sinatra.

Paul then discussed various topics, including how he was affected by Linda's death. 'I didn't expect to be sitting here being asked about her death. It was just a terrible blow for me and the kids, and all her family.' He discussed the Beatles and John Lennon saying, 'He was a complex guy, because he had a lot of tragedy in his life. I think he was very guarded, and the wit and everything was the shell that came down. But, having said that, he was a very lovable guy, very warm-hearted and a great friend.' Discussing how they got in contact again he said, 'We had some really good conversations, and thankfully, for me, we were really good friends by the time he died. I would hate to have left it on another note.'

At the close of the interview, Parkinson said, 'It was every bit the event I expected it to be. It was worth waiting for.'

Parnes, Larry

Major British music impresario of the 1950s who once booked the Silver Beatles to back Johnny Gentle on a tour of Scotland in 1960. In 1983 he filed a suit against Paul and the BBC over comments made by

Paul on his *Desert Island Discs* appearance in January 1982. Paul had said that the group had never been paid for their Scottish tour.

The legal dispute was eventually settled on the 28 July 1984 edition of the programme when Roy Plomley made a formal apology, although pointing out that Paul had only meant it as a joke.

Parsons, Alan

A recording manager and technician. He originally applied for a job at Abbey Road Studios. He was hired and within weeks was working as technical assistant at the *Abbey Road* recording sessions.

In an interview with the German edition of *Penthouse*, published in May 1995, he recalled the first time he met the Beatles.

'I will probably never forget it. The Beatles had just moved into their new "Apple" studio and had technical problems. I was sent there, entered the wrong room, and there they were sitting. All four of them, including George Martin, their producer. I stood there very astonished and had to force myself to keep breathing. After I successfully connected all wires at the right places, the studio was kind of ready to kick off working. Immediately the Beatles cried out in Abbey Road, "Can we put this boy into service as a technical assistant until we've finished our LP?" And that's how destiny created the opportunity to look inside the Beatles' frying pan.'

The date he helped to get the Apple studio working was Thursday 23 January 1969.

Parsons was later to form the Alan Parsons Project and also became, for a time, manager of the Abbey Road Studios.

He remained friendly with Paul and after the Beatles had broken up, Paul hired him as technical assistant on his first solo album *McCartney*. Parsons recalled, 'He played all the instruments himself, and we were in the studio day and night. That was the start of our friendship. Later, in 1973 – meanwhile I'd become Abbey Road's chief technician – Paul claimed my services for *Red Rose Speedway*.'

Party

A closing track from the *Run Devil Run* album lasting 2 minutes and 38 seconds and recorded at Abbey Road Studios on Thursday 4 March 1999 with Paul on lead vocal and bass guitar, Dave Gilmour on electric guitar, Pete Wingfield on piano and Ian Paice on drums.

It's actually 'Let's Have a Party', the number Elvis Presley sang in the movie 'Loving You'.

The Beatles used to perform it early in their career at a time when they didn't always get the words of a song right. They had thought there was a line, 'I never kissed a goo' and always sang it like that. When Paul began to record it for *Run Devil Run* one of his backing musicians asked what a 'goo' was, so Paul looked up the actual words to the song and it was 'I never kissed a goon'.

Party at the Palace

An event that took place in the grounds of Buckingham Palace during Queen Elizabeth II's Golden Jubilee celebrations on 3 June 2002.

Two million people had entered a lottery to get tickets for the all-star concert, for which only 12,500 tickets were available.

Performers at the event included Brian Adams, Queen, Eric Clapton, Brian Wilson, Ray Davies, Rod Stewart, Phil Collins, Shirley Bassey, Ricky Martin, Tony Bennett, Tom Jones, Cliff Richard, Joe Cocker, Ozzy Osbourne, Elton John and Steve Winwood.

The backing band included Paul 'Wix' Wickens and Phil Collins. The Corrs performed 'The Long And Winding Road' and Joe Cocker performed 'With A Little Help From My Friends'.

Dame Edna Everage introduced Paul, who was the final act to appear. He opened by singing his own composition, 'Her Majesty', before performing an acoustic version of 'Blackbird'. As a tribute to George Harrison, Eric Clapton joined Paul on 'While My Guitar Gently Weeps', following an announcement by Sir George Martin about the Beatles' impact on British music and the contribution made by George Harrison. His touring band then backed Paul when he performed 'Sgt Pepper's Lonely hearts Club Band' coupled with 'The End'.

Paul then asked the crowd to sing along with him on 'All You Need Is Love', saying, 'I think you just might know it.' The song had actually been chosen as the Jubilee anthem and had been sung throughout the country that day.

The Queen then walked on stage with other members of the royal family, and Prince Charles made a speech.

Paul then turned to the audience and said: 'I said to Her Majesty: "Are we doing this again next year?" and she said, "Not in my garden." ' He asked them if they wanted another song and said: 'Good, you're getting one.' He then performed 'Hey Jude'.

On finishing the song he said: 'You don't want to go home; I don't want to go home; so, even though the TV show is over, let's do another. Give me my bass.' He then performed 'I Saw Her Standing There'. This number wasn't included in the two-hour BBC television coverage of the event.

Following the concert, Paul said: 'It was just fantastic. It's been a really buzzy day. When I was singing I just suddenly realised there were people in the Mall, all over Britain and all over the world listening. That's a big audience.'

The live broadcast had an estimated worldwide audience of 200 million

Two DVDs of the Jubilee events were issued on BBC/Opus Arte and Naxos of America, *Prom At the Palace* and *Party at the Palace*.

Party at the Palace included an eight-page booklet, lasted approximately three hours and was issued by BBC/Opus Arte OA 0857 D (DVD) and on OA 0862 V (VHS).

Party Party (promotional film)

The promotional video for the number required 600 hours of animation works by director Peter Brookes and his three assistants. The four painted 4,500 images on 16mm film, completing it in 12 days. The animation was then intercut with snippets from 'Put It There' to complete the promotional film.

Party Party (single)

This was a number which was credited to P McCartney/L McCartney/McIntosh/Stuart/Whitten/Wickens.

This track, which had previously been unreleased, was added as a bonus one-sided vinyl single to the *Flowers In The Dirt (World Tour Pack)*, issued in the UK on Parlophone R6238 on Thursday 23 November 1989 and in America as a CD single on Sunday 15 January 1990. Five hundred copies of a 12″ edition were also pressed specially for British disc jockeys under the catalogue number 12 RDJ 6238. It was also included in a two-CD special *Flowers In The Dirt* package issued in Japan in March 1990.

Paul

A magazine published in America in 1964 by SMH Publications. It was part of a series of separate publications on each member of the Beatles.

Paul And Friends – The PETA Concert For Party Animals (DVD)

A DVD release of the 1999 Peta concert. The contents include 'The Skin Trade' by Pamela Anderson-Lee, 'Cheap Tricks' by Alex Baldwin, 'Fur Farming' by Stella McCartney, 'Puppy Mills' by Charlize Theron, 'North Carolina Pig Farm Investigation' by James Cromwell, 'Teach Yourself', a music video by Raw Youth and a public service announcement compilation. Music was supplied by Sarah McLachlan who performed 'Angel' to a background of still photographs of Paul and Linda; 'Love Shack' and 'Rock Lobster' by the B-52s; 'Roam' by the B-52s with Chrissie Hynde and Sarah McLachlan; 'I'll Stand By You' by Chrissie Hynde and the B-52s; and Paul McCartney and his band performing 'Honey Hush', 'Brown Eyed Handsome Man', 'No Other Baby', 'Try Not To Cry', 'Lonesome Town' and 'Run Devil Run'.

Other celebrities appearing in the DVD include Jamie Lee Curtis, Ellen DeGeneres, Margaret Cho, Andy Dick, Anne Hecke, Ricki Lake, Bill Maher, Brian McKnight, Kathy Najimy and Alicia Silverstone.

'Paul is Dead'

A bizarre chapter in the Beatles' story arose when rumours that Paul had died in a car accident led to newspaper and magazine features, radio phone-ins, even a television special relating to the alleged death of Paul and his replacement by a double. The Beatles were then alleged to have introduced into their recordings various clues that Paul had died.

On 12 October 1969 Russ Gibbs, who was a disc jockey on the Detroit radio station WKNR-FM, received a phone call from someone referring to himself simply as Tom, who suggested that, if he listened to certain parts of Beatles recordings, he would find references to the death of Paul.

Listening to the programme at the time was an aspiring journalist, Fred LaBour, who had been asked to review the *Abbey Road* album for the *Michigan Daily*. He recalled: 'This guy was saying that if you played part of "Revolution No. 9" backward, they were saying "Turn me on, dead man", and that in "I Am The Walrus" – or was it "Strawberry Fields Forever"? – you could hear "I buried Paul", and that it all meant that Paul was dead. I was astonished at the craziness of this, so the next day I led off the review with those and a bunch of other observations I made up. It was a satire on seeing things that weren't there, but people took it seriously.'

In his review of the album, LaBour claimed that on the *Abbey Road* album cover the group were leaving a cemetery and that John was dressed as a minister, Ringo as an undertaker and George as a gravedigger, and pointed out that Paul was out of step with the others, which apparently meant that it was in fact either his corpse, or, more popularly, a substitute who'd had plastic surgery. According to the rumours, proof positive of the impostor theory was the fact that Paul was holding a cigarette in his right hand and everyone knew that the real Paul McCartney was left-handed.

Most of his 'clues' could actually be checked out and disregarded as wrong. For instance, the reference to John's lyrics 'Here's another clue for you, the walrus was Paul' on 'Glass Onion', led LaBour to say that 'walrus' was Greek for 'corpse', which was easily disproved.

Gibbs continued to fuel the rumours on his show and suggested that Paul had been involved in an argument with the other members of the Beatles at Abbey Road Studios on 9 November 1966 and had stormed out of the session, driven away in his Aston-Martin and been decapitated in a crash. Brian Epstein had hushed up the death and replaced Paul with a lookalike. Gibbs said that clues could be found on subsequent Beatles albums, including *Abbey Road*. He pointed out that Paul was barefoot in the picture, which indicated a Mafia (or Grecian) sign of death.

Other clues relating to the *Abbey Road* album arose when fans discovered that the registration number of a Volkswagen car in the background included 28IF, which indicated that Paul would have been 28 'IF' he had lived. In fact, Paul was 27.

Paul would recall: 'I just turned up at the photo session. It was a really nice hot day and I think I wore sandals. I only had to walk around the corner to the crossing because I lived pretty nearby. I had me sandals off and on for the session. Of course, when it comes out people start looking at it and they say: "Why has he got no shoes on? He's never done that before." OK, you've never see me do it before but in actual fact it's just me with me shoes off. Turns out to be some old Mafia sign of death or something.'

Tim Harper, another journalist, had a feature entitled PAUL IS DEAD appearing in the college newspaper in Des Moines, Iowa, on 17 September. The article was then featured in the 21 October 1969 edition of the *Chicago Sun-Times*.

Alan Bennett of the New York radio station WMCA-AM actually flew to London to follow up the clues and said: 'The only way McCartney is going to quell the rumours is by coming up with a set of fingerprints from a 1965 passport which can be compared to his present prints.'

Various singles relating to the rumours were released, including 'St Paul', 'Paulbearer', 'So Long Paul' and 'Brother Paul'.

Further articles appeared claiming that Paul had been replaced by a double; names varied from William Campbell to Billy Shears. There was a *Paul Is Dead* magazine issued, a National Lampoon satire and even a television programme hosted by a noted defence attorney F Lee Bailey.

Fans began finding clues in previously released albums such as *Sgt Pepper*, *Rubber Soul*, *The Beatles Yesterday And Today*, *Revolver* and *The Beatles*.

In the case of the *Sgt Pepper* album they pointed to the fact that a cardboard cutout of the comedian Issy Bonn had his hand slightly raised over Paul's head, which they alleged was an Indian sign of death. They said that the flowers on the sleeve represented a symbolic grave.

In the centrefold of the album Paul is wearing a badge with the initials 'OPD', which fans suggested meant 'Officially Pronounced Dead'. The patch on Paul's sleeve does sport such initials, but they stood for 'Ontario Provincial Police'. Paul was given the official patch while the Beatles were appearing in Toronto on Tuesday 17 August 1965. The back cover had an image of George, John and Ringo with a back view of Paul. Fans said that this was because someone substituted for the dead Paul. This wasn't so, as other pictures from the same session reveal that it was Paul in the photograph.

Twenty-six years after the 'Paul is Dead' affair began, Paul issued an album, *Paul Is Live*, repeating his Abbey Road zebra crossing, taking great pains to reproduce items from the original scene, even having some of them computer-generated. This time the registration number of the Volkswagen was 51 IS, referring to Paul's current age and the fact that he was very much alive.

The affair has caused Paul some amusement over the years and in an episode of *The Simpsons* an animated Paul, with Paul's actual voice, says, 'Oh, by the way, I'm alive.'

Paul Is Dead (film)

A German film written and directed by Hendrik Handloegten who originally wrote it as a film school thesis. A teenager hears the 'Paul is Dead' rumours on the radio and sets out with friends to discover more of the death clues. The 75-minute film was shown at the Sundance Film Festival in America in January 2001.

Paul Is Live (album)

All 24 tracks on this album were recorded during the 1993 New World Tour in either Australia or the USA by former Beatles engineer Geoff Emerick. He commented, 'What we captured was the energy that came from the stage. With this album you really get the feeling of being there, because we've captured the ballsiness.'

The album was released in Britain on Monday 15 November 1993 and in America on Tuesday 16 November on Capitol CDP 7243. A five-track sampler CD was issued in Europe by Parlophone on PMLIVE1, but was immediately withdrawn, partly because of an error on the cover artwork. The sampler contained five tracks: 'Magical Mystery Tour', 'Biker Like An Icon', 'My Love', 'Paperback Writer' and 'Live And Let Die'.

Paul's PR man Geoff Baker provided sleeve notes for the sampler in which he pointed out that both the title and album sleeve photograph was a parody on the 'Paul is Dead' rumours sparked off by, among other things, the *Abbey Road* album cover. Computer artwork placed the 1993 Paul into the original Abbey Road shot of 1969.

For the sleeve photograph Paul engaged photographer Iain Macmillan, who had taken the original *Abbey Road* cover shot.

In the new image, instead of the Beatles, Paul's only companion on the crossing now is an Old English sheepdog, the latest in a line of such pals he's had since Martha.

Commenting on the parody, Paul said, 'Back in the sixties the wild rumour was that I was dead because of certain alleged "clues" in the *Abbey Road* sleeve. Because I was barefoot, it being a scorching summer's day, it was taken as a bizarre Mafia sign of death. Then they said that because part of the number plate of the Volkswagen parked behind us read 28IF, it meant I – being 27 at the time – would have been 28 IF I'd lived.

'So we're having a little parody of that on the sleeve of *Paul Is Live*. This time I've got my boots on (veggie Doc Martens, by the way, so they're not dead either). The original Volkswagen is still there. This time the number reads 51 IS.

'It was strange to go back to the Abbey Road crossing again. The déjà vu hit in. It was a summer's day again. The cops held the traffic again. The crowd of surprised onlookers gaped again. But the only difference was, instead of the Beatles, it was one man and his dog – but, please, don't start reading anything into that.'

He was to add, 'But there is absolutely no significance in the fact that, on the *Paul Is Live* sleeve, I am on the crossing with a dog – except that, on this New World Tour, we're supporting animal rights.' Paul also said, 'As I've said, it's all just a bit of light-hearted parody of the crazy rumours that were dismissed as nonsense at the time of *Abbey Road*. The idea for the title came to me after I received a letter from a young Hollywood film director, who had written to tell me about a movie she is planning for next year called *Paul Is Dead*. Apparently the film is about this girl having a breakdown and being institutionalised. She told me that during her breakdown, this image of me would come to her in her dreams and help her work through it. That set me thinking about the album title.'

Comparing the covers of *Abbey Road* and *Paul Is Live*, Paul also said, 'There's another coincidence, as the guy who made my original suit that I wore on the *Abbey Road* shot – which was thought at the time to be an "Oxfam suit", but was in fact a Savile Row suit – this guy, Edward Sexton, is the same tailor who made the suit I wore for the sleeve of *Paul Is Live*, and who has also made the stage clothes for me, and the band, on the New World Tour.'

Paul Is Live (video)

The home video *Paul Is Live* was issued in Britain on Monday 21 March 1994 on Picture Music International MVN 4912453. The 85-minute film included a pre-concert 'home movie' in which there were excerpts from 'A Quiet Moment' 'Sexual Ealing', 'Jam 18', 'Jam 22' and 'Liverpool Suite'. There was also some animal welfare footage in the 'home movie' section which resulted in the video being given a '15' certificate, which meant that anyone under fifteen years of age couldn't buy it.

It was directed by Aubrey Powell and produced for MPL by Steven J Swartz with video remix by Kevin Godley and Jerry Charter.

The track listing was: 'Drive My Car', 'Let Me Roll It', 'Looking For Changes', 'Peace In the Neighbourhood', 'All My Loving', 'Good Rockin' Tonight', 'We Can Work It Out', 'Hope Of Deliverance', 'Michelle', 'Biker Like An Icon', 'Here There And Everywhere', 'Magical Mystery Tour', 'C'mon People', 'Lady Madonna', 'Paperback Writer', 'Penny Lane', 'Live And Let Die', 'Kansas City', 'Let It Be', 'Yesterday' and 'Hey Jude'.

A 72-minute *Paul Is Live* video was issued By Vap Video in Japan on VPVR-60736 on 1 January 1994. The same company also released a laserdisc of it on VPLR-70352 on 1 February. The release featured twenty tracks: 'Drive My Car', 'Let Me Roll It', 'Looking For Changes', 'Peace in The Neighbourhood', 'All My Loving', 'Robbie's Bit', 'Good Rockin' Tonight', 'We Can Work It Out', 'Hope Of Deliverance', 'Michelle', 'Biker Like An Icon', 'Here There And

Everywhere', 'My Love', 'Magical Mystery Tour', 'C'mon People', 'Lady Madonna', 'Paperback Writer', 'Penny Lane', ' Live and Let Die' and 'Kansas City'.

Paul Is Live In Concert On The New World Tour

A 70-minute video that tied in with the release of the *Paul Is Live* album. This comprised footage from several of the concerts on the tour, edited in to fit the overdub-free soundtrack of the album. Aubrey Powell directed the video and the 'video remix' was by Kevin Godley and Jerry Chater.

Paul, Les

A legendary guitar player who also revolutionised the design of guitars. He was born on 9 June 1915 in Wankesha, Wisconsin, USA. Les Paul also introduced innovations in studio recording and had a series of chart hits with his wife Mary Ford. On Saturday 16 April 1988 he gave Paul a special custom-built left-handed guitar when Paul was visiting New York. He'd originally intended presenting it to him at the Rock 'n' Roll Hall of Fame event on 20 January, but Paul (McCartney) had decided not to attend at that time.

Paul McCartney (single)

Title of a single by Manchester band Laugh that was issued on the Remorse label on LOSS 5 on Friday 14 August 1987. The record sleeve featured a picture of a walrus.

Paul McCartney (single)

Title of a single by singer/songwriter Tony Hazzard, issued on the Bronze label.

Paul McCartney (TV documentary)

A documentary produced by Ardent Productions that was first screened on the Biography Channel on Saturday 3 November 2001. It included an exclusive interview with Paul.

Paul McCartney, The

A rose named after Paul. This was a gift EMI Records made to Paul on his 47th birthday on 18 June 1989. It was a medium-pink hybrid tea rose grown in France which was described as 'a vibrant pink with a strong fragrance'. As the Paul McCartney it was officially registered in Meillard, France in 1995.

Paul McCartney and Friends (DVD)

A DVD from Image Entertainment of the PETA Concert featuring five songs from the *Run Devil Run* album. It was issued in America on 4 September 2001.

Paul McCartney and Friends (event)

A fundraising evening held at St James' Palace, London in the presence of Prince Charles the Prince of Wales, on Thursday 23 March 1995, in aid of the Royal College of Music.

RCM director Janet Rimmerman said, 'This will be a memorable one-off occasion. Paul McCartney has had a considerable influence on classical music. His interest in classical music is part of the broadening out and cross-fertilisation of different musical genres which is taking place at the moment.'

Paul said that he had decided to premiere his new piece, *A Leaf* at the RMC because he 'was glad to be given the chance to help young aspiring musicians. In today's competitive world, it is very difficult for people to get a good start. I hope this concert will help give musicians of the future a much needed boost, and the rest of us an enjoyable evening.'

The orchestral night included performances from Paul, Elvis Costello and the Brodsky Quartet, soprano Sally Burgess and baritone Willard White.

Tickets were limited to 300, sent to the college's subscribing members, by invitation only, requiring a donation of £250 each.

Paul was Master of Ceremonies and began the evening by announcing, 'Your Royal Highness, my lords, ladies, gentlemen – and the rest of us – thank you for your generous support for the Royal College of Music. I'm here to support the young musicians of the future, so thanks for coming, and for caring. We've got a varied programme tonight – and thanks to all the talented performers . . . for showing up sober!'

He then announced the first artist describing her as 'an ex-student of the Royal College of Music, the 22-year-old daughter of Dmitri Alexeyev, performing a new piano piece wot I wrote!'

This main performance of the evening was the world premiere of Paul's composition *A Leaf*, a solo performance by the Russian pianist Anya Alexeyev, a former prize-winning student at the college. The ten-minute solo piano suite had been specially written by Paul for the occasion.

At the end of the piece, Paul said 'Fantastic!' He then introduced 'a friend called Willard'. This was baritone singer Willard White who reprised selections of his work on Paul's *Liverpool Oratorio* before singing 'We're all Dodging'.

Paul then introduced Sally Burgess who was joined by the New London Children's Choir as she and Willard sang the schoolroom song from the Oratorio. Sally next sang a ballad from the Oratorio, 'Do You Know Who You Are'. She next sang a number from the musical *Showboat*, 'Can't Help Loving That Man'.

Next were the Brodsky Quartet who had formerly teamed up with Elvis Costello on his album *The Juliet Letters*. They performed 'Harold In Islington' and were joined on stage by Costello, who Paul introduced as 'someone I've written a few songs with over the last few years'.

Together with the quartet he performed some of the songs from *The Juliet Letters* and they then went on to perform some popular numbers such as 'God Only Knows'.

Elvis was joined on stage by Paul and announced, 'If I sing any wrong notes, you have to blame him, 'cause I got my musical education from singing along with his records.'

The two performed 'Mistress And Maid', which they had co-written and which was included on the *Off The Ground* album and they also sang John Lennon's 'One After 909'.

Paul then sang 'For No One', accompanied by the Brodsky Quartet with Michael Thompson on French horn. He then played an up-tempo version of 'Lady Madonna' on the piano. Paul then asked the quartet to take a bow before singing 'Yesterday'.

After the enthusiastic applause, Prince Charles took the stage to say, 'I hope you agree with me that we've been incredibly lucky this evening. Personally, I'm enormously grateful to Paul McCartney for having given up so much time and put so much into this evening.

'When I was at school in the sixties, I remember getting out of an airplane, coming back from school in Scotland to London Airport. As I got out, a strong gust of wind blew, and my hair fell over my head like this.' He indicated a fringe-like effect. 'In the papers the next day, it said: "Prince Has Beatles hairstyle". I could do it in those days, I can't do it now.'

He referred to the importance of the evening in raising funds for the students, saying, 'One of the great requirements is for video recording equipment so that all the students can see what they look like when they're playing. This makes a huge difference to their technique.

'The wonderful thing about this evening is that it reminds one that the music he wrote with John Lennon never fades; it is still just as good as it always was. That's the test of real music, I think.'

The Prince turned to Paul and said, 'In recognition of everything you've done, in particular for the Royal College of Music, the College wanted to offer you an honorary fellowship, which I hope you'll come and accept when they give out degrees.'

The hour-long performance was followed by a vegetarian dinner.

The concert was broadcast in Britain by *Classic FM* at Easter.

A Leaf was a piano piece that was difficult to play, which is probably why Paul himself did not want to perform it on this occasion. EMI's classical division released a version of *A Leaf* in Britain on 24 April. Lady Elizabeth Arnold, chairperson of the invitation committee for the gala evening described the piece as 'absolutely wonderful. It's a soliloquy piece. You can hear this little leaf drifting around.'

Paul McCartney Band, The

The name Paul chose for his group, which backed him on the 1989/90 World Tour. They were: Paul McCartney, vocals, bass; Hamish Stuart, guitar, bass, vocals; Linda McCartney, keyboards, vocals; Robbie McIntosh, lead guitar, vocals; Chris Whitten, drums; and Paul 'Wix' Wickens, keyboards, synthesisers.

Prior to deciding on that name, Paul had initially considered several others, including the Flowers In The Dirt, Game Play, Lumpy Trousers and Paul McCartney's Think Tank.

The group were originally assembled by Paul in July 1987 to record the album *Flowers In The Dirt*, and were then reunited for the world tour which began on 26 September 1989 and toured Norway, Sweden, Germany, France, Italy, Switzerland, Spain, Holland, United States, Canada, Brazil, Japan, Britain, New Zealand and Australia.

Paul McCartney: Beyond The Myth

An audio cassette/CD issued by Laserlight in 1995, part of a series of cassettes of interviews compiled and collated by Geoffrey Giuliano, and packaged as a Beatles audio set, taking advantage of the massive worldwide publicity for *The Beatles Anthology*. The tape was produced by Giuliano, Fred Betschen and David St Onge and contained no music, only interviews.

The tracks were:

1. Introduction by author (Giuliano). 2. Paul's younger brother, Mike McCartney. 3. Mike McCartney. 4. Paul McCartney. 5. Cavern club compere, Bob Wooler. 6. Beatles personal assistant, Alistair Taylor. 7. Early Beatles compere, 'Father' Tom McKenzie. 8. Mike McCartney. 9. Cavern doorman, Paddy Delaney. 10. Paul McCartney. 11. Paul McCartney. 12. Apple executive, Peter Brown. 13. Bonzo Dog Doo-Dah Band Member, Roger Ruskin Spear. 14. Bonzo Dog Doo-Dah Band Member, Neil Innes. 15. Roger Ruskin Spear. 16. Neil Innes. 17. Bonzo Dog Doo-Dah Band drummer, 'Legs' Larry Smith. 18. Paul McCartney. 19. Mike McCartney. 20. Denny Laine. 21. Denny Laine. 22. Steve Holly. 23. Mike McCartney. 24. Denny Laine. 25. Paul McCartney. 26. George Harrison. 27. Paul McCartney. 28. More exclusive reminiscences from Paul McCartney and Julia Baird (bonus track).

Paul McCartney Collection, The

The title given to the back catalogue of Paul McCartney/Wings releases, remastered for Parlophone by Peter Mew. They were issued on both CD and cassette to tie in with Paul's New World Tour. In addition to the sixteen titles there was also a promotional sampler containing tracks from all the albums. They were released in two sections. The first set was issued on Monday 7 June 1993. It comprised *McCartney*, Parlophone 7 89239 2, with no bonus tracks; *Ram*, Parlophone 7 89139 2 with the addition of 'Another Day' and 'Oh Woman, Oh Why'; *Wild Life*, Parlophone 7 89237 2, with the addition of 'Give Ireland Back To The Irish', 'Mary Had A Little Lamb', 'Little Woman Love' and 'Mama's Little Girl'; *Red Rose Speedway*, Parlophone 7

89238 2 with the addition of 'C Moon', 'Hi, Hi, Hi', 'The Mess' and 'I Lie Around'; *Band On The Run*, Parlophone 7 89240 2 with the addition of 'Helen Wheels' and 'Country Dreamer'; *Venus And Mars*, Parlophone 7 89241 2 with the addition of 'Zoo Gang', 'Lunch Box'/'Odd Sox' and 'My Carnival'; *Wings At The Speed Of Sound*, Parlophone 7 89140 2 with the addition of 'Walking In The Park With Eloise', 'Bridge On The River Suite' and 'Sally G'; and *London Town*, Parlophone 7 89265 2 with the addition of 'Girls' School' and 'Mull Of Kintyre'.

The second set was released on Monday 9 August 1993. It comprised *Wings Greatest*, Parlophone 7 89317 2 with no bonus tracks; *Back To The Egg*, Parlophone 7 89136 2 with the addition of 'Daytime Nighttime Suffering', 'Wonderful Christmastime' and 'Rudolph The Red-Nosed Reggae'; *McCartney II*, Parlophone 7 89137 2 with the addition of 'Check My Machine', 'Secret Friend' and 'Goodnight Tonight'; *Tug Of War*, Parlophone 7 89266 2 with no bonus tracks; *Pipes Of Peace*, Parlophone 7 89267 2 with the addition of 'Twice In A Lifetime', 'We All Stand Together' and 'Simple As That'; *Give My Regards To Broad Street*, Parlophone 7 89268 2 with the addition of 'No More Lonely Nights' (extended version) and 'No More Lonely Nights' (special dance mix); *Press To Play*, Parlophone 7 89269 2 with the addition of 'Spies Like Us' and 'Once Upon A Long Ago' (long version); and *Flowers In the Dirt*, Parlophone 7 89138 2 with the addition of 'Back On My Feet', 'Flying To My Home' and 'Loveliest Thing'.

Paul McCartney Collection CD Sampler, The

An 19-track promotional-only Paul McCartney sampler CD that was not for sale in regular record shops. It was issued in 1993 in a CD-single jewel case with the catalogue number CDPMCOLDJ 1 and different from previous compilations in that it included several album tracks that weren't considered classic McCartney cuts.

The track listing was: 'Every Night', 'Maybe I'm Amazed', 'Too Many People', 'Tomorrow', 'C Moon', 'Let Me Roll It', 'Treat Her Gently', 'Lonely Old People', 'Beware My Love', 'Girlfriend', 'Another Day', 'Live And Let Die', 'Daytime Nighttime Suffering', 'Waterfalls', 'Ballroom Dancing', 'The Man', 'No More Lonely Nights', 'Footprints' and 'You Want Her Too'.

Paul McCartney – Composer, Artist

A book crediting Paul as author, published by Pavilion Books in 1981 in both hard and soft covers. In many ways this was a disappointment because pre-publicity had led people to believe that the book was Paul's equivalent of George Harrison's *I, Me, Mine*.

A book of Paul's songs on which he had actively worked with the publishers should have resulted, it was felt, in something better than this.

Personal comments from Paul on all the numbers, some incisive background as to how he came to write the songs, some replicas of the material (papers, tissues, menu cards) on which he had originally penned his ideas and so on would have produced a publication which provided some insight on Paul as 'composer/artist'.

In fact, what is given is a hundred-word introduction, three photos of Linda, forty-seven doodles and forty-eight songs.

Described as 'an extra-special glimpse into McCartney's creative mind ... revealed through songs and never-before-published drawings', it fails to deliver. The music and lyrics are as beautiful as ever – but they are available in many songbooks.

This is, in fact, a glorified songbook. The spidery drawings don't even illustrate the actual songs they are placed alongside and the majority of them are merely sketches of faces, while the general standard of the drawings is uneven, to say the least.

Paul actually sent a special collector's edition of the book to the Artists For Animals group, which is an anti-vivisection organisation. The idea was for them to auction it and raise funds for their cause. It proved to be an embarrassing move because they had to send the book back.

Their spokeswoman Viv Smith commented, 'We don't criticise Paul. He's a compassionate guy who gives a lot of support to animal causes. But if we were to auction the book we would be accused of animal exploitation because it is bound in skin!'

Paul McCartney – Freeze Frame

A 30-minute TV programme aired in some ITV areas of Britain late in the evening of Friday 7 September 1984.

A film of Paul and George Martin during the recording of *Tug Of War* was followed by a conversation in which Paul discussed the album. The programme also included four complete Macca videos: 'Take It Away', 'Coming Up', 'Tug Of War' and 'Ebony And Ivory'.

Paul McCartney: From Liverpool To Broad Street

A two-hour radio programme on Paul's career, syndicated in America to coincide with the release of *Give My Regards To Broad Street*.

Paul McCartney Fun Club, The

Also known as the Wings Fun Club, it was founded by Paul and Linda as the only official fan club. A glossy news magazine *Club Sandwich* was issued and the club also provided a mail order service with special offers for fans. Paul also invited members to special recordings and appearances. In 1989 McCartney's Fun Club had 7,000 UK and 3,000 US members. The club was officially disbanded due to Linda's death and a letter of notice was sent to each member on 2 October 1998.

Paul McCartney Goes Too Far

This was to be the title of an album of his avant-garde music, which Paul once considered releasing, but decided against.

Paul McCartney In The World Tonight

A one-hour documentary surrounding the making of the *Flaming Pie* album which was produced and directed by Geoff Wonfor and edited by Andy Matthews. Wonfor had suggested the idea to Paul and the documentary features Paul discussing the individual songs, with shots of him recording them in the studio. There is also a tour of the studio and details of the preparation of the artwork for the album cover, designed by Rick Ward. Mark Lewisohn and Geoff Baker then interview Paul who discusses the songs, track by track. Paul is seen taking *Oobu Joobu* producer Eddy Pumer around his Mill studio, giving a demonstration of the various instruments there.

Filming of the documentary began in February 1997 and was completed on Friday 11 April with the rooftop concert Paul gave on top of his MPL building in Soho, although this segment wasn't used in the documentary. In fact, 35 hours of material was edited out of the final one-hour special.

'Paul McCartney In The World Tonight' was previewed to the British national press at the BAFTA headquarters in Piccadilly, London on Tuesday 13 May 1997 and then received its television premiere on VH-1 in America on Friday 16 May and its British premiere on ITV on Sunday 18 May.

An insight into the *Flaming Pie* album was given during the VH-1 documentary with the question-and-answer session conducted with Paul by his publicist Geoff Baker:

Geoff: Is this new album, *Flaming Pie*, timed for release to coincide with certain important anniversaries this year?

Paul: No, it's not *timed* to fit in with those anniversaries, that's just coincidence. But it's true, there *are* these big anniversaries: the album is out on 12 May, which is around the time, thirty years ago, of the release of *Sgt Pepper* and it's also the thirtieth anniversary, that week, I believe, of me and Linda meeting for the first time.

Geoff: Isn't it the fortieth anniversary this July of you meeting John, for the first time?

Paul: No, it can't be, because I'm not even that old.

Geoff: But you did meet him forty years ago. And here you are, forty years on, and one of you gets knighted. Wonder what you'd have thought of that back then?

Paul: We'd have collapsed in fits of laughter, the mere idea of it was so unthinkable, that we'd have thought it was a joke. Maybe we might have looked at a posh sports car and thought, 'Umm, maybe one day,' but a knighthood, no way. It would just be an impossible dream.

Geoff: So does that mean that Linda's Lady Linda or Lady McCartney now?

Paul: It's both isn't it. The nice thing about it really is when me and Linda are sitting away on holiday, watching the sunset. I turn to her and say, 'Hey, you're a *lady*.' It's a giggle, but it's nice because you get to make your girlfriend a lady, although she always was anyway.

As for myself, it's like a school prize. You don't go after it but if you do some good drawings, then you can get the art prize and they give it you because they think you're all right. And that's the way I take it, really. It's just something nice that's offered and it'd be rude to turn it down, wouldn't it?

Geoff: Is it four years since the last studio album, since *Off The Ground*?

Paul: Yes. Actually, after the last album we were all gearing up to do the *Anthology* and someone from EMI gave me the message that 'we don't need an album from you for a couple of years because we're doing the *Anthology*'. And at first I was a little pissed off. I thought, 'Oh yeah, ye of little faith. Typical record company!' But then I thought, 'They're right.' Number one, I wanted to concentrate on the *Anthology*, did a lot of work there getting it right. And also it would be very unseemly for any one of us to release a solo album in the middle of all that. Also stupid, to try to go against the Beatles sales. So I waited, worked on the *Anthology* and all the while I kept writing, as I do.

Geoff: Are all the songs on the album written by you?

Paul: Yes, apart from those that aren't. 'Listen To Be Bad' I wrote with Steve Miller and 'Really Love You' I wrote with Ringo. It's our first composition together, I think, we just sort of made that one up on the spot.

Geoff: Is Ringo playing drums on the album, then?

Paul: Yeah, just on a couple of tracks, 'Really Love You' and 'Beautiful Night'. The only other drummer, on all the other tracks, is me. I sort of learned how to do that, way back before Ringo joined the Beatles. When we didn't have a drummer, or when one didn't turn up, it was always me who got lumbered with that.

Geoff: So there are a lot of other musicians on this album?

Paul: It's basically me and a bunch of pals – Ringo, Steve Miller and Jeff Lynne in various combinations but not all of them together on any one track. So it's a bit of a solo effort, really, getting back to *McCartney* and *Ram*.

Geoff: Anybody else?

Paul: Yes, there's a couple of members of my family.

Geoff: Who's producing?

Paul: I co-produced most of the tracks with Jeff Lynne, eight of them. My old friend George Martin produced 'Calico Skies' and 'Great Day' with me and the others were produced by me and the seat of my pants. It's pretty much a home-made album.

Geoff: There's been a rumour going round that this album was going to be called *Don't Sweat It*. Is that true?

Paul: No. The album's called *Flaming Pie*. But 'Don't Sweat It' is the attitude with which we made this album. I've been telling everyone involved in the promotion of the album not to sweat it and there's to be no waking up in the middle of the night worrying about this album, because it's just an album. If you like it, you like it, if you don't – don't buy it.

Geoff: What brings you to that frame of mind?

Paul: Just having all the time and the freedom and the relaxation of doing the *Anthology*. Just having two years off, basically, but wanting to do music. So all the music that I did was just for my own pleasure. Normally you ring a producer and say, 'Right, put aside two months, six weeks at the least to get it together.' And then there's the mixing and then there's the overdubbing bit, and it can get very boring. It can get very horrible, actually. You can just think, 'I wish I could just have a day off.'

So I rang up Jeff Lynne, told him I had a bunch of songs and said could he come over. He said, 'How long? A month or six weeks or so?' I said, 'No, two weeks. We might get bored with each other after that.'

If you look at a Beatles album and look down the track list, they're all good little songs. So I thought I'd make an album where there wouldn't be a stiff on the track list – as far as I was concerned, anyway. I wanted to make sure that I liked every song on this album.

One of my theories is that the enjoyment you have in the studio communicates itself to people. If I'm having fun, which I am, maybe it'll sound like fun.

Geoff: Is there anything else, besides the influence of the *Anthology*, that has given you this calm, more relaxed approach?

Paul: Drugs. There's these drugs you can take, every morning you get up. Forty in each foot. Not easy but, boy, it gets you so relaxed.

Geoff: Much of the guitar on this album is heavier than you've recorded before. Have you got a new guitarist?

Paul: Not as such because I'm not playing with a band on this album. As I said, Steve Miller's on a few of the tracks and I love Steve's guitar playing. I'd been told that he was very difficult to produce because he's said to be very fussy, a great perfectionist. Somebody told me that he can sometimes take up to three hours to decide what guitar to use. But I found him very comfortable to work with. I'd just say, 'Whack that guitar up, Steve. Bloody hell, that sounds good,' and we got on with it.

My guitar playing on this album is a bit heavier than you may have heard before. Linda's into all that. When Linda and I first met she'd say, 'I didn't know you played heavy guitar like that, I love that,' and she'd get me to play like that at home.

So I did. It's a little naïve, my guitar style. It's not amazingly technical, it's a little bit like Neil Young; I feel a bit of affinity with Neil. We drove up to see him at the Phoenix Festival last year and I know that we like similar things, like he's a big Hendrix fan too.

Geoff: Does anyone else play guitar on the album besides you and Steve Miller and Jeff Lynne?

Paul: My son, James, plays on 'Heaven On A Sunday'. That was great to do. He's getting really good on the guitar now and I thought it would be a nice idea to record with him. When you've known someone for twenty years, you read them and they read you, so you can trade licks.

So we did; I played the acoustic sort of part, like an old blues guy, and I left the young Turk to play the hot electric stuff.

Of course, as a dad, I was just so proud, it's just brilliant to be playing with your kids. He came up with some very nice phrases.

Geoff: Have you been keeping your eye on him over the years, waiting for this moment?

Paul: People have often asked me if any of my kids are musical and I've always said that yes, they are all musical, but I've never pushed them into music because of that 'he's the son of, she's the daughter of,' syndrome. I always feel a bit sorry for kids coming into that. So I decided I would never push them into it but if any of them had a passion for it then I won't stand in their way, I'd support them.

James got a guitar when he was about nine or ten and he's been playing it ever since, for about ten years now. He's got steadily better and better and he loves it. He used to come home from school and go straight to his guitar.

He hasn't had a tutor. I said to him early on exactly what my dad said to me. 'Son, if you want to learn, get proper lessons.' He said to me, 'You didn't, Dad,' which is exactly what I said to my dad. So the saga continues.

No, he wanted to teach himself I suppose, seeing that I'd done it that way and it seemed all right for me and of course I couldn't stand in the way of that.

Geoff: Talking of family, didn't Linda influence the speed of writing a couple of songs?

Paul: Yeah, 'Same Days' and 'Young Boy' were written against the clock on a couple of little bets that I made with myself while Linda was working on her vegetarian cookery projects.

Sometimes I'll drive Linda to one of her cookery assignments and I'd driven her to a photo session she was doing at a farmhouse in Kent. As she got on with that, I kept out of the way, I asked the lady of this house if I could borrow a room and she let me use her son's bedroom upstairs.

So I went up there with my acoustic guitar and I made up a little fantasy for myself to write a song in the time that Linda would be doing this photo session. I knew she'd be about two hours doing the shoot. And that was 'Some Days'. I wrote the whole song in that time.

Normally you might get most of it down and think you'll finish it up next week or whatever. But I thought I'd finish up the whole song so that when Linda would say, 'What did you do? Did you get bored?' I could say, 'Oh, I wrote this song. Wanna hear it?'

It's just a little game that I play with myself. John and I used to play this game and I don't think it ever took us more than three hours to write a song. And I did the same with 'Young Boy', I wrote that against the clock too. And that was when Linda was doing another veggie cooking thing for the press.

We were in Long Island then and Linda was cooking a lunch with Pierre Franey for an article in the *New York Times*. So while she cooked lunch, which was Vegetable Soup, Aubergine Casserole and Applesauce Cake, I went off into a little back room with my guitar and started playing some chords and a song came up. Actually, it started as, 'He's just a poor boy . . . he's just a poor boy looking for a way to find love.' But *poor* boy reminded me too much of like an Elvis song, so I made it *young* boy, which I liked better. So I started making up this song thinking about all the young people I know who are in that position, a lot of my kids' friends.

I remember that position myself. I remember thinking as a kid, 'There's somebody out there who's for me, but how am I ever going to meet her? There's three hundred bloody million of them, how the hell am I ever going to meet the right one?' It's very perplexing at that age.

Anyway, they got on with the lunch and then they came in and said, 'What have you been doing?' 'Oh, funny you should say that. I've written a song.' I really just do it for that moment, because I know that people don't know how you write songs.

Then I went to Idaho, where Steve Miller's got a studio, and we recorded the song with just me and him doing the track.

I hadn't seen Steve since one night in the sixties when there had been an unfortunate Allen Klein meeting with the Beatles in the middle of all our troubles. I'd resisted their efforts to sign some business deal. I thought we should think about it. It all got a bit heated and they all went off with Allen Klein and I was left at the studio and Steve stuck his head around the door and said, 'Hi man, does that mean the studio's free?'

He asked me if I fancied doing something together in the studio: I said, 'OK, but just let me drum.' I wasn't in a very good mood after that meeting and I just wanted to thrash something. So we developed this process that we've used now on *Flaming Pie*. I drummed, Steve played some guitar. I put bass on it, he played a little more guitar solos. He sang it, I sang some harmonies. And by about three or four in the morning on that Beatles occasion out at Olympic Studios in Barnes we'd done a track, which was called 'My Dark Hour'.

I played the track recently to my son and he liked it and that reminded me, so I rang up Steve, who we played with in '93 when we did the Earth Show at the Hollywood Bowl, we got our friendship going again, and I told him I had this song called 'Young Boy' and I thought we could do it together.

So I went out to Sun Valley, to Steve's place. I took Geoff Emerick, my engineer, our old Beatles engineer, and we did the same process that we'd done with 'My Dark Hour'. It was good. It was like falling back into an old habit.

Geoff: Talking of Beatles links with these new songs, what's the story behind the title track 'Flaming Pie'?

Paul: Over the years there's been some conflict of memory over who actually thought of the name the Beatles. George and I have a very clear memory about that. We were at Gambier Terrace in Liverpool, where John and a couple of art school mates had a first-floor apartment. We used to stay there; it was so exciting as kids, kipping out on an old mattress. It was exciting – stroke – *tiring* listening to Johnny Burnette records, staying up all night doing wild teenage things.

Anyway, one night John and Stu (Stuart Sutcliffe) came out of the flat, we were walking towards the Dingle and John and Stu said to me and George, 'Hey, we've had an idea for what to call the band – the Beatles, with an A.' George and I were kind of surprised and John said, 'Yeah, me and Stu thought of it.'

This is what George and I remembered, but over the years some people have thought that John had single-handedly come up with the idea for the name the Beatles and, as their reason for that, they've cited a bit of writing that John did for a publication called *Mersey Beat* in the early sixties.

John wrote this piece for *Mersey Beat* called 'Being A Short Diversion On The Dubious Origins Of Beatles', in which at one point he wrote, 'there were three little boys called John, George and Paul ... Many people ask what are Beatles? Why Beatles? How did the name arrive? It came in a vision. A man appeared on a flaming pie and said unto them, "From this day on you are Beatles with an A".'

Obviously John hadn't had a vision. It was a joke. It was a joke in the Goon humour of the time. However, certain people maybe didn't understand that humour and over the years they have truly believed that John really did have this vision. Which he didn't.

It's quite easy to see the joke, in the language. 'It came in a vision.' OK at that point. But, 'a man said unto them'. Now when you say 'unto' you start to go into the joke, because it's biblical. 'A man appeared on a flaming . . .' OK, now if you said chariot or phoenix then that would still be all right – a flaming chariot. But the minute you mention 'pie' then humour has crept in in a big way. And, of course, if John had had a vision at the age of twelve, how come his first band was called the Quarry Men?

Anyway, when I was doing 'Souvenir' on this album with Jeff Lynne we decided we wanted some raw, heavyish guitar and while the engineers were getting the sound I started vamping riffs. Jeff joined in and I began shouting a bit of a melody. We decided to stick it on the tape, just as it might be handy later.

At the same time, Jeff and I had been talking about old recording techniques and how, in the Beatles, we'd record two songs in the morning, go down to the pub for an hour, and record another two songs in the afternoon. So, just as an exercise, we decided that we should try that and try to record a complete song, using this jam that we'd taped, in just four hours. Just for the hell of it.

I then had the problem of thinking of some words and I was out horse riding with Linda, just musing some words, and I was going to start the song, 'making love underneath the moon, shooting stars in a purple sky . . .' So I was thinking of a rhyme for 'sky' and, as you do, went through the alphabet . . . 'bye' . . . 'cry' . . . and I got to 'pie'. I thought, 'No, no, no, that's a joke.' But then this story came back to me – 'pie' . . . 'There's no way we would work that in, is there?' And I suddenly thought, 'Oh, flaming pie!'

So Jeff and I did it, in our four hours. I sang it live and we got it all mixed in the time. Then, when I was looking for an album title, I mentioned *Flaming Pie* and everyone I mentioned it to just sort of smiled.

Geoff: There's a line in 'The World Tonight' that sounds rather Beatley too, that line 'I go back so far I'm in front of me'. What's 'The World Tonight' about?

Paul: People talk about this mystery thing about songwriting. Where does the song come from? This started off, 'I saw you sitting in the centre of a circle, everybody wanted something from you' and I still haven't figured who I really mean by that. It's not anyone in particular, it's a lot of people. There's a lot of us sitting in the centre of a circle with everyone wanting something from you. We all know that one.

The words aren't about anyone specific, they were just gathering thoughts and that line, 'I go back so far I'm in front of me', I don't know where that came from. It's one of those that if I'd be writing with John, I might have questioned it, but I think he would have said, 'OK, leave that one in. We don't know what it means but we know what it means.'

Geoff: Is it true that there will be a TV documentary screened around the release of *Flaming Pie*?

Paul: Yes. I was asked to make it with Geoff Wonfor, the director of the *Anthology*. However, unlike the *Anthology*, we didn't take a couple of years to film it. In fact we knocked it off in under a month, a couple of days here, a few more there. That's very much the way I like to do things now. I don't like to wait around. It's like with writing 'Young Boy' or 'Some Days', knock 'em off in a couple of hours. It's more fun like that. Working like that reminds me of something my dad used to say – D.I.N., Do It Now.

Geoff: Have they made a radio show for *Flaming Pie* too?

Paul: Yeah. A couple of years back in the USA they aired this radio show called *Oobu Joobu* which was a series of programmes that I presented myself and which I'd recorded at spare moments over the years. That was a lot of fun to do and it seemed very popular, so we kind of did that again with me hosting a show, just a one-off this time, talking about the new album.

Geoff: You mentioned that you are painting these days. What does painting give you that music doesn't?

Paul: When I turned forty, everyone said life begins at forty, so I looked around for a couple of days and nothing appeared to begin. So I thought I had better start some stuff. So I started jogging a little bit, because I'd never done that before. That was good fun. Then I thought that I would love to paint, as I have always liked drawing – at school I did get a little art prize, nothing major, but I've always liked to fiddle around that area.

But I'd always had this big block in my head, that it was *those* people who paint and not us. I didn't see it as my place to paint. I never even dreamed about it. But when I got to forty I thought now it was time to get down to an art shop and buy a canvas or two – which was odd for me, the thought of me buying a canvas was like being arrogant. It was like an ego trip.

So I bought a canvas, a few paints and a couple of brushes and I just started and I discovered that I really enjoyed it. And what painting gives me is very similar to what music gives me; if your day isn't going that great it's lovely to go into a room with a guitar and *make* the day go great by making some music and getting involved in the magic of that.

Painting's a bit similar for me. And so I've been doing it for about fourteen years now and I just love it. If I'm on tour, in the middle of all that craziness, I'll just have a day off sometimes and do a painting. It's like a therapy. I can put my feelings into it. It's a freedom thing for me, which in many ways is very similar to music.

Geoff: You recently returned to the Liverpool Institute for Performing Arts, but this time to meet with the students reportedly for a master class. How did it feel to go back to your old school as a master?

Paul: Well I didn't think like a master, that's for sure. That's that terrible thing about Us and Them. When I was at school there were some teachers who were quite nice and groovy, who you could get on with and you felt like they respected you as a person instead of just being someone to hit about the ears. So I felt more like one of those good older guys, hopefully, and I just kicked around some ideas for a project with the students.

It felt very good. I tried to get them to give me their ideas because I've always said that if I come in to give a songwriting class, which this wasn't, the first thing that I'll have to say is that I don't really know anything about how to do it. Because I don't, and I also don't *want* to know how to do it. Because the minute I know *how* to write a song I'll be bored. To me, writing a song is like magic. Every time it happens. It's like, 'who lit that candle?' I'm always like *amazed* by it and that's what I follow. It's not like I'm doing it, it's doing it and I'm merely following it.

Geoff: You said a few years ago that you doubted if you'd ever achieve all that you wanted to. But now, with the knighthood, the paintings, the symphonic piece, the world tours, are you getting close to achieving what you want?

Paul: Since I was forty, I have decided to try to do all of those things that you thought you'd never do. There's always something more, although at the moment I couldn't tell you what it is.

But there's lots of little things that I'm doing that I always wanted. I've got a little sailboat now because I've always wanted to sail. It's not a yacht, it's literally just a one-man sailboat. I love that and that's another of those things that if you were brought up where I was brought up, you didn't go sailing. *They* sailed. We rolled our trousers up and paddled.

And one of the things I'm discovering about myself is that because I never had any lessons with music, I like that primitive approach in discovering other things. I like not knowing and working it out for myself. And I think you also get a bit of an original take on it; if it's out of a book fifty thousand people could have read that book, but if you work it out yourself you sometimes learn things that although you may later find out you would have learned from a book, you've got a bit of an original angle on it.

It's a good feeling out there in the wind; it's just you, the boat and the sail and it's very quiet and I think the first primitive men who sailed, it must have been a bit like this. It's fascinating for me.

I can't think of too many more ambitions. I'm knocking them off one by one. But there will always be something.

Geoff: Have you always tried to retain that primitive approach to your work?

Paul: Yeah, me and John started off writing songs and didn't know how to do it. Nobody said to us, 'This is how you do it.' So we just tried and the first few songs you can tell that we were trying because they weren't that good. We had to learn our way.

I like the primitive approach because it makes it more exciting.

And also, there's no rules. No one's told you the rules yet. George Martin always used to say, 'Oh Paul, you're not supposed to double a third.' But because it was a rule, we'd say, 'George, double it, we don't care what it is, if it's a rule not to do it, do it.' So George would have to do all this terrible stuff we'd force him into, but it meant that our songs weren't like the next man's.

And sometimes when you did it, 'posh journalists' would write about 'the Aeolian cadences and panatonic clusters'. We'd say, 'What's he talking about?' and they'd say it's the end of 'She Loves You'. So we were obviously coming up with it, without knowing. It's just that they had the *names* for it all, they had all the technique and the rules. And we were just winging it, just flying out there and having fun.

Geoff: With all these various and numerous projects that you get involved in, do you feel that you have room in your life for your life?

Paul: No. Definitely not. Sometimes you feel that there's not enough time in a day to fit in all that you want, but I have a pretty good go at it because I enjoy working. Some people call me a workaholic but I don't really think that I am because I *enjoy* it. I always assume that workaholics work too hard and don't really enjoy it. I like working, there's a lot of people out of a job and who want a job, so I'm always grateful to be in work. I like teamwork.

But I like my time off too, because of the balance. So I like to go off into the woods and just make a path through the woods with an axe or a chain saw. Then it's just me and my life, doing something that I want to do that I don't have to do really. I like to go off on an hour's horse ride with Linda: that's often why I'm late for things, because I can't get down off that horse quick enough.

I get a lot done, that's for sure. But when it gets too crazy and hectic I try to just stop it and I want to get back and make some music. Somebody said to me recently, 'Oh, I see you still enjoy your music then?' But it hadn't occurred to me that anyone would think that I could ever go off it.

Geoff: The National Trust of Britain has bought your old home in Liverpool for the posterity of the nation. How did you feel about that?

Paul: If, when we were kids, me and John were wandering around with guitars slung over our shoulders walking down from Forthlin Road to Menlove Avenue, where he lived, and back again, if you'd just ever said that it'd be a National Trust house ... well, the idea is still fairly laughable. It's only a little terraced house. There's no way we'd have believed that would happen. If somebody had predicted it, we'd just have thought they'd had a few too many drinks.

But it's great. I love it, it's an honour. Someone chooses your house and sticks a plaque on it and reckons its famous. Though, if you listen to the National Trust reasons for doing this, it's not bad; because it's from where we launched to Hamburg and the guy next door, Mr Richards, made our jackets, our purple jackets that we took to Hamburg. In that area John and I showed my Dad the final version of 'She Loves You' and we used to rehearse 'To Know Him Is To Love Him' or 'To Know Her Is To Love Her', as we changed it to. And I wrote the tune 'When I'm Sixty-Four' on the family piano there when I was fifteen or sixteen.

I think the National Trust is thinking of the house as a bit of a tourist attraction, because the tourist buses go past there anyway. Actually, when I go up to Liverpool with the kids I get in my car and I like to drive myself. So I was driving myself around Liverpool one evening, I drove down Forthlin Road and I pulled up right outside the house and I was telling the kids, 'that was my room there, my Dad planted a mountain ash right there, he used to have a favourite lavender bush right here and the ginger tom cat from next door used to come out and pee in the lavender'.

Anyway, I'm sitting there, telling the kids all these stories, we're crouched down in the car and some bloke walks past, leans down to the car window and says, 'Yeah, he did used to live there.'

Geoff: We mentioned your new classical piece, what is it and when will it be heard?

Paul: EMI, which is my record company, celebrates its one hundredth anniversary this year and to mark that they commissioned me to write a piece which has become what they call a 'symphonic poem'. It's called *Standing Stone*, it's four movements and will be performed by the London Symphony Orchestra at the Albert Hall in London on 14 October. I've written it myself, just me, a computer and a little help from my friends.

Geoff: Are you still playing your old Hofner bass?

Paul: I played my Hofner throughout the making of this album and it's my favourite bass again. I love the lightness of the Hofner, it's like it's made of balsa wood and you can really move around with it instead of being weighed down as you are with some other models, which are like playing some big chunk of heavy oak.

But on one of the songs on the album, 'The Song We Were Singing', I'm playing the Bill Black double bass. Bill Black was the bass player with Elvis and I'm such a fan of Elvis and Bill that Linda bought me Bill's bass as a birthday present a few years ago. She quietly tracked it down without me knowing. A birthday pressie! Are you kidding me! It's like an icon, really. It's the wrong way round for me, because Bill was right-handed, but I always try to give it a go. I can't really play the stand-up bass, the bull bass, you need a different set of chops. You need bigger hands. But I try; I can just about play 'Heartbreak Hotel'.

Geoff: *Flaming Pie* is said to have a very relaxed feel to it. Is this because a lot of the album was written while you were on holiday, even though most people don't work on holiday?

Paul: As I said, because of my obligation to the Beatles *Anthology* projects, I didn't have to produce an album. I thought *great*, what a lovely, lazy couple of years. So then the only music I made was for the fun of it. I always say that if I had to retire I'd still do this as a hobby and so it was; I was taking time out, having holidays, not scheduled to be in a studio and the songs just came to me, I couldn't stop them.

I get like that on holidays. I know that on holiday you are supposed not to work but, as I say, the songs just came to me. Holidays are when I'm most relaxed. For me they are the equivalent of being a teenager – you know what it's like, that time when you've got nothing to do except maybe do a gig in the evening. It's like that, like being in a band but the band's not big yet. You ring up John, you go up to his place and play guitar and then it's, 'Now what shall we do? Oh, dunno, suppose we could go to the pictures.' It's like having endless deserts of time. And this, having the *Anthology* and holidays, was a bit like that for me.

So these songs were written purely for fun. There's not one of them that was written with the idea of 'this is for my next album' in mind. I couldn't stop them – like 'Calico Skies', that came after we were in America in the wake of Hurricane Bob. Bob had blown out all the power and so as I couldn't play records I just sat around with my acoustic as Linda cooked meals over a wood fire. Our family loves all that simplicity and while Linda was cooking up these wood-fire meals – once for twenty people – I was sitting about providing the acoustic soundtrack to it all. And 'Calico Skies' came out of that relaxation, it was just a simple little powercut memory.

Geoff: One of the distinct elements of *Flaming Pie* is that you are playing all these instruments – guitar, bass, piano, drums –

yourself and in that it appears that you are going back to what you did with your first solo album after the Beatles, *McCartney*.

Paul: People are often saying to me, 'We want to hear you on record, we don't want to hear you and lots of other people, we just want to hear you.' So I thought, 'Well, great, I'll do that, I'll drum then,' because I did it on *McCartney* and I did it on *Band On The Run*. And one of my great compliments was off Keith Moon, when he and John and others were going through that manic lost weekend episode. I went out to see them and Keith Moon asked me who drummed on *Band On The Run*. I said it was me and Keith said 'Fucking great'. Coming from Keith, that was high praise for me.

Geoff: Was it difficult to get back to this spirit of simplicity that you can hear on *Flaming Pie*.

Paul: It was very easy for this album to get back to that and I'm not sure why. I think probably because I was listening to a lot of early Beatles stuff, seeing how quick we were, hearing the directness of it and all that. But in recent years it has been hard because one tends to equate something being complex with being good and, similarly, something being simple with being not good. As I've said before, the melody of 'Yesterday' came to me in my sleep. You can't get much simpler than that. And when I first did 'Yesterday' I told people the tune had come to me in a dream – but maybe I shouldn't have done that, because it makes it seem too simple. Maybe I should have said that it was a song I'd been working on for eight months, in Tibet.

I think that the natural thing in a career is to view it as a progression. I've got my feel and throughout my career I have made efforts to try to get away from it and go in some other direction. I'm willing to try all these other things because you've got to, just to see if they are any better.

But on this album I've started thinking that I don't really need to go in another direction. And somebody pointed out to me that a lot of what those new groups are doing is *'your sound'*. So it's actually mad if I don't do it and just let everybody else do it and admire how well they sound when they do it.

Geoff: You mentioned the calls on you to heavily promote the album, are you heeding them?

Paul: I had a lot of fun making this album. I really enjoyed making it and what I basically want to do now is to have a good time. So I've started to say to myself, 'What's it been worth to do all that Beatles career, earn all this money and get all that fame if at some point I don't go, "Now I can have a good time"?'

If I keep on going on like some manic preacher for the rest of my life, it just seems so pointless.

Geoff: But does the industry, the great rock and roll industry, allow that in this day and age?

Paul: Exactly. When we started out in the business, the suits were in charge. The Beatles changed all that and turned that over. But I feel that the suits are back in charge now and I want to be subversive and break that lock.

In my mind now I don't make a record for the industry. I make a record for the kid in the bedroom who's been out on the bus to buy the record. He's read the sleeve notes on the way home and he's back in his bedroom hearing it. Whether that kid is in Minnesota, Kansas City, Rotherham or Speke, I identify very strongly with that kid. I've been that kid.

Somebody recently said to me how much they'd love it if the record industry could learn from the Beatles *Anthology* what we'd learned from the *Anthology* and I say right on to that. It's absolutely where it needs to go now. It's like suing Neil Young for not having a hit is the *wrong* way to go, business people, and letting the talent flow and not putting too many demands on it is the *right* way to go. It really is; you've got to nurture talent instead of beating them about the head. You've got to give them a bit of freedom.

It's like I've been saying to people, with this album I really don't give a shit if it is a hit or not. I've been saying that and I *mean* it. Sure, everyone likes to have a hit, but not at the expense of having fun.

Paul McCartney: In The World Tonight

A 72-minute DVD or videocassette, released in November 1997, which was a documentary on the recording of *Flaming Pie* and featured studio footage and performances of 'In The World Tonight', 'Oobu Joobu', 'Little Willow', 'Beautiful Night' and 'Calico Skies'.

There was also a 55-minute DVD issued by Rhino Home Video in America in 1998 on R2 4462. It was described as: 'An intimate look at the making of Paul McCartney's 1997 Grammy-nominated album, *Flaming Pie*, with a little help from friends Ringo Starr, Steve Miller, Jeff Lynne and George Martin.'

Paul McCartney Job, The

The name by which the Newhaven CID referred to the 1984 plot to kidnap Linda McCartney. Detectives said that they had uncovered a kidnap plot in which Linda was to be snatched in a military-style operation on a country lane near the Sussex farm. The kidnappers intended to hold her hostage in a woodland lair and demand £10 million ransom. Paul was reluctant to discuss the matter, commenting; 'Any talk of a kidnap plot is bound to give ideas to all sorts of nutters.'

Paul McCartney – Live At The Cavern

The show that was originally broadcast live over the Internet and later broadcast in the US on the satellite channel Direct TV in 2000. It was later broadcast as a 45-minute programme on PBS (Public Broadcast Service) TV in America on Tuesday 5 December 2000.

The documentary opens with Paul's limousine arriving at the rebuilt Cavern club in Mathew Street and then the onstage performance begins.

Paul McCartney Live At The Cavern Club 1999

A 63-minute video featuring the concert, together with two of Paul's music videos, 'No Other Baby' and 'Brown Eyed Handsome Man', together with a 22-minute interview with Paul conducted by Jools Holland, which was issued in America on 19 June 2001 by Image Entertainment.

A DVD version (ID0384MPDVD) was also available with an interview with Laura Gross first distributed as an infomercial on cable TV, plus text biographies of members of the band and three pages of text on the Cavern club.

The releases were issued in Britain on 25 June.

Paul McCartney – The Man

A radio interview with Paul that was recorded on Tuesday 6 March 1984 at AIR Studios in London by Radio Leicester for syndication to local BBC radio stations throughout Britain.

Paul McCartney: The Man, His Music, His Movies

A 30-minute American television special screened on several US stations during April 1984. It was scripted by Rick Sublett, produced by Gayle Hollenbaugh and narrated by Tom Bosley. The programme included interviews with Paul about the making of *Give My Regards To Broad Street*, in addition to some clips from the movie. The show was part of a series called *On And Off Camera*. There was a brief history of the Beatles using clips from 'The Compleat Beatles' documentary and music from 'Ballroom Dancing', 'Yesterday' and 'The Long And Winding Road'.

Paul McCartney – The New World Sampler

A 17-track 2-CD in-store promotional record produced by Capitol in America in February 1993 which featured one CD of up-tempo numbers and one of mid-tempo songs.

The tracks were: 'Hope Of Deliverance', 'Maybe I'm Amazed', 'Get On The Right Thing', 'Off The Ground', 'Venus And Mars'/'Rock Show'/'Jet' live from *Wings Over America*, 'Biker Like An Icon', 'Helen Wheels', 'Twenty Flight Rock' from *Choba B CCCP*, 'I've Had Enough', 'Looking For Changes', 'Smile Away', 'Magneto And Titanium Man', 'Stranglehold', 'I Owe It All To You', 'Rockestra Theme', 'C'Mon People' and 'Golden Slumbers'/'Carry That Weight'/'The End' – the *Tripping The Live Fantastic* medley.

Paul McCartney Night

An evening devoted to Paul on VH1 on Thursday 10 August 2000. It began with the screening of 'Paul McCartney Live In The New World', followed by PETA's Millennium Concert in which Paul performs 'Honey Hush', 'Brown Eyed Handsome Man', 'No Other Baby', 'Try Not To Cry' and 'Run Devil Run', followed by Paul 'Live At The Cavern'. Paul then selected his ten favourite songs (see 'Top Ten' for details).

Paul McCartney Paintings

Title of the exhibition of Paul's paintings which opened at the Kuntforum Lyz Gallery, St Johann Street in the university town of Siegen in Germany on Saturday 1 May 1999. It ran until Sunday 25 July 1999.

Paul had been passionate about art since he was a child and used to paint his own birthday and Christmas cards. He also designed some of the Beatles album sleeves.

In London in the mid-60s, under the influence of gallery owner Robert Fraser, he became an art collector and particularly likes the work of René Magritte.

Paul also became acquainted with the Dutch painter Willem de Kooning, based in New York, who was a client of Paul's father-in-law. When Paul had turned forty, he was encouraged by de Kooning to take up painting and soon had his own work studios in his homes in the south of England, Arizona and Long Island. An added incentive was a Christmas present from Linda – René Magritte's own easel. Since 1983 Paul has produced nearly 600 abstract paintings.

It was Wolfgang Suttner, Cultural Events Officer for the Siegen-Wittgenstein district of Westphalia, who was responsible for Paul deciding on holding the exhibition in Siegen and Suttner and Paul selected 73 paintings for exhibition.

Discussing his decision to exhibit in Siegen, Paul said, 'Wolfgang was the first person to approach me seriously. Many people said, "We'd like to give you an exhibition," and I said, "You haven't seen the pictures!" They said, "That's OK" – they were just willing to exhibit the celebrity. Wolfgang was the first person who came up and said, "I'd like to look at your pictures and examine them." So he took a very serious approach, and that's how it wound up here. This is where he lives, Siegen, this is his gallery. I think it's good, because it's my first experience too, to see if I like it. And then if an offer comes for London or New York, I'll maybe do that then.'

Suttner was to say, 'His talent completely overshadows the artistic efforts of other stars who try to paint. Paul gave me his OK to the exhibition, as Siegen was the birthplace of Peter Paul Rubens.'

The exhibition was mainly for Paul to receive some feedback about his work as none of the paintings were for sale. The exhibition also featured a sound/visual installation that was called 'Feedback' which sported six monitor sculptures designed by Paul, which displayed a video of him playing original music on guitar.

The paintings, which were in oils and acrylic, covered landscapes, portraits and abstracts and included several paintings of Linda. There were also paintings of John Lennon, David Bowie and the Queen of England, the latter entitled *A Salute To The Queen*. Other titles included *John's Room*, *Yellow Linda With Piano*, *Egypt Station*, *Sea God* and *Tara's Plastic Skirt*.

The official exhibition guide commented, 'Most of the paintings on show are autonomous pictures with a strong emphasis on material and composition. In his pictures, McCartney – who is an admirer not only of Willem de Kooning, but also of René Magritte – brings together expressive and surreal elements in a synthesis determined by colour processes: the material qualities of the paint and accidental marks on the canvas are taken up and incorporated.'

The 142-page catalogue was more in the style of a paperback book and contained 82 reproductions of the paintings with text in German and a separate English translation. There were introductory pieces by Brian Clarke and Barry Miles, a critique by Christoph Tannert and a lengthy interview with Paul in which he discusses 34 of the paintings.

Paul was to say, 'One thing I have learned is that the more precise you try to be about a thing, the less you achieve. You can go too wooden, you can lose the spirit of the thing.'

Paul had travelled to Siegen a few days before the opening of the exhibition and held a press conference on Friday 30 April 1999 during which he answered questions about his paintings before signing a number of limited edition prints of his work. A reception was held in the gallery that evening with Stella, James and Heather in attendance, along with Paul's brother Mike, Sir George Martin and former Wings member Denny Laine.

Paul McCartney: Rediscovering Yesterday

A BBC Radio 2 programme broadcast on Thursday 18 June 1992.

Brian Matthew narrates it and the hour-long documentary was to celebrate Paul's fiftieth birthday.

Paul McCartney's Musical Ways

A documentary by Telefiction and Zaq Productions written by Gerry Waxler and narrated by Teddy-Lee Dillon. The music was by Carl Abut, a Canadian composer who admired the music of the film *The Family Way*, originally issued in 1966, when he discovered it almost thirty years later. As a result he received permission to re-arrange the variations and themes based on Paul's original score for the film, which starred Hayley Mills.

Polygram released his album of the music called *The Family Way, Variations Concertantes Opus 1* in 1996. The following year a 53-minute documentary was produced called 'Paul McCartney's Musical Ways', which was screened on the Bravo cable channel in Canada and the US. It told the story of Abut's project and included interviews with George Martin, Elvis Costello, Jerry Hadley and Paul.

Paul McCartney's Theme From The Honorary Consul

A single by guitarist John Williams released on Island Records IS 155 on Monday 19 December 1983. This was a version of Paul's instrumental title music for the film *The Honorary Consul*, starring Richard Gere and Michael Caine.

The film was directed by John McKenzie, who had directed Paul's promotional video for 'Take It Away' in June 1982.

In America the film underwent a title change to *Beyond The Limit*.

Paul McCartney's Town Hall Meeting

An event that took place on Saturday 17 May 1997. This was organised by the American music channel VH-I as part of their 'Paul McCartney Week' and was transmitted live simultaneously in Europe and America from Bishopsgate Memorial Hall in east London.

John Fugelsang hosted the event and questions had been gathered from fans during the previous week for Paul to answer and fifty of them were submitted to Paul. The question and answer session included a question from American President Bill Clinton.

Paul had arrived at the hall at 1.30 p.m. and during the afternoon watched coverage of the FA Cup Final. The audience of 100 comprised 50 American contest winners, 25 members of Paul's fan club and 25 friends and family. Paul brought an acoustic guitar and played part of a number called 'Bishopsgate', which he said he'd written backstage.

Immediately following the 60-minute programme, Paul went to the first floor of the hall and conducted a 30-minute 'Netcast'.

Paul McCartney's Working Classical

An album by the London Symphony Orchestra and the Loma Mar Quartet. Produced by John Fraser, it was issued on EMI Classics 7243 5 56897 2 6 on 19 November 1999.

Paul was executive producer of this 14-track album of short classical pieces, which he composed. The engineers were Arne Akselberg, Keith Smith and Eddie Klein. The titles were: 'Junk' (quartet), 'A Leaf' (orchestra), 'Haymakers' (quartet), 'Midwife' (quartet), 'Spiral' (orchestra), 'Warm And Beautiful' (quartet), 'My Love' (quartet), 'Maybe I'm Amazed' (quartet), 'Calico Skies' (quartet), 'Golden Earth Girl' (quartet), 'Someday' (quartet), 'Tuesday' (orchestra), 'She's My Baby' (quartet) and 'The Lovely Linda' (orchestra).

Working Classical, Paul's third major album of classical music, saw its first public performance take place at the Philharmonic Hall in Liverpool on Saturday 26 October 1999. The concert was also recorded then and was screened in America on PBS Television in March 2000. It included three new orchestral works played by the London Symphony Orchestra conducted by Andrea Quinn – 'A Leaf', 'Spiral' and 'Tuesday'. There were also string quartet arrangements of his popular love songs, written with Linda in mind – 'Maybe I'm Amazed', 'Junk' and 'My Love', played by the Loma Mar Quartet. The quartet comprised Krista Bennion Feeney on first violin, Anca Nicolau on second violin, Joanna Hood on viola and Myron Lutzice on cello.

Paul attended the concert and after the rendition of 'The Lovely Linda' he joined the orchestra on stage for a standing ovation.

Paul was to say, '*Working Classical* is a pun because I don't like to get too serious – but I'm also very proud of my working-class roots. A lot of people like to turn their backs, especially when they get a little bit elevated in life – but I am always keen to remind other people and myself of where I'm from.'

At the actual recording session, Paul surprised the quartet by supplying them with two new compositions, which he'd written especially for the occasion – 'Haymakers' and 'Midwife'.

The album was issued only two weeks after the *Run Devil Run* album and, commenting on the contrast between the two, Paul said, 'I enjoy the fact that I can work both ways. I'm Gemini and we are supposed to like this and that; it's slightly schizophrenic. I got involved in orchestra music because I wanted to stretch myself. But I didn't want to lose my roots. I'm always working class, I'm always from Liverpool and my roots are always in rock 'n' roll – but I like the odd cello.'

When *Working Classical* was released in America it topped the Billboard classical charts for nine weeks.

Paul McCartney Special, The

A television special that was originally produced for the BBC, where it was screened several times, and conceived as a promotional special for the album *Press To Play*.

It was Richard Skinner of the BBC who persuaded Paul to agree to some in-depth interviews, which took place at Abbey Road Studio Two. Scattered in between the interviews are promotional clips, videos and concert footage.

The Abbey Road interviews were filmed on Friday 18 July 1986 and the special first aired on BBC 1 on Friday 29 August 1986 and followed on BBC 2 on Saturday 20 December 1986 under the name 'McCartney'.

MPL Communications Inc then issued it as a 60-minute home video on MC 2008 on Friday 6 November 1987 in America and on Friday 27 November 1987 in Britain under the title 'The Paul McCartney Special'. The blurb on the video read: 'Filled with rare music and newsreel clips, this is a personal, in-depth retrospective of one of rock's most influential recording artists. McCartney chronicles his life and times, including his relationship with John Lennon, the Beatles and their break-up, his solo career, Wings, the making of *Press To Play* and everything in between.'

Paul McCartney Story, The (TV special)

Filmed simply as *McCartney* at Abbey Road Studios on Wednesday 16 July 1986, this was a TV special produced as an MPL/BBC co-production. It was essentially made to promote Paul's new album *Press To Play* and included him performing the number 'Press'.

The special was initially screened on BBC 1 on Friday 29 August 1986 and then in an extended version lasting 59 minutes on BBC 2 on Tuesday 30 December 1986.

The clip of Paul performing 'Press' was also included in the TV chat show *Wogan* on Friday 1 August 1986.

The special was eventually released as a home video called 'The Paul McCartney Story' in 1989.

See also 'McCartney' (TV special).

Paul McCartney Week

A week of programming by the American music channel VH-I that began on Monday 12 May 1997. Highlights included the Wednesday 14 May programming which presented a 60-minute 'The Paul McCartney Video Collection' which screened ten of Paul's promotional videos; Friday 16 May which saw the worldwide premiere of the documentary 'Paul McCartney In The World Tonight' and Saturday 17 May which saw the screening of 'Paul McCartney's Town Hall Meeting' and the 1979 'Wings Over The World' MPL documentary, seen for the first time since its original transmission eighteen years previously, together with the concert film *Rockestra*.

Paul The Fearless Signalman

The character Paul played in the Beatles Christmas Show at the Finsbury Park Astoria over Christmas 1963. Originally, Paul was cast as Handsome Paul the Signalman, but asked if the name could be changed in case people considered him big-headed!

Pavarotti, Luciano

The acclaimed Italian tenor. Paul met him on Monday 27 October 1997 at the Alexander Palace during the *Gramophone* Awards.

Pavarotti was being acclaimed for his work on behalf of Bosnian orphans. He asked Paul if he would help him to open a music school in Bosnia. Paul said, 'Luciano is a great singer and talent, and I would be very happy to collaborate.' Pavarotti was to say, 'I just finished making him an offer, and he is just finished telling me he is thinking about it.'

The surrounding press corps thought they had a scoop and pressed

Paul for more comments, but he simply told the Reuters representative, 'We have no plans – you have got no scoop.'

Paul wasn't involved in the project and the school opened in Mostar, Bosnia on 21 December 1997.

Peace In The Neighbourhood
A track penned by Paul, lasting 5 minutes and 5 seconds, which was included on the *Off The Ground* album.

A live version of the number, lasting 4 minutes and 54 seconds, recorded at Boulder, Colorado on 26 May 1993, was included on the *Paul Is Live* album.

Peasmarsh
The village in East Sussex where Paul bought a house after deciding to move his family out of central London. All his children were educated in the local school, which had been founded in 1841. Apart from Lower Gate Farm, Paul has another house in the area and he also bought Hog Hill Mill in nearby Icklesham.

Paul's favourite bar in the area was said to be the Bull in Rye.

Peebles, Andy
A Radio One disc jockey who conducted the final BBC interviews with John Lennon, which were published in book form as *The Lennon Tapes*.

A pre-recorded interview, which Andy had conducted with Paul, was transmitted on Sunday 18 April 1982, when they discussed the new *Tug Of War* album, track-by-track. The interview was also broadcast on the New York station WNEW FM on 2 June.

Penina
A song written by Paul when he was on holiday in Portugal. 'Penina' was the name of the hotel where he was staying.

Singer Carlos Mendes heard Paul singing the number and liked it so much that Paul allowed him to have the song to record.

That version was issued in Portugal on 18 July 1969 on Parlophone QMSP 16459. The flipside was 'Wings Of Revenge'.

The following year a Dutch band Jotte Herre also recorded it and it was issued in Holland on Philips 369 002 PF. At the time, Paul had forgotten to inform Northern Songs about the number and the fact that he'd let someone record it without telling them about it.

Penny Lane
'Penny Lane', along with 'Strawberry Fields Forever', was the first track originally slated for an album about the Beatles' memories of Liverpool and their childhood there. However, EMI were pressing for a release of a single and George Martin decided to issue the two tracks as a double A-side.

It was issued in Britain on 17 February 1967 and received its first radio play on Tuesday 31 January on Radio London. EMI issued the first 250,000 in special colour-picture sleeves.

Although one of the Beatles' strongest singles, it failed to reach No. 1 in Britain, being held at the No. 2 spot by Engelbert Humperdinck's version of 'Release Me'. Humperdinck had been a last-minute replacement on *Sunday Night at the London Palladium*, the TV show with the biggest ratings in Britain at the time, and his rendition of 'Release Me' saw it shoot straight to the top of the charts. George Martin regretted that he had made the single a double A-side, splitting the sales, which could have been another reason why it didn't reach the top of the charts.

Derek Taylor was to comment, 'What a fuss there was in the British music press and in the Schadenfreudian columns of some of the regular press: "Beatles Fail to Reach the Top", "First Time in Four Years", "Has the Bubble Burst?"'

Frieda Kelly, their fan club secretary, said, 'The single was released without the usual A and B-sides because the Beatles wanted you to decide which of the two you like better. An awful lot of John's special fans prefer "Strawberry Fields", but our fan-club mail shows that "Penny Lane" is the overall winner by a short head – and we've got to admit that "Penny Lane" is one of the most catchy songs the Beatles have ever done.'

In America it was issued on 13 February 1967 where it topped the charts and remained in the Top 40 for nine weeks.

Paul composed the number on the piano at his Cavendish Avenue house, jotting down notes of what he remembered of the street – the ladies who stood and sold flags for charities, the barber shop Bioletti's, the Penny Lane cake shop, the Liverpool Victoria Insurance Company office, Winter's fashion store, Woolworths, the fire station, the bus terminus at a big dilapidated roundabout. Paul remembered the barber's shop with hairstyle photos. Of his lyrics he said: 'It's part fact, part nostalgia for a great place, blue suburban skies as we remember it.'

It has been suggested that the song might have been inspired by the Dylan Thomas poem 'Fern Hill', which Paul had been reading at the time, which concerned nostalgic reminiscences of childhood.

Paul said, 'Penny Lane is a bus roundabout in Liverpool and there is a barber's shop showing photographs of every head he's had the pleasure to know. Well, no, that's not true, they're just photographs of hairstyles, but all the people who come and go, stop and say hello. There is a bank on the corner, so we made up the part about the banker in his motorcar. We put in a joke or two, "Fish and finger pie". The women would never dare say that, except to themselves. Most people wouldn't hear it, but "finger pie" is just a nice joke for the Liverpool lads who like a bit of smut.' Another line was a phallic inference – the reference to the fireman who 'keeps his engine clean'.

John came over and helped him with the third verse.

Paul also had the idea of using a 'fantastic high trumpet' that he'd heard at a concert of Bach's *Brandenberg Concerto* on BBC 2's *Masterworks* on Wednesday 11 January. He said, 'I got the idea of using trumpets in that pizzicato way on "Penny Lane" from seeing a programme on television. I didn't know whether it would work, so I got the arranger for the session into the studio, played the tune on the piano and sang how I wanted the brass to sound. That's the way I always work with arrangers.'

The person who played the piccolo trumpet was David Mason of the London Symphony Orchestra.

A live version of the number, lasting 3 minutes and 3 seconds, recorded on 26 May 1993 at Boulder, Colorado, was included on the *Paul Is Live* album.

Perkins, Carl

One of the original American rock-'n'-roll legends. Carl was born on 9 April 1932 in Lake City, Tennessee. He signed with the legendary Sun Records, and wrote and recorded the classic rocker 'Blue Suede Shoes' and a number of other rock-'n'-roll standards.

A serious car accident in 1956, in which his brother and manager were killed, left him hospitalised for a year. His career suffered a number of setbacks and he compounded his problems by drinking too much. He rose from the doldrums when Chuck Berry invited him to tour with him in Britain in 1964 when he met the Beatles for the first time. He met and chatted with Paul at a party in London and his career, personal life and finances were boosted when the Beatles recorded three of his numbers: 'Matchbox', 'Honey Don't' and 'Everybody's Trying To Be My Baby'. With the royalties he was able to buy his parents a farm.

Over the years he kept in touch with Paul, visiting him whenever he was in England. One year, on 9 April , Carl's birthday, he arrived in his hotel room to discover a large box with a blue ribbon around it. When he opened it he found a cake in the shape of a guitar and the message 'Happy Birthday! We love you, Paul, Linda and kids.'

In 1981 he received a phone call from Paul, who asked him what he was doing. Carl said, 'Nothing much' and Paul said he was going to make an album called *Tug Of War* in Montserrat with Stevie Wonder and Ringo and would Carl like to join them as he had a song he'd like Carl to do.

Carl had no idea where Montserrat was, but Paul said he'd fix up everything with his travel agent. Carl received tickets, took a plane to Nashville, then flew to Antigua. There was a private plane there and the pilot said, 'Are you Carl Perkins? I come for you. Paul McCartney sent me for you.' They then flew to Montserrat where Paul and Linda were waiting on the airstrip for him.

Carl had been so delighted with the invitation that the night before he left the island he sat down and composed a number 'My Old Friend', in tribute to Paul.

Paul had composed the number 'Get It' for the two of them to record, but said to him, 'To be truthful, we don't have to do this one if you don't want to. I have others.'

Carl liked the number and they went ahead and recorded it. During the sessions they had a jam in which they played a number of Perkins's classics, including 'Honey Don't', 'Boppin' The Blues' and 'Lend Me Your Comb'.

Paul recorded all the jam sessions, in addition to studio conversations for his personal collection.

Carl played the number 'My Old Friend' on the day he was to leave Montserrat. Paul was moved and said, 'I love it.' He called Linda in to listen to it and she loved it too. He then asked Carl if he had to leave that day and persuaded him to stay and record the number. Carl said they recorded it and 'he (Paul) played bass, organ, rhythm guitar and drums on it. I played a couple of guitar parts and we both sang on the song.'

A few weeks later Carl received a call from Paul who asked him if he'd mind if he did the treatment on the record, saying, 'I hear violins and horns, and I'd really like to make it a big record.'

Carl told him, 'I don't mind if you put the Queen in there.'

Perkins was to say that the number meant more to him than any other song he'd written, including 'Blue Suede Shoes'. On the track Paul added backing vocals and played organ, rhythm guitar, drums and bass, but didn't use it on *Tug Of War*.

'Get It' was featured on the album and was also issued as the flipside of the 'Tug Of War' single. Carl also included the number, with Paul's vocals, on his own album *Go Cat Go*, released in America on the Dinosaur label in 1996.

Sadly, Perkins died on 19 January 1998.

Perry, Lee 'Scratch'

A famous Jamaican record producer who had a four-track studio, which he called Black Ark Studios, in the backyard of his home in Kingston, Jamaica. On Monday 20 June 1977 Paul hired Perry to produce three numbers with Linda, which he'd intended to include on a solo album of hers.

The numbers were 'Sugartime', 'Mr Sandman' and 'Dear Hearts And Gentle People'.

PETA

An acronym for 'People for The Ethical Treatment of Animals', one of several charities which Paul has supported.

PETA and PAWS (Performers for Animal Welfare) received the

proceeds from the sale of the 13-track album *Animal Magnetism*, issued in 1995. It featured the song 'White Coated Man', penned by Linda McCartney and Carla Lane on which Linda sang lead vocal. Other artists included the Pretenders, Pat Travis, Linda Rondstadt, Edgar Winter and Steve Walsh.

At the end of 1996 Paul and Linda were presented with an award from PETA at a ceremony in Los Angeles. Linda's acceptance speech was her first public appearance since she received treatment for cancer.

In 1997 Paul took part in another PETA publicity campaign. An advertisement appeared in *New Yorker* magazine for 'Paul's furs', which seemed to offer furs for sale with a message reading: 'Before you buy, let us show you our lively collection of fox, mink and raccoon. You'll be astonished and could save thousands.'

There was a phone number and when people called Paul's voice would answer saying, 'Hello. You've reached Paul's furs. Please leave your name and address for your free video to arrive.'

The video had a 'Paul's Furs' label on it, but when it was played it showed graphic scenes of animals in traps and being killed on fur farms.

It naturally caused some controversy and PETA issued a statement by Paul in which he said, 'Prospective customers will see who pays the ultimate price for fur: the animals.'

Following Linda's death, Paul vowed to continue carrying on her crusade for animals' rights. He gave an interview to the PETA magazine *Animal Rights* in 1998. Paul commented, 'Animal rights is too good an idea for the next century to be suppressed. It's time we get nice. I want people to be reassured that we're going to keep this torch burning.

'Over the years, because I had the luxury of Linda taking the front role on animal issues, some people would occasionally make out that I wasn't really committed and that I was a secret meat-eater in the background. Just to prove that's not the case, I thought, rather than do some general interviews about how much I miss her, which the newspapers would like, I should do it with the PETA magazine because that's where it's at.'

The PETA Awards is an annual gala and awards ceremony held by PETA. A special PETA tribute to Linda McCartney took place on Saturday 18 September 1999 at Paramount Studios in Hollywood; it was called the PETA Millennium Gala.

In the New York Street area of the studio there was a reception for donors who had paid $350, with live music from the Royal Crown Revue. There was a second reception near the Bronson Gate where 800 donors had paid approximately $1,250.

Two thousand people attended the gala, each paying a minimum of $350 and the event raised $1million.

The B-52s and Chrissie Hynde performed and then Paul took to the stage at 12.30 a.m., backed by Dave Gilmour and Mick Green on guitar, Pete Wingfield on keyboards and Ian Paice on drums. Paul then performed six numbers from his *Run Devil Run* album: 'Honey Hush', 'Brown Eyed Handsome Man', 'No Other Baby', 'Try Not To Cry', 'Lonesome Town' and 'Run Devil Run'.

There was a video of the event 'Paul McCartney & Friends: PETA's Millennium Concert' which included acts such as the B-52s, Sarah McLachlan and Chrissie Hynde. Paul performed his set with his *Run Devil Run* backing band. After a false start with 'Brown Eyed Handsome Man', he said, 'We're gonna start that again 'cause that wasn't awfully good. A little discrepancy there. And we're not having that, are we lads? We're not coming all the bloody way from England and having discrepancies!'

There was also a VH1 special of the concert that only featured three of the numbers performed by Paul – 'Honey Hush', 'Brown Eyed Handsome Man' and 'Run Devil Run'.

The main event was the first annual Linda McCartney Memorial Award, which Sir Paul presented to actress Pamela Anderson Lee for her animal rights work.

Sarah McLachlan performed 'Angel', which was accompanied by a film of Linda. Paul then made a speech.

Paul's daughter Stella was present and she was also honoured for her anti-fur work.

At the PETA Gala at the Waldorf-Astoria, New York on 8 September 2001, hosted by Pamela Anderson, Paul accepted a humanitarian award and also presented the Linda McCartney Memorial Award to Chrissie Hynde.

Some controversy was caused in 2001 when Paul backed a PETA campaign to prevent children drinking milk because PETA was opposed to dairy farming.

Pets

Both Paul and Linda loved animals and had numerous pets. In 1968, when she and Paul first became close in London, Linda bought her Old English sheepdog, Martha. Paul bought his father a racehorse, Drake's Drum, in 1964. Paul had a horse called Honour and Linda had an Irish thoroughbred mare called Cinnamon and an Appaloosa stallion called Lucky Spot. Other Appaloosas they were to own included Malice Pina and Mr Tibbs and Paul's horse Blankit. The children had ponies. Heather's was called Coconut, Mary's Cookie and Stella's Sugarfoot. They had a Dalmatian called Lucky and a Labrador called Jet. They also had another Dalmatian called Captain Midnight, a Yellow Labrador called Poppy and a collie called Murdoch. James also had a sheepdog called Arrow. Their cats included Jo and Scotty.

They also included their farmyard animals as pets, particularly since Dragonfly was the lamb that inspired them to turn vegetarian in 1970.

They had two cows called Lavender and Vanessa, two of the many animals they have saved from slaughter.

A number of the pets have inspired songs – Martha, Jet and Arrow.

Piano Tape, The
A 61-minute tape that Paul recorded at one sitting on Sunday 14 July 1974. He played a selection of songs on a piano, a number of which have never been released. The tape eventually emerged on a bootleg album called *The Piano Tape*. During the hour session, Paul ran through 26 numbers.

They were: 'Million Miles'; 'Mull Of Kintyre'; 'I'll Give You A Ring'; 'Baby You Know It's True'; 'Women Kind'; 'Getting Closer'; 'In My Dreams'; 'Rockestra Theme'; 'Now That She Is Mine (Letting Go)'; 'Call Me Back Again'; 'Lunch Box/Odd Sox'; 'Treat Her Gently/Lonely Old People'; 'You Gave Me The Answer'; 'Waiting For The Sun To Shine'; 'She Got It Good'; 'Blackpool'; 'Sunshine In Your Hair'; 'Girlfriend'; 'I Lost My Little Girl'; 'Upon A Hill'; 'Sea'; 'Love Is Your Road'; 'Sweet Little Bird'; 'Partners In Crime'; 'Suicide'; and 'Dr Pepper'.

Piazza San Marco
The famous Venetian square where Wings appeared before 30,000 people on 25 September 1976.

The occasion was a UNESCO-organised series of major events to raise funds for the Venice restoration.

Paul agreed to add the date to Wings' schedule and generously also offered to pay for the equipment and transport costs himself. UNESCO (United Nations Educational, Scientific and Cultural Organisation) provided the hotel accommodation and organised the actual evening, erecting the scaffolding for the stage and preparing the seating. There was some irony in the event; the press pointed out that Wings did more to destroy the city than to restore it due to the fact that the heavy lorries containing their equipment cracked some paving stones in the ancient square.

Paul commented, 'I can't think of a more beautiful place to stage a concert.'

Seating had been arranged for 15,000 people, with some tickets costing £10. However, thousands more poured into the square, effectively doubling that number. Approximately £54,000 was raised by the concert, which, after all expenses had been deducted, brought the fund a handsome donation of £25,000.

At the climax of the evening, seven lasers were used to provide a spectacular visual display as they alighted on the walls of the cathedral at the far end of the square in the shape of a butterfly.

Picasso's Last Words
A track from the *Band On The Run* album lasting 5 minutes and 50 seconds. Paul was on holiday near Montego Bay, Jamaica in 1973 and

he and Linda joined actor Dustin Hoffman and his wife for dinner. Hoffman was in Jamaica filming *Papillon*. He was intrigued by the songwriting process and asked Paul if he could write about any subject. Paul said he could, so Hoffman showed him a copy of *Time* magazine dated 23 April 1973, which featured an article, 'Pablo Picasso's Last Days And Final Journey'. Paul was intrigued by Picasso's last words which were, 'Drink to me, drink to my health ... you know I can't drink anymore.' Paul then wrote the song in front of Hoffman who was to comment, 'It's right under childbirth in terms of great events in my life.'

Pilchard

The name of a play that Paul and John attempted to write in their early days of collaboration.

Paul later described it as 'a sort of precursor of *The Life Of Brian*, about a working-class weirdo who was always upstairs praying. It was a down-market Second Coming. But we had to give it up because we couldn't actually work out how it went on, how you actually filled up all the pages.'

In 1963 John said, 'I had a bash at writing a serious play with Paul. It was about Jesus coming back to earth today, and living in the slums. We called the character Pilchard. It all fell through in the end, but we aim to do at least one big play or musical together. That's our ambition – a West End production with our own words and music.'

Pipes Of Peace (album)

Paul's follow up to *Tug Of War*. He was originally going to call the album *Tug Of War II*. In a Radio One interview with Simon Bates on 16 June 1983 he said, 'It's a sequel to *Tug Of War* and I was going to call it *Tug Of War II* but I thought the Rocky thing of *Rocky I*, *Rocky II* and *Rocky III* was really boring, so I've called it *Pipes Of Peace*.'

Some tracks for *Tug Of War* were never included on the album and Paul thought, 'What would be the opposite of a tug of war? Peace pipes, pipes of peace and stuff.'

In fact he composed a number called 'Tug Of Peace' for the album, and his feelings for the concept of an album about love and peace are evident in the quote by Indian poet Rabindranath Tagore, which he placed on the sleeve: 'In love all of life's contradictions dissolve and disappear.'

Paul continued his collaboration with George Martin to produce this eleven-track album that was originally released simultaneously in Britain and America on Monday 31 October 1983. The British release was on Parlophone PCTC 1652301.

Tracks were: 'Pipes Of Peace', 'Say Say Say', 'The Other Me', 'Keep Under Cover', 'So Bad', 'The Man', 'Sweetest Little Sorrow', 'Average Person', 'Hey Hey', 'Tug Of Peace', 'Through Our Love'.

There was no detailed listing on the album of the musicians who participated, but Paul was the principal artist and Michael Jackson duetted with him on 'Say Say Say'. Ringo Starr was also a guest drummer and Linda provided backing vocals and keyboards.

An array of other musicians was featured on different tracks. They included: Steve Gadd, drums; Denny Laine, vocals, guitar, keyboards; Dave Mattacks, drums; Eric Stewart, vocals, guitar; Hugh Burns, guitar; Stanley Clarke, bass; Gary Herbig, horn; Jerry Hey, horn; James Kippern, tabla; Chris Hammersmith, harmonica; Ernie Watts, sax; Nathan Lamar Watts, bass; Geoff Whitehorn, guitar; David Williams, guitar; Gavyn Wright, violin. George Martin produced the album and Geoff Emerick was the engineer.

The album received a critical mauling from the British music press. The *New Musical Express* commented: 'A dull, tired and empty collection of quasi funk and gooey rock arrangements ... with McCartney cooing platitudinous sentiments on a set of lyrics seemingly made up on the spur of the moment.

Melody Maker commented that it was 'slushy', 'watery-weak', 'congratulatory self-righteous' and 'wince-inducing.'

The album reached No. 4 in the British charts and No. 16 in the American.

The title track provided Paul with a No. 1 Christmas hit and a stunning video.

On Wednesday 29 February 1984 it became the first Beatle-related CD to be issued by EMI on CDP 7460182. It was issued on CD in America on the same day.

A remastered CD version was issued on 9 August 1999 on Parlophone CD 7 891372, with three bonus tracks: 'Twice In A Lifetime', 'We All Stand Together' and 'Simple As That'.

Pipes Of Peace (promotional film)

The promotional film received the award for 'Best Video' in the 1983 British Rock and Pop Awards broadcast live on BBC Television on Tuesday 21 February 1984. Paul was on holiday at the time of the awards, but recorded a video message that was screened at the event. Keith MacMillan, who had directed the promotional film, collected the award on his behalf.

Pipes Of Peace (single)

The single credited simply to Paul McCartney was issued in Britain on Parlophone R6064 on Monday 5 December 1983 where it reached the top of the charts.

'So Bad' was on the flip.

It was also released in Germany on Odeon 1C0061655287.

When it was released in America on Columbia 39149 on Monday 5 December 1983 the A and B-sides were reversed.

The American version was also the one issued in France on Pathe Marconi/EMI 1655287.

Playhouse Theatre

A BBC theatre situated in Northumberland Avenue, London. Paul began four days of rehearsals with his Paul McCartney Band at this venue on Monday 24 July 1989. On Wednesday 26 and Thursday 27 July he performed concerts for an invited audience who included 400 members of the Wings Fun Club, in addition to staff members from MPL and EMI Records. The shows began at 5 p.m. Their repertoire for both shows was the same: 'Figure Of Eight', 'Jet', 'Rough Ride', 'Got To Get You Into My Life', 'Band On The Run', 'We Got Married', 'Put It There', 'Hello Goodbye', 'Things We Said Today', 'Can't Buy Me Love', 'Summertime', 'I Saw Her Standing There', 'This One', 'My Brave Face', 'Twenty Flight Rock', 'The Long And Winding Road', 'Ain't That A Shame', 'Let It Be' and 'Coming Up'.

At a press conference at this venue, which took place between 1 p.m. and 3 p.m. on 27 July 1989, Paul announced the line-up of his Paul McCartney Band and the dates for his European and British tour. Paul and his band also performed 'Midnight Special', 'Twenty Flight Rock' and 'This One'.

A filmed excerpt from their performance of 'This One' was included on *Entertainment Tonight* on 31 July.

Poetry

Paul first began to write poetry whilst at Liverpool Institute. One of his first efforts was called 'The Worm Chain Drags Slowly'. He was to comment, 'When I was a teenager, for some reason I had an over-whelming desire to have a poem published in the school magazine. I wrote something deep and meaningful – which was promptly rejected – and I suppose I have been trying to get my own back ever since.'

The person who was a great influence on his reading habits then was his English tutor at Liverpool Institute, Alan Durband.

Paul was to say, 'I did A-level English at the Inny, which is my scholastic claim to fame, and we had Alan "Dusty" Durband, a lovely man, who showed us the dirty bits of Chaucer, you know, the Miller's Tale, and the Nun's Tale, which were dirtier than anything we were telling each other. He had studied under FR Leavis at Oxford, and he brought a rich pool of information to us guys, and when we would listen, which was occasionally, it was great. He introduced us to Louis MacNeice and Auden, both of whom I liked. It was a great period of my life and I enjoyed it.'

He decided to write poetry again when he heard of the death of his childhood friend Ivan Vaughan and said, 'After having written so many song lyrics with and without John Lennon, I wrote a poem on hearing of the death of my dear friend Ivan Vaughan,' and added, 'It seemed to me that a poem, rather than a song, could perhaps best express what I was feeling.'

The result was the poem 'Ivan', which inspired Paul to take up writing poetry again.

After the publication of his poetry in *Blackbird Singing* edited by Adrian Mitchell, Paul began a series of poetry readings, insisting that the first one be in Liverpool because it was the city that put the poetry in him.

Commenting on Paul's ability as a poet, Mitchell described him as a popular poet rather than an academic one. He observed, 'A few song-writers, although they know you can get away with banal nothingness in pop lyrics, have a vision and try to convey it to us. A few manage to write truthfully about the world – as Paul does in 'Penny Lane', 'She Came In Through The Bathroom Window' and 'Eleanor Rigby'. Paul takes risks, again and again, in all his work. He's not afraid to take on the art of poetry – which is the art of dancing naked. Paul knows the value of words, how they can help us to enjoy living and loving. He also knows how words can work during the deepest grief – not just as therapy, but as a way of speaking to and for others who have lost their loved ones.'

In 2001 Paul said that the favourite poem he had written was 'Her Spirit'.

Poetry Olympics Marathon, The

An event which took place during 'National Poetry Day' on Thursday 4 October 2001 at the Queen's Theatre, Shaftesbury Avenue, London, with Paul topping the bill.

This was Paul's first poetry recital in London and he read poems and lyrics from his book *Blackbird Singing*. In addition, he read a previously unheard poem called 'Sweet Little Girl Next Door'.

Other poets on the bill included Patience Agbabi, Tom Pickard, Fran Landesman, Inge Elsa Laird, Lemn Sissay, Frieda Hughes, Adrian Mitchell and Michael Horovitz.

Portugal

Bruce Welch of the Shadows had bought a holiday home in Albufeira in southern Portugal and in 1963 told Paul that he was free to use the villa at any time. Paul forgot about it but was reminded once again when he bumped into Welch in 1965. Welch said he was going to his home in Portugal for a break and once again offered Paul its use at any time.

When Paul and Jane Asher met up with Welch again at the Pickwick Club in London and the offer was repeated Paul, who had been through a hectic schedule of work, arranged to visit Portugal for the first time and Paul and Jane flew out on 27 May 1965. They took a one-and-a-half-hour flight to Lisbon (Faro airport had not opened at the time) and had a five-hour journey by road. During the car journey the words to 'Yesterday' began to flow. He'd had the tune in his mind almost for years and now the words just seemed to pop into his head. As soon as they arrived at the Welch villa Paul immediately asked him if he had a guitar. Welch said, 'I could see he had been writing lyrics on the way down; he had the paper in his hand as he arrived.'

Welch handed him a 1959 Martin model 0018, which Paul had to play upside down due to being left-handed. He began to sing the song immediately and asked Welch, 'What do you think of this?'

Bruce and his wife had packed and were ready to leave, and as they left for London, Paul and Jane settled down to their holiday, during which Paul completed his classic, 'Yesterday'.

In December 1968 Paul, Linda and Heather arrived unexpectedly at Hunter Davies's holiday home in the Algarve, in the region of southern Portugal. It was literally the middle of the night. Beatles official biographer Hunter woke up to hear someone shouting his name very loudly and demanding to be let in.

Earlier that evening, back in London, Paul had decided impulsively that he wanted to take up Hunter's open invitation to visit him, and so chartered a jet to fly him, his new girlfriend and her daughter out to Faro, the nearest airport. They stayed about ten days with the Davies's, who, as Hunter recalls, were a little bemused as when they had left England earlier that year (Hunter was on a year's sabbatical after completing *The Beatles* book) Paul had been engaged to Jane Asher.

Post House Hotel, Bristol

A hotel situated just outside Bristol where Paul held a press conference on Thursday 11 September 1975 following Wings' appearance at the Hippodrome, Bristol the previous evening. Here is an excerpt of the question and answer session:

Question; Just what keeps you going?
  Paul: Drugs! No, I just like the music.
  Question: Have you seen the Beatles lately?
  Paul: We run into each other and stuff. We're just good friends.
  Question: Is Wings really a logical development from the Beatles?
  Paul: Well, I've always written songs, but with the Beatles we only ever rehearsed for three days at the most. With this band we rehearse a lot.
  Question: Are you looking forward to playing in Cardiff?
  Paul: Of course.
  Question: Why did you decide to go back on the road?
  Paul: Well, either we sit at home and do it, or we play in front of people. Now it's a pleasure to do it and we want to keep on working.
  Question: Will Wings ever become as big as the Beatles?

Paul: I think it could be, funnily enough. The whole thing is bigger now. We're having a great time – we like to play music and people like to come and hear it.

Question: How different is Wings from the Beatles?

Paul: They scream at our concerts, but they don't scream as much. People used to come and scream and didn't hear any of the music. Now they can.

Question: Do you want to bring back the Beatles?

Paul: It wasn't within my power to bring back the Beatles. It was a four-way split and we all wanted to do different things. We're all very good friends. John is keeping very quiet at the moment, while fortunately I'm out working . . . I like it.

Powell, Aubrey

Cambridge-born Powell was originally asked to design an album cover by Pink Floyd. He teamed up with Storm Thorgerson in a company they named Hipgnosis and they became influential and innovative designers of album sleeves for a range of artists including Paul McCartney and Led Zeppelin.

Since 1985 he decided to cease designing sleeves and set up a film company with Storm and he continues to specialise in directing, writing, and producing documentaries, commercials and music-related films.

He directed 'Paul McCartney – Movin' On' also 'Live In The New World' and 'Going Home' (aka 'From Rio To Liverpool'), the latter winning a cable equivalent of an Emmy award.

Powell, Colin

The American Secretary of State in 2001 when Paul and Heather Mills met up with him on 19 April of that year.

The couple wished to discuss their campaign against land mines with him.

They commented, 'We had a really good meeting and Secretary of State Colin Powell was very helpful. We basically explained to him our point of view, a lot of which he agreed with. He was very supportive about this whole thing and there are reasons to be very hopeful for the future.'

Powell pointed out to Paul and Heather that the United States had contributed $500 million to the mine clearing programmes – including Heather's own 'Adopt A Landmine' programme.

Following their meeting with Powell, they held a press conference, which was broadcast on the CNN programme *Inside Politics* in which Paul discussed the crusade to ban landmines which Heather and himself were involved in.

Power Cut

A number that Paul wrote during the miners' strike in Britain in 1972 when there were widespread power cuts. It was the final number of a four-number 11-minute 15-second medley that closed the *Red Rose Speedway* album and was 3 minutes and 50 seconds in length. Paul sang lead vocal and played piano, celeste and Mellotron. Linda played electric piano, Denny Laine electric guitar and vocal, Henry McCullough electric guitar and vocal and Denny Seiwell drums.

Power of Music, The

A 40-minute BBC documentary broadcast on BBC 1 on Wednesday 26 October 1988. The documentary was about the benefits of music therapy and Paul appeared with Dr Clive Robbins at the Nordoff-Robbins Music Therapy centre in Camden, London.

Earlier that year, Paul had received a Silver Clef award from Nordoff-Robbins for the help he had given to the organisation over the years and he was also to perform for their benefit at Knebworth in 1990.

During the documentary Paul performed four numbers, three of them on acoustic guitar. The three were 'You Are My Sunshine', 'Acoustic Guitar Improvisation' and 'Martin Can Sing, Peter Can Play'. The electric guitar number was 'Give Me Your Love'.

The documentary was repeated on BBC 2 on 12 April 1993.

Power, Jonathan

A former Liverpool Institute school friend of Paul's. When they first met, Paul befriended him, buying him an ice-lolly and offering him a cigarette. Later in life Powell became involved in Amnesty International and wrote a book *Like Water On Stone – The Story Of Amnesty International*, which Paul helped to promote at a ceremony at LIPA in Liverpool on Friday 20 July 2001.

Following the graduation ceremony for 200 students, Paul spoke about Amnesty International and Power followed him, saying, 'Between us we have had forty years of righting wrongs and forty years of writing songs. Today I think the world is a better place.'

Power Station Studios

New York recording studios where Paul began recording several songs, produced by Phil Ramone, from Monday 25 August until Friday 29 August 1986. At the sessions he was backed by Billy Joel's group who comprised Liberty Devitto, drums; Russell Javors, rhythm guitar; Doug Stegmeyer, bass; Mark Rivera, percussion and wind instruments; and David Brown, lead guitar.

Ramone continued the sessions in October of that year at Paul's home studios in Sussex.

Praying Mantis Heart

A demo which Paul recorded in his Rude Studio in Scotland in 1978. An excerpt from the number was heard on Part 13 of the *Oobu Joobu* radio series.

Presley, Elvis

The most famous solo singer in popular music history, born Elvis Aaron Presley on 8 January 1935 in Tupelo, Mississippi. He died on 16 August 1977.

When Brian Epstein once said that the Beatles would become bigger than Elvis, everyone laughed at him. Eventually, the Beatles achieved more No. 1 chart hits than Elvis did, although a posthumous re-recording of Elvis's topped the charts in 2002.

In 1967 Paul told Beatles biographer Hunter Davies, 'Every time I felt low I just put on an Elvis record and I'd feel great, beautiful. I'd no idea how records were made and it was just magic. "All Shook Up!" Oh, it was beautiful!'

In an interview in *Melody Maker* on Saturday 14 September 1968, Paul said, 'I'd love to produce an album for Elvis. His albums haven't been produced very well and as I am a fan of his I think I'd be able to produce him well.'

Asked why the Beatles didn't include Elvis on the cover of their *Sgt Pepper* album, Paul told their press agent Tony Barrow, 'Elvis was too important and too far above the rest even to mention. I think we all assumed everyone felt that way, so we didn't put him on the list because he was more than merely a fave rave fab gear pop singer, he was Elvis the King.'

The Beatles actually met with Elvis on Friday 27 February 1965 at his Hollywood home in 565 Perugia Way, Bel Air, Beverly Hills.

Recalling the historic moment, Paul said, 'He met us at the door. The thing that always sticks in my mind is that he had the first remote control switcher for a telly I had ever seen. He was switching channels, and we were, like, "Wow! How are you doing that?"'

Commenting on Elvis, he said, 'I really liked him. He didn't talk much, and he looked great. He was a really cool, casual guy. He was also playing bass, so that was great for me. "You're trying to learn bass are you son? Hey, I play bass too. Sit down, let me show you a few things." I couldn't give him any hints, but I could, at least, talk knowledgably about it. I felt a bond with him, like, "Hey, I play bass too".'

During the recording of the *London Town* album, Paul wrote a number that he specifically intended for Elvis Presley, 'Name And Address', although Elvis died before Paul could send him a demo of the song.

Press

A track from the *Press To Play* album lasting 4 minutes and 43 seconds. It was released as a single simultaneously in Britain and America on Monday 14 July 1986. The UK release was on Parlophone R 6133. There was also a 12″ disc in a picture sleeve on Parlophone 12R 6133, containing an alternative mix to the track by Julian Mendelssohn and American producer Burt Bevans. The American release was on Capitol B-5597.

The flipside was 'It's Not True'.

The record reached No. 22 in the British charts and No. 21 in the American.

The British single was replaced on Saturday 20 July 1986 by another mix of the number labelled 'video edit'.

It was also released in Germany on Parlophone 1C006 2013417.

Press To Play

An album co-produced by Paul and Hugh Padgham, with a special contribution from Eric Stewart. There was a cover photograph of Paul and Linda taken by famous Hollywood photographer George Hurrell.

The album was released in Britain on Monday 1 September 1986 on Parlophone PCSD 103 and cassette TC-PCSD 103. It was released in America on Capitol on Friday 23 August 1983. The album reached No. 8 in the British charts and No. 30 in the American.

A mid-price CD version was issued in Britain on Monday 4 January 1988.

The tracks were: Side One: 'Stranglehold' (penned by Paul and Eric Stewart), 'Good Times Coming'/'Feel The Sun' (penned by Paul), 'Talk More Talk' (penned by Paul), 'Footprint' (penned by Paul and Stewart) and 'Only Love Remains' (penned by Paul). Side Two: 'Press' (penned by Paul), 'Pretty Little Head' (penned by Paul and Stewart), 'Move Over Busker' (penned by Paul and Stewart), 'Angry' (penned by Paul and Stewart) and 'However Absurd' (penned by Paul and Stewart).

Apart from Paul, Linda and Stewart other musicians on the album included Jerry Marotta, Carlos Alomar, Eddie Rayner, Phil Collins, Pete Townshend, Nick Glenni-Smith, Dick Morrissey, Ray Cooper, Simon Chamberlain, Graham Ward, Lennie Pickett, Gary Barnacle, Gavin Wright and John Bradbury.

Voices providing vocal harmony on the various tracks included Linda and James McCartney, Kate Robbins, Eddie Klein, John Hammel, Matt How, Steve Jackson and Ruby James.

Pretty Little Head (remix)

A number, 5 minutes and 13 seconds in length, composed by Paul in collaboration with Eric Stewart and initially included on the *Press To Play* album. Paul described the song as 'a bit like abstract art', mentioning that it originally began as an instrumental number and then he added some exotic lyrics to it.

It was released as a single in several formats.

The initial single was issued in Britain on Parlophone R6145 on Monday 27 October 1986 with 'Write Away' on the flipside and reached No. 76 in the charts. Paul McCartney and Hugh Padgham produced the disc. There were also maxi singles containing three tracks in the 7" and 12" format.

A 12" version was issued on the same day with a longer remix of the

A-side by John Potoker. It had the same B-side as the single, together with a bonus track, 'Angry', a remix by Larry Alexander that was three seconds longer than the album version.

All three numbers were co-written by Paul and Stewart.

The record failed to chart and three weeks later Paul issued his first ever cassette single, which contained the same tracks as the 12″ version. There was a picture sleeve with a photograph taken by Linda McCartney.

The musicians on 'Pretty Little Head' were Paul on guitars, bass, keyboards and vocal, Eric Stewart on guitars and vocals, Jerry Marolta on vibraphone and drum programming and Carlos Alomar on guitar.

There was a longer remix of 'Pretty Little Head' on the 7″ release which was done by John 'Tokes' Potokey, with the B-side a remix of 'Angry', the same version issued as the flipside in America on 'Stranglehold' on Wednesday 29 October 1986.

The single was released in Germany on Parlophone 1C006-2015217.

There was also a limited edition of 2,000 copies of a cassette single issued in Britain on Parlophone TCR 6145.

Pride Of Britain British Achievers Awards

A ceremony organised by the *Daily Mirror* newspaper and Virgin to acknowledge outstanding achievements. The 1999 ceremony took place at the Dorchester Hotel, London and Paul presented the Linda McCartney Award For Animal Welfare to Juliet Gellatley, founder and director of Viva, a vegetarian charity, who Paul had personally chosen as recipient of the award.

Paul said, 'It has been a very emotional occasion. I never expected it to be like this. What a day this has been. It has been such an inspiration. The point about these awards is that you don't usually see this side of people. You normally see the other side. I have been choked up. This shows how many good people there are in the world. Linda would have been well chuffed with the award created in her name. I have been crying all year and now I come here. I just want to thank *Mirror* readers for creating this category and dedicating it to my lovely Linda. I know she would be proud.'

On presenting the award to Gellatley, he said, 'I chose Juliet because she deserves more publicity for her work. The point is that a few years ago Juliet would not have been at an awards ceremony like this, but vegetarianism is now the way of the future.'

It was at this event that Paul was to meet his future wife, Heather Mills.

Prime Time

A New Zealand television show. On the afternoon of 25 March 1993, the day after Wings had arrived in New Zealand for their concert at Western Springs Stadium, Linda was interviewed for the show. She discussed her 24-year marriage to Paul, the confidence she now felt as a member of Wings and gave the interviewer a copy of her vegetarian cookbook to pass on to the Prime Minister of New Zealand.

Prince, Tony

A disc jockey who recorded a special interview with Linda McCartney at Elstree Studios in March 1976. This was broadcast by Radio Luxembourg on *The Royal Rock Show* (because Tony was known as the 'Royal Ruler') on Saturday 20 March from 11 p.m. until midnight.

Prince's Trust 10th Birthday Charity Gala

Event held at Wembley Arena, London on Friday 20 June 1986, providing Paul with his first indoor concert appearance for six and a half years.

Elton John introduced Paul as 'someone who's inspired us all'. Paul then performed 'I Saw Her Standing There' and 'Long Tall Sally' and then introduced Mick Jagger and David Bowie, who performed 'Dancing In The Street'. Paul then returned to perform the finale, 'Get Back', where he was joined by most of the other artists from the show, including Elton John, Eric Clapton, Midge Ure, Mark Knopfler, Ray Cooper, Howard Jones, Bryan Adams, Mark King, John Illsley, Tina Turner and Paul Young.

The concert was filmed and presented as a 90-minute special on BBC 2 on Saturday 28 June 1986 and Wednesday 31 December 1986. There was also a two-hour Radio One stereo broadcast on Sunday 6 July. *The Old Grey Whistle Test* was to show the 'Get Back' sequence on Tuesday 24 June and Friday 27 June 1986. Excerpts were also shown in America on *Entertainment Tonight* on Wednesday 23 July 1986. A home video of the show was also released in Britain and America.

The capacity 8,000 audience had bought their tickets before Paul's appearance had been announced – as this was the tenth anniversary of the Prince's Trust. The concert is a regular charity event to raise money for young people and was attended by Prince Charles and Princess Diana.

Private Property

A song Paul wrote for Ringo to perform, 2 minutes and 43 seconds in length, which was included on the *Stop And Smell The Roses* album, issued on RCA LP 6022 on Friday 20 November 1981. On the track Paul plays bass and piano and adds some backing vocals. Howie Casey also plays sax. It was also released as a single in America in 1982 on Boardwalk Records 7-11-134 as a follow-up to 'Wrack My Brain'.

Proby, PJ

An American singer, born in Texas, real name James Marcus Smith, who was first brought over to Britain by producer Jack Good to appear on the 'Around The Beatles', 1964 Redifusion special.

Proby admitted that he nearly caused problems when he was introduced to Paul because of his temper. He said, 'Jack Good had told the Beatles a bunch of lies about me being the lead singer in Rosie & the Originals and so Paul asked me to sing their hit for them. So I said, "Rosie & the Originals? They're coloured people and I ain't coloured, you ******* sing it!"

'So Paul and I got off to a bad start. But when he introduced me on the show, he described me as their best mate and I was so flabbergasted, I almost couldn't sing, but I was made all over the world. Anybody who'd done that show and had the launch I had would've made it anyway.'

Proby also recorded a Lennon and McCartney number, mainly written by Paul, called 'That Means A Lot'. John Lennon commented, '"That Means a Lot" is a ballad which Paul and I wrote for our film, but we found we just couldn't sing it. We made a real hash of it. So we thought we'd give it to somebody who could sing it well, and decided on Proby.'

Professor Longhair

The name used by blues pianist Henry Roeland Byrd, who led an R&B revival in New Orleans in the 1970s and was known as the 'king of Rhumboogie'.

It was while they spent some time in New Orleans in the mid-1970s on material for the *Venus And Mars* album that Paul and Linda first met Professor Longhair.

On 24 March 1975 Paul invited the legendary pianist to perform at a special party he was hosting with Linda on the *Queen Mary* at Long Beach in California.

Arrangements were made to record his set and his manager Allison Kaslow was to comment: 'Byrd had no idea who Paul McCartney was, he had never heard of the Beatles. Even though he had been to Europe and all across the country, his world was right there on Rampart Street with his family.'

An album of the performance, entitled *Live On The Queen Mary*, was issued in the UK on 23 March 1978 on Harvest SHSP 4086 and in America on 24 July 1978 on Harvest SW 1179 under the auspices of MPL Communications and sporting an album cover photograph taken by Linda. This was to tie in with the Professor's first London concert at the New Theatre, Drury Lane on 26 March 1978.

Professor Longhair died of a heart attack on 29 January 1980 at the age of 61.

The album was reissued on the Stateside label on 10 March 1986 on SSL 6004. The cassette version was on TC-SSL 6004.

PS I Love You

A song penned by Paul early in 1962 that the Beatles recorded on the Beatles second proper session on Tuesday 11 September 1962. Andy

White played drums, Ringo played maracas. It was issued in Britain as the flipside of their debut single on Parlophone R 4949 on 5 October 1962.

Paul was later to acquire the rights to the song and he chose to revive it in a medley with 'Love Me Do' in 1990.

PS Love Me Do

A medley of the only two Beatles songs that Paul has the publishing rights to. His MPL Company acquired the numbers from the EMI music publishing subsidiary Ardmore & Beechwood in the 1980s.

He put the song together in 1987 during recording sessions with producer Phil Ramone and initially included it as a special bonus disc in the special CD tour pack of *Flowers In The Dirt* in April 1990, which was issued in Japan to coincide with his tour there. The disc also contained some of the B-sides to Paul's records: 'The Long And Winding Road', 'Loveliest Thing', 'Rough Ride', 'Ou Est Le Soleil', 'Mamma's Little Girl', 'Same Time Next Year' and 'Party Party'. The CD also contained a 28-second message from Paul to the Japanese fans.

Pseudonyms

Paul didn't relish pseudonyms as much as John Lennon, although on the Silver Beetles' first tour, when they backed singer Johnny Gentle in Scotland, Paul decided on using the name Paul Ramon. George called himself Carl Harrison in tribute to Carl Perkins, Stuart Sutcliffe called himself Stu De Stael after one of his favourite painters and although it was said that John Lennon called himself Johnny Silver, he has always denied this.

It was odd that they decided on stage names for this particular tour because they were never advertised by name. All the bills for the tour read 'Johnny Gentle and his Group'.

Paul used the name Bernard Webb when he penned the song 'Woman' for Peter and Gordon as he wanted to see how well a number of his would do without the magic of the McCartney name. He also used the alias A Smith on the number.

When he produced the track 'I'm An Urban Spaceman' for the Bonzo Dog Doo-Dah Band, he used the pseudonym Apollo C Vermouth. Apollo is obviously linked with 'Spaceman' because of the American Apollo space missions.

Paul was also to use the Paul Ramon name many years later when he recorded 'My Dark Hour' with Steve Miller in 1969.

When Paul, Linda and family flew to New York on 4 January 1985 to escape the winter weather in Britain, Paul used the name Mr Winters.

Clint Harrigan was a name used when Paul penned a sleeve note for *Wild Life* and *Thrillington*.

Ian Iachimore was the pseudonym Paul assumed when friends

wanted to contact him by letter in order to differentiate them from the vast fan mail that came his way. He claimed it was the sound of his own name played backwards on a tape recorder. The original manuscript for *Paperback Writer* ended with the words, 'Yours sincerely, Ian Iachimore'.

Paul also helped the underground newspaper *International Times* financially and was acknowledged by having his 'secret name' included in the credit box: Iachimore.

Billy Martin was a pseudonym Paul used when he was recording part of his *McCartney* debut album at Morgan Studios in February 1970.

Martin was not the Liverpool Billy Martin, who ran a famous dance studio in Liverpool, but Billy Martin the New York Yankees second baseman who later became their manager.

Pumer, Eddie

A former member of the 1960s band Kaleidoscope, who later became known as Fairfield Parlor. He became the producer of Paul's 1995 radio series *Oobu Joobu*.

Pure Gold

A number penned by Paul, lasting 3 minutes and 15 seconds, that was recorded during Ringo Starr's album sessions at Sunset Sound Studios in Los Angeles while Paul was awaiting the start of his American tour. It was released on Ringo Starr's *Ringo's Rotogravure* album in 1976.

The musicians were: Ringo Starr on lead vocals and drums, Lon Van Eaton on guitar, Klaus Voormann on bass, Jim Keltner on drums, Jane Getz and John Jarvis on keyboards, George Devens on congas, Paul and Linda McCartney on background vocals, Vini Poncia on harmony vocals and Gene Orloff, concert master for strings.

Put It There (documentary)

A documentary by MPL, filmed between February and April 1989, mainly at Paul's home studio in Sussex. Among the numbers recorded were a new version of 'The Long And Winding Road', plus new numbers 'Rough Ride' and 'Party Party'.

Directed by Geoff Wonfor, it was about the making of *Flowers In The Dirt*. The special was premiered in Britain on BBC 1 on Saturday 10 June 1989 and in America on the Showtime channel on 11 November 1989.

The documentary was also issued as a Polygram Home Video for MPL Communications Ltd in the UK on 19 December 1989. A laser disc version was also issued in America in March 1990.

The 66-minute documentary featured musical contributions from Paul and Linda, Hamish Stewart, Wix, Robbie McIntosh, Chris Whitten and Elvis Costello.

The numbers featured were 'C Moon'/'My Brave Face', 'Elvis

Costello's My Brave Face', 'My Brave Face', 'Rough Ride', 'Figure Of Eight', 'Fool On The Hill', 'Things We Said Today'/'I Saw Her Standing There', 'The Long And Winding Road', 'How Many People', 'The Day Is Done', 'This One', 'Put It There', 'Songs From Choba BCCCP', 'Distractions', 'Party Party' and 'Let It Be'.

Put It There (single)

A fourth single by Paul from the *Flowers In The Dirt* album. It was issued in Britain on Parlophone 6246 on Friday 5 January 1990 where it reached No. 32 in the charts.

'Mama's Little Girl' was on the flipside.

The title was based on a favourite saying of Paul's father, Jim McCartney and 'put it there' referred to a hearty handshake. Paul wrote the number during two 30-minute sessions while on a skiing holiday in Zermatt, Switzerland.

There were five different configurations issued. The CD and 12" versions included an extra track, 'Same Time Last Year'. The 12" version on 12R 6246 did not include a free print of Paul's cover artwork although the edition numbered 12RS 6246 did.

A cassette-only version was issued in America on Capitol 4J44570 on Tuesday 1 May 1990.

A version of this number, lasting 2 minutes and 43 seconds, was included on the *Tripping The Live Fantastic* album. It was recorded live at the Scandinavium, Gothenburg, Sweden on 28 September 1989 during the 1989/90 World Tour.

Putnam, Norbert 'Curly'

A premier country music songwriter, born on a mountain named after his family in Princeton, Alabama. He has received 36 BMI awards for his songs such as 'D-I-V-O-R-C-E' and he was composer of the Tom Jones hit 'The Green Green Grass Of Home'.

Curly owned a 133-acre ranch near Nashville, Tennessee where Paul, Linda and the kids, plus Wings (Mark 3) stayed for two weeks from 6 July 1974, practising in Putnam's garage and recording in the evening at Buddy Killen's Soundshop Recording Studios.

Que Sera, Sera

A number by Jay Livingston and Ray Evans which Paul recorded as a Mary Hopkin single in August 1969, with 'Fields Of St Etienne' by Bernard Gallagher and Graham Lyle on the flip.

It was issued in France on Friday 19 September 1969 on Apple 16 and in America on Monday 15 June 1970 on Apple 1823.

Queen Mary

The famous British ocean liner, which is now permanently docked at Long Beach, California. On Monday 24 March 1975 Paul and Linda held a special party for 200 invited guests to celebrate the end of two months of recording for the *Venus And Mars* album.

George Harrison was among the guests and it was believed that this was the first time the two ex-Beatles had met socially following the break-up of the Beatles.

Also present was Peter Grant, manager of Led Zeppelin, together with members of the group; Mickey Dolenz and Davy Jones of the Monkees; former Apple friends Derek Taylor and Mal Evans; Cher; Joni Mitchell; Carole King; Ryan and Tatum O' Neal; Marvin Gaye; Bob Dylan; the Faces; Phil Everly; the Jackson Five; Paul Williams; Tony Curtis; Rudy Vallee; Dean Martin and David Cassidy.

Music was provided by Professor Longhair and the Meters. Professor Longhair (Henry Byrd) had his performance recorded by Paul and it was later issued as an MPL album in 1978 called *Live On The Queen Mary*.

The Meters (one of the members was Art Neville, later of the Neville Brothers) also had their set recorded during the evening. It wasn't issued as an album until late in 1992 when it was released by Sequel

(NEX CD 220) called *Uptown Rest! – The Meters Live On The Queen Mary*. In the introduction to their set, Paul, Linda and Wings are mentioned.

Quickly, Tommy

A young Liverpool singer signed up by Brian Epstein. Epstein provided him with the Remo Four, one of Liverpool's top groups, as a backing band and gave him John Lennon's 'No Reply' to record.

Quickly was slightly drunk at the session and couldn't manage the song. After seventeen takes he abandoned the attempt. Epstein then gave him the Paul McCartney number 'Tip Of My Tongue'. The number had been added to the Beatles' repertoire in 1962 and the group actually recorded it on Monday, 26 November 1962, but George Martin didn't consider it suitable for release. The Tommy Quickly version was issued in Britain on Piccadilly 7N 35137 on 30 July 1963, but failed to enter the charts.

Quinn, Aidan

The actor who appeared as Paul in the VH1 movie *The Two Of Us*, first transmitted in 2000.

Prior to filming, in his search for authenticity, Quinn spent a day and a half in Liverpool. Ian Hart, a fellow actor who had played John Lennon in *The Hours And The Times* and *Backbeat* accompanied him. Quinn commented, 'I went to Liverpool as soon as I got the job and grabbed Ian, who's a friend of mine, and he was my tour guide. We went and did the whole Beatles thing. But I still might fall flat on my face.'

RADD

An organisation originally called Rock Artists Against Drunk Driving, but has now become known as Recording Artists, Actors and Athletes Against Drunk Driving. RADD aims to increase the public's awareness of drunk driving during holiday periods, enlisting a large number of businesses in providing free rides home for drivers who have had just enough to drink to make them unfit to drive home.

Paul had appeared in the organisation's video 'Drive My Car' and also secured the use of 'Drive My Car' for RADD without them having to pay royalties. As a result they intended to present him with their 'Sterling Silver Founder's Award' at their awards dinner on 24 January 1997, but the dinner was postponed until May and then cancelled.

RADD finally caught up with Paul to present the award when he was in New York in November 1997 for the Carnegie Hall performance of *Standing Stone*. RADD Chairman David Niven Jr and its President Erin Meluso presented Paul with the award during the rehearsals at the Riverside Methodist Church. In addition to the award they presented him with a gift, a guitar custom-made by Linc Luthier.

Paul then videotaped another commercial for them in which he begins singing 'Drive My Car' and then says, 'You can't drive my car or anyone else's if you've been drinking.'

The commercial was launched as a TV spot on Tuesday 25 November during 'National Drunk And Drugged Driving Prevention Month'.

Radio Gosh

A radio station at Great Ormond Street Children's Hospital in London. During October 1983 Paul volunteered to give the station an exclusive 40-minute interview, which was broadcast to the patients. He even recorded some jingles for them. At around the same time he recorded a one-hour special for the British Hospital Radio Association.

Radio Special Promo Mix

A CD, limited to 500 copies only, which was issued in Brazil in 1994 to tie-in with the release of the *Paul Is Live* video. It was issued on EMI 9951 360 and contained a live version of 'Biker Like An Icon' from 1993, the medley 'PS Love Me Do', 'The Long And Winding Road' from the Rio concert and 'Things We Said Today' from the 1991 *Unplugged*.

RAI TV

An Italian television station. Immediately prior to Paul's appearance at the Forum, Assage, near Milan, Italy on Thursday 18 February 1993, he was interviewed for the station by Andrea Barbato. The interview was broadcast on RAI TV at 5.30 p.m. on Sunday 28 February.

Barbato began: 'The Beatles changed our lives. What is it like having that responsibility?' Paul answered: 'Responsibility? It's a funny thing, but a good thing. I was lucky. It is a nice part of people's lives. I like playing music. The fact that people have grown up with my music is great.'

Highlights from the interview were:

Barbato: After eight years of triumph, the Beatles split up. What was the real cause of this separation?

Paul: Broadly speaking, it was a matter of business. At the beginning, we were friends, then as time passed, it became a business – we ended up having to spend our time discussing the financial aspect of things, and that's what split us apart.

Barbato: Is there any chance of a reunion with George and Ringo?

Paul: A documentary is being prepared in England, in ten parts. George, Ringo and I have been asked to record an instrumental piece for the soundtrack of the film. I think we're going to do it this year. But we aren't planning to get back together for a tour or anything like that, just for this soundtrack.

Barbato: How did you feel when you heard about John's death, and how do you remember him now?

Paul: I felt awful, as everyone did. I had been one of his best friends. It was a terrible shock. The killer was the most stupid man in the world – I still think that – there was no reason behind what he did. I have very good memories of John. I was lucky to have the chance to speak to him on the phone just before he died. We talked of everyday life, of problems at home, with the children. His son, Sean, was five years old. We talked about work, about money . . . everyday things. John was wonderful.

Barbato: In your concerts you have the chance to see the youth of today, and compare them with the youth of the sixties. Is there much difference between them?

Paul: There isn't much difference, though they do dress differently. When we started out, we were very young too. Only John was married. There was a kind of romantic attachment with our fans, which lasted for a time – a crazy sort of time! Then people grew up and matured. The situation now is still wild during a big show, and the audiences are great. Today's young people look like parents did in the sixties, but I still love them so much.

Barbato: What do you teach your children, and are you afraid of spoiling them with all your money?

Paul: When Linda and I got married, she came from a rich family, whereas I came from a poor English family. She didn't like the way rich people brought up their children – lots of money, but not much love. So we tried to bring them up in an ordinary way. We didn't give them much money – just the same as their friends at school got from their parents. We didn't send them to Eton or somewhere like that, we kept them close to us. They are all growing up now, but they are down-to-earth, they have no problems speaking to anybody, they aren't haughty, they are open and get on well with people.

Barbato: Do you think that the environment is the major political problem in Europe these days?

Paul: I would say it's a world problem. We are the only animal that soils its own nest. We polluted the sea, and the air – we go to the beach and risk getting skin cancer. We have gone too far. We should take a few steps back from the edge. Politicians everywhere should immediately start trying to eliminate any kind of pollution, otherwise there won't be any world left for them to do their politics in.

Barbato: Do you think that songs have a political value and can change the world?

Paul: I think so. A song like "All You Need Is Love" gave everybody a lot of hope. "We Shall Overcome" was important for the human rights movement. "Give Peace A Chance" helped put a stop to the Vietnam war. It gives people something to think about, and to aim for. On my new album, there are a couple of protest songs: one of them is "Looking For Change", about animal experiments like making monkeys smoke until they die of cancer. We already know smoking is dangerous for our health, so these experiments aren't needed.

Barbato: If you could have three wishes, what would they be?

Paul: To have more wishes!

Barbato: Finally, Paul, how much longer do you think you'll keep on singing and performing?

Paul: I don't know. When I was eighteen, I used to say I will play until I'm twenty-four, then until I was thirty. When I was thirty, I said until I'm forty, and then fifty. Now I'm fifty, I plan to sing for ever!

Rainclouds

A number Paul was said to have worked on during the day following John Lennon's murder. He'd co-composed the number with Denny Laine and Paddy Maloney played aeolian harp on it. This was one of the numbers performed at the *Tug Of War* rehearsals at Pugin's Hall, Tenterdon, Kent on 30 October 1980 and was one of seven songs recorded during the *Tug Of War* sessions that were not included on the album. It appeared as the B-side of 'Ebony And Ivory'.

Ram

The album was issued by Apple and featured a cover photograph by Linda of Paul holding a ram by the horns outside their home in Scotland. John Lennon was later to satirise this picture when he included a postcard inside the *Imagine* album of himself holding a pig by the ears. On the cover there is also a design spelling out 'Lily' (which means 'Linda I love you') and on the reverse of the sleeve is a picture of two beetles copulating.

Ram was Paul's second album since leaving the Beatles, issued in 1971. In Britain it was released on Friday 21 May on Apple PAS 10003, where it was to reach the No. 1 spot, and in the States on Monday 17 May on Apple SMAS 3375 where it got to No. 2, being held off the top spot by Carole King's *Tapestry*.

Paul recorded the album in New York between January and March. Sessions actually began on Monday 10 January at the former Columbia Studios of A&R.

The New York Philharmonic Orchestra was featured on the album, and Paul's backing musicians included Dave Spinozza and Hugh McCracken on guitars and Danny Seiwell on drums.

The album tracks were: 'Too Many People', 'Three Legs', 'Ram On', 'Dear Boy', 'Uncle Albert/Admiral Halsey', 'Smile Away', 'Heart Of The Country', 'Monkberry Moon Delight', 'Eat At Home', 'Long Haired Lady', 'Ram On' (reprise) and 'The Back Seat Of My Car'.

Paul was to comment, 'Linda was very present all the way through, we've been writing many more songs together and we're developing as a harmony team.'

Ram was the only Wings album that was officially attributed to both Paul and Linda.

Ram On

A track from the *Ram* album which, interestingly, features the use of a ukulele as the main instrument.

Ramon, Paul

The pseudonym Paul used when the Silver Beetles toured Scotland as a backing band to Johnny Gentle. Paul couldn't remember why he chose that particular surname, but he thought it was rather glamorous. So much so, that he was to use it again, many years later, when he recorded a track with the Steve Miller band, 'My Dark Hour', in 1969.

Ramone, Phil

An American child prodigy who began playing the violin at the age of three and who appeared on a Royal Command Performance before Queen Elizabeth II at the age of ten.

Ramone was educated at the Julliard School of Music in New York and opened his independent recording studio, A&R Recording, in New York in 1961.

He has recorded numerous major artists including Frank Sinatra, Barbra Streisand, Billy Joel, Paul Simon, Ringo Starr and Julian Lennon.

He first worked with Paul in September 1985 when he was one of the three producers of the 'Spies Like Us' single. The single was recorded over four nights at Paul's studio, the Mill, in Sussex. Ramone was there to aid with the mixing and after an eight-hour mixing session he left for Compass Point studios in Nassau to record Julian Lennon's 'The Secret Value Of Daydreaming'.

Over the years he has produced Paul on a number of occasions including 'Ram', 'Stranglehold', 'Only Love Remains', 'Spies Like Us'. 'Once Upon A Long Ago' and 'P.S. Love Me Do' in 1987.

Paul was with Ramone in Long Island shortly before the release of *Press To Play* and decided to go into the studio with him for some exploratory recordings. They began recording at New York's Power Station studios between Monday 25 August and Friday 29 August 1986 and completed 'Beautiful Night' and 'Loveliest Thing'. Paul was supported by two members of Billy Joel's backing band: Liberty Devitto on drums and David Brown on lead. The other musicians were noted New York session men David LeBolt on keyboards and Neil Jason on bass.

Ramone resumed recording Paul in England at Paul's home studio in Rye, Sussex in March 1987, completing the sessions in early July. The numbers recorded during this period, known as the 'Phil Ramone sessions' were 'Back On My Feet', 'Love Comes Tumbling Down', 'Once Upon A Long Ago', 'This One', 'Atlantic Ocean', 'Love Mix', 'Return To Pepperland', 'Sgt Pepper's Lonely Hearts Club Band', 'Big Day,' 'Christian Bop' and 'Peacocks'.

Julian Mendelsohn, John Hudson and James Guthrie did remixing of certain titles. Nigel Kennedy played on one of the tracks.

Ramones, The

An American band who took their name from Paul's alias.

The group formed in Forest Hills, New York in 1974 and their bass guitarist Douglas Colvin suggested it. He called himself Dee Dee Ramone. Jeffrey Hyman, the group's lead vocalist, who became known as Joey Ramone, commented, 'When we met he was calling himself Dee Dee Ramone and he was a big fan of Paul McCartney. Paul used to check into hotel rooms under the alias of, like, Paul Ramon, so Dee Dee kind of adopted it as our surname to create a sense of unity. Then everyone could have their unique personality within their own thing almost like the Beatles kind of did to some degree.'

Ranachan Rock

An unreleased instrumental, recorded in 1978.

Ransome-Kuti, Fela

A radical Nigerian musician and political dissenter. When Paul travelled to Lagos, the Nigerian capital, to record *Band On The Run*, he went to listen to Ransome-Kuti and his band at the musician's own club. Ransome-Kuti had recently been released from jail.

Paul enjoyed his music very much but Ransome-Kuti made an unpleasant attack on Paul, accusing him of stealing from Nigerian musicians and coming to Lagos with the intention of exploiting black music.

Paul commented, '(He) accused us of stealing black African music. So I had to say, "Do us a favour, Fela, we do OK. We're all right as it is. We sell a couple of records here and there. African music is very nice – but you're welcome to it!" He did have a great band, though.'

In fact, Paul was later to tell Paul Gambaccini: 'They (the Nigerian musicians) are brilliant, it's incredible music down there. I think it will come to the fore. And I thought my visit would, if anything, help there, because it would draw attention to Lagos and people would say, "Oh, by the way, what's the music down there like?" and I'd say it was unbelievable. It is unbelievable. When I heard Fela Ransome-Kuti for the first time it made me cry, it was that good.'

Ransome-Kuti was actually the creator of Afro-Beat, a fusion of soul and jazz. He died of heart failure, brought about by AIDS, on Saturday 2 August 1997.

Rapido

A French show screened on BBC 2. Paul pre-recorded an interview for the show in Paris on Thursday 3 December 1987. Antoines De Caunes, the French presenter, interviewed him for 42 minutes. During the interview Paul discussed his latest album *Flowers In The Dirt*, George's Handmade Films, the Nike commercial featuring the music of 'Revolution' and his recordings of rock-'n'-roll songs for Russian release.

Ten minutes of the interview was broadcast on *Rapido* the following day, Friday 4 December as part of a Beatles special.

BBC 2 transmitted the edition of *Rapido* with Paul's interview on Wednesday 10 May 1989. It was repeated on Saturday 13 May 1989.

Razzmatazz

An afternoon children's programme from Tyne-Tees Television, which was broadcast on the ITV network. Paul made a pre-recorded interview for the show to promote his latest release *Pipes Of Peace*, which was transmitted on *Razzmatazz* on Tuesday 13 December 1983.

Real Buddy Holly Story, The

A home video issued to coincide with the 1986 Buddy Holly Week, which was the fiftieth anniversary of Holly's birth.

The video utilised the BBC 2/MPL production of the Buddy Holly documentary screened on BBC 2's *Arena* programme on 12 September 1985. This time it included 25 minutes of extra footage, bringing its length to 90 minutes.

The video also utilised the Quarry Men recording of Holly's 'That'll Be The Day', from 1958.

It was issued in Britain by Picture Music International on VHS: MVN 99 1126 2 and on Beta: MXN 99 1126 4 on Tuesday 26 August 1986. Two audio videocassettes containing 28 Buddy Holly tracks were also part of the package.

The home video was issued in America on Monday 21 September 1987.

Real Love

'Real Love' was the second Beatles single issued in 1996 utilising tapes John Lennon had made during the 1970s. In the press release accompanying the single, Paul was to write, 'It was good fun doing it. Unlike "Free As A Bird", it had all the words and music and we were more like "sidemen" to John, which was joyful and I think we did a good job.'

The release also commented, 'The surviving Beatles decided to use as little state-of-the-art equipment as possible to give a timeless Beatles feel to the single. To enhance this effect, Paul McCartney used a stand-up double bass originally owned by Elvis Presley's bassist, the late Bill Black. Both Paul and George used six-string acoustic guitars to augment the electric instruments and Ringo used his Ludwig drum kit. The result is a bona fide organic Beatles single with ageless appeal.'

It was issued in Britain on Monday 4 March 1996 and caused controversy when Radio One decided not to put it on its playlist, effectively banning the single. They must not have considered that it had 'ageless appeal'. The station's press officer Polly Ravenscroft commented, 'We have played "Real Love" a few times, but no, it's not on the playlist.'

In response to the record not being played on Radio One, Paul wrote an 800-word article for the *Daily Mirror* which was published on 9

March 1996, 'Is Radio One saying that its judgement is better than almost all the British public? Is it saying that all the people who bought the record and yesterday put it at No. 4 in its first week don't know what they like? It's not just young people who pay the licence fee to pay Radio One's wages. People of all ages pay that fee, so how come they don't get a look-in? You can't put an age limit on good music.'

Other comments were, 'The Beatles don't need our new single "Real Love" to be a hit – it's not as if our careers depend on it. We've done all right over the years, and if Radio One feels that we should be banned now it's not exactly going to ruin us overnight.'

Ninety-one per cent of the *Daily Mirror* readers voted that they wanted to hear the single on the radio and the *Mirror* urged readers to ring or send a fax to Trevor Dann of Radio One, saying, 'Give Dann a hard day's night by telling him exactly what you think.'

Really Love You

A track on the *Flaming Pie* album. This was the first song to be credited to McCartney/Starr as it arose out of a jam session during the recording. Ringo was very surprised to discover the co-songwriting credit. It was produced by Paul and Jeff Lynne. The engineers were Geoff Emerick and Jan Jacobs assisted by Keith Smith. Recording began on 14 May 1996 and Paul sang lead vocals and backing vocals and played bass guitar, electric guitar and Wurlitzer piano. Jeff Lynne sang backing vocals and played electric guitar. Ringo Starr played drums.

Paul said, 'When I played it back to Ringo, he said, "It's relentless, it's relentless." He's a one with words.'

Red Rose Speedway

Wings' second album and Paul's fourth post-Beatles LP, issued in America on Apple SMAL 3409 on 30 April 1973 where it topped the charts for three weeks. It was issued in Britain on Apple PCTC 251 on 4 May and reached No. 4 in the UK charts.

The 12-track album, lasting 42 minutes and 22 seconds, was recorded in March and October 1972 at Morgan Studios, Olympic Studios, Trident Studios, Island Studios and Abbey Road Studios and credited to Paul McCartney and Wings. The other musicians were Linda McCartney, Denny Laine, Denny Seiwell and Henry McCullough. Paul produced it and the engineers included Alan Parsons, Richard Lush, Dixon Van Winkle, Tim Geeland, Glyn Johns and David Hentschel.

The original album was going to be a double one, but Paul was persuaded to abandon that idea. The album's title was inspired by the McCartney's housekeeper, Rose, and Paul is featured on the cover with a rose in his mouth and a gleaming Harley Davidson motorcyle in the background.

The gatefold sleeve featured lyrics to the songs and included a twelve-page booklet with photographs of Wings on the road and drawings and paintings by noted artists Alan Jones and Eduardo Paolozzi. The back cover of the album featured a message to Stevie Wonder in Braille: 'We love you'.

Tracks were: Side One: 'Big Barn Bed', 'My Love', 'Get On The Right Thing', 'One More Kiss', 'Little Lamb Dragonfly'. Side Two: 'Single Pigeon', 'When The Night', 'Loop (First Indian on the Moon)' and a medley made up of four unfinished songs: 'Hold Me Tight'/ 'Lazy Dynamite'/ 'Hands of Love'/ 'Power Cut'.

John Lennon said that this was the last of Paul's albums that he listened to.

Reeve, Christopher

An American actor who first came to fame as the star of the *Superman* films. He was involved in a tragic accident, which paralysed him, but his courage and refusal to knuckle under to the situation earned him international admiration.

Paul wrote a letter to him:

Dear Christopher,

I am so glad to hear news of your continued recovery because you have always been someone rather special in our household. I refer particularly to the time when my son was quite young and we met you on a flight from London to America. When I told you he was a huge Superman fan, you were kind enough to give him a big wave when he turned around to look at you. That's the kind of thing that means a lot to soppy old parents like us, and something we won't forget in a hurry.

On behalf of the whole family, I send our very best wishes to you and your family, and hope that, with the help of a laugh or two from Robin Williams, your recovery will be a speedy one.

Best of luck and, once again, thanks for the simple gesture which meant so much.

Love,
Paul McCartney.

Paul also contributed a video message to the ABC TV programme 'Christopher Reeve: A Celebration Of Hope' on Sunday 1 March 1998. He also sent a new version of himself performing 'Calico Skies' from the *Flaming Pie* album.

Reggae Moon

A demo disc, which Paul recorded at his Scottish Rude Studios in 1978, part of which was aired on the *Oobu Joobu* radio series.

Religion

Paul and Mike's mother had been reared as a strict Roman Catholic. By marrying the Protestant Jim McCartney she broke faith with her religion, despite the fact that the wedding ceremony took place in St Swithin's Roman Catholic Church. Jim and Mary promised the priest that the two boys would be formally baptised into the Roman Catholic faith. They were also circumcised.

However, Jim McCartney prevailed by having the boys attend a secular school rather than a Roman Catholic one. They also attended a Church of England church rather than a Catholic church and Paul became a choirboy at St Barnabas' Church, near Penny Lane.

Although christened a Roman Catholic, Paul now lists himself as 'C of E'.

Rembrandt

The five-bedroom house that Paul bought in July 1964 for £8,750. It was situated in Baskervyle Road, Heswall, Cheshire, overlooking the River Dee estuary and fifteen miles from Liverpool. The house even had its own wine cellar. A further £8,000 was spent on central heating, furnishing and decorations. The removal of furniture from Forthlin Road took place at midnight to escape the fans that gathered outside the house during the day.

Paul had bought the house ostensibly for his father Jim to live in, as Jim had retired as a cotton salesman that year. It would also be a home for his brother Mike, and Paul would be able to use it on his visits to Merseyside for his regular family reunions with aunties, uncles, cousins and other relatives.

Paul had discussed the move from 20 Forthlin Road with his father following his return from his American concert tour that year. Jim told him, 'I like the idea of Heswall, over the water, on the Wirral.'

It was stockbroker country and Jim had worked as a gardener there in his youth.

Paul spent as much money on improvements and renovations to the house as he'd spent on the purchase price and also chose the furniture, which included a grand piano.

After moving in, Mike was to say, 'Surrounded by all these rich trappings, we soon became accustomed to our new fairy bubble, and settled in with alarming ease. Dad and I were like two little Lord Fauntleroys in our ivory castle, as snug as two bugs in a rug.'

Paul also sent regular cheques for the upkeep of the house.

Paul and Jane Asher kept twin moped bikes at 'Rembrandt' and used to drive around the Wirral peninsula on them. One evening Paul decided to ride over to Bebington by himself to visit a cousin. Although it was a journey of only a few miles, Paul had an accident and smashed the bike into a kerb and was flung head over heels over the handlebars. He had a badly cut lip that needed stitches and a local doctor attended to the lip and also to some damage above one eye.

Remember Live Aid

A radio dramatisation of the famous 'Live Aid' charity extravaganza which was broadcast on BBC Radio Four on Saturday 15 July 1995, the tenth anniversary of the event. Actor Peter O'Meara played Bob Geldof and portrayed him trying to convince Paul that he should take part in the event. Paul played himself in his first dramatic role on radio.

Replica Studios

Paul obviously had great affection for EMI's No. 2 Studios at Abbey Road, where so many Beatles and Wings records had been made. However, he became frustrated when he discovered he couldn't record there late in 1978 because Cliff Richard had booked the studio for months to record his album *Rock And Roll Juvenile*. He decided to build an exact replica of Studio 2's mixing room in the basement of MPL's London offices, together with panelled walls for recording, hence the name Replica Studios.

The studios were completed in 1978, ready for *Back To The Egg*, part of which was recorded at Replica. Paul recorded there between December 1978 and February 1979 and after his album was completed Replica Studios was dismantled.

Respect For Animals

A charity aimed at discouraging people from wearing fur.

Jude Law and his wife Sadie Frost directed an advertisement for the charity that was screened nationwide in British cinemas in 2002 among the trailers for *Ocean's Eleven*. The all-star cast of the advert included Sir Paul and his daughter Stella, plus Mel C and George Michael.

Return Of The Saint

A projected film. In 1972 producer Anthony Spinner offered Paul the role of a rock star who is kidnapped. Paul was interested provided he could compose the music and also direct, but plans fell through and the film was never made.

Return To Pepperland

A tribute to *Sgt Pepper*, which Paul recorded, with Phil Ramone producing, in June 1987. The *Sgt Pepper* album was to be issued as a CD in June 1987. The song had originally been planned as a September 1987 release as an EP with 'Love Comes Tumbling Down' and 'Beautiful Night'. It was then considered as a bonus track for the CD single release of 'The World Tonight' in 1997, but was also dropped.

Reverse

An unreleased instrumental number by Paul, which he recorded in Abbey Road Studios in 1975.

Revolution 9

A number penned by John Lennon and featured on *The Beatles* double album in November 1968. The number is over eight minutes in length and is experimental. John used thirty tape loops to provide an unusual effect.

He was to comment, 'All the things were made with loops, I had about thirty loops going. I fed them into one basic track and one loop, chopping it and making it go backwards and things like that to get the sound effects.'

The avant-garde number, which was mastered solely by John, was to become associated with the many 'clues' put forward to prove that Paul was dead.

In this instance, fans claimed that when the track was played backwards, the words 'Turn me on, dead man, turn me on, dead man,' could be heard – in their eyes yet another nail in Paul's coffin.

Rhone, Dorothy

A girl who attended Liverpool Institute for Girls at the same time Paul was at Liverpool Institute. She lived in the Childwall area of Liverpool and became Paul's first serious girlfriend. They went 'steady' for three years.

Dot, together with her sisters Anne and Barbara and brother Billie, lived with their parents and, together with their mother Jessie, had an unpleasant home life, owing to the fact that their father was an alcoholic.

Paul first met Dot in September 1959 at the Casbah Club in Hayman's Green, West Derby, Liverpool, where the Quarry Men had their first residency. The two became lovers in December of that year. Dot had been a virgin and the two had made love when Paul's father Jim and his brother Mike were absent from the house in Forthlin Road.

After leaving school, Dot had jobs as a chemist's assistant and a bank clerk. It was during her time as a bank clerk that she discovered she was pregnant. She informed her parents and Paul informed his father, who told Paul that they would have to get married. Abortions were not considered in those days. Jim McCartney began to make arrangements for the two to be married in a register office, but, three months into the pregnancy, Dot had a miscarriage and the wedding was cancelled.

Dot and Cynthia Powell, John Lennon's girlfriend, became close friends and they were both invited to Hamburg to join their boyfriends, who were performing at the Top Ten Club in April 1961. Cynthia stayed with Astrid Kirchherr, a friend of the Beatles, and Dot and Paul stayed on a houseboat owned by Rosa Hoffman, the 'toilet-frau' at the club where the group played.

Several months after the German trip, Cynthia invited Dot to move into a room next door to hers in a rented accommodation. While there, Paul told Dot that their affair was over.

Heartbroken, within a year she emigrated to Canada and a year later married a German businessman, Werner Becker.

Rhythm Of Life, The

A three-part BBC television series by George Martin about twentieth-century music that began on Monday 29 December 1997. In the third and final part of the series on Monday 5 January 1998, Paul was featured discussing his songwriting and providing examples with excerpts from 'I Lost My Little Girl' and 'Lady Madonna'.

Rice, Tim

Co-writer of *Jesus Christ: Superstar*, *Evita* and other hit stage musicals, who also became a radio and television celebrity, panellist and interviewer.

In 1980 he interviewed Paul for the Independent Television network which was screened by Thames Television on Monday 4 August and by Granada TV on Monday 27 October. It was also featured on a number of TV channels around the world.

Richardson, Sir Ralph

A well-loved and much-respected British actor who was born in Cheltenham in 1903. He made his first major appearance on the London stage in 1926 in *Yellow Sands* and developed into one of Britain's leading film and theatre actors, receiving much acclaim for his many roles for the Old Vic Company.

His film career stretched from the 1930s to the 1980s and included dozens of movies ranging from *Things To Come* to *Dr Zhivago*.

Paul's film *Give My Regards To Broad Street* was Sir Ralph's last, as he died a few months after filming was completed.

Discussing how he first approached him, Paul commented: 'I've found out over the years that the best people in any field are the most approachable, so I wasn't nervous. I was a bit nervous about *acting* with him, but he was such a wonderful actor he made me look better. He did it all *for* me.'

Director Peter Webb was to add: 'Ralph's is a small role but so is that of the wizard in *The Wizard Of Oz*. It's crucial. In the scenes they play together, Old Jim, in a sense, is Paul's inner voice telling him to have faith and continue the quest. Ralph quickly caught on to this element in the story, and it enabled him to develop the role as only a great actor can. He loved the part with its simple straightforward dialogue capable of being given subtle nuances. It was the kind of dialogue he liked'.

Discussing how he felt about appearing with Sir Ralph, Paul said: 'I was frightened to do it, because he's a big, famous, old British actor, and that's intimidating because a person's image does walk ahead of them. He made it easy. He had a twinkle in his eye all the time. I thought my script might not be to his liking, and I said, "Look, this isn't Shakespeare or Chekov, so we can change it if you like."'

Sir Ralph wouldn't have any of that, and he complimented Paul's script by saying, 'Thank you, dear boy, not a comma out of place.'

Sir Ralph's appearance is only brief. Paul, worried that his friend Harry has disappeared with the master tapes of his new recordings, knocks on Old Jim's door. Jim lives above a pub and opens the door, his pet monkey in his hands. He welcomes Paul into his room, which is full of old *Picture Post* magazines and a wireless set, a room still decorated in the style of the 1940s.

When asked by Paul, Jim mentions that he'd seen Harry the previous evening in the pub – and he did have a large blue box with him. Old Jim advises: 'You're always running around. If you didn't run around so much you might get a better view of the world, you know.' After a short chat Paul leaves saying: 'Thanks all the same, Jim, I've got to be off.' With a twinkle in his eye, Jim replies: 'You've been off for years.'

Linda was able to take a photographic session with the actor and has a good set of shots of Paul and Sir Ralph together.

Rickenbacker

An American make of guitar. Paul bought a Sunburst Rickenbacker 4000 stereo bass guitar in America in 1965. It was a specially built model for left-handers. Paul used it mainly on recording sessions and didn't play it on stage until the Wings tours. The Dutch artists known collectively as the Fool painted a colourful design on the guitar. Paul also used the instrument in 'Magical Mystery Tour', on the 'Our World' television show and in the promotional video 'Hello Goodbye', recorded at the Saville Theatre. Paul later had the Fool design removed.

Riding Into Jaipur

A track from the *Driving Rain* album. It is 4 minutes and 8 seconds in length and was recorded on 16 February 2001. The number was issued as the B-side to the single 'From A Lover To A Friend' on 29 October 2001.

Rinse The Raindrops

The closing track of the *Driving Rain* album – and the longest at 10 minutes and 8 seconds. The number was recorded on 19 February 2001.

Roach Avenue

An area of Liverpool on the Knowsley Estate that became Paul's third home when his family moved there for a short time immediately after Mike McCartney was born in 1944.

Robber's Ball

A number recorded at Lympne Castle in May 1979, which had originally started out as a jam session with Laurence Juber. Paul penned the lyrics in ten minutes and it was recorded with Paul on drums and Juber on guitar.

Robbie's Bit (Thanks Chet)

A number by Robbie McIntosh lasting 1 minute and 56 seconds that was recorded live at the Blockbuster Pavilion, Charlotte. It was included on the *Paul Is Live* album.

Robbins, Betty

Paul's cousin, who was twelve years older than him. When Paul and his brother Mike were very young, Betty, more familiarly referred to as Bett, often looked after the two youngsters in the little terraced house in Boaler Street, next door to the shop where her mother ran a sewing repairs business. Since the terraced house had no garden, they all often had to stay indoors for several hours at a time and Bett used to entertain them with music. She had a banjolele, which she used to play for them. She was to show Paul how she played and would say that if he put his fingers into the instrument's triangle he got a D-seventh on that one chord. She then taught him three basic chords of two songs, 'The Man From Arizona' and 'Has Anybody Seen My Gal'. She next taught him 'Ragtime Cowboy Joe'.

Bett also had a record collection that interested Paul, particularly records by Peggy Lee. Other records Bett had which Paul enjoyed included 'All The Things You Are' by Frank Sinatra, 'Star Eyes' by Al Martino, 'The Folks Who Live On The Hill' by Peggy Lee and 'Laura' by the Woody Herman Orchestra. He also loved the *Beauty And The Beat* album by Peggy Lee and George Shearing.

Bett also played him some light classical music such as *Peer Gynt Suite*, *Scheherazade*, *Holberg Suite* and *La Calinda*.

It was Bett who gave Paul Peggy Lee's versions of 'Fever' and ''Til There Was You', which he included in the Beatles act and sang on the *With The Beatles* album.

Bett was married to comedian Mike Robbins and the two of them became Redcoats at Butlin's holiday camp in Pwhelli. It was Mike who encouraged Paul and Mike McCartney to get on stage in a talent contest at Butlin's in 1957.

The couple were then to run a pub called the Fox and Hounds, where Paul and John visited in 1960. They helped in the bar and played an acoustic set on Saturday night and Sunday afternoon as the Nerk Twins, playing numbers such as 'The World Is Waiting For The Sunrise' (a hit for Les Paul and Mary Ford). Mike paid them £5 each, which was a lot of money in those days.

Bett and Mike later became publicans of the Bow Bells on Ryde, the Isle of Wight and Paul and John also visited them there. The trip was said to have inspired the number 'Ticket To Ride'.

Robbins, Jane

The sculptress daughter of Paul's cousin. In 2000 Paul commissioned Jane to create a life-size statue of Linda cradling a dog in her arms. The statue was originally to have been placed in the Linda McCartney Memorial Gardens near the Mull of Kintyre. The £20,000 bronze statue was completed but for some reason it was decided not to place it in the gardens.

Discussing her commission, Jane said, 'I went to see Paul about another matter when he asked if I could do it. I knew Linda and the sort of person she was, so I am in a good position to produce something that Paul's going to be pleased with.'

Robbins, Kate

Paul's cousin, who has become a recording artist in her own right and has occasionally guested as a backing vocalist on some of Paul's records.

Paul took a hand early in her career and produced her recording 'Tomorrow', the song from the musical *Annie*, which was part of his own MPL publishing catalogue.

The single was released in Britain on Anchor ANC 1054 on 30 June 1978, but was unsuccessful.

Her biggest hit was 'More Than In Love', a song featured on the television soap opera *Crossroads*, which brought her to a No. 2 position in the British charts when the single was issued on RCA in May 1981.

Kate was to have more success as a television celebrity, comedienne and impressionist.

In 1994 she presented a slot, 'Tiny Tots', on GMTV. She is the mother of two girls and a boy.

Robert F Kennedy Memorial Stadium

The Washington DC venue where Paul appeared on Wednesday 4 July and Friday 6 July 1990 during the final leg of his world tour. A combined audience of 91,892 attended the shows. Paul and his party arrived early at the venue on 4 July, Independence Day, to enable Paul to watch the semi-final of the football World Cup in his dressing room – a satellite dish had been ordered specially. There were only slight changes to the tour repertoire, with Paul dropping the Lennon medley and singing 'Happy Birthday' as a tribute to 4 July, America's 214th birthday. On the 6 July show Paul omitted 'Happy Birthday' and performed the Lennon medley – he also told the audience that Washington had been the scene of the Beatles' first American concert.

A special reception was also held, attended by Paul and Linda, costing $250, with funds going to Friends Of The Earth.

The Hard Rock Café in Washington celebrated National Secretaries Day with a contest in which ten secretaries tossed typewriters from a second-floor balcony onto a target labelled 'Boss'. Four tickets to Paul's concert went to the winner.

Rock & Roll Remembers

A syndicated American radio series, hosted by Dick Clark. A four-hour programme dedicated to Paul was syndicated in this series between Friday 17 October and Sunday 19 October 1986.

Rock 'n' Roll Hall of Fame

The Beatles were inducted into the 'Rock 'n' Roll Hall of Fame as a group in 1988.

The event took place on Wednesday 20 January at the Grand Ballroom in the Waldorf-Astoria, New York.

It was the third annual induction ceremony and the choices for induction into the Hall of Fame were the Beatles, the Beach Boys, Bob Dylan, the Supremes, the Drifters and Berry Gordy Jr.

George Harrison and Ringo Starr were in attendance, as was Yoko Ono with Julian and Sean Lennon. Among the other artists present were Little Richard, Elton John, Bruce Springsteen, Ben E King, Paul Simon and Mick Jagger.

Paul was conspicuous by his absence and a fax, sent from MPL was read out: 'After twenty years the Beatles still have some business differences which I had hoped would have been settled by now. Unfortunately, they haven't been, so I would feel like a complete hypocrite waving and smiling with them at a fake reunion.'

When the Beach Boys were being inducted, Mike Love attacked Paul by saying, 'Paul McCartney couldn't be here tonight because he's in a lawsuit with Ringo and Yoko. He sent a telegram to a high-priced attorney who's sitting out there. Now, that's a bummer because we're talking about harmony, right? And it's a shame Ms Ross can't make it, right? The Beach Boys did a hundred and eighty performances last year. I'd like to see the mop-tops top that!'

When George Harrison spoke he said, 'I don't have too much to say because I'm the quiet Beatle. It's too bad Paul's not here because he's the one who's had the speech in his pocket. We all know why John's not here: we know he'd be here. It's really hard to stand here representing the Beatles. It's what's left, I'm afraid. We all loved John very much and we love Paul very much.'

When a representative of Rogers & Cowan, Paul's press agency, was asked if they had been anticipating his arrival, she said, 'Paul decided months ago that he wasn't coming. He was damned if he came and damned if he didn't. He couldn't win either way. Don't quote me, but Paul is not going to let himself be roped into any Beatles reunion. Especially not while Yoko is going around acting like the Fourth Beatle. No siree. Paul only does what Paul damn well wants to. He *is* the Chief Beatle, after all.'

John Lennon, as a solo artist, was inducted into the Rock 'n' Roll Hall Of Fame at the Waldorf-Astoria on Wednesday 19 January 1994. Yoko Ono attended the event with Sean and Paul was pictured hugging Yoko.

Paul and Linda entered with Bruce Springsteen and his wife and were joined at their table by Eric Clapton, Yoko Ono, Sean Lennon and John F Kennedy Jr.

Paul made the induction speech for John and, in a press conference following the event, announced that the three surviving Beatles were to go into the recording studio to make a record together. He also said, 'It's a privilege to come along and do this. John, no matter what people thought of him from minute to minute, was a very, very beautiful person. And it's an honour to be able to do this with Yoko and Sean. It's just a lot of fun and it's a privilege, 'cause he was some serious dude.' Asked why had picked 'Beautiful Boy' as his favourite song by John, he said, 'Well, you know, I've got kids and I know that emotion, and I think John captured it perfectly in that song.'

When he was asked if he found his 'Dear John' letter difficult to write, he said, 'It was wonderful. It wasn't hard at all. I mean, the thing is, you must remember, I'm a Number One John Lennon fan and I love him to this day. I always did love him. Even when we were bitching and going through our problems, which we all went through – and even though Yoko and I, you know, for a long time were bitching at each other.' Yoko interrupted him then to say, 'I didn't know that.' Paul continued, 'Hmmm. Maybe we *weren't* bitching at each other! But we still know that the man we're talking about tonight, the man who's been honoured tonight, was a seriously incredible dude.'

Later that evening Paul visited Yoko at the Dakota and she gave him four of John's home demo discs for the planned recording of a new Beatles single.

Paul's induction speech went as follows:

Dear John,

I remember when we first met at Woolton, at the village fete. It was a beautiful summer day and I walked in there and saw you on stage. And you were singing 'Come Go With Me' by the Del-Vikings. But you didn't know the words so you made them up . . . 'Come go with me to the penitentiary.' It's not in the lyrics.

I remember writing our first songs together. We used to go to my house, my dad's home, and we used to smoke Typhoo tea with the pipe my dad kept in a drawer. It didn't do much for us but it got us on the road. We wanted to be famous.

I remember the visits to your mum's house. Julia was a very handsome woman, very beautiful woman. She had long red hair and she played a ukulele. I'd never seen a woman that could do that. And I remember having to tell you the guitar chords because you used to play the ukulele chords.

And then on your twenty-first birthday you got one hundred pounds off one of your rich relatives up in Edinburgh, so we decided we'd go to Spain. So we hitchhiked out of Liverpool, got as far as Paris, and decided to stop there for a week. And eventually got our hair cut by a fellow named Jurgen and that ended up being the 'Beatle haircut'.

I remember introducing you to my mate George, my schoolmate, and getting him into the band by playing 'Raunchy' on the top deck of a bus. You were impressed. And we met Ringo, who'd been working the whole season at Butlin's camp – he was a seasoned professional – but the beard had to go, and it did.

Later on we got a gig at the Cavern club in Liverpool which was officially a blues club. We didn't really know any blues numbers. We loved the blues but we didn't know any blues numbers, so we had announcements like 'Ladies and gentlemen, this is a great "Big" Bill Broonzy number called "Wake Up Little Susie". And they kept passing up little notes, 'This is not the blues, this is not the blues. This is pop.' But we kept on going.

And then we ended up touring. It was a bloke called Larry Parnes who gave us our first tour. I remember we all changed names for that tour. I changed mine to Paul Ramon, George became Carl Harrison and, although people think you didn't really change your name, I seem to remember you were Long John Silver for the duration of that tour.

We'd been in a van touring later and we'd have the kind of night where the windscreen would break. We would be on the motorway going back to Liverpool. It was freezing so we had to lie on top of each other in the back of the van creating a Beatle sandwich. We got to know each other. These were the days we got to know each other.

We got to Hamburg and met the likes of Little Richard, Gene Vincent . . . I remember Little Richard inviting us back to his hotel. He was looking at Ringo's ring and said 'I love that ring.' He said, 'I've got a ring like that. I could give you a ring like that.' So we all went back to the hotel with him – we never got the ring.

We went back with Gene Vincent to his hotel room once. All was going fine until he reached in his bedside drawer and pulled out a gun. We said, 'Er, we've got to go, Gene, we've got to go.' We got out quick.

And then came the USA – New York City – where we met up with Phil Spector, the Ronettes, Supremes, our heroes, our heroines. And then later in LA we met up with Elvis Presley for one great evening. We saw the boy on his home territory. He was the first person I ever saw with a remote control on a TV. Boy! He was a hero, man.

And then later, Ed Sullivan. We'd wanted to be famous, now we were getting really famous. I mean imagine meeting Mitzi Gaynor in Miami!

Later, after that, recording at Abbey Road. I still remember doing 'Love Me Do'. You officially had the vocal 'Love me do' but because you played the harmonica, George Martin suddenly said in the middle of the session, 'Will Paul sing the line "Love me do"?', the crucial line. I can still hear it to this day – you would go 'Whaaa whaa', and I'd go 'Loove me doo-oo'. Nerves, man.

I remember doing the vocal to 'Kansas City' – well, I couldn't quite get it, because it's hard to do that stuff. You know, screaming out the top of your head. You came down from the control room and took me to one side and said, 'You can do it, you've just got to scream, you can do it.' So, thank you. Thank you for that. I did it.

I remember writing 'A Day In The Life' with you, and the little look we gave each other when we wrote the line 'I'd love to turn you on.' We kind of knew what we were doing, you know. A sneaky little look.

After that there was this girl called Yoko. Yoko Ono. She showed up at my house one day. It was John Cage's birthday and she said she wanted to get hold of manuscripts of various composers to give to him, and she wanted one from me and you. So I said, 'Well, it's OK by me, but you'll have to go to John.' And she did.

After that I set up a couple of Brunnell recording machines we used to have and you stayed up all night and recorded 'Two Virgins'. But you took the cover yourselves – nothing to do with me.

And then, after that there were the phone calls to you. The joy for me after all the business shit that we'd gone through was that we were actually getting back together and communicating once again. And the joy as you told me about how you were baking bread now. And how you were playing with your little baby, Sean. That was great for me because it gave me something to hold on to.

So now, years on, here we are. All these people. Here we are, assembled to thank you for everything that you mean to all of us.

This letter comes with love, from your friend Paul.

John Lennon, you've made it. Tonight you are in the Rock 'n' Roll Hall of Fame.

God bless you.

Paul was then inducted into the Rock 'n' Roll Hall of Fame himself at the fourteenth annual ceremony of the event at New York's Waldorf-Astoria Hotel on Monday 15 March 1999.

When he was first informed, Paul said, 'I am very excited and honoured. Rock 'n' roll has played a huge part in my life and in that of my lovely Linda – so this one's for her.'

Paul dedicated his award to his late wife, saying, 'I love New York because New York gave me Linda! This one's for you, baby!' He also said to the organisers, 'You've got John and me in this – what about George and Ringo?' This referred to the fact that although the Beatles were inducted in 1988, only John and Paul of the Beatles had been inducted as solo artists.

Other inductees that day were Sir George Martin, the late Dusty Springfield, Billy Joel, Bruce Springsteen and Curtis Mayfield.

Neil Young inducted Paul, saying, 'Out he stepped from the shadow of the Beatles, and there he was. It kind of blew my mind.'

Eric Clapton, Bono and Bruce Springsteen then joined Paul on stage as they performed 'Let It Be', followed by rock standards such as 'Blue Suede Shoes' and 'What'd I Say'.

Paul's daughter Stella had accompanied him and sported a T-shirt reading 'About f***ing time!'

The following year Paul was the presenter at the induction of former Apple signing James Taylor at the Waldorf-Astoria event on 6 March.

Paul, who sat at Taylor's table, was to say:

OK, well, I haven't got any big long speech, you'll probably be glad to hear. I'm just gonna remember a couple of things from way way ago in the sixties when we were starting a new record label called Apple. Before it was a computer. And we were looking for talent. So we sent out this message, come all ye talented ones unto us. And they ... well, a few of them did. A lot of others came along with it, too. But it was a great time, it was a crazy time, and my friend Peter Asher one day came to the office, and he showed up and he said, 'I've got this guy from New York.' You know, 'Go on, come on, let's have a listen,' you know. And for once, it was someone really great. Which I must say we didn't really expect.

But it was this kind of haunting guy who could really play the guitar. And really sing beautifully. And, as I found out later, he'd been through a lot of troubles just recently, and he'd pulled himself out of them all, and he'd come over from New York, straightened himself out and got to England. And we were just lucky to run into him; he was lucky to run into us, I suppose. He started singing and it was just so beautiful that right there and then we said, 'OK, he's on Apple.' And so he was one of our very first artists on Apple.

So, as I say, I'm not going to go on too much about him except to say that I love him. And he's a really beautiful guy. We had a lot of good times back then ... I think! And I'm just very honoured this evening to induct him into the rhythm 'n' blues, rock 'n' roll, ballad, jazz, slow foxtrot award here tonight. And you know, you gotta do all those categories 'cause we all know you can't really call it one thing. Rock 'n' roll is too sort of slim for what's been going on tonight. So, it's too deep, you know? Especially I think, the trouble ... really, you can't put it into words. It's what Eric and Robbie just did and what James is about to do. And what

Bonnie did and Melissa, is really why we're all in it, you know, we're not really words people, we're *singers,* man. And players. So I just want to thank everyone who voted for him and it's my honour to induct him, but first of all, we're gonna have a look at the clip . . .

A video clip of James Taylor's was screened and Paul continued: 'Yes, James! OK, so I'm proud of this guy . . . so I'd like to now induct James Taylor into the Rock 'n' Roll Hall of Fame.'

Rock Around The World
Title of a radio interview Paul gave to disc jockey Alan Freeman, which was syndicated on Friday 11 and Saturday 19 April 1975. During the programme Paul sang a few songs a cappella. One was the first verse of 'Suicide', a number he was actually to send to Frank Sinatra. The others were the Vikings' hit 'Come Go With Me', which the Quarry Men used to perform, and the Bill Justis hit 'Raunchy', which allegedly was the number which helped George Harrison become a member of the Quarry Men.

Rock For Kampuchea
A television production of the 1979 Hammersmith Odeon 'Concerts For The People Of Kampuchea'. Excerpts from Paul and Wings' performance were included in the special, which premiered in Britain on the ITV network on Sunday 4 January 1981. Three Wings performances were featured: 'Got To Get You Into My Life', 'Every Night' and 'Coming Up', together with three Rockestra numbers, 'Lucille', 'Let It Be' and 'The Rockestra Theme'.

Rocker
'Rocker' was the name Paul gave to this brief jamming session by the Beatles during the *Get Back* sessions. It was also known as 'Instrumental 42'. Glyn Jones included it in his version of the *Get Back* recordings, but Phil Spector left it out when he used the tapes to prepare *Let It Be.*

Rockestra, The
A rock orchestra created by Paul. It was originally used for two numbers on the *Back To The Egg* album, 'The Rockestra Theme' and 'So Glad To See You'. Paul invited a host of noted rock musicians to join Wings and their brass section at Abbey Road Studios on Tuesday 3 October 1978 to make the recordings.

The line-up of musicians was: Pete Townshend (of the Who), Dave Gilmour (of Pink Floyd), Hank Marvin (of the Shadows), Laurence Juber and Denny Laine on guitars; Ronnie Laine (formerly with the Small Faces), John Paul Jones (of Led Zeppelin) and Bruce Thomas (of

Elvis Costello's Attractions) on bass; Tony Ashton (of Ashton, Gardner & Dyke), Gary Brooker (of Procol Harum) and Linda McCartney on keyboards; John Bonham (of Led Zeppelin), Kenny Jones (of the Small Faces) and Steve Holly on drums; Morris Pert, Speedy Acquaye and Tony Carr on percussion; and Thaddeus Richard, Tony Dorsey, Howie Casey and Steve Howard on brass. During the sessions a special film of the occasion was taken for posterity, intended for showing as a television item. Director Barry Chattington was in charge of the film crew, who were using five 35mm Panavision cameras. Paul was to edit the 80,000 feet of film taken that day into 5,500 feet, which made a 40-minute film called *Rockestra*. However, the film was never released, although a 15-minute excerpt was screened on Monday 11 June at the *Back To The Egg* launch party.

Paul was to say: 'I asked the fellow who was going to do the film if he could film it like they film wildlife. You know, they sit back off wildlife and just observe it and they just let it go on with its own thing and when you try and film our session it's a bit like the same sort of thing. If everyone notices the cameras and lights, they all freeze up and won't talk naturally and they all get embarrassed. So they put all the cameras behind a big wall and no one could see the cameras and a lot of them didn't even know it was being filmed.' Then he joked, 'John Bonham had no idea it was filmed – in fact he is suing us!'

The Rockestra was to be gathered together for one special surprise appearance. Dr Kurt Waldheim, Secretary General of the United Nations, had contacted Paul regarding the tragedy in Kampuchea, where millions of people were starving. As a result, 'The Concerts For The People Of Kampuchea' were organised at the Hammersmith Odeon, London, in December 1979.

Paul and Wings appeared on the bill on Saturday 29 December, with Elvis Costello & the Attractions and Dave Edmunds and Nick Lowe in Rockpile. At the end of the Wings set the Rockestra took to the stage. Musicians included Pete Townshend, Dave Edmunds, James Honeyman-Scott, Billy Bremner, John Bruce Thomas, Gary Brooker, John Bonham, John Paul Jones, Kenny Jones, Bruce Thomas, Rockpile and Robert Plant.

They performed 'The Rockestra Theme', 'Lucille', with Paul on lead vocals, 'Let It Be' on which Pete Townshend had an exceptional solo spot and 'Rockestra Theme' again.

There was much anticipation aroused by the concert due to persistent rumours that the Beatles would be re-forming for a special appearance that evening.

The concerts were filmed for television and were screened in certain ITV regions on Sunday 4 January 1981 in 'Rock For Kampuchea', an edited version of highlights from the four concerts. There was also an album issued in America on Atlantic K60153 on Monday 30 March 1981 and in Britain on Friday 3 April 1981 that featured Paul, Wings and the Rockestra. Apart from the three Rockestra numbers from the concert, the album included Wings performing 'Got To Get You Into My Life', 'Every Night' and 'Coming Up'.

Rockline

A radio show broadcast on KLOS-FM in Los Angeles. Paul appeared live for ninety minutes on the show on Monday 29 May 1989.

Paul appeared on the show again on Friday 26 October 1990. During the interview he also played an acoustic version of 'Matchbox'.

Rockshow

Paul's first feature-length film produced for the cinema. Lasting 102 minutes, it featured the Wings concert at the Kings Dome, Seattle on 10 June 1976. An audience of 67,000 people watched the concert. Some numbers were edited in from film of other locations on the tour.

Altogether there were twenty-three numbers in the film, a further six having been edited out of the finished print.

Songs included 'Venus And Mars', 'Yesterday', 'Band On The Run', 'Let Me Roll It', 'The Long And Winding Road', 'Maybe I'm Amazed', 'Jet' and 'Bluebird'.

The film was made by Paul's company MPL and edited by Robin Clark and Paul Stein. The amplification system used during the film was capable of generating 15,000 watts.

The movie was premiered at New York's Ziegfield Theater on Wednesday 26 November 1980, but the European Charity Premiere at the Dominion Theatre, Tottenham Court Road, London, proved to be the star-studded event. It took place on Wednesday 8 April 1981, was attended by Paul and was graced by the Earl and Countess of Snowdon. The charity premiere was in aid of the Snowdon Award Scheme for Physically Handicapped Students and was attended by a host of stars including comedian Billy Connolly, musicians Mike Oldfield, Steve Harley, Phil Lynott, Eric Stewart and Gary Glitter, Trevor Eve (who portrayed Paul in the stage play *John, Paul, George, Ringo . . . and Bert*) and luminaries from the world of politics, fashion and theatre.

Rockshow was distributed in Britain by Miracle International and in America by Miramax Films.

It then became available on home video in Dolby stereo sound on Thorn EMI on Monday 12 October 1981 on VHS TVD 90 03342 and Betamax- TXB90 0334 4, although the tracks 'Call Me Back Again', 'Lady Madonna', 'The Long And Winding Road', 'Picasso's Last Words', 'Blackbird' and 'My Love' were omitted from the home video versions.

Rocky Raccoon

A number by Paul from *The Beatles* double album, which is a mock-country song that Paul attempts to sing in a Southern accent. It tells the tale of young Rocky from the hills of Dakota whose girlfriend Lily

McGill runs off with a nasty character, Danny. The track includes the sound of saloon gunfire.

The number was written during the sojourn at the Maharishi's ashram in Rishikesh, India and Paul had the inspiration when he, John Lennon and Donovan Leitch were playing their guitars on the roof of one of the ashram buildings.

The Western-style song had an original working title of 'Rocky Sassoon'. Paul had some assistance from Donovan and John, although John was to comment, 'Paul wrote it, couldn't you guess? Would I go to all that trouble about Gideon's Bible and all that stuff.'

The song was recorded at Abbey Road Studios in one complete session on 15 August 1968. A version was also included on the Beatles' *Anthology 3* CD in October 1996.

Roddenberry, Gene

The creator of *Star Trek* and several other science-fiction series.

In November 1976 Paul got together with Roddenberry to work on a science-fiction musical film starring Wings. Roddenberry had approached Paul while he was recording at Abbey Road Studios. The proposed musical about an invasion from space was intended as a vehicle in which the group could show their acting as well as their musical talents and an announcement about the project was given to the press. Unfortunately, nothing came of it.

Rode All Night

A rough version of this number was recorded during the *Ram* sessions and the refrain was later incorporated into 'Giddy', a number given to Roger Daltrey.

Rodrigo

A Spanish composer. For the annual Proms in 1996, the BBC Proms '96 programme included a free CD in which 21 celebrities had voiced their appreciation of a classical composer. Paul had selected Rodrigo.

He commented, 'When I was a teenager, my father gave me a trumpet for my birthday. I tried to master it because he himself had played trumpet at an early age, and he taught me a little. I realised that it was going to be difficult for me to sing with this thing stuck in my mouth so I asked if he minded if I traded it in for a guitar. Which I did. I think that first guitar, a Zenith, started my love of the instrument. A piece like Rodrigo's *Guitar Concerto* is therefore a very special piece of music to me, and I think to hear it performed on 12 August at the Royal Albert Hall is going to be a very special evening indeed.

'The composer of the piece, Rodrigo, was born in Spain around about the time my father was born in Liverpool, and when the *Concerto de Aranjuez* was being premiered it was around the time I was being born in Liverpool – a couple of years before. I think this is a very beautiful piece of music. Its melody has always stuck with me, particularly the slower movement, which is quite famous. It's a very haunting melody, and although it's simple, the whole piece, it's very memorable. So there's one to remember: Rodrigo, John Williams, the Albert Hall, the Proms – a great institution.'

Rose, Charlie

An American talk-show host. Charlie Rose interviewed Paul for the 92nd Street YMHA Concert at Kaufmann Concert Hall, 1395 Lexington Avenue, New York on Tuesday 24 April 2001. The event, with tickets at $20 each, was sold out in advance, so a satellite feed was set up.

Rosetta

An old jazz standard composed by Earl 'Fatha' Hines and Henri Woods that Paul rediscovered. He called Brian O'Hara of the Fourmost and suggested it be their next single for CBS. He also offered to produce the single for them.

'Rosetta' was released on Friday 21 February 1969 on CBS 4041, with 'Just Like Before' on the flip. Mike McCartney plugged the disc and Bill Harry acted as PR.

Sadly, it never made the charts.

Rough Ride

A track from the *Flowers In The Dirt* album, originally recorded in October 1984.

A version of this number lasting 4 minutes and 49 seconds was included on the *Tripping The Live Fantastic* album. It was recorded live at the Palais Omnisport de Bercy in Paris on 10 October 1989 during the 1989/90 World Tour.

Paul was to say it was 'me trying to be Big Bill Broonzy'. He added, 'I'd seen a blues programme, and I thought, well these guys do a song and it's all one chord, two verses and a little guitar riff. That's all I had and it grew from nothing.'

Royal Court Theatre

A Liverpool theatre which saw the launch of Wings' 1979 UK tour with a free concert on 23 November with new group members Laurence Juber and Steve Holly.

The theatre had been threatened with closure due to financial problems earlier that year and Paul had donated £5,000 to the venue. At the city council a motion by Conservative members to thank Paul for his generosity was voted down by the Labour councillors. One of them was Roy Stoddard, who commented, 'I don't see why Paul McCartney should be singled out for special praise. The Beatles could have given a million and not missed it. They made their millions and we have not seen them since.'

The free concert was held in honour of Paul's former school, the Liverpool Institute. Pupils and staff were invited and Paul was to say: 'It's my way of saying "Thank you" for some very happy years. Everyone seems to knock their schooldays but for me they have fond memories.'

Wings also played to full houses at the Royal Court for the next three days.

Regarding the ungenerous comments by Roy Stoddard: this was actually typical of Liverpool councillors, particularly Labour, who had been lambasting the Beatles for years and refusing permission for a variety of tributes ranging from statues to street names. Eventually they had to bow to the inevitable and such tributes have become beneficial to the city's tourist industry.

Eddie Roderick was another councillor who, in January 1984, following press coverage of Paul's drug charge in Barbados, wanted the offer that had been made to Paul of the Freedom of the City to be withdrawn. Roderick said, 'He has brought shame on the city.' His request fell on deaf ears and Paul received the honour on 28 November 1984 in a ceremony held before the premiere of *Give My Regards To Broad Street*.

Royal Iris

The famous Liverpool ferryboat that was available for dances and parties and proved to be a popular showboat on the Mersey. When Paul made his appearance in Liverpool with Wings in November 1979, he took the group for a thirty-minute cruise on the boat at a cost of £150. He was to comment that the Beatles 'played in the salon of the *Royal Iris* for a fiver each – and we weren't asked back!'

He was joking, of course, because they appeared on the *Royal Iris* on four different occasions.

The ferry was taken out of service and ended up moored at Greenwich, London.

Royal Rock Show, The

A Radio Luxembourg series hosted by disc jockey Tony Prince, who interviewed Linda McCartney at Elstree Studios in March 1976. The interview was broadcast on Saturday 20 March between 11 p.m. and midnight.

Linda mentioned the new Wings album of the time, *Wings At The Speed Of Sound*, and discussed the problems of travelling extensively on a two-month tour with her children, coping as a wife, mother and musician. She said she was pleased with the education that her children were receiving: 'Heather is very worldly, just having gone with us everywhere we've gone.'

She mentioned that her children were just ordinary kids: 'They're not affected, posh or anything.'

Discussing photography, she reiterated that she was no relation to the Eastman-Kodak family, and said that she usually only carried one camera around with her, always loaded. She discussed her father and his profession in New York, pointing out that Paul had wanted him to look after his personal business affairs, but that he'd never attempted to get involved in managing the Beatles.

She discussed her diaries, in particular the Nashville diary and her diary of Polaroid photographs, then mentioned her forthcoming book *Linda's Pictures*.

Prince then led her into details of her background and how she became a photographer. She recalled seeing Paul for the first time at the Bag Of Nails club in London and their first dates, then discussed the track about her on the new album, 'Cook Of The House'.

She told of her struggles to develop her musical ability and the criticisms she received in the early stages. Like any normal couple they had their 'barnies', she said, and mentioned the recent Scandinavian tour and the trouble they'd had in finding drummers for Wings. For the future she wanted Paul and herself to become involved in some films and television work and liked the idea of acting in movies.

Linda was asked about the superstars who were leaving England because of the swingeing taxes introduced by Harold Wilson's government and though she thought it was silly of the government to drive so many people away, she maintained she and Paul would remain in England, 'because I don't believe money should rule your life. I like England and Scotland.'

She mentioned that the people in the music industry stimulated work and brought a lot of money into England, but with the new tax regulations a lot of this would be lost to America.

Linda admitted liking the English countryside – and the people: 'they're very sort of ordinary people, rather than laid-back people. I'm normally a laid-back person myself.'

On nights off Paul and Linda would watch telly, have a good meal and put their feet up, she said, and mentioned that when they were at their farm in Scotland, 'we listen to music, watch telly, paint a bit, draw a bit. Just talk. Go out for a walk.' They still discussed the Beatles, she said, and had just phoned John Lennon a few days previously; John and Paul were mates but George and Ringo weren't seeing eye to eye. Of her relationship with Yoko, she commented, 'Oh, I get on with her great! Much to people's surprise. I think she is really a nice, good person . . . she's not pushy or anything.'

Royal Variety Command Performance

Paul appeared on the Royal Variety Command Performance at the Theatre Royal, Drury Lane, London on Monday 24 November 1986. It was 23 years earlier that Paul had performed at a Royal Command Performance with the Beatles.

Highlights of the show were screened on BBC TV on Saturday 29 November. In the royal box was Queen Elizabeth the Queen Mother, the Duchess of York, Princess Alexandra, the Hon Mrs Angus Ogilvy and the Hon Angus Ogilvy.

Paul was introduced on stage by David Frost and he sat at a grand piano and sang 'Only Love Remains', backed by Linda McCartney and Tessa Niles on vocals, Eric Stewart on acoustic guitar, Jamie Talbot on saxophone, Graham Ward on drums, Preston Heymen on percussion and Nick Glennie-Smith on synthesiser.

Rude Studios

The name Paul gave to the studios he had built on his farm on the grounds of Kintyre in Campbeltown, Scotland. It had a four-track recorder and was described as 'a wood-lined, tin-roofed shack'. It was here, in 1975, that he produced and recorded *Holly Days*. He later changed the name to Spirit of Ranachan Studios, which was situated in a larger barn.

Dock Sweetenham had prepared the studio in the mid-1970s as a small four-track studio.

During 1977 Paul recorded numerous demos here, including ones for numbers such as 'Suicide', 'Love Awake', 'Winter Rose', 'The Pound Is Sinking', 'Dress Me Up As A Robber', 'Twelve Of The Clock', 'Down San Francisco Way', 'Giddy', 'Girls' School', 'With A Little Luck', 'Purple Afternoon', 'London Town', 'Café On The Left Bank', 'Famous Groupies', 'Children Children', 'Girlfriend' and 'Don't Let It Bring You Down'.

Rudolph The Red-Nosed Reggae

A number, which Paul recorded at Abbey Road Studios in 1975. He recalled that he was 'just recording some crazy music for some far-out film some fellow was doing.' During a break in the session, Paul began talking to the deliveryman from a music rental company he'd hired. He discovered that the man could play the fiddle and asked him to get his instrument and join in with him on the session for the 'Rudolph' number. After the session the man disappeared without giving his name to Paul. The number ended up as the flipside of 'Wonderful Christmastime' in 1979. Later, the identity of the fiddler was established: his name was Bob Loveday.

Run Devil Run (album)

Paul was to say, 'This album is something I've wanted to do for years, and Linda was always very keen that I should do it. So I thought it would be the right thing to do.'

Run Devil Run was released in the US on Tuesday 5 October 1999 on Capitol CDP 5-22351-2 and in Britain on Monday 4 October. Chris Thomas and Paul produced it at Abbey Road Studios between 1 March and 5 May 1999. Geoff Emerick and Paul Hicks were the engineers. Dave Fine took the cover photograph. Musicians included: Paul McCartney on electric guitar, bass guitar, percussion and vocals; Ian Paice on drums and percussion; Peter Wingfield on organ; Dave Gilmour on electric guitar, steel guitar and backing vocals; Mick Green on electric guitar; Chris Hall on accordion; and Dave Mattacks on drums, percussion, piano and Wurlitzer.

Ian Paice was to comment, 'Paul wanted to make the album the same way that the Beatles cut their early records. So he went to the same studio, Number Two at Abbey Road, and he followed exactly the same routine. The rule was that we got there at 10 a.m., like the Beatles used to, and have a cup of tea. Then we'd start work at ten-thirty, stop for lunch at 1 p.m.; and then work through to five-thirty, when we went home. We did that for five days, and in that time we recorded twenty tracks.'

The tracks were: 'Blue Jean Bop' (originally recorded by Gene Vincent), 'She Said Yeah' (previously recorded by the Animals and the Rolling Stones), 'All Shook Up' (recorded by Elvis Presley), 'Run Devil Run' (one of Paul's own numbers), 'No Other Baby' (recorded by Chad And Jeremy), 'Try Not To Cry' (a McCartney original), 'Movie Magg' (previously recorded by Carl Perkins), 'Brown Eyed Handsome Man' (the Buddy Holly classic), 'What It Is' (another composition by Paul), 'Coquette' (recorded by Fats Domino), 'I Got Stung' (recorded by Elvis Presley), 'Honey Hush' (recorded by Joe Turner), 'Shake A Hand' (recorded by Faye Adams) and 'Let's Have A Party' (recorded by Wanda Jackson).

There was a special limited edition boxed set of eight singles from *Run Devil Run* issued in Britain and Germany on Parlophone 523 221 on Monday 6 December 1999.

They were: 'Blue Jean Bop'/'She Said Yeah' on Parlophone 5232301. 'All Shook Up'/'Run Devil Run' on Parlophone 5232311. 'No Other Baby'/'Lonesome Town' on Parlophone 5232321. 'Try Not to Cry'/'Movie Magg' on Parlophone 5232331. 'Brown Eyed Handsome Man'/'What It Is' on Parlophone 5232341. 'Coquette'/'I Got Stung' on Parlophone 5232351. 'Honey Hush'/'Shake A Hand' on Parlophone 5232361 and 'Party'/'Fabulous' on Parlophone 5232371.

Parlophone also issued a 7,000 limited edition box set of 7″ singles from the *Run Devil Run* album on 7 December 1999 on Parlophone TPM 701A.

Strictly for promotional use, Parlophone also issued a 7″ single of 'Run Devil Run'/'Blue Jean Bop' on RDR 003.

Run Devil Run (song)

An original rock-'n'-roll song by Paul that he penned on the suggestion of co-producer Chris Thomas when they were discussing the album of rock-'n'-roll covers, which eventually adopted the title *Run Devil Run*. The number lasted 2 minutes and 37 seconds. It was recorded at Abbey Road Studios on Wednesday 3 March 1999 and featured Paul on lead vocal and bass guitar, Dave Gilmour on electric guitar and lap steel guitar, Mick Green on electric guitar, Peter Wingfield on piano and Ian Paice on drums.

Paul recalled that he was in Atlanta with his son James when he came across a voodoo shop in which a bottle of bath salts in the window display was called 'Run Devil Run'. He remembered that when he was trying to think of a title for a song while on holiday.

Rupert And The Frog Song

A home video cassette with the full title 'Paul McCartney's Rupert And The Frog Song'. It was issued in Britain by Virgin Video in November 1985 on VVC (VHS and Beta).

The 15-minute animation of the Rupert story is the main item in the 25-minute video, which also features the short films *Seaside Woman* and *The Oriental Nightfish*.

The video became the No. 1 hit that Christmas and Britain's best-selling music video up until then, selling 200,000 copies during the year. Paul picked up the award for 'Best Selling Video Of The Year' at the British Video Awards on Thursday 16 October 1986; it received the BAFTA as 'Best Animated Short Film'; and the theme song won the Ivor Novello Award as 'Best Film Theme Or Song of 1984'.

Geoff Dunbar directed the film for MPL Communications and Paul provided the voice of Rupert with other vocal contributions coming from Windsor Davies and June Whitfield. In the story Rupert sets out on a hike and encounters a tree full of butterflies. He then follows some frogs into a 'frogs only' cavern and witnesses a performance by the frog chorus. Rupert then saves the frog king and queen by warning them as an owl swoops down on them. He then returns home to tell his mother of his adventure.

Paul is credited with writing the storyline although Alan F Murray, a University of Edinburgh professor, says that the storyline was loosely based on 'Rupert And The Water Lily', which first appeared in the 1958 Rupert annual and features an Alfred Bestall picture of a frog chorus.

Rupert Bear

A popular British children's character created for the *Daily Express* newspaper by Mary Tourtel in 1920.

He is a white bear who walks upright and wears a red cardigan, checked yellow trousers with scarf to match and white boots. He lives in Bear Cottage on Nutwood Common with his parents, Mr and Mrs Bear.

Rupert Bear annuals regularly sell in the region of 175,000 copies per year, and over 50 million have been sold worldwide. The strip has been running in the *Daily Express* newspaper for decades. Rupert is also the mascot of the Muscular Dystrophy campaign in Britain.

Paul used to read Rupert Bear annuals as a child and rediscovered the character when he started reading the stories to his stepdaughter Heather. In April 1970 one of the first things Paul did on leaving the Beatles was to buy the film rights to Rupert. His new company McCartney Productions Ltd handled it.

Paul says that he thinks of Rupert as a twelve-year-old boy and at the time commented, 'I've bought up the film rights for Rupert The Bear, the cartoon character from the *Daily Express*. As a kid I loved that strip – I've still got all the old Rupert annuals at home.'

He originally began to develop the idea of an eight-minute featurette of Rupert with animator Oscar Grillo and actually penned about eleven songs for a full-length animated movie.

In 1980 he recorded 'We All Stand Together' at AIR Studios. George Martin produced the sessions on 31 October and 3 November. A 38-piece orchestra, the St Paul's Choir and the Kings Singers, backed Paul.

He completed a script himself called 'Rupert And The Frog Chorus' and worked with Geoff Dunbar, an award-winning British designer who actually animated the final project. This turned into a 13-minute film, which Geoff also directed.

In the story Rupert leaves Bear Cottage one morning and sets off on a walk. On the way he encounters a tree full of butterflies. He discovers a waterfall, finds a secret passage and witnesses a huge gathering of frogs. He is enchanted as they begin to sing and their king and queen arise out of a cascade. Two mischievous black cats and a large owl upset the magical moment. The congregation scatters but they are unharmed by the interlopers. Rupert returns home to tell his mother of the adventure.

The cartoon was a great success when it was included on the bill with *Give My Regards To Broad Street* and Paul's single 'We All Stand Together' was a chart hit.

In the programme 'The Rupert Bear Story', first broadcast on Channel 4 television in Britain on 8 December 1982, Paul described his nostalgic feelings for Rupert. Hosted by Terry Jones, the programme paid tribute to 89-year-old Alfred Bestall, the artist who drew Rupert's adventures from 1935–1965. He recalled how he was reading Rupert to Heather 'and as I was going through the story I kept sort of thinking "Wow! this is amazing you know. I never really realised there was this in it." Because I knew in this image we'd got from our youth I kept seeing all these little glass bubbles with just one little lever so that they looked timeless . . . very modern.'

He was recalling images of Rupert flying around the world in a little glass ball.

Other people in the documentary included Sir Hugh Casson, President of the Royal Academy; Dr John Rae, headmaster of Westminster School; artist Anthony Green; and architect Richard Rogers.

In 1987, when Paul was recording the original soundtrack demos, he recorded his original storyline for a Rupert feature film:

Once upon a time there was a young bear called Rupert. He lived with his mother and father in the village of Nutwood.

One day he's exploring in the woods when he's surprised by a black-winged stallion leading a herd of white flying horses.

They tell Rupert of a secret mission that the King of the Birds has for him and the stallion says they've been sent to take him to the King. So Rupert sits on the leader's back and off they gallop.

After a long run they leap off the edge of a high cliff and start to climb towards the clouds. As the huge clouds part, they see the palace of the King of the Birds.

The King explains that the North wind has gone out of control and is about to freeze the whole world over. Rupert agrees to help and flies away carried by a giant bird. But they meet icy winds which freeze the bird's wings over and he has to drop Rupert, who manages to parachute down near a tropical island.

After a celebration with the natives where Rupert meets Sailor Sam, they set off the next day across the sea. A great storm blows up and their small boat is tossed by giant waves. They're washed up on the shore and are taken by friends home to Nutwood.

After a visit by Dr Lion, Rupert begins to feel better and one day he goes for a walk in the countryside, whistling in the meadow.

Rupert now decides to carry on with his mission and with the help of the Professor he sets off in a special flying bubble to seek the advice of the Wise Goat of the mountains. After many adventures, he meets Jack Frost, but they're both buried by a massive avalanche of snow and ice. The friendly South wind rescues them and after a fierce battle they and all their helpers defeat the North wind.

The balance between the winds is restored and Rupert and his friends say goodbye and return home for tea.

On 5 September 1988, while appearing on the BBC 2 programme *DEF II* he recalled, 'A long time ago I used to read my daughter Rupert at bedtime. One of the stories had him in a glass ball and there was just one little control. I thought, this is like *Star Wars*, it's amazing.'

Paul also mentioned Rupert in his 1990 tour programme when he wrote, 'I ended up going down to see Sir Max Aitken who was head of the *Daily Express* at the time, in his big office down in Fleet street, and said, "Look Max, baby, we've got to keep Rupert in England because if the Yanks get hold of him . . . they'll make him talk like Winnie the

Pooh and he'll be a little American Rupert." So I said, "You've got to let someone like me do it." I gave him all the big spiel and he was impressed ... so that was how we got the animation rights to do Rupert.'

Paul had been eager to see a feature film of his original story and commissioned various writers, including Terry Jones and Willis Hall to complete the scripts, but he never got round to doing the film.

Canada's Nelvana produced a 65-episode animated series in 1991–96, which was syndicated to 28 countries. Unfortunately, unlike Paul's 'Rupert And The Frog Song', which maintained Rupert's Englishness, the Nelvana cartoons Americanised Rupert and his friends and gave them mid-Atlantic accents.

Rupert The Bear

An unreleased soundtrack for a projected animated feature film of Rupert The Bear that has appeared on various bootleg albums such as *Rupert The Bear*. Paul recorded it at the Spirit of Ranachan Studio in Campbeltown, Scotland with Wings in July 1978.

There were twelve numbers recorded: 'Rupert's Song' (version one), 'Tippi Tippi Toes' (parents' theme), 'Flying Horses', 'When The Wind Is Blowing', 'The Palace Of The King Of The Birds', 'Sunshine, Sometime', 'Sea/Cornish Wafer', 'Storm', 'Nutwood Scene', 'Walking In The Meadow', 'Sea Melody', 'Rupert's Song' (version two).

Rushes

The Fireman, Paul's secret project with producer Youth, released a new album *Rushes* on Hydra Records, a new EMI label established specially for this release, on Monday 21 September 1998. It was Paul's first new work since Linda's death.

The press handout read, in part: 'The Fireman brings bison for trancing in the streets. The Fireman understands darsh walls and emerdeen sky. Do you? The Fireman knows a lemon's peal. And the power of the equinox.'

The CD cover sported a full-frontal female nude, with a zodiac design overlay.

The track listing was: 'Watercolour Guitars', 5 minutes 48 seconds; 'Paloverde', 11 minutes 57 seconds; 'Auraveda', 12 minutes 49 seconds; 'Fluid', 11 minutes 20 seconds; 'Appletree Cinnabar Amber', 7 minutes 12 seconds; 'Bison', 2 minutes 40 seconds; 'Watercolour Rush', 1 minute 44 seconds; 'Fluid', 11 minutes 19 seconds; and 'Bison', 7 minutes 55 seconds.

Russell, Willy

The award-winning Liverpool playwright whose first major stage play *John, George, Paul, Ringo ... and Bert* won the *Evening Standard* award as comedy of the year. Russell also received an award for *Blood*

Brothers and penned several other television plays based in Liverpool, some, like *Educating Rita* and *Shirley Valentine* being adapted into motion pictures.

Paul commissioned him to write a film script for a movie tentatively titled *Band On The Run*. Willy completed the project, but the film was never made.

Rye Memorial Care Centre

A hospital in Paul's locality in East Sussex, which was built largely as a result of his efforts.

In 1990 there was an announcement that the town hospital, which had been built during the First World War, was to be closed. Paul and Linda became involved in a campaign to prevent the closure or build an alternative. The need for the hospital in the area became apparent when a 16-year-old asthma patient died before he could reach the nearest available hospital following the closure.

Paul and Linda lobbied officials of the National Health Service, the local authority, social services and even marched through the town centre to protest at the closure.

He used a considerable donation from his £110,000 prize from the Royal Academy of Music in Sweden to help towards the building fund of the new centre, which eventually cost £5 million.

Paul and Linda joined 150 building workers and VIPs for the topping-off ceremony on Thursday 6 April 1995 when the final brick was placed on the new centre, which opened that summer.

The new mini-hospital contained 25 beds and a day-care centre.

Sacrée Soirée

A French television show. Paul and his band appeared on the programme on Wednesday 31 May 1989. In the show he appeared for 23 minutes during which he performed 'My Brave Face' with the band and was interviewed. George Martin was also on the show and '*Besame Mucho*' from the Decca auditions on New Year's Day 1962 was played.

Saint Paul

Another American single inspired by the 'Paul is dead' rumours. Recorded by Terry Knight and issued in 1969 on Capitol 2506 with 'Legend of William and Mary' on the flip.

Saint Vincent Estate '89

An Italian TV show on the RAI station. While promoting his new *Flowers In The Dirt* album, Paul and his group flew to Rome on Thursday 15 June 1989 to appear on the programme, which took place at the Teatro Delle Vittorie before a live audience. Paul and his group also mimed to 'My Brave Face' and 'This One'.

The programme was then screened on Friday 16 June 1989.

Sally

A number composed by W Haines/H Leon/L Towers, which was much associated with Gracie Fields, the famous singer from Lancashire. Paul's version of the number, lasting 2 minutes and 3 seconds was included on the *Tripping The Live Fantastic* album. It was recorded during a soundcheck at Wembley Arena, London on 21 January 1990 during the 1989/90 World Tour.

Sally G

A track which Paul wrote in Nashville in July 1974, inspired by country music singer Diane Gaffney and a visit to the red-light district 'Printer's Alley'. The number was recorded on Tuesday 9 July 1974 between 6 p.m. and midnight at the Soundshop Recording Studios. Paul invited a number of country music musicians to join him on this country track including the pedal steel and slide guitar player Lloyd Green and Johnny Gimble, fiddle player with Bob Willis and the Texas Playboys.

It was also the first Wings single to feature Geoff Britton and Jimmy McCulloch.

It was issued in Britain and America as the flipside of 'Junior's Farm'. The British single was issued on Friday 25 October 1974 and the American one on 4 November 1974.

The single was re-released on Wednesday 5 February 1975 with 'Sally G' as the A-side. Paul commented, 'We flipped the single and I thought it might seem like we were trying to fool the public, but it isn't. It's only to get a bit of exposure on that song. Otherwise, it just dies a death, and only the people who bought 'Junior's Farm' get to hear 'Sally G'. I like to have hits, this is what I am making records for.'

It was also the last single to appear on the original Apple label.

Same Time Next Year

A song Paul wrote and recorded as the title track for the film *Same Time Next Year* in 1988, a movie that starred Alan Alda and Ellen Burstyn. The number was rejected in favour of 'The Last Time I Felt Like This' by Marvin Hamlisch, because it was said that Paul's number 'gave away too much of the plot'. Paul's 'Same Time Next Year' was eventually issued on 5 February 1990 as a bonus track on the CD and 12″ vinyl singles of 'Put It There'.

Paul recorded the number at Rak Studios on 5 May 1978, with Laurence Juber making his first appearance as a member of Wings; it was co-produced by Paul and Chris Thomas. The following day it was completed at Abbey Road Studios with a 68-piece string section, in an arrangement by Paul and Fiachra Trench.

San Ferry Anne

A number Paul wrote and recorded for the *Wings At The Speed Of Sound* album. It was 2 minutes and 6 seconds in length.

San Francisco Blues

Originally a single by Ramblin' Jack Elliott. During the MTV *Unplugged*, Robbie McIntosh played it on slide guitar.

San Remo Festival, The

Paul appeared at the annual San Remo Music Festival in Italy on Saturday 27 February 1988 when he featured as the headline attraction and on stage performed 'Once Upon A Long Ago' and 'Listen To What The Man Said' during a 14-minute spot. He lip-synched both songs for a television show. The appearance also gave him the opportunity of performing in public with his new band: Hamish Stuart, guitar/bass; Chris Whitten, drums; Gary Barnacle, saxophone; Andrew Chater, violin; and Linda McCartney on keyboards. George Harrison was also present at the festival and on Friday 26 February received a 'Best Video Of The Year' award for 'When We Was Fab'.

Saturday Night Live

An American TV show on the NBC network.

In a tongue-in-cheek manner, Lorne Michaels had been making offers for the Beatles to re-form and appear on the show.

On Saturday 24 April 1976 Paul and Linda dropped in to see John and Yoko at the Dakota apartments. John had been watching television and they all saw Michaels make his offer once again, saying, 'Hi, I'm Lorne Michaels, the producer of *Saturday Night*. Right now we're being seen by approximately twenty-two million viewers, but please allow me, if I may, to address myself to four very special people – John, Paul, George and Ringo: the Beatles.

'Lately, there have been a lot of rumours to the effect that the four of you might be getting back together. That would be great. In my book, the Beatles are the best thing that ever happened to music. It goes deeper than that, you're just not a musical group, you're part of us, we grew up with you. It's for this reason that I'm inviting you to come on our show.

'Now, we've heard and read a lot about personality and legal conflicts that might prevent you guys from reuniting, that's none of my business. You guys will have to handle that. But it's also been said that no one has yet come up with enough money to satisfy you. Well, if it's money you want, there's no problem here. The National Broadcasting Company authorises me to authorise you a cheque for $3,000. Here, can you get a close-up of this?'

Michaels holds the cheque up to the camera and it is made out to 'The Beatles'.

'As you can see, verifiably, a cheque made out to you, the Beatles, for $3,000. All you have to do is sing three Beatle tunes. 'She Loves You, Yeah, Yeah, Yeah'. That's $1,000 right there. You know the words, and it'll be easy. Like I said, this cheque is made out to 'The Beatles'. You divide it anyway you want. If you want to give Ringo less, that's up to you. I'd rather not get involved. I'm sincere about this. If it helps you to reach a decision to reunite well, it's a worthwhile investment. You have agents, you know where I can be reached. Just think about it. OK? Thank you.'

John said that they were amused by it and thought it would be funny if the two of them turned up at the studio. They almost took a cab to

Saturday Night Live but decided they felt too tired. Paul and Linda left them while John and Yoko settled down to watch 'The Time Machine' on television.

Michaels repeated the offer on the Saturday 22 May 1976 edition of the show, upping the offer from $3,000 to $3,200.

On the Saturday 2 October 1976 edition of the show he said, 'Hi, I'm Lorne Michaels. Several months ago I made a bona fide offer of $3,000 to the Beatles to perform on *Saturday Night*. For months there was no response and then about two weeks ago, I got a long-distance phone call from Eric Idle, tonight's host, in London saying that if I would let him come over and host the show, he would bring the Beatles with him. Well, in my excitement, I agreed and foolishly sent him the cheque for $3,000. You see, he said the Beatles wanted the money in advance so that they could buy some new clothes to wear on the show. Well, when I met Eric at the airport last Monday, I noticed that he was alone. So I said, "Where are they, I mean the Beatles." He said that their new clothes weren't ready yet, so they were going to catch a later flight. I still didn't think anything was wrong, until yesterday, when a telegram arrives saying, "Can't come now, Ringo's pants too long Stop Please send more money for alterations Stop Signed the Beatles."

'When I showed the telegram to Eric, he said he would call London immediately and he did, and convinced John, Paul, George and Ringo to send over a film instead. Well, twenty minutes ago, the film arrived from England. I just saw it and it's . . . quite good, only it's not the Beatles, it's the Rutles. Evidently, Eric had a bad phone connection to London and, well, anyway . . . it's halfway through the show and Eric's already spent the $3,000, so ladies and gentlemen, here are the Rutles . . . the fabulous Rutland sound, created by the fab four, Dirk, Stig, Nasty and Barry, who created a musical legend that will last a lunchtime.'

Paul and Linda were guests on the programme on Saturday 17 May 1980. Billy Crystal, in the guise of a character of his invention called Father Guido Sarducci, talked to them by satellite as they were outside the MPL offices in London. 'Sarducci' also sang a 'Beatles Medley'. A clip of 'Coming Up' also received its American premiere on the show.

During his New World Tour, Paul and his band appeared on the show on Saturday 13 February 1993. Paul initially chatted to Lorne Michaels about the $3,000 offer *Saturday Night Live* made for a Beatles reunion many years earlier. Paul and his band performed three numbers, 'Biker Like An Icon', 'Get Out Of My Way' and 'Hey Jude'. Linda joined him on a spoof song 'I Love My Sweatshirt' and he also appeared in some comic sketches such as 'The Mimic' and was subject to a spoof interview with Chris Farley.

Saturday Shake Up

A children's TV show produced by Tyne-Tees Television. On Friday 7 December 1979 Wings were interviewed for the show backstage at the

City Hall, Newcastle. It was added to clips from 'Old Siam Sir', 'Goodnight Tonight' and 'Wonderful Christmastime' to produce a 24-minute segment, which was titled 'Flying With Wings' and screened on Saturday 22 December 1979.

Saturday Superstore
A BBC 1 Saturday-morning show for youngsters, hosted by disc jockey Mike Read. Paul appeared on the show for forty minutes on Saturday 7 December 1985 during which he participated in an audience phone-in and introduced two of his promotional videos – for 'Spies Like Us' and 'We All Stand Together'.

He returned to the show on Saturday 13 December 1986 and was interviewed by Mike Read once again. Paul answered viewers questions by phone and his appearance lasted for 28 minutes.

Save The Child
A single issued by Angel/Capitol in the States on Tuesday 12 November 1991, the first and only American single from the *Liverpool Oratorio*. In the UK it was the second single following 'The World You're Coming Into'.

'Save The Child' was issued in three formats in the UK on Monday 18 November, with 'The Drinking Song' on the flip. They were the 7″ vinyl version on KIRIS 2 or 2 04513 7, the compact disc on KIRICD 2 or 2 04513 2 and the cassette on KIRITC 2 or 2 04513 4.

Say Say Say (promotional film)
The promotional film for the video was directed by Bob Giraldi who had earlier directed a Michael Jackson promotional film for 'Beat It'.

The promotional film cost half a million dollars to produce and was filmed in Los Alamos, California between Tuesday 4 October and Friday 7 October 1983.

The promotional film was premiered on *The Tube*, a Channel 4 programme on Friday 28 October 1983.

Say Say Say (single)
A single by Paul McCartney and Michael Jackson, issued in America on Columbia/MPL 38-04 168 and in Britain on Parlophone R6062. It was released simultaneously in Britain and the US on Monday 3 October 1983. The number was produced by George Martin and was also included on the *Pipes Of Peace* album.

The 7″ single was a four-minute version, with 'Ode To A Koala Bear' on the flipside. The 12″ version, with a remix by 'Jellybean' Benitez, was nearly two minutes longer and, apart from 'Ode To A Koala Bear', also has a 7-minute instrumental version on the flipside.

The review in the music paper *Melody Maker* read: 'Ebony and Ivory back together in perfect harmony but for what? Mutual bank accounts?' The *New Musical Express* review read, 'Far closer to a

Wingsoid rocker than anything that Jackson had attempted over the past few years – but still falls short of even the pitiful standard set by last year's collaboration.'

It was released in Germany on Odeon 1C006-1652527.

The number was included on a charity disc compilation, *Let's Beat It*, with proceeds donated to the TJ Martell Foundation for Leukemia in New York. It was issued on Monday 1 July 1985 by Epic Records on EPC 26345 and on cassette 40-26345.

Scene Special

A Granada Television show. Paul recorded an interview for the show on Wednesday 18 January 1967 that was transmitted on Thursday 7 March 1967. Paul discussed the 'underground' scene and Pink Floyd performed 'Interstellar Overdrive'.

Schwartz, Francie

A Pennsylvanian-born, New York City-educated brunette who arrived in Britain in 1968 seeking backers for a film script she had written. She took it along to the Apple office in Wigmore Street and Paul noticed her in the reception lounge. They chatted for a while and he said she could make herself useful in the Apple offices. She gave Paul her address in London and he came to see her one Monday morning.

She was to comment, 'He settled right into a chair with me on his lap. The kisses started . . . and later we visited friends in the country and ran barefoot in the rain.'

The first time she and Paul made love was in her King's Road flat immediately after Mike McCartney's wedding. Paul had been to lunch there a week earlier.

The brief affair had begun while Paul was still courting Jane Asher, who was currently away on tour. According to stories of the time, Francie had become a regular visitor to Paul's Cavendish Avenue house when, about three weeks into the arrangement, Jane turned up. Her tour of the provinces with the Old Vic had ended ahead of schedule.

Margot Stevens, one of the Apple Scruffs (the group of fans who hung around the Beatles' homes, offices and recording studios), spotted Jane arriving in her car and pressed the Entryphone, warning Paul of her arrival. He didn't believe her. Jane, who had her own key, entered the house and found Francie dressed only in Paul's dressing gown. She left.

Later that evening her mother arrived in an estate car and took away some of Jane's belongings, while Paul was recording the White Album. Mrs Asher left a note for Paul and he was to tell Francie that he'd said to Mrs Asher, 'I've met someone who's offering something that Jane couldn't.'

She was watching TV with Paul, his father Jim and his wife Angie and stepdaughter Ruth the night Jane publicly announced their engagement was over.

Francie began living in Cavendish Avenue, doing the cooking, cleaning and entertaining house guests such as John and Yoko. She also attended recording sessions at Abbey Road.

Soon after, the fling with Francie was over and she wrote a piece in the *News of the World* newspaper, saying: 'He (Paul) hadn't formally ended his friendship with Jane Asher, so at first it was a secret.'

She returned to America where she sold the story of her affair to *Rolling Stone* magazine entitled 'Memories Of An Apple Girl'.

She then wrote a book called *Body Count* for *Rolling Stone* publishers Straight Arrow, concerning her various love affairs. She devoted a full chapter to her short affair with Paul, whom she described as: 'A little Medici prince pampered and laid on a satin pillow at a very early age.'

Scott, Tom

A horn player who has appeared on sessions for Paul, George Harrison and Ringo Starr. Scott provided the sax solo on 'Listen To What The Man Said'.

Scottish Exhibition And Conference Centre

The Glasgow venue for Paul's Saturday 23 June 1990 appearance on his 1989/90 World Tour. The concert, called 'Get Back To Glasgow', had originally been planned as an open-air show, but it was moved indoors when it was believed that the ticket sales were waning. However, the actual concert drew a capacity audience of 9,300. Paul performed 'Mull Of Kintyre' on this show for the only time on the entire tour and the Campbeltown Pipers accompanied him. A proportion of the proceeds for this show went to local charities, including the Yorkhill Children's Trust, Scottish Women's Aid, the Simon Community for the Homeless and the Scotcare charitable consortium.

Scouseology Awards

The Scouseology Awards are presented in Liverpool each year to people who have made a contribution to life on Merseyside. Whilst Paul was in Liverpool at the end of June 1991 for the premiere of *Paul McCartney's Liverpool Oratorio* at the Anglican Cathedral, Liverpool, he received the Scouseology award as 'Scouse Personality Of The Year'. Paul said, 'I'm chuffed. This means more to me than all these music paper awards. This is the people of Liverpool voting for me. This is Scousers saying, "You're OK, Macca." It is great to be back home and what a fantastic place the Cathedral is. To think I was nearly a choirboy here myself, but they turned me down.'

The awards, sponsored by Whitbread and the *Liverpool Echo*, were presented to Paul by Arthur Johnson, the *Echo* marketing manager and Phil Young of Scouse Promotions. Young was in the same class as Paul at the Joseph Williams County Primary School.

Although a prominent Liverpool figure is awarded a 'Scouse Of The Year' award at the annual events, Paul was given their highest accolade in 1997 when they gave him a 'Lifetime Achievement' award. Paul was unable to attend the event but sent a message of thanks.

Sea Dance
An instrumental track by Paul, which Wings recorded at the Sea Saint Studios in New Orleans in January 1975 during the *Venus And Mars* sessions. The track wasn't used.

Seaside Woman (film)
In 1980, a 34-minute animated film based on the song and made by Oscar Grillo was entered in the Cannes Film Festival. It won first prize in the Short Film Competition, and due to this success, A&M reissued the single on Friday 18 July 1980 on A&M AMS 7548. Director Oscar Grillo was awarded the *Palme d'or du Festival international du film*.

Seaside Woman (song)
A reggae-inspired number written by Linda McCartney following a trip to Jamaica.

She was inspired to write it following the controversy over her co-writing songs with Paul. Linda commented, 'We were getting sued by a publisher, saying that I was incapable of writing. So Paul said, "Get out and write a song." So I wrote "Seaside Woman", which is a reggae number. So then I thought, "We need a B-side for it", so we went in and recorded a number called "Oriental Goldfish", which turned out so good that we thought, "Now we've got two A-sides", so now we needed two B-sides.'

She recorded it with backing from Wings members at AIR Studios on 27 November 1972 and Paul produced the session. It was decided to use the name Suzy and the Red Stripes in reference to the local Jamaican beer, Red Stripe and Suzy because Linda was referred to by that name in Jamaica because she liked a reggae version of the number 'Suzi Q'. However, the single, although recorded in 1972, wasn't issued until 1977 when it was released in America on Tuesday 31 May 1977 on Epic 3-50403. The flipside was another joint McCartney composition, 'Side To Seaside'. Epic was to re-release it in 1979 and 1980.

In Britain it wasn't released until Wednesday 17 August 1979 on A&M AMS7461.

On 7 July 1986 EMI released it on 7″ on EMI 5572 and 12″ on 12 EMI 5572 in a remix by engineer Alvin Clark. EMI produced a special promotional video for the release.

It was released in Germany on EMI 1A 006-201352.

Second Coming Of Suzanne, The
A film script by Michael Barry, son of American actor Gene Barry. British record producer Mickie Most at one time considered filming the

story, which concerned Jesus Christ's return to Earth in contemporary times – as a woman! One of the plum roles was that of Lee Simons, a pop star poet – and Most wanted Paul for the part. A story in the music press on Wednesday 9 September 1970 announced that Most had approached Paul about the role.

Most said, 'Paul's a hard guy to contact, but Apple are trying to get him for me. The chances are if he likes the script, he'll do it. Paul once told me that every film script offered to the Beatles was another *Help!* and that he wanted to do something different. This film is different.'

On Sunday 13 September 1970 Apple issued a statement that Paul would not be appearing in the film.

'The Second Coming Of Suzanne' was never made.

Secret Friend

The flipside of the limited edition 'Temporary Secretary' issued as a single in Britain only on 15 September 1980. At 10 minutes and 24 seconds it was the longest song Paul ever recorded. It had been produced during the *McCartney II* sessions, but not included on the album.

See, Joseph Melville

Linda McCartney's first husband. Born in New York, he moved to Tucson in 1960 after graduating from Princeton. He met Linda at Arizona University when he took his master's degree in geology. Linda was studying art history. He married Linda Eastman in 1962 and they had a daughter, Heather. Much of See's work involved travelling regularly while studying the indigenous people of Mexico and he believed the travelling contributed to the breakdown of his marriage. Discussing the split, he said, 'I started becoming interested in native peoples, travel and seeing the geology of the world and Linda started developing her photography and her appreciation of art. Slowly we began to spend more time apart.'

The marriage foundered in 1964 and Linda later married Paul, who adopted Heather.

It's said that See was the inspiration for the character of Jo Jo in the 1969 hit 'Get Back', penned by Paul. Paul refers to Jo Jo having left his home in Tucson, Arizona, for some California grass. Despite this, Paul insists that Jo Jo was a fictional character and says that a number of people have claimed to be Jo Jo, but that he had no particular person in mind when he wrote it.

See was devastated when Linda left him. He never remarried and remained fond of her until she died.

He was known as Melville to his friends and he remained good friends with the McCartneys over the years and began to get acquainted with his daughter Heather again from 1990. Paul and Linda encouraged him to keep in contact with Heather, and he said,

'Linda once said we were all a family. When you were around Paul and Linda you were happy because they made people happy.'

On Sunday 19 March 2000 he was found dead at his home in Tucson, from a self-inflicted shotgun wound. It was less than two years after Linda's death from breast cancer. His friends said he had been troubled for some time and Debra Zeller, an art historian who was a close friend, commented, 'Linda's death hit him really hard. He began to realise he was mortal too.'

A number of newspapers reported that the verdict of suicide might have been a premature one as the police were treating the death as suspicious. Sheriff's Deputy Deanna Copus commented, 'It's still very much an open case – there are suspicious circumstances and homicide police are still investigating.'

See was 62 years old when he died.

Seiwell, Denny

An American session drummer, born in Leighton, Pennsylvania, whose father had also been a drummer.

At the age of seven Denny began to play snare in the local Boy's Orchestra and was later to join the army as a bandsman.

In the 1960s, on leaving the army, he moved to Chicago where he played jazz with various outfits before moving on to New York, where he also played in jazz clubs and did a lot of session work with artists such as James Brown and John Denver.

Early in January 1971 Denny attended auditions for Wings in a New York basement. Paul said that he found Denny 'lying on a mattress one day in the Bronx. You know how all these people pass them by in *Midnight Cowboy*? Well, we thought, we'd better not, so we picked him, put him on a drum kit, and he was all right!'

Recalling the audition, Denny commented, 'A lot of the boys were really put out at being asked to audition. Paul just asked me to play, he didn't have a guitar, so I just sat and played. He had a certain look in his eyes. He was looking for more than a drummer, he was looking for a certain attitude too. I just played. I always say that if you can't get it on by yourself you can't get it on with anyone.'

He got the job and recorded the *Ram* sessions between January and March 1971. Paul then asked him if he would be interested in joining the band with him and Denny agreed.

Together with his French wife Monique, he left New York to move into Paul's farm to await the Wings formation. He and Monique were later to buy a house in London and a farm in Scotland, just like Paul and Linda.

Some say the official formation of Wings took place on 3 August 1971 during the *Wild Life* sessions; others put it a month later when Stella was born, saying that Paul actually thought of the name 'Wings' at this time.

Denny recorded two Wings albums, *Wild Life* and *Red Rose Speedway* and drummed on the singles 'Mary Had A Little Lamb', 'Hi-Hi-Hi' and 'Give Ireland Back To The Irish'. He toured with the band in Britain and Europe in 1972 and 1973.

His reasons for leaving the group are not clear. When he phoned Paul to tell him he was quitting three hours before the band were due to fly out to Lagos, Nigeria, to record *Band On The Run* he gave his reason as the fact that he did not want to go to Africa. He quit on 30 August 1974, five days after Henry McCullough. McCullough said he was unhappy with the band because he felt Linda didn't belong in it. Seiwell is also said to have been unhappy about Linda's involvement.

Send Me The Heart
A track which Denny Laine co-wrote with Paul in Nashville in 1973 and which was recorded with Buddy Emmens on steel guitar and Paul on bass. It was included on Denny Laine's album *Japanese Tears*.

Sgt Pepper's Lonely Hearts Club Band (album sleeve)
Contrary to popular opinion, all the characters on the cover of the *Sgt Pepper* album weren't personally chosen by the Beatles to represent their heroes and influences. Robert Fraser and Peter Blake asked each member of the Beatles to write down ten choices on a piece of paper. Ringo didn't bother to make any choices, George picked mainly Indian gurus and a number of choices by John and Paul were left out or vetoed. A great number of the seventy-plus characters were chosen by Fraser and Blake, so the cover isn't representational of the Beatles' heroes after all.

Paul chose Karlheinz Stockhausen. The composer couldn't be contacted as he was sailing in the Pacific, but his image was used anyway.

Paul also added Fred Astaire to his list. Astaire had been one of his favourites when he was a child and he loved to watch Hollywood musicals at the cinema. One of his favourite songs was Astaire's 'Cheek To Cheek'.

Commenting on his early influences, Paul had said, 'I like the Astaire films they show on television. I think, wow, great, boy can they dance. Boy, can they arrange tunes. They were only doing what we're doing now, but some of the time they were much better at it.'

Other choices by Paul included Brigitte Bardot and William Burroughs.

Sgt Pepper's Lonely Hearts Club Band (album)
The suggestion for the front of sleeve came from Paul who said they could show people, living or dead, who the Beatles respected. 'We want all our heroes together. If we believe this is a very special album for us, we should have a lot of people who are special to us on the sleeve with us.'

He also said, 'Why don't we make the whole album as though the Pepper band really existed, as though Sergeant Pepper was doing the record?'

Paul appeared to be the prime mover behind the album and John Lennon was to say, 'He (Paul) said that he was trying to put some distance between the Beatles and the public – and so there was this identity of Sergeant Pepper. Intellectually, that's the same thing he did by writing "he loves you" instead of "I love you". That's just his way of working.'

Paul also thought of having the group wear Salvation Army uniforms, but was talked out of it and they eventually wore costumes made by Maurice Berman, the theatrical costumiers.

Paul was not happy with press reports that he considered exaggerated George Martin's contribution and said, 'We got offended by this. We don't mind him helping us, it was great, but it's not his album, folks, you know!' The first song was Paul's 'When I'm Sixty-Four'.

The Sgt Pepper Band was the Beatles' alter ego. Paul was to comment, 'We were getting a little fed up of being the Beatles, because everything we did had to be the Beatles, and I felt we were getting trapped in this whole idea of "what kind of songs does John do? What does George do? Paul does the ballads." It was all getting bloody predictable. I said, "Why don't we pretend that we're another band?" That's what I did, it freed us to make those slightly more daring decisions than you'd normally make.'

Paul played some of the album tracks for Bob Dylan. Paul recalled, 'He said "Oh, I get it, you don't want to be cute any more." That summed it up, that was sort of what it was. The cute period had ended and it was now . . . it started to be art.'

Sgt Pepper's Lonely Hearts Club Band (film)

An American movie, which was based on the Beatles' album and screened in 1978. The film starred Peter Frampton and the Bee Gees. The Robert Stigwood Organisation, who produced the film, originally offered Paul the leading role of Billy Shears, but he turned it down.

Sgt Pepper's Lonely Hearts Club Band (song)

John Lennon was to say, 'Paul wrote it after a trip to America. The whole West Coast long-named group thing was coming in, you know, when people were no longer called the Beatles or the Crickets. They were suddenly called Fred And His Incredible Shrinking Grateful Airplanes. He got influenced by that and came up with the idea of us doing us as somebody else. He was trying to put something between the Beatles and the public. It took the "I" out of it some.'

Their road manager at the time, Mal Evans, claimed to have had some input in the song and was said to have received some of the royalties.

Mal commented, 'I stayed with him for four months and he has a music room at the top of his house with his multi-coloured piano and we were up there a lot of the time. We wrote 'Sgt Pepper' and also another song on the album, 'Fixing a hole'. When the album came out, I remember it very clearly, we were driving somewhere late at night. There was Paul, Neil Aspinall and myself and the driver in the car, and Paul turned round to me and said, "Look Mal, do you mind if we don't put your name on the song? You'll get your royalties and all that, because Lennon and McCartney are the biggest things in our lives. We are really a hot item and we don't want to make it Lennon-McCartney-Evans. So, would you mind?" I didn't mind, because I was so in love with the group that it didn't matter to me, I knew myself what had happened.'

Paul commented, 'I was just thinking of words like Sergeant Pepper and Lonely Hearts Clubs, and they came together for no reason. But, after you've written it down, you start to think. "There's this Sergeant Pepper who has taught the band to play, and got them to play, so that, at least, they found one number." They're a bit of a brass band in a way, but also a bit of a rock band because they've got the San Francisco thing.'

The number was recorded at Abbey Road on 1 April 1967.

A version of this number, lasting 6 minutes and 23 seconds, was included on the *Tripping The Live Fantastic* album. It was recorded live on 23 November 1989 at the Great Western Forum, Los Angeles during the 1989/90 World Tour.

Shadow Cycle

A 21-minute short animation film based on the last musical score written by Linda McCartney.

Made by Klacto Animation for MPL, it is described as: 'A work of love and emotional fantasy intertwined with the cycle of life and death, represented by the reflecting shadows of the characters as they travel through their life's journey.'

The film received its British premiere at the London Film Festival in November 2001.

John Harle orchestrated the music by Linda and Paul and Oscar Grillo wrote the scenario. The latter also designed and directed the film.

Shake A Hand

A track from the *Run Devil Run* album lasting 3 minutes and 52 seconds. It was recorded at Abbey Road Studios on Tuesday 2 March 1999 with Paul on lead vocal, bass guitar and electric guitar, Dave Gilmour on electric guitar, Mick Green on electric guitar, Pete Wingfield on piano and Hammond organ, and Ian Paice on drums.

During the Beatles' early trips to Hamburg they frequented a pool hall which had a jukebox in it and the Beatles used to play the records and take down the words of the songs, as they couldn't afford to buy records at the time. They took down the words of this Little Richard record and it became one of Paul's favourites – although he never did buy the actual record.

Shallow Grave

A number, originally called 'Short Shallow Grave', which was co-penned by Paul and Elvis Costello in 1991. The number was to appear on Elvis Costello's album *All This Useless Beauty* in 1996.

She Came In Through The Bathroom Window

Paul wrote this song on 13 May 1968 while in New York.

It first turned up on the Beatles *Let It Be* sessions on 22 January 1969, and eventually ended up as part of the *Abbey Road* medley, being recorded as one song with 'Polythene Pam' on 25 July 1969.

The number was based on an incident when fans tried to break into his home in St John's Wood and originally was simply called 'Bathroom'. Paul initially wanted Joe Cocker to record the number, which he did, following the release of the Beatles' version.

She Said Yeah

A song Paul chose to record for his *Run Devil Run* album. It was his favourite Larry Williams number and ran for 2 minutes and 6 seconds. It was recorded at Abbey Road Studios on Friday 5 March 1999. It featured Paul on lead vocal and bass guitar, Dave Gilmour on electric guitar, Mick Green on electric guitar, Pete Wingfield on piano and Ian Paice on drums.

Paul remembered that he'd also interested Mick Jagger in the number, playing it to him one day in a music room – and Mick then went and recorded the number with the Rolling Stones.

She's A Woman

Paul penned this rocker literally on the spot during a recording session on 8 October 1964, during the *Beatles For Sale* sessions and it was issued as the flipside of 'I Feel Fine' in Britain on Parlophone R 5200 on 27 November 1964 and in America on Capitol 5327 on 23 November.

John Lennon was to comment, 'That's Paul's with some contribution from me on lines, probably. We put in the words 'turns me on'. We were so excited to say 'turn me on' – you know, about marijuana and all that, using it as an expression.'

The number wasn't included on *Beatles For Sale* and didn't turn up as a track on an official album release in Britain until 2 December 1978 on *Rarities*. *Rarities* was a 'free' album included with *The Beatles Collection* package, a boxed set of all twelve original EMI studio albums, plus the additional *Rarities*. However, it was included on the

American album *Beatles '65* issued on Capitol ST 2228 on 15 December 1964.

A stereo version was included on *The Beatles Box* issued by World Records, a subsidiary of EMI on SM 701-SM 708 in December 1980. A slightly longer stereo version was included in *The Beatles Collection* issued on BEP 14 on 7 December 1981, a boxed set of the Beatles EP collection.

In America, Capitol reissued the 'If I Fell'/'She's A Woman' single on Capitol Starline A-6286 on 30 November 1981.

It was also included on the *Past Masters. Volume One* CD release, issued on Tuesday 8 March 1988.

In addition to singing lead vocal, Paul also played piano on the track.

The Beatles performed the song on their Christmas show in 1964 and on their subsequent tours. The number was included on *Beatles At The Hollywood Bowl* and *Beatles Rarities*.

The version included on Volume Two of *The Beatles Live At The BBC* was a track taken from their *Top Gear* radio broadcast of 26 November 1964.

A concert version of the number was included as the final track on the first half of the Beatles' *Anthology 2*.

She's Given Up Talking
A track from the *Driving Rain* album. The number lasts for 4 minutes and 57 seconds and was recorded on 17 February 2001.

She's Leaving Home
Paul was inspired to write this number after reading a story in the national newspapers about a girl who had run away from home.

He was to say, 'It's a much younger girl than Eleanor Rigby, but the same sort of loneliness. That was a *Daily Mirror* story again. This girl left home and her father said, "We gave her everything. I don't know why she left home." But he didn't give her that much, not what she wanted when she left home.'

The story was actually in the *Daily Mail* newspaper on 27 February 1967. The headline ran: 'A-Level Girl Dumps Car And Vanishes'.

It concerned a 17-year-old girl, Melanie Coe, who had been studying for her A levels at Skinner's Grammar School in Stamford Hill, London. She then ran away from home leaving her car, diamonds and a mink coat behind. Her father John Coe commented, 'I cannot imagine why she should run away, she has everything here.'

The Beatles recorded the number at Abbey Road on 17 March 1967 and overdubbed the vocals on 20 March 1967. The Beatles didn't play on the number. Paul and John sang it with a string backing: Sheila Bromberg on harp; Erich Gruenberg, Derek Jacobs, Trevor Williams and Jose Luis Garica on violins; John Underwood and Stephen Shingles on violas; Dennis Vigay and Alan Dalziel on cellos; and Gordon Pearce on double bass.

Paul asked George Martin to arrange the number for strings and harp, but Martin had a recording session with Cilla Black scheduled. Paul was eager to go ahead with the number and hired Mike Leander to arrange it. George Martin was to say, 'I couldn't understand why he was so impatient all of a sudden. It obviously hadn't occurred to him that I would be upset.' Paul said, 'He was busy, and I was itching to get on with it. I was inspired. I think George had a lot of difficulty forgiving me for that. It hurt him; I didn't mean to.'

Arranger Mike Leander was to comment, 'This record will alter everyone's approach to record making. I have new thoughts myself now every time I go into the studio. Apart from my contribution, this is a work of art, but I am terrified of the next one.'

People have claimed that 'the man from the motor trade' mentioned in the lyrics referred to Terry Doran, a friend of the Beatles who was a car salesman. Paul has denied this.

She's My Baby
A song for Linda, 3 minutes and 6 seconds in length, from the *Wings At The Speed Of Sound* album. Paul re-arranged the number for Linda's memorial services. He also re-recorded it for his *Working Classical* album.

Shears, Billy
A make-believe character created for the *Sgt Pepper* project. On the album, Ringo was Billy Spears.

The character was fleshed out by the many wild stories in the 'Paul is Dead' campaign of 1969. One American 'underground' paper, *Rat Subterranean News*, ran a full-page story written by Lee Merrick and proclaiming that Billy Shears had become a substitute for the dead Paul McCartney.

Shrimpton, Stephen Walmsley
Former managing director of MPL, who was Paul's right-hand man for a time. He joined the company in January 1980.

Stephen was born in Melbourne, Australia, and joined EMI Australia in 1969 as national marketing and sales manager, eventually rising to the post of managing director in April 1974. He got to know Paul when he was in charge of the entire Wings product in Australia.

Stephen intended to return to Australia after the filming of *Give My Regards To Broad Street* – in which Australian actor Bryan Brown portrayed a character based on him – but Paul talked him into remaining with the company, although he eventually resigned in 1986 and moved to America to accept a senior position with Warner Brothers in Los Angeles. His replacement, Bob Mercer, lasted barely a month.

Silly Love Songs

Paul wrote this number in reply to the criticism that he was writing 'sentimental slush', saying, 'Originally, I wrote this song at about the time when the kind of material I did was a bit out of favour, and you had Alice Cooper doing "No More Mr Nice Guy", and that kind of parody. I rather picked up a feeling in the air that ballads were regarded as soppy and love as too sentimental.

'I thought, so what's wrong with silly love songs? I was striking a blow for nice, sentimental love songs.'

It was 5 minutes and 53 seconds in length and issued in Britain on Capitol R6014 on Friday 30 April 1976 and topped the charts and was issued in the US on Capitol 4256 on Thursday 1 April 1976 where it also hit the No. 1 spot.

'Cook Of The House' was on the flip.

It was also released in Germany on Capitol 1C600-97683, in France on Parlophone 2C006-97683 and in the USSR on Melodia C62 20413004.

Silvey, Susie

Name used by a strippogram girl who turned up at Paul's fortieth birthday celebrations at Elstree Film Studios on Friday 18 June 1982.

Her appearance at the studios was totally unexpected.

As she explained: 'I told a girlfriend I wanted to do a singing telegram for him, but didn't know if I dared. She dared me to! So I took all the gear along to the studio where Paul was making 'Take It Away'. Just before lunch, I slipped into my fishnets, suspenders and black-lace corset and covered it with a dress I could easily peel off when the moment came. I was shaking like a leaf. As Paul started to leave the set for lunch, I ran after him, and shouted "Paul!" He spun around and as he did so, I took off my dress and stood there in front on him in my gear, singing a special version of "All You Need Is Love". Then I gave him a birthday congratulations telegram. He thought it was amazing.'

Simon Bates Show, The

A Radio One show hosted by Simon Bates. Paul and Linda appeared on the show on Wednesday 1 May 1991. The couple actually phoned in to the show after they'd heard Bates having an on-air tasting of Linda's vegetarian foods and Bates had also been playing tracks from Paul's forthcoming *Unplugged – The Official Bootleg*.

Simon Mayo Show, The

A Radio One show hosted by Simon Mayo. Paul phoned up the programme on Tuesday 15 December 1992 to talk about his new single. Paul had talked about the planned *Beatles Anthology* in New York on Friday 11 December and said, 'We've talked for years and years about doing this thing – "One of these days we'll set the story straight and do it our way." I saw George yesterday in California and we're getting together, you know, for this thing – so it's bringing us together. And there's a chance we might write a little bit of music for it. So it's good. But rather than put huge pressure on us and say, "The Beatles are re-forming!" and "Do they need Julian?" or "What do they need?" and all that stuff, it'll probably happen a lot more naturally.' Because of this, Mayo asked Paul if he was getting together with George and Ringo, but Paul was reluctant to add anything to what he'd said before.

Simple As That

This was originally put down as a home demo in August 1980 under the title 'It's As Simple As That'. Paul then produced it following his *Press To Play* sessions in 1985 as 'Simple As That'. It included backing vocals from Paul's kids – Mary, Stella and James – and was originally released on the Phoenix House charity album *The Anti-Heroin Project – It's A Live-In World* (AHP-LP) in November 1986. It was also included on the 1993 EMI CD of *Pipes Of Peace*.

Simpsons, The

The Simpsons cartoon series featured many Beatles references and several references to Paul. In Season Two an opening sequence to one of the episodes featured a Paul McCartney gravestone, a parody of the 1960s 'Paul is Dead' rumours. In another episode, at Stanley and Martha Peterson's wedding, their vows include two lines from 'Martha My Dear'. In one of the episodes of Season Seven 'Golden Slumbers' is featured in Homer's dream sequence. Season Five has an episode in which one character reveals, 'My greatest achievement was getting Paul McCartney out of Wings.'

Paul and Linda agreed to appear in animated form in the American cartoon and to provide their own voices in the episode 'Lisa The Vegetarian', first screened in the US on 15 October 1995. It was the first episode of Season Seven and the two introduce Lisa to vegetarianism after a meeting at Apu's roof garden. When Lisa meets them she exclaims, 'Wow! Paul McCartney! I read about you in history class.'

Singalong Junk

An instrumental version of Paul's number 'Junk', lasting 2 minutes and 34 seconds, which was included on Paul's 1970 album *McCartney*. He completed the recording at Morgan Studios in London playing electric guitar, bass drum, sizzle cymbal and Mellotron.

Single Pigeon

A track on the *Red Rose Speedway* album, recorded at Olympic Studios and lasting 1 minute and 52 seconds. Paul sang lead vocal and played piano. Linda provided vocals, Denny Laine was on drums, Henry McCullough on acoustic guitar and Denny Seiwell on bass.

Sir Paul McCartney's Liverpool

An album of Paul's compositions in a classical style by Quatuor La Flute Enchantee Quartet, issued on ATMA Classique ACD 2 2137 in May 2000. The album was suggested and authorised by Paul.

It contained selections from *The Family Way* film score, the *Liverpool Oratorio Suite*, 'A Leaf' and a classical arrangement of 'Distractions', the track from *Flowers In The Dirt*.

Quatuor La Flute Enchantee Quartet are four flute players from Quebec, Canada.

The project had its origin in 1995 when Michel Laverdiere first interviewed Paul regarding his interest in classical music. In 1997 Laverdiere sent Paul a recording of Linda's 'Appaloosa' and Paul suggested a recording of a transcription of the Oratorio. The project grew from there.

75 Sir Thomas White Gardens, Everton, Liverpool

Address in a tenement building which became Paul's third Liverpool home when his mother and father moved into a ground-floor flat there. They left their house in Wallasey to be nearer the place where Jim McCartney had found a job as an inspector with the Liverpool Corporation cleansing department. The building has since been demolished.

Six O Clock

A track on the album *Ringo* penned by Paul and Linda McCartney. The album, produced by Richard Perry, was issued in America on Apple SWAL 3413 on 2 November 1973 and in America on Apple PCTC 252 on 9 November 1973.

The musicians were Ringo Starr on lead vocal and drums, Paul McCartney on piano, synthesiser, background vocals and string and flute arrangements, Linda McCartney on background vocals, Klaus Voormann on bass, and Vinio Poncia on acoustic guitar and percussion.

Sixty Minutes

An American current affairs series produced for CBS Television. Paul appeared on the programme on Wednesday 24 October 2001, mainly discussing the 11 September World Trade Center tragedy.

Paul was interviewed by veteran reporter Dan Rather.

Commenting on the tragedy and the concert held to raise funds for the families of the victims, Paul said, 'I wanted to do something. Like a lot of people, I felt helpless. I'm not a firefighter but my dad was in World War Two. He was a volunteer firefighter in Liverpool, which got a lot of heavy bombing.'

He continued, 'My parents' generation went through World War Two, so I know how they dealt with it. And it was with humour, it was with courage, it was with strength.'

He said, 'They had to have something to keep their courage up, so they did. There was a lot of humour, a lot of music. And if it was good enough for them, I think it's good enough for us.'

Earlier that week Rather took Paul back to the old studio where the Beatles had first recorded the *Ed Sullivan Show* in February 1964 and showed him a tape of the original performance. Paul seemed bemused. 'Good group. Wow. You had to take me back there, didn't you?' He mentioned how it didn't feel like that much time had passed. 'It's one of those staggering things about life, you can just literally seem a few years ago. And it isn't – it's a long time ago. But I have memories. Very exciting for us as Liverpool lads to come to America and then to suddenly be involved in something like that. A really big show. And then the reaction to it, I love. I still meet people who say, "I know where I was, I was in our sitting room" and their dads invariably say, "Those are wigs. They're wearing wigs." You look at it now. It looks pretty short, it looks pretty tame.'

Paul recalled the Shea Stadium appearance and the fact that the sound system wasn't very good. 'If we thought we were playing well, it was a little bit annoying, because the people who came to hear couldn't hear us. If we were not in a very good mood, and not playing very well, it was a blessing.'

On the subject of grief, Paul said, 'All I can really say is that I think it's important to let it out, and not to hold it in. That was really the single most important thing I found. As a guy, you like to think you're tough, you can take these things, and you can give me your best shot. But, of course, when you lose someone it's not really possible. You can put it inside yourself and hide it if you want, but I don't think that's a good thing. So, for me, what I found was to talk to people. A lot. Not worry about crying like a baby sometimes if that's what you had to do. And not worried about who was looking at you. And just really let it all out.'

Discussing Linda he said, 'After Linda died I didn't really do anything. Some people said to me, "Get back to work. That's what you should do, put yourself into work!" I just couldn't, I thought, "I don't want to." Didn't seem like the thing to do. After I'd sort of spent the year grieving, I said, "You know what? I'm really blessed to have thirty years with that girl. She's such an amazing woman. And it's not everyone has thirty great years of married life. So I looked at the positive aspects of it, tried to kind of rationalise it. And felt that that helped me.'

Skydome

A venue in Toronto, Canada where Paul appeared on Thursday 7 December 1989. The show had originally been scheduled to take place at the Maple Leaf Gardens, but was changed. Ringo Starr was a member of the audience. On the day of the show, Paul held a press conference.

After he was introduced he was asked:

Q: Paul, there have been a lot of problems with the sound system in the Skydome. Have you done a sound check so far?

Paul: No, we haven't done a sound check so far.

Q: What do you think of the facility?

Paul: I haven't actually had a look, but it looks good from the outside. I'm sure it will be great, you know.

Q: Paul, can you talk about your decision to be sponsored by Visa and why you went that way?

Paul: Yeah, well, the thing is, as you probably know like all tours these days use sponsors, right. I think like most big tours this size are going to get sponsored by someone and really, all we were doing was sticking out for a sponsor that we could kind of keep our integrity with, so that I didn't actually have to hold up anything and say I recommend this. And it was put to me that the way these particular people were going to do it would be similar to the campaign they did on the Olympics, which you didn't really get the feeling that the Olympics were sponsoring the card company; it was the other way around. You felt like they were kind of promoting the Olympics – and I think when you see the campaign you won't ever actually see me turn to the camera and say, 'Hey, don't go anywhere without one of these.' It's not that kind of a deal.

I mean, you know, I figure we're living in a capitalist society, you know, all you guys are being paid, aren't you? You know, I don't see – suddenly out of this mist, suddenly this idea that you shouldn't take money. Where's this idea come from? I mean even the communists are kind of giving up on this idea now, and they seem to say, like, as if we never got paid in the sixties or something, or we never accepted money. We never did commercials, you know, and this is not me really doing a commercial. This is a commercial about the tour with these people and they are under-writing the travel expenses. I personally don't see anything wrong with it, I don't see anything wrong even with the Stones' deal, which people think is a real sell-out, or the Who. I wouldn't personally do one of those beer commercials and stuff 'cause, you know, I'm not really into commercials. I think on a tour of this size, I think it's allowed in our society to accept money.

Q: Will this commercial be seen in Canada?

Paul: I'm not sure, I'm not really that into it, you know. The point is, in the economics of a tour like this, just getting from place to place is a big expense and so these days most people accept some kind of sponsorship. So we held out for one of the obvious ones and we've gone with this one, which is, I think, when you see the actual commercials, you'll agree there is no real sell-out.

Q: Do you still feel strongly against using your music in other commercials for other products?

Paul: Yeah. I mean I see a difference here, you know, in this thing. I wish I had the commercial to show you and I haven't even seen it and stuff. I think there is a difference using songs like 'All You Need Is Love' to kind of promote a product and, you know, using them sort of like in a movie or something. I think actually once they get identified with a specific product, like all the things that people have been doing for soft drinks, I think there is a difference and that kind of commercial I wouldn't do.

I was talking to someone yesterday. I have been offered a lot of money to hold up a whisky bottle in Japan, you know, that I don't want to do though, 'cause that is what I call a commercial. I think if these people you are talking about, Visa, want to film us, film this show, the tour show, moments from the show, show me getting in and out of limos and then talk about their card without me ever actually turning to the viewer and saying, 'Yes, this card . . .' In fact, we are kind of religious about it, we do sound checks where we advertise all the other cards!

Q: Let's talk about recording studios themselves. Could you tell me how you view recording from back in the Beatles days to now? I mean, is it more fun? You've spent thirty years in the studio.

Paul: Well, the main difference is it used to be a lot quicker to record, you know. We recorded the first Beatles album in a day from ten o'clock in the morning to ten o'clock at night. We did 'Twist And Shout' last because if we'd done it first we couldn't have done any of the others, you know, John's voice would have gone. So you know one day for an album was pretty fast. Now it takes one day to switch on the machines, load the computer, find out where the on/off switch is, that's the main difference, I think, it just takes forever now to record one song whereas you used to do a whole album in a day. But the nearest I got to it recently was doing the Russian album. I did a lot of rock and roll songs. We did eighteen songs in a day and it was really good. I think it's more fun to record that way, very spontaneous you know, and immediate. The other is like – God, it's like, honest it's terrible – you get this computer downtime, the other great fun thing you get, you probably all get it too. It's like, 'take five hours, guys, we're just going to fix the computer,' which was introduced to make things cheaper and quicker.

Q: Paul, what kind of music will you play . . . ?

Paul: Wait and see.

Q: We know you're doing some Beatles songs.

Paul: Yeah, we do sixteen Beatles songs, fifteen non-Beatles – mine, and a couple of rock-'n'-roll things.

Q: You've given us years and years of music and I'm sure everybody in here feels very dear to the music, I understand that next year for the first time you are going to co-write a book about yourself. Is it a deal with Pioneer Books?

Paul: I'm not really sure which deal it is you're talking about. I've got a friend of mine from the sixties who recently approached me, he wants to do a book on Alan Ginsberg and it would concentrate on the art rather than which toothpaste I use, you know, so that's probably it.

Q: Can I ask you what I read in a British magazine? It's called *Twenty Years On His Own*, Pioneer Books, apparently co-written. Is that bogus?

Paul: Well, I don't know really and I'm not co-writing a book with anyone, so maybe it is bogus. These things do spring up you know.

Q: Paul, on your last album you worked with six producers and one person you keep going back to is George Martin. What is it about George Martin that he provides that you can't?

Paul: I know his address! No, really, I love George Martin, he's a marvellous man. He's a great musician, we get on very well. I've known him a long time, so I can sit down and in half an hour we can kind of do something very constructive. I don't have to go through meeting him and getting to know him, checking out our chemistry and stuff, plus he's a great musician.

Q: Paul, I realise that perhaps there's no other way to do this, but I'm just wondering if you could comment on venues of this size and the fact that so many people walk away from these concerts thinking that they got ripped off because the sound was bad.

Paul: Well, I mean, I can't really tell you about that one till tonight. I mean, I don't know. I don't like going to shows in this size of hall normally so we'll have to see how we do on this. I haven't done one of these in quite a while. The last thing I did was Seattle Kingdome, which went down very well, nobody, I don't think, complained. I've got a suspicion nobody's going to complain after tonight, but I'm not going to count my chickens. I saw Genesis at Wembley, the football stadium in England, and I couldn't tell whether Phil Collins was on the stage or not. I think that's a problem, you know, and also you suddenly found that you've come out and you're watching telly all evening, when you thought you were going to a concert and you're watching this big screen. I could have stayed at home and done that. I would have been warmer. But we're trying to address those problems, we'll see. We've tried to make the show good wherever we are, even if it's in a pub or a venue this size. The idea is that the music should be good enough to satisfy you, so we'll see how you feel tomorrow. I hope no one feels ripped off.

Q: Why are you coming and playing venues of this size?

Paul: I'm not having to play venues this size. The promoter just says, 'Would you like to play the Skydome?' and I say, 'Yes'. Well, you know, I'll play anything. Like I say, I'll play a little club or a little pub, or anything. If there's a venue there I normally haven't got anything against them and I'll say the Seattle Kingdome was very good.

Q: Songwriting. Apparently Elvis Costello is a big Beatles fan, I'm told. When you worked with him on *Flowers* . . .

Paul: Yeah, he is a Beatles fan and also, I suspect, he is a John fan, you know. 'Cause often guys with glasses kind of identified with John. Well, I mean, that's true, but he's similar to John in a number of ways and it wasn't a deterrent, it was good to work with him mainly just 'cause he's a good writer and he's got a very strong opinion, that's the main thing.

Q: Why didn't he come on the tour?

Paul: I don't know.

Q: Did you ask him?

Paul: No. Maybe that's why.

Q: Paul, you support Friends Of The Earth. Could you tell us a little bit about the environmental issues that are close to your heart.

Paul: Really, all that's happened with me is like a lot of people. Probably. Probably all the people in this room. This has been the year when finally people have realised that, like, it's catching up with us. I know about ten years ago some scientists produced a thing called 'Blueprint For Survival' where they warned about all this global warming. But, I think, well the politicians will fix it up; our government will do something about it. But it never looked this serious until this year when they actually told us there's a hole in the sky. I think that's what got me. This hole in the ozone layer, that it's getting wider unless someone, you know, stops using CFCs and stuff. And then you go to places like LA and you see the smog hanging over and you think, you know, so all of these things basically have led me to think about this tour. Either we just go around the world having a bit of fun, making some money and making music for the fans or, at the end of it all we come off it all and we think, 'OK, there was a little bit more than that to it.' So that's when we decided to hook up with the Friends Of The Earth, and all I'm really doing is, I don't know that much about it, you know, I'm a father of four, I want to go to a lake and I'd like it to be clean, please, so I can swim in it. I hate the idea that it's all crap in it. Similarly, you go out to sunbathe, it used to be a great thing to do, now you've got to put on block 79, you know, before you go anywhere and I think it's crazy, you know. We're the only species on earth as far as I can see that soils its own nest and we're getting even more far out. So what I normally do in these press conferences is ask, 'Will anyone who doesn't want to clean the world and doesn't want to save the planet, please put his or her hand up now,' and, you know, obviously no hands go up. So it's just common sense to me and I've got a platform here with these concerts and press conferences like this where I can actually get to talk to radio and TV and journalists and push home the fact that people like Friends Of The Earth do want it cleaned up. They don't want spills like Exxon – and if it spills they want it cleaned up, not half cleaned up, like it was. So I mean, to me, it's nothing more than common sense.

Q: It's been thirteen years since your *Wings Over America* tour and twenty years since you performed some of the songs actually on stage. Have you ever forgotten any of the words?

Paul: Ever? Better question – have I ever remembered them? Yeah, there's always, like, about a line a night. I go, 'Oh God, you know, I wish I . . .' Yeah, there's a lot of words to remember in a two-hour show, you know, and I must admit some of them elude me occasionally. It's funny, I was in Europe and the audience is there, I think this was in Spain, and I had two instances: one where I got it right and one where they got it right, 'cause often they know it better than me, 'cause they've heard these records and, like, they've been listening to them where maybe I haven't for the last twenty years.

I'm not through yet, do you mind! Hang on, I'm telling a story here – whose life is it anyway? I'll tell you what, just quickly then, just very brief on this long-winded story I'm about to go on. There was this girl in the audience that I saw and I was doing 'I Saw Her Standing There' and I saw her saying, 'I'll never dance with a number'. So I thought, right, well I've got that line, that's one for me and I was doing that one right and I looked over here and I was doing, 'I'll never dance with another' and this other guy was doing, 'She'll never dance with another' – oops, he was right. So you know, it kind of works out about equal. Sorry, go ahead.

Q: Well, 'Motor Of Love' from *Flowers In The Dirt*, I hear that as a religious hymn. Were you trying to lend yourself to a different audience?

Paul: No. I have this thing that I do which is kind of quasi-religious. I did it in 'Let It Be' where I talk about Mother Mary. In fact, the Mother Mary I'm talking about is my own mother, and that song happened because in the sixties one night I was a bit sort of freaked out, which happened often in the sixties, those crazy days, he said, admitting everything. But I was a bit sort of freaked out and I was having a dream and my mother came to me, she died when I was fourteen, she came to me in this dream and said it was alright, and it really did make me feel a lot better when I woke up. So I wrote the song, 'In my darkest hour Mother Mary comes to me'. So that was that one and that got interpreted as being a bit religious, you know, you can take it that way if you want, it works both ways. And in this song 'Motor Of Love' that you're talking about, I talk about Heavenly Father. I'm actually talking about my dad, 'Heavenly Father look down from above'. My dad who hopefully went up top when he died in '76. I do that, the word Father, generally in my mind I'm talking about my father, but I recognise the ambiguity.

Q: I hear my church choir doing that.

Paul: Well, that is the nice thing, that if anyone wants to put a religious meaning on it, I've no problem with that.

Q: About Friends Of The Earth again. Is it just a platform to raise awareness? Are they getting any money directly?

Paul: Well, that's happened. Yeah, there are one or two people. The commercial firm you mentioned earlier which I don't really want to go on about 'cause I'm not really sponsoring these people, but they've given a large donation. Part of their deal was to give a large donation to Friends Of The Earth, and we'll be giving donations at the end of the tour. Mainly, it is – like a guy in Italy asked 'Paul, is it publicity or is it genuine?' I said it's both. It's publicity certainly, you can't say this isn't publicity, all these cameras here, but it is genuine. As I say, there's no one in this room who doesn't want it all cleaned up. I don't go on about it. I try not to preach. People get bored with people preaching, but I just do one announcement in the show and I just say to them, you know, go home, have a little think about it. If you get a chance to vote, just tell your politicians you want to live in a clean world. That's really all I do, you know, but I think it makes a lot of sense. I think you've got to have somebody saying it and with Friends Of The Earth, they haven't got enough exposure. They're a little fringe group, you know, like Greenpeace has got more exposure, so someone like me can command this kind of attention. It's not for me I'm doing it, it's for us all.

Q: Any chance of changing George's mind and having him work with you and Ringo?

Paul: Well, I don't know. I hear George has sort of said there will not be a Beatles reunion. I mean, as far as we're concerned, there can't be a Beatles reunion because John died and that was the Beatles, you know. I don't think any of us would be interested in substituting someone for John, even Julian, which has been suggested. It wouldn't be the Beatles, it would be a group. It just wouldn't be the Beatles, there can't be a Beatles reunion. So I think that's probably what George is talking about, I've only heard this second-hand through these press conferences, but there is a film that we might get around to in a couple of years that we've been meaning to do and there might possibly be some involvement there where we play together – me, George and Ringo. Now we wouldn't call it a Beatles reunion, but you probably would.

Q: Any possibility of turning these concerts into live album sets, like *Wings Over America*?

Paul: Yeah, there is a distinct possibility, seeing as we're recording it every night. Yeah, I don't know when that would happen but, you know, we are recording and the tapes go back to England and get mixed so maybe some time next year there might be.

Q: Did you write a song about Friends Of The Earth?

Paul: Yeah, I did have a think about that, yeah. I did start writing something along the lines of, 'I'm a Friend of the Earth', but I didn't get far with it.

Q: Can you say something about the nineties?

Paul: Say something about the nineties? The nineties is going to be the time when people finally realise we've got to clean this world up and the nineties is going to be the time when we do it, in order to have a clean twenty-first century. That's my wish, anyway, you know. Optimistic?

Filming also took place at the concert and was included in the *Get Back* movie, released in September 1991. Executive producer was Canadian-born Jake Eberts, who said that Skydome had been chosen as a location, 'because it's the first time on this tour he has played to an audience of sixty thousand. We wanted an indoor location and to capture a large audience. In Europe, he played arenas seating between six and ten thousand and in the US it's been mainly fifteen thousand-seaters.

SMA

A home demo recorded at Rude Studios in Scotland in 1978, by both Paul and Linda.

It was a punk-type song on which Linda sang and the lyrics were based on the list of ingredients in the formula of the baby food SMA that they'd been feeding to James. The demo was included in Part 10 of the *Oobu Joobu* radio series.

Smile Away

A track on the *Ram* album. It was also issued as a flipside of 'Eat At Home', although that particular single wasn't issued in either Britain or America. However, it was released as a single in various other countries, including Japan and Germany.

Smith, Cissy
The brother of John Lennon's uncle, George Smith. He was a teacher at Liverpool Institute and taught Paul handwriting and English.

So Glad To See You Here
A number originally penned by Paul in 1979 for his Rockestra. On Wednesday 4 and Thursday 5 February 1987 Paul produced a version with Duane Eddy for the American guitarist's new Capitol Records album, *Duane Eddy*. The recording took place at Paul's East Sussex studio and Paul also played bass guitar. Other musicians performing on the recording were Jim Horn and Larry Knechtal.

So Graham Norton
Graham Norton is an Irish chat-show host on Channel 4. His popular *So Graham Norton* show featured an appearance by Paul in May 2001 when Channel 4 also screened the 'Wingspan' documentary.

So Like Candy
A number co-written by Paul and Elvis Costello (Declan McManus), featured on the 1991 Elvis Costello album *Mighty Like A Rose*.
   It was also issued on the 1999 *Working Classical*.

Solters & Roskin
An American publicity firm who Paul originally hired to promote the American leg of the Wings World Tour in 1975/76. However, when he discovered that they also represented 'The International Committee To Reunite the Beatles', he fired them.

Some People Never Know
The first track on the second side of the *Wild Life* album. A lengthy track at over six minutes, with lots of acoustic guitar work. Paul played bass guitar, guitars, keyboards and vocals, Linda added vocals, Denny Laine played guitar and vocals and Denny Seiwell played drums. The number, produced by Paul and Linda, was engineered by Tony Clark and Alan Parsons and ran for 6 minutes and 36 seconds.

Somedays
A track from the *Flaming Pie* album, which Paul wrote in two hours. It was produced by Paul and Jeff Lynne and engineered by Geoff Emerick and Jan Jacobs with assistance from Keith Smith. Recording began on 1 November 1995 with Paul singing lead vocal and playing acoustic guitar, Spanish guitar and bass guitar. There was orchestral accompaniment, orchestrated by George Martin and conducted by David Snell, which was added on 10 June 1996. The other musicians were: Keith Pascoe, Jackie Hartley, Rita Manning and Peter Manning on violins; Christian Kempen and Martin Loveday on cellos; Peter Lake and

Levine Andrade on violas; Andy Findon on alto flute; Martin Parry and Michael Cox on flutes; Gary Kettel on percussion; Skaila Kanga on harp; and Roy Carter on oboe and cor anglais.

Paul wrote it when he drove Linda to a photo session in Kent and says, 'I knew that Linda would be about two hours doing the shoot, so I set myself a deadline to write a song in that time. And this was it. I wanted to finish it so that when Linda had finished and would say, "What did you do? Did you get bored?" I could say, "Oh, I wrote this song. Wanna hear it?" It's just a little game that John and I used to play, and I don't think it ever took us more than three or so hours to write a song.'

The number was also reworked and included on the 1999 CD *Working Classical*.

Song We Were Singing, The

The opening track on the *Flaming Pie* album and the first number that Paul taped during his initial sessions for the album. It was penned by Paul in Jamaica in January 1995 and lasted 3 minutes and 54 seconds. The number was produced by Paul and Jeff Lynne and engineered by Geoff Emerick and Jan Jacobs with assistance from Keith Smith.

Recording began at Paul's studio in Sussex on 6 November 1995 and Paul sang lead vocal and harmony vocal and played electric guitar, acoustic guitar, bass guitar, double bass and harmonium, while Jeff Lynne sang harmony vocal and played electric guitar, acoustic guitar and keyboard. The double bass Paul played was the one used by Bill Black, bass guitarist for Elvis Presley.

Commenting on the track, Paul said, 'I was remembering the sixties, sitting around late at night, dossing, smoking, drinking wine, hanging out. We were taking a sip, seeing the world through a glass, talking about the cosmic solution. It's that time in your life when you get a chance for all that.'

Songwriters, The

A series of eight BBC 1 TV programmes screened in the summer of 1978, written by Tony Staveacre and directed by Keith Cheetham.

Songwriters in the series included Noel Coward, Lionel Bart and Tim Rice and Andrew Lloyd Webber.

The 55-minute programme on 27 July 1978 featured 'Lennon and McCartney'. It covered their career from their first meeting at Woolton village fete until the dissolution of their partnership. The series had been filmed in a small studio on a limited budget, but employed colourful videotape effects and montages of album covers and photographs to good effect.

The first part of the programme dealt with their early career in Liverpool and Hamburg and excerpts from *Mersey Beat*, *Twilight Of*

The Gods by Wilfred Mellers, the *Daily Mirror* and the *Evening Standard* were quoted.

Unfortunately, the artists chosen to sing the Lennon and McCartney numbers were rather pedestrian and middle-of-the-road and included Sheila White, Vicki Brown, Peter Blake, Marti Webb and Paul Jones.

South Bank Show, The

An arts programme on London Weekend Television, hosted by Melvyn Bragg.

Paul made his first appearance on the show on its debut screening on Sunday 15 January 1978 when he was subjected to a detailed interview that spotlighted his songwriting career. It was titled 'Paul McCartney: Songsmith'.

The interview was actually filmed on Friday 2 December 1977 and Paul also discussed a number of subjects ranging from his childhood to the Beatles' success in America. Among the songs he chatted about were 'Eleanor Rigby', 'Yesterday' and 'When I'm Sixty-Four'. Paul was also shown recording the guitar and vocal parts to 'Mull Of Kintyre', playing piano on 'I Lost My Little Girl' and he jammed with Denny Laine on 'Lucille'.

Paul played a piano impression he called 'Melvyn Bragg In The Parlour Having Tea', did short a cappella renderings of 'Too Bad About Sorrows', 'Scrambled Egg' and 'Michelle' and whistled 'From Me To You'. Various clips from performances were also shown in the 30-minute programme.

Another special edition of the show on Sunday 14 October 1984 devoted 48 minutes to the film *Give My Regards To Broad Street* and featured filmed interviews with Paul and George Martin during the making of the movie and behind-the-scenes coverage of the recording of the songs. His new versions of Beatles songs such as 'Eleanor Rigby', 'For No One' and 'Yesterday' were publicly broadcast for the first time.

The show was also transmitted in America under the title 'The Making Of *Give My Regards To Broad Street*'.

Souvenirs

A song Paul composed while on holiday in Jamaica. The bluesy number was recorded in February 1996 and included on the *Flaming Pie* album. The number lasted 3 minutes and 42 seconds and was penned by Paul, produced by Paul and Jeff Lynne, and engineered by Geoff Emerick and Jan Jacobs, assisted by Keith Smith.

Recording began on 19 February 1996. Paul sang lead vocal, backing vocal and played drums, piano, harpsichord, acoustic guitar, electric guitar and bass guitar. Jeff Lynne provided backing vocal and played acoustic guitar, electric guitar and keyboard. Kevin Robinson played trumpet, Chris 'Snake' Davis saxophone and Dave Bishop baritone saxophone.

Paul had originally cut a demo of this number when he was in Jamaica and when they were about to record this he commented, 'I said to Jeff, "Let's take this demo but instead of what we normally do – take all the information off and renew it, and wreck it – let's make sure that everything that's going on is at least as good and has the flavour of the demo." This song's a little favourite of mine. I'm looking forward, I hope, to an R&B singer doing it. I would have loved it as a single, but I knew that no one on earth would ever have chosen it as a single.'

Spector, Phil

A legendary record producer, born Harvey Phillip Spector in the Bronx, New York on 26 December 1940.

At the age of seventeen he had his first chart-topping hit with the million-seller 'To Know Him Is To Love Him', by the Teddy Bears. He penned the song and was a member of the group, although he was to gain his fame as a record producer, noted for his distinctive 'wall of sound', which was the use of a massive sound using many musicians and instruments – keyboards, choirs, strings, percussion, guitars and so on.

He also produced a string of hits by a variety of groups such as the Crystals, Ronettes and Righteous Brothers, including 'He's A Rebel', 'Da Doo Ron Ron', 'Then He Kissed Me', 'Baby I Love You' and 'You've Lost That Lovin' Feelin''.

Regarded as something of an eccentric figure, as some geniuses are, he retired from the music industry for a while in frustration at the lack of American success of his production of 'River Deep, Mountain High' by Ike & Tina Turner.

Spector had had an earlier social association with the Beatles and John Lennon asked him to produce 'Instant Karma' for him.

At the time the Beatles had hours and hours of tapes from the *Get Back* sessions, a projected album of that title, which they were undecided what to do with. John, together with George Harrison and Allen Klein, then commissioned Spector to make an album from the tapes, although they didn't let Paul know about their decision.

On 23 March 1970 Spector moved into Abbey Road Studios, initially working from Room Four, to remix the tapes.

Spector also commissioned a number of arrangers to add to some of the tapes and gave Richard Hewson the tapes of Paul's 'The Long And Winding Road' and George's 'I, Me, Mine'. Spector instructed him, 'I want it orchestrated with a massive orchestra.'

Hewson recalled, 'So I lined up an orchestra with what I thought was a massive orchestra. All through the night, Spector kept ringing up saying, "Let's have some more violins. Let's have three harps instead of one," and all that.'

Recording began at seven in the evening of Wednesday 1 April 1970. Ringo played drums at this session, which is noted as the one in which he was the last member of the Beatles to play at the last Beatles recording session.

Apart from Ringo, the mass of musicians included eighteen violins, four violas, four cellos, a harp, three trumpets, three trombones, two guitars and fourteen singers.

Hewson said, 'There were so many musicians in the end that we couldn't get them all in! We actually, literally, had to shut the door and say that's enough.'

The musicians began to become annoyed at the antics of the eccentric producer, who kept making them play the parts over and over again. Hewson recalls, 'He kept going, "Let's have another take." He didn't even want to listen to the playback; he just wanted to play it over and over again. The guys were saying, "We played it. We can't play it any better." It wasn't that difficult music for those guys. They're brilliant musicians. The first reading through is pretty well perfect, and the second one is right on. Eventually, after the tenth time, they got fed up and left.'

Ringo continued to play. Hewson said, 'He was very cheery, and he didn't seem to mind. He kept drumming every time we took a tape.'

This production was actually contrary to what Paul had in mind for the album as a whole, to keep the whole thing simple, as if the Beatles had played the album live.

In particular, this was his vision of 'The Long And Winding Road'.

Paul presented his point of view in an interview in the *London Evening Standard* on 24 April 1970 when he expressed his distaste at what Spector had done to the numbers.

He said, 'The album was finished a year ago, but a few months ago American record producer Phil Spector was called in by John Lennon to tidy up some of the tracks. But a few weeks ago, I was sent a remixed version of my song 'The Long And Winding Road' with harps, horns, an orchestra, and a woman's chorus added. No one had asked me what I thought. I couldn't believe it. The record came with a note from Allen Klein saying he thought the changes were necessary. I don't blame Phil Spector for doing it, but it just goes to show that it's no good me sitting here thinking I'm in control because obviously I'm not. Anyway, I've sent Klein a letter asking for some things to be altered, but I haven't received an answer yet.'

Paul never received an answer.

When Paul was at the Q Awards at the Park Lane Hotel in London to receive a Best Songwriter Award for *Flaming Pie* on Tuesday 4 November 1997, there was also a special award for Phil Spector. When Spector got up to make a speech, Paul walked out, presumably because he has never forgiven him for what he did to 'The Long And Winding Road'.

Speedy Prompt Delivery Service

The Liverpool firm where Paul worked for a fortnight in December 1960 following his return from the first Hamburg trip. His father had suggested that he find himself a job so he went to the local office of the labour exchange and was given a job for the firm, which he called SPD, spending his time as second man in the back of a lorry delivering parcels, mainly in the area of the Liverpool docks.

Paul told Hunter Davies in *The Beatles: The Authorised Biography*: 'I used to sit on the back of the lorry and helped to carry parcels. I was so buggered sometimes. I fell asleep in the lorry when we went to places like Chester. I was with them about two weeks and felt very worldly having a job and a few quid in me pocket. But I got laid off. The Christmas period was over and there wasn't so much work.'

Spies Like Us (promotional film)

Director John Landis decided on an *Abbey Road* cover spoof for the promotional film, which he also directed. Paul told him, 'If you're going to do it as a parody of the album cover, you might as well get a few of the in-jokes in there. So there's the Volkswagen with "281F" there. Dan took his shoes off for the shot on the crossing, all that stuff.'

The promotional film opens with Paul arriving at Abbey Road Studios on a bike, disguised in glasses and a thin moustache. A truck pulls up with Dan Aykroyd in the back. Another Paul, this time disguised with a bowler hat and handlebar moustache, drives up in a limo while Chevy Chase, in deerstalker hat and Inverness cape, alights from a bus.

Inside the studio a figure in a Prince Charles mask takes it off to reveal he is Paul. Three different Pauls, each in different outfits, begin to play guitar, bass and drums while Aykroyd is at the studio console and Chase on keyboards. They are then joined by two blondes who are also in the film – Vanessa Angel and Donna Dixon (who is married to Dan Aykroyd). The promotional film was also intercut with scenes from the film.

Spies Like Us (song)

Spies Like Us was a spy-spoof feature film starring Dan Aykroyd and Chevy Chase. Director John Landis has asked Paul to write a theme for *Spies Like Us*. After he'd been shown rough footage from the film, which he liked, Paul wrote and recorded the number in a week.

He said, 'John Landis rang me and said he wanted an up-tempo rock-'n'-rolly thing.' Paul added, 'I thought I might have done a Bondy song – the 75-piece orchestra, more melodic, with maybe an Eastern touch, the known ingredients for a "spy" type of song. I think one of the fun things about what I'm doing now is varying those things a bit.'

Paul's eponymous song is only heard on the closing sequences of the movie, but the single was released in Britain on Parlophone R6118 on Monday 18 November 1985. The flipside was the Wings recording of 'My Carnival', previously unreleased although recorded in New Orleans as far back as 1975. There was also a three-track 12" single issued on Monday 2 December on 12R 6118 which contained 'Spies Like Us (Party Mix)', 'Spies like Us (Alternative Mix)' and 'My Carnival'. A 7″ picture disc on RP 6118 was also issued. The record proved to be a Top Ten chart entry in the States (Capitol B-5436), when it became the first release under Paul's new contract with Capitol and, taking in the 65 entries with the Beatles, became Paul's 100th single to enter the *Billboard 100* chart, although it only reached No. 13 in the British charts. A promotional video was released which included footage from the movie and shots of Paul in various disguises at Abbey Road Studios.

Dan Aykroyd and Chevy Chase also appeared in the Abbey Road sequence on Paul's video.

Paul, who recorded the number in September 1985, played all the instruments on 'Spies Like Us', with the exception of the synthesiser, which was played by Eddie Rayner of Split Enz. The backing vocals were by Linda, Kate Robbins, Ruby James and Eric Stewart.

It was produced by Paul, Hugh Padgham and Phil Ramone.

Musicians on 'My Carnival' were Paul, Linda, Denny Laine, Jimmy McCullough, Joe English, George Porter and Benny Spellman.

Paul's recording of the title song was not included on the soundtrack album, which consisted solely of Elmer Bernstein's music score.

It was released in Germany on Parlophone 1C006-2009407.

Like a number of Paul's singles, there was a plethora of different variations. A 12″ picture disc was issued on Parlophone 12 RP 6118 on Tuesday 2 December 1986 and a 7″ version, cut to shape, was issued on Parlophone RP 6118 a week later.

Spike

An album by Elvis Costello, issued in Britain on the Warner Brothers label as an album on 6 February 1989 on WX 238. There was also a cassette (W 238C) and a compact disc (925848-2).

There were two tracks on the album co-written by Paul and Costello. They were 'Veronica' and 'Pads, Paws and Claws'.

Spin It On

A song written by Paul which was issued as the flipside of 'Old Siam Sir' in Britain on 1 June 1979 and as the flipside of 'Getting Closer' in America on 5 June. A few days later it appeared as the fourth track of a *Back To The Egg* TV special and Wings performed the number as part of their repertoire on their British tour in 1979.

Spinetti, Victor

A British comic actor who appeared in more Beatles movies than anyone else, apart from the Beatles themselves.

Victor became a close friend of the group and appeared in a small cameo role in Paul's video of 'London Town'.

The two of them took part in the 'recruiting scene' in 'Magical Mystery Tour'.

Victor had been asked to become a member of the actual tour party but he was appearing in a play at the time. However, he managed to get enough time off to appear in this scene, in which the character he plays is based on his role in the film *Oh, What A Lovely War!*

Spinning On An Axis

A track from the *Driving Rain* album lasting 5 minutes and 16 seconds. It was recorded on 21 February 2001.

Spinozza, Dave

A New York session musician, one of several hired by Paul to play on the *Ram* album. Paul was impressed with his work and offered him a job in Wings, but Spinozza turned him down, content to remain a session musician.

Spiral

A piano piece composed by Paul which made its debut in the *Standing Stone* programme at the Royal Albert Hall, London on 14 October 1997. Composer Richard Rodney Bennett provided the orchestral arrangements. Paul was to say, 'I felt frightened that, as a composer, he might take over. I knew I had to do the work myself and get my ideas on to the computer, so that the piece was me. Then I could relax and allow other people to point out where "me" hadn't worked or where maybe "me" could be improved.'

Spirit Of Ranachan Studio

A studio Paul used on his land in Campbeltown, Scotland. It is not to be confused with his Rude Studio. It was a barn that Paul converted into a studio using the Rak Records 24-track mobile unit.

Spirits Of Ancient Egypt

A number from the *Venus And Mars* album, which Wings performed during their *Wings Over America* tour with Denny Laine on lead vocals.

The song had its inspiration in 1974 when Paul was dining with Chet Atkins in Nashville. Atkins suggested to Paul that he read a book about the Great Pyramids, which motivated Paul into writing the song.

Spud

In 1997 a pop group of 16-year-olds from Ealing called Spud were spotted in a London club by Julian Temple, who was to direct the video of 'Beautiful Night'. He invited them to take part in the video.

The boys were currently studying for their A levels at Drayton Manor High School. Guitarist Gareth Johnson was to comment,

'We've been gigging around London for the past six months and now we're playing with Paul and Ringo. Talk about dreams coming true.'

The four-piece outfit spent a day filming at the Nightingale Estate, Hackney with Paul and Linda, in the sequence where Paul is standing in the forecourt of a tower block as 40 TV sets were thrown out of the 18th-floor window to crash all around him.

The group were also filmed playing with Ringo.

St John's
One of the American Virgin Islands where Paul and Wings went to record in the summer of 1977. While moored there they were fined. Paul explained, 'It's a National Park. One of the rules is you must not play amplified music. I think they meant trannies. But we had a whole thing going. You could hear it for miles. We got fined fifteen dollars.'

St Swithin's
A Roman Catholic church in the Gill Moss area of West Derby in Liverpool. Paul's father James was married to his mother Mary at the church on 15 April 1941. At the time Paul's dad, who was a cotton salesman, was 39, and had been living at 58 Fieldton Road, West Derby.

Standing Stone (album)
Standing Stone, Paul's second major classical work, was released on EMI Classics (CDC 5564842) on Monday 6 October 1997. The full title is *Standing Stone – A Symphonic Poem*. Lawrence Foster conducted the 300-piece London Symphony Orchestra. It was released in America in November and held the No. 1 spot in the *Billboard* classical chart for nine weeks.

Paul was to comment, 'It's not actually a symphony. It's a symphonic poem. Symphonies are in four parts, but they tend not to have a story. Once it has a story, it tends to be called a tone poem. But a lot of people would think that it was just a poem if you called it a tone poem, so symphonic poem suggests that there's some music in it.'

Paul was more specific in the booklet which was enclosed with the CD, relating how he'd spent much of the past four years composing his second large-scale classical work. He comments, 'Unlike the *Liverpool Oratorio*, which features prominent roles for four solo singers, *Standing Stone* relies entirely on colours and effects drawn from orchestral and choral forces. With no soloists to propel the "story" and to help keep me on track throughout the writing of about 75 minutes of music, I wrote a poem in which I try to describe the way Celtic man might have wondered about the origins of life and the mystery of human existence.'

Standing Stone (orchestral work)
A symphonic poem by Paul, which marked EMI Records' centenary and was premiered at the Royal Albert Hall on Tuesday 14 October

1997, where it received a standing ovation following the 75-minute performance. The evening's performance was in aid of the Music Sound Foundation.

Richard Lyttleton, the president of EMI Classics, had originally commissioned the four-movement work in 1993.

Paul was to say that the origin of the *Standing Stone* poem came about following the death of his friend Ivan Vaughan from Parkinson's Disease. He said, '"Jive with Ive, the ace on the bass" was his intro when we played together. Ivan was very important to me. Poetry seemed the right way to express what I felt about his death. Later, I decided to write an epic poem that would serve as the framework for *Standing Stone*. I realised that I wasn't going to write a symphonic work where you take a theme and develop it throughout a movement, partly because I simply didn't know how to do that.'

The theme is basically that of the history of life on earth via the ancient standing stones of the Celts. It relates the tale of an early man who sails on a crystal ship to a distant land where the inhabitants welcome him and he saves them from invaders and falls in love.

Paul was aided in this ambitious work by a number of people, including Steve Lodder, a jazz musician who wrote down the initial keyboard sketches on cassette tapes. Paul then used an electronic keyboard linked to a computer with software that translated what he played into printed music. The computer print-outs were then put into readable form by composer David Matthews.

Other help came from saxophonist John Harle. Paul commented, 'He advised me on the architecture of the piece, helping me shape the sketches I'd made. He also made sense of the second movement's 'Lost at sea' section, translating what was on the computer into recognisable notation, and worked on the 'Trance' section in the third movement.'

The 300-piece London Symphony Orchestra and Chorus, conducted by Lawrence Foster, performed the work.

The performance was in two parts and prior to the staging of the symphony, four other classical pieces by Paul were performed. They were *Stately Horn*, played by the Michael Thompson Horn Quartet, *Inebriation* by the Brodsky Quartet and *A Leaf* and *Spiral*, both performed by the London Symphony Orchestra.

Paul and Linda were in the front row of the stalls and at the end of the performance Paul went on stage to be greeted by thunderous applause. Also in the audience was Ringo Starr.

The American premiere took place at Carnegie Hall in New York on Wednesday 19 November 1997 and a live webcast was broadcast at 9 p.m., sponsored by Mercedes Benz.

The proceeds from this concert were donated to the Save The Music Foundation and the Liverpool Institute of Performing Arts.

The live webcast featured an interview and also allowed questions that had been submitted in advance. The concert and interview was broadcast by National Public Radio on over 350 radio stations throughout America

The National Public Radio interview was recorded during rehearsals at New York's Riverside Church and was broadcast shortly before the performance. Also, immediately before the concert, Martin Goldsmith interviewed Paul in Carnegie Hall.

Standing Stone was performed by the Orchestra of St Luke's and the New York Choral Artists.

Stardust

An evergreen number by the late Hoagy Carmichael. Paul arranged the number for Ringo for his 1970 album *Sentimental Journey*.

Starr, Ringo

Richard Starkey was born in the front bedroom of a tiny terraced house at 9 Madryn Street, the Dingle, Liverpool on 7 July 1940.

His father was Richard Starkey, his mother Elsie (née Gleave), who was one of fourteen children. Both parents worked in a bakery. Father and son were sometimes referred to as 'Big Ritchie' and 'Little Ritchie', although the father–son relationship wasn't to last and Richard Starkey left his wife and son in 1943. He did visit his son Ritchie at the children's hospital in Myrtle Street and Ritchie recalled: 'He came once to see me in hospital with a little notebook to ask me if I wanted anything.'

Ritchie Jr's early life was plagued by ill health, which severely affected his education.

Soon after his parents had divorced, he moved with his mother into another terraced house at the nearby No. 9 Admiral Grove and began to attend St Silas's Infant School. He was six years old when he suffered a severe stomach ailment. He recalls: 'I felt an awful stab of pain. I remember sweating and being frightened for a while.' The little boy was rushed to the Children's Infirmary in Myrtle Street with a ruptured appendix, which developed into peritonitis, and he was taken into the special care unit, where he sank into a coma for two months.

He returned to school the following year, where some of the other pupils dubbed him 'Lazarus'.

In 1953 his mother remarried, to a painter and decorator called Harry Graves, whom Ritchie referred to as 'my stepladder'. It was Harry who bought Ritchie his first drum kit during a visit to Romford. It cost him almost £10 and he lugged it to Liverpool on the train.

The youth moved on to Dingle Vale Secondary School when he was eleven years old, but was still absent for long periods owing to various illnesses, and wasn't allowed to take the Eleven-Plus exam. As a result he became the only member of the Beatles not to be educated at a grammar school.

In 1953, Harry took his wife and stepson to visit his parents in

Romford and Ritchie was caught in a thunderstorm, having refused to wear a raincoat, and caught a chill, which developed into pleurisy.

Once again, he returned to the Myrtle Street Hospital. The pleurisy had affected his lungs so much that he was sent to Heswall Children's Hospital in the Wirral, where he remained for almost two years.

On leaving school, he needed to get a job, so he returned to Dingle Vale to receive a certificate confirming that he'd left the school. 'They didn't even remember I'd been there,' he recalled.

For a while he worked as a delivery boy with British Rail, but he failed the medical and was seeking another job two months later, ending up as a barman on a Mersey ferry. Finally, his stepfather manager to secure him a job at HH Hunt & Sons as an apprentice engineer.

Although he possessed a drum kit, Ritchie had no dreams of becoming a musician. He was to recall: 'I remember by mum saying a neighbour was in a band and why didn't I have a go? I thought it was a jazz group, I was mad on jazz. When it turned out to be a silver band, playing in the park and sticking to the marches and all that, I chucked it in. I lasted just one night.'

Ritchie became friends with a fellow worker, Eddie Miles, and, together with three other apprentices, they formed the Eddie Clayton Skiffle Group. The line-up was Eddie Miles on guitar/vocals (he called himself Eddie Clayton because he thought it sounded better than his real name), Ritchie Starkey on drums, Roy Trafford on tea-chest bass, John Dougherty on washboard and Frank Walsh on guitar. Ritchie's grandfather lent him £50 to buy a new drum kit and the group made their debut at the Peel Street Labour Club.

When the group disbanded in 1958, Ritchie joined the Darktown Skiffle Group. It was during this time that he met up with a group leader called Rory Storm, who told him he was looking for a drummer.

Rory, whose real name was Alan Caldwell, led a band called the Raving Texans. Ritchie decided to join them and made his debut with the group on 25 March 1959 at the Mardi Gras in Mount Pleasant.

The group then had various name changes until they settled on Rory Storm & the Hurricanes. The line-up of the group was Rory Storm (vocals), Johnny Byrne (rhythm guitar), Charles O'Brien (lead guitar), Wally Eymond (bass guitar/vocals) and Ritchie Starkey (drums). It remained that way until August 1962, when Ritchie became a member of the Beatles.

Despite changing the name from the Raving Texans, Rory was obviously still fond of a Western theme – at the time there were numerous Western series on television. He decided to call Byrne Johnny Guitar, after the title of the 1954 Joan Crawford Western; Ritchie became Ringo Starr; and Charles was renamed Ty after Ty Hardin, star of the *Bronco* series. Rory also thought that Lou Walters was a more suitable name for Wally.

The group also changed from a skiffle band to a rock 'n' roll, band which caused problems at the Cavern Club, where rock 'n' roll was banned. In January 1960 the group were still including a number of skiffle songs in their repertoire and appeared at the Cavern on a bill with the Cy Laurie Jazz Band on Sunday 2 January, and the following Saturday were appearing there again supporting the Saints Jazz Band and Terry Lightfoot's New Orleans Jazz Band.

On Sunday January 10 Ray McFall began his Liverpool Jazz Festival in an attempt to put Liverpool and jazz on the map. During that week top trad bands such as that of Acker Bilk appeared, together with modern jazz outfits, country-music bands and skiffle groups. When Rory Storm & the Hurricanes appeared again on Sunday 17 January, on a bill with Micky Ashman's Jazz Band and the Swinging Bluegenes, they began their set with 'Cumberland Gap'. Then they decided to switch to a rock-'n'-roll set and played 'Whole Lotta Shakin' Goin' On'. The jazz fans became furious and started pelting the group with copper coins. The Hurricanes continued the show but were drowned out by a booing audience. When they came off stage, a furious McFall fined them six shillings (30 pence) for daring to play rock-'n'-roll music. The group were able to collect all the coins from the stage, which more than compensated for the fine.

The group appeared at the Liverpool Stadium on 3 May 1960 on a bill with Gene Vincent. This was the show that aroused Larry Parnes's interest in Liverpool groups and led to the Wyvern Club auditions. In the audience were John Lennon, Stuart Sutcliffe and Pete Best. Best remembered being particularly impressed by the showmanship displayed by Rory Storm and the group.

The auditions at the Wyvern Club were set up ostensibly for Parnes to find a Liverpool band to back Billy Fury. The Hurricanes didn't audition because they already had a lead singer, Rory Storm, although Rory turned up at the auditions, not to perform, but just to have his photo taken with Billy Fury! It would have been interesting if the Hurricanes had auditioned because Ringo had been in the same class as Billy Fury at St Silas's.

In May the group were offered a summer season at Butlin's in Pwllheli in the Rock 'n' Calypso Ballroom, from July to September.

Despite the Butlin's offer of £25 each per week, some members of the group had to consider the risks they were taking in becoming fully professional. Ritchie was the most reluctant member: he was an apprentice at Henry Hunt's, making school climbing frames at the time. He didn't want to go to Butlin's, but Rory decided to persuade him.

It was during this period that Rory insisted that Ringo have his own five-minute spot, 'Starrtime', during which he sang numbers such as the Shirelles' 'Boys' and 'Alley Oop'.

At Butlin's, the act began to shape up far more professionally and they were playing for sixteen hours a week.

There was a write-up on Ritchie's appearance with the group published in the *South Liverpool Weekly News* on 25 August 1960. Under the heading RICHARD REALISES A BOYHOOD AMBITION, it read:

Richard Starkey always wanted to be a drummer. From when he was a small boy he was always tapping his fingers.

He has been in hospital twice, and has had 12 operations, several of them major ones.

When he came out last time after two years spent mostly in bed, he looked around for something to do – and started his fingers tapping again.

So he saved up and spent £10 on a second hand drum kit and set about teaching himself to play.

After two months' hard practice he joined a group. And now, with a new drum kit costing £125, he is entertaining hundreds of teenagers at a Pwllheli (North Wales) holiday camp as a member of Rory Storm's Hurricanes.

All five of them Liverpool lads are packing the camp's rock and calypso ballroom each evening for three-hour jive sessions.

Working a 16 hour week they spend their spare time joining in all the fun of the camp, swimming, sport and sunbathing.

'It's was good as a holiday – and we get paid for it,' said 20-years-old Richard – he lives in Admiral Grove, Dingle – during a break in the rock session.

His suntanned face broke into a smile as he added: 'It's fabulous.'

Richard – he plays under the name Ringo Starr – is the second ex-pupil of St. Silas C. of E. School, Dingle, to make a professional career in rock and roll.

The first – Ronnie Wycherley, now carving a niche for himself as Billy Fury.

It is the group's biggest contract so far: before they filled dates at Liverpool jazz clubs and had a spot in a rock show at Liverpool Stadium in May, which starred Gene Vincent and was to have featured Eddie Cochran. But he was killed a few days before.

Led by ex-cotton sampleman Rory Storm (his real name is Alan Caldwell) whose home is at 54 Broadgreen Road, Stoneycroft, the group has been playing together for just 10 months.

The other members – Lou Walters, 22 (bass guitar and vocal), Ty Brian, 19 (lead guitarist), Johnny Guitar, 20 (rhythm guitar and vocal), and Richard, all belonged to other groups before that.

When they finish their 13-week engagement at Pwllheli in a few days, the lads plan a holiday in London.

And later they hope to go on the Continent to seek dates there.

Said Richard: 'There is too much competition here. Rock and roll is beginning to wane.'

He added: 'But I like the life. I certainly don't want to give it up.'

A local coffee-bar owner, Allan Williams, had taken a group called Derry Wilkie & the Seniors down to the 2 I's coffee bar in Soho, where they were allowed to play. They were spotted by the Hamburg club owner Bruno Koschmeider, who earlier that year had visited the 2 I's and booked some local musicians, who were to form a group and call themselves the Jets, for his club, the Kaiserkeller. He was now seeking a group to replace them and was impressed by the Seniors and, in particular, the dynamism of their lead singer, Derry Wilkie.

As the British rock-'n'-roll groups were proving so popular, Koshmeider contacted Williams for another band to appear at his club, beginning in August 1960. Williams sought Rory Storm & the Hurricanes, but they were already booked for their summer season in Butlin's. He next approached Gerry Marsden, leader of Gerry & the Pacemakers, who turned him down. In desperation he asked the Beatles, who agreed.

When the Beatles arrived, with their new drummer Pete Best, they were shuttled off to a poky little former strip joint at the bottom end of the Grosse Freiheit called the Indra. Koshmeider told them to 'mach shau', as Derry Wilkie, an amazing showman, was doing at the Kaiserkeller.

Owing to noise complaints, the police told Koshmeider he had to stop the rock-'n'-roll shows at the Indra and move the Beatles down to the Kaiserkeller.

In October 1960 the Hurricanes, having finished their Butlin's season, were off to Hamburg, replacing Derry & the Seniors at the Kaiserkeller. They were paid more than either the Seniors or the Beatles.

They were also billed above the Beatles and alternated with them on the daily twelve-hour stretch, which the groups had to play. So each band did 90 minutes on and 90 minutes off.

It was during this eight-week season, that Allan Williams was so impressed with Lou Walters's voice that he offered to pay for the Hurricanes to make a disc. On Saturday 18 October 1960, the recording session took place at the Akoustik Studio. Three of Wally's ballads were recorded: 'Fever,' 'September Song' and 'Summertime'. John, Paul and George played on 'Summertime' and it was the first time that John, Paul, George and Ringo actually performed together.

The events substantiate the evidence that Allan Williams never actually managed the Beatles. The coffee-bar owner did act as their agent, but never actually managed them. If he did, why were the Hurricanes his first choice for Hamburg? Why would he pay for the Hurricanes to make a record, but refuse to pay for the Beatles to make one? If he was booking groups into the Kaiserkeller why would he allow the Hurricanes to be billed above the Beatles?

It was in Germany that George Harrison referred to Ringo as 'the nasty one with his little grey streak of hair'.

Journalists have often thought that the Beatles first met Ringo in Hamburg. This isn't so, as Rory and Ringo were often to be found hanging around the Jacaranda club at the same time as John Lennon and co., and were a well-known outfit in Liverpool.

At one time Ringo considered joining the Seniors, but on 30 December 1961 he left for Germany to back Tony Sheridan at the Top Ten Club in Hamburg, enticed by the lure of a large fee, a flat and the use of a car. However, he found Sheridan's eccentric style of performing too hard to cope with (he'd often change songs in the middle of a performance without telling his backing band) and returned to the Hurricanes. While he was absent from the group, Derek Fell from the Blackpool group the Executioners replaced him.

Ringo was also becoming disenchanted with Liverpool and his role as a musician and wrote to the Chamber of Commerce in Houston, Texas, in search of a job.

During the Skegness season, Ringo received a letter from Kingsize Taylor offering him £20 a week if he would join them in Germany as a replacement for Dave Lovelady, who was leaving the group to complete his studies. Ringo agreed. Then, one day, John Lennon and Paul McCartney turned up at the camp and offered Ringo £25 a week if he'd join them. The extra £5 sealed it and Ringo agreed to become a Beatle as from August 1962.

Johnny Guitar says that John and Paul turned up at ten one morning and knocked on their caravan door, saying they wanted Ringo to join them. Rory told them that the Hurricanes couldn't work without a drummer and they hadn't finished their season. Paul told him that Brian Epstein had said they could have Pete Best. Rory went to Liverpool but Pete Best was too upset. Rory then returned to Skegness and used relief drummers.

Ringo made his debut with the Beatles on Saturday 18 August 1962 at the Horticultural Society dance at Hulme Hall, Port Sunlight. He'd spent two hours rehearsing with the group. The following day the Beatles were at the Cavern, where the mood was initially ugly, with the audience shouting 'Pete for ever, Ringo never!' and George Harrison being given a black eye. However, by the end of the gig that night, it seemed that the audience had accepted Ringo.

Although there had been comments about his looks – and it was once said, 'Why get an ugly-looking cat when you can get a good-looking one' – he did seem to fit in with the group and, under instructions from Epstein, shaved off his beard. The silver streak in his hair vanished and the local hairdresser at Horne Brothers gave him a Beatle cut. He initially didn't consider himself a Beatle because of his looks and once said: 'I have a face which makes people laugh.' While he was a member of Rory Storm & the Hurricanes, looks didn't seem to matter, but in the Beatles there were three handsome guitarists. Ringo, however, was redeemed by his sense of humour, natural warmth and general air of friendliness.

Feelings were mixed about the two drummers. Pete had been the most popular member of the Beatles in Liverpool, but Ringo had been well known as a member of Rory Storm & the Hurricanes. Now, sans Best, local audiences were concentrating on the three guitarists/vocalists Lennon, McCartney and Harrison.

There was actually nothing wrong with Best's drumming, as Paul McCartney was to admit decades later in his *Wingspan* documentary. Another local singer, Billy Kramer, was also to comment: 'I didn't think the Beatles were any better with Ringo Starr. I never doubted his ability as a drummer but I thought they were a lot more raw and raucous with Pete.'

Paul and Ringo generally got on well together, although Ringo once described Paul as 'pleasantly insincere'.

They also used to holiday together and Ringo was to comment: 'Paul and I went to Corfu for a week, and then to Athens. We were living in chalets. We used to get up about ten in the morning and go sunbathing. After a few days we travelled around a bit, to the island of Rhodes, then back to Athens. We had a great time at the hotel we stayed at there. We couldn't understand a word of the songs the hotel band were playing, so on the last night Paul and I did a few rockers like "What'd I Say?" Then we went round to a local bar with some people we knew and did the same act again!'

The Beatles decided to feature Ringo singing at least one song on each Beatles album. When Paul was discussing writing the number 'With A Little Help From My Friends' for Ringo, he commented: 'It was a challenge for us because we actually had to write in a key for Ringo and you had to be a little tongue-in-cheek. Ringo liked kids a lot; he was very good with kids. In this case, it was a slightly more mature song, which I always liked very much.'

The vocals Ringo performed on Beatles albums included 'Boys' on *Please Please Me*, 'I Wanna Be Your Man' on *Meet The Beatles*, 'Honey Don't' on *Beatles For Sale*, 'Act Naturally' on *Help!*, 'What Goes On' on *Rubber Soul*, 'Yellow Submarine' on *Revolver*, 'With A Little Help From My Friends' on *Sgt Pepper's Lonely Hearts Club Band*, 'Don't Pass Me By' on *The Beatles* and 'Octopus's Garden' on *Abbey Road*.

In 1963 Paul said: 'We're thinking about Ringo doing some dancing on stage. It would only be for certain numbers, but it's an idea we're working on. We all mess around on drums a bit and we could take his place now and again. Mind you, we could never be as good as Ringo. He's the best drummer we've ever had. We hear rumours that he's leaving, but there's absolutely no truth in them.'

Once, when Paul tried to talk to Ringo during one of Ringo's moments of depression, he said: 'Don't you tell me what's going on inside my head.'

When the Beatles made their initial impact in America, Ringo emerged as one of the most popular members of the group, as evidenced by the number of tribute records that were released: 'Ringo', 'Ringo Beat', 'Ringo Bells', 'Ringo Boy', 'Ringo Comes To Town', 'Ringo – Deer', 'Ringo Did It', 'Ringo For President', 'Ringo, I Love you', 'Ringo, I Want To Know Your Secret', 'Ringo Dingo', 'Ringo, Ringo Little Star', 'Ringo's Dog', 'Ringo's Jerk', 'Ringo's Walk' and 'R (Is for Ringo)'.

Ringo married Maureen Cox on 11 February 1965 and the couple would have three children: Zak, Jason and Lee. The pair were divorced in July 1973 and Maureen died after being diagnosed with leukaemia on Friday 30 December 1994. He went on to marry the actress Barbara Bach, with whom he appeared in the film *Caveman* on 27 April 1981.

There was disharmony during the recording of *The Beatles* (the one that was commonly known as the White Album). Apple's Pete Brown recalls Ringo spending most of the time in the studio playing cards with Neil Aspinall and Mal Evans, and commented: 'It was a poorly kept secret among Beatle intimates that after Ringo left the studio Paul would often dub in the drum tracks himself. When Ringo returned to the studio the next day he would pretend not to notice that it was not his playing.'

On Thursday 22 August 1968 Paul told Ringo off for not getting his drum part right on 'Back In The USSR'. Paul said: 'I'm sure it pissed Ringo off when he couldn't quite get the drums to "Back In The USSR" and I sat in. It's very weird to know that you can do a thing someone else is having trouble with. If you get down and do it, just bluff right through it, you think: What the hell! At least I'm helping. Then the paranoia comes in: But I'm going to show him up! I was very sensitive to that.'

Ringo walked out on the group. Later, he recalled: 'I felt I was playing like shit. And those three were really getting on. I had this feeling that nobody loved me; I felt horrible. So I said to myself: "What am I doing here? Those three are getting along so well and I'm not even playing well." That was madness, so I went away on holiday to sort things out. I don't know, maybe I was just paranoid. To play in a band you have to trust each other.'

Ringo returned to the recording studio on Thursday 5 December 1968 and found that Paul had placed bouquets of flowers over his drum kit. He recalled: 'When I came back everything was all right again. Paul is the greatest bass player in the world. But he is also very determined: he goes on and on to see if he can get his own way. While that may be a virtue it did mean that musical disagreements inevitably arose from time to time.'

Ringo was to appear in numerous films and television specials and series. The films included *A Hard Day's Night*, *Help!*, *Candy* (1968); *The Magic Christian* (1969); *Weekend of Champions* (1970); *Blindman* (1971); *200 Motels* (1971); *Born To Boogie* (1972); *Son of Dracula* (1972); *That'll Be The Day* (1973); *Harry and Ringo's Night*

Out (1974); *Lisztomania* (1975); *Sextette* (1978); *The Last Waltz* (1978); *The Kids Are Alright* (1979); *Caveman* (1981); *The Cooler* (1982); *Give My Regards To Broad Street* (1984). His TV specials included *Ringo* (1978) and he appeared in a miniseries, *Princess Daisy*, with his wife Barbara.

When Allen Klein entered the scene, Ringo sided with John and George, despite warnings they'd received from previous clients of his. Ringo commented that Klein was 'a powerful man and also, no matter what anyone says, he's fair'.

Owing to advice that the only way he could rid himself of Klein was to call for the dissolution of the Beatles, Paul decided to apply to the High Court. He also recorded a solo album and then found that Klein didn't want it released at a time that might clash with the Beatles' *Let It Be* album.

In February 1970 Ringo arrived at Paul's Cavendish Avenue house and spoke into the intercom.

Inside, Paul greeted him, although he was obviously aware of why he was there. It was obviously to persuade him to hold back the release of his solo album *McCartney*. Ringo handed him two letters, one from John, one from George, which they wanted him to read. Ringo also told him that Allen Klein had said he couldn't put out the solo album yet because *Let It Be* was due to be released in May.

Paul was furious and turned on Ringo. 'This is the last straw. If you drag me down, I'll drag you down,' he shouted.

Ringo was to recall, 'To my dismay, he went completely out of control, shouting at me, prodding his fingers towards my face, saying "I'll finish you all now", and "you'll pay". He told me to put my coat on and get out.

'While I thought Paul had behaved a bit like a spoiled child, I could see the release date of his record had a gigantic emotional significance for him. Whether he was right or wrong to be so emotional, I felt that since he was our friend, and since the date was of such immense significance to him, we should let him have his own way.'

During his solo years, Ringo had various ex-Beatles write or perform with him on his albums. Paul and Linda wrote 'Six O Clock' for him to record on his 1973 album *Ringo* and the number featured Paul on piano and synthesiser. For Ringo's *Stop And Smell The Roses* album in 1981 Paul produced the numbers 'Private Property', 'Attention' and 'Sure To Fall'. Paul also provided bass, piano and percussion sounds. Paul had written both 'Private Property' and 'Attention' and he, Linda, Sheila Casey and Lezlee Livrano Price provided backing vocals on all three tracks. At Paul's suggestion they also made a short promotional film called *The Cooler*, which was entered in the Short Film category at the Cannes Film Festival in May 1982.

In 1989 Ringo formed his first All-Starr Band and has been touring regularly ever since with various different All-Starr Band personnel.

In 1995 Ringo teamed up with Paul and George once again to work on the *Anthology* project and he was to work again with Paul on the *Flaming Pie* album.

Stars In Their Lives

An ITV show in which Heather Mills appeared on Sunday 22 October 2000. The programme discussed Heather's charity work. During the last ten minutes of the show Heather and Paul publicly declared their love for each other and discussed their relationship for the first time – and also gave each other an on-air kiss.

Discussing their first meeting, Paul said, 'When I saw her at that award show I thought, "Wow, she looks great." A very beautiful, true fine woman. That was the first impression and then when I heard her speak, I was very impressed. So I found out her telephone number and rang her up and said, "We should talk about some charity stuff".' Heather then said: 'I couldn't believe it. I was a bit naïve, actually, and I just thought here's a guy who does a lot of work for charity. I thought he was very cute but it didn't enter my head that he fancied me. At the end of one of the last meetings, I got into a lift and just felt these eyes in my back. I turned round and saw him peeping. I said, "I think you're eyeing up my bum".' On TV, Paul answered, 'I was.' Heather continued, saying, 'I love him.' Paul said, 'On national telly?' Heather replied, 'You started it. I was going to say nothing tonight about it.' Then Paul admitted, 'Yeah, I love her.' Heather described how they were together at Halloween when Paul had carved twenty pumpkins with smiley faces. She said, 'I just started crying that he'd done this for me. That was the icing on the cake. He's the most romantic man I've ever met.'

Stella May Day

An instrumental by Paul which he recorded and produced on 1 May 1995 at Hog Hill Mill for a presentation at his daughter Stella's fashion graduation show at Central St Martin's School of Art. The final show took place at the Business Design Centre, Islington and Paul wrote 'Stella May Day' especially for this show. The guitar instrumental was played over the PA system as Naomi Campbell, Kate Moss and Yasmin le Bon modelled Stella's designs.

Step Inside Love

A number Paul wrote specially as the theme tune of Cilla Black's television series, *Cilla*. During the recording of 'I Will' at Abbey Road on Monday 16 September 1968, Paul, playing an acoustic guitar, performed a brief version of the number for his fellow Beatles. This recording was to surface on the Beatles *Anthology 3*, released in October 1996. Paul made a demo for Cilla at his St John's Wood home and gave it to her. Cilla then recorded it at

Abbey Road Studios on 28 February 1968 and it was rush-released as a single on Parlophone R5674 on 9 March 1968, with 'I Couldn't Take My Eyes Off You' on the flipside, and reached No. 8 in the British charts. It was the third number by Paul that Cilla had recorded.

It wasn't actually released until the series was almost over because Paul had written it at the last moment.

Cilla commented, 'I recorded "Step Inside Love", Paul McCartney's theme of my BBC TV series, and it was released on 9 March 1968. Paul used to write simple songs, but they were difficult to arrange and get the sound you wanted. On the first recording Paul played it on guitar, but the key didn't suit me – and I had to have it taken up. Then the second version was disappointing. I just couldn't get my teeth into it. But we did a great recording in the end.'

Cilla was also to say that Paul was upset when she sang the song live on her television show and forgot the lyrics. She commented: 'Paul thought the producers had made me change the words and he wasn't happy over that. Actually I was so nervous I was making them up as I went along!'

It was issued in America on Bell 726 on 6 May 1968.

In July 1997 a three-CD retrospective *1963–1973: The Abbey Road Decade* was issued on EMI Zonophone (8 57053 2). This contained a number of versions of the song, including a demo with a vocal by Cilla and acoustic guitar backing by Paul, the original single by Cilla and an Italian version.

Steve Wright Show, The

A Radio One show hosted by disc jockey Steve Wright. Paul turned up out of the blue on Wednesday 13 June 1990 and took part in the show during which he was interviewed by Wright, played acoustic versions of 'Matchbox' and 'Bluebird' and even read weather and traffic reports. Wright also played the medley 'PS Love Me Do' which had been recorded at Paul's live performance at the Tokyo Dome earlier that year.

Stevens, Joe

An American photographer who Paul hired in 1972 to document the Wings tour of Europe. The New Yorker had been living in London working for various 'underground' publications. Due to difficulties with obtaining a work permit for him, he was nicknamed Captain Snaps and a company called Women's Tango Lessons Ltd was formed to collect the profits from the sale of the photographs, which were then to be divided between Paul, Linda and Stevens.

Captain Snaps once mentioned how Paul did not want to hear any talk of the Beatles at the time, saying, 'I think he'd been almost brain-damaged for a while from having been Paul of the Beatles.'

Stewart, Eric

A guitarist born in Manchester on 20 January 1945 who was originally a member of the Mindbenders and later joined 10cc.

Eric played on some tracks on the *Tug Of War* album and was then asked to play on the *Pipes Of Peace* sessions. He was also featured on the *Give My Regards To Broad Street* album and appeared in the film.

In an interview with the Dutch fanzine *Beatles Unlimited*, Eric discussed how he was first asked to play on the *Tug Of War* sessions: 'I meet Paul fairly often and we've known each other ever since way back when he was with the Beatles and I was with the Mindbenders. We used to play at the Cavern together. We used to play the same kind of music, American R&B, and we're both from the North, we have the same accent, the same sense of humour.

'After I had a car accident a while back, Paul phoned me up to see if I was all right. I said I was, but in fact I was still rather messed up and still had to use drugs and all that. But Paul asked me if I felt like playing on his new LP so I said, "Great!"'

When he was a member of 10cc Eric played on Mike McGear's solo album *McGear* on the tracks 'The Man Who Found God On The Moon' and 'Givin' Grease A Ride'. Paul produced the album and that was when Eric and he renewed their acquaintance.

10cc disbanded in 1983, but the members: Eric, Graham Gouldman, Kevin Godley and Lol Creme, recorded a reunion album. It contained a song part-composed by Paul, 'Don't Break The Promises', which was originally co-written by Paul and Stewart during the *Press To Play* period in 1985/86, but not included on the album. Gouldman later contributed to the number, as it is a shared three-man copyright.

For the *Press To Play* album, Paul and Stewart wrote six of the tracks together. He was only the third person Paul had written with since the break-up of the Beatles, the other two being Linda and Denny Laine.

In the summer of 1986 it was reported that he had been asked to tour with Paul, but Paul stated that he and Stewart had fallen out over the fact that he hadn't let Stewart produce an album.

Stockton Wood Road Primary School

A large primary school built in the Speke area of Liverpool after the war. It was close to where Paul and his younger brother lived at the time and was the first primary school they attended, with Mike enrolling one year after Paul. The headmistress was to comment that Paul was a quiet young man and a quick learner. Within a short time the school had taken on so many pupils that, at over 1,500, it had the largest primary school enrolment in Britain.

Paul and Michael moved on to the Joseph Williams Primary School because of the overcrowding.

In 1993, when Paul discovered that burglars had ransacked the school, both he and his brother Mike donated signed copies of their books to raise money in an auction to replace stolen toys. Paul's signed copy was of his *Paul McCartney: Composer and Artist* book.

Stop And Smell The Roses

An album by Ringo Starr. When he began recording it at the Superbear recording studios situated 2,700 feet up a mountain, close to Nice on the French Riviera, between Friday 11 July and Monday 21 July 1981, he was joined for the initial sessions by Paul and Linda, who brought their children along. At the time the album went under the working title of *Can't Fight Lightning*. Paul produced four of the album tracks and also penned two of the numbers for Ringo, 'Private Property' and 'Attention'. Other musicians present were Lloyd Green on steel guitar, Laurence Juber on guitar, Howie Casey on sax and Sheila Casey and Linda on backing vocals. The engineer was Peter Henderson.

While there, Paul, Linda and Juber recorded one of Linda's songs 'Love's Full Glory', although it wasn't released.

Stop And Smell The Roses was issued in America on Boardwalk NBI 33246 on Monday 26 October 1981 and in Britain on RCA LP 6022 on Saturday 21 November 1981. There were ten tracks with compositions and production credits being shared by Paul, George, Harry Nilsson, Ron Wood, Stephen Stills and Ringo.

Stranglehold

This was the first number Paul and Eric Stewart wrote together and it was the opening track on the *Press To Play* album, lasting 3 minutes and 36 seconds. Recording began at Paul's Hog Hill Mill studio in April 1985 with Paul, Eric and session drummer Jerry Marotta.

On Wednesday 29 October 1986 the 'Stranglehold' single was issued on Capitol B-5636 with 'Angry (remix)' on the flip. Paul and Eric Stewart wrote both sides. The video for 'Stranglehold', directed by Bob Giraldi, was released a month later.

On the same day a different Macca single was issued in Britain, 'Pretty Little Head', a remix by Larry Alexander.

A music video of the number was filmed in Nogales, Arizona in October 1986 in a derelict restaurant, the Halfway Station. Musicians included Duane Sciaqua on guitar, Jerry Marotta on drums, Lenni Pickett on baritone, Neil Jason on bass, Alex Foster on baritone and Stan Harrison on alto. Apart from performing 'Stranglehold', the group also jammed on several numbers, including 'Fortune Teller', 'Tequila', 'Cactus Club' and 'Love Is Strange'.

Stuart, Hamish

A guitarist, born in Glasgow on 8 October 1949. He joined a band called the Webb at school when he was twelve years old and has been a performer ever since. During the late 1960s the bands he played in included the In-Crowd.

Stuart moved down to London as vocalist with a band called the Scots of St James, but returned to Glasgow after a few months to join Dream Police. He then became a guitarist rather than a lead singer. The band recorded three singles for Decca and built up a following with regular appearances at the Marquee, but disbanded due to their lack of success on record.

The next band he formed was called Berserk Crocodiles, which lasted until he formed the Average White Band in May 1972 and made twelve albums with the group. The Average White Band disbanded in 1982 and Hamish became a session musician performing on records for over two-dozen artists ranging from Aretha Franklin to Diana Ross. He also wrote a number of hit songs for artists who included the Temptations and Diana Ross.

In 1987, while he was in a band called Easy Pieces, he was invited to Paul's studio in Sussex where he met up with Paul, Nicky Hopkins and Chris Whitten. During the session a McCartney/Stuart composition resulted, 'The First Stone'.

Hamish was then invited to join Paul's sessions with Elvis Costello and then spent the next six years performing with Paul's band, appearing on two world tours and on albums such as *Tripping The Live Fantastic*, *Flowers In The Dirt* and *Off The Ground*. He was also to play on Linda's tribute album, *Wide Prairie*.

After leaving Paul, he formed his own outfit, the Hamish Stuart Band, appearing on the London club circuit and releasing his first solo album *Sooner Or Later* in September 1999.

Subiaco Oval

Venue in Perth, Australia where Paul appeared on Friday 5 March 1993 when opening the Australasian arm of his New World Tour. His band comprised himself, Linda, Blair Cunningham, Robbie McIntosh, Hamish Stuart and Paul 'Wix' Wickens. His basic repertoire comprised 'Drive My Car', 'Coming Up', 'Get Out Of My Way', 'Another Day', 'All My Loving', 'Let Me Roll It', 'Peace In The Neighbourhood', 'Off The Ground', 'I Wanna Be Your Man' and 'Can't Buy Me Love'. There was an acoustic set with 'Robbie's Bit', 'Good Rockin' Tonight', 'We Can Work It Out', 'Every Night', 'And I Love Her', 'Hope Of Deliverance', 'Michelle', 'Biker Like An Icon', 'Here, There And Everywhere', 'Yesterday', 'My Love', 'Lady Madonna', 'Live And Let Die', 'Let It Be', 'Magical Mystery Tour', 'C'Mon People', 'The Long And Winding Road', 'Paperback Writer', 'Fixing A Hole', 'Penny Lane' and 'Sgt Pepper's Lonely Hearts Club Band'. Encores were 'Band On The Run', 'I Saw Her Standing There', 'Mull Of Kintyre' and 'Hey Jude'.

The ABC TV Channel and Channel 9 both screened part of the 'Live And Let Die' performance the following day.

Sugartime

A track originally recorded on 20 June 1977 at the Black Ark studios in Kingston, Jamaica as part of Paul's idea of having Linda release a solo album. The number had been penned by Odis Echols and Charlie Phillips and had originally been a chart hit for the McGuire sisters in March 1958. Linda added her vocals to the track at Rude Studios in Scotland in August 1977 and the number was first heard on the radio series *Oobu Joobu*. Following Linda's death, Paul did further work on the track on 7 July 1998 at his Hog Hill studio and it was included on Linda's posthumous album 'Wide Prairie' in 1998.

Suicide

In the days before the Beatles were successful, Paul originally wrote this number with Frank Sinatra in mind. He said that he wrote it in bed just before dropping off to sleep. He always had a pencil and paper by the side of his bed and says that he has the ability to write in the dark. He was later to regard the number as 'horrible'.

Then, when the Beatles were recording at Abbey Road, Frank Sinatra phoned and asked to speak to Paul. Sinatra asked him if he had a song for him. Paul quickly made a demo of 'Suicide' and sent it to him. Apparently, Sinatra thought Paul was taking the mickey and said, 'Is this guy having me on?'

A few seconds of the song were heard on the *McCartney* album and other snippets are to be found on bootleg recordings.

In 1993 Paul was to comment, 'Before rock 'n' roll, for John and I, our accolade would have been to write for Sinatra. For the first couple of years we just thought like that. Then rock 'n' roll came in and blew everything out of its way! There was life before rock 'n' roll, and there was a lot of music I like there. Cole Porter and people like that are still great favourites of mine.'

In 1994 Paul turned down the opportunity of appearing on Frank Sinatra's *Duets* album.

Sullivan Stadium, Foxboro

A venue near Boston, Massachusetts. On Tuesday 24 July 1990 Paul appeared there during his World Tour and was interviewed backstage by the Boston station WBCN. On Wednesday 25 July 1990 an additional performance was held at this venue, with invitations limited to an audience of 800. Paul and the band mimed to the recording of a Philadelphia show to allow close-up shots to be filmed for the planned concert film, 'Get Back'.

Summit, The (album)

A charity album in aid of the 'Year Of The Child', issued in Britain on K-Tel NE 1067 on Friday 11 January 1980. Various artists contributed tracks to the album and Paul's contribution was his recording of 'Jet'.

Summit, The (venue)

A venue in Houston, Texas where Wings appeared on Tuesday 4 May during the American leg of their Wings World Tour 1975/76.

During the concert a piece of scaffolding fell onto the stage, narrowly missing Paul, but injuring his roadie Trevor Jones who was taken to hospital and given thirteen stitches.

10 Sunbury Road, Anfield, Liverpool

Paul's first home where he was brought to following his birth at Walton Hospital.

Sunday Beatle

A special supplement of the *Sunday Mirror* in Sydney, Australia. In June 1963 it ran a special competition to link up with Paul's 22nd birthday, in conjunction with the Sydney *Daily Mirror*, and offered the 'chance of a lifetime'.

Under the headline 'You ... Could Go To Paul's Birthday Party', the competition announced that a selection of girls between the ages of sixteen and twenty-two could win the opportunity of attending Paul's birthday party on Thursday 18 June at the Sheraton Hotel, Sydney. Initially, the girls had to submit a fifty-word essay on the theme: 'Why I Would Like To Be A Guest At A Beatle's Birthday Party'. There were 10,000 entries and the finalists had to attend an interview at the hotel before a panel of judges who included Derek Taylor, Irish comedian Dave Allen, editor of the *Sunday Mirror* Hugh Bingham and Leicester Warburton and Blanch d'Alpuget, also from the *Sunday Mirror*.

There were seventeen winners and fifteen runners-up. The latter were invited to meet the Beatles after their concert on the Friday evening.

The girls invited to Paul's Thursday bash were: Glennys Smith; Jenny Lamb; Sandra Linklater; Caroline Styles; Ines Truse; Evelyn Mac; Patricia Thompson; Christine Buetter; Claire Hogben; Caroline Keirs; Carmel Stratton; Anne-Marie Alexander; Marcia McAmeny; Delphine Dockerill; Jannette Carroll; Nancy Haddow and Sandra Stevenson.

Jannette Carroll, who was only sixteen at the time, commented: 'As we were leaving Paul shook all our hands and by this time I was even braver so I said, "I'm not used to shaking boys' hands on their birthday," and offered him my cheek. He very gently took my chin, turned my face around and gave me a beautiful kiss right on the lips. I know it sounds corny, but for about two weeks I washed every part of my face but my lips.'

The party took place around midnight, after their show was over, and as the Beatles entered the room, Paul was heard to say, 'Ee, it's a proper do, isn't it?'

Sunshine, Sometime

A number Paul wrote for his Rupert Bear project, surprisingly more than a decade before he produced his animated movie. He penned the number and recorded it during the *Ram* sessions.

Rupert Bear had been a childhood favourite of Paul's and he had suggested in 1968 that it should be a Beatles project and was to comment they should have done a Rupert The Bear film instead of *Yellow Submarine*.

He'd bought the rights to the character in April 1970 only days after the Beatles had dissolved and began to write songs for the project straight away.

Super Furry Animals

A band from Wales, formed in Cardiff 1993, who comprise Gruff Rhys, vocals, guitar; Dafydd Ieuan, drums, vocals; Cian Ciaran, keyboards, vocals; Guto Pryce, bass; and Huw Bunford, guitars, vocals, cello.

Paul first met the group in February 2000 at the *NME* Brat Awards when he accepted a prize of 'Best Band Ever' on behalf of the Beatles. Cian told Paul to give him a call if he wanted anything remixing.

Paul did and they first collaborated on *Liverpool Sound Collage*, along with Youth. The album was made specially for Peter Blake's 'About Collage' exhibition at the Tate Liverpool and was nominated for a Grammy in 2001 for 'Best Alternative Musical Album'.

Paul can also be heard munching celery on a track of the Super Furry Animals album *Rings Around The World*, released in 2001. Discussing Paul's participation in an interview with the *NME*, Gruff Rhys commented, 'He's on the record chewing celery in time to the rhythm of "Receptacle For The Respectable". That's a song in four parts, it goes from sixties harmony pop to early seventies glam rock in the Bacharach balladry, then goes death metal. It's not an obvious single.'

Superbowl

Paul performed along with 500 young people at the 36th Superbowl, the climax of the American Football season, at the Louisiana Stadium in New Orleans on 3 February 2002.

This was a further performance in aid of the families of the firemen and policemen who were killed on 11 September 2001. Paul commented, 'As a sports fan I am thrilled to have the opportunity to be involved in the Superbowl and as a musician I am honoured to add my voice to the message of tribute that this year's Superbowl will carry.'

The Superbowl was watched by an audience of 150 million in America and 800 million further people throughout the world.

The Superbowl pre-game entertainment was extended from one hour to three hours under the title 'Heroes, Hope and Homeland' and was a strongly patriotic presentation, beginning with the Boston Pops

Orchestra and including performers such as No Doubt and the Barenaked Ladies. Paul appeared at the finale and was preceded by performances of 'America The Beautiful' and 'The Star Spangled Banner'.

Sure To Fall (In Love With You)

A number penned by Carl Perkins, Quinton Claunch and William Cantrell, recorded by Perkins and issued in 1956 on Sun 235.

Paul produced Ringo Starr's version of the number on Ringo's 1981 album *Stop And Smell The Roses*.

Sutcliffe, Stuart

The Beatles' original bass guitarist, who was born in Edinburgh on 23 June 1940. In 1956, at the age of sixteen, he became a student at Liverpool College of Art, where Bill Harry introduced John Lennon to him. Stuart's best friend was Rod Murray, with whom he shared a flat initially in Percy Street and then in Gambier Terrace. John felt his group needed a bass guitarist and offered both Stuart and Rod the position. Having little money, they couldn't afford a guitar, so Rod began making one. Stuart had entered one of his paintings in the John Moores Exhibition and, when John Moores himself bought it, Stuart obtained a guitar on hire purchase when he placed a deposit on a Hofner President at Frank Hessy's music store.

It was Stuart who suggested the name 'Beetles' because he felt they should choose the name of an insect as Buddy Holly's backing group the Crickets had done.

When the Beatles made their debut in Hamburg in 1960 they initially played at a club called the Indra. At one time the club owner, Bruno Koschmeider, took Stuart from the Beatles to include him in a group with Howie Casey at the Kaiserkeller. When the Beatles attracted a crowd of artistic students to their performances, it was generally Stuart who made a mark on them, and one of the students, Astrid Kirchherr, fell in love with him. As a result, when the Beatles returned to Liverpool, Stuart remained in Hamburg for a time with Astrid. He returned to Liverpool in late February and then joined the Beatles at their March season at the Top Ten Club in Hamburg.

Stuart had enrolled at the State High School of Art Instruction in Hamburg and was living at Astrid's home. It seemed that his passion for art was becoming more important to him than his being a member of the Beatles.

There was also, arguably, some friction between Stuart and Paul, as Paul wanted to take over as the group's bass player.

During their Top Ten season they performed with Tony Sheridan, which produced a slight problem: there were too many guitarists in the group – so Paul played piano.

The drummer Pete Best found that Paul was beginning to niggle

Stuart, particularly regarding his relationship with Astrid, and remembers that it ended in fisticuffs.

He says that Paul kept winding Stuart up. 'On this particular night Astrid was there and Paul said something. I don't actually know what the remark was because Paul was playing piano on the other side of the drum rostrum. Stu took his bass off and it wasn't with a view to giving it to anyone. He put it down and, the next thing, the two of them were swinging at one another.' Stuart left soon after that.

Following a fall down the attic steps of Astrid's home, Stuart began to experience headaches and died on Tuesday 10 April 1962.

Over the years, probably originating from inaccurate information in Allan Williams's book *The Man Who Gave the Beatles Away*, people who had never seen him or heard him play began to write in books and articles that he was a lousy bass guitarist.

Yet, when he had originally stayed behind in Hamburg when his fellow Beatles returned to Liverpool in December 1960, George Harrison wrote to him: 'Come home sooner, as if we get a new bass player for the time being, it will be crummy, as he will have to learn everything. It's no good with Paul playing bass, we've decided, that is if he had some kind of bass and amp to play on.'

In a 1964 interview in *Beat Instrumental* in which he was discussing guitars, Paul said: 'I believe that playing an ordinary guitar first and then transferring to bass has made me a better bass player because it loosened up my fingers. NOT that I'm suggesting that EVERY bass player should learn on ordinary guitar. Stuart Sutcliffe certainly didn't, and he was a great bass man.'

Pauline Sutcliffe, his younger sister, was to tell Bill Harry: 'According to Stuart's letters and conversations with him he thought he was progressing quite well and loved it and thought he was quite innovative as a bass player. He thought himself good enough to do session work after he left them and – I've got letters – he was asked to be in other groups.'

Klaus Voormann, who was once considered as a replacement for Paul in the Beatles, took up the bass guitar because Stuart, whom he regarded as his favourite bass player, inspired him.

Suzy and the Red Stripes

Name given to some recording and animated projects surrounding Linda McCartney, which originated in November 1972 when Paul and Wings used the title while recording 'Seaside Woman' at AIR Studios in London. Linda had been called 'Suzy' when they were in Jamaica because she loved the reggae version of 'Suzy Q'. The Red Stripe referred to Jamaican beer.

Further Suzy and the Red Stripes sessions took place in Paris in November 1973 with Paul, Linda, Denny Laine, Jimmy McCulloch and Davey Lutton.

Sweet Baby

A track recorded at Strawberry Studios in Stockport, Cheshire during the *McGear* sessions, which Paul produced. It was omitted from the *McGear* album but used as the flipside of the first single from the album, 'Leave It' (Warner Bros K 16446). It was also included as a bonus track when *McGear* was later issued as a CD on the See For Miles label. The song had originally been called 'All My Lovin'' and had been recorded by Mike with Paul on acoustic guitar and Linda on keyboards. The number had been inspired by the birth of Mike's daughter Abbi. The song was retitled as it was obviously too close to Paul's 'All My Loving'.

Tadpoles
A single by the Bonzo Dog Doo-Dah Band, produced by Paul and issued in Britain on Friday 1 August 1969 on Liberty LBS 83257, with 'I'm The Urban Spaceman' on the flip.

Take It Away (promotional film)
The filming of the promotional video for 'Take It Away' took place at EMI's Elstree Studios in Boreham Wood and was directed by John MacKenzie.

Six hundred members of the Wings Fun Club were invited along as a live audience to the filming, which took place on Wednesday 23 June 1982.

The band comprised Paul on bass, Eric Stewart on lead, George Martin on electric piano, Ringo and Steve Gadd on drums, Linda on tambourine and the horn section from the Q Tips.

In between the various takes of 'Take It Away' Paul and his band played several numbers to entertain the audience, including 'Lucille', 'Bo Diddley', 'Peggy Sue', 'Send Me Some Lovin'', 'Twenty Flight Rock', 'Cut Across Shorty', 'Reeling And Rocking', 'Searching' and 'Hallelujah I Love Her So'.

The promotional film made its debut on *Top Of The Pops* on Thursday 15 July 1982.

Take It Away (single)
A single by Paul which was issued in Britain on Parlophone 6056 on Monday 21 June 1982 where it reached No. 14 in the charts and in America on Columbia 18-02018 on Saturday 3 July 1982 where it reached No. 10 in the charts.

'I'll Give You A Ring' was on the flip.

It was released in Germany on Odeon 1C006-64845T.

The number was originally written with Ringo Starr in mind. Paul recalled, 'I was writing some songs for Ringo and "Take It Away" was in amongst those songs. I thought it would suit me better. The way it went into the chorus and stuff, I didn't think it was very Ringo.'

Talk More Talk

A track on the *Press To Play* album lasting 5 minutes and 17 seconds that Paul describes as 'surrealist'.

Tarrant County Convention Center

Venue in Fort Worth, Texas where Wings opened the American leg of their 1975/76 World Tour, called *Wings Over America*. The 14,000-seater venue was sold out and before Wings could begin their set, the audience gave them a 15-minute standing ovation.

The group had been rehearsing in Fort Worth and the tour had been delayed for almost a month due to Jimmy McCulloch's fractured finger. The line-up of the band comprised Paul, Linda, Denny Laine, McCulloch and Joe English, together with a horn section comprising Howie Casey on saxophone, Tony Dorsey on trombone, Steve Howard on trumpet and flugelhorn, and Thaddeus Richard on saxophone, clarinet and flute.

Their repertoire comprised: 'Venus And Mars', 'Rock Show', 'Jet', 'Let Me Roll It', 'Spirits Of Ancient Egypt', 'Medicine Jar', 'Maybe I'm Amazed', 'Call Me Back Again', 'Lady Madonna', 'The Long And Winding Road', 'Live And Let Die', 'Picasso's Last Words', 'Richard Cory', 'Bluebird', 'I've Just Seen A Face', 'Blackbird', 'Yesterday', 'You Gave Me The Answer', 'Magneto And Titanium Man', 'My Love', 'Listen To What The Man Said', 'Let 'Em In', 'Time To Hide', 'Silly Love Songs', 'Beware My Love', 'Letting Go' and 'Band On The Run.' The encores were 'Hi, Hi, Hi' and 'Soily'.

Jimmy McCulloch sang lead vocal on 'Medicine Jar' and Denny Laine sang lead vocal on 'Spirits Of Ancient Egypt', 'Richard Cory' and 'Time To Hide'.

Taste Of Honey, A

A song which Paul sang lead vocal on during their Cavern days and which was included on their concert performances in 1962 and 1963. Ric Marlow and Bobby Scott had penned it and Lenny Welch had recorded a version in America. The Beatles recorded the number at Abbey Road on Monday 11 February 1963 and it was included on their *Please Please Me* album. Herb Alpert & the Tijuana Brass was to have an instrumental hit with the number in America in 1965.

During some performances, John changed the chorus to 'A Waste Of Money'.

Tavener, Sir John

A British classical composer, born in 1944, who Ringo Starr had introduced to Apple. Ringo had been having building work on his property carried out by Roger Tavener, who told Ringo about his brother. Ringo heard a tape of the BBC recording of Tavener's first long work *The Whale* which had been performed at the Royal Albert Hall, and immediately got in touch. Tavener was signed to Apple Records and they issued his *The Whale* and *Celtic Requiem*.

On 4 May 2000 Paul travelled to New York by Concorde specially to appear at a concert at the church of St Ignatius Loyola. Interviewed by WNYC radio, Paul mentioned that he was initially reluctant to appear when invited by Sir John Tavener, but said, 'He was keen for me to do it, and I trust him.' Accompanied by Heather Mills, Paul chatted to Mia Farrow, who sat close to him and Tavener. Paul then read parts of a short poem 'In the Month of Athyr', which Taverner had set to music, with a chorus singing the rest.

Tavener was to say he was 'touched that Paul McCartney is also journeying across the sea on Concorde to read a Greek poem'. The concert was broadcast live on the WNYC *New Sounds Live* programme.

Taylor, Alistair

Originally a personal assistant to Brian Epstein at his NEMS branch in Whitechapel, Liverpool. When Bill Harry arranged for Brian Epstein to visit the Cavern club to see the Beatles on 13 December 1961, Alistair accompanied him. It was Alistair's signature that witnessed the first Beatles management contract, and he also turned down Epstein's offer of 2½ per cent of the Beatles contract. Later, owing to asthma problems suffered by his wife, Lesley, Alistair decided to move to healthier climes down South and left Epstein's employ to join Pye Records.

A casual meeting with Epstein at Pye resulted in Alistair's rejoining NEMS. He recalls that the member of the Beatles he was closest to was Paul and it was Paul who coined the term 'Mr Jobworthy' for him because he was responsible for arranging so many things for them. He was also known as 'Mr Fixit'.

Following Epstein's death, Alistair remained in the Beatles' employ and, when Apple was launched, John Lennon suggested he become general manager of the company. Paul arranged for Alistair to pose for the photograph used in the initial advertisements, designed by Paul, who featured Taylor as a one-man band, dressed in bowler hat and suit.

Paul also wrote the copy for the ad, which read:

This man has talent. One day he sang his songs to a tape recorder (borrowed from the man next door). In his neatest handwriting he wrote an explanatory note (giving his name and address) and, remembering to enclose a picture of himself, sent the tape, letter and photograph to Apple Music, 94 Baker Street, London W1. If you were thinking of doing the same thing yourself – do it now! This man now owns a Bentley!

Alistair has written no fewer than three biographies describing his experiences with the Beatles. The first *Yesterday: The Beatles Remembered*, was a positive memoir with no rancour, despite the fact that he was unceremoniously sacked from Apple when Allen Klein took over the reins. Alistair attempted to contact members of the group by phone, but none of them would talk to him. Paul was to comment on the sacking in the *Daily Mail* when he said: 'It isn't possible to be nice about giving someone the sack.'

He worked for Dick James Publishing as a press officer for a while, and then became project manager at Morgan Grampian Publications. He later took on a number of labouring jobs and said: 'I've shovelled lead, made machine knives, washed pots in pubs. I'm not proud or very well qualified.'

His second book, *A Secret History*, published in 2001, saw him take a more bitter tone concerning his relationship with the Beatles, possibly because he was not even mentioned in *The Beatles Anthology*. His co-writer Stafford Hildred, wrote: 'He arranged flights, deflected paternity suits, lent money and often a shoulder to cry on. He bought islands, cars and houses for the Fab Four ... he was a grief counsellor for Paul McCartney when Jane Asher dumped him because she came home early and found him in their bed with another woman ... and he had been effectively airbrushed out of official Beatles history.'

In his book Alistair claims that he helped Paul to co-write 'Hello Goodbye' at Cavendish Avenue and says: 'Those were the seeds of a Beatles number one, written, I will always believe, by Taylor and McCartney.'

He admits that he never got on with Linda and has a number of negative things to say about her in his book.

He published his third biography a year later in 2002.

Teatro Tendo

A venue in Naples, Italy, the name meaning 'tent theatre' in English. Paul and his band (Paul, Linda, McIntosh, Stuart, Wickens, Cunningham) made several 'surprise' appearances between May and July 1991 and this was one of them. They flew into the city, appeared in concert and then flew back to England following the show.

Paul had recently filmed the MTV *Unplugged* show and decided on two 45-minute sets, the first acoustic, followed by an electric set. The brief tour of venues in Britain and Europe was referred to as the 'Surprise Gigs' Tour.

They appeared at the theatre on Wednesday 5 June 1991. During the show Paul played harmonica on stage for the first time during the performance of a new number 'The River'. He also introduced a second new track during the set, 'The World Is Waiting For The Sunrise'. Paul hadn't played this particular number for decades. In fact, the previous performance was with John Lennon when the two were at a pub run by Paul's cousin and they played a set under the name the Nerk Twins. Another number they performed at Naples, but not at the other ' surprise' concerts was 'Singing The Blues'.

Teddy Boy

A number by Paul, which the Beatles originally recorded during the *Get Back* sessions. They performed it for the first time at Abbey Road Studios on Friday 24 January 1969. Paul re-recorded it for his debut solo album *McCartney*, so the Beatles version was dropped from *Let It Be*. However, it was eventually to surface on the Beatles *Anthology 3* CD in October 1996.

Paul wrote the number in India and after the version with the Beatles had been scrapped he completed the song in Scotland and London, initially recording it at home and then at Morgan Studios. The number, 2 minutes and 22 seconds in length, features Linda on harmonies and Paul playing guitar and bass.

Tell Me If You Can

A number Tony Sheridan claims he co-wrote with Paul in Hamburg. Sheridan recorded a version of the number in 1964, without Paul's permission.

Tell Me What You See

A number penned by Paul and recorded by the Beatles at Abbey Road on 18 February 1965. It was included as a track on the *Help!* album and was also featured on the American *Beatles IV* and on *Love Songs*.

Temporary Secretary

A track on the *McCartney II* album, 3 minutes and 13 seconds in length. It was also issued as a 12″ single in Britain, limited to an edition of 25,000, with 'Secret Friend' on the flip on Parlophone 12 R 6039 on 15 September 1980.

The cover on the front of the sleeve depicted a bespectacled 'temp' sitting on Paul's lap in a drawing by Jeff Cummins of Hipgnosis. The reverse illustration was a photograph of Paul taken by David Thorpe.

The Mr Marks referred to on the number referred to Alfred Marks, the founder of the Alfred Marks Agency, a company providing temporary secretaries (or 'temps') to local businesses.

TFI FRIDAY

A Channel Four series hosted by Chris Evans and produced by Ginger television. Paul appeared on the show on Friday 27 June 1997. The previous day he'd spent the afternoon at the show's venue, the Riverside Studios in Hammersmith, rehearsing the two songs he would be performing, 'Flaming Pie' and 'Young Boy', also laying down the guitar, drums and bass parts which would back him during his performance.

Evans had actually been trying to get Paul to appear on his show for over a year and received confirmation after he'd sent Paul a fax: 'You would (a) have a great time; (b) have a great time; (c) have a f****** great time.'

Paul appeared in the second part of the show in which Chris Evans took faxes from various celebrities who had asked Paul a question. They included Ringo Starr, former footballer George Best, comedian Frank Carson and cook Delia Smith. At the end of the show Paul and Evans climb into a waiting speedboat and set off down the River Thames.

Paul and Evans returned for an after-show party, attended by Paul's daughters Mary and Stella.

Thames At Six

A television show that included a section called 'Nicky Horne's Music Scene'. The five-minute piece included an interview with Paul on Monday 19 May 1980. Paul was promoting his *McCartney II* album and also discussed his recent Japanese drug bust, saying, 'It was very stupid. We'd been to America and the attitude to drugs over there is very different and it led me to take a real casual approach. Most people taking that kind of thing into the country would give it to the roadies, that's the common practice. That just shows that I wasn't really thinking about it. I was taking my opinion of it instead of the legal opinion of it, and I just didn't really think much about it, you know, till the fellow pulled it out of the suitcase and he looked more embarrassed than me. He wanted to put it back and forget the whole thing, you know.'

Horne asked him, 'What thoughts went through your head when you realised it could be seven years?'

Paul said, 'The first thing you do is ask to see your British Consul. You always think, "He'll get me out." Well, he turned up with a flat cap on, he didn't look like a consul at all, our man in Havana or something. He said, "Well Paul, there's a fellow in here who had a lot less than you had and he's done three months already, so you could have seven years' hard labour to look forward to." I thought, "What!" and my jaw dropped. You're worried about how long it's going to last; you're just not worried about the immediate conditions. It's not *Bridge On The River Kwai* you know, it's not that bad. The immediate worry during the time is what's going to happen to Linda and the kids. Those are the main worrying things.'

Thank You Darling

A Wings number that was first performed live at their Nottingham University debut in February 1972. The studio recording was originally intended for the *Red Rose Speedway* album, but wasn't used.

That Day Is Done

One of the songs Paul co-wrote with Elvis Costello for the album *Flowers In The Dirt*, and it's also the song in which the phrase 'flowers in the dirt' comes from. Paul described it as a sad song because it was written when Elvis's grandmother was dying in Ireland.

That Means A Lot

A number by Paul and John, which the Beatles recorded during the *Help!* album sessions on Saturday 20 February and Tuesday 30 March 1965. They weren't happy with the result and didn't release it.

John was to say, 'The song is a ballad which Paul and I wrote for the film but we found we just couldn't sing it. In fact, we made a hash of it, so we thought we'd better give it to someone who could do it well.'

When the Beatles were making their 'Around The Beatles' TV special, PJ Proby was one of the guests and he asked Paul if he had a number to give him. Paul let him have 'That Means A Lot'. Proby recorded it at Abbey Road Studios on Wednesday 7 April 1965, with Ron Richards producing. He issued the number as a single in the US on 5 July 1965 on Liberty 55806. It was issued in the UK on 17 September 1965 on Liberty 10215 and was a minor hit for him, reaching No. 30 in the British charts. The number was also included on his album *PJ Proby*, issued in the US on Liberty LST 7421 on 23 August 1965.

That's Alright Mama

Paul's version of the Elvis classic, which became part of the fiftieth anniversary film and album tribute to the Sun Records label in 2001. Paul recorded the track early in May 2000 with Scotty Moore and DC Fontana, two of Elvis's backing musicians on the original record, with Ahmet Ertegun producing. The number was included in a fiftieth anniversary film and album tribute to the Sun Records label in 2001. It was also included as part of a two-hour tribute to the label on American TV in December 2001.

That Would Be Something

A track on Paul's first solo album *McCartney*, 2 minutes and 37 seconds in length, which was written in Scotland in 1969 and included as the second track on the album. On it, Paul plays guitar, tom-tom, cymbal and bass. He taped the number at Cavendish Avenue and then mixed the track at Abbey Road Studios on 22 February 1970.

Paul explained, 'I had only one mike, as the mixers and VU meters hadn't arrived.' Paul had originally recorded a version during the Beatles January 1969 sessions for *Let It Be*.

The Grateful Dead were to record the number several years later and Paul also performed the number on his *Unplugged* sessions.

Thatcher, Margaret

The first female Prime minister of the UK and former leader of the Conservative Party.

Paul and Linda's opinions over the years seemed to suggest that the couple favoured socialism. During the 1981 industrial dispute over nurses' salaries, Paul actually sent a telegram to Margaret Thatcher in November.

It read: 'What the miners did for Ted Heath, the nurses will do for you.'

This referred to the fact that the Conservative government had been brought down by the miners' strike in 1972. Paul's prediction didn't come true.

In 1984 Paul and Linda met Mrs Thatcher and said afterwards, 'When we were talking to Mrs Thatcher, we said how in a lot of council houses the plumbing was bad, the paint and ceilings were cracking. Why don't they take people on the dole, who want to work, and give them jobs repairing council homes? Maggie Thatcher said, "Oh, the unions wouldn't allow me to do that."'

Theatre Antique

A 2,000-seater open-air Roman amphitheatre in Chateauvallon, in the South of France. This was the venue chosen by Paul to stage his first scheduled concert since the Beatles' final tour of 1966 with his new band Wings, who had made their live debut some months before with a series of impromptu concerts at British universities and colleges. The concert took place on Sunday 9 July 1972.

The Theatre Antique was the launching pad for a five-week tour of France, Germany, Switzerland, Norway, Belgium and the Netherlands.

When asked why he hadn't included Britain on the tour, Paul commented, 'We will play in Britain some time or other, but not right now. The audiences are very critical in Britain and we're a new band just starting out, no matter what any one us have been through individually before. We have to get worked-in before doing any big shows in Britain and America.'

At the backstage press conference Paul also commented on a number of matters. When discussing the fact that he turned down an invitation from George Harrison to appear at 'The Concert For Bangla Desh' the previous year, he said, 'If I'd gone there I know for certain it would have been played up as "Hey! The Beatles are back together again!" It may have only been for one night, but the whole world would have taken it as the truth. But it's ended!'

When Paul was asked why he and the band were travelling around on a double-decker bus, he answered, 'It mainly came about when we were on holiday and we were trying to get healthy before a tour. We suddenly thought, "Wait a minute", if we're going to be in Europe in summer going to places like the South of France, we thought it'd be silly to be in some box all day gasping for air. So we came up with this idea to have an open deck. We've got mattresses up there so we can just cruise along – fantastic! Just lie around, get the sun and keep healthy.'

The line-up was Paul, Linda, Henry McCullough on lead, Denny Laine on rhythm and Denny Seiwell on drums. All five wore dark stage-suits with bell-bottom trousers with gold braiding. Numbers in the first half included 'Eat At Home', 'Smile Away', 'Bip Bop', 'Mumbo', 'Blue Moon Of Kentucky', '1882', 'I Would Only Smile' (vocal by Denny Laine) and 'The Mess'. There was a ten-minute intermission and numbers performed in the second half of the show included 'Best Friend', 'Soily', 'I Am Your Singer' (a duet with Paul and Linda), 'Seaside Woman' (a solo by Linda), 'Say You Don't Mind' (vocal by Denny Laine), 'Henry's Blues' (a Henry McCullough guitar spotlight number), 'Give Ireland Back To The Irish', 'Cottonfields', 'My Love', 'Mary Had A Little Lamb', 'Maybe I'm Amazed' and 'Hi, Hi, Hi'.

There's Only One Paul McCartney
An hour-long BBC programme timed to celebrate Paul's sixtieth birthday, screened on 2 June 2002. It featured a host of celebrities paying tribute to him, and they included Cilla Black, Ben Elton, Bob Geldof, Elvis Costello, Dustin Hoffman, Bono, Travis and Paul's cousin Kate Robbins. There was also archive footage.

Things We Said Today
A number that Paul wrote while on holiday in the Bahamas in May 1964 with Jane, Ringo and Maureen. They'd rented a yacht named *Happy Days*. In one of the cabins below deck Paul began writing the song one afternoon on an acoustic guitar then completed the rest on the deck.

Paul commented, 'I wrote this on acoustic. It was a slightly nostalgic thing already, a future nostalgia. We'll remember the things we said today, sometime in the future, so the song projects itself into the future. It was a sophisticated little tune.'

It was recorded at Abbey Road Studios on 2 June 1964 and issued as the B-side of 'A Hard Day's Night' on 10 June 1964.

A version of this number lasting 5 minutes and 2 seconds was included on the *Tripping The Live Fantastic* album. It was recorded live at the Palacio des Sportes, Madrid, Spain on 2 November 1989 during the 1989/90 World Tour.

Thingumybob

The theme tune of a television series *Thingumybob*, composed by Paul, who also produced the John Foster and Sons Ltd Black Dyke Mills Band recording of the number. The single was issued in Britain on 6 September 1968 on Apple 4 and on 26 August 1968 in America on Apple 1800.

'Yellow Submarine' was on the flip.

This Is Your Life

A popular television show that, in Britain, once had a weekly audience of 20 million viewers.

Eamonn Andrews, a former Irish boxer who won the Irish Junior Middleweight title, originally hosted it. He worked in an insurance office in his native Dublin for a time before moving to London to present the BBC's *Sports Report*. In 1951 he became host of *What's My Line?*, a popular television show, before moving in 1964 to independent television to host *The Eamonn Andrews Show*, Britain's first late night chat-show.

In the 1960s he took over as host of Thames Television's series *This Is Your Life*. Among the many guests he spotlighted were Arthur Dooley, George Martin and John Conteh.

Conteh was 22 years old at the time and had won the World Light-Heavyweight Championship title 36 days previously.

Paul had featured him on the cover of his *Band On The Run* album and had attended the Championship fight after sending John a telegram reading: 'You made me number one. Now you be number one.'

Because of this, Andrews decided that Paul and Linda could help him to spring the surprise on the new champion. On Wednesday 6 November 1974, Paul and Linda lured the unsuspecting Conteh to Abbey Road Studios on the pretext that Linda wanted to take some photographs of him and Paul together. Andrews hid behind an acoustic screen; when John was settled at the piano with Paul, he jumped out with his famous red book and photographer Stan Allen snapped away. Conteh was then driven to the television studios for the programme and a live link was kept open with Abbey Road to enable Paul and Linda to pay their own tribute on the show.

Paul was also to record a message for Gerry Marsden when the leader of Gerry & the Pacemakers was a recipient of the red book.

This One (promotional film)

The 1989 promotional video was directed by Tim Pope and was an attempt to produce a visual psychedelic effect with changing colours and blurred images to promote the release of the single. Paul, Linda and the band were seen dressed in various colourful costumes with Paul wearing a bowler hat at one stage and a halo and coloured glasses in another.

This One (single)

A single that was issued in Britain on Monday 17 July 1989 on Parlophone R6223 where it reached No. 18 in the charts. On that day there was a 7", a 12", a cassette and a CD version of the number, the second *Flowers In The Dirt* single to be issued in the UK.

It was released in America in cassette form only on Capitol 4JM44438 on Wednesday 2 August 1989, but only managed to reach No. 94 in the charts.

The flipside was 'The First Stone'.

In addition, on Monday 24 July 1989 'This One' was issued in a limited edition box with 'The Long And Winding Road' on the flip. A 7" vinyl promotional version was issued in America on Wednesday 2 August 1989.

There was a four-track CD single also issued on Britain on Parlophone CDR 6223 with 'This One', 'The First Stone', 'I Wanna Cry' and 'I'm In Love Again'.

In Britain there were no less than seven different figurations of 'This One', which would have cost a fan in the region of £18 to buy. They included a postcard pack, which comprised the single and six postcards, one for each member of the band. There was also a different flipside to this limited edition – a version of 'The Long And Winding Road' taken from the TV special 'Put It There'.

The single was released in Germany on Parlophone 1C006-203448-7.

A version of this number lasting 4 minutes and 29 seconds was included on the *Tripping The Live Fantastic* album. It was recorded live at the Palace of Auburn Hills, Detroit, Michigan on 1 February 1990 during the 1989/90 World Tour.

Thomas, Chris

A British record producer who had recorded various acts, including the Sex Pistols and Badfinger. Thomas was originally an assistant engineer to George Martin and Paul hired him to co-produce *Back To The Egg* with him. 'Daytime Nightime Suffering', the flipside of 'Goodnight Tonight', was also co-produced by Paul and Chris.

Chris also produced Paul's album *Run Devil Run*.

3 Legs (promotional film)

Paul produced two promotional films in Scotland for the *Ram* tracks *3 Legs* and *Heart Of The Country*, both edited by Ray Benson, who had been involved in the editing of the *Magical Mystery Tour* film. The *3 Legs* promotional film includes scenes of Paul and Linda riding horses on their land on the Mull of Kintyre.

Both promos were screened as part of the 'album' slot on *Top Of The Pops* on Thursday 24 June 1971. *The Heart Of The Country* promotional film was made only a few days before the *TOTP* screening and included scenes of Paul and Linda walking along a beach with their sheepdog Martha.

3 Legs (song)

A bluesy track from the *Ram* album, with backing vocals by Linda.

Thrillington

An orchestral version of *Ram*, which was recorded at Abbey Road Studios on 15–17 June 1971. It was eventually issued on Regal Zonophone EMC 3175 on 29 April 1977. Attributed to Percy 'Thrills' Thrillington, an orchestra leader, the material was arranged and conducted by Richard Hewson and mixed by Tony Clark and Alan Parsons.

The cover design by Hipgnosis featured artwork by Jeff Cummins depicting a ram in an evening suit playing a violin, sitting in front of a music stand. The back cover showed a view of a recording session in a studio; the figure with a ram's head is discussing the music with the seated musicians, and Paul's head is reflected in the glass pane of the studio window. This picture is based on an actual photograph taken during the *Ram* sessions when the standing figure was Paul.

The album was an MPL production with the credit: 'Produced by Percy "Thrills" Thrillington', so we may assume that Percy is a pseudonym for Paul. The biographical blurb below the photograph reveals: 'Percy "Thrills" Thrillington was born in Coventry Cathedral in 1939. As a young man he wandered the globe. His travels took him to Baton Rouge, Louisiana in the US where he studied music for five years. He later moved to LA where he gained expertise in conducting and arranging as well as the marketing end of the music business. Eventually his path led to London where his long ambition to form his own orchestra was finally realised. On this record Percy takes all the songs from Paul and Linda McCartney's *Ram* album and, with the help of some of London's best orchestra and "big band" musicians, forges the pop music themes into new orchestral versions. He is assisted by Richard Hewson, who arranged and conducted. When McCartney heard what "Thrills" was doing he even gave the project his seal of approval.'

Musicians appearing on the 11-song album included Clem Cattini on drums, Roger Coulan on organ, Vic Flick on guitar, Herbie Flowers on bass, Steve Grey on piano, and Jim Lawless on percussion. Also featured on five tracks were the Swingle Singers, and recorders played by the Carl Dolmetsch Family were overdubbed onto a number of the tracks.

The tracks were 'Too Many People', '3 Legs', 'Ram On', 'Dear Boy', 'Uncle Albert/Admiral Halsey', 'Smile Away', 'Heart Of The Country', 'Monkberry Moon Delight', 'Eat At Home', 'Long Haired Lady', 'Ram On' and 'The Back Seat Of My Car'. A single of 'Uncle Albert/Admiral

Halsey'/'Eat At Home' was issued as a single in Britain but failed to register.

Through Our Love
A love song to Linda, which is included as the final track on the *Pipes Of Peace* album.

Thumbin' A Ride
A Jerry Leiber and Mike Stoller composition recorded by Jackie Lomax. Paul produced it on his wedding eve, Tuesday 11 March 1969. It became the flipside of the Lomax single 'New Day', issued in America on Apple 1807 on Monday 2 June 1969. It was also used as the flipside to the Jackie Lomax single 'How The Web Was Woven', issued in Britain on Friday 6 February 1970 on Apple 23.

Till There Was You
A song penned by Meredith Wilson which was written for the musical *The Music Man*, which made its Broadway debut in 1957, when it was originally sung by Robert Preston and Barbara Cook, who also performed it on the cast album.

Paul had actually liked Peggy Lee's version of the number and introduced it into the Beatles' act and it became a staple of their early repertoire. They played it on their Liverpool and Hamburg appearances and included it on their shows from 1961 to 1964, including their Royal Command Performance on 4 November 1963, their *Ed Sullivan Show* debut on 9 February 1964 and their Washington and Carnegie Hall concerts in February 1964. They also performed it during their Decca Records audition. A version is also to be found on the *Live At The Star Club, Hamburg* recordings.

The Beatles recorded the number on 18 and 30 July 1963 and it was included on the *With The Beatles* album.

It was while the Beatles were recording 'Till There Was You', that their manager Brian Epstein mentioned that on one take there seemed to be a flaw in Paul's voice. John bellowed, 'We'll make the records. You just go on counting the percentages!'

Tilton, Milt
Veteran musician, known as 'the Judge'. He played stand-up bass on 'Little Woman Love', on *Wild Life*. He was 65 years old at the time. Denny Seiwell recommended him. He had played in Cab Calloway's band for fifteen years.

Time To Hide
A number recorded at the *Wings At The Speed Of Sound* sessions. Denny Laine was on lead vocal and the number was included in Wings live shows during 1976. It was 4 minutes and 32 seconds in length.

Timon

A Merseyside singer who was one of the artists to record for Apple in the early days. However, the numbers he recorded were never released because George Harrison didn't like them. On one track, called 'Something New Everyday', produced by Peter Asher, Paul plays piano.

Tiny Bubble

A track from the *Driving Rain* album. It lasts for 4 minutes and 21 seconds and was recorded on 25 February 2001.

Tiswas

A British children's Saturday morning television show. Wings appeared on the programme on Saturday 1 December 1979. The group had recorded it on Wednesday 28 November.

They were interviewed by Sally James and then appeared in a comedy sketch with Chris Tarrant and John Gorman during which they sang 'The Bucket Of Water Song'.

The Wings excerpt lasted four minutes.

Today

An NBC TV series. Paul began recording a four-part interview for the programme in order to promote his new album *Press To Play* on Monday 18 August 1986. The interviews were screened between Monday 25 August and Thursday 28 August 1986.

Together

A number composed by Paul, Linda, Hamish Stuart, Robbie McIntosh, Paul 'Wix' Wickens and Chris Whitten. A version lasting 2 minutes and 17 seconds was recorded during a soundcheck at the Rosemont Horizon, Chicago, Illinois on 5 December 1989 during the 1989/90 World Tour.

Tokyo Dome

Japanese baseball stadium with a 50,000 capacity where Paul was booked to do a series of six concerts between Saturday 3 March and Tuesday 13 March 1990 as the fifth leg of his worldwide tour. Initially he was concerned that the authorities would prevent him from appearing at the concerts due to his previous conviction there on a drugs offence.

The concert on Friday 9 March was transmitted live on closed circuit TV at Kyousai Hall, Sapporo; Sendai Denryoku Hall, Sendai; Ceremony Hall, Niigata; Aichi Kousei Nenkin Kaikan, Nagoya; Suita Mei Theatre, Osaka; Takamatsu Olive Hall, Takamatsu; Matsuyama City Sougou Community Centre, Matsuyama; Hiroshima Mima Koudou, Hiroshima; Papyon 24 Gas Hall, Hakaya and Melpark Hall Kumamoto, Kumamoto. All the venues were fully booked and attendees were handed a free copy of a Paul McCartney CD.

The Tokyo Dome concerts on Friday 9 March, Sunday 11 March and Tuesday 13 March saw Paul perform the debut of his medley 'PS Love Me Do'. The 9 March performance was filmed on video and later screened at the John Lennon Memorial Concert at the Pier Head, Liverpool on Saturday 5 May 1990.

On Wednesday 10 November 1993 Paul arrived at Narita Airport, Tokyo, the scene of his arrest in 1980, for the Japanese leg of his New World Tour. There were over 200 fans and around 50 journalists waiting for him at the airport and Paul said '*Konnichiwa*', which means 'Hello' in Japanese and '*Ossu!*' which means 'Hi!' The following day Paul met some of his fans in the offices of Fuji Television. Paul and the band then did a two-hour soundcheck at the Tokyo Dome on Friday 12 November.

Paul had three dates at the indoor stadium, where he performed the same repertoire as in Europe: 'Drive My Car', 'Coming Up', 'Looking For Changes', 'Jet', 'All My Loving', 'Let Me Roll It', 'Peace In The Neighbourhood', 'Off The Ground', 'Can't Buy Me Love', 'Robbie's Bit', 'Good Rockin' Tonight', 'We Can Work It Out', 'I Lost My Little Girl', 'Ain't No Sunshine', 'Hope Of Deliverance', 'Michelle', 'Biker Like An Icon', 'Here There And Everywhere', 'Yesterday', 'My Love', 'Lady Madonna', 'Let It Be', 'Magical Mystery Tour', 'C'Mon People', 'Live And Let Die', 'Paperback Writer', 'Back In The USSR', 'Penny Lane', 'Sgt Pepper', 'Band On The Run', 'I Saw Her Standing There' and 'Hey Jude'.

During the performance he also spoke a few words in Japanese to the audience: '*Minna genkikai?*', which means 'Are you all in good spirits?' and '*Mata kite yokattago*', which means 'It's nice to come back to Japan'.

Fuji Television videotaped the Friday 12 November show which they screened as part of a 90-minute special on Christmas Eve 1993.

Sunday 14 November saw another capacity audience at the venue and more Japanese words from Paul, such as his description of the audience as '*sugoi!*', which means '*Marvellous*'. As he left the stage he said, '*Mata kimasu!*' – 'We'll come back'.

The Monday 15 November show also saw a capacity 50,000 audience

Too Bad About Sorrows

One of Paul's early compositions, which was included in the Quarry Men's set. The Beatles never recorded the number in its entirety, although part of it was played during the *Let It Be* sessions in 1969 and Paul mentioned it when Melvyn Bragg interviewed him for *The South Bank Show* in 1977.

Too Many People

The opening track on the *Ram* album, which was also used as the flip-side of the American single 'Uncle Albert/Admiral Halsey'. This is another track that received some scathing comment from John Lennon.

Tomorrow
A number composed by Paul, which was included on Wings' debut album *Wild Life*.

Tomorrow
A song from the musical *Annie*. Paul, who owns the publishing rights to all the *Annie* numbers, produced a record of his cousin Kate Robbins singing the song. It was issued in Britain on Anchor Records in 1978.

Tonight
The long-running NBC TV American late evening chat show. Paul and John first appeared on the *Tonight* show on Tuesday 14 May 1968. During that interview, regular host Johnny Carson was away and they were interviewed by baseball star Joe Garagiola.

On that occasion Paul was with John Lennon on a trip to New York to discuss with the media the Beatles' plans for setting up their Apple Corps organisation. They taped the show in the early evening and it was transmitted hours later from midnight to 1.00 a.m. The guest immediately before Paul and John had been 66-year-old Tallulah Bankhead, a famous star of the silent screen. The appearance wasn't too successful as Garagiola seemed at a loss regarding what to ask them and Bankhead was quite garrulous. She attempted to tell Paul and John how beautiful they were and John was to say that she was 'pissed out of her head'.

Paul put forward his concept that Apple would be: 'a controlled weirdness, a kind of western communism. We want to help people, but without doing it like a charity.' He said, 'We always had to go to the big men on our knees and touch our forelocks and say, "Please can we do so-and-so . . . ?" We're in the happy position of not needing any more money, so for the first time the bosses aren't in it for a profit. If you come to me and say, "I've had such and such a dream", I'll say to you, "Go away and do it".'

Following the show he'd arranged to meet Linda Eastman at Nat Weiss's apartment, as he didn't want them to be seen together or photographed in case Jane Asher heard about it. During his brief stay he also baby-sat for Heather.

Paul recorded an interview on the *Tonight* show on Monday 15 October 1984 that was transmitted on Tuesday 23 October.

It attracted the biggest number of studio-audience applications ever for the show. Paul was there to discuss his movie *Give My Regards To Broad Street* and he also picked up an acoustic guitar to play 'Yesterday' and 'You Are My Sunshine'.

This time Paul was interviewed by Johnny Carson, who asked, 'Do you still compose music, Paul?'

Top Ten

In 1990 Paul revealed to a Japanese TV crew his all-time top ten favourite records. They were: (1) 'God Only Knows', the Beach Boys. (2) 'Sex Machine', James Brown. (3) 'Cheek To Cheek', Fred Astaire. (4) 'Flamingo', Duke Ellington. (5) 'Baby Let's Play House', Elvis Presley. (6) 'Love Me Do', the Beatles. (7) 'We Got Married', Paul McCartney. (8) 'Long Tall Sally', Little Richard. (9) 'Daytime Nighttime Suffering', Wings. (10) 'That'll Be The Day', Buddy Holly.

Paul repeated these same top ten records as his favourites in a *Daily Star* series of articles in June 1992.

TOTP2

A BBC 2 series, which presents vintage and themed material from the *Top Of The Pops* archives. On 23 and 26 May 2001, Paul hosted a special edition of the show, which featured ten clips of Wings numbers, with Paul commenting on each of the songs.

They were 'Hi, Hi, Hi', 'C Moon', 'My Love', 'Maybe I'm Amazed', 'Band On The Run', 'Live And Let Die', 'Silly Love Songs', 'Mull Of Kintyre', 'With A Little Luck' and 'Coming Up'.

Tours

Wings Tours.

The group made their public debut before 700 students at Nottingham University on Wednesday 9 February 1972. They then began a tour of British universities:

Thursday 10 February. Goodridge University, York.
Friday 11 February. Hull University.
Sunday 13 February. Newcastle-Upon-Tyne.
Monday 14 February. Lancaster University.
Wednesday 16 February. Leeds Town Hall.
Thursday 17 February. Sheffield.
Friday 18 February. Manchester.
Monday 21 February. Birmingham University.
Tuesday 22 February. Swansea University.
Wednesday 23 February. Oxford University.

Wings then began a seven-week European tour called 'Wings Over Europe'. John Morris, their tour manager at the time, was to comment, 'We have no specific plans to play Britain. Paul wants to play small halls and most of the capacities here are less than 3,000. He wasn't interested in playing the monstrous places which he probably could have filled.' The group then travelled for two weeks in July in a double-decker bus.

Their repertoire included 'Smile Away', 'The Mess', 'Hi, Hi, Hi', 'Mumbo', 'Bip Bop', 'Say You Don't Mind', 'Seaside Woman', 'I Would Only Smile', 'Blue Moon Of Kentucky', 'Give Ireland Back To The Irish', 'Henry's Blues', '1882', 'I Am Your Singer', 'Eat At Home',

'Maybe I'm Amazed', 'My Love', 'Mary Had A Little Lamb', 'Soily', 'Best Friend', 'Long Tall Sally', 'Wild Life' and 'Cottonfields'. Linda sang 'Seaside Woman', Denny Laine sang 'Say You Don't Mind' and Henry McCullough performed 'Henry's Blues'.

'Long Tall Sally' was included as the encore and was the only number that Paul performed which he'd also performed as a member of the Beatles. He said, 'The Beatle thing's a bit close for me right now to play.'

The dates were:

Sunday 9 July. Theatre Antique, Chateau Vallon Centre Culturelle.
Wednesday 12 July. Juan Les Pins, France.
Thursday 13 July. Arles Theatre Antique, France.
Sunday 16 July. Olympia, Paris, France.
Tuesday 18 July. Circus Krone, Munich, Germany.
Wednesday 19 July. Offenbach Hall, Frankfurt, Germany.
Friday 21 July. Congress Halle, Zurich, Switzerland.
Saturday 22 July. Montreux Pavilion, Montreux, Switzerland.
Sunday 23 July. Montreux Pavilion, Montreux, Switzerland.

Paul had initially considered a brief UK tour taking in cities such as London, Manchester and Glasgow, but decided against it. A planned gig in Lyons on 14 July was cancelled due to poor sales.

There was a break in the tour because Paul and Linda flew to New York on 26 July to see the Rolling Stones at Madison Square Garden – it was also Mick Jagger's birthday. They then resumed the tour in Denmark, with a new tour opening number, 'Eat At Home'.

Tuesday 1 August. KB Hallen, Copenhagen, Denmark.
Friday 4 August. Messuhalli, Helsinki, Finland.
Saturday 5 August. Turku Idraets, Turku, Finland.
Monday 7 August. Tivoli Gardens, Stockholm, Sweden.
Tuesday 8 August. Oerebro Idretis Hall, Oerebro, Sweden.
Wednesday 9 August. Oslo, Norway.
Thursday 10 August. Skandinavium Hall, Gothenburg, Sweden.
Friday 11 August. Lund Olympean, Lund, Sweden.
Sunday 13 August. Odense Flyns Farum, Sweden.
Monday 14 August. Aarhus Wejlby Denmark.
Wednesday 16 August. Hanover, Germany.
Thursday 17 August. Evenmanten, Gronnegan, Rotterdam, Holland.
Friday 18 August. Doelan, Rotterdam, Holland.
Saturday 19 August. Turship, Breda, Holland.
Sunday 20 August. Congresgebouw, the Hague, Holland.
Monday 21August. Congresgebouw, the Hague, Holland.
Tuesday 22 August. Cine Roma Borgerhaut, Antwerp, Belgium.
Thursday 24 August. Deutschland Halle, Berlin, Germany.

The 22 August show was originally scheduled to be at the Cirque Royal, Brussels, but was changed to Antwerp.

At the end of the European tour, Paul commented, 'The main thing I didn't want was to come on stage, faced with the whole torment of five rows of press people with little pads, all looking at me and saying, "Oh well, he is not as good as he was." So we decided to go out on that university tour which made me less nervous, because it was less of a big deal. So we went out and did that, and by the end of that tour I felt ready for something else, so we went into Europe. I was pretty scared on the European tour, because that was a bit more of a big deal. Kind of, "Here he is, ladies and gentlemen. Solo!"

'I had to go on there, with a band I really didn't know much about, with all new material. We had decided *not* to do Beatle material, which was a killer of course. We had to do an hour of other material, but we did not have it then. I didn't even have a song then that was mine. I felt that everybody wanted Beatle stuff, so I was pretty nervous about that. By the end of the European tour I felt a bit better. By then, there was enough of a repertoire to do it. I wouldn't mind doing Beatle songs, just through nostalgia, and yet you don't want to live on your laurels. You want to try and create a whole new thing, so that you say, "Well this is me." Then you do the Beatle stuff, once you've established yourself. That's the way I felt, really.'

Wings made their first official tour of Britain when they opened at the Bristol Hippodrome on Friday 11 May 1973. Paul was to comment, 'The way we tour now, it seems easier. It's not actually more organised, but we get days off every now and then, so it's quite good. It hasn't ground me into the ground, anyway.'

The tour was originally to last for two months but was reduced from thirty dates to seventeen. The group's repertoire comprised: 'Big Barn Bed', 'Soily', 'When The Night', 'Wild Life', 'Seaside Woman', 'Go Now', 'Little Woman Love', 'C Moon', 'Live And Let Die', 'Maybe I'm Amazed', 'Say You Don't Mind', 'My Love', 'The Mess', 'Hi, Hi, Hi' and 'Long Tall Sally'.

Linda performed 'Seaside Woman' and Denny Laine sang lead on 'Go Now' and 'Say You Don't Mind'.

The support act was Brinsley Schwarz, who were promoting their latest album *Nervous On The Road*.

The other dates were:

Saturday 12 May. New Theatre, Oxford.
Sunday 13 May. Capitol Theatre, Cardiff.
Tuesday 15 May. Winter Gardens, Bournemouth.
Wednesday 16 May. Hard Rock, Manchester.
Thursday 17 May. Hard Rock, Manchester.
Friday 18 May. Empire Theatre, Liverpool.
Saturday 19 May. Leeds University.
Monday 21 May. Guildhall, Preston.
Tuesday 22 May. Odeon, Newcastle.
Wednesday 23 May. Odeon, Edinburgh.

Thursday 24 May. Green's Playhouse, Glasgow.

Friday 25 May. Odeon, Hammersmith, London.

Saturday 26 May. Odeon, Hammersmith, London.

Sunday 27 May. Odeon, Hammersmith, London.

The second part of the British tour could be called a mini-tour, as it only comprised four dates.

Wednesday 4 July. City Hall, Sheffield.

Friday 6 July. Odeon, Birmingham.

Monday 9 July. Odeon, Leicester.

Tuesday 10 July. City Hall, Newcastle.

During the Newcastle gig the band brought out a birthday cake for Denny Seiwell, and Denny Laine and Henry McCullough sang 'Happy Birthday'. Brinsley Schwarz joined them on stage for the encore 'Long Tall Sally'. This was the last date this line-up of Wings played together.

In 1975, Wings undertook a 13-date tour of the UK with a two-hour show featuring approximately 30 numbers. They included, 'Soily', 'Venus And Mars', 'Rock Show', 'You Gave Me The Answer', 'Magneto And Titanium Man', 'Letting Go', 'Spirits Of Ancient Egypt', 'Medicine Jar', 'Call Me Back Again', 'Listen To What The Man Said', 'Jet', 'Bluebird', 'Let Me Roll It', 'Picasso's Last Words', 'My Love', 'Maybe I'm Amazed', 'Little Woman Love', 'C Moon', 'Live And Let Die', 'Junior's Farm', 'I've Just Seen A Face', 'Yesterday', 'Blackbird', 'Lady Madonna' and 'The Long And Winding Road'. Denny Laine sang lead on 'Go Now', 'Spirits Of Ancient Egypt' and 'Richard Corey'.

To coincide with the tour a single was issued on 12 September; 'Letting Go'/'You Gave Me The Answer', both from the *Venus And Mars* album.

Wings were supported on the tour by a horn section comprising Howie Casey on tenor sax, Thaddeus Richard on clarinet and soprano sax, Tony Dorsey on brass trombone and Steve Howard on trumpet.

The tour dates were:

Tuesday 9 September. Gaumont, Southampton.

Wednesday 10 September. Hippodrome, Bristol.

Thursday 11 September, Capitol, Cardiff.

Friday 12 September, Free Trade Hall, Manchester.

Saturday 13 September, Hippodrome, Birmingham.

Monday 15 September, Empire Theatre, Liverpool.

Tuesday 16 September, City Hall, Newcastle.

Wednesday 17 September, Odeon, Hammersmith, London.

Thursday 18 September, Odeon, Hammersmith, London.

Saturday 20 September, Usher Hall, Edinburgh.

Sunday 21 September, Apollo, Glasgow.

Monday 22 September, Capitol, Aberdeen.

Tuesday 23 September, Caird Hall, Dundee.

Two Rolls-Royces and a luxury coach transported the entourage who also included Paul's manager Brian Brolly, Paul and Linda's three children, Denny Laine's son and Tony Dorsey's daughter, with a nanny and tutor for the children, in addition to publicity man Tony Brainsby and various wives, chauffeurs and bodyguards. In the evenings, Paul usually had a film show organised for everyone in his party with movies such as *The French Connection*, *Blazing Saddles* and *Play It Again, Sam*.

Next Wings toured Australia in November 1975 with the same basic repertoire and 'Hi, Hi, Hi' and 'Soily' as the encores. They were seen by a total of 72,000 people.

The dates were:

1 November. Entertainment Centre, Perth.

4 November. Apollo Stadium, Adelaide.

5 November. Apollo Stadium, Adelaide.

7 November. Hordern Pavilion, Sydney.

8 November. Hordern Pavilion, Sydney.

10 November. Festival Hall, Brisbane.

11 November. Festival Hall, Brisbane.

13 November. Myer Music Bowl, Melbourne.

14 November. Myer Music Bowl, Melbourne.

Wings were next due to appear at three sell-out concerts at the Budokan Stadium in Tokyo, Japan on 19, 20 and 21 November.

However, on 11 November, the Justice Minister of Japan announced that Paul would not be allowed in the country due to his previous drug busts. He then went on a brief holiday to Hawaii.

Paul's next tour was a European one in March 1976. Apart from himself and Linda, the other musicians were Wings members Denny Laine, Jimmy McCulloch and Joe English with the horn section comprising Howie Casey on saxophone, Tony Dorsey on trombone, Steve Howard on trumpet and flugelhorn, and Thaddeus Richard on saxophones, clarinet and flute.

Their basic repertoire comprised: 'Venus And Mars', 'Rock Show', 'Jet', 'Let Me Roll It', 'Spirits Of Ancient Egypt', 'Medicine Jar', 'Maybe I'm Amazed', 'Call Me Back Again', 'Lady Madonna', 'The Long And Winding Road', 'Live And Let Die', 'Picasso's Last Words', 'Richard Cory', 'Bluebird', 'I've Just Seen A Face', 'Blackbird', 'Yesterday', 'You Gave Me The Answer', 'Magneto And Titanium Man', 'My Love', 'Let 'Em In', 'Silly Love Songs', 'Beware My Love', 'Letting Go', 'Listen To What The Man Said' and 'Band On The Run'. The encores were 'Hi, Hi, Hi' and 'Soily'.

Paul's father died on 18 March as the tour was about to start, but Paul decided to carry on with the tour.

The dates were:

20 March. Falkoner Theatre, Copenhagen.

21 March. Falkoner Theatre, Copenhagen.

23 March. Deutschlandhalle, West Berlin.

25 March. Ahoy Sportpaleis, Rotterdam, the Netherlands.
26 March. Pavilion, Paris.
Jimmy McCulloch fractured a finger in Paris and the American tour, which was due to start on 8 April, had to be postponed for two weeks. The dates were:
3 May. Tarrant County Convention Center, Fort Worth, Texas.
4 May. The Summit, Houston, Texas.
7 May. Olympia Stadium, Detroit, Michigan.
8 May. Olympia Stadium, Detroit, Michigan.
9 May. Maple Leaf Gardens, Toronto, Canada.
10 May. Richfield Coliseum, Richfield, Ohio.
12 May. The Spectrum, Philadelphia, Pennsylvania.
14 May. The Spectrum, Philadelphia, Pennsylvania.
15 May. Capitol Centre, Landover, Maryland.
16 May. Capitol Centre, Landover, Maryland.
18 May. Omni Coliseum, Atlanta, Georgia.
19 May. Omni Coliseum, Atlanta, Georgia.
21 May. Nassau Coliseum, Uniondale, New York.
22 May. Boston Garden, Boston, Massachusetts.
24 May. Madison Square Garden, New York City.
25 May. Madison Square Garden, New York City.
27 May. Riverfront Coliseum, Cincinnati, Ohio.
29 May. Kemper Arena, Kansas City, Missouri.
31 May. Chicago Stadium, Chicago, Illinois.
1 June. Chicago Stadium, Chicago, Illinois.
2 June. Chicago Stadium, Chicago, Illinois.
4 June. St Paul Civic Centre, St Paul, Minnesota.
7 June. McNichols Sports Arena, Denver, Colorado.
10 June. Kingdome, Seattle, Washington.
13 June. Cow Palace, San Francisco, California.
14 June. Cow Palace, San Francisco, California.
16 June. Sports Arena, San Diego, California.
18 June. Community Center Music Hall, Tucson, Arizona.
21 June. The Forum, Los Angeles, California.
22 June. The Forum, Los Angeles, California.
23 June. The Forum, Los Angeles, California.
In 1979 Wings toured Great Britain. The repertoire included: 'Got To Get You Into My Life', 'Getting Closer', 'Every Night', 'Again & Again & Again', 'I've Had Enough', 'No Words', 'Cook Of The House', 'Old Siam Sir', 'Maybe I'm Amazed', 'The Fool On The Hill', 'Let It Be', 'Hot As Sun', 'Spin It On', 'Twenty Flight Rock', 'Go Now', 'Arrow Through Me', 'Wonderful Christmastime', 'Coming Up', 'Goodnight Tonight', 'Yesterday', 'Mull Of Kintyre' and 'Band On The Run'.
The dates were:
23 November. Royal Court, Liverpool, a free concert for students of Paul's old school, Liverpool Institute.

24 November. Royal Court, Liverpool.
25 November. Royal Court, Liverpool.
26 November. Royal Court, Liverpool.
28 November. Apollo, Manchester.
29 November. Apollo, Manchester.
1 December. Gaumont, Southampton.
2 December. New Conference Centre, Brighton.
3 December. Odeon, Lewisham.
5 December. Rainbow Theatre, London.
7 December. Wembley Arena, London.
8 December. Wembley Arena, London.
9 December. Wembley Arena, London.
10 December. Wembley Arena, London.
12 December. Odeon, Birmingham.
14 December. City Hall, Newcastle.
15 December. Odeon, Edinburgh.
16 December. Odeon, Edinburgh.
17 December. Apollo, Glasgow.

Wings then reappeared for another live appearance less than a fortnight later in one of a series of charity concerts for the United Nations emergency relief fund for the people of Kampuchea.

29 December. Odeon, Hammersmith.

Paul was not to tour again for another ten years, by which time Wings had been disbanded.

The Paul McCartney World Tour, 1989/90.

Pre-tour rehearsals took place at the Playhouse Theatre, London on 26 and 27 July 1989 and in the Lyceum Theater, New York on 21 and 24 August. A press conference preceded the rehearsal on 24 August and a further rehearsal was held at Elstree Borehamwood Studios in London on 21 September.

Paul had discussed returning to touring: 'There's no doubt about it, I'm a ham. As much as I *try* to retire, I keep thinking, "Well, that's not me." I do like being at home. But I've realised that I can't *just* do that. My character is now set to such an extent that I do like getting a little bunch of musicians together and getting out there for the crowds.'

The band line-up was: Paul McCartney, guitar, keyboards, bass guitar, vocals, piano; Linda McCartney, keyboards, vocals; Chris Whitten, drums; Hamish Stuart, bass guitar, guitar, vocals; Paul 'Wix' Wickens, keyboards; and Robbie McIntosh, guitar, vocals.

The basic tour repertoire was as follows. First half: 'Figure Of Eight', 'Jet', 'Rough Ride', 'Got To Get You Into My Life', 'Band On The Run', 'Ebony And Ivory', 'We Got Married', 'Maybe I'm Amazed', 'The Long And Winding Road', 'Fool On the Hill' and 'Sgt Pepper's Lonely Hearts Club Band'. Second half: 'Sgt Pepper' (reprise), 'Goodday Sunshine', 'Can't Buy Me Love', 'Put It There'/'Hello

Goodbye', 'Things We Said Today', 'Eleanor Rigby', 'Back In The USSR', 'I Saw Her Standing There', 'This One', 'My Brave Face', 'Twenty Flight Rock', 'Coming Up', 'Let It Be', 'Ain't That a Shame', 'Live And Let Die', 'Hey Jude', 'Yesterday', 'Get Back' and 'Golden Slumbers'/'Carry That Weight'/'The End'.

This was the longest tour ever undertaken by an ex-member of the Beatles, lasting from late September 1989 to the end of July 1990. The American publication *Amusement Business* presented it with an award for the highest grossing show of 1990. The two concerts at Berkeley Memorial Stadium alone brought in $3,550,560.

The tour dates were:

European Leg:

26 September 1989. Drammenshallen, Drammen, Norway.

28 September. Scandinavium, Gothenburg, Sweden.

29 September. Isstadium, Stockholm, Sweden.

30 September. Isstadium, Stockholm, Sweden.

3 October. Sporthalle, Hamburg, Germany.

4 October. Sporthalle, Hamburg, Germany.

6 October. Festhalle, Frankfurt, Germany.

7 October. Festhalle, Frankfurt, Germany.

9 October. Palais Omnisport de Bercy, Paris, France.

10 October. Palais Omnisport de Bercy, Paris, France.

11 October. Palais Omnisport de Bercy, Paris, France.

16 October. Westfalenhalle, Dortmund, Germany.

17 October. Westfalenhalle, Dortmund, Germany.

20 October. Olympiahalle, Munich, Germany.

21 October. Olympiahalle, Munich, Germany.

22 October. Olympiahalle, Munich, Germany.

24 October. Palaeur, Rome, Italy.

26 October. Palatrussardi, Milan, Italy.

27 October. Palatrussardi, Milan, Italy.

29 October. Hallenstadion, Zurich, Switzerland.

30 October. Hallenstadion, Zurich, Switzerland.

2 November. Palacio des Sportes, Madrid, Spain.

3 November. Palacio des Sportes, Madrid, Spain.

5 November. La Halle Tony Garnier, Lyons, France.

7 November. Ahoy Sportpaleis, Rotterdam, Netherlands.

8 November. Ahoy Sportpaleis, Rotterdam, Netherlands.

10 November. Ahoy Sportpaleis, Rotterdam, Netherlands.

11 November. Ahoy Sportpaleis, Rotterdam, Netherlands.

First American Leg:

23 November. Great Western Forum, Los Angeles, California.

24 November. Great Western Forum, Los Angeles, California.

27 November. Great Western Forum, Los Angeles, California.

28 November. Great Western Forum, Los Angeles, California.

29 November. Great Western Forum, Los Angeles, California.

3 December. Rosemont Horizon, Chicago, Illinois.

4 December. Rosemont Horizon, Chicago, Illinois.

5 December. Rosemont Horizon, Chicago, Illinois.

7 December. Skydome, Toronto, Ontario.

9 December. Forum, Montreal, Quebec.

11 December. Madison Square Garden, New York City, New York.

12 December. Madison Square Garden, New York City, New York.

14 December. Madison Square Garden, New York City, New York.

15 December. Madison Square Garden, New York City, New York.

First British Leg:

2 January 1990. NEC International Arena, Birmingham.

3 January. NEC International Arena, Birmingham.

5 January. NEC International Arena, Birmingham.

6 January. NEC International Arena, Birmingham.

8 January; NEC International Arena, Birmingham.

9 January. NEC International Arena, Birmingham.

11 January. Wembley Arena, London.

13 January. Wembley Arena, London.

14 January. Wembley Arena, London.

16 January. Wembley Arena, London.

17 January. Wembley Arena, London.

19 January. Wembley Arena, London.

20 January. Wembley Arena, London.

21 January. Wembley Arena, London.

23 January. Wembley Arena, London.

24 January. Wembley Arena, London.

26 January. Wembley Arena, London.

Second American Leg:

1 February. Palace of Auburn Hills, Detroit, Michigan.

2 February. Palace of Auburn Hills, Detroit, Michigan.

4 February. Civic Arena, Pittsburgh, Pennsylvania

5 February. Civic Arena, Pittsburgh, Pennsylvania.

8 February. Worcester Centrum, Worcester, Massachusetts.

9 February. Worcester Centrum, Worcester, Massachusetts.

12 February. Riverfront Coliseum, Cincinnati, Ohio.

14 February. Market Square Arena, Indianapolis, Indiana.

15 February. Market Square Arena, Indianapolis, Indiana.

18 February. The Omni, Atlanta, Georgia.

19 February. The Omni, Atlanta, Georgia.

Japanese Leg:

3 March. Tokyo Dome, Tokyo.

5 March. Tokyo Dome, Tokyo.

7 March. Tokyo Dome, Tokyo.

9 March. Tokyo Dome, Tokyo.

11 March. Tokyo Dome, Tokyo.

13 March. Tokyo Dome, Tokyo.

Third American Leg:
  29 March. Kingdome, Seattle, Washington.
  31 March. Memorial Stadium, Berkeley, California.
  1 April. Memorial Stadium, Berkeley, California.
  4 April. Sun Devil Stadium, Tempe, Arizona.
  9 April. Rupp Arena, Lexington, Kentucky.
  12 April. Tampa Stadium, Tampa, Florida.
  14 April. Joe Robbie Stadium, Miami, Florida.
  15 April. Joe Robbie Stadium, Miami, Florida.
  20 April. Maracana Stadium, Rio de Janiero, Brazil.
  21 April. Maracana Stadium, Rio de Janiero, Brazil.
Second British Leg:
  23 June. Scottish Exhibition and Conference Centre, Glasgow.
  28 June. King's Dock, Liverpool.
  30 June. Knebworth Park, Knebworth, Hertfordshire.
Fourth American Leg:
  4 July. Robert F Kennedy Stadium, Washington DC
  6 July. Robert F Kennedy Stadium, Washington DC
  9 July. Giants Stadium, East Rutherford, New Jersey.
  11 July. Giants Stadium, East Rutherford, New Jersey.
  14 July. Veterans Stadium, Philadelphia, Pennsylvania.
  15 July. Veterans Stadium, Philadelphia, Pennsylvania.
  18 July. University of Ohio Stadium, Aimes, Iowa.
  20 July. Cleveland Municipal Stadium, Cleveland, Ohio.
  22 July. Carter-Finley Stadium, Raleigh, North Carolina.
  24 July. Sullivan Stadium, Foxboro, Massachusetts.
  26 July. Sullivan Stadium, Foxboro, Massachusetts.
  29 July. Soldier Field, Chicago, Illinois.

The appearance at Knebworth was a concert in aid of Nordoff-Robbins, which was broadcast live on BBC radio, filmed for TV and recorded for a live album. The Scottish Exhibition Centre was an indoor arena with a 9,300 capacity. The King's Dock event was an open-air concert.

The Guinness Book of Records acknowledged that Paul's concert at the Maracana Stadium, Rio De Janeiro, Brazil on 21 April 1990 broke the world attendance record for a rock concert, with 184,000 people in the stadium. Free concerts had drawn more in the past, but this was a paying audience.

The 9 March 1990 appearance at the Tokyo Dome, Japan was broadcast live by closed-circuit TV to venues in ten other Japanese cities – Fukuoka, Hiroshima, Kumamoto, Matsuyama, Nagoya, Niigata, Osaka, Sapporo, Sendai and Takamatsu.

Paul's tour in North America accounted for six of the top box-office takes of 1989/90. The American magazine *Amusement Business* published the figures. The No. 1 grossing booking was $3,550,580 for two shows at the Memorial Stadium, Berkeley on 31 March and 1

April. The No. 3 grossing booking was $3,415,165 for the Giants Stadium, East Rutherford concerts on 9 and 11 July. The No. 6 grossing booking was £3,107,980 for the Veterans Stadium, Philadelphia concerts on 14 and 15 July. The No. 10 grossing booking was $2,862,300 for the Joe Robbie Stadium, Miami concerts on 14 and 15 April. The No. 11 grossing booking was $2,756,760 for the Robert F Kennedy Memorial Stadium, Washington DC concerts on 4 and 6 July and the No. 12 grossing booking was $2,578,110 for the Foxboro Stadium, Foxboro concerts on 24 and 26 July.

The tour had lasted 45 weeks and had performed 102 concerts at 46 venues, with an audience of 2.8 million.

Incidentally, when on tour, Paul's backstage requests for food and drink are for Johnny Walker Red Label, Coca-Cola, non-French mineral water (in protest at their nuclear policy in the Pacific), selection of cheeses, herbal tea, Earl Grey Tea, vegetarian curry, vegetarian rice and pasta dishes, cheese and herb dips, strictly no meat.

During 1991 Paul and his band appeared in six surprise concerts. These were inspired by Paul's appearance on MTV's *Unplugged* series, which resulted in Paul releasing *Unplugged – The Official Bootleg*, which the concerts promoted. The first half of the show comprised an acoustic set, as in *Unplugged*; the second set, an electric one, featured numerous numbers performed on the recent world tour.

The acoustic set numbers were: 'Mean Woman Blues', 'Be-Bop-A-Lula', 'We Can Work It Out', 'San Francisco Bay Blues', 'Every Night', 'Here There and Everywhere', 'That Would Be Something', 'And I Love Her', 'She's A Woman', 'I Lost My Little Girl', 'Ain't No Sunshine', 'Hi-Heel Sneakers', 'I've Just Seen a Face', 'The World Is Waiting For The Sunrise' and 'Good Rockin' Tonight'.

For the last four gigs, beginning at St Austell, Paul introduced a skiffle-type number called 'Down By The River', which followed 'That Would Be Something'. During the number he played harmonica – and not one with a harness, but a harmonica held up by one of the roadies! Paul also played drums on 'Ain't No Sunshine'.

The second set featured 'My Brave Face', 'Band On The Run', 'Ebony And Ivory', 'I Saw Her Standing There', 'Coming Up', 'Get Back', 'The Long And Winding Road', 'Ain't That A Shame', 'Let It Be', 'Can't Buy Me Love' and 'Sgt Pepper's Lonely Hearts Club Band'.

The first of the six gigs took place at the Zeleste Club, Barcelona, Spain on Wednesday 8 May. This was followed by: The Mean Fiddler, London on Friday 10 May; Teatro Tendo, Naples, Italy on Wednesday 5 June; Cornwall Coliseum, St Austell, England on Friday 7 June; Cliffs Pavilion, Westcliffe-on-Sea, Essex on Friday 19 July; and the Falkoner Theatre, Copenhagen, Denmark on Wednesday 21 July 1991.

The New World Tour 1993 was seen by 1,700,000 fans. Rehearsals began during January 1993 at Pinewood Studios.

Paul's repertoire for this tour was: 'Drive My Car', 'Coming Up', 'Get Out Of My Way', 'Another Day', 'All My Loving', 'Let Me Roll It', 'Peace In The Neighbourhood', 'Off The Ground', 'I Wanna Be Your Man', 'Robbie's Guitar Solo', 'Good Rockin' Tonight', 'We Can Work It Out', 'And I Love Her', 'Every Night', 'Hope Of Deliverance', 'Michelle', 'Biker Like An Icon', 'Here There And Everywhere', 'Yesterday', 'My Love', 'Lady Madonna', 'Live And Let Die', 'Let It Be', 'Magical Mystery Tour', 'The Long And Winding Road', 'C'Mon People', 'Paperback Writer', 'Fixing A Hole', 'Penny Lane' and 'Sgt Pepper's Lonely Hearts Club Band'. The encore numbers were 'Band On The Run', 'I Saw Her Standing There' and 'Hey Jude'.

Prior to the concerts a warm-up tape was played featuring the following numbers and artists: 'Let 'Em In' by Shinehead; 'Wolf Is Dead' by Daniel Lentz; 'Strawberries, Oceans, Ships, Forest' by the Fireman; 'Vespers Of The Blessed Virgin' by Monteverdi; 'A Quiet Moment' by Paul McCartney; 'Sexual Healing' by Paul McCartney; 'Liverpool Suite 2' by Paul McCartney; 'Jam 22' by Paul McCartney; 'Liverpool Suite 5' by Paul McCartney; 'Monkberry Moon Delight' by Screaming Jay Hawkins; 'My Love' by Junior Walker; 'I Got A Feeling' by Liebach; 'Live And Let Die' by Guns N' Roses; 'Deliverance' by Paul McCartney (a Steve Anderson remix); and 'Luck Be A Lady Tonight' by Marlon Brando.

The three September dates at the 18,000-seater Earls Court arena were added to the tour, making it the first time Paul had appeared at the venue. Normally he would have appeared at Wembley arena, but that particular venue was booked up at the time.

The first leg of the tour was Europe, although there were only a couple of dates in two countries.

Thursday 18 February. The Forum, Assage, near Milan, Italy.

Friday 19 February. The Forum, Assage, near Milan, Italy.

Monday 22 February. The Festehalle, Frankfurt, Germany.

Tuesday 23 February. The Festehalle, Frankfurt, Germany.

The second leg of the tour covered Australia and New Zealand between the dates 5–27 March. They were:

Friday 5 March. Subiaco Oval, Perth, Australia.

Tuesday 9 March. Cricket Ground, Melbourne, Australia.

Wednesday 10 March. Cricket Ground, Melbourne, Australia.

Saturday 13 March. The Adelaide Oval, Adelaide, Australia.

Tuesday 16 March. The Entertainment Centre, Sydney, Australia.

Wednesday 17 March. The Entertainment Centre, Sydney, Australia.

Saturday 20 March. The Entertainment Centre, Sydney, Australia.

Monday 22 March. Parramatta Stadium, Sydney, Australia.

Tuesday 23 March. Parramatta Stadium, Sydney, Australia.

Saturday 27 March. Western Springs Stadium, Auckland, New Zealand.

The third leg of the tour took place in North America. During this leg of the tour there were minor changes in the repertoire. The dates were:

Wednesday 14 April. Sam Boys Silver Bowl, Las Vegas.
Friday 16 April. The Hollywood Bowl, Los Angeles, California.
Saturday 17 April. Anaheim Stadium, Anaheim, California.
Tuesday 20 April. Aggie Memorial, Las Cruces, New Mexico.
Thursday 22 April. The Astrodome, Houston, Texas.
Saturday 24 April. Louisiana Superdome, New Orleans.
Tuesday 27 April. Liberty Bowl, Memphis, Tennessee.
Thursday 29 April. Busch Memorial Stadium, St Louis, Missouri.
Saturday 1 May. Georgia Dome, Atlanta, Georgia.
Wednesday 5 May. Riverfront Stadium, Cincinnati, Ohio.
Friday 7 May. Williams-Bryce Stadium, Columbia, South Carolina.
Sunday 9 May. Citrus Bowl, Orlando, Florida.
Friday 21 May. Winnipeg Stadium, Winnipeg, Manitoba, Canada.
Sunday 23 May. HHH Metrodome, Minneapolis, Minnesota.
Wednesday 26 May. Folsom Field Stadium, Boulder, Colorado.
Saturday 29 May. Alamodrome, San Antonio, Texas.
Monday 31 May. Arrowhead Stadium, Kansas City, Missouri.
Wednesday 2 June. County Stadium, Milwaukee, Wisconsin.
Friday 4 June. Pontiac Silverdome, Pontiac, Detroit, Michigan.
Sunday 6 June. CN Exhibition Stadium, Toronto, Ontario, Canada.
Friday 11 June. Giants Stadium, East Rutherford, New Jersey.
Saturday 12 June. Giants Stadium, East Rutherford, New Jersey.
Sunday 13 June. Veterans Stadium, Philadelphia, Pennsylvania.
Tuesday 15 June. Blockbuster Pavilion, Charlotte, North Carolina.

America's *Amusement Business* magazine reported on some of the grosses made by several of Paul's US concerts. Fulsom Field, Boulder, Colorado on 25 May sold 37,245 of its 39,137 seats, grossing $1,210,463. The Alamodrome, San Antonio, New Mexico concert on 29 May sold out and grossed £1,513,200. The Arrowhead Stadium, Kansas City gig on 31 May drew a capacity audience of 42,934, grossing $1,132,576. The County Stadium, Milwaukee show drew a capacity audience of 47,013 and grossed $1,527,923. The Exhibition Stadium, Toronto, Canada show on 6 June sold 32,442 of its 40,000 seats and grossed $1,178,940 Canadian dollars. The Pontiac Silverdome, Michigan concert on 4 June drew a capacity 49,378 audience and grossed $1,291,778. The Giants Stadium, New Jersey concert drew a capacity audience of 53,013 and grossed $1,722,923. The Veterans Stadium, Philadelphia on 13 June drew a capacity audience and grossed $1,288,394.

The fourth leg of the tour saw a return to Europe. Dates were:
Friday 3 September. The Waldbuehne, Barling, Germany.
Sunday 5 September. The Stadhalle, Vienna.
Monday 6 September. The Stadhalle, Vienna.
Thursday 9 September. Olympiahalle, Munich, Germany.

Saturday 11 September. Earl's Court, London.
Tuesday 14 September. Earl's Court, London.
Wednesday 15 September. Earl's Court, London.
Saturday 18 September. Westfalenhalle, Dortmund, Germany.
Sunday 19 September. Westfalenhalle, Dortmund, Germany.
Tuesday 21 September. Westfalenhalle, Dortmund, Germany.
Thursday 23 September. HM Schleyer-Halle, Stuttgart, Germany.
Saturday 25 September. Scandinavium, Gothenburg, Sweden.
Monday 27 September. Spektrum, Oslo, Norway.
Tuesday 28 September. Spektrum, Oslo, Norway.
Friday 1 October. Globen Arena, Stockholm, Sweden.
Sunday 3 October. Maimarkthalle, Mannheim.
Tuesday 5 October. HM Schleyer-Halle, Stuttgart, Germany.
Wednesday 6 October. Festhalle, Frankfurt, Germany.
Saturday 9 October. Ahoy Sportpaleis, Rotterdam, Holland.
Sunday 10 October. Ahoy Sportpaleis, Rotterdam, Holland.
Wednesday 13 October. Palais Omnisports de Bercy, Paris, France.
Thursday 14 October. Palais Omnisports de Bercy, Paris, France.
Sunday 17 October. Flanders Expos, Ghent.
Wednesday 20 October. Zenith, Toulon, France.
Friday 22 October. Palasport, Florence, Italy.
Tuesday 26 October. Palau San Jordi, Barcelona, Spain.
Wednesday 27 October. Palau San Jordi, Barcelona, Spain.
The final leg of the tour took place in Tokyo, Mexico and Brazil and lasted from 12 November until 16 December.

The numbers performed during this final part of the tour included 'Drive My Car', 'Coming Up', 'Looking For Change', 'Jet', 'All My Loving', 'Let Me Roll It', 'Peace In The Neighbourhood', 'Off The Ground', 'Good Rockin' Tonight', 'We Can Work It Out', 'I Lost My Little Girl', 'Ain't No Sunshine', 'Hope Of Deliverance', 'Michelle', 'Biker Like An Icon', 'Here, There And Everywhere', 'Yesterday', 'My Love', 'Lady Madonna', 'C'mon People', 'Magical Mystery Tour', 'Let It Be', 'Live And Let Die', 'Paperback Writer', 'Back In The USSR', 'Penny Lane', 'Sgt Pepper's Lonely Hearts Club Band', 'Band On the Run', 'I Saw Her Standing There' and 'Hey Jude'.

The dates were:
Friday 12 November. Tokyo Dome, Japan.
Sunday 14 November. Tokyo Dome, Japan.
Monday 15 November. Tokyo Dome, Japan.
Thursday 18 November. Fukyoka Dome, Tokyo, Japan.
Friday 19 November. Fukyoka Dome, Tokyo, Japan.
Thursday 25 November. Autodromo Hermanos Rodriquez, Mexico City, Mexico.
Saturday 27 November. Autodromo Hermanos Rodriquez, Mexico City, Mexico.
Thursday 3 December. Pacaembu Stadium, Sao Paulo.

Saturday 5 December. Paulo Leminski Rock, Curitiba, Brazil.
Thursday 10 December. Estadio River Plate, Buenos Aires.
Friday 11 December. Estadio River Plate, Buenos Aires.
Saturday 12 December. Estadio River Plate, Buenos Aires.
Wednesday 16 December. Estadio Nacional, Santiago.

In 1994 he was to comment, 'One of the things about touring is when you see people out there actually crying. It's a big choker. Now I can accept the emotion that happens in concerts because I'm more able to accept emotion. Having had kids, having gone through this and that, you're more able to get in touch with your emotions. When you get out in front of an audience and they like it, it's very obvious. They just cheer and clap and smile and weep and it's the payoff; you actually get the feedback that you wrote the song for. It's an affirmation that what you're doing is OK.'

Paul's 'Driving USA' Tour in 2002 found him backed by Rusty Anderson on guitar and Abe Laboriel on drums, both musicians who backed him on the *Driving Rain* album. Paul 'Wix' Wickens was on keyboards and Brian Ray on guitar and bass. Musical director was David Kahne.

There was some controversy about Paul postponing the European leg of the tour to include extra dates in America. An EMI spokesman was to comment, 'It has sparked anger here, and is sure to infuriate fans.'

Apparently Paul's financial advisers informed him that he could earn more money in America where he could charge twice as much for tickets as in Europe. The production costs would also be lower. (Considering Paul was worth more than £711,000,000, a sum he could never possibly spend, why would he wish to compromise his European fans just to earn some extra money?) Paul denied that a European tour had been cancelled, saying, 'We are looking at European dates now. And it's not like this is my last tour.'

The *Sun* newspaper ran a report saying that the American tour was being extended at the expense of a European tour in May as originally announced and quoted 'a senior EMI source' as saying, 'The phrase money-grabber is being used. He would still have made a profit in Europe, though nowhere near what he will make in the US.'

The American promoters said, 'There has been such overwhelming excitement from all over the States to see Paul play, we felt it was fairer to the fans to ask him to extend the schedule to enable even more of America to get the chance to see what is set to be one of the rock-'n'-roll events of all time.'

There were also criticisms from fans about the high ticket prices, the lack of a free programme which had been given out with previous tours and a ban on fans taking photographs, which resulted in cameras being confiscated.

Commenting on the high prices, Paul said, 'I just let the promoters do that. I say "what do things cost?" and they tell me, and I'm always shocked. Is the suggestion that I do it for free? I suppose I do already have a lot of money. But these promoters have a living to make. And you know what, I really don't mind earning money. I never have and never will. It's our capitalistic ethic.'

The repertoire was: 'Hello Goodbye', 'Jet', 'All My Loving', 'Getting Better', 'Coming Up', 'Let Me Roll It', 'Lonely Road', 'Driving Rain', 'Your Loving Flame', 'Blackbird', 'Every Night', 'We Can Work It Out', 'Mother Nature's Son', 'Vanilla Sky', 'You Never Give Me Your Money', 'Fool On The Hill', 'Here Today', 'Eleanor Rigby', 'Here There And Everywhere', 'Band On The Run', 'Back In The USSR', 'Maybe I'm Amazed', 'C Moon', 'My Love', 'Can't Buy Me Love', 'Freedom', 'Live And Let Die' and 'Hey Jude'. Encore numbers included 'The Long And Winding Road', 'Lady Madonna', 'I Saw Her Standing There', 'Yesterday', 'Sgt Pepper (Reprise)' and 'The End'.

The dates were:

1 April. The Oakland Arena, Oakland.
3 April. The San Jose Arena, San Jose.
6 April. MGM Grand, Las Vegas.
10 April. The United Center, Chicago.
13 April. Air Canada Center, Toronto.
16 April. First Union Center, Philadelphia.
17 April. Continental Arena, Rutherford.
19 April. Fleet Center, Boston.
23 April. MCI Center, Washington.
26 April. Madison Square Garden, New York.
29 April. Guna Arena, Cleveland.
1 May. Palace At Auburn Hills, Detroit.
4 May. The Staples Center, Los Angeles.
5 May. The Pond, Anaheim.
7 May. Pepsi Arena, Denver.
9 May. Reunion Arena, Dallas.
12 May. Phillips Arena, Atlanta.
15 May. Ice Palace, Tampa.
18 May. National Center, Fort Lauderdale.

Paul opened the second leg of his 2002 American tour on 21 September at the Bardley Center, Milwaukee. It covered 23 shows and ended on 29 October.

The band for the tour remained the same: Abe Laboriel Jr on drums, Rusty Anderson and Brian Ray on guitars and Paul 'Wix' Wickens on keyboards. Paul McCartney was to comment: 'This band is too good to just be put up on a shelf; we're having too much fun to want to stop playing now.

The itinerary was:

21 September: The Bradley Center, Milwaukee.
23 September: The Xcel Energy Center, Minneapolis.
24 September: The United Center, Chicago.
27 September: The Hartford Civic Center, Hartford.

28 September: The Boardwalk Hall, Atlantic City, New Jersey.
1 October: The Fleet Center, Boston.
4 October: The Gund Arena, Cleveland.
5 October: The Conseco Field House, Indianapolis.
7 October: The Sports Center, Raleigh.
9 October: The Savvis Center, St Louis.
10 October: The Schottenstein Center, Columbus.
12 October: The New Orleans Arena, New Orleans.
13 October: The Compaq Center, Houston.
15 October: The Ford Center, Oklahoma City.
18 October: The Rose Garden, Portland.
19 October: The Tacoma Dome, Tacoma.
21 October: The Arco Arena, Sacramento.
22 October: The Compaq Arena, San Jose.
25 October: The Arrowhead Pond, Anaheim.
26 October: The MGM Garden Grand Arena, Las Vegas.
28 October: The Staples Center, Los Angeles, CA.
29 October: The America West Arena, Phoenix.

Ticket prices varied but usually ranged from $50 to $250. Las Vegas tickets were $125, $225 and $300 and in Atlantic City $100, $150 and $250.

It was said that Paul would then appear at three concerts at the Auditorio Nacional in Mexico, followed by three appearances at the Tokyo Dome.

Tripping The Live Fantastic

Paul listened to the tape of the 1990 tour in his home studios. For the previous tour triple album, *Wings Over America*, he'd overdubbed and remixed the tracks to an extent that fans believed he'd lost much of the live atmosphere of the concerts. This time Paul had learned to leave a lot of the roughness of the live performances as they stood, producing a warts-and-all souvenir of the major concert tour.

The live album from Paul's world tour was issued in Britain and America on Monday 5 November 1990. The 37-track compilation was produced by Paul with Peter Henderson and mixed by Bob Clearmountain.

The vinyl triple album was released on Parlophone PCST 7346, the double cassette on TC-PCST 7346 and the double CD on CD-PCST 7346.

The tracks were: Side One: 'Showtime', 'Figure Of Eight', 'Jet', 'Rough Ride', 'Got To Get You Into My Life', 'Band On The Run', 'Birthday'. Side Two: 'Ebony And Ivory', 'We Got Married', 'Inner City Madness', 'Maybe I'm Amazed', 'The Long And Winding Road', 'Crackin' Up'. Side Three: 'The Fool On The Hill', 'Sgt Pepper's Lonely Hearts Club Band', 'Can't Buy Me Love', 'Matchbox', 'Put It There', 'Together'. Side Four: 'Things We Said Today', 'Eleanor Rigby', 'This

One', 'My Brave Face', 'Back In The USSR', 'I Saw Her Standing There'. Side Five: 'Twenty Flight Rock', 'Coming Up', 'Sally', 'Let It Be', 'Ain't That A Shame', 'Live And Let Die', 'If I Were Not Upon The Stage', 'Hey Jude'. Side Six: 'Yesterday', 'Get Back', 'Golden Slumbers'/'Carry That Weight'/'The End', 'Don't Let The Sun Catch You Crying'.

The highest position it reached in the American charts was No. 26.

Tripping The Live Fantastic – Highlights!
An edited 17-track CD version of Paul's triple album of the 1990 tour, which was released simultaneously in Britain and America on Monday 19 November 1990.

The tracks on the American release were: 'Got To Get You Into My Life', 'Birthday', 'We Got Married', 'The Long And Winding Road', 'Sgt Pepper's Lonely Hearts Club Band', 'Can't Buy Me Love', 'Put It There', 'Things We Said Today', 'Eleanor Rigby', 'My Brave Face', 'Back In The USSR', 'I Saw Her Standing There', 'Coming Up', 'Let It Be', 'Hey Jude', 'Get Back', 'Golden Slumbers'/'Carry That Weight'/'The End'.

It reached No. 141 in the American charts.

Tropic Island Hum
The title tune of a projected 15-minute animated short, which Paul eventually hoped to turn into a feature-length animated film. It centred on two characters, a squirrel and a one-legged frog, with Paul providing the voices for both of them. He recorded the tune at AIR Studios on Tuesday 1 December 1987, with George Martin producing.

Trumpet
The first musical instrument Paul owned, which his father bought for him. Paul was to say, 'I was never keen about learning to play the trumpet, but I liked the guitar because I could play a proper tune on it after learning a few basic chords. Unlike the trumpet, I could sing at the same time as I played and I could do my impersonations.'

In an interview with Tony Webster in the September 1964 issue of *Beat Instrumental*, Paul commented, 'The very first musical instrument I played was a trumpet, a rather battered old thing which was given to me when I was fourteen years old. My father says he gave it to me because I'd always seemed interested in music from the time I was a 'tiddler', and he thought it would be a suitable instrument for me to learn to play. 'Course, I immediately fancied myself as Louis Armstrong, but I only got as far as learning "The Saints Go Marching In" before I got fed up with it. It used to hurt my lip and I didn't fancy the thought of walking around like a beat-up boxer, so I decided to buy myself a guitar.'

In 1996, when Paul made a spoken introduction about the classical music composer Rodrigo on a CD given away with the 'BBC Proms '96' programme, he said, 'When I was a teenager, my father gave me a trumpet for my birthday. I tried to master it because he himself had played trumpet at an early age, and he taught me a little. I realised that it was going to be difficult for me to sing with this thing stuck in my mouth, so I asked if he minded if I traded it in for a guitar. Which I did. I think that first guitar, a Zenith, started my love of the instrument.'

Paul exchanged his trumpet at Rushworth & Dreaper's music store for a £15 acoustic Zenith guitar.

Try Not To Cry

Another original song by Paul, which he included on his *Run Devil Run* album. It was produced by Paul and Chris Thomas at Abbey Road Studios, was 2 minutes and 40 seconds in length and was engineered by Geoff Emerick and Paul Hicks. It was recorded on Friday 5 May 1999. The musicians were Paul on lead vocal, bass guitar and percussion, Dave Gilmour on electric guitar, Mick Green on electric guitar, Dave Mattacks on drums and percussion, and Geraint Watkins on piano.

A promotional CD was issued in America in September 1999 on Capitol DPRO 7087 6 13852 29.

T-Shirt

A record by the Crickets which was produced by Paul, who also played piano and contributed backing vocals to the track, which was released by CBS Records on Monday 5 September 1988 to tie in with Paul's annual Buddy Holly Week. The 7″ version was issued on CBS TSH 1 and the 12″ on CBS TSH T1. The number was also included on the Crickets' new album, also called *T-Shirt* and issued on 3 October 1988 by CBS on CBS 462876.

The song had been penned by Jim Imray, winner of the competition organised by MPL for the previous year's Buddy Holly Week, which held a competition to find a Buddy Holly-type song. The flipside was a Jerry Allison number, 'Holly Would', which the Crickets produced themselves.

Tube, The

A Channel 4 TV show produced by Tyne-Tees Television. On Friday 16 December 1983 actress Leslie Ash interviewed Paul for the programme. Leslie met Paul outside the Oxford Street studios of AIR and the two took a cab and were taken to Regent's Park where Ash continued the interview while Paul walked with her around the Regent's Park Zoo.

A pre-recorded interview with Paul was also shown on the Friday 7 December 1984 edition of the programme.

On Thursday 11 December 1986 Paul and Linda's car burst into flames when they were on their way to the Tyne-Tees television studios in Newcastle, although both were unharmed.

Before transmission Paul performed one mimed and one live version of 'Only Love Remains'. Then went on to sing 'Whole Lotta Shakin'' and 'Baby Face'. He asked the audience what he should sing next, but there were so many requests he sang another verse of 'Whole Lotta Shakin''.

An embarrassing episode occurred when Paul was interviewed by thirteen-year-old Felix Howard. During the interview Howard completely 'dried up' and was unable to ask Paul another question, so Paul had to virtually continue the interview himself, turning the tables by asking Howard a question. Paul's segment lasted approximately fourteen minutes and was transmitted the next day, Friday 12 December 1986. It was repeated on Sunday 14 December 1986.

Tuesday (film)

A thirteen-minute animation film produced by Paul and directed by Geoff Dunbar that made its debut at the 58th Venice Festival where 140 films were screened between 29 August and 8 September 2001. Paul and Heather attended the *Tuesday* premiere, appropriately screened on Tuesday 4 September 2001. It was then shown at film festivals in Toronto and New York.

The film was based on a children's book by American writer David Weisner.

Paul said, 'I was given the book as a present and was really taken by it. Mostly it's a kids story, but it translates to adults because of its surreal quality.'

In the story, one Tuesday thousands of frogs take off on their lily pads and fly through the night over a town in Middle America on their way to reach the *Late Night With David Letterman* show.

Dustin Hoffman's voice tells viewers that the events are real and that they should remember there is always another Tuesday. Paul is also heard as the voice of a frog and apart from producing, he composed the musical score.

Paul added, 'The whole premise is that you should believe in the impossible and you shouldn't give up believing. It's like a metaphor for life. I think sometimes people grow up and they start to think, "Oh, it couldn't happen to me!" Whereas I've always thought it definitely could happen to me.

'Anything might happen. You just have to remember that.'

The number 'Tuesday', which Paul wrote for the film, was reworked for inclusion on the *Working Classical* album.

Tug Of War (album)

This follow-up to *McCartney II* was released simultaneously in Britain and America on Monday 26 April 1982, in Britain on Parlophone PCTC 259, and in the States on Columbia TC 37462.

Part of the album was recorded on the island of Montserrat, where George Martin had a studio. George co-produced part of the album with the aid of engineer Geoff Emerick. Paul invited a number of guest musicians to play on *Tug Of War*.

The artists performing on each track are as follows:

'Take It Away': Paul on piano, bass, acoustic guitar, vocals; Steve Gadd and Ringo Starr on drums; George Martin on electric piano; and Paul, Linda and Eric Stewart on backing vocals.

'Somebody Who Cares': Paul on acoustic and Spanish guitars and vocals; Stanley Clarke on bass; Steve Gadd on drums and percussion; Denny Laine on guitar and synthesiser; Adrian Brett on pan pipes; and Paul, Linda and Eric Stewart on backing vocals.

'What's That You're Doing?': Paul on bass, drums, electric guitar and vocals; Stevie Wonder on synthesisers and vocals; and Paul, Linda and Eric Stewart on backing vocals.

'Here Today': Paul on guitar and vocals; Jack Rothstein and Bernard Partridge on violins; Ian Jewel on viola; and Keith Harvey on cello. The number was Paul's tribute to John Lennon.

'Ballroom Dancing': Paul on piano, drums, bass, electric guitar, percussion and vocals; Denny Laine on electric guitar; Jack Brymer on clarinet gliss; and Paul, Linda and Eric Stewart on backing vocals.

'The Pound Is Sinking': Paul on acoustic guitar, electric guitar, synthesisers and vocals; Stanley Clarke on bass; Denny Laine on acoustic guitar; and Paul, Linda and Eric Stewart on backing vocals.

'Wanderlust': Paul on piano, bass, acoustic guitars and vocals; Adrian Sheppard on drums and percussion; Denny Laine on bass; and Paul, Linda and Eric Stewart on backing vocals. There was further music from the Philip Jones Brass Ensemble.

'Get It': Paul on acoustic guitar, percussion, vocals, synthesisers and bass; and Carl Perkins on electric guitar and vocals.

'Be What You See': Paul on guitar and vocoder.

'Dress Me Up As A Robber': Paul on vocals, guitar and bass; Dave Mattacks on drums and percussion; Denny Laine on synthesiser and electric guitar; George Martin on electric piano; and backing vocals by Paul and Linda.

'Ebony And Ivory': Paul on bass, guitar, synthesisers, vocals, vocoder, percussion; with backing vocals by Paul and Stevie Wonder. See also 'Wonder, Stevie'.

Paul considered 'Wanderlust' his favourite track on the album.

Tug Of War (single)

The single, credited to Paul McCartney, was issued in Britain on Parlophone R6057 on Monday 20 September 1982 and in America on Columbia 38-03235 on Sunday 26 September 1982. It reached No. 55 in the American charts, but made no impression on the British charts.

'Get It' was on the flip.

It was released in Germany on Odeon 1C006-64935 and in France on Pathe Marconi/EMI 2C008-64935.

Musicians backing Paul on the track included Denny Laine and Eric Stewart on electric guitars and Campbell Maloney on military snares.

Turpentine

When Paul made his decision to form a band of his own in 1971, the name he originally came up with was Turpentine. An elderly fan was horrified and talked him out of it. Paul thought again and came up with Wings.

Twentieth Century Blues

A tribute album in memory of Noel Coward, who died in 1973.

Coward was a major figure of twentieth-century entertainment history, winning fame as a playwright, songwriter and actor. In 1998, on the 25th anniversary of his death, Neil Tennant of the Pet Shop Boys organised the album *Twentieth Century Blues* to raise money for the Red Hot AIDS Charitable Trust. Among the artists contributing to the album were Robbie Williams, Marianne Faithfull, the Divine Comedy and Elton John.

There is also a track by Paul, his rendition of Coward's 'Mad About The Boy'.

It was issued in the UK on 1 April 1998.

Twenty Flight Rock

A number popularised by the late Eddie Cochran and the first song to unite Paul and John.

When they first met at Woolton parish church, following an introduction by a mutual friend, Ivan Vaughan, Paul impressed John by his ability to not only play the piece, but to write down all the lyrics from memory.

Recollecting the incident to Hunter Davies for *The Authorised Biography*, Paul commented, 'I showed them (the Quarry Men) how to play "Twenty Flight Rock" and told them all the words. They didn't know it. Then I did "Be-Bop-A-Lula", which they didn't know properly either. Then I did my Little Richard bit, went through the whole repertoire in fact.

'I remember this beery old man getting nearer and breathing down me neck as I was playing. "What's this old drunk doing?" I thought. Then he said "Twenty Flight Rock" was one of his favourites. So I knew he was a connoisseur.'

John also talked to Davies about the number and said, 'I was very impressed by Paul playing "Twenty Flight Rock". He could obviously play the guitar. I half thought to myself – he's as good as me. I'd been kingpin up to then. Now, I thought, if I take him on, what will happen?

It went through my head that I'd have to keep him in line, if I let him join. But he was good, so he was worth having.'

The number was composed by Fairchild/Cochran and a version by Paul lasting 3 minutes and 9 seconds was included on the *Tripping The Live Fantastic*. It was recorded live at Wembley Stadium, London on 13 January 1990 during the 1989/90 World Tour.

24 Hours

A CBS News networked show which filmed a documentary surrounding Paul's December 1989 concerts in Chicago.

Producer Nancy Duffy originally went to Milan, Italy during the European arm of Paul's tour and on Thursday 26 October 1989 met Paul and his current manager Richard Ogden to discuss the proposal. She returned to New York, then travelled to Rotterdam on Tuesday 7 November to finalise the arrangement.

The basic idea was to interview Paul and to present footage of his concerts at Chicago's Rosemont Horizon on Sunday, Monday and Tuesday, 3–5 December 1989. In the final broadcast only fifteen minutes of music was used, on Paul's insistence, including new material from *Flowers In The Dirt* and Beatles songs.

Duffy was to say: 'Paul was ordinary, friendly and unaffected for a star of his stature. He and Linda couldn't have been nicer. They were just like someone you'd meet at a party.'

Bernard Goldberg, a 23-year-old, was assigned to interview Paul for the programme, which was expanded from its normal hour to a length of 90 minutes.

An aspect of the programme, which Paul hadn't known was taking place, was the filming of a fan as she tried to meet Paul. The crew followed the fan, Joy Waugh, as she travelled round Chicago in her attempt to meet her idol. Then, when it looked as if she was going to be successful, being present as Paul's limo pulled out of the under-ground car park of the hotel, with his window rolled down, the cameraman rushed forward to film Joy seeing Paul – and tripped over a kerb and fell down onto the street!

The programme was initially aired on Thursday 25 January 1990. When Paul's PRs saw the footage of Joy they contacted her and arranged for her to meet him, flying Joy and her husband Bob to see his concert at the Centrum, Worcester, Massachusetts on Thursday 9 February 1990.

Twice In A Lifetime

Paul wrote and performed the title song for the 1985 film, starring Gene Hackman, Ann Margret and Ellen Burstyn. Four songs written by producer David Foster and Paul were scrapped.

The story concerned a married man having an affair with a younger woman, which leaves his family in chaos. It was based on a British TV drama penned by Colin Welland and starring Bill Maynard.

Paul had originally penned 'Theme From Twice In A Lifetime' in 1978 and re-recorded it in April 1983. It is heard at the end of the Ann Margret movie.

Twice The Price

A BBC Radio Merseyside show hosted by disc jockey Peter Price, which transmitted a pre-recorded interview Price had conducted with Paul on Thursday 25 January 1973.

Twiggy

A model, recording artist and actress, who was born Lesley Hornby in September 1949.

Twiggy was to become one of the leading models of the Swinging Sixties. In her first autobiography *Twiggy*, she mentions that the first record she ever bought was 'Please Please Me' and that she went to see the Beatles at Finsbury Park Astoria in 1963. She said, 'I screamed my head off for Paul.'

It was film producer Ken Russell who was responsible for introducing Twiggy, the young model, to Paul. Russell had found a William Faulkner story, 'The Wishing Tree', the tale of a musician and a young girl, and he wanted Paul to do the music for it. He also wanted to star the 17-year-old Twiggy in the movie and arranged a lunch date for them to all to meet. This was then followed by a dinner at the White Tower, a Greek restaurant. Paul started to think up songs for the film while they were sitting there. Nothing came of that particular film project, although Russell later directed *The Boyfriend*, with Twiggy as the star.

Granada Television then decided to make a documentary 'Twiggy In Russia'. Twiggy's manager Justin de Villeneuve had asked Paul to write a song for the documentary. In early May 1968 visas were refused due to the invasion of Czechoslovakia. One evening at Mr Chows restaurant in London, when Paul was having dinner with Twiggy and de Villeneuve, he reminded them of it and said he'd written a number. He then belted out 'Back In The USSR'.

Soon after their original meeting, Twiggy had gone up to stay with Paul's father and stepmother at their home in Heswall, Cheshire. Over dinner Paul told them he was looking for new singers for Apple Records. Twiggy asked if he'd watched *Opportunity Knocks* the previous evening. It was a television talent show hosted by Hughie Green. Paul hadn't seen it. Twiggy mentioned that a talented young singer called Mary Hopkin had impressed her. They then all sat around the dinner table and began writing cards voting for her, they must have written about a hundred, which were then posted off. Mary won it, Paul watched the programme, then phoned her up and sent a car down to Wales to fetch her. The result was 'Those Were the Days', which topped the charts.

At one time Twiggy was going to make a musical set on a cruise liner in the 1930s. It was called *Gotta Dance*. Paul wrote a number especially for her to sing in the film called 'Gotta Sing, Gotta Dance'. The film was never made and the song was never recorded. However, Paul was to use the number for a spectacular sequence in his television special 'James Paul McCartney'.

As a recording artist in her own right, Twiggy has issued over a dozen singles and half a dozen albums although, strangely enough, considering Paul wrote 'Back In The USSR' and 'Gotta Sing, Gotta Dance' for her, she never recorded the numbers.

She is married to actor Leigh Lawson.

Two Of Us (song)

A number penned by Paul that was originally called 'On Our Way Home'. It was under this title that he produced the New York trio Mortimer performing the number in April 1969. It was scheduled to be released by Apple Records, but was never issued. The number was later to re-emerge under the new title 'Two Of Us' in the film *Let It Be* and was recorded by the Beatles for the album on 31 January 1969.

Linda provided some insight into the song when she said, 'As a kid, I loved getting lost. I would say to my father, "Let's get lost." But you could never seem to be able to get really lost. All signs would eventually lead back to New York or wherever we were staying. When I moved to England to be with Paul, we would put Martha, Paul's sheepdog, in the back of the car and drive out of London. And as soon as we were on the open road, I'd say, "Let's get lost," and we'd keep driving without looking at any signs. Hence the line in the song, "Two of us going nowhere." Paul wrote that on one of those days out.'

Two Of Us, The (TV movie)

A VHI movie, filmed in Toronto, Canada, that was first screened in America on 1 February 2000 at 9 p.m. It was directed by Michael Lindsay-Hogg and was a fictional tale speculating on a fictional event in 1976 where Paul drops into the New York Dakota building (where John and Yoko lived) on an unexpected visit and spends the evening chatting with John, six years after the Beatles' break-up.

It starred Aidan Quinn as Paul and Jared Harris as John. When describing it, Quinn said, 'In the movie they fight, argue, laugh, reminisce and fight again. It focuses on that period when they were coming out of that estrangement.'

Quinn was also a little apprehensive that both he and Harris might not come across as an authentic John and Paul. He said, 'I'm just scared that I really shouldn't have done it, that I'm not really right for it. Jared looks and sounds nothing like John Lennon, and I look and sound nothing like Paul.'

Mark Stanfield, a 40-year-old Beatles fan, conceived the idea for the film, which became the first script he ever wrote.

The title was obviously inspired by Paul's song 'Two Of Us'.
Incidentally, Harris is the son of actor Richard Harris.

Two Of Us, The (parody)

In 2000, *Saturday Night Live* did a parody of VH1's 'The Two Of Us'. It was set many years after the Beatles had disbanded, when John and Paul team up again to open a fried-chicken restaurant. Yoko then intervenes to say they should sell Tariyaki Fried Chicken. Paul objects to Yoko's interference and leaves, complaining about her 'bloody avant-garde chicken recipes. I'm going vegetarian.' There's a happy ending as the two resolve the problem, team up and the skit ends with a customer shouting, 'Hey McCartney, you tard, where's my coleslaw?'

Tynan, Kenneth

A major figure in the British theatrical world during the 1960s. Paul went to one or two parties hosted by Tynan in which a cross section of 'Swinging London' celebrities would be in attendance. Tynan was also one of the signatories to the cannabis advert in *The Times* in which the Beatles were involved.

On the invitation of Laurence Olivier, Tynan became the artistic director of the National Theatre in 1962.

A few years later he invited Paul to compose music for an all-male National Theatre production of *As You Like It*. Paul declined.

Tynan wrote to him on 18 September 1964:

Dear Mr McCartney,

Playing 'Eleanor Rigby' last night for about the 500th time, I decided to write and tell you how terribly sad I was to hear that you had decided not to do *As You Like It* for us.

There were four or five tracks on *Revolver* that are as memorable as any English songs of this century – and the maddening thing is that they are all in exactly the right mood for *As You Like It*. Apart from E Rigby I am thinking particularly of 'For No One' and 'Here, There And Everywhere'. (Incidentally, 'Tomorrow Never Knows' is the best musical evocation of LSD I have ever heard.)

To come to the point: won't you reconsider?

We don't need you as a gimmick because we don't need publicity; we need you simply because you are the best composer of that kind of song in England. If Purcell were alive, we would probably ask him, but it would be a close thing. Anyway, forgive me for being a pest, but do please think it over.

Paul replied that the reason he could not do the music was because, 'I don't really like words by Shakespeare.' He ended his letter, 'Maybe I could write the National Theatre Stomp sometime, or the Ballad of Larry O.'

Tynan seemed keen on interviewing Paul. With some suggestions of possible subjects for him to write about, he proposed in a letter dated 7 November 1966: 'Interview with Paul McCartney – to me, by far the most interesting of the Beatles and certainly the musical genius of the group.'

But on 5 January 1970, he wrote: 'I'm saddened to have to tell you that Paul McCartney doesn't want to be written about at the moment – at least, not by me. I gather that for some time now the Beatles have been moving more and more in separate directions. Paul went to a recording session for a new single last Sunday, which was apparently the first Beatles activity in which he'd engaged for nearly nine months. He doesn't quite know where his future lies, and above all he doesn't want to be under observation while he decides. I quite understand how he feels, but coming on top of the Pinter turndown, it's a bit of a blow.'

Tynan also wrote to John Lennon on 16 April 1968:

'Dear John L.

'You know that idea of yours for my erotic review – the masturbation contest? Could you possibly be bothered to jot it down on paper? I am trying to get the whole script in written form as soon as possible.'

John replied: 'You know the idea, four fellows wanking – giving each other images – descriptions – it should be ad-libbed anyway – they should even really wank which would be great . . .'

Lennon did indeed end up writing a sequence included in Tynan's review, which came to be known as *Oh, Calcutta!*

Incidentally, it was Tynan who described the *Sgt Pepper* album as 'a decisive moment in the history of Western civilisation'.

Udo, Seijuro

The Japanese promoter who organised the Wings tour of Japan in 1980, a task which had taken him over two years. When the tour had to be cancelled due to Paul's arrest on drugs charges, Udo accused Paul of betraying him, claiming that the cancellation had cost him £200,000. Paul compensated him for the full amount.

Ullman, Tracey

A talented British actress who also forged a successful career for herself as a hit recording artist. Critics first noticed her versatility when she did comic character impersonations in the BBC TV series *Three Of A Kind*.

Tracey made her film debut in *Give My Regards To Broad Street*, in which she portrayed Sandra, a young working-class woman.

Commenting on her role in *Give My Regards To Broad Street*, she said, 'I have to cry right the way through the film and generally look dreadful. McCartney's character has to comfort me all the while and because he was a childhood hero of mine that was very nice.'

Paul appeared in the video film of her single 'They Don't Know'. She simply rang Paul and asked him if he'd do an afternoon's work appearing on her video. She said, 'Hey, Paul, I've been in your film, now you be in mine.' And he agreed. He is seen driving a car with her as the passenger. She said Paul was paid 'forty-three pounds and luncheon vouchers for his work'.

The single reached No. 2 in the British charts in October 1983.

Uncle Albert/Admiral Halsey

A single credited to Paul and Linda McCartney and issued in America on Monday 2 August 1971 on Apple 1837. It topped the charts. 'Too Many People' was on the flip.

Paul had an Uncle Albert who died when Paul was young. Paul recalled him as a good bloke who used to get drunk and stand on the table and read passages from the Bible. Admiral Halsey was an American admiral.

Unforgettable

Also known as *Paul's Christmas Album*, a recording which Paul made for his fellow Beatles in the mid-1960s. Only four copies of the album were pressed. He said, 'It was like a magazine programme: full of weird interviews, experimental music, tape loops, some tracks I knew the others hadn't heard. It was just a compilation of odd things.' There were also excerpts of Nat King Cole singing 'Unforgettable'.

Unplugged (album)

Unplugged – The Official Bootleg was a 17-track album from Paul's Friday 25 January 1991 taping for MTV's *Unplugged* series. Paul had originally considered calling it simply *Bootleg*.

There was a limited worldwide pressing of only 250,000 copies in all formats, with only 45,000 available in Britain. It was released in Britain on Monday 20 May 1991 and in America on Friday 4 June 1991. The limited edition was mostly in compact disc and cassette, but with some vinyl. Although it entered the British charts at No. 7, its chart stay only lasted three weeks due to the limited pressing. It had a short run in the American charts, with its highest placing at No. 14.

It was while he was driving away from his performance at Limehouse Studios in north London that the idea struck Paul. He said, 'I figured that as *Unplugged* would be screened around the world there was every chance that some bright spark would tape the show and turn it into a bootleg. So we decided to bootleg the show ourselves. We heard the tapes in the car driving back. By the time we got home, we'd decided we'd got an album – albeit one of the fastest I've ever made.

'It was a good laugh because, just like the bootleggers, we didn't mess with the tapes and try to clean it up – as a producer would with a proper album. We're just putting it out as it happened.'

The album featured Paul's new band for the first time on record, with Blair Cunningham replacing Chris Whitten on drums.

Paul and his band performed 22 different numbers for the recorded show, 14 of which were included on the MTV broadcast and 17 on the album.

The tracks were: Side One: 'Be-Bop-A-Lula', 'I Lost My Little Girl', 'Here, There And Everywhere', 'Blue Moon Of Kentucky', 'We Can Work It Out', 'San Francisco Bay Blues', 'I've Just Seen A Face', 'Every Night', 'She's A Woman'. Side Two: 'Hi-Heel Sneakers', 'And I Love Her', 'That Would Be Something', 'Blackbird', 'Ain't No Sunshine', 'Good Rockin' Tonight', 'Singing The Blues', 'Junk'.

There were three extra tracks included which weren't featured on

MTV's edited screening, but which Paul had performed that night. They were 'San Francisco Bay Blues', 'Hi-Heel Sneakers' and 'Ain't No Sunshine'.

Paul made a special request and as a result the vinyl releases for the world appeared on Hispavox, EMI's Spanish label (Hispavox 7964131). The sleeve note was also in Spanish.

CD (Capitol CDP 7964132) and cassette releases (C4-96413), were issued in the US by Capitol and in the UK by Parlophone and featured sleeve notes in English.

This was actually Paul's second official bootleg. He recorded *Choba B CCCP* in 1988, which was released only in the Soviet Union.

Of *Unplugged – The Official Bootleg* he said, 'This is number two in a series of "bootlegs". The Russian one was a good experience, so I'm happy to be doing it again. This time we're having the vinyl version printed in Spain, complete with Spanish sleeve notes, so linguists beware! I don't know what it'll actually mean: we'll probably end up with a title that's Spanish for "Madam, that's my luggage".'

Each sleeve of the package was individually numbered and featured a black-and-white photograph of Paul and the band performing and there was an insert booklet with photos, credits and liner notes.

In 1996 a CD-Rom 'MTV Unplugged' was released featuring various artists from the MTV series. Paul's performance of 'Things We Said Today' was included. The disc was released by Viacom New Media via Sony (VNM 1008).

Unplugged (TV show)

A popular MTV series in which rock musicians performed acoustically, without electronics or amplification.

Paul recorded an *Unplugged* concert for two-and-a-half hours on the tiny stage at Limehouse television studios, Wembley, London before an audience of 200 invited friends on the evening of Friday 25 January 1991.

Paul had dug deep into his blues and rockabilly roots for the performance and synthesisers, Stratocasters and that Hofner bass were left at home as the band busked it. Paul played a six-string acoustic, lead guitarist Robbie McIntosh played six- and twelve-string acoustics and steel guitar, Hamish Stuart played an acoustic bass, Paul 'Wix' Wickens tinkled on a stand-up piano and an accordion, Linda McCartney played a hand-pumped Indian harmonium and Paul's new drummer – ex-Pretender Blair Cunningham – kept to a simple kit.

Among the highlights of the show, which aired on MTV on Wednesday 3 April, was the first-ever TV performance of 'I Lost My Little Girl', which was the first song Paul ever wrote when he was a schoolboy of fourteen years old. During 'Ain't No Sunshine', Paul switched roles and

Hamish sang lead vocal, Robbie played the bass, Linda played percussion, Blair played triangle – and Paul beat the drums.

The numbers Paul performed were: 'Matchbox', 'Midnight Special', 'I Lost My Little Girl', 'Here There And Everywhere', 'San Francisco Bay Blues', 'We Can Work It Out', 'Blue Moon Of Kentucky', 'I've Just Seen A Face', 'Every Night', 'Be-Bop-A-Lula', 'She's A Woman', 'And I Love Her', 'The Fool', 'Things We Said Today', 'That Would Be Something', 'Blackbird', 'Hi-Heel Sneakers', 'Good Rockin' Tonight' and 'Junk'.

Paul then took over on drums while Hamish took over on vocals for 'Ain't No Sunshine'.

They reverted back to previous form while Paul tried again with 'We Can Work It Out', which hadn't worked out when he'd played it earlier on, and closed with 'Singing The Blues'.

Following the MTV transmission there was a short programme 'Last Word' which included an interview with Paul and some clips from his 1989/90 tours. The *Unplugged* show was also simultaneously broadcast on American radio.

It was shown on Danish television on Tuesday 23 July 1991 and Channel Four screened the programme in Britain on 18 August 1991.

Up Close

An MTV series. Paul together with his group – Linda, Hamish, Blair, Robbie and Wix – recorded two shows for the *Up Close* series at the Ed Sullivan Theater, New York on Thursday 10 December and Friday 11 December 1992.

Paul had enjoyed his previous MTV show *Unplugged* the previous year and was pleased at the opportunity given to promote his new single 'Hope Of Deliverance' and the *Off The Ground* album.

To the announcement: 'Ladies and gentlemen: please welcome Paul McCartney!' Paul and his group appeared on stage with Paul saying, 'Thank you. Good evening.' He then explained what the show was about: '*Unplugged*, no, sorry, *Up Close*, is a new MTV series,' and then performed 'Twenty Flight Rock'.

Welcoming the audience to the theatre, he referred to the fact that this was the very theatre the Beatles made their American television debut in on 9 February 9 1964, saying, 'I got the strangest feeling of déjà vu. I feel like I've been here, I don't know what it was. Some previous life, probably!'

He then performed 'Get Out Of The Way'.

Following a rendition of 'Fixing A Hole', Paul said, 'Hang on, I think I've got to have some make-up,' and a make-up girl ran on stage to attend to it.

Paul and the group then performed 'Looking For Changes'.

Paul then said, 'Seems like yesterday to me, but then it would,' and began to play 'Penny Lane'.

Changing to an acoustic guitar he then played another track from the new album, 'Biker Like An Icon', then 'I Owe It All To You' and 'Big Boys Bickering'. Due to some four-letter words used in the last song, MTV wouldn't use 'Big Boys Bickering' in the broadcast.

Paul tuned his guitar and performed 'Michelle', followed by 'Jingle Bells'.

The next numbers were 'Hope Of Deliverance' and 'Can't Buy Me Love', before a short break during which Paul changed to an electric guitar to play 'Peace In The Neighbourhood'. The make-up girl then came on stage for a second time to attend to him.

The title track to the new album, 'Off The Ground', came next, with Paul announcing that his daughter Mary had thought of the title. He next announced, 'This is a new version of a song you've heard before,' and launched into 'I Wanna Be Your Man'.

Paul said, 'This is one of the songs we did on tour a couple of years ago, and this one goes back more than twenty years,' and then performed 'Sgt Pepper'.

On finishing the number he said, 'Thank you, you're a great crowd.' The make-up girl came on the stage for a third time and Paul encouraged the audience to applaud her. A piano was brought onto the stage and Paul sat down at it to perform 'My Love'. Then he performed 'C Moon', followed by 'Lady Madonna' and 'C'Mon People'.

He then announced, 'We've only got one more song to do, so get your booing in now,' and was greeted by a chorus of boos. 'It's been a great pleasure,' he said, 'we've enjoyed it, coming here to New York to play for you. You've been lovely, a great crowd as usual . . . here's one that got covered,' and he played 'Live And Let Die'.

At the end of the number Paul and the group left the stage and, due to the cheers, he returned for a moment to say, 'That's it!'

The programme was first broadcast by MTV in America on Wednesday 3 February 1993 at 10 p.m. EST (Eastern Standard Time) and in Europe on MTV on Wednesday 24 February. It was also screened on BBC 1 on Monday 12 April 1993.

Used To Be Bad

A track from the *Flaming Pie* album, written by Paul and Steve Miller and lasting 4 minutes and 12 seconds. It was produced by Paul and engineered by Geoff Emerick and Jan Jacobs with assistance from Keith Smith. It was recorded on 5 May 1995 at Paul's home studio, the Mill, with Paul on lead vocal, drums and bass guitar. Steve Miller also sang most of the lead vocal part and played electric guitar.

Paul commented, 'Steve came to England saying, "I want to get you singing Texas blues." That sounded like a good offer and he turned up with millions of little blues riffs. It was just a jam, really, with Steve wacking out these riffs, I got on the drums and we just went for it – a little duet, sung on one mike, from a jam. And we did it in one take.'

Valentine Day

The third track on Paul's debut album *McCartney* in 1970, lasting 1 minute and 40 seconds. Paul ab-libbed on the number and recorded it at his Cavendish Avenue home, playing guitar, drums, electric guitar and bass. The final mix was completed at Abbey Road Studios on 22 February 1970.

Vanilla Sky

Paul received a Golden Globe Award nomination for composing 'Vanilla Sky', theme song for the film of the same name. Director Cameron Crowe had approached Paul, who wrote the song in four days. He said, 'All I had to do was watch forty minutes of the film to agree. I saw Cruise acting his heart out, and I thought Cameron Diaz and Penelope Cruz also delivered great performances. It's very exciting being nominated for a Golden Globe.'

He received an award for the song at the seventh annual Critics' Choice Awards, held in Beverly Hills, on Friday 11 January 2002.

He also won an award for the number at the 59th Golden Globes Award ceremony that took place on Sunday 20 January 2002 at the Beverly Hilton Hotel, Beverly Hills, California.

The song was also nominated for an Academy Award as Best Original Song in 2002 and Paul performed it at the Oscars ceremony, although it didn't win.

When he was told of the nomination, Paul said, 'This is fantastic news, it's a great honour to be considered for an award such as this. We are thrilled and would like to thank all of the people responsible.'

Paul had previously been nominated for an Oscar for 'Live And Let Die' in 1971.

'Vanilla Sky' was in the repertoire of his Drivin' USA tour in 2002 and when he performed the number on stage he was joined by Rusty Anderson on a six-string acoustic guitar and Paul 'Wix' Wickens playing the flute part on keyboard.

Vaughan, Ivan

The friend who first introduced Paul to John Lennon. Ivan was born on the same day as Paul.

Ivan's house in Vale Street, Woolton, backed onto John Lennon's home 'Mendips' in Menlove Avenue and the two were firm friends from an early age and attended Dovedale Primary School.

When John then went to Quarry Bank School and Ivan enrolled at Liverpool Institute, Ivan was in the same class as Paul and they became great friends. It was Ivan who asked Paul to accompany him on 6 July 1957 to meet John Lennon and see his group the Quarry Men perform at the Woolton village fete. They both arrived on their bikes and Ivan took Paul into the village hall where he introduced him to John.

In subsequent years, Paul and Ivan remained in touch with each other, Paul with his success as a Beatle, Ivan with his career as a teacher following his graduation from Cambridge. At one time Paul and John invited Ivan to run an Apple School, but the venture was never realised.

It was Ivan's wife Janet who helped Paul with some of the French words for 'Michelle'.

Tragically, Ivan developed Parkinson's Disease, which is incurable. His courageous fight against the disease came to the attention of Jonathan Miller, who produced a BBC 2 documentary, simply called 'Ivan'. It was broadcast on BBC 2 on 3 December 1984. Paul had also allowed the programme to use his composition 'Blackbird' free of charge.

Paul was devastated by the news of Ivan's illness and invited him to spend Christmas with the family at their home in Sussex that year.

Ivan's book, *Living with Parkinson's Disease* was published in 1986. He died in 1994.

After Ivan's death Paul began to write poetry. He said, 'I couldn't write a song about somebody dying, so I just started on this poem. It was a farewell, and it went from there.' In his book *Blackbird Singing* he has a poem simply titled 'Ivan'. This is 27 short lines in length and covers his life from birth to death.

Ivan also inspired Paul's *Standing Stone*. At a press conference conducted prior to the Albert Hall premiere of *Standing Stone* on Tuesday 14 October 1997, Paul said that the original of the *Standing Stone* poem which provided the focus for the symphonic poem, came about following Ivan's death. He said, '"Jive with Ive, the ace on the bass" was his intro when we played together. Ivan was very important to me. Poetry seemed the right way to express what I felt about his death. Later, I decided to write an epic poem that would serve as a framework for *Standing Stone*. I realised that I wasn't going to write a symphonic work where I had to take a theme and develop it throughout a movement, partly because I simply didn't know how to do that.'

Vaughan, Jan
The wife of Paul's childhood friend Ivan Vaughan. Jan was a French-language teacher and when Paul was composing 'Michelle' he sought her help.

Jan was to say: 'Paul asked me if I could think of a French girl's name, with two syllables, and then a description of the girl, which would rhyme. He played me the rhythm on his guitar and that's when I came up with "Michelle, Ma belle." Some days later, he phoned me up and asked me if I could translate the phrase, "These are words that go together well".'

Paul confirmed this. Soon after writing the song he commented, 'I just fancied writing some French words and I have a friend whose wife taught French and we were sitting around and I just asked her, you know, what we could figure out that was French. We got words that go together well. It was mainly because I always used to think the song always sounded like a French thing, and I can't speak French really, so we worked out some actual words.'

Vegetables
Paul attended a Beach Boys recording session on Tuesday 11 April 1967 and can be heard chewing vegetables on a track called 'Vegetables', which was issued as a track on the Beach Boys album *Smiley Smile*. This was issued in the US on 18 September 1967 and in the UK on 20 November 1967. It was also suggested that Paul had played bass guitar on 'On Top Of Old Smokey', but this track was never released.

Brian Wilson was to say, 'That was when Paul McCartney came to the session. He was dressed in a white suit with red patent leather shoes. He was very handsome and a little crazy, and I said, "You look good!" He played "She's Leaving Home" for me and my ex-wife, so we got a special trip that night. We were eating vegetables while we were recording, to get the feeling.'

In May 2002 Paul won a radio phone-in Beatles quiz.

He was driving in Los Angeles and turned to the local radio station where disc jockey Chris Carter was hosting a Beatles breakfast show. He asked, 'What Beach Boys song does Paul appear on eating a carrot?'

There were dozens of wrong answers, so a frustrated Paul stopped the car to enable him to telephone the station and give them the correct answer, 'Vegetables'. He won a bag of goodies – signed by Paul McCartney! He told the disc jockey to give them away and then requested that he play 'Here Today', the number Paul wrote in tribute to John Lennon.

Carter was to say, 'It was quite a surprise when Paul called up but this is a Beatles show so we were very honoured. It's nice to know he obviously tunes in. He's very pleasant to talk to and he told us to keep up the good work. There's not many megastars in the world who would do that.'

Vegetarianism

Paul first became a vegetarian following an incident at his farm in Scotland. The family was sitting down to a Sunday dinner of roast lamb when Paul looked out of the window and spotted a small lamb outside.

'It really brought it home that we could probably do without this,' he said. 'Linda is a crazy animal lover, we have lots of pets, and as a kid I used to run around with my *Observer Book Of Birds* in my pocket.

'So from then on we stuck to eating things where nothing had to lose a life. One Christmas, Linda even managed to make a kind of macaroni turkey: you could cut it into slices just like the real thing.

'I know it sounds a bit corny, but we really value being vegetarians, and it doesn't seem too daft because our place is a nut house anyway!'

On another occasion, Paul said, 'If slaughterhouses had glass walls, everyone would be a vegetarian. We feel better ourselves about the animals, knowing we're not contributing to their pain.'

Paul and Linda became patrons of the Vegetarian Society in 1995. Linda commented, 'Being a vegetarian is about life, not ending it,' while Paul said, 'I'm convinced that the vegetarian way is the way of the future for many people and Linda and I are pleased to be a part of it.'

In 1998 National Vegetarian Week in Britain was held in tribute to Linda.

Following the death of Linda, Paul gave his first interview to Juliet Gellatley, the founder and director of Viva (Vegetarians International Voice For Animals) who had persuaded the major supermarkets to stop taking 'exotic' meats such as kangaroo and ostrich. He also presented her with 'The Linda McCartney Award For Animal Welfare'.

He also said, on Linda's death, 'She was unique and the world was a better place for knowing her. The tribute she would have liked best would be for people to go vegetarian.'

Paul is also active in his campaign to promote vegetarianism. During National Vegetarian Week in 1999 a leaflet was issued, 'Go Veggie With Paul McCartney and Viva'. Viva had issued the leaflet, which contained text by Paul and several of Linda's recipes.

Paul wrote, 'Going veggie saves animals and people, protects the environment and is one of the healthiest things you can do. Linda became the spokesperson on vegetarianism largely because she had the time available. I'd be off making music somewhere but in fact she was speaking for both of us – for all our family.

'I really worry that good people around the world might think that we've lost a powerful voice. Well, we have, but my voice is there now and I'm trying to use it.'

He also commented, 'The science is now overwhelming – vegetarians suffer less from a whole string of diseases and they live longer. It is an ideal diet for everyone.'

Talking further about vegetarianism, he wrote, 'It's always been and will always be compassion for animals. That's it! It's respect for our fellow species. We're just another animal yet we think we're so clever, know so much, but what have we done? We're heading towards disaster and won't even acknowledge it. From the biggest to the smallest we have beaten all the other animals into submission. Couldn't we be magnanimous in victory? Isn't it time to see if there's anything they can teach us before we obliterate the whole lot of them and ourselves as well.

'We can't go cramming creatures into battery cages, broiler sheds, pig pens and so on. Where's the compassion? For the sake of the animals, support Viva!'

On National Vegetarian Week that year, he commented, 'It's magnificent that National Vegetarian Week is now in its seventh year. There was a time when you couldn't imagine anything like this happening. Since it began more and more people have made every week vegetarian week and I hope more people will join us and realise the bonus of cooking with kindness.'

The International Vegetarian Union also posthumously awarded Linda the Mankar Trophy in honour of her significant contribution to the cause of vegetarianism. Paul accepted the award in December 1999.

Stella McCartney became a patron of the Vegetarian Society in September 2000, commenting, 'It is a great honour for me to be a patron of the Vegetarian Society. It is a brilliant organisation and you can support them by going veggie now.'

At the Gala Ball and Vegetarian Society Awards on Friday 19 June 2001 at the Grosvenor House Hotel, London, Mary McCartney accepted the Vegetarian Society Achievement award on behalf of her late mother.

Paul wrote a two-page foreword to a 2001 book by Susan Shumaker and Than Shaffel called *Vegetarian Walt Disney World And Greater Orlando*, which was a guide to vegetarian restaurants in the area. Paul was to write, 'As any travelling vegetarian can tell you, this series has been sorely needed for quite some time. Veggies on the road often have to make a special effort to eat right, what with steak houses and fast-food chains dominating the landscape.'

On 14 September 2001, when the vegetarian group 'Viva!' held their annual conference in Atlanta, Georgia, Paul sent a video he had made especially for them. In it he said, 'There's a whole host of things threatening the planet, but government and big business don't seem to do anything about it. But you can, and you don't need anyone's permission. You can help end the appalling cruelty to animals. You can save the environment, and you can improve your own health, just by going vegetarian.'

According to PETA, 850,000,000 animals are killed annually for food.

They are the Eloi, we are the Morlocks.

However, vegetarians are twice as likely to become anaemic as meat-eaters due to a lack of iron and vitamin B12. B12 is the nutrient that is needed for cells to divide and mature properly and comes mostly from animal foods. Therefore, strict vegetarians who eat no meat or dairy foods need to take B12 supplements or brewer's yeast.

Venus And Mars (album)

The title is supposed to refer to how people relate to star signs, but critics assumed it referred to Paul and Linda.

The album was the first McCartney LP to carry the MPL logo and was the first recorded product by an ex-Beatle not to be issued on Apple.

It was released in Britain on Parlophone PCTC 254 on 30 May 1975 and reached the No. 1 position in the charts. In America it came out on Capitol SMAS 11419 on 27 May 1975 and also reached the No. 1 spot.

Some tracks were recorded at Abbey Road Studios with Geoff Britton on drums, namely 'Love in Song', 'Letting Go' and 'Medicine Jar'.

The band then flew separately to New Orleans, moved into the Latin Quarter and recorded further tracks at the Sea Saint studios.

Geoff had been feeling that both Denny Laine and Jimmy McCullogh had been voicing their dislike of him to Paul. His fears seem to have been borne out, as Paul and Linda came to his room and told him he was no longer a member of the group.

He was to comment in an interview with Chris Welch: 'When I first joined I was promised royalties and we talked in telephone numbers. Then it became session fees and bonuses. But it was a waste to have let such a golden opportunity become such a bad experience. Maybe I should have given Jimmy McCulloch and Denny Laine the pasting they deserved. Maybe Jimmy wouldn't be dead now and we'd all be still in Wings.'

Joe English replaced him and the sessions, which spread from January to April, moved on to the Wally Heider studios in Los Angeles.

When the album was completed there was a celebratory party held on the *Queen Mary* in Long Beach Harbour with guests who included Michael Jackson, Joni Mitchell, Bob Dylan, Cher, Tatum O'Neil, Davy Jones and George Harrison.

The tracks on the album were: 'Venus And Mars', 'Rock Show', 'Love

In Song', 'You Gave Me The Answer', 'Magneto And Titanium Man', 'Letting Go', 'Venus And Mars Reprise', 'Spirits Of Ancient Egypt', 'Medicine Jar', 'Call Me Back Again', 'Listen To What The Man Said', 'Treat her Gently', 'Lonely Old People' and 'Crossroads Theme'.

Commenting on their recording part of the album in New Orleans, Paul said, 'The album doesn't sound very New Orleansy to me. I couldn't tell you. It's just your opinion. Everybody says something different about every track anyway. We just wanted to record in America and find a musical city. There's not that many. Only New York, Nashville and Los Angeles and I'd never been to New Orleans, except on tour when we never saw anything except the inside of a trailer. The only thing I remembered about New Orleans was the vibrator bed in the motel. And it was sweating hot.'

Venus And Mars (single)
The single was released with a 'Rockshow' medley and 'Magneto And Titanium Man' on the flipside. The Wings single was issued in Britain on Capitol R6010 on 28 November 1975 and in the US on Capitol 4175 on 27 October 1975 where it reached No .12 in the charts.

It was released in Germany on Capitol 1 C600-97142 and in France on Capitol 2C006-97142.

Veronica
A number co-written by Paul and Elvis Costello, credited to McCartney-McManus (Elvis's real name is Declan McManus). It was included on the Costello album *The Spike* and also released as a single. The single was issued in Britain by Warner Brothers on 20 February 1989 on a 7″ disc (W 7558), a 12″ (W 7558T), a 3″ compact disc (W 7558CD) and a 5″ compact disc (W 755CDX).

Vertical Man
Ringo Starr's album, issued on Tuesday 16 June 1998. It included 'What In The . . . World', with Paul on bass and 'La De Da' with Paul on backing vocals.

Videography
A selection of some of the many videos associated with Paul.
1973: James Paul McCartney.
1975: Wings Live In Melbourne.
1979: Rock Show
1979: *Back To The Egg*.
1980: *Seaside Woman*.
1981: *Concert For Kampuchea*.
1982: McCartney Today.
1982: The Cooler.
1984: Paul McCartney: Freeze Frame.

1984: *Give My Regards To Broad Street*.
1984: Paul McCartney: The Man, His Music, And His Movies.
1985: *Rupert And The Frog Song*.
1986: McCartney.
1989: Put It There.
1990: From Rio To Liverpool.
1991: *Get Back*.
1993: Paul McCartney Up Close.
1993: Movin' On.
1997: *Standing Stone*.
1997: Paul McCartney: In The World Tonight.
1999: Here, There & Everywhere, A Concert For Linda.
1999: Paul McCartney Live At The Cavern Club.

Virgin Islands

A group of islands in the West Indies. Paul and Ringo hired a yacht called *Happy Days* when they took a holiday in the Virgin Islands with Jane Asher and Maureen Cox in 1964. While he was on the yacht, Paul penned the number 'Things We Said Today', which was featured in the movie *A Hard Day's Night*.

The islands were also where the second set of sessions for the *London Town* album was recorded on a yacht. Denny Laine had the idea after seeing Rod Stewart record on a yacht moored off the California coast.

Paul chartered the *Fair Carol* and engaged the engineers from Record Plant, who'd arranged the Stewart sessions, to convert her into a floating recording studio complete with a 24-track machine. Accommodation for the twenty-strong party was provided on the *El Toro*, where Paul, Linda and family stayed, and on the *Samala* and the *Wanderlust* where Wings, their families and the recording crew stayed. Other bits of necessary equipment were also stowed on these boats. All four yachts were moored in a bay off the island of St John's.

The sessions lasted from 1–31 May 1977 during which time nine tracks were recorded, seven of which were used on the album. Work tended to start at nightfall, as there were naturally too many distractions during the day – sunbathing, swimming and sight-seeing! Everybody had a wonderful time, but as Paul was later to tell Rosie Horide of *Beatles Monthly*, there were problems. 'The Virgin Islands were really great. The thing was that it's a big problem getting a studio on a boat like that just for a whim. OK, it's a great idea – and a lot of people would like to record on a boat, I'm sure. But the great problem was that we might get out there and find that the salt water had gone for the machines or that the machines just didn't work.'

Wings were also fined $15 by the National Park Commission for breaking the rule: 'No amplified music after 10 p.m.'

Voice

A CD single by Heather Mills, released on Monday 13 December 1999 with Heather on vocals and Paul McCartney on backing vocals and guitar. Paul also produced two dance mixes at his own studio.

Heather had told Paul she was making a record and mentioned she needed a singer. She said, 'Paul said, "I'll do it, love," and I couldn't believe it. I was worried to begin with because I thought he might have felt forced into saying it because he was getting so involved in the charity (Adopt A Minefield). But I know now he would never say something he didn't mean.

'When he offered, I didn't want him to feel pressurised into it but I knew he had done it from the heart and I wouldn't have accepted his help if it wasn't.'

Pinnacle Records issued it in Britain on CODARCD 004.

On the record Heather relates the story of a young girl who is an amputee and the prejudice she encounters.

She recorded part of the single in Greece where her sister Fiona runs the dance-music label Coda in Athens. Nikko Patrelakis produced the track, which also featured violinist Stamos Semsis and pianist Jonathan Elvey. When Heather visited Paul's studio in Peasmarsh he added guitar and backing vocals. He also produced a remix of the track.

There was a press launch for the single at the IMAX cinema in Waterloo, London on Tuesday 23 November 1999, which Paul attended.

A promotional video of the single was screened on which Heather narrated the story of the disabled girl. It was a controversial promotional film because it showed pictures of limbless children intercut with shots of Heather dancing and saying, 'I'm so flexible with my false leg now that I can dance with Michael Jackson,' and then her leg comes off and goes flying across the dance floor.

Voormann, Klaus

The son of a Berlin doctor who, in 1960, drifted into the Kaiserkeller club in Hamburg after hearing an exciting sound. The group on stage was Rory Storm & the Hurricanes, but Klaus was more impressed with the next band to appear – the Beatles. He then brought his girlfriend Astrid Kirchherr and fellow student Jurgen Vollmer to see the group. Klaus became a very close friend of the Beatles and was particularly influenced by the group's bass guitarist Stuart Sutcliffe, to the extent that he became a bass guitarist himself.

Klaus was later to join a band with two Liverpool musicians, Paddy Chambers, former member of Faron's Flamingos, and Gibson Kemp, who'd replaced Ringo Starr in the Hurricanes and later married Klaus's former girlfriend Astrid. The group was called Paddy, Klaus & Gibson and they were initially managed by Tony Stratton Smith, then by Brian Epstein.

Klaus designed the cover of the *Revolver* album, for which he won a Grammy, and married actress Christine Hargreaves, who was then a regular in the soap *Coronation Street*. He joined Manfred Mann and over the years became associated with the individual members of the Beatles on various recording projects, including the Plastic Ono Band, with whom he appeared in Toronto, Canada, in 1969.

When Paul instigated the legal action that heralded the end of the Beatles as a business partnership, John and George considered replacing Paul with Klaus.

The *Daily Mirror* ran a story by Don Short on 20 March 1971 headlined 'The New Beatles' in which the subheading ran: 'John, George, Ringo . . . Now Comes Klaus'.

An Apple spokesman commented, 'Paul refuses to return to the group, so what are they to do?'

The name they were to adopt was said to be the Ladders.

The group never came into existence. Klaus recorded sessions for solo projects with John, George and Ringo and in the 1980s returned to live in Hamburg.

He later decided to abandon his career as a musician to concentrate on graphic art and was commissioned to design the *Anthology* CD covers.

Wait

A number that Paul composed in Bermuda during the filming of *Help!* He wrote it in the company of actor Brandon DeWilde. John was possibly to make a contribution to it at a later date.

The song was actually included on the *Rubber Soul* album and was recorded on 17 June and 11 November 1965.

See 'DeWilde, Brandon'.

Wait In The Dark

A number that Paul composed while on holiday with his family in Jamaica in January 1995, although it remains unreleased.

Walker Art Gallery

The Walker Art Gallery in Liverpool was built in 1877.

Following Paul's 'Driving USA' Tour he returned to England to attend the exhibition of his works at the Walker Art Gallery, which opened on Friday 24 May 2002. He'd attended a private viewing, accompanied by Heather, his bride-to-be, at the Gallery the previous day.

The exhibition included seventy paintings and sculptures that Paul has created over a period of twenty years, including portraits of Linda, John Lennon and Larry King, with a 1988 painting called *The Kiss* showing Paul and Linda kissing. The King print is one of two works incorporating digital photography. There were also some sculptures made from driftwood. They came from his homes in Britain and America and none of them were allowed for sale, although 25 signed copies of each of the three pictures in the exhibition were sold at £1,000 each.

Paul commented, 'I felt that only people who'd gone to art college were allowed to paint. A lot of the time all I want to do is paint.'

Paul's exhibition broke records at the gallery, whose previous record was of 1,000 visitors a day for an exhibition of drawings by Leonardo da Vinci. Prior to that the 'Art Of The Beatles' exhibition which took place there from 4 May to 30 September 1984 attracted the largest crowds in recent times.

Michael Simpson, the former curator of modern art at the Walker Art Gallery, selected the works in the exhibition although by the time of the exhibition he had moved to run the new Imperial War Museum in Manchester.

Sadly, British critics in particular have been unkind to Paul's work with one describing them as 'dreadful daubs defying description'.

Critic Brian Sewell wrote, 'His work has no merit. It is rubbish. What is worse, the man thinks he is a genius. He will be walking on water next,' while Robin Simon, editor of the *British Art Journal* commented, 'I was shown examples of his work last year without having any idea who had painted them – which is, of course, how one should always review art. What I saw was a dog's dinner.'

However, there were some positive reviews. Phil Key was to write: 'McCartney paints in a semi-abstract fashion using a bright palette, taking on several influences and often with his heart worn well on his sleeve.

'They are works of emotion – lots of personal references abound – and no more so than in works like *The Kiss* and *Yellow Linda with Piano* . . . it is certainly an enjoyable show, nothing here to frighten the horses and a lot of it is pure pleasure.'

Paul was in good company at the gallery. On the same floor as his exhibition there was another new exhibition, 'Turner's Journey Of The Imagination', with works of William Turner, Britain's finest landscape painter.

Paul explained why he had chosen the Walker Art Gallery to hold his exhibition. 'I feel comfortable here. I like Liverpool. Some people kind of leave their home town and turn their backs on it, but it's not the way it has been with me. I have a lot of family here. I like to reach Liverpool off the motorway. I like the people. I like to come back here. I feel a bit safe here.'

Walking In The Park With Eloise

A number that was originally composed by Paul's father James in the early 1950s under the title 'Eloise', although it had never been written down.

While Wings were recording in Nashville during June and July 1974, Chet Atkins, who was working on the sessions, suggested that Paul record it.

The session took place on 16 July 1974 at the Soundshop recording studios and the musicians were Paul on bass, Denny Laine on acoustic guitar, Geoff Britton on drums, Chet Atkins on electric guitar, Floyd

Cramer on piano, Bobby Thompson on banjo, Bill Puitt on clarinet, Don Sheffield on trumpet and Dennis Good on trombone.

The number, 3 minutes and 7 seconds in length, was issued under the name the Country Hams in Britain on EMI 2220 on Friday 18 October 1974 with 'Bridge Over The River Suite' as the flip. It was released in America on Monday 2 December 1974 on EMI 3977.

When Paul made his appearance on *Desert Island Discs* he said that the record was one of his all-time favourites, so EMI re-released it on Wednesday 3 March 1982.

Walking Man
A James Taylor album issued by Warner's in 1974. Paul provided backing vocals on the tracks 'Rock 'n' Roll Is Music Now' and 'Let It All Fall Down'.

Walton Hospital
Situated at 107 Rice Lane, Liverpool. Paul was born here on 18 June 1942 in a private ward, the first child of Mary and James McCartney. Paul's mother had once been a nursing sister in the hospital's maternity unit.

Wanderlust
A number lasting 3 minutes and 49 seconds on the *Tug Of War* album. Among the musicians who backed Paul on the track were Denny Laine on electric guitar and Adrian Shepherd on drums and percussion.

Warm And Beautiful
A number on the 1976 *Wings At The Speed Of Sound* album, which Paul wrote for Linda. Two euphoniums were used on the track. Paul was to re-arrange the number for *Working Classical*. It was 3 minutes and 12 seconds in length.

Water From The Wells Of Hope
An album by Johnny Cash, issued on Monday 19 September 1988. Paul made a guest appearance on the album.

Waterfalls (cottage)
A two-bedroom cottage near Rye, Sussex that Paul and Linda bought in June 1974 from Mr Jim Huggs for £40,000. The property included 160 acres of farmland and a number of animals and pets – 11 horses and ponies, 10 sheep, 18 pheasants, ducks and hens, 3 dogs and an aviary of budgerigars.

Waterfalls (promotional film)
The promotional film, filmed in June 1980, featured Olaf, a polar bear from Chipperfields Circus. The animal (eight-foot high when standing)

was hired to appear in the video with Paul to promote the 'Waterfalls' single. The video was made inside an aircraft hanger and one and a half tons of polystyrene was used as snow. The promotional film was eventually shown twice on independent TV.

There were actually six promos made of the number, produced by Keef & Co. One version was seen on the TV programme 'Meet Paul McCartney'; another was screened on the ATV Saturday morning show *Tiswas* on 14 June 1980. The promotional film was also due to be shown on *Top Of The Pops*, but didn't appear due to a technician's strike.

Waterfalls (single)

The title of a track that first appeared on *McCartney II* in May 1980. It was then issued as a single in Britain on Friday 14 June 1980 on Parlophone R6037 where it went to No. 7 in the charts. It was issued in America on Tuesday 22 July on Columbia 1-11335 where it struggled to reach No. 106. The picture sleeve on both sides of the Atlantic featured a painting of a waterfall by Christian Broutin; the back cover featured a photograph of Paul by Linda. The flipside of the single was 'Check My Machine'.

The single was issued in Germany on Odeon 1C600-63969.

Waterspout

A number recorded during the *London Town* sessions, but not included on the album. It was almost issued on the proposed *Cold Cuts* in 1981 and the 1987 release *All The Best*.

Watkins, Geraint Meurig Vaughan

A Welsh pianist, born in Abertridwr, South Wales on 5 February 1951 (although some reports say 2 February). After leaving Portsmouth Art College he appeared with various groups including Juice In The Loose, Red Beans And Rice and the Balham Alligators. He also became an in-demand session musician, appearing with numerous major names. On the *Run Devil Run* album he played piano on the tracks 'All Shook Up', 'Lonesome Town' and 'Try Not To Cry'.

Wealth

Paul's wealth not only comes from his records and concert tours, but also from the four companies which he owns outright or has a stake in, such as MPL Communications, MacLen, Macsolo and Apple.

In *The Sunday Times Guide To The Richest 1000 People In Britain*, published on Sunday 7 April 2002, Paul came in at No. 34 with £717 million. They reckon that his companies made about £4.8 million profit in the preceding year on sales of £17.1 million. They also pointed out the £138 million that he inherited from Linda.

The magazine also referred to Heather Mills' comment, 'If I were going to go out with anyone for their money, I would be with someone a lot richer.' Such a quote has left her open to a great deal of press comment.

We All Stand Together

The song which brought George Martin and Paul together again in the recording studios. The number was penned for the soundtrack of a short animated featurette 'Rupert and the Frog Song' about Rupert Bear. Martin produced it in his AIR Studios on Friday 31 October and Monday 3 November 1980. The King's Singers and the St Paul's Boys Choir backed Paul.

'We All Stand Together' was eventually released in Britain on Parlophone R6086 on Monday 5 November 1984 and rose to No. 3 in the British charts. It was also issued in Germany on Parlophone IA 2004547.

A cut-to-shape picture disc was also issued on Monday 3 December 1984 on Parlophone RP 6086.

The flipside was a humming version of the song, credited to Paul McCartney and the Finchley Frogettes.

Incidentally, in the 1958 edition of the Rupert annual, there is a picture of a frog conducting a frog orchestra with two cats and an owl in the background.

Webb, Bernard

A pseudonym Paul used for the number 'Woman', which was recorded by Peter and Gordon.

Paul was to comment, 'I tried to write a song under another name, just to see if it was the Lennon and McCartney bit that sold our songs. I called myself Bernard Webb and I was a student in Paris and was very unavailable for interviews. Peter and Gordon made it a big hit and then it came out that it was me. I realised that when I saw a banner at a concert saying, "Long Live Bernard Webb".'

Webb, Peter

The director of the feature film *Give My Regards To Broad Street*. David Puttnam had suggested to Paul that he should contact Peter, who had only previously directed television commercials.

Commenting on *Broad Street*, Peter said: 'I liked the Runyonesque feel and its irony, which I understand. It's a totally imaginary story. What I've attempted to do is to make a film that is as original as the music within it, and as inventive. There's a mystical element in McCartney's music. The movie has a dreamlike quality. Its strength is its simplicity.'

Webb had won several awards for his television commercials, which includes ones for John Courage Ale, Ovaltine and Hovis.

The Yorkshire-born director said, 'I had worked with Paul six months earlier on a different project, and I knew that there wouldn't be any problem. Paul has a good visual sense and quite a grasp of cinematic construction. There is none of that star stuff about him, he respects professionalism. We never had any real arguments, but there were naturally some disagreements. I lost some and I won some as you would with anyone. Musically, I relied on him heavily, but even there he was flexible. One song we were doing fell a little short of what we wanted dramatically, and I told him. He went home that weekend and wrote me another chorus.'

We Can Work It Out

It has been suggested that Jane Asher was once again Paul's inspiration when he wrote this song. And John once again helped him with the song's middle section.

The number had the distinction of being the very first Beatles double A-side with 'Day Tripper' and it was issued in Britain on 3 December 1965 on Parlophone R5389, leaping straight to the top of the charts. In America it was issued on 6 December 1965, where it sold a million copies and also topped the charts.

It was included on *A Collection Of Oldies (But Goldies)*, *The Beatles 1962–1966*, *The Beatles Box*, *20 Greatest Hits* and the American album *Yesterday And Today*. This is also a number that has been recorded by dozens of different artists, including Dionne Warwick, George Burns, Petula Clark, Deep Purple, Humble Pie, Johnny Mathis, Melanie, Johnny Nash, Sam & Dave and Caterine Valente. Stevie Wonder had the most successful version in 1971 when his single reached No. 9 in America and No. 22 in Britain. The Beatles performed the song on their British tour in 1965.

A live version of the number lasting 2 minutes and 40 seconds was recorded at the East Rutherford concert, New Jersey on 11 June 1993 and included on the *Paul Is Live* album.

We Got Married

An initial version of this number was first co-produced by Paul and David Foster on 1 December 1984. A version of this number, lasting 6 minutes and 38 seconds, was included on the *Tripping The Live Fantastic* album. It was recorded live at Wembley Arena, London on 16 January 1990 during the 1989/90 World Tour.

Weep For Love

A Wings track recorded at Lympne Castle, Kent in 1979, which Denny Laine included on his album *Japanese Tears*. Paul, Linda and Steve Holly are heard singing in the background and there is a guitar solo by Laurence Juber.

Welcome To The Soundcheck

A 42-second link from the sound check of a concert rehearsal, which was included on the *Paul Is Live* album.

Weller, Paul

Weller, former leader of the Jam and Style Council, was once said in the 1970s to be the greatest musical genius since Lennon and McCartney. In 1995 for a time he also went out with Paul's daughter Mary. He was estranged from his wife at the time.

Paul teamed up with Weller and Noel Gallagher of Oasis on 4 August 1995 at Abbey Road Studios to record 'Come Together' for a charity album called *Help*, which was in aid of victims of the war in Bosnia. The trio used the name the Mojo Filters.

'Come Together' was also issued as a single in three formats on 4 December 1995. These comprised a 7″ on Go! Discs GOD 136 with 'A Minute's Silence' by the Beautiful South on the flip; a cassette on GODMC 136 with the same two tracks and a CD on GOSCD 136 with 'Is It Me?' by Dodgy and 'In The Name Of The Father' by Black Grape.

Discussing recording with Paul McCartney, Weller said, 'He was jamming all day with all of us, doing "Green Onions" and "Time Is Tight", playing the drum kit, playing through one song he'd written on the way up from his farm or whatever, we were jamming on that. At one point that was going to go on the album. We ran out of time, unfortunately.'

We Love You

A single by the Rolling Stones that was issued in Britain on Decca F12654 on 18 August 1967, and in America on London 905 ten days later. Paul and John Lennon provided backing vocals.

We're All Paul Bearers

Another American 'Paul is Dead' novelty disc issued in 1969 on Viking 1004 by Zacharias and the Tree People. It featured 'We're all Paul Bearers Pt II' on the flip.

We're Open Tonight

A track on the *Back To The Egg* album, which Paul wrote in Scotland. It was originally intended to be the title of the album, but Linda suggested *Back To The Egg*.

Western Springs Stadium

The venue in Auckland, New Zealand where Paul paid his first visit to New Zealand since 1964 when he performed a concert on Saturday 27 March 1993. Paul had arrived in New Zealand on Thursday 25 March and rehearsed at the stadium the following day. He and Linda were staying at a house called 'Waimanu' in Herne Bay, Auckland while the band lodged at the Regent Hotel and the crew stayed at the Hyatt Kingsgate Hotel. Paul also held a press conference at the venue. The sole New Zealand artist on the concert was singer Annie Crummer, who opened the show. When Paul introduced the band he sang 'Happy Birthday' to Wix, as it was his birthday that day. His daughter Mary was also on stage, videoing the crowd. His performance of 'Mull Of Kintyre' saw him backed by the Continental Airlines Pipe Band. Following their concert they held a party at the Regent Hotel until 3.30 a.m. It was their last concert of their Australasian Tour and they returned to Britain the following day.

Wetten Dass

A celebrity game show on the German television channel ZDF. On 11 December 1999 Paul appeared on the programme discussing his early days in Hamburg, recalling the times when the Beatles performed at the Kaiserkeller, Top Ten and Star Club. He also plugged a new book *Hamburg Days* by Klaus Voormann and Astrid Kirchher.

What Do We Really Know?

A number from Mike McCartney's 1974 album *McGear* which was produced by Paul. Paul also wrote it and can be heard singing alongside Mike.

What It Is

A track from the *Run Devil Run* album lasting 2 minutes and 23 seconds. It was recorded at Abbey Road Studios on Thursday 4 March 1999 with Paul on lead vocal, bass guitar and electric guitar, Dave Gilmour on electric guitar, Mick Green on electric guitar, Peter Wingfield on piano and Ian Paice on drums.

It was his third original number on the album and he wrote it for Linda.

What's That You're Doing?

A song Paul co-wrote with Stevie Wonder. It took place during the recording sessions at George Martin's AIR Studios on the Island of Montserrat on Thursday 26 February 1981 for the 1982 *Tug of War* album and was included on the finished album.

Stevie was one of the artists who'd agreed to contribute backing vocals. They wrote the song together during a joint jam session. Stevie and Paul both sang lead vocals on the finished version, which was 6 minutes and 21 seconds in length. Paul, Linda and Eric Stewart provided backing vocals.

Paul also played drums and later overdubbed bass, electric guitar and vocals while Andy Mackay of Roxy Music provided the sax sound.

When I'm Sixty-Four

Paul originally conceived the basic idea for this song in the late 1950s, and was to say: 'I wrote the tune when I was about fifteen, I think, on the piano at home.' He later said he'd written it when he was sixteen. During 1966 he remembered the unfinished number and added a new set of verses in honour of his father's 64th birthday, which fell in June 1966. And it became the first number completed for the *Sgt Pepper* album (as 'Penny Lane' and 'Strawberry Fields Forever' had been taken off the album).

It was recorded at Abbey Road Studios on 6 December1966 and overdubs were added on 8, 20 and 21 December.

When asked to comment on the number in a *Playboy* interview, John Lennon said, 'I would never even dream of writing a song like that.'

When The Night

A track on the *Red Rose Speedway* album lasting 3 minutes and 41 seconds. Paul sang lead vocal and played piano while Linda played electric bass piano and provided harmonies. Denny Laine was on acoustic guitar and harmonies, Henry McCullough on acoustic guitar and harmonies and Denny Seiwell on drums and harmonies.

When We Was Fab

A George Harrison number, released on 30 January 1988. George invited Paul to appear in his promotional film. However, Paul wasn't available to appear in the video. He said, 'I suggested that he put someone else in a walrus costume and tell everyone that it was me. We've always had fun with the walrus thing. We don't lay many false trails but the walrus has always been one of them.'

Whitten, Chris

A drummer, born in Wimbledon on 26 March 1959. He attended Leeds College of Music and joined a band called Gary Boyle in December 1977. He then joined several other bands and backed various solo artists before becoming a member of Paul McCartney and his Band in 1987.

The other outfits following Gary Boyle were the Shakers, Rank & File, Mecca Band, Live Wire, Out, the Catch, the Waterboys and Julian Cope.

In 1990 he said, 'I played in sort of punky rock bands before I did this, and I thought, "McCartney, yeah, there will be some ballads, it should be a fairly easy gig to breeze your way through." And I end up thrashing me guts out every night.'

Whitten decided to leave Paul McCartney and his Band and later toured with Dire Straits. Discussing his decision to leave Paul, he said, 'I realised that I had been with McCartney for three years, which is a long time. I'm a session player at heart, I love the diversity of playing with all kinds of artist, in all kinds of styles. Since the end of the tour was coming up, I decided the time was right.'

Why Don't We Do It In The Road?

During the *The Beatles* double album sessions, Paul took Ringo aside and recorded this rocker with him. Several years later John was to say how disappointed he was that Paul hadn't consulted him and George about recording the number with him. He was to say, 'I can't speak for George, but I was always hurt when Paul would knock something off without involving us.'

In 1981 Paul commented, 'There's only one incident I can think of which John has publicly mentioned. It was when I went off with Ringo and did "Why Don't We Do It In The Road?". It wasn't a deliberate thing. John and George were tied up finishing something, and me and Ringo were free, just hanging around, so I said to Ringo, "Let's go and do this."

'I did hear John some time later singing it. He liked the song, and I suppose he'd wanted to do it with me. It was a very John sort of song anyway. That's why he liked it, I suppose. It was very John, the idea of it, now me. I wrote it as a ricochet off John.

'Anyway, he did the same with "Revolution 9". He went off and made that without me. No one ever says all that. John is now the nice guy and I'm the bastard.'

In an interview regarding the various Beatles songs that had been written John commented, 'That's Paul's. He even recorded it by himself in another room. We came in and he'd made the whole record. Him drumming. Him playing the piano. Him singing. Still, I can't speak for George, but I was always hurt when Paul would knock something off without involving us. But, that's just the way it was then.'

The number was recorded at Abbey Road Studios on 9 October 1968 and overdubs were added on 10 October. During the *Let It Be* sessions, John jokingly inserted the line 'Why don't you put it on the toast?' in between numbers.

Wickens, Paul 'Wix'

A keyboards player in the Paul McCartney band.

Born Paul Wickens in Brentwood, Essex on 27 March 1955, he has always been known as 'Wix'.

Educated at St Paul's College, Gloucester, he originally had ambitions to become a PE teacher but decided on becoming a musician and formed a band called the Young Ones in 1977. In 1980 he joined Kevin Coyne and appeared on four albums with the band.

Wix considers himself a studio musician and has worked with various artists in recording studios. He has also been involved with a number of bands, spending eighteen months with the Waterboys. He toured America with U2 and also spent two and a half years playing in a band led by Julian Cope.

Wix first became involved with Paul at the time of the recording of the Russian album in July 1987. He then did some TV shows with Paul for 'Once Upon A Long Ago' and then he began to work on the album with Paul and Hamish Stuart and, as they needed some guitar work, Robbie McIntosh became involved halfway through the album.

Wide Prairie (album)

A posthumous solo album by Linda McCartney featuring sixteen tracks, thirteen of them original songs by Linda that she'd recorded over a period of years together with three of her favourite rock and roll and R&B numbers. The tracks were recorded in England, America, France and Jamaica between November 1972 and March 1998.

Paul produced the record on which their son James is also featured playing lead guitar, and Paul also sang backing vocals and played a variety of instruments.

The album was released in Britain by EMI on Monday 26 October 1998 and in America by Capitol on Tuesday 27 October 1998.

Paul was to say, 'A couple of years ago, a fan wrote to Linda saying she had enjoyed "Seaside Woman" and asked if there were any more tracks of her available. That letter made us decide to gather all the music she had recorded through the years and put it on one album.'

He pointed out that the title track had originally been intended for a planned *Cold Cuts* album of his own. He said the number was about 'Linda's fantasy. Her passion for horses and riding started as a gradual thing and remained with her all her life.' He said that 'I Got Up' was 'typical of Linda's unwillingness to put up with other people's bullshit. She hated worlds like "should" and "compromise".' On the cover of the 1950s number 'Poison Ivy' he said, 'She had a lasting affection for doo-wop music, having spent many hours under the bedclothes with a transistor radio glued to her ear.' On the track 'The Light Comes From Within', which was finished a month before Linda's death, Paul said, 'This was Linda's answer to all the people who had ever put her down, and that whole dumb male chauvinist attitude, that to her had caused so much harm in our society. God bless her . . . my baby literally had the last word.'

The tracks were: 'Wide Prairie', 'New Orleans', 'The White Coated Man', 'Love's Full Glory', 'I Got Up', 'The Light Comes From Within', 'Mr Sandman', 'Seaside Woman', 'Oriental Nightfish', 'Endless Days', 'Poison Ivy', 'Cow' 'B-Side To Seaside', 'Sugartime', 'Cook Of The House' and 'Appaloosa'.

In his sleeve notes to the album, Paul wrote, 'During the last couple of years of her life, we were required to make many trips up to London for one treatment or another. We always put the journey time to good use. She and I talked a lot about this album and the lyrics to some songs were finished on such trips.'

Her friend Carla Lane penned the lyrics to two of Linda's songs, 'Cow' and 'The White Coated Man'. The first was about a cow that a farmer was about to send to the abattoir and the second about a little puppy who is in a cage and naively believes that the vivisectionist in the white coat is his friend.

Carla was to comment: 'She worked at it until the end. She wanted to get the record out no matter what she was going through. This is the bravest album ever made.'

The single 'Wide Prairie' was issued in Britain as a single on Monday 9 November 1998 and issued in America on Tuesday 10 November.

Paul went on the Internet on 17 December 1999 to discuss the album, saying that his favourite song was 'The Light Comes From Within'. He said, 'Because of the feisty way Linda hits back at her critics and detractors. I also love the ballads "Endless Days" and "Love's Full Glory". And for other reasons to do with animal welfare I love "The White Coated Man".'

He also said that 'Love's Full Glory' 'wasn't a surprise for a special occasion. It was true that after I'd written "My Love", Linda liked the idea of working on a follow-up. She wasn't playing a piano, but a mini-Moog. She had a wonderful melody on there.'

Paul also explained how Linda composed the song 'Endless Days'.

'She worked on the song in her own session and brought it in. There it was, done without my participation. I think it's a sweet song. A bit emotional for me, that is.'

He also revealed that there was one more song by Linda that hadn't seen the light of day, which he might make a recording of.

Discussing the controversial lyrics of 'The Light Comes From Within', he said, 'Those lyrics are full of tongue-in-cheek anger. Yeah, they were in response to a long string of slights. In the early days, a lot of people were jealous. People were upset when she joined Wings – they thought we should have had "stars" and not "my old lady" on stage.'

Wide Prairie (film)

Shortly before Linda died of breast cancer she collaborated on a short animated film with Oscar Grillo called *Wide Prairie*. It received its world premiere at the Edinburgh Film Festival on Wednesday 19 August 1998 on the same bill as *The Horse Whisperers*.

The film was based on a song that Linda had written and recorded. Grillo was to comment, 'It was so evocative. Beautiful images. She rode at night and felt the stars and open sky were so close she was riding in the skies.'

The film was a surreal animated tale about a woman who longs to escape the drudgery of everyday life by riding horses with her lover.'

Sheila Whitaker, the former director of the London Film Festival called the film 'beautiful' and said, 'It's a song that Linda performed in a country and western style and it's about family, freedom of the range and all that kind of thing. And it's great fun.

'The animation visualises the song and it is very nice, very warm –

and it makes you come out feeling good basically. It's about six minutes long and it's very well animated.'

Wild Honey Pie

A recording Paul made during *The Beatles* double album recording sessions. The song had its origins at a singalong at the Maharishi's ashram in India and Paul was the only member of the Beatles on the track.

John, George and Ringo weren't around when Paul recorded this brief number at Abbey Road Studios.

Paul sang, played guitar and bass drum and also double-tracked. At only 53 seconds in length, it is the shortest cut on *The Beatles White Album*. When Paul had originally penned the song in India, he had never really intended recording it. However, both Jane Asher and Pattie Harrison liked it and encouraged him to record it. He commented: 'This was just a fragment of an instrumental which we weren't sure about, but Pattie liked it very much so we decided to leave it on the album.'

It's not to be confused with another number by Paul, recorded later the same year, called 'Honey Pie'.

Wild Life (album)

The first Wings album. It was issued in Britain on Apple PCS 7142 on 3 December 1971 where it reached the position of No. 11 in the charts. In America it came out on Apple SW 3386 on 7 December, reached. No 10 in the charts and achieved Gold Disc status.

Paul had written the material for the album with Linda, and then decided to form a group that they could take on the road and selected Denny Laine and Denny Seiwell as the basis of the four-piece Wings.

Paul said, 'Denny (Laine) came round to see me and we played something together, just rehearsing, and it sounded great. We had a very short rehearsal time. We just banged out a few chords and played what we wanted.'

He also commented, 'It's very simple stuff on the album. Tony Clarke engineered it for us, and we told him we wanted it fat and funky.'

The entire album was recorded in the studios in a three-day period during August 1971, which left the group open to criticism for the haste in which it was recorded.

The only song that Paul and Linda didn't pen was 'Love Is Strange', which had provided the Everly Brothers with a hit in 1965. The tracks on the album were: 'Mumbo', 'Bip Bop', 'Love Is Strange', 'Wild Life', 'Some People Never Know', 'I Am Your Singer', 'Tomorrow' and 'Dear Friend'.

Responding to critics, Paul was to say, 'When *Wild Life* came out, all the critics said that it was rubbish, so I started thinking like them that it was rubbish. But when I heard it later, I really liked it and I still think it's quite good. OK, I didn't make the biggest blockbuster of all time. But I don't think you need that all the time. We did *Wild Life* very quickly. You see, *Wild Life* was inspired by Dylan, because we heard that he'd just been in the studios and he just took one week to do an album. So we came in and thought, "Great, we'll do it a bit like that and we'll try to get just the spontaneous stuff down and not to be too careful with this one." So it came out like that and a few people thought that we could have tried a bit harder, but I'd like to see them do it.'

Linda was to say, 'We've put the rock songs on one side and the slow ones on the other. That's so you can play it at parties. When you want to dance you play Side One, when you want to croon you play Side Two.'

Although the album was completed rapidly in Abbey Road Studios in August, it wasn't released until December. Paul was not pleased with Allen Klein's control of Apple and didn't want the album issued by Apple. However, the company had the right to release it and it was issued by them, although it was the first Beatles-related album not to sport the famous Apple Granny Smith logo.

Wild Life (song)

The title track of Wings' debut album that the group began to perform live in 1972. Paul said he was inspired to write the song following a visit to a game park in Ambosali, near Nairobi on a safari holiday in November 1966. He recalled it as place 'where the animals have the right of way over you'.

Wild Prairie Maid

A number recorded by Linda McCartney and Wings during a session in Paris in 1974. They used the pseudonym Suzy and the Red Stripes.

Williams, Angie

Paul's stepmother. Angela Williams was a widow who married Jim McCartney on 24 November 1964. She was 34 years old and Jim was 62. Jim proposed on the couple's third meeting and Angela was initially hesitant as she had a four-year-old daughter, Ruth, and Jim was more than 25 years her senior.

They settled in the McCartney home 'Rembrandt' in Hoylake on the Wirral, the house that Paul had bought.

Following Jim's death, Angie attempted to make a living for herself by setting up a pop-group agency in Liverpool, but Paul was angry at her use of the family name. In 1981 she moved south with her daughter and reverted to the surname Williams.

That same year she told her 'story' in a series of articles ghosted by Tony Barrow, the Beatles' former PR. The articles appeared in the *Sun* newspaper and were highly critical of Paul and his attitude towards her, causing further estrangement between them.

Angie later sold Paul's birth certificate and a furious Paul told the *Sunday Mirror* in November 1995 that by doing so she had betrayed his father.

Angie told the same newspaper, 'We don't exist. Paul has written us out of his life. It's heartbreaking. I write and send Christmas cards, but never receive a reply.'

At the time Angie was living in Nashville. She said, 'I got on fine with Paul at the beginning and he loved Ruth. Paul was twenty-two then and she was like a new toy for him. Ruth was four when I married Jim. We changed her name to McCartney by deed poll.'

She said that Jim had received a £7,000 a year allowance from Paul, but after Jim's death in March 1976 – 'Zilch. Nothing.'

They were hit by hard times and Angie and her daughter moved to America. She sold the birth certificate in America but claimed it was only a copy.

She added, 'I have always regretted selling the birth certificate, but it put a Christmas turkey on the table, and it was about the only thing I had to sell at that stage. I know that I have done some silly things in my life, but I'd just like to say to Paul that it's time to heal the hurt now for the sake of his father.'

In answer, Paul said, 'She was my dad's second wife, and after he died, she fell out with me and all our Liverpool family. She then sold my birth certificate, which I didn't think you could do, and she sold a story to the newspapers – and here she is running to the newspapers again.

'I might say that she sold my birth certificate without saying anything to me or letting me know that she was putting it up for sale at auction. So some bugger has got my birth certificate now, and I don't know who that is. I consider that to be an act of betrayal towards my father. I'm no different from any other member of the human race, and we all know people like this. As far as I'm concerned it's all over between us and that is the opinion of the rest of our family. I don't wish Angie and Ruth ill, but I and the family generally consider that she married my dad for money and she's just in it for the money.'

Williams, Elizabeth
Paul's great-grandmother. She married James McCartney in 1864.

Wilson, Brian
Brian Wilson, born on 20 June 1942, was the leader and composer for the Beach Boys and Paul admired his work and was particularly enthusiastic about the album *Pet Sounds*.

Paul and Linda visited Brian on his 34th birthday on 20 June 1976 at his brother Carl's beachside home. Some footage of the visit was included on the 1985 documentary 'The Beach Boys: An American Band'.

Paul and Linda attended the Beach Boys concert in Anaheim, California on Saturday 10 July 1976. The concert was something special as Brian was appearing live on stage with the group for the first time in twelve years. Other celebrities in the audience included Jan and Dean, Tony Kaye, Rod Stewart, Leo Sayer and Jesse Ed Davis.

A conversation between Wilson and Paul was heard in the *Oobu Joobu* radio series in 1995. Producer Eddy Pumer commented, 'Brian goes on about how he just flipped over the lyrics of "The Long And Winding Road" and then he sings a bit of "Hey Jude", and starts messing with it. Paul does a scat of "California Girls", too. They mess around with three or four songs, including "She's Leaving Home".'

Paul inducted Brian Wilson into the Songwriter's Hall of Fame in a ceremony in New York City on Thursday 15 June 2000. He said:

I'm very honoured to be here as a songwriter. I've always loved the fact that I am. Tonight, I'm even prouder. I think one of the things when you first write a song and it comes out of you, there's a magic moment when you just think 'Oh, yeah. Wow. That's it. I've done it.'

And so many people, the great writers and performers here tonight, know that moment. Another great moment is when you realise the effect it has on other people. I think a lot of the great writers here tonight have had people come up to them and say, 'You saved my life, man.' You know, 'I was going through college and it was hell, but I heard your stuff, you know.'

I'd have a headache and I'd put on a certain record and (Paul makes a sound) no headache at the end of the record. And the person I'm going to honour, induct him into this great Hall of Fame tonight, has had that effect on me many times.

In the sixties particularly, he wrote some music, when I played it, it made me cry. And I don't quite know why. It wasn't necessarily the words or the music . . . there was just something so deep in it that there's only certain pieces of music can do this to me. Just reaching down in me and I think it's a sign of great genius to be able to do that with a bunch of words and a bunch of notes.

And I would take, in later years, I would take my kids aside, and say, 'Listen to this bit of music here.' And they would watch my crying, and they understood. They're at an age now where they're ready to cry at that stuff.

So there you go, that's why I'm here tonight . . . to honour this particular gentleman who I have so much respect for. I think, personally, he's one of your great American geniuses, so I feel honoured as a fellow songwriter and as a fellow bass player . . . yo dude . . . just to be part of this whole thing.

You know, all the writers here, I just get thrilled and this man, he deserves to be in the Hall of Fame, that's for sure. So thank you, sir, for everything you've done for me, for making me cry, for having that 'thing' you can do with your music. You just put those notes and those harmonies together, stick a couple of words over the top of it and you've got me. Any day. Ladies and gentlemen, Brian Wilson.

On 13 June 2001 Paul turned up at the Greek Theater, Los Angeles for the Brian Wilson and Paul Simon Concert. Brian introduced Paul to the audience, stating that the next song 'God Only Knows' was one of Paul's favourite songs. Paul also took to the stage to sing 'I've Just Seen A Face' with Paul Simon.

57 Wimpole Street, London

The home of Jane Asher's family. It had five bedrooms, four reception rooms, five bathrooms and two kitchens. The Asher family moved into the premises in 1957 from a flat in nearby Portland Street.

Paul moved in during November 1963. He'd been sharing a flat in Green Street, Mayfair with the other members of the group, and happened to mention to Jane's mother that he didn't like it there. She suggested that he move into their five-storey house, saying, 'Why don't you stay here for a little while.' Paul later commented, 'Margaret Asher cooked, I liked the family – and I hadn't been happy in Green Street because I was used to a family situation.'

Paul settled in a small room at the top of the house, which he described as 'a bit of an artist's garret, right next to Peter Asher's room. It was one of those huge Wimpole Street houses and Jane lived a couple of floors down, next to her mum and dad.'

Paul's room contained a bed, an easy chair, a record player, a small piano and overlooked the rear of the house. It was self-contained as it had its own bathroom. Peter Asher was in the bedroom next door and Jane and her sister Claire in the rooms below on the next floor.

Among the songs he composed in the Wimpole Street house were 'I Want To Hold Your Hand' and 'Yesterday'.

Winedark Open Sea

A track from the *Off The Ground* album, penned by Paul and lasting 5 minutes and 25 seconds.

Wingfield, Pete

A British pianist who became part of Paul McCartney And Friends in 1999, participating in the recording of the *Run Devil Run* album and making live appearances such as the famous 'Live At The Cavern Club' performance.

Pete was born in Kiphook, Hampshire on 7 May 1948 and formed his first band, Jellybread, while still at Sussex University. During his career he has appeared on numerous recordings for a variety of artists

including the Hollies, BB King, Freddie King, Nazareth, Chris Rea, the
Everly Brothers and Elton John.

Wings (band)

After the birth of Stella in September 1971, Paul was saying, 'I can't
wait to get back on stage again. Television and recording are not
enough. I want to do concerts again and get back to playing live for the
fans and I want Linda to be there on stage beside me.'

He thought of the name Wings while waiting outside the operating
theatre at King's College Hospital for Stella's birth.

Paul decided to form a backing group and initially wanted to start up
in a small way, appearing at colleges. He commented, 'You don't fight
Cassius Clay on your first time out.' He was also to say, 'Don't ever call
me ex-Beatle McCartney again. The Beatles were my old job.'

Discussing the origin of the name, he said, 'We were thinking of all
sorts of names. We had a new group and we had to think of a name.
We had a letter from an old gentleman in Scotland which said, "Dear
Paul, I see you are looking for a name for your group. I'd like to suggest
'the Dazzlers'." So we were nearly the Dazzlers, with the big sequinned
jackets. But we thought, "No, we need something a little more earthy,"
so we thought of Turpentine. But I wrote to the guy in Scotland and
told him that and he wrote back, "I don't think you'll be calling yourselves Turpentine because that's something used to clean paint off," so
we thought of Wings.

'I thought of the name Wings when Linda was in hospital having Stella
and I had persuaded the hospital to let me have a camp bed in her room
to be with her. I wanted something that would become a catch phrase
like the Beatles. You know, people would say things like, "We've got
beetles in the kitchen," and there would be some crack about it being
us. Anyway, I was thinking for some reason of wings of a dove, wings
of angels, wings of birds, wings of a plane. So I said to Linda, "How
about Wings?" It was at a time when most people would be thinking
about a name for a child, and there we were talking about a pop group.'

He said, 'The whole idea behind Wings was to get a touring band, so
that we were just like a band, instead of the whole Beatles myth.'

The first new member was Denny Laine, former member of the
Moody Blues. Next in line was an American session drummer Denny
Seiwell, who had recorded with Paul on his second album *Ram*. Paul
also asked Hugh McCracken and David Spinozza, who had also been
involved in performing on the *Ram* album, but they both turned him
down. All three musicians were successful session men, but Seiwell
decided to take up the offer.

Linda was the fourth member. When there were questions about
Linda's being in his band Paul said, 'Sod 'em, it's my band and I'll have
who I want in it.' Linda said, 'It was good copy at the time to slag
everything. It never really brought me down much.'

Discussing their early work together, he said, 'Linda did kind of appear out of nowhere and to most people she was just some chick. I just figure she was the main help for me on albums at the time. She was there every day helping on harmonies and all that stuff.'

The group then went into the recording studios in August 1971 where they recorded Wings' debut album *Wild Life*, issued in December.

Wild Life received a critical mauling in the media – although it did enter the Top Ten on both sides of the Atlantic. Paul was to comment, 'I don't care if people don't like it . . . I like it. I've got an awful lot to live up to, that's the problem. But I know I'm good. If I'm in the right mood I can write a solid gold hit.'

A launch party was held for the album at the Majestic Ballroom, London and there was also a press conference at Abbey Road Studios where Paul told the media that the album had been made in two weeks and most of the tracks recorded in one or two takes. He said the object was to achieve a 'live' feel to the album.

When Paul decided that the group should go on the road, performing at small gigs, he decided he needed another guitar player and recruited Henry McCullough, former member of Joe Cocker's Grease Band. His first recording as a member of Wings took place on 1 February 1972 when Wings recorded 'Give Ireland Back To The Irish', a debut single which created a great deal of controversy following the events of 'Bloody Sunday'.

A week after the recording session, on Tuesday morning, 8 February 1972, Paul, Linda, Heather and Mary McCartney, Denny Laine, Denny Seiwell and Henry McCullough left London by car and caravan, travelling in a small truck with instruments and amplifiers. They turned off the M1 at Hatherton because Paul thought it sounded like Heather. They arrived at Ashby de la Zouch, but found no village hall was available and ended up in Nottingham. They'd had no destination in mind. McCullough then remembered a year he was with the Grease Band and they had performed at Nottingham University, so they drove to the campus and Paul said to the first two students he met, 'How's about us giving you a concert here tomorrow?'

At midday next day they were on stage performing in one of the college halls. It was Paul's first in front of a live audience since Candlestick Park in August 1966.

The posters, hurriedly written, had announced, simply: 'Today! Guest group – Paul McCartney and Wings! Admission 50p'.

The numbers they played were: 'Lucille', 'Long Tall Sally', 'Blue Moon Of Kentucky', plus tracks from *Wild Life* such as 'Some People Never Know', 'My Love', 'The Mess I'm In', 'Henry's Blues' and 'Seaside Woman'. They gave a ninety-minute performance and had a ten-minute break in between.

'Henry's Blues' was a showcase for McCullough and 'Seaside

Woman' was eventually issued as a single in 1977 under the name Suzy
& the Red Stripes.

The next day they appeared at York, then Hull, Newcastle,
Lancaster, Leeds (played at the Town Hall), Sheffield, Manchester,
Birmingham, Swansea and Oxford.

The Birmingham University paper *Redbrick* reported, 'It took a
moment before the audience realised it was really them. The
McCartney aura filled the stage, with all eyes on him.'

Paul said, 'I felt very much alone. For all of thirteen or fourteen years
I'd been in a group, with my mates – four of us who'd been firm friends
since schooldays. Now I had something to prove and I had to do it on
my own, I had to do everything without their help.

'When the Beatles broke up, it was a little difficult, it was like a
messy divorce and I didn't want to do anything that might seem to be
associated with the ex-wife, so to speak, so I avoided doing material I'd
done earlier with the group.'

It was obvious after the university gigs that the group needed far
more rehearsals before embarking on a proper tour and they began
rehearsing at Emerson, Lake & Palmer's Manticore Studios, situated in
a former Odeon cinema in Fulham.

The group's next single was 'Mary Had A Little Lamb'.

During the summer of 1972 Paul decided that Wings should tour
Europe in a double-decker bus, although they encountered problems in
Sweden when they were busted for smoking cannabis – fortunately
only receiving a fine.

The tour lasted for seven weeks and took in twenty-six cities.

They had already begun work on their next album following the
university tour, but completed most of the recordings during October
and the sessions also resulted in their next single, 'Hi, Hi, Hi'/ 'C
Moon', released in December 1972.

The second album was *Red Rose Speedway*, issued in 1973, with the
album being credited to Paul McCartney and Wings. The same month
saw the release of the single 'My Love'/'The Mess'. The album topped
the American charts and was promoted in Britain via a tour and the TV
screening of the 'James Paul McCartney' special.

In May 1973 they began their first tour of Britain as headliners, with
Brinsley Schwarz as a support band. With the exception of 'Long Tall
Sally' and Denny Laine featuring on 'Go Now', the repertoire
comprised virtually all Wings material.

In the meantime, the Wings theme for the new James Bond film 'Live
And Let Die' was issued as a single in June.

When Paul was anxious to get into the studios to record his next
album, EMI studios were booked, so he decided to travel to Nigeria to
record in the EMI studios there. On the eve of departure, McCullough
and Seiwell decided to leave the band. McCullough said he left because
of Linda. 'I wouldn't have Linda in the band. She doesn't have a

musical head on her.' Paul, Linda and Denny Laine arrived in Lagos, with Wings reduced to a trio, with Paul playing on bass, guitar, drums and synthesiser. The result was the acclaimed *Band On The Run* album, which was issued in April 1974 and reached the top on both sides of the Atlantic and became Wings' first platinum disc.

By this time Paul had hired a new drummer, Geoff Britton, and had found a replacement for McCullough in Jimmy McCulloch, a former member of Thunderclap Newman and Stone the Crows.

In the meantime new singles had been issued, 'Helen Wheels'/'Country Dreamer' in November 1973, 'Jet'/'Let Me Roll It' in February 1974 and 'Band On The Run'/'Nineteen Hundred And Eighty-Five' in April 1974.

In early Wings interviews, Paul had said that he wouldn't be able to tour America due to his drug busts, but he finally received his American visa in December 1973.

In June 1974 the band travelled to Nashville for their first American recording sessions, which resulted in two singles, both issued later that year – 'Junior's Farm'/'Sally G' (in November) and 'Walking In The Park With Eloise'/'Bridge Over The River Suite' (December). 'Eloise', which had been based on a song by Paul's father Jim McCartney, was issued under the name the Country Hams.

For the sessions, Paul recruited two famous country artists, Chet Atkins and Floyd Cramer.

On their return to England they began rehearsing for their first world tour, with their rehearsals being filmed for a documentary 'One Hand Clapping', which wasn't actually released.

There were tensions in the band between Britton and McCulloch and by the time they arrived in New Orleans for more recording sessions in January 1975, Britton left, to be replaced by Joe English (this meant that McCullough was replaced by McCulloch and Britton was replaced by English!).

This was the line-up that recorded the next two Wings albums: *Venus And Mars*, issued in 1975 and *Wings At The Speed Of Sound* issued in 1976.

The albums gave some of the other members the opportunity to shine. Laine sang lead on three vocals, including one he had penned himself, 'Time To Hide', while McCulloch also performed two lead vocals on numbers he had co-written with Colin Allen. English sang lead on 'Must Do Something About It' and Linda tackled lead vocals on 'Cook Of The House'.

In the meantime, singles issued included 'Listen To What The Man Said'/'Love in Song' in May 1975 and 'Letting Go'/'You Gave Me The Answer' in September.

Their world tour kicked off in Britain in September 1975 and continued in Australia during November. There was a break for a few months while they completed the *Wings At The Speed Of Sound* sessions and the tour resumed in March 1976 with European dates. When Wings appeared in Denmark, Paul and Linda took Heather, Mary and Stella with them and turned up at the Palace and said, 'Hello, we're the McCartneys and we've come to see the Queen.' Unfortunately, she wasn't in the palace that day!

In May the tour hit the United States and was to result in the album *Wings Over America*, although it was to prove the group's only tour of the States. It was during this tour that Paul introduced five Beatles numbers into the repertoire. They followed it up with a brief tour of Britain and Europe.

They had been disappointed with the problems relating to a proposed tour of Japan. Despite the fact that the Japanese embassy had signed their visas and David Bailey was making a film of Wings' Japanese visit, the Japanese Minister of Justice said that Wings could not tour the country due to Paul's record of drug convictions. Paul commented, 'I suppose he'd say it was my fault for having smoked some of the deadly weed.'

A proposed tour of America also had to be cancelled. After the group had performed a concert in Paris, McCulloch had an accident and broke a finger on his left hand and was unable to play for several weeks.

Other Wings singles were 'Venus and Mars'/'Rockshow'/'Magneto And Titanium Man' issued in October 1975, 'Silly Love Songs'/'Cook Of The House' issued in April 1976, 'Let 'Em In'/'Beware My Love' in June 1976 and 'Maybe I'm Amazed'/'Soily' in February 1977.

During 1977 the Suzi & the Red Stripes single 'Seaside Woman' was released (in May), along with Denny Laine's album *Holly Days*, produced by Paul.

The *Wings Over America* album was issued in 1977 and in May the group travelled to the Virgin Islands where they were to begin recording in a mobile studio on the boat the *Fair Carol*.

By September Jimmy McCulloch, who had been showing some disenchantment with the group, left, intending to join the Small Faces. He was unsuccessful and was found dead two years later on 27 September 1979 of a suspected drug overdose.

Joe English had also become somewhat unsettled and he also left Wings to join a band called Sea Level and later to become involved in Christian music.

The double A-side 'Mull Of Kintyre'/'Girls' School' was issued early in November 1977 with 'Mull Of Kintyre' becoming the big British Christmas chart-topper, while 'Girls' School' was the A-side issued, not very successfully, in America.

In January 1978 Paul and Linda, together with Denny Laine, returned to the recording studio to complete their new album *London Town*, which was issued in May, along with the single 'With A Little Luck'/'Backwards Traveller'/'Cuff Link'.

During the sessions, two new musicians were added to the line-up, guitarist Laurence Juber and drummer Steve Holly. By the spring they were both officially members of Wings.

In June 1978 the group began recording at Paul's Campbeltown studio, the Spirit of Ranachan. The same month a new single 'I've Had Enough'/'Deliver Your Children' was released. A further single 'London Town'/'I'm Carrying' was issued in August 1978.

The album sessions continued at Lympne Castle in Kent in September and on 3 October Wings became part of 'Rockestra', a rock orchestra formed by Paul for recordings at Abbey Road. Members included Howie Casey, Pete Townshend, Ronnie Lane, John Paul Jones, Kenney Jones, John Bonham, Ray Cooper, Gary Brooker and Dave Gilmour.

The 'Rockestra' tracks were 'So Glad To See You Here' and 'Rockestra Theme'.

As a new album hadn't been completed, EMI issued a compilation, *Wings Greatest* including ten hit singles plus 'Another Day' and 'Uncle Albert/Admiral Halsey'.

In March 1979 the television documentary 'Wings Over The World' was screened, together with a single 'Goodnight Tonight'/'Daytime Nighttime Suffering'.

The release was on a different label from either Capitol or Apple – Columbia, who issued the single in both a 7″ and 12″ format.

In May the new album *Back To The Egg* was issued, which Paul co-produced with Chris Thomas.

June saw the single 'Getting Closer' issued in America and 'Old Siam Sir' in Britain, with 'Spin It On' as the flip.

In August 1979 'Getting Closer'/'Baby's Request' was issued in Britain and 'Arrow Through Me'/'Old Siam Sir' in America.

On 23 November Wings began their final tour in Liverpool and performed a free concert in aid of Paul's old school, Liverpool Institute.

Twelve days after the last date on the tour, Wings appeared at the Odeon, Hammersmith to participate in the Concert For Kampuchea, amid unsubstantiated rumours that the Beatles would be making an appearance. However, Paul did put together a 'Rockestra', which included Robert Plant, James Honeyman-Scott and Dave Edmunds.

In January 1980 Wings flew to Japan for the beginning of a second world tour, but Paul was arrested at the airport for possession of marijuana and spent nine days in jail, while the concerts, which had all sold out, were then cancelled.

Due to the cancellation, Wings literally disintegrated. Juber and Holly left for London and Denny Laine went to Cannes, signed a new record deal and issued a single called 'Japanese Tears', exploiting the situation of Paul's arrest.

On his return home, Paul completed a solo album and single. The single, 'Coming Up', topped the American charts and entered the British Top Ten. Later in the year the animated film *Seaside Woman* was released and won first prize in the short film category at the Cannes Film Festival and the 'Rockshow' concert film was also issued.

In July Paul worked with Ringo Starr on Ringo's album *Stop And Smell The Roses* and Linda, Laurence Juber and Howie Casey were brought in for the three tracks which Paul produced.

There was a brief reunion of Wings in October to work on a projected collection of Paul's to be called *Cold Cuts*, which was never released because it was pre-empted by a bootleg version.

In 1980 Paul began sessions for his next album, which initially looked like a Wings album as Linda, Denny Laine, Laurence Juber and Steve Holly joined him. However, George Martin, who was producing the album, talked Paul into dispensing with the idea of a Wings album, so Steve Holly and Laurence Juber left.

Wings were wound up on 27 April 1981.

In 2001 when Paul announced he was going to tour again he was asked if he would ever re-form Wings. He said, 'You can't re-form Wings for the same reason that you can't re-form the Beatles, because a very important member of each band wouldn't be there. With the Beatles it is John, and with Wings it is Linda.'

Wings – The Birth Of A Band

Following Wings' British tour in 1975 BBC Radio One dedicated an entire show to the group on Sunday 5 October. Entitled 'Wings – the Birth of a Band' it was part of the *Insight* series and was transmitted at 5 p.m. Paul was interviewed by Paul Gambaccini.

Wings At The Speed Of Sound

An album, recorded in January and February 1976 that was first issued in Britain on Parlophone PAS 10010 on Friday 9 April 1976 and in America on Capitol SW 11525 on Thursday 25 March 1976. Paul produced it and the engineer was Pete Henderson.

It got to No. 1 in both the UK and US charts. This was despite problems in Los Angeles relating to airplay. The album was premiered in America on WNEW, a New York station and the Los Angeles station KHJ-FM played it 24 hours before the other Los Angeles stations received their copy. This caused some pique with the other stations, a number of which refused to play the album.

Tracks on the album were: 'Let 'Em In', 'The Note You Never Wrote', 'She's My Baby', 'Beware My Love', 'Wino Junko', 'Silly Love Songs', 'Cook Of The House', 'Time To Hide', 'Must Do Something About It', 'San Ferry Anne' and 'Warm And Beautiful'.

Each member of Wings was given the opportunity to take lead vocals. Denny Laine was lead vocalist on 'The Note You Never Wrote' and 'Time To Hide'; Jimmy McCulloch sang his own composition 'Wino Junko'; Linda sang 'Cook Of The House' and Joe English was lead vocalist on 'Must Do Something About It'.

The horn section on the album included Tony Dorsey on trombone, Howie Casey on saxophone, Steve Howard on trumpet and flugelhorn, and Thadeus Richard on saxophones, clarinet and flute.

The re-release in 1993 featured three bonus tracks: 'Walking In The Park With Eloise', 'Bridge Over The River Suite' and 'Sally G'.

On Friday 19 March 1976, prior to a short European tour, Paul held a press conference at his London offices where he answered questions about some of the album's tracks.

Q: What is the origin of the doorbell used to introduce 'Let 'Em In'?

Paul: Well, as it happens, it is our actual doorbell which our drummer bought us, so it has a group significance, and it seemed a good introduction to the album.

Q: What was the origin of 'Cook Of The House'?

Paul: Well, we were in Adelaide and rented a house to stay at rather than a hotel, and after the gig each night, Linda and I would get dropped off and sit up in the kitchen and have a late-night bite. They had these pots of sage and onion – all the condiments of the season – that's a joke that, condiments of the season. Well all this stuff was lined up and it was a kind of freak song and I took everything I saw and tried to work it into a song. Every line in the song was actually in the kitchen.

Q: What were the sizzling noises heard in the introduction?

Paul: We went round to our house with the mobile unit and Linda decided to cook a meal and get cooking sounds recorded and then fed the meal to us and the engineers. We all had a laugh and a drink. The mobile was outside the house and we just ran wires into the kitchen. Take one. Bacon frying. The first British cooking on record. There are chips at the end, which is great because it sounds like applause. If you get any questions you can tell them it was an E-flat bacon pan and Selmer chips.

Wings Fun Club

A fan club that was launched in the early 1970s and continued despite the demise of the group Wings. For the enrolment fee a member received an introductory package, including a membership card, a set of postcards, two posters, some back issues of the magazine *Club Sandwich* and a year's subscription to the magazine. There were also numerous club offers available to members, including a range of merchandise such as books, tracksuits, calendars, photographs, sheet music, magazines and T-shirts. The magazine was suspended after Linda's death.

Wings Greatest

With this album, Paul became the last member of the former Beatles to issue a compilation album. It was issued in America on Wednesday 22

November on Capitol S00-1905 and in Britain on Wednesday 1 December 1978 on Parlophone PCTC 256. Two of the numbers, 'Another Day' and 'Uncle Albert/Admiral Halsey' weren't even Wings singles, but recordings by Paul and Linda. Five of the numbers had reached No. 1 in America and all but one of the numbers had reached the Top 10. The number that failed to make a dent in the American charts was 'Mull Of Kintyre'.

The tracks were: Side One: 'Another Day', 'Silly Love Songs', 'Live And Let Die', 'Junior's Farm', 'With A Little Luck' and 'Band On The Run'. Side Two: 'Uncle Albert/Admiral Halsey', 'Hi, Hi, Hi', 'Let 'Em In', 'My Love', 'Jet' and 'Mull Of Kintyre'.

The album reached No. 5 in the UK charts and Number 29 in the US.

Angus Forbes photographed the statue featured on the cover in Switzerland.

To coincide with the British release, Paul had a 30-second television commercial issued. A man in a bath sings 'Mull Of Kintyre' out of tune, a chef sings 'Silly Love Songs' in a restaurant, two secretaries sing 'Jet' and a dustman sitting in his truck sings 'Band On The Run' with Paul, Linda and Denny driving up alongside him and Paul saying, 'You're a bit flat, mate,' and the driver replying, 'Funny, I only checked them this morning.'

Wings Live In The Studio

An EP that was proposed but never released. On Monday 9 September 1974 at Abbey Road Studios, a six-track acetate was made of previous recordings from Thursday 15 August for the documentary film 'One Hand Clapping'. The numbers were: 'Jet', 'Let Me Roll It', 'Junior's Farm', 'My Love', 'Little Woman Love'/'C Moon'/'Little Woman' (a medley) and 'Maybe I'm Amazed'.

Wings Over America

A triple album set, produced by Paul, which was recorded live in America between 3 May and 23 June 1976 during the Wings tour of America.

It was released on both sides of the Atlantic on 10 December 1976, in America on Capitol SWCO 11593 and in Britain on Capitol PCSP 720.

Side One opened with a medley, then comprised: 'Venus And Mars', 'Rock Show', 'Jet', 'Let Me Roll It', 'Spirits Of Ancient Egypt' and 'Medicine Jar'. Side Two: 'Maybe I'm Amazed', 'Call Me Back Again', 'Lady Madonna', 'The Long And Winding Road' and 'Live And Let Die'. Side Three: a medley, 'Picasso's Last Words', 'Richard Corey', 'Bluebird', 'I've Just Seen A Face', 'Blackbird' and 'Yesterday'. Side Four: 'You Gave Me The Answer', 'Magneto And Titanium Man', 'Go Now', 'My Love', 'Listen To What The Man Said'. Side Five: 'Let 'Em In', 'Time To Hide', 'Silly Love Songs' and 'Beware My Love'. Side Six: 'Letting Go', 'Band On The Run', 'Hi, Hi, Hi' and 'Soily'.

Ninety hours of recordings on 24-track had been made during the course of the tours and these were edited at Abbey Road Studios by Phil McDonald, Jack Maxson, Mark Vigars and Tom Walsh.

Wings Over The World

A 90-minute TV film of Wings' 1975/76 tour made by Jack Priestley, who also worked on the film of the band's final appearance, called 'The Last Waltz'.

The MPL-produced film included interviews with the McCartney family at home, and scenes from Scotland, Australia and America.

Subtitled 'Paul McCartney Sings His Greatest Hits', it included the numbers 'The Long And Winding Road', 'Yesterday', 'Maybe I'm Amazed', 'Silly Love Songs', 'Let 'Em In', 'Band On The Run' and 'Live And Let Die'. It was originally screened in America as a CBS TV special at 11.30 p.m. on Friday 16 March 1978 and repeated on Friday 6 April 1979. A shorter version, at 75 minutes, was screened in Britain on BBC 2 on Sunday 8 April 1978 and repeated on BBC 1 on Monday 24 December.

Wingspan

A forty-track, two-disc retrospective of Wings' recording career, issued in Britain on 7 May 2001 and in America the following day. The collection contained seventeen million-selling singles and twenty-four tracks from nine No. 1 albums. It was issued in three versions: a double CD, four LPs and 2 cassettes.

The compilation was issued to coincide with the two-hour broadcast in America of an ABC TV special of the same name on 11 May, which was also broadcast in the UK on Channel Four on Saturday 19 May.

The two discs were called *Hits* and *History* (catalogue No. 5328762). Disc One, *Hits*, is 73 minutes and 37 seconds in length. The tracks are: 'Listen To What The Man Said', 'Band On The Run', 'Another Day', 'Live And Let Die', 'Jet', 'My Love', 'Silly Love Songs', 'Pipes Of Peace', 'C Moon', 'Hi, Hi, Hi', 'Let 'Em In', 'Goodnight Tonight', 'Junior's Farm' (DJ edit), 'Coming Up', 'No More Lonely Nights'.

Disc Two, *History*, is 77 minutes and 29 seconds in length. The tracks are: 'Let Me Roll It', 'The Lovely Linda', 'Daytime Nighttime Suffering', 'Maybe I'm Amazed', 'Helen Wheels', 'Bluebird', 'Heart Of The Country', 'Every Night', 'Take It Away', 'Junk', 'Man We Was Lonely', 'Venus And Mars', 'Rock Show' (single edit), 'Back Seat Of My Car', 'Rockestra Theme', 'Girlfriend', 'Waterfalls', 'Tomorrow', 'Too Many People', 'Call Me Back Again', 'Tug Of War', 'Bip Bop – Hey Diddle', 'No More Lonely Nights' (play out version).

The four-album set has the catalogue No. 5328501.

Wingspan earned Paul his 21st American gold disc since leaving the Beatles in 1970. This includes 11 as a solo artist and 10 with Wings.

Wingspan (TV special)

A two-hour television special that made its debut on the TV network ABC in the US on 11 May 2001. The documentary was produced and directed by Paul's daughter Mary and her husband Alistair Donald, who had been working on the project for the previous three years.

He was to say, 'Making "Wingspan" initially involved months of searching through archives and collections around the world to compile the best footage, photographs, and audio available. We discovered a lot of excellent, rare and never-seen material. I wanted to have Paul tell us the story of Wings as the on-screen link. This meant that not only could he give the footage an authoritative perspective, but also that he could provide Linda's view, which is essential, as the story of Wings is equally the story of a marriage and a family.'

To coincide with the TV special was the release of a two-CD set with forty songs by Wings on 8 May.

Commenting on the film, Paul said, 'I always thought you could not follow the Beatles. "Wingspan" is the story and soundtrack of how we set about to do it.'

Paul's spokesman Geoff Baker said that the film shows 'the trauma of the break-up of the Beatles and how that led to the brink of a breakdown. And for the first time, Paul has revealed his experiences in prison – when he was jailed in Tokyo in 1980 on possession of cannabis.'

Discussing the idea behind the back-to-basics band, Baker also said, 'Instead of arriving at stadium concerts in police-escorted limousines, the members of Wings drove themselves to small halls unannounced and uninvited and were paid for their impromptu gigs in fifty-pence pieces.'

Wino Junko

A number penned by McCullough/Allen, with Jimmy McCullough on lead vocal, which was a track on the *Wings At The Speed Of Sound* album.

Winter Rose

This number was among several demos made at Paul's Rude Studios in 1977. He recorded the number again at the Spirit of Ranachan studio in July 1978 and Paul would place it with 'Love Awake' as a medley on the *Back To The Egg* album. Paul recorded the Black Dyke Mills Band on the track 'Winter Rose' at Abbey Road Studios on Sunday 1 April 1979.

With A Little Help From My Friends

A track from the *Sgt Pepper's Lonely Hearts Club* album. Paul said he'd write something for Ringo. The working title was 'Bad Finger Boogie'. He worked on it with John at Weybridge, a part of the songwriting process that was witnessed by the Beatles' biographer Hunter

Davies, although it's generally credited that Paul wrote most of the song.

The number was recorded at Abbey Road on 29 and 30 March 1967.

Joe Cocker also recorded a version of the number and topped the British charts with it in November 1968 in what people regard as the best version of the number. Ritchie Haven was also one of many other artists to record the song and prior to performing it at one concert he described it as 'my favourite song in the whole universe'.

Although the working title 'Bad Finger Boogie' was abandoned, the name Badfinger was given to Apple group the Iveys.

With A Little Luck (single)

A song that Paul wrote in Scotland, originally began recording during a Wings trip to the Virgin Islands in 1977, and completed at a recording session in London.

It was first issued in America on Capitol 4559 on Monday 20 March 1978 and rose to the No. 1 position. It didn't fare so spectacularly in Britain when it was issued on Parlophone R 6019 on Thursday 23 March, although it climbed to the No. 7 position.

The flipside was a medley, comprising 'Backwards Traveller' and 'Cuff Link', the latter originally called 'Off-The-Cuff-Link'. Paul plays drums on the track.

The number was also featured on *London Town*, released later the same month, and on *Wings Greatest*, issued on 1 December 1978.

The number was played at the end of the Farrah Fawcett feature film *Sunburn*.

It was issued in Germany on EMI Electrola 1C600-60639.

With A Little Luck (promotional film)

The promotional film for this *London Town* track was filmed before an audience of fifty fans on 24 March 1987 at Twickenham Studios, directed by Michael Lindsay Hogg. It was to see the introduction of a guest drummer Steve Holly, who was then to become a member of Wings.

Without Walls

A Channel 4 arts programme. Paul appeared in a special edition of the show subtitled 'This Is Tomorrow' on Sunday 21 June 1992. The programme looked at the career of artist Richard Hamilton who had worked with Paul on the designs for *The Beatles* double album sleeve and the accompanying collage poster.

Wogan

A BBC 1 TV show hosted by Irish disc jockey Terry Wogan. Paul appeared on *Wogan* on Friday 1 August 1986. The show was live and was filmed at the BBC Television Theatre, Shepherd's Bush, London. Paul was interviewed for fifteen minutes and a clip of him performing 'Press' was also screened. The promotional film of 'Press' had been filmed by Philip Davey at Abbey Road Studios on Friday 18 July 1986.

Paul, together with Linda, also recorded another *Wogan* show on Thursday 19 November 1987, which was broadcast the following day. The appearance lasted for 36 minutes during which Paul performed 'Jet' and 'Listen To What The Man Said'. A promotional film of 'Once Upon A Long Ago' was also screened. Following the performance, Russian journalist Artemy Troitsky interviewed Paul.

Paul also appeared on Wogan on Friday 14 December 1990. Wogan introduced Paul:

Wogan: Wherever they wander, the great and the good, they end up back at Shepherd's Bush. This man has come back from a world tour that started in Oslo before 5,000 and finished in Chicago before 55,000. In between, there were 184,000 at the Maracana Stadium in Rio. A slightly smaller but select group here – for 'All My Trials' – Paul McCartney.

Paul and the band performed 'All My Trials' and then Paul joined Wogan.

Wogan: Well, that was some score – 184,000 people at Maracana.

Paul: Yeah, at least that.

Wogan: Weren't you terrified standing there?

Paul: I thought it was going to look like miles and miles and miles of people, but because it's a little compact stadium it didn't actually look like that many people – but, yes, it was terrifying.

Wogan: Now this latest single of yours – bit of a storm in a teacup over this, isn't there?

Paul: Yes, it became like, sort of, a political thing. In actual fact, we just started off liking the song and then put a video to it and suddenly it seemed to have a more powerful message because we used things like homeless people in the video to show the trials and then the timing was right when Maggie got dumped. Remember that, which we couldn't have possibly known about as, you know, you plan these things weeks in advance. So the left-wing newspaper got hold of it and ran it and then the right-wing newspaper countered it, and then Jonathan King climbed aboard and all hell broke loose.

Wogan: Doesn't it make you wonder why you bother?

Paul: No, Terry. It's funny, you know. Some people said to me, 'Look, you've got a lot of money; you're disqualified from talking about the homeless, because you're well off. Which I think is mad, you know. Probably the more money you've got, the more you've got to talk about the homeless, I would have thought.

Wogan: Money of course is not the answer, is it – flinging money at it.

Paul: Actually, yes, but I mean flinging a little bit of publicity at it, I don't think hurts, really, because the alternative is to ignore it.

Wogan: You're still winning awards. Did I see you'd just won an award for having the best teeth or something?

Paul: No, it was a good behaviour award from Wandsworth.

Wogan: This week there were two awards.

Paul: Yes, this big crowd in Rio and in America we were the top box-office thing. But I'm playing it down, Terry.

Wogan: Are you?

Paul: Modestly he said, well, yes we did win it. Yes it was marvellous at this venerable age of mine to be still winning awards.

Wogan: Did it change your attitude a bit and make you say: 'I'm going to tour every ten minutes from now on'?

Paul: Well, maybe once a year, maybe not ten minutes. I thought when we started the tour that I'd be totally knackered at the end of it and that I'd hate audiences forever. In fact, I think I ended up a bit fitter at the end of the tour than when we started and so, yeah, we're thinking of doing it in maybe a year's time.

Wogan: You said in your programme for the tour, you rediscovered the Beatles songs in a sense – the ones that you had written and you were able to bring the audience in as well on all those participation songs. Did that make a difference to your concert, did you feel it gave it something else?

Paul: Yeah, it was good. When the Beatles broke up, all of us didn't want to deal with the Beatles music because it was kind of painful reminders of what had gone down. But enough water had gone under the bridge, so I felt it was time to bring them out and unpack them and I realised that I hadn't done quite a few of them ever, you know, because the Beatles weren't touring. Songs like 'Hey Jude' and 'Sgt Pepper' I'd never actually sung to an audience. So that was quite a buzz.

Wogan: You're about to work with Carl Davis on this symphony thing as well?

Paul: I'm not about to, I've been working about a year with the man.

Wogan: Anything happening?

Paul: Yeah, we've been working like loonies for about a year now. It's for the Royal Liverpool Philharmonic Orchestra. They've commissioned me to write a piece for their 150th anniversary, so some very old people in that orchestra! So it was a great opportunity for me, because I've kind of flirted with that stuff with 'Yesterday' and 'Eleanor Rigby' and things like that. I like so-called classical instruments. But this is a really big challenge. This is like the whole bit, it's an oratorio for the whole orchestra, the whole chorus: oratorio. You're wondering what it is, aren't you, Terry?

Wogan: I thought it was a character in *Hamlet*.

Paul: No, the fellow who shot Moby Dick.

Wogan: We were talking about families earlier and you're a family man. Would you agree with that, about keeping your distance from your family? I know everyone has their own ideas.

Paul: I hate to tell you this, but I wasn't listening.

Wogan: Oh great.

Paul: Oh, that's marvellous. Invite him on the show and he doesn't even listen.

Wogan: Don't pay any attention. They were saying . . .

Paul: What were they saying, Terry?

Wogan: They were saying that the secret of a happy family Christmas was not necessarily . . .

Paul: Don't go!

Wogan: No, get together for dinner or lunch, but possibly have a cigar outside in the garden afterwards on your own.

Paul: Yes, I think that's right in some families, you know. Occasionally you need your space. I'm very lucky I've got a very close family. I think it's time for a lot of people and occasionally me, but I'm very lucky I've got a very close family. I quite like having the kids around and I hear the theme music, so thank you very much, Terry Wogan, it's been lovely having you on my programme tonight. Over to you, Tel.

Wogan: Thank you. I'm very glad to get the chance to wish you all goodnight. Thanks to everybody and thank you for joining us. Hope you enjoyed the programme.

(The Maggie referred to was Margaret Thatcher who had just been ousted as prime minister and the reference to 'families' was part of a discussion by earlier guests Jamie Lee Curtis and John Cleese.)

Wogan With Sue Lawley

Immediately following a European promotional tour for his new album *Flowers In The Dirt*, Paul appeared on this show on Friday 19 May 1989. Sue Lawley was deputising for the usual host Terry Wogan on the chat show, although Paul wasn't the subject of an interview, but performed 'My Brave Face' and 'Figure Of Eight' from the album.

Woman (song)

A number that Paul wrote for Peter and Gordon. It was the A-side of their single, issued in America on 10 January 1966 on Capitol 5579, and in Britain on 11 February 1966 on Columbia DB 7834. The flipside was 'Wrong From The Start'. The number was also included on the duo's album of the same name, issued in March of that year. Paul used the pseudonym Bernard Webb when he wrote the song because he was interested to see if a number of his could be successful without using the McCartney name. Webb was said to be an aspiring songwriter and a student in Paris. Paul also used the pseudonym A Smith in connection with the single.

When it reached the charts Paul admitted that he'd written it.

'Woman' reached No. 14 in the American charts and No. 18 in Britain.

'Woman' was also the opening track on Peter and Gordon's album *Woman*, issued in America on 7 March 1966 on Capitol ST 2477, and on their British album *Peter and Gordon*, issued on 17 June 1966 on Columbia SCX 6045, and also on *The Best Of Peter And Gordon*, issued in America on 5 July 1966 on Capitol Starline ST 2549. It was the flipside of Peter and Gordon's 'I Don't Want To See You Again' single, also penned by Paul, issued in America on 1 May 1967 on Capitol Starline 6155.

Woman was also the title of a 16-track album by Paul's brother Mike. It was issued in Britain on Island ILPS 9191 on 21 April 1972. Mike produced it himself and co-wrote most of the songs with Roger McGough. The cover of the album features a photograph of Mary McCartney, mother of Paul and Mike.

The number is not to be confused with a John Lennon song of the same title.

Paul mentioned that the Beatles had actually done a version of the number. He said, 'We did a much better one, the first time we did it. The first time we ever did it, we did it very dry. It was little with about eight violins. It really sounded like a string quartet, you know. We were very fussy at the time. We thought, "This was the one", but we just chucked it and jacked it in, and let them go and do it again. It got turned into a mammoth Peter and Gordon treatment; only Gordon couldn't get the high notes. It was a great song, though. I wonder if Peter has still got our original thing?'

Wonder, Stevie

Stevie was blind when he was born in Saginaw, Michigan on 13 May 1950.

He was twelve years old when he signed with Motown and his single 'Fingertips' topped the US charts.

On the back cover of Paul's *Red Rose Speedway* album is the Braille message to Stevie: 'We love you.'

When Paul gathered together some famous guest artists to record on the island of Montserrat, Stevie accepted his invitation to record 'Ebony And Ivory'. Paul had wanted to do the number with a black artist and Stevie was his first choice. They recorded the song the day after Stevie arrived on the island with Paul playing piano and bass, Stevie on drums and synthesiser, and both of them sharing the vocals.

Paul was to say, 'I'm a hero for life with the locals for taking Stevie to the island. They were quite interested in me, but not very excited. But Stevie Wonder! It was pandemonium. He is like a god to them.'

As a thank you to Paul, Stevie penned a song about the island.

'Ebony And Ivory' provided Stevie with his first British chart-topper. However, Motown Records refused to allow Stevie to receive full billing on the release and the credit had to read Paul McCartney *with* Stevie Wonder rather than Paul McCartney *and* Stevie Wonder.

Wonderful Christmastime

A single issued in Britain on Parlophone R 6029 on Friday 16 November 1979 and in America on Columbia 1-11162 on Tuesday 20 November 1979.

The Christmas number, written and produced by Paul, was the first single that was credited solely to Paul McCartney since the release of 'Another Day' in 1971.

It failed to make a dent in the American charts. However, the single reached the position of No. 7 in Britain.

The flipside was 'Rudolph the Red-Nosed Reggae'. This was a number originally penned by John David Marks and recorded by Gene Autry in 1949.

Paul performed the number on stage during the Wings British tour of 1979 when artificial snow added to the effect. Imprinted on the record itself are two messages. On 'Wonderful Christmastime' there are the words 'Lift a glass to . . . Xmas '79'; and on the flip: 'Love from Rudi! Xmas '79'.

Paul was also to tell a story relating to the violinist playing on the B-side. When Paul was rehearsing the number in June 1975 a violin was delivered to the studio. Paul then decided that the violin should be used on the track. He asked the man who delivered the instrument whether he would play it and the man agreed. After the session the man left without leaving his name and all initial attempts by Paul to find him and give him his session fee failed. However MPL finally tracked him down and he received a cheque for his contribution.

The picture sleeve features a picture of Paul in a Santa Claus hat but sans beard.

The single was also issued in Germany on Odeon 1C600-63435.

Working Classical

See *Paul McCartney's Working Classical*.

World Tonight, The (documentary)

An MPL documentary on the making of Paul's *Flaming Pie* album, directed by Geoff Wonfor. It received its world premiere in America on

VH-1 on Friday 16 May 1997 and its European premiere in Britain on the ITV network on Sunday 18 May 1997.

The documentary was issued on home video on the PNE label on 6 October 1997.

World Tonight, The (single)

A track from the *Flaming Pie* album composed by Paul during a holiday in America in 1995. At 4 minutes and 6 seconds in length, it was the second single to be released from the album and was issued in Britain on Parlophone RP 6472 on Monday 7 July 1997. 'Born To Be Bad' was on the flip. It was also the first single to be released from the album in America.

There were two CDs and a 7″ picture disc released. The picture disc on Parlophone RP 6472 had 'Used To Be Bad' on the flip. The first CD, CD1 on CDRS 6472 also contained 'Used To Be Bad' and 'Oobu Joobu Part Three'. 'Oobu Joobu Part Three' contained 'Intro Chat', 'Oobu Joobu Main Theme', 'Squid', 'Paul McCartney Talks About The World Tonight', 'Link' and 'Oobu Joobu Main Theme'. CD2 on CDR 6472 included 'Really Love' and 'Oobu Joobu Part Four'. 'Oobu Joobu Part Four' contained 'Intro Chat', 'Oobu Joobu Main Theme', 'Link', 'Don't Break The Promise', 'Paul McCartney Talks About Reggae Music', 'Link' and 'Oobu Joobu Main Theme'.

The maxi-single issued in America on 6 May 1997 on Capitol 8-58650-2 had the tracks 'The World Tonight', 'Looking for You' and 'Oobu Joobu Part One'.

Paul originally wrote the number during a holiday he was taking in 1995. He was to comment, 'The lyrics were just gathering thoughts. Like 'I go back so far, I'm in front of me' – I don't know where that came from, but if I'd been writing with John he would have gone "OK. Leave that one in, we don't know what it means but we do know what it means".'

It was co-produced by Paul and Jeff Lynne and engineered by Geoff Emerick and Jan Jacobs, assisted by Keith Smith.

Recording began on 13 November 1995 with Paul on lead vocal, vocal harmony and drums, bass guitar, electric guitar, acoustic guitar, piano and percussion. Jeff Lynne provided harmony vocal and electric guitar, acoustic guitar and keyboard.

Paul was also to say, 'It's got a bit of a tougher riff on it. Actually, there's a bit more of my heavier guitar on this album. When Linda and I first met, she'd say, "I didn't know you played heavy guitar like that, I love that." But I've always done quite a bit of that for myself.

'So when it came to this album Linda said, "Really play guitar, don't just get someone to play it." It's a little naïve, my guitar style, it's not amazingly technical. It's a bit like Neil Young. In fact, I still haven't done the guitar as much as she wanted. But next album . . .'

It was rumoured that there was a secret message on this recording, that if you played it backwards between 2.38 and 2.41 the words 'Save the animals fur, Linda Eastman' could be heard.

World You're Coming Into, The
A CD single issued in 1991 featuring Kiri Te Kanawa performing excerpts from the *Liverpool Oratorio* composed by Paul McCartney and Carl Davis. There were three tracks, the first two from 'Movement 7 – Crises'. They were 'Introduction – Allegro Molto' and 'The World You're Coming Into', with Kiri Te Kanawa (soprano) and Jeremy Budd (treble). Track three, '*Tres Conejus*' was from 'Movement 2 – School' and featured Sally Burgess (mezzo-soprano), Jerry Hadley (tenor) and Willard White (bass). Backing was by the Royal Liverpool Philharmonic Orchestra, conducted by Carl Davis.

World Without Love
A number Paul wrote in the Forthlin Road house when he was only sixteen. He originally offered it to Billy J Kramer, who turned it down. He then gave it to Peter and Gordon after slightly altering the lyrics. The single was released in the UK on Friday 28 February 1964 on Columbia DB 7225 and reached the No. 1 position in May, knocking 'Can't Buy Me Love' off the top. It was issued in America on 27 April 1964 on Capitol 5175 and reached No.1 in America in June.

The *New Musical Express* review of the single read: 'Here's a disc which could easily register, if only because of its Beatle associations. A nostalgic medium-pacer, it's not one of John and Paul's greatest songs, but it's still quite effective. And a powerful Geoff Love backing, with thudding beat and added organ, deserves full marks.'

It was re-released in America on 15 December 1965 on Capitol Starline 6076 and was also the opening track on the album *Woman*, issued in America on 7 March 1966 on Capitol ST 2477 and on *Peter And Gordon*, an album issued in Britain on 17 June 1966 on Columbia SCX 6045 and also on *The Best Of Peter And Gordon*, issued in America on 5 July 1966 on Capitol Starline ST 2549.

It was also included on the double album *Alan Freeman's History Of Pop Vol 2*, issued in Britain on 29 March 1974 on Arcade ADEP 9/10.

Wright, Maggie
A young British actress who appeared as Paul's girlfriend, Maggie the Lovely Starlet, in 'Magical Mystery Tour'.

Yale Bowl, New Haven

An arena in Connecticut, with a 63,000 capacity, where Paul was originally to appear on Sunday 29 July 1990 on the final leg of his world tour.

There was a history of hostility towards rock concerts at this venue and in previous years planned concerts by Michael Jackson, Bruce Springsteen, the Who and Simon and Garfunkel had been cancelled due to opposition from the council and local citizens.

The city council originally vetoed the concert due to complaints from residents in the nearby Westville neighbourhood. The local Board of Aldermen then decided to allow it after voting 19–6 to approve the show although they had presented MPL with a list of twenty restrictions that they said had to be adhered to. Despite this, there were still complaints.

Billboard magazine was to comment, 'The same neighbourhood that feared it would be overrun during concerts has gladly lent its front lawns as parking lots for the Yale-Harvard football matches.'

On 1 April 1990, prior to Paul's concert at Berkeley Memorial Stadium, Paul's manager Richard Ogden said that they had discovered that only 50 people had voiced objections while 60,000 wanted the concert to go ahead. However, it had been decided not to do the show.

Ogden commented, 'I have closely followed the events in New Haven over the past few weeks, both through official channels and by communications with my wife's family who live in the area, and I have decided that the strength of local opposition was formidable enough to have us reconsider the proposed New Haven show. Paul is very sensitive to community concerns of this sort and has no desire to be the catalyst for such a deep and divisive controversy within the city.'

He was to add, 'Fortunately, as a contingency plan, we held tickets for the July twenty-fourth and twenty-fifth shows at Boston's Sullivan Stadium and these will go on sale immediately to fans in the New Haven area.'

Yates, Kerry

An Australian journalist whose meeting with Paul benefited her career.

Glenn A Baker relates the event in his book *The Beatles Down Under*.

Kerry was seventeen years old and working for *Women's Weekly* when the Beatles arrived in Sydney in June 1964. She was among the large group of reporters and photographers waiting in a corridor in the Sheraton hotel, hoping to get a story on Paul as he was celebrating his 22nd birthday.

Paul decided to have a few words with the press, but as soon as he saw Kerry he went straight to her and invited her to his room for an interview.

Kerry commented, 'I had long blonde hair and a pink sweater and I must have stood out from all the grey and brown suits because Paul made a beeline right for me and invited me up to his room. He let my photographer take shots of him surrounded by his presents and the next week we ran one of them on the front cover with my "exclusive" story inside. For years I've been asked what I had to do to get that scoop, which really did help my career. I know that everyone wants to know but I'm not saying if I did it or if I didn't.'

Years Roll Along, The

A song that Paul wrote in the late 1950s, which was never recorded. When he wrote a letter to a local journalist in 1959 attempting to get some publicity for the Quarry Men, Paul mentioned the title of the number.

Yellow Roads Of Texas

One of several numbers created in a jam session during Wings' second trip to Lympne Castle, Kent in May 1979.

Yellow Submarine

Paul was to comment, 'I was lying in my bed one night, and, just before I went to sleep, I had this idea about a yellow submarine. It just came into my mind, so, the next day I started writing it and finished it up. This was written as a commercial song, a kids' song. People say, "Yellow Submarine? What's the significance? What's behind it?" Nothing! I knew it would get connotations, but it was just a children's song. Kids get it straight away. I just loved the idea of kids singing it. I was playing with my little stepsister the other day, looking through a book about Salvador Dali, and she said to me, "Oh look. A soft watch." She accepted it. She wasn't frightened or worried. Kids have got it. It's only later that they get messed up. With "Yellow Submarine", the whole idea was "if someday I come across some kids singing it, that will be it".'

Another time he recalled, 'I was just drifting off to sleep and there's that nice twilight zone as you drift off. I remember thinking that it would be a good idea to write a children's song. I thought of images and the colour yellow came to me and a submarine came to me and I thought "That's kind of nice; like a toy, very childish yellow submarine."

Donovan also helped Paul with some of the lyrics and said, 'I helped Paul with the lyrics for "Yellow Submarine". He came round to my apartment and parked his Aston Martin in the middle of the road with the doors open and the radio blaring. He walked away from the car and came up to my apartment and played me "Eleanor Rigby" with different lyrics and he also said that he had another song that was missing a verse. It was a very small part and I just went into the other room and put together "Sky of blue, sea of green". They had always asked other people for help with a line or two, so I helped with that line. He knew that I was into kids' songs and he knew I could help. I'm sure he could have written the line himself but I suppose he wanted someone to add a line and I added a line.'

John Lennon was to say, '"Yellow Submarine" is Paul's baby. Donovan helped with the lyrics. I helped with the lyrics too. We virtually made the track come alive in the studio, but based on Paul's inspiration, Paul's idea, Paul's title.'

The song was an ideal vehicle for Ringo, providing him with his first vocal A-side on a Beatles single, and was recorded on 28 May and 1 June 1966 and included on the *Revolver* album.

The number became the inspiration for the animated movie *Yellow Submarine* and was also included on the *Yellow Submarine* soundtrack album issued on Parlophone CDP7 46445 2. A version in which Ringo makes a spoken word introduction was included on Volume Two of *The Beatles Anthology*.

'Yellow Submarine' was also issued as a single in the US on 8 August 1966 on Capitol 5715 with 'Eleanor Rigby' and reached No. 2 in the charts. It was issued in Britain on 5 August on Parlophone R5493 and topped the charts.

Yesterday

One of Paul's most famous compositions, of which there have been over 2,500 versions by a wide variety of artists of almost every musical genre, including Elvis Presley, Frank Sinatra, Ray Charles, Tammy Wynette, Placido Domingo, Howard Keel, Liberace and Erroll Garner. Only four versions have actually reached the charts: those by the Beatles, Matt Monro, Ray Charles and Marianne Faithfull.

Billy J. Kramer said that at one point in his career when he was looking for a new song he travelled to Blackpool to see Paul and ask him if he had a suitable number. Paul played him 'Yesterday', but Billy said he turned it down because he didn't think it was right for him. Chris Farlowe also says that he turned the number down, telling Paul, 'It's not for me. It's too soft. I need a good rocker, a shuffle or something.'

Although Paul says he played 'Yesterday' to both artists, he said it wasn't with the intention of giving them the song to record.

Paul began writing it when he was 21 and it was the first time a Beatle had made a solo recording.

In 1980 Paul said 'I really reckon "Yesterday" is probably my best song. I like it not only because it was a big success, but because it was one of the most instinctive songs I've ever written. I was so proud of it. I felt it was an original tune – the most complete thing I'd ever written. It's very catchy without being sickly.'

Paul woke up one morning, late in 1963 in the attic bedroom of the Ashers' house at 57 Wimpole Street with the melody in his head and set some nonsense words to the tune, which had the working title of 'Scrambled Egg'. He said, 'I just fell out of bed and the bones of the melody were there. I had a piano by the side of my bed and just got up and played the chords.'

He was later to state, 'It was the only song I ever dreamed.'

He later went along to Alma Cogan's flat and played her the tune on the piano. He was to ask her 'This is something I've written; does this remind you of anything?' He was still working on it when he was visiting the family home in the Wirral and Ruth McCartney recalls Paul walking around the house singing 'Scrambled eggs, Oh, you've got such lovely legs, scrambled eggs. Oh, my baby how I love your legs.'

Paul was unsure whether he'd actually created the melody or had heard the tune somewhere before. He played it to his fellow Beatles as a new composition and recalled, 'It was like handing in something you'd found at the police station and waiting to see if anyone claimed it. After two weeks they hadn't in this case so I felt entitled to collect it and call it my property.'

In January 1964 while they were in Paris, staying at the George V Hotel, Paul played it to George Martin, while it was still under the working title of 'Scrambled Eggs'. Martin recalls, 'Paul wanted a one-word title except that he thought the word "Yesterday" was perhaps too corny. I persuaded him that it sounded fine to me.'

Paul was still working on the number when the Beatles were filming their second feature *Help!* at Twickenham Studios, playing it constantly on piano. This irritated director Richard Lester who told him, 'If you play that bloody theme one more time I'll have the piano taken off the set. Either finish the song properly or give up on it.'

Ray Coleman was to write an entire book dedicated to the song in 1995 which was called *Yesterday and Today*.

Beatles publisher Dick James was to tell Coleman that he heard Paul playing it at the Twickenham Studios during the filming of *Help!*

He was to say, 'Paul said to me, "Come and listen to this. It's my latest tune, we'll be recording it soon, I've got an idea but I haven't worked out the lyrics yet." And he switched on the Hammond organ and very quietly just held the keys and used the bass part. Paul, in his construction of the song, always seemed to feature the bass before almost any other part of the melody. He played the left hand on the bass of the organ, and used the words "Scrambled Eggs" as the title. Funny words, but you really didn't have to be a great musician or even a music man to know that it was one of the greatest melodies that your ears had ever heard.'

The song was recorded in June 1965. In his book *All You Need Is Ears*, George Martin was to write 'I started to leave my hallmark on the music when a style started to emerge which was partly of my making. It was on "Yesterday" that I started to score their music. It was on "Yesterday" that we first used instruments or musicians other than the Beatles and myself.'

Paul had said, 'We tried ways of doing it with John on organ but it sounded weird, and in the end I was told to do it as a solo. I was never comfortable doing that, especially with the others.'

The next step was the use of a string quartet and Martin recalled, 'And that, in the pop world in those days, was quite a step to take. We started breaking out of the phase of using just four instruments and went into something more experimental, though our initial experiments were severely limited by the fairly crude tools at our disposal and had simply to be moulded out of my recording experience.'

When recalling that the number had been a tune without words for quite a long time, he pointed out that the working title 'Scrambled Eggs' had three syllables, as did 'Yes-ter-day'. He took his time to work out the lyrics, saying they were 'not too sickly but certainly it was always going to be a love song. I'm hip to the fact that people like a love song. I like ballads and I know people like them too.'

Recording of the number began on Monday 14 June 1965 at Abbey Road's No. 2 Studio with Paul playing 'Yesterday' on acoustic guitar and vocal. George Harrison was also present at the recording. The number was completed on Thursday 17 June with the overdubbing, an additional vocal track by Paul – and the presence of a string quartet comprising Tony Gilbert on first violin, Sidney Sax on second violin, Francisco Gabarro on cello and Kenneth Essex on voila.

Initially, Paul talked to the quartet, explaining his ideas, with such instructions as 'No vibrato. I don't want vibrato.' He recalled, "When they dropped the vibrato it sounder stronger. Before, it had sounded quite classical enough. Now it was no longer like the old gypsy violinist playing round a camp fire.'

Martin considered that the number was a solo Paul McCartney

effort and thought that it should be released as such. He even approached the Beatles' manager Brian Epstein to discuss it. He said, 'I actually went to Brian and said: "What are you going to call this? Is it Paul McCartney?" And he looked at me very sternly and said: "No. It is the Beatles." He did not want to divide his holy quartet. Though it wasn't the Beatles at all, it had to remain so, as part of their recordings. I don't think it irritated Paul at the time because he considered himself to be a Beatle above all other things.'

When the Beatles appeared on *Blackpool Night Out* on Sunday 1 August 1965, Paul performed 'Yesterday.' Apparently John Lennon was not pleased with Paul getting what amounted to a solo spot and was shouting out sarcastic comments when Paul was rehearsing the number. When Paul was about to play it, George Harrison introduced him with the word's 'We'd like to do something now that we've never ever done before. It's a track off our new LP and this song's called "Yesterday". So for Paul McCartney of Liverpool, opportunity knocks!'

Matt Monro, a leading British ballad singer watched the *Blackpool Night Out* television show and the next day phoned George Martin asking him when the number was being issued as a single. Martin told him that there were no plans for it to be released as a single – Brian Epstein had vetoed it. Monro then said he wanted to record it and, as Martin was his own recording manager, asked him to score it for him.

Martin recalled, 'That was most difficult because I had already scored it for Paul and I didn't want to do it any other way. I did re-score it for Matt, and produced his record with a string orchestra. We had a French horn and I changed the harmonies. All the things Paul would hate were there, but it worked for Matt Monro.'

Paul was keen on Marianne Faithfull recording the number and even attended her recording session on 11 November 1965.

When the Beatles began touring in June 1965, Paul initially didn't play 'Yesterday' because he thought it might upset John. However, Capitol Records wanted to issue it as a single in America and asked if Paul could perform it on *The Ed Sullivan Show*, which the Beatles recorded on Saturday 14 August 1965. George Harrison announced, 'We'd like to carry on with a song from our new album in England and it will be out in America shortly. And it's a song featuring just Paul, and it's called "Yesterday".' Paul sang it and was accompanied by a pre-taped track featuring three violins. When Paul finished the number, John announced, 'Thank you Paul, that was just like him.' The show was screened on 12 September 1965.

'Yesterday' was included on the *Help!* album, but was not released as a Beatles single in Britain until 1970. It was the title song on their British EP, released on GEP 8948 on 4 March 1966 with the tracks 'Yesterday', 'Act Naturally', 'You Like Me Too Much' and 'It's Only Love'. However, it was issued in many other countries and topped the charts in America, Hong Kong, Finland, Norway and Belgium.

It was included on the compilation album *A Collection of Beatles Oldies (But Goldies)* issued on Parlophone PCS 7016 on 10 December 1966. It was also included on *The Beatles 1962–1966* issued on Parlophone PCSP 717 on 19 April 1973. It was finally released as a single in Britain on Parlophone R 6013 on 8 March 1976 with 'I Should Have Known Better' on the flip. It was also the opening track on the mail order set issued by World Records as *The Beatles Collection* in 1977 and was also the opening track on *The Beatles Ballads*, issued on Parlophone PCS 7214 on 20 October 1980.

The American single was issued on Capitol 5498 on 13 September 1965 with 'Act Naturally' on the flip and was a million-seller there within ten days. It was also included on the American album *Yesterday and Today* issued on Capitol ST2553 on 20 June 1966 and was the opening track on the American album *Love Songs*, issued on Capitol SKBL 11711 on 21 October 1977.

'Yesterday' received the Ivor Novello Award as 'The Outstanding Song Of The Year' in 1966 and was the most performed song in America for eight consecutive years from 1965–1973.

Paul continued to use the number during his solo years and included it on his Wings 1975/6 tour, his British tour of 1979, also as an encore on his 1989/90-world tour and his 1993 tour. It also surfaced on the *Wings Over America* album. He also decided to include it in his *Give My Regards to Broad Street* feature film and it was part of the movie soundtrack album which was issued on 22 October 1984.

At the Dorchester Hotel, London, in November 1993 Paul was to receive an award for the 6 millionth American radio play, which was said to be 'the most performed song ever on US radio and television.'

He said, 'I asked as a favour if I could have my name before John's on the Anthology credit for "Yesterday" and Yoko refused.

'I could question her but I'm a civil person and life isn't long enough. I'd prefer to walk in the park, have fun.

'At one time Yoko earned more from "Yesterday" than I did. It doesn't compute, especially when it's the only song that none of the Beatles had anything to do with.'

During April 1998 he performed the number for a BBC 2 television tribute to Spike Milligan on his eightieth birthday. He played an acoustic version on guitar, slipping in part of Milligan's 'Ying Tong Song' into it.

Another version of this number, lasting two minutes and seven seconds, was recorded live for the *Tripping The Live Fantastic* album on 9 February 1990 at the Worcester Centrum, Worcester, Massachusetts during the 1989/90 World Tour.

Ying Tong Song

One of the nonsense songs created by the Goons, the cult British comedy group comprising Peter Sellers, Spike Milligan, Harry Secombe and Michael Bentine. On 18 April 1998, the night after Linda's death, a programme celebrating Spike Milligan's eightieth birthday, 'Happy Birthday Spike', was screened in Britain on BBC 2 with a pre-recorded piece from Paul in which he mentioned Spike's huge influence on the Beatles' sense of humour and sang a version of 'Yesterday', mixing it with the 'Ying Tong Song'.

You Gave Me The Answer
A track on the *Venus And Mars* album. It was also used as the flip of the 'Letting Go' single and was included on the *Wings Over America* album. Paul performed the number during the Wings World Tour of 1975/76 and often dedicated this particular number to actor/dancer Fred Astaire.

You Know I'll Get You Baby
One of several numbers Paul recorded in July 1979 during sessions for *McCartney II*, which weren't used on the album. Paul had originally intended issuing a double album and 'You Know I'll Get You Baby' had been planned for Record Two.

You Never Give Me Your Money
A number penned by Paul for the Beatles 1969 album *Abbey Road*. It was recorded at Olympic Studios on 6 May, with overdubbing at Abbey Road on 1, 11, 15, 30 and 31 July and 5 August 1969. The theme was inspired by the financial problems at Apple.

Paul commented, 'This was me directly lambasting Allen Klein's attitude to us. No money, just funny paper. All promises and it never works out. It's basically a song about no faith in a person.'

You Won't See Me
A track on the *Rubber Soul* album.

Paul was to comment, 'It was one hundred per cent me, as I recall, but I was always happy to give John a credit because there's always a chance that, on the night of the session, he might have said, "That'd be better" to me. It was very Motown flavoured. It's got a James Jameson feel. He was the Motown bass player.'

The Beatles recorded it on Monday 22 November 1965 and it was the last session for the album.

Paul wrote and performed the song on the piano and Mal Evans played Hammond organ in the recording studio.

It was inspired by a row Paul had had with Jane Asher.

You'll Never Walk Alone
A number from the Rodgers and Hammerstein musical *Carousel* that became a No. 1 British hit for Gerry & the Pacemakers. It also became an anthem at Liverpool FC where the fans sang the song en masse. The

gates outside the football ground now sport the message 'You'll Never Walk Alone'.

Following the fire in the stands of a football match at Bradford City ground in which 55 people died, Gerry Marsden set out to make a charity record to raise funds for the bereaved families. He amassed a group of artists that he called the Crowd and issued the record on Friday 24 May 1985.

Paul had been invited to take part, but couldn't attend the actual recording session. However, he recorded a seventeen-second telephone message of sympathy that was included on the B-side of the record, entitled 'Messages'.

Young Boy

A track from the *Flaming Pie* album lasting 3 minutes and 54 seconds. It was penned and produced by Paul and engineered by Geoff Emerick and Jan Jacobs, assisted by Keith Smith and Frank Farrell.

Recording began on 22 February 1995 and Paul sang lead vocal and played drums, bass guitar, acoustic guitar and Hammond organ. Steve Miller provided backing vocal and played electric guitar and rhythm guitar.

It was issued in the UK on Parlophone RP 6462 on Monday 28 April 1997 in three different formats, a 7″ picture disc and two different CDs.

Trevor Dann of the BBC, who'd originally vetoed 'Real Love' from being played on Radio One in 1998, banned 'Young Boy' from *Top Of The Pops* on the grounds that it was not new music.

'Looking For You' was on the flip.

Commenting on the number, Paul said, 'This was another written against the clock. I wrote it in the time that it took Linda to cook a lunch for a feature in the *New York Times*. It was great to renew my sixties friendship with Steve Miller.'

Paul had originally recorded with Miller in London in the 1960s and said, 'I rang up Steve, said I had this song, how about it? He's got this studio in Sun Valley, Idaho, and we went out there. Working with him was like falling back into an old habit. We worked on "Young Boy" over three days at his place and it was fun, we didn't sweat it. It's very straightforward, just a song straight from the shoulder.'

Paul was also to say that he was inspired to write the number by his son James. He commented, '"Young Boy" is just about a young guy looking for a way to find love and basically I suppose I was thinking of my own son, who's nineteen, though he'd kill me for saying that.

'It's for anyone around that age, looking for love. I remember the feeling well.

'I remember thinking, "There's three hundred million people out there and one of them is the right one for me." But you don't know if you'll ever meet them or how you'll do it. It's a pretty scary feeling. So this song is for all those people.'

Your Loving Flame

A track on the *Driving Rain* album lasting 3 minutes and 43 seconds. It was recorded on Tuesday 19 June 2001 and mixed by David Leonard. A string quartet was overdubbed on the track. The musicians were: David Campbell, viola; Matt Funes, viola; Joel Derouin, violin; and Larry Corbett, cello.

Your Mother Should Know

The theme number for the conclusion of the *Magical Mystery Tour* film, which was a spectacular finale. The Beatles were to descend a gigantic winding staircase, dressed in white evening suits. As they reached the bottom of the stairs they joined a huge gathering of more than 200 people including 160 members of the Peggy Spencer Formation Dancing team and 24 girl cadets from the Women's Air Force.

The sequence was filmed at West Malling's Air Station and Paul was to say, 'That was the shot that used most of the budget!'

Apple's Alistair Taylor commented, 'The idea for this sequence was because Paul was, very much, into the Busby Berkeley school of thought. That's why he had the Peggy Spencer Formation Team there.

'The hour before we were due to film in this aircraft hangar, the generator blew. Every light, the sounds, everything went. So, it was panic stations. It was a Sunday and we couldn't get hold of the people we hired the generator from. So, a guy brilliantly made a wooden cog, because it was a wooden cog that had gone in the generator and we, thankfully, got it going again. But it blew again, and by this time it was getting near dusk and all the invited villagers started drifting off. Children in prams and the other, older children started going. So, the final scene in *Magical Mystery Tour* was just a tenth of the people that should have been there.'

Paul had actually composed the number inspired by songs of the 1930s and even included the line, 'a song that was a hit before your mother was born'.

Due to the fact that the Abbey Road Studios were fully booked, the number was recorded at Chappell Recording Studios at 52 Maddox Street, London W1. The sessions took place on Tuesday and Wednesday 22 and 23 August 1967. There were some sessions recording this particular song at Abbey Road Studios, but the Chappell Studios recordings were the ones used on the *Magical Mystery Tour* releases.

Your Way

A track from the *Driving Rain* album. The number lasts for 2 minutes and 55 seconds and was recorded on 18 February 2001.

You're Sixteen

A number written by Robert and Richard Sherman that had given Johnny Burnette a million-seller in 1960 and Ringo Starr a multi-million seller in February 1974. It was also included on the *Ringo* album.

The track included a kazoo passage by Paul. Producer Richard Perry had played Paul the tapes of the album and Paul felt that the number needed something extra. He played the kazoo, a small mouth instrument which can produce a tinny sound that people used to imitate with a comb wrapped in paper, but which in this instance sounded almost like a saxophone.

Yvonne's The One

A number Paul penned in collaboration with Eric Stewart that was originally made as a demo disc in February 1985 under the title 'So Long Yvonne'. It was included on the *Press To Play* album. Stewart was to say the song was inspired by a postcard he'd received from Nick Mason of Pink Floyd. It was re-recorded by Adrian Lee, with Paul on rhythm, and issued as one of the tracks on 10cc's *Mirror Mirror* album when it was issued in Europe and Japan in 1995, although the track wasn't included on the American release.

Zappa, Frank

Founder of the Mothers of Invention, Zappa arrived in London in September 1967 to appear at the Royal Albert Hall and to promote his new album *Absolutely Free*. During his stay in London he used the Indica bookshop as his unofficial office, with the co-operation of Paul's friend Barry Miles.

Zappa told Miles that for his next album he would like the cover to be a parody of the *Sgt Pepper* cover and wanted to contact Paul for his permission. Miles arranged it. Zappa phoned Paul and asked him if he had any objection to the proposal and Paul told him that he didn't mind, but he didn't know if there were any copyright problems and it was EMI who should actually be approached. Paul then gave him his blessing.

The album *We're Only In It For The Money* satirising the *Pepper* cover was issued on MGM Verve and no permission was sought. As a satirical piece it did not need permission to be given.

Paul was puzzled when, some years later, Zappa claimed that Paul said he wouldn't allow him to do it, yet he'd given Zappa his blessing.

When Apple launched their experimental and spoken-word label Zapple, Zappa mistakenly believed it had been named for him. It hadn't. It was a name John Lennon came up with.

Zappa died in December 1993.

Zeleste Club

An 1800-seat venue in Barcelona, Spain and one of the six venues Paul decided to appear at during his 'Surprise Gigs' tour between May and July 1991 with himself, Linda, Robbie McIntosh, Hamish Stuart, Paul 'Wix' Wickens and Blair Cunningham playing a 45-minute acoustic set followed by a 45-minute electric set.

The tours were basically intended to enhance the promotion for his album *Unplugged – The Official Bootleg*.

Paul and the band flew into Barcelona on Wednesday 8 May 1991 and returned to the UK immediately following the concert.

The acoustic set comprised: 'Mean Woman Blues', 'Be-Bop-A-Lula', 'We Can Work It Out', 'San Francisco Bay Blues', 'Every Night', 'Here, There And Everywhere', 'That Would Be Something', 'And I Love Her', 'She's A Woman', 'I Lost My Little Girl', 'Ain't No Sunshine', 'I've Just Seen A Face', 'Hi-Heel Sneakers' and 'Good Rockin' Tonight'. The electric set comprised: 'My Brave Face', 'Twenty Flight Rock', 'Band On The Run', 'Ebony And Ivory', 'I Saw Her Standing There', 'Get Back', 'Coming Up', 'The Long And Winding Road', 'Ain't That A Shame' and 'Let It Be'. The two encores were 'Can't Buy Me Love' and 'Sgt Pepper's Lonely Hearts Club Band'.

Zenith

The first guitar Paul owned and one that he still possesses. He'd been presented with a trumpet by his father, but wasn't too keen on the instrument because he couldn't play it and sing at the same time, so he swapped the trumpet for a Zenith guitar. Initially, he had difficulty playing it, until he realised that a left-handed player had to reverse the strings, which he did.

Zoo Gang, The

A British ITV television series starring Lili Palmer, Brian Keith and John Mills, which was first screened in 1974. Paul penned the title song for the series and recorded it with Wings. It was on the flipside of the 'Band On The Run' single, issued on 28 June 1974 on Apple R 5997.

A band called Jungle Juice released a version of Paul's 'Zoo Gang' in Britain one month before Wings issued a version of their own. The record was released on Pye-Bradley BRAD 74071 on 24 May 1974.

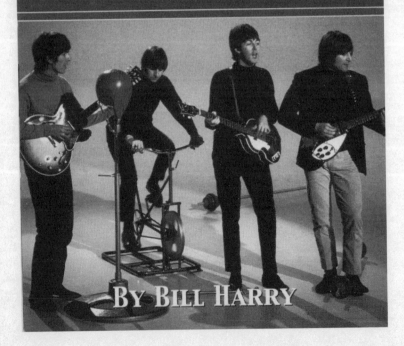

THE
BEATLES
ENCYCLOPEDIA
REVISED AND UPDATED

BY BILL HARRY

THE JOHN
LENNON
ENCYCLOPEDIA

BY BILL HARRY